NTC's
Dictionary
of
BRITISH
SLANG
and
COLLOQUIAL EXPRESSIONS

Ewart James

NTC Publishing Group
NTC/Contemporary Publishing Company

Library of Congress Cataloging-in-Publication Data
James, Ewart, 1942-
    NTC's dictionary of British slang and colloquial expressions /
Ewart James.
     p. cm.
   Includes index.
   ISBN 0-8442-0838-8. — ISBN 0-8442-0839-6 (pbk.)
   1. English language—Great Britain—Slang—Dictionaries.
2. Figures of speech—Dictionaries. I. Title.
PE3729.G7J36 1996
427'.941—dc20   96-35537
                                   CIP

Published by NTC Publishing Group
A division of NTC/Contemporary Publishing Group, Inc.
4255 West Touhy Avenue, Lincolnwood (Chicago), Illinois 60646-1975 U.S.A.
Copyright © 1997 by NTC/Contemporary Publishing Group, Inc.
Printed in the United States of America
International Standard Book Number: 0-8442-0838-8 (cloth)
                                        0-8442-0839-6 (paper)
18   17   16   15   14   13   12   11   10   9   8   7   6   5   4   3   2   1

Contents

About this Dictionary

Within this dictionary you can find the most frequently-heard slang and colloquial expressions of modern Britain. In a comprehensive but highly readable manner we are introduced to the everyday language of the cities and counties of Britain; to the special words used by both criminals and police; to the talk of Essex girls and Sloan Rangers; to the extensive vocabulary of drinkers and drug users; to the vast repertoire of sexual terms—euphemistic, comic and blatant—that are in everyday use in almost every corner and certainly every pub of these islands. Not least, we shall meet and delight in the informal linguistic glories of Cockney rhyming slang, wonderful examples of hobson-jobson and unique contributions from around the regions of Britain.

Pervading the book are many naturalised Americanisms, because without doubt the most powerful single influence on the development of British English in the twentieth century has come from across the Atlantic Ocean, and any collection of modern British slang that ignored this huge fact would be guilty of a serious oversight.

In 1901 G. K. Chesterton wrote that, "...all slang is metaphor, and all metaphor is poetry." Perhaps so, but this does not really tell us what slang does or where it comes from, or how it is associated with yet different from colloquial language. In the hierarchy of linguistic acceptability, slang is superior to cant— the secret jargon of the underworld—-but inferior to colloqui alism. How can we tell what is slang and what is colloquial? There is no easy formulistic way to do this. The answer is elusive because the boundary between the slang and the colloquial is elusive. Indeed, the division between what might be called formal and informal language—which includes both slang and colloquial—is itself elusive.

Often terms emerge into use as slang, progress to colloquialisms and in due course are endowed with the sometimes dubious virtue of formal status as standard English. However, sometimes the formal can move over time into informality and slang; some words and expressions can remain in use as slang for many centuries, while others are tried out (as it were) as slang, fail the test of permanent acceptability and vanish with little or no trace.

For centuries, underworld cant has been a significant source of popular slang. Sex, money and drink are the traditional large topics of slang, now joined by multitudes of coinings from the drug culture. Taboo topics, especially sexual ones, provide a happy area for the creation of euphemistic slang and taboo words themselves, although not true slang, have been included in this dictionary. Youth culture is responsible for the coinage of many entries and clever or humorous or insulting—or all three—nicknames for individuals and groups have delivered many more.

Not all slang or colloquial expressions refer to taboo topics, or are insults, or are humorous. Many are no more than the terminology of common everyday speech in the British Isles. Throughout, examples have been given in naturalistic language, with grammatical correctness taking second place to authenticity. The examples should be taken as representative of slang usage and not of standard formal English.

The grammar and syntax of each expression are best determined from the examples that accompany each entry. The notion of "part of speech" is relevant to the function of individual words. The words within the clauses and phrases that are entries in the dictionary can be given part-of-speech labels, but it is the grammar and syntax of the entire phrase that is important. Each expression in the dictionary is assigned a "function code" that serves to indicate the functional potential of the entry expression. These codes represent function independently from form. That is to say, expressions that function the same get the same label. For instance, nouns, noun compounds, noun phrases and noun clauses are all marked *n.* for "nominal."

Unlike standard English, few slang or colloquial expressions are standardized in spelling or punctuation. Standard dictionaries differ considerably as to whether a standard English compound is printed as one word, two words or a hyphenated word. The spelling of slang entries is even more variable. This dictionary usually represents slang expressions in the form in which they were found in print, except for rhyming compounds, e.g., "fat-cat" or "funny-money," which are always hyphenated.

The entries come from many sources. Many have been collected and submitted by students and other individuals. Much of the latest material has come directly from television and a lesser amount from contemporary radio. Standard reference works have been used to verify the meanings and spellings of older material. A surprising amount of old material has been verified in reruns of old movies. Many attestations have come from contemporary journalism, especially human interest and Sunday supplement material. Few of the examples are verbatim quotes of the original. Some are concocted, and many more have been edited to exemplify an expression's meaning more concisely than the original quote. The examples exist to illustrate meaning, not to prove the earliest date of print or broadcast dissemination.

This is not a polite book; every human frailty is exposed within its covers and if such things offend you then you should look no further. Political correctness and slang do not make natural bedfellows. But those of us who delight in humanity's infinite capacity for inventive metaphor will find a veritable treasure trove of poetry here.

Read on and see for yourself how right G. K. Chesterton was.

Guide to the Use of the Dictionary

1. Entries are alphabetized according to an absolute alphabetical order that ignores all hyphens and spaces. Entries beginning with numerals precede the alphabetic entries.

2. The first step in finding an expression is to try looking it up in the dictionary. Entries that consist of two or more words are entered in their normal order, such as **chill someone's action**. Phrases are never inverted or re-ordered.

3. If you do not find the expression you want, or if you cannot decide on the exact form of the expression, look up any major word in the expression in the *Phrase-Finder Index*, which begins on page 499. There you will find all the multiword expressions that contain the word you have looked up. Pick out the expression you want, and look it up in the dictionary.

Terms and Abbreviations

□ marks the beginning of an example.

acronym an abbreviation consisting of a set of initials pronounced as a single word, as with *UNESCO*, the **U**nited **N**ations **E**ducational, **S**cientific, and **C**ultural **O**rganization.

backslang a slang expression created by reversing a standard English expression. This may be based on either the written (letter-by-letter) or the pronounced version of the expression.

black typically used or originated by immigrants or the descendants of immigrants from Africa or the Caribbean.

cant the jargon of criminals, originally a secret form of speech employed by denizens of the underworld.

catch phrase an expression that is meant to catch attention because of its cleverness or aptness.

combining form a sense of a word used only in combination with another word.

computer jargon the terms and expressions used by people who operate computers. This includes a special keyboard vocabulary made up of initialisms, such as IMHO = in my humble opinion, which are used in no other domain.

crude normally not suitable in public speech and often considered offensive; best avoided.

deliberate spoonerism a deliberate interchanging of initial consonants in a pair of words, such as "queer old dean" for "dear old queen."

disguise an expression that is similar in pronunciation or form, but not in meaning, to the expression for which it stands. A disguise is EUPHEMISTIC in that its pronunciation or form suggests the expression for which it is a disguise. RHYMING SLANG and BACKSLANG are also types of disguise.

euphemism a EUPHEMISTIC expression.

euphemistic relatively refined and having no negative connotations.

exclam. exclamation.

eye-dialect a term which is the phonetic written form of a slang or dialectal pronunciation of a standard English expression.

hobson-jobson a process by which unfamiliar, usually foreign, expressions are substituted with familiar ones which sound similar but are unrelated in meaning. The name "hobson-jobson" originated from a garbled anglicisation of the exclamation *"Ya Hasan, ya Husayan!"* uttered by Islamic troops of the British Indian Army when on parade during the 19th century. Hasan and Husayan were grandsons of Mohammed.

initialism an abbreviation consisting of the initial letters of the words being shortened. The letters are pronounced one by one, as with "BBC."

interj. interjection

interrog. interrogative.

jargon the specialized terminology of an occupation; shoptalk.

mod. modifier. Expressions serving to modify, restrict or qualify (adjectives, adjective phrases, adverbs, adverb phrases, etc.) are marked *mod.*

n. nominal. Expressions functioning as nominals (nouns, noun phrases, etc.) are marked *n.*

offensive occurring in public speech but often considered offensive by individuals so described; use with care.

phr. phrase.

police from the speech of police officers.

prep. preposition.

pro. pronoun.

pseudo-Latin a form of wordplay where an expression is made to look and sound as if it were Latin although it is not.

racially offensive insulting to the group referred to, not acceptable in public speech and usually considered very offensive; always avoid if possible.

rhyming slang a form of slang where a standard English expression, or its conventional slang equivalent, is replaced by another which rhymes with it but is unconnected in meaning. The replacement may be expanded, the original rhyming portion dropped and the process repeated from that point. This can result in expressions which lack any apparent connection with their meanings. For example, the rhyming slang term "china" is linked to "friend" as follows: china [plate] ≈ [mate] = friend, where "≈" means that the expressions on either side are linked by rhyme rather than meaning, "=" means that the expressions on either side are linked by meaning rather than rhyme, and a word or phrase contained within [square brackets], as here, is one necessary for the link between entry and meaning, but is not part of either and is thus silent, although it may not have been at an earlier stage in the evolution of the term to its present-day status. These symbols and this syntax are used throughout the dictionary to show the linkage of rhyming slang expressions.

securities market(s) having to do with the stock markets, the bond markets or the sale of other financial instruments.

sent. sentence.

taboo not acceptable in public speech and usually considered very offensive; always avoid if possible.

term of address an expression that can be used to address someone directly.

underworld from the speech of criminals and often, by osmosis, police officers.

vb. verb.

aardvark *n.* hard work. (A pun.) □ *What they expect from us here is too much like aardvark.* □ *If you don't like aardvark you won't last long around here.*

abortion *n.* something exceptionally ridiculous or ugly. □ *A little bit absurd? Naw, it was a total abortion!* □ *The dress was not so much pleasing to look at as an abortion.*

above *mod.* more than. □ *There were above twenty people at Mary's party.* □ *We're trying to score above average.*

above oneself *mod.* conceited; overbearing. □ *John has been getting above himself ever since he got his new job.* □ *I can't stand people who are as above themselves as that.*

above one's weight *mod.* beyond one's capability or class; too expensive for one. □ *I'm afraid that car's a bit above my weight.* □ *Have you got another similar, cheaper one that's not above my weight?*

above stairs *mod.* upstairs. □ *All the bedrooms are above stairs.* □ *June went above stairs to her room.*

abso-bloody-lutely *mod.* absolutely; emphatically. □ *Do I like pizza? Abso-bloody-lutely!* □ *We are abso-bloody-lutely sick to death of your wishy-washy attitude.*

Absolutely. *interj.* "Yes, for certain." □ *Absolutely. There can be no doubt about it.* □ *That's right. Absolutely!*

accidentally-on-purpose *mod.* deliberate, but meant to look like an accident. □ *Then, I accidentally-on-purpose spilt water on him.* □ *I knew it was done accidentally-on-purpose. That kind of thing doesn't just happen.*

AC-DC AND **AC/DC** *mod.* bisexual. (Crude. An initialism.) □ *I didn't realise at first that we were in an AC-DC bar!* □ *Clare said Tom is AC/DC, but I don't believe it.*

Ace! *interj.* "Excellent!" □ *I hear you've won again, Joan. That's really ace!* □ *Ace! That's the way to do it!*

ace *mod.* best; top-rated. □ *She is an ace reporter with the newspaper.* □ *Frank is an ace swimmer.*

ace up one's sleeve *n.* something important held in reserve. □ *The twenty pound note I keep in my shoe is the ace up my sleeve.* □ *Mary's beautiful singing voice was the ace up her sleeve in case everything else failed.*

achers *n.* the testicles. (Taboo. Normally with *the* and in the plural. Compare with ACRES.) □ *He turned sideways to protect his achers.* □ *Thud, right in the achers. Ye gods, it hurt!*

acid *n.* lysergic acid diethylamide (L.S.D.). □ *Acid and pot! That's all you think about.* □ *Freddy got hold of some bad acid and freaked out.*

acid house (party) *n.* a kind of teens' entertainment involving the combination of electronic music with hallucinogenic drugs like L.S.D. or ECSTASY. □ *The police raided another acid house party there last night.* □ *There were hundreds of teenagers at that acid house.*

acid test *n.* a very thorough test. (From a test for determining true gold using acid.) □ *We put your invention to the acid test, and—I am extremely sorry to tell you—it failed miserably.* □ *I'll take this home to my kids and let them give it the acid test. If it survives them, it's a winner.*

acker(s) AND **yacker(s)** *n.* cash; low value bank notes. (Originally this was military slang, from a corruption of the Arabic word *fakka*, meaning "coin." An example of hobson-jobson.) □ *The dosser asked Reginald if he had any acker to spare.* □ *I don't think Reginald knows what yackers means; he's never had to deal in such trivial sums.*

acres *n.* the testicles. (Taboo. Normally with *the* and in the plural. Compare with ACHERS.) □ *He got hit right in the acres.* □ *Thud, right in the acres. Ye gods, it hurt!*

act a part *vb. phr.* to pretend or play a part. □ *I'm tired of acting a part for you.* □ *Be yourself; you don't have to act a part for my sake.*

action 1. *n.* excitement; activity in general; whatever is happening. □ *This place is dull. I want some action.* □ *How do I find out where the action is in this town?* **2.** *n.* a share of something; a share of the winnings or of the booty. (Compare with PIECE OF THE ACTION.) □ *I did my share of the work, and I want my share of the action.* □ *Just what do you do to earn any of the action?*

action man *n.* an enthusiastic participant in physical exercises and military activities; anyone who is excessively macho or over-enthusiastic. □ *The trouble with Ken is that he's such an action man.* □ *Yes, a little of an action man like him can go a long way.*

Adam *n.* ECSTASY, a hallucinogen similar to L.S.D. □ *You can get some good Adam in this part of town.* □ *Adam is just one of a dozen drugs with similar formulas.*

Adam and Eve *vb. phr.* to believe. (Rhyming slang.) □ *I don't think you Adam and Eve me, do you?* □ *Yes, of course I Adam and Eve what you say.*

Adam's ale AND **Adam's wine** *n.* water. □ *I'm so thirsty! A drink of Adam's ale would be most welcome.* □ *A pitcher of Adam's wine had been placed on the table.*

Adam's wine See ADAM'S ALE.

addict *n.* someone showing a marked preference for something or someone. (A combining form not related to drug addiction.) □ *Sam is a real opera addict. He just loves the stuff.* □ *My uncle is a detective-story addict.*

admass *n.* that portion of the population who are supposedly influenced by advertising. □ *Do you think the admass will go for this slogan?* □ *Whatever the admass may think, I'm not impressed.*

admin 1. *mod.* administrative. □ *It's an admin question: do we do it this way or the other?* □ *There's supposed to be a good admin reason for doing things the way we do.* **2.** *n.* administration. □ *Someone from admin wants to speak to you.* □ *The admin of this company is not very good.*

admin block *n.* administration building. □ *I work in the admin block.* □ *That's the admin block over there.*

advert *n.* an advertisement. □ *Joan placed an advert for her old car in the newspaper.* □ *Mike read the advert and thought it sounded just like the sort of car he wanted.*

aereated *mod.* livid with rage. □ *Calm down! Don't get so aereated!* □ *Helen got really aereated when she heard that Mary won the essay prize.*

African lager *n.* stout. (Racially offensive. Stout is a dark, full-bodied beer made with roasted malt. Lager is light beer.) □ *African lager is good for you, it's full of nutrients.* □ *Fancy a drink of African lager?*

African Woodbine *n.* a marijuana cigarette. (Racially offensive. Woodbine was a brand of cheap cigarette.) □ *What does African Woodbine cost around here?* □ *Have you any spare African Woodbine?*

afters *n.* the last course of a meal. □ *For afters, Mary ordered ice cream.* □ *After we had finished the afters, we were served with coffee.*

afterthought *n.* the youngest child of a large family, especially if much younger than all the rest. □ *I suppose you could say that Petra is an afterthought, as she's ten years younger than her sister.* □ *Petra may be an afterthought, but she's our favourite.*

aggro 1. *n.* aggravation. □ *Don't give me all that aggro!* □ *Charlie says the* police have been giving him aggro again. **2.** n. deliberate violence or the threat of it, often by groups of youths. □ Some youths have been causing a lot of aggro in the neighbourhood. □ Charlie says the police threatened him with aggro. **3.** n. a problem or difficulty. □ I've had a lot of aggro trying to make that TV work. □ Jane is having aggro with her tax return.

agony aunt n. a journalist, normally a woman, who answers readers who write to an AGONY COLUMN about their personal problems. □ Margaret may be agony aunt on the Daily Press, but she can't sort out her own life. □ Ann told David she wanted a divorce after she found out that he wrote to an agony aunt about their problems.

agony column n. a column in a newspaper or magazine written as a joint enterprise between an AGONY AUNT and her readers. □ Margaret may write an agony column on the Daily Press, but can't sort out her own life. □ Ann told David she wanted a divorce after the letter he wrote about their problems was published in an agony column.

agree to disagree phr. to agree, after discussion, that agreement is not possible. □ We have accomplished nothing except that we agree to disagree. □ The two political parties agreed to disagree in 1971, and that was the last agreeable thing either one of them did.

agricultural mod. [of play in cricket] clumsy, poor quality or inelegant. (Such as the play to be expected from a small rural team.) □ Peter is a bit of an agricultural batsman. □ What can you expect from the team from Little Haddam except agricultural play?

ahead of the game mod. being early; having an advantage in a competitive situation; having done more than necessary. (Especially with get or keep.) □ Without a mobile telephone, I found it hard to get ahead of the game. □ If being ahead of the game is important to you and to your business, lease a mobile telephone from us.

aim Archy at the Armitage See POINT PERCY AT THE PORCELAIN.

aim for the stars AND **reach for the stars** vb. phr. to aspire to something; to set one's goals high. □ Aim for the stars, son. Don't settle for second best. □ Set your sights high. Reach for the stars!

air dancing n. death by hanging. □ Air dancing is just a euphemism people use to make hanging people seem more acceptable. □ If more people experienced air dancing there would be less crime.

airhead n. a stupid person. (Someone with air where there should be brains.) □ What is that loony airhead doing there on the roof? □ Some airhead put mustard in the ketchup squeezer.

airs and graces 1. n. a man's braces. (US suspenders. Rhyming slang.) □ Bert stood at the top of the stairs in his airs and graces, the very picture of sartorial elegance. □ What have you done with me airs and graces, woman? **2.** n. artificial or pretentious behaviour. □ No more of your airs and graces, just get on with it! □ Why do you always put on these airs and graces?

airy-fairy 1. mod. fairy-like or insubstantial. □ That material is so airy-fairy, you can see right through it. □ Something as airy-fairy as that will just blow away. **2.** mod. impractical; trivial; vague; pointless; of wishful thinking. □ Haven't you outgrown that kind of airy-fairy thinking yet? □ Her ideas are too airy-fairy. □ I don't care to hear any more of your airy-fairy ideas.

aled(-up) mod. intoxicated due to drink or drugs. □ All four of them went out and got themselves comprehensively aled. □ Sally was aled-up after only a few drinks.

Alf's peed again. interj. "Be seeing you." (From the German auf Wiedersehen, by hobson-jobson.) □ Right, I'm on my way. Alf's peed again! □ "Alf's peed again," she cried out, and left.

alilie n. a false alibi. (Police.) □ You're going to have to come up with a more convincing alilie than that, Otto. □ Some of the alilies you hear round here are really imaginative.

alky AND **alkie** n. a drunkard; an alcoholic. □ You see alky after alky all up *and down Maxwell Street.* □ *Some alkie came in and asked for twenty pence.*

alley cat *n.* a sexually immoral woman. (Crude.) □ *That slut! She's just an alley cat!* □ *I don't think Zoe is an alley cat.*

all-found *mod.* everything provided. (Accommodation and food supplied free by an employer.) □ *You'll get all-found lodgings while you're away on this project.* □ *With all-found accommodation, I can save a lot of money!*

all gas and gaiters *phr.* pompous verbosity. □ *Oh, you can ignore him; he's all gas and gaiters.* □ *It's all gas and gaiters here today.*

all mouth and trousers AND **all piss and wind** *phr.* making much noise and fuss, but achieving little or nothing. (Crude. All piss and wind is taboo.) □ *Roger is just all mouth and trousers. Ignore him.* □ *As usual, it was all piss and wind.*

all-nighter *n.* something that lasts all night, like a party or study session. □ *After an all-nighter studying, I couldn't keep my eyes open for the exam.* □ *Sam invited us to an all-nighter, but we're getting a little old for that kind of thing.*

all of a doodah *mod.* nervous. □ *Oh, you've got me all of a doodah!* □ *They're all of a doodah now, but it'll be all right later.*

all over bar the shouting *phr.* all over except trivial details. □ *Well that's it, all over bar the shouting.* □ *Just when we thought it was all over bar the shouting, the whole business started up again.*

all over someone *phr.* making a great fuss of someone. □ *It was disgusting! She was all over him!* □ *I don't know why she should be all over someone she hardly knows.*

all over the place AND **all over the shop** **1.** *mod.* everywhere. □ *You can find examples of it all over the place.* □ *Jack has been all over the shop in his time.* **2.** *mod.* chaotic. □ *What a mess! It's all over the place.* □ *The stuff was all over the shop but he's started sorting things out.*

all over the shop See ALL OVER THE PLACE.

all piss and wind See ALL MOUTH AND TROUSERS.

All right. 1. *interj.* "Yes."; "I agree." □ *All right, I'll do it.* □ *All right. I'm coming.* **2.** *mod.* for sure; for certain. □ *He's the one who said it, all right.* □ *I was there, all right.*

all-rounder *n.* a person able to perform several activities well. (Especially in sports.) □ *Brian is a real all-rounder.* □ *There are very few all-rounders in a place like this.*

all serene *mod.* all right; everything fine. □ *Is everything all serene?* □ *Yes, it's all serene now.*

all set *phr.* "all ready." □ *Well I'm all set.* □ *I'm all set too.*

all the best *phr.* "good wishes"; "good luck." □ *All the best at your job interview.* □ *All the best with your new job.*

all the hours God gives us *n.* all the time that is available. □ *We're very busy, working all the hours God gives us.* □ *Even with all the hours God gives us, it's going to be tight.*

all the rage *n.* the current fad; an irresistible fad. □ *Get a haircut like mine! It's all the rage!* □ *It may be all the rage but I think it looks terrible on me.*

all to buggery See ALL TO COCK.

all to cock AND **all to buggery** *mod.* seriously incorrect; badly wrong; totally destroyed. (Taboo.) □ *It's all to cock again.* □ *It's all useless, all to buggery!*

all-up *mod.* finished; ruined. □ *That's it all-up. We can go home now.* □ *The business went all-up last year.*

almond (rocks) AND **army rocks** *n.* socks. (Rhyming slang.) □ *You should've seen the multicoloured almonds he was wearing.* □ *So I pulled on me army rocks and went off to work.*

alphabet soup *n.* initialisms and acronyms in general. □ *The names of these government offices are just alphabet soup.* □ *Just look at the telephone book! You can't find anything because it's filled with alphabet soup.*

also-ran *n.* someone of no significance. (From horse-racing.) □ *Oh, he's just another also-ran.* □ *Ignore the also-rans.*

amateur AND **enthusiastic amateur** *n.* a woman who provides free what a prostitute requires to be paid for. (Crude.) □ *It's difficult for the pros to compete with the amateurs.* □ *No, I'd not say she's a prostitute; an enthusiastic amateur, more like.*

amber nectar *n.* [Australian] beer. (Especially lager. Normally with *the.*) □ *A glass of the amber nectar would be most welcome.* □ *Another pint of the amber nectar?*

ambisextrous *mod.* bisexual. □ *I wouldn't say he was bisexual; let's just say ambisextrous.* □ *There's a lot of these ambisextrous people in this pub.*

(ambulance) chaser *n.* a lawyer or entrepreneur who hurries to the scene of an accident to try to get the business of any injured persons. □ *The insurance companies are cracking down on ambulance chasers.* □ *Two minutes after the spectacular accident, seven chasers with police radios showed up and began harassing the victims.*

Americanese *n.* the variety of English spoken in the United States. □ *No, he doesn't speak proper English. Americanese, more like.* □ *Americanese is full of words that are unfamiliar to most British people.*

American sock *n.* a condom. (Crude. Compare with FRENCH LETTER.) □ *"Forget it without an American sock!" she said.* □ *I've got an American sock somewhere.*

ammo *n.* ammunition □ *There they were, trapped in a foxhole with no ammo, and with enemies all over the place. What do you think happened?* □ *I don't know. They sent out for ammo, maybe?*

amps *n.* amphetamines. □ *I never do any drugs except maybe a few amps now and then, and the odd downer, and maybe a little grass on weekends, but nothing really hard.* □ *Paul is on a roller coaster of amps.*

amusements *n.* the rides and sideshows at a carnival or fair. □ *Johnny loves trying out all the amusements.* □ *Amusements seem to be getting more and more expensive and high-tech all the time.*

anarf *n.* fifty pence. (Half of one Pound Sterling.) □ *That'll be two anarf quid, squire.* □ *Anarf? For what?*

anchor *n.* a brake. (Often with *the*, usually plural.) □ *He slammed on the anchor and we slid to a halt.* □ *I think this car needs new anchors.*

ancient history *n.* someone or something completely forgotten, especially past romances. (Compare with HISTORY.) □ *Bob? I never think about Bob anymore. He's ancient history.* □ *That business about joining the army is ancient history.*

and change *phr.* plus a few pennies; plus a few hundredths. (Used in citing a price or other decimal figure to indicate an additional fraction of a full unit. Compare with CHANGE.) □ *This one only costs ten quid and change.* □ *The London Stock Exchange was up seven points and change to break the record for the third time this week.*

And how! *exclam.* a strong agreement; an emphatic concurrence. (Often used ironically.) □ *I am really pleased you are here, and how!* □ BILL: *I am pleased you're here.* BOB: *Me, too! And how!*

Andrew *n.* the Royal Navy. □ *Paul's joined the Andrew.* □ *The Andrew are always looking for the right kind of people.*

angel 1. *n.* a financier of a theatrical production. □ *Who was the angel for your new play?* □ *Martin had been hoping for an angel to see his production through, but all the usual rich suckers seemed to have disappeared.* **2.** *n.* a helpful person. □ *Be an angel and answer the door.* □ *You were an angel to look after the kids while I was away.* **3.** *n.* a (female) nurse. □ *Where would sick people be without these angels?* □ *She may be an angel to the patients but away from the hospital she has a ferocious temper.*

angel dust *n.* the common name for phencyclidine (P.C.P.). □ *Angel dust is becoming quite a problem in this town.* □ *I thought that angel dust and stuff like that was a problem of the sixties.*

angels on horseback *n.* oysters wrapped in bacon slices. □ *Mmmm! I* *just love angels on horseback.* □ *We're having some angels on horseback this evening.*

angle 1. *n.* a selfish or ulterior motive. □ *Okay, Ted, I know you better than to think that you are doing this out of the kindness of your heart. What's your angle?* □ *I don't have any angle. I have reformed.* **2.** *n.* a slant; a bias; a focus. □ *Let's try to get a good angle on this news story so the wire service will buy it from us.* □ *I think that by studying the Maya I will be able to develop a new angle on why they disappeared.*

animal *n.* a male who acts like a beast in terms of manners, cleanliness or sexual aggressiveness. (Crude. Also a term of address.) □ *You are an animal!* □ *Stop picking your nose, animal.*

ankle-biter *n.* a small child. □ *The place was full of ankle-biters.* □ *Why won't this ankle-biter leave me alone?*

annihilated *mod.* very intoxicated due to drink or drugs. □ *The boys came in annihilated and their father had plenty to say to them.* □ *Pete and Gary went out and got annihilated.*

anorak *n.* a student considered to be dull, conventional and unfashionably dressed. □ *Exciting? Let's just say everyone calls him an anorak.* □ *Sometimes the anoraks get the best degrees.*

another peep (out of you) *n.* another complaint, word or sound from someone. (Usually in the negative.) □ *I don't want to hear another peep out of you!* □ *I've heard enough! Not another peep!*

an' that *phr.* an implicit request for assurance added to the end of statements. (Compare with Y'KNOW.) □ *Well, you know what I mean, don't you, an' that?* □ *Why don't you speak to her, an' that?*

anti *mod.* against someone or something. (Usually with the force of a preposition.) □ *I'm not anti the proposal, I just have some questions.* □ *Four are in favour, and two are anti.*

any amount *n.* large quantities. □ *Yes, there's any amount, even enough for you.* □ *I wouldn't do that for any amount of money.*

Any joy? 1. *interrog.* "Have you succeeded?" □ *Any joy yet?* □ *If you have*

any joy, tell me. **2.** *interrog.* "Have you had any luck?" □ *Any joy with the lottery?* □ *I've never had any joy in my life.*

any road *mod.* anyhow; anyway. □ *Any road, I said to her that that was enough.* □ *She continued any road.*

Anytime. *interj.* "You are welcome."; "Happy to oblige." (Sometimes said in response to "Thank you.") □ MARY: *Thanks for the lift.* PAUL: *Anytime. Think nothing of it.* □ TOM: *You've been a real friend, Sally. I can't thank you enough.* SALLY: *Anytime.*

Any work going? *interrog.* "Is there any work available?" □ *Have you got any work going?* □ *Is there any work going?*

ape *n.* a hoodlum or strong-arm man, especially if big and strong. (Underworld.) □ *Tell your ape to let me go!* □ *You take your apes and get out of here!*

ape hangers *n.* long steering handles on a bicycle or motorcycle. □ *Who is that guy riding the bike with ape hangers?* □ *Aren't ape hangers sort of dangerous?*

app *n.* a computer software application. (Computer jargon.) □ *Ted bought a new app for word processing and he says it's great.* □ *Ted's killer app can run circles around your old WordSun program.*

apple core *n.* twenty Pounds Sterling. (Rhyming slang, linked as follows: apple core ≈ [score] = twenty pounds.) □ *That'll cost you an apple core, mate.* □ *I'm not handing over apple core for that thing!*

apple fritter *n.* bitter beer. (Rhyming slang. This is the most common draught beer sold in English pubs, usually served at room temperature.) □ *A pint of your apple fritter, bartender!* □ *Fancy an apple fritter, mate?*

apple-pie bed *n.* a bed with sheets folded short, so that one cannot get into it. □ *Children love surprising each other with apple-pie beds.* □ *An apple-pie bed is a common practical joke.*

apple-pie order *mod.* perfect condition. □ *There! In apple-pie order!* □ *I want this room in apple-pie order.*

apple-polisher *n.* a flatterer. □ *Doesn't that wimpy apple-polisher know how* stupid he looks? □ Everybody at work seems to be an apple-polisher but me.

apples 1. *n.* the testicles. (Taboo. Normally with *the* and in the plural.) □ He turned sideways to protect his apples. □ Thud, right in the apples. Ye gods, it hurt! **2.** *n.* the female breasts. (Taboo. Normally with *the* and in the plural.) □ My apples aren't all I might have wished for. □ There she was, bold as brass, with her apples on full display.

apples and pears *n.* stairs. (Rhyming slang.) □ She stood at the top of the apples and pears, shouting at him. □ Right, you two! Up the apples and pears and straight to bed!

apples and rice *mod.* nice. (Rhyming slang. Used ironically.) □ Oh that's apples and rice, I must say! □ Very apples and rice, I don't think. Get lost!

April showers *n.* flowers. (Rhyming slang.) □ Harry brought me a bunch of April showers! □ He's got that stall selling April showers outside the tube station, right?

Are we away? *interrog.* "Shall we go?"; "Let's go." (Really a command to depart expressed as a question.) □ Well, it's late. Are we away? □ The car's warmed up. Are we away?

Argie *n.* an Argentinean. □ Norah's married to an Argie. □ We met two Argies down the pub last night.

argy-bargy 1. *n.* an argument. □ I've just had a big argy-bargy with Sandra. □ No more argy-bargies, you two! **2.** *vb.* to argue. □ If you want to argy-bargy, go somewhere else. □ Stop argy-bargying now!

arm and a leg *n.* a large amount of money. □ That'll cost me an arm and a leg. □ A million Pounds! Now that's what I'd call an arm and a leg!

arm-twister *n.* someone who uses strong persuasion. □ I hate to seem like an arm-twister, but I really need your help on this project. □ My aunt works as an arm-twister collecting overdue bills for the telephone company.

arm-twisting *n.* powerful persuasion. □ The boss is very good at arm-twisting. □ If nice talk won't work, try a little arm-twisting.

army and navy *n.* gravy. (Rhyming slang.) □ Bert likes his army and navy. □ Why do they always drown my food in army and navy?

army rocks See ALMOND (ROCKS).

(a)round the bend AND **round the twist** *mod.* crazy; beyond sanity. (Compare with DRIVE SOMEONE AROUND THE BEND.) □ I think I'm going around the bend. □ She sounds like she's round the twist already.

arrow *n.* a throwing dart in the game of darts. □ It's my turn to throw. Where are my arrows? □ He threw each arrow perfectly.

'Arry Stottle See HARRY.

arse 1. *n.* the anus; the buttocks. (Taboo. A highly offensive word to most people. There are many additional meanings and constructions using this word. It is in fact Standard English, but virtually all applications of it are not.) □ Get off your arse and on with your work! □ Still, it was funny when she slipped in the mud and landed on her arse. **2.** *n.* a despicable or objectionable person. (Taboo.) □ Get out of here, you arse! □ What an arse that woman is.

arse about AND **arse around** *vb. phr.* to behave in a foolish fashion. (Taboo.) □ Quit arsing about and get on with your work. □ These two are always arsing around.

arse about face *mod.* facing in the wrong direction. (Taboo.) □ OK men, let's turn about as we are all arse about face once again. □ This is all arse about face, and we'll have to do it again.

arse around See ARSE ABOUT.

arse-bandit AND **chocolate-bandit; trouser-bandit** *n.* a male homosexual. (Taboo.) □ I hear that you-know-who is an arse-bandit. □ So what if he's an trouser-bandit? He can still vote, can't he?

arse-end 1. *n.* the rear portion of some object. (Taboo.) □ The arse-end of the bus was blocking my driveway. □ What have you done to my house's arse-end, you little idiot? **2.** *n.* the final portion of some process. (Taboo.) □ We're down to the arse-end now, boss! □ Get over there and make sure they don't screw up right at the arse-end.

arsehole 1. *n.* the anus. (Taboo.) □ Someone kicked him on the arsehole. □ With luck, his arsehole will hurt for a long time, that creep! **2.** *n.* an odious individual. (Taboo.) □ I don't care if that arsehole is the Pope in person. Get him out of here! □ You really can be a total arsehole at times, Rodney! **3.** *vb.* to fawn; to obsequiously flatter. (Taboo.) □ Stop arseholing and get on with what you're paid to do. □ He always arseholes like that if he thinks he may get a fat tip.

arse-licker *n.* an exceptionally obsequious or toadying person. (Taboo.) □ What an arse-licker you are! □ Just get out of my sight, you arse-licker!

arse over elbow AND **arse over tits** *mod.* head over heels. (Taboo.) □ I fell arse over elbow on the steps. □ Take care not to go arse over tits here, Walter.

arse over tits See ARSE OVER ELBOW.

arse up AND **cock up; screw up; fuck up** *vb. phr.* to ruin something; to bungle something. (Taboo.) □ I hope I don't arse up things this time. □ I really fucked-up before.

arse-up AND **cock-up; fuck-up; piss-up; screw-up** *n.* a mess; a blunder; an error; utter confusion. (Taboo.) □ This dish is the chef's arse-up, not mine. □ Well, you certainly managed to create a screw-up there!

Artful Dodger *n.* a lodger. (Rhyming slang. The Artful Dodger was a character in Dickens's novel *Oliver Twist*.) □ So what's the missus up to with the Artful Dodger? □ If that Artful Dodger shows his face here again he won't have any face for long, I promise!

artic *n.* an articulated lorry. □ There's an artic parked outside our front door. □ That's Maggie's new boyfriend's artic.

article *n.* a contemptible person. □ You little article! □ Get that article out of here!

arty-crafty AND **arty-farty** *mod.* pretentiously artistic. (Taboo.) □ I don't like

this arty-crafty stuff. □ It may be arty-farty to you, but he's just sold it for a million pounds.

arty-farty See ARTY-CRAFTY.

ASAP AND **A.S.A.P.** *mod.* as soon as possible. □ Harry, I need that report ASAP! □ I'll be with you A.S.A.P.

(as) daft as a brush *mod.* completely crazy. □ Tom is as daft as a brush, but fun. □ They're all as daft as a brush in there.

(as) dry as dust *mod.* exceptionally dull, boring and uninteresting. (See also DRY-AS-DUST.) □ The whole series of lectures really were as dry as dust. □ Why do you have to make an interesting topic as dry as dust?

(as) dull as dishwater *mod.* very dull. □ She's pretty, but dull as dishwater. □ Life can be as dull as dishwater.

as ever was *mod.* unchanged. □ Some things remain as ever was. □ There! As ever was, despite all your worries.

as it goes *phr.* "as it happens." □ I'm a dentist, as it goes. What's it to you? □ As it goes, I'm going to Manchester tomorrow.

ask for it See ASK FOR TROUBLE.

ask for trouble AND **ask for it** *vb. phr.* to encourage trouble; to bring on trouble. □ I don't want to ask for trouble. I have enough already. □ Saying something like that is just asking for it.

as long as one's arm *mod.* very long. □ Bruno? He's got a criminal record as long as your arm. □ The fish that got away was as long as my arm.

(as) near as dammit *mod.* very close indeed; very nearly; almost. (Crude.) □ Come on! We're as near as dammit, just another inch or so! □ We're not going to give up when we're as near as dammit to agreement, are we?

(as) nutty as a fruitcake *mod.* very silly or stupid. □ The whole idea is as nutty as a fruitcake. □ Tom is as nutty as a fruitcake. They will put him in a nuttery one fine day.

as one lives and breathes *mod.* with absolute certainty. □ As one lives and breathes, you never ever went to Alaska, did you? □ Well as I live and breathe, it's Harry Smith!

as per usual *phr.* "as usual." □ *As per usual, Mike's late.* □ *And Richard has no money, as per usual.*

as quick as dammit AND **soon as dammit** *mod.* as soon as possible; very rapidly. (Crude.) □ *I need you here as quick as dammit.* □ *When? As soon as dammit, that's when!*

as rare as hen's teeth See AS SCARCE AS HEN'S TEETH.

as safe as houses *mod.* as safe as can be. □ *Don't worry, you'll be as safe as houses here.* □ *Well, I don't feel as safe as houses.*

as scarce as hen's teeth AND **as rare as hen's teeth** *mod.* exceptionally rare; non-existent. □ *Jobs are as scarce as hen's teeth these days.* □ *Qualified people are as rare as hen's teeth nowadays.*

(as) sick as a parrot **1.** *mod.* spectacularly nauseous. (See (AS) THICK AS A PARROT.) □ *Oh lord, I'm sick as a parrot!* □ *He really was sick as a parrot after that curry.* **2.** *mod.* exceptionally dissatisfied. □ *Unhappy? I was as sick as a parrot!* □ *That decision of yours made me sick as a parrot.*

assist the police with their enquiries *vb. phr.* to be questioned by the police. (A common euphemism employed in official statements.) □ *A man is assisting the police with their enquiries into the theft.* □ *Assisting the police with their enquiries, eh? Sounds bad for him.*

as sure as death See AS SURE AS GOD MADE LITTLE GREEN APPLES.

as sure as eggs is eggs See AS SURE AS GOD MADE LITTLE GREEN APPLES.

as sure as fate See AS SURE AS GOD MADE LITTLE GREEN APPLES.

as sure as God made little green apples AND **as sure as death; as sure as eggs is eggs; as sure as fate; as sure as hell; as sure as I'm standing here; as sure as you live** *mod.* absolutely certain. (HELL is crude.) □ *I'm as sure as God made little green apples that he's the one.* □ *You as sure as hell better get yourself over here really fast.*

as sure as hell See AS SURE AS GOD MADE LITTLE GREEN APPLES.

as sure as I'm standing here See AS SURE AS GOD MADE LITTLE GREEN APPLES.

as sure as you live See AS SURE AS GOD MADE LITTLE GREEN APPLES.

(as) thick as a parrot *mod.* spectacularly stupid. (This is a pun on AS SICK AS A PARROT.) □ *It was unbelievable; he really is as thick as a parrot.* □ *Are you really thick as a parrot or is it all just a very clever act?*

as thick as a short plank AND **as thick as two short planks** *mod.* exceptionally dim-witted; highly obtuse. □ *Dumb? As thick as a short plank, more like.* □ *Oh, I'd not say she was stupid. As thick as two short planks, yes, but stupid? Never!*

as thick as two short planks See AS THICK AS A SHORT PLANK.

astronomical **1.** *mod.* extremely expensive; descriptive of any very large number. □ *The prices here are astronomical!* □ *The market indexes have all reached astronomical heights for the second time.* **2.** *mod.* vastly huge. (Especially of numbers or money.) □ *What an astronomical price!* □ *There's an astronomical pile of mail waiting for you.*

(as) ugly as sin *mod.* very ugly. □ *This car's as ugly as sin, but it's cheap and dependable.* □ *My old dog may be as ugly as sin but he's completely faithful, too.*

at a good bat *mod.* at a high speed. □ *The car was moving at a good bat.* □ *"Yes," said the policeman, "it was going at a good bat. Too good."*

at a loose end *mod.* nervous and anxious; bored with nothing to do. □ *Tom usually plays at solving puzzles whenever he's at a loose end.* □ *I'm at a loose end at weekends.*

at a pinch *mod.* if absolutely necessary. □ *I suppose that's possible at a pinch.* □ *At a pinch we could do that.*

at a snail's pace *mod.* very slowly. □ *Things are moving along at a snail's pace here, but we'll finish on time—have no fear.* □ *Poor old Willy is creeping along at a snail's pace because his car has a flat tyre.*

at full stretch **1.** *mod.* at full capacity. □ *The network is now operating at full stretch.* □ *But we're already working at* *full stretch, boss!* **2.** *mod.* at the maximum extent possible. □ *We were working at full stretch.* □ *By working at full stretch, we'll get it done.*

Athens of the North *n.* Edinburgh. (Normally with *the*. Compare with AULD REEKIE and MODERN ATHENS.) □ *Why do they call Edinburgh "the Athens of the North?"* □ *I think "Auld Reekie" is a better name for Edinburgh than "the Athens of the North."*

at it *mod.* indulging in sexual intercourse. (Crude.) □ *Charles and Mary are upstairs at it, since you ask.* □ *They are always at it!*

Attaboy! See THAT'S MY BOY!

at the crease AND **at the wicket** *mod.* batting. (Cricket.) □ *It's my turn at the crease.* □ *I love my time at the wicket.*

at the minute *mod.* right now, at this instant. (Irish usage.) □ *Just at the minute, I'm not quite ready.* □ *Come on! Right now, at the minute!*

at the races *mod.* streetwalking as a prostitute. (Crude.) □ *There are a lot of girls at the races in this part of town.* □ *The rozzers hauled her in because she looked as if she was at the races.*

at the wicket See AT THE CREASE.

attract *vb.* to steal. □ *Otto tends to attract car stereos and things like that.* □ *Watch out, he'll attract anything not nailed down.*

Auld Reekie *n.* Edinburgh. (Literally, this means "Old Smokey." Compare with ATHENS OF THE NORTH and MODERN ATHENS.) □ *I think "Auld Reekie" is a better name for Edinburgh than "the Athens of the North."* □ *Why do they call Edinburgh "Auld Reekie?"*

Aunt Nelly *n.* the stomach. (Rhyming slang, linked as follows: Aunty Nelly ≈ [belly] = stomach.) □ *Fred's at home today with a bad pain in his Aunt Nelly.* □ *I think large Aunt Nellies are most unsightly.*

Aunt Sally *n.* someone who is subject to unreasonable or persistent attack. □ *Why are they making an Aunt Sally of him?* □ *He's not an Aunt Sally! He's just plain wrong!*

aunty *n.* an elderly passive male homosexual. (Crude.) □ *She came to the dance with a real aunty.* □ *Tom is getting to be such an aunty.*

Aunt(y) Beeb AND **Beeb** *n.* the BBC (Normally with *the*.) □ *Aunty Beeb won't ever show that.* □ *The Beeb showed it last night.*

aurora metropolis *n.* night-time light pollution due to street lighting, etc., from urban areas. (Pseudo-Latin.) □ *You can see the aurora metropolis of a large city from dozens of miles away.* □ *The aurora metropolis filled the whole of the southern horizon.*

Aussie AND **Ozzie** *n.* an Australian. (Offensive.) □ *There's nothing but Aussies in that pub.* □ *What's wrong with an Ozzie?*

Awa' tae fuck! *exclam.* "Go away!"; "Leave me!" (Taboo. Scots usage.) □ *That's it! Awa' tae fuck!* □ *Awa' tae fuck, you creep!*

away *mod.* in prison. (Underworld.) □ *My cousin is away for a year.* □ *The judge wanted to put him away for two years, but decided on one instead.*

Away an bile yer heid! AND **Away an take a running jump at yersel!; Away an raffle yer doughnut!** *exclam.* "Get lost!"; "Don't bother me!" (Scots usage.) □ *I've had enough of yer nonsense; away an bile yer heid!* □ *Away an raffle yer doughnut! I've better things to do.*

Away an raffle yer doughnut! See AWAY AN BILE YER HEID!

Away an take a running jump at yersel! See AWAY AN BILE YER HEID!

away fixture *n.* an away game or match. (Sports.) □ *The next away fixture is in Manchester.* □ *I'm going to Manchester for the away fixture.*

away team *n.* a visiting team. (Sports.) □ *The away team are from Bristol.* □ *We beat the away team 4 to 1.*

awkward customer *n.* a difficult person to deal with. □ *Here comes another awkward customer.* □ *How can you tell the awkward customers from the rest?*

awkward squad 1. *n.* a group of raw recruits. (Military.) □ *Right, you awkward squad. We're going to turn you into soldiers!* □ *Would you believe that that was the awkward squad just a few* *weeks ago?* **2.** *n.* any group not pre-pared to go along with accepted ways. □ *This lot are another awkward squad.* □ *The awkward squad have gone on strike again.*

axe 1. *n.* an economy drive. (Always with *the.*) □ *The coffee machine went in the last axe.* □ *They're going to have another axe soon.* **2.** *n.* a job dismissal; the sack. (Always with *the.*) □ *I've been given the axe.* □ *If you get the axe, phone this number.*

B

B.A. See SWEET FANNY ADAMS.

baby 1. *n.* a project thought of as an off-spring. (Always with a possessor.) □ *Whose baby is the Johnson account?* □ *You give the report. This project is your baby.* **2.** *n.* a lover; one's sweetheart. (Also a term of address.) □ *Come over here and kiss me, baby.* □ *Look, baby, I think we can work this out.*

baby blues *n.* postnatal depression. □ *After the birth, she got the baby blues.* □ *Baby blues sounds like a joke, but it can be serious.*

Babylon 1. *n.* the establishment; the government. (In the view of journalism/media people. Always with *the*.) □ *I hate the present-day Babylon.* □ *When the Babylon changes, nothing changes here.* **2.** *n.* the police. (In the view of black Cockneys. Always with *the*.) □ *Get away, get away! The Babylon are outside!* □ *Hey man, the Babylon pick on us just because of our colour.*

baby's head *n.* steak and kidney pudding. (From its appearance.) □ *Fancy some baby's head?* □ *Baby's head is always my favourite dish!*

baby's pram *n.* jam. (Rhyming slang.) □ *Pass me the baby's pram, please mum.* □ *Jane makes her own baby's pram, you know.*

baccy *n.* tobacco. □ *Got any baccy?* □ *Here's some baccy.*

back *n.* a toilet. □ *Where's the back?* □ *The back? Oh, it's along that passageway.*

backbone *n.* courage; integrity. □ *If you had any backbone, you would be able to deal with this.* □ *She lacks backbone, that's all.*

backchat *n.* an ill-considered or rude reply or replies. □ *Now that's what I call backchat!* □ *Less of your backchat!*

backdoor man 1. *n.* a male adulterer. (Taboo.) □ *His wife found out he was a backdoor man and divorced him.* □ *Backdoor men have more fun...until they are caught.* **2.** *n.* a male homosexual. (Taboo.) □ *Tell that backdoor man to get out of here.* □ *He doesn't like being called a backdoor man.*

backer *n.* a supporter; a financier of a play, political campaign, etc. □ *I had a lot of generous backers for the play.* □ *I was hoping for a backer, but the project was too chancy.*

backfire *vb.* to release intestinal gas anally; to cause a noise or smell associated with this. (Crude.) □ *Whew! Somebody backfired!* □ *It was noisy when Dave backfired, so no one heard.*

backfire (on someone) *vb. (phr.)* to rebound or to work in reverse. (Used to describe a scheme or plan that has an opposite effect to the one intended.) □ *I hope this plan doesn't backfire on me.* □ *Her attempt to frame Bill for the crime backfired.*

backhanded compliment *n.* an unintended or ambiguous compliment. □ *Backhanded compliments are the only kind he ever gives!* □ *And I think his backhanded compliments are all given by accident, too!*

backhander *n.* a clandestine, improper or secret payment such as a bribe or informal gratuity. □ *Imagine! She offered me a backhander to give her company the contract!* □ *So, just how big a backhander did you get from her?*

back in action *mod.* healthy and getting around once more. □ *Once I got well, I was back in action again immediately.* □ *When will she be back in action again?*

backlash *n.* a negative reaction or response. □ *Was there any backlash to your suggestion?* □ *We weren't prepared for the backlash we got.*

back of beyond *n.* the middle of nowhere. □ *Out of the way? It's the back of beyond!* □ *Well, maybe it is back of beyond, but at least you'll not have to be polite to the neighbours.*

back-pedal AND **back-track** *vb.* to retract from a previously held position. □ *He's going to have to back-pedal on this.* □ *Now he is back-tracking as hard as he can.*

backroom boys 1. *n.* the hidden experts (originally and typically scientists and engineers but by extension, now any kind of specialists) who arrange things, devise new equipment or make malfunctioning systems work. □ *I see the backroom boys have come up with a great new computer* □ *Leave it to the backroom boys; they'll figure out the answer.* **2.** See also BOYS IN THE BACKROOM.

backseat driver *n.* an annoying passenger who tells the driver how to drive; someone who tells others how to do things. □ *I don't need any backseat driver on this project.* □ *Stop being a backseat driver!*

backside *n.* the buttocks; one's rear. □ *She fell right on her backside.* □ *There is some mustard or something on your backside.*

backslapper *n.* someone who is excessively friendly and outgoing. □ *At election time, county hall is filled with backslappers and baby-kissers.* □ *This backslapper of a used car salesman comes up to me and tells me he's got something that will last me a lifetime.*

back to square one *phr.* "back to the beginning." (Often with *go*.) □ *Well, it looks like it's back to square one.* □ *We've got to get this done without going back to square one.*

back to the salt mines *phr.* "back to the workplace." □ *Well, it's Monday morning. Back to the salt mines.* □ *Break's over! Back to the salt mines, everybody.*

back-track See BACK-PEDAL.

backward about coming forward *mod.* shy. □ *Is he not rather backward about coming forward?* □ *Backward about coming forward? No, not Otto!*

backward thought *n.* reconsideration; a second thought. □ *I've just had a backward thought.* □ *What is your backward thought, Alan?*

bad *mod.* suitable; excellent; good. (Black.) □ *I got some new silks that are really bad.* □ *Look at those really bad shoes on that guy.*

Bad cess to you! *exclam.* "Here's wishing you bad luck." (Irish usage.) □ *Bad cess to you, you arrogant and incompetent clown!* □ *If that's what you think, then bad cess to you, too!*

baddy AND **baddie** a bad person; a criminal. □ *You can always tell who is the baddy in cowboy films; he wears a black hat.* □ *Mary has become such a baddie that no one speaks to her anymore.*

bad egg *n.* a repellent person. □ *You're not such a bad egg after all.* □ *She's a real bad egg.*

bad fist *n.* a bad job. □ *I don't want to make a bad fist of this.* □ *You'll not make a bad fist!*

bad form *n.* improper or impolite behaviour. □ *Placing your feet on the boss's desk would definitely be considered bad form.* □ *Bad form is a bad idea around here.*

bad job *n.* a bad state of affairs or outcome. □ *No, that's too much of a bad job! Do it again.* □ *Oh, what a bad job.*

bad-mouth *vb.* to speak ill of someone or something. □ *I wish you would stop bad-mouthing my car.* □ *Harry bad-mouths everything he doesn't understand.*

bad news *mod.* [of a person] unpleasant; unfortunate. □ *That poor guy is really bad news.* □ *It's bad news Freddy on the phone again.*

bad patch *n.* a difficult period. □ *I was sorry to hear of your bad patch.* □ *Are you over your bad patch yet?*

bad penny *n.* something or someone undesirable that keeps reappearing or cannot be got rid of. □ *Like a bad penny, it keeps turning up.* □ *Go away! Why do you want to be like a bad penny?*

bad show 1. *n.* a misfortune. □ *Oh, what a bad show.* □ *Bad show! Better luck next time!* **2.** *n.* something done or presented badly. □ *That was a bad show; we must do better next time.* □ *Another bad show like that and there won't be another time.*

bad trip *n.* a bad experience with a drug. □ *My first experience was a bad trip, and I never took another.* □ *The guide is supposed to talk you down from a bad trip.*

baffle someone with bullshit *vb. phr.* to confuse or impress someone with a lengthy, confusing, complex, but ultimately meaningless or spurious explanation. (Taboo. Compare with BLIND WITH SCIENCE.) □ *If things look bad, baffle them with bullshit. It never fails.* □ *Look, instead of trying to baffle us with bullshit, why not just explain in a few words what really happened?*

bag 1. *vb.* to capture and arrest someone. (Underworld.) □ *They bagged the thief with the loot still on him.* □ *We'll be able to bag the alleged killer when we have more evidence.* (See BAGGED.) **2.** *n.* an ugly woman. (Derogatory.) □ *Tell the old bag to mind her own business.* □ *She has turned into an absolute bag.* **3.** *vb.* to obtain something. □ *I'll try to bag a couple of tickets for you.* □ *See if you can bag one of the red ones.* **4.** *vb.* to claim ownership. (Childish.) □ *Bags the big one!* □ *I've already bagged the big one.* **5.** *vb.* to claim the right to be first. (Childish.) □ *Bags, I go first!* □ *Stop bagging first place all the time, Johnny.*

bagged *mod.* arrested. □ *"You are bagged," said the officer, clapping a hand on the suspect's shoulder.* □ *"I'm not bagged yet, copper!" shouted the crook.*

bagman *n.* a tramp. □ *Two old bagmen wandered slowly down the lane.* □ *The bagman asked politely for some work to do in return for food.*

bag of bones *n.* an extremely skinny person or animal. □ *I'm just turning* into a bag of bones. □ *Get that old bag of bones off the racetrack!*

bag of wind See WINDBAG.

bags *n.* a large quantity. □ *There's plenty! Bags!* □ *We need bags of the stuff.*

bail out *vb. phr.* to resign or leave; to get free of someone or something. □ *I can't take any more. I'm going to bail out.* □ *Albert bailed out just before he got fired.*

bait AND **bate** *n.* anger, fury or bad temper. □ *Watch her foul bait today.* □ *Bait? Who says I've got a bait? I'll flay them alive!*

baked *mod.* sunburned. □ *I was out in the sun so long I got baked.* □ *If you would use some lotion, you wouldn't get so baked.*

baked bean *n.* the Queen; any queen. (Rhyming slang.) □ *Sally likes to watch the baked bean on the telly.* □ *Which particular baked bean are you talking about?*

Baker day *n.* an in-service training day for teachers. (After Kenneth Baker, Secretary of State for Education at the time these were established.) □ *He's not here today, it's a Baker day.* □ *How many Baker days are there each year?*

baldy AND **baldie 1.** *n.* a bald person. □ *There's a baldy coming up to the front door.* □ *That baldie is your Uncle Jim.* **2.** *n.* a bald-headed man. □ *I'm getting to be an old baldie.* □ *I turned into a baldy in my twenties.*

ball *n.* a wild time at a party; a good time. (Compare with HAVE A BALL.) □ *We really had a ball last night.* □ *Your birthday party was a ball!*

ball and bat AND **this and that** *n.* a hat. (Rhyming slang.) □ *Why are you wearing that ridiculous ball and bat?* □ *I'm going to buy myself a new this and that.*

ball and chain *n.* a wife. (Mostly jocular.) □ *I've got to get home to my ball and chain.* □ *My ball and chain is angry with me.*

ball is in someone's court *phr.* to be someone else's move, play or turn. (Always with *the.*) □ *The ball's in your court now. You do something.* □ *I can't do anything so long as the ball remains in John's court.*

ball o' chalk See PENN'ORTH (OF CHALK).

ballocks AND **bollocks** 1. *n*. the testicles. (Taboo. Normally with *the* and in the plural.) □ *He turned sideways to protect his ballocks.* □ *Thud, right in the bollocks. Ye gods, it hurt!* 2. *exclam.* "Nonsense!"; "This is untrue!" (Taboo.) □ *That is just ballocks!* □ *Bollocks! You're quite wrong about that.*

ball of chalk See PENN'ORTH (OF CHALK).

balloon *n*. a braggart, blowhard or pretentious person. (Scots usage.) □ *He's just a balloon; ignore what he says.* □ *Who does this old balloon think he is?*

balloon car *n*. a saloon bar. (Rhyming slang.) □ *The balloon car's the more expensive area of a traditional pub.* □ *Originally, women were allowed into the balloon car only.*

balls 1. *n*. the testicles. (Taboo. Normally with *the* and in the plural.) □ *He got hit right in the balls.* □ *The teacher preferred "testicles" to "balls," if they had to be mentioned at all.* 2. *n*. nonsense. (Taboo.) □ *That is just balls.* □ *You say it's balls, but how do you know?* 3. *n*. courage. (Taboo. Originally applied to males only but now, occasionally and raffishly, to women, too.) □ *Well, he's got balls; I'll say that.* □ *She's got balls too, if you see what I mean.*

ballsed up *mod*. confused; mixed up. (This is hyphenated before a nominal. Compare with BALLS-UP.) □ *That bitch is so ballsed up she doesn't know anything.* □ *This is really a ballsed-up mess you've made.*

balls-up See ARSE-UP.

bally *mod*. BLOODY. (Crude. A euphemism for or variation on BLOODY.) □ *Get your bally car out of my way!* □ *That was bally stupid!*

baloney AND **boloney** *n*. nonsense. (Also as an exclamation.) □ *Don't give me all that baloney!* □ *That's just a lot of boloney. Don't believe it for a minute.* □ *Baloney! You're crazy!*

bamboozle *vb*. to deceive someone; to confuse someone. (See BAMBOOZLED.) □ *Don't try to bamboozle me! I know*

what I want! □ *The crooks bamboozled the old man out of his life savings.*

bamboozled *mod*. deceived; confused. □ *This stuff certainly has me bamboozled.* □ *I don't know who's more bamboozled, you or me.*

bampot *n*. a foolish or crazy person. (Scots usage.) □ *Ye bampot! You've buttered the tablecloth!* □ *Look, ye big bampot, I've had just about enough of yer blethering. (Look you big fool, I've had just about enough of your silly talk.)*

banana 1. *n*. a fool. □ *Tell that banana in the front row to shut up.* □ *What banana put this thing on upside down?* 2. AND **tummy banana** *n*. the male sexual organ. (Taboo. Childish.) □ *Johnny! Put your banana away!* □ *The naked infant ran through the room, tummy banana wobbling up and down.*

bananas crazy. (See also GO BANANAS.) □ *You are driving me bananas!* □ *You were bananas before I ever showed up on the scene.*

band in the box *n*. venereal disease. (Rhyming slang, linked as follows: band in the box ≈ [pox] = venereal disease.) □ *All right, it's true, I've got the band in the box.* □ *Getting the band in the box tends to restrict your love life, you know.*

B and T AND **bum and tit** *n*. hetrosexual activity in general, from a male perspective. (Taboo.) □ *I really could use some B and T tonight.* □ *If you're looking for bum and tit, try that pub there.*

bang 1. *n*. the degree of potency of the alcohol in liquor. □ *This stuff has quite a bang!* □ *The bang is gone from this wine.* 2. *n*. an injection of a drug; any dose of a drug. □ *I need a bang pretty fast.* □ *If Max doesn't have a bang by noon, he gets desperate.* 3. *vb*. to inject a drug. □ *They were in the back room banging away.* □ *She banged herself and went on with her work.* 4. *n*. a drug RUSH. □ *One snort and the bang will knock you over.* □ *There was one sudden bang and then nothing.* 5. *vb*. to perform sexual intercourse. (Crude.) □ *One look and he knew she had already been banged that evening.* □ *There are* *some teenagers in the back room, banging.* **6.** *n.* an act of sexual intercourse. (Crude.) □ *I think really, she's gasping for a bang, you know.* □ *A good bang would probably do her the power of good, in fact.*

banger 1. *n.* a noisy old car. □ *Where did you get that old banger?* □ *What do you mean, a banger? This is a genuine vintage car.* **2.** *n.* a sausage. □ *Have you got any bangers?* □ *Mike always likes a banger or two at breakfast.* **3.** *n.* a firecracker or other noisy fireworks. □ *On Guy Fawkes Night there'll be lots of bangers going off.* □ *My dog gets frightened by the noise of bangers.*

bangers and mash *n.* a dish of sausages and mashed potatoes. □ *A serving of bangers and mash over here, please!* □ *Bangers and mash are always acceptable.*

bangles 1. *n.* the female breasts. (Crude. Normally with *the* and in the plural.) □ *My bangles aren't all I might have wished for.* □ *With bangles like that, she can go anywhere she likes.* **2.** *n.* the testicles. (Taboo. Normally with *the* and in the plural.) □ *The teacher preferred "testicles" to "bangles," if they had to be mentioned at all.* □ *He got hit right in the bangles.*

bang like a shit-house door *vb. phr.* [for a woman] to enthusiastically indulge in sexual intercourse. (Taboo.) □ *Keen? She bangs like a shit-house door.* □ *There she was, banging away like a shit-house door.*

bang off *mod.* immediately; without delay; right now. □ *I'll be there bang off.* □ *Hurry! I need this bang off.*

bang on 1. *vb. phr.* to harangue, nag or remonstrate with someone in an especially lengthy manner. □ *Why are you always banging on?* □ *Because banging on is the only way to get you to do anything.* **2.** AND **smack on** *mod.* exactly correct; right on the target. □ *Bang on! That's it, exactly.* □ *I'll try to get it smack on the next time, too.*

bang someone up *vb. phr.* to lock away, especially in jail. □ *Otto's been banged up for two years.* □ *They banged Otto up for about twenty years.*

bang the drum for someone or something AND **beat the drum for someone or something** *vb. phr.* to promote or support someone or something. □ *I spent a lot of time banging the drum for you, you know.* □ *That politician is only here to beat the drum for his special interests.*

bang to rights AND **dead to rights** *mod.* caught in the middle of a criminal act. □ *We caught her bang to rights with the loot still on her.* □ *There he was, dead to rights with the gun still smoking.*

banjaxed 1. *mod.* demolished; ruined. (Irish usage.) □ *My car is totally banjaxed. What a mess!* □ *Everything I worked for is now banjaxed.* **2.** *mod.* utterly defeated; totally unable to continue. (Irish usage.) □ *Well, I can do no more. I'm banjaxed.* □ *The rest of us are all banjaxed too.* **3.** *mod.* amazed; startled; disbelieving. (Irish usage.) □ *No! I'm banjaxed! That's amazing!* □ *We were all banjaxed by the news.* **4.** *mod.* intoxicated due to drink or drugs. (Irish usage.) □ *Joe and Arthur kept on knocking them back till they were both banjaxed.* □ *She's sort of banjaxed right now.*

banjo 1. *n.* a sandwich, especially a very large one. (Originally military.) □ *A round of banjos here, please!* □ *I don't know how he can put away so many of these banjos.* **2.** *n.* any food obtained by pilfering. (Originally military.) □ *Where did you get that banjo?* □ *He had a huge stash of banjo he was selling to the locals.*

banjoed *mod.* completely intoxicated due to drink or drugs. □ *She just sat there and got banjoed.* □ *All four of them went out and got themselves comprehensively banjoed.*

banker 1. *n.* a route regularly requested by taxi-driver's clients. □ *A couple more bankers and I'm finished for the day.* □ *Heathrow to the City is a typical banker.* **2.** *n.* a business transaction that is reliably profitable. □ *Every one of these sales is a banker.* □ *Bankers may be boring, but they'll make you rich.*

banker's hours *n.* short working hours. □ *When did you start keeping banker's* *hours?* □ *There aren't many bankers who keep banker's hours these days.*

barb *n.* a barbiturate; a barbiturate capsule. □ *Old Joey is hooked on barbs.* □ *Have you got a barb I can use?*

Barbie doll *n.* a pretty, giddy girl or woman. □ *She's just a Barbie doll.* □ *Ask that little Barbie doll if she wants a drink.*

barclay *vb.* to masturbate. (Rhyming slang, linked as follows: Barclay[s Bank] ≈ [wank] = masturbate. Barclays Bank is a major British retail bank.) □ *If he gets frustrated enough, he barclays.* □ *Timmy's mother caught him barclaying in the garden shed.*

bareback riding AND **rough riding** *n.* sexual intercourse without a condom. (Taboo.) □ *Bareback riding is a good way to get AIDS, of course.* □ *Do you do rough riding, love?*

barf *vb.* to empty one's stomach; to vomit. (Crude.) □ *Who barfed on the driveway?* □ *The doctor gave him some stuff that made him barf it up.*

bargaining chip *n.* something to be used in negotiations □ *I want to use this incident as a bargaining chip in future negotiations.* □ *I need a few bargaining chips to use when we get down to drawing up the contract.*

barking (mad) *mod.* completely crazy. □ *You're barking mad!* □ *I think I am going barking.*

barmy *mod.* stupid; crazy. □ *Some barmy fool called to tell us that the sky is falling in.* □ *Why not start a barmy ideas contest?*

Barnaby Rudge *n.* a judge. (Rhyming slang. Barnaby Rudge was a character in Dickens's novel of the same name.) □ *I'll be up before the Barnaby Rudge tomorrow.* □ *That Barnaby Rudge ain't wearing no wig!*

barnet *n.* hair. (Rhyming slang, linked as follows: Barnet [Fair] ≈ hair. Barnet is an district in north London.) □ *Me barnet's a right mess.* □ *There's nuffink wrong with yer barnet, luv.*

barney *n.* a loud argument. □ *We could hear their barney halfway down the street.* □ *Quit that barney!*

barrel (along) *vb. (phr.)* to travel in a dangerous, rapid way, in the manner of

a rolling barrel. □ *Ton-up boys barrel along on motorbikes.* □ *If you must barrel like that you'll get booked.*

barrel of fun *n.* a tremendous amount of fun. □ *Tracy is just a barrel of fun on dates.* □ *We had a barrel of fun at your party.*

bar steward *n.* an odious individual. (Crude. A deliberate spoonerism of "bastard." Compare with PHEASANT PLUCKER.) □ *You really can be a bar steward at times, Rodney!* □ *I don't care if that bar steward is the Pope in person. Get him out of here!*

bash 1. *n.* a wild party; a night on the town. □ *What a bash! I'm exhausted!* □ *There's a big bash over at Willy's place.* **2.** *n.* an attempt. □ *Is that the best bash you could manage?* □ *Although he's been making bashes at it all day long he's no closer to a solution.* **3.** *vb.* to work as a prostitute. (Crude.) □ *If you try to bash around here the cops will pick you up.* □ *A lot of them bash to feed a drug habit.*

bashed *mod.* crushed; struck. □ *His poor car was bashed beyond recognition.* □ *I'll straighten it out if it gets bashed.*

basher *n.* someone regularly engaged in carrying out uninteresting or boring duties. □ *It must be very boring being a basher.* □ *Well, a lot of bashers don't seem to worry about that.*

bashing 1. *n.* criticizing; defaming. (A combining form that follows the name of the person or thing being criticised.) □ *I am sick of your college-bashing!* □ *I hope you'll excuse the broker-bashing, but some of these guys don't play fair.* □ *On T.V. they had a long session of candidate-bashing, and then they read the sports news.* **2.** *n.* prostitution. (Crude.) □ *Bashing is probably the biggest business in this part of town.* □ *Joan almost took up bashing to pay for a habit.*

bash someone's head in AND **do someone's head in** *vb. phr.* to beat someone. □ *Talk nice to him, or he'll bash your head in.* □ *I was afraid that the cop was going to do my head in.*

bash someone up *vb. phr.* to beat someone up; to assault someone. □

They've arrested the yobs who were bashing up people in the streets. □ *Mummy, some big boys bashed me up!*

basinful *n.* a sufficient, or more than sufficient amount of trouble or worries. □ *That's it, I've had a basinful; I'm off.* □ *It won't be long before you've had a basinful of that.*

basket *n.* a BASTARD. (Crude. A euphemism.) □ *Why you dirty little basket! I'll get you!* □ *So I told that basket what he could do with his money...*

basket case 1. *n.* a person who is a nervous wreck. □ *After that meeting, I was practically a basket case.* □ *The waiting was so intense that I was a real basket case.* **2.** *n.* a person who is totally physically disabled. □ *Have you seen Gerry? He looks like a basket case.* □ *He's been no more than a basket case ever since his illness.* **3.** *n.* a venture or project that is damaged beyond hope or recovery. □ *After that crazy decision, the whole project is a basket case.* □ *His business was turned into a basket case when his biggest customer went bust.*

bassalony *n.* a hazelnut. □ *Fancy some bassalonies?* □ *There was a single bassalony on his plate. Just one!*

bastard *n.* a very serious or difficult problem or predicament. (Taboo. Compare with BUGGER.) □ *That's a real bastard. What do we do now?* □ *Let's get this bastard sorted now!*

bat 1. *n.* a step, pace or speed. □ *You'll get the best results if you can maintain a regular, steady bat.* □ *Try to increase your bat a little; we would rather like to get there this year, you know.* **2.** *n.* a price. □ *I'm not paying a bat like that for this.* □ *Come on then, what bat do you really want for it?*

bat and wicket *n.* a ticket. (Rhyming slang.) □ *Well, I've got me bat and wicket and I'm going on holiday tomorrow!* □ *You need a bat and wicket to get on the train, love.*

bat an eyelid *vb. phr.* to show visible emotion. (Always used in a negative context.) □ *When the police told him of the death of his mother, he did not bat an eyelid.* □ *He didn't bat an eyelid again, even when they charged him*

with her murder.

bat around *vb. phr.* to dabble or dawdle to no purpose. □ *If they didn't bat around, they'd get it done with time to spare.* □ *Stop batting around and get on with your work!*

bate See BAIT.

bats AND **batty** crazy. (Compare with HAVE (GOT) BAT'S IN ONE'S BELFRY.) □ *You're bats!* □ *You are driving me batty!*

battered *mod.* intoxicated due to drink or drugs. □ *Boy, I was really battered. I'll never drink another drop.* □ *Those guys really were completely battered at the party.*

battered fish *n.* a fish fried in batter. □ *Harry always appreciated a nice plate of battered fish and some chips.* □ *I think the batter is what makes battered fish so good.*

battle-axe *n.* a belligerent (old) woman. (Derogatory.) □ *Tell the old battle-axe she can go to blazes.* □ *I can handle a battle-axe. Send her on in.*

battle cruiser *n.* a public house or pub. (Rhyming slang, linked as follows: battle cruiser ≈ [boozer] = pub(lic house).) □ *He's down the battle cruiser, as usual.* □ *That's not a bad little battle cruiser you've got there, mate.*

batty See BATS.

bawl someone out *vb. phr.* to harangue, nag or remonstrate with someone in an especially loud manner. □ *Please stop bawling out that poor girl.* □ *Unfortunately, bawling her out seems to be the only way to get her to do anything.*

bazoomas See BAZOOMBAS.

bazoombas AND **bazumbas; bazoomas; bazungas** *n.* the female breasts. (Crude. Normally with *the* and in the plural.) □ *"Nice bazoombas,"* he thought, *as she walked past.* □ *There she was, bold as brass, with her bazungas on full display.*

bazungas See BAZOOMBAS.

BBFN *sent.* "Bye-bye for now." (Computer jargon. Written only. An initialism used in computer communications. Compare with TTFN.) □ *OK, I'll be back later. BBFN.* □ *BBFN. Gotta go.*

be a bit much *vb. phr.* to be more than enough; to be more than good taste allows. □ *That was a bit much, Paul. After all there is such a thing as good taste.* □ *Your birthday card was a bit much, but thank you just the same.*

be a bit off *vb. phr.* to be somewhat unfair or unreasonable. □ *That was really a bit off, you know.* □ *If you're going to be a bit off like that, I'll not be coming back here!*

be a bit slow upstairs See BE A BIT THICK.

be a bit thick 1. *mod.* to be unacceptable or unreasonable. □ *Hey! That's a bit thick! You can't do that!* □ *I thought the explanation was a bit thick, but what could I do?* **2.** AND **be a bit slow upstairs** to be dim-witted or stupid. □ *Harry's a bit slow upstairs, you know.* □ *All of us can seem to be a bit thick at times.*

Be a devil. *sent.* "Take a chance." □ *Go on! Be a devil!* □ *Oh, let's be a devil just for once.*

be a drag (on someone) *phr.* to be a burden (to someone). □ *I wish you wouldn't be such a drag on your friends.* □ *I don't want to be a drag on everybody else.*

beak 1. *n.* a nose. □ *What a beak on that guy!* □ *I want some glasses that sit in just the right place on my wonderful beak.* **2.** *n.* a judge or magistrate. □ *I'll be up before the beak tomorrow.* □ *The beak ain't wearing a wig!* **3.** *n.* a school headmaster. □ *The beak asked the teacher what she thought she was doing.* □ *If you do that again, I'll send you to see the beak!*

bean-counter *n.* a statistician; an accountant. □ *When the bean-counters get finished with the numbers, you won't recognise them.* □ *The bean-counters predict a recession sometime in the next decade.*

beanfeast AND **beano** *n.* a celebration, party or jolly time. □ *What time do we have to be at that beanfeast on Saturday night?* □ *What a fancy beano! They even have glass glasses!*

beano See BEANFEAST.

beanpole *n.* a skinny person. □ *I'm getting to be such a beanpole.* □ *I used to be a beanpole. Look at me now—both of me!*

beardie *n.* a man with a beard. □ *Who was the beardie I saw you with yesterday?* □ *The man who ran away was certainly a beardie.*

beatnik *n.* a member of the Bohemian subculture that flourished in the 1950s. (The *nik* is from Russian via Yiddish. Pronounced BEET-nik.) □ *Those beatniks back in the fifties were something to behold.* □ *So this beatnik comes up to me and mumbles something I can't hear.*

beat someone's brains out *vb. phr.* to beat someone severely. □ *She threatened to beat my brains out.* □ *Those thugs nearly beat his brains out.*

beat the drum for someone or something See BANG THE DRUM FOR SOMEONE OR SOMETHING.

beaut 1. *n.* someone or something excellent, not necessarily beautiful. (Australianism.) □ *Boy, this fishing rod's a beaut!* □ *This is a beaut of a day!* **2.** *n.* a particularly attractive or beautiful woman. (Australianism.) □ *Have you seen Gerry's new girlfriend? She's a beaut!* □ *He told Sarah that he thought her a real beaut, but she continued to ignore him.*

beautiful *mod.* very satisfying; excellent. □ *This wine is really beautiful!* □ *Gosh, this place is beautiful. You get your own sink and toilet right in the room and good strong bars to keep the riffraff out.*

beauty sleep *n.* sleep; the sleep one requires. (Usually mentioned by non-beautiful men as a joke.) □ *You really need some beauty sleep. Take a look at yourself!* □ *I've got to get home and get my beauty sleep.*

beaver away at something *vb. phr.* to work consistently and well. □ *Oh, they're beavering away at that right now.* □ *Keep beavering away at it until we solve it.*

beddy-byes *n.* sleep. (Juvenile.) □ *I need some beddy-byes before I get started again.* □ *I could use beddy-byes before I have to get to work.*

bed of roses *n.* a luxurious situation; an easy life. □ *Who said life would be a bed of roses?* □ *If I had a million quid, now that'd be a bed of roses.*

bedroom eyes AND **come-to-bed eyes**
1. *n.* seductive eyes. □ *Beware of bedroom eyes. They mean trouble.* □ *She
batted those come-to-bed eyes at me,
and I knew I was a goner.* **2.** *n.* an alluring or seductive look or glance, usually from a woman to a man. (See also
COME-HITHER LOOK.) □ *She stared at
him with her bedroom eyes, giving him
that age-old come-on.* □ *Who could resist come-to-bed eyes like these?*

bedsit(ter) *n.* a bed sitting room (US
studio apartment). □ *After they broke
up, he moved into a bedsitter.* □ *I don't
think you'll find living in a bedsit very
glamorous.*

bedworthy *mod.* sexually desirable.
(Taboo.) □ *Harry thinks Susan is very
bedworthy.* □ *Susan does not think
Harry is bedworthy at all.*

bee 1. *n.* a euphemistic abbreviation for
bastard. (Crude.) □ *Get out, you bee!*
□ *Yes, he really is a bee.* **2.** *n.* a euphemistic abbreviation for BUGGER.
(Crude.) □ *Why does that bee always
have to interfere?* □ *That's a bee!*

Beeb See AUNT(Y) BEEB.

Bee Em *n.* a BMW car. □ *Like my new
Bee Em, darling?* □ *I'm rather partial
to Bee Ems.*

beef 1. *vb.* to complain. □ *Stop your
beefing!* □ *What's he beefing about
now?* **2.** *n.* a complaint. □ *This time
I've got a really serious beef.* □ *A serious beef will make a change, sir.*

beef bayonet AND **meat dagger; mutton dagger** *n.* the male sexual organ.
(Taboo.) □ *Myra says beef bayonets are
disgusting but then Myra's strange.* □
*Only small boys wave their mutton dag-
gers about like that, Wayne. Put it
away!*

beef curtains *n.* the female breasts.
(Taboo. Normally with *the* and in the
plural.) □ *All you think about is beef
curtains!* □ *There she was, bold as
brass, with her beef curtains on full display.*

beef something up *vb. phr.* to add
strength or substance to something. □
*Let's beef this up with a little more on
the drums.* □ *They beefed up the offer
with another thousand pounds.*

been had AND **was had 1.** *phr.* [of a
woman] subjected to sexual intercourse. □ *I've been had, and now I'm
going to have a baby.* □ *When she said
she was had, I didn't know it was on her
honeymoon.* **2.** *phr.* been mistreated,
cheated or dealt with badly. (Compare
with TAKEN.) □ *Look at this shirt! I was
had!* □ *I've been had by that lousy gyp
joint.*

**Been there, done that, got the tee-
shirt.** *sent.* "That's an old-fashioned or
outmoded activity, place, object or interest which is no longer of any interest
or use." □ *Climb Mount Everest? Been
there, done that, got the tee-shirt.* □ *So
you work in the insurance business, eh?
Been there, done that, got the tee-shirt.*

beeper *n.* a portable telephone signalling device. □ *I sometimes have
somebody call me during a meeting so
my beeper will go off and get me out of
it.* □ *My beeper went off, and I had to
leave the meeting.*

beer and skittles *n.* something very
easy to do; an easy time of it. □ *Did
you think life was all beer and skittles?*
□ *All you want is beer and skittles.
Don't you know you have to work hard
for what you want?*

beer belly AND **beer gut** *n.* a large
belly. □ *You're going to end up with a
real beer belly hanging over your belt if
you don't let up on that stuff.* □ *Look at
the beer gut on that guy.*

beer from the wood *n.* draught beer
drawn from a wooden cask. □ *I prefer
beer from the wood.* □ *Beer from the
wood has a special flavour.*

beer gut See BEER BELLY.

beer token See DRINKING TOKEN.

beer voucher See DRINKING TOKEN.

bees (and honey) *n.* money. (Rhyming
slang.) □ *Sorry, I can't afford it, I've no
bees and honey.* □ *How much bees do
you need, squire?*

bee's knees *n.* someone or something
that is perfect. □ *That's just the bee's
knees!* □ *It's the bee's knees. I could not
ask for more!*

Beetle *n.* the original Volkswagen car.
□ *We wanted to buy a Beetle, but
decided on another make of car.* □ *I*

remember when people used to put big windup keys on their Beetles to make them look like windup toys.

beetle about *vb. phr.* to scurry around. ☐ *She's always beetling about.* ☐ *Why do you have to beetle about all the time?*

beetle-crusher *n.* a large shoe or boot. ☐ *She pulled on her beetle-crushers and left the room, despondent.* ☐ *These beetle-crushers really do nothing for your appearance, Cynthia.*

beetle off *vb. phr.* to scurry away. ☐ *Sorry, I've got to beetle off now.* ☐ *I beetled off before my presence was noticed.*

beezer *n.* a cheerful person. ☐ *He's a pleasant enough old beezer.* ☐ *The beezer was waiting outside the office.*

be for it *vb. phr.* to be in immediate danger of punishment or other trouble. ☐ *You're for it when they catch you!* ☐ *I'll be for it if I get caught.*

beggar belief *vb. phr.* to strain credulity beyond breaking point; to be unbelievable. ☐ *What you tell me beggars belief!* ☐ *That's fantastic! It beggars belief!*

beggar my neighbour *mod.* unemployed. (Rhyming slang, linked as follows: beggar my neighbour ≈ [labour] = [(no) work] = unemployed.) ☐ *Harry's beggar my neighbour again.* ☐ *That beggar my neighbour guy next door was looking for you.*

behind *n.* the posterior; the buttocks. ☐ *I've got a boil on the behind that's driving me crazy.* ☐ *She needs some jeans that will flatter her behind.* ☐ *With her behind, they'll have to flatten a lot before they do any flattering.*

behind bars *mod.* in jail; in prison. ☐ *You belong behind bars, you creep!* ☐ *I've got something here that will keep you behind bars for years.*

belay *vb. phr.* to cancel. (Nautical.) ☐ *Belay that, Number one!* ☐ *I better belay that order, I suppose.*

belch 1. *n.* a BURP; an upwards release of stomach gas. ☐ *That was the loudest belch I've ever heard.* ☐ *What I really need is a good belch.* **2.** *vb.* to bring up stomach gas. ☐ *They swallow beer by the can and see who can belch the*

loudest. ☐ *I belched, and everybody stared.*

Believe you me! *exclam.* "You should believe me!" ☐ *Believe you me, that was some cake!* ☐ *This is a fine picnic. Believe you me!*

be light (of) something *mod.* lacking something; short of something. ☐ *Yes, he's light of something all right: brains, I think.* ☐ *The balance sheet's light about £100,000.*

bell *n.* a telephone call. ☐ *I'll give you a bell.* ☐ *She's been waiting all day for that bell.*

bells and whistles *n.* unneccessary or fanciful embellishments and decorations; frills. ☐ *I like computers that have all the latest bells and whistles.* ☐ *All those bells and whistles add to the cost, y'know.*

Bell's palsy *n.* the result of drinking too much whisky. ☐ *Bell's palsy is named for a well-known brand of Scotch.* ☐ *There's no denying it, he shows all the signs of Bell's palsy.*

belly *n.* the underside of an aircraft's fuselage. ☐ *He looked around under the huge belly of the 747, uncertain what he was expecting to find.* ☐ *There's some superficial damage to the belly near the tail, Captain.*

bellyache 1. *vb. phr.* to complain. ☐ *You are always bellyaching!* ☐ *Don't bellyache to me about it!* **2.** *n.* a stomachache. ☐ *Mummy, I have a terrible bellyache!* ☐ *That stuff will give you a fine bellyache, you'll see.*

belly button *n.* the navel. ☐ *Because the dress had a transparent midriff you could see her belly button.* ☐ *Do dogs have belly buttons?*

belly flop 1. *n.* a failed dive where there is a loud noise when the flat of the stomach hits the water. ☐ *Wow, I never knew that a belly flop hurts!* ☐ *A belly flop gets zero points in a diving competition.* **2.** *vb.* to dive into the water so that the flat of the stomach hits the water, usually making a loud noise. ☐ *Sam belly flopped again.* ☐ *I get so embarrassed when I belly flop!*

bellyful *n.* something that is more than enough; more than one needs. ☐ *I've* *had a bellyful of your excuses.* □ *You've given us all a bellyful. Now, good night.*

belly laff See BELLY LAUGH.

belly-landing *n.* the landing of an aircraft with its undercarriage retracted. □ *There's no choice, we're going to attempt a belly-landing.* □ *The belly-landing was all right as these things go, but I don't recommend them as a pastime.*

belly laugh AND **belly laff** *n.* a loud, deep, uninhibited laugh. □ *I don't want to hear giggles when I tell a joke. I want long belly laughs.* □ *I let out a loud belly laff at the vicar's joke. This turned out to be a bad idea.*

belly up AND **belly-up 1.** *mod.* dead. □ *What a disaster! All of the farmer's cattle were belly up following the flood.* □ *I hear old Ann went belly-up last week. Well, she was 97.* **2.** *mod.* wrecked; damaged beyond repair. □ *That's the end. This company is belly up.* □ *Despite Harry's attempts at repair, the TV remained obstinately belly-up.* **3.** *mod.* upside down. □ *After the collision the bus lay belly up in the middle of the road.* □ *The dead fish floated belly-up in the pool.*

belt 1. *n.* a blow with the fist or hand. □ *Quiet or I'll give you a belt in the chops.* □ *I got a belt in the gut for my trouble.* **2.** *vb. phr.* to strike someone. □ *Quiet or I'll belt you one!* □ *Don't belt me!* **3.** *vb.* to travel rapidly; to rush about. □ *She belted past me a few miles back. What's up?* □ *We were belting down the motorway when this cop car spotted us.*

belt and braces *n.* especially strong security or safety. □ *Right, let's take no chances; we'll have some real belt and braces here!* □ *Don't you think that's a bit too much like belt and braces, sir?*

belt (down) *vb. (phr.)* to rain hard. □ *I hate driving when it's belting down.* □ *It was really belting so we went to the pictures.*

belt out *vb. phr.* to play or sing music loudly, and not necessarily too harmoniously. □ *Well, we were really belting it out last night!* □ *If you belt out that so-called music of yours in the middle of the night again I'll call the police.*

Belt up! *exclam.* "Shut up!" □ *Why don't you just belt up!* □ *Belt up! I can't hear the music!*

belt up *vb. phr.* to be quiet; to shut up. □ *I'm trying to sleep! Please belt up.* □ *Will you please just belt up.*

be mother *vb. phr.* to take responsibility for dispensing tea at (typically) a family meal. □ *I'll be mother. Milk or sugar?* □ *Sally found herself being mother, as usual.*

Be my guest. *sent.* "Please go in front of me."; "Please make yourself comfortable in my home." □ *John stood aside at the open door and said to Walter, "Be my guest."* □ *Be my guest. Help yourself to whatever you need.*

bender 1. *n.* a drinking binge. □ *Her benders usually last about ten days.* □ *Paul is off on a bender again.* **2.** *n.* a heavy drinker; a drunkard. □ *This bender comes up to me and nearly kills me with his breath, asking for a match.* □ *In the dim light I could make out a few of the regular benders, but Harold wasn't there.* **3.** *n.* a passive male homosexual. (Taboo.) □ *Tell that bender to get out of here.* □ *He doesn't like being called a bender.*

bend one's elbow AND **bend the elbow; lift one's elbow** *vb. phr.* to take a drink of an alcoholic beverage; to drink alcohol to excess. □ *He's down at the pub, bending his elbow.* □ *Oh, Paul gets lots of exercise. He's lifting his elbow thirty times a day.*

bend over backwards AND **fall over backwards; lean over backwards** *vb. phr.* to make every possible effort, even beyond that which is reasonable; to help or to be fair. □ *I've been bending over backwards for you, and now you want yet more?* □ *He seems to just expect me to lean over backwards and then some.*

bend someone *vb.* to divert or pervert someone from an honest path. □ *You'll never bend her, she's completely straight.* □ *How did you ever get bent like this, Harry?*

bend something *vb.* to physically damage something. □ *I've bent my dad's car.* □ *I hope you did not bend my car, son.*

bend the elbow See BEND ONE'S ELBOW.

bend the law *vb. phr.* to cheat a little bit without technically breaking the law; to keep within the letter of the law while acting against its spirit. (Jocular.) □ *I didn't break the law. I just bent the law a little.* □ *Nobody ever got arrested for bending the law.*

benny *n.* a Benzedrine™ capsule or tablet. □ *Have you got a benny or two you could spare me?* □ *A couple of bennies will chase away the blues.*

bent 1. *mod.* dishonest; criminal; corrupt. □ *I'm afraid that Paul is a little bent. He cheats on his income tax.* □ *A lot of those officeholders get bent while in office—if they weren't before.* **2.** *mod.* homosexual. (Crude.) □ *So what if he's bent? He can still vote, can't he?* □ *Tom is getting to be so bent.*

bent shot *n.* a male homosexual. (Crude. Scots usage.) □ *Tom is getting to be such a bent shot.* □ *He doesn't like being called a bent shot.*

berk AND **burk** *n.* a fool or idiot. (Crude. Rhyming slang, linked as follows: Berk[shire Hunt] ≈ [cunt] = fool. The BURK alternative has come into use mainly due to confusion with BURKE.) □ *Don't be such a berk, Joe. No one believes that story any more.* □ *I felt like a complete burk when I found out that I'd boarded the wrong train.*

be sitting pretty *vb. phr.* to be in a very pleasant and secure position. □ *If I get the job, I'll be sitting pretty for a long time.* □ *She married a millionaire, and now she's sitting pretty.*

best-case scenario *n.* the best outcome considered. (Compare with WORST-CASE SCENARIO.) □ *Now, let's look at the best-case scenario.* □ *In the best-case scenario, we're all dead eventually—but then that's true of the worst-case scenario also.*

Best of British (luck). *sent.* "You're going to fail of course, but good luck anyway." A way of apparently wishing someone good luck, while in fact making an ironic or sardonic comment on their minute or non-existent chance of success. □ *Win the Nobel Prize? Best of British luck.* □ *Best of British with your man-powered ornithopter. Is your insurance fully up-to-date?*

better half *n.* one's wife, and occasionally, one's husband. □ *My better half disapproved of the film.* □ *I've got to go home to my better half.*

Better luck next time. *sent.* "I wish you luck when you try again." □ *So you screwed up. Better luck next time.* □ *You blew it, you stupid twit. Better luck next time.*

betty *n.* a picklocking tool used by a burglar. □ *He slipped the betty in between the door and its frame, and in seconds the doorway was clear and they could enter.* □ *Otto found it rather difficult to explain to the policeman why he was carrying a betty around at 3:00 a.m.*

between hell and high water *phr.* in considerable difficulty; faced with a serious dilemma. (Crude.) □ *Let's face it, we're between hell and high water here.* □ *Yes, we are between hell and high water, but we must make a choice or it will just get worse.*

between you, me and the bedpost See BETWEEN YOU, ME AND THE GATEPOST.

between you, me and the gatepost AND **between you, me and the bedpost** *phr.* "just between you and me." □ *Between you, me and the gatepost, things are going to get worse before they get better.* □ *They're worse than you think now, just between you, me and the bedpost.*

bev *vb.* to drink. (Compare with BEVVY.) □ *Let's bev and talk.* □ *What would you like to bev?*

bevvy 1. *vb.* to drink heavily. (Scots usage. Compare with BEV.) □ *Ma man's awa bevvying as usual. (My husband's away drinking as usual.)* □ *Let's go an bevvy the nicht. (Let's go and drink this evening.)* **2.** *n.* a session of heavy drinking. (Scots usage.) □ *Fancy a bevvy the nicht? (Fancy some serious drinking this evening?)* □ *When Wully's away on a bevvy, he's really away.*

beyond it 1. *mod.* exhausted; unable to continue. □ *I'm sorry, my father's* *beyond it.* □ *It's been a long day and I'm beyond it.* **2.** *mod.* incapacitated by drink. □ *Brian was beyond it before closing time.* □ *If you get beyond it you'll be kicked out of the pub.*

beyond the pale *mod.* outside or beyond the bounds of acceptable behaviour. (Derived from the historic Dublin Pale, once considered the only civilised part of Ireland.) □ *Well! That sort of behaviour is beyond the pale, of course.* □ *If you get beyond the pale you'll be kicked out.*

BF See BLOODY FOOL.

bhong See BONG.

bible-basher *n.* an evangelistic Christian. □ *There's a lot of bible-bashers around here.* □ *Watch what you say, she's a bit of a bible-basher.*

bicarb *n.* bicarbonate of soda, used for an upset stomach. (Pronounced BYE-carb.) □ *I really could use a little bicarb after that chili she served.* □ *I can't stand that sweet-tasting stuff. I want bicarb.*

biccy See BIKKY.

bicky See BIKKY.

bicycle AND **(town) bike** *n.* a promiscuous woman; a prostitute. (Taboo. From association with RIDE.) □ *Joan almost became a bicycle to pay for a habit.* □ *A lot of the town bikes are hooked on something or other.*

biddy *n.* a woman. □ *There's a biddy here asking for you.* □ *Ask the biddy what she wants, please.*

biff 1. *n.* a blow. □ *The biff on the nose gave Fred a nosebleed.* □ *Tom got a biff in the gut for his trouble.* **2.** *vb.* to hit someone. □ *Tom biffed Fred on the hooter.* □ *Fred got biffed, and that really made him angry.*

big ben 1. *n.* ten Pounds Sterling. (Rhyming slang. Big Ben is the bell of the clock in the tower of the House of Commons in London.) □ *All right, here's a big ben. Don't spend it all in one shop.* □ *Can you lend me a big ben 'till payday?* **2.** *n.* the numeral 10; ten of anything. (Rhyming slang.) □ *I'll give you a quid for big ben of them.* □ *Big ben? You've got that many?*

Big Brother 1. *n.* a personification of a putative totalitarian state. (From George Orwell's *1984*.) □ *Big Brother has changed the tax laws again.* □ *Now Big Brother has fixed it so you can't even babysit without paying taxes.* **2.** *n.* anyone—such as police, parents, teachers—who personify or are said to personify a totalitarian regime. □ *Big Brother is keeping me at home for a week.* □ *Big Brother says the paper is due tomorrow, or else.*

big cheese *n.* the boss; the key figure; the leader. □ *Here's a note from the big cheese telling me to come in for a chat.* □ *The big cheese is giving everyone a bonus at the end of the year.*

Big deal! *exclam.* "So what!" □ *So he snores! Big deal! Snore back!* □ *She says to me, "Your socks don't match." And I says back, "Big deal!"*

big deal *n.* something really important. □ *Don't make such a big deal out of it!* □ *This isn't a big deal as I see it.*

big drink of water AND **long drink of water** *n.* a very tall, thin person. □ *Tim really is a big drink of water.* □ *Kate grew into a long drink of water.*

big end 1. *n.* the large end of an internal combustion engine's connecting rod. □ *The big end had gone, I was told.* □ *How much does a big end cost?* **2.** *n.* the buttocks. □ *The dog bit her in the big end.* □ *She fell right on her big end.*

biggie *n.* something or someone important. □ *This one's a biggie. Treat him well.* □ *As problems go, this one's a biggie.*

big girl's blouse 1. *n.* an ineffective or pathetic man. □ *There's a big girl's blouse here looking for you.* □ *The big girl's blouse sat on the bench and waited for him.* **2.** *n.* an effeminate man; a passive male homosexual. (Crude.) □ *Gay? I'd call him a big girl's blouse.* □ *So what if he's a big girl's blouse? He can still vote, can't he?*

big H *n.* heroin. (Always with *the*.) □ *So Marty scores a bag of big H, and we get out the stuff to shoot.* □ *Lay off the big H, Harry! You'll end up hooked.*

bigheaded *mod.* conceited. □ *Now don't get bigheaded, but you are the top drummer in my books.* □ *Look at him swagger. He's so bigheaded.* □ *What a bigheaded jerk!*

big league *mod.* professional; BIG TIME. (From soccer and other sports.) □ *He works for one of the big league accounting firms.* □ *When I'm a big league star, I'll send you free tickets.*

big M *n.* one million Pounds Sterling. □ *Frank opened the suitcase and we all stared at the contents. "Yes," he said, breaking the silence, "That's what a big M looks like."* □ *He dreams all day of winning the big M in the lottery.*

big mouth *n.* a person who talks too much or too loudly; someone who tells secrets. (Also a term of address.) □ *Okay, big mouth! Shut up!* □ *Tell that big mouth to be quiet.*

big name *n.* a famous and important person. □ *Lots of big names were there lending their support to the cause.* □ *One of the big names invited for the event cancelled at the last minute.*

big-name *mod.* famous; important. □ *Some big-name star I've never heard of was there pretending to serve dinner.* □ *These big-name football players make millions.*

big noise *n.* an important person. □ *If you're such a big noise, why don't you get this queue moving?* □ *She's the big noise in Westminster right now.*

big of someone 1. *mod.* magnanimous of someone. □ *That is really big of you, Fred.* □ *It was big of Tom to come back and apologize.* **2.** *mod.* nice of someone. (Often sarcastic.) □ *A whole pound. Wow, that is really big of you!* □ *Three daisies he gave me! "Oh, that's big of you!" I said, fluttering my eyelashes.*

big on someone or something *vb. phr.* to be very interested or fond of someone or something. □ *Marty's really big on Jack now.* □ *If you were half as big on me as I am on you, that would be great!*

big P *n.* the release of a prisoner from prison on parole. (Always with *the*.) □

Now this lot are really well-behaved 'cause they're all hoping for the big P. □ *He smiled. It was the big P, at last!*

big shot *n.* a very important person. □ *So, you really think you're a big shot.* □ *I'm no big shot, but I do have some influence around here.*

Big Smoke AND **Great Smoke; Smoke** *n.* London. (Normally with *the*.) □ *I'm off up to the Big Smoke for a business meeting.* □ *I don't like going to the Smoke, but when I must, I must.*

big spender *n.* someone who spends much money. (Often sarcastic.) □ *The big spender left me a whole quarter tip!* □ *It's the big spenders who get themselves into money trouble.*

big stink *n.* a major issue; a scandal; a big argument. □ *There was a big stink made about my absence.* □ *Don't make such a big stink about it.*

big talk *n.* boasts; exaggerated claims. □ *No more big talk. I want action!* □ *I heard nothing but big talk since you got here.*

big time *n.* the high level of success. □ *I've finally reached the big time!* □ *When the pressure in the big time got to be too much, the guy simply retired.*

big top 1. *n.* a circus tent; the circus, in general. □ *The best acts take place under the big top.* □ *And now, one of the greatest acts under the big top.* **2.** *mod.* having to do with the circus. □ *Big top life doesn't appeal to me at all.* □ *One big top experience like that was enough to last me a lifetime.*

big wean *n.* a childish adult. (Scots usage.) □ *Dinny be such a big wean, Wully. Pull yersel thegither. (Don't be so childish, William. Pull yourself together.)* □ *Wully is aye such a big wean. (William is always so childish.)*

bigwig *n.* an important person; a self-important person. □ *The bigwig in charge of that sort of thing will be in tomorrow.* □ *Some bigwig in a pinstripe suit waltzed through and asked me to leave.*

bike 1. *n.* a motorcycle; a bicycle. □ *How much did that new bike of yours set you back?* □ *You have to wear a*

helmet with a bike that size, don't you?
2. See also BICYCLE.

bike it *vb. phr.* to cycle. □ *He's biking it back home just now.* □ *Bike it over there and tell him we need to talk.*

biker *n.* a motorcycle rider. □ *Four bikers roared by and woke up the baby.* □ *That biker is wearing about a dozen earrings.*

bikky AND **biccy; bicky** *n.* a biscuit. (Childish.) □ *Can I have a bikky, mummy?* □ *Now eat up your bicky, Johnny.*

bilge *n.* nonsense. □ *You're talking utter bilge again—as usual.* □ *What bilge that is!*

Bill See OLD BILL.

bill and coo *vb. phr.* to kiss and cuddle. (In the manner of love birds.) □ *Keep an eye on those kids. They aren't going to be satisfied with billing and cooing forever, you know.* □ *If they bill and coo enough now, maybe they will remember how to when they're older.*

Billingsgate pheasant AND **Yarmouth capon** *n.* a red herring; misleading information; a false clue. □ *I'm afraid that that has turned out to be no more than a Billingsgate pheasant.* □ *We can't afford any more Yarmouth capons; let's get it right!*

Billingsgate talk *n.* foul language. (Billingsgate is London's 1,000-year-old fish market.) □ *I don't want to hear any more of your Billingsgate talk.* □ *That Billingsgate talk just makes me sick.*

Bill shop *n.* a police station. (See OLD BILL.) □ *He's gone to the Bill shop to complain.* □ *They've so much business here they're building a new Bill shop.*

bimbette *n.* a teenage BIMBO. □ *She's far too young for him. She looks like a bimbette!* □ *Who's the bimbette with you, John?*

bimbo 1. *n.* the posterior or bottom. (Dated.) □ *He slipped on the ice and landed on his bimbo.* □ *Sit yourself down on your bimbo and pay attention.* **2.** *n.* a glamorous, but silly or empty-headed young woman. □ *All right, she's a bimbo, but she still has rights. Have a heart!* □ *Now that bimbo is a star in*

the movies. **3.** *n.* a sexually available young woman. (Crude.) □ *Joan is such a bimbo. That's the third guy she's gone out with this week alone!* □ *On Saturday night the young men go into the town looking for bimbos.*

Bimmer *n.* a BMW car. □ *When I'm rich I'm going to get a Bimmer.* □ *I think Bimmers are rather over-rated.*

bin *n.* a cell in a police station or prison. (Usually with *the*.) □ *Bert's in the bin again.* □ *Whose in that bin, Sarge?*

bind *n.* a complication, problem or nuisance. □ *I've got a little bind here I didn't anticipate.* □ *That's a bit of a bind! And I had thought we had nearly resolved this business.*

binder *n.* a bore or tiresome person. □ *What's a binder like that doing around here?* □ *I'm sorry but we really don't need another binder working here.*

bind someone *vb.* to bore or tire someone. □ *My goodness, that fellow binds me!* □ *I think Walter has bound Dad into sleep again!*

bin end *n.* the last bottle in a wine bin, often sold at a discount. □ *The bin end was a particularly fine white French wine, so I bought it.* □ *I like to be the bin end because it's so cheap.*

binge 1. *n.* any spree of self-indulgence: emotional, gluttonous, etc. □ *About Christmas time I start a month-long eating binge.* □ *The crying binge started when Marty got off the train.* **2.** *vb.* to drink heavily. □ *He has been binging since June.* □ *She binges about once a month and is stone cold sober the rest of the time.* **3.** *n.* a drinking or drug-taking spree. □ *Larry is the type who likes a good binge every now and then.* □ *A coke binge can cost a lot of cabbage.*

Bingo! *exclam.* "Yes!"; "That's right!" (From the game "Bingo." Pronounced BING-go.) □ *Bingo! I've got the answer!* □ *And we put this little gismo here, another one here, and bingo! We're done.*

bin something *vb.* to throw away something. □ *Oh, I binned that ages ago.* □ *If it's no use to you, just bin it.*

bint *n.* a girl or woman. (Crude. From the Arabic for "daughter.") □ *Who was* that bint I saw you with last night? □ That "bint" was my wife!

bird 1. *n.* an attractive woman; a pretty girl. □ I like the bird you were with last night. □ What a bird! I want that one. **2.** *n.* an aircraft. □ I like this bird. She's a dream to fly. □ The bird crashed on takeoff. **3.** *n.* jail. □ A couple of days of bird would do you fine. □ Take it easy. I don't want to end up in bird. **4.** *n.* a dismissive response from an audience. (Theatrical. Rhyming slang, linked as follows: bird = [goose-hiss] ≈ [hiss and boo] = dismissive response. Also, "hiss" rhymes with "dismiss." Compare with RICHARD (THE THIRD).) □ They give him the bird in the Royal last night and the play's been taken off. □ They reckon if you didn't get the bird at the Glasgow Empire there must be something wrong with you! **5.** *vb.* to bird-watch. □ He birds every weekend, if he can. □ A lot of people bird in that marsh area.

birdbrain *n.* a stupid-acting person. □ You silly birdbrain. Stop it! □ I'm such a birdbrain. I forgot my driver's licence, officer.

birdbrained *mod.* stupid. □ I've never heard such a birdbrained idea in my life. □ Look, you birdbrained idiot, you are dead wrong!

bird cage *n.* a dormitory or place of residence for women, e.g., nurses, military personnel, etc.) □ That's the bird cage there. Steer clear, if you know what's good for you my lad! □ Henry was caught trying to break into the bird cage last night.

birder *n.* a bird-watcher. □ There are a lot of birders here today. □ The birders tend to use that area over there.

bird's nest *n.* the room occupied by an individual resident within a BIRD CAGE. □ Paul claims she let him into her bird's nest in the nurse's home, but I don't believe it. □ Her bird's nest was tiny. I don't know how she was supposed to manage.

bird-watcher *n.* a girl-watcher; someone, usually a man, who enjoys watching women go by. □ Harry is a dedicated bird-watcher. □ You bird-watchers should just mind your own business.

bish *n.* a mistake or error. □ No more bishes, please! □ What a foolish bish that turned out to be!

bit 1. *n.* a woman. □ I'm afraid I do not know the bit. □ Why is that bit walking through our office? **2.** *n.* the smallest possible unit of information. (Computer jargon. Originally an abbreviated merging of "binary" and "digit.") □ It may be tiny, but one wrong bit can crash your computer. □ When you look at all the millions of bits there, it's amazing these things ever work.

bitch 1. *vb.* to complain. □ You are always bitching! □ If I couldn't bitch, I would blow my top. **2.** *n.* a difficult thing or person. □ Life's a bitch. □ This algebra problem is a real bitch. **3.** *n.* a derogatory term for a woman. (Crude.) □ That stupid bitch doesn't know anything about this. □ You bitch! Stop it!

bitch of a person or thing *n.* a really difficult person or thing. (Crude.) □ What a bitch of a day! □ He is really a bitch of a boss.

bitchy *mod.* spiteful; moody; rude; complaining. (Crude.) □ Don't be so bitchy! □ Who needs a house full of bitchy kids?

bite 1. *vb.* to accept a deception; to fall for something; to respond to a come-on. □ I knew somebody would bite. □ We put up a sign advertising free pop, but nobody bit. **2.** *vb.* [for someone or something] to be bad or threatening. □ Watch out for Gloria. She bites! □ My dad bites, but don't worry, he's in a good mood.

bite the bullet *vb. phr.* to accept something difficult and try to live with it. □ You are just going to have to bite the bullet and make the best of it. □ Jim bit the bullet and accepted what he knew had to be.

Bite your tongue! *exclam.* "Be sorry you said that!"; "Take back what you said!" □ Me a thief? Oh, bite your tongue! □ Why do you say that this will fail? Bite your tongue!

bit of a barney *n.* a modest or minor argument or fight. (Always with *a*.) □ It *was just a bit of a barney; we're friends, really.* □ *Oh, we have a bit of a barney now and then.*

bit of a lad AND **quite a lad 1.** *n.* a man continually chatting up women. □ *The girls say he's not just a bit of a lad, but a real nuisance.* □ *Being a quite a lad is one thing, but this is too much.* **2.** *n.* a spirited young man. □ *Well, he is quite a lad, isn't he?* □ *Although a bit of a lad, he's very smart, too.*

bit of all right 1. *n.* a satisfactory condition or situation. □ *Yeh, this set-up's a bit of all right, innit?* □ *Now if I was set up in a bit of all right like that, I'd just be quiet.* **2.** *n.* an unexpected pleasant event; good luck. (Always with *a.*) □ *Well that was a bit of all right. We should be all right now.* □ *Just one little bit of all right would be nice!*

bit of all right AND **bit of crackling; bit of crumpet; bit of fluff; bit of homework; bit of skirt; bit of stuff; bit of tail; bit of tickle; bit of tit** *n.* a sexually attractive or co-operative woman, from the male perspective. (Crude. Always with *a.*) □ *A bit of all right? I'll say she is!* □ *Harry's out looking for a bit of crumpet tonight.* □ *I like the look of that bit of tit.*

bit of Braille *n.* the sexual groping of a woman by a man. (Taboo. Always with *a.*) □ *Fancy a bit of Braille, darling?* □ *No I do not fancy any bit of Braille from you. Sod off!*

bit of crackling See BIT OF ALL RIGHT.

bit of crumpet See BIT OF ALL RIGHT.

bit of fluff See BIT OF ALL RIGHT.

bit of homework See BIT OF ALL RIGHT.

bit of meat AND **meat injection** *n.* an act of sexual intercourse. (Taboo.) □ *Fancy a bit of meat, love?* □ *He wanted to give her a meat injection but was rebuffed.*

bit of nonsense AND **bit on the side 1.** *n.* a mistress; an illicit girlfriend. (Always with *a.*) □ *Oh, she's just the boss's bit of nonsense.* □ *So I'm just his bit on the side am I? We'll see about that!* **2.** *n.* an illicit sexual affair. (Crude. Always with *a.*) □ *It was just a bit of nonsense, and now we've parted.* □ *If you want a bit on the side, don't look for it in your own back yard.*

bit of skirt See BIT OF ALL RIGHT.

bit of spare 1. *n.* a married man's mistress. (Always with *a.*) □ *She's Mr Big's bit of spare. Don't touch.* □ *That was Otto's new bit of spare, that was.* **2.** *n.* anyone, male or female, who is available sexually. (Crude. Always with *a.*) □ *He came to the pub looking for a bit of spare.* □ *She looks like a tasty bit of spare.*

bit of stuff See BIT OF ALL RIGHT.

bit of tail *n.* sodomy, either homosexual or heterosexual. (Taboo. Always with *a.* See BIT OF ALL RIGHT.) □ *I could hear them, quite clearly, talking about giving her a bit of tail.* □ *They say he's inclined towards, you know, a bit of tail now and again.*

bit of the action See PIECE (OF THE ACTION).

bit of the other *n.* an act of sexual intercourse. (Crude. From the male perspective. Usually with *a.*) □ *A little bit of the other would probably do her the power of good, in fact.* □ *I think really, she's gasping for a bit of the other, you know.*

bit of tickle See BIT OF ALL RIGHT.

bit of tit See BIT OF ALL RIGHT.

bit on the side See BIT OF NONSENSE.

bit previous 1. *mod.* too soon; before required. (Always with *a.*) □ *I think we've got here a bit previous, dear.* □ *If you don't slow down we'll be ready a bit previous.* **2.** *mod.* not wanted; not following the customary rules. (Usually with *a.* See OUT OF ORDER.) □ *No, no, you're a bit previous. That's not the way we do things around here.* □ *That's a bit previous. We don't want it here.*

bits and bobs *n.* bits and pieces. □ *We ended up with nothing but bits and bobs to work on.* □ *I have some more bits and bobs here.*

biz *n.* equipment used for injecting drugs. □ *She always has her biz with her, just in case, you know.* □ *I don't know what I'd do if I lost my biz.*

blab *vb.* to tell a secret; to reveal something private in public. □ *I'll tell you if you promise not to blab it.* □ *Tiffany blabbed the whole thing.*

blabbermouth *n.* someone who talks too much and tells secrets. □ *You are* *such a blabbermouth!* □ *See if you can get that blabbermouth to keep quiet.*

black 1. *mod.* [of coffee] without cream or milk. (See BLACK OR WHITE?) □ *I'd like mine black, please.* □ *Black coffee, good and hot, please.* **2.** *vb.* to boycott, especially a business, especially by a trade union. □ *The unions blacked the company because it refused to increase pay.* □ *Union blacking sometimes works, and sometimes does not.* **3.** *n.* Guinness™ porter beer. (From it's very dark colour.) □ *How about another black before you go, Patrick?* □ *Give my friend here a black.*

black and blue *mod.* bruised, physically or emotionally. □ *I'm still black and blue from my divorce.* □ *What is that black and blue area on your leg?*

black and tan *n.* stout or porter beer mixed with ale in equal proportions. (See BLACK VELVET.) □ *Give my friend here a black and tan.* □ *How about a black and tan before you go, Charlie?*

black and white *n.* night. (Rhyming slang.) □ *What were you up to during the black and white?* □ *I was being ill all black and white, that's what I was up to.*

black beauties See BLACK BOMBERS.

black bombers AND **black beauties** *n.* amphetamines. □ *Where can I get black bombers around her?* □ *Charlie always keeps a stash of black beauties.*

black-coated workers *n.* prunes. (A pun on "work," in the sense that prunes, which are dark-coloured, cause the human digestive system to "work." In other words, constipation is avoided or overcome.) □ *He likes his black-coated workers. Keeps things moving along, he says.* □ *Oh no, no black-coated workers for me!*

blackleg *n.* a scab or strike-breaker; a betrayer of fellow workers, etc. □ *We're refusing to work with that blackleg.* □ *They brought in blacklegs to break the strike.*

blacklist 1. *n.* a list of banned people; a list of people undesirable to some group. □ *Am I on your blacklist?* □ *I hear they keep a blacklist of all the people they disagree with.* **2.** *vb.* to put

someone's name on a list of undesirables. □ *They blacklisted me for not belonging to the right—which is to say, left—organisations.* □ *Nobody else I know was blacklisted.*

black maria AND **magic bus; meatwagon; paddy wagon** *n.* a police or prison vehicle used to transport prisoners. □ *It took two black marias to carry away the people they arrested.* □ *The cop put the woman in handcuffs and then called for the paddy wagon.*

Black or white? *interrog.* (See BLACK, sense 1.) "Do you want coffee with or without cream?" □ *Coffee's here. Black or white?* □ *Black or white coffee?*

blackout 1. *n.* a loss of consciousness. □ *I don't know what happened. I think I had a blackout.* □ *Well, it was a rather convenient blackout, I must say!* **2.** *n.* total censorship; complete suppression of all news. □ *There was a complete blackout before the attack.* □ *I don't know why, but there's a news blackout.*

black-top *n.* the bitumen-based material used as the wearing surface material on roadways. □ *The black-top started to melt in that heat wave.* □ *They're laying new black-top on that road.*

black velvet 1. *n.* Guinness™ porter beer mixed with champagne. (Irish usage. See BLACK AND TAN.) □ *Black velvet for my friends, barman!* □ *That's a good excuse for some more black velvet, don't you think?* **2.** *n.* sexual intercourse with a black woman. (Racially offensive.) □ *Harry always liked some black velvet.* □ *I think talking about black velvet like that is disgusting.* **3.** *n.* a black woman considered as a sex-object. (Racially offensive.) □ *What a luscious piece of black velvet that woman was!* □ *She's not just black velvet! She's a human being!*

blackwash *vb.* to make something look worse than it really is; to emphasise something bad. □ *Look, things are hard enough without the likes of you blackwashing them.* □ *Well, it looks as if the blackwashing has started.*

bladder of lard *n.* a playing card. (Rhyming slang.) □ *Come on, what's* *that bladder of lard we can see in your hand?* □ *Have you got any other bladders of lard hidden away?*

blade *n.* a knife. □ *Bring your blade over here and cut this loose.* □ *What are you carrying a blade for?*

blagger 1. *n.* a violent thief or mugger. □ *I was stopped by a blagger.* □ *The police caught the blagger.* **2.** *n.* a scrounger. □ *The blaggers who hang around outside the railway station were rounded up by the police today.* □ *Since John lost his job he's turned into nothing more than a blagger.*

blag someone *vb.* to mug someone, to rob someone in a violent way. □ *A gang of youths were prowling around blagging people.* □ *He blagged an old lady and got put away for six months.*

blag something *vb.* to steal or to scrounge something. □ *He blagged some food from the little man again, you know!* □ *Why do you keep blagging money off me?*

blah-blah *phr.* gibberish; incessant chattering. (Onomatopoetic. It can be repeated many times.) □ *Why all this blah-blah-blah?* □ *She's going blah-blah on the phone all the time.*

blankety-blank AND **blankity-blank** *mod.* damned. (From the former practice of printing blank spaces in place of banned words.) □ *I'm tired of your blankety-blank bad humour.* □ *Get this blankity-blank cat out of here!*

blank someone *vb.* to ignore someone. □ *Why are you blanking me?* □ *The hostess and all the guests blank him, until he began to wonder if he was invisible or something.*

blast 1. *vb.* to shoot someone with a gun. □ *The speeding car drove by, and somebody tried to blast him with a machine gun.* □ *The squaddies blasted away at the terrorist till there was nothing left.* **2.** *vb.* to attack or criticise someone or something verbally. □ *She really blasted the plan, right in front of the board.* □ *He blasted on and on at his brother until we all left in embarrassment.* **3.** *n.* a verbal attack. □ *The opposition MP levelled a blast of criticism at the government.* □ *The govern-*

ment delivered a huge blast at their critics during the debate in the House. **4.** *n.* the kick or RUSH from taking or injecting a drug. □ *That stuff really gives me a blast.* □ *With a blast like that, folks are going to get hooked fast.*

blasted *mod.* damned. □ *I asked her to get her blasted stockings off the shower curtain.* □ *Shut your blasted mouth!*

Blast it! *exclam.* "Damn it!" □ *Blast it! We've missed again!* □ *Another price rise! Blast it!*

blazes 1. *n.* Hell. □ *You can go straight to blazes as far as I care.* □ *It's as hot as blazes here.*

bleat *vb.* to make a feeble protest. □ *Oh stop bleating, will you!* □ *There's Harry, making his usual bleats.*

bleeder *n.* an unattractive or disreputable person. (Crude.) □ *This bleeder is offensive most of the time.* □ *Who's the bleeder with the enormous mustache?*

bleed for someone *vb. phr.* to sympathise with someone. (Often used sarcastically.) □ *I really bleed for you, but there's nothing I can do.* □ *We bleed for you, we really do.*

bleeding AND **blessed** *mod.* BLOODY. (A euphemism or variation. Crude.) □ *Get that bleeding dog out of my nice house!* □ *Oh my, what a blessed mess!*

bleed like a (stuck) pig *vb. phr.* to bleed profusely. □ *It was a terrible accident; the driver bled like a stuck pig.* □ *If someone suffers that sort of rupture they will bleed like a pig, so be warned.*

bleed someone *vb.* to drain someone of money through extortion or continuous demands for payment. (Compare with BLEED SOMEONE WHITE.) □ *You can't bleed me anymore. I'm skint.* □ *I'm going to bleed you till I get what I deserve.*

bleed someone dry See BLEED SOMEONE WHITE.

bleed someone white AND **bleed someone dry** *vb. phr.* to take all of someone's money; to extort money from someone. (Compare with BLEED SOMEONE.) □ *The creeps tried to bleed me white.* □ *Max got some pictures of*

Fred and Paul together and tried to bleed both of them dry.

blessed See BLEEDING.

blighter *n.* an insignificant man. □ *What does the blighter want?* □ *He's a rather surprising blighter.*

Blighty *n.* England. (From the Hindi *bilayati*, meaning "foreign," by hobson-jobson.) □ *After all these years in far-flung corners of the globe dreaming of Blighty, all he wanted was to come home.* □ *When he eventually got back to Blighty, I think the reality was a bit of a shock.*

blimey AND **corblimey; gorblimey** *exclam.* a euphemistic abbreviation of "God blind me," once a popular curse. (Crude.) □ *Blimey, that's a nice car.* □ *Well, gorblimey, I'm not interested in that!*

blimp *n.* an obese person. (Offensive. Also a term of address. Originally the name of a World War I observation balloon.) □ *Look at that blimp who just came in.* □ *This enormous blimp managed to get on the plane, but couldn't get into a seat.*

blind (along) *vb. (phr.)* to drive heedlessly and very rapidly, especially without looking ahead. □ *If you blind along like that you'll have a serious accident.* □ *Don't blind like that, please. It makes me very nervous.*

blind drunk *mod.* very intoxicated due to drink. □ *You came in blind drunk last night. What's going on?* □ *Joe and Arthur kept on knocking them back till they were both blind drunk.*

blinder *n.* an extensive drinking session. □ *I think the boys are off on another blinder.* □ *I'm getting to be too old for these blinders.*

blind hedge *n.* a ditch. □ *Mind that blind hedge!* □ *Woops. Help your father out of the blind hedge, James.*

blinding AND **blinking; blooming** *mod.* BLOODY. (Crude. A euphemism.) □ *Why don't you take your blinding job and shove it?* □ *That's a blooming stupid idea.*

blindingly stupid *mod.* very stupid indeed. □ *I have never seen anyone so blindingly stupid. What a dunce!* □ *She is blindingly stupid. Totally clueless.*

blind man's holiday *n.* a dark night. □ *It's a regular blind man's holiday out there, you know.* □ *It usually is a blind man's holiday in the country when the moon's not up.*

blind with science *vb. phr.* to confuse or impress with a lengthy or complex explanation, especially a technical or scientific-sounding one. (Compare with BAFFLE SOMEONE WITH BULLSHIT.) □ *I'm blinded with science. What's really going on here?* □ *Well, now you've got me really blinded with science.*

blinking See BLINDING.

blip 1. *n.* anything quick and insignificant; a one-off, not-repeated event of little importance. □ *It was nothing, just a blip. The press blew it out of proportion.* □ *It wasn't really a fight. It was just a blip.* **2.** *n.* an intermittently appearing or flashing light on a computer or radar screen. □ *A blip caught the controller's eye for an instant.* □ *Did you see that blip, Freddy?*

blissed (out) AND **blissed-out** *mod.* in a state of euphoria or emotional bliss. □ *After the second movement, I was totally blissed out.* □ *What a blissed-out dame!* □ *I know a gal who can get blissed from a sunset.*

bliss out *vb. phr.* to become euphoric or ecstatic. (See BLISSED (OUT).) □ *I blissed out just because it is spring and I am with you.* □ *I always bliss out from talk like that, but I still love Wally.*

blister *n.* an irritating person. (Offensive.) □ *What a blister that woman can be.* □ *Get out of here, you blister!*

blistering *mod.* BLOODY. (Crude. A euphemism.) □ *That car is blistering fast.* □ *Who's the blistering fool who did this?*

blithering idiot *n.* a crazy person; a totally disoriented person; a fool. □ *How can you be such a blithering idiot?* □ *You blithering idiot! You've buttered the tablecloth!*

blob 1. *n.* an ulcer. □ *I think you've got a little blob here, Mr Simpson.* □ *That's an ugly blob; I want rid of it.* **2.** *n.* the victim of a fatal highway accident. (Police slang.) □ *There were two blobs lying in the road.* □ *How many blobs* *were there this time?* **3.** *n.* a score of zero runs scored by a cricket batsman. □ *Another blob again I see, Gerald. Sorry.* □ *I really must try to do better than a blob next time.*

blobs AND **love blobs 1.** *n.* the female breasts. (Crude. Normally with *the* and in the plural.) □ *Cor, look at the blobs on that, Fred!* □ *There she was, bold as brass, with her love blobs on full display.* **2.** *n.* the testicles. (Taboo. Normally with *the* and in the plural.) □ *The teacher preferred "testicles" to "love blobs," if they had to be mentioned at all.* □ *He got hit right in the blobs.*

blobwagon *n.* an ambulance attending a road traffic accident. (Police and medical.) □ *Send for a blobwagon!* □ *When the blobwagon got there, it was too late.*

blockbuster 1. *n.* something enormous, especially a film or book that attracts a large audience. □ *That blockbuster should make about twenty million.* □ *I need two blockbusters like that to pay for the last flop.* **2.** *mod.* exciting and successful. □ *The new blockbuster film made about a zillion pounds in a month.* □ *With a blockbuster novel like that in print, you should make quite a bundle.*

blockhead *n.* a stupid person. □ *Without a blockhead like you to remind me of the perils of stupidity, I might be less efficient than I am.* □ *Why did he call me a blockhead? I didn't do anything.*

bloke *n.* a man. (As distinct from a woman. Reputedly derived from a secret word used by gypsies.) □ *Ask that bloke if he needs any help.* □ *Why do we need this bloke?*

blokey *mod.* rumbustiously masculine. □ *Oh, he's very friendly in a blokey sort of way.* □ *I feel sort of out of place among all that blokey heartfulness.*

blondie *n.* a fair-haired man. □ *I like the look of this blondie.* □ *The blondie was not there.*

bloodbath *n.* a massacre; a great disaster. □ *What a bloodbath! The whole town collapsed after the factory went bust.* □ *There was a blood bath at the office when the manager fired twenty people.*

bloody *mod.* very. (An intensifier.) □ *Well, that's bloody unlikely, I'd say.* □ *He can be bloody annoying at times, I agree.*

bloody fool AND **BF** *n.* a very foolish person. □ *I felt like such a bloody fool when I found out that I'd got onto the wrong train.* □ *Tell that BF in the front row to shut up.*

bloody mary *n.* a drink consisting of tomato juice and vodka. □ *Can I have a bloody mary, please?* □ *I do like this bloody mary.*

bloody-minded *mod.* deliberately awkward, perverse or unhelpful. □ *Why do you always have to be so bloody-minded?* □ *He may be bloody-minded, but I'm afraid he's right.*

bloomer *n.* a mistake. □ *Rubbing my nose in it is not going to correct the bloomer.* □ *So I made a bloomer! I wish you'd stop going on about it!*

blooming See BLINDING.

blootered *mod.* very intoxicated due to drink. (Scots usage.) □ *Shuggy's blootered again.* □ *They were all so blootered they couldny stan up. (They were all so drunk they could not stand up.)*

blot one's copybook *vb. phr.* to make a mistake; to create a bad impression or damage one's reputation. □ *How could I ever have blotted my copybook like that?* □ *I don't intend to blot my copybook.*

blotter *n.* lysergic acid diethylamide, or LSD, an hallucinogenic drug sold on bits of blotting paper. □ *Most of the acid around here is blotter.* □ *Blotter can cost one to five pounds a pop.*

blotto *mod.* intoxicated due to drink or drugs. □ *Let's go out and get blotto.* □ *She just lay there—blotto.*

blow *vb.* to squander or waste money; to spend money. □ *Mary blew forty bucks on a second-hand radio.* □ *We will blow it all at a fancy restaurant.*

blow 1. *n.* a setback; an attack. □ *It was a real blow to our prestige.* □ *Acme Systems Industries suffered a blow to its plans to acquire A.B.C. Steel Widgets.* **2.** *vb.* to play a musical instrument, not necessarily a wind instrument. □ *Boy,* *listen to her blow.* □ *When he blows, everybody listens.* **3.** *vb.* to SNORT any powdered drug; to take snuff. □ *Those guys spend all their time blowing coke.* □ *Are you blowing something good?* **4.** *vb.* to smoke marijuana. □ *He sits there blowing by the hour. How can he afford it?* □ *They say that blowing that much will affect your brain.* **5.** *n.* cannabis; marijuana. □ *You can get some good blow in this part of town.* □ *What does blow cost around here?*

blow a fuse AND **blow one's fuse; blow a gasket; blow one's top; blow the lid off** *vb. phr.* to explode with anger; to lose one's temper. □ *Come on, don't blow a fuse.* □ *Go ahead, blow a gasket! What good will that do?*

blow a gasket See BLOW A FUSE.

blower *n.* a telephone. □ *The blower's been very busy all day today.* □ *The blower was ringing off the hook when I came in.*

blowhard *n.* a braggart; a big talker. □ *You're just a big blowhard.* □ *When and if this blowhard finishes, let's go.*

blow job *n.* an act of oral sex upon a man. (Taboo.) □ *That girl standing at the corner does provide blow jobs if you pay enough.* □ *Fancy a blow job, darling?*

blown away *mod.* dead; killed. (Underworld.) □ *Four of the mob were blown away when the cops got there.* □ *That guy was blown away weeks ago.*

blow off (some) steam AND **let off (some) steam** *vb. phr.* to release emotional tension by talking or getting angry. □ *Don't worry. She's just blowing off steam.* □ *Let off some steam. Get it out of your system.*

blow one's fuse See BLOW A FUSE.

blow one's own horn AND **toot one's own horn** *vb. phr.* to brag. □ *Gerry certainly likes to toot his own horn.* □ *"I hate to blow my own horn," said Bill, lying through his teeth.*

blow one's top See BLOW A FUSE.

blow-out 1. *n.* an extravagant party, drinking session or meal. □ *I haven't had a blow-out like that in years.* □ *That was a blow-out at Tom's the other night.* **2.** *n.* a loss of temper; a burst of

fury. □ *You only have to look at them to see that they've been having a terrible blow-out.* □ *Don't work yourself up into a having a blow-out.*

blowse *vb.* to sniff glue. □ *Why do these kids blowse?* □ *They blowse for kicks.*

blowser *n.* a glue sniffer. □ *There's a lot of blowsers around here.* □ *Little Paul's a blowser already, and he's just twelve.*

blow someone *vb.* to perform oral sex upon a man. (Taboo.) □ *Please, will you blow me?* □ *She blew him again, just because he asked.*

blow someone away 1. *vb. phr.* to kill someone; to shoot someone. (Underworld.) □ *The boss said we was to blow you away if you gives us any trouble.* □ *We blow away guys like you every day.* **2.** *vb. phr.* to overwhelm someone; to amaze someone. □ *That music really blew me away.* □ *The whole idea just blew her away.*

blow someone out of the water *vb. phr.* to utterly destroy someone. (As a ship is blown up by a torpedo.) □ *This is too much. I'm gonna blow that guy out of the water.* □ *How does it feel to be blown out of the water like that?*

blow someone's cover *vb. phr.* to reveal someone's true identity; to ruin someone's scheme for concealment. □ *The dog recognised me and blew my cover.* □ *I didn't mean to blow your cover.*

blow someone's mind 1. *vb. phr.* to greatly impress someone; to overwhelm someone. □ *This whole business is just about blowing her mind, you know.* □ *It is wonderful news; it really blows my mind!* **2.** *vb. phr.* to intoxicate someone, usually with drugs. □ *This stuff will blow your mind.* □ *That acid blew my mind.*

blow the gaff *vb. phr.* to expose or tell a secret by accident. □ *Why did you have to blow the gaff?* □ *Blowing the gaff at this very moment is particularly awkward.*

blow the lid off See BLOW A FUSE.

blow the lid off something *vb. phr.* to expose something secret or dubious. □

I must blow the lid off these dirty deal-ings. □ *She's undoubtedly going to blow the lid off our activities.*

blow the whistle See WHISTLE-BLOW.

blow (up) *vb. (phr.)* to exaggerate or boast. □ *I do wish you would not blow up things like that. It's not that impor-tant.* □ *Oh, he's always blowing, that one.*

blow up 1. *vb. phr.* to burst into anger. □ *I just knew you'd blow up.* □ *So she blew up. Why should that affect you so much?* **2.** *n.* an angry outburst; a fight. (Usually BLOWUP.) □ *After the third blowup, she left him.* □ *One blowup after another. Yuck!* **3.** *n.* an enlarged version of a photograph, map, chart, etc. (Usually BLOWUP.) □ *Here's a blow up of the scene of the crime.* □ *Kelly sent a blowup of their wedding picture to all her relatives.*

blue 1. *mod.* pertaining or relating to the Conservative Party (in the UK). □ *He's another blue individual, if ever I saw one.* □ *The blue vote is slipping away this time round.* **2.** *mod.* de-pressed; melancholy. □ *I'm feeling sort of blue.* □ *That music always makes me blue.* □ *I'm in a blue mood.* **3.** *n.* an am-phetamine tablet or capsule, especially a blue one. □ *How are blues different from reds and yellows?* □ *I'm sort of wired. You got any blues?* **4.** *n.* a police officer; the police. □ *The blues will be here in a minute.* □ *One blue isn't enough to handle this job.* **5.** *n.* a wild party. □ *Sam invited us to a blue, but we're getting a little old for that kind of thing.* □ *After a blue, I couldn't keep my eyes open the following day.* **6.** See also BLOW.

blue around the gills AND **green around the gills** *mod.* ill; nauseated. □ *You are looking a little blue around the gills.* □ *How about a little air? I feel a little green around the gills.*

blue balls *n.* a jocular name for intense male sexual frustration. (Taboo.) □ *I've got to find a woman to treat these blue balls of mine, soon!* □ *Blue balls is what they say you get if you are getting nothing, if you know what I mean.*

bluebottle *n.* a policeman. (From the colour of his uniform.) □ *See that blue-bottle over there? He lifted me once.* □ *The bluebottles will catch up with you some day.*

blue chip 1. *n.* the stock of large, reli-able companies. (Securities markets. See GILT-EDGED.) □ *The blue chips took another nose dive in today's trading.* □ *I buy nothing but blue chips.* **2.** *mod.* of reliable investments. (Securities mar-kets.) □ *The blue chip rally ran for a third day.* □ *It was another blue chip led sell off.*

blue-eyed boy *n.* a favourite person. □ *What does the blue-eyed boy want?* □ *Even a blue-eyed boy like that has to earn a living.*

bluefoot *n.* a prostitute. (Crude.) □ *The Old Bill hauled her in because she looked like a bluefoot.* □ *There are a lot of bluefoots around here in the cen-tre of town.*

blue funk *n.* a state of blind panic or ab-ject terror. □ *I'm glad I've got over my blue funk.* □ *You've got to get out of your blue funk, calm down and get back to work.*

blue in the face *mod.* pale from ex-haustion or exertion. □ *I laughed until I was blue in the face.* □ *She worked hard enough to be blue in the face.*

blue moon *n.* a spoon. (Rhyming slang.) □ *Hoy, waiter! Where's me blue moon then?* □ *You're supposed to lick the blue moon clean Nigel, not yer ac-tual bowl.*

blue murder *n.* loud cries of alarm; a great noise. □ *What a noise! The child was crying blue murder.* □ *There was someone yelling blue murder all day long.*

blue-nosed *mod.* religiously or morally severe; censorious. □ *Don't you think that's a rather blue-nosed attitude about nothing very much.* □ *We have very blue-nosed neighbours, so we try to be careful.*

blue o'clock *n.* the wee small hours; the dead of night. □ *Why are you up at blue o'clock?* □ *She came home at blue o'-clock; I wonder why?*

blunderbuss *n.* a baby's pram. (A pun.) □ *If you're having a baby, you'll need a blunderbuss.* □ *Well, my aunt bought me a blunderbuss for the new baby.*

blunt end *n.* a landlubber's term for the stern of a ship. (Compare with SHARP END.) □ *I think the blunt end is the bit at the back of the boat.* □ *The two of them stood at the blunt end, watching the island disappear over the horizon.*

b.o. AND **BO** *n.* (bad) body odour. (Crude. An initialism.) □ *Boy, oh boy! Do you have b.o.!* □ *Now here is a product that will end your worries about BO.*

board of green cloth 1. *n.* a billiards table. □ *The balls were set up for play on the board of green cloth again.* □ *Here was the board of green cloth, ready for another game of billiards.* **2.** *n.* a card table. □ *The four sat silently around the board of green cloth. No one spoke.* □ *A game of whist? Right, let's get out the board of green cloth.*

boat race *n.* a face. (Rhyming slang.) □ *Why are you looking at me like that? Is there something wrong with me boat race?* □ *The woman had a very unusual boat race, you know.*

bob (and dick) 1. *mod.* unwell. (Rhyming slang, linked as follows: Bob (and Dick) ≈ [sick] = unwell.) □ *God, I feel really bob and dick!* □ *I told you that curry would make you bob.* **2.** *n.* the male sexual organ. (Taboo Rhyming slang, linked as follows: Bob (and Dick) ≈ [prick] = penis.) □ *The doctor told him he'd got something wrong with his bob and dick.* □ *That's all very well Myra, but where would the world be without bobs?*

bobby *n.* a policeman. (From the given name of Sir Robert Peel, who founded the Metropolitan Police in 1829.) □ *The bobby broke up the fight.* □ *These two bobbies drove around in their car picking on innocent people like me.*

bobby-dazzler *n.* an excellent or unusual person or thing. □ *This is a bobby-dazzler of a day!* □ *Mary's got herself a bobby-dazzler of a new job.*

Bob's your uncle! *exclam.* "Everything's just fine!" (Reputedly this expression refers to Robert Cecil, Lord Salisbury, who was British Prime Minister for most of the last 20 years of the 19th century; he had a propensity to appoint family members to his Cabinet.) □ *There, Bob's your uncle!* □ *Suddenly, Bob's your uncle and everything's fine again.*

bod 1. *n.* someone who is intrusive, supercilious or tedious. (An abbreviation of "body.") □ *So this bod, a total stranger, turns round and tells Mary that he thinks her skirt doesn't suit her!* □ *Frank's a funny old bod, always pontificating on the topic of the day—whatever it happens to be.* **2.** *n.* a person. (An abbreviation of "body.") □ *How many bods are coming over tonight?* □ *Who's the bod with the tight slacks?*

bodge *vb.* to botch or bungle. □ *I really bodged this before.* □ *I hope I don't bodge it up this time.*

bodgy *mod.* not functioning properly; inferior. □ *That sort of behaviour is really too bodgy to be acceptable, you know.* □ *Sorry, it's too bodgy for me.*

bodice ripper *n.* a romantic novel containing much titillation, which is aimed at female readers. □ *Margo just devours bodice rippers, reading one after the other.* □ *I can't get into reading bodice rippers. Sorry.*

body count 1. *n.* the total of dead bodies after a battle. □ *The body count at Hill 49 was three.* □ *The body count seems to go down during the rainy season.* **2.** *n.* a count of people present. □ *The body count was about forty-five at the meeting.* □ *The body count seems to go down each month.*

body of the kirk *n.* the main group or party, where most people are seated or are to be found. (Originally Scots usage, now general. "Kirk" is Scots for "church." Normally with *the*.) □ *Don't be shy, come on into the body of the kirk.* □ *The body of the kirk thought we should do that.*

body-snatcher *n.* a stretcher-bearer. □ *He's got a job as a body-snatcher at the* *local hospital.* □ *The body-snatchers carried her of to the ambulance.*

b.o.f. See BORING OLD FART.

BOF See BORING OLD FART.

boff *n.* the buttocks. □ *There is some mustard or something on your boff.* □ *She fell right on her boff.*

boffer 1. *n.* a sexually willing girl. (Taboo.) □ *Know of any boffers in the pub tonight?* □ *She's a boffer, I'm sure.* **2.** *n.* a masturbator. (Taboo.) □ *Some filthy boffer has been here before us!* □ *These cinemas showing dirty films are full of boffers.*

boffin *n.* a research scientist. □ *The boffins have discovered a way to transmit smells as well as sound and pictures to your television.* □ *You have to be very clever to be a boffin, son.*

boffing *n.* sexual intercourse. (Taboo.) □ *After that boffing, she felt cheap.* □ *They were talking about, you know, boffing.*

boffing (off) *n.* masturbation. (Taboo.) □ *At least with boffing you don't have to be polite first.* □ *Boffing off is a very popular teenage pastime, you know.*

boff someone 1. *vb.* to punch someone. □ *I was afraid she was going to boff me.* □ *Ted boffed Harry playfully.* **2.** AND **bonk someone** *vb.* to perform sexual intercourse. (Taboo. Originally from the male perspective; now, raffishly, also from the female.) □ *I'm telling you he was in there, boffing her!* □ *If he wants to bonk someone, it should be his wife.*

bog *n.* a toilet. (Crude. Compare with BOG-TROTTER, sense 2.) □ *I must use your bog!* □ *Help yourself. The bog's through there.*

boggin *mod.* stinking. (Scots usage.) □ *I don't know what had been going on but the whole place was boggin.* □ *Oh my, what a boggin mess.*

bog-ignorant *mod.* very ignorant or stupid. (Offensive. From the supposed stupidity of the supposedly bog-dwelling Irish.) □ *I think that was the most bog-ignorant suggestion yet heard. Next?* □ *Get out, you bog-ignorant Irish git!*

Bog off! *exclam.* "Go away!"; "Get lost!" □ *Bog off! I don't want to go out with you!* □ *Can't you take a hint? Get lost! Just bog off, won't you!*

bog off *vb. phr.* to leave; to go away. □ *Look, why don't you just bog off?* □ *You know, I finally told him to bog off and he did!*

bog-roll *n.* a roll of toilet paper. (Crude.) □ *We need a bog-roll in here!* □ *There should be a bog-roll in the cupboard.*

bog seat *n.* a toilet seat. (Crude.) □ *Lift the bog seat!* □ *Put down the bog seat!*

bog-standard *mod.* standard; normal; unmodified. □ *Yes, that's the bog-standard model you have there.* □ *I'm just looking for a bog-standard one; nothing fancy.*

bog-trotter 1. *n.* an Irish vagabond; any Irishman. (Offensive.) □ *Where are all these bog-trotters coming from?* □ *Irish people are called bog-trotters because ignorant English people think the whole of Ireland is one big bog.* **2.** *n.* anyone who is a frequent visitor to the toilet. (Crude. Compare with BOG.) □ *Harry's a real bog-trotter!* □ *He's a bog-trotter because of his illness.*

bog-up *vb. phr.* to make a mess of things. □ *I think I've bogged-up again.* □ *Why do you always bog-up anything that matters?*

bogus *mod.* phony; false; undesirable. □ *I can't eat any more of this bogus food.* □ *This class is really bogus.*

bogy *n.* a policeman. □ *Think about how the bogy on the beat is affected by this cold.* □ *The bogy stopped at the door, tried the lock and moved on.*

boiled *mod.* intoxicated due to drink. □ *All four of them went out and got themselves comprehensively boiled.* □ *She's boiled at the moment.*

boiler *n.* an unattractive or stupid woman, especially an older one. □ *I'm afraid she really is an old boiler.* □ *The boiler seemed to be unable to understand what was happening.*

boiler-maker *n.* a drink consisting half of draught mild beer and half of bottled brown ale. □ *Boiler-makers are sort of* *dated now, aren't they?* □ *He ordered a boiler-maker and came over to join us.*

bollock *n.* a dance; a ball. (Crude.) □ *So what did you think of that bollock we were at at the weekend?* □ *I don't like bollocks like that where everybody gets drunk or worse.*

bollocking AND **rollocking** *n.* a severe chastisement. □ *I think you can be sure that if you don't behave you will experience a right bollocking.* □ *We could hear the rollocking at the other end of the building.*

bollocks See BALLOCKS.

bollocky starkers See STARK NAKED.

boloney See BALONEY.

bolshie 1. *mod.* awkward; unhelpful. □ *He always was a bolshie little tyke.* □ *"Bolshie" is an abbreviation of "Bolshevist," a member of the radical section of the Russian Socialist Party, which, led by Lenin, took power in the Russian Revolution of 1918.* **2.** *mod.* foul-tempered. □ *Do what I ask or I'll get really bolshie with you.* □ *What a bolshie person she can be.*

B.O.L.T.O.P. AND **BOLTOP** *phr.* "Better on lips than on paper." (An initialism is sometimes written on love letters, set beside a paper kiss, an "X." Also an acronym.) □ *XXXX B.O.L.T.O.P.* □ *Love and kisses. BOLTOP.*

bomb 1. *vb.* to fail. □ *My first try bombed, but things got better.* □ *It bombed the minute the first curtain went up.* **2.** *n.* a great success. □ *What a bomb! The whole thing was just wonderful.* □ *I'm sure it's going to be a great bomb.* **3.** *n.* a very large sum of money. □ *She gets paid a bomb to worry about stuff like that.* □ *To me, £400 is a bomb.* **4.** *n.* a very old car. □ *Why are you driving a bomb like that, Paul?* □ *Have you seen the way that bomb was being driven?* **5.** AND **dive bomb** *vb.* to cover a wall with graffiti. □ *I see that wall's been bombed again.* □ *So, who's been dive bombing on these wall now?*

bombed *mod.* very intoxicated due to drink or drugs. □ *Those guys really* were completely bombed at the party. □ *You came in bombed last night. What's going on?*

bomber 1. *n* a large marijuana cigarette. □ *Where did you get that bomber you're smoking?* □ *A bomber would be just a bit too much for me.* **2.** AND **boomer** *n.* a nuclear missile submarine. □ *I used to watch the bombers slide out of Faslane and into the Firth of Clyde.* □ *My husband is on the crew of a boomer, so he's away for months at a time.* **3.** AND **dive bomber** *n.* someone who sprays graffiti. □ *I see we've got a bomber at work around here again.* □ *Who's the dirty little dive bomber that wrote that on the wall?*

bomb out *vb. phr.* to fail to appear. □ *The second interviewee bombed out.* □ *Now don't you bomb out, too. Make sure you get there!*

bomb-proof *mod.* impregnable against danger. □ *I'm sure we're bomb-proof on this, sir.* □ *How can we become bomb-proof here?*

bombshell *n.* a stunning piece of news that is "dropped" without warning. □ *I am still recovering from your bombshell of yesterday.* □ *After you left us with the bombshell about your marriage to that Christmas tree farmer in Wales, we began to realise that it's your life and you should do what you want.*

bonce 1. *n.* a large glass marble used for playing various games. □ *The children like to use a bonce when they play marbles.* □ *Bonces made of multicoloured glass can be very pretty.* **2.** *n.* the head. □ *Put your hat on your bonce, and let's go.* □ *That's using your bonce!*

bone box *n.* the mouth. □ *Have I ever told you that you have an ugly bone box?* □ *Shut your bone box and get on with your work.*

bone dome *n.* a protective helmet worn by motorcyclists, aviators, etc. □ *It's an offence to ride on a motor bike without wearing a bone dome.* □ *He grabbed his bone dome and climbed into the cockpit of the Tornado.*

bonehead 1. *n.* a stupid or stubborn person. □ *You are such a bonehead* when it comes to buying cars. □ *Why am I married to the world's greatest all-time bonehead?* **2.** *n.* a boxer. □ *With a bonehead like him we can make serious money.* □ *I tell you, Mr Big, this one is a real bonehead.*

boneheaded *mod.* stupid; stubborn. □ *Of all the boneheaded things to do!* □ *Don't be so boneheaded.*

bone idle *mod.* very lazy; completely idle or unproductive. □ *Your problem is that you are bone idle.* □ *Take your bone idle brother and move out!*

bone-orchard AND **bone-yard** *n.* a cemetery. □ *That is a very pleasant bone-orchard.* □ *Does it really matter how comfortable a bone-yard looks?*

boner *n.* a silly error; a gaffe. □ *Well, that was a bad boner.* □ *What a boner! You must be embarrassed.*

bone-yard See BONE-ORCHARD.

bong AND **bhong 1.** *n.* a marijuana smoking device that cools the smoke by passing it through water. □ *This bong is really getting sort of nasty.* □ *Fill up your bong and let's get going.* **2.** *vb.* to smoke marijuana or other drugs with a BONG or other device. □ *You can't just bong for the rest of your life!* □ *Wanna go bong a bowl?* **3.** *n.* a puff or HIT of marijuana taken through a BONG. □ *I'll take two bongs, and then I gotta go.* □ *I only got one bong!*

bonk *n.* a bang or a thumping sound. □ *What was that loud bonk?* □ *There was a bonk, and then silence.*

bonkers AND **crackers** *mod.* insane; crazy. □ *Get this bonkers brother of yours out of here!* □ *I think I am going crackers.*

bonk oneself *vb.* to strike a part of one's own body upon some other object. □ *He bonked his head on the shelf.* □ *I bonked my arm.*

bonk someone 1. *vb.* to strike someone. □ *I bonked John upon the shoulder.* □ *He wouldn't move, so I bonked him.* **2.** See also BOFF SOMEONE.

bonk something *vb.* to hit something. □ *I wish you would not bonk your pillows all night long.* □ *The car bonked into the tree.*

boob 1. *n.* a stupid person; a rural oaf. □ *You boob! What have you done?* □ *Why did I marry a boob like you?* **2.** *n.* a screw-up or stupid error. □ *What a foolish boob that turned out to be!* □ *No more boobs, please!*

boob job *n.* a plastic surgery operation to change the appearance of one's breasts. (Crude.) □ *After my boob job I felt I had something to be proud of.* □ *Don't you need some boobs first before you can have a boob job done on them, then?*

boo-boo 1. *n.* an error. (Compare with MAKE A BOO-BOO.) □ *It's only a small boo-boo. Don't excite yourself.* □ *Another boo-boo like that, and you are through.* **2.** *n.* the buttocks. (Childish.) □ *Still, it was funny when she fell on the mud and landed on her boo-boo.* □ *There is some mustard or something on your boo-boo.*

boobs *n.* the female breasts. (Crude. Normally with *the* and in the plural.) □ *My boobs aren't all I might have wished for.* □ *With boobs like that, she can go anywhere she likes.*

boob tube *n.* a woman's tight strapless dress top. □ *I don't think she suits that boob tube.* □ *She came out to see me wearing a boob tube.*

booby hatch AND **booby hutch** *n.* a mental hospital. (Named after a former mental hospital at Colney Hatch, north London.) □ *I was afraid they would send me to the booby hatch.* □ *She spent years in the booby hutch and it shows.*

booby hutch See BOOBY HATCH.

booby-prize AND **wooden spoon** *n.* a prize, usually mythical, awarded to the last in a race, competition, etc. □ *I see Simon's won the booby-prize again this year.* □ *Well, I would not like to say that you've come last, but here's your wooden spoon.*

booby trap 1. *n.* a concealed trap. (Both literal and figurative.) □ *This clause in the contract is a real booby trap. Let's rewrite it.* □ *Some kind of booby trap in the warehouse kept the robber from getting away.* **2.** *vb.* to install a concealed trap in a place. (Usually BOOBY-

TRAP.) □ *The agents booby-trapped the cellar.* □ *They booby-trapped the lift so it turned into a cell if you didn't know the code to open the door.*

booed and hissed *mod.* intoxicated due to drink. (Crude. Rhyming slang, linked as follows: booed and hissed ≈ [pissed] = drunk. Compare with BRAHMS AND LISZT and MOZART.) □ *Joe and Arthur kept on knocking them back till they were both booed and hissed.* □ *Boy, I was really booed and hissed. I'll never drink another drop.*

book *vb.* to charge someone with a crime. □ *The copper booked him for vagrancy.* □ *She looked really shabby and suspicious and they wanted to book her for something, but didn't know what.*

bookie *n.* a bookmaker; one who accepts bets on horse races, etc. □ *Max was a bookie till he got into drugs.* □ *My bookie wants his money on the spot.*

boomer See BOMBER.

boot 1. *n.* a dismissal or ejection. □ *I got the boot even though I had worked there for a decade.* □ *Seven people got the boot there this week.* **2.** *vb.* to start the operating system of a computer. (Computer jargon.) □ *I tried to boot the thing, but it just sat there.* □ *It booted all right, but when I tried to run the application it just beeped at me.* **3.** *n.* money. □ *How much boot do you need, then?* □ *Sorry, I can't afford it, I've no boot.* **4.** *n.* a car tyre. (Usually in the plural.) □ *I'm looking for a new set of boots for my car.* □ *You'll get a good price for boots here.*

booter *n.* a merchant or trader at a CAR BOOT SALE. □ *This booter was selling used false teeth, would you believe!* □ *Harry's working weekends as a booter.*

bootie See BOOT-NECK.

boot is on the other foot *phr.* "things have changed around." (Usually with *the.*) □ *Well, the boot is on the other foot so watch out!* □ *Now that the new management has taken over, the boot is on the other foot.*

boot-neck AND **bootie** *n.* a member of the Royal Marines. □ *I'd never be a*

boot-neck if I could help it! □ *Who's that bootie Marti's with tonight?*

boot sale See CAR BOOT SALE.

boot someone out AND **turf someone out** *vb. phr.* to throw someone out; to kick someone out. □ *Are you going to boot me out?* □ *I don't turf anybody out. Bruno does that. Bruno, come here.*

bootsy *n.* an hotel porter. □ *The bootsy here will be happy to carry your luggage to your room, madam.* □ *The bootsy put the luggage down in the room and stood silently with his hand out, waiting.*

booze 1. *vb.* to drink alcohol to excess; to go on a BASH. (Compare with BOOZE-UP.) □ *Let's go out boozing.* □ *Stop boozing for a minute and listen to me, guys.* **2.** *n.* an alcohol beverage. (Slang since the 1500s.) □ *I don't care for booze. It makes me sneeze.* □ *Where's the booze?*

booze-artist *n.* a drunkard; an alcoholic. (Crude. See also PISS ARTIST is taboo. Compare with BOOZE.) □ *Sorry, anyone downing a whole bottle of gin every day is a booze-artist so far as I'm concerned.* □ *That pub is full of booze-artists.*

boozer 1. *n.* a pub. (Compare with BOOZE.) □ *You'll find Frank in the boozer, as usual.* □ *I don't like that boozer, let's try this one instead.* **2.** *n.* a drunkard. (Compare with BOOZE.) □ *Some old boozer froze to death last night.* □ *You are going to turn into a real boozer if you don't let up on your drinking.*

booze-up *n.* a drinking session; a party when much alcohol is consumed. (Compare with BOOZE.) □ *Are you going to Charlie's booze-up tonight?* □ *After that booze-up, I feel as if I've got two heads this morning.*

boozy 1. *mod.* intoxicated due to drink. (Compare with BOOZE.) □ *She was really boozy and Molly had to take her home.* □ *Everybody was quite boozy and singing by the time the food arrived.* **2.** *n.* a drunkard. (Irish usage. Compare with BOOZE.) □ *If getting rid of a bottle of gin a day makes you a* *boozy, she's a boozy.* □ *There was an old boozy asleep across the front entrance to the office when I got here this morning.* **3.** *mod.* involved with large quantities of alcoholic drink. (See BOOZE.) □ *Now that's what I'd call a boozy do!* □ *If it had been any more boozy we could have swum in the stuff!*

bop 1. *vb.* to strike someone or something. □ *I bopped the car on the bonnet and made a dent.* □ *Are you trying to get bopped on the hooter?* **2.** *vb.* to dance. □ *Come on darling, let's bop.* □ *We bopped for hours, yet somehow were not exhausted.*

bo-peep *n.* sleep. (Rhyming slang.) □ *I could use about another hour of bo-peep.* □ *It's about time to get some bo-peep.*

borassick *mod.* broke; entirely without money. □ *Me? Lend you money? I'm borassick!* □ *I was borassick by the end of the week, but it was well worth it.*

bore someone to tears AND **bore the pants off someone** *vb. phr.* to bore someone exceedingly. □ *You bore me to tears, since you ask!* □ *The lecture bored the pants off everybody.*

bore the pants off someone See BORE SOMEONE TO TEARS.

boring old fart AND **b.o.f.; BOF; bof 1.** *n.* any older person, especially if male. (FART is taboo. Teens.) □ *Calling your boss a boring old fart is not a good way to win a promotion.* □ *The b.o.f. is telling us how he personally won World War Two. Again.* **2.** *mod.* outdated; unfashionable. (FART is taboo. Teens.) □ *I can't stand any more of this boring old fart stuff. Let's go!* □ *Don't be so bof, Gerald! No one cares about that anymore.*

borrow *vb.* to steal. (A jocular euphemism.) □ *Can I borrow a paper clip?* □ *Someone borrowed my car last night.*

borrow and beg *n.* an egg. (Rhyming slang.) □ *A sausage and borrow and beg please, mate.* □ *I'm telling you, he balanced a borrow and beg on the end of his nose!*

bosh *n.* nonsense; idle talk. (Also an exclamation, BOSH!) □ *That's enough of your bosh!* □ *Oh, bosh! You don't know what you're talking about.*

bosom buddy *n.* a very close male or female friend. □ *We are bosom buddies, but we can still get into a big fight every now and then.* □ *Oh, yes, Sharon is my bosom buddy.*

boss 1. *mod.* excellent; powerful; superior. □ *That is a boss tune.* □ *This rally is really boss.* **2.** *n.* one's wife. (Jocular. Usually with *the.*) □ *The boss is angry with me.* □ *I've got to get home to the boss.*

boss-eyed 1. *mod.* blind in one eye. □ *Yes, our cat's been boss-eyed ever since a fight with the next-door cat a few years ago.* □ *There's another boss-eyed cat over there.* **2.** *mod.* cross-eyed. □ *Look at that boss-eyed lady, mummy!* □ *Don't stare, dear. She can't help being boss-eyed, you know.* **3.** *mod.* one-sided. □ *Well, that's a very boss-eyed way of looking at this problem.* □ *Your boss-eyed attitude shows, you know.* **4.** *mod.* misaligned. □ *The machine is boss-eyed and would be very dangerous to use like that.* □ *We've got to fix that boss-eyed track before it will work properly.*

boss shot 1. *n.* a bad guess. □ *Yes it was a boss shot, but then I really had no idea.* □ *I hope this is not another of your boss shots.* **2.** *n.* a failed attempt. □ *Oh no, another boss shot!* □ *That last boss shot was particularly disastrous.* **3.** *n.* a mess. □ *What a boss shot you've made of this!* □ *We don't need any more boss shots, you know.* **4.** AND **duff shot** *n.* a failure to strike a target when firing a gun, throwing a dart, etc. □ *Oh, sorry. Another boss shot, I'm afraid.* □ *I must not make another duff shot.*

bossy-boots *n.* a domineering or bossy woman or child. □ *Please get that bossy-boots out of here!* □ *This particular bossy-boots has just been sacked, as it happens.*

bother(ation) *n.* violence; crowd trouble. (Police.) □ *There's some botheration down here, sarge.* □ *Help PC223 sort out that bother.*

both sheets in(to) the wind AND **four sheets in(to) the wind; three sheets**

in(to) the wind; two sheets in(to) the wind *mod.* intoxicated due to drink. □ *She's both sheets in the wind at the moment.* □ *She's not just three sheets to the wind—she's got them all in the wind.*

both-way bet *n.* a bet where one backs a horse to either win or to be placed. □ *He said I should take a both-way bet on that bottle of sauce.* □ *No Lavinia, you can't have a both-way bet in a one-horse race.*

bottle *n.* courage or self-confidence. □ *Oh, he's got lot of bottle all right.* □ *It must take a lot of bottle to do that.*

bottle and stopper *n.* a policeman. (Rhyming slang, linked as follows: bottle and stopper ≈ [copper] = policeman.) □ *The bottle and stopper stopped at the door, tried the lock and moved on.* □ *Think about how the bottle and stopper on the beat is affected by this cold.*

bottle of beer *n.* an ear. (Rhyming slang.) □ *Look at the huge bottle of beers on her!* □ *Allow me to take you to one side and have a word in your bottle of beer, sonny.*

bottle of sauce *n.* a horse. (Rhyming slang.) □ *He said I should take a both-way bet on that bottle of sauce.* □ *Who ever told you that that bottle of sauce had any hope of winning?*

bottle of Scotch *n.* a watch. (Rhyming slang.) □ *That's an new bottle of Scotch on your wrist, innit?* □ *Where did you get your bottle of Scotch, then?*

bottle of water *n.* a daughter. (Rhyming slang.) □ *Careful there, mate! That's old Bert's bottle of water!* □ *Me bottle of water's coming round later today.*

bottle out *vb. phr.* to loose one's nerve. □ *I'm afraid he's going to bottle out rather than take the risk.* □ *Don't you dare bottle out on me again!*

bottle party *n.* a party where guests bring drink to add to the common stock. □ *What a fancy bottle party! They even have glass glasses!* □ *What time do we have to be at that bottle party on Saturday night?*

bottom 1. *n.* the buttocks. □ *Ted fell on his bottom and just sat there.* □ *My bottom is sore from sitting too long.* **2.** *vb.* to clean especially thoroughly. □ *You better bottom this properly if you want to get paid.* □ *I have bottomed the thing twice now, and still she wants it cleaner!*

bottomless pit 1. *n.* a very hungry person. □ *The guy is a bottomless pit. There just isn't enough food in town to fill him up.* □ *I've got two boys, and they're both bottomless pits.* **2.** *n.* an endless source of something, usually something troublesome. □ *This house is a bottomless pit. Keeping it up is endless.* □ *Our problems come from a bottomless pit. There is just no end to them.*

bottom line 1. *n.* the grand total; the final figure on a balance sheet. (Securities markets. Always with *the*.) □ *The company's bottom line is in bad shape.* □ *If the bottom line is positive, everything is okay.* **2.** *n.* the result; the NITTY-GRITTY; the SCORE. □ *The bottom line is that you really don't care.* □ *Well, when you get down to the bottom line, it's only money that matters.*

bottom of the barrel *n.* the location of persons or things of the very lowest quality. (Usually with *from.* Compare with SCRAPE THE BOTTOM OF THE BARREL.) □ *That last secretary you sent me was really from the bottom of the barrel.* □ *I don't need any candidates from the bottom of the barrel.*

bottom of the garden *n.* the point in a rear garden that is farthest from the house. □ *There was a shed at the bottom of the garden.* □ *They wandered off down to the bottom of the garden, I think.*

bottom out *vb. phr.* to reach the lowest or worst point of something. □ *All my problems seem to be bottoming out. They can't get much worse.* □ *Interest rates bottomed out last February.*

Bottoms up! *sent.* "Let us drink up!" (A drinking toast.) □ *Well, bottoms up.* □ *They all raised their glasses, and the host said, "Bottoms up!"*

bounce 1. *vb.* [for a cheque] to be returned from the bank because of insufficient funds. Compare with RUBBER CHEQUE.) □ *The cheque bounced, and I* *had to pay a penalty fee.* □ *If your cheque bounces, you'll have to bring us cash.* **2.** *vb.* [for a bank] to refuse to honour a cheque. □ *They bounced another of my cheques today.* □ *The bank won't bounce any more cheques because I closed the account.* **3.** *n.* pep; energy. □ *All these kids have a lot of bounce.* □ *I never have any bounce when I wake up early.* **4.** See also CHUCK OUT.

bouncer 1. *n.* a cheque which is returned unpaid. □ *His cheque turned out to be a bouncer, I'm afraid.* □ *That's about the twentieth bouncer he's issued recently.* **2.** AND **minder** *n.* a strong man hired to eject unruly people from a bar or similar place. (People supposedly bounce when thrown out. Compare with CHUCKER-OUT.) □ *I saw the bouncer looking at me, and I got out of there fast.* □ *He was the biggest minder I've ever seen.*

bouncers *n.* the female breasts. (Crude. Normally with *the* and in the plural.) □ *All you think about is bouncers!* □ *Cor, look at the bouncers on that, Fred!*

bounty bar *n.* a black person. (Offensive.) □ *So this bounty bar drives away in a BMW!* □ *Why should a BMW not belong to a bounty bar?*

bovver *n.* bother; trouble. (Eye-dialect. Typical spoken English in London and surrounding area. Used in writing only for effect. Used in the examples of this dictionary.) □ *There's been some bovver down at the pub, I hear.* □ *Bert's in a spot of bovver with the rozzers again.*

bovver boot *n.* a heavy boot, often with a metal toe cap, worn by BOVVER BOYS or SKINHEADS. □ *Traditionally, it's yer bovver boy what wears yer bovver boots.* □ *Why do you wear bovver boots?*

bovver boy *n.* a violent troublemaker. □ *There was a group of bovver boys standing around outside the pub.* □ *Little Archie's turned into a regular bovver boy, I'm afraid.*

bow and arrow 1. *n.* a sparrow. (Rhyming slang.) □ *Aw, look at the little bow and arrow over there.* □ *Some-*

one just shot the pretty bow and arrow with a bow and arrow! **2.** *n.* a barrow. (Rhyming slang.) □ *A man passed by, pushing a bow and arrow.* □ *The bow and arrow was loaded down with fresh fruit.*

bowler *n.* a bowler hat. □ *Very few British businessmen still wear the traditional bowler.* □ *Once bowlers seemed to be compulsory in business.*

bowler-hat *vb.* to retire from the army. □ *The colonel was bowler-hatted last year.* □ *I don't want to bowler-hat just yet.*

bowling green *n.* a fast-moving railway line. □ *This one's a bowling green; don't fool around near the track.* □ *Trains pass here at over 130 m.p.h.; it's a regular bowling green!*

bowl someone out 1. *vb. phr.* to dismiss a batsman. (Cricket.) □ *I was bowled out.* □ *This bowler is good; he will bowl out one batsman after another.* **1.** *vb. phr.* to dismiss an entire side. (Cricket.) □ *We were all bowled out one after the other.* □ *That bowler bowled out the whole side.*

bow-wow 1. *n.* an ugly woman; a DOG. (Derogatory.) □ *What a bow-wow!* □ *I would have chosen a better nose if I had been given a chance, but—all in all—I'm not such a bow-wow.* **2.** *n.* a dog. (Juvenile.) □ *The bow-wow frightened me.* □ *We're going to get you a bow-wow!*

box 1. *n.* a coffin. □ *I want the cheapest box they sell.* □ *Put him in a box and put the box in a hole. Then the matter is closed.* **2.** See also IDIOT BOX.

box clever *vb. phr.* to behave shrewdly. □ *I tried to box clever, but she was too smart for me.* □ *Box clever with this one; he's out to trip you up.*

boxed in *mod.* in a bind; having few alternatives. □ *I really feel boxed in around here.* □ *I got him boxed in. He'll have to do it our way.*

boxed-up *mod.* imprisoned. □ *The judge wanted to have him boxed-up for two years, but decided on one instead.* □ *My cousin is boxed-up for a year.*

box someone in *vb. phr.* to put someone into a bind; to reduce the number of someone's alternatives. □ *I don't want to box you in, but you are running out of options.* □ *I want to box in the whole staff, so they'll have to do it my way.*

boy *n.* heroin. □ *She's on boy now. Soon she'll be hooked for good.* □ *The boy in this town is so watered down, you can joy pop for years and never get hooked.*

boy in blue *n.* stew. (Rhyming slang.) □ *Any more of that great boy in blue, love?* □ *Me Harry always likes me boy in blue.*

boyo 1. *n.* a boy or man. (Welsh usage. Also a form of address.) □ *The boyo sat on the bench and waited for him.* □ *There's a boyo here looking for you.* **2.** *n.* an IRA (Irish Republican Army) terrorist. (Irish usage.) □ *There are a number of boyos living around here, I think.* □ *They say Sean is a boyo, but I don't know.*

Boy, oh boy! See OH, BOY!

boys in blue *n.* the police; policemen. □ *The boys in blue are looking for you.* □ *You can depend upon the boys in blue to sort things out around here.*

boys in the backroom AND **backroom boys** *n.* any private male group making decisions, usually politicians. □ *The boys in the backroom picked the last parliamentary candidate.* □ *The backroom boys have decided too many things in the past. Their day is over.*

boys on ice *n.* lice. (Rhyming slang.) □ *The first thing is to check for boys on ice on everyone.* □ *I'm afraid every one of these refugees have boys on ice.*

bozo *n.* a clown; a fool. (Also a term of address. Pronounced BOE-zoe.) □ *Look, you bozo, I've had enough of your jabber.* □ *Those bozos are at it again. Spend, spend, spend.*

bra-burner *n.* a nickname for a woman who supported the women's liberation movements of the 1960s and 1970s. (Crude.) □ *Didn't the bra-burners give way to whale-savers in the seventies?* □ *Mike wants to know if the bra-burners took them off first.*

Brahms and Liszt *mod.* intoxicated due to drink. (Taboo. Rhyming slang, linked as follows: Brahms and Liszt ≈ [pissed] = drunk. Compare with BOOED AND HISSED and MOZART.) □ *Tracy gets a little Brahms and Liszt after a drink or two.* □ *Tipsy? Brahms and Liszt, more like!*

brain *vb.* to hit someone hard upon the head. □ *I ought to brain you for that!* □ *She almost brained me with her umbrella.*

brainbox *n.* a very intelligent person. □ *Here was one brainbox that was different from the others, he thought.* □ *I don't think I could take another brainbox like that today.*

brainchild *n.* someone's good idea viewed as an offspring of the brain. □ *Is this your brainchild? Because it won't work.* □ *Listen to this one. It's my best brainchild yet.*

brain drain *n.* the movement of intellectuals from one country to another where pay and job opportunities are better. □ *It looks like the brain drain of the sixties is reviving with more and more academics leaving Britain to join American universities.* □ *Where there is a good education system, there will always be a brain drain.*

brains *n.* the person(s) in charge of thinking something through. □ *Who's the brains around this outfit?* □ *Bruno is not what you would call the brains of the organisation.*

brainstorm *vb.* to try to think up good ideas, especially as a group. □ *Let's brainstorm this around for a little while.* □ *They are in the meeting room now, brainstorming.*

brain-teaser AND **brain-twister** *n.* a puzzle or mystery. □ *Can you help me with this brain-teaser?* □ *This Maltese falcon case is a real brain-twister.*

brain-twister See BRAIN-TEASER.

brand new See BRAND SPANKING NEW.

brand spanking new AND **brand new; spanking new** *mod.* completely new. □ *My car is spanking new.* □ *Look at that brand spanking new car!*

brass 1. *n.* cheekiness. □ *Why, the brass of her!* □ *Less of your brass, you young pup!* **2.** *n.* money. □ *I don't make enough brass to go on a trip like that!*

□ *It takes a lot of brass to buy a car like that.* **3.** *n.* a badge, medallion or ornament. □ *Right, you go round the building and polish all the brass you can find.* □ *Remember to wear your brass at the parade tomorrow.* **4.** *n.* a prostitute. (Crude. Rhyming slang, linked as follows: brass [rail] ≈ [tail] = prostitute.) □ *There was a brass standing right on that corner.* □ *Clare dresses like a brass.*

brass band *n.* a hand. (Rhyming slang.) □ *He had a brass band on him like a gorilla.* □ *Get your brass bands off me glass.*

brassed (off) *mod.* angry; disgusted. □ *You look so brassed off at the world. Smile!* □ *I'm not brassed in the least, really.*

brass farthing *n.* the least possible money. □ *Look, I don't have so much as two brass farthings to rub together.* □ *I'm afraid there is not even one brass farthing left in that account.*

brass monkey's weather *n.* very cold weather. (Crude. Derived from the picturesque description of such weather as being "...so cold it would freeze the balls off a brass monkey.") □ *Cor! Real brass monkey's weather today, innit?* □ *In brass monkey's weather like this he prefers to stay indoors.*

brass neck AND **hard neck; neck** *n.* cheek; impudence. □ *The brass neck! Who does she think she is?* □ *Any more neck like that and he'll get everything he deserves.*

brass something out *vb. phr.* to brazen something out. □ *What else could I do but brass it out?* □ *I tried to brass the situation out but did not have the nerve.*

brass tacks AND **tin tacks** *n.* the essential details; the serious business. (Rhyming slang, linked as follows: brass/tin tacks ≈ [facts] = essential details/serious business.) □ *Now that we are talking brass tacks, how much do you really want for this watch?* □ *Since we haven't got down to brass tacks yet, would it be unethical for me to buy you lunch?*

brass up *vb. phr.* to pay up. □ *Come on, brass up!* □ *Time to brass up, is it?*

brat *n.* a child. □ *She is a most irritating brat.* □ *Is this brat yours?*

brave and bold *mod.* cold. (Rhyming slang.) □ *I won't go out in brave and bold weather.* □ *Why does it have to be so brave and bold?*

bread and butter 1. *n.* one's livelihood. □ *It's bread and butter to me. I have to do it.* □ *I can't give it up. It's my bread and butter.* **2.** *n.* a gutter. (Rhyming slang.) □ *John! The bread and butter's overflowing again!* □ *I've got to get the ladder out to fix the bread and butter.*

bread and butter letter *n.* a letter thanking the host or hostess upon returning from a visit. (Compare with COLLINS.) □ *Well, that's nice. Only Mrs Harris has had the courtesy to send a bread and butter letter.* □ *I must write a bread and butter letter to Mrs Jackson to thank her for last night's wonderful dinner party.*

bread (and honey) *n.* money. (Rhyming slang. Compare with DOUGH.) □ *I need to get some bread and honey to live on.* □ *You got any bread you can spare?*

bread and lard *mod.* hard. (Rhyming slang.) □ *Cor, that's a bread and lard job you've got there!* □ *The ice was really bread and lard.*

break 1. *n.* a chance; an opportunity. □ *Come on, give me a break!* □ *I got my first break in show biz when I was only twelve.* **2.** *vb.* [for a news story] to unfold rapidly. (Journalism.) □ *As the story continues to break, we will bring you the latest.* □ *Something is breaking on the Wilson murder. Get over to the crime scene, quick.*

Break a leg! *exclam.* "Good luck!" (A special theatrical way of wishing a performer good luck. Among theatricals, saying the actual words "good luck" is reputed to be a jinx.) □ *"Break a leg!" shouted the stage manager to the heroine.* □ *Let's all go and do our best. Break a leg!*

Break it up! *exclam.* "Stop it!" (An order to two or more people to stop doing something, such as fighting.) □ *All right you two, break it up!* □ *She told the boys to break it up or get sent to the headmaster's office.*

break the back of someone *vb. phr.* to require someone to take on some task or responsibility greater than that with which they can cope. □ *That task would break the back of these poor people, sir.* □ *My workload is going to break my back one day.*

break the back of something *vb. phr.* to achieve the largest or hardest part of some problem or task. □ *We've almost broken the back of this problem.* □ *Come on, we're not going to give up now we've almost broken the back of our little task.*

break the ice 1. *vb. phr.* to be the first one to do something. □ *No one wants to break the ice. Oh well, I suppose I'll have to be the first as usual.* □ *Well, I think we should break the ice and start dancing.* **2.** *vb. phr.* to attempt to become friends with someone. □ *He tried to break the ice, but she was a little cold.* □ *A nice smile does a lot to break the ice.*

breakup *n.* the end of a school's summer term and the start of summer vacation. □ *It was breakup, and we were going on our summer holidays.* □ *Just before breakup, we had school prize-giving day.*

breathe down someone's neck *vb. phr.* to be very near to someone; to have almost caught up with someone. □ *All right, all right, I'm going as fast as I can. Do you have to breathe down my neck?* □ *Stop breathing down people's necks like that; it puts them off.*

breather *n.* a rest period; a lull. □ *I really need a breather.* □ *As soon as we've had a breather, it's back to work.*

breeze *n.* an outburst of bad temper. □ *That one remark was enough to cause the whole subsequent breeze.* □ *What a breeze that was! I thought murder might be done!*

brekkies *n.* breakfast. (Jocular or childish.) □ *Anyone want brekkies?* □ *Ah, brekkies! What do we have?*

brew 1. *n.* tea; occasionally, coffee. □ *I could use a nice brew.* □ *This is my kind of brew: hot, black and strong.* **2.** *n.* beer; a can, bottle or glass of beer. □ *Can I have a pint of brew, please?* □

This is my favourite brew. Isn't it delicious at room temperature?

brewed *mod.* intoxicated due to drink. □ *She just lay there, brewed.* □ *Those guys really were completely brewed at the party.*

brewer's droop *n.* temporary impotence induced by excessive consumption of beer. □ *Doris was soon to discover that Frank had returned from his evening in the pub with a severe case of brewer's droop.* □ *I'm afraid it takes depressingly little beer to give me brewer's droop.*

brew up *vb. phr.* to make tea. □ *I'm exhausted! Let's brew up.* □ *Come in, we were just brewing up.*

Brian *n.* a name that supposedly typifies a boring, dull or uninteresting person. □ *The Brian was waiting outside the office for him.* □ *He's a pleasant enough Brian, if that's not a contradiction in terms.*

brick 1. *n.* a solid and reliable person. □ *We really could use another brick like him working here.* □ *We're so lucky having a brick like her around here.* **2.** *n.* a kilogram of marijuana. □ *If the fuzz find a brick on you you'll go away for a long time.* □ *How much do you think a brick is worth on the street?*

brickie *n.* a bricklayer. □ *We need more brickies if we're to get this thing built on time.* □ *There's a brickie here to see you.*

bride *n.* a prostitute. (Crude.) □ *Do you think she's a bride or just too friendly?* □ *This bride comes up to me and acts like she's met me before.*

bridge widow *n.* a wife left alone while her husband plays bridge. (See GOLF WIDOW and COMPUTER WIDOW.) □ *Why don't you come along to the next meeting of the Bridge Widows?* □ *There's a lot of us bridge widows around here, especially at weekends.*

brief 1. *n.* material pertaining to legal case-work performed by a barrister. □ *I've got an interesting brief for you to consider.* □ *I'm not sure how we stand on that brief.* **2.** *n.* a criminal barrister. □ *Get me my brief!* □ *The brief says he'll be here in an hour.*

bright and breezy *mod.* cheery and alert. □ *You look all bright and breezy. What happened?* □ *Bright and breezy people on a day like this make me sick.*

bright as a button *mod.* very intelligent; alert. □ *Oh, she's as bright as a button!* □ *I need someone as bright as a button on this job.*

bright bastard *n.* a know-all; a SMART ALEC. (Taboo. Compare with ILLEGITIMATE GLOW-WORM.) □ *I hate these bright bastards who think they know all the answers.* □ *What you really hate, Otto, is that that particular bright bastard usually is right.*

bright-eyed and bushy-tailed *mod.* alert and ready to do something; as alert and as active as a squirrel. □ *You look all bright-eyed and bushy-tailed this morning.* □ *The child—bright-eyed and bushy-tailed—woke everyone up at dawn.* □ *Tell that bright-eyed and bushy-tailed brat to shut up!*

Brighton Pier *mod.* a male homosexual. (Crude. Rhyming slang, linked as follows: Brighton Pier ≈ [queer] = homosexual.) □ *She came to the dance with a real Brighton Pier.* □ *Tom is getting to be such an obvious Brighton Pier.*

bright spark *n.* a lively, cheerful person. □ *Even a bright spark like that has to earn a living.* □ *What does the bright spark want?*

brill *mod.* excellent; thrilling. □ *Boy, this fishing rod is brill.* □ *This wine is really brill!*

bring-down *n.* something that depresses someone. □ *The news was a terrible bring-down.* □ *Just to see your face was a bring-down.*

bring home the bacon *vb. phr.* to earn a livelihood; to earn money to buy food. □ *When I have to bring home the bacon, I hope I have an interesting job.* □ *I have to bring home the bacon for six kids.*

bring someone down 1. *vb. phr.* to terminate one's own or someone else's drug experience. □ *It took a lot to bring her down.* □ *We brought down the two of them carefully.* **2.** *vb. phr.* to depress someone. □ *The news really brought*

me down. □ *The failure of the business brought down the staff.*

bring someone low *vb. phr.* to humiliate or ruin. □ *Now that sort of disaster always brings me low.* □ *Why do you try to bring low your friends?*

bring someone off *vb. phr.* to induce an orgasm in someone. (Taboo.) □ *He brought off the girl again.* □ *Oh God, he's bringing me off!*

bring someone on *vb. phr.* to excite someone sexually. (Taboo.) □ *She tried to bring on Martin, but he remained true to Robert.* □ *This kind of music brings me on.*

bring someone to book *vb. phr.* to charge someone with a crime, especially when this is done by the police. □ *They are determined to bring Mr Big to book.* □ *The only ones they ever bring to book are the little men.*

bring something up 1. *vb. phr.* to mention something. (Standard English.) □ *Why did you have to bring that up?* □ *Then they brought up the question of money.* **2.** *vb. phr.* to vomit something up; to cough something up. (Crude.) □ *See if you can get him to bring up the penny.* □ *I did, and he brought up a 5p coin instead!*

briny *n.* a poetic name for the sea. (Normally with *the.*) □ *He looked out over the vastness of the briny.* □ *His plane crashed into the briny, I'm afraid.*

Bristol fashion See SHIPSHAPE AND BRISTOL FASHION.

bristols *n.* the female breasts. (Crude. Normally with *the* and in the plural. Rhyming slang, linked as follows: Bristol [Citie]s ≈ [titties] = breasts. Normally with *the* and in the plural. Bristol City is a soccer club. Compare with TALE OF TWO CITIES.) □ *There she was, bold as brass, with her bristols on full display.* □ *My bristols aren't all I might have wished for.*

Brit *n.* a British person. □ *I don't think I could take another Brit like him today.* □ *There was one Brit in that crowd, but he stood out from the rest.*

Brixton briefcase *n.* a GHETTOBLASTER. (Potentially racially offensive. Brixton, in south London, has a large population of immigrants from the Caribbean and Africa.) □ *Turn off your Brixton briefcase for a moment and just listen to what I have to tell you.* □ *When you get several Brixton briefcases all together the noise is indescribable.*

broad brush *mod.* generally, without any detail. □ *This is the broad brush picture.* □ *I only have broad brush information; no detail.*

broads *n.* playing-cards. □ *Get out the broads and we'll have a game.* □ *What do you like to play with your broads?*

broadsman *n.* a card sharper. □ *Broadsmen can make a lot of money out of the dupes they persuade to play with them.* □ *That friendly old card partner you've found is a broadsman, I'm sure.*

broke *mod.* without money; bankrupt. □ *I was broke by the end of the week, but it was well worth it.* □ *Me? Lend you money? I'm broke, too!*

broken reed *n.* an unreliable person. □ *He's just a broken reed.* □ *I'm not going to trust my business to a broken reed like him.*

brolly *n.* an umbrella. □ *I'm taking my brolly as it looks like rain.* □ *He opened his brolly and walked out into the rain.*

broody 1. *mod.* pensive; silent and sullen. □ *Why is she always so broody?* □ *She's a strange, broody person.* **2.** *mod.* [of a woman] wishing for a child. □ *I think Marie has been getting broody again since little Susan began to grow up.* □ *She's thirty and broody, worried she may never be a mother.*

brothel creepers *n.* thickly-soled suede shoes. (Crude.) □ *The trouble with brothel creepers is that they make the wearer so silent.* □ *He put on his brothel creepers and went out into the rain.*

brown bread *mod.* dead. (Rhyming slang.) □ *Me missus is brown bread, mate.* □ *He put the brown bread cat in the rubbish bin.*

browned off 1. *mod.* angry. (Compare with BROWN SOMEONE OFF.) □ *I am really browned off at you!* □ *The boss is browned off—to say the least.* **2.** AND **cheesed off** *mod.* bored or fed up. □ *I*

am very browned off today. □ *Why are you always so cheesed off?*

brown hatter *n.* a male homosexual. (Taboo.) □ *He doesn't like being called a brown hatter.* □ *Does Tom have to be such a blatant brown hatter?*

brownie 1. *n.* ECSTASY, a hallucinogen similar to L.S.D. (Usually in the plural.) □ *You can get some good brownies in this part of town.* □ *Brownies are just one of a dozen drugs with similar formulas.* **2.** *n.* a male homosexual. (Taboo.) □ *I hear that you-know-who is a brownie.* □ *She came to the dance with a brownie.*

brownie points *n.* imaginary credit for doing something well. □ *How many brownie points do I get for not frowning when you take my picture?* □ *No brownie points for you, you twit!*

browning *n.* the act of sodomy; anal intercourse. □ *Unprotected browning may be a principle reason for the spread of AIDS.* □ *Browning is not something you talk about in public.*

brown job *n.* a soldier. (From the colour of the uniform.) □ *Who's the brown job Mart's with tonight?* □ *I'd never be a brown job if I could help it!*

brown-nose *vb.* to curry favour with someone; to be a sycophant. □ *Don't you brown-nose me!* □ *Don keeps brown-nosing, and the professor pretends not to notice.*

brown-noser *n.* a sycophant; one who flatters for self-serving motives. □ *You are just a plain old brown-nose.* □ *That brown-noser actually gave the boss a bottle of wine for her birthday.*

brown someone off *vb. phr.* to make someone angry. (Compare with BROWNED OFF.) □ *That whole business with the cab really browned me off.* □ *I'm afraid I'm going to brown off everyone, but here goes anyway.*

bruiser 1. *n.* a big tough-looking man. □ *That big bruiser must weigh a ton.* □ *They call that 22-stone bruiser "The Fridge."* **2.** *n.* a boxer. □ *He may be a bruiser, but he's as gentle as a kitten.* □ *The two heavy-weight bruisers really went for each other in the ring.*

Brum *n.* Birmingham. □ *He comes from Brum.* □ *I'm off to Brum for a business meeting tomorrow.*

brummagem *mod.* cheap, counterfeit or fake. (From *Birmingham.*) □ *This is all brummagem stuff; it's useless.* □ *No brummagem goods, please!*

brummagem screwdriver AND **Chinese screwdriver** *n.* a hammer. (From "Birmingham.") □ *It looks as if these screws were put in with a brummagem screwdriver.* □ *Pass me my Chinese screwdriver, please.*

Brummie AND **Brummy** *n.* a native, citizen or inhabitant of Birmingham. □ *There's a guy who sounds like a Brummy here to see you.* □ *I don't know any Brummies.*

brush 1. *n.* an encounter; a CLOSE SHAVE. □ *My brush with the bear was so close I could smell its breath—which was vile, I might add.* □ *It seemed like a brush with death.* **2.** *n.* a woman's pubic hair. (Taboo.) □ *He got arrested trying to look up women's skirts in the hope of seeing their brush.* □ *What do you mean, you can see my brush? Oh my god, I've forgotten my knickers!*

brush-off *n.* a rejection. (Compare with GIVE SOMEONE THE BRUSH-OFF.) □ *I see you've given Moira the brush-off.* □ *That's a brush-off, I take it?*

Brussels Sprout *n.* a boy scout. (Rhyming slang.) □ *Were you ever a Brussels Sprout?* □ *What is that Brussels Sprout doing here?*

BTW *interj.* "by the way." (Computer jargon. Written only. An initialism used in computer communications.) □ *BTW, have you heard about the new communications software upgrade?* □ *I am, BTW, very interested in what you said about the high cost of software.*

bubbies *n.* the female breasts. (Crude. Normally with *the* and in the plural.) □ *There she was, bold as brass, with her bubbies on full display.* □ *With bubbies like that, she can go anywhere she likes.*

bubble AND **double bubble** *n.* overtime. □ *There's lots of bubble while this rush lasts.* □ *I'm working double bubble tonight again.*

Bubble (and Squeak) *n.* a Greek. (Offensive. Rhyming slang.) □ *Donna's new boyfriend is a Bubble and Squeak, I hear.* □ *Who's this Bubble you're going into business with?*

bubble and squeak 1. *n.* meat, vegetables and potatoes chopped up and then fried together. □ *Bubble and squeak is an old favourite in the East End of London.* □ *It's called bubble and squeak because that's what it's supposed to do while it's cooking.* **2.** *vb. phr.* to speak. (Rhyming slang.) □ *Why did you have to bubble and squeak just then?* □ *Listen to him bubbling and squeaking on and on about nothing!*

bubble on someone See YOP ON SOMEONE.

bubbly *n.* champagne. (Often with *the*.) □ *I'd like a big glass of bubbly, if you don't mind.* □ *The bubbly will brighten up any party.*

bucket and pail *n.* a jail. (Rhyming slang.) □ *Get me out of this terrible bucket and pail!* □ *Do you want to talk, or do you want to spend a little time in the bucket and pail?*

bucket shop 1. *n.* a location where informal and speculative share dealing is conducted. □ *I never go near bucket shops.* □ *Is there a bucket shop around here?* **2.** *n.* an agency selling heavily discounted airline tickets. □ *Sally found a really good holiday flight bargain at the bucket shop.* □ *The bucket shop in High Street was closed after some tickets it sold turned out to be worthless.*

Buck House *n.* Buckingham Palace. □ *You'll find Buck House at the end of the Mall.* □ *Buck House is where the Royal Family lives when they're in London.*

bucks See DOLLARS.

buckshee 1. *mod.* extra or free. (From the Persian *baksis*, meaning "gift," by hobson-jobson.) □ *That particular one is buckshee.* □ *If it's buckshee, there has to be a catch.* **2.** *n.* a bribe. □ *He took the buckshee and won't get in our way.* □ *Someone in here has been taking buckshee.*

buck up *vb. phr.* to cheer up; to perk up. □ *Come on, now, buck up. Things can't* *be all that bad.* □ *She began to buck up when I showed her the results of the tests.*

budgie *n.* a small Australian parakeet or parrot, the budgerigar. (Formally *melopsittacus undulatus*, it is a very popular household pet in Britain.) □ *My pet budgie has died.* □ *My Aunt Joan has a budgie, too.*

buffer See OLD BUFFER.

bug 1. *n.* a flaw in computer software. (Computer jargon. Compare with DEBUG.) □ *As soon as I get the bugs out, I can run my program.* □ *There is a little bug still, but it hardly causes any problems.* □ *That's not a bug, it's a feature!* **2.** *n.* a spying device used to listen to someone's conversation. □ *I found a little bug taped under my chair.* □ *The MI5 agents put bugs everywhere.* **3.** *vb.* to install hidden listening devices such as concealed microphones. (Compare with DEBUG.) □ *Who bugged my office?* □ *We'll have to bug Mr Big's own office if we're ever going to get what we need.* **4.** *vb.* to listen, using hidden devices, secretly. (Compare with DEBUG.) □ *This room is bugged.* □ *I bugged the place myself, before I defected.*

Bugger! *exclam.* a powerful expletive. (Taboo.) □ *Bugger! Why did you do that?* □ *Bugger, it's worked this time!*

bugger 1. *n.* a very serious or difficult problem or predicament. (Taboo. Compare with BASTARD.) □ *This is a bugger! What do we do now?* □ *If we don't get this bugger sorted out, the whole project will fail.* **2.** *n.* a sodomite. (The official, legal word for this sort of person. Nevertheless, it is normally taboo outside a courtroom.) □ *He is, quite literally, a bugger.* □ *When a judge calls you a bugger, Simon, he is not swearing at you.*

bugger about *vb. phr.* to fuss around; to waste time; to fool about. (Taboo.) □ *That's enough buggering about.* □ *Instead of buggering about, could you try working for a change?*

bugger all *n.* absolutely nothing. (Taboo.) □ *When I looked, there was bugger all there.* □ *I have bugger all money, and there's an end to it.*

buggeration factor *n.* a complicating factor, a delaying factor or a problem. (Taboo.) □ *Unfortunately, you've forgotten the buggeration factor.* □ *This whole business is full of buggeration factors, one after the other.*

buggered for something *mod.* lacking something. (Taboo.) □ *All right, so we're buggered for one little screw. Get one!* □ *Why is it buggered for something so stupid and obvious, then?*

Bugger it! AND **Bugger me!** *exclam.* "Curse it"! (Taboo.) □ *I've been trying to make this computer work all day. Bugger it!* □ *Bugger me, is that the best you can do?*

buggerlugs *n.* a pejorative term of address sometimes used rafishly as a friendly greeting. (Taboo.) □ *Hello, you old buggerlugs! How are you?* □ *What's that buggerlugs up to now?*

Bugger me! See BUGGER IT!

Bugger off! See FUCK OFF!

bugger off 1. *vb. phr.* to go away; to get lost. (Taboo.) □ *I wish that pest would be good enough to bugger off and leave me in peace.* □ *I thought I'd better bugger off before they discovered I was not supposed to have been there in the first place.* **2.** See also FUCK OFF.

bugger's muddle AND **sods' holiday** *n.* a bad muddle or confusion. (Taboo.) □ *No more bugger's muddle like that, thank you very much.* □ *We cannot afford any more of these sods' holidays; is that clear?*

bugger (up) *vb. (phr.)* to spoil or ruin. (Taboo.) □ *The whole project's buggered now!* □ *Try not to bugger up this one too.*

buggery 1. *n.* the act of sodomy; anal intercourse. (The official, legal word for this act. Nevertheless, it is normally taboo outside a courtroom.) □ *Buggery is not something you talk about in public.* □ *They say unprotected buggery may be a principle reason for the spread of AIDS.* **2.** *n.* ruination; oblivion; destruction. (Taboo.) □ *Oh no! It's all going to buggery!* □ *We will all face buggery soon, unless you can come up with a solution.*

buggin's turn *n.* selection by rote rather than merit. □ *We do these thing by buggin's turn round here.* □ *It's buggin's turn: you're next!*

bugladders *n.* side-whiskers or sideburns. □ *He's the fellow with the great big bugladders.* □ *I don't trust men with bugladders.*

bugs bunny *n.* money. (Rhyming slang.) □ *Sorry, I can't afford it, I've no bugs bunny.* □ *How much bugs bunny do you need, then?*

built for comfort *mod.* [of a woman] pleasantly plump. (Crude. From the point of view of a man.) □ *Now Tina's one girl who was clearly built for comfort rather than speed.* □ *I like girls who are built for comfort.*

built like a brick shithouse *mod.* well-built; either strong or attractive. (Taboo.) □ *That guy's built like a brick shithouse.* □ *This garage is built like a brick shithouse. It'll last for years.*

bulge *n.* a nose. □ *How did you get a bulge like that?* □ *He threatened to punch me right on the bulge!*

bulge-duster *n.* a handkerchief. □ *There was a bulge-duster sticking out of his top pocket.* □ *He removed his bulge-duster and blew his nose.*

bulge the onionbag *vb. phr.* to score a goal during a game of soccer. □ *Yes, he's bulged the onionbag again! What a goal!* □ *Right lads, let's go out there and bulge the onionbag.*

bull 1. *n.* nonsense; bullshit. □ *That's just a lot of bull.* □ *Don't give me that bull! I won't buy it.* **2.** *n.* the bull's-eye of a target. □ *Aim at the bull and gently squeeze the trigger.* □ *I hit the bull!* **3.** *n.* otherwise pointless routine tasks imposed upon troops supposedly as a means of imposing military discipline. □ *If you join the army, you'll find out all about bull.* □ *I don't think there's anything like as much bull in the army nowadays.*

bull and cow *n.* a row; an argument. (Rhyming slang.) □ *No more bull and cows, you two!* □ *I've just had a big bull and cow with Sandra.*

Bulldog Breed *n.* the British, as seen by the British. (Normally with *the*.) □ *I'm afraid I don't think the Bulldog Breed is quite so bulldog-like anymore.* □ *Of course we're the Bulldog Breed, as tough and determined and resilient as ever.*

bullock *vb.* to pawn something. (Rhyming slang, linked as follows: bullock['s horn] ≈ pawn.) □ *He had no money and had to bullock something.* □ *Why did you ever think to bullock that?*

bull session *n.* a session of casual conversation. □ *The guys were sitting around enjoying a bull session.* □ *The bull session ran on late into the night.*

bull's-eye *n.* a hard, large, spherical, peppermint-flavoured sweet or candy. □ *Mummy, can I have a bull's-eye?* □ *I love bull's-eyes. I always have, ever since I was little.*

bum *n.* the buttocks. □ *Bob fell down on his bum.* □ *I was so angry. I wanted to kick him in the bum as he left.*

bum and tit See B AND T.

bum bag *n.* a small bag attached by a belt around the waist. □ *Why are you wearing a bum bag?* □ *A bum bag is very handy way to secure your valuables as you travel about.*

bumbledom *n.* pompous or officious rules or regulations, or the application of these. (From an officious character called "Bumble," in Dickens's novel *Oliver Twist*.) □ *I've just experienced a classic case of bumbledom at the local council office.* □ *I think they're sent away to learn how to be better at bumbledom.*

bum boy AND **bum chum** *n.* a passive male homosexual. (Taboo.) □ *Tell that bum boy to get out of here.* □ *He doesn't like being called a bum chum.*

bum chum See BUM BOY.

bumf AND **bumph 1.** *n.* toilet paper. (Crude.) □ *We need some bumf in here!* □ *There should be some bumph in the cupboard.* **2.** *n.* trashy literature. □ *He never reads anything but bumf.* □ *Where do you get that bumph?*

bum-freezer *n.* a short coat or jacket. □ *You'll discover why they're called bum-freezers if you wear one on a really cold day.* □ *He stood there in his bum-freezer and shivered.*

bummer *n.* a disagreeable thing or person. □ *My coach is a real bummer.* □ *That game was a bummer like you wouldn't believe.*

bummer AND **bum trip** *n.* a bad drug experience. □ *She almost didn't get back from a bum trip.* □ *This bummer comes from mixing pills.*

bumpers *n.* the female breasts. (Crude. Normally with *the* and in the plural.) □ *My bumpers aren't all I might have wished for.* □ *Cor, look at the bumpers on that, Fred!*

bumph See BUMF.

bump someone *vb.* to remove someone from an aircraft flight, usually involuntarily, because of overbooking. □ *They bumped me, but gave me something to make up for it.* □ *Is this airline in the habit of bumping old ladies?*

bump someone off *vb. phr.* to kill someone. (Originally underworld. Compare with KNOCK SOMEONE (OFF).) □ *What am I supposed to do, bump her off?* □ *The gang bumped off the witness before the trial.*

bump tummies See PLAY BOUNCY-BOUNCY.

bum's rush *n.* the ejection of an individual from a particular location or organisation. □ *I got the bum's rush at that bar. Do I look that bad?* □ *Give this tart the bum's rush. She can't pay for nothing.*

bum trip See BUMMER.

bunce 1. *n.* a windfall or unexpected profit. □ *Well, here's a nice bit of bunce.* □ *We made a lot of bunce out of that deal.* **2.** *n.* commission; profit. □ *No, that's just my regular bunce.* □ *I need that weekly bunce to live on.*

bunce someone *vb.* to overcharge someone. □ *Those car repair places can bunce you if you don't watch out.* □ *You are trying to bunce me. I won't pay it!*

bunch of fives 1. *n.* a handful of five pound notes. □ *He showed me a bunch of fives and said, "Okay, how much if I pay cash?"* □ *He put a bunch of fives into the top pocket of my shirt and said that there were plenty more to be had if I asked no questions.* **2.** *n.* the fist. □

How would you like a bunch of fives right in the kisser? □ *He ended up with a bunch of fives in the gut.*

bundle *n.* a large amount of money. (Compare with LOSE A BUNDLE and MAKE A BUNDLE.) □ *He still has a bundle he made from the sale of his house.* □ *You must think I have a real bundle.*

bundle of joy *n.* a baby. □ *We are expecting a bundle of joy next September.* □ *When your little bundle of joy arrives, things will be a little hectic for a while.*

bundle of nerves *n.* a very nervous person. □ *I'm just a bundle of nerves. I wish this were over.* □ *Paul's been a bundle of nerves ever since he had the accident.*

bun fight *n.* a tea party. □ *The bun fight was most enjoyable.* □ *What a boring bun fight!*

bung 1. *vb.* to bribe or tip someone. □ *I'm sure you can bung at least one of them, if you try hard enough.* □ *Why do you want one of them bunged?* **2.** *vb.* to fling or throw something. □ *She was bunging all her old clothes away.* □ *When I said you should get rid of it I did not mean you should literally bung it out the window.*

bungaloid *mod.* like a bungalow. □ *It's a single-story, bungaloid structure.* □ *He hides all day in his bungaloid office.*

bungaloid growth *n.* an infestation of bungalows. □ *There has been a bungaloid growth to the west of the town.* □ *We're not going to allow any more bungaloid growth around this area.*

Bungalow Bill *n.* a slow-witted man. (Implying·that there is nothing much going on upstairs.) □ *What does this dumb Bungalow Bill want?* □ *I don't think the Bungalow Bill really knows what he wants.*

bung-full AND **chock-full** *mod.* full to the top. □ *The boot's bung-full. There's no more room.* □ *The new musical is just chock-full with laughs.*

bungie-jump See BUNGI-JUMP.

bungie-jumping See BUNGI-JUMPING.

bungi-jump AND **bungie-jump; bungy-jump** *vb.* to jump from high places in order to be rescued from certain death by an elastic line attached to the feet. □ *I bungi-jump every chance I get.* □ *I could never bungy-jump, no matter what.*

bungi-jumping AND **bungie-jumping; bungy-jumping** *n.* the apparently suicidal sport of jumping from high places in order to be rescued from certain death by an elastic line attached to the feet. □ *I think bungi-jumping is crazy.* □ *Bungy-jumping is an increasingly popular sport.*

bung something over *vb. phr.* to pass or hand something to someone. □ *Bung that manual over, please.* □ *He asked me to bung the thing over.*

bungy *n.* a rubber eraser. □ *I've lost my bungy.* □ *Here, take my bungy; I never need it.*

bungy-jump See BUNGI-JUMP.

bungy-jumping See BUNGI-JUMPING.

bunk off *vb. phr.* to play truant, especially from school. □ *Do you have a problem with kids bunking off at this school?* □ *No, no one bunks off here.*

bunk-up *n.* a furtive act of sexual intercourse. (Taboo.) □ *Fancy a quick bunk-up, love?* □ *I think really, she's gasping for a bunk-up, you know.*

bunny 1. *n.* a rabbit. □ *The children have a pet bunny.* □ *I'm afraid your pet bunny has been eaten by my pet cat.* **2.** *vb.* to talk or chatter. (Rhyming slang, linked as follows: bunny = [rabbit (and pork)] ≈ [talk] = chatter. Compare with RABBIT.) □ *Why must you bunny like that?* □ *Oh, they're always bunnying about something.*

Bunter *n.* any grossly overweight youth. (Offensive. Sometimes used as a term of address. From a fictional schoolboy, Billy Bunter, who appeared in a large number of stories written by Frank Richards between 1910 and the outbreak of World War II.) □ *Fat? He was, let's face it, a real Bunter.* □ *Don't you dare call me Bunter!*

burger 1. *n.* a hamburger sandwich; a hamburger patty. □ *Are you ready for another burger?* □ *He's cooking burgers out on the grill right now.* **2.** *n.* EC-STASY, a hallucinogen similar to L.S.D. (Usually in the plural.) □ *You can get*

some good burger in this part of town. □ *Burger is just one of a dozen drugs with similar formulas.*

burk See BERK.

burke *vb.* to suppress or hush up. (Possibly derived from Burke and Hare, two Edinburgh murderers who smothered their victims in order to sell their bodies for dissection by medical students.) □ *Now, that ought to burke you.* □ *If he comes in here, I'll burke him all right.*

B.U.R.M.A. AND **BURMA** *phr.* "Be upstairs ready my angel." (The initialism is sometimes written on love letters. Also an acronym.) □ *Don't ever forget, B.U.R.M.A.* □ *BURMA, forever.*

burn 1. *n.* a cigarette. □ *Gimme a burn, okay?* □ *Fred just stood there with a burn on his lower lip and his hands in his pockets.* **2.** *vb.* to smoke a cigarette. □ *I need to burn a fag. Just give me a minute.* □ *This nicotine fiend needs to burn one for a fix!* **3.** *n.* blackmail. (Always with *the.*) □ *They've got the burn on me.* □ *The burn is disgusting.*

burnt offering *n.* burned food; a badly cooked meal. □ *Everything I try to cook turns out to be a burnt offering.* □ *All I have to look forward to after work is a burnt offering.*

burnt out 1. *mod.* exhausted. □ *I'm burnt out after all that partying.* □ *I don't want to work with burnt out people. I need energy.* **2.** See also CHEESED OFF.

b(u)roo *n.* an unemployment office. (Scots usage.) □ *He went and joined the queue outside the buroo.* □ *The broo's where you go if you dinny hae a job. (The unemployment office is where you go if you do not have a job.)*

burp 1. *vb.* to bring up stomach gas. □ *She burped quietly behind her hanky, so no one would notice.* □ *Try not to burp at the table, Johnny.* **2.** *n.* a BELCH; an upward release of stomach gas. □ *The burp did not go unnoticed.* □ *What can you do when you make a burp in church?*

Burton(-on-Trent) *n.* rent. (Rhyming slang.) □ *That money is for the Burton-on-Trent.* □ *How much is your Burton?*

bury the hatchet *vb. phr.* to make peace. (From an alleged American

Indian practice.) □ *I'm sorry. Let's stop arguing and bury the hatchet.* □ *Tom and I buried the hatchet and we are good friends now.*

bushed *mod.* completely exhausted. □ *Poor Ted really looks bushed.* □ *I feel too bushed to go to work today.*

bushel *n.* the throat. (Rhyming slang, linked as follows: bushel [and peck] ≈ [neck] = throat.) □ *I've got a real sore bushel today.* □ *Otto grabbed him by the bushel. He nearly croaked.*

bush telegraph AND **jungle telegraph** *n.* a rumour. (Compare with GRAPEVINE.) □ *I heard on the bush telegraph that Sam is moving north.* □ *The jungle telegraph was right. He's already left.*

business *n.* the best; the genuine one. (Always with *the*.) □ *Now this is the best; the real business.* □ *She always has the business.*

business end of something *n.* the place or point of something where the action is. □ *I found myself looking into the business end of a pistol.* □ *Harry burned himself on the business end of a soldering iron.*

business girl *n.* a prostitute. (Crude.) □ *Joan almost became a business girl to pay for a habit.* □ *A lot of business girls are hooked on something or other.*

busker *n.* a street performer, especially of music. □ *There was a busker playing outside the window.* □ *Some of these buskers make quite a lot of money.*

busk it *vb. phr.* to improvise, especially in a musical context. □ *Let's busk it and see how it goes.* □ *If you're going to be busking it, could you use that room over there?*

bust *n.* a riotous drinking party. □ *There was a big bust in the park until two in the morning.* □ *There was no beer at the bust. Only wine.*

bust a gut *vb. phr.* to make an extreme effort. □ *The poor guy has really been busting a gut to get this.* □ *Don't bust a gut. It's never worth it.*

bust someone *vb.* to arrest someone. □ *I hear they've bust someone for the Smithfield job.* □ *I don't intend letting them bust me.*

busty *mod.* of a woman with large breasts. (Crude.) □ *Now Mary is what you'd call busty.* □ *There's a really busty barmaid at the local pub now.*

busy *n.* a detective. □ *I'm the busy that will catch up with you some fine day, Mr Big.* □ *See that busy over there? He lifted me once.*

but *interj.* a general emphasis sometimes added at the end of a statement, especially but not exclusively one containing a contradiction. (Scots and Irish usage.) □ *Ah don't care what he thinks, but.* □ *The food's good and expensive, but.*

butch 1. *mod.* dominant and masculine, in a homosexual context, either male or female. (Crude.) □ *That's a real butch haircut, Claude.* □ *Really, Clare. How butch!* **2.** *n.* a dominant or masculine male or female homosexual. (Crude.) □ *Tom is getting to be such a butch.* □ *He doesn't like being called butch.*

butchers *n.* a look or glance. (Rhyming slang, linked as follows: butcher's [hook] ≈ look. Usually used with *take a*.) □ *Take a butchers at that, John.* □ *He took a butchers at the girl, but didn't recognise her.*

butterfingers *n.* someone who cannot hold on to things. (Also a term of address.) □ *I'm such a butterfingers. I dropped my papers.* □ *Hang on to this tight, butterfingers!*

buttoned up See SEWN UP.

buttonhole *vb.* to accost someone; to make someone listen to one. (As if grabbing someone by the coat lapel to keep them from getting away.) □ *The guy buttonholed me on my way out, and started asking me a lot of questions.* □ *See if you can buttonhole a cop and get some directions.*

Button it! AND **Button (up) your lip!**; **Button up!** *interj.* "Silence!"; "Be quiet!" □ *Button it! We don't want that story getting out.* □ *When I say "Button it," Button it! Okay?*

buttons *n.* a page boy dressed in livery. □ *Ask the buttons to get me a newspaper.* □ *Imagine. Still with buttons in this day and age!*

button something up See SEW SOMETHING UP.

Button up! See BUTTON IT!

Button (up) your lip! See BUTTON IT!

butty *n.* a sandwich made using a buttered bread roll rather than two slices of bread. (North of England usage.) □ *He sat there, eating a butty.* □ *Can I have a butty, mum?*

buy 1. *n.* a purchase. □ *Boy, this is a great buy.* □ *What a buy, two for the price of one.* 2. *n.* a drugs purchase made by an undercover police officer. □ *One buy and they've got you.* □ *Are buys legal?*

buy it AND **buy the farm** *vb. phr.* to die; to get killed. □ *For a minute, I thought I was going to buy it.* □ *He bought the farm when his plane crashed during a training flight.*

buy something *vb.* to believe or agree to something. □ *Nobody'll buy that story.* □ *It sounds good to me, but will your wife buy it?*

buy the farm See BUY IT.

buy time *vb. phr.* to postpone an event. □ *You are just doing this to buy time.* □ *Maybe I can buy some time by asking for a continuance.*

buzz 1. *vb.* to signal someone with a buzzer. □ *I'll buzz my secretary.* □ *Did you buzz, Gloria?* 2. *n.* a thrill. □ *I got a real buzz out of that.* □ *The dancers gave the old man a buzz.* 3. *n.* the initial effects of drinking alcohol or taking certain drugs. □ *Sam got a little buzz from the wine, but he still needed something stronger.* □ *She knocked back her drink and leaned back, waiting for the buzz.* 4. *n.* a rumour. □ *The buzz is that we've got the contract.* □ *What's the latest buzz in the Paris office?* 5. *n.* a telephone call. □ *There was a buzz for you earlier.* □ *This is your buzz, Simon.*

buzz along *vb. phr.* to drive or move along rapidly. □ *We were buzzing along at about seventy when we heard a siren.* □ *"You were buzzing along at eighty-two miles per hour," said the cop.*

buzzing *mod.* intoxicated due to drink. □ *Sally was buzzing after only a few drinks.* □ *She was really buzzing and Molly had to take her home.*

Buzz off! *interj.* "Go away!" □ *Stop bothering me! Buzz off!* □ *Buzz off! I've no time just now.*

buzzword *n.* a specialist word; a technical word; a jargon word. □ *Your constant use of buzzwords makes your work sound quite trivial.* □ *What's the latest buzzword?*

by a long chalk *mod.* by a long way. □ *You've missed by a long chalk.* □ *Not by a long chalk! No way!*

by a short head 1. *mod.* in a horse race, leading or winning by a very small margin. (Referring to the length of a horse's head.) □ *Silent Runner won the 3:30 at Doncaster by a short head.* □ *The horse won by a short head only but still, it won!* 2. *mod.* very slightly ahead or better than. □ *If Paul is better than Peter, then it's only by a short head.* □ *The difference may only be by a short head, but that's enough here.*

by-blow 1. *n.* a blow at something which is not the main or intended target. □ *He took the opportunity and gave me a by-blow anyway.* □ *It was just a by-blow. Sorry about that.* 2. *n.* an illegitimate child. □ *The by-blow is playing in the garden.* □ *So, just how many by-blows do you have now?*

By gum! *exclam.* "By God!" (A euphemism or disguise.) □ *By gum, that's a lot of money!* □ *By gum, I'm glad it's not me in there!*

By jove! *exclam.* "By Jupiter!" (A euphemism or disguise.) □ *I'll tell him what I think of this all right, by jove!* □ *By jove, that was a clever trick!*

by return *mod.* by return of post. □ *Please reply by return.* □ *The answer came back by return.*

byte *n.* a sequence of eight BITS; a unit of information equivalent to one single alphanumeric character. (Computer jargon. Derived from BIT and "bite.") □ *That byte represents the letter "K," and this one "O."* □ *Harry can actually read these bytes that all look meaningless to me; now that's real programming!*

C

C *n.* cocaine. □ *C seems to be what they're calling cocaine nowadays.* □ *What's the price of C around here?*

cab *n.* a taxi-cab. □ *There are never any cabs when it rains.* □ *We hailed a cab and got on board.*

cabbage 1. *n.* money. (Originally underworld. Compare with LETTUCE.) □ *How much cabbage you want for this heater?* □ *I don't make enough cabbage to go on a trip like that!* **2.** *n.* someone who is inactive, disinterested or apathetic. □ *I'm sorry but I feel like a cabbage just now.* □ *Just ignore the cabbages.* **3.** *n.* someone who is brain-dead as the result of illness, accident, etc. (See CABBAGE PATCH.) □ *I think we have to face facts; he's a cabbage now.* □ *I don't accept that anybody can be reduced to a sort of cabbage.*

cabbagehead *n.* a fool; a stupid person. □ *What cabbagehead put this thing on upside down?* □ *I'm such a cabbagehead. I posted my pay cheque back to the office by mistake.*

cabbage patch *n.* a hospital intensive care unit. (See CABBAGE, sense 3.) □ *A lot of nurses work in the cabbage patch.* □ *Visiting the cabbage patch is always so depressing.*

cabbie AND **cabby** *n.* a taxi driver. (Also a term of address.) □ *Ask the cabbie if he can change a twenty pound note.* □ *I say, cabby, do you know the way to St. Joseph's Hospital?*

caca AND **cack; kak; kaka 1.** *vb.* to defecate. (Juvenile. Crude.) □ *Jimmy kakad in his nappy!* □ *It's time you learnt to caca in the potty.* **2.** *n.* excreta. (Childish. Crude. From the Latin *cacare*.) □ *There's fresh cack in the*

front garden. □ *Don't worry. It's just dog kaka.*

cack See CACA.

cack-handed 1. *mod.* left-handed. □ *So I'm cack-handed. So what?* □ *Paul doesn't like people commenting on his being cack-handed.* **2.** *mod.* clumsy or incompetent. □ *Well, that's a cack-handed way of going about it.* □ *Why are you always so cack-handed?*

cadge *vb.* to obtain by begging. □ *There was a tramp trying to cadge money outside on the pavement.* □ *They managed to cadge a couple of quid out of me, I'm afraid.*

cafe au lait *mod.* of a person of mixed race. (Offensive.) □ *She's sort of, you know, cafe au lait.* □ *A really gorgeous cafe au lait girl came into the restaurant.*

caff *n.* a cafe. □ *I'm hungry and here's a caff; lets' use it.* □ *The caff was deserted; when we ate there we discovered why.*

cagey *mod.* sneaky; shrewd; cautious. □ *Bert is pretty cagey today.* □ *He's too cagey for me. I don't trust him at all.*

cake-hole AND **fag-hole** *n.* the mouth. □ *Put this in your cake-hole and chew it up.* □ *Shut your fag-hole!*

cake-walk 1. *n.* money obtained very easily. □ *Hey Mike, interested in some a cake-walk?* □ *Well, that money was a cake-walk. Any more where it came from?* **2.** *n.* any problem or task easily dealt with. □ *Well, what a cake-walk that was!* □ *I don't trust cake-walks like that; I feel we must have missed something.*

cakey *mod.* simple-minded. (Scots usage.) □ *She dizny act like she's cakey.*

(She does not behave as if she's simple-minded.) □ *Morag is mair than jist a cakey wee lassie, ye ken! (Morag is more than just a stupid little girl, you know!)*

calf-love AND **puppy-love** *n.* an infatuation or crush between teenagers. □ *Is it really love or just puppy-love?* □ *Look at them together. It may be calf-love, but it looks wonderful.*

call Charlie AND **call Hughie; call Ralph; call Ruth; call Earl** *vb. phr.* to empty one's stomach; to vomit. (Crude. Onomatopoetic from the sound of retching. See also CRY HUGHIE.) □ *Fred spent an hour in the loo calling Hughie.* □ *Oh boy! I have to go and call Ruth.*

call Earl See CALL CHARLIE.

call Hughie See CALL CHARLIE.

call it a day *vb. phr.* to stop; to quit. □ *All right you two, call it a day.* □ *We've decided to call it a day.*

call of nature See NATURE'S CALL.

call Ralph See CALL CHARLIE.

call ralph See CRY HUGHIE.

call Ruth See CALL CHARLIE.

call ruth See CRY HUGHIE.

call someone to the bar *vb. phr.* to become a barrister. (See also CALL WITHIN THE BAR. Usually passive.) □ *Wilma's legal career is going well and she expects to be called to the bar next year.* □ *After I was called to the bar, I really began to enjoy life again.*

call someone within the bar AND **take (the) silk** *vb. phr.* to become a King's or Queen's Counsel; to become a senior barrister. (See also CALL TO THE BAR. Usually passive.) □ *Senior barristers are called within the bar to become Queens' Councils.* □ *I hear he's been taken silk.*

call up *n.* military conscription. □ *There has been no call up in Britain for over a third of a century.* □ *Sometimes I think bringing back the call up would be a good idea.*

Cam and Isis *n.* the Universities of Cambridge and Oxford taken together. (A somewhat poetic rendition, constructed from the names of the rivers they stand upon. Compare with OXBRIDGE and CAMFORD.) □ *Graduates*

of *Cam and Isis share a certain mentality which some think is bad for British business.* □ *I don't know whether he went to Oxford or Cambridge but it was one or the other. Let's just settle for Cam and Isis, eh?*

Camford *n.* an alternate combined name to the better-known OXBRIDGE for the Universities of Cambridge and Oxford taken together. (Compare with CAM AND ISIS and OXBRIDGE.) □ *I don't know whether he went to Oxford or Cambridge but it was one or the other. Let's just settle for Camford, eh?* □ *There is a sort of Camford mentality which some think is bad for British business.*

camp 1. *mod.* overdone or affected; exaggeratedly or absurdly theatrical. □ *Most camp entertainment is pretentious and overdrawn.* □ *Who needs camp films?* **2.** *mod.* of effeminate male homosexual behaviour, especially when exaggerated. (Crude.) □ *What a camp way of walking!* □ *He's so camp, I could scream!*

camp about See CAMP IT UP.

camp it up AND **camp about 1.** *vb. phr.* to overact. □ *Can you make it a little more lively without camping it up?* □ *She's so dull that she could camp it up and still look half asleep.* **2.** *vb. phr.* [for a homosexual male] to overdo effeminancy; to act too effeminately in public. (Crude.) □ *Can't you even walk across the room without camping it up?* □ *John just loves to burst into the most sedate hotel in town and camp it up in the lobby.*

can 1. *n.* prison. (Usually with *the.*) □ *Otto's in the can, and will be there for some time I think.* □ *Have you ever been in the can?* **2.** *vb.* to decide against using something. □ *They've canned that idea.* □ *The building project has been canned.*

cancer stick *n.* a tobacco cigarette. (From the notion that cigarette smoking is a major cause of lung cancer. Old but recurrent.) □ *Kelly pulled out his ninth cancer stick and lit it up.* □ *A lot of people are addicted to cancer sticks.*

canned *mod.* having to do with prerecorded laughter or applause that is added to the sound track of a television program. □ *Canned laughter really sounds phony.* □ *The dialogue was funny enough that they didn't need to have the laughter canned.*

cannon *vb.* to collide. □ *We cannoned into each other on the stairs.* □ *Try to avoid cannoning, all right?*

cannot see (any) further than the end of one's nose See SEE NO FURTHER THAN THE END OF ONE'S NOSE.

can of worms *n.* an intertwined set of problems; an array of difficulties. (Often with *open*.) □ *This whole business is a real can of worms.* □ *When you brought that topic up, you opened a whole new can of worms.*

can't say boo to a goose *phr.* timid or shy. □ *Martin really can't say boo to a goose.* □ *If you can't say boo to a goose, don't risk it.*

can't say fairer *phr.* as reasonable as possible. □ *Oh now, we can't say fairer than that, can we?* □ *I can't say fairer. It's up to you.*

can't win (th)em all *phr.* [one should] expect to lose every now and then. □ *It doesn't really matter. You can't win them all.* □ *Well, I can't win 'em all.*

Cape of Good Hope *n.* soap. (Rhyming slang.) □ *What have you done with the Cape of Good Hope, woman?* □ *Some Cape of Good Hope, please; I want to wash.*

caper 1. *n.* a criminal job: theft, kidnapping, blackmail, etc. (Underworld.) □ *Who did you work with on that bank caper?* □ *The rozzers turned up right in the middle of the caper.* **2.** *n.* any stunt or event; a trick or a swindle. □ *That little caper the kids did with the statue from the town square was a dandy.* □ *Another caper like that and I call your parents.*

capital *n.* cash; money. □ *I'm a little short of capital right now.* □ *Do you think I could borrow a little capital until pay-day?*

Captain Cook AND **cook 1.** *n.* a book. (Rhyming slang.) □ *Any good Captain Cooks to read?* □ *Hey, leave me cook alone!* **2.** *n.* a look. (Rhyming slang.) □

He took a Captain Cook at the girl, but didn't recognise her. □ *Take a cook at that, Walter.*

captain of industry *n.* a corporation officer; a capitalist. □ *The captains of industry manage to hang on to their money no matter what.* □ *It's fun to see those captains of industry drive up in their Rollers.*

car boot sale AND **boot sale** *n.* a sale, usually at the weekend or a public holiday, of used or home-made goods, originally from the boot of a car. □ *Fancy visiting the car boot sale this Sunday?* □ *He goes to boot sales in the hope of finding a bargain.*

carcass *n.* one's body; a large or heavy body. □ *He hauled his carcass out of the car and lumbered into the bank.* □ *Set your carcass on a chair, and let's chew the fat.*

card *n.* a funny person. □ *Tracy is such a card. She makes me laugh.* □ *Gee, Fred. You're a card. Somebody's going to have to take you on one day.*

cardboard box *n.* venereal disease. (Rhyming slang, linked as follows: cardboard box ≈ [pox] = venereal disease.) □ *Getting cardboard box does tend to restrict your love life, since you ask.* □ *A dose of the cardboard box is not really funny, you know.*

cards *n.* an employee's documents, which are normally held by their employer. □ *I knew I was being sacked because he told me I could just go and collect my cards.* □ *When you come to work here, we will keep your cards in the main office.*

carpet *vb.* to reprimand. □ *I'm afraid that after that little exhibition, you will have to be carpeted.* □ *I was really carpeted this morning.*

carpet-biter *n.* someone who has or tends to have uncontrollable rages. □ *Boy! What a carpet-biter!* □ *Take care, this guy can be a real carpet-biter, you know.*

carriage paid *mod.* having delivery costs prepaid. (Often hyphenated before a nominal.) □ *You can send it back, carriage paid.* □ *A carriage-paid parcel just arrived for you.*

carrier *n.* a narcotics seller or transporter. □ *The carrier has the most dangerous job of all.* □ *You'll never see an old carrier.*

carrot top *n.* a person with red hair. (Also a term of address.) □ *Sam is a carrot top with the most beautiful hair I've ever seen.* □ *Hey, carrot top, where are you going?*

carry *vb.* to carry drugs on one's person. □ *If you get busted while you're carrying, you are in big trouble with the man.* □ *You gotta learn when you can carry and when you can't.*

carry all before one 1. *vb. phr.* [for a woman] to be very pregnant. □ *I can see she's carrying all before her again.* □ *Then this woman, carrying all before her, started to complain too.* **2.** *vb. phr.* [for a woman] to have very large breasts. (Crude.) □ *There she came, carrying all before her as usual.* □ *Now you might say that Mary is carrying all before her.*

carry-on 1. *n.* a love affair. □ *It seems Jane and Jack are having a carry-on.* □ *Right, there shall be no carry-ons between staff personnel, okay?* **2.** *n.* dubious behaviour. □ *What sort of carry-on is going on here?* □ *I think there had been some kind of carry-on just before we arrived.* **3.** *n.* a confused or excited environment. □ *What a carry-on that place has become.* □ *I could not work in a carry-on like that.*

carry one's bat *vb. phr.* to remain in play as a batsman at the end of an innings. (Cricket.) □ *At least, he carried his bat.* □ *It's important for the team that Simon carry his bat tonight.*

carry someone *vb.* to do someone's work for them. □ *If you imagine I'm going to carry you, think again.* □ *How did she talk you into carrying her?*

carry the can *vb. phr.* to take responsibility or blame; to be blamed, especially for the faults of others. □ *Otto'll carry the can. Otto always carries the can.* □ *I don't want to carry the can for this.*

carry weight *vb. phr.* to have influence. □ *I don't carry much weight around here, but Walter does.* □ *Tom carries weight with the mayor. Ask him.*

carsey AND **carzey; kahsi; kharsie; khazi 1.** *n.* a water closet; a toilet. (Crude. Probably derived from *casa*, meaning "house" in Spanish, which was a slang term for a brothel in 17th and 18th century London.) □ *Where's the carsey?* □ *The khazi? Oh, it's along that passageway.* **2.** *n.* a communal toilet. (Crude. Typically found in military barracks and similar places.) □ *If you want a smoke, go to the carzey.* □ *I went to the kharsie for a quick smoke and met the captain doing the same thing!*

cart someone *vb.* to arrest someone. (Scots usage.) □ *The polis carted Wully again. (The police arrested William again.)* □ *What have they carted him for this time?*

cartwheel *n.* an amphetamine tablet or capsule. □ *Have you any cartwheels?* □ *I hear that Wally's on cartwheels now.*

carved in stone *mod.* permanent or not subject to change. (Often in the negative.) □ *Now, it isn't carved in stone yet, but this looks like the way it's going to be.* □ *Is this policy carved in stone?*

carve someone *vb.* to slash someone with a razor. □ *This guy's crazy; he'll carve you!* □ *Some lunatic has carved someone in the park.*

carve something up *vb. phr.* to ruin someone's chances. □ *You've carved up my chances.* □ *She's saying he's carved up all her plans.*

carve-up 1. *n.* a fight; a war. □ *Right men, this is it; the real carve-up.* □ *I'm glad the inevitable carve-up has come at last, really.* **2.** *n.* the value of a will. □ *When mother died, all he was interested in was the carve-up.* □ *Always asking about the carve-up is really sick, Otto.* **3.** *n.* a swindle. □ *Gerry has a new money-making carve-up, but he hasn't made any yet.* □ *What sort of carve-up did you get ripped off with?*

carving knife *n.* a wife. (Rhyming slang.) □ *I'd better ask the carving knife.* □ *Wlll your carving knife let you out to the pub tonight?*

carzey See CARSEY.

case the joint 1. *vb. phr.* to look over a location in order to work out how to break in, what to steal, etc. (Underworld.) □ *First of all you've got to case the joint to see where things are.* □ *You could see he was casing the joint the way he looked around.* **2.** *vb. phr.* to look a place over. □ *The dog came in and cased the joint, sniffing out friends and foes.* □ *The old lady entered slowly, apparently casing the joint for the face of someone of her era, and finally took a seat.*

cash cow *n.* a dependable source of money; a good investment. □ *I put most of my money in a cash cow that pays out once a month.* □ *Mr Wilson turned out to be the cash cow we needed to start our repertoire company.*

casher *n.* a trouser pocket containing cash. (Pickpocket's cant.) □ *Alf's out looking for cashers to lighten.* □ *People really don't take proper care of their cashers; it's almost too easy.*

casualty *n.* a hospital casualty or emergency department. □ *Casualty is very busy today.* □ *There are a lot of traffic accident victims in casualty.*

cat *n.* a vicious or malicious woman. (Compare with CATTY.) □ *Watch out! She's a really spiteful cat when crossed.* □ *Mary can be such a cat, you know.*

cat and mouse *n.* a house. (Rhyming slang.) □ *That's a nice cat and mouse.* □ *Whose cat and mouse is that?*

catch 1. *n.* a drawback, difficulty or problem. □ *Okay, that sounds good, but what's the catch?* □ *There's no catch. It's all on the up and up.* **2.** *vb.* to view something; to attend something. □ *We'll take the girls to catch a film after we eat.* □ *Did you catch "Gone with the Wind" on TV?* **3.** *vb.* to become infected with a disease. □ *I appear to have caught a cold.* □ *Joe has had to go home. He seems to have caught a really bad dose of the flu.* **4.** *vb.* to rapidly eat something such as a sandwich or other snack, between other events. □ *I'm in a hurry and will catch a sandwich on the way.* □ *We caught a snack on the way here.*

catch a cold 1. *vb. phr.* to become infected with gonorrhoea. (Military

slang.) □ *I did not plan to catch a cold, you know.* □ *Perhaps you would like to explain how you managed to catch a cold?* **2.** *vb. phr.* to get into financial difficulties. □ *If you're not sure about us catching a cold, just look at all these bills we've to pay. Somehow.* □ *We've caught a cold and just have to cut back spending.*

catch (one) with one's trousers down *vb. phr.* to be discovered or exposed in an embarrassing or awkward situation. □ *It is most embarrassing to be caught with one's trousers down.* □ *Well, they certainly caught us with our trousers down that time.*

catch someone on the rebound *vb. phr.* to become engaged or married to a recently-jilted person. □ *I think she caught him on the rebound.* □ *Well, I wouldn't mind catching someone like her on the rebound or on any other occasion either, come to that.*

catch up *vb. phr.* to cease using drugs; to withdraw from a drug addiction. □ *Well, I did it. I caught up.* □ *I managed to catch up two years ago and have never looked back.*

cat's miaow See CAT'S PYJAMAS.

cat's mother *n.* an insignificant female person. □ *I'm just the cat's mother, eh?* □ *Who do you think I am? The cat's mother?*

cat's pyjamas AND **cat's whiskers; cat's miaow** *n.* someone or something that is ideal or excellent. □ *This wine is really the cat's pyjamas!* □ *Boy, this fishing rod is the cat's miaow.*

cat's whiskers See CAT'S PYJAMAS.

cattle (truck) *vb. (phr.)* to perform sexual intercourse. (Taboo. Rhyming slang, linked as follows: cattle (truck) ≈ [fuck] = copulate.) □ *Let's go somewhere quiet and cattle truck.* □ *Want to cattle?*

catty *mod.* spiteful; snotty. (Compare with CAT.) □ *You know how catty Mary is—almost as catty as Gloria—well, she told me something about you that really shocked me.* □ *How can anybody be so catty?*

Cavalier *n.* an uncircumscribed male. (Compare with ROUNDHEAD.) □ *Oh,*

Otto's not Jewish; he's a Cavalier. □ *Just how do you know that Otto is a Cavalier, Maya?*

Cave! *exclam.* "Look out!" (Juvenile. From the Latin *cave*, meaning "beware.") □ *Cave! Here comes the teacher!* □ *He shouted "Cave!" but too late; the policeman saw what happened.*

cave man *n.* a strong, virile man. □ *He's sort of a cave man, big and hairy.* □ *I don't care for cave men.*

cease trading *vb. phr.* to go out of business. □ *That company ceased trading a long time ago.* □ *If the bank does not help, we'll have to cease trading immediately.*

ceiling inspector *n.* a willing or frequent female sexual partner. (Crude.) □ *Oh, Maggy is a ceiling inspector all right. You'll see!* □ *There are plenty of ceiling inspectors in the pubs of this town—if that's all you want.*

celeb *n.* a celebrity. (Pronounced suh-LEB.) □ *They hired a few celebs to pitch for their new computer.* □ *They said there were celebs all over the place, but nobody I recognised.*

century *n.* one hundred Pounds Sterling. (Underworld.) □ *I got a couple of centuries for driving these guys home from the bank.* □ *Here's a century for your trouble, young man.*

cert *n.* a certainty. □ *Oh yes, she's a dead cert all right.* □ *How do you know she's a cert?*

cessy *mod.* foul; disgusting. □ *If you must be cessy, do so somewhere else thank you.* □ *That's really cessy, don't go in there.*

chain and locket *n.* a pocket. (Rhyming slang.) □ *Get yer hand out of yer chain and locket, son.* □ *Any change in your chain and locket?*

chain-smoker *n.* someone who smokes cigarette after cigarette. □ *She was a chain-smoker for thirty years, and then suddenly, boom. She's gone.* □ *There are fewer chain-smokers now than there were just a few years ago.*

Chalfonts *n.* hemorrhoids. (Rhyming slang, linked as follows: [the] Chalfonts = [Chalfont St. Giles] ≈ [piles] = haem-orrhoids. Usually with *the*.) Chalfont St. Giles is one of a group of villages in an area of Buckinghamshire, near London, known collectively as the Chalfonts.) □ *Our Bert suffers terribly from the Chalfonts, you know.* □ *A bad dose of the Chalfonts is sheer hell.*

chalk and cheese *n.* diametric opposites. □ *I've never seen two people who were more like chalk and cheese.* □ *These two choices really are like chalk and cheese.*

chalkie *n.* a schoolteacher. □ *We got a new chalkie at school today.* □ *The chalkie told the children not to do that.*

chalk up *vb. phr.* to score a point in any game, but particularly darts. □ *I chalked up another forty and moved in to the lead again.* □ *How much did he chalk up in that game?*

champers AND **shampers** *n.* champagne. (Compare with POO and SHAMPOO.) □ *I could live on shampers.* □ *My dad sent us a bottle of French champers.*

champion *mod.* excellent. □ *Your news is really champion, you know.* □ *What a champion idea that was.*

chancer *n.* someone who takes chances; a bluffer. □ *He's just a chancer; ignore him.* □ *Who's this chancer and who does he think he's kidding?*

Chance would be a fine thing. *sent.* "If only I could." □ *Me win the lottery? Chance would be a fine thing.* □ *I'd like to have been one of the astronauts that went to the moon, but chance would be a fine thing.*

change *n.* money. (Compare with AND CHANGE.) □ *It takes a lot of change to buy a car like that.* □ *I don't have the change to get one of those videotape machines.*

channel fleet *n.* a street. (Rhyming slang.) □ *There he was, walking down the channel fleet.* □ *She stood on the channel fleet and cried.*

channel hop AND **channel surf; channel zap** *vb. phr.* to use a remote control to move quickly from one television channel to another, pausing only a short time on each channel. □ *I* *wish you wouldn't channel hop!* □ *Channel zapping is a way to keep up with a number of television programmes at the same time.*

channel hopper AND **channel surfer; channel zapper** *n.* a person who CHANNEL HOPS. □ *My husband is a confirmed channel surfer. I can't understand why he does it.* □ *Channel surfers try to keep up with many programmes at one time.*

channel surf See CHANNEL HOP.

channel surfer See CHANNEL HOPPER.

channel zap See CHANNEL HOP.

channel zapper See CHANNEL HOPPER.

chap *n.* a man or boy. □ *Why do we need this chap?* □ *Ask the chap if he needs any help.*

Chapel *n.* nonconformists. □ *Oh, these people are Chapel, you know.* □ *A lot of Chapel live around here.*

chappie *n.* a diminutive form of CHAP. □ *Ask these chappies what they want.* □ *I say you chappie, what's up?*

chapter and verse *mod.* in the finest detail. (From the "chapter and verse" organisation of the Bible.) □ *He could recite, chapter and verse the law concerning state-funded libraries.* □ *She knew her rights, chapter and verse.*

char 1. *n.* a charwoman. □ *The char gets here about four in the morning, since you ask.* □ *We could use a char around here.* **2.** *n.* tea. (From the Chinese cha, meaning "tea," hobson-jobson.) □ *Fancy a cup of char, Tony?* □ *I think I'll make us some char.*

charge *n.* a dose or portion of a drug. □ *I need a charge to tide me over.* □ *Just a little charge till I can get to my dealer.*

charity-bang *n.* a woman providing free sexual favours in a situation where payment might be expected. (Taboo.) □ *Well, if all else fails, Sonia is always willing to be a charity-bang.* □ *The ladies under that street lamp are making threatening noises about the charity-bang.*

Charlie *n.* cocaine. □ *They're selling Charlie quite openly in the street now.* □ *Is there a house where I can buy some Charles somewhere close?*

charlie 1. *n.* a fool. □ *How can you be such a charlie?* □ *That poor charlie thinks he can convince them.* **2.** *n.* a night watchman. □ *Otto reckons the charlie'll be no problem.* □ *What do we do about the charlie if he tries to set off the alarm?* **3.** *n.* the female sexual organ. (Taboo. Rhyming slang, linked as follows: Charlie [Hunt] ≈ [cunt] = female sexual organ.) □ *He got arrested trying to look up women's skirts in the hope of seeing their charlie.* □ *If your dresses get any shorter, we'll all be able to see your charlie.*

charlies *n.* the female breasts. (Crude. Normally with *the* and in the plural.) □ *My charlies aren't all I might have wished for.* □ *All you think about is charlies!*

charmer *n.* a seducer. □ *You always have to act like some half-arsed charmer chatting up every female in sight like it really mattered! Grow up!* □ *Willard is such a charmer! Too bad he's married.*

Charming(, fucking charming)! *exclam.* an ironic or sarcastic response to an insult or an unpleasant or difficult situation. (CHARMING, FUCKING CHARMING! is taboo.) □ *Charming, fucking charming! I leave my car for ten minutes and come back to two slashed tyres and a parking ticket!* □ *Well that's just charming! What are you trying to do? Drive people out of town?*

charming wife *n.* a knife. (Rhyming slang.) □ *What are you carrying that charming wife for?* □ *Bring your charming wife over here and cut this loose.*

chartered libertine *n.* a person who does whatever he or she likes. □ *Here was one chartered libertine that was different from the others, he thought.* □ *I don't think I could take another chartered libertine like that today.*

charts *n.* the trade magazine rankings of current pop music. □ *The big one is back on the charts this week. Give it a listen.* □ *Number five on the charts again this week—it's "My Blue Heaven" with the Andrews Sisters.*

chaser 1. *n.* an alcoholic drink taken after a non-alcoholic one; beer, water or some similar liquid drunk after a SHOT of hard liquor. (Compare with WASH.) □ *I could use a little chaser with this soft stuff.* □ *I'd like a double scotch and a beer chaser.* **2.** See also AMBU-LANCE CHASER.

chase someone *vb.* to closely super-vise someone in order to ensure that what they are doing is performed time-ly and well. □ *Chase them; make sure it happens as we require.* □ *I'm already chasing them, sir.*

chase the dragon *vb. phr.* to inhale opium fumes through a straw. □ *Harry thinks that chasing the dragon sounds like real fun.* □ *Chasing the dragon may sound good, but it smells awful.*

chat *n.* a manner of speaking; a way of using language. □ *I don't think I like that sort of chat, okay?* □ *Oh, that's just chat for "difficult."*

chat show *n.* a television or radio pro-gramme consisting of people being in-formally interviewed. □ *She just loves all these chat shows.* □ *I can't stand chat shows.*

chat someone up *vb. phr.* to talk infor-mally to someone, with an ulterior mo-tive. □ *I think I'll try chatting her up.* □ *He chat up the girl, and then they left together.*

chattering classes *n.* certain verbose members of the middle classes. (Nor-mally with *the*.) □ *Most members of the chattering classes appear to be of a lib-eral disposition and often of a preten-tiously artistic bias.* □ *How come the chattering classes seem to have a char-tered right to appear on the television?*

cheapie 1. *n.* a cheaply made article. (Compare with EL CHEAPO.) □ *I don't want a cheapie. I can afford better.* □ *It broke. I suppose it was a cheapie.* **2.** See CHEAP SHOT.

cheap shot AND **cheapie** *n.* a remark that takes advantage of someone else's vulnerability. □ *It's easy to get a laugh with a cheap shot at cats.* □ *People who wouldn't dare utter anything nega-tive about blacks, Irish or women just love to take a cheapie at yuppies.*

cheapskate *n.* a miserly person; a very cheap person. □ *A 5 percent tip! What a*

cheapskate! □ *I don't think of myself as a cheapskate, but I do try to watch my cash flow.*

check out the plumbing AND **visit the plumbing** *vb. phr.* to go to the toilet. □ *I think I'd better check out the plumbing before we go.* □ *I want all you children to visit the plumbing as soon as we get there.*

cheeks *n.* the buttocks. (Usually with *the*.) □ *There is a bit of mustard or something on your cheeks.* □ *She fell right on her cheeks.*

cheerio AND **cheers 1.** *n.* a toast made upon drinking. □ *Well, cheerio! Good luck!* □ *Cheers, and thanks.* **2.** *exclam.* good wishes upon arriving or depart-ing. □ *Cheerio, see you Monday.* □ *So long; cheers.* **3.** *exclam.* an expression of thanks. □ *That's helpful; cheerio.* □ *Cheers. That's very handy.*

cheers See CHEERIO.

cheesecake *n.* pictures of sexually at-tractive young women, typically wear-ing very few or no clothes. (Crude.) □ *The walls of his room are covered in cheesecake.* □ *Cheesecake is always going to sell.*

cheesed (off) *mod.* angry; disgusted. □ *Clare was really cheesed off at the but-ler.* □ *The butler was cheesed at the cook.*

cheesed off See BROWNED OFF.

Cheese-head *n.* a Dutch person. (Of-fensive.) □ *The Dutch are called Cheese-heads because their country pro-duces so much cheese.* □ *I see there's a lot of Cheese-heads in town today.*

cheese-paring *mod.* excessively eco-nomical. □ *What a miserable, cheese-paring affair it was.* □ *You could not be more cheese-paring if you tried, could you?*

cheeser *n.* a person with smelly feet. □ *Cor! He's a right cheeser!* □ *I can't stand cheesers.*

cheque-book journalism *n.* the pur-chase by newspapers or TV companies of exclusive rights to stories. □ *There is something sordid about much of cheque-book journalism, don't you think?* □ *Why is there more and more cheque-book journalism all the time?*

cherries *n.* greyhound racing. (Rhyming slang, linked as follows: cherry [hogs] ≈ [dogs] = greyhound racing. Usually with *the*.) □ *He spent all his money on the cherries and now he's broke.* □ *I'm off to the cherries tomorrow. Wish me luck!*

cherry ace *n.* a face. (Rhyming slang.) □ *His cherry ace was hidden behind a long white beard.* □ *I know that cherry ace. Who is he?*

cherry-picker *n.* an effeminate man; a passive male homosexual. (Crude.) □ *She came to the dance with a cherry-picker.* □ *I hear that you-know-who is a cherry-picker.*

cherry-ripe *n.* nonsense. (Rhyming slang, linked as follows: cherry ripe ≈ [tripe] = nonsense.) □ *What cherry-ripe that is!* □ *You're tailing cherry-ripe again—as usual.*

chestnuts *n.* the female breasts. (Crude. Normally with *the* and in the plural.) □ *Cor, look at the chestnuts on that, Fred!* □ *There she was, bold as brass, with her chestnuts on full display.*

chesty **1.** *mod.* prone to or presenting the symptoms of any one of a number of chest diseases. □ *I've always been a bit chesty.* □ *If you are chesty then you've got to take special care of yourself in cold weather.* **2.** *mod.* of a woman possessing large breasts. (Crude.) □ *Chesty girls are usually very popular with men, but not with other women.* □ *At 40 inches, I suppose we could say that Kathy is chesty.*

chew someone's ball(ocks) off *vb. phr.* to castigate someone severely. (Taboo.) □ *The creep! I'll chew his ballocks off!* □ *Don't let him chew your balls off. It was not your fault.*

chew something over *vb. phr.* to think something over. □ *I'll have to chew it over for a while. I'm not sure now.* □ *Don't chew it over too long. The offer is only good till Friday.*

chew the fat **1.** *vb. phr.* to revive an old disagreement or argument. □ *Do we have to chew the fat over that again?* □ *Here we are, chewing the fat yet again!* **2.** AND **chew the rag** *vb. phr.* to chat or gossip. □ *Put your carcass down onto the chair, and let's chew the fat for a while.* □ *We were just chewing the rag. Nothing important.*

chew the rag See CHEW THE FAT.

chick **1.** *n.* a young male prostitute. (Crude.) □ *There are a lot of chicks around here in the centre of town.* □ *A lot of chicks are hooked on something or other.* **2.** *n.* a girl; a girlfriend. □ *Hands off my chick if you know what's good for you!* □ *What a beautiful chick she is.*

chicken **1.** *n.* a coward. □ *Come on, let's go. Don't be a chicken.* □ *He's no fun. He's a chicken.* **2.** *n.* cowardice. □ *You must be chicken if you're scared to do that.* □ *Dan's just chicken.* **3.** *n.* an underage girl considered as an actual or potential sexual partner. (Crude.) □ *When pornographers talk about chickens they mean very young girls.* □ *Some of the chickens in these videos are as young as eleven or twelve.* **4.** *n.* a game where young people challenge each other to perform increasingly dangerous acts. □ *These teenagers had been playing chicken with the traffic on the motorway when young Alf got killed.* □ *Standing in the path of an oncoming vehicle until the last possible moment is called "playing chicken." I call it "exceptionally stupid."* **5.** *n.* a young boy who is subjected to the advances of pederasts. (Crude.) □ *Little Joe was a chicken until he was rescued from the streets.* □ *He's got a new, even younger, chicken that moved in with him just last week.*

chicken feed *n.* a small amount of anything, especially of money. (Compare with FOR PEANUTS.) □ *Of course I can afford it. It's just chicken feed.* □ *It may be chicken feed to you, but that's a month's rent to me.*

chicken-hearted *mod.* cowardly. □ *Yes, I'm a chicken-hearted softie. I hope you don't want to make something of it.* □ *He's chicken-hearted, but I still love him.*

chicken out (of something) *vb. phr.* to manage to get out of something, usually because of fear or cowardice. □

Come on! Don't chicken out now! □ *Freddy chickened out of the plan at the last minute.*

chief *n.* the person in charge. (Also a term of address.) □ *Okay, chief, where to now?* □ *Have you got a couple of quid to pay the toll, chief?*

chief cook and bottle washer See HEAD COOK AND BOTTLE WASHER.

chiefy *n.* the person in charge of a military unit. □ *The chiefy was waiting outside the office for him.* □ *He's a pleasant chiefy.*

chilled *mod.* magnificent; fabulous. □ *Your pad is not what I'd call chilled, but it's certainly all right.* □ *What a chilled stereo that is!*

chillum *n.* a pipe or device used for the smoking of marijuana. □ *He keeps a chillum in his stash.* □ *Ernie has a chillum with him that he's trying to sell.*

china *n.* a friend. (Rhyming slang, linked as follows: china [plate] ≈ [mate] = friend.) □ *Hello there, china!* □ *Of course Bert's my china.*

China white AND **Chinese white 1.** *n.* pure or nearly pure heroin; it can be deadly. □ *Beware of that China white.* □ *You never see Chinese white anymore. There's too many other kinds of junk for anybody to bother with it.* **2.** *n.* fentanyl, a synthetic narcotic analgesic. □ *That Chinese white can paralyse your lungs.* □ *All the users I know of stay away from China white.*

Chin-chin! 1. *exclam.* a toast made upon drinking. □ *Chin-chin, and thanks!* □ *Well, chin-chin! Good luck!* **2.** *exclam.* good wishes upon arriving or departing. □ *Well, chin-chin Charlie, I hope all goes well!* □ *Chin-chin! What a lovely morning.*

Chinese burn *n.* pain inflicted by holding a victim's arm with both fists close together, and then twisting them in opposite directions. (Juvenile.) □ *If you tell on me, I'll give you a Chinese burn.* □ *The bully gave the little girl such a bad Chinese burn, she had to go to hospital.*

Chinese screwdriver See BRUMMAGEM SCREWDRIVER.

Chinese white See CHINA WHITE.

Chinkie AND **Chinky 1.** *n.* a Chinese person. (Racially offensive.) □ *Why can you not be polite to Chinkies?* □ *Y'know, Otto, if you call a Chinaman a Chinky, he's likely to get nasty.* **2.** *mod.* Chinese. (Racially offensive.) □ *Tell Otto there's a awful lot of Chinky people in the world, please.* □ *I really like Chinky food.* **3.** *n.* a Chinese restaurant. (Racially offensive.) □ *Harry and me are off to the Chinky for a meal. Want to come with us?* □ *Are there a lot of Chinkies around here?*

chinless wonder *n.* a foolish upperclass person, usually male. □ *That chinless wonder thinks he can convince them.* □ *Sorry, he's still a genuine chinless wonder.*

chin someone *vb.* to hit someone. □ *He chinned me as I walked over to my car.* □ *Harry's livid and out to chin you for what you did.*

chip *vb.* to indulge in banter. □ *Oh, you're just chipping again!* □ *Would I chip with you, Mavis?*

chip butty *n.* a buttered bread roll sandwich filled with French fried potatoes. (North.) □ *A chip butty consists of a double helping of carbohydrate, with added grease; healthy eating this is not.* □ *But on the other hand, a chip butty tastes great, especially when you're ravenous!*

chipper *n.* a fish and chip shop. (Scots usage.) □ *A new chipper opened in our street.* □ *If you're going round the chipper, could you get me some chips, please?*

chippery *n.* banter. □ *We just had some pleasant chippery after you left.* □ *What's all this chippery about.*

chippy 1. *n.* a fish and chip shop. □ *Fancy something from the chippy tonight, love?* □ *I'm just off down to the chippy.* **2.** *mod.* resentful and arrogant in an irritating way. □ *Why do you always have to be so chippy?* □ *If you were less chippy you'd get more done.* **3.** AND **chips** *n.* a carpenter or joiner. (Also a term of address.) □ *Tell our chippy to come up here and put in a new floorboard.* □ *Tell me, chips, how fast can you build a coffin?*

chips See CHIPPY.

chisel *vb.* to extort (money). □ *Lefty tried to chisel forty quid out of me.* □ *He's always chiseling. That's his thing.*

chit AND **chitty** **1.** *n.* a bill or tabulation of charges that one signs rather than pays at the time. □ *I don't have any cash. Can I sign a chitty for it?* □ *Fred came in to pay for his chitties about once a week.* **2.** *n.* a memorandum. □ *Did you receive my chit on that topic.* □ *Yes, I think your chitty is in my file.* **3.** *n.* a note recording money that is owed. □ *According to this chit, you owe the company 50.* □ *I left a chitty for the 20 I had to borrow yesterday.*

chitchat **1.** *n.* a short, friendly conversation. □ *I'd like to have a little chitchat with you when you have time.* □ *We had a chitchat about the problem, and I think things will work out.* **2.** *n.* talk; idle talk □ *That's enough chitchat. Please get to work.* □ *Please stop the chitchat there in the back row.*

chitty See CHIT.

chiv See SHIV.

chivvy someone AND **hassle someone** *vb.* to harass someone; to bother someone; to give someone a difficult time. □ *Listen, please don't chivvy me. I've had a hard day.* □ *Please get this woman to stop hassling me!*

chiz *n.* a swindle or cheat. □ *What a chiz! I'm calling the police.* □ *I lost a fortune in that share chiz.*

choc *n.* chocolate. □ *If it's made with choc I'll love it.* □ *He can't stand choc.*

choc-ice *n.* a chocolate-covered ice cream bar. □ *There were some ten children sitting in a row, all eating choc-ices.* □ *Would you like a choc-ice, Johnny?*

chocker *mod.* disgusted, fed up or near to tears. □ *I'm chocker, really chocker!* □ *Fed up? I'm chocker!*

chock-full See BUNG-FULL.

chock up *vb. phr.* to cram in or make completely full. □ *Come on, we can really chock up this bin.* □ *Why has this cupboard been chocked up like this?*

chocoholic *n.* a person who craves chocolate. (Patterned on *alcoholic.*) □ *Cake, ice cream, pie—make it choco-*late. *I'm a chocoholic and I'm glad.* □ *I have a real treat for you chocoholics— triple chocolate cheesecake.*

chocolate-bandit See ARSE-BANDIT.

chocolate box *mod.* of popular art, particularly paintings, which are excessively sentimental or trashily pretentious. (Compare with KITSCH.) □ *This stuff is too chocolate boxy for me.* □ *A lot of people like chocolate box art.*

chocolate drop *n.* a coloured immigrant child. (Racially offensive. Juvenile.) □ *Johnny, you really must not call Ahmid a chocolate drop!* □ *I heard him call them chocolate drops.*

choke *vb.* to shock or disgust. □ *It's so vile it makes you choke.* □ *It really choked me.*

choked *mod.* shocked; disgusted □ *I was choked by that.* □ *He was choked, too.*

chokey *n.* prison. □ *"Welcome to your local chokey," said the warder.* □ *He knew he was going to end up in chokey.*

chomp *vb.* to eat; to chew. □ *Stop chomping and listen to me.* □ *You're always chomping. You're going to get fat.*

chompers AND **choppers** *n.* the teeth. (Always plural.) □ *I may be on my last legs, but my chompers are still my own.* □ *That horse has a nice set of choppers.*

choosey *mod.* fussy; particular. □ *She's very choosey, so take care.* □ *What a choosey customer!*

chop **1.** *n.* a brand or trademark. (From the Hindi *chap*, meaning "stamp," by hobson-jobson.) □ *Don't you recognise the chop on that car?* □ *Mr Big's chop is all over this job.* **2.** *n.* the act of killing. (Normally with *the.*) □ *Oh don't worry, I'll soon find someone willing to carry out a chop.* □ *Mr Big needs a chop done.* **3.** *n.* a job dismissal; the sack. (Always with *the.*) □ *The firm just gave me the chop!* □ *Give him the chop; he's no use.* **4.** *n.* a blow with the fist. (Boxing.) □ *He chopped me in the stomach. Lord, It hurt!* □ *One good chop and you have him, Robert!*

chop and change *vb. phr.* to vacillate. □ *Please don't keep chopping and changing, but just decide once and for* *all.* □ *Why must you always chop and change?*

Chop-chop! *interj.* "Hurry up!"; "Move faster!" (From pidgin English, a Chinese term meaning "chop quick.") □ *Chop-chop! We're late!* □ *Come on, all of you! Chop-chop!*

chopper 1. *n.* a helicopter. □ *That chopper that reports on the traffic for the radio goes over my house every morning at six a.m.* □ *I never want to fly in a chopper. Those things scare me.* **2.** *n.* the male sexual organ. (Taboo.) □ *Men keep their brains in their choppers!* □ *Unlike Myra, Sharon thinks of little else but choppers.* **3.** *n.* a tail. □ *Happy? He was a pleased as a dog with two choppers, I tell you.* □ *Tell your kid to stop pulling on my cat's chopper.*

choppers See CHOMPERS.

chop someone *vb.* to hang; to execute. □ *We just heard. He's to be chopped.* □ *They will chop him all right.*

chop something *vb.* to abbreviate, terminate or dispense with something. □ *They chopped our plan yesterday.* □ *Management have just chopped that project.*

chow *interj.* "Hello."; "Goodbye." (From the Italian colloquialism *ciao*, meaning, "at your service.") □ *Chow, Charlie; how are you today?* □ *So I said "Chow" and left.*

Christmas! *exclam.* "Christ!" (Crude. A euphemism and disguise.) □ *Oh Christmas! How could I forget!* □ *Christmas, Margaret! That's the third time this week!*

Christmas crackered *mod.* exhausted. (Rhyming slang, linked as follows: Christmas crackered ≈ [knackered] = exhausted. See KNACKERED. A Christmas cracker is a brightly coloured paper tube that is pulled apart by people sitting together at Christmas dinner, to cause a loud noise and release a small toy, a paper hat and other trivia.) □ *John, you look really Christmas crackered.* □ *I'm really Christmas crackered after all that running.*

chrome-dome *n.* a shiny, bald head; a man with a bald head. (Also a rude term of address.) □ *The guy with the chrome-dome suddenly grasped his chest and made a face.* □ *Hey, chrome-dome, you're blinding me!*

chronic *mod.* severe or very bad. □ *We have a chronic situation here, and I don't know what to do.* □ *No matter how chronic it may look, I'm sure we can work out a solution.*

chuck 1. *vb.* to eat excessively when withdrawing from drug addiction. □ *When I stopped cold turkey I really chucked for a long while.* □ *Chucking is better than drugs any day.* **2.** *n.* a familiar form of address. (North of England usage.) □ *Got a light, chuck?* □ *Look chuck, I'll get you, you wait!*

chucker-out(er) *n.* a strong man hired to eject unruly people from a bar or similar place. (Compare with BOUNCER. See also MINDER.) □ *He was the biggest chucker-outer I've ever seen.* □ *I saw the chucker-out looking at me, and I got out of there fast.*

Chuck it! *interj.* "Cease!"; "Stop it!"; "Give up!" □ *Oh come on! Chuck it!* □ *Chuck it! That's enough!*

chuck it in AND **chuck one's hand in 1.** *vb. phr.* to quit; to give up; to cease trying. (Compare with THROW IN THE TOWEL.) □ *I was so depressed, I almost chucked it in.* □ *If I didn't have to keep the job to live, I'd have chucked my hand in long ago.* **2.** *vb. phr.* to die. □ *The parrot chucked it in before I got it home.* □ *I was afraid I'd end up chucking my hand in.*

chuck one's hand in See CHUCK IT IN.

chuck someone (out) *vb. (phr.)* to exonerate; to clear of guilt. □ *Somehow, Mr Big was chucked out once more.* □ *This court has too many cases chucked.*

chuck someone out AND **bounce someone** *vb. (phr.)* to eject or refuse admittance to someone. □ *I got chucked out of the pub last night.* □ *If he comes back, bounce him again, Otto.*

chuck something (out) *vb. (phr.)* to throw a case out of court. □ *The other side got their case chucked out.* □ *I'm afraid the judge says he'll chuck it.*

chuck (up) *vb. phr.* to empty one's stomach; to vomit. (Crude. Compare with UPCHUCK.) □ *Who chucked up on the driveway?* □ *The doctor gave him some stuff that made him chuck.*

chuff 1. *n.* the buttocks. □ *Get off your chuff and on with your work!* □ *Still, it was funny when she fell on the mud and landed on her chuff.* **2.** *n.* an anal release of intestinal gas; a noise or smell associated with this. (Crude.) □ *The trouble with Joe is that he lets go of these chuffs all the time.* □ *I've told you before Joe—no more of these chuffs.*

chuffed 1. *mod.* satisfied or delighted. □ *I'm pleased you're chuffed.* □ *Don't get too chuffed yet.* **2.** *mod.* flattered. □ *She appeared really chuffed at the compliment.* □ *I really wanted to deflate that silly chuffed fool.*

chum *n.* a pal; a good friend. □ *This is my old chum, Walter.* □ *We've been chums for years. Went to school together.*

chummy 1. *mod.* friendly. □ *I'm glad to see that you are a little more chummy this morning.* □ *Don't get too chummy with me. I'm a real son of a bitch.* **2.** *n.* a prisoner. (Police slang.) □ *How's chummy in Cell 3?* □ *OK, bring chummy through here.*

chump 1. *n.* the head. □ *Turn your chump around and take a look at this.* □ *He's distinctive because he has a particularly large chump.* **2.** *n.* a stupid person; a gullible person. □ *You are such a chump.* □ *See if that chump will loan you some money.*

Chunnel *n.* a popular name for the Channel Tunnel. (Normally with *the.*) □ *We travelled to France through the Chunnel.* □ *Without doubt, the Chunnel is the best way to get across in bad weather.*

chunter (on) *vb. (phr.)* to grumble; to speak inarticulately. □ *Please don't chunter like that; come right out with it!* □ *Why must you always chunter on?*

churn out *vb. phr.* to manufacture, produce or deliver in a routine or mechanical manner. □ *They were selling the things as fast as they could churn them out.* □ *I had not realised they were churned out in such vast numbers.*

cig See CIGGY.

ciggy AND **cig; ciggie** *n.* a cigarette. □ *How about a ciggy before we take off?* □ *Where is my packet of ciggies?*

cinch *n.* something very easy to do or achieve. □ *No problem! It was a cinch!* □ *What a cinch. Anybody can do it.*

circs *n.* circumstances. □ *Whatever the circs, I won't do that.* □ *The circs better be very special before I could forgive that.*

(circular) file *n.* a wastepaper basket. □ *That letter went straight into the circular file.* □ *Most of the junk mail sits here until I can put it into file 13.*

Circus *n.* a nickname for the British secret service. (Normally with *the.*) □ *Were you ever in the Circus?* □ *It's for you to discover who was and was not in the Circus.*

cissie AND **cissy; sissie; sissy 1.** *n.* an effeminate man; a passive male homosexual. (Crude.) □ *He doesn't like being called a cissie.* □ *Tell that sissy to get out of here.* **2.** *mod.* effeminate; homosexual. (Crude.) □ *He's so cissie, I could scream!* □ *What a sissie way of walking!*

City of Dreaming Spires *n.* Oxford. (Normally with *the.*) □ *Martin is now working in the City of Dreaming Spires, as they call the place.* □ *It's called the City of Dreaming Spires because of the number you can see as you approach it.*

city slicker *n.* a smart and sophisticated city dweller. □ *He's a real city slicker, that one.* □ *We don't have any of them city slickers in this village.*

civvies *n.* civilian clothes as distinct from a uniform. (Military slang.) □ *I feel sort of funny in civvies.* □ *I joined up again because I couldn't stand the thought of civvies and stuff like that.*

civvy *n.* a civilian. (Military slang.) □ *What did the civvy want, corporal?* □ *Sorry, no civvies beyond this point.*

civvy street *n.* civilian life. (Military slang.) □ *What will you do when you get back on civvy street, Archie?* □ *I wish I was on civvy street right now.*

clack (on) *vb. (phr.)* to chatter at length. □ *She does clack on, doesn't she?* □ *Look, just stop clacking. OK?*

clag *n.* a cloud. □ *There's not a clag in the sky!* □ *Here comes a clag, full of nice wet rain.*

claggy *mod.* [of clothes] wet and uncomfortable. □ *I hate this dress. It's so claggy.* □ *I must get out of these claggy clothes.*

clam up *vb. phr.* to get quiet. □ *The minute they got him inside the cop-shop, he clammed up.* □ *You'll clam up too if you know what's good for you.*

clanger *n.* a blunder. □ *So I made a clanger! I wish you'd stop going on about it!* □ *Rubbing my nose in it is not going to correct the clanger.*

clap *n.* gonorrhoea. (Taboo. Normally with *the*. See CLAPPY.) □ *Max has had the clap a dozen times.* □ *A case of the clap can change your life for a while.*

clapped out 1. *mod.* [of people] tired or worn out. □ *Why are you always so clapped out?* □ *I am clapped out today.* **2.** *mod.* [of equipment] worn out or broken. □ *There's your problem: a clapped out lynch pin.* □ *Is that clapped out car of yours still working?*

clappers *n.* the testicles. (Taboo. Normally with *the* and in the plural.) □ *Thud, right in the clappers. Ye gods, it hurt!* □ *He turned sideways to protect his clappers.*

clappy *mod.* infected with gonorrhoea. (See CLAP.) □ *Watch it, she's clappy.* □ *Do you really want to go with a clappy dame like that?*

(clap)trap *n.* the mouth. □ *How do we get her claptrap closed so the rest can talk?* □ *Why don't you just shut your trap for a moment and listen?*

claptrap *n.* nonsense talk; something worthless. □ *This is enough claptrap. I'm leaving.* □ *I know claptrap when I see it, and your play was claptrap.*

claret *n.* blood. □ *The sight of all that claret would make me sick.* □ *I discovered that Otto get's squeamish at the sight of claret, too!*

clash *n.* a formally arranged battle between gangs of hooligans. (Scots usage.) □ *There was a huge clash not far from here last night.* □ *Can't the police stop these clashes?*

class *n.* high style; elegance. □ *The dame's got class, but no brains.* □ *Class isn't worth much around here these days.*

classy *mod.* elegant; dandy. □ *Pretty classy place you got here.* □ *How much does a classy car like this cost?*

clatter someone *vb.* to hit someone. □ *Fred got clattered, and that really made him angry.* □ *Tom clattered Fred on the hooter.*

claw-hammer suit AND **penguin suit** *n.* a man's formal evening suit, complete with tails. □ *There he stood, in his claw-hammer suit. What a laugh!* □ *Do I have to wear this ridiculous penguin suit, Mavis?*

clean 1. *mod.* not using drugs; not involved with drugs. □ *There's a success story. Greg is a clean guy if I ever saw one.* □ *I've been clean for more than a month now.* **2.** *mod.* sober; not intoxicated with drugs at the moment. (Almost the same as sense 1.) □ *He's clean right now, but he'll get the call in an hour or two.* □ *Just being clean for a day is an accomplishment.* **3.** *mod.* not breaking any law. (Police and underworld.) □ *I'm clean, officer. You can't charge me with anything.* □ *This guy is clean. Let him go.* **4.** *mod.* not carrying a weapon. (Police and underworld.) □ *I frisked him. He's clean.* □ *Bugsy's gang was clean except for Bugsy himself who had a small pistol.* **5.** *mod.* cleared by the national security services for employment on sensitive work. □ *OK, you're clean.* □ *If you're not clean there's no way you can work there.*

clean bowl someone *vb. phr.* to bowl out or dismiss a batsman by directly hitting the wicket, without first touching either the bat or the player's body. (Cricket.) □ *Harris has never been clean bowled by anyone ever.* □ *Well, someone clean bowled him that time!*

clean-cut *mod.* having to do with a person who is neat and tidy. □ *He's a very clean-cut guy, and polite too.* □ *He's sort of clean-cut looking, but with bushy hair.*

cleaned out *mod.* broke; with no money. □ *I'm cleaned out. Not a penny left.* □ *Tom's cleaned out. He's broke. He'll have to go home.*

clean one's act up *vb. phr.* to reform one's conduct; to improve one's performance. □ *We were told to clean our act up or move on.* □ *I cleaned up my act, but not in time. I got kicked out.*

clean someone out *vb. phr.* to get all of someone's money. □ *The bill for supper cleaned me out, and we couldn't go to the flicks.* □ *The robbers cleaned out everybody on the train.*

clean sweep *n.* a broad movement clearing or affecting everything in the pathway. (Usually figurative.) □ *The boss and everybody in the front office got fired in a clean sweep from upstairs.* □ *Everybody got a pay rise. It was a clean sweep.*

clean up (on something) *vb. phr.* to make a lot of money on something. □ *The promoters cleaned up on the product.* □ *If we advertise, we can clean up.*

clear *vb.* to earn a specific net amount of money. □ *She cleared a cool forty thousand on that Wilson deal.* □ *We just want to clear a decent profit. Nothing greedy.*

clear as mud *mod.* not clear at all. (Often with *as.*) □ *All of this is clear as mud to me.* □ *I did all the reading, but it's still as clear as mud.*

clear out *vb. phr.* to leave; to depart. □ *Time for you people to clear out. It's just midnight.* □ *The boss gave me till next week to clear out. I've been fired.*

clever *mod.* nice; pleasant. (Usually employed in the negative.) □ *Well I don't think that was so clever; I won't be going back to that hotel again.* □ *The weather's not too clever today.*

clever clogs AND **clever dick** *n.* someone who gives the impression of knowing everything; a SMART ALEC. □ *That clever clogs isn't of much use to our committee.* □ *Pete is such a clever dick!*

clever dick See CLEVER CLOGS.

clever Mike *n.* a bicycle. (Rhyming slang, linked as follows: clever Mike ≈ [bike] = bicycle.) □ *What do you want with a clever Mike like that?* □ *I'm rather chuffed with my new clever Mike.*

click 1. *n.* a kilometre. □ *A click is about five eighths of a mile.* □ *We've got about ten more click to go.* **2.** *vb.* [for a woman] to become pregnant. □ *I hear Sally has clicked.* □ *When I clicked, I wondered what to do.* **3.** *vb.* to succeed; to have good luck. □ *Everything just clicked!* □ *Sometimes it clicks and it's great!*

click (with someone) *vb. (phr.)* to catch on with someone; to intrigue someone; to become popular with someone. □ *The pink hair and multiple earrings never really seemed to click with many kids.* □ *Sam and Mary are getting along fine. I knew they'd click.*

climb the wall(s) *vb. phr.* to do something desperate when one is anxious, bored or excited. □ *He was home for only three days; then he began to climb the wall.* □ *I was climbing the walls to get back to work.*

clinch *vb.* to settle something; to make something final. □ *I was able to clinch the deal, and I got a pay rise for it.* □ *I want to clinch this contract before the weekend.*

clincher *n.* the final element; the straw that broke the camel's back. □ *The clincher was when the clerk turned up the volume.* □ *Eating garlic by the bushel was the clincher. I had to get a new roommate.*

clink *n.* jail. □ *We'll throw you in the clink if you don't talk.* □ *One night in the clink was enough.*

clip 1. *vb.* to cheat someone. □ *That guy in there clipped me for a fiver.* □ *I didn't clip you or anybody else!* **2.** *n.* a music video; a short film. □ *This next clip is something you'll recognise.* □ *Stay tuned for more great clips.* **3.** *vb.* to hit with the hand. □ *"If you don't shut up I'll clip you on the ear," the mother shouted in exasperation.* □ *She clipped her crying child on the ear. The little girl cried louder than ever.* **4.** *n.* a fast rate; a high speed. □ *By travelling at a good clip, we managed to get there* *before the wedding started.* □ *You were moving at a pretty good clip when you ran into the lorry.*

clip-ons *n.* dark glasses that clip onto ordinary spectacles. □ *She clipped on her clip-ons and sat back to enjoy the sun.* □ Q: *Where are my clip-ons? I can't find them anywhere.* A: *You're wearing them, Mum.*

clipped *mod.* cheated. □ *When Marty counted his change, he found he'd been clipped.* □ *You weren't clipped by me. I just made a mistake.*

clippie *n.* a bus conductress. □ *When I was young, I worked as a clippie.* □ *They were called clippies from their propensity to clip passenger's tickets.*

clip someone's wings *vb. phr.* to restrain someone; to reduce or put an end to a teenager's privileges. □ *One more stunt like that and I'm going to clip your wings for a couple of weeks.* □ *Her father clipped her wings for getting into trouble with the police.*

clit(ty) *n.* the female sexual organ. (Taboo.) □ *A woman who shows her clitty is just the lowest.* □ *They dance completely nude in there, with clit and everything on view.*

cloakroom *n.* a toilet. (A euphemism.) □ *Where's the cloakroom?* □ *The cloakroom is through here.*

cloaks *n.* a cloakroom. □ *The cloaks is through that way.* □ *He hung his coat up in the cloaks, I think.*

clobber 1. *n.* personal clothes or possessions. □ *I've lost all my clobber!* □ *What's all that clobber doing lying around here?* **2.** *vb.* to hit or to beat up. □ *I ought to clobber you really hard.* □ *She clobbered him over the head with her bouquet.* **3.** *vb.* to defeat in a decisive manner. □ *Let's face it, they clobbered us.* □ *Right men, we're going to go out there and clobber them.*

clobber up *vb. phr.* to dress smartly. □ *We all got clobbered up before the party.* □ *Oh good, I like clobbering up.*

clock 1. *n.* a face. □ *The woman had a very unusual clock, you know.* □ *Why are you looking at me like that? Is there something wrong with my clock?* **2.** *n.*

the period of 36 hours following cautioning and arrest of a suspect by the police. (Police slang. This is the maximum time a suspect can be held by the police without being charged and brought before a magistrate.) □ *We've got to charge him or let him go inside the clock, y'know.* □ *Clock has already started for Smith.* **3.** *vb.* to hit someone, especially on the face. □ *He just clocked me, constable.* □ *Did you clock this gentleman, sir?* **4.** *vb.* to look at someone in an aggressive and threatening manner. □ *Don't clock me!* □ *Why are you clocking him like that?* **5.** *vb.* to move back the number of driven miles registered on the odometer of a vehicle so that it appears to have been used less extensively than is actually the case. □ *I think this car's been clocked!* □ *I resent that! I would never dream of clocking a milometer.*

clock in AND **clock on** *vb. phr.* to record one's arrival at a set time. □ *He clocked in three minutes late.* □ *When they clock on, give each of them one of these envelopes.*

clock off See CLOCK OUT.

clock on See CLOCK IN.

clock out AND **clock off** *vb. phr.* to record one's departure at a set time. □ *Don't clock off early if you want to keep on working here.* □ *He clocked out three minutes early.*

clock someone *vb.* to see or recognise someone. □ *Just then I thought I clocked someone in the crowd.* □ *He clocked me! He did!*

clock watcher *n.* someone—a worker or a student—who is always looking at the clock. □ *There are four clock watchers in our office.* □ *People who don't like their jobs can turn into clock watchers.*

clodhopper 1. *n.* a policeman. (Rhyming slang, linked as follows: clodhopper ≈ [copper] = policeman.) □ *The clodhoppers are here looking for you again, Joe.* □ *What have you been doing to interest the clodhoppers this time?* **2.** *n.* a stupid person; a rural oaf. □ *Some clodhopper came into town and fell in* with the wrong crowd. □ *You wouldn't know it, but that clodhopper is worth about two million quid.*

clogger *n.* a soccer player who regularly injures other players. □ *Watch that one over there; they say he's a clogger.* □ *Who was that great big clogger they had on their team?*

cloggie *n.* a clog dancer. □ *Do you like watching cloggies doing their thing?* □ *I don't know. I've never seen a cloggie, except in a photograph.*

clog(gy) **1.** *n.* a Dutch person. (Offensive.) □ *I see there's a lot of Cloggies in town today.* □ *The Dutch are called Clogs because they are all supposed to wear wooden clogs.* **2.** *n.* the Dutch language. (Offensive.) □ *Do you speak Cloggy?* □ *Why bother learning Clog? Most Dutch people speak English.*

clone **1.** *n.* an unthinking follower of the latest fashions. □ *Oh, when it comes to clothes, she's just another clone.* □ *Look at all these stupid clones.* **2.** *n.* a stereotypical homosexual man. (Crude.) □ *Why does he work so hard to look like he's a clone?* □ *She came to the dance with a clone.*

close call See CLOSE SHAVE.

close shave AND **close call** *n.* a narrow escape. □ *Wow, that was a close shave.* □ *The car passed this near to us—a real close call.*

closet *mod.* secret; concealed. □ *Marty is a closet chocolate fiend.* □ *I'm a closet hard rock fan.*

close to the knuckle AND **near (to) the knuckle** *mod.* almost indecent. (May be hyphenated before a nominal.) □ *That dress of hers was, well, a bit close to the knuckle.* □ *Another one of your near-the-knuckle jokes again eh, Albert?*

closet queen *n.* a secret passive male homosexual. (Crude.) □ *So what if he's a closet queen? He can still vote, can't he?* □ *Gay? No, I'd call him a closet queen.*

clot *n.* a fool or blockhead. □ *You clot! You've buttered the tablecloth!* □ *Who's the clot in the bright orange trousers?*

cloth-eared AND **wooden-eared** **1.** *mod.* not listening or prepared to listen.

□ *Oh, he's only cloth-eared when it suits her.* □ *For once don't be so cloth-eared and listen to what I have to say!* **2.** *mod.* partially deaf. □ *You don't have to shout. I'm not cloth-eared, you know.* □ *Just listen, you wooden-eared old sod!*

cloth ears AND **wooden ears** **1.** *n.* one who does not or will not listen. □ *I hate cloth ears who only hear what they want to hear.* □ *Don't be a wooden ears. Listen!* **2.** *n.* someone who is partially deaf. □ *Susan's a cloth ears...I said, Susan is a cloth ears!* □ *How can a wooden ears hear what people are saying?*

clotheshorse *n.* someone who is obsessed with clothing and looking good in them. □ *Her brother is the real clotheshorse.* □ *Mary is such a clotheshorse! Look at her now.*

clothes-peg *n.* an egg. (Rhyming slang.) □ *How much for a dozen clothes-pegs, love?* □ *Did you remember to get the clothes-pegs, Harry?*

clout **1.** *n.* influence; power. □ *You have the clout with the mayor. You try it.* □ *I don't have any clout at all.* **2.** *n.* a powerful blow. (Compare with WALLOP.) □ *Boy, that was some clout you landed on him.* □ *I don't want another clout like the last one.*

clown *n.* a fool. □ *Some clown seems to have dropped our paper in a puddle this morning.* □ *Tell that clown in the front row to shut up.*

clown around *vb. phr.* to act silly; to mess around. □ *Please stop clowning around and get to sleep.* □ *We were just clowning around. We didn't mean to break anything.*

cludge **1.** *n.* a toilet. (Crude. Scots usage.) □ *I must use yer cludge.* □ *After that pie, they were a' lined up to use the cludge!* **2.** See also KLUDGE.

cludgy See KLUDGY.

clued up *mod.* alert; knowledgeable. □ *If he says so, it's so; he's pretty clued up, you know.* □ *Ask Harry. He's usually clued up.*

clueless **1.** *mod.* unskilled at something. □ *He was not just a poor worker;*

he was really clueless! □ *Sorry, I'm to-tally clueless about this.* **2.** *mod.* stupid; ignorant. (Compare with CLUELESS-NESS.) □ *She is so dense. Totally clue-less.* □ *I have never seen anyone so completely clueless. What a dunce!*

cluelessness *n.* total stupidity. (Compare with CLUELESS.) □ *I just shake my head in wonder at the cluelessness of my fellow humans.* □ *This place is just infested with juvenile cluelessness!*

cluster *n.* the testicles. (Taboo. Normally with *the* and in the plural.) □ *He got hit right in his cluster.* □ *Thud, right in the cluster. Ye gods, it hurt!*

clutch *n.* any form of dancing that involves the partners holding each other together closely. □ *I only dance when it's some sort of clutch.* □ *A clutch: now that's a real dance.*

coal and coke *mod.* broke. (Rhyming slang.) □ *Tom's coal and coke. He's broke. He'll have to go home.* □ *I'm coal and coke. Not a penny left.*

coals to Newcastle *n.* something sent to or received at a location where that thing is already in surplus. □ *Isn't importing whisky into Scotland not a bit like coals to Newcastle?* □ *No more coals to New-castle nonsense, please. The factory that makes these things is in this very town and we already have more of them than we know what to do with.*

coasting *mod.* intoxicated with drugs. □ *Boy, was she coasting!* □ *She says she only lives for coasting now.*

cobblers *n.* the testicles. (Taboo. Rhyming slang, linked as follows: cob-bler's [awls] ≈ [balls] = testicles. Normally with *the* and in the plural. See also LOAD OF OLD COBBLERS at LOAD OF CODS(WALLOP).) □ *He got hit right in the cobblers.* □ *The teacher preferred "testicles" to "cobblers," if they had to be mentioned at all.*

Cobblers to you! *interj.* "Balls to you!"; a generic insult. (Crude.) □ *Well, if that's what you think, cobblers to you!* □ *Cobblers to you! I'm off.*

cock 1. *n.* the male sexual organ. (Taboo.) □ *He made some joke about a cock, but nobody laughed.* □ *The streaker covered his cock as he ran*

across the field. What sort of streak is that? **2.** *n.* nonsense. □ *Don't give me that cock! I won't buy it.* □ *That's just a lot of cock.* **3.** *vb.* to perform sexual intercourse. (Taboo.) □ *He's, shall we say, rather keen to cock.* □ *Fancy being cocked, love?* **4.** *n.* cheek; impudence. □ *Any more cock like that and he'll get everything he deserves.* □ *The cock of the woman! Who does she think she is?* **5.** See also POPPYCOCK.

cock and hen *n.* ten Pounds Sterling. (Rhyming slang.) □ *These things cost more than just a few cock and hen, you know!* □ *Have you got a cock and hen you can spare me?*

cock a snook (at someone) 1. *vb. phr.* to make a gesture of contempt. □ *Look at that! That man cocked a snook at me!* □ *I cocked a snook at that stuckup bitch with my two fingers.* **2.** *vb. phr.* to make obvious one's contempt for someone; to defy someone. □ *He cocked a snook at me by just ignoring my request.* □ *I don't care if he does think I'm cocking a snook at him, I'm doing it any way!*

cock-broth *n.* chicken soup. □ *Fancy a bowl of cock-broth?* □ *There's nothing better than some cock-broth on a cold day.*

cock(er) *n.* a male companion or friend. □ *Who's your cock, Albert?* □ *The two cockers left the pub, each one preventing the other from falling over.*

cock-eyed *mod.* slightly intoxicated due to drink or drugs. □ *I felt a little cock-eyed by then, but this didn't stop me from having more.* □ *You came in cock-eyed last night. What's going on?*

Cockney *n.* a native of the east end of London. □ *Cockneys have their own distinct way of speaking, and make a lot of use of rhyming slang.* □ *"Cock-ney" began as an insulting mediaeval nickname for a town dweller, and orig-inally meant "cock's egg."*

cock someone up *vb. phr.* to perform sexual intercourse upon someone, from the male perspective. (Taboo.) □ *He was cocking her up like it was going out of fashion.* □ *Of course I love you. Now, can I cock you up?*

cock something up *vb. phr.* to make a mess of something. □ *If you must cock something up, try to make it something that doesn't matter.* □ *Why must you cock everything up?*

cock-sparrow *n.* a barrow. (Rhyming slang.) □ *The cock-sparrow was loaded down with fresh fruit.* □ *A man passed by, pushing a cock-sparrow.*

cock-teaser AND **prick-teaser** *n.* a woman who excites or entices a man sexually, and then fails to deliver on her implied promise. (Taboo.) □ *No, I'm not a cock-teaser. In the dark I thought you were someone else.* □ *Otto does not like prick-teasers.*

cock-teasing AND **prick-teasing** *n.* exciting or enticing a man sexually, and then failing to deliver on the implied promise. (Taboo.) □ *When I said no, he accused me of cock-teasing.* □ *No, I'm not prick-teasing. In the dark I thought you were someone else.*

cock that won't fight *n.* a plan or proposal that cannot work. (Often with *a*.) □ *That's a cock that won't fight; forget it.* □ *Your cock that won't fight has just been agreed by the board.*

cock up See ARSE UP.

cock-up See ARSE-UP.

cocky *mod.* over-confident; impudent. □ *He gets some pretty cocky ideas.* □ *Ken can be rather cocky sometimes.*

coco(nut) *n.* a black person, especially one seen as an "Uncle Tom." (Racially offensive. Called this because a coconut is black on the surface but white under the skin.) □ *Would you believe, the coconut tells the Babylon where to find her?* □ *If that coco comes back here he'll be sorry, man!*

cod *n.* a trick, hoax or parody. □ *Don't you try to fool me with a cod like that!* □ *That was a really, really dumb cod!*

cod roe *n.* money. (Rhyming slang, linked as follows: cod roe ≈ [dough] = money. Compare with DOUGH and BREAD.) □ *It takes a lot of cod roe to buy a car like that.* □ *I don't make enough cod roe to go on a trip like that!*

cods *n.* the testicles. (Taboo. Normally with *the* and in the plural.) □ *The teacher preferred "testicles" to "cods,"*

if they had to be mentioned at all. □ *He turned sideways to protect his cods.*

cod's wallop See CODSWALLOP.

codswallop AND **cod's wallop** *n.* utter nonsense. (See LOAD OF CODS.) □ *Boy, he can certainly churn out codswallop by the ton!* □ *That's just a lot of cod's wallop. Ignore it.*

coffin nail *n.* a cigarette. □ *No more coffin nails for me.* □ *Every coffin nail you smoke takes a little off the end of your life.*

cog *n.* a gear (on a car, etc.). □ *Don't crash the cogs!* □ *There's something wrong, I can't change cog.*

cog box *n.* a gear box. □ *Me car needs a new cog box.* □ *What's wrong? Cog box gone?*

coin it (in) *vb. phr.* to make vast sums of money rapidly. □ *If we advertise, we can coin it in.* □ *The promoter is coining it on this product.*

coke *n.* cocaine. □ *You can get some good coke in this part of town.* □ *Where can I get coke around here?*

cold *mod.* [of stolen goods that are] untraceable. □ *They'll never find it now it's cold.* □ *That stuff ain't cold yet. Watch it!*

cold call *vb.* to call a sales prospect from a list of persons one has never met. □ *The salesman cold called a number of people each evening for two months.* □ *Things have to be pretty bad before the senior partners at a major brokerage firm start cold calling people to get business.*

cold feet *n.* a wave of timidity or fearfulness. □ *Suddenly I had cold feet and couldn't sing a note.* □ *You sort of expect a chicken like that to have cold feet.*

cold fish *n.* a dull and unresponsive person. □ *I hate to shake hands with a cold fish like that. He didn't even smile.* □ *I hate going out with a cold fish.*

cold-meat job *n.* a case involving a corpse. (Police.) □ *There's a cold-meat job in Watson Street, Inspector.* □ *He's on his way to the cold-meat job right now.*

cold shoulder *vb.* to ignore someone; to give someone a cool reception. □

The hostess cold shouldered me, so I spilt my appetisers in the swimming pool. □ *Tiffany cold shouldered the guy who was coming on strong at Roberta.*

cold sober *mod.* sober; completely sober. □ *Of course I'm cold sober!* □ *He had a hangover and wanted more than anything to be cold sober and alert.*

cold steel *n.* a bayonet. (Military.) □ *Cold steel is very effective; they don't like it up them, you know!* □ *Remember men, that cold steel will certainly concentrate the mind of the enemy.*

cold turkey *mod.* of stopping something suddenly without tapering off. (Said especially and originally of stopping an addictive drug intake, but now applied more generally.) □ *Martha stopped cold turkey and survived.* □ *I stopped smoking cigarettes cold turkey and ended up in hospital.*

collar 1. *n.* an arrest. □ *It was a tough collar, with all that screaming and yelling.* □ *I made the collar in broad daylight.* **2.** *n.* a lie. (Rhyming slang, linked as follows: collar [and tie] ≈ lie.) □ *That's just a collar. Ignore it.* □ *Boy, he can certainly churn out collars by the hour!*

collared *mod.* arrested. □ *Willard Babbit? Oh, yes. He's collared. Got him last night.* □ *Would you believe? I got collared while we was sitting there stuck in the middle of a traffic jam.*

collar someone *vb.* to arrest someone. (Police.) □ *The cops collared her as she was leaving the hotel.* □ *The rozzers tried to collar Max too, but he moved away too fast.*

collect *vb. phr.* to visit someone and then to proceed to another place with them. □ *He's going to collect Simon first.* □ *Hello, I'm here to collect Simon.*

collect a gong *vb. phr.* to win a medal. □ *He goes to the Palace next week to collect a gong.* □ *Collecting a gong was not the most important objective of my career, you know.*

collins *n.* a letter thanking the host or hostess upon returning from a visit. (From a character in Jane Austin's novel *Pride and Prejudice.* Compare with BREAD AND BUTTER LETTER.) □ *I must write a collins to Mrs Jackson to thank her for last night's wonderful dinner party.* □ *Well, that's nice. Only Mrs Harris has had the courtesy to send a collins.*

collywobbles *n.* an apprehensive feeling. □ *She's got the collywobbles again.* □ *Why the collywobbles, dear? What happened?*

colour of someone's money *n.* evidence of the genuineness and quantity of one's money. □ *Well, I could tell if we might make a deal if I could see the colour of your money.* □ *Let me see the colour of your money first. Then we'll talk.*

combo *n.* a small group of musicians; a small band, especially a jazz or dance band. (From "combination.") □ *Andy started his own combo and made money from day one.* □ *You can make a good living with a combo.*

come AND **cum** *n.* semen. (Taboo.) □ *There were stains of come on the bed.* □ *Cum is messy stuff.*

come a clover *vb. phr.* to fall over. (Derivation: fall over = over = clover = come a clover.) □ *I came a clover on a flagstone outside my house.* □ *Don't come a clover!*

come across 1. *vb. phr.* to be compliant. □ *Oh, she'll come across, just you wait; she'll do what we want.* □ *Come on, come across!* **2.** *vb. phr.* to agree; to yield. □ *He came across to our point of view.* □ *How can we get him to come across?*

come across someone or something *vb. phr.* to meet or find someone or something accidentally. □ *The other day I came across a book I had not read for ages.* □ *Fancy coming across you again after all those years!*

come across with something 1. *vb. phr.* to give or lend something. □ *He's come across with the things he promised.* □ *Could you come across with some of these things?* **2.** *vb. phr.* to confess; to speak out. □ *Eventually, he came across with the full story.* □ *If you come across with it, I'll be able to help you.*

Come again? *phr.* "Please repeat." □ *Eh? Come again?* □ *Please come again? I didn't understand that.*

come apart (at the seams) 1. *vb. phr.* to disintegrate; to cease to function as a coherent entity. □ *I'm afraid the whole operation was clearly coming apart at the seams.* □ *It was hardly surprising that the thing came apart, considering the pressure it had to operate under.* **2.** *vb. phr.* to fail catastrophically. □ *It began to look as if the whole project was coming apart at the seams.* □ *Please don't come apart just yet, she found herself willing the ancient motor car.*

come away *vb. phr.* to become detached. □ *The door handle came away in my hand.* □ *Our ship came away from the land and sailed out into the ocean.*

come back *vb. phr.* to repeat. □ *Why are you coming back again?* □ *Please stop coming back on yourself over and over again.*

comeback *n.* a return to a former state. □ *The ageing singer tried to sober up and make a comeback.* □ *Her comeback was not a financial success, but it improved her spirits.*

come clean with someone (about something) *vb. phr.* to admit (something) to someone. □ *I wish you'd come clean with me about this problem.* □ *You're gonna have to come clean eventually.*

come down *vb. phr.* to begin to recover from the effects of alcohol or drug intoxication. □ *She came down slowly, which was good.* □ *It was hard to get her to come down.*

come-down *n.* a letdown; a disappointment. □ *The loss of the race was a real come-down for Willy.* □ *It's hard to face a come-down like that.*

come (down) hard *vb. phr.* to threaten or to attack in an aggressive manner. □ *Any more of this, and I'll come down so hard you won't know what hit you.* □ *You've got to come hard to have any effect on these people.*

come down hard *vb. phr.* to come out of a drug use session badly. □ *Mike came down hard, and it took them a long time to calm him down.* □ *Some kids who come down hard will need treatment, but none of them get it unless they look like they are in a real bad way.*

come down on someone hard AND **come down on someone like a ton of bricks** *vb. phr.* to be especially angry with someone; to reprimand someone with great force. □ *The teacher came down on the wayward pupil hard.* □ *Misbehave and he'll come down on you like a ton of bricks.*

come down on someone like a ton of bricks See COME DOWN ON SOMEONE HARD.

come-hither look AND **glad eye** *n.* an alluring or seductive look or glance, usually from a woman to a man. (See also BEDROOM EYES.) □ *Although she'd mastered the come-hither look, she was not ready for what came next.* □ *Norah gave him the glad eye and smiled inwardly at the look of surprised confusion on his face..*

come it *vb. phr.* to behave aggressively or presumptuously. □ *Don't you come it with me!* □ *He tried to come it but I got the better of him.*

come (off) AND **cum** *vb. (phr.)* to have a sexual orgasm. (Taboo.) □ *These walls are so thin, you can actually hear them cry out when they come off!* □ *Most prostitutes learn to fake cumming.*

Come off it! AND **Get off it! 1.** *exclam.* "Stop acting so arrogantly!" □ *Oh, you're just one of us. Come off it!* □ *Get off it, Tony. Who do you think you are? The President of the United States?* **2.** *exclam.* "Give up your incorrect point of view!" □ *Get off it! You're wrong, and you know it.* □ *You are arguing from a foolish position. You're dead wrong. Come off it!*

come off something *vb. phr.* to fall off something. (Such as a horse, for example.) □ *A lot of people come off motorbikes going round that dangerous corner.* □ *He broke his hip when he came off his horse.*

Come on! *exclam.* "You are wrong!"; "Don't be absurd!" □ *Come on! This is* *a good set of clubs!* □ *Come on! Wasteful spending occurs at all levels of all governments! Nobody is innocent!*

come on *vb. phr.* to commence menstruating. (Crude.) □ *Sue doesn't go swimming when she's coming on.* □ *Kim's just come on and in a bad mood.*

come-on 1. *n.* a sexual invitation. (Crude.) □ *She stared at him with her bedroom eyes, giving him that age-old come-on.* □ *Who could resist a come-on like that?* **2.** *n.* a lure; bait. □ *Forty people responded to the come-on published in the Sunday paper.* □ *It has to be a come-on. Nobody is going to give away a decent colour TV just for listening to a sales pitch.*

come on strong *vb. phr.* to seem aggressive; to impress people initially as very aggressive and assertive. □ *She has a tendency to come on strong, but she's really a softie.* □ *The new prime minister comes on strong at first.*

come out 1. *vb. phr.* to go on strike. □ *The entire workforce came out today.* □ *If they come out I'll close the plant down and sack them all.* **2.** *vb. phr.* to make a public declaration of homosexuality. □ *Well, I'm pleased Larry's come out at last.* □ *Bruno? Come out? Come on!*

come out ahead *vb. phr.* to end up with a profit or some other benefit. □ *I never seem to come out ahead at the end of the month.* □ *We'll come out ahead in the end. Just you wait.*

come out in the wash *vb. phr.* to be dealt with in the normal chain of events. (As if someone were counselling someone who had caused a clothing stain.) □ *All of these things will come out in the wash.* □ *Whatever it is, it'll come out in the wash. Don't worry.*

come out on top *vb. phr.* to end up to the better; to win. □ *Tim always has to come out on top—a classic poor loser.* □ *She made all the wrong moves and still came out on top.*

come over queer *vb. phr.* to feel ill suddenly. □ *Mary was come over queer and had to go home.* □ *If you come over queer like that again, I want to know.*

come round *vb. phr.* to make an informal visit. □ *Your aunt is coming round.* □ *Why don't you come round for a drink?*

come the innocent *vb. phr.* to pretend innocence. □ *Don't you come the innocent with me, my lad!* □ *He's coming the innocent, but we'll get to the truth.*

come the old soldier with someone 1. *phr.* to wheedle, importune or take liberties with someone. □ *Don't you come the old soldier with me!* □ *He tried to come the old soldier with us but we disabused him of that in short order.* **2.** *phr.* to dominate or impose one's own views upon someone, by virtue of presumed superior knowledge or experience. □ *Don't come the old soldier with me. I know better than that.* □ *Although he tried to come the old soldier with the doctor, he got nowhere.*

come through *vb. phr.* to survive or succeed. □ *If you can come through that, you're very clever or very lucky.* □ *There! We came through!*

come to a sticky end *vb. phr.* to be murdered; to die in some particularly gory way. □ *If you go on like that you'll come to a sticky end.* □ *I knew he'd come to a sticky end.*

come-to-bed eyes See BEDROOM EYES.

come to no harm *vb. phr.* to be unharmed. □ *The main thing is, she come to no harm.* □ *As long we come to no harm it's all right.*

come to stay 1. *vb. phr.* to arrive for a long visit. □ *Your aunt has come to stay for a month or two.* □ *Can I come to stay this summer?* **2.** *vb. phr.* to come to reside permanently. □ *Uncle Jack will be coming to stay with us from now on.* □ *I was most unhappy when I came to stay at our new home.*

Come to that. *phr.* "Since you mention that..."; "That reminds me..." □ *Come to that, when are you planning on paying me?* □ *Now it comes to that I think we can cope.*

come to the wrong shop *vb. phr.* to ask something in the wrong place. □ *Woops! I've come to the wrong shop, haven't I!* □ *This is the vet's surgery. If you want your toothache attended to, you've come to the wrong shop.*

come under the hammer *vb. phr.* to auction (something). □ *The house at the corner is coming under the hammer next week.* □ *What's come under the hammer this week, then?*

come undone See COME UNGLUED.

come unglued AND **come undone; come unravelled; come unstuck; come unstrung 1.** *vb. phr.* to go wrong. □ *I think your wonderful scheme has come unglued, Mary.* □ *Oh boy, how did our plan come unstrung like that?* **2.** *vb. phr.* to become extremely nervous or disorganised; to lose control. □ *I think the poor man just become unglued under the pressure.* □ *Just be careful not to come unstrung when things get difficult.*

come unravelled See COME UNGLUED.

come unstrung See COME UNGLUED.

come unstuck See COME UNGLUED.

come up for air *vb. phr.* to pause for a break. □ *The kissers—being only human—had to come up for air eventually.* □ *They were taking in money so fast at the box office that there wasn't any time to come up for air.*

comeuppance *n.* a well-deserved rebuke. □ *He finally got the comeuppance that he's needed for so long.* □ *I gave her a comeuppance she'll never forget.*

comfy *mod.* comfortable. □ *This is a very comfy chair.* □ *I find myself in a not too comfy position with regards to your further employment here.*

coming out of one's ears *mod.* in great abundance. □ *Mr Wilson has money coming out of his ears.* □ *Borrow some paper from Chuck. He's got it coming out of his ears.*

commie *n.* a communist. □ *What are the commies up to now?* □ *Commies? What commies? Haven't you noticed how they've all vanished since 1989?*

common *n.* common land. □ *Anyone can walk on the common; after all, it's common land!* □ *The large open space in front of you there is the village common.*

common (dog) *n.* common sense. □ *Anyone with an ounce of common dog should be able to do that, Otto.* □ *The problem with common is that it's not common at all.*

common or garden *mod.* normal or usual. □ *Oh, that's just the common or garden kind.* □ *Really, any old common or garden one will do.*

company man *n.* a man who always sides with his employers. □ *Ken's a company man—he'll always take management's side.* □ *You can depend on a company man to do as he is told.*

computerese *n.* computer jargon. □ *I haven't got a clue. He spoke nothing but pure computerese.* □ *I don't speak your computerese. Plain English only, please!*

computer widow *n.* a wife left alone while her husband works (or plays) at his computer. (See GOLF WIDOW and BRIDGE WIDOW.) □ *Ever since he got that thing, I've been turned into a sort of computer widow.* □ *I see they're starting a local branch of Computer Widows.*

con 1. *vb.* to swindle or deceive someone. □ *Don't try to con me. I know the score.* □ *Bruno conned him out of his money.* **2.** SEE CONFIDENCE TRICK.

con artist See CON MAN.

conchie *n.* a conscientious objector. □ *Otto was a conchie in the war, you know.* □ *Otto? The only things he was ever a conchie about were hard work and honest effort.*

confessional *n.* an interview room at a police station. (Police. Usually with the.) □ *Into the confessional, chummy!* □ *It's amazing what they try to deny they said in the confessional.*

confidence trick AND **con trick; con** *n.* a swindle where the perpetrator persuades the victim to trust him or her. □ *They pulled a real dirty confidence trick on that old lady.* □ *This is an okay con you've got going here.*

conflab *n.* a discussion. □ *We're having a conflab on the situation now.* □ *What's this conflab about?*

congratters *n.* congratulations. □ *Congratters! Well done.* □ *Just to say congratters on your new baby.*

conk AND **konk 1.** *n.* a large or particularly obtrusive nose. □ *Have you seen the size of that guy's conk?* □ *Joan bonked Pete on his big red konk.* **2.** *n.* the head. □ *Harry's distinctive hairy* *conk hove into view.* □ *Where'd you get that nasty bump on your konk?*

conker *n.* the hard, round nut that is the fruit of the horse-chestnut tree. □ *Conkers are horse-chestnut nuts threaded with and suspended from strings. They are then swung at each other in turn until one or the other is smashed, the surviving being the victor.* □ *Jimmy has a great collection of conkers this autumn.*

conkers *n.* a game played by children, particularly in the autumn. □ *The children were outside, playing conkers.* □ *Conkers is popular with children at this time of the year.*

conk out 1. *vb. phr.* [for someone] to collapse. □ *I was so tired I just went home and conked out.* □ *I was afraid he would conk out while he was driving.* **2.** *vb. phr.* [for something] to break down; to quit running. □ *My car finally conked out.* □ *I hope my computer doesn't conk out.*

con man AND **con artist** *n.* someone who makes a living by swindling people. □ *Gary is a con artist, but at least he's not on the dole.* □ *He looks like a con man, but really he's just a sweetie.*

connection AND **connexion** *n.* a seller of drugs; someone who is a source for drugs. □ *Max's connection got lifted.* □ *This connexion you keep taking about—is he dependable?*

connexion See CONNECTION.

constant screamer *n.* a concertina. (Rhyming slang. Here, the concertina referred to is the musical instrument.) □ *My uncle used to play the constant screamer.* □ *Constant screamers are kinda rare nowadays.*

constipated *mod.* reluctant to part with money. □ *When it comes to handing out money, she's as constipated as they get.* □ *Come on, you constipated old miser. It's a good cause.*

con trick See CONFIDENCE TRICK.

conversion job *n.* a heavy beating. □ *After a conversion job like that, the guy spent two weeks in the hospital.* □ *Bruno gave the guy a terrible conversion job.*

coo AND **cor** *exclam.* "God." (A euphemism and disguise.) □ *Coo, she's a*

real looker! □ *Cor, what's young Alf done now?*

cook See CAPTAIN COOK.

cookie *n.* a prostitute. (Crude. Scots usage.) □ *There was a cookie standing right on that corner.* □ *There are a lot of cookies around here in the centre of town.*

cooking *mod.* busy. □ *The phone was cooking for more than an hour.* □ *I was cooking and couldn't get to the phone.*

cook something up 1. *vb. phr.* to create a falsehood; to lie. □ *Where did he cook up that one up?* □ *We're going to have to cook up some sort of plausible explanation.* **2.** *vb. phr.* to prepare drugs for injection. □ *Just as soon as it's cooked up, she'll inject it.* □ *Would you believe it? They were cooking up right there, where everyone could see.*

cook the books *vb. phr.* to prepare a set of false accounts. □ *Cook the books? No, not Jane. She's as honest as the day is long.* □ *Jane's been fired for cooking the books.*

cool 1. *mod.* unabashed; unruffled; relaxed. (Compare with *keep one's cool* and *lose one's cool.*) □ *She is so cool, no matter what happens.* □ *Keep cool and everything will be all right.* **2.** *mod.* [of music] mellow or smooth. □ *This stuff is so cool, I'm just floating.* □ *Doesn't he blow a cool trumpet?* **3.** *mod.* no less than (some amount of money). □ *He earns a cool million every year.* □ *She cleared a cool forty thousand on the Wilson deal.*

cool, calm and collected *mod.* cool; unabashed. □ *Albert is almost always cool, calm and collected.* □ *Before a race I am anything but cool, calm and collected.*

cooler 1. *n.* jail. (Usually with *the.*) □ *Do you want to talk, or do you want to spend a little time in the cooler?* □ *Get me out of the cooler!* **2.** *n.* a prison cell. □ *It was when the heavy door slammed shut that it really got through. He was in the cooler.* □ *It was a grim, cold, unwelcoming little room, this cooler.*

Cool it! *exclam.* "Calm down!" □ *Take it easy! Cool it!* □ *Come on, cool it, man!*

cool off *vb. phr.* to calm down. □ *It's all right. Cool off, now!* □ *I knew things would cool off eventually.*

cool one's heels AND **kick one's heels** *vb. phr.* to be left waiting, typically with nothing to do. □ *We were left to cool our heels for over two hours!* □ *I'm sorry you had to kick your heels for so long.*

coon *n.* a black person. (Racially offensive.) □ *He said he was not a racist, he just hated coons!* □ *Don't call black people coons, please. It is very offensive and racist.*

co-op *n.* a co-operative store. □ *Most co-ops are turned into supermarkets nowadays.* □ *I'm afraid I don't shop in the co-op very often.*

cop 1. *n.* an arrest. □ *It was a smooth cop. No trouble, no fuss.* □ *"All right, gov, it's a fair cop," said the burglar, "I'll come quietly."* **2.** *vb.* to arrest or capture. □ *The policeman copped him and told him his rights.* □ *They copped Brian with the evidence right on him.* **3.** *n.* a police officer. (See also COPPER.) □ *Why does this cop want to talk to you?* □ *The cop's not going away 'till he sees you.*

cop a feel on someone *vb. phr.* to touch or fondle someone sexually. (Taboo.) □ *He copped a feel on her, yet she said nothing.* □ *She actually said he could cop a feel on her if he liked!*

cop a packet AND **get a packet** *vb. phr.* to become badly injured, to be wounded severely. (Originally military.) □ *Me uncle copped a packet in Normandy.* □ *If you want to get a packet or worse, just stand up in that shallow trench, son.*

cop a plea *vb. phr.* to plead guilty to a lower charge. □ *He's copping a plea and admitting to manslaughter.* □ *If you cop a plea, I think you could get off with a fine.*

cop car *n.* a police car. □ *There was a cop car blocking the end of the street.* □ *Two plainclothes men got out of the cop car.*

cope (with it) AND **cope (with things)** *vb. phr.* to manage one's life or business in a satisfactory way. □ *Don't worry, I can cope with it.* □ *Leave me be! I'll cope!*

cope (with things) See COPE (WITH IT).

cop it 1. *vb. phr.* to be found out; to be caught. □ *He copped it right in the middle of the attack, sir.* □ *If they try that here they'll copped it for sure.* **2.** *vb. phr.* to be made to endure; to be punished. □ *You're just going to have to cop it until we get this sorted.* □ *You'll cop it for that behaviour, I promise.* **3.** *vb. phr.* to become pregnant. □ *Has she copped it again?* □ *Zoe has been trying to cop it for months, you know.*

cop one's whack *n.* to get what one deserves. (Scots usage. In the sense of punishment or reward.) □ *I suppose I copped my whack when the car I stole crashed and I was hurt.* □ *How did you ever cop yourself a whack like that?*

cop (on to) something *vb. phr.* to understand or become aware of something. □ *I think I'm copping on to the significance of this at last.* □ *Try to cop what I'm saying, Otto.*

cop out 1. *vb. phr.* to give up and quit, to CHICKEN OUT (OF SOMETHING). □ *Why do you want to cop out just when things are going great?* □ *I couldn't cop out on you guys if I wanted to.* **2.** *n.* a poor or unconvincing excuse to get out of something. (Also in the forms COP-OUT or COPOUT.) □ *This is just a silly cop out.* □ *That's not a good reason. That's just a cop-out.*

copped *mod.* arrested. □ *Jed got himself copped for speeding.* □ *I was copped for doing absolutely nothing at all.*

copper *n.* a police officer. (Originally underworld. Because the COPPER "cops" or "takes." See also COP.) □ *See that copper over there? He lifted me once.* □ *The coppers will catch up with you some day.*

cop shop *n.* a police station. □ *They hauled everybody off to the cop-shop.* □ *The pigs down at the cop-shop tried to act like they didn't know who Martin was.*

copycat *n.* someone who mimics or copies the actions of others. □ *Don't be such a copycat. Find a style that suits you.* □ *Jim is a real copycat. He can say anything you say, just the way you say it.*

cor See COO.

corblimey See BLIMEY.

corey *n.* the male sexual organ. (Taboo.) □ *Only a small boy waves his corey about like that, Wayne. Put it away!* □ *Myra says coreys are disgusting but then Myra's strange.*

Corgi and Bess *n.* the annual television broadcast made by Queen Elizabeth on Christmas Day. (Her pet corgi dogs are usually in evidence.) □ *What do we call a Corgi and Bess if the corgis don't turn up?* □ *Corgi and Bess is the highlight of Christmas day for Aunt Mary.*

Cor love a duck! See LORD LOVE A DUCK!

corned (beef) *mod.* deaf. (Rhyming slang. Scots usage; in Scotland "deaf" is pronounced DEEF.) □ *Auld Willie's been corned beef ever since he was a lad, y'know.* □ *Are you corned? Yes, you! I'm talking to you!*

corned beef *n.* a thief. (Rhyming slang.) □ *We are the police. We are here to catch a corned beef, madam.* □ *This little toe-rag is just another corned beef.*

corner shop *n.* a small local convenience shop. □ *Jimmy, run down to the corner shop and get me some sugar.* □ *Do you not have a corner shop near here?*

Cornish (pasty) **1.** *n.* a pastry turnover containing seasoned meats and vegetables. □ *Alfred has a Cornish pasty every day for lunch.* □ *I like the occasional Cornish, too.* **2.** *n.* a wide, thickly-soled heavy-duty man's shoe. □ *A lot of the older working men around here still wear Cornish pasties.* □ *The Cornish was a practical solution to a practical pedestrian problem.*

corny **1.** *mod.* concerning humour which is dated, feeble or trite. □ *This corny dialogue has to be revised before I'll act in that play.* □ *Don't be corny. This is serious.* **2.** *mod.* concerning overdone or excessive sentimentality. □ *The love scenes were real out-and-out corny, but nobody laughed.* □ *Harry always laughs at corny rubbish in a film.* **3.** *mod.* outdated; old-fashioned. □ *Don't be so corny, daddy. No*

one says "wireless" nowadays. □ *What a corny old dress she was wearing!* **4.** *mod.* trivial; insignificant. □ *It was just a corny little place.* □ *He came up with this stupid, corny suggestion; it was pathetic, really.*

corporation cocktail *n.* milk which has had coal gas (or similar) bubbled through it. (The result is a cheap but potentially deadly intoxicant. The corporation in question is British Gas plc, formerly British Gas Corporation.) □ *Once upon a time, corporation cocktails were the tipple of choice among the denizens of this salubrious neighbourhood.* □ *There are few people trying the corporation cocktail now, principally because the natural gas that is supplied nowadays does not work like the old coal gas supply did.*

corridors of power *n.* government departments and agencies, and the people who inhabit them. (Normally with *the*.) □ *It's in the corridors of power that the real governing goes on.* □ *Where are these famous corridors of power, anyway?*

cosh **1.** *n.* a bludgeon or blackjack. □ *"All right son, why are you carrying a cosh?" the policeman asked him.* □ *He took out a cosh and threatened me.* **2.** *vb.* to bludgeon. □ *He tried to cosh me but I managed to run off.* □ *Have you ever been coshed?*

cosmic *mod.* excellent; superb. □ *Mary's got herself a cosmic new job.* □ *This is a cosmic day!*

Costa del Crime *n.* the south-eastern coastal region of Spain. (The name is a play upon Spain's *Costa del Sol.* Compare with COSTA GERIATRICA.) □ *The area is called the Costa del Crime because of the large number of fugitives from British justice reputed to be in hiding there.* □ *I hear Mr Big's retiring—to the Costa del Crime, of course.*

Costa Geriatrica *n.* the southern coastal region of England. (See COSTA DEL CRIME.) □ *They call it the Costa Geriatrica because of the many retired people living there.* □ *The name Costa Geriatrica is a play made upon Spain's Costa Brava.*

cost a packet AND **cost the earth** *vb. phr.* to be very expensive or costly. □ *It'll cost a packet to do that.* □ *I don't care if that painting costs the earth. Buy it!*

cost the earth See COST A PACKET.

cosy 1. *mod.* handy; convenient. □ *Next door, eh? Well that's cosy, I must say.* □ *I think they had a cosy little arrangement going there.* **2.** *vb.* to perform sexual intercourse. (Crude.) □ *She seems to think that saying she's "cosying" makes it all right.* □ *I want to cosy with him.*

cotics *n.* narcotics. □ *You can get some good cotics in this part of town.* □ *Is Willy doing cotics again?*

cottage *n.* a urinal. □ *What do you expect in a toilet except a cottage?* □ *What a disgusting cottage that is in there!*

cottage AND **fairy glen** *n.* a public toilet habitually used as a place of assignation by male homosexuals. (Crude.) □ *Watch it! That one's the local fairy glen, you know.* □ *Why do these people have to use this place as a cottage?*

cottaging 1. *n.* the habit of spending the weekend at a second home in the country. □ *We go cottaging in Suffolk most weekends.* □ *This area is full of houses belonging to people who do a lot of cottaging.* **2.** *n.* the practice of homosexuality. (Crude.) □ *I think they've gone off for a spot of quiet cottaging, if you know what I mean.* □ *They're always cottaging! It's disgusting!*

cottier *n.* thread. □ *This shop sells a great deal of cottier.* □ *Without cottier there would be no cloth.*

cotton wool on top *mod.* unburdened with excessive intelligence. □ *She's, well, rather cotton wool on top, you know.* □ *We do not need any more of these cotton wool on top people in here.*

couch potato *n.* a lazy individual, addicted to television-watching. □ *All he ever does is watch TV; he's become a real couch potato.* □ *Couch potatoes can tend to become very fat and unhealthy, you know.*

cough 1. *vb.* to confess to a crime. (Police.) □ *Are you going to cough?* □ *All*

right, all right. I'll cough to the break in but not the assault. **2.** *n.* useful or general information. (Police.) □ *Here's some cough you might find handy.* □ *Well, that is useful cough!*

cough and stutter AND **mutter and stutter** *n.* butter. (Rhyming slang.) □ *I like cough and stutter on me bread. Don't you?* □ *Half a pound of mutter and stutter, please.*

cough something up *vb. phr.* to produce something which someone has requested, often money. □ *Come on, buster, cough it up, now!* □ *You owe me seven stereo amplifiers. Now, cough them up!* □ *Cough up what you owe me!*

could not organise a piss-up in a brewery *mod.* incapable of organising anything successfully. (Taboo.) □ *Otto could not organise a piss-up in a brewery.* □ *She could not organise a piss-up in a brewery if her life depended on it.*

couldn't half *phr.* most certainly could. □ *I couldn't half go a pint.* □ *She couldn't half.*

council house *n.* a family dwelling owned by and rented from a local authority. □ *We live in a council house.* □ *There were once a lot of council houses over there.*

counter *n.* sexual intercourse with a prostitute, viewed as a business transaction. (Crude.) □ *She said she needed about ten counters tonight to pay the money-lender tomorrow.* □ *I wonder if the gingers actually enjoy these counters?*

country cousin *n.* a dozen. (Rhyming slang.) □ Q: *How many eggs?* A: *A country cousin, please.* □ *There's about a country cousin of people here to see you, Claire.*

county *n.* the landed gentry and other leading citizens within a county. □ *The county are so superior, you'd think they own the place.* □ *To a large extent, the county do own the place.*

couple of bob *n.* a small, non-specific sum of money. (Usually with *a*. Literally, two shillings in old currency or ten pence in new currency. "Bob" was a slang term for a shilling.) □ *I'm afraid* there is not even a couple of bob left in that account. □ Of course I can afford it. It's just a couple of bob.

Cousin Jack *n.* a Cornishman, especially a tin miner. □ *Ivor's a Cousin Jack; he comes from Penzance.* □ *What have you got against Cousin Jacks?*

Cousins *n.* Americans; the US Government; the United States. (Normally with *the*. A term used in British government circles rather than among the general public. It is not necessarily meant in a complimentary way.) □ *Do we know what the Cousins really want?* □ *We never know what the Cousins are really after.*

cover in *vb. phr.* to cover or roof over. □ *We have to cover in this trench before nightfall.* □ *Why did you cover in the box, Jean?*

cover-up *n.* an act of concealing something. □ *The cover-up attracted more attention than whatever it was that it was covering up.* □ *The candidate accused her opponent of a cover-up.*

cow AND **mare; moo(-cow); sow** *n.* a woman, especially a particularly fat or coarse one. (Crude.) □ *That fat cow can hardly get herself through the door.* □ *Wouldn't you think a sow like that would go on a diet?*

cow and calf **1.** *n.* a half. (Rhyming slang.) □ *Surely a cow and calf's enough.* □ *It's just a cow and calf, but I want it all.* **2.** *n.* one Pound and fifty pence; formerly, thirty shillings. (Rhyming slang, linked as follows: cow and calf ≈ half [of one Pound Sterling].) □ *That'll be a cow and calf, missus.* □ *He wanted me to pay a cow and calf for this worthless thing!*

cowboy **1.** *n.* a reckless and independent man; a reckless driver. □ *Come on, you cowboy, let a professional have a go at repairing this.* □ *Some cowboy in an ancient pick-up cut in in front of me.* **2.** *n.* an unqualified, incompetent or reckless business person. □ *Even a cowboy like that has to earn a living. I think.* □ *What does the cowboy want?* **3.** *n.* an unqualified, incompetent or reckless construction worker. □ *I can see by this mess that you've had some*

cowboy working on this. □ *Watch out for cowboys; they'll rip you off.*

cowboy outfit *n.* an incompetent or ineffective business, especially in construction. □ *That firm of builders is utterly terrible. I think they must be the original cowboy outfit.* □ *We don't want any cowboy outfits working on this project.*

cowhorns *n.* tall curved handles upon a bicycle or motorcycle. □ *Are you sure these cowhorns are safe?* □ *I just love riding it with these cowhorns.*

cozzer AND **cozzpot** *n.* a policeman. □ *See that cozzer over there? He lifted me once.* □ *The cozzpots will catch up with you some day.*

cozzpot See COZZER.

crab *n.* a pubic louse. (Taboo. Usually plural.) □ *He's scratching like he's got the crabs.* □ *The old wino and his crabs wandered into the flophouse for a little peace and quiet.*

crabby *mod.* bad-tempered. □ *That's the sort of stupidity that makes me crabby!* □ *Watch out, he's really crabby today.*

crack **1.** *n.* a joke; a SMART-ALEC remark. □ *Another crack like that and your nose will be a little flatter than it is.* □ *Who made that crack?* **2.** *n.* a try or attempt that may or may not succeed. □ *Have another crack at it.* □ *One more crack and I'll have it.* **3.** *n.* crystalline, smokable cocaine. □ *This crack seems to have become the drug of choice for users of all ages.* □ *Crack became popular when it became easy and cheap to process. It's been around for years in medicinal form.* **4.** *vb.* to break down and talk under pressure. (Underworld.) □ *They kept at her till she finally cracked and talked.* □ *We knew you'd crack in the end.* **5.** *mod.* [of a person] excellent or top-flight. □ *The dealer's crack salesman was no help at all.* □ *With our crack staff, we can have everything worked out in no time.* **6.** *vb.* to break into something. (Underworld.) □ *We almost cracked the safe before the alarm went off.* □ *His speciality is cracking car trunks and stealing tyres.*

crack a stiffie *vb. phr.* to have an erection. (Taboo.) □ *I cracked a stiffie as* *soon as she walked in the room!* □ *If you can't crack a stiffie, you should see the doctor.*

crack down on someone *phr.* to stop or prevent someone committing a crime. □ *The police cracked down on Tommy real hard.* □ *Did cracking down on you like that make any difference?*

crack down on something *vb. phr.* to stop or prevent acts which are criminal. □ *The police are going to crack down on car theft around here.* □ *If they would just crack down on crime, like in the old days.*

cracked up to be *mod.* supposed to be. □ *This pizza isn't all it's cracked up to be.* □ *I wanted to find out whether this stuff was what it is cracked up to be.*

cracker 1. *n.* a sexually attractive person. (Crude.) □ *Now he's what I'd call a real cracker!* □ *A delicious cracker of a girl came into the office today.* **2.** *n.* a dry, thin unsweetened biscuit often eaten with cheese. □ *He likes a few crackers with his cheese.* □ *Can I have another cracker, please?*

crackers See BONKERS.

crackhead *n.* a user of CRACK. □ *They brought an eight-year-old crackhead in for treatment.* □ *Crackheads are becoming a very serious problem in this country.*

crack house *n.* a house or dwelling where CRACK is sold and used. □ *The police are continuing their efforts to close down crack houses in the area.* □ *In one dilapidated area of the inner city, there is a crack house on just about every street corner.*

cracking *mod.* exceptionally good. □ *What a cracking idea that was.* □ *Your news is really cracking.*

crack it *vb. phr.* to solve a difficult problem. □ *At last, I think we've cracked it!* □ *We don't have long to crack it, you know.*

crack on *vb. phr.* to talk endlessly. □ *Oh, he'll crack on till doomsday.* □ *The old friends cracked on for ages about old memories and old friends.*

crack one's face *vb. phr.* to smile. □ *Try cracking your face, just for once.* □ *Come on, now. Crack your face.*

crackpot 1. *n.* an insane person; one with strange or crazy ideas or plans. □ *Some crackpot called to tell us that the sky is falling in.* □ *I'm no crackpot! I saw some of the sky floating in the lake. If it had fallen on land, someone might have been killed.* **2.** *mod.* having to do with crazy things, mainly ideas. □ *We need the occasional crackpot idea around here just so we'll have something to compare your ideas to.* □ *Why not start a crackpot ideas contest?*

crack up 1. *vb. phr.* to have a nervous breakdown. □ *The poor guy cracked up. It was too much for him.* □ *You would crack up, too, if you had been through all he went through.* **2.** *vb. phr.* to praise. (Normally employed in a negative context, such as NOT ALL IT'S CRACKED UP TO BE.) □ *Why crack up that rubbish?* □ *He tried to crack the plan up, but failed.*

cradle-snatch *vb.* to date or marry someone much younger than oneself. □ *She likes younger men, and doesn't appear to mind being accused of cradle-snatching.* □ *Who have you cradle-snatched tonight, Donna?*

cradle-snatcher *n.* one who dates or marries someone much younger than oneself. □ *Well, he's forty and she's seventeen. I think that makes him a cradle-snatcher, but Harry thinks that just makes him lucky.* □ *I wonder if cradle-snatchers tend to have more coronaries?*

crafty 1. *mod.* clever; cunning. □ *She is really crafty. Glad she came along.* □ *That was well done, Tom. You're crafty.* **2.** *mod.* sly; secret. □ *Well, you're a crafty one!* □ *That was very crafty. How did you do it?*

cram *vb.* to study hard at the last minute for an examination. □ *She spent the night cramming for her exam.* □ *If you would study properly all the time, you wouldn't need to cram.*

cramp one's style *vb. phr.* to prevent or limit one's ability to do one's best. □ *Are you trying to cramp my style?* □ *They think the church next door sort of cramps Mr Big's style.*

crank *mod.* eccentric. □ *We had four crank phone calls threatening to blow up the Tower of London.* □ *A crank letter promised us a million pounds if we would play "My Blue Heaven" for two hours each morning.*

crap 1. *n.* faeces. (Crude.) □ *There's dog crap on the lawn.* □ *Don't step in that crap.* **2.** *vb.* to defecate. (Crude.) □ *Your dog crapped on my lawn!* □ *I have to crap; then I'll be right with you.* **3.** *n.* junk; worthless matter. □ *Why don't you just throw this crap away?* □ *Get your crap off my bed!*

crappy *mod.* bad; lousy; junky. □ *This has really been a crappy day!* □ *Shut your crappy mouth!*

crash 1. *vb.* to gain access to a party or other event uninvited. (Compare with CRASH PAD and CRASHER.) □ *Some clown tried to crash the rally, but my dad called the cops.* □ *The boys who tried to crash also broke a window.* **2.** *vb.* to spend the night. (Compare with CRASH PAD and CRASHER.) □ *I crashed at a friend's place in town.* □ *D'you have a place I can crash?* **3.** *vb.* to fail or break down, usually without warning and usually disastrously. (Computer jargon. It may refer to the computer itself or the software running on it.) □ *"This computer crashes every time I hit that particular key." "So why do you hit it?"* □ *My Macintosh is much more reliable; it hasn't crashed since I got it.* **4.** *n.* a total, usually catastrophic, failure. (Computer jargon. It may refer to the computer itself or the software running on it.) □ *Most of my data was lost in the crash.* □ *Crashes are to teach you to back up your data.* **5.** *vb.* [for a stock market] to lose a significant portion of its value in a short time. □ *The market crashed and scared the stuffing out of everybody.* □ *When the bond market crashed, the press didn't even realise it.* **6.** *n.* a collapse of a stock market. □ *After the crash, a lot of people swore off the market for good.* □ *A crash like that was too much for a lot of people.*

crash course *n.* a very intensive, short course of tuition in some specific topic. □ *He's on a crash course this week.* □ *Perhaps we need to send you on a crash course.*

crasher 1. *n.* a person who attends a party uninvited. (Compare with CRASH.) □ *The crashers ruined the party, and my dad called the police.* □ *The crashers were no more rude than the guests.* **2.** See also CRASHING BORE.

crashing bore AND **crasher; crusher** *n.* an exceptionally tedious or boring person or thing. □ *I don't think I could take another crashing bore like that today.* □ *One crusher was no different from the others, he thought.*

crash pad *n.* a place to stay the night on short notice. (Compare with CRASH.) □ *I've got a crash pad in London for emergencies like this.* □ *I've got to find a crash pad for tonight.*

crate *n.* an aircraft, especially a dilapidated or older one. □ *You're not seriously going to fly in that old crate?* □ *This crate gets me into the air and back down again in one piece. That's good enough.*

crawl *vb.* to behave in an excessively toadying or sycophantic way. □ *Why do you have to crawl to anyone in authority?* □ *I was not crawling!*

crawling *mod.* sycophantic. □ *What a crawling toady he is.* □ *I'm not crawling!*

crawling with it *mod.* exceptionally wealthy. □ *There are not many people crawling with it like him.* □ *Ken is crawling with it because of the money his uncle left him.*

crawling with someone or something *mod.* covered with someone or something; alive with someone or something. □ *The place was crawling with police.* □ *The room was just crawling with ants.*

crazy *n.* a crazy person. □ *The guy's a crazy, and he keeps coming in here asking for money.* □ *I think the crazies are taking over the world.*

creaking gate *n.* an invalid who neither recovers nor gets worse. □ *It's terrible; she's been a creaking gate for months now and we don't know what to do.* □ *I hope I'm never a creaking gate like that.*

cream 1. *vb.* [for a woman] to become sexually excited. (Taboo.) □ *I don't know if she liked it, but I can tell you she was certainly creaming.* □ *If you're going to cream like that, go and do it somewhere else, thank you!* **2.** *vb.* to smash up. □ *Someone has creamed my stereo.* □ *If you drop that you'll cream it.* **3.** *vb.* to steal small or insignificant items from one's place of work on a regular basis without being noticed. □ *It may appear harmless to cream, but it's still theft.* □ *Everyone creams nowadays, it seems.*

cream puff *n.* the huff; a fit of petty anger. (Rhyming slang. Scots usage.) □ *Oh, she's having a cream puff again.* □ *We've no time for you and your cream puffs just now.*

creased *mod.* exhausted; unable to continue. □ *I feel too creased to go to work today.* □ *Poor Ted really looks creased.*

creat See CREATE FUCK.

create fuck AND **create hell; create** *vb. phr.* to make a considerable fuss or to complain very loudly. (FUCK is taboo; HELL is crude.) □ *He was there when I got back, creating fuck.* □ *If you don't sort this out right now, I'll create hell and that's a promise!* □ *I'm just going to stand here and create until you do something about this.*

create hell See CREATE FUCK.

creep 1. *n.* a weird or eerie person. □ *Charlie is such a creep when he's stoned.* □ *I thought Charlie was a bit of a creep anyway, but when he got into black magic I had no doubts.* **2.** *n.* a toady; sycophant. □ *That creep actually gave the boss a bottle of wine for her birthday.* □ *You are just a plain old creep.* **3.** *vb.* to burgle a house while it is occupied. □ *Otto once tried creeping but he always got caught.* □ *We've been creeped!*

creepy-crawly *n.* an insect. □ *Is that a creepy-crawly?* □ *Susan screams when she sees a creepy-crawly.*

crem *n.* a crematorium. □ *Aunt Mavis's funeral was at the crem.* □ *That's the crem, where Aunt Mavis is now.*

crew *n.* a group of aggressive youths. □ *Watch that crew, they're out looking for trouble.* □ *I don't like the look of that crew over there.*

crib 1. *vb.* to plagiarise. □ *Smith! You cribbed these answers, didn't you?* □ *I didn't crib nuffink, sir.* **2.** *vb.* to grumble; to complain. □ *Why do you always have to crib?* □ *There he is, cribbing us usual.* **3.** *n.* an aid to cheating in an examination, such as written notes. □ *I'm afraid there's no doubt that Smith took a crib into the examination with him, headmaster.* □ *If I had a crib, where is it then, sir?*

cricket *mod.* fair; reasonable; acceptable. (See also KOSHER. See negative examples at NOT CRICKET.) □ *Is it really cricket to play under two different names?* □ *Who cares if it's cricket!*

crikey AND **cripes; cringe; crumbs** *exclam.* "Christ." (Crude. A euphemism and disguise.) □ *Crikey, I hope we get there on time.* □ *Well crumbs, I didn't think it mattered so much.*

crimper *n.* a hairdresser. □ *Would you ever guess that Bert was once a lady's crimper?* □ *The crimper looked like a right nancy.*

cringe See CRIKEY.

cringe someone *vb.* to embarrass someone. □ *Why did you have to cringe me like that?* □ *He really made him cringe.*

crinkle See CRINKLY.

crinkly 1. AND **crumblie** *n.* a senile or very old person. (Offensive. Also a term of address.) □ *Take care where the crinklies are crossing the road.* □ *Just remember we'll each of us be a crumblie ourselves one day, with luck.* **2.** AND **crinkle** *n.* a banknote; paper money. □ *That'll be 15 please, sir. Or 10 in crinkles, if you like.* □ *How much crinkle do you need, then?* □ *Sorry, I can't afford it. I've no crinkly.*

cripes See CRIKEY.

crisp *vb.* to die by arson. □ *I really would hate to be crisped in a fire. What a way to go.* □ *Three people crisped in that big fire last night.*

criss-cross *n.* a crossword puzzle. □ *I like to complete the criss-cross every morning while having my breakfast.* □ *I don't enjoy criss-crosses.*

critical *mod.* seriously or dangerously ill. □ *He is still critical following the accident.* □ *Yes, he's very ill. Critical, in fact.*

croak *vb.* to die; to expire; to succumb. □ *I was afraid I'd croak.* □ *The parrot croaked before I got it home.*

croaker AND **writer** *n.* a doctor who writes prescriptions for drug addicts. □ *Try Dr Fraser. They say he's a croaker.* □ *Why are there all these police cars around that writer's surgery?*

crowd *vb.* to pressure or threaten someone. □ *Don't crowd me!* □ *Max began to crowd Bruno, which was the wrong thing to do.*

crowie *n.* a old woman. □ *Ask the crowie what she wants, please.* □ *There's a crowie here asking for you.*

crown *vb.* to hit someone on the head. □ *The clerk crowned the robber with a champagne bottle.* □ *The bride, at the end of her patience, crowned the stuttering cleric with her bouquet, shouted "I do," and began kissing the groom.*

crucial *mod.* excellent or wonderful. □ *What a crucial idea that was.* □ *Your news is really crucial, you know.*

crud **1.** *n.* a repellent person. (Rhymes with "mud.") □ *Don't be such a crud!* □ *That crud kept trying to paw me!* **2.** *n.* nastiness; junk; worthless matter. □ *This is just crud. Get rid of it.* □ *Get all that old crud out of the attic so we can have room for newer stuff.*

cruddy *mod.* nasty; awful. □ *What is this cruddy stuff on my plate?* □ *It's just chocolate mousse, and it's not cruddy.*

crumblie See CRINKLY.

crumbs See CRIKEY.

crummy *mod.* lousy; bad; inferior. □ *You know, this stuff is pretty crummy.* □ *It's worse than crummy.*

crumpet **1.** *n.* a woman considered as a sex object. (Crude.) □ *I don't think many women would think that being described as a crumpet is much of a compliment.* □ *I think she's a really nice bit of crumpet.* **2.** *n.* women in general, considered as sex objects. (Crude.) □ *Any crumpet around here, mate?* □ *It's Saturday night and as usual the boys are out looking for crumpet.*

crumpet run *vb.* to drive a vehicle through an area or along a street, for the purpose of looking at the girls. □ *All evening long, these cars crumpet run through here.* □ *Why do you have to crumpet run, Otto?*

crunch *n.* the moment of crisis or of the most severe testing. □ *We seem to be in a crunch of one kind or another all the time.* □ *The budget crunch meant we couldn't take holidays in Florida any more.*

crush **1.** *n.* a large crowded social event. □ *My birthday party was a real crush.* □ *There's quite a crush down here, folks.* **2.** *n.* an infatuation. □ *These crushes are becoming serious, I fear.* □ *She's always having a crush for some pop idol or other.*

crusher **1.** *n.* a policeman. □ *The crusher broke up the fight.* □ *These two crushers drove around in their car picking on innocent people like me.* **2.** See also CRASHING BORE.

crust *n.* the head. □ *Where'd you get that nasty bump on your crust?* □ *Harry's distinctive hairy crust hove into view.*

crusty *mod.* feisty; gruff. □ *Geoff is a crusty old man.* □ *Unlike most crusty, avuncular old men, Geoff hasn't a single redeeming quality.*

cry hughie AND **call ruth; call ralph; cry ralph; cry ruth** *vb. phr.* to empty one's stomach; to vomit. (Crude. See also CALL CHARLIE.) □ *He is in the loo crying hughie.* □ *I think I have to cry ruth! Stop the car!*

cry in one's beer *vb. phr.* to feel sorry for oneself. □ *She calls up, crying in her beer, and talks on and on about her problems.* □ *Don't cry in your beer. Get yourself straightened out.*

cry ralph See CRY HUGHIE.

cry ruth See CRY HUGHIE.

crystal *n.* Methedrine™. □ *I hear that Wally's using crystal. Is that true?* □ *Max has lots of crystal right now.*

cry stinking fish *vb. phr.* to belittle or disparage the efforts of oneself, one's family, friends or fellow workers. □ *Do you have to go around crying stinking fish?* □ *To cry stinking fish is not a* *good way to be popular with the people closest to you.*

cuckoo *mod.* insane. □ *The poor girl is just cuckoo, that's all.* □ *How did I ever get involved in this cuckoo scheme, anyway?*

cuckoo-farm See FUNNY-FARM.

cuddle and kiss *n.* a girl. (Rhyming slang, linked as follows: cuddle and kiss ≈ [miss] = girl.) □ *Jack's round at his cuddle and kiss.* □ *So this cuddle and kiss asks what I thought of the international situation!*

cufflink *n.* a Chinese person. (Rhyming slang, linked as follows: cufflink ≈ [Chink] = Chinese.) □ *Y'know, Otto, if you call a Chinaman a cufflink, he's likely to get nasty.* □ *Why can you not be polite to cufflinks?*

cufuffle See KAFUFFLE.

cum See also COME; COME (OFF).

cunt 1. *n.* the female sexual organ. (Taboo. A highly offensive word to most people. There are many additional meanings and constructions using this word. It is in fact Standard English, but virtually all applications of it are not.) □ *Get your hand off my cunt, Sunshine!* □ *Who do think you are, going for my cunt like that?* **2.** *n.* a despicable person, not necessarily female. (Taboo.) □ *Get out of here, you stupid cunt!* □ *What a cunt that woman can be.*

cunt face *n.* a spectacularly ugly person. (Taboo.) □ *What a cunt face you are!* □ *Just get out of my sight, you cunt face!*

cunt hat See FANNY HAT.

cunt-hooks AND **twat-hooks** *n.* the fingers. (Taboo.) □ *Get your cunt-hooks out of there before I break them off!* □ *She looked at them carefully and realised for the first time that he really did have very ugly twat-hooks.*

cunt-struck *mod.* of a man sexually smitten with women in general or with one particular woman. (Taboo.) □ *Well, if you really want to know, I think he was cunt-struck with her.* □ *Oh, he used to get cunt-struck with every woman who wandered past.*

cup *n.* a cup of tea. □ *Lovely, I could really use a cup.* □ *A cup would be lovely.*

cup of tea *n.* something preferred or desired; that which really suits one. (Often employed in a negative context.) □ *This drug scene stuff is just not my cup of tea.* □ *Driving children around all afternoon is not my cup of tea.*

cuppa *n.* a cup of tea. (Rhyming slang, linked as follows: cuppa ≈ cup o' = cup of [tea]. Compare with MUGGO.) □ *I sat down and had a lovely cuppa.* □ *A cuppa is always welcome.*

curl up and die *vb. phr.* to retreat and die. (Often figurative.) □ *I was so embarrassed, I thought I would just curl up and die.* □ *The old cat, finishing up the last of its nine lives, just curled up and died.*

curp AND **kirp** *n.* the male sexual organ. (Taboo. Backslang, from PRICK.) □ *That's all very well Myra, but where would the world be without curps?* □ *The doctor said he's got something wrong with his kirp.*

Currant Bun *n.* the Sun. (Rhyming slang. *The Sun* is a daily newspaper. Usually with *the.*) □ *I once tried to read the Currant Bun but couldn't find anything much more than pictures to look at.* □ *My next-door neighbour reads the Currant Bun every day.*

currant bun 1. *n.* a son. (Rhyming slang.) □ *That's Mr Big's currant bun, you know.* □ *He stood there with his currant bun.* **2.** *n.* the sun. (Rhyming slang.) □ *The currant bun was shining bright, high in the sky.* □ *The light from the currant bun was right in his eyes.* **3.** *mod.* on the run. (Rhyming slang. Refers to running from the police, etc.) □ *Otto's on the currant bun again.* □ *Going currant bun won't help; they'll still find you, sooner or later.*

current form *n.* the present performance of, for example, a sports team. □ *On current form they're set to win.* □ *Their current form is dire.*

curse *n.* the menses. (Crude. Always with *the.*) □ *The curse struck this morning.* □ *Oh, the woes of the curse!*

curse rag AND **rags** *n.* a sanitary towel. (Crude.) □ *I've got a curse rag on, you pig!* □ *Why do I need rags? Why do you think?*

curtain climber *n.* a young child. □ *I wish she would try to control that curtain climber of hers.* □ *I hope you like curtain climbers. There are several here this afternoon.*

curtains *n.* death. (Originally criminal.) □ *It's curtains for you if you don't come across.* □ *Okay, Barlowe, this time it's curtains.*

cushy 1. *mod.* soft; easy. (From "cushion.") □ *He's got sort of a cushy job.* □ *That's a cushy kind of life to lead.* **2.** *mod.* safe. □ *Oh, you're cushy there. No one will notice.* □ *Is there somewhere cushy around here where I'll be all right?*

custard and jelly *n.* television. (Rhyming slang, linked as follows: custard and jelly ≈ [telly] = television.) □ *He watched the custard and jelly all day long.* □ *I try to get through the day without watching any custard and jelly.*

cut 1. *mod.* intoxicated due to drink or drugs. (Compare with HALF-CUT.) □ *She's too cut to drive.* □ *He got cut on beer, which is unusual for him.* **2.** *n.* a share of the loot or the profits. (Originally underworld.) □ *I want my cut now.* □ *You'll get your cut when everybody else does.* **3.** *n.* a single song or section of music on a record. □ *This next cut is one everybody likes.* □ *Let's listen to another cut of the same album.*

cut along *vb. phr.* to depart. □ *All right, cut along now Smith.* □ *The teacher told me to cut along, sir.*

cut and run *vb. phr.* to stop what one is doing and flee. □ *The cops were coming, so we cut and run.* □ *At the first warning, we cut and run.*

cut corners *vb. phr.* to do something more easily; to take shortcuts; to save money by finding cheaper ways to do something. □ *They're always finding ways to cut corners.* □ *I won't cut corners just to save money. I put quality first.*

cutie *n.* a smart girl. □ *Oh, she's a cutie all right!* □ *You'll never outsmart a cutie like that, Otto.*

cutie-pie *n.* a good-looking or attractive girl or young woman. □ *Now there's a really attractive cutie-pie.* □ *Look at her, isn't she a cutie-pie?*

cut it See CUT THE MUSTARD.

Cut it out! *exclam.* "Stop it!" □ *That's enough! Cut it out!* □ *Get your hands off me! Cut it out!*

cut loose *vb. phr.* to let go; to become independent. □ *It was hard to cut loose from home.* □ *I suppose it's time I cut loose.*

cut no ice (with someone) *vb. phr.* to have no influence on someone; to fail to convince someone. □ *I don't care who you are. It cuts no ice with me.* □ *So you're the boss's daughter. That still cuts no ice.*

cut off a slice *vb. phr.* to perform sexual intercourse. (Taboo.) □ *Want to cut off a slice?* □ *Let's go somewhere quiet and cut off a slice.*

cut one's losses *vb. phr.* to do something to stop a loss of something, often money. □ *I knew I had to do something to cut my losses, but it was almost too late.* □ *Sell some of the high-priced stuff to cut your losses.*

cut one's own throat *vb. phr.* to do something that harms oneself. □ *If I do that, I'd be cutting my own throat.* □ *He's just cutting his own throat, and he knows it.*

cut-rate *mod.* cheap; low-priced. □ *I don't want any cut-rate stuff.* □ *Where are your cut-rate sweaters?*

cut someone down to size *vb. phr.* to bring someone back to a more modest appreciation of their own importance or worth. □ *Did you hear how she cut him down to size?* □ *Been cut down to size, eh?*

cut someone in (on something) *vb. phr.* to permit someone to share something. □ *You promised you would cut me in on this caper.* □ *We can't cut you in this time. There's not enough to go round.*

cut something fine *vb. phr.* to conduct some activity just within the practical or legal limits. □ *You may get away with this, but boy are you cutting this fine.* □ *Why cut it so fine if you don't absolutely have to?*

cut something out *vb. phr.* to cease doing something. □ *We cut stealing out for a week or two, I suppose.* □ *Cut that smoking out!*

Cut the cackle! *exclam.* "Stop talking and get on with what you are supposed to be doing!" □ *Cut the cackle, you lot!* □ *If you don't cut the cackle now, you'll get into trouble.*

Cut the comedy! *exclam.* "Get serious!"; "Stop acting silly!" □ *That's enough, you lot. Cut the comedy!* □ *Cut the comedy and get back to work!*

cut the mustard AND **cut it** *vb. phr.* to be able to do something that supposedly requires youth or vigour. □ *Do you really think he can still cut the mustard?* □ *She's not too old to cut it.*

cut up (about someone or something) *mod.* emotionally upset about someone or something. □ *She was all cut up about her divorce.* □ *You could see how cut up she was.*

cut up rough *vb. phr.* to exhibit resentment, bad temper or anger. □ *Otto really cut up rough when he was told.* □ *Don't cut up rough; you'll get fired.*

D

dab hand *n.* an expert; a skilled amateur. □ *Jim's a dab hand with computers.* □ *No one could ever call me a dab hand at this sort of thing.*

dabs AND **darbies** *n.* fingerprints. □ *They found a good set of dabs on the window.* □ *Why did they want my darbies?*

dad *n.* one's father; any father; any old man; any man ten or so years older than the user. (Also a term of address. Capitalised when referring to one's own father.) □ *Dad, can I use the car tonight?* □ *Well, dad, how's it going?* □ *Is your dad all right? Can he make it?*

daddy *n.* a dominant male homosexual. (Crude.) □ *He doesn't like being called a daddy.* □ *So what if he's a daddy? He can still vote, can't he?*

daddy of them all AND **grand-daddy of them all** *n.* the biggest or oldest of all; the patriarch. □ *This old fish is the granddaddy of them all.* □ *This one is the daddy of them all. It's been here since the place was built.*

daffodil AND **daisy** *n.* an effeminate man; a passive male homosexual. (Crude.) □ *He doesn't like being called a daffodil.* □ *She came to the dance with a daisy.*

daffy-headed *mod.* lacking intelligence. □ *I think you could say he's, well, sort of daffy-headed.* □ *Who's that daffy-headed clown in there?*

daft *mod.* stupid, crazy or foolish. □ *Don't be daft. That's impossible.* □ *I'm not daft. I just can't make it work.*

daft as a brush *mod.* completely crazy. (See AS DAFT AS A BRUSH.) □ *Tom is as daft as a brush, but fun.* □ *They're all as daft as a brush in there.*

daft as a yett (on a windy day) *mod.* completely crazy. (Scots usage; *yett* is Scots for "gate.") □ *Yon Sandy is daft as a yett on a windy day.* □ *She may be as daft as a yett but she's rolling in money.*

dag *n.* a stupid or unpleasant person. (Australianism. Crude. Originally a very old, now archaic, Standard English word for a portion of sheep dung that had become dried and affixed to the wool at the rear of a sheep. See DAGGY.) □ *Mike is a real dag; he's that way all the time.* □ *If you like dags, you'll love Mike.*

Dagenham dustbin *n.* a car made by Ford. □ *Ford cars are sometimes called Dagenham dustbins because there is a large Ford plant at Dagenham, Essex.* □ *I got into my old Dagenham dustbin and set off to work.*

daggy 1. *mod.* unpleasantly or disagreeably ill or hung-over. (Australianism. Crude. See DAG.) □ *Boy, do I feel daggy today. But what a time we had last night!* □ *The trouble with drinking like Mike does is that you feel daggy every morning.* **2.** *mod.* stupid; unpleasant. (Australianism. Crude. Compare with DAG.) □ *Mike is so daggy when he's been drinking.* □ *Mike is daggy all the time; he's just a natural-born dag.*

dago *n.* a Spanish or South American person. (Offensive.) □ *Y'know, Otto, if you call a dago a dago, he's likely to get nasty.* □ *Why can you not be polite to dagoes?*

daily *n.* a cleaning woman visiting daily. □ *Why is our daily walking through our office in the middle of the* *day?* □ *I know we have a daily but I'm afraid I've never seen her.*

daily grind *n.* the tedious pattern of daily work. (Compare with RAT RACE.) □ *Well, it's Monday. Time to start another week of the daily grind.* □ *This daily grind really gets me down.*

Daily (Mail) 1. *n.* a story, especially a hard-luck story. (Rhyming slang, linked as follows: Daily (Mail) ≈ [tale] = story. *The Daily Mail* is a newspaper published in London.) □ *I listened to his Daily Mail and gave him five quid.* □ *It's certainly a very sad Daily. In fact, it's almost a pity he made it all up.* **2.** *n.* the buttocks. (Rhyming slang, linked as follows: Daily (Mail) ≈ [tail] = buttocks.) □ *She fell right on her Daily Mail.* □ *There is some mustard or something on your Daily.* **3.** *mod.* [of a woman] sexually available or attractive. (Crude. Rhyming slang, linked as follows: Daily (Mail) ≈ [tail] = woman.) □ *She certainly looks like a Daily Mail girl to me!* □ *Now that woman is really Daily!* **4.** *n.* a sexually available or attractive woman. (Crude. Rhyming slang, linked as follows: Daily (Mail) ≈ [tail] = woman.) □ *Now that's what I'd call a Daily!* □ *A Daily Mail? I'll say she is!* **5.** *n.* court bail. (Rhyming slang, linked as follows: Daily (Mail) ≈ [bail].) □ *I don't know how he ever got Daily Mail.* □ *I'd never give him Daily, not ever!* **6.** *n.* beer. (Rhyming slang, linked as follows: Daily (Mail) ≈ [ale] = beer.) □ *Can I have Daily Mail please?* □ *I do like this Daily they have in here.* **7.** *n.* a nail. (The kind that gets hammered into wood, etc. Rhyming slang, linked as follows: Daily (Mail) ≈ nail.) □ *He hammered at the Daily Mail, but it would not go in.* □ *Pass the Dailies, mate.* **8.** *n.* a fingernail. (Rhyming slang, linked as follows: Daily (Mail) ≈ [nail] = fingernail.) □ *Oh look, I've split me Daily Mail!* □ *How did you do that to yer Daily?* **9.** *n.* the post. (Rhyming slang, linked as follows: Daily (Mail) ≈ [mail] = post.) □ *Anything in the Daily Mail for me today?* □ *The postman handed her her Daily.*

dairies *n.* the female breasts. (Crude. Normally with *the* and in the plural.) □ *My dairies aren't all I might have wished for.* □ *With dairies like that, she can go anywhere she wants.*

daisy See DAFFODIL.

daisy-cutter 1. *n.* a perfect landing by an aircraft. □ *This boy's a good pilot; look, another daisy-cutter!* □ *He made a daisy-cutter and taxied to the terminal.* **2.** *n.* a cricket ball that fails to rise when it is delivered. □ *Watch out for these daisy-cutters.* □ *A daisy-cutter is sneaky because it gets under the defences, as it were.*

daisy roots *n.* boots. (Rhyming slang.) □ *Why are you in your daisy roots? Is it muddy out?* □ *I find these daisy roots uncomfortable.*

daks *n.* a pair of men's trousers. (Originally a trade name.) □ *He pulled on his daks and stood up.* □ *Woman, what have you done with all my daks?*

damage *n.* the cost; the amount of a bill (for something). (Compare with BAD NEWS.) □ *Okay, waiter. What's the damage?* □ *As soon as I pay the damage, we can go.*

damager *n.* a manager. (Rhyming slang.) □ *Have you seen our new damager yet? I'll give him a week!* □ *Damager? Yeh, that's about the right name for him.*

dame *n.* a girlfriend. (Scots usage. Note: *not* an import from the US, but *originally* Scots, from whence it was exported to the US. The word has been used in Scotland in this sense for over 200 years. Yet further back, of course, it derives, via French, from the Latin *domina*, meaning "mistress"—as do the Standard English meanings of the word.) □ *Ma dame isny happy about aw ma bevvyin an' that. (My girlfriend is not happy about all my drinking and so on.)* □ *I'm ayeways getting hame ower late, says the dame. (I'm always getting home too late, says my girlfriend.)*

damn all *n.* absolutely nothing. (Crude.) □ *I have damn all to do these days.* □ *I assure you, there is damn all here!*

damp See WET.

Dan 1. *n.* the janitor or attendant at a public toilet for men. (Crude.) □ *Dan, Dan, the shit-house man!* (Taboo.) □ *That's an unfortunate cry the kids shout when they see the Dan.* **2.** *n.* a Roman Catholic. (Offensive. Also a term of address. Scots usage. From "Daniel," a given name once common among Irish Roman Catholics. Compare with JUNGLE JIM and TIM.) □ *Willy thinks the Dans are taking over these days.* □ *Willy actually moved house because a Dan moved in next door!*

dance the Tyburn jig *vb. phr.* to hang by the neck until dead. (Tyburn—now called Marble Arch—was London's principal place of public execution until 1783.) □ *You'll dance the Tyburn jig in the morning, me lad!* □ *No one dances the Tyburn jig in Britain today, since capital punishment was abolished some years ago.*

dandiprat *n.* a dwarf. □ *Who's that dandiprat over there?* □ *The fellow can't help being small, and you should not call him a dandiprat.*

danger *n.* a chance or likelihood. (Scots usage. Ironic.) □ *There's no danger of him getting here on time.* □ *Is there any danger of us getting paid today?*

dangler *n.* the male sexual organ. (Taboo.) □ *Unlike Myra, Sharon thinks of little else but danglers.* □ *Men keep their brains in their danglers!*

danglers *n.* the testicles. (Taboo. Normally with *the* and in the plural.) □ *He got hit right in the danglers.* □ *Thud, right in the danglers. Ye gods, it hurt!*

dangle the Dunlops *vb. phr.* to lower the undercarriage of an aircraft. □ *Time to dangle the Dunlops, skipper.* □ *It's a good idea to dangle the Dunlops before attempting to land, laddie.*

danny *n.* an unmarked police car. □ *Watch it! That's a danny!* □ *The danny drove forward, blocking my exit.*

darbie 1. *n.* a hand. (Rhyming slang, linked as follows: darbie ≈ [Derby Band] = hand. A *Derby Band* was a bond made to a moneylender in 17th century London. *Derby* is pronounced DAR-by. Always in the plural.) □ *Show me yer darbies, son. What 'ave you*

been doing to get 'em so mucky? □ *He grabbed me by the darbies and told me to do what he said.* **2.** *n.* a handcuff. (Rhyming slang, linked as follows: darbie ≈ [Derby Band] = handcuff. Always in the plural.) □ *The constable slipped the darbies on me as quick as get out.* □ *My hands were locked together behind my back in his darbies and I felt a kind of claustrophobia coming over me.*

darbies See DABS.

Darby and Joan 1. *n.* a long and happily married elderly couple. □ *Are they not a lovely Darby and Joan?* □ *Do you think we will be a Darby and Joan one day?* **2.** *n.* a telephone. (Rhyming slang, linked as follows: Darby and Joan ≈ (tele)phone.) □ *You'll find a Darby and Joan over in that corner.* □ *He's got one of them portable Darby and Joans.*

Darby and Joan club *n.* an old age pensioners' club. □ *I think she spends more and more time at the Darby and Joan club.* □ *The Darby and Joan club is very popular with the old folks.*

dark blue 1. *n.* a present or former student of Harrow School. □ *All our family have been dark blues.* □ *The most famous dark blue was Sir Winston Churchill.* **2.** *n.* a present or former student of Oxford University. □ *George is a dark blue.* □ *If I were a dark blue, I would really appreciate my good fortune.*

dark horse 1. *n.* an unknown entrant into a contest; a surprise candidate for political office. □ *The party is hoping that a dark horse will appear before the election.* □ *You'd be surprised at how eagerly people will vote for a dark horse.* **2.** *mod.* previously unknown. □ *Who would vote for a dark horse candidate?* □ *A dark horse player can win if all the others are creeps.*

darling *mod.* generous; sweet. □ *Thank you, that was most darling of you.* □ *What a darling man.*

dart *n.* a paper aeroplane. □ *When the teacher opened the classroom door he found the air thick with flying darts.* □ *Some darts can make very good fliers, but most are lousy.*

dash 1. *exclam.* "damn." (A euphemism and disguise.) □ *Oh dash, there's the turnoff.* □ *Where's the dashed cat?* 2. *n.* money. □ *I don't make enough dash to go on a trip like that!* □ *It takes a lot of dash to buy a car like that.*

Dash it! *exclam.* "Damn it!" (A euphemism and disguise. See DASH.) □ *Dash it, I forgot again.* □ *Well dash it Susan, I don't care any more.*

Dash it all! *exclam.* "Oh, phooey!"; "To hell with it all!" (See DASH.) □ *Oh, dash it all! I'm late.* □ *I broke it! Dash it all!*

day after the fair *n.* when it is too late. (Normally with *the.*) □ *Once more, you get here the day after the fair. How do you do it?* □ *He made his offer the day after the fair, I'm afraid: just too late.*

daylight robbery AND **highway robbery** *n.* outrageous overpricing; a bill that is much higher than normally acceptable but must be paid. (As if one had been accosted and robbed on the open road or in broad daylight.) □ *But this is daylight robbery. I demand to see the manager.* □ *Four thousand pounds! That's highway robbery!*

day one *n.* the first day. □ *You haven't done anything right since day one! You're fired!* □ *She was unhappy with her new car even on day one.*

day person *n.* a person who prefers to be active during the daytime. (Compare with NIGHT PERSON.) □ *I am strictly a day person. Have to be in bed early.* □ *The Count insisted that he was not a day person, and had to remain indoors with curtains drawn closed until nightfall.*

day's a-dawning *n.* the morning. (Rhyming slang.) □ *Day's a-dawning, and bitter cold!* □ *Good night. See you in the day's a-dawning.*

day-tripper *n.* a tourist who makes excursions lasting just one day. □ *At about 4:00 p.m. the day-trippers start thinning out.* □ *Being a day-tripper is hard on your feet sometimes.*

dead 1. *mod.* quiet and uneventful; boring. □ *The day was totally dead.* □ *What a dead day!* □ *Things were really dead around here this summer.* 2. *mod.*
very tired. □ *I am just dead from all that jogging.* □ *I went home from the office, dead as usual.* 3. *mod.* dull; lifeless. □ *This meal is sort of dead because I am out of onions.* □ *The band didn't turn up at Mary's party, which was kinda dead as a result.* 4. *mod.* [of an issue] no longer germane; no longer of any importance. □ *Forget it! It's a dead issue.* □ *The project is dead. Don't waste any more time on it.*

dead-and-alive *mod.* monotonous or boring. □ *I've never been in such a dead-and-alive place.* □ *Unexciting? It was dead-and-alive!*

dead and gone 1. *mod.* [of a person] long dead. □ *Old Gert's been dead and gone for quite a spell.* □ *When I'm dead and gone, I hope folks remember me at my best.* 2. *mod.* [of a thing] gone long ago. □ *That kind of thinking is dead and gone.* □ *Horse and buggy days are long dead and gone now, Harry.*

deadbeat 1. *n.* someone who doesn't pay debts or bills. □ *Some deadbeat with the same name as mine is ruining my credit rating.* □ *Pay up! Don't be a deadbeat.* 2. *n.* a scrounger or vagrant. □ *Since John lost his job he's turned into a complete deadbeat.* □ *The deadbeats who hang around outside the railway station were rounded up by the police today.*

dead cert *n.* an absolute certainty; an easy thing to do. □ *It's a dead cert. I foresee no problems.* □ *The job was not a dead cert, but we did it on time.*

dead chuffed AND **real chuffed** *mod.* very satisfied or pleased. □ *He was dead chuffed to win.* □ *I'm real chuffed to win this!*

dead drunk *mod.* very intoxicated due to drink. □ *They were both dead drunk. They could only lie there and snore.* □ *Martin is dead drunk again.*

dead duck *n.* someone or something doomed to failure or disaster. □ *This whole plan was a dead duck from the beginning.* □ *Archie is a dead duck because he flunked astronomy.*

dead easy 1. *mod.* very easy. □ *This whole job is dead easy.* □ *It was so* *dead easy, Frank did it with one hand.* **2.** *n.* a woman who is willing to have sex with any man. (Crude.) □ *I wouldn't say Maggy is dead easy but she is amazingly popular with the Rugby club.* □ *Some girls think that you can be popular if you are dead easy.*

dead-end kid *n.* a youth with no future, usually a male. □ *Kelly wasn't your typical dead-end kid.* □ *Max was a dead-end kid from the day he was born.*

dead from the neck up 1. *mod.* stupid. (With a non-functioning brain.) □ *Beavis seems dead from the neck up.* □ *She acts like she is dead from the neck up.* **2.** *mod.* no longer open to new ideas. □ *My uncle is dead from the neck up. A real fossil.* □ *Everyone on the board of directors is dead from the neck up.*

deadhead *n.* a stupid, boring or useless person. □ *Who's the deadhead in the tartan trousers?* □ *Boy, are you a real deadhead!*

dead head AND **dead loss** *n.* a useless person. (Crude.) □ *You dead head! Why have you done that!* □ *Some dead loss forgot to get petrol today and the car has run dry.*

dead in the water *mod.* stalled; immobile. (Originally nautical.) □ *This whole company is dead in the water.* □ *The project is dead in the water for the time being.*

dead issue AND **dead letter** *n.* an issue that doesn't matter anymore. □ *The boss's plan for our pay rise is a dead issue.* □ *This contract is a dead letter. Forget it!*

dead letter 1. *n.* a letter that cannot move through the post office because the addressee does not exist or because the address is wrong or illegible. (Standard English.) □ *Every now and then they open the dead letters to see if they can figure out who they were meant for.* □ *Sometimes dead letters have return addresses in them.* **2.** See also DEAD ISSUE.

dead loss 1. *n.* any job or other activity which is not useful. □ *I quit because the job was a dead loss, that's why.* □ *I've not got the time for dead losses like that.* **2.** See DEAD HEAD.

deadly dull *mod.* very dull indeed. □ *The lecture was deadly dull, and I went to sleep.* □ *Her story was really deadly dull. I am sorry I was awake for part of it.*

dead man See DEAD SOLDIER.

dead marine See DEAD SOLDIER.

dead meat *n.* someone who is already dead or about to die. (Criminal.) □ *Get out before you end up as dead meat.* □ *Too late, he's dead meat already.*

dead on *mod.* exactly right; on target. □ *That's a good observation, Tiffany. You are dead on.* □ *Your criticism is dead on!*

dead one See DEAD SOLDIER.

deadpan *mod.* [of a face that is] expressionless. (Compare with PAN.) □ *He has a great deadpan expression.* □ *Remember the deadpan face she used to put on?*

dead ringer (for someone) AND **ringer (for someone)** *n.* someone who is an exact duplicate or double of someone else. □ *You are exactly a dead ringer for my brother.* □ *Isn't he a ringer for Charlie?*

dead soldier AND **dead man; dead marine; dead one** *n.* an empty bottle of spirits or beer. (Often plural. Compare with SOLDIER.) □ *Throw your empty soldiers in the rubbish bin, please.* □ *A dead one fell off the table and woke up all the drunks.*

dead to rights See BANG TO RIGHTS.

dead to the world *mod.* sound asleep. □ *After all that exercise, he's dead to the world.* □ *He's dead to the world, and I can't rouse him.*

dead trouble *n.* very serious trouble. (Always with *in.*) □ *You're in dead trouble, my lad!* □ *I'll be in dead trouble if I get caught.*

Dear John letter *n.* a letter a woman writes to her boyfriend in the forces telling him that she does not love him anymore. □ *Bert got a Dear John letter today.* □ *Sally sends a Dear John letter about once a month.*

death on someone or something *mod.* causing the death or destruction of someone or something. □ *This kind of road is just death on tyres.* □ *Rich,* *sweet food like this is death on my teeth.*

deb *n.* a young girl being introduced into London's upper-class society for the first time. (An abbreviation of the French *debutante*, meaning "beginner.") □ *Cynthia is going to be a deb this coming season.* □ *What do debs actually do all the rest of the year, anyway?*

debag *vb.* to remove a man's trousers as a prank. □ *Philip got debagged at his stag party last night.* □ *I wish they wouldn't debag people.*

deb's delight *n.* an upper-class young man who is considered a socially acceptable marriage partner for the daughters of upper-class families. (See DEB.) □ *I think Basil is what they call a deb's delight.* □ *If that's a deb's delight, then I'm glad I'm not a deb.*

debug 1. *vb.* to rectify or remove flaws in computer software. (Computer jargon. Compare with BUG.) □ *Harry here is good at debugging software.* □ *I don't know how long I will be. It takes as long to debug code as it takes.* **2.** *vb.* to discover and remove hidden listening devices. (Compare with BUG.) □ *The conference room has been debugged for tomorrow's meeting.* □ *We better debug the rest of the building.*

decent *mod.* good; very good. □ *This is some pretty decent jazz.* □ *Your threads are decent, all right.*

decider *n.* the round of a sport or game—often an additional one after a draw—that determines the victor. □ *I think this will have to go to a decider next week.* □ *Are you going to be at tonight's decider?*

deck 1. *n.* an aircraft runway. (Aviation. Always with *the*.) □ *Yes, I see the deck now.* □ *OK Tower, We're lined up with the deck.* **2.** *n.* the ground. (Originally aviation. Always with *the*.) □ *We got the plane down on the deck eventually.* □ *He stood on the deck, looking up at the sky.* **3.** *n.* a floor. (Always with *the*.) □ *The deck was covered in Persian carpets.* □ *The child likes to play on the deck of her bedroom.* **4.** *n.* a small quantity of drugs. □ *The cops found a deck on her.* □ *They usually just caution people with decks.*

decoke *vb.* to decarbonise the cylinders of an internal combustion engine. □ *Your car needs to be decoked, mister.* □ *Decoke it then, please.*

dee-aitch *n.* the head. (Backslang.) □ *Harry's distinctive hairy dee-aitch hove into view.* □ *Where'd you get that nasty bump on your dee-aitch?*

deejay See DISK JOCKEY.

deep-sea diver *n.* a five Pound note. (Rhyming slang, linked as follows: deep-sea diver ≈ [fiver] = five Pound note.) □ *I'll take a deep-sea diver for my trouble, squire.* □ *It cost a few of deep-sea divers to get driving home in a taxi.*

deep-sea fisherman *n.* a card sharper on an ocean-going liner or cruise ship. □ *That friendly old card partner you've found is a deep-sea fisherman, I'm sure.* □ *Deep-sea fishermen can make a lot of money out of the suckers they find on board.*

deep shit *n.* very severe trouble. (Taboo.) □ *Boy, I'm in deep shit if this ever comes out!* □ *There's still more deep shit to come for that politician, I think.*

def *mod.* excellent. □ *Man, this music is def.* □ *This wine is really def!*

default *vb.* to return to a preselected option defined by a computer program when the operator fails to choose an alternative. (Computer jargon.) □ *Don't default here.* □ *When you defaulted you wiped out all my data!*

deff out *vb. phr.* to lose contact with one's girl friends after acquiring a steady boyfriend. (Teens.) □ *Maureen had deffed out within a week of meeting Tony.* □ *I won't deff out on you like Maureen did, girls.*

degree of frost *n.* the number of degrees below freezing. (Refers to the Fahrenheit system of temperature measurement, not the Celsius one.) □ *There were ten degrees of frost last night.* □ *If there are thirty degrees of frost, that's really cold!*

dekko *n.* a glance or quick look. □ *Take a dekko at that!* □ *He took a quick dekko but saw nothing unusual.*

Delhi belly *n.* a picturesque name for diarrhoea, as suffered by tourists in India. (Named for New Delhi, the capital city of India and once the scene of many an outbreak of this affliction.) □ *I've got a touch of the Delhi belly and will have to miss the Taj Mahal.* □ *I've got something you can take for Delhi belly.*

demo 1. *n.* a demonstration (of something). □ *Can I have a demo of this model?* □ *Hey, Harry, give this man a demo.* **2.** *n.* a car or other machine or device that has been used by a dealer for demonstration purposes. □ *I can give you a demo for half price.* □ *Do you have any demos?* **3.** *vb.* to demonstrate something (to someone). □ *Let me demo this for you so you can see how it works.* □ *Will someone please demo this computer?* **4.** *mod.* concerning demolition. □ *The demo people started knocking down that old warehouse today.* □ *There's going to be a lot of demo work round here soon.* **5.** *n.* a public meeting or march, held for political reasons. □ *There was a big demo in London at the weekend.* □ *We went on a demo too, but in Birmingham.*

demob 1. *vb.* to demobilise or disband an army, etc. □ *After the war was over, the army was demobbed.* □ *We are demobbing the army.* **2.** *vb.* to discharge an individual from an army, etc. □ *My son's been demobbed at last!* □ *When do you think I'll get demobbed, sir?*

Dennis the Menace *n.* ECSTASY, a hallucinogen similar to L.S.D. □ *You can get some good Dennis the Menace in this part of town.* □ *Dennis the Menace is just one of a dozen drugs with similar formulas.*

dented AND **dinted** *mod.* damaged. □ *My car is dented!* □ *I can't drive a dinted car!*

denture adventure *n.* a visit to the dentist. □ *I've got toothache, so it's denture adventure time.* □ *I could not say that I exactly enjoy denture adventures.*

derro *n.* a vagrant; someone who has fallen on really bad times. (An abbreviation of *derelict.*) □ *By midnight the derros had gone wherever they go to* sleep, *and we got that part of town to ourselves.* □ *There are always a lot of derros hanging around that part of town.*

derry *n.* a derelict building. □ *That derry is dangerous, Tommy; don't play near it.* □ *They're going to pull down the derry at last, I hear.*

designer jury *n.* a jury "designed" by the careful use of challenges by defence lawyers. □ *It will be interesting to see how this designer jury behaves.* □ *Some people think designer juries give an unfair advantage to the defence.*

des res *n.* a desirable residence. (Estate agent's jargon.) □ *There's a nice-looking des res up for sale on Charles Street, I see.* □ *Would you call this place a des res?*

destroyed *mod.* drug intoxicated. □ *Wow, what happened to Tracy? She looks destroyed.* □ *These kids who take angel dust are destroyed most of the time.*

detox *n.* the detoxification of an alcoholic or drug addict. □ *It's time you went away for a detox.* □ *I don't want a detox!*

deuce 1. *n.* two Pounds Sterling. □ *Can you lend me a deuce 'till payday?* □ *All right, here's a deuce. Don't spend it all in one shop.* **2.** *n.* bad luck. (An old word for the Devil.) □ *What rotten deuce.* □ *Once we've got the deuce behind us it must get better, right?*

deuce to pay *n.* big trouble. (Literally, "the Devil to pay." Normally with *the.*) □ *There will be the deuce to pay when this comes out.* □ *I had the deuce to pay at the time of course, but that's all behind us now.*

devil *n.* junior legal counsel. □ *She keeps a whole bunch of devils to handle that sort of thing.* □ *I've got a devil who can help us out of this scrape.*

devil of a time *n.* a very difficult time. (Always with *a.*) □ *I had a devil of a time with my taxes.* □ *This cold has been giving me a devil of a time.*

devil's own *mod.* very difficult. (Always with *the.*) □ *I had the devil's own job with these tax forms.* □ *My gout is giving me the devil's own time.*

dew-drop *n.* a drop of clear liquid upon the end of the nose. □ *The old man must have had a cold, as a dew-drop was visible on his nose.* □ *His dew-drop fell into my drink!*

dial *n.* a face. □ *I know that dial. Who is he?* □ *His dial was hidden behind a long white beard.*

dib *n.* a partly-smoked cigarette. □ *He produced a dib from his pocket and relit it.* □ *I threw my dib away and turned to look him in the eye.*

dibs and dabs *n.* body or pubic lice. (Taboo. Rhyming slang, linked as follows: dibs and dabs ≈ [crabs] = (body/pubic) lice.) □ *I'm afraid every one of these refugees have dibs and dabs.* □ *The first thing is to check for dibs and dabs on everyone.*

dicey *mod.* risky; delicate; chancy; TOUCH AND GO. (Pronounced DISE-ee.) □ *Things are just a little dicey right now.* □ *I'm working on a dicey deal in the City just now.*

dick 1. *n.* the male sexual organ. (Taboo.) □ *She told some dirty joke about a dick, but everybody just sat there and looked straight ahead.* □ *He covered his dick and stooped down, then reached up to pull down the blind.* **2.** *n.* a declaration. (A corrupted abbreviation.) □ *What a strange dick to make!* □ *Do you want to make a dick too, Mr Arrow?* **3.** *n.* a man. □ *The dick was not there.* □ *I like the look of this dick.* **4.** *vb.* to look. □ *I better dick at this.* □ *What are you dicking at, eh?*

dickbrained *mod.* exceptionally stupid. (Taboo.) □ *Let's not come up with another dickbrained plan. This one has to make sense.* □ *Now that is really a dickbrained idea.* □ *It's not dick-brained!*

dickens *n.* the Devil. (A euphemism.) □ *She was in a dickens of a temper after losing the argument.* □ *I felt bad about what had happened but what the dickens could I do?*

dicker *n.* a lookout. □ *Otto, you're the dicker.* □ *Why am I always the dicker?*

dick(-head) *n.* an idiot; a fool. (Taboo. Originally only male, but raffishly, now sometimes female also. Compare with LOMBARD.) □ *You really are a complete dick-head!* □ *What stupid dick put this thing here in the way?*

dickless Tracy *n.* a policewoman. (Crude.) □ *Oh no, not another dickless Tracy!* □ *Well, there's one dickless Tracy with more balls than you, Frank.*

dickory dock *n.* a clock. (Rhyming slang.) □ *The dickory dock in the kitchen has broken.* □ *Wind your dickory dock before you forget.*

dicky 1. *mod.* unreliable; likely to collapse or to fail. □ *I'm afraid this car of mine's a bit dicky.* □ *He's got a dicky heart, you know.* **2.** *mod.* unwell. □ *Carol is a bit dicky today, I'm afraid.* □ *Oh dear, I feel rather dicky.*

dicky bow *n.* a bow tie. □ *Tom's the one in the dicky bow.* □ *I like men who wear a dicky bow.*

dicky-diddle *vb.* to urinate. (Crude. Rhyming slang, linked as follows: dicky-diddle ≈ [piddle] = urinate.) □ *I've got to dicky-diddle. Back in a minute.* □ *He just went out to dicky-diddle.*

dicky dido *n.* the female sexual organ. (Taboo.) □ *They dance completely nude in there, with dicky dido and everything on view.* □ *What do you mean, you can see my dicky dido? Oh my god, I've forgotten my knickers!*

dicky (dirt) *n.* a shirt. (Rhyming slang.) □ *Where's me dicky dirts, woman?* □ *Otto looked good in that colourful new dicky you got him.*

dicky seat 1. *n.* the driver's seat on a horse-drawn carriage. □ *He got up into the dicky seat and drove off.* □ *A new driver sat in the dicky seat that day.* **2.** *n.* an extra seat at the rear of a vehicle that folds away when not in use. □ *You don't see many dicky seats nowadays.* □ *There was once a dicky seat in almost every car.*

diddle 1. *vb.* to cheat someone; to deceive someone. □ *The clerk diddled me with my change so I reported her.* □ *That's a good place to get diddled. You've got to watch them in there.* **2.** *vb.* to perform sexual intercourse. (Taboo.) □ *I didn't think they'd diddle right there in the film.* □ *I'm tired of* *hearing who has diddled whom in Hollywood.* **3.** *vb.* to sexually stimulate a woman manually. (Taboo.) □ *She actually said he could diddle her if he liked!* □ *He was diddling her, yet she said nothing.*

diddy 1. *n.* an idiot. (Scots usage.) □ *Morag is no jist a diddy, ye ken! (Morag is not just an idiot, you know!)* □ *She dizny act like she's diddy.* **2.** *mod.* small. (Childish.) □ *What a diddy little car!* □ *Have you not got any diddy ones?*

didn't oughter AND **dirty daughter** *n.* water. (Rhyming slang.) □ *A pitcher of didn't oughter had been placed on the table.* □ *I'm so thirsty! A drink of dirty daughter would be most welcome.*

Did one buggery! AND **Did one fuck!; Did one hell!** *interj.* a violent refutation. (Taboo.) □ *Did I buggery! That's a lie!* □ *Don't accuse me! Did I hell!*

Did one fuck! See DID ONE BUGGERY!

Did one hell! See DID ONE BUGGERY!

die laughing *vb. phr.* to die from laughter due to someone or something being extremely humorous. (Figurative.) □ *The whole audience died laughing.* □ *Laugh? I could have died!*

die on someone 1. *vb. phr.* [for a patient] to die under the care of someone. □ *Get that medicine over here fast before this guy dies on us.* □ *Come on, mister, don't die on me!* **2.** *vb. phr.* [for something] to cease running or working for someone. □ *My car died on me, and I couldn't get it started again.* □ *My stereo died on me, and I had to listen to the radio.*

diff *n.* difference. □ *Aw, come on! What's the diff?* □ *The diff is about twenty pounds worth of repairs, that's what.*

different *mod.* unusual; exotic. (Used as a ambiguously polite or sarcastic dismissive description of something that one has been asked to admire but in truth cannot. Compare with FABULOUS and INTERESTING.) □ *Well, it's...uh...different!* □ *Let's just say it was a very different way to decorate a home.*

dig (at) someone *vb. phr.* to annoy or irritate someone. □ *Digging at them*

like that is not going to correct the mistake. □ *So I made a mistake! I wish you'd stop digging me.*

digs *n.* a furnished dwelling, usually rented. (Such as might be occupied by a student, for example.) □ *You've got some pretty good digs here.* □ *Nice digs. Do you like it here?*

dike AND **dyke** *n.* a lesbian, especially one with masculine traits. (Crude.) □ *Why does she work so hard to look like a dike?* □ *Who's the dyke in the cowboy boots?*

dikey AND **dykey** *mod.* lesbian, especially if with masculine traits. (Crude.) □ *She looks so dykey in these cowboy boots.* □ *Why does she work so hard to look dikey?*

dildo *n.* a stupid person, usually male. (Taboo. A DILDO is an artificial male sexual organ.) □ *Hank can be such a dildo sometimes.* □ *You silly dildo!*

dilly 1. *mod.* amazing; wonderful. □ *Your news is really dilly, you know.* □ *What a dilly idea that was.* **2.** AND **dimbo; dink** *n.* a foolish or dim-witted person. □ *You total dilly! You've buttered the tablecloth!* □ *How can you be such a complete dink?*

dim *n.* a partially blind person. □ *He's a pleasant dim.* □ *The dim was waiting outside the office for him.*

dimbo See DILLY.

dimmo *n.* an unintelligent person. □ *What's a dimmo like that doing around here?* □ *I'm sorry but we really don't need another dimmo working here.*

dimwit *n.* an oaf; a dullard. (Offensive. Also a term of address.) □ *Oh, Dave, you can be such a dimwit!* □ *Come on, now, you're not really a dimwit.*

din-din(s) *n.* dinner; any meal. (Jocular or childish.) □ *Ah, din-dins! What do we have?* □ *Anyone want din-din?*

ding-a-ling *n.* an eccentric person; a crank. □ *This ding-a-ling comes up and asks me for a pound for the orphans. I tell her I've already got all the orphans I can use at any price.* □ *Who's the ding-a-ling who painted the windows stuck?*

dingbat *n.* an eccentric person; a crank. □ *Who's the dingbat who painted the* *windows stuck?* □ *You don't want to go in there. The place is full of dingbats.*

ding-dong 1. *n.* a song. (Rhyming slang.) □ *Oh yes, I love that old ding-dong.* □ *Now there's a ding-dong that brings back old memories, eh?* **2.** *n.* a fight; a quarrel. □ *That was some ding-dong last night.* □ *Who's going to win the ding-dong, I ask?*

ding-dong (bell) *phr.* Hell. (Rhyming slang.) □ *What the ding-dong bell is going on here?* □ *It's as hot as ding-dong down here.*

dinge *n.* a black person. (Racially offensive. From *dingy.*) □ *Why should a BMW not belong to a dinge?* □ *So this dinge drives away in a BMW!*

dinghy *n.* a motorcycle sidecar. □ *You don't see many motorbikes with dinghies nowadays.* □ *Here he comes, with his girl in the dinghy.*

dink See DILLY.

dinky 1. *mod.* dainty; delicately pretty; neat. □ *Yes, it is dinky.* □ *That is a pretty dinky car you have there.* **2.** *mod.* small; undersized. □ *What a dinky little car you've got!* □ *I'll take the dinky one. I'm on a diet.*

Dinna fash yersel. AND **Never fash yer hied. 1.** *exclam.* "Don't trouble yourself." (Scots usage.) □ *Dinna fash yersel on ma account lassie, I'll be fine.* □ *He said never fash yer hied, it'll be aw richt.* **2.** *phr.* "Don't get excited, keep calm." (Scots usage.) □ *Och dinna fash yersel, it'll come oot aw richt. (Oh, don't excite yourself, it'll come out all right.)* □ *Ah telt ye never to fash yer hied as I had it aw weel in haund. (I told you that you did not need to exert yourself as I had it all well in hand.)*

dinner lady *n.* a woman who serves lunch at school. □ *The dinner lady is ready to serve lunch, I think.* □ *Please ask the dinner lady to tidy up before she goes home!*

dinner pail *n.* a container for a packed lunch. □ *He went off to work every morning with his dinner pail.* □ *Anyone seem my dinner pail?*

dinted See DENTED.

dip 1. *vb.* to become indebted. □ *Yeh, all right, I've been dipped by you.* □

He's put me into his dip. **2.** *n.* an act of sexual intercourse. (Taboo.) □ *She seems to think that calling it "dip" is all right.* □ *I could use a good dip about now.* **3.** AND **dipper; dipster** *n.* a pickpocket. (Underworld.) □ *Watch out for dips at the racetrack.* □ *The dipster tried to make a snatch, but the dupe turned around at the wrong time.* **4.** AND **dipstick; dipshit** *n.* an awkward lout. (Taboo.) □ *Why are you acting like such a dip?* □ *Don't be such a dipshit, Walter.* □ *Is there a convention of dipsticks or something here today?* **5.** *n.* a foolish or crazy person. (Taboo.) □ *Oh, I feel such a dipstick! I should have realised that.* □ *What a dipshit Paul is. What's he trying to do—lose us the contract?*

dip one's wick *vb. phr.* to perform sexual intercourse, from the male perspective. (Taboo. Compare with WICK.) □ *He's, shall we say, rather keen to dip his wick.* □ *I think really, she's gasping for you to dip your wick, you know.*

dip out 1. *vb. phr.* to be unlucky. □ *Trust me to dip out.* □ *When I dip out, I just pick myself up and try again.* **2.** *vb. phr.* to avoid or escape some duty or responsibility. □ *I know you tried to dip out. Don't try it again.* □ *We've got to dip out of this place.*

dipper See DIP.

dippy *mod.* crazy; eccentric. □ *Who is that dippy chick with the lamp shade on her head?* □ *Tom is dippy, but fun.*

dipshit See DIP.

dipso *n.* a drunkard; an alcoholic. (An abbreviation of "dipsomaniac.") □ *Oh, I didn't realise she was a dipso.* □ *She's sort of a closet dipso.*

dipster See DIP.

dipstick See DIP.

dirt *n.* scandal; incriminating secrets; DIRTY LINEN. □ *What's the dirt on Tracy?* □ *I don't want to know about anybody's dirt!*

dirt cheap *mod.* very cheap. □ *I picked this thing up dirt cheap.* □ *Get one of these while they're dirt cheap.*

dirty 1. *mod.* obscene. □ *You have a dirty mind.* □ *The movie was too dirty for me.* □ *How would you know what's* *dirty and what's not?* **2.** *mod.* low and sneaky. □ *What a dirty trick!* □ *That was really dirty!* □ *What a dirty thing to do!* **3.** *mod.* a general-purpose intensifier. □ *There's a dirty big car just drawn up outside our house.* □ *He let out a dirty great laugh when he heard.*

dirty daughter See DIDN'T OUGHTER.

dirty deal *n.* an unfair deal. □ *That was a dirty deal. I feel cheated.* □ *I got a dirty deal at that shop, and I won't go back.*

dirty dog *n.* a lecherous man. (Often used jocularly.) □ *I saw you with that new girl, you dirty dog.* □ *That dirty dog tried to get fresh with me!*

dirty joke *n.* an obscene joke. □ *Fred told a dirty joke that shocked almost everyone.* □ *No dirty jokes around here. We get enough of that on television.*

dirty laundry See DIRTY LINEN.

dirty linen AND **dirty laundry; dirty washing** *n.* scandal; unpleasant private matters. □ *I wish you wouldn't put our dirty linen out for everyone to see.* □ *I've heard enough about her dirty washing.*

dirty look *n.* a frown meant to show displeasure with something that has been said or done. □ *I gave him a dirty look, and he took his arm off my shoulder.* □ *What is that dirty look meant to mean?*

dirty mac brigade *n.* lecherous old men as a group. □ *I think almost the entire audience were in the dirty mac brigade.* □ *Why do there seem to be so many members of the dirty mac brigade in this part of town?*

dirty-minded *mod.* having a tendency to see the lewd or obscene aspects of anything; having a tendency to place an obscene interpretation on the words and actions of others. □ *Trevor is sort of dirty-minded, but he wouldn't do anything really vile.* □ *He's a vile, dirty-minded jerk.* □ *Most of those guys are dirty-minded.*

dirty old man *n.* a lecherous old man. (Usually jocular.) □ *Jimmy, you are getting to be a dirty old man!* □ *What a terrible joke. You are a dirty old man!*

dirty washing See DIRTY LINEN.

dirty weekend *n.* a weekend spent with one's lover rather than one's spouse. □ *I think they're off to Paris for a dirty weekend.* □ *Do people still go on dirty weekends?*

dirty word *n.* a swear word; a taboo word; an informal word concerned with sex or excreta. □ *No dirty words are allowed on this computer bulletin board.* □ *Some kid grabbed the microphone and yelled a dirty word into it.*

dirty work **1.** *n.* menial work; hard or difficult work. □ *Why do I always get stuck with the dirty work?* □ *We should share the dirty work evenly.* **2.** *n.* sneaky or underhand activities. □ *I hear that Sam is up to his old dirty work again.* □ *He is a master at dirty work.*

dischuffed *mod.* dissatisfied; displeased. □ *I think it is important for you to know that I am dischuffed indeed by your performance.* □ *A dischuffed boss is a dangerous boss.*

disc jockey See DISK JOCKEY.

dish *n.* a good-looking or attractive girl or young woman. (Compare with DISHY.) □ *Look at her, isn't she a dish?* □ *Now there's a good-looking dish.*

dish someone or something *vb. phr.* to demolish, destroy or defeat someone or something. □ *Why did you dish that project?* □ *You've dished me!*

dish someone out of something *tv.* to be deprived of something by cheating. □ *He still considers himself dished out of promotion.* □ *Don't try to dish me out of that one, too!*

dish something out **1.** *vb. phr.* to serve up food to people. □ *I'll dish it out, and you take it to the table.* □ *Careful how you dish out the mashed potatoes. There may not be enough.* **2.** *vb. phr.* to distribute information, news, etc. □ *The press secretaries were dishing reports out as fast as they could write them.* □ *The company dishes out propaganda on a regular basis.* **3.** *vb. phr.* to give out trouble, scoldings, criticism, etc. □ *The boss was dishing criticism out this morning, and I really got it.* □ *The teacher dished out a scolding to each one who was involved in the prank.*

dishy *mod.* attractive. (Usually sexually. Compare with DISH.) □ *Now that woman is really dishy!* □ *She certainly looks dishy to me!*

disk jockey AND **deejay; disc jockey; D.J.; jock** *n.* a radio announcer who introduces music from phonograph records. (The abbreviations are initialisms.) □ *The disk jockey couldn't pronounce the name of the singing group.* □ *I was a D.J. for a while, but didn't like it.*

Disneyland *n.* anywhere that does not function as promised or is noticeably inefficient. (Scots usage. See also DIZNY.) □ *They call this place Disneyland because this dizny work and that dizny work and he dizny work...* □ *Shuggy works at Disneyland. Well, to call it "work" is an exaggeration.*

Ditch *n.* the English Channel. (Always with *the*.) □ *We stood there looking over the Ditch at France.* □ *We sailed to France across the Ditch.*

ditch 1. *vb.* to dispose of someone or something; to abandon someone or something. □ *The crooks ditched the car and continued on foot.* □ *All right, which one of you animals ditched their dirty socks behind the radiator?* **2.** *vb.* [for an aircraft] to make a forced landing on water. □ *Look's like we'll just have to ditch the old bird.* □ *He's going to ditch over there in that bay.*

dither *n.* a state of confusion, hesitation or agitation. (Compare with IN A DITHER.) □ *It's hard to break out from a dither like that. Maybe a good night's sleep would help.* □ *I'm in such a dither; I don't know what to do next.*

div *n.* a stupid old person. (Criminal.) □ *These divs are easy targets for all the small-time crooks around.* □ *Divs are just too tempting.*

dive *n.* a low drinking establishment; a cheap bar. □ *I don't think I want to spend the whole evening in this dive.* □ *You know, this dive ain't so bad after all.*

dive bomb See BOMB.

dive bomber 1. *n.* someone—such as a vagrant—who collects cigarette ends from the pavement with a view to smoking them. □ *It was a cold night and no one was to be seen but a lonely dive bomber slowly working her way along the street.* □ *We don't want dive bombers around here, they're bad for the image of our town.* **2.** See also BOMBER.

divvy *n.* a share of something. (Particularly those earned by a co-operative venture. Compare with DIVVY SOMETHING UP.) □ *How much is my divvy?* □ *Give me my divvy so I can go home.*

divvy something up *vb. phr.* to divide something up. (Compare with DIVVY.) □ *We had to divvy my aunt's things up after her death.* □ *They divvied up the fish and drove back to town.*

dizny *phr.* "does not." (Scots usage. See also DISNEYLAND.) □ *It dizny matter, wur no going, okay? (It does not matter, we are not going, all right?)* □ *Ah telt ye he dizny want ony tea. (I told you he does not want any tea.)*

dizzy *mod.* stupid; scatterbrained. □ *The prof is a little dizzy, but entertaining.* □ *Who is that dizzy bird?*

D.J. See DISK JOCKEY.

DJ *n.* a dinner jacket. □ *You'll be expected to wear a DJ at tonight's event.* □ *Everyone stood there in DJs—except me.*

do 1. *n.* a party; a social event. □ *We had a smashing time at your little do.* □ *I'm having a do for a friend this weekend. Would you like to come?* **2.** *vb.* to use a drug or drugs in general. (Compare with DO DRUGS.) □ *Is Tracy doing coke again?* □ *Tracy never stopped doing. She just switched from coke to speed.* **3.** *n.* a swindle or hoax. □ *Another do like that and I call your parents.* □ *That little do the kids did with the statue from the town square was a dandy.* **4.** *n.* a battle. □ *That was some tough do. Someone had to lose.* □ *It's going to be some do but we'll win.*

d.o.a. AND **DOA 1.** *phr.* "dead on arrival." (Hospitals. Initialism.) □ *The kid was d.o.a., and there is nothing anybody can do about that.* □ *Do you want to end up DOA?* **2.** *n.* a person who is dead on arrival at a hospital. □ *They brought in two DOAs Saturday night.*

□ *Drugs increase the number of d.o.a.s considerably.*

do a beer AND **do a drink; do a drop; do a one** *vb. phr.* to take an alcoholic drink. □ *I'll do a beer, thanks.* □ *Do me a drop, too.*

do a Bertie *vb. phr.* to turn Queen's evidence in a criminal trial. (From a certain Bertie Small, who did this.) □ *Mick would never do a Bertie on you.* □ *Mike has done a Bertie.*

do a bunk AND **do a Michael; do a mick(e)y; do a runner** *vb. phr.* to depart rapidly, disappear or escape. □ *He did a bunk before he was fired.* □ *Time for us all to do a runner, I think. They'll be home soon.*

do a drink See DO A BEER.

do a drop See DO A BEER.

do a flanker AND **pull a stroke; pull a fast one; pull a flanker; work a flanker** *vb. phr.* to trick; to outwit; to deceive; to evade. □ *You can try to do a flanker on me if you like, but I'm on to your tricks.* □ *Don't try to work a flanker on me!*

do a good turn to someone *vb. phr.* to give a woman sexual pleasure, as seen from the male perspective. (Taboo.) □ *Cor, I fancy giving her a good turn!* □ *I here Otto's willing to do a good turn to any of us girls!*

do a Houdini *vb. phr.* to escape. (After the feats of the late Harry Houdini.) □ *There was no time to do a Houdini, so we had to talk to Mrs Wilson.* □ *Lefty tried to do a Houdini.*

do a job on someone or something 1. *vb. phr.* to ruin someone or something; to give someone or something a thorough working over. □ *The cops did a job on Robbie, but he still wouldn't talk.* □ *There's no need to do a job on me, man, I'll tell you everything I know—which is nil.* □ *That punch sure did a job on my nose.* **2.** See also DO A NUMBER ON SOMEONE.

do a left *vb. phr.* to turn left. □ *When you get to the end of the road, do a left.* □ *He did a left and disappeared.*

do a line with someone *vb. phr.* to go out with a girl. □ *Why are you doing a line with someone like her?* □ *I'd love*

to do a line with Zoe, if only she'd have me!

do a message AND **do the messages** *vb. phr.* to run an errand. (Scots, Irish and North of England usage.) □ *I sent Jimmy to do a message for me.* □ *She's out at the supermarket doing the messages.*

do a Michael See DO A BUNK.

do a mick(e)y See DO A BUNK.

do a mischief to someone *vb. phr.* to injure someone. □ *If you're not careful you'll do a mischief to someone.* □ *Sorry, but you've done a mischief to yourself with that motorbike.*

do a moon job See MOON.

do a number on someone AND **do a job on someone** *vb. phr.* to harm or deceive someone. □ *The Inland Revenue really did a number on me.* □ *My friendly local plumber did a job on me cleaning out my drain.*

do a one See DO A BEER.

do a right *vb. phr.* to turn right. □ *He did a right and disappeared.* □ *When you get to the end of the road, do a right.*

do a runner 1. *vb. phr.* to leave (a restaurant, for example) without paying. □ *I think the customer at that table over there is planning to do a runner.* □ *The diner did a runner so we called the police.* **2.** See also DO A BUNK.

do a show *vb. phr.* to go to a theatrical entertainment. □ *We'll do a show while we're in London.* □ *I'd rather like to do a show, too.*

do a starry *vb. phr.* to sleep under the stars. □ *Other people would rather die than do a starry.* □ *Other people love doing a starry.*

do as you like *n.* a bicycle. (Rhyming slang, linked as follows: do as you like ≈ [bike] = bicycle.) □ *You have to wear a helmet with a do as you like that size, don't you?* □ *How much did that do as you like set you back?*

doat *n.* a person that deserves to be doted upon. (Irish usage.) □ *His mother has always seen him as a poor wee doat.* □ *Even someone who's treated like a doat is entitled to their own point of view.*

dob *n.* a small lump or dollop. □ *There was a dob of the stuff on the plate, but I wasn't going to eat it.* □ *All right, give me a dob.*

do bird AND **do chokey; do porridge** *vb. phr.* to serve time in prison. □ *Oh, I'm sure he'll have to do bird for this.* □ *Otto's doing chokey again.* □ *You should do porridge for that.*

do chokey See DO BIRD.

dock asthma *n.* theatrically expressed surprise or disbelief displayed by the accused in court. (Police and criminal slang.) □ *Terry's denial was interrupted by long gasps of dock asthma.* □ *It was the most convincing diplay of dock asthma the judge had seen for many a year.*

doctor *vb.* to spay or castrate an animal. □ *Sally suggested that someone ought to doctor Beavis—if he isn't doctored already.* □ *Get somebody to doctor your cat!*

doddle 1. *n.* some action or activity that is easily carried out or trouble-free. □ *Don't worry; it was a doddle.* □ *Don't tell them it'll be a doddle, they don't need to know that.* **2.** *n.* money obtained without effort. (Scots usage.) □ *That money was a doddle, wasn't it?* □ *Hey Jimmy, interested in another doddle like that last one?* **3.** *vb.* to win with ease; to walk it. □ *Well, winning that was a doddle.* □ *It's a doddle. Of course we can do this!*

dodge *n.* a swindle; a deception. □ *What sort of dodge did you get ripped off with?* □ *Gerry has a new dodge to make money, but he hasn't made any yet.*

dodgem car *n.* a small electrically-powered fairground bumper car. □ *We had a great time driving on the dodgem cars.* □ *Dad! Can we go on the dodgem cars?*

dodgy 1. *mod.* tricky or difficult. □ *What you want will be very dodgy.* □ *It was dodgy job, but we managed.* **2.** *mod.* chancy. □ *The place was in a real tizzy. Everything was dodgy.* □ *It was dodgy for a while, but we are out of the woods now.* **3.** *mod.* evasive. □ *Why are you being so dodgy? Answer the ques-*

tion! □ *I think he's being dodgy because he's got something to hide.* **4.** *mod.* unreliable; untrustworthy. □ *The whole plan looks very dodgy to me.* □ *Careful! That chair's very dodgy and may collapse under you.*

dodgy boiler *n.* a woman perceived to be the carrier of a sexually transmitted disease. (Crude.) □ *The story is that Maggie is a dodgy boiler.* □ *Well, I don't know if she's a dodgy boiler, but don't believe every rumour you hear.*

dodgy gear AND **dodgy kit** *n.* stolen goods. □ *All right, then tell us where this dodgy gear came from?* □ *We found a huge pile of dodgy kit in his house.*

dodgy kit See DODGY GEAR.

do drugs *vb. phr.* to take drugs; to use drugs habitually. (Compare with DO, sense 2.) □ *Rich doesn't do drugs, and he doesn't drink.* □ *Marty started doing drugs when he was very young.*

do for someone 1. *vb. phr.* to serve as housekeeper for someone. □ *She does for the elderly gent in the big house.* □ *I do for people because it makes some money for me.* **2.** *vb. phr.* to clean someone's house on a regular basis. □ *He has a woman who comes in every day to do for him.* □ *Mrs Wilson does for a couple of the old folks who have houses around here.* **3.** AND **do someone in** *vb. phr.* to kill someone. □ *That fellow did for his girl, you know.* □ *Someone had done in that poor old lady.*

dog *n.* an ugly or unattractive girl or young woman. □ *I'm no dog, but I could wish for some changes.* □ *So she's not a film star; she's not a dog either!*

dog and bone *n.* a telephone. (Rhyming slang, linked as follows: dog and bone ≈ (tele)phone.) □ *The dog and bone was ringing off the hook when I came in.* □ *The dog and bone's been very busy all day today.*

dog-eat-dog *mod.* cruel; highly competitive. □ *This is a dog-eat-dog world.* □ *It's dog-eat-dog out there.*

dog (end) *n.* a cigarette end. □ *There was a tramp nosing around, seemingly* *looking for dog ends.* □ *He emptied his pockets, which were full of old dogs.*

do-gooder 1. *n.* a busybody concerned with the social improvement of others, whether or not desired or required by the recipients. (Usually derogatory.) □ *The do-gooders are demanding a bigger cut of the pie.* □ *I don't consider myself a do-gooder, but I try to help people.* **2.** *n.* a social worker, as seen by their so-called "clients." □ *Your do-gooder was looking for you.* □ *Why can't these do-gooders go and do good to someone else for a change?*

do-goodery *n.* what social workers do. □ *All that do-goodery must be very boring.* □ *Let's face it, you only do do-goodery because you like to pry into other people's business.*

dog-out *vb. phr.* to keep watch. □ *Bert, you go and dog-out while we get on with things here.* □ *Instead of dogging-out, Bert went and let the dog out, which barked and attracted attention...*

dogs 1. *n.* greyhound racing. (Normally with *the*.) □ *I'm off to the dogs tomorrow. Wish me luck!* □ *He spent all his money on the dogs and now he's broke.* **2.** *n.* the feet. (Normally plural.) □ *My dogs are killing me today.* □ *Doctor, please take a look at my dogs.*

dogsbody 1. *n.* a junior naval officer. □ *In this ship, dogsbodies just have to do what everybody else tell them.* □ *He may be dogsbody but he's still an officer of the Royal Navy.* **2.** *n.* a drudge; an insignificant person. □ *Why does everybody treat me like a dogsbody?* □ *Because you are a dogsbody, that's why.* **3.** *n.* a pudding consisting of peas. □ *I see we're having dogsbody today.* □ *I've never tried dogsbody. What's it like?*

dog's breakfast AND **dog's dinner** *n.* a mess; a shambles. □ *What a dog's breakfast this place has become.* □ *Why do you have to make a dog's dinner of every place you live at?*

dog's dinner See DOG'S BREAKFAST.

doings *n.* the things required. □ *Have you got the doings, dear?* □ *Without all the doings, we can't do anything.*

do-it-yourself *n.* masturbation. (Taboo.) □ *Do-it-yourself is a very popular teenage pastime, you know.* □ *At least with do-it-yourself you don't have to be polite first.*

dole *n.* payment made by the state to unemployed people. □ *He's come to collect his dole.* □ *You get the dole through there.*

dole something out *vb. phr.* to distribute or hand out. □ *Right, it's time to dole out the work for the week.* □ *He doled out the little food remaining; it did not come to much.*

dolie *n.* an unemployed person. □ *Four hundred dolies turned up for that one job interview.* □ *I don't think I could take another dolie again today.*

doll *n.* a good-looking or attractive girl or young woman. □ *Who's the doll I saw you with last night?* □ *That doll was my sister, you pratt.*

dollars AND **bucks** *n.* Pounds Sterling; money. □ *How many bucks does this thing cost?* □ *I don't have any dollars on me.*

dollop *n.* an undifferentiated lump, especially of food. □ *I can't eat these dollops of so-called food.* □ *Well, that dollop is potatoes, that dollop is peas, that dollop is spaghetti...I think.*

doll up *vb. phr.* to dress attractively or well. □ *Get dolled up, darling. We're going out.* □ *What are you getting dolled up for?*

dolly 1. *mod.* pretty or attractive. □ *Norah really is quite dolly.* □ *Boy! What a dolly that girl next door is!* **2.** *n.* a cricket ball that is easy to hit or catch. □ *Here comes a dolly for you, Charles!* □ *Oh, Charles! Missing a dolly!*

do me good 1. *n.* a cigarette. (Rhyming slang, linked as follows: do me good ≈ [Woodbine] = cigarette.) ("Woodbine" was a brand of cigarette especially popular with troops on the Western Front during World War I.) □ *Where is my packet of do me goods?* □ *How about a do me good before we take off?* **2.** *n.* wood. (Rhyming slang.) □ *We need more do me good to finish this job.* □ *There's a great pile of do me good in the garden next door.*

Donald Duck *n.* sexual intercourse. (Taboo. Rhyming slang, linked as follows: Donald Duck ≈ [fuck] = sexual intercourse.) □ *I think he's hoping for a little bit of the old Donald Duck when he takes her home.* □ *There were a couple of teenagers in the back room, having a Donald Duck.*

done by mirrors AND **done with mirrors** *mod.* illusory; purposefully deceptive. □ *The whole budgetary process is done with mirrors.* □ *The self-review was done by mirrors and didn't come off too bad.*

done for *mod.* doomed; in serious trouble; dead. □ *I'm sorry, this whole scheme is done for.* □ *I knew I was done for.*

done over 1. *mod.* beaten up; successfully assaulted. □ *We done over the other guys good and proper, and they knew it.* □ *Harry felt that Mike would get the idea if he was done over a bit.* **2.** *mod.* frisked or searched. □ *He looked at his done over flat and sighed.* □ *Why were you done over? What were they looking for?*

done thing *n.* the acceptable way of doing things. (Normally with *the*.) □ *This is the done thing.* □ *That is not the done thing.*

done to a turn *mod.* well-cooked; nicely cooked. □ *The entire meal was done to a turn.* □ *The turkey was done to a turn; thanks Mary.*

done with mirrors See DONE BY MIRRORS.

dong(er) *n.* the male sexual organ. (Taboo.) □ *Men keep their brains in their dongers!* □ *Unlike Myra, Sharon thinks of little else but dongs.*

donkey's ages See DONKEY'S YEARS.

donkey's years AND **donkey's ages** *n.* a very long time. □ *I haven't seen you in donkey's years.* □ *It's been donkey's ages since we talked.*

donnybrook *n.* a big argument; a brawl. (Irish usage.) □ *There was a big donnybrook at the concert, and the police were called.* □ *Who started this donnybrook?*

Don't ask. *sent.* "The answer is so depressing, you don't even want to hear it." □ *How am I? Don't ask.* □ *This has been a horrible day. How horrible, you say? Don't ask.*

Don't ask me. *sent.* "I don't know either." (With the emphasis on *me*.) □ *I don't know. Don't ask me.* □ *Don't ask me. I wasn't there.*

don't care tuppence *mod.* totally disinterested. □ *I don't care tuppence, really.* □ *Why should you worry? You don't care tuppence either.*

Don't I know it! *exclam.* "It is really true—I know it for a fact!" □ *It's bad all right. Don't I know it!* □ *Late? Don't I know it. Any later than this and it'll be early again.*

don't make a fuss *n.* a bus. (Rhyming slang.) □ *I saw him on the don't make a fuss this morning.* □ *Waiting for the don't make a fuss, eh?*

Don't make me laugh! *exclam.* "That is a stupid suggestion!" □ *You a judge? Don't make me laugh!* □ *Don't make me laugh. Tom could never do that.*

Don't start! *exclam.* "Do not complain!" □ *Yes, I know it's a mess. Don't start!* □ *Don't start, I'm sorting it out.*

Don't you wish! *exclam.* "I'm sure you wish it were true." □ *You think you'll win? Don't you wish!* □ *There's no school tomorrow? Don't you wish!*

doodad AND **doodah** *n.* someone or something for which the correct name has been forgotten or was never known. □ *I lost my—you know—my doodad—my watch!* □ *Did you get one of these doodads I asked for?*

doodah See DOODAD.

doodle *vb.* to draw or write aimlessly while listening or purporting to be listening to others, as at a meeting. □ *He sat there doodling all day long.* □ *Try to concentrate instead of doodling.*

doofer AND **dufer** *n.* a (found or borrowed) cigarette saved for smoking at another time. (It will "do for" later.) □ *Sam always has a doofer stuck behind his ear.* □ *He took two fags, one to smoke and the other as a dufer.*

doolally 1. *mod.* insane. □ *Anyone who would want to marry Frank has to be doolally.* □ *Jane's got this doolally idea that she's going marry Frank.* **2.** *mod.* eccentric. □ *Sally is just naturally doolally.* □ *Sometimes what you say is completely doolally!*

doolander *n.* a heavy blow. ☐ *She landed a real doolander on his thigh.* ☐ *She tried to take a doolander at me!*

do oneself proud *vb. phr.* to have done a very fine job. ☐ *That's super! You've done yourself proud!* ☐ *I feel like I've done myself proud.*

do one's fruit AND **do one's nut** *vb. phr.* to become furiously angry. ☐ *I'd do my fruit if that happened to me, I can tell you!* ☐ *Boss, there's a customer out here doing his nut.*

do one's nut See DO ONE'S FRUIT.

do one's (own) thing *vb. phr.* to do what one wants; to do what pleases oneself no matter what others think. ☐ *She's going to start doing her own thing for a change.* ☐ *I've always done my thing, and I don't see a great amount of benefit from it.*

doon the stank *mod.* squandered or lost forever. (Scots usage. "Stank" is Scots for "drain" or "gutter.") ☐ *It's gone, lost doon the stank.* ☐ *If you do that, everything we have worked for will be doon the stank.*

do-or-die *mod.* obstinate continuance upon a course of action, whatever the risks. ☐ *He has an obsessive do-or-die attitude.* ☐ *Whatever it took, I was determined to get there, do-or-die.*

doormat *n.* a weak-willed person who is abused by others. ☐ *I always feel like a doormat.* ☐ *Why do people treat me like a doormat?*

doorstep *vb.* to sell or canvas door-to-door. ☐ *Don't you doorstep me!* ☐ *Can you make any money doorstepping?*

door to door *n.* a door. (Rhyming slang.) ☐ *He's at the old door to door.* ☐ *I knocked on yer door to door, but no one answered.*

dope 1. *n.* drugs in general; marijuana. ☐ *Lay off the dope, will ya?* ☐ *How much dope do you do in a week anyway?* **2.** *n.* false or deliberately deceptive information. ☐ *I don't want any more of your dope. What really happened?* ☐ *It's just a load of dope. We need help.* **3.** *n.* information in general. ☐ *All right, what's the real dope on this?* ☐ *I already gave him all the dope.*

dope (it) up *vb. phr.* to be taking drugs. ☐ *All his money goes on doping it up.* ☐ *Let's go and dope up.*

dop(e)y *n.* a drug addict. ☐ *I am not a dopey!* ☐ *This area is full of dopies.*

do porridge See DO BIRD.

do right by someone *vb. phr.* to behave honourably or properly with regard to someone. ☐ *If you do right by me, I'll do right by you.* ☐ *I thought you said you'd do right by me?*

dork 1. *n.* a foolish, strange or offensive person—possibly all three combined. (Offensive. Also a term of address.) ☐ *Ye gods, Sally! You are a dork!* ☐ *Here comes the king of dorks again.* **2.** *n.* the male sexual organ. (Taboo.) ☐ *Myra says dorks are disgusting but then Myra's strange.* ☐ *Only small boys wave their dorks about like that, Wayne. Put it away!*

dorky *mod.* foolish, strange or offensive. (Offensive.) ☐ *That is a really dorky idea. Just forget it.* ☐ *I wouldn't be caught dead wearing that dorky hat.*

dorm *n.* dormitory. ☐ *Which dorm do you live in?* ☐ *Fred lives in a mixed dorm.*

do's and don'ts *n.* the rules; the things that should be done and things that should not. ☐ *I must admit that a lot of the do's and don'ts don't make much sense to me either.* ☐ *Better learn the do's and don'ts immediately.*

dosh *n.* money. ☐ *Sorry, I can't afford it, I've no dosh.* ☐ *How much dosh do you need, then?*

do someone *vb.* to arrest someone. ☐ *The rozzers tried to do Frank too, but he moved away too fast.* ☐ *The cops did her as she was leaving the hotel.*

do someone down *vb. phr.* to harm someone. ☐ *Don't do your family down like that.* ☐ *I'm sorry about your difficulty, but don't do me down because of that.*

do someone in See DO FOR SOMEONE.

do someone over 1. *vb. phr.* to search someone; to frisk someone. ☐ *I was done over by the police but they found nothing.* ☐ *Harry pushed Mike up against the wall and held him still while* *he did him over. When he found the money, he ran off down the street.* **2.** AND **do the business on someone** *vb. phr.* to beat someone up. □ *Mummy, some big boys did me over!* □ *They've arrested the yobs who were doing the business on people in the streets around here.*

do someone's head in See BASH SOMEONE'S HEAD IN.

do someone up like a kipper *vb. phr.* to steal from someone by trickery; to cheat. □ *Oh we did the little creep up like a kipper all right, Martin.* □ *I keep being done up like a kipper by people who seem to see me as a soft target.*

do something up *vb. phr.* to zip or button up something (such as a coat, for example.) □ *I did up my coat and walked out.* □ *"Do up your jacket first!" she called to him.*

doss **1.** *n.* a bed. □ *Get out of that doss and get up and get going!* □ *Well, it's time I was getting into the old doss.* **2.** *vb.* to sleep. □ *Just let me doss!* □ *You can doss over there.*

doss down *vb. phr.* to sleep rough. □ *If you don't have a choice, you doss down.* □ *I'd been dossed down for some time when he arrived.*

dosser **1.** *n.* a tramp or other person without proper accommodation. □ *The dosser was waiting outside the office for him.* □ *Even a dosser like that has to earn a living.* **2.** See also DOSS-HOUSE.

doss-house AND **dosser** *n.* a cheap hotel or lodging house for vagabonds, tramps, etc. □ *There's a doss-house at the end of the street.* □ *Some very strange people seem to inhabit these dossers.*

dossy *mod.* silly; simple-minded. □ *Y'know, maybe that's not so dossy.* □ *Come on, don't be dossy.*

Do tell. *interrog.* "Is that so?" (A disinterested way of holding up one end of a conversation.) □ *So, you're a dentist. Do tell.* □ *Do tell. I've never heard that before. Nice talking to you.*

do the business *vb. phr.* to perform sexual intercourse. (Taboo.) □ *There were a couple of teenagers in the back*

room, doing the business. □ *One look and he knew she had already done the business that evening.*

do the business on someone See DO SOMEONE OVER.

do the dirty on someone **1.** *vb. phr.* to play a low trick on someone. □ *Mr Big did the dirty on Otto.* □ *Otto was so dumb he didn't ever realise Mr Big had done the dirty on him.* **2.** *vb. phr.* to impregnate a girl and then abandon her. □ *If you do the dirty on my sister I'll kill you.* □ *When her brother found out I'd done the dirty on Sophia, I had to run!*

do the honours *vb. phr.* take charge of pouring and serving drinks. □ *Will you do the honours, Harry?* □ *Ask Harry. He's doing the honours.*

do the Knowledge *vb. phr.* to systematically learn the KNOWLEDGE. □ *It can take years to do the Knowledge properly.* □ *I'm doing the Knowledge at the moment.*

do the lot *vb. phr.* to lose all one's money. □ *Would you believe, I've done the lot on a horse.* □ *It's kind of hard to feel sorry for someone who does the lot gambling, you know.*

do the messages See DO A MESSAGE.

do the (religious) dodge on someone *vb. phr.* to pretend to be religious in order to gain some advantage or favour from someone. □ *He's going from door to door, doing the religious dodge on little old ladies to get money from them.* □ *I have no time for people who do the dodge on trusting people like that.*

do the ton *vb. phr.* to reach 100 mph. □ *We did the ton on the motorway today.* □ *The policeman said he thought the car was doing the ton when it hit the bridge abutment.*

do the trick *vb. phr.* to do or provide exactly what is needed. □ *This about does the trick.* □ *Does this little thingumabob do the trick?*

do time *vb. phr.* to serve a sentence in prison; to serve a specific amount of time in prison. (Underworld.) □ *Lefty had done time on a number of occasions.* □ *You'd better talk and talk fast if you don't want to do time.*

dots *n.* sheet music. □ *Right, who's got the dots?* □ *You can buy the dots for this in that music shop in High Street.*

dot someone *vb.* to hit or strike someone. □ *I got heavily dotted by Harry yesterday.* □ *Harry dotted him one right on the jaw.*

dotty *mod.* crazy, eccentric or absurd. □ *Now you're being dotty.* □ *There's a dotty old woman asking for you.*

double *n.* a drink containing two measures of spirits. □ *Make mine a double, bartender.* □ *Sam usually has two doubles on the way home.*

double-barrelled name *n.* a hyphenated surname. □ *Oh, he's got a double-barrelled name—Dekewer-Eagle or something absurd like that.* □ *Jack thinks double-barrelled names so often sound ridiculous because of the ridiculous people who have them.*

double bubble See BUBBLE.

double-choked *mod.* extremely disgusted. □ *Heavens, we were all double-choked, I think.* □ *I don't want to be double-choked again.*

double cross 1. *vb.* to betray someone. (Originally a more complicated switching of sides in a conspiracy wherein the DOUBLE-CROSSER sides with the victim of the conspiracy—against the original conspirator.) □ *Don't even think about double crossing me!* □ *Max double crossed Mr Big a few years back.* **2.** *n.* a betrayal. (See comments with sense 1.) □ *He always remembered that double cross.* □ *It's the one double cross that Max was sorry about.*

double-crosser *n.* a person who betrays someone. (Often with *dirty.* See DOUBLE CROSS.) □ *You dirty, low-down double-crosser, you!* □ *Max is the classic double-crosser.*

double-decker 1. *n.* a bus seating passengers upon two levels or decks. □ *I like to travel in double-deckers.* □ *Some double-deckers don't have tops.* **2.** *n.* a sandwich with two layers of fillings. □ *He put away a giant double-decker and a glass of milk.* □ *How can anybody eat a double-decker that is so thick?*

double Dutch *n.* gibberish; unintelligible speech. □ *It sounded as if they were talking double Dutch.* □ *Well, it's all double Dutch to me anyway.*

double event *n.* a glass of whisky together with a glass of beer. (Scots usage.) □ *A double event for me please, bartender!* □ *That's the fourth double event he's had within an hour.*

double take *n.* a surprised second look at something, due to disbelief or surprise. □ *I did a double take and blushed.* □ *Fred did a double take, then realised it was Tracy.*

double up (with laughter) *vb. phr.* to laugh so hard that one bends over. □ *We all just doubled up with laughter.* □ *I doubled up when I heard the punch line.*

doubt *vb.* to suppose or suspect. □ *I doubt that that must be true after all.* □ *We all began to doubt that something was wrong after that.*

dough *n.* money. (Compare with BREAD.) □ *I got a lot of dough for that ring I found.* □ *I need some dough to buy groceries.*

dout AND **dowt** *n.* a cigarette end. □ *I threw my dout away and turned to look him in the eye.* □ *He produced a dowt from his pocket and relit it.*

do well *vb. phr.* to live well or prosper. □ *Now there's one couple who're doing well.* □ *I'll do well when I've made the money to fund it, not before.*

down 1. *mod.* depressed; melancholy. (Compare with DOWN WITH SOMETHING.) □ *I feel sort of down today.* □ *We're all a little down.* **2.** *mod.* inoperative. (Computer jargon. Said of other equipment too, by osmosis.) □ *The system is down. Come back later.* □ *How long has it been down?* **3.** *vb.* to eat or drink something down quickly. □ *He downed a soft drink and burped like a thunderclap.* □ *She downed her sandwich in record time.* **4.** *vb.* to throw someone down, as in wrestling; to knock someone down as in a fight. □ *Wilbur downed his opponent and won the match.* □ *Paul downed the guy with one blow.* **5.** *mod.* behind in the score achieved in a game. □ *We're three goals down with two minutes to play.* □ *They're two goals down, and it looks* *like the village team has won.* **6.** See also DOWNER.

down among the dead men *mod.* very intoxicated due to drink. □ *Boy, I was really down among the dead men. I'll never drink another drop.* □ *She's down among the dead men at the moment.*

down and out *mod.* destitute. □ *He's really down and out and needs help.* □ *How did you manage to get so down and out so fast?*

down-and-out *n.* someone who is impoverished. □ *There were a couple of down-and-outs sleeping under the railway bridge.* □ *The down-and-out touched Martin for a fiver.*

downer 1. *n.* a depressing event; a boring situation. □ *These cloudy days are always downers.* □ *Her 60th birthday party was a real downer, I'm afraid.* **2.** AND **down; downie** *n.* a barbiturate or a tranquillizer. □ *She favours downers.* □ *Too much booze with those downers, and you're dead.*

downie See DOWNER.

download *vb.* to transfer data from a remote computer to a local one by electronic means. (Computer jargon. Compare with UPLOAD.) □ *I wonder if they could download that data to us now?* □ *Joad will download it to you now.*

down on someone *mod.* having prejudice or hostility towards someone. □ *Why are you always so down on him?* □ *She's really down on Brian. What has he done?*

down the chute See DOWN THE DRAIN.

down the drain AND **down the pan; down the tubes; down the chute** *mod.* gone; wasted; ruined. □ *Well, there's 400 quid down the drain.* □ *A lot of money went down the tubes on that deal, and all for nothing.* □ *That's it! Down the pan, just like that.* □ *Oh, its all down the pan now.*

Down the hatch! *exclam.* "Let's drink it!" (A drinking toast.) □ *Down the hatch! Have another?* □ *Bottoms up! Down the hatch!*

down the pan See DOWN THE DRAIN.

down the pub *mod.* at the pub. □ *I'm off down the pub, okay?* □ *Are you coming down the pub later?*

down the tubes See DOWN THE DRAIN.

down time *n.* the time when a computer is not operating. (Computer jargon. Compare with UP TIME.) □ *I can't afford a lot of down time in the system I buy.* □ *We had too much down time with the other machine.*

down tools *vb. phr.* to cease work. □ *At the end of the working day they will down tools and go home.* □ *They've downed tools and are talking about striking.*

down to the ground *mod.* completely, utterly or entirely. □ *He was fed up, right down to the ground.* □ *Why are you so rotten all the way down to the ground?*

down under *n.* the antipodes; particularly Australia and New Zealand. □ *I've always wanted to visit down under.* □ *We spent Christmas down under.*

down with something *mod.* unwell; in bed due to illness. (Compare with DOWN.) □ *I was down with the flu for two weeks.* □ *Fred and his wife were down with colds for weeks at a time.*

downy *mod.* shrewd or knowing. □ *He's a downy one all right; you won't fool him.* □ *We need a downy individual in that job.*

dowt See DOUT.

D'Oyly Carte *n.* an anal release of intestinal gas; a noise or smell associated with this. (Crude. Rhyming slang, linked as follows: D'Oyly Carte ≈ [fart] = intestinal gas.) □ *Oh lord! Who made that D'Oyly Carte?* □ *The pungent scent of a recent D'Oyly Carte hung in the air.*

Do you get my drift? AND **Get my drift?** *interrog.* "Do you understand me?" □ *Get my drift? Should I explain it again?* □ *Do you get my drift, or shall I run through it again?*

dozy *mod.* lazy or stupid. □ *Who is that dozy fellow leaning on the bar?* □ *He may look dozy, but he knows what he's doing.*

Dracula *n.* a hospital pathologist. (Because of the blood samples taken.) □ *Here comes Dracula, looking for your blood.* □ *You'll find Dracula in the path lab along there.*

drag 1. *n.* something dull and boring. □ *This day's a drag.* □ *What a drag. Let's go somewhere interesting.* **2.** *n.* a puff of a cigarette. □ *He took a big drag and scratched at his tattoo.* □ *One more drag and he coughed for a while. Then he stubbed out the fag.* **3.** *vb.* to pull or puff on a cigarette. □ *She dragged a couple of times and sat in the fug for a while.* □ *When she dragged a fag, you could see her relax and get straight.* **4.** *vb.* to race a car against someone; to race someone in a car. □ *I'm planning to drag you at the fairgrounds next Saturday. Better be there.* □ *I don't drag anybody anymore. I lost my licence.* **5.** *n.* women's clothing worn by male homosexuals, transvestites and female impersonators. □ *There's a shop in the clone-zone selling nothing but drag.* □ *I bet you don't know that George has a huge wardrobe of drag.* **6.** *n.* an annoying person; a boring person. □ *Gertie could be a real drag when she wanted.* □ *The whole project was a drag from start to finish.*

dragged out *mod.* exhausted; worn out. □ *I feel so dragged out. I think I'm short of vitamins or something.* □ *After the game, the whole team was dragged out.*

drag one's heels *vb. phr.* to be slow or reluctant. □ *You must not drag your heels over this, we must get finished.* □ *Why was he dragging his heels?*

drag queen *n.* an effeminate male homosexual who wears women's clothing. (Crude.) □ *Tell that drag queen to get out of here.* □ *I hear that you-know-who is a drag queen.*

drag up *vb. phr.* [for a man] to wear women's clothing. (Crude.) □ *I see Simon is dragging up again.* □ *I don't understand why a man would want to drag up.*

drain 1. *n.* someone or something that exhausts one. □ *Harry is such a drain on me.* □ *What a drain these meetings are.* **2.** *vb.* to wear someone out. □ *Arguing like that drains me, really drains me.* □ *Your constant bickering is meant to drain my resistance till I submit. Is that it?*

drain one's radiator AND **drain one's snake** *vb. phr.* [for a man] to urinate. (Crude.) □ *I'm just going to drain my radiator.* □ *Well, draining one's snake does relieve the pressure of all that beer!*

drain one's snake See DRAIN ONE'S RADIATOR.

Drat! *exclam.* "Damn!" □ *Drat! I'm late!* □ *Oh, drat! Another broken nail!*

draw 1. *n.* cannabis; marijuana. □ *You can get some good draw in this part of town.* □ *What does draw cost around here?* **2.** *n.* tobacco. (Prisoner's slang.) □ *Any draw, mate?* □ *You'll find prisoners can become obsessed about draw.* **3.** *vb.* to smoke a cigarette. □ *This nicotine fiend needs to draw a cigarette for a fix!* □ *I need to draw a fag. Just give me a minute.* **4.** *vb.* to smoke marijuana. □ *Want a draw, man?* □ *He was in his room, drawing.*

draw the bow *vb. phr.* to make a guess. □ *Go on, what do you think? Draw the bow.* □ *If you really want me to draw the bow on this...*

draw the long bow *vb. phr.* to exaggerate. □ *I wish I could stop her drawing the long bow as she does.* □ *If you keep drawing the long bow, no one will believe anything you say.*

dream *n.* a charming or delightful person. □ *What a dream she would be to date.* □ *She's a real dream.*

dreck *n.* dirt; garbage; faeces. (Crude. From German via Yiddish.) □ *What is all this dreck in the corner?* □ *I've had enough of this dreck around here. Clean it up, or I'm leaving.*

drecky *mod.* filthy; extremely unpleasant. (Crude.) □ *Oh that's really drecky!* □ *What a drecky place.*

dreg *n.* a useless person. (Offensive. Also a term of address.) □ *What a dreg that woman can be.* □ *Get out of here, you dreg!*

dressed to kill *mod.* dressed in fancy or stylish clothes that are intended to impress someone. □ *She is always dressed to kill.* □ *I'm never dressed to kill. I just try to be neat.*

dressed to the nines *mod.* dressed very stylishly with nothing overlooked.

□ *She showed up for the picnic dressed to the nines.* □ *Clare is usually dressed to the nines in order to impress people.*

drink *n.* the sea. (Always with *the.*) □ *His plane crashing in the drink, I'm afraid.* □ *He looked out over the vastness of the drink.*

drinkies *n.* a drinks or cocktail party. □ *That was some drinkies at Tom's the other night.* □ *I haven't had a drinkies like that in years.*

drinking token AND **beer token; drinking voucher; beer voucher** *n.* a one Pound coin. □ *Have you got a few drinking tokens you can spare?* □ *These things cost more than just a beer voucher or two.*

drinking voucher See DRINKING TOKEN.

drink (money) **1.** *n.* blackmail money. □ *I've got to pay them drink money or else!* □ *Gimme the drink you owe me!* **2.** *n.* money paid by the police for information supplied. □ *If it's good information, you'll get your drink* □ *How much drink money is this news worth?*

Drink up! *exclam.* "Finish your drink!"; "Finish that drink, and we'll have another!" □ *Okay, drink up! It's closing time.* □ *Drink up, and let's get going.*

drinkypoo *n.* a little drink of wine or spirits. □ *Wouldn't you like just one more drinkypoo of Madeira?* □ *Just a little drinkypoo, my dear.*

drip **1.** *n.* an oaf; a NERD. □ *Oh, yuck. He's such a drip* □ *Bob is a drip, I suppose, but he's a harmless one.* **2.** *n.* a soppily sentimental person. □ *Even a drip like that has to earn a living.* □ *What does the drip want?* **3.** *n.* a spotty, immature youth. □ *Who's that drip I saw Linda with?* □ *I don't like him, he's a drip!*

dripper *n.* an old prostitute past her "sell-by date." (Taboo.) □ *The Old Bill hauled her in because she looked like a dripper.* □ *Does Clare not realise that she dresses like a dripper?*

driver **1.** *n.* the captain of a ship. □ *Yes madam, I am the driver of this ocean liner, as you put it.* □ *Wake the driver. I think there's a problem that needs his presence on the bridge.* **2.** *n.* the pilot of an aircraft. □ *If I were you, I would*

not call the captain the driver. □ *Who's the driver in that thing?*

drive someone around the bend AND **drive someone bonkers; drive someone nuts** *vb. phr.* to drive someone crazy. (Compare with AROUND THE BEND.) □ *This tax stuff is about to drive me nuts.* □ *Gert tried to drive us all around the bend.*

drive someone bonkers See DRIVE SOMEONE AROUND THE BEND.

drive someone nuts See DRIVE SOMEONE AROUND THE BEND.

drive someone up the wall *vb. phr.* to frustrate someone; to drive someone to distraction. □ *These days of waiting drive me up the wall.* □ *Staying in the house drove us all up the wall.*

droops *n.* a feeling of lassitude. (Always with *the.*) □ *You're not going to get much from Albert today as he's got the droops.* □ *Oh, I've got the droops; I can't be bothered.*

droop-snoot *n.* an adjustable nose of an aircraft. □ *The Concorde has a droop-snoot which can be lowered in order that the pilot can see what is happening when landing.* □ *They gave this one a droop-snoot so the pilot could see where he was going on the ground.*

droopy-drawers *n.* an indecisive or disorganised girl. □ *Come on, droopy-drawers. Make up your mind!* □ *She's not a real droopy-drawers; she's not as disorganised as she looks.*

drop **1.** *vb.* to knock someone down. □ *Jim dropped Willard with a single punch to his shoulder.* □ *The swinging board hit him and dropped him.* **2.** *n.* a small drink or serving of liquor. □ *I'll take just another drop of that whisky, if you don't mind.* □ *Can I give you another drop?* **3.** *n.* a place where drugs are left to be claimed by the recipient. □ *The police discovered the drop and waited for the runner.* □ *They switched drops constantly just in case of discovery.* **4.** *n.* a tip or gratuity. □ *So, how big a drop did you give the waiter?* □ *Imagine! She offered a drop to her doctor!* **5.** *n.* a bribe. □ *So, how big a drop were you offered by the contractor?* □ *Imagine! She offered* *them a drop to give her company the contract!*

drop a bombshell *vb. phr.* to reveal startling information. □ *Tracy came in and dropped a bombshell with her news.* □ *You really dropped a bombshell this afternoon!*

drop a brick *vb. phr.* to reveal indiscreet or embarrassing information. □ *I really dropped a brick when I blurted out about Tony's divorce in front of everyone.* □ *Well! That was not a helpful thing to say. Do you always go around dropping bricks?*

drop a clanger *vb. phr.* to commit a serious blunder. □ *Woops! I dropped a clanger there, didn't I?* □ *Try not to drop any more clangers, Ivan.*

drop (a pup) *vb. (phr.)* to give birth. □ *Samantha dropped a pup last week.* □ *When do you drop?*

Drop dead! *exclam.* "No!"; "Get lost!"; "Go away and don't bother me!" □ *I don't care. Just drop dead!* □ *Drop dead! Get lost!*

drophead **1.** *n.* a convertible car. □ *I'm rather partial to dropheads.* □ *Like my new drophead, darling?* **2.** *n.* the removable fabric roof of a convertible car. □ *I only remove the drophead when there's no danger of rain.* □ *The drophead's not been off this car since it was new.*

Drop it! *exclam.* "Forget it!"; "Never mind!" □ *Never mind! Just drop it!* □ *Drop it! I should never have brought it up.*

drop off the twig AND **hop off (one's twig)** *vb. phr.* to die. □ *He dropped off the twig when his plane crashed during a training flight.* □ *For a minute, I thought I was going to hop off my twig.*

drop of the hard stuff *n.* a drink of spirits. □ *Graham always liked drop of the hard stuff.* □ *A drop of the hard stuff sounds tempting just now.*

drop one AND **drop one's guts; drop one's lunch** *vb. phr.* to release intestinal gas anally; to cause a noise or smell associated with this. (Taboo.) □ *If you absolutely must drop one, would you have the goodness to go somewhere else to do it?* □ *I could not believe it! He just dropped his lunch right there, without warning or apology.*

drop one's guts See DROP ONE.

drop one's lunch See DROP ONE.

drop on someone (from a (very) great height) **1.** *vb. phr.* to punish or reprimand someone with great severity. □ *When I catch him I will drop on him from a very great height all right. That's a promise!* □ *The boss really dropped on Charlie!* **2.** *vb. phr.* to land someone in very severe trouble or difficulties. □ *If you let me down I'll drop on you from a very great height.* □ *Don't fail, or it will all drop on you.*

drop out to withdraw from a conventional lifestyle. □ *Sometimes I just want to drop out and raise pigs or something.* □ *Ted dropped out and bought a farm.*

drop-out AND **dropout** **1.** *n.* someone who has dropped out of university, etc. □ *Dropouts find it very hard to get a job.* □ *Some dropouts make great successes of themselves, but not very many.* **2.** *n.* someone who has withdrawn from a conventional lifestyle. □ *I've been a drop-out for twenty years and have no intention of ever dropping in again.* □ *Well, you'll see when you meet her that she's a bit of a dropout.*

dropped *mod.* arrested. □ *Harry's just been dropped by the rozzers.* □ *If you want to be dropped, just keep on behaving like that.*

drop someone *vb.* to knock someone down; to punch and knock down a person. □ *Fred dropped Brian with one punch to the jaw.* □ *Max lost his cool and dropped Brian.*

drop someone in it See DROP SOMEONE IN THE SHIT.

drop someone in the shit AND **drop someone in it** *vb. phr.* to betray someone; to expose someone to danger. (Taboo.) □ *Now you've really dropped me in the shit!* □ *Sorry; I did not intend to drop you in it like that.*

drop someone or something like a hot potato *vb. phr.* to disassociate oneself with someone or something instantly. □ *When we learnt of the conviction, we* *dropped him like a hot potato.* □ *I dropped the idea like a hot potato.*

drop the ball *vb. phr.* to fail at something; to allow something to fail. □ *I didn't want to be the one who dropped the ball, but I knew that someone would screw up.* □ *Sam dropped the ball, and we lost the contract.*

drop them *vb. phr.* [for a woman] to make herself sexually available. (Crude. Refers to what she is prepared or expected to do with her knickers or panties.) □ *Linda will drop them at the least excuse.* □ *"Drop them, darling!" is not the most romantic or subtle way to sweep a girl off her feet, Otto.*

drown something *vb.* to overdilute spirits by adding too much water. □ *Don't drown that perfectly good whisky!* □ *The English always drown the stuff.*

druggie AND **druggy** *n.* a drug addict or user. □ *That druggy loves to hang about around here.* □ *There are too many druggies in this neighbourhood.*

drum 1. *n.* a night-club. □ *We went to a drum with a jukebox for entertainment.* □ *It was a nice little drum, with a combo und a canary.* **2.** *n.* a brothel. (Crude.) □ *He was found dead in some cheap drum late last night.* □ *The police raided the drum and took away the madam and all the girls.* **3.** *vb.* to drive very fast. □ *We were really drumming along the motorway when this cop car signals us to stop.* □ *If you drum along like that you'll have a serious accident.* **4.** *n.* a house; a place of residence. □ *The burglar's drum was chock full of stolen goods.* □ *Is this your drum?* **5.** *vb.* to sell door-to-door. □ *Can you make any money drumming?* □ *I've tried it and I can't drum. I just can't do it.*

drum and fife 1. *n.* a knife. (Rhyming slang.) □ *Swiftly and silently his drum and fife found its way up under Rocko's ribs. All over a silly bit of skirt.* □ *I could tell from the way his cuff had broken that there was a drum and fife strapped to his leg.* **2.** *n.* a wife. (Rhyming slang.) □ *I've got to go home to my*

drum and fife. □ *My drum and fife disapproved of the film.*

drummer 1. *n.* a thief; a burglar. □ *This little toe-rag is just another drummer.* □ *We are the police. We are here to catch drummers, madam.* **2.** *n.* a door-to-door salesman. □ *There's a drummer at the door.* □ *I tried being a drummer for a while but hated it.*

drumming *n.* thieving; burglary. □ *There's a lot a drumming in this area.* □ *He was actually doing a drumming when we arrested him, sarge.*

drum up *vb. phr.* to make tea by the side of the road. □ *A couple of tramps were drumming up in the lay-by.* □ *This would be a good place to drum up.*

dry 1. *mod.* having to do with a region or district where alcoholic beverages cannot be purchased. (Compare with WET.) □ *Some counties in Wales are still dry on Sundays.* □ *Some small towns are dry, but not many.* **2.** *n.* a Conservative politician favouring right-wing, free-enterprise and individualistic policies. (Compare with WET.) □ *Being a dry was particularly popular during the Prime Ministership of Margaret Thatcher, who is reputed to have invented the usage.* □ *Him? Oh yes, he's a really dry dry.*

dry-arsed *mod.* safe again after danger. (Taboo.) □ *Well at least we're dry-arsed again!* □ *You were very lucky to get out of that dry-arsed.*

dry as a basket *mod.* very thirsty. □ *Got a pint? I'm as dry as a basket.* □ *Being as dry as a basket, I took a long cool drink of water.*

dry-as-dust *mod.* dull; lifeless. (See also AS DRY AS DUST.) □ *I can't take another one of his dry-as-dust lectures.* □ *All her ideas are dry-as-dust.*

dry-hump *vb.* to simulate sexual intercourse. (Taboo.) □ *I thought they were doing the real thing but it turned out to be no more than dry-humping.* □ *I don't care if you were just dry-humping. You're not doing it here!*

dry old stick *n.* an old man with a dry sense of humour. □ *There's some dry* old stick here looking for you. □ *The dry old stick sat on the bench and told a series of very funny stories.*

dry run AND **dummy run** *n.* a rehearsal. (Military, not theatrical, in origin.) □ *Right men, we'll have a dry run for the big op tomorrow.* □ *How did the dummy run go, Colonel?*

dry-shave *vb.* to delude someone. □ *Don't let him dry-shave you.* □ *The scoundrel dry-shaved me!*

Dry up! *exclam.* "Shut up!"; "Go away and don't bother me!" □ *Oh, dry up! I've heard enough.* □ *Dry up and get lost!*

dry up *vb. phr.* to forget one's lines while on stage. (Theatrical.) □ *It must be terrible to dry up like that on first night.* □ *She dried up and then just stood there for ages.*

dub out See DUB UP.

dub someone up *vb. phr.* to incarcerate or jail someone. □ *Don't let them dub me up!* □ *They dub people up for that sort of thing, you know.*

dub up AND **dub out** *vb. phr.* to pay out money. □ *Come on, dub up!* □ *Just how much do you expect me to dub out this time?*

duchess *n.* a costermonger's wife. (A costermonger is a man who sells fruit and vegetables from a barrow, on the street; a barrow-boy.) □ *You could tell she was a real duchess, covered from head to toe in pearlies.* □ *The costermonger and his duchess were very interesting people.*

duck *n.* a score of zero in some sports, especially cricket. □ *I'm afraid I scored a duck again.* □ *Well, a duck isn't the end of the world.*

duck and dive *vb. phr.* to hide. (Rhyming slang.) □ *It's too late to duck and dive, Boris. The police are here.* □ *He's ducking and diving to avoid his creditors.*

duck (out) *vb. (phr.)* to avoid someone or something. □ *Clare is ducking out of her responsibility.* □ *You can't duck this investigation. They're on to you.*

duck-pond *n.* the Atlantic Ocean. (Always with *the.*) □ *Oh, he's across the duck-pond just now, on business in New York.* □ *People think nothing of hopping over the duck-pond nowadays.*

ducks AND **ducky** *n.* darling, dear, etc. (A familiar form of address to or from a woman.) □ *Hello ducks, fancy some fun tonight?* □ *Fancy going down the pub, ducky?*

duck's disease *n.* short legs. □ *You may have just a touch of duck's disease my love, but to me they are lovely little legs nevertheless.* □ *You can tell which one is Harry. He's the one with duck's disease.*

ducky 1. *mod.* cute; charming. □ *Isn't she ducky?* □ *What a ducky girl she is.* **2.** See also DUCKS.

duck(y) bumps *n.* gooseflesh; goose pimples. (Jocular.) □ *It was so cold I was covered in ducky bumps in no time.* □ *I could feel duck bumps all over as I realised the full audaciousness of my idea!*

dud *n.* a failure; something that fails to perform as intended. □ *The whole idea turned out to be a dud.* □ *The play was a dud from start to finish.*

dufer See DOOFER.

duff 1. *mod.* counterfeit, broken, useless or worthless. □ *I don't want any more of your duff radios.* □ *What a duff deal that turned out to be.* **2.** *vb.* to fail to strike a golf ball. □ *Woops! I've duffed that shot.* □ *He's a terrible golfer, duffing just about every other swing he takes at a ball.*

duffer 1. *n.* an unskilled golfer. □ *Those duffers up ahead are holding up the game.* □ *Don't call me a duffer!* **2.** *n.* a foolish oaf; a bumbler. □ *Some old duffer is weeding our garden for us. He's lost, I think.* □ *Pete's just a duffer—he's not really serious at it.* **3.** *n.* a useless or ineffective person. □ *I don't think I could take another duffer like that today.* □ *Barlow wondered why the firm had to employ all these useless duffers.* **4.** *n.* a harmless or unimportant man. □ *What does the duffer want?* □ *He's a rather surprising old duffer.*

duff shot 1. *n.* a failed attempt to strike a golf ball. □ *I don't think you're supposed to see duff shots at the European Open.* □ *That's Harry's fifth duff shot* *so far and we're still on the first hole. I don't think he's all that good at golf.* **2.** *n.* a fluffed or lost opportunity. □ *Well, that was a duff shot.* □ *I can't afford another duff shot like the last.* **3.** See BOSS SHOT.

duff up *vb. phr.* to beat up. □ *He did not hesitate to duff up Willy.* □ *If you duff up people, you can expect trouble.*

dugs *n.* old or flaccid female breasts. (Crude. Normally with *the* and in the plural.) □ *There she was, bold as brass, with her dugs openly flapping in the breeze.* □ *Once, my dugs were considered one of my best features.*

Duke of Kent *n.* rent. (Rhyming slang.) □ *How much is your Duke of Kent?* □ *That money is for this month's Duke of Kent.*

dukes *n.* the fists. (Rhyming slang, linked as follows: Duke [of York] ≈ [fork] = [finger] = [hand] = fist. Always in the plural.) □ *Okay, sunshine, put up your dukes.* □ *The guy's got bigger dukes than you'd believe.*

dumb blonde *n.* a girl who combines extreme prettiness with extreme stupidity. □ *Joe always finds dumb blondes irresistible.* □ *It's not the blondeness of dumb blondes he likes, so much as their dumbness.*

dumb-dumb AND **dum-dum** *n.* a stupid oaf; a dullard. □ *You can be such a dumb-dumb without even trying.* □ *Marvin is no dum-dum. He just looks that way.*

dumbo *n.* a stupid oaf. (Also a rude term of address.) □ *Come on, dumbo, move out of the way.* □ *Who's the dumbo in the luminous green trousers?*

dum-dum See DUMB-DUMB.

dummy run See DRY RUN.

dummy up *vb. phr.* to keep silent. □ *Look, just dummy up while I do the talking.* □ *Why have you dummied up? Have you lost the power of speech?*

dump 1. *n.* an act of defecation. (Crude.) □ *He said he needed a dump.* □ *He had a dump and then came back.* **2.** *n.* a low or cheap establishment. □ *I want out of this dump.* □ *My mum didn't bring me up to spend the rest of my days in a run-down dump like this.*

dunk *vb.* to perform sexual intercourse, from the male perspective. (Taboo.) □ *One look and he knew she had already been dunked that evening.* □ *There were a couple of teenagers in the back room, dunking.*

dunkie *n.* a woman viewed as a sex object. (Crude.) □ *So this dunkie I'd been eyeing up came right up to me and said, "It's £20 for a short time, darling."* □ *Now there's a nice dunkie walking down the street.*

Dunlop (tyre) *n.* a liar. (Rhyming slang.) □ *The fact is, he's just a Dunlop tyre.* □ *Anyone who told you that is a Dunlop.*

dunny 1. *n.* a cellar. (Scots usage.) □ *We keep aw sorts o' strange things down oor dunny.* □ *The polis found him hiding in a dunny.* **2.** *n.* an underground passageway. (Scots usage, related to the Standard English "dungeon.") □ *She widna go doon the dunny 'cos it was too dark.* □ *Dinny make me go back doon the dunny, Daddy! (Don't make me go back down that underground passageway, Father!)*

dupe 1. *n.* a potential victim of a confidence trick; a PATSY. □ *The crooks found a good dupe and started their scheme.* □ *I don't want to be a dupe for anybody.* **2.** *vb.* to trick someone; to swindle someone. □ *You tried to dupe me!* □ *I did not try to dupe you. It was an honest mistake.*

Durex *n.* a condom. (Crude. A trademarked name for those that are made by the London Rubber Company, but used generically.) □ *There's a machine selling Durex through the back.* □ *He bought a packet of Durex and left.*

dust 1. *n.* a powdered drug: heroin, phencyclidine (P.C.P.), cocaine; fine cannabis. □ *It's the dust that can really do you damage.* □ *Willy got hold of some kind of dust and took it to the police.* **2.** *n.* money. □ *It takes a lot of dust to buy a car like that.* □ *I don't make enough dust to go on a trip like that!*

dustbin lid *n.* a child. (Rhyming slang, linked as follows: dustbin lid ≈ [kid] = child.) □ *Is this dustbin lid yours?* □ *She is a most irritating dustbin lid.*

dusters *n.* the testicles. (Taboo. Normally with *the* and in the plural.) □ *He turned sideways to protect his dusters.* □ *Thud, right in the dusters. Ye gods, it hurt!*

dust-up *n.* a fight. □ *Mark got into bit of a dust-up with Brian.* □ *There was a dust-up at the party that ruined the evening for everyone.*

dusty *n.* an old person. □ *He's a pleasant dusty.* □ *The dusty was waiting outside the office for him.*

dusty answer *n.* an unsatisfactory or brusquely negative reply. □ *He offered a her dusty answer and did not hang around for her reaction.* □ *I think you've just got your answer, and it's a dusty answer indeed.*

Dutch courage *n.* false courage derived from drinking spirits. □ *Some Dutch courage, and he was ready to face anything.* □ *I'd never have made it through without a little Dutch courage.*

dutch(ess) *n.* a wife; a mother. □ *I'd better ask the duchess.* □ *Will your dutch let you out to the pub tonight?*

Dutch kiss *n.* an act of sexual intercourse. (Taboo.) □ *I think really, she's gasping for a Dutch kiss, you know.* □ *A good Dutch kiss would probably do her the power of good, in fact.*

Dutch treat *n.* an outing for two or more where the cost is split among the participants, either evenly or in proportion to what is consumed. (Compare with GO DUTCH.) □ *I propose a Dutch treat to celebrate the day.* □ *We had a Dutch treat, which gave us a chance to get to know one another better.*

Dutch uncle *n.* someone who gives avuncular advice; a man who gives advice with the directness of one of one's own relatives. □ *If I can be a Dutch uncle for a minute, I could give you some good advice.* □ *Dutch uncles can be as big of a pain as parents.*

dweeb *n.* an unpopular or foolish person. (Schoolchildren's term.) □ *Don't call Bob a dweeb! Even if he is one.* □ *The dweebs get all the best marks so why work?*

dyke See DIKE.

dykey See DIKEY.

dynamite 1. *n.* anything potentially powerful, such as a drug, news, a person, etc. □ *This new girl is really dynamite!* □ *The story about the scandal was dynamite and kept selling papers for a month.* **2.** *n.* self-raising flour. (It causes cakes, etc., to "blow up"...or, at least, to rise.) □ *Mum sent me out to the supermarket for some dynamite so she could bake a cake.* □ *Well, you can't bake properly without dynamite.*

E *n.* ECSTASY, a hallucinogen similar to L.S.D. □ *You can get some good E in this part of town.* □ *E is just one of a dozen drugs with similar formulas.*

eager-beaver *n.* a person who tackles something with more enthusiasm than wisdom. □ *Rocko is an eager-beaver when it comes to collecting money for the business.* □ *The eager-beavers were trying to buy tickets yesterday!*

eagle-eye *n.* an eye or eyes with very keen vision. □ *Keep your eagle-eye trained on the entrance.* □ *My eagle-eye tells me there's trouble over there.*

ear-bash AND **ear'ole; ear-hole; ear-wig** **1.** *vb.* to harangue, nag or remonstrate. □ *Why are you always ear-bashing me?* □ *Because ear-wigging is the only way to get you to do anything.* **2.** *vb.* to talk to (or at) someone at great length. □ *He ear-bashed me for hours about that!* □ *I think I probably deserved being ear-wigged, but not all night.* **3.** *vb.* to overhear a conversation; to eavesdrop. □ *If you try to ear-bash me again, you could well find yourself lacking an ear.* □ *There's Bert, always trying to ear-wig someone else's conversation.*

ear basher AND **ear-holer; ear-wigger** **1.** *n.* a haranguer, nagger or remonstrator. □ *You quite enjoy being an ear basher, don't you?* □ *If you want to be an ear-wigger, please go and be one to someone else.* **2.** *n.* someone who is overly loquacious. □ *I wish that ear basher would just shut up for a change.* □ *Look, you ear-wigger, please be quiet and give my ears a rest!* **3.** *n.* an overhearer of a conversation; an eavesdropper. □ *I'd take care not to discuss anything important within range of that ear basher, if I were you.* □ *That ear-wigger seems to pick up every detail that matters.*

ear-bashing AND **ear-holing; ear-wigging** **1.** *n.* a haranguing, nagging or remonstration. □ *Now that was a real ear-bashing!* □ *If you want another ear-wigging, just be as stupid as that all over again.* **2.** *n.* a long talk to (or at) someone. □ *That was some ear-bashing.* □ *I think I probably deserved an ear-wigging, but not an all night one.* **3.** *n.* the overhearing of a conversation; eavesdropping. □ *Take care, a lot of ear-bashing goes on around here.* □ *I can't stand ear-wigging.*

earful **1.** *n.* a scolding. □ *Her mother gave her an earful when she finally got home.* □ *Tom got an earful for his part in the prank.* **2.** *n.* a tremendous amount of gossip. □ *I got a big earful about Sally.* □ *I can give you an earful about the mayor.*

ear-hole See EAR-BASH.

ear-holer See EAR-BASHER.

ear-holing See EAR-BASHING.

early bath *n.* a departure or termination which is unexpectedly early. (Originally a sporting metaphor.) □ *He was forced to take an early bath when they found out he was cooking his expenses.* □ *Arthur said he'd had enough and was taking an early bath.*

early bird **1.** *n.* a person who gets up early. □ *I never miss sunrise. I'm an early bird.* □ *The early birds saw the corpse on the street and called the coppers.* **2.** *n.* a person who arrives early. □ *The early birds get the best seats.* □ *There were some early birds who arrived before the tea things were laid.*

3. *mod.* having to do with early arrival. □ *Early bird arrivals will be given a free cup of coffee.* □ *The early bird special this week is a free six-pack of cola for the first 100 visitors.*

early days *n.* too soon for something to have yet happened. □ *Hold on, it's early days yet!* □ *I know it's early days, but I think we may be on to something here.*

early door *n.* a prostitute. (Rhyming slang, linked as follows: early door ≈ [whore] = prostitute.) □ *Another early door went off with him in his car.* □ *Don't worry, there's always another early door available around this area.*

earner *n.* a profit made by criminal activities. (Criminal cant. Compare with NICE LITTLE EARNER.) □ *He got an earner out of that last burglary.* □ *To make an earner from stuff you steal, you've got to find a buyer.*

ear'ole See EAR-BASH.

earth to someone *phr.* "Hello someone, are you listening?" (A means of getting the attention of someone who is ignoring you or who is daydreaming. As if one were on the earth, trying to contact someone in a spaceship.) □ *Earth to Mum! Earth to Mum! What's for dinner?* □ *Earth to Fred! Are you asleep? Say something, Fred!*

ear-wig See EAR-BASH.

ear-wigger See EAR-BASHER.

ear-wigging See EAR-BASHING.

ease *vb.* to take time off or to relax. (Police slang.) □ *The policeman took five minutes to ease.* □ *Don't even think of easing when the sergeant is around.*

easts and wests *n.* the female breasts. (Crude. Rhyming slang. Normally with *the* and in the plural.) □ *Cor, look at the easts and wests on that, Fred!* □ *My easts and wests aren't all I might have wished for.*

Easy! **1.** *interj.* "Slow up!"; "Relax!" □ *Easy! It'll be okay.* □ *That's it, slowly...easy!* **2.** *exclam.* a cry of joy or derision, often heard chanted by crowds at sporting events, etc. □ *Easy! Easy! We won again!* □ *We won the Cup! Easy!*

easy *mod.* easy to please; flexible. □ *Don't worry about me. I'm easy.* □ *Fred's easy. He'll eat anything.*

easy as pie *mod.* very easy indeed. □ *There! That was as easy as pie, wasn't it?* □ *It may seem as easy as pie to you.*

easy as taking pennies from a blind man See EASY AS TAKING TOFFEE FROM A CHILD.

easy as taking toffee from a child AND **easy as taking pennies from a blind man** *phr.* "very easy indeed." □ *Stealing the car was as easy as taking toffee from a child.* □ *Well, it may look as easy as taking pennies from a blind man, but I fear there are complications.*

easy as you know how *mod.* quite easy. □ *Oh, in the end it was easy as you know how.* □ *There's no problem; you'll find it easy as you know how.*

Easy does it. 1. *phr.* "Calm down."; "Relax." □ *Cool it, man, easy does it.* □ *Easy does it! Relax and slow down!* **2.** *phr.* "Be gentle."; "Handle with care." □ *Easy does it. Go slow, and you won't dent anything.* □ *Easy does it. Two people can handle this heavy old thing if they go carefully.*

easy mark AND **easy meat** *n.* a woman who is easily persuaded to perform sexual intercourse. (Crude.) □ *Know of any easy marks in the pub tonight?* □ *Oh, Maggy is easy meat all right. You'll see!*

easy meat 1. *n.* something that is easy to obtain. □ *That money was easy meat, wasn't it?* □ *If you're looking for easy meat, take a walk through these doors.* **2.** See also EASY MARK.

easy money *n.* money earned or gained with little or no difficulty. □ *Do you know where I can get some easy money?* □ *All you people want is easy money. Don't you want to work for it?*

easy-peasy *mod.* very easy. (Childish.) □ *Simple! Easy-peasy, even!* □ *How do you manage to make everything look so easy-peasy?*

eat *vb.* to be bothered or worried by something. □ *What's eating you, Bill?* □ *Nothing's eating me. I'm just the nervous type.*

eater *n.* fruit suitable to be eaten raw. (Typically apples.) □ *Yes, these apples* *are eaters.* □ *There was an eater or two there a moment ago.*

eat one's hat *vb. phr.* to do something extraordinary. □ *If she wins, I'll eat my hat.* □ *I'll eat my hat if our advertisement actually brings us the sort of person we want.*

eat one's heart out 1. *vb. phr.* to suffer from sorrow or grief. □ *She has been eating her heart out over that creep ever since he ran away with Tracy.* □ *Don't eat your heart out. You really didn't like him that much, did you?* **2.** *vb. phr.* to suffer from envy or jealousy. (Usually a command.) □ *Yeah, this one's all mine. Eat your heart out!* □ *Eat your heart out! I won it fair and square.*

eat shit *vb. phr.* to submit to degradation, usually verbal. (Taboo.) □ *All right! All right, you're right, I'm eating shit. What more can you want?* □ *If you've got this one wrong too he'll make you eat shit, you know.*

eat someone out *vb. phr.* to perform oral sex upon a woman. (Taboo.) □ *If you think you're going to eat me out you've another think coming!* □ *There he was, eating her out!*

eat something up *vb. phr.* to consume something rapidly, such as food or money.* □ *Running this household eats my income up.* □ *The car really eats up petrol.*

eat up *vb. phr.* to eat in enjoyment. (Usually a command.) □ *Come on, now. Sit down and eat up!* □ *Eat up! There's plenty more where this came from.*

eau-de(-Cologne) *n.* the telephone. (Rhyming slang, linked as follows: eau-de(-Cologne) ≈ (tele)phone.) □ *My mobile eau-de-Cologne went off, and I had to leave the meeting.* □ *I'll have somebody call me during the meeting on me eau-de to get me out of it.*

ecilop *n.* the police. (Criminal's backslang.) □ *The ecilop are looking for you. What have you done?* □ *If the ecilop turn up, I'm not here, okay?*

eckles AND **exes** *n.* expenses incurred in the course of work. □ *He made a profit out of his eckies.* □ *I can't approve these exes.*

ecnop *n.* a prostitute's pimp. (Crude. Backslang, from PONCE.) □ *Well, the truth is Simon is her ecnop.* □ *the ecnop turned and came after the punter.*

eco freak AND **eco nut** *n.* someone with strong concerns about the environment and conservation. (Mildly derogatory. From "ecology.") □ *They call me an eco freak, which is okay by me.* □ *It's we eco nuts who think about the future of our planet.*

eco nut See ECO FREAK.

Ecstasy *n.* a hallucinogen similar to L.S.D. □ *Chemicals with names like "Ecstasy" are being put on the streets every day.* □ *Ecstasy is just one of a dozen drugs with similar formulas.*

edge *n.* antagonism; mutual dislike. □ *There has always been an edge in their relationship.* □ *The edge between these two has developed into out-and-out hatred.*

edgy *mod.* nervous; anxious and uncertain. □ *I feel sort of edgy about the race.* □ *I'm just an edgy fellow.* □ *Don't let yourself get so edgy.*

edie *n.* a low-class or cheap prostitute. (Crude.) □ *There was a edie standing right on that corner.* □ *There are a lot of edies around here in the centre of town.*

eefink *n.* a knife. (Backslang.) □ *I could tell from the way his cuff broke that there was a eefink strapped to his leg.* □ *Swiftly and silently his eefink found its way up under Rocko's ribs. All over a silly bit of skirt.*

Eeh-oop! *exclam.* an expression of surprise. (North of England usage.) □ *Eeh-oop! What are you 'ere for?* □ *Eeh-oop, that's a surprise!*

eelacs *n.* scales. (Backslang.) □ *Where you put the eelacs to weigh this lady's fish, Sid?* □ *I think he's nobbled the eelacs.*

Ee-mocing pu! *exclam.* "Coming up!" (Backslang.) □ *Watch out! Ee-mocing pu!* □ *"Ee-mocing pu!" "You what?"*

eenob *n.* a bone. (Backslang.) □ *He took a nasty knock on his eenob there, wot really hurts.* □ *Any eenobs for the dog?*

eff-all *mod.* FUCK-ALL. (Crude. Euphemistic.) □ *I tell you, there's eff-all there.* □ *I've been with left with eff-all to do for the rest of today.*

effing and blinding *mod.* swearing; using coarse language. (Crude.) □ *Here he comes, effing and blinding as usual.* □ *You can go around effing and blinding all you want but it makes no difference.*

Eff off! *exclam.* "FUCK OFF!" (Crude. Euphemistic.) □ *Why don't you just eff off!* □ *Eff off! I've had enough of you!*

egg and spoon *n.* a black person. (Racially offensive. Rhyming slang, linked as follows: egg and spoon ≈ [coon] = black person.) □ *He said he was not a racist, he just hated egg and spoons!* □ *Don't call black people eggs and spoons, please. It is very offensive and racist.*

egghead *n.* an intellectual person. □ *The eggheads aren't exactly taking over the world.* □ *My uncle was an egghead, but nobody in our family thought he knew very much.*

egg someone on *vb. phr.* to encourage. □ *Don't egg him on. He needs no encouraging.* □ *I was egged on to do it.*

ego trip *n.* a public expression of one's feelings of importance or superiority. □ *He's on another ego trip. Pay no attention.* □ *Sorry, I suppose that made it look as if I'm on another ego trip.*

ego tripper *n.* a person who habitually goes on an EGO TRIP. □ *Not another ego tripper standing for Parliament?* □ *You have to be an ego tripper to be a politician.*

E.G.Y.P.T. AND **EGYPT** *phr.* "eager (to) grab your pretty tits." (Crude. An initialism sometimes written on love letters. Also an acronym.) □ *I love you. E.G.Y.P.T., Harry.* □ *You bet I'm EGYPT! Wait 'till I get home; you'll see!*

Egyptian PT *n.* sleeping. (Offensive. Originally World War II military slang from the Middle East.) □ *Awake? Not exactly. She's getting in some Egyptian PT.* □ *Look, you can't go around talking about Egyptian PT; it's racist, you know.*

ejaculatorium *n.* a room set aside at a sperm bank for the production of sperm. (Crude. Pseudo-Latin.) □ *They say there are interesting magazines to read in the ejaculatorium.* □ *Do they really call that room an ejaculatorium?*

ekker *n.* exercise, particularly at university or school. □ *The truth was, he just loathed ekker.* □ *Every Thursday, the afternoon was given over to ekker of all sorts.*

elbow-bending *n.* drinking liquor; drinking liquor to excess. □ *She spends quite a bit of time at elbow-bending.* □ *That's a lot of elbow-bending for one sitting.*

elbow-grease *n.* effort. □ *Put out a little elbow-grease.* □ *All this job needs is a little more elbow-grease.*

el cheapo 1. *mod.* cheap. (Mock Spanish. Compare with CHEAPIE.) □ *The el cheapo brand won't last.* □ *Is this the el cheapo model?* **2.** *n.* the cheap one; the cheapest one. □ *I don't want one of those el cheapos.* □ *I can only afford the el cheapo.*

electric soup *n.* a particularly powerful alcoholic punch or fortified wine. (Scots usage.) □ *For goodness sake, that's really some electric soup you've got there!* □ *Any more o' yon electric soup?*

elephant *mod.* intoxicated due to drink. (Rhyming slang, linked as follows: elephant's [trunk] ≈ drunk.) □ *She was really elephant and Molly had to take her home.* □ *Joe and Arthur kept on knocking them back till they were both elephant.*

elevenses *n.* a light refreshment or snack taken mid-morning. □ *Do you take elevenses here?* □ *We stop for elevenses every day, about ten-thirty.*

eliminated *mod.* killed. □ *Mr Big wanted Max eliminated.* □ *When Max is eliminated, there will be no competition.*

eliminate someone *vb.* to kill someone. □ *We will eliminate you.* □ *They eliminated the main opposition very rapidly, in fact.*

Elmer *n.* a (male) American tourist in Britain. □ *The Elmer says he's looking* for the *Loch Ness Monster, dad.* □ *Do you think we should tell the poor Elmer that he's unlikely to find Nessie in Putney Reservoir?*

e-mail AND **email 1.** *n.* a message sent by electronic mail. (Computer jargon.) □ *There's an e-mail for you from Frank.* □ *Send him an email.* **2.** *vb.* to send a message by electronic mail. (Computer jargon.) □ *Frank has emailed you.* □ *E-mail him.* **3.** *mod.* concerning a message sent by electronic mail. (Computer jargon.) □ *There's an e-mail message for you from Frank.* □ *Send an email message to him.*

embalmed *mod.* very intoxicated due to drink. □ *By morning they were all embalmed.* □ *Bob was too embalmed to stand up.*

embalming fluid *n.* phencyclidine (P.C.P.). □ *What does embalming fluid cost around here?* □ *I handed her the embalming fluid and she rushed off to use it.*

embrocation *n.* spirits or beer; any alcoholic drink. □ *How about a little embrocation, landlord?* □ *Can I interest you in some embrocation before lunch?*

[emoticon] See SMILEY.

empties *n.* empty bottles. □ *Throw your empties in the rubbish bin.* □ *Whose empties are these, and how many are there?*

end *n.* the final insult; too much; the last straw. (Normally with *the.*) □ *This is just the end. I'm leaving.* □ *When she poured her drink down my back, that was the end.*

end to end *mod.* [of a couple] engaged in sexual intercourse. (Taboo.) □ *They were end to end, right there at the back of the room!* □ *Some people get end to end in public, sort of!*

English disease 1. *n.* syphilis. (Normally with *the.*) □ *The French called syphilis the English disease back in the 16th century.* □ *Syphilis? Ah, the English disease!* **2.** *n.* bronchitis. (Normally with *the.*) □ *The rest of Europe called bronchitis the English disease back in the 19th century.* □ *Because Britain was the first country that burned vast quantities of coal, bronchi-*

tis was much commoner there than elsewhere at that time. **3.** *n.* class conflict. (Normally with *the.*) □ *The rest of Europe called class conflict the English disease in the early years of the 20th century.* **4.** *n.* economic failure. (Normally with *the.*) □ *The rest of Europe called economic failure the English disease from the end of World War II until the mid-1980s.* **5.** *n.* labour conflicts and strikes. (Normally with *the.*) □ *The rest of Europe called labour conflicts and strikes the English disease from the end of World War II until the mid-1980s.* **6.** *n.* violent and outrageous behaviour by soccer fans. (Normally with *the.*) □ *The rest of Europe calls violent and outrageous behaviour by soccer fans the English disease in the 1990s.)*

enough to be going on with AND **something to be going on with** *mod.* sufficient for the moment. □ *Seven courses and twenty bottles of wine will be enough to be going on with, I assure you.* □ *Could we have something to be going on with, until the while thing is ready?*

enough to make a cat laugh *mod.* very funny. □ *Funny? It was enough to make a cat laugh!* □ *Harry's jokes can be funny enough to make a cat laugh at times.*

enthusiastic amateur See AMATEUR.

erdy *n.* a person without imagination, someone who is conventional and earthbound. (Usually in plural. From the German *Erde*, meaning "earth" or "the Earth.") □ *What's a erdy like that doing around here?* □ *I'm sorry but we really don't need another erdy working here.*

erk 1. *n.* an unpopular person. □ *What does the erk want?* □ *Even a erk like that has to earn a living.* **2.** *n.* in the Royal Air Force, an aircraftsman. □ *Come on you erks! There's work to do!* □ *There were a number of erks milling about outside the mess.* **3.** *n.* in the Royal Navy, a naval rating. □ *"What did that erk want?" the captain asked the officer.* □ *Look son, erks have to obey pigs in this navy.*

Errol (Flynn) *n.* the chin. (Rhyming slang.) □ *He punched me right on the*

Errol Flynn. □ *You can tell it's Harry 'cos he's the one with the huge Errol.*

esclop See SLOP.

essence of pig-shit *n.* an exceptionally attractive woman. (Taboo. A raffish allusion to HAPPY AS A PIG IN SHIT. Normally with *the*.) □ *Oh yes, he actually called her the essence of pig-shit!* □ *Well I dunno about calling her essence of pig-shit to her face, but she is certainly a looker!*

Essex girl *n.* a superficial and brainless young woman. (The butt of many sexist jokes, and the worthy partner for ESSEX MAN. Essex is a county adjacent to London.) □ *Essex girls are typically presented as empty-headed and with too much money.* □ *We've got some real Essex girls living around here, I can tell you.*

Essex man *n.* a prosperous but ignorant young man. (The worthy partner for ESSEX GIRL. Essex is a county adjacent to London.) □ *The typical Essex man made a lot of money for no good reason in a few years in the City.* □ *Essex men are a sort of living caricature for all that's gone wrong with Britain over the last few years.*

Establishment *n.* a social group exercising or perceived to be exercising control over the rest of the population. (Normally with *the*.) □ *The Establishment is reputedly resistant to change and to consist of such people as senior politicians, civil servants, generals and so forth.* □ *He many not be a member of the Establishment himself, but he appears to know the people who matter.*

Euro *mod.* European. □ *Brussels wants a common Euro position agreed on this.* □ *Apparently the new common Euro currency is to be called the Euro.* •

Eurobabble *n.* the specialist jargon used in documents and other writings concerned with or emanating from the European Union. □ *Have you ever tried to read the Eurobabble that comes out of Brussels?* □ *So, what does that mean in Eurobabble?*

Eurobin *n.* a large, wheeled rubbish bin. □ *You can usually see Eurobins at the foot of these tower blocks.* □ *Someone tried to block the entranceway with a Eurobin.*

Eurocrat *n.* a civil servant who works for the European Union. □ *Wilbur got a job in Brussels as a Eurocrat.* □ *Eurocrats have a reputation for being out of touch, interfering and overpaid.*

Eurodollar *n.* US currency held in a European bank. □ *There's an awful lot of Eurodollars in circulation today.* □ *Mr Big advised me to keep as much capital as I can in Eurodollars.*

evens See EVEN-STEPHEN(S).

even-Stephen(s) AND **even-Steven(s); evens; Stephens; Stevens 1.** *n.* a bet with even odds. (Rhyming slang.) □ *I think the chances are even-Stephens.* □ Q: *Can you win?* A: *It's about Stevens.* **2.** *n.* an equal trade or swap—one without anything else involved for either party. (Rhyming slang.) □ *All right, that's even-Stephens. I'll go along with that.* □ *If we are to divide this up, it's got to be Stevens.* **3.** *mod.* evenly divided. (Rhyming slang.) □ *He made the two piles of diamonds even-Steven and then let me chose which one I wanted.* □ *The cake is not exactly cut even-Stephen.* **4.** *mod.* even; balanced. (Rhyming slang.) □ *Now we're even-Stevens.* □ *Now that we've given each other black eyes, are we even-Stephen?*

even-Steven(s) See EVEN-STEPHEN(S).

ever so 1. *mod.* very or extremely. □ *That was ever so stupid, you know.* □ *You're ever so lovely, my love.* **2.** *phr.* "very much." □ *Thanks ever so!* □ *That's ever so generous of you.*

ever so much of something *n.* a vast quantity of something. □ *We have ever so much of the stuff, we don't know what to do with it.* □ *The orphanage can use ever so much of these toys.*

ex *n.* a former spouse or lover. □ *My ex is in town, but we don't talk much anymore.* □ *Her ex remarried.*

ex-con *n.* a former convict. □ *Watch out, he's an ex-con, you know.* □ *You'd never guess Charlie's an ex-con, would you?*

excuse-me *n.* a dance where it is permitted to change partners. □ *The next* *dance will be an excuse-me, ladies and gentlemen.* □ *Since it was an excuse-me, I suppose I should not have been surprised to find I was dancing with Roger.*

Excuse my French. See PARDON MY FRENCH.

exec *n.* an executive. □ *The execs are well-treated around here.* □ *They are even firing the execs now.*

exes See ECKIES.

exob *n.* a box. (Backslang.) □ *What's in the exob, Gov?* □ *Mum, Sid's just come in with a great big exob.*

expat *n.* an expatriate; particularly, a European living in Africa, the Middle East, Far East, etc. □ *There are a lot of British expats in every corner of the world.* □ *I was an expat in the Middle East for many years.*

expensive care unit *n.* a hospital intensive care unit. □ *Visiting the expensive care unit is always so depressing.* □ *A lot of nurses work in the expensive care unit.*

extract the Michael See TAKE THE PISS.

extract the urine See TAKE THE PISS.

ex-works *mod.* of the condition and price of goods as they are when they leave the place where they are made. □ *Well that's the price ex-works. If you want the thing delivered, that's extra.* □ *The ex-works price is the cheapest you'll find, normally.*

eyeball 1. *vb.* to look hard at someone or something. □ *I eyeballed the contract and saw the figures.* □ *The two eyeballed each other and walked on past.* **2.** *n.* surveillance. (Police.) □ *Another night of eyeball and I'll go crazy.* □ *Eyeball is really boring.*

eyeball to eyeball *mod.* face to face. □ *They approached each other eyeball to eyeball and frowned.* □ *Let's talk more when we are eyeball to eyeball.*

eyeful *n.* a good-looking or attractive girl or young woman. □ *Boy! What an eyeful that girl next door is!* □ *Norah really is quite an eyeful.*

eye-opener *n.* a real surprise. □ *Her confession was a real eye-opener.* □ *This day has been an eye-opener for me.*

Eyetie *n.* an Italian person. (Offensive.) □ *Why can you not be polite to Eyeties?* □ *Y'know, Otto, if you call a Eyetie a Eyetie, he's likely to get nasty.*

eyewash *n.* pretentious talk intended to confuse or deceive. □ *Oh, come on! That's just a lot of eyewash!* □ *It's not eyewash! It's true!*

FA See SWEET FANNY ADAMS.

fab *mod.* fabulous. □ *What a fab stereo that is!* □ *Your pad is not what I'd call fab. Just okay.*

fabulous *mod.* wonderful; exotic. (Used as an ambiguously polite or sarcastic dismissive description of something that one has been asked to admire but in truth cannot. Compare with DIFFERENT and INTERESTING.) □ *"Well, it's…uh…fabulous!"* □ *Oh yeh, it's really, you know, fabulous.*

face *n.* a well-known person; an easily-recognised individual. □ *When that face appeared in the crowd, John knew he was among friends.* □ *She's certainly a face, but she's not a pleasant person for all that.*

face fungus AND **fungus** *n.* whiskers; a beard. (Compare with FUNGUS-FACE.) □ *If John would shave off that face fungus, he'd look a lot better.* □ *What do you need all that fungus for anyway?*

face like the back (end) of a bus AND **face that would stop a clock; face like the side of a house** *n.* a spectacularly unattractive visage. (Normally used of a woman or girl.) □ *Memorable? I'll say, she's got a face like the back end of a bus.* □ *You could say that when you looked into her eyes, time stood still, but then it is a face that would stop a clock.*

face like the side of a house See FACE LIKE THE BACK (END) OF A BUS.

face that would stop a clock See FACE LIKE THE BACK (END) OF A BUS.

face the music *vb. phr.* to receive the rebuke that is due one. □ *You had better go in and face the music now.* □ *You*

are going to have to face the music eventually.

facilities *n.* the toilet. □ *Where are the facilities around here?* □ *Can I use your facilities?*

facts of life 1. *n.* an explanation of human reproduction, especially as presented to a child. (Always with *the.*) □ *No one ever explained the facts of life to me. I read books about it.* □ *She is so naive. She doesn't even know the facts of life.* **2.** *n.* the truth about life's difficulties. □ *You had better face up to the facts of life and get a job.* □ *They taught me everything in college except the facts of life.*

fade AND **walk** *vb.* [for people] to disappear; to depart. □ *Time for us all to fade, I think. They'll be home soon.* □ *He walked before he was fired.*

faff *n.* fuss. □ *Don't make such a faff! It's almost sorted.* □ *Why do you have to turn the simplest things into such a faff?*

faff about AND **faff around; flap around** *vb. phr.* to hesitate, dither or fuss about. □ *Instead of faffing about, could you try working for a change?* □ *That's enough flapping around.*

faff around See FAFF ABOUT.

fag 1. *n.* a cigarette. □ *Hey, mate, gimme a fag.* □ *Go and buy your own fags!* **2.** *n.* an unwanted or dreary task; drudgery. □ *I hate all this fag.* □ *Two more hours of fag, then freedom for the rest of the day!*

fag-ash Lil *n.* a girl or woman who smokes, especially one who smokes heavily. □ *The fag-ash Lil stood at the door, cigarette dangling from the corner of her mouth.* □ *"I'm in perfect* *health," the fag-ash Lil said, between her spluttering and bronchial coughing.*

fag-end 1. *n.* a cigarette butt. □ *He produced a fag-end from his pocket and relit it.* □ *I threw my fag-end away and turned to look him in the eye.* **2.** *n.* a useless or left-over portion or part. □ *I want a complete one, not a fag-end!* □ *We've only got a fag-end left here. Get a new one.*

fagged out *mod.* exhausted. □ *I'm really fagged out after all that running.* □ *John, you look really fagged out.*

fag-hole See CAKE-HOLE.

fag it *vb. phr.* to smoke (a cigarette, etc.). □ *Let's go outside and fag it, eh?* □ *Are we allowed to fag it in here?*

fag out *vb. phr.* to exhaust or tire. □ *Are you trying to get me fagged out or something?* □ *Anyone attempting that will soon be fagged out.*

fail *n.* a failing grade or mark on an examination test. (Compare with PASS.) □ *Did you get a pass or fail?* □ *Oh no! I've got a fail in French yet again!*

faintest AND **remotest 1.** *n.* the least idea. (Always in the negative. Always with *the*.) □ *I haven't the faintest what he's talking about.* □ *Maggy doesn't have the remotest of what this is all about.* **2.** *n.* the least chance. (Always in the negative. Always with *the*.) □ *You don't have the remotest of a job there. Look elsewhere!* □ *He's very ill. There's not the faintest that he'll pull through.*

fainting fits *n.* a woman's breasts. (Crude. Normally with *the* and in the plural. Derivation: fainting fits ≈ [tits] = breasts.) □ *All you think about is fainting fits!* □ *With fainting fits like that, she can go anywhere she likes.*

fair cop *n.* a clean arrest. □ *All right guv, it's a fair cop. I'll come quietly.* □ *That was no fair cop; I was set up!*

fair crack of the whip *phr.* a reasonable opportunity to participate or contribute. □ *We all would like a fair crack of the whip.* □ *I'd like to let you have a fair crack of the whip.*

fair dos *n.* equitable shares. □ *Oh come on, fair dos! We all deserve the same.* □ *No, Jack gave us all fair dos I must say.*

fair few AND **good few** *n.* a large number. (Always with *a.*) □ *There were a fair few folks at the church this morning.* □ *It'll take a good few payments like that to clear your debts.*

fair jiggert *mod.* very tired. (Scots usage.) □ *Just leave me be, I'm fair jiggert.* □ *He'll be fair jiggert when he gets back.*

fair skint *mod.* almost or entirely without money. (Scots usage.) □ *Have yous yins ony money, cos I'm fair skint agin. (Have any of you any money, because I'm almost or entirely without money again.)* □ *As usually, Shuggy's fair skint.*

fair treat *n.* a very pleasurable experience. □ *Today was a fair treat. When can we do that again?* □ *The office party was a fair treat, I suppose.*

fair-weather friend *n.* a temporary friend; one who is insincere or unreliable in times of difficulty. □ *I need something more than a fair-weather friend to help me through all this.* □ *When it came to the moment of truth, Simon turned out to be no more than a fair-weather friend.*

fairy *n.* an effeminate man; a passive male homosexual. (Crude.) □ *I hear that you-know-who is a fairy.* □ *Who goes around calling people fairies?*

fairy glen See COTTAGE.

fairy story See FAIRY TALE.

fairy tale AND **fairy story** *n.* a simplistic and condescending explanation for something; a lie. □ *I don't want to hear a fairy tale, just the facts, ma'am.* □ *What you're telling me sounds like a fairy story. Come back when you can be more straightforward.*

fake it *vb. phr.* to pretend (to do something). □ *If you don't know the right notes, just fake it.* □ *I can't fake it anymore. I've got to be honest with you.*

falderal AND **folderol** *n.* nonsense; fuss; complications. □ *I've had about enough of your falderal.* □ *Stop that folderol and get down to work!*

fall 1. *vb.* to be arrested. □ *Mr Big said that somebody had to fall for it, and he didn't care who.* □ *Lefty didn't want to* *fall for a job he didn't do.* **2.** *vb.* to go or be sent to prison for a specified period. □ *You'd better talk and talk fast if you don't want to fall.* □ *Lefty has fallen on a number of occasions.*

fall down on the job *vb. phr.* to fail badly. □ *He fell down on the job and had to be replaced.* □ *If anyone falls down on the job around here, they're out immediately.*

fall for it *vb. phr.* to become pregnant. □ *When I fell for it, I wondered what to do.* □ *I hear Sally has fallen for it.*

fall for someone *vb. phr.* to be romantically or sexually attracted to someone. □ *Yes, I think he's lovely and I've quite fallen for Patrick.* □ *I think she's rather fallen for him.*

fall guy *n.* a scapegoat; a SUCKER. □ *Gerry wasn't going to let himself become the fall guy again.* □ *Oh no, you don't make me your fall guy this time. Find some other sucker!*

falling-down drunk *mod.* very intoxicated due to drink. □ *Poor Fred is falling-down drunk and has no way to get home.* □ *She's not just tipsy; she's falling-down drunk.*

falling-out *n.* a disagreement. □ *Tom and Bill had a falling-out yesterday and now they're ignoring each other.* □ *Eventually they patched up their little falling-out.*

fallout *n.* the results of something; the FLAK from something. □ *The fallout from this afternoon's meeting was not as serious as some expected.* □ *It's not the crisis itself, but the fallout from the crisis that concerns us all.*

fall over backwards See BEND OVER BACKWARDS.

falsies *n.* false or artificially enhanced female breasts. (Crude.) □ *I'm telling you, she's wearing falsies.* □ *The thing was, her falsies were so obviously false!*

family jewels AND **wedding kit; wedding tackle** *n.* the testicles. (Taboo. Normally with *the* and in the plural.) □ *He got hit right in the family jewels.* □ *The teacher preferred "testicles" to "wedding tackle," if they had to be mentioned at all.*

fan *n.* an enthusiastic devotee of a particular activity, sporting team, performer, etc. (Originally, an abbreviation of "fanatic.") □ *Of course fans are fanatic. That's what the word means.* □ *Everywhere he looked, there was as sea of screaming teenage girl fans.*

fancy *vb.* to desire or be attracted towards, especially sexually. □ *He looked like he really fancies Sally.* □ *Fred fancies Martha, I've heard.*

Fancy meeting you here. *sent.* "Just imagine meeting you here!"; "I am surprised to meet you here!" □ *Well, hello, Tom. Fancy meeting you here!* □ *Fancy meeting you here, Bill. How have you been?*

fancy parts *n.* a feminine euphemism for the male sexual organ. (Crude. Always with *the.*) □ *She says she saw his fancy parts!* □ *There she was, bold as brass, touching his fancy parts.*

Fancy that! *exclam.* "Imagine that!" □ *So, you're a bus driver now. Well, fancy that!* □ *Fancy that! There's a piece of pie left in the fridge.*

fancy woman *n.* a mistress. □ *Have you got a fancy woman?* □ *What a question! Of course I've not got a fancy woman.*

fang *n.* a tooth. □ *Where can I find a good dentist? It's my fangs.* □ *I have a painful fang, I'm afraid.*

fang bosun *n.* a ship's dentist. □ *He had to go to see the fang bosun about his toothache.* □ *Most of the time, fang bosuns don't have much to do.*

fanny *n.* the female sexual organ. (Taboo. Note: this word *never* means "buttocks" in Britain!) □ *If your dresses get any shorter, we'll all be able to see your fanny.* □ *He got arrested trying to look up women's skirts in the hope of seeing their fannies.*

fanny adams See SWEET FANNY ADAMS.

fan(ny) belt AND **puss(y) pelmet** *n.* a very short mini skirt. (Taboo.) □ *You're not going anywhere in that fan belt, young lady!* □ *Here comes Maya, wearing a pussy pelmet.*

fanny hat AND **cunt hat** *n.* a trilby. (Taboo. A trilby is a soft, felt hat with an indented crown.) □ *It's called a* *fanny hat because of the dent in the hat's crown.* □ *You look ridiculous in that cunt hat.*

fare 1. *n.* the client of a professional male prostitute. (Crude.) □ *A lot of the renters bring their fares here.* □ *His pimp told him he'd find plenty of fares in this part of town.* **2.** *n.* a taxicab driver's passenger. □ *Cabbies can spend hours just cruising around looking for a fare.* □ *He picked up a fare who wanted to go to the airport.*

far gone 1. *mod.* late in time. □ *My goodness, I had no idea it was as far gone as that. We must go.* □ *Of course the time for that had far gone by the time we got there.* **2.** *mod.* intoxicated due to drink or drugs. □ *Larry's far gone and looking sick.* □ *Lord, she is really far gone!*

farmers *n.* hemorrhoids. (Rhyming slang, linked as follows: Farmer [Giles] ≈ [piles] = haemorrhoids.) □ *She's got to go into hospital to get her farmers dealt with.* □ *When the wife's got the farmers she gets in a foul mood.*

far out 1. *mod.* great; extraordinary; COOL. □ *This jazz is really far out!* □ *Do you want to hear some far out heavy metal?* **2.** *mod.* intoxicated due to drink or drugs. □ *How'd you get so far out?* □ *Three beers, and Wally was really far out.*

fart 1. *n.* an anal release of intestinal gas; a noise or smell associated with this. (Taboo. This word is in fact Standard English, but virtually all applications of it are not.) □ *Who caused that fart?* □ *Did I hear a fart?* **2.** *n.* an obnoxious or stupid person. (Taboo.) □ *Who's the stupid-looking fart with the enormous moustache?* □ *Who called me an old fart?* **3.** *vb.* to release intestinal gas anally; to cause a noise or smell associated with this. (Taboo.) □ *Who farted?* □ *Somebody farted.*

fart about AND **fart-arse around; fat-arse around** *vb. phr.* to dawdle or waste time. (Taboo.) □ *Stop farting about and get on with your work!* □ *If they didn't fat-arse around, they'd get it done with time to spare.*

fart-arse around See FART ABOUT.

fart-catcher *n.* a male homosexual. (Taboo.) □ *She came to the dance with a fart-catcher.* □ *Does he not care that he looks like a fart-catcher?*

farting shot *n.* an expressive way of registering one's contempt while departing. (Taboo. A pun. See PARTING SHOT.) □ *He fired a loud farting shot as he left the room.* □ *I suppose that odour is what we might call Otto's farting shot.*

fart-sack *n.* a sleeping bag; a bed. (Taboo.) □ *Well, it's time I was getting into the old fart sack.* □ *Get out of that fart sack and get up and get going!*

fast one *n.* a clever and devious trick. (Compare with PULL A FAST ONE.) □ *That was a fast one. I didn't know you were so devious.* □ *This was the last fast one like that you'll ever pull on me.*

fat-arse around See FART-ARSE AROUND.

fat-cat 1. *n.* someone who is ostentatiously and smugly wealthy. □ *I like to watch the fat-cats go by in their rollers.* □ *I'm no fat-cat. I'm usually financially embarrassed, in fact.* **2.** *mod.* having to do with wealth or a wealthy person. □ *You'll never see me driving any of those fat-cat cars.* □ *I just have a bank account. No fat-cat investments.*

fat chance *n.* no hope or chance whatever. (Sarcastic.) □ *Fat chance I'll ever get a new car.* □ *Me, get a job? Fat chance.*

fathead *n.* a stupid person; someone who has fat where brains ought to be. □ *You can be such a fathead!* □ *Paul, you are being a perfect fat-head.*

fatheaded *mod.* stupid. □ *Now that is a really fatheaded idea.* □ *It's not fatheaded!* □ *Let's not come up with another fatheaded plan. This one has to make sense.*

fatso AND **fatty** *n.* a fat person. (Offensive. Also a term of address.) □ *Hey, fatso! Go on a diet!* □ *Okay fatty, you get the biggest piece of cake because there's more of you to feed.* □ *Some fatso tried to get on the plane and couldn't even get through the door!*

fatty See FATSO.

favourite *mod.* excellent; ideal. □ *This is a favourite day!* □ *Mary's got herself a favourite of a new job.*

fax-up *vb. phr.* to send a fax to the wrong recipient. □ *Woops, we've faxed-up here, I think.* □ *This confidential information must not be faxed-up, all right?*

feart *mod.* afraid; scared. (Scots usage.) □ *Feart? Me? Am no feart! (Scared? Me? I'm not afraid!)* □ *She dizny act like she's feart.*

fearty *n.* a coward. (Scots usage.) □ *Come oan, ye're jist a fearty like a' the rest. (Come on, you're just a coward like all the rest.)* □ *Why do we get all the fearties here?*

feather-bed someone *vb. phr.* to make someone very comfortable. □ *Now, we're not going to feather-bed you, you know.* □ *I don't expect you to feather-bed me.*

feathers *n.* pubic hair. (Taboo. Always plural.) □ *A woman who shows her feathers is just the lowest.* □ *They dance completely nude in there, with feathers and everything on view.*

fed-upness *n.* the condition of being fed up. □ *There's a lot of fed-upness around here. You better explain what's happening.* □ *There's enough fed-upness among the people working here to cut with a knife.*

fed (up) to the back teeth with something or someone *phr.* extremely bored or dissatisfied with something or someone. □ *I am fed up to the back teeth with him and in the end I told him as much!* □ *We are all fed to the back teeth with nonsense like this.*

fed up (with something or someone) *mod.* bored or dissatisfied with something or someone, typically too much of something or someone. □ *I'm fed up with all this rain. When will it stop?* □ *Joe got fed up waiting for you and went out to the pub.*

feed *n.* a comedian's straight man. □ *The comic's feed kept getting his lines wrong and had to go.* □ *The trouble with the replacement feed was that the audience found him funnier than the comic.*

feed one's face *vb. phr.* to put food in one's mouth; to eat (something). □ *You're always feeding your face. You're going to get fat.* □ *Stop feeding your face and listen to me.*

feeling no pain *mod.* numbed by alcohol and feeling nothing; drunk. □ *Since she fell off the wagon she has been feeling no pain.* □ *He drank the whole thing, and he's feeling no pain.*

feel like death warmed up AND **feel like nothing on earth; feel like shit** *vb. phr.* to feel very ill. (FEEL LIKE SHIT is taboo.) □ *Oh dear, I feel like death warmed up.* □ *Carol feels like shit today, I'm afraid.*

feel like nothing on earth See FEEL LIKE DEATH WARMED UP.

feel like shit See FEEL LIKE DEATH WARMED UP.

feel someone's collar *vb. phr.* to arrest someone. (Police.) □ *The cops want to feel Harry's collar.* □ *Let's feel this hooligan's collar.*

feel someone up *vb. phr.* to caress intimately; to pet sexually. (Taboo.) □ *If you try to feel me up I'll scream!* □ *He felt her up, yet she said nothing.*

fem(me) *n.* a passive, feminine lesbian. (Crude.) □ *It's not obvious to most people that these femmes are lesbian.* □ *That little quiet one is Donna's new fem.*

fence 1. *vb.* to deal in stolen goods; to sell stolen goods.. □ *Oh, we know Harry's been fencing for years. All we need now is the proof.* □ *How did they manage to fence a unique painting like that?* **2.** *n.* a dealer in stolen goods. □ *Oh, we know Harry's a fence, Inspector. The hard bit is to prove it.* □ *There's another big-time fence around here and I want him!*

festering fool AND **festering idiot** *n.* an impossibly stupid person. (Scots usage.) □ *Get awa' ye festering fool!* □ *What a festering idiot!*

festering idiot See FESTERING FOOL.

fetch up *vb. phr.* to empty one's stomach; to vomit. (Crude.) □ *I think I'm going to have to go and fetch up.* □ *See if you can get him to fetch up.*

fib 1. *vb.* to tell a small lie. (Childish.) □ *Stop fibbing and tell me the truth.* □

Did you fib to the teacher? **2.** *n.* a small lie. □ *It was just a little fib. I'm sorry.* □ *Is this another one of your fibs?*

fibber *n.* a liar. (Childish.) □ *Harry can be a fibber sometimes. You've got to watch him.* □ *Jimmy is turning into a little fibber.*

fiddle 1. *vb.* to swindle, cheat or lie. □ *Bruno fiddled him out of his money.* □ *Don't try to fiddle me. I know the score.* **2.** *n.* a difficult or frustrating task. □ *The task I was given was a fiddle, for sure.* □ *This job is a real fiddle.*

fiddler *n.* a swindler, cheater or liar. □ *That filthy fiddler told the police where I was.* □ *Harry is a certified fiddler. Don't trust him with a penny!*

field of wheat *n.* a street. (Rhyming slang.) □ *She stood on the field of wheat and cried.* □ *There he was, walking down the field of wheat.*

fife and drum *n.* a buttock. (Rhyming slang, linked as follows: fife and drum ≈ [bum] = buttock. Always in the plural.) □ *She needs some jeans that will flatter her fifes and drums.* □ *With fifes and drums like hers, they'll have to be flattened a lot before jeans will do any flattering.*

FIFO *phr.* "first in, first out," the first items placed in the stack are the first items to be retrieved. (Computer jargon. Pronounced FI-fo. Compare with GIGO and LIFO.) □ *Of course the wrong thing came out. That register is FIFO.* □ *Oh, I thought this thing was FIFO, and I put the stuff in the wrong order.*

fifty-fifty *mod.* even or equal. □ *The chances of success are about fifty-fifty.* □ *Even at fifty-fifty, it's probably worth it, you know.*

fifty-two See FIVE-TO-TWO.

file 13 See CIRCULAR FILE.

filleted See GUTTED.

fill someone in *vb. phr.* to inform or advise. □ *I already filled him in on this.* □ *All right, now fill us in with the rest of the story.*

fill the bill AND **fit the bill** *vb. phr.* to fit or suit a requirement or need. □ *Does this one fill the bill?* □ *This about fits the bill.*

filth *n.* the police. (Normally with *the*.) □ *Here comes the filth!* □ *The filth are out to get me, you know.*

filthy lucre *n.* money. (In fact from the King James Version of the Bible: Titus, Chapter 1 Verse 11: "…teaching things which they ought not, for filthy lucre's sake.") □ *I certainly could use a little of that filthy lucre.* □ *I don't want to touch any of your filthy lucre.*

filthy (rich) 1. *mod.* very wealthy. □ *There are too many filthy rich people now.* □ *Ken is filthy because of the money his uncle left him.* **2.** *n.* people who are very wealthy. □ *The filthy rich can afford that kind of thing, but I can't.* □ *I sort of feel sorry for the filthy…but not that sorry.*

financially embarrassed *mod.* broke. □ *I'm a bit financially embarrassed at the moment.* □ *Gary found himself financially embarrassed when the time came to pay the bill.*

find 1. *n.* a person worth getting to know. □ *The find was waiting outside the office for him.* □ *He's a real find.* **2.** *vb.* to steal. (A euphemism.) □ *Otto has gone out to find a car for the bank job.* □ *Otto found a Mercedes.*

find one's feet *vb. phr.* to learn how to perform a new task or cope with a new situation. □ *It was still the first week and I was still trying to find my feet.* □ *Once you find your feet, you'll love it here.*

find something *vb. phr.* to obtain a job. □ *I'm pleased to hear you've found something at last. Does the work suit you?* □ *Of course there are jobs! All you have to do is look and you'll soon find something.*

fine and dandy *n.* brandy. (Rhyming slang.) □ *He handed me a glass of find and dandy and we sat down.* □ *Any more of that find and dandy, squire?*

fine print AND **small print** *n.* the details, especially of a contract or agreement. □ *I want to know the fine print before I agree to anything.* □ *So what does the small print say?*

fine weather for ducks *phr.* very wet weather. □ *Raining? I'll say! It was fine weather for ducks.* □ *I looked out the* *window and saw it was fine weather for ducks. I reached for my umbrella.*

finger 1. *vb.* to point someone out; to identify someone (as having done something, been somewhere, etc.). □ *Pete fingered Marty as being the one who arrived first.* □ *Nobody would dare finger Rocko as the one who did it.* **2.** *n.* someone who identifies criminals for the police; a police informer. (Underworld.) □ *Tracy has become a finger for the rozzers.* □ *Yep, she turned finger after her last holiday.*

fingers 1. *n.* a pickpocket. □ *The fingers tried a snatch, but the punter turned around at the wrong time.* □ *Watch out for fingers at the racetrack.* **2.** *n.* a policeman. □ *Think about how the fingers on the beat is affected by this cold.* □ *The fingers stopped at the door, tried the lock, and moved on.*

finish up *vb. phr.* to end up. □ *I don't want to finish up on the scrapheap.* □ *That's a terrible way to finish up.*

fink *vb.* to think. (Eye-dialect. Typical spoken English in London and surrounding area. Used in writing only for effect. Used in the examples of this dictionary.) □ *I don't give a tinker's what you fink, mate. I want me money!* □ *There's too much finking at them universities, I reckon. It must be bad for you.*

finnip *n.* a five Pound note. □ *Burnside slipped him a finnip and faded into the fog.* □ *For a finnip, the tramp led Burnside to the place where the crate still lay in the alley.*

fire away *vb. phr.* to start asking questions; to start talking. □ *Okay, I'm ready. Fire away.* □ *The detective fired away at him for almost an hour.*

fireball *n.* an energetic and ambitious person; a go-getter. □ *That fellow is a real fireball when it comes to sales.* □ *I don't want to hire some young fireball. I need wisdom and thoughtfulness.*

fireman's hose *n.* a nose. (Rhyming slang.) □ *I want some glasses that sit in just the right place on my wonderful fireman's hose.* □ *What a fireman's hose on that guy!*

fire-proof *mod.* invulnerable. □ *It's good to be fire-proof!* □ *You really*

think no one can touch you, that you're fire-proof, eh? We'll see!

fireworks 1. *n.* excitement. □ *When the fireworks are over, come in and we'll talk.* □ *What're all the fireworks about around here?* **2.** *n.* trouble; a display of temper. □ *After Bruno's fireworks, we calmed down a little.* □ *Cut out the fireworks, Sally. Calm down and get back to work.*

firkin 1. *n.* something for which the correct name has been forgotten or was never known. □ *What're you supposed to do with this firkin?* □ *Hand me that firkin with the copper base, will you?* **2.** *mod.* FUCKING. (Crude. A euphemism.) □ *Get that firkin cat out of here!* □ *I can't stand firkin swearing.*

firm 1. *n.* a criminal gang. □ *Mr Big's firm is getting really dangerous these days.* □ *There's a rival firm around here, too.* **2.** *n.* a squad of detectives. □ *The firm will catch up with you some day.* □ *Inspector Burnside's firm like to think they always get their man.* **3.** *n.* a group of doctors, nurses and other medical professionals who work together as a team. □ *I joined Professor McLean's firm last week.* □ *It's important to be looked after by the right firm.*

firmware *n.* those parts of computer software which have been etched permanently into a memory chip within a computer so that it is always present when the computer is switched on. (Computer jargon. Compare with LIVE-WARE, VAPOURWARE and WETWARE.) □ *The basic operating system is in firmware.* □ *Firmware's okay, but when there's a bug there it's a bitch to work around.*

fish-eaters *n.* a knife and a fork. (Especially when used for eating a fish dish.) □ *It's not often we get the fish-eaters out around here.* □ *We are supposed to use fish-eaters for eating a fish, you know.*

fishing *n.* the art of gathering information while appearing to be doing something else. □ *She's not really any good at fishing. It was obvious what she was up to.* □ *It's amazing what you can learn by means of fishing*

fishy *mod.* dubious; questionable; likely to be improper or illegal. (Compare with SMELL FISHY.) ☐ *Something here is fishy.* ☐ *That was a pretty fishy story you told us.*

fist 1. *n.* a hand. ☐ *If your fists so much as brush by my jacket again, you are finished!* ☐ *Get your fist off my car!* **2.** *n.* handwriting. ☐ *Well, I could read his fist—just about.* ☐ *Try to write in a reasonable fist if you can.*

fitba' *n.* the game of football (soccer) as it is called in Glasgow. (Scots usage. Eye-dialect.) ☐ *Oor Willie's fitba' crazy.* ☐ *Are you going to the park for a game of fitba', Willie?*

fit someone up *vb. phr.* to frame an innocent person for a crime. (Police.) ☐ *The police here are always fitting people up.* ☐ *No they're not; they only fit up people when they can't find genuine evidence.*

fit the bill See FILL THE BILL.

fit-up 1. *n.* a temporary stage. ☐ *He climbed onto the fit-up and declaimed the whole of Hamlet's soliloquy.* ☐ *We built the fit-up over there, but then we were told to move it.* **2.** *n.* the framing of an innocent person for a crime. (Police.) ☐ *It's a fit-up!* ☐ *No, it's not a fit-up, Otto. The evidence is overwhelming.*

fit-up company *n.* a travelling theatrical company. ☐ *I spent many years travelling around with a fit-up company.* ☐ *There are very few fit-up companies left; I blame television.*

fiver *n.* a five pound note. (Compare with TENNER.) ☐ *This thing only cost me a fiver.* ☐ *Give him a fiver, and let's get away from here.*

five-to-two AND **fifty-two** *n.* a Jewish person. (Offensive. Rhyming slang.) ☐ *Don't call Jewish people five-to-twos, please. It is very offensive and racist.* ☐ *He said he was not a racist, he just hated this particular fifty-two!*

fix 1. *n.* a dose of a drug, especially for an addict who is in need of drugs. (It "fixes" the suffering of withdrawal.) ☐ *It was clear that the prisoner needed a fix, but there was nothing the fuzz would do for him.* ☐ *Max arranged to get a fix into the jug.* **2.** *vb.* to neuter, castrate or spay an animal, especially a pet. (Jocularly of people.) ☐ *Get somebody to fix your cat!* ☐ *Sally suggested that the vet ought to fix Beavis—if he isn't fixed already.* **3.** *vb.* to influence the outcome of a contest or election, with the implication that this has been done improperly or illegally. ☐ *Who fixed this race?* ☐ *Bruno knows what it takes to fix an election—cash.* **4.** *n.* an implicitly improper or illegal scheme to influence the outcome of a contest or election. ☐ *Something is wrong with this game. I smell a fix.* ☐ *Bruno planned a great fix, but the cops got wise.* **5.** *n.* a repair made to a computer or software running on a computer. (Computer jargon.) ☐ *This little fix should make the whole program run faster.* ☐ *I wrote a beautiful fix to make the program more efficient; now it won't run at all.* **6.** *n.* a "cure" for a social ill. (Compare with QUICK FIX.) ☐ *There is no easy fix for a problem like this.* ☐ *Some people think there is no fix at all.* **7.** *n.* a bribe. ☐ *Someone in here has been taking fixes.* ☐ *He took the fix and won't get in the way.*

fixed 1. *mod.* doped; intoxicated. ☐ *Max is comfortable now that he's fixed.* ☐ *He was fixed and broke—in a real mess, I'd say.* **2.** *mod.* bribed. ☐ *Don't worry, the night watchman is fixed.* ☐ *The cop is fixed and won't give you guys any trouble.* **3.** *mod.* having the outcome pre-arranged. (Implicitly by improper or illegal means. Said of a contest or election.) ☐ *The election was fixed, and we are going to protest.* ☐ *It was not fixed!* ☐ *The race was supposed to be fixed, but we won anyway.* **4.** *mod.* [of an animal] neutered, castrated or spayed. ☐ *Now that the cat is fixed, she seems even more bad-tempered.* ☐ *I wouldn't buy anything but an already-fixed dog.*

fixed up *mod.* provided with a date. ☐ *Sam got fixed up with Martha.* ☐ *Okay, Sam is fixed up with a date for Saturday.*

fixer *n.* an agent for a performer, actor, etc. ☐ *He's a pretty pathetic small-time* *fixer for small-time artists.* □ *What a despicable little fixer he is.*

fix someone up 1. *vb. phr.* to provide someone with accommodation, etc. □ *Yes, I'll fix him up for a few weeks.* □ *Could you fix another person up as well?* 2. *vb. phr.* to provide someone with an acceptable companion of the opposite sex. □ *Oh, I can fix you up if you want.* □ *He tried to fix me up with a girl.* 3. *vb. phr.* to murder someone. (Irish usage.) □ *Watch it! Otto would fix you up you as soon as look at you.* □ *I'm gonna fix you up once and for all.*

fixture *n.* a planned sporting event. □ *The next big fixture is on Saturday.* □ *Are you planning to attend the fixture?*

fixtures and fittings *n.* the fixed furnishings of a house or an apartment. (Typically consisting of such things as built-in furniture, light fittings and, possibly, carpets and curtains.) □ *Does your price for the house include the fixtures and fittings?* □ *I don't like the fixtures and fittings, I'm afraid.*

flab *n.* obesity or flabbiness. □ *Fight that flab!* □ *She looks as if she's nothing but flab!*

flabbergasted *mod.* surprised; astonished; dumbfounded. □ *We were flabbergasted by your proposal.* □ *They all sat there flabbergasted.*

flack See FLAK.

flaff around *vb. phr.* to behave in a confused or agitated way. □ *Don't flaff around, tell me what's really wrong.* □ *If you flaff around like this we can't help.*

flag day *n.* menstruation time. (Crude.) □ *Sue doesn't go swimming when it's her flag day.* □ *Kim's having her flag day and is in a foul mood.*

flak AND **flack** *n.* complaints; criticism; negative feedback. □ *Why do I have to get all the flak for what you did?* □ *We're getting a lot of flack for that news broadcast.*

flaked out AND **flakers** *mod.* unconscious; exhausted; tired out. □ *Tom? He's upstairs flakers from work.* □ *There are too many flaked out people working at dangerous machines.*

flake (out) *vb. (phr.)* to pass out from exhaustion; to fall asleep. □ *I just flaked out. I had had it.* □ *After jogging, I usually flake for a while.*

flakers See FLAKED OUT.

flak(e)y *mod.* eccentric; crazy. □ *The whole set up in there is really flakey.* □ *She's flaky, but nice.*

flame *vb.* to write an excited and angry note on a computer bulletin board. (Computer jargon.) □ *Barb is flaming again. It doesn't take much to set her off.* □ *Stop flaming a minute and try to explain your position calmly.*

flaming *mod.* enraged; livid. □ *He's come back, and he's really flaming.* □ *I was flaming! I could have screamed.*

Flaming heck! AND **Flaming hell!** *exclam.* an expression of disappointment, anger or both. (Crude. Euphemisms for "fucking hell.") □ *Flaming heck, why should we do that?* □ *Why the flaming hell should we do that?*

Flaming hell! See FLAMING HECK!

flanker *n.* a trick, sharp practice or a swindle. □ *What sort of flanker did you get ripped off with?* □ *Gerry has a new money-making flanker, but he hasn't made any yet.*

flannel 1. *n.* nonsense. □ *You're talking flannel again—as usual.* □ *What flannel that is!* 2. *n.* flattery. □ *All he has said is just so much flannel, you know.* □ *Oh, it's not flannel. He is such a sincere young man.* 3. *n.* a small washcloth. □ *So I picked up the flannel and started on the dishes.* □ *There was just one filthy flannel.* 4. *vb.* to flatter. □ *I'll say this; he certainly knows how to flannel.* □ *Why must you flannel all the time to everybody?*

flannelled fools *n.* a humorous or derisive term for people who play cricket. □ *Have you ever stopped to watch these flannelled fools and their strange game?* □ *If you ever wonder why they're called flannelled fools, just watch a while.*

flap 1. *n.* an argument; a minor scandal. □ *I'm sorry about that flap we had yesterday, but it was all your fault.* □ *Who started this flap anyway?* 2. *vb.* to panic; to become excited. □ *Don't flap,* *it'll be all right.* □ *Aunt Flora's flapping again.* **3.** *n.* a panic; an excitement. □ *Try not to start a flap in there.* □ *A flap will not help. Calm down.*

flap around 1. *vb. phr.* to rush about in an aimlessly manner. □ *If you flap around about like that you'll miss something important.* □ *Stop flapping around about and just listen for a moment!* **2.** See also see FAFF ABOUT.

flapjack *n.* a lady's powder compact. □ *I think I've left my flapjack in the ladies' room.* □ *She flipped open her flapjack and powdered her nose.*

flaps 1. *n.* the ears. (Always with *the.*) □ *He was grabbed by the flaps and forcibly removed from the premises.* □ *Pull back your flaps, this is worth hearing!* **2.** *n.* the female sexual organ. (Taboo. Always in the plural, always with *the.*) □ *A woman who shows her flaps is just the lowest.* □ *They dance completely nude in there, with flaps and everything on view.*

flash 1. *mod.* flashy, garish. □ *Look at that flash git over there.* □ *If you did not dress so flush you would not attract so many comments from passers-by.* **2.** *vb.* to display something briefly. □ *You'd better not flash a wad like that around here. You won't have it long.* □ *The WPC flashed her badge and nicked him.* **3.** *n.* lysergic acid diethylamide, or LSD, an hallucinogenic drug. □ *You can get some good flash in this part of town.* □ *What does flash cost around here?*

flasher *n.* someone, usually a man, who briefly exhibits his sexual organ. (Crude.) □ *The cops caught the flasher and took him away.* □ *Sarah said she thought she saw a flasher in the library.*

Flash Harry *n.* a man who dresses in an expensive and flashy manner but lacks taste or elegance. □ *Take a look at this Flash Harry.* □ *That Flash Harry you mentioned was not there.*

flashing *n.* the practice of briefly exhibiting one's sexual organ in public. (Crude.) □ *There was a flashing at the cricket match this afternoon.* □ *Have you ever been present at a flashing, Martha?*

flash (it) See FLASH ONE'S MEAT.

flash of light *n.* a gaudily dressed person, particularly a woman. (Rhyming slang, linked as follows: flash of light ≈ [bright] = gaudy.) □ *I'm sorry but we really don't need another flash of light working here.* □ *What's a flash of light like that doing around here?*

flash one's meat AND **flash (it)** *vb. phr.* to briefly exhibit one's sexual organ in public. (Taboo.) □ *The guy flashed his meat and moved on down the street.* □ *She flashed briefly, providing the show that people came to see, and left the stage.*

flash the ash *vb. phr.* to offer a cigarette. □ *He flashed the ash but not one other person around the table was interested.* □ *I don't think you should flash the ash here; it's the annual meeting of the Campaign To End Smoking.*

flat-back *vb.* to perform sexual intercourse, from the female perspective. (Taboo.) □ *She was flat-backing, right there at the back of the room!* □ *All men want to do is flat-back you and forget you.*

flat-backer *n.* a prostitute. (Crude.) □ *The Old Bill hauled her in because she looked like a flat-backer.* □ *Clare dresses like a flat-backer.*

flat (broke) *mod.* having no money at all. □ *Sorry, I'm flat broke. Not a penny on me.* □ *You may be flat broke, but you'll find a way to pay your electricity bill or learn to live in the dark.*

flatfoot *n.* a police officer, especially one on foot patrol. □ *Think about how the flatfoot on the beat is affected by this cold.* □ *The flatfoot stopped at the door, tried the lock and moved on.*

flatmate *n.* a roommate or housemate. □ *I'll have to see if my flatmate agrees first.* □ *Alan's flatmate is a girl, you idiot!*

flat out *mod.* at top speed. □ *They drove the thing flat out for an hour.* □ *If we run flat out, we can get there before dusk.*

flat-out *mod.* all-out. □ *If we make an flat-out effort we can still win.* □ *It's important that we keep this going flat-out.*

flat spin 1. *n.* an almost horizontal spin by an aircraft. □ *Oh lord, he's gone into a flat spin!* □ *Fear not, he knows how to get out of a flat spin.* **2.** *n.* panic or excitement. □ *I was in a flat spin for a while, I'm afraid.* □ *Try not to get into a flat spin again, Arthur.*

flatten *vb.* to knock someone down with a blow. □ *Max flattened the kid with a jab to the nose.* □ *Wilbur will flatten his opponent.*

flatters *mod.* flat. □ *I say, your lawn is really flatters, eh?* □ *What a flatters tummy you have, Belinda.*

flat top *n.* an aircraft carrier. □ *The flat top was bouncing up and down like a cork in the stormy sea.* □ *Landing on a flat top in a storm at night is either unforgettable or unsurviveable, they say.*

flavour of the month *n.* a sarcastic name for the current fashion. □ *So, are tartan ties flavour of the month?* □ *Why do you always have to wear the flavour of the month, then?*

flea-bag 1. *n.* a cheap, low-quality, hotel. □ *I won't stay in this fleabag for one minute.* □ *Harry never stays in fleabags. He's too proud. Bruno doesn't care.* **2.** *n.* a bed. □ *I was so tired I could hardly find my flea-bag.* □ *Somebody put a spider in my flea-bag.* **3.** *n.* a unattractive dog. □ *Why do you keep a flea-bag like that?* □ *The ugly old flea-bag frightened me.*

flea-pit *n.* a rundown or dilapidated cinema. □ *If you think I'm going to sit and watch a film in a flea-pit like that, think again.* □ *Our local cinema really was a flea-pit by the time it closed down.*

flea powder *n.* drugs of inferior quality. □ *This stuff is terrible; real flea powder!* □ *Have you nothing better than this flea powder?*

fleece *vb.* to cheat someone; to steal everything from someone. (Underworld.) □ *Brian fleeced the kids of a lot of money.* □ *Rich never tried to fleece anybody.*

fleeing *mod.* very intoxicated due to drink or drugs. (Scots usage.) □ *Shuggy came hame fleeing agin last night.* □ *I got there late and everyone was already fleeing.*

Fleet Street *n.* the collective name for London's newspapers. (Fleet street was the centre of London's printing business from about 1500 onwards. Newspapers offices began moving out in the 1980s and by the mid-1990s all had left. However this is still their collective name.) □ *Let's see what Fleet Street makes of this in tomorrow's papers.* □ *I think the whole of Fleet Street is outside wanting to interview you, sir.*

flick *n.* a film; a movie. □ *That was a pretty good flick, eh?* □ *Let's go see that new Woody Allen flick.*

flies' cemetery *n.* a cake consisting of a layer of currants sandwiched between shortbread layers. □ *I love flies' cemetery.* □ *Have another slice of my aunt's delicious flies' cemetery.*

flight deck *n.* the female breasts. (Crude. Normally with *the* and in the plural.) □ *My flight deck isn't all I might have wished for.* □ *Cor, look at the flight deck on that, Fred!*

flim *n.* any banknote which has a face value of five Pounds Sterling. □ *He put a number of flims into the top pocket of my shirt and said that there are plenty more to be had if I asked no questions.* □ *That'll be 15 please, sir. Or 10 in flims, if you prefer.*

flimflam 1. *n.* nonsense; deception. □ *Beware of the flimflam they will try to pull on you.* □ *I can spot flimflam a mile away.* **2.** *vb.* to cheat or deceive (someone). □ *Don't try to flimflam me. I wasn't born yesterday, you know.* □ *She is flimflamming over at the village fair this week.* **3.** *n.* idle chatter; trivia. □ *We talked a lot of flimflam but did not get down to business.* □ *I didn't come here to listen to flimflam. Tell me what you are really after.*

flimsy 1. *n.* thin paper. □ *The fragile crockery was all wrapped up in flimsy.* □ *Where did you find all that flimsy?* **2.** *n.* a copy made on thin paper. □ *Make a flimsy of this and send it off to the head office.* □ *He opened a box which turned out to be full of some very interesting flimsies.* **3.** *n.* women's underwear made from very fine material. □ *She stood there in nothing but her* flimsies. □ *Oh, I don't think I could wear a flimsy like that!* **4.** *n.* a conduct certificate issued to a naval officer by his or her superior at the end of their time spent under that command. □ *I've got my flimsy!* □ *He took the flimsy and filed it away carefully.*

flip 1. *vb.* to go crazy. □ *Oh boy, I've got so much to do, I may just flip.* □ *The guy flipped. He was the nervous type.* **2.** *n.* a short pleasure flight in an aircraft. □ *We just went up for a flip.* □ *They don't allow flips around here. Being on the final approach-path into a major international airport might just have something to do with it, yes.* **3.** *n.* a brief tour. □ *Come on, let's go for a flip round the area.* □ *Fancy a flip somewhere today?* **4.** *mod.* flippant; glib. □ *His talk is flip, but his action is gross.* □ *He is a flip operator.*

flip-flop *n.* a rubber-soled sandal held on by a toe-thong. □ *You can hear people in flip-flops before you see them.* □ *Where are my flip-flops?*

flip one's lid AND **flip one's top; flip one's wig.** *vb. phr.* to become extremely emotional, almost insane. (See FLIP.) □ *All right! Try not to flip your lid!* □ *Really, she flipped her wig when she heard about it.*

flip one's top See FLIP ONE'S LID.

flip one's wig See FLIP ONE'S LID.

flip (out) *vb. (phr.)* to lose control of oneself. □ *I almost flipped out when I heard about it.* □ *He got so angry that he flipped.*

flipping *mod.* FUCKING. (Crude. A euphemism.) □ *Get this flipping dog out of here!* □ *What's the flipping idea?*

flip side *n.* the "other" side of a gramaphone record. □ *On the flip side, we have another version of "Love Me Tender" sung by Sandy Softly.* □ *You really should listen to the flip side sometime.*

flit(ting) See MOONLIGHT FLITTING.

float *n.* the money retained in the till of a shop, etc. □ *He went to the bank every morning to get a new float.* □ *The float was usually about £100.*

float around AND **knock around** *vb. phr.* to wander around aimlessly, or to

no purpose. □ *I think I'll knock around a few months before looking for another job.* □ *We're just knocking around and keeping out of trouble.*

floater 1. *n.* a government stock certificate considered to be acceptable collateral for a loan. □ *Yes, the bank will accept floaters.* □ *What's the face value of your floater?* **2.** *n.* an error. □ *What a floater! You must be embarrassed.* □ *Well, that was a bad floater.* **3.** *n.* an uncommitted voter. □ *He won't say which party he supports; put him down as a floater.* □ *There's an awful lot of floaters around here.* **4.** *n.* a drowned corpse. (Police, etc.) □ *There's a floater in the river.* □ *We've got to get the floater onto dry land first.* **5.** *n.* a sausage in soup. □ *Floaters are always acceptable to Otto.* □ *A serving of soup and floater came next.* **6.** *n.* a spot before the eyes. (Always used in the plural.) □ *Harold's gone to see his doctor about these floaters he's been getting.* □ *Are floaters serious?*

flob *vb.* to spit. (Childish.) □ *Angry? I could've flobbed!* □ *None of your flobbing in here!*

flog *vb.* to sell. □ *So, what are you trying to flog me today?* □ *We've got to flog this stuff now before people find out it's stolen.*

floored *mod.* knocked to the floor by a blow. □ *Wilbur was floored by his opponent.* □ *The guy was floored and didn't move a muscle-ever again.*

floosie *n.* a promiscuous woman; a prostitute. (Crude.) □ *Tracy was enraged when Rocko called her a floosie.* □ *"I didn't call you a floosie," said Rocko. "I said you were boozy."*

flop *n.* a failure. □ *What do you mean your life has been a flop?* □ *The play was a flop. The entire audience—all five of them—left during the second act.*

flophouse *n.* a very cheap hotel inhabited by vagrants. (Crude.) □ *This place is a flophouse! I won't stay here for a moment.* □ *All some of those guys look for in life is a flop in a flophouse.*

flopper-stopper *n.* a brassiere. (Crude.) □ *With tiny boobs like mine, I hardly need a flopper-stopper at all.* □ *Susan's* *huge bazoombas require huge flopper-stoppers, too.*

flowers (and frolics) *n.* the testicles. (Taboo. Rhyming slang, linked as follows: flowers (and frolics) ≈ [bollocks] = testicles. Normally with *the* and in the plural.) □ *The teacher preferred "testicles" to "flowers and frolics," if they had to be mentioned at all.* □ *He got hit right in the flowers.*

flowery (dell) *n.* a prison cell. (Rhyming slang.) □ *You won't find Jerry here; he's found himself back in the flowery dell!* □ *Another two years in the flowery. He felt utterly depressed.*

fluff 1. *n.* nonsense. □ *That's just a lot of fluff.* □ *Don't give me that fluff! I won't buy it.* **2.** *n.* a good-looking or attractive girl or young woman. □ *Now there's a really attractive bit of fluff.* □ *Look at her, isn't she a real fluff?* **3.** *vb.* to break wind. □ *Do you absolutely have to fluff all the time?* □ *That's disgusting, fluffing like that!*

Fluff off! *exclam.* "FUCK OFF!" (Crude. A euphemism.) □ *Fluff off! I don't want to go out with you!* □ *Can't you take a hint? Get lost! Just fluff off, won't you!*

fluff one's duff *vb. phr.* to masturbate. (Taboo.) □ *Well, fluffing your duff may be enough for you, but I want the real thing.* □ *You're not going to fluff your duff here!*

flummery *n.* a meaningless or pointless gesture; empty words. □ *No more flummery, please. What are the facts?* □ *All you ever get there is flummery.*

flummox *vb.* to bewilder or confuse. □ *Please do not try to flummox me any more than I am already.* □ *It was all the maths that flummoxed me, I'm sure.*

flummoxed *mod.* confused; silenced. □ *Well, now you've got me really flummoxed.* □ *I'm flummoxed. What's going on here?*

flump 1. *n.* a sudden dull noise. □ *There was a loud flump, and then silence.* □ *What is making these flumps?* **2.** *vb.* [for an aircraft] to land heavily. □ *You really flumped it that time, my lad. You're lucky we still have an undercarriage.* □ *Flumping the aircaft is not popular with the owners, you know.*

flunk *vb.* to fail an examination. □ *I flunked history again.* □ *I flunked all my exams except history.*

flunkey 1. *n.* a flatterer. □ *Who is that obsequious little flunkey?* □ *What a flunkey you are!* **2.** *n.* a snob. □ *I don't want to listen to that flunkey anymore.* □ *Mr Wilson is a flunkey, and people would tell him so if he didn't have so much money.*

flush *mod.* wealthy; with plenty of money. □ *Today I am flush. By tomorrow, I'll be broke.* □ *I'm not exactly flush, but I can pay the bills.*

fly *mod.* cunning; alert; knowing. □ *This fellow is fly; there's no question about it.* □ *We don't need any more fly people like you around here.*

fly a kite 1. *vb. phr.* to propose a plan that is known to be doubtful. □ *I know it's not certain to work, but I think it's worth flying a kite.* □ *Why did you fly such a ridiculous kite, John?* **2.** *vb. phr.* to smuggle things in or out of prison. □ *My girl will fly a kite for me.* □ *They caught a warder trying to fly a kite.* **3.** *vb. phr.* to write a letter begging for money. □ *It's sad to see a man like that reduced to flying a kite like this.* □ *You'd be surprised how often you do get money when you fly a kite.*

fly-boy AND **fly man** *n.* a man who lives by his wits or cunning. □ *There are a lot of fly-boys around here, so watch out.* □ *How can anyone ever trust a fly man like him?*

fly-by-night *mod.* undependable; dishonest. □ *Bruno seems like such a fly-by-night character.* □ *He's not fly-by-night at all.* □ *Don't do business with fly-by-night people.*

fly-by-nights *n.* tights; pantyhose. (Rhyming slang. Always used in the plural.) □ *I see you forgot to put on your fly-by-nights this morning, Mary.* □ *She was wearing multi-coloured fly-by-nights.*

flying *mod.* very intoxicated due to drink or drugs. □ *Tipsy? Flying, more like!* □ *Boy, I was really flying. I'll never drink another drop.*

fly man 1. *n.* a professional criminal. (Scots usage.) □ *Watch that one; he's a* *fly man all right.* □ *Yon fly man canna be trusted ta cross the road.* **2.** See also FLY-BOY.

fly-tipping *n.* the practice of secretly dumping rubbish at unapproved locations or without obtaining permission. □ *There's a lot of fly-tipping going on around here.* □ SHE: *Fly-tipping should be made a crime!* HE: *It is; the problem is catching people at it.*

foaming (at the mouth) *mod.* livid with rage. □ *Angry? He was foaming at the mouth!* □ *I really was foaming when I heard!*

foggiest (idea) *n.* a very vague or hazy idea. (Usually in the negative. Always with *the.*) □ *I'm sorry I don't know. I haven't the foggiest.* □ *I don't have the foggiest idea of how to do this.*

folderol See FALDERAL.

folding money AND **folding stuff** *n.* paper money (bank notes) as distinct from coins. □ *Sorry, I don't have any folding money with me. Can you pay?* □ *"Thank you, thank you," said the comedian as he finished his act, "Please just throw folding stuff, it hurts less."*

folding stuff See FOLDING MONEY.

fold (up) *vb. (phr.)* to fail; to close. □ *The play folded in the second week.* □ *I'm afraid that business folded up some time ago.*

folks *n.* one's parents. (Always with the possessive.) □ *I'll have to ask my folks if I can go.* □ *Her folks are sort of angry with her.*

folksie *mod.* concerned with folk-singing and folk music. □ *They're very folksie, you know.* □ *Folksie folk like other folk who are folksie.*

foodie *n.* someone obsessed about food. □ *Of course he's a foodie! Have you ever seen him not eating?* □ *The foodies all sit over there, near the kitchen.*

foot *n.* feet. (This is the plural of "foot," the measure of length and not the thing at the bottom of one's leg.) □ *This door is six foot nine tall.* □ *How many foot long is your new boat, John?*

foot-and-mouth disease *n.* the habitual making of faux-pas. □ *Unfortunately Harry makes remarks like that all the time. He seems to suffer from foot-and-*

mouth disease. □ *Oh no! My foot-and-mouth disease is showing again!*

footer AND **footy** *n.* the game of football. (Soccer.) □ *Anyone for a game of footer?* □ *The lads are playing footy in the park.*

footling *mod.* unimportant; trivial. □ *He came up with a stupid, footling suggestion; it was pathetic, really.* □ *It was just a footling little place.*

Footsie *n.* The Financial Times Stock Exchange Index. □ *How's the Footsie's behaving?* □ *The Footsie's gone up nicely today.*

footslog *n.* a very lengthy or exhausting march or walk. □ *Yes, It's a footslog but well worth it.* □ *That was a long footslog today.*

foot-slogger *n.* an infantryman. (Military.) □ *The foot-sloggers marched all day.* □ *Who'd be a foot-slogger?*

footy See FOOTER.

for all I know *phr.* "as far as I know"; "I really don't know." □ *For all I know, they just did it for a lark.* □ *She came in late because she had an accident, for all I know.*

for (all) one's trouble *phr.* in spite of one's efforts; in very poor payment for one's efforts. □ *He got a punch in the jaw for his trouble.* □ *For all her trouble, she's got little to show for it.*

forbidden fruit *n.* something that is attractive because it is denied to one. (From the "Garden of Eden" in the Bible. See comments at FILTHY LUCRE.) □ *A new car became Ralph's forbidden fruit.* □ *Booze was forbidden fruit for Garry.*

for chicken feed See FOR PEANUTS.

For Christ's sake! *exclam.* an expression of surprise or irritation. (Taboo.) □ *For Christ's sake! What is the trouble now!* □ *For Christ's sake Harry, you can't do that!*

For crying out loud! *exclam.* an expression of surprise or irritation. □ *You can't do that, for crying out loud!* □ *For crying out loud! You'll break it if you do that!*

foreigner *n.* illicit work carried out at one's regular workplace for personal benefit. □ *They found out about Brian's* *foreigner, and now he's unemployed.* □ *It seems everyone here does foreigners.*

forever and a day *phr.* "forever more." □ *Is this going to go on forever and a day?* □ *I know it seems like forever and a day, but really it's just one week.*

for free *mod.* free from monetary charge; gratis. □ *And I get all this for free?* □ *Is all this really mine for free?*

For fucks sake! *exclam.* an expression of surprise or irritation. (Taboo.) □ *Oh, for fucks sake! I quit!* □ *For fucks sake get out of here now!*

Forget it! 1. *exclam.* "Never mind, it wasn't important!" □ *Forget it! It wasn't important.* □ *I had an objection, but just forget it!* **2.** *exclam.* "Never mind, it was no trouble at all!" □ *No trouble at all. Forget it!* □ *Forget it! It was my pleasure.*

for good and all AND **once (and) for all** *mod.* finally; conclusively; in order to finally remove any doubt. □ *I'm gonna take care of you for good and all!* □ *I would like to get this ridiculous problem settled once for all.*

fork and knife *n.* a wife. (Rhyming slang.) □ *My fork and knife disapproved of the film.* □ *I've got to go home to my fork and knife.*

for keeps *mod.* forever. □ *Does that mean I'm going to have this scar for keeps?* □ *This is yours for keeps. Enjoy it.*

for kicks *mod.* for fun; for a thrill. □ *We just did it for kicks. We didn't mean to hurt anyone.* □ *Let's drive over to Wally's place, just for kicks.*

form 1. *n.* a criminal's prison or police record. □ *Does Otto have form?* □ *Form? You bet Otto has form.* **2.** *n.* a procedure. □ *There's a form for this sort of thing.* □ *All right, what's the form?* **3.** *n.* a situation. □ *What kind of form do you have there now?* □ *So how do we get ourselves out of this form we're in, eh?*

fornicating *mod.* lying; infuriating. (Crude. A euphemistic variant of "fucking.") □ *That's just a lot of fornicating rubbish. Ignore it.* □ *I've heard enough of your fornicating.*

for openers AND **for starters** *phr.* "to begin with." □ *Well for openers, you've got all the important facts wrong.* □ *Could you sort this one out for starters, please.*

for peanuts AND **for chicken feed** *mod.* for practically no money at all. (Compare with CHICKEN FEED.) □ *I won't work for peanuts.* □ *You surely don't expect me to do this for chicken feed, do you?*

For Pete's sake! AND **For pity's sake!; For the love of Mike!** *exclam.* "Good grief!" □ *For Pete's sake! How've you been?* □ *For pity's sake! Ask the man to come in out of the cold!*

For pity's sake! See FOR PETE'S SAKE!

for real *mod.* genuine; not imaginary. □ *Ken is really strange. Is he for real?* □ *This whole day just isn't for real.*

for starters See FOR OPENERS.

For sure! *exclam.* "Certainly!"; "Without doubt!" □ *That's how it is here for sure!* □ *For sure, I mean what I say.*

for sure *mod.* for certain; without doubt. □ *He's finished for sure.* □ *For sure I'll go.*

Forth Bridge job *n.* anything requiring constant and unending attention. (For the reason for this, see PAINT THE FORTH BRIDGE.) □ *I think you're taking on a Forth Bridge job there, Simon.* □ *What a full-time, never-ending Forth Bridge job that turned out to be!*

for the best *mod.* with the best intent. □ *It may not seem so now, but this is for the best.* □ *It's for the best if you go.*

for the hell of it *mod.* because it is slightly evil; for no good reason. (Crude.) □ *The kids broke the window just for the hell of it.* □ *We just drove over for the hell of it.*

For the love of Mike! See FOR PETE'S SAKE!

forty winks *n.* a nap; a sleep. □ *I could use forty winks before I have to get to work.* □ *Before I get started again I need forty winks.*

fossil *n.* an old-fashioned person. □ *Some old fossil called the police about the noise.* □ *Oh, Ted, you are such a fossil!*

fouled up *mod.* messed up; ruined; tangled up. □ *This is a really fouled up mess.* □ *You really are fouled up, you know.*

foul mouth *n.* a person who uses obscene language habitually. □ *Terry, don't be such a foul mouth.* □ *Sally is turning into a real foul mouth.*

foul up 1. *n.* a blunder; an error. (Usually FOUL-UP.) □ *That was a fine foul-up! Is that your speciality?* □ *I can produce a serious foul up with both hands tied behind my back.* **2.** *vb. phr.* to blunder; to MESS UP. □ *Please don't foul up again. Okay?* □ *The goal-keeper fouled up in the first half, and that lost us the game.*

four-eyes *n.* someone who wears glasses. (Also a rude term of address.) □ *Well, I've got to the age where I'm a four-eyes.* □ *Hey, four-eyes, bet you can't see this!*

four-letter man *n.* an obnoxious man. □ *He's a real four-letter man.* □ *What does the four-letter man want?*

four-letter word *n.* a word commonly considered unacceptable, which often happens to have four letters. □ *None of your four-letter words in here, thank you.* □ *The air was thick with four-letter words, I tell you.*

fourpenny one 1. *n.* a scolding. □ *Tom got a fourpenny one for his part in the prank.* □ *Her mother gave her a fourpenny one when she finally got home.* **2.** *n.* a push or shove. □ *I gave him a fourpenny one and he just fell over, honest!* □ *What was that fourpenny one for, eh?*

four sheets in(to) the wind See BOTH SHEETS IN(TO) THE WIND.

fox someone *vb.* to delude or puzzle someone. □ *I'm just not going to be foxed.* □ *Are you trying to fox me?*

frame AND **frame-up** *n.* a scheme where an innocent person is made to take the blame for something; incrimination caused by contrived evidence. (Underworld.) □ *Brian must have been the victim of a frame-up, otherwise they'd never have caught him.* □ *The frame would have worked if it weren't for one little thing.*

frame someone *vb.* to cause an innocent person to be blamed for a crime; to contrive evidence so that someone appears to be guilty. (Originally underworld.) □ *Jimmy tried to frame his sister for painting the cat yellow.* □ *You won't frame me and get away with it!*

frame-up See FRAME.

France and Spain *n.* rain. (Rhyming slang.) □ *Oh no, France and Spain again.* □ *Don't just stand out there in the France and Spain!*

Franglais *n.* a supposed language which consists of an exotic (and comic) mixture of English and French. □ *Travelling in France with Charles is embarrassing, as he speaks a sort of Franglais.* □ *Sometimes Franglais is really very funny.*

frank *mod.* obscene; pornographic. (Crude. A euphemism.) □ *Psst! Want to buy some frank photographs?* □ *Frank? Disgusting, I'd call it.*

frank and fearless *n.* a discussion. (From the cliché.) □ *Time for a frank and fearless, eh?* □ *OK, we'll have a frank and fearless now.*

fraught *mod.* risky; dangerous. □ *Your plan is, let's say, fraught.* □ *You really are in a fraught situation here, you know.*

freak (out) 1. *vb. (phr.)* to panic; to lose control. □ *I was so frightened, I thought I would freak.* □ *Come on, relax. Don't freak out.* **2.** *n.* a bad drug experience; a psychotic reaction to the drug L.S.D. (Usually FREAK-OUT or FREAKOUT.) □ *The poor kid had a freak-out and never really recovered.* □ *Some of them get turned off drugs by a really good freak-out.*

freak someone out *vb. phr.* to shock or disorient someone. □ *The whole business freaked me out.* □ *I didn't mean to freak out everybody with the bad news.*

freaky *mod.* strange; eccentric. □ *I get a freaky feeling whenever I hear that music.* □ *What a freaky film!* □ *That's really freaky.*

Fred *n.* a Tom and Jerry cartoon film. (From the name of the producer, Fred Quimby, whose name appeared during the opening titles of all the original se-ries.) □ *We all enjoy watching Freds.* □ *There was a Fred showing on the TV when we arrived.*

freebase 1. *vb.* to smoke a pure extract of cocaine. □ *Richy has never free-based in his life.* □ *Richy won't free-base, smoke or anything.* **2.** *n.* a smokable, pure extract of cocaine. □ *Max is real big on free base.* □ *Bruno likes freebase, too.*

freebaser *n.* a user of FREEBASE. (Drugs.) □ *Of course Max is a freebas-er! What doesn't he do?* □ *Some of these freebasers have heart attacks.*

freebasing *n.* using FREEBASE as a recreational drug. □ *Richy refuses to try freebasing.* □ *He saw what freebasing did to his brother.*

freebie AND **freebee; freeby** *n.* some-thing given away free. □ *They gave me a freebie with my purchase.* □ *I expect a freebee when I spend a lot of money like that.*

freeby See FREEBIE.

free-for-all See FREE FOR ALL.

free for all AND **free-for-all** *n.* a brawl; a general fight. □ *A free for all started on the beach over near the refreshment stand.* □ *The cops broke up the free-for-all.*

freeze *n.* the act of ignoring someone; the COLD SHOULDER. □ *Everybody seems to be giving me the freeze.* □ *I got the freeze from Julie. What did I do wrong?*

freeze someone out *vb.* to lock some-one out socially. □ *We didn't want to freeze you out. You failed to pay your dues, however.* □ *They froze out the newcomers.*

freezing cold *mod.* very cold. □ *It's freezing cold out there.* □ *I won't go out in freezing cold weather.* □ *Why does it have to be so freezing cold?*

French *n.* an act of oral sex upon a man. (Taboo.) □ *If you want to have French you better find another girl, buster!* □ *Fancy French, darling?*

Frenchie See FRENCH LETTER.

Frenchies *n.* French knickers. (Crude.) □ *There's a little shop just round the corner where you can buy new Frenchies, Ella.* □ *All her Frenchies*

were there on display, drying in her bathroom.

French kiss 1. *n.* kissing using the tongue; open mouth kissing. □ *What's French about a French kiss?* □ *The last thing he expected from Jane was a French kiss.* **2.** *vb. phr.* to kiss some-one using the tongue. □ *Kids like to try to French kiss each other at an early age. It's part of growing up.* □ *He tried to French kiss me, but I stopped him.*

French leave *n.* absent without permis-sion. □ *It seems he's taken French leave.* □ *If he's on French leave, sack him!*

French letter AND **Frenchie; froggie; frog-skin** *n.* a condom. (Crude. Com-pare with AMERICAN SOCK.) □ *I've got a French letter somewhere.* □ *"Forget it without a frog-skin!" she said.*

French letter on the prick of progress *phr.* anything or anyone that slows down or stops movement or develop-ment. (Taboo.) □ *You really are a French letter on the prick of progress, you reactionary!* □ *No, that'll never do; it would be like a French letter on the prick of progress.*

French loaf *n.* four Pounds Sterling. (This is an example of that rare beast, rhyming slang that depends upon back-slang to make the connection. In the following, *ruof*—or *roaf*—is backslang for *four*. The rhyming slang linking is thus : French loaf ≈ [ruof] = four Pounds Sterling.) □ *A French loaf? For that?* □ *Burnside slipped him a French loaf and faded into the fog.*

French someone *vb.* to perform oral sex upon a man. (Taboo.) □ *Give me 20 and I'll French you.* □ *That one will French anyone who pays.*

fresh 1. *mod.* cheeky; impudent. □ *Ken can be rather fresh sometimes.* □ *Kids get some pretty fresh ideas.* **2.** *mod.* somewhat aggressive sexually; prone to caress too eagerly. □ *Don't get fresh with me, Sunshine!* □ *He got fresh, so I slapped him.*

fresher *n.* a freshman. □ *Bob's a fresh-er at the university now.* □ *There was a gaggle of fresher in the bar.*

Friar (Tuck) *n.* sexual intercourse. (Taboo. A euphemism. Rhyming slang, linked as follows: Friar (Tuck) ≈ [fuck] = sexual intercourse.) □ *They were talking about, you know, Friar Tuck.* □ *She seems to think that calling it "Friar" makes all right.*

fricking *exclam.* FUCKING. (Crude. A euphemism.) □ *The fricking dog's chasing the cat again!* □ *Get that fricking animal out of here!*

fridge *n.* a refrigerator. □ *Put this in the fridge so it won't spoil.* □ *What's in the fridge tonight for dinner?*

fridge-freezer *n.* a unit combining the features of a refrigerator and a freezer. □ *She put the shopping away in the fridge-freezer.* □ *There's a fridge-freezer in the kitchen.*

frig *vb.* to masturbate. (Taboo.) □ *Someone has frigged or something in here!* □ *Girls frig as well as boys, you know.*

frigging 1. *mod.* FUCKING. (Taboo. A euphemism.) □ *Who made this frigging mess?* □ *I smashed up my frigging car!* **2.** *mod.* damnably. (Taboo.) □ *What a frigging stupid thing to do!* □ *That is a frigging dumb thing to do!*

frightener *n.* a scare. □ *Gosh, that was a right frightener, wasn't it?* □ *She does not like frighteners.*

frighten the hell out of someone AND **frighten the pants off someone; frighten the living daylights out of someone; frighten the shit out of someone; scare the hell out of someone; scare the living daylights out of someone; scare the pants off someone; scare the shit out of someone** *vb. phr.* to frighten someone badly, suddenly or both. (All are crude. SHIT is taboo.) □ *These figures frighten the hell out of me.* □ *The door blew shut and scared the shit out of me.* □ *It takes a lot to scare the pants off a hardened criminal.*

frighten the living daylights out of someone See FRIGHTEN THE HELL OUT OF SOMEONE.

frighten the pants off someone See FRIGHTEN THE HELL OUT OF SOMEONE.

frighten the shit out of someone See FRIGHTEN THE HELL OUT OF SOMEONE.

Fringe *n.* the Edinburgh Fringe Festival. (Normally with *the*. An informal collection of theatrical and other artistic events, exhibitions and so forth, taking place alongside the official Edinburgh Festival, but not part of it.) □ *Are you going to the Fringe this year?* □ *We saw a number of very strange events at the Fringe, but that's normal.*

fringe theatre *n.* a theatrical performance that exceeds or challenges current mainstream practices. □ *Do you often go to the fringe theatre?* □ *There is a group near us that often puts on fringe theatre.*

frisk someone 1. *vb.* to search someone quickly, as by the police or customs. □ *The cops frisked us all.* □ *"Right," the big rozzer said, "Frisk him!"* **2.** *vb.* to pick someone's pockets. (Criminal's cant.) □ *He frisked a wealthy-looking pedestrian.* □ *I've been frisked!*

frit *mod.* frightened; terrified. □ *She's a very frit person; try not to frighten her off.* □ *I feel a little frit every time I have to fly.*

Frog 1. *n.* a French person. (Offensive.) □ *Y'know, Otto, if you call a French person a Frog, he's likely to get nasty.* □ *Why can you never be polite to Frogs?* **2.** *n.* the French language. (Offensive.) □ *Why bother learning Frog? Most French people speak English.* □ *Do you speak Frog?*

frog and toad *n.* a road. (Rhyming slang.) □ *He was driving along the frog and toad when it happened.* □ *I hate travelling on that frog and toad.*

froggie See FRENCH LETTER.

froggy *mod.* French. (Potentially offensive.) □ *Do you like froggy wine?* □ *He's not sure about their wine, but Mike certainly likes froggy girls!*

frog in the throat *n.* a boat. (Rhyming slang.) □ *We sailed away in his frog in the throat.* □ *Three men sat in their frog in the throat out there for hours, just fishing I think.*

frog-skin See FRENCH LETTER.

frogspawn *n.* a sago or tapioca pudding. (Childish. Sago is a common children's "milk pudding" that is popular in Britain.) □ *Yuch! I hate frogspawn!* □ *Now, you eat up all your frogspawn. It's really yummy.*

from a child *mod.* since infancy or childhood. □ *Oh, he's been like that from a child.* □ *From a child she brought me up.*

from A to Z *mod.* of a complete and wide variety. □ *We have just about everything from A to Z.* □ *She ordered everything on the menu from A to Z.*

from here on in *phr.* "from this point forward." □ *From here on in we do it my way.* □ *I want everything clear from here on in.*

from Land's End to John O'Groats *phr.* the whole length of Great Britain. (It is commonly—but wrongly—supposed that Land's End and John O'Groats are the points farthest apart on the British mainland.) □ *To travel from Land's End to John O'Groats is supposed to be the longest journey you can make on the island of Great Britain.* □ *Just how far do you intend to walk? From Land's End to John O'Groats?*

from the year dot *mod.* from the very beginning; from the earliest times. □ *We've done it that way from the year dot.* □ *Nothing had changed from the year dot.*

front 1. *n.* a respectable or legitimate deportment, style or appearance; an outward form which is bluff or pretence. □ *Jan can put up a good front, but most of us know the real Jan.* □ *The front she put up collapsed as she heard the bad news.* **2.** *n.* a seemingly legitimate business behind which criminals operate their real business. □ *The restaurant is just a front.* □ *What we need is a convincing front.*

front bottom AND **front passage** *n.* the female sexual organ. (Taboo. Mock-childish.) □ *The door to the shower room flew open and the girl screamed, trying to cover her front bottom.* □ *If your dresses get any shorter, we'll all be able to see your front passage.*

front man 1. *n.* a respectable and well-known man who represents a less respectable person or organisation. □ *The former adviser now serves as a front*

man for a large foundation. □ *The front man came out and made an announcement.* **2.** *n.* a man who lures victims into a criminal trap of some sort. □ *Bruno is not a very convincing front man.* □ *The front man persuaded her to give him her credit card number.*

front passage See FRONT BOTTOM.

front runner *n.* the person or thing thought most likely to win or succeed. □ *The press found out some juicy secrets about the front runner and made them all public.* □ *Who is the front runner in the race to be MP?*

frot *vb.* to surreptitiously rub one's fully-clothed body up against that of another for purposes of sexual stimulation. (Crude. From the French *frotter*, meaning "to rub.") □ *Apparently there are people who frot every day on the Tube.* □ *I can't understand people who frot.*

froth-blower *n.* a beer-drinker. □ *Harry's certainly a froth-blower.* □ *Oh, there's a lot of froth-blowers around here!*

fruit *n.* a blatantly homosexual male. (Crude.) □ *So what if he's a fruit? He can still vote, can't he?* □ *He doesn't like being called a fruit.*

fry someone (up) *vb. (phr.)* to electrocute someone. □ *They're going to fry me up tonight.* □ *They fried Otto!*

fry-up 1. *n.* an electrocution. □ *I was not at Otto's fry-up.* □ *That's where they do the fry-ups.* **2.** AND **grease-up** *n.* the preparation and serving of fried food. □ *I could use a big fry-up.* □ *OK, let's have a grease-up.*

fubsy *n.* a short and fat person. □ *Even a fubsy like that has to earn a living.* □ *What does the fubsy want?*

fuck 1. *vb.* to perform sexual intercourse. (Taboo. A highly offensive word to most people. There are many additional meanings and constructions using this word. It is in fact Standard English, but virtually all applications of it are not.) □ *Two dogs were fucking out on the lawn.* □ *He actually said in public that he had—you know—fucked her.* **2.** *n.* a woman viewed strictly as a sex object. (Taboo.) □ *Joan is a good fuck.*

□ *I don't think many women would consider being called a "fuck" is much of a compliment.*

fuckable *mod.* acceptable as a sexual partner. (Taboo.) □ *Oh yes, she is most certainly fuckable.* □ *Lord, what a fuckable piece of crumpet!*

Fuck-a-duck! *exclam.* an expression of intense surprise or irritation. (Taboo.) □ *Oh fuck-a-duck, that can't be true!* □ *Fuck-a-duck! Don't be absurd!*

fuck-all *n.* nothing whatever. (Taboo.) □ *I assure you, there is fuck-all here!* □ *I have fuck-all to do these days.*

fucked 1. *mod.* [of objects] ruined; useless; damaged beyond repair. (Taboo.) □ *The thing is just completely fucked.* □ *If it's fucked, get another one.* **2.** *mod.* [of people] exhausted; defeated; unable to continue. (Taboo.) □ *I've been working hard all week and I'm fucked. OK?* □ *That's it! I'm fucked, I give up.*

fucker *n.* a person, usually a man. (Not necessarily derogatory. Taboo.) □ *Well, you old fucker, what the hell are you doing here?* □ *What a useless fucker you are!*

fucking *mod.* damnable. (Taboo.) □ *Get that fucking idiot out of here!* □ *What the fucking hell do you think you are doing?*

Fucking arseholes! AND **Fucking hell!** *exclam.* a strong expression of disbelief. (Taboo.) □ *Fucking arseholes, that's just ridiculous!* □ *What? They did what? Fucking hell!*

Fucking hell! See FUCKING ARSEHOLES!

fuck like a stoat *vb. phr.* to participate vigorously and eagerly in sexual intercourse. (Taboo. Said of a woman.) □ *Let's go somewhere quiet and fuck like a stoat.* □ *Want to fuck like a stoat, darling?*

Fuck me! *exclam.* a strong expletive, with a shade of humour. (Taboo.) □ *Fuck me, it's worked this time!* □ *Fuck me! Why did you do that?*

Fuck me gently! *exclam.* an expression of amazement or surprise. (Taboo.) □ *Well, fuck me gently! That's amazing!* □ *Really? Fuck me gently, but that's hard to swallow!*

fuck off AND **bugger off; piss off** *vb. phr.* to depart. (Taboo.) □ *How can I*

put this politely? *Will you be so kind as to fuck off!* □ *I don't know where he is, he just pissed off.*

Fuck off! AND **Bugger off!; Piss off!** *exclam.* "Go away!"; "Leave me!" (Taboo.) □ *Fuck off, you creep!* □ *I told you; piss off!*

Fuck this for a game of soldiers! AND **Sod this for a game of soldiers!** *exclam.* "I've had enough!"; "I quit!" (Taboo.) □ *I've had enough. Fuck this for a game of soldiers!* □ *Sod this for a game of soldiers! I'm off.*

fuck up See ARSE UP.

fuck-up See ARSE-UP.

Fuck you! *exclam.* a strong condemnation. (Taboo.) □ *Fuck you! Why did you have to do that?* □ *Fuck you! I don't care any more!*

fudd *n.* the female sexual organ. (Taboo.) □ *What do you mean, you can see my fudd? Oh my god, I've forgotten my panties!* □ *He got arrested trying to look up women's skirts in the hope of seeing their fudds.*

fuddy-duddy *n.* a stuffy person; an quaint or old-fashioned person. □ *Pay no attention to him. He's just an old fuddy-duddy.* □ *There seems to be a convention of fuddy-duddies in the park today.*

fug *n.* stale or smoky air. □ *There was a terrible fug in the room when we got there.* □ *We got rid of the fug by opening the widow.*

fuggy *mod.* stale or airless. □ *It was so fuggy; I could hardly breath.* □ *This far too fuggy for me.*

Fujiama *phr.* "Fuck you Jack, I'm all right!" (Taboo. Almost an initialism.) □ *Well, Fujiama! I don't care.* □ *Fujiama is a hell of an attitude.*

full *mod.* intoxicated due to drink. □ *You came in full last night. What's going on?* □ *They were both full. They could only lie there and snore.*

full belt AND **full bore; full tilt** *n.* maximum speed. □ *She passed me at full belt me a few miles back. What's up?* □ *We were going along the motorway at full tilt when this cop car spotted us.*

full blast See FULL BOTTLE.

full bore See FULL BELT.

full bottle AND **full blast** *mod.* as fast or as loud as possible. □ *As soon as he got onto the motorway, he put his foot down and was travelling at full bottle.* □ *The whistle blew full blast and woke everyone up.*

full marks 1. *n.* the highest possible examination score. □ *Congratulations! You scored full marks!* □ *If he got full marks, how could anyone fail?* **2.** *n.* a recognition of excellence. □ *Well, I think you deserve full marks for that performance.* □ *Work like that really is worth full marks.*

full of beans *mod.* lively; high spirited; energetic. □ *What a wonderful day! I feel so full of beans this morning!* □ *It's wonderful to see John so full of beans again after the difficult time he had.*

full of crap AND **full of hot air; full of it; full of shit; full of wind** *mod.* full of nonsense. (Crude. SHIT is taboo.) □ *You're full of crap. I don't believe you.* □ *Here's Harry, full of shit as usual.* □ *Aw, you're just full of it! Be quiet!*

full of hot air See FULL OF CRAP.

full of it See FULL OF CRAP.

full of shit See FULL OF CRAP.

full of wind See FULL OF CRAP.

Full stop! AND **Period!** *exclam.* "That is all."; "Finally, without exception, extenuation or extension." □ *Right that's it, full stop!* □ *I'm not saying one more word, period!*

full tilt See FULL BELT.

full whack *n.* the full price. □ *I had to pay the full whack.* □ *I never pay full whack—on principle!*

fun and games 1. *n.* a pleasant time; a period spent in amusement. □ *That's enough fun and games. Let's get on with the business.* □ *You spend too much time with fun and games!* **2.** *n.* a sexual or romantic dalliance. (Crude.) □ *Everybody knows about your fun and games with Paul last night, Jane.* □ *I see Jane's at her fun and games again with a new man.*

funbags *n.* the female breasts. (Crude. Normally with *the* and in the plural.) □ *There she was, bold as brass, with her funbags on full display.* □ *All you think about is funbags!*

fundy *n.* a religious fundamentalist. □ *Are you a fundy?* □ *I think fundies are...shall we say...unusual.*

fungus See FACE FUNGUS.

fungus-face AND **fungus-features** *n.* a bearded man. (Compare with FACE FUNGUS.) □ *Who's the fungus-face in the striped blazer?* □ *Hey, fungus-features! Who is that behind all the fuzz?*

fungus-features See FUNGUS-FACE.

funk 1. *n.* cowardice; terror. □ *She suffers from a terrible funk whenever she has to give a talk.* □ *The dog was in such a funk that it was crying.* **2.** *vb.* to exhibit cowardice or fear. □ *If she seems to funk at all, get her out of there fast.* □ *Don't you dare funk again!*

funk hole *n.* a pretext used to avoid an unpleasant duty or responsibility. □ *He tends to use his work as a funk hole to avoid domestic responsibilities, I think.* □ *You find being a mother a great funk hole to get away from the real world, don't you Mavis?*

funk-hole AND **hid(e)y-hole** *n.* a hiding place used during periods of particular danger. □ *I think Otto's gone into his funk hole.* □ *Where do you think his hidey-hole is?*

funk something *vb.* to shrink or evade a duty, responsibility or challenge. □ *No more funking will be tolerated around here; all right?* □ *He funked out of that one, somehow.*

funky 1. *mod.* smelly; disgusting. □ *That's really funky, don't go in there.* □ *If you must be funky, do so somewhere else thank you.* **2.** *mod.* fashionable. (Of popular music.) □ *I love his funky style, don't you?* □ *His music was funky but not really for me.*

funnies *n.* the comic strips found in newspaper. (Always with *the*.) □ *I was sitting there reading the funnies.* □ *Give me the page with the funnies please.*

funny *n.* an intelligence officer. (Police jargon. Could refer to a member of the Security Service, formerly MI5—Military Intelligence Department Five—which is responsible for counter-intelligence and security within the UK; the Secret Intelligence Service, formerly MI6—Military Intelligence Department Six—which is responsible for overseas intelligence and espionage; or Special Branch—the section within the police that is responsible for political security and the protection of important individuals within the UK.) □ *He's not a real copper, he's a funny.* □ *I think Harry's been invited to become a funny, but he's not saying of course.*

funny business See MONKEY BUSINESS.

funny-farm AND **cuckoo-farm; laughing academy** *n.* an insane asylum; a mental hospital. □ *I think they ought to send you to the funny-farm.* □ *He's too far gone for the cuckoo-farm.*

funny-money AND **mick(e)y-mouse-money** *n.* any substitute money: counterfeit money, foreign currency; military script, etc. □ *I don't want any funny-money. Real British Pounds Sterling or forget it.* □ *Who'll change this mickey-mouse-money back into the real thing?*

funny stuff See MONKEY BUSINESS.

fusspot *n.* a person who is inclined to fuss. □ *I don't think I could take another fusspot like that today.* □ *What's a fusspot like that doing around here?*

fuzz *n.* the police. □ *The fuzz is onto you.* □ *The fuzz are at the back of the house as well as the front. I think they mean business.*

fuzz-ball *n.* an anal release of intestinal gas; a noise or smell associated with this. (Crude.) □ *The pungent scent of a recent fuzz-ball hung in the air.* □ *Oh lord! Who made that fuzz-ball?*

FWIW *interj.* "for what it's worth." (Computer jargon. Written only. An initialism used in computer communications.) □ *FWIW, I understand exactly what you are saying.* □ *I think you are just too sensitive, FWIW.*

G

G *interj.* "grin." (Computer jargon. Written only. An initialism used in computer communications. Shows that the writer is grinning or happy. Can be in various forms, including, "(G)"; "<G>"; "g"; "(g)" and "<g>".) □ *I suppose you are not interested in what I was saying to you. <G>.* □ *When are you going to learn to spell? (g).*

gab 1. *n.* mindless chatter; gossip. □ *I like to listen in on other people's gab.* □ *Enough of this gab—on with the show!* 2. *vb.* to chatter; to gossip. □ *Can you stop gabbing just for a minute?* □ *We like to gab. Leave us alone.*

gaff 1. *n.* a cheap public amusement hall or theatre. □ *Don't you go near that gaff again, my lad!* □ *They are always having fights in that gaff. I don't know how it keeps its licence.* 2. *n.* a building that is someone's home. □ *I stood outside his gaff and waited.* □ *Where's your gaff, son?* 3. *vb.* to cheat. □ *She gaffs every single customer that comes her way; she doesn't know any other way to operate.* □ *Don't try to gaff me. I wasn't born yesterday, you know.* 4. *n.* a criminal venture. □ *The cops turned up right in the middle of the gaff.* □ *The whole gaff was a stupid idea in the first place anyway.* 5. See also GUFF.

gaffer 1. *n.* an old man; a rustic old man. (Possibly from *godfather.*) □ *Nobody out there but some old gaffer with a cane.* □ *The old gaffer smiled and moved on.* 2. *n.* a foreman; the boss. □ *If Joe says we lift these boxes, we lift these boxes; he's the gaffer.* □ *The gaffer asked if anyone wanted extra work at the weekend.* 3. *n.* the commanding officer of a Royal Navy ship.

□ *Wake the gaffer. I think there's a problem that needs his presence on the bridge.* □ *Yes madam, I am the gaffer of HMS Valiant, as you put it.*

gag 1. *n.* a joke; a trick. □ *She tells the best gags.* □ *What a great gag! Everybody will love it.* 2. *vb.* to retch or choke, especially with much noise. (Standard English.) □ *The food was so horrible I almost gagged on it.* □ *Don't eat so fast. You'll gag.* 3. *in.* to empty one's stomach; to vomit. (Crude. Youth usage.) □ *Willy gagged his whole dinner.* □ *One look at the food, and I almost gagged there and then.*

gaga 1. *mod.* senile. □ *Try not to look as if you've gone gaga.* □ *I think she's gaga, but what do you expect at age 90?* 2. *mod.* crazy; eccentric. □ *Sometimes what you say is completely gaga!* □ *Sally is just naturally gaga.*

gage *n.* marijuana. □ *I certainly could use some gage right now.* □ *She had gage on her when she was arrested.*

galley-arsed *mod.* suffering from the effects of a curry. (Taboo.) □ *That vindaloo has left me galley-arsed.* □ *I get galley-arsed every time I go to that Indian restaurant.*

gall(o)us *mod.* bold; cheeky; unmanageable. (Scots usage.) □ *What a gallous idiot you are!* □ *Get awa' ye gallus fool!*

galumph (around) *vb. (phr.)* to walk about in an awkward or noisy manner. □ *I spent all day galumphing around, looking for a present for Ted.* □ *Stop galumphing long enough to eat some dinner.*

gam *n.* an act of oral sex upon a man. (Taboo.) □ *The punter was looking for* *a gam.* □ *That girl standing at the cor-ner does gams if you pay enough.*

game 1. *mod.* willing to do something. □ *Is anybody game for some pizza?* □ *I'm game, what about you?* **2.** *n.* prosti-tution. (Crude. Always with *the.*) □ *That's what it's called around here, love. The game.* □ *"The truth? Well, Mary really likes it on the game. Power without responsibility..."* *"Yes, I know that one,"* *he said, sadly.*

game ball *mod.* in good health; in good form. □ *Yes of course I'm a game ball; I've never felt better.* □ *We need a game ball in this job as it will take a lot of effort.*

gammy 1. *mod.* injured. □ *Tom's gammy and needs some help.* □ *Fred had a little accident, and he's pretty gammy.* **2.** *mod.* permanently lame. □ *He's sort of gammy since that football game.* □ *I've got a gammy leg, you know. I'll catch up with you later.*

gamp *n.* a large umbrella. (From Mrs Sarah Gamp in Dickens's *Martin Chuzzlewit*, who had such an umbrella.) □ *She opened her gamp and walked out into the rain.* □ *I'm taking my gamp as it looks like rain.*

gams *n.* a woman's legs, especially if attractive. □ *Is she the one with the gor-geous gams?* □ *Look at the gams on that bird!*

gam someone *vb.* to perform oral sex upon a man. (Taboo.) □ *There she was, gamming him!* □ *If you think I'm going to gam you, you've another thing coming!*

gander *n.* a look. (Compare with TAKE A GANDER (AT SOMEONE OR SOMETHING).) □ *Let me take a gander at it and see if it's done right.* □ *We should all take a gander to see what one is like.*

Gandhi's revenge *n.* a picturesque name for diarrhoea or similar, inflicted upon a visitor to a foreign land. (Indian variety.) □ *I had a little touch of Gand-hi's revenge the second day, but other than that we had a wonderful time.* □ *Most people blame Gandhi's revenge on the water.*

gang-bang AND **gang-rape 1.** *n.* an act of group rape. (Taboo.) □ *The fuzz was* around investigating that gang-bang on the next block. □ *There were reports of a gang-rape in the prison.* **2.** *vb.* to rape in a group. (Taboo.) □ *The pack of thugs set out to gang-bang some inno-cent woman.* □ *Why do they have to go gang-raping young girls?*

gang-rape See GANG-BANG.

ganja AND **ganjah** *n.* marijuana; mari-juana resin. □ *It's the ganja that gives the stuff its kick.* □ *Can you get ganjah by itself?*

ganjah See GANJA.

gannet *n.* someone who gobbles down large quantities of food; a greedy per-son. (Crude. From the perceived propensity of the sea-bird of this name to consume whole fish in such a man-ner.) □ *Get out of here, you gannet!* □ *Of course he's a gannet! Have you ever seen him not eating?*

gantry 1. *n.* the area behind a bar when bottles of spirits are displayed upside down with optics attached ready for dispensing. (Scots usage.) □ *A pub's gantry is the very heart of the place.* □ *He reached over to the gantry and poured a measure.* **2.** *n.* the range of spirits, especially malt whiskies, avail-able in a pub. (Scots usage.) □ *What's that new malt you've got on the gantry tonight?* □ *The gantry in this pub is huge.*

gap site *n.* a plot of land between build-ings that is considered large enough to accommodate another building. □ *We found a lovely little gap site in Southern Street.* □ *They're building a new house in that gap site.*

garbage *n.* jumbled or meaningless computer code. (Computer jargon.) □ *All I get is garbage on the screen.* □ *If you put garbage into the computer, you'll get garbage out.*

gargle 1. *vb.* to drink any alcoholic drink. □ *They sat and gargled for an hour or two.* □ *Let's go out and gargle for a bit.* **2.** *n.* spirits or beer; any alco-holic drink. □ *Would you like some more gargle?* □ *Pour me a little of that gargle, if you please.*

gargler *n.* a drinker; a drunkard. □ *You are going to turn into a gargler if you* *don't let up on your drinking.* □ *Some old gargler froze to death last night.*

garn *exclam.* an expression of disbelief. (Derived from "go on.") □ *Really? Garn!* □ *Garn, that's all crap.*

gas 1. *vb.* to talk nonsense; to make idle chat. □ *Pay no attention. She's just gassing.* □ *Stop gassing for a minute and listen.* **2.** *n.* a joke; a humorous predicament. □ *You may think my predicament was a gas, but I certainly did not.* □ *I don't think that gas was funny.*

gash 1. *mod.* pointless, broken or useless. □ *What a gash deal that turned out to be.* □ *I don't want any more of your gash promises.* **2.** *mod.* additional, extra or not required. □ *There's a gash TV set in the bedroom, if you want to borrow it.* □ *Why have we got all these gash chairs in here?* **3.** *mod.* unattached; available. (Of a woman.) □ *Now there is one woman who is gash for you!* □ *She certainly looks like a gash girl to me!* **4.** *n.* the female sexual organ. (Taboo.) □ *They dance completely nude in there, with gash and everything on view.* □ *A woman who shows her gash is just the lowest.* **5.** *n.* a girl or woman. (Taboo.) □ *Get a look at that gash over there.* □ *If you louts call me a gash again I'll give both of you new gashes of your own to contemplate!*

gasper *n.* a cigarette. □ *Got a gasper, pal?* □ *He got out the gaspers and passed them around.*

gasping *mod.* desperate. □ *She was gasping for it.* □ *Oh him! He's always gasping for something or another.*

gassed *mod.* intoxicated due to drink. □ *Joe and Arthur kept on knocking them back till they were both completely gassed.* □ *By morning they were all gassed.*

gate-crasher *n.* an uninvited guest at a party or other social event. □ *Tim's party was ruined by a bunch of gate-crashers.* □ *Since you ask, the gate-crasher was far and away the most lively and interesting person present.*

gates of Rome *n.* home. (Rhyming slang.) □ *It's not much but it's me gates of Rome.* □ *There, after all these years, I was in my gates of Rome once more.*

gauch out AND **gouch out** *vb. phr.* to pass out under the influence of drugs. □ *After taking the stuff, Gary gauched out.* □ *After the fix, Gert waited patiently to gouch out.*

Gawd love a duck! See LORD LOVE A DUCK!

gawk AND **gawp** *vb.* to stare in a blatant or stupid manner. □ *Don't gawk, it's rude!* □ *Why is everybody always gawping at me?*

gawker AND **gawper** *n.* someone who GAWKS or GAWPS. □ *There was a gawker looking in the shop window for hours.* □ *I hate gawpers.*

gawp See GAWK.

gawper See GAWKER.

gay 1. *n.* a homosexual, normally male but not exclusively. (Crude. Used by homosexuals to describe themselves.) □ *He doesn't like being described as a gay.* □ *Then why does he apparently work so hard to look like he is a gay?* **2.** *mod.* homosexual, normally male but not exclusively. (Crude. Used by homosexuals to describe themselves.) □ *Moira has found this wonderful gay hair stylist that she swears by now.* □ *Who cares if he's gay? He can still vote, can't he?* **3.** *mod.* sexually lax; immoral. (Crude.) □ *These are really gay; anything goes there.* □ *When I say they are gay, I do not mean they are homosexual; I mean they are immoral.*

gay deceivers *n.* false or artificially enhanced female breasts. (Crude.) □ *I'm telling you, these are gay deceivers.* □ *Unfortunately, her gay deceivers did not do very much deceiving.*

gazump *vb.* to raise a selling price, usually of a house or other property, after informally accepting an offer to buy at a lower price. □ *They tried to gazumph the price just before exchanging contracts.* □ *I just knew that that seller was going to gazump us!*

gazumper 1. *n.* someone who raises a selling price after informally accepting an offer to buy at a lower price. □ *If I ever get hold of that dirty gazumper...* □ *Well, I suppose the gazumper was* *pleased with himself.* **2.** *n.* a swindler. □ *I don't want anything to do with a gazumper like him.* □ *What an obvious gazumper that fellow is.*

gazump someone *vb.* to short-change a customer. □ *Hoy! You gazumped me!* □ *If you try to gazump customers, you'll be fired on the spot.*

gazunder 1. *vb.* to lower an offer price after informally making a higher one. (Coined by merging GAZUMP with "under.") □ *I'm amazed! He actually tried to gazunder us!* □ *People try to gazunder most frequently when the housing market is slow.* **2.** *n.* a chamber-pot. (Because it *gazunder* the bed.) □ *You don't see very many gazunders nowadays.* □ *Gazunders used to be very common before en-suite bathrooms.*

GBG *interj.* a "great big grin." (Computer jargon. Written only. An initialism used in computer communications. Shows that the writer is grinning, joking or happy. Often enclosed, "<GBG>.") □ *I think you are just talking nonsense <GBG>.* □ *You are really odd! <GBG>.*

gear 1. *mod.* excellent. □ *This jazz is really gear!* □ *Now that's what I'd call a gear pizza!* **2.** *n.* clothes. □ *I feel sort of funny in this gear.* □ *Where did you get gear to wear like that?* **3.** *n.* ridiculous talk. □ *Look, that's enough of your gear.* □ *No more gear, let's get serious.* **4.** *n.* stolen goods. □ *We found a huge pile of gear in his house.* □ *All right, then tell us where this gear came from?* **5.** *n.* marijuana. □ *I've got the gear, man.* □ *You get good gear in this part of town.* **6.** *mod.* homosexual. (Crude. Rhyming slang, linked as follows: gear ≈ [queer] = homosexual.) □ *So what if he's gear? He can still vote, can't he?* □ *Why does he always work so hard to look like he's gear?*

gee-gee *n.* a childish name for a horse. □ *Look at that gee-gee, daddy!* □ *Can I have a gee-gee too, Mummy?*

Gee (whiz)! *exclam.* "Gosh!" (An abbreviation of JESUS!, although not always recognised as such.) □ *Gee whiz! What a mess!* □ *Gee, do I have to?*

geezer *n.* a man. □ *Why do we need this geezer?* □ *Ask the geezer if he needs any help.*

gelly AND **jelly** *n.* gelignite, a type of powerful explosive. □ *Pat's the one who knows how to get the best results with gelly.* □ *The jelly was packed into a tight crate at the back of the van, and sweating dangerously.*

gelt *n.* money. (From German via Yiddish.) □ *How much gelt do you need, then?* □ *Sorry, I can't afford it, I've no gelt.*

gender-bender *mod.* concerning something that obscures sexual distinctions. (Crude.) □ *Those gender-bender hairstyles can be confusing.* □ *He always wears gender-bender clothes.*

gentleman of the road AND **knight of the road** *n.* a tramp. (A euphemism.) □ *There's a knight of the road asleep in our garage.* □ *Some so-called gentleman of the road are no gentleman at all.*

gentleman's gentleman *n.* a gentleman's personal servant; a butler. □ *He's that gentleman's gentleman's gentleman.* □ *The gentleman's gentleman was waiting for him in the drawing room.*

gents' *n.* a men's toilet. (An abbreviation of "gentlemens'." Often with *the.*) □ *Is there a gents' somewhere close?* □ *Joe has gone to the gents'.*

genuine article *n.* the real thing rather than a substitute. □ *Is this the genuine article or some cheap local substitute?* □ *I'll take the genuine article, thanks.*

George Raft *n.* a draught. (Rhyming slang.) □ *There's a terrible George Raft blowing from that window.* □ *He caught a chill from a George Raft and is in bed.*

George (the Third) 1. *n.* an act of defecation. (Crude. Rhyming slang, linked as follows: George (the Third) ≈ [turd] = [shit] = defecation.) □ *He had a George and then came back.* □ *He said he needed a George the Third.* **2.** *n.* a bird. (Rhyming slang.) □ *What sort of George the Third was that?* □ *So this George was caught by the cat, then.*

Gerrof! See GET OUT!

Gestapo *n.* the police. (Offensive. Always with *the.* From the well-known

German abbreviation for *Geheime Staatspolizei*, the "Secret State Police" of the Nazi regime, and that organisation's invidious reputation.) □ *The Gestapo are after me!* □ *No friend of mine ever talks to the Gestapo!*

get AND **git** *n.* a foolish person. □ *Please don't call me a get. I do my best.* □ *Who's the git in the bright orange trousers?*

get a bad name *vb. phr.* to acquire a bad reputation. □ *I don't intend to get a bad name.* □ *How could I ever have got a bad name like that?*

get a bit *vb. phr.* to perform sexual intercourse, from the male perspective. (Taboo. Usually with *a.*) □ *I'm hoping to get a bit tonight.* □ *You'll always get a bit from Fiona, the girl who can't say no.*

get a fix *vb. phr.* to buy drugs; to take a dose of drugs. □ *Gert had to go home to get a fix.* □ *What did Tracy mean when she said she had to get a fix fast?*

get a grip on one's knickers *vb. phr.* to take control of oneself. □ *Look, it's not the end. Get a grip on your knickers!* □ *So I got a grip on my knickers and it was all right after that.*

get a jump See HAVE A JUMP.

get a load off one's mind *vb. phr.* to say what one is thinking; to speak one's mind; to talk something out. □ *I'm sorry, but I just had to get a load off my mind.* □ *I think you'll feel better once you get a load off your mind.*

get along with you AND **get away with you** **1.** *phr.* "I don't believe you." □ *Get along with you! What really happened?* □ *I don't believe you. Get away with you.* **2.** *phr.* "Don't be silly." □ *Oh get along with you; I could never do that!* □ *Me? Never! Get away with you!* **3.** *phr.* "Go away." □ *Oh, get along with you. I can't be bothered.* □ *Get away with you. You're just being a nuisance.*

get a packet See COP A PACKET.

get a rise AND **have a rise** *vb. phr.* to have an erection. (Taboo.) □ *Joe can't get a rise any more, you know.* □ *I had a rise as soon as she walked in the room!*

get a toehold *vb. phr.* to work one's way into some association or relationship. □ *As soon as I get a toehold in the company, I'll be more relaxed.* □ *Once you let him get a toehold, you'll never get rid of him.*

Get away! *exclam.* "Stop being a pest!"; "I don't believe you!" □ *Don't bother me! Get away!* □ *Get away! Nobody is that stupid!*

getaway 1. *n.* a quick or short holiday trip. □ *We took a little getaway to Greece.* □ *What you need is a weekend getaway.* **2.** *n.* an escape from the law or other undesirable consequence of an action. (Originally underworld.) □ *Lefty made a quick getaway.* □ *There was no time to make a getaway, so we had to talk to Mrs Wilson.*

get away with something 1. *vb. phr.* to succeed unexpectedly or unjustifiably. □ *Somehow we'll get away with it!* □ *We got away with it, but I don't know how—or why.* **2.** *vb. phr.* to just succeed and no more. □ *I think we'll just about get away with it.* □ *Well, we just got away with it again, but by the skin of our teeth this time.*

get away with you See GET ALONG WITH YOU.

get behind someone or something *vb. phr.* to support someone or something. □ *Let's all get behind the party in the next election.* □ *Everybody got behind Todd and cheered him on.*

get by 1. *vb. phr.* to evade undesirable notice. □ *Just how do you intend to get by the police patrols, Otto?* □ *He got by the whole elaborate security system and escaped from the prison.* **2.** *vb. phr.* to cope, just, on limited income or other resources. □ *I'm getting by, but just.* □ *There's more to life than simply getting by, surely.* **3.** *vb. phr.* to live in comfort. (Ironic.) □ *Oh, I think they get by very nicely, thank you.* □ *We get by, we get by.*

get cracking *vb. phr.* to get moving or get on with things. □ *Right, let's get cracking as we're running out of time.* □ *Tom certainly got cracking on the project, I must say!*

get down to it AND **get stuck in** *vb. phr.* to begin hard and earnest work. □

Right men, let's get down to it. □ *We'll get stuck in right after lunch.*

get down to some serious drinking *vb. phr.* to settle down to a long session of drinking. □ *Well, now we can get down to some serious drinking.* □ *When the kids go to bed, let's get down to some serious drinking.*

get down to the nitty-gritty *vb. phr.* to get down to the heart of the matter. (Compare with NITTY-GRITTY.) □ *Stop messing around and get down to the nitty-gritty.* □ *If we could only get down to the nitty-gritty and stop wasting time.*

get hot *vb. phr.* to become busy or hectic. □ *Things always get hot around here toward the end of the month.* □ *When things start getting hot, we have to hire more people.*

get in on the act *vb. phr.* to become involved in something with someone else. (The involvement is not necessarily welcome.) □ *Everybody wants to get in on the act.* □ *Why are you trying to get in on the act?*

get into bed with someone *vb. phr.* to work closely with as business partners; to merge businesses. □ *Have you heard? The company's getting into bed with Acme Industries?* □ *I want you two to get into bed with each other and sort this problem out.*

get into something *vb. phr.* to become deeply involved with something. □ *I got into computers when I was still at school.* □ *When did you get into foreign films?*

get it 1. *vb. phr.* to understand a joke; to understand a point of information. □ *Sorry. I don't get it.* □ *Don't you get it?* **2.** *vb. phr.* to get punished. □ *I just know I'm going to get it when I get home.* □ *You're going to get it all right!*

get it in the neck 1. *vb. phr.* to receive a severe or fatal blow. □ *When the new store opened, it was soon clear that the old one had got it in the neck.* □ *If you people don't get organised fast, you're all going to get it in the neck.* **2.** *vb. phr.* to receive severe punishment or criticism. □ *You are going to get it in the neck for that remark.* □ *Jimmy was*

afraid he'd get it in the neck for being late.

get it on *vb. phr.* to perform sexual intercourse. (Taboo.) □ *Come on, baby, let's get it on.* □ *I don't want to get it on with you or any other creep.*

get it out *vb. phr.* to tell (someone) about a problem; to pour out one's grief. □ *Come on, get it out. You'll feel better.* □ *He would feel better if he could get it out.*

get it together AND **get organised; get sorted out** *vb. phr.* to become ordered; to tidy up; to get mentally adjusted. □ *When I get it together again, I'll try to go back to full-time education.* □ *Try to get sorted out and come back to work next week, okay?*

get it up *vb. phr.* to have an erection. (Taboo.) □ *If you can't get it up, you should see the doctor.* □ *Joe can't get it up any more, you know.*

get it wrong *vb. phr.* to misunderstand. □ *Oh Otto, you've got it wrong again!* □ *Why do you have to get it wrong every time?*

Get knotted! AND **Get lost!** *exclam.* "Go away!"; "Leave me!" □ *Get knotted, you're bothering me!* □ *Quit following me. Get lost!*

get laid *vb. phr.* to perform sexual intercourse. (Crude.) □ *Sally just wants to get laid.* □ *Let's go somewhere quiet and get laid.*

Get lost! See GET KNOTTED!

Get my drift? See DO YOU GET MY DRIFT?

get no change *vb. phr.* to get no help. □ *You'll get no change from that quarter.* □ *I got no change there.*

get nowhere fast *vb. phr.* to make very poor or no progress. □ *We are getting nowhere fast around here.* □ *I'm getting nowhere fast in this job. I quit.*

Get off it! See GET OUT!, COME OFF IT!

get off someone's back *phr.* to cease to irritate or annoy someone. □ *Look, I think you should get off his back now.* □ *Get off my back, will you!*

get off with (someone) *vb. phr.* to seduce someone; to perform sexual intercourse with someone. (Crude.) □ *You'll never get off with him, Samantha.* □

Getting off with the right person is all they think of at that age.

get one right here *vb. phr.* to affect one deeply in a specific way. (Usually accompanied with a hand gesture showing exactly where one is affected: the heart = lovingly, the stomach or bowels = sickeningly.) □ *That sort of thing gets me right here.* □ *Pete clasped his hand to his chest and said, "That sort of thing gets me right here."*

get one's act together AND **get one's shit together; get one's stuff together** **1.** *vb. phr.* to become ordered; to tidy up; to get one's possessions organised. (SHIT is taboo.) □ *Let me get my act together, and I'll be right with you.* □ *I'll get my stuff together and be right with you.* **2.** *vb. phr.* to calm down and get mentally organised. (SHIT is taboo.) □ *As soon as I get my act together, I can be of more help.* □ *Get your stuff together and start living again.*

get one's books AND **get one's cards** **1.** *vb. phr.* to be fired from a job. □ *Why did I get my books?* □ *I want you to make sure this character gets his cards right now.* **2.** *vb. phr.* to get oneself fired from a job. □ *Simon got his books when he told his boss what he really thought.* □ *Getting your cards from that great job was really, really stupid, you oaf!*

get one's cards See GET ONE'S BOOKS.

get oneself spliced *vb.* to get oneself married. □ *I hear you got yourself spliced, Paul.* □ *When did you two get yourselves spliced, then?*

get one's end away AND **get one's end in** *vb. phr.* to perform sexual intercourse. (Taboo. Refers to a male.) □ *He really wanted to get his end away.* □ *How do you get one's end in around here?*

get one's end in See GET ONE'S END AWAY.

get one's head down **1.** *vb. phr.* to lie down to rest or to go to sleep. □ *He's got his head down through there.* □ *I'm just going to get my head down for half-an-hour.* **2.** *vb. phr.* to concentrate upon the task in front of one. □ *I'm very busy and must get my head down* □ *If you get your head down, you can soon be finished.*

get one's knickers in a twist **1.** *vb. phr.* to become angry. □ *I'm trying not to get my knickers in a twist, but it's hard.* □ *Now, don't get your knickers in a twist. Relax.* **2.** *vb. phr.* to become confused. □ *Please try to avoid getting your knickers in a twist once more.* □ *I'm sorry but I've got my knickers in a twist again, I think.* **3.** *vb. phr.* to become excited and upset. □ *Don't get your knickers in a twist. It's going to be all right.* □ *She really had her knickers in a twist, I tell you.*

get one's leg over AND **get one's oats** *vb. phr.* to perform sexual intercourse. (Taboo.) □ *Where do you go to get your leg over around here?* □ *Come on love! I've got to get my oats tonight!*

get one's monkey up *vb. phr.* to become very angry. □ *Now you're getting his monkey up.* □ *Don't get his monkey up.*

get one's nose out of joint *vb. phr.* to feel slighted by something someone has done; to take offence at something. (Compare with PUT SOMEONE'S NOSE OUT OF JOINT.) □ *You get your nose out of joint too easily about stuff like that.* □ *Now, don't get your nose out of joint. She didn't mean it.*

get one's oats See GET ONE'S LEG OVER.

get one's rocks off *vb. phr.* to obtain sexual satisfaction; to have an orgasm. (Taboo.) □ *There was Mary and me getting our rocks off and these creeps next door were banging on the wall and shouting to complain about the noise. I mean, what noise?* □ *It was disgusting! Just through the wall and we could here every sound as they were getting his rocks off!*

get one's shit together See GET ONE'S ACT TOGETHER.

get one's stuff together See GET ONE'S ACT TOGETHER.

get one's teeth into something *vb.* to get started doing something. □ *I can't wait to get my teeth into that Wallace job.* □ *Here, get your teeth into this and see if you can't manage this project.*

get one's walking papers *vb.* to be fired or dismissed from work. (From the paperwork associated with ceasing employment.) □ *I hope I don't get my walking papers today. I need this job.* □ *Well, I got my walking papers today.*

get one's wind up AND **put one's wind up** *vb.* to induce terror or fear. □ *What you said has really got his wind up, I'm afraid.* □ *Well, something's put her wind up.*

get one's wires crossed *vb.* to be at, or to be talking at, cross-purposes with another person. □ *We appear to have got our wires crossed. Let's clear things up.* □ *I'm sorry but we really don't need getting our wires crossed around here.*

get on someone's tits AND **get on someone's wick** *vb. phr.* to irritate or annoy someone; to get on someone's nerves. (Crude. See also WICK.) □ *You know, you are really beginning to get on my tits!* □ *I left because I could see I was getting on his wick.*

get on someone's wick See GET ON SOMEONE'S TITS.

get on to someone *vb. phr.* to contact someone by telephone. □ *I'll just get on to her and ask.* □ *Hello, Jane! I've been meaning to get on to you about that all morning!*

get on to someone or something *vb. phr.* to become suspicious of someone or something. □ *The police have got on to them by now, I hear.* □ *Otto's getting on to the idea that not every advertisement is telling the literal truth.*

get organised See GET IT TOGETHER.

Get out! AND **Get off it!; Gerrof!** *exclam.* "That's ridiculous!" (GERROF is an abbreviated form of GET OFF IT.) □ *That's absurd! Get out!* □ *Gerrof! That can't be true!*

get-out clause *n.* an exclusion or loophole in a legal document such as a contract or insurance policy. □ *I'm afraid he's inserted a killer get-out clause just here.* □ *Get-out clauses are one good reason for reading the small print.*

get out of something *vb. phr.* to evade some responsibility, task or duty. □ *I know you; you're just trying to get out of attending the wedding.* □ *Of course not, I would not want to get out of the wedding.*

get (out) while the going is good AND **get out while the going's good** *vb. phr.* to leave while it is still safe or possible to do so. □ *I told her to get out while the going was good.* □ *I could tell now was the time to get out while the going's good.*

get out while the going's good See GET (OUT) WHILE THE GOING IS GOOD.

get shacked See SHACK UP (WITH SOMEONE).

get shot of someone or something *vb. phr.* to get rid of someone or something. □ *Get shot that work soon, and we'll sort you out.* □ *He got shot of Harry very quickly.*

get smart (with someone) *vb. phr.* to be cheeky or insulting to someone; to talk back to someone. □ *Don't you get smart with me!* □ *If you get smart again, I'll thump you right on the hooter.*

get someone *vb.* to move or impress someone. □ *I think my presentation really did get them!* □ *Did your talk get him?*

get someone by the balls AND **get someone by the short and curlies; have someone by the balls; have someone by the short and curlies 1.** *vb. phr.* to have someone completely under one's control. (Taboo.) □ *"When you have someone by the balls, their hearts and minds will follow." (LBJ, discussing Vietnam.)* □ *Oh, he'll agree. We have him by the short and curlies now.* **2.** *vb. phr.* to capture someone's close and undivided personal attention. (Taboo.) □ *Once you get someone by the balls, son, they'll listen.* □ *What I said then soon had him by the short and curlies!*

get someone by the short and curlies See GET SOMEONE BY THE BALLS.

get someone going *vb. phr.* to get someone excited; to get someone talking excitedly. □ *I really got him going on the subject of politics.* □ *The whole business really makes me mad. Don't get me going.*

get (someone) out of one's pram *vb. phr.* to cause someone to become very excited or angry. □ *Well, that news really get him out of his pram!* □ *Now,* *don't get out of your pram when you hear my news.*

get someone's goat *vb. phr.* to irritate someone. □ *Don't let Mary get your goat. She's just irritable today.* □ *Everybody seems to be getting my goat today.*

get some shut-eye *vb. phr.* to get some sleep. □ *I need to get home and get some shut-eye before I do anything else.* □ *We all could use some shut-eye.*

get something cracked *vb. phr.* to solve a problem or difficulty; to learn a skill. □ *I've got it cracked!* □ *After I get it cracked, the rest'll be easy.*

get something off one's chest *vb. phr.* to confess. □ *If you can get it off your chest, I'll be able to help you.* □ *Come on, don't be shy! Get it off your chest!*

get sorted out See GET IT TOGETHER, GET ORGANIZED.

get stroppy *vb. phr.* to become angry. □ *Oh, Willy is always getting stroppy about something.* □ *Willy can get stroppy when he talks about the accident.*

get stuck in See GET DOWN TO IT.

Get stuffed! *exclam.* "Go away!"; "Get lost!" □ *You're despicable. Get stuffed!* □ *Why don't you just get stuffed!*

get that way *vb. phr.* to get into that condition. □ *Whatever happened? How did you get that way?* □ *If you get that way again I'll kick you out of the house.*

get the bullet AND **get the chop 1.** *vb. phr.* to be killed. □ *The boss told Rocko to make sure Barlowe got the bullet.* □ *Barlowe was sure he could avoid getting the chop from Rocko.* **2.** See also GET THE SACK.

get the chop See GET THE BULLET, GET THE SACK.

get the dirty end *vb. phr.* to come off the worst. □ *There was no doubt that Stuart had got the dirty end of this deal.* □ *Next time he took more care to avoid getting the dirty end.*

get the drift *vb. phr.* to comprehend or understand what is going on. □ *I think I've got the drift now.* □ *Don't worry, he'll get the drift eventually.*

get the drop on someone *vb. phr.* to gain an advantage over someone. □ *Why are you always out to get the drop*

on me? □ *I'm sorry but we really don't try to get the drop on people around here.*

get the goods on someone *vb. phr.* to learn the truth about someone. □ *Well, I've got the goods on him at last.* □ *How did you get the goods on him?*

get the hell out (of here) *vb. phr.* to depart as rapidly as possible. (Crude.) □ *Time for us all to get the hell out of here, I think. They'll be home soon.* □ *He got the hell out before he was fired.*

get the horn AND **raise a gallop** *vb. phr.* to achieve an erection. (Taboo. Normally used in the negative.) □ *Joe can't raise a gallop any more, you know.* □ *I got the horn as soon as she walked in the room!*

Get the message? *interrog.* "Do you understand?"; "Are you able to figure out what is meant?" □ *Things are tough around here, and we need everyone's co-operation. Get the message?* □ *We don't need lazy people around here. Get the message?*

get the push 1. *vb. phr.* to be sent away. □ *Sent to Australia? You mean, I'm getting the push?* □ *What did I do to get the push like this?* **2.** See also GET THE SACK.

get the road See GET THE SACK.

get the sack AND **get the bullet; get the chop; get the push; get the road; get the wallop** *vb. phr.* to be dismissed from one's employment. □ *Poor Tom got the sack today. He's always late.* □ *I was afraid that Sally was going to get the wallop.*

get the show on the road AND **get this show on the road** *vb. phr.* to get (something) started. (Compare with ON THE ROAD.) □ *Let's get started! Get the show on the road!* □ *Get this show on the road. We don't have all day.*

get the staggers *vb. phr.* to lose one's ability or talent. (Sports.) □ *Well, I don't think he's going to be running in the Olympics after getting the staggers like he has.* □ *Oh no, I've got the staggers; I'm finished now.*

get the wallop See GET THE SACK.

get this show on the road See GET THE SHOW ON THE ROAD.

get through 1. *vb. phr.* to contact by telephone. □ *I think there's something wrong with the phone, as I can't get through.* □ *I want to report a fault. No-one can get through to our number.* **2.** *vb. phr.* to successfully make (someone) listen or understand. □ *Do you understand? Have I got through to you yet?* □ *Try to get through to him. It's important.*

Get to fuck (out of here)! *exclam.* "Go away!"; "Leave me!" (Taboo.) □ *I'm far too busy. Get to fuck out of here!* □ *That's it! Get to fuck!*

get-together *n.* an informal gathering. □ *Do you want to come to our little get-together?* □ *What's the reason for this particular get-together?*

get tore into someone *vb. phr.* to attack someone vigorously. (Scots.) □ *Come on! Get tore into them!* □ *The two teams were really getting tore into each other by half time.*

get tore in to something *vb. phr.* to set about a task vigorously. (Scots usage.) □ *Soon he was really getting tore in to his new task.* □ *Get tore in to it and the job will soon be complete.*

get-up *n.* an elaborate style of dress. □ *It was some get-up.* □ *Why are you in a get-up like that?*

get up someone's nose *vb. phr.* to greatly irritate someone. □ *So I made a mistake! I wish you'd stop getting up my nose about it.* □ *Getting up his nose is not going to correct the mistake.*

Get weaving! *exclam.* "Get moving!" □ *Get weaving! We're late!* □ *Hurry up! Get weaving!*

get weaving 1. *vb. phr.* to get started. □ *Let's get weaving on this.* □ *The sooner we get weaving, the sooner we'll get there.* **1.** *vb. phr.* to move along quickly. □ *We better get weaving now.* □ *We can still do it if we get weaving.*

get with it *vb. phr.* to modernise one's attitudes and behaviour. □ *Get with it, Martin. You can't go on like this any longer.* □ *You really have to get with it, Ernie.*

get yin's jotters *vb. phr.* to be dismissed from one's employment. (Scots

usage.) □ *We wur aw gin oor jotters the day. (We were all sacked today.)* □ *Yous yins do than yince mair and yous all'll get yer jotters. OK? (If you lot do that once more you'll all get sacked, is that clear?)*

get your finger out AND **get your skates on** *phr.* "hurry up, get a move on." □ *Come on, all of you! Get your finger out!* □ *Get your skates on! We're late!*

get your skates on See GET YOUR FINGER OUT.

gey wheen *n.* a large number. (Scots usage.) □ *There's a gey wheen o' folk at the game today.* □ *That's a gey wheen of money to pay out!*

ghettoblaster AND **ghetto box** *n.* a portable stereo radio. (Racially offensive. Often carried on the shoulder, especially by black people.) □ *Hey, turn down that ghettoblaster in here!* □ *You can't bring that ghetto box on this bus!*

ghetto box See GHETTOBLASTER.

Gib *n.* Gibraltar. (See ROCK.) □ *Have you ever been to Gib?* □ *Well, at least Gib's still British.*

g.i.b. AND **GIB** *mod.* good in bed. (Crude. An initialism.) □ *They say she's g.i.b.* □ *The priest asked me what GIB means!*

giddy limit *n.* someone or something that is at, or just beyond, the acceptable. (Always with *the.*) □ *That's it! That's just beyond the giddy limit!* □ *Whee! She's the giddy limit!*

Giddy up! *exclam.* "Move faster!" (Said to a horse to start it moving. Also said to people or things as a joke.) □ *Giddy up, Charlie! It's time to start moving.* □ *Let's get going, chum. Giddy up!*

gift of the gab 1. *n.* the ability to speak well in public; the ability to persuade people verbally. (Always with *the.*) □ *Gary has the gift of the gab, but it doesn't get him anywhere because he doesn't know where to go.* □ *I wish I had the gift of the gab. I'm just so shy.* **2.** *n.* the ability to speak fluently or loquaciously in an extemporaneous situation. (Always with *the.*) □ *No, she's really got the gift of the gab, her.* □ *I don't think anyone would accuse Otto of having the gift of the gab.*

gig 1. *n.* a onetime job; an engagement. (Musicians.) □ *I had a gig up north, but couldn't get there on time.* □ *The gig was cancelled because of the snow.* **2.** *vb.* to play or perform. (Musicians.) □ *I didn't gig at all last week. I'm getting hungry for a job.* □ *I'm happiest when I'm gigging.*

giggle 1. *n.* a group of schoolgirls. □ *He looked up and saw a giggle of girls walking across the park.* □ *That giggle should all be at school just now.* **2.** *n.* a trivial but amusing person or thing. □ *Well yes, she is just something of a giggle I suppose.* □ *Even giggles have to earn a crust—probably by being amusing if that's possible.*

giggle (and titter) *n.* beer. (Rhyming slang, linked as follows: giggle (and titter) ≈ [bitter] = beer.) □ *Have another pint of giggle and titter, Charlie.* □ *Hey, that's good giggle you've got here!*

giggle factory *n.* a lunatic asylum. □ *They're going to send you to the giggle factory one fine day.* □ *That judge spent three years in the giggle factory, y'know.*

GIGO *phr.* "garbage in, garbage out." (Computers. Acronym. If you get garbage out of a computer, it's because you put garbage in. Compare with FIFO and LIFO.) □ *The program failed, and I know it's my fault. You know, GIGO.* □ *GIGO is my theme song. I get out just what I deserve.*

gilt-edged 1. *n.* the stock of the largest and most reliable companies. The most secure and reliable investments. (Securities markets. See BLUE CHIP.) □ *Gilt-edged seem like the only safe bet these days.* □ *She has a large portfolio of gilt-edged.* **2.** *mod.* of especially reliable investments. (Securities markets.) □ *The gilt-edged rally ran into the sand almost immediately.* □ *It was gilt-edged stock that was leading the sell off.*

gimlet *n.* half a glass of whisky. (Irish usage.) □ *Come on, let's have more than a mere gimlet.* □ *He was nursing a gimlet in that corner all evening; that's all.*

gimme *phr.* "give me." (Eye-dialect. Typical spoken English. Used in writing only for effect. Used in the examples of this dictionary.) □ *Do you wanna gimme the thingy and lemme go ahead with my work?* □ *Gimme another one.*

Gimme a break! See GIVE ME A BREAK!

gimmer *n.* a gossipy old woman. (North of England usage. From an obsolete dialect word in the North of England, meaning "old sheep.") □ *I just could not get the old gimmer to stop talking.* □ *Who's that gimmer living next door to you?*

gimp 1. *vb.* to limp about. □ *I've been gimping a little bit since my accident.* □ *I'll gimp over there as soon as I can. It'll take a while on these crutches.* **2.** *n.* a fool; a mentally deficient person. (Use with caution.) □ *Lefty never reads a newspaper because he's a gimp.* □ *The gimp came past, muttering something incoherent under his breath.* **3.** *n.* a cripple. □ *I would not say he's a gimp, but he has great difficulty with walking.* □ *You can't go around calling people with walking difficulties gimps!*

gimpy *mod.* crippled; lame. □ *I've got a gimpy leg. I'll catch up in a minute.* □ *He's sort of gimpy since that football game.*

gin and It *n.* a drink consisting of gin and vermouth. ("It" is an abbreviation of "Italian," which is where vermouth comes from.) □ *I often enjoy a gin and It in the evening.* □ *You know how a gin and It disagrees with you, my dear.*

gin dive AND **gin palace** *n.* a low-class pub or tavern. □ *Fred hit every gin palace on the way home.* □ *You'll find Bob slumming it in some gin dive in the East End.*

ginger *n.* any sort of carbonated soft drink. (Scots usage. Compare with SKOOSH.) □ *See's a boatle o' that ginger, hen. (May I have a bottle of that carbonated soft drink, miss.)* □ *Gauny hae a ginger, pal? (Would you like a carbonated soft drink, my friend?)*

ginger (beer) 1. *n.* a male homosexual. (Crude. Rhyming slang, linked as follows: ginger (beer) ≈ [queer] = homosexual.) □ *She came to the dance with a ginger beer* □ *Tell that ginger to get out of here.* **2.** *n.* a ship's engineer. (Rhyming slang.) □ *This is Scotty. He's* our ginger beer. □ *The ginger told the captain it would be about two hours before the ship could be ready to sail.*

ginger (girl) *n.* a prostitute who robs her clients. (Crude.) □ *Joan nearly became a ginger girl to pay for her habit.* □ *A lot of gingers are hooked on something or other.*

ginny *mod.* addicted to gin. □ *Everybody knows she's ginny.* □ *My sister's ginny, and I want to help her.*

ginormous *mod.* vast or huge. □ *A ginormous aircraft flew low over the village.* □ *Why are lawyer's fees always so ginormous?*

gin palace See GIN DIVE.

Gippo AND **Gyppo; Gippy; Gyppy 1.** *n.* a Gypsy. (Offensive.) □ *Y'know, Otto, if you call a Gippo a Gippo, he's likely to get nasty.* □ *Why can you not be polite to Gyppies?* **2.** *n.* an Egyptian. (Offensive.) □ *He said he was not a racist, he just hated Gippos!* □ *Don't call Egyptian people Gyppies, please. It is very offensive and racist.*

Gippy See GIPPO.

Gippy tummy AND **Gyppo tummy; Gyppy tummy** *n.* a picturesque name for diarrhoea or similar, inflicted upon a visitor to a foreign land. (Egyptian variety.) □ *Most people blame Gippy tummy on the water.* □ *I had a little touch of Gyppo tummy the second day, but other than that we had a wonderful time.*

girl 1. *n.* a woman; a young woman. (Objectionable to some as demeaning to women.) □ *A bunch of us girls got together for coffee today.* □ *Would you girls care to come over to my house next week?* **2.** *n.* a male prostitute. (Crude.) □ *Lets face it, he's a girl!* □ *The girl turned and ran the moment he saw Otto.* **3.** *n.* cocaine. □ *My sister's using girl, and I want to help her.* □ *Were do you buy girl around here?*

Girl Friday *n.* a girl who is a useful assistant in an office. □ *And here's our new Girl Friday, Susan.* □ *She was fed up being Girl Friday; she wanted some real responsibility.*

girlie magazine *n.* a magazine featuring pictures of naked or near-naked women. (Crude.) □ *The girlie maga-*

zines were hidden under the counter. □ *Some creepy character asked Sally if she would pose for a girlie magazine.*

girlie show *n.* a theatrical performance featuring naked or near-naked women. (Crude.) □ *Bob and Pete went into town and tried to get into a girlie show.* □ *The whole performance turned out to be nothing but a girlie show.*

gismo AND **gizmo** *n.* a gadget. (Pronounced GIZ-moe.) □ *What is this silly little gismo on the bottom for?* □ *This gizmo turns it on.*

git See GET.

giveaway *n.* something that reveals a fact that was meant to be concealed. (Often with *dead*.) □ *The way he was walking was a giveaway to the fact that he was the one who was injured.* □ *The look on her face was a dead giveaway.*

give away (the) change *vb. phr.* to let slip confidential information. □ *Woops! I think I just gave away the change!* □ *Don't give away change tonight if you value your skin.*

give head *vb. phr.* to perform oral sex upon a man. (Taboo.) □ *She actually likes giving head, you know.* □ *Why won't you give head?*

Give it a rest! *exclam.* "Shut up!" (The "it" is a mouth. Compare with GIVE ME A REST!) □ *I've heard enough. Give it a rest!* □ *Give it a rest! You talk too much.*

give it away *vb. phr.* to be willing to indulge in sexual intercourse with anyone. (Crude. Refers to a woman.) □ *Mary just gives it away.* □ *Some girls think that you can be popular if you give it away.*

give (it) the gun *vb. phr.* to race the engine of a vehicle. □ *Give it the gun, Bert, so I can see where that oil's leaking from.* □ *Why do you always have to give the gun all the time when you're driving?*

give it to someone *vb. phr.* to perform sexual intercourse. (Taboo. From the male perspective.) □ *Come on Harry, give it to her!* □ *I've just got to give it to someone tonight!*

Give it up! *exclam.* "Quit now!"; "Enough is enough!" □ *Oh, give it up!*

You can't do it right. □ *Give it up! You can't bowl!*

Give me a break! AND **Gimme a break! 1.** *exclam.* "That is enough!"; "Stop it!" □ *Do you have to go on and on? Give me a break!* □ *Give me a break, you guys! That's enough!* **2.** *exclam.* "Don't be so harsh!"; "Give me a chance!" □ *I'm sorry! I'll do better! Give me a break!* □ *I was only late once! Give me a break!* **3.** *exclam.* "I don't believe you!"; "You don't expect anyone to believe that!" □ *You say a gorilla is loose in the city? Gimme a break!* □ *Tom said he was late again because the back stairs caved in. His boss said, "Gimme a break!"*

Give me a rest! *exclam.* "Lay off!"; "That is enough!" (Compare with GIVE IT A REST!) □ *Haven't I told you everything you need to know? Give me a rest.* □ *Give me a rest! I've heard enough.*

give one one's character *vb. phr.* to inform someone in full unpleasant detail just exactly what you really think of them. (Scots usage.) □ *If you go back there she'll give you your character all right!* □ *What do I really think of him? Oh, I'll give him his character, if that's really what you want.*

give one's bum an airing *vb. phr.* to use the toilet. (Taboo.) □ *Won't be a moment. Just got to give me bum an airing.* □ *He's giving his bum an airing.*

give over *vb. phr.* to desist or cease. □ *Oh give over. I've had enough.* □ *If you don't give over I'll call the police.*

give someone a bell AND **give someone a shout** *vb. phr.* to telephone someone. □ *You'd better give her a bell to find out what's up.* □ *Harry asked for you to give him a shout.*

give someone a (good) talking to *vb. phr.* to scold someone; to lecture someone sternly. □ *I think I'll have to give Pete a good talking to.* □ *The teacher gave Jimmy a talking to.*

give someone an earful *vb. phr.* to scold someone. □ *I'm going to give Ralph an earful for doing that.* □ *Sally gave Sam an earful for the way he treated Mary.*

give someone a shout See GIVE SOMEONE A BELL.

give someone a thrill *vb. phr.* to perform sexual intercourse upon someone. (Taboo.) □ *I'm sure she wants me to give her a thrill!* □ *Fancy me giving you a thrill, love?*

give someone gyp *vb. phr.* to experience pain or discomfort. (Probably derived from "gee-gee," a command to a horse to speed up, which was once often reinforced with the use of the spur or whip; hence the pain or discomfort.) □ *Oh no, not him. Every time I meet him he gives me gyp.* □ *Get this sorted out now or I'll really give you gyp.*

give someone hell 1. *vb. phr.* to bawl someone out; to scold someone severely. (Crude.) □ *The boss just gave me hell about it.* □ *I'm really going to give Tom hell when he gets home.* **2.** *vb. phr.* to trouble someone. (Crude.) □ *My arthritis is giving me hell in this weather.* □ *This problem is giving us hell at the office.*

give someone in charge *vb. phr.* to hand someone over to the police. □ *Our neighbour gave the burglar in charge.* □ *Give Otto in charge! He's a crook!*

give someone or something a miss *vb. phr.* to fail to visit someone or something. □ *I'm trying to give Lavinia a miss this week.* □ *If I were you, I'd give France a miss this year.*

give someone or something the (old) heave-ho *vb. phr.* to evict or dismisss someone. □ *I thought my job was secure, but today I got the old heave-ho.* □ *If your fridge does not refrigerate any more, then give it the old heave-ho.*

give someone stick *vb. phr.* to subject someone to severe criticism or retribution. (Compare with TAKE STICK.) □ *Do that again and I'll give you stick all right!* □ *He was really giving her stick; I had to stop it.*

give someone the benefit of one's thoughts See GIVE SOMEONE THE SIDE OF ONE'S TONGUE.

give someone the big E See GIVE SOMEONE THE ELBOW.

give someone the brush-off AND **give someone the frozen mitten** *vb. phr.* to repel someone; to ignore someone. (Compare with BRUSHOFF.) □ *Sam was afraid that Mary was going to give him the brush-off.* □ *The manager gave her the frozen mitten when she asked for a raise.*

give someone the chop See GIVE SOMEONE THE SACK.

give someone the elbow AND **give someone the big E** *vb. phr.* to dismiss or send away someone. □ *I'm afraid he gave Simon the elbow.* □ *Give that creep the big E.*

give someone the frozen mitten See GIVE SOMEONE THE BRUSH-OFF.

give someone the nod 1. *vb. phr.* to signal agreement by nodding. (Not slang.) □ *I gave Pete the nod, and he started the procedure.* □ *Just give me the nod when you are ready.* 2. *vb. phr.* to choose someone. (Compare with *get the nod.*) □ *The committee gave Frank the nod for the job.* □ *They gave her the nod.*

give someone the pip *vb. phr.* to annoy someone greatly. □ *That remark gave her the pip, once she realised what it meant.* □ *The whole business began to give her the pip after a while.*

give someone the raspberry *vb. phr.* to make a rude noise with the lips at someone. (Compare with RASPBERRY.) □ *The audience gave him the raspberry, which gave him some second thoughts about his choice of career.* □ *Even after his fabulous play during last night's game, they gave him the raspberry.*

give someone the sack AND **give someone the chop** *vb. phr.* to dismiss someone from employment. □ *They had to give Paul the sack because he was so unproductive.* □ *I was afraid they would give me the chop.*

give someone the shits 1. *vb. phr.* to scare oneself badly. (Taboo.) □ *What a fright! You nearly give me the shits there!* □ *Watch this, it'll really give them the shits.* 2. *vb. phr.* to scare someone very greatly. (Taboo.) □ *Don't do that! Are you trying to give me the*

shits? □ *It gave him the shits when he heard that Otto was after him.*

give someone the side of one's tongue AND **give someone the benefit of one's thoughts** *vb. phr.* to harangue, nag or remonstrate. □ *I'll certainly give her the side of my tongue if she shows her face in here again!* □ *I'm here to give you the benefit of my thoughts, so shut up and listen!*

give someone the slip *vb. phr.* to escape from a pursuer. □ *We were on his tail until he gave us the slip.* □ *I can give her the slip in no time at all.*

give someone the word *vb. phr.* to warn someone. □ *Give Otto the word; the cops are on to him.* □ *I gave him the word but I think he ignored me.*

give someone what for *vb. phr.* to scold or beat up someone. □ *Boy, they were really giving the other side what for!* □ *He'll give you what for if you don't behave.*

give something a bash AND **give something a go; give something a tumble** *vb. phr.* to attempt to achieve something. □ *Well, I'm prepared to give it a bash!* □ *Yes, I'd like to give the thing another a tumble.*

give something a go See GIVE SOMETHING A BASH.

give something a miss *vb. phr.* to stop doing or to fail to do something. □ *I'm going to give drinking a miss from now on.* □ *It would be a good idea for all of you to give smoking a miss, too.*

give something a tumble See GIVE SOMETHING A BASH.

give the game away *vb. phr.* to reveal a secret. □ *If you do that you'll give the game away!* □ *I don't want to give the game away, but...*

gizmo See GISMO.

glad eye See COME-HITHER LOOK.

glad rags *n.* one's best clothes. (Compare with RAG.) □ *You look pretty good in your glad rags.* □ *I'll get on my glad rags, and we'll go out tonight.*

glaikit *mod.* thoughtless; stupid. (Scots usage.) □ *Morag is mare than jist a glaikit wee lassie, ye ken! (Morag is more than just a stupid little girl, you* know!) □ *Do you always have to look so glaikit?*

glam *mod.* glamorous. □ *Some glam blonde sang a couple of songs, and then the band played again.* □ *He has a real glam place nowadays.*

Glasgow boat *n.* a coat. (Rhyming slang.) □ *That's a ridiculous Glasgow boat; I won't wear it.* □ *Anyone seen me Glasgow boat?*

Glasgow capon *n.* salt herring. □ *Do you eat Glasgow capon?* □ *No, I can't stand Glasgow capon. Sorry.*

Glasgow kiss AND **Southend kiss** *n.* a head butting. □ *If you've experienced a Glasgow kiss, you'll not forget it in a hurry.* □ *He'll give you a Southend kiss as soon as look at you.*

Glasgow Ranger AND **Queen's Park Ranger** *n.* a stranger. (Rhyming slang. Glasgow Rangers and Queen's Park Rangers are both well-known soccer clubs.) □ *I saw her in the pub with a Glasgow Ranger.* □ *Who was that Queen's Park Ranger you were with?*

glass *n.* diamond. (Criminals.) □ *What's this glass worth, eh?* □ *Not much. This glass of yours really is glass.*

glasshouse *n.* a military prison. □ *If you think civvie prison is bad, just try the glasshouse.* □ *Some of these people have been in the glasshouse for years, on and off.*

glazed over *mod.* suffering from extreme alcoholic intoxication. □ *She has had too much. She's glazed over.* □ *Fred looks a little glazed over. I think he's done for.*

gleg in the uptak *mod.* quick-witted; quick on the uptake. (Scots usage.) □ *Yon yin's gleg in the uptak aw richt. (That person is quick-witted all right.)* □ *You may be gleg in the uptak, but you're wrong this time.*

glitch *n.* a defect; a BUG. □ *There is a glitch in the computer program somewhere.* □ *I'm afraid there's a glitch in our plans.*

glitterati *n.* the flashier, glamorous and more publicity-conscious members of the entertainment and artistic firmament. □ *A lot of the glitterati are ex-*

pected at the premier tonight. □ *You can tell the glitterati from the rest of us by the way the flashbulbs flash when they get out of their cars.*

glitz *n.* flashiness and phoney glamour. □ *The place was a morass of eager sales creeps and nauseating glitz.* □ *The glitz was blinding, and the substance was invisible.*

glitzy *mod.* fashionable; glamorous. □ *It was a real glitzy place to hold a meeting.* □ *Some glitzy blonde sang a couple of songs, and then the band played again.*

glooms *n.* a fit of depression. (Irish usage. Always with *the*.) □ *The glooms? If you don't get yourself sorted out in short order I'll give you the glooms all right!* □ *I think it would be smart to leave him alone just now; he's got the glooms.*

Glorious Twelfth AND **Twelfth** *n.* August 12, which is the first day of the grouse-shooting season. (Normally with *the*.) □ *We hope to be in Scotland in time for the Glorious Twelfth.* □ *The bag on the Twelfth was rather poor this year.*

glory days *n.* a former time of maximum influence, power or wealth. □ *That was in his glory days; he's not nearly so vigorous now.* □ *In my glory days, I could have taken you all on—and won.*

glossy *n.* a magazine, often with artistic pretensions, that is printed on glossy paper. □ *The table in the dentist's waiting room was covered with glossies.* □ *She picked up a glossy and sat there quietly, reading it.*

glow *n.* a mild state of drug or alcohol intoxication. □ *She had a nice glow, but was by no means stewed.* □ *What was supposed to be a nice glow turned out to be a terrifying hallucination.*

glueie *n.* a teenager who sniffs glue. □ *Terry was just another glueie who overdosed.* □ *Why do these glueies do it?*

glug *n.* a gulp or shot of liquor. □ *Have another glug of this moonshine.* □ *I took one glug and spat it out.*

Glums *n.* the musical show called "Les Miserables." (Always with *the*.) □ *Mrs*

Stuart has been to see the Glums over twenty times. □ So she likes the Glums, then?

gnat's piss *n.* a weak or insipid drink. (Taboo.) □ *Sorry, this stuff is just like gnat's piss. □ Don't waste your money on that gnat's piss.*

go 1. *n.* a try (at something). □ *Let me have a go at it this time. □ I'd like to have another go at it, if I can.* **2.** *vb.* to urinate. (Crude. A euphemism.) □ *I gotta go! □ Jimmy's gonna go in his pants!*

go about together *vb. phr.* to go out with each other. □ *I see Sally and Bill are going about together now. □ That pair have been going about together for years!*

go a bundle on someone *vb. phr.* to think highly of someone. (Always in the negative.) □ *I'm afraid I did not go a bundle on Susan. No, not at all. □ Apparently Susan didn't go a bundle on you either, since you didn't ask.*

go-ahead *n.* permission to proceed; the signal to go ahead. (Compare with SAY-SO.) □ *We're ready to go as soon as we get the go-ahead. □ I gave him the go-ahead, and the tanks started moving in.*

goalie *n.* a goal-keeper. (Soccer.) □ *My uncle Willie's a goalie in the local team. □ That goalie was useless! He let in all these goals!*

go all the way *vb. phr.* to perform sexual intercourse; to carry caressing all the way to sexual intercourse. (Crude.) □ *Did they go all the way? □ He keeps wanting me to go all the way.*

Go (and) fuck yourself! AND **Go and piss up your kilt!** *exclam.* an insulting and brusque synonym for "No!" (Taboo.) □ *Absolutely not! Go and fuck yourself! □ That is a stupid and insulting suggestion. Go and piss up your kilt!*

Go (and) jump in the lake! See GO AND TAKE A FLYING LEAP AT YOURSELF!

Go and piss up your kilt! See GO (AND) FUCK YOURSELF!

Go and take a flying leap at yourself! AND **Go (and) jump in the lake!; Take a flying leap at yourself!; Take a flying leap!; Jump in the lake!** *exclam.*

"Get lost!"; "Go away!" □ *Oh, go and take a flying leap at yourself! Get out of my life! □ Go and jump in the lake!! You're a pain in the neck.*

go ape (over someone or something) *vb. phr.* to become very excited over something. □ *I just go ape over chocolate. □ Sam went ape over Mary.*

go (a)round the houses *vb. phr.* to avoid or to delay coming to the point. □ *Instead of going around the houses yet again, could we finally come to the point, please? □ Why did you go round the houses instead of just coming right out and asking?*

gob 1. *n.* the mouth. □ *Shut your gob and get on with your work. □ Have I ever told you that you have an ugly gob?* **2.** *n.* a slimy lump. □ *I can't eat these gobs of so-called food. □ There was a gob of the stuff on the plate, but I wasn't going to eat it.*

go ballistic AND **go into orbit** *vb. phr.* to become very excited, usually in anger. □ *Oh boy, the manager was so angry I thought she was going to go ballistic. □ The entire staff went into orbit when they got the news.*

go bananas *vb. phr.* to go mildly crazy. (See also BANANAS.) □ *Sorry, I just went bananas for a minute. □ I thought he was going to go bananas.*

gobbledygook *n.* nonsense; officialese or government gibberish. □ *I can't understand all this gobbledygook. □ They must have a full-time staff to dream up all this gobbledygook.*

gobble someone *vb.* to perform oral sex upon a man. (Taboo.) □ *He actually came right out and asked, you know, for me to gobble him! □ So did you gobble him then?*

go belly up AND **turn belly up 1.** *vb. phr.* to fail. □ *I sort of felt that the whole thing would go belly up, and I was right. □ The computer—on its last legs anyway—turned belly up right in the middle of an important job.* **2.** *vb. phr.* to die. (As a fish does when it dies.) □ *The cat was friendly for a moment before she turned belly up. □ Every fish in Greg's tank turned belly up last night.*

gob job *n.* an act of oral sex upon a man. (Taboo.) □ *Fancy a gob job, darling?* □ *They say that girl standing at the corner will do a gob job on you if you pay her enough.*

gobshite *n.* a despicable person. (Crude.) □ *What a gobshite you are!* □ *Just get out of my sight, you gobshite!*

gobslutch *n.* a person with disgusting or filthy personal habits. (Crude.) □ *You gobslutch, that's just disgusting!* □ *If you're going to be a gobslutch, you can be one somewhere else.*

gobsmacked AND **gobstruck** *mod.* flabbergasted, entirely astonished or dumbstruck. □ *Clearly, he was gobsmacked by the news.* □ *What she said really gobstruck me.*

gobstopper *n.* a large sweet that fills the mouth and is made of hard material. □ *I love gobstoppers. I always have, ever since I was little.* □ *Mummy, can I have a gobstopper?*

gobstruck See GOBSMACKED.

go by the book *vb. phr.* to follow the rules exactly. □ *Around here we go by the book. All right?* □ *I will only go by the book, so there!*

go cold on someone or something *vb. phr.* to lose enthusiasm for someone or something. □ *No, I've gone cold on that idea.* □ *She's gone cold on him, I'm afraid.*

God love her *n.* mother. (Rhyming slang.) □ *When does your God love her get home?* □ *I'll have to ask me God love her if I can come out to play.*

go down 1. *vb. phr.* to leave university without a degree. □ *If I don't pass these degree exams I'll have to go down.* □ *Roger went down after five years at the college.* **2.** *vb. phr.* to be accepted. (Compare with SWALLOW.) □ *We'll just have to wait for a while to see how all this goes down.* □ *The proposal didn't go down very well with the manager.* **3.** *vb. phr.* to be arrested. (Underworld.) □ *Lefty didn't want to go down for a job he didn't do.* □ *Mr Big said that somebody had to go down for it, and he didn't care who.* **4.** *vb. phr.* to be sent to prison. □ *He'll go down for ten years.* □ *"You're going down for sure," said the judge.*

go down a bomb See GO LIKE A BOMB.

go down a treat AND **go down well** *vb. phr.* to greatly enjoy something, especially food or drink. □ *That looks as if it would go down a treat.* □ *It really went down well.*

go down for the gravy AND **go down on someone** *vb. phr.* to perform oral sex on someone. (Taboo.) □ *She went down for the gravy again, because he asked.* □ *That one will go down on anyone who pays.* □ *I'll go down on you for £20, mister.*

go downhill *vb. phr.* to decline. □ *This company is going downhill at a great rate.* □ *Things began to go downhill rapidly when the council cut the maintenance budget.*

go down in flames *vb. phr.* to fail spectacularly. (Compare with SHOOT SOMEONE OR SOMETHING DOWN IN FLAMES.) □ *The whole team went down in flames.* □ *I'd hate it if all your planning was to go down in flames.*

go down like a lead balloon AND **go over like a lead balloon 1.** *vb. phr.* to fail utterly. □ *The joke went down like a lead balloon.* □ *I'm afraid your plan went over like a lead balloon.* **2.** *vb. phr.* to be totally rejected. □ *My plan went down like a lead balloon.* □ *The alternative will go over like a lead balloon too, you'll see!*

go down on someone See GO DOWN FOR THE GRAVY.

go down the tube(s) *vb. phr.* to fail totally; to be ruined. □ *The whole project is likely to go down the tubes.* □ *All my plans just went down the tube.*

go down well See GO DOWN A TREAT.

go down with something *vb. phr.* to become infected with a disease. □ *I think I'm going down with something.* □ *The poor dear seems to have gone down with the measles.*

God rep *n.* a chaplain or padre. (Normally with *the*.) □ *The God rep's a good guy.* □ *He had to go and see the God rep about something or other.*

gods 1. *n.* the highest gallery level of a theatre. (Normally with *the*.) □ *Sitting in the gods is an experience you have to experience at least once.* □ *The* *cheapest seats are in the gods, of course.* **2.** *n.* the people sitting on the highest gallery level of a theatre. (Normally with *the*.) □ *He prefers to sit among the gods, as they are—he says—a nicer bunch.* □ *There were few gods in the top balcony that evening.*

God's acre *n.* a cemetery. □ *When I end up in God's acre, I want everything to go on without me.* □ *Fear not, everything will go on without you. God's acre is full of indispensable people.*

God slot *n.* a time set aside for religious programmes on television. □ *She's addicted to every God slot on TV.* □ *So when are all these God slots anyway?*

go Dutch *vb. phr.* [for two people] to split the cost of something, such as a meal. (Compare with DUTCH TREAT.) □ *How about dinner tonight? We'll go Dutch, okay?* □ *Yes, let's go Dutch.*

goer *n.* a woman considered sexually willing and available. (Crude.) □ *She's a goer, I'm sure.* □ *I wouldn't say Susan's a goer, but you never know your luck.*

gofer *n.* a person who runs errands for others. □ *Here was one gofer that was different from the others, he thought.* □ *I don't think I need another gofer today.*

go for a burton **1.** *vb. phr.* to be killed, particularly in battle. □ *A large number of our best went for a burton taking that hill, and for what?* □ *If we try to take that hill like we did the last one, a lot more of us will go for a burton for sure.* **2.** *vb. phr.* to become broken or destroyed. □ *I'm afraid the thing's gone for a burton.* □ *If you drop it, it will assuredly go for a burton.*

go for broke *vb. phr.* to choose to risk everything; to try to succeed against great odds. □ *I feel lucky today. I'll go for broke.* □ *We decided to go for broke, and that is exactly how we ended up.*

go for it *vb. phr.* to try for something. □ *Go on, go for it. It's worth trying.* □ *It looked like something I wanted to do, so I decided to go for it.*

go for one's life *vb. phr.* to run as fast as one possibly can. □ *If you go for your*

life you might just still catch that train. □ *Yes, he really was going for his life.*

go-getter *n.* an aggressively energetic person. □ *Willy is a real go-getter. He'll go places.* □ *Sally likes people to think she's a go-getter.*

goggle box *n.* a television set. □ *A huge goggle box sat there, dominating the room.* □ *She flicked off the goggle box as we entered.*

go-go girl *n.* a young woman who performs provocative dances for the entertainment of customers in a public house or strip-tease club. (From the French *a gogo*, meaning "whatever you wish," or "galore.") □ *I worked as a go-go girl for a while.* □ *Those go-go girls have changed their style.*

go great guns *vb. phr.* to be going forward very vigorously or successfully. □ *Everything is going great guns around here. We're busy and making lots of money.* □ *The project is finally going great guns, just as we planned.*

go haywire **1.** *vb. phr.* [for someone] to go berserk; to become erratic or seriously mentally disturbed. □ *I thought for a minute that Pete was going to go haywire.* □ *Sorry, I suppose I must have just gone haywire for a minute.* **2.** *vb. phr.* [for something] to go out of control; to break down or become disorganised. □ *My stereo's gone haywire again.* □ *I'm afraid my car's steering's gone haywire. It's too dangerous to drive.*

going like a train *vb. phr.* to be moving very fast; to be working very effectively or well. □ *Oh, everything's going like a train now.* □ *We were really going like a train down the motorway by this time.*

going over **1.** *n.* a disagreeable examination or interrogation. □ *After a thorough going over, the doctor pronounced me alive.* □ *I gave your car a good going over, and I fixed a lot of little things.* □ *The cops gave Willy a thorough going over, but he admitted nothing.* **2.** *n.* a beating. □ *Bruno gave the guy a terrible going over.* □ *After a going over like that, the guy spent two weeks in the hospital.*

goings-on *n.* happenings; events. □ *There are certainly some strange goings-on around here.* □ *Some big goings-on in the town centre tied up the traffic.*

go into a huddle *vb. phr.* to hold a secret meeting. □ *Right, I think we better go into a huddle.* □ *What was said once you all went into a huddle?*

go into dry dock *vb. phr.* to stay for some time in hospital. □ *I'm going into dry dock for that operation next week.* □ *Sorry, but you must go into dry dock right away.*

go into orbit See GO BALLISTIC.

gold digger *n.* a woman who pays attention to a man solely because of his wealth. □ *Sam called Sally a gold digger, and she was devastated.* □ *"You little gold digger!" cried Sam.*

gold dust *n.* cocaine. □ *Snorting gold dust is a fool's game.* □ *He took the packet of gold dust and left, without a word.*

golden handcuffs *n.* monetary inducements to stay in a job. (Usually for highly paid executives in large corporations.) □ *The company provided a variety of golden handcuffs to keep its execs happy through a take-over.* □ *The golden handcuffs included a half million in severance pay for one of the directors.*

golden handshake *n.* a gratuity or bonus paid to a senior employee or executive upon leaving the employment of a company. □ *Imagine! She offered a golden handshake to him just to go away!* □ *So, how big a golden handshake did you get from them?*

golden oldie *n.* a hit tune from earlier years that is still popular. □ *Oh yes, I remember that golden oldie!* □ *I suppose it's only us oldies who remember golden oldies like these nowadays.*

golden opportunity *n.* a very good opportunity. □ *This is my golden opportunity, and I can't pass it up.* □ *You get a golden opportunity like this very rarely.*

gold watch *n.* whisky, (Rhyming slang, linked as follows: gold watch ≈ [Scotch] = whisky.) □ *A wee drop of the gold watch is always acceptable round here.* □ *He said thank you with a bottle of gold watch, since you ask.*

golf widow *n.* a wife left alone while her husband plays golf. (See COMPUTER WIDOW and BRIDGE WIDOW.) □ *There's a lot of us golf widows around here, especially at weekends.* □ *Why don't you come along to the next meeting of Golf Widows Anonymous?*

go like a bomb AND **go down a bomb** **1.** *vb. phr.* to be greatly successful in business. □ *The sale was going like a bomb when I turned up.* □ *I think his plan will go down a bomb.* **2.** *vb. phr.* to function very well. □ *I think the whole thing is going like a bomb!* □ *It was a tremendous success, going down a bomb.*

go like a rabbit *vb. phr.* to perform sexual intercourse frequently and enthusiastically. (Crude.) □ *The two of them were going at it like rabbits!* □ *One look and he knew she was going to go like a rabbit.*

go like the clappers **1.** *vb. phr.* to travel very rapidly. □ *Go like the clappers! We're very late!* □ *If we're to get there on time we must go like the clappers.* **2.** *vb. phr.* to work very hard. □ *If you go like the clappers you should be finished on time.* □ *We must go like the clappers. There is no time to lose!*

golly(-wog) *n.* a black person. (Racially offensive.) □ *Don't call black people gollies, please. It is very offensive and racist.* □ *He said he was not a racist, he just hated golly-wogs!*

go mental *vb. phr.* to go crazy; to go insane. □ *Don't go mental, Jane. Just calm down and think about it.* □ *Another day in that history class and I know I will go mental.*

go native *vb. phr.* to become assimilated with the local inhabitants. □ *He left to live in Nigeria and went native, I hear.* □ *Why did you go native anyway?*

gone *mod.* intoxicated due to drink or drugs. □ *Those girls are gone—too much to drink.* □ *Ted is really gone under.*

gone an' dunnit *n.* a hat. (Rhyming slang, linked as follows: gone an' dunnit ≈ [bunnit] = hat. Scots usage. *Bunnit* is the Scots dialectal form of *bonnet* and *dunnit* is the Scots dialectal form of *done it*.) □ *Now yon's a gone an' dunnit with a difference.* □ *Do you have to wear a gone an' dunnit like that?*

gone by *mod.* [of a person] too old. □ *He's far too gone by for this sort of work.* □ *He's pleasant enough, but gone by.*

goner *n.* someone or something finished or nearly finished. □ *This one's a goner. Let's just chuck it out.* □ *The horse was a goner, so it had to be destroyed.*

gone time *mod.* past or after an expected time or duration. □ *It's gone time. Get on with it.* □ *We can't wait any longer as it's gone time now.*

gong *n.* a military medal. □ *What a lot of gongs you have, uncle.* □ *I got that gong for the Falklands.*

gonk *n.* a prostitute's derisory name for a client. (Crude.) □ *Don't worry, there's always another gonk.* □ *Another gonk went off with her in his car.*

gonna *phr.* "going to." (Eye-dialect. Typical spoken English. Used in writing only for effect. Used in the examples of this dictionary.) □ *What time are you gonna be home?* □ *I'm gonna get you, you little squirt!*

goo *n.* some sticky substance; GUNGE. □ *What is this goo on my shoe?* □ *There is some sort of goo on my plate. Is that meant to be my dinner?*

good few See FAIR FEW.

good for a giggle AND **good for a laugh** *phr.* possibly worthless, but may be amusing. □ *He did what?...well, at least it's good for a giggle.* □ *That may be good for a laugh but it's not the real solution.*

good for a laugh See GOOD FOR A GIGGLE.

good form *n.* the proper way to behave. □ *We are looking for good form around here, you understand.* □ *What's the good form on this situation then?*

good-for-nothing 1. *mod.* worthless. □ *Let's get rid of this good-for-nothing car right now.* □ *Tell your good-for-nothing brother to find another place to live.* **2.** *n.* a worthless person. (Also a

rude term of address.) □ *Tell the good-for-nothing to leave.* □ *Look you good-for-nothing, just get up and go out and get a job.*

Good for you! See GOOD ON YOU!

Good heavens! *exclam.* a mild exclamation of amazement, shock, etc. □ *Good heavens! I didn't expect you to be here.* □ *Good heavens, there's a man at the window!*

good job *n.* a fortunate circumstance. □ *It's a good job you stayed at home today.* □ *What a good job I caught you when I did.*

good jump See JUMP.

good kick *n.* a soccer player who can kick the ball especially well. □ *He's a good kick. I want him on our team.* □ *Who's that good kick on the other team?*

good looker *n.* a person with an attractive appearance. □ *Fred is not exactly a good looker, but he is pleasant enough.* □ *Mary is certainly a good looker and I would like to go out with her.*

Good on you! AND **Good for you!**; **Good show!** *exclam.* "Well done!"; "Congratulations!" □ *Good on you! That's just what we want!* □ *Good show! I'm glad you won.*

Good show! See GOOD ON YOU!

good trip *n.* a good session with L.S.D. or some other drug. □ *Paul said he had a good trip, but he looks like hell.* □ *One good trip deserves another. At least that's what my guru says.*

good wicket 1. *n.* a cricket game that's going well. □ *We've got a good wicket today.* □ *A good wicket makes all the difference.* **2.** *n.* a good situation to be in. □ *Well, that's a good wicket to be in!* □ *I'm looking for a good wicket.*

goody two-shoes AND **Miss Goody Two-shoes** *n.* someone, usually female, who is well-behaved and virtuous to the point of nauseousness. (Also a term of address.) □ *I'm no goody two-shoes. I just like to keep my nose clean.* □ *Well, Miss Goody Two-shoes, so you condescended to sit with us.*

goof *n.* a foolish oaf. □ *Sometimes I'm such a goof. I really messed up.* □ *Don't be a goof. Get with it.*

go off at half-cock *vb. phr.* to proceed before everything is ready. (Compare with HALF-COCKED.) □ *I waited because I didn't want to go off at half-cock.* □ *The boss insisted we went off at half-cock and the result is the mess you see about you.*

go off someone or something *vb. phr.* to start to dislike or lose interest in someone or something. □ *She really has been going off him for some time now.* □ *Naw, I've gone off that idea.*

go off the boil *vb. phr.* to lose the initiative; to lose interest. □ *I think he's gone off the boil for that plan.* □ *If you don't keep up interest the public will go off the boil.*

go off the deep end *vb. phr.* to succumb to emotion, particularly to fly into a rage of anger. □ *I saw what he had done, and I just went off the deep end. I was in a blind rage and didn't know what I was doing.* □ *I was afraid that when John learnt that Mary had left him he would go off the deep end, and he did.*

googly *n.* a ball bowled so that it spins in the opposite way to that expected. (Cricket.) □ *Take care, he does a deadly googly.* □ *I can't cope with googlies.*

googly-merchant *n.* a bowler of GOOGLIES. (Cricket.) □ *This bowler is a real googly-merchant.* □ *If he's a googly-merchant I'm a gonner.*

goolie AND **gooly** *n.* a testicle. (Taboo. Normally with *the* and in the plural.) □ *Thud, right in the goolies. Ye gods, it hurt!* □ *He turned sideways to protect his goolies.*

Go on! **1.** *exclam.* an expression of disbelief. □ *Go on! You don't really know what you are talking about!* □ *Go on! You weren't even there.* **2.** *exclam.* an expression of encouragement. □ *Go on! What happened next?* □ *Go on! You'll love it when you get there.*

go on *vb. phr.* to commence bowling. (Cricket.) □ *Can you go on now please, Harold?* □ *Well, we went on and bowled the lot out, one after the other!*

go on a bit *vb. phr.* to talk at somewhat excessive length. □ *You do go on a bit, don't you?* □ *She went on a bit, it's true.*

go on (and on) about someone or something *vb. phr.* to talk about someone or something endlessly. □ *He just went on and on about the trouble he was having with the post office.* □ *Why do you have to go on about your sister so?*

go on at someone *vb. phr.* to irritate or nag someone persistently. □ *Tom is always going on at Frank.* □ *Stop going on at me!*

goopy *n.* a fool. □ *Who's the goopy in the bright orange trousers?* □ *I felt a right goopy when I found out that I'd got onto the wrong train.*

goose **1.** *n.* a silly oaf; an oaf. □ *Oh, I'm such a silly goose!* □ *What a goose you are!* **2.** *vb. phr.* to poke something, such as a finger, in someone's anus, or between their legs, or to attempt at this. (Crude.) □ *Freddy goosed me!* □ *If you goose me again I will not be responsible for the painful death you will suffer!* **3.** *n.* the poking of something, such as a finger, in someone's anus, or between their legs, or an attempt at this. (Crude.) □ *Harry is a master of the rude goose.* □ *He tried to give me a goose!*

goose and duck *n.* a lorry. (Rhyming slang.) □ *There are too many geese and ducks using this small residential road.* □ *Why is there a huge goose and duck parked outside our house?*

goose girl *n.* a lesbian. (Crude.) □ *Don't you know? Sandra's a goose girl.* □ *You'll find nothing but goose girls in that pub.*

goosegog *n.* a gooseberry. □ *Goosegogs make you...well, you know.* □ *My wife makes goosegog jam every year.*

goose('s neck) *n.* a cheque. (Rhyming slang.) □ *All right, I'll take your goose.* □ *I'm afraid my goose's neck'll bounce.*

go out like a light *vb. phr.* to lose consciousness very suddenly or quickly. □ *She's very tired and will go out like a light.* □ *I went out like a light last night and feel so rested now.*

go over big *vb. phr.* to be very successful. □ *I'm sure this will go over big with the folks at home.* □ *Well, it didn't go over very big with the boss.*

go overboard **1.** *vb. phr.* to do far more than is necessary; to go too far. □ *He* has a tendency to go overboard at these parties. □ Now don't go overboard for us. We're nothing special. **2.** vb. phr. to be very enthusiastic. □ Harry's gone overboard for his new computer. Again. This happens every time he gets one. □ Don't go overboard yet! There are some problems with this idea, too.

go over like a lead balloon See GO DOWN LIKE A LEAD BALLOON.

go over the top vb. phr. to exceed reasonable limits, particularly of dress or behaviour. (See OVER THE TOP. From World War I, when "going over the top" meant climbing up out of a trench and into no-man's-land with a view to charging at the enemy, but quite probably getting shot dead in the process. Since then, it has become a euphemism for doing anything that is excessive, especially if outrageous, stupid or suicidal.) □ Work for a living? You don't have to go over the top, Otto! □ There's Martin, going over the top again.

go places vb. phr. to become very successful. □ I knew that Sally would go places. □ I really want to go places in my career.

go public 1. vb. phr. to sell to the public shares of a privately owned company. (Securities markets. Technically, to transform a private limited company into a public limited company. Compare with TAKE SOMETHING PUBLIC.) □ The company decided not to go public because the economy was so bad at the time. □ We'll go public at a later time. **2.** vb. phr. to reveal something to the public. (Especially with with, as in the examples.) □ It's too early to go public with the story. □ Just let me know when we can go public with this.

go racing vb. phr. to attend a horse racing meet. □ They've all gone racing today. □ Fancy going racing tomorrow?

gorblimey See BLIMEY.

Gordon Bennett! exclam. an exclamation of surprise or annoyance or both. (Reputed to be a euphemism for CORBLIMEY or GORBLIMEY. James Gordon Bennett was a Scots-born New York newspaper baron who lived from 1795 to 1892. He founded and edited the New York Herald, and it was his identically-named son who sent Stanley to Africa to seek out Livingstone. Nevertheless he is now largely forgotten in both his native and adopted lands, yet somehow or other his name is preserved as a sort of oath uttered when something particularly irritating or annoying happens without warning. Apparently Mr Bennett was in the habit of announcing his arrival in a restaurant by yanking away the cloths of any tables he passed, which might have something to do with this strange immortality.) □ Gordon Bennett! What has that idiot done now! □ Gordon Bennett, will you just stop pestering me!

gorilla n. one thousand Pounds Sterling. (Compare with MONKEY, PONY and SCORE.) □ Who the blazes is going to be daft enough to give you a gorilla for that? □ This car is worth at least twenty gorillas.

gormless mod. foolish or witless; none too smart. □ You gormless fool, you've wrecked it! □ Then this gormless idiot comes up and asks her for a dance.

go round the haystack vb. phr. to visit the toilet. (Rhyming slang, linked as follows: go round the haystack ≈ [back] = toilet.) □ Just a moment while I go round the haystack. □ Gotta go round the haystack!

go short of something vb. phr. to do without something. □ I'm afraid we'll just have to go short of food until we get back to base, Captain. □ I don't see why we should have to go short of anything.

go something vb. to use something. □ I could go a cup of tea. □ This company could go a serious injection of cash.

go spare 1. vb. phr. to become extremely angry or upset. □ Now don't go spare! It's not as terrible as it looks. □ Are you surprised she went spare when she saw it? **2.** vb. phr. to become surplus or no longer required. □ These ones in the corner are going spare. □ If you have any that go spare, we'll take them. **3.** vb. phr. to go to waste. □ It's a shame that all that food had to go spare. □ There's four hundred quid going spare here you know.

gospel (truth) *n.* the honest truth. □ *He's speaking the gospel truth. You can trust him.* □ *You've gotta believe me. It's gospel!*

goss *n.* gossip. (Teens.) □ *Enough of this goss—on with the show!* □ *I like to listen in on other people's goss.*

go stag *vb. phr.* to go to a party without a date. (Said of a male.) □ *He decided to ignore her and go stag.* □ *A bunch of the lads got together and went stag to the dance.*

go steady *vb. phr.* to be together as a courting couple or as boyfriend and girlfriend. □ *They've been going steady for over a year now.* □ *Are you still going steady with Robert?*

go straight *vb. phr.* to stop breaking the law. □ *Lefty thought about going straight once, but pulled himself out of it.* □ *I think I'll give all this up and go straight—some day.*

Gotcha! AND **Gotcher!** *exclam.* "I got you!"; "I've caught you!" □ *Gotcha! (Front page headline of the* Sun *newspaper after the Royal Navy's nuclear-powered submarine* HMS Conqueror *torpedoed and sank the Argentinean cruiser* General Belgrano *with the loss of 368 lives, during the Falklands War of 1982.)* □ *"Gotcher!" said the policeman, as he grabbed the burglar climbing through the window.*

Gotcher! See GOTCHA!

goth(ic) *n.* a species of rock music aficionado. □ *Gothics are particularly disposed to adopting a cadaverous style of dress, make up and general appearance.* □ *A number of goths often gather in that cafe over there.*

go through (something) like a dose of salts *vb. phr.* to carry out some process very rapidly or efficiently. (From the ability of a strong laxative to move through the digestive tract with great rapidity.) □ *The new girl is very effective. She went through the paperwork like a dose of salts.* □ *Ratification of the treaty went through Parliament like a dose of salts.*

go through the motions *vb. phr.* to appear to be doing something without actually doing it; to conform for the sake of appearances. □ *Well, they're going through the motions, but everyone knows it's hopeless.* □ *Do we have to go through the motions all over again?*

go through the roof AND **hit the roof** *vb. phr.* to become extremely angry. □ *She really went through the roof when she found out what happened.* □ *My dad'll hit the roof when he finds out about this.*

Go to blazes! AND **Go to the devil!** *exclam.* "Go away!"; "Get lost!" □ *Go to blazes! Stop pestering me!* □ *I'm sick of your complaining. Go to the devil!*

go to earth *vb. phr.* to hide. (As an animal does in its burrow.) □ *He's gone to earth to avoid his creditors.* □ *It's too late to go to earth, Boris. The police are here.*

go to pay the water bill *vb. phr.* to urinate. (Crude.) □ *He just went out to go to pay the water bill.* □ *I've got to go to pay the water bill. Back in a minute.*

go to the country *vb. phr.* to call a general election. □ *The prime minister has decided to go to the country.* □ *We will go to the country next month.*

Go to the devil! See GO TO BLAZES!

go to the loo *vb. phr.* to urinate. (Crude.) □ *Well, going to the loo does relieve the pressure of all that beer!* □ *I'm just going to the loo.*

go to town *vb. phr.* to do something with gusto; to do something with great speed and energy. □ *The main office is really going to town on collecting overdue payments.* □ *My goodness, our team is really going to town.*

got something off pat *vb. phr.* to have learned something perfectly. □ *As soon as I got the wording off pat, they changed the words.* □ *The secret of effective speechmaking is not to get the exact words off pat, but to get the meaning off pat in your mind so that when you stand up you know what message you want to impart. The words will come easily then.*

Got you. *sent.* I understand you. □ *OK. Got you.* □ *I've got you now.*

gouch out See GAUCH OUT.

go underground *vb. phr.* to go into hiding; to begin to operate in secret. □ *The entire operation went underground, and we heard no more about it.* □ *We'll go underground if we have to. Nothing will stop the movement.*

go up the steps *vb. phr.* to appear on trial at the OLD BAILEY. □ *Otto goes up the steps today.* □ *I don't want to have to go up the steps.*

go up to town *vb. phr.* to visit London. □ *I have to go up to town for a few days, my dear.* □ *Sometimes I wonder what he does when he goes up to town.*

governor AND **guv; guv'nor** 1. *n.* one's employer. (Also a term of address.) □ *My governor told me to move these boxes.* □ *What do you want done next, guv?* 2. *n.* one's father. □ *My governor insisted I got a job.* □ *I'll ask my guv'nor if I can go.*

go walkabout *vb. phr.* [for celebrities such as politicians or royalty] to go on an informal tour; to mingle with a crowd. (Australianism.) □ *The Queen went walkabout when she arrived in the crowded square.* □ *Every time one of these people goes walkabout, the security people get a few more grey hairs.*

go walkies *vb. phr.* [for a small child or pet] to go for a walk; to be taken for a walk. □ *Want to go walkies, Jimmy?* □ *He's gone walkies with the dog.*

go west 1. *vb. phr.* [for something] to be destroyed. □ *If the company goes west, we'll all be looking for new jobs.* □ *Well, there's another good idea gone west.* 2. *vb. phr.* [for someone] to be killed or to die. □ *Don't look. He's gone west, I'm afraid.* □ *I don't like this; another good man gone west.*

gowp 1. *vb.* to throb with pain. (Scots usage.) □ *The doctor wants to know if it gowps, Sheena.* □ *After that heavy blow his arm really gowped.* 2. *vb.* to ache. (Scots usage.) □ *I really gowp for that lassie.* □ *She's richt gowping in her hied. (She has a very bad headache.)*

gozz *n.* a gossip session, especially on the telephone. □ *Is this gozz going to go on all night?* □ *If you must have gozzes like that, get your own phone.*

grab a pew AND **take a pew** *vb. phr.* to take a seat; to sit down. □ *Come in,*

Fred. Just grab a pew anywhere you see a chair. This place is a mess. □ *Just take a pew, and we'll have our little talk.*

graft 1. *n.* hard work or effort. □ *It's called graft; try it sometime.* □ *None of these young ones know what hard graft really means.* 2. *n.* shady dealings or corruption, especially bribery. □ *The amount of graft going on in here is beyond belief.* □ *How can we stop this epidemic of graft?*

grafter 1. *n.* a hard worker. □ *You won't be sorry, he's a real grafter.* □ *I only want grafters working on this.* 2. *n.* a criminal. □ *Greg has become such a grafter that no one speaks to him anymore.* □ *There's nothing but grafters in that pub.*

gran *n.* a grandmother. □ *The kids love visiting their gran.* □ *I love my gran.*

grand *n.* one thousand Pounds Sterling. □ *That car probably cost about twenty grand.* □ *Four grand for that thing?*

grand-daddy of them all See DADDY OF THEM ALL.

grand slam *n.* a complete and triumphal success. □ *One more grand slam like that and we'll be happy.* □ *Congratulations on your grand slam.*

Granite City *n.* Aberdeen. (Normally with *the*.) □ *The Granite City is Britain's oil capital.* □ *Aberdeen is called the Granite City because it is built upon and from granite.*

Granite Jug *n.* Dartmoor Prison. (It was built upon and from granite. Normally with *the*. See JUG (AND PAIL).) □ *Have you ever been in the Granite Jug?* □ *Otto's in the Granite Jug, and will be there for some time I think.*

granny annexe AND **granny flat** *n.* part of a private residence used as a self-contained apartment, usually by an elderly relative. □ *We built a granny annexe for the wife's mother but then she died.* □ *The granny flat was there when we bought the house.*

granny bond *n.* a government savings certificate available to pensioners only. □ *When she died, they found out that she had a fortune in granny bonds.* □ *My aunt buys a granny bond every week.*

granny flat See GRANNY ANNEXE.

grapevine *n.* a secret or informal means of communication, often mouth-to-mouth, often of rumours. (Compare with BUSH TELEGRAPH.) □ *I heard on the grapevine that Sam is moving north.* □ *The grapevine was right. He's already left.*

grass 1. *n.* marijuana. □ *These kids managed to find this grass somewhere.* □ *Almost everyone knows that grass means marijuana.* **2.** AND **grasser** *n.* a police informer. □ *What did the grass say?* □ *Harry's a grasser.*

grasser See GRASS.

grasshopper *n.* a policeman. (Rhyming slang, linked as follows: grasshopper ≈ [copper] = policeman.) □ *The grasshopper stopped at the door, tried the lock, and moved on.* □ *Think about how the grasshopper on the beat is affected by this cold.*

grass on someone *vb. phr.* to inform, especially to the police or other authorities. □ *Mike was grassed on by Joe, and now Mike's in the slammer.* □ *Joe grassed on Mike, and now Joe's in the hospital.*

grassroots 1. *n.* the ordinary mass of people, especially when considered as voters; the ordinary members of a trade union, political party, etc. □ *We really haven't heard anything from the grassroots yet.* □ *The grassroots are not going to go for these fancy ideas of yours, you know.* **2.** *mod.* having to do with or originating with the ordinary mass of people or voters, ordinary members of a trade union, political party, etc. □ *Grassroots pressure forced Smith to change his views on that topic.* □ *Politicians love to create grassroots movements.* **3.** *n.* the source; the fundamental level or source. □ *At the grassroots nothing has changed.* □ *The basic, grassroots principles are unchanged behind all the new features added in recent years.*

graveyard shift *n.* the night shift of work in a factory, usually starting at about midnight. □ *I'd prefer not to work the graveyard shift.* □ *The pay is pretty good on the graveyard shift.*

gravy AND **gravy train** *n.* extra or easy money; easy profit. □ *Virtually every penny that came in was pure gravy— no expenses and no materials costs at all.* □ *After I pay expenses, we're on the gravy train with the rest.*

gravy train See GRAVY.

grazer *n.* someone who frequently eats small amounts throughout the day. □ *Doris is a real grazer, always with a snack.* □ *Do grazers get fatter than other people?*

GR&D *interj.* "grinning, running and ducking." (Computer jargon. Written only. An initialism used in computer communications. Describes what one might be doing after having written a mischievous message. Sometimes enclosed, "<GR&D>.") □ *I'm GR&D, but I'm glad I said it.* □ *I suppose that you got just the kind of answer that you deserve.* <GR&D>.

grease monkey *n.* a mechanic. □ *Leave it to the grease monkeys; they'll fix it.* □ *This is Mac. He's our grease monkey.*

greaser *n.* a rough and aggressive male, usually with long, greased-down hair. □ *Who's the greaser who just swaggered in?* □ *Donna has been going out with a real greaser.*

grease-up See FRY-UP.

greasy spoon *n.* any untidy, unappetising and possibly unhygenic cafe or restaurant. □ *Let's eat at the greasy spoon on the High Street. The food is grotty, but the people-watching is good.* □ *I wouldn't be caught dead in a greasy spoon like that.* □ *If you keep on eating at greasy spoons like that, you probably will be caught dead—from a coronary.*

greatest *n.* the very best. (Normally with *the*.) □ *Elvis is the greatest!* □ *That lunch was the greatest.*

Great Scott! *exclam.* "Good grief!" □ *Great Scott! What happened?* □ *I'm late again! Great Scott!*

Great Smoke See BIG SMOKE.

great unwashed *n.* a snobbish name for the proletariat. (Normally with *the*.) □ *Charles would really like to have nothing whatever to do with the great* unwashed. □ *The trouble with the great unwashed is that there are so many of them.*

Great Wen *n.* London. (Normally with *the. Wen* is an archaic word for a wart.) □ *"There it is," he said, pointing to the left side of the aircraft, "the whole of the Great Wen laid out before you." □ We have business in the Great Wen, my lad; we have business there.*

Greek to someone *n.* something incomprehensible to someone; something as mysterious as Greek writing. □ *I don't understand this. It's all Greek to me. □ She said it was Greek to her, and that it made no sense at all.*

green around the gills See BLUE AROUND THE GILLS.

Green Berets *n.* the Royal Marines. (Normally with *the.*) □ *"The Green Berets are a fine body of men," said Margaret. □ "She should know about the Green Berets' bodies," thought Margaret's companion, "she's inspected as many as she can at the closest possible quarters."*

green fingers *n.* the wonderful ability to garden and grow pot plants. □ *Helen has green fingers and can work wonders with plants. □ If I had green fingers, I could grow my own roses.*

green goddess *n.* a military fire engine. (Named for its colour.) □ *When the civilian firemen went on strike, they brought in green goddesses. □ I used to drive a green goddess.*

green light *n.* the signal to go ahead with something; the OKAY. (See GO-AHEAD.) □ *She gave the green light to the project. □ When we get the green light, we'll start.*

green welly *n.* a sort of up-market wellington boot. (A wellington boot is a rubber or plastic waterproof boot that usually covers the shin. It was invented by the Duke of Wellington.) □ *Wearing green wellies is usually a sign that you don't belong in the countryside. □ You've got to admit that a green welly looks smarter than an ordinary one.*

green welly brigade *n.* upper-class city-dwellers who weekend in the country. (Normally with *the.*) □ *Our village*

seems to be being invaded by the green welly brigade. □ *The green welly brigade arrives every Friday evening and leaves every Monday morning.*

Gregory (Peck) 1. *n.* a bank cheque. (Rhyming slang.) □ *"Don't worry," he smiled, "a Gregory Peck will be just fine." □ I made my Gregory out and handed it to him.* **2.** *n.* the neck. (Rhyming slang.) □ *Have you noticed? Harry's got a really thick Gregory Peck. □ Look, you are a real pain in the Gregory. OK?*

gremlin *n.* a mischievous spirit or imp responsible for the failure of all kinds of mechanisms. □ *Gremlins are often found in new aircraft. □ There's some sort of gremlin that prevents it from working.*

grey *n.* a conventional, middle-aged person. (Teens.) □ *I'm sorry but we really don't need another grey here, man. □ What's a grey like that doing around here?*

grey area *n.* an area suffering economic deprivation. □ *Most of the north of England seems to be a grey area these days. □ Grey areas can get special help from the government.*

grice *vb.* to watch trains, as a hobby or pastime. □ *There are a lot of people gricing on that bridge most Saturdays. □ What's the fascination in gricing?*

gricer *n.* an enthusiastic watcher of trains. □ *There they are; the gricers are out in force today. □ Why does anyone want to be a gricer?*

grim *mod.* unpleasant. □ *What a grim place. □ Oh, that's really grim!*

grind *n.* sexual intercourse. (Taboo.) □ *I think really, she's gasping for a grind, you know. □ A good grind would probably do her the power of good, in fact.*

grind 1. *vb.* to perform sexual intercourse. (Taboo.) □ *I think you could get a grind there, Barry. □ They were having a grind like it was going out of fashion.* **2.** *n.* a woman viewed as a sex object. (Taboo.) □ *Look at the grind in this place, Martin! □ This particular grind will break your fingers if you touch her again. Is that clear, you creep?* **3.** *vb.* to masturbate. (Taboo.) □

Timmy's mother caught him grinding in the garden shed. □ If he gets frustrated enough, he grinds.

grip 1. *n.* a traveller's handbag. □ *Don't forget your grip! □ I picked up my grip and boarded the train.* **2.** *vb.* to fascinate. □ *I find he grips me. □ Grip me with another of your wonderful tales, James.*

gripe 1. *vb.* to complain. □ *I bet she's come here to gripe once again. □ I've never known her not to be griping about something or another.* **2.** *n.* a complaint. □ *What's your gripe today? □ That's one of the most original gripes I've heard for some time, I'll say that.*

gripped AND **riveted** *mod.* fascinated. □ *She was gripped by his story. □ She sat there, riveted.*

gripped at the knickers *mod.* nervous; neurotic. □ *The poor woman was really gripped at the knickers with fright. □ Don't get gripped at the knickers dear. It'll be all right.*

gripping AND **riveting** *mod.* fascinating. □ *What a gripping story. □ That is absolutely riveting.*

grit *n.* courage; nerve; endurance. □ *It takes a lot of grit to do something like that. □ Well, Pete has lots of grit. He can do it.*

grizzle 1. *n.* the fretful cry of a young child. □ *The child's grizzle has been there in the background all night now. □ How can anyone ignore grizzle for so long?* **2.** *vb.* to whine or complain. □ *Some people grizzle because they don't have anything else to do. □ Come on, don't grizzle all the time!*

grocer's shop *n.* an Italian person. (Offensive. Rhyming slang, linked as follows: grocer's shop ≈ [Wop] = Italian.) □ *He said he was not a racist, he just hated this particular grocer's shop! □ Y'know, Otto, if you call an Italian a grocer's shop, he's likely to get nasty.*

grockle *n.* a tourist. (Cornish.) □ *There are too many grockles in Cornwall. □ Cornwall is very popular with grockles, especially in the summer.*

grog *vb.* to spit. (Scots usage.) □ *None o' yer groggin in here! □ Angry? I could've grogged!*

grog-blossom *n.* a pimple cause by excessive drinking. □ *There has never in all the annals of medicine been such a severe outbreak of grog-blossoms. □ Why does he have to sit there picking at his grog-blossom?*

groggy 1. *mod.* tired; semi-conscious. □ *He was too groggy to care what happened to him. □ I'm still groggy by ten in the morning.* **2.** *mod.* intoxicated due to drink; in a drunken stupor. □ *John was a little groggy—from the grog, of course. □ He was too groggy to drive.* **3.** *mod.* unwell. □ *Carol is a bit groggy today, I'm afraid. □ Oh dear, I feel rather groggy.*

grog-shop *n.* a low-class public house. (Originally one frequented by sailors used to their daily ration of grog, a concoction of rum and water once served them on Royal Navy ships.) □ *They are always having fights in that grog-shop. I don't know how it keeps its licence. □ Don't you go near that grog-shop again, my lad!*

groid See NEGROID.

groise *n.* a hard-working student; a SWOT. (Childish.) □ *Jimmy's no groise; he doesn't know the meaning of homework, I think. □ It's the groises who do well in later life.*

groovy *mod.* pleasant; COOL. □ *Man, this music is groovy. □ What a groovy day!*

grope *vb.* to fondle sexually, especially in a crude way or against a person's wishes. (Crude.) □ *He groped her, yet she said nothing. □ If you try to grope me I'll scream!*

gross *mod.* crude; vulgar; disgusting. (Slang only when overused.) □ *This food is gross! □ What a gross thing to even suggest.*

grot *n.* junk; dirt; filth. □ *I've had enough of this grot around here. Clean it up, or I'm leaving. □ What is all this grot in the corner?*

grotty 1. *mod.* ugly, dirty or disgusting. □ *If you must be grotty, go and do so somewhere else, thank you. □ That's really grotty, don't go in there.* **2.** *mod.* grotesque; highly undesirable. □ *Let's not see another grotty movie tonight. □ What is this* *grotty stuff they serve here?* □ *It's not grotty!*

ground 1. *n.* the floor of a room. □ *The ground was strewn with all sorts of discarded rubbish.* □ *We had to sit on the ground because there were no chairs.* **2.** AND **patch** *n.* the area that a police officer patrols or is responsible for. □ *The officer looked over his new ground and shuddered.* □ *It's a pretty grim patch, but it's all mine.*

ground bones *n.* powdered milk. □ *I keep some ground bones in there in case we run out of the liquid kind.* □ *Oh, I prefer ground bones actually.*

group-grope *n.* a group of people engaged in sexual activities; a sexual orgy. (Crude.) □ *That party turned into a hopeless group-grope.* □ *The group-grope was broken up by you-know-who.*

groupie *n.* a young woman who follows a band seeking romance with the band members. □ *Would you believe that Sally was a groupie when she was 19?* □ *You mean all those young girls are groupies?*

grouse *vb.* to complain or grumble. □ *Paul is always grousing about something.* □ *Stop grousing and look on the good side of things.*

Grovel, grovel! *interj.* an expression of abject apology, often jocular. □ *All right, grovel, grovel! I was wrong.* □ *Grovel, grovel! I should not have said that!*

grub *n.* food. □ *Hey, this grub's pretty good.* □ *What time's grub?*

grubby *mod.* unclean; untidy; unshaven. □ *Pete looks sort of grubby today. What's wrong?* □ *Who's that grubby guy?* □ *I feel grubby, and I want a shower.*

Grub Street *n.* hack writers as a class. (From an actual, physical Grub Street—which has long since been renamed Milton Street—in London where such people used to congregate.) □ *I hear half of Grub Street is offering to ghost your autobiography.* □ *Not half. Only two denizens of Grub Street have approached me.*

grue *n.* fear; terror. □ *Just thinking of that gives me the grue every time.* □ *She gets the grue whenever she has to give a talk.*

gruesome-twosome *n.* two people or things that are always seen together. (Jocular. Neither the things nor the people have to be "gruesome.") □ *Well, it's the gruesome-twosome. Come in and join the party.* □ *The gruesome-twosome will both star in tonight's game.*

grumble and grunt 1. *n.* the female sexual organ. (Taboo. Rhyming slang, linked as follows: grumble and grunt ≈ [cunt] = female sexual organ.) □ *The door to the shower room flew open and the girl screamed, trying to cover her grumble and grunt.* □ *A woman who shows her grumble and grunt is just the lowest.* **2.** *n.* unattractive but available women, from the male perspective. (Taboo.) □ *I see Brian's got himself a real grumble and grunt tonight!* □ *She may be only a grumble and grunt to you, but to me she's my sister.*

grumbly *n.* a clumsy or dull person. □ *Even a grumbly like that has to earn a living.* □ *What does the grumbly want?*

grungy *mod.* dirty; smelly; unwashed. □ *A strange, grungy smell hung over the whole area.* □ *The trouble is that the grungy little tyke usually has good information.*

gubbins 1. *n.* a fool. □ *You gubbins! You've buttered the tablecloth!* □ *Those gubbins are at it again. Spend, spend, spend.* **2.** *n.* machinery. □ *But what's all this gubbins for, Martin?* □ *Get this gubbins working; that's what you're paid for!* **3.** *n.* rubbish. □ *You've certainly got a lot of gubbins here.* □ *What are we supposed to do with this gubbins?*

gucky *mod.* nauseating; disgusting. □ *If you're going to be gucky, you can do so somewhere else.* □ *You pig, that's just gucky!*

guest beer *n.* a beer from one brewery on sale in a public house owned by another. □ *How about a guest beer before you go, Charlie?* □ *Give my friend here a guest beer.*

guestimate *n.* a rough calculation; a calculated guess. □ *If you really want me to make a guestimate on this...* □ *Go on, what do you think? What's your guestimate?*

guff AND **gaff** *n.* nonsense. □ *Boy, he can certainly churn out guff by the ton!* □ *No more gaff out of you, okay?*

GUI *phr.* a "graphical user interface." (A type of computer control system that uses an orderly layout on the screen with icons and menus that are controlled by a computer mouse. GUI is a technical acronym.) □ *Some of the older programs that lack a GUI require a lot less memory to run.* □ *Many new computer users find it much easier to use a GUI than to type in arcane commands.*

guinea-pig *n.* someone upon whom an experiment is tried. □ *What made me angry was that I did not know I was being used as a guinea-pig.* □ *Oh, it's always easy to find another guinea-pig.*

gum *n.* opium. □ *He still smokes gum.* □ *Max deals mostly in gum, but can get you almost anything.*

gump See GUMPTION.

gumption AND **gump** **1.** *n.* initiative; enterprise. □ *She figured it out for herself; that's what I call real gump!* □ *He's the right one, with loads of gumption.* **2.** *n.* common sense. □ *Come on! Use your gumption!* □ *If you'd any gump you've seen that was ridiculous.*

gum up the works *vb. phr.* to bring some process to a halt; to break a mechanism. □ *Please try not to gum up the works again.* □ *Oh no, that's really gummed up the works.*

gun **1.** *vb.* to race an engine. □ *See how loud it is when I gun it?* □ *Gun the thing again and let me hear it.* **2.** *n.* a member of a hunting or shooting party. □ *He's to be a gun in Lord Symon's shooting party this weekend.* □ *His Lordship regrets that he is unable to be a gun on this occasion.* **3.** *n.* a hypodermic syringe. □ *What'll I do? I broke my gun.* □ *The addict caught some strange disease from a dirty gun.*

gun for someone *vb. phr.* to be looking for someone, not necessarily with a gun, but certainly not to impart bonhomie and good news. □ *Brian is gunning for Mark.* □ *The French prof is gunning for you.*

Gunga Din and squatter's daughter *n.* gin and water. (Rhyming slang.) □ *He*

gave me a Gunga Din and squatter's daughter and left me alone.* □ *Like another Gunga Din and squatter's daughter, mate?*

gunge *n.* any messy or sticky substance. □ *What sort of gunge is that?* □ *We opened the jar, and found it was full of some disgusting gunge.*

gunge something up *vb. phr.* to clog up with GUNGE. □ *Who gunged up the sink again?* □ *Gunging up one long-range oil pipeline with impurities can cost millions of pounds to repair.*

gung-ho *mod.* zealous; enthusiastic. □ *We're really gung-ho about the possibilities of this product.* □ *Pete always seems so gung-ho about everything.* □ *He's a gung-ho sort of guy.*

gungy *mod.* messy; sticky; spoiled; ruined or worn out; nasty. □ *Get your gungy feet off the sofa.* □ *All that gungy stuff is blocking the drain.*

gunk *n.* any nasty, messy stuff. □ *What is this gunk on the counter?* □ *Get this gunk off the floor before it dries on for keeps.*

guppie *n.* a green YUPPIE. (From the abbreviation and merging of "green," signifying environmental concern, etc., with "yuppie.") □ *These guppies make me sick, trying to tell the rest of us how to behave.* □ *Most people in the countryside don't have much time for guppies.*

gurk *vb.* to belch. □ *Try not to gurk at table, Johnny.* □ *She gurked quietly behind her hanky, so no one would notice.*

gut *n.* a particularly large or protruding belly or stomach. (The word is Standard English in the straight-forward sense of the belly or the intestines, when used without reference to size.) □ *What a gut that guy has.* □ *Tom poked Bill right in his gut.*

gutless *mod.* cowardly. □ *What a gutless individual he turned out to be.* □ *Yes he's gutless, but I still love him.*

gut-rot *n.* any cheap or inferior alcoholic drink, especially wine. □ *Lord! That stuff is just gut-rot!* □ *Any more of that gut-rot?*

guts **1.** *n.* the belly; the intestines. □ *Ted poked Frank right in the guts.* □

I've got some kind of pain in the guts. **2.** *n.* the inner workings of anything. □ *There's something wrong in the guts of this clock.* □ *My tape recorder needs all new guts.* **3.** *n.* courage; bravado. □ *Man, she's got guts!* □ *It takes guts to do something like that.*

gutsy *mod.* courageous; enthusiastic. □ *She certainly is a gutsy young thing.* □ *Ernie's acting sort of gutsy today. What happened?* □ *She's not so gutsy as you might think.*

gutted AND **filleted** *mod.* distraught; completely disillusioned. □ *The footballer was gutted by the defeat.* □ *He knew he'd be filleted if they lost again.*

guttered *mod.* very intoxicated due to drink. (Scots usage.) □ *Weel missus, he's nay say much happy as guttered. (Well madam, he's not so much happy as extremely drunk indeed.)* □ *The way ah see it, if ye drink an' end up in the gutter, ye're guttered, right?*

gutter press AND **sewer press** *n.* disreputable newspapers and other publications that concentrate on scandal and sensational items. □ *Just ignore the gutter press, my dear.* □ *The trouble is that the sewer press does have a loud voice and are difficult to ignore.*

guv' See GOVERNOR.

guv'nor See GOVERNOR.

guy 1. *n.* a fellow; a man or boy. (Always male, whether singular or plural.) □ *Come on you guys, let's get going!* □ *The guys are ready to go out and are asking if the girls are ready, too.* **2.** *n.* an effigy of Guy Fawkes. □ *Penny for the guy, mister?* □ *The children have built a huge bonfire to burn the guy on the 5th of November.*

guzzle *vb.* to eat or drink in great quantities. □ *Stop guzzling for a while and pay attention.* □ *Don't guzzle all that food down at once or you'll make yourself ill.*

guzzle-guts *n.* someone who is particularly greedy, especially for food. □ *Of course he's a guzzle-guts! Have you ever seen him not eating?* □ *The guzzle-guts all sit over there, near the kitchen.*

guzzler *n.* a heavy eater or drinker. □ *Harry is getting to be quite a guzzler.* □ *A couple of guzzlers in the restaurant were carrying on a low conversation when Barlowe came in.*

gyke *n.* a gynaecologist. □ *I hear he's a very good gyke.* □ *That gyke helped me greatly with my last baby.*

gyp *vb.* to swindle; cheat. □ *Hey! Give me my money back! I've been gypped!* □ *That purchase was a total gyp. They must have seen you coming.*

Gyppo See GIPPO.

Gyppo tummy See GIPPY TUMMY.

Gyppy See GIPPO.

Gyppy tummy See GIPPY TUMMY.

Gypsy's (kiss) *n.* an act of urination. (Crude. Potentially racially offensive. Rhyming slang, linked as follows: Gypsy's (kiss) ≈ [piss] – urinate.) □ *Come on, I've gotta stop here for a Gypsy's kiss.* □ *He went out to take a Gypsy's.*

Gypsy's warning *n.* the morning. (Rhyming slang. Potentially racially offensive.) □ *Good night. See you in the Gypsy's warning.* □ *Gypsy's warning, and it was bitter cold.*

H *n.* heroin. □ *Now he's shooting H.* □ *First it was M.; now it's H.*

habit *n.* an addiction to a drug. □ *She has to steal to support her habit.* □ *There are many treatment programmes to help people with drug habits.*

hack **1.** *vb.* to work enthusiastically on a computer as a hobby. □ *Dave has hacked away at his computer to produce a magnificent new game.* □ *I like to hack on my computer.* **2.** *vb.* to write clumsy or inefficient computer programs. □ *I can hack a program for you, but it won't be what you want.* □ *Well, I can hack a bit myself.* **3.** *vb.* to make unauthorised access into a computer's files. □ *Security's so good, it's impossible for anyone to hack into our computer.* □ *Wanna bet? Someone hacked into the computer and destroyed all our files last night.* **4.** AND **hackette** *n.* an uninspired or uninspiring male (hack) or female (hackette) professional writer, particularly a journalist, who writes mediocre material to order. □ *This novel shows that even a hack can get something published these days.* □ *That hackette can't even write her name!*

hacked off **1.** *mod.* angry; annoyed. □ *Willy was really hacked off about the accident.* □ *Oh, Willy is always hacked off about something.* **2.** *mod.* very bored. □ *Jill has nothing to do now and is really quite hacked off.* □ *I get hacked off when its quiet.*

hacker **1.** *n.* an enthusiastic and skilled computer hobbyist. □ *Dave may only be 12 years old, but he's an amazing hacker!* □ *Hackers can become more than a little obsessive.* **2.** *n.* a sloppy or inefficient computer programmer. □

This program was written by a real hacker. It's a mess, but it works. □ *I may be a hacker, but I get the job done.* **3.** *n.* a generally unsuccessful person. □ *Poor Pete is just a hacker. He'll never get anywhere.* □ *Hackers keep trying, but they never succeed.* **4.** *n.* a computer operator who makes unauthorised access to files. □ *No hacker's ever going to break into my system.* □ *Really? Some hacker broke into your system over the weekend and all your data is lost.*

hackette See HACK.

hack it *vb. phr.* to endure something; to succeed despite difficulties. □ *It's hard, but I'm sure I can hack it.* □ *I'm afraid you can't hack it. It just isn't working out.*

had See TAKEN.

had a basinful *phr.* had enough; had as much as one can stand. □ *I've had a basinful. I'm off.* □ *That's it, I've had a basinful.*

haggis-basher *n.* a Scotsman. (Offensive.) □ *Why can you not be polite to haggis-bashers?* □ *Y'know, Otto, if you call a Scotsman a haggis-basher, he's likely to get nasty.*

hail and hearty *n.* a party. (Rhyming slang.) □ *After a hail and hearty, I couldn't keep my eyes open the following day.* □ *Sam invited us to a hail and hearty, but we're getting a little old for that kind of thing.*

hail and rain *n.* a train. (Rhyming slang.) □ *There are hail and rains passing here all the time.* □ *Take the hail and rain—that's the easy way to get there from here.*

hail jing-bang AND **hall rickmatiok; hale jing-bang; hale rickmatick** *n.*

everything and/or everybody. (Normally with *the*. Scots usage.) □ *He's brought the hail jing-bang with him!* □ *The hale rickmatick were wrong.*

hail rickmatick See HAIL JING-BANG.

hail smiling morn *n.* an erection. (Taboo. Rhyming slang, linked as follows: hail smiling morn ≈ [horn] = erection. Compare with SEPTEMBER MORN.) □ *Here I come, complete with a real fine hail smiling morn!* □ *Fear not my lovely, it shall be hail smiling morn for you!*

hair-do 1. *n.* a dressed and styled feminine hair. □ *How do you like my new hair-do?* □ *Is that hair-do supposed to be the fashion nowadays?* **2.** *n.* the process of having feminine hair dressed and styled. □ *I'm away for a hair-do.* □ *My hair-do will take a couple of hours at least.*

hair of the dog (that bit one) *n.* a drink taken (usually the following morning) to counteract a hangover. □ *You know how a hair of the dog that bit you always makes you worse, my dear.* □ *I often find a hair of the dog in the morning helps.*

hair-raiser *n.* an exciting, thrilling or frightening book or film. □ *I'm very glad that film's over. It was a real hair-raiser!* □ *I think you might find this book quite a hair-raiser, too.*

hairy 1. *mod.* hazardous; difficult. □ *That was a hairy experience!* □ *Boy, that's hairy!* □ *What a hairy trip that was!* **2.** *n.* a low-class, sluttish young woman. (Crude. Scots usage.) □ *Who's that wee hairy ah seen you with last night? (Who was that sluttish young woman I saw you with last night?)* □ *She may look like a hairy, but Morag has an advanced degree in computing.* **3.** *n.* a prostitute. (Crude. Scots usage.) □ *The police brought her in because she looked like a hairy.* □ *Clare dresses like a hairy.*

hairy-arsed *mod.* masculine and tough. (Taboo.) □ *Do you have to be so hairy-arsed all the time?* □ *Brian is a real hairy-arsed old boy, isn't he?*

hairy-fairy *n.* an effeminate man; a passive male homosexual. (Crude.) □ *He doesn't like being called a hairy-fairy.* □ *Why does he work so hard to look like he's a hairy-fairy?*

hale jing-bang See HAIL JING-BANG.

hale rickmatick See HAIL JING-BANG.

half *n.* half a pint. (Usually beer, when ordered in a pub.) □ *Just make mine a half, thanks.* □ *Come on, you must have more than just a half!*

half (a) bar AND **half a nicker** *n.* half of one Pound Sterling. □ *Lend us a half bar for the fruit machine, mate.* □ *Come on, even you can afford this; it's only half a nicker!*

half-a-dollar *n.* twelve and a half pence (formerly two shillings and six pence). (This dates from the 19th century, when there were four US Dollars to the Pound for many years.) □ *For half-a-dollar, what have you go to lose?* □ *What does half-a-dollar buy you nowadays?*

half a mo *n.* half a moment. □ *Half a mo, what did you say?* □ *I'll be there in half a mo.*

Half-a-mo! *exclam.* "Wait a moment!" □ *Hold on! Half-a-mo!* □ *Half-a-mo! Can we have a word?*

half a nicker 1. *n.* a vicar. (Rhyming slang.) □ *Most of the time, our half a nicker don't seem to have much to do.* □ *I went to see the half a nicker for some advice.* **2.** See also HALF (A) BAR.

half-arsed *mod.* foolish; ineffective. (Taboo.) □ *Don't bring me any more of your half-arsed efforts.* □ *My last one looked half-arsed at first, but it worked, didn't it?*

half a stretch *n.* six months in prison. □ *He's doing half a stretch this time.* □ *Half a stretch doesn't sound much, until you actually have to bear it yourself.*

half a ton *n.* fifty Pounds Sterling. □ *Can you lend me half a ton 'till payday?* □ *All right, here's half a ton. Don't spend it all in one shop.*

half-baked *mod.* badly thought out; partially planned; incomplete. (Compare with HALF-COCKED.) □ *Was that half-baked scheme the best you could come up with?* □ *It would have been approved if it weren't so obviously half-baked.*

half-blind *mod.* intoxicated due to drink. □ *Fred got himself half-blind in no time at all.* □ *Get that half-blind jerk out of here!* □ *Four cans of beer and she was half-blind.*

half-brass *n.* an enthusiastic amateur prostitute who does not always charge for her services. (Crude.) □ *Some men think that if they can find a friendly half-brass they're on to a good thing.* □ *The professional girls really hate the half-brasses.*

half-canned AND **half-pissed** *mod.* somewhat intoxicated due to drink. (Taboo.) □ *Bruno's a really nice person when he's half-canned.* □ *I felt half-pissed, but that didn't stop me from having more.*

half-cocked *mod.* unprepared; not fully ready. (Derived from the cocking of the firing lever of a gun to make it fireable. Compare with GO OFF AT HALF-COCK and HALF-BAKED.) □ *So he's half-cocked. So what?* □ *Everything you do goes off half-cocked.*

half-cut *mod.* partly intoxicated due to drink. □ *Everybody was half-cut and singing by the time the food arrived.* □ *Tracy gets half-cut after just a drink or two.*

half-inch *vb.* to steal. (Rhyming slang, linked as follows: half-inch ≈ [pinch] = steal.) □ *Everyone half-inches nowadays, it seems.* □ *It may seem harmless to half-inch from your employer, but it's still theft.*

half-pint *mod.* [of a person] short. □ *I don't think I could take another half-pint individual like that today.* □ *I may only be half-pint in height, but I'll still beat you in the brains department; you'll see!*

half-pissed See HALF-CANNED.

half-seas-over *mod.* somewhat intoxicated due to drink. □ *I felt half-seas-over, but that didn't stop me from having more.* □ *By morning they were all half-seas-over.*

half-stewed *mod.* intoxicated due to drink. □ *Poor Fred was half-stewed and still had to give a speech.* □ *We were half-stewed and had a lot of drinking yet to do.*

half under **1.** *mod.* semi-conscious. □ *I was half under and could hear what the doctor was saying.* □ *I was afraid the surgeon would start cutting me open while I was still only half under.* **2.** *mod.* intoxicated due to drink. □ *He was half under and could barely stand up.* □ *It only took four beers and she was half under.*

Halt, tomatoes, turds! *interj.* a parody of a sentry's command to halt at British military bases in Cyprus, where the English *halt*, Greek *stamata* and Turkish *dur* all have to be called out. (Taboo. Hobson-jobson.) □ *All right you lot! Halt, tomatoes, turds!* □ *Halt, tomatoes, turds! Only if you like, of course.*

ham **1.** *n.* an over-histrionic actor; a bad actor. □ *What a ham! A real showoff.* □ *The cast was an assemblage of hams.* **2.** *n.* an amateur radio operator. □ *My brother is a ham, and he helped a lot during the emergency.* □ *The hams helped by providing communication to the outside world.*

ham-fisted See HAM-HANDED.

ham-handed AND **ham-fisted** *mod.* lacking dexterity; clumsy. □ *If I wasn't so ham-handed, I could probably fix the thing myself.* □ *He is the most ham-fisted guy I've ever seen.*

hammered *mod.* intoxicated due to drink or drugs. □ *Boy, old Fred was really hammered.* □ *She got so hammered she couldn't see.*

Hampden roar *n.* the score, particularly of a soccer match. (Rhyming slang. Scots usage.) □ *Hampden Park, in Glasgow, is Scotland's national football stadium, where international and significant national games are played. The noise of up to 80,000 spectators cheering, known as the "Hampden roar," can reputedly be heard all over the city.* □ *What's the latest Hampden roar, Jimmy?*

hamps See HAMPSTEADS.

hampsteads AND **hamps** *n.* the teeth. (Rhyming slang, linked as follows: Hampstead [Heath] ≈ teeth.) □ *That horse has a nice set of hampsteads.* □ *I may be on me last legs, but me hamps are still all me own.*

handbag someone vb. [for a woman] to attack or hit someone. □ *Mrs Thatcher had a reputation for handbagging her opponents.* □ *If you come any closer, young man, I'll handbag you!*

handful n. a difficult thing or person. □ *Little Jimmy is a handful.* □ *His dad can be a handful, too, especially after the pub shuts.*

hand-in-glove mod. suiting one another naturally or perfectly. □ *These two go hand-in-glove.* □ *Now you can see how these two parts of the mechanism fit together hand-in-glove.*

hand it to someone vb. phr. to acknowledge someone's excellence or superiority (at something). □ *Well, I have to hand it to you. That was great!* □ *He had to hand it to her for her excellent performance.*

hand job n. masturbation. (Taboo.) □ *A hand job is a very popular teenage pastime, you know.* □ *At least with a hand job you don't have to be polite first.*

handlebars n. a moustache that resembles a pair of handlebars. □ *I was amazed at the size of his handlebars.* □ *I don't trust men with handlebars.*

handles See (LOVE) HANDLES.

handle (someone or something) with kid gloves AND **treat (someone or something) with kid gloves** vb. phr. to handle with care; to treat gently. □ *Don't worry, I'll handle this with kid gloves.* □ *After this news we must treat her with kid gloves.*

hand-me-downs n. second-hand clothes. □ *Where did you get hand-me-downs to wear like that?* □ *I feel sort of funny in these hand-me-downs.*

hand-out 1. n. a free meal to the hungry. □ *There are hand-outs available at the Salvation Army, you know.* □ *A huge queue formed outside the place when word got round about the hand-outs.* **2.** n. money gifted to the poor. □ *The woman is always making hand-outs.* □ *The orphanage just got a huge hand-out.*

handout 1. n. a gift of money, food or other goods to a needy person. □ *I don't want a handout, just a loan.* □ *Give him a handout and send him on his way.* **2.** n. an information sheet (of paper) "handed out" to people. □ *As I can see on your handout, 40 percent of those who started never finished.* □ *I didn't get a handout.*

hand over fist mod. repeatedly and energetically, especially with taking in money in a great volume. □ *We were taking in fees hand over fist, and the people were queued up for miles.* □ *The money was coming in hand over fist.*

hands down mod. easily; unquestionably. □ *She won the contest hands down.* □ *They declared her the winner hands down.*

handsome mod. excellent; very satisfactory. □ *This wine is really handsome!* □ *Boy, what a handsome fishing rod this is.*

hands-on 1. mod. concerning a training session where novices learn by actual use of the device—such as a keyboard or control panel—that they are being taught to use. □ *Please plan to attend a hands-on seminar on the new computers next Thursday.* □ *After three weeks of hands-on training, I still couldn't add two and two.* **2.** mod. concerning an executive or manager who participates directly in operations. □ *We expect that he will be the kind of hands-on president we have been looking for.* □ *John is a hands-on manager. I wish he would stay in his office.* **3.** mod. concerning an activity or process requiring actual personal use of the keyboard by the operator. (Computer jargon.) □ *This new application requires a hands-on operator at all times.* □ *Hands-on experience is what counts.*

Hands up! AND **Stick 'em up!** exclam. "Raise your hands in the air; this is a robbery!" (Underworld and Western.) □ *Hands up! Don't anybody move a muscle. This is a robbery.* □ *"Stick 'em up! Give me all your valuables." "We can't give you anything with our hands up in the air."*

Hang about! exclam. "Wait for a moment!" □ *Hang about! We need to talk!* □ *I won't be long. Hang about!*

hang around vb. phr. to loiter; to fritter away time doing nothing. □ *Don't* *just hang around. Get busy with some-thing.* □ *Move. Don't just hang around. There's work to be done.*

hang in there *vb. phr.* to keep trying; to persevere. □ *Hang in there. Keep try-ing.* □ *If I just hang in there, maybe things will get better.*

Hang it all! *exclam.* "Damn it all!" □ *Oh, hang it all! I'm late.* □ *He's late again! Hang it all!*

hang on *vb. phr.* to wait. □ *We hung on as long as we could.* □ *If you could just hang on for a moment please...*

hang one on *vb. phr.* to get very intox-icated due to drink or drugs. □ *Fred was fed up and went out to hang one on.* □ *Fred hangs one on about once a month.*

hang up *n.* a problem or concern; an obsession. (Usually HANG-UP.) □ *She's got some serious hang-ups about cats.* □ *I don't have any hang ups at all. Well, almost none.*

hanky AND **hankie** *n.* a handkerchief, especially if lacy and feminine. □ *Do you have a hanky I can borrow?* □ *Here, use my hankie.*

hanky-panky 1. *n.* sexual play; sexual misconduct or infidelity. (Crude.) □ *Sam and Mary are up to a little hanky-panky, I've heard.* □ *"There's some hanky-panky going on in the store-room." "What, again?"* **2.** *n.* funny business; deceitfulness. □ *There's some hanky-panky going on in the treasur-er's office.* □ *I am going to get this hanky-panky straightened out right now.*

happening *n.* a significant artistic or in-spirational event. □ *The concert was a real happening.* □ *Well, that class is hardly a happening, but it's never dull either.*

happy *mod.* intoxicated due to drink. □ *She seems a little happy. Must have had a few already.* □ *She's not happy, she's stewed.*

happy as a pig in shit *mod.* ecstatical-ly happy; entirely content; in the utmost comfort. (Taboo. See ESSENCE OF PIG-SHIT.) □ *Pleased? He was as happy as a pig in shit!* □ *I'm as happy as a pig in shit with that news!*

happy as a sandboy AND **happy as Larry** *mod.* carefree; very happy. □ *Now he has his new computer, he's happy as a sandboy.* □ *Clearly if you're happy as Larry, you don't understand the gravity of our predicament.*

happy as Larry See HAPPY AS A SANDBOY.

happy camper *n.* a happy person. (Often used in the negative.) □ *Fred flunked algebra and he is not a happy camper.* □ *I am not a happy camper. I am tired, hungry and I need a shower.*

happy chappie *n.* someone who is de-lighted with their situation. (Always used in the negative, or ironic.) □ *I don't think he's a happy chappie, doc-tor.* □ *What a collection of happy chap-pies you are I must say!*

happy clappy *n.* a member of certain kinds of evangelical churches, where congregations regularly participate in services with frequent bursts of ap-plause, which can appear meaningless to the casual observer. □ *There was a convention of happy clappies in our town last week.* □ *What does a happy clappy actually do—apart from clap, that is?*

happy pills *n.* tranquillizers. □ *She asked the doctor for some happy pills.* □ *She is now hooked on happy pills.*

harbour *mod.* all right. (Rhyming slang, linked as follows: harbour [light] ≈ (all) right.) □ *Don't worry, it's all harbour again now.* □ *It's fine; it's all harbour.*

hard 1. *mod.* having to do with an ad-dictive drug. (Compare with SOFT.) □ *Gert's on hard stuff now.* □ *Hard drugs are easier to get than ever before.* **2.** *mod.* tough. (Akin to *hardhearted* and *hard as nails*.) □ *Sally is really hard. She can stand anything.* □ *Only the hard guys get through basic training.* **3.** *n.* hard labour performed in conjunc-tion with a prison sentence, as a form of punishment. □ *You are sentenced to four years hard.* □ *I got four years hard for that.*

hard at it *mod.* working hard. □ *There they all are, hard at it.* □ *"I like to see all my workers hard at it," said Mr Big.*

hardboiled *mod.* tough; sharp; astute. □ *She is a hardboiled old girl.* □ *Do* *you have to be so hardboiled all the time?*

hard case *n.* a young male rowdy or gang member whose behaviour is difficult to restrain or moderate. □ *Geoff has turned into a hard case. He's fighting us at every turn.* □ *The hard case we dealt with last week is back again.*

hard cheese AND **hard lines** *n.* hard luck. □ *Now that's really hard cheese.* □ *We have had our share of hard lines.*

hard core 1. AND **hard porn** *n.* strong pornography. (Crude.) □ *They keep the hard core in a secret room at the back of the shop.* □ *You can't get the real hard porn here.* **2.** AND **hard-core** *mod.* extreme; entrenched. (Compare with SOFT CORE.) □ *She spent some time teaching hard core illiterates in a medium-sized town.* □ *There are too many cases of hard-core poverty in that area.*

hard done by *mod.* mistreated or illserved. □ *I'm hard done by!* □ *You don't know the meaning of hard done by.*

hardheaded *mod.* realistic; determined. □ *Gary is a real hardheaded guy.* □ *Anybody that hardheaded is going to get what they want, despite everyone else.*

hard hit *vb.* to defecate. (Taboo. Rhyming slang, linked as follows: hard hit ≈ [shit] = defecate.) □ *Just where do you go to hard hit around here?* □ *He had to go and hard hit.*

hard lines See HARD CHEESE.

hard neck See BRASS NECK.

hard-nosed *mod.* stern and businesslike; unsympathetic. (Compare with SOFT-NOSED.) □ *She's pretty hardnosed and tends to put people off.* □ *It takes a hard-nosed manager to run a place like this.*

hard-on *n.* an erection. (Taboo.) □ *You can't walk along the street with a hardon!* □ *Here I come, hard-on and all!*

hard porn See HARD CORE.

hard sell *n.* a high-pressure attempt to sell something. □ *I didn't want to listen to any hard sell, so I bought it from a mail order place.* □ *I'm afraid I'm very susceptible to the hard sell.*

hard stuff 1. *n.* whisky. (Always with *the.*) □ *I could go a glass or three of*

the hard stuff. □ *The hard stuff was certainly flowing that evening, I can tell you.* **2.** *n.* morphine. □ *I think Otto's on the hard stuff again.* □ *That hard stuff is dangerous.*

hard ticket *n.* a tough man. (Scots usage.) □ *Yon hard ticket canna be trusted ta cross the road without thumping you.* □ *Watch that one; he's a hard ticket all right.*

hard to swallow AND **hard to take in** *mod.* difficult to believe. □ *Your story is pretty hard to swallow, but I am beginning to believe it.* □ *The news was hard to take in.*

hard to take in See HARD TO SWALLOW.

hard up 1. *mod.* short of money. □ *Freddie said he was hard up and couldn't afford to take Mary out.* □ *Mary was too hard up to go out last night.* **2.** *mod.* desperate for companionship. □ *Freddie said he was hard up and needed a date.* □ *Mary must be hard up to date a creep like that.*

harf *mod.* half. (Eye-dialect. Typical spoken English in London and surrounding area. Used in writing only for effect. Used in the examples of this dictionary.) □ *Y'know, that idea ain't harf bad!* □ *Harf a pinta milk, mate!*

harpic *mod.* crazy; demented. (From the advertising for Harpic, a household cleaning agent, that claimed it would "clean round the bend.") □ *I'm not really as harpic as I seem.* □ *I'm not harpic. I just can't make it work.*

Harris tweed *n.* amphetamines. (Rhyming slang, linked as follows: Harris tweed ≈ [speed] = amphetamines.) □ *By now, he was well away on Harris tweed.* □ *I could use some Harris tweed.*

harry *mod.* BLOODY. (Crude. A euphemism.) □ *Who's the harry fool who did this?* □ *What the harry hell are you doing here?*

Harry AND **'Arry Stottle** *n.* a bottle. (Rhyming slang, linked as follows: Harry = 'Arry Stottle ≈ [Aristotle] = bottle.) □ *What's in that Harry?* □ *Pass me the 'Arry Stottle mate.*

Harry hoof *n.* a male homosexual. (Taboo. Scots usage. Rhyming slang, linked as follows: Harry hoof ≈ [poof] = homosexual.) □ *So what if he's a Harry hoof? He can still vote, can't he?* □ *Tell that Harry hoof to get out of here.*

Harvest Moon *n.* a black person. (Racially offensive. Rhyming slang, linked as follows: Harvest Moon ≈ [coon] = black person.) □ *So this Harvest Moon drives away in a BMW!* □ *Why should a BMW not belong to a Harvest Moon?*

has-been 1. *mod.* former; burnt-out. □ *Some has-been singer croaked through "Rule Britannia."* □ *Now I'm a has-been football player, and nobody even knows my name.* **2.** *n.* someone who used to be important; a person whose career has ended. □ *Marty is just a has-been. There's no future for him.* □ *Some old has-been was trying to host a late-night talk show.*

hash *n.* hashish; cannabis in general. □ *The amount of hash that moves into this city in a single day would astound you.* □ *Hash is still the favourite first drug other than alcohol.*

hash-head *n.* a smoker of cannabis. □ *You can't stay a hash-head all your life.* □ *Kelly was almost a hopeless hash-head.*

hassle *n.* a dispute; a bother. □ *The whole thing was a real hassle.* □ *It's a hassle every time I come here.*

hassle someone See CHIVVY SOMEONE.

hatchet job *n.* destructive criticism of someone. (Usually in print.) □ *Did they really deserve a hatchet job like that?* □ *You are going to get a terrible hatchet job after that remark.*

hatchet man *n.* the person appointed to tell others within an organisation that they have been sacked, etc. □ *He's pleasant as hatchet men go, I suppose, if that's possible.* □ *The hatchet man was waiting outside the office for him.*

hate someone's guts *vb. phr.* to dislike someone intensely. □ *The plain truth is she hates his guts.* □ *You hate her guts, don't you?*

haul 1. *n.* the proceeds from a theft; loot. (Underworld.) □ *They divvied up the haul from the bank job.* □ *The cops thought they must have got a pretty*

good haul. **2.** *n.* the proceeds from any activity: a performance, a fishing trip, a collection of goods or money for charity, etc. □ *They got a good haul from the benefit.* □ *They surveyed the haul of cans and packages and decided they had done a pretty fair job.*

have *vb.* to swindle someone. □ *You tried to have me!* □ *I was not trying to have you. It was an honest mistake.*

have a ball *vb. phr.* to have an exciting time. (Compare with BALL.) □ *I plan to have a ball while I'm there.* □ *Come on, everybody! Let's have a ball!*

have a bash *vb. phr.* to make an attempt. □ *Come on, have a bash!* □ *If you want to have a bash come through here.*

have a bit (off with someone) *vb. phr.* to perform sexual intercourse. (Taboo.) □ *One look and he knew she had already been having a bit off with someone that evening.* □ *There were a couple of teenagers in the back room, having a bit.*

have a crack at something See TAKE A CRACK AT SOMETHING.

have a fit See THROW A FIT.

have a go *vb. phr.* to try to prevent a crime; to try to apprehend a criminal. (By a member of the public rather than a police officer.) □ *Only nuts have a go nowadays.* □ *It's when you have a go that you discover if they have a gun.*

have a go at someone *vb. phr.* to attack. □ *If you have a go at people, you can expect trouble.* □ *He did not hesitate to have a go at Willy.*

have a go at something *vb. phr.* to attempt something. □ *I hear you're going to have a go at writing a book.* □ *If I don't have a go at it now I never will.*

Have a heart! *exclam.* "Be compassionate!"; "Be kind!" □ *Have a heart! Give me another chance.* □ *Come on! Have a heart!*

have a heart *vb. phr.* to have a weak heart. (Medical.) □ *Take care with the old fellow, he has a heart.* □ *People with a heart can drop at any time.*

have a jump AND **get a jump** *vb. phr.* to perform sexual intercourse, from the male perspective. (Taboo.) □ *They were having a jump like it was going out of* *fashion.* □ *I think you could get a jump there, Barry.*

have an early night *vb. phr.* to go to bed early. □ *I'm tired and I'm having an early night tonight.* □ *If you have to get up so early tomorrow, perhaps you should have an early night?*

have a price *vb. phr.* to have a chance. (See PRICE.) □ *Look, you have a price here. Take it!* □ *You don't have a price.*

have a quickie AND **take a quickie 1.** *vb. phr.* to have a drink. □ *Fancy having a quickie?* □ *We took a quickie in that pub.* **2.** *vb. phr.* to urinate. (Crude.) □ *I've got to take a quickie. Back in a minute.* □ *He just went out to have a quickie.* **3.** *vb. phr.* to perform sexual intercourse. (Taboo.) □ *There were a couple of teenagers in the back room, having a quickie.* □ *Two dogs were taking a quickie out on the lawn.*

have a rise See GET A RISE.

have a roll *vb. phr.* to perform sexual intercourse. (Taboo.) □ *They were having a roll like it was going out of fashion.* □ *I think you've a good chance of having a roll there, Barry.*

have a run off *vb. phr.* to urinate. (Crude.) □ *I'm just going to have a run off.* □ *Well, having a run off does relieve the pressure of all that beer!*

have a scene with someone *vb. phr.* to flirt or have an affair with someone. □ *She only wants to have a scene with me.* □ *Those two have been having a scene for months.*

have a slate loose *vb. phr.* to be somewhat mentally unstable. □ *This child's has a slate loose, I think.* □ *I feel like I must have a slate loose.*

have (a) sticky palm 1. *vb. phr.* to have a tendency to steal. (Usually in the plural.) □ *That particular employee is now an ex-employee after we found out he had sticky palms.* □ *Harry has a sticky palm; don't leave things lying around.* **2.** *vb. phr.* to be susceptible to bribes. □ *You'll find that there's someone on late shift who has a sticky palm.* □ *I knew someone would have sticky palms.*

have a tiger by the tail *vb. phr.* to have become associated with someone or something powerful and potentially

dangerous. (*Have got* can replace *have*.) □ *You have a tiger by the tail there. You bit off more than you could chew.* □ *You've had a tiger by the tail ever since you took office.*

have a whale of a time *vb. phr.* to have an exciting time; to have a big time. □ *We had a whale of a time at your party.* □ *Yes, we really had a whale of a time.*

have a word with someone *vb. phr.* to beat someone up. (A euphemism.) □ *I asked Otto to have a word with him and I don't think he'll be bothering us again.* □ *Otto better have a word with that other creep as well.*

have (got) a big mouth *vb. phr.* to speak loudly; to tell secrets; to be indiscreet. □ *Boy, do you have a big mouth!* □ *He has got a big mouth. Don't tell him anything you don't want everybody else to know.*

have (got) all one's marbles *vb. phr.* to have all one's mental faculties; to be mentally sound. (Compare with LOSE ONE'S MARBLES.) □ *I don't think he has all his marbles.* □ *Do you think Bob has got all his marbles?*

have (got) a monkey on one's back *vb. phr.* to have a drug addiction. □ *Jenny has got a monkey on her back.* □ *Do you think she wants to have a monkey on her back?*

have (got) an ace up one's sleeve *vb. phr.* to have something useful in reserve; to have a secret or unexpected trick in reserve. □ *I still have an ace up my sleeve that you don't know about.* □ *I don't have an ace up my sleeve. If it doesn't work, it doesn't work.*

have (got) an itch for something *vb. phr.* to have a desire for something. □ *I have got an itch for some ice cream.* □ *We had an itch for a good film, so we went.*

have (got) ants in one's pants *vb. phr.* to be nervous and anxious. □ *He seems to have got ants in his pants before each game.* □ *All kids've got ants in their pants all the time at that age.*

have (got) a screw loose *vb. phr.* to be silly or eccentric. □ *He's sort of strange. I think he's got a screw loose.* □ *Yes, he has a screw loose somewhere.*

have (got) a short fuse *vb. phr.* to be easy to anger. □ *He's got a short fuse, so watch out.* □ *Tracy has a short fuse and is likely to lose her temper at any time.*

have (got) a skinful *vb. phr.* to have drunk too much alcohol; to be intoxicated due to drink. (Compare with SKINFUL.) □ *Pete had a skinful and just sat there quietly for a while. Then he quietly fell over.* □ *What is wrong with her is that she has got a skinful, that's what.*

have (got) a yellow streak down one's back *vb. phr.* to be cowardly. □ *I think that Wally has got a yellow streak down his back. That's what's wrong.* □ *If you have a yellow streak down your back, you don't take many risks.*

have (got) bad vibes *vb. phr.* to have bad feelings (about someone or something). (Compare with HAVE (GOT) GOOD VIBES.) □ *I've got bad vibes about Helen.* □ *I know everything will go wrong. I have bad vibes. I just know.*

have (got) bats in one's belfry *vb. phr.* to be eccentric or insane. (Compare with BATS.) □ *You must really have bats in your belfry if you think I'll put up with that kind of stuff.* □ *Pay no attention to her. She has got bats in her belfry.*

have (got) egg on one's face *vb. phr.* to be embarrassed by something one has done. (As if one went out in public with a dirty face.) □ *I was completely wrong, and now I have egg on my face.* □ *She's really got egg on her face!*

have (got) good vibes *vb. phr.* to have good feelings (about someone or something). (Compare with HAVE (GOT) BAD VIBES.) □ *I've got good vibes about Helen.* □ *I know everything will go all right. I have good vibes. You'll see.*

have (got) it made *vb. phr.* to have succeeded; to be set for life. □ *I have a good job and a nice little family. I have it made.* □ *He's really got it made.*

have (got) one foot in the grave *vb. phr.* to be near death. □ *I feel like I've got one foot in the grave.* □ *Uncle Ben has one foot in the grave, but he's still cheery.*

have (got) something on the brain *vb. phr.* to be obsessed with something. □

You've just got girls on the brain, you silly twit. □ *I have money on the brain, I suppose.*

have got to *vb. phr.* to have to. □ *Look, the thing is you have got to agree to this.* □ *I have got to go right now.*

have (got) what it takes *vb. phr.* to have the skills, power, intelligence, etc., to do something. □ *I know I've got what it takes.* □ *I suppose I don't have what it takes to be a composer.*

have (had) it 1. *vb. phr.* to be mortally wounded. (Military.) □ *If you go out into that firefight, you're almost sure to have had it.* □ *My great uncle had it during the Battle of the Somme.* **2.** *vb. phr.* to be passed one's best. □ *I've had it! I'll never get anywhere now!* □ *He thinks he's had it and he's right.*

have had it 1. *vb. phr.* to be too late. □ *Basil's had it again. He can never get himself going fast enough.* □ *If you don't get here right now you'll have had it.* **2.** *vb. phr.* to have been killed. □ *I'm afraid the whole family have had it.* □ *Why has he had it? What happened?*

have had it (up to here) (with someone or something) *vb. phr.* to have had enough of someone or something. □ *I've had it up to here with you. Goodbye.* □ *I'm off; I've had it with these people.*

have it away *vb. phr.* to escape from prison. □ *You'll never have it away from this place.* □ *Oh yeh? I'll have it away. You'll see.*

have it (away) with someone AND **have it off with someone** *vb. phr.* to perform sexual intercourse with someone. (Taboo.) □ *I'l have it away with her tonight.* □ *You can always have it off with Fiona, the girl who can't say no.*

have it off with someone See HAVE IT (AWAY) WITH SOMEONE.

have it taped *vb. phr.* to have everything well under control. □ *Don't worry, we have it taped.* □ *You say you have it taped, but I see no sign of that.*

have kittens 1. *vb. phr.* to become extremely upset or worried. □ *When I heard the news, I had kittens.* □ *I almost had kittens when I heard that Mary was pregnant.* **2.** *vb. phr.* to be surprised. □ *I nearly had kittens when I heard.* □ *She had kittens when she heard about the wedding.*

have money to burn *vb. phr.* to have plenty of money. □ *Oh don't worry about that, I have money to burn!* □ *I wonder what it's like to have money to burn?*

have-nots *n.* the poor; those who have little or nothing. (Always with *the*. Compare with HAVES.) □ *The have-nots seem never to be able to get ahead.* □ *What's in it for the have-nots?*

have one in the oven *vb. phr.* to be pregnant. □ *She's got one in the oven, I'm sure.* □ *I hear that Tracy has one in the oven.*

have one's chips 1. *vb. phr.* to be unable to avoid punishment; to be unable to avoid losing a struggle. □ *It's no use, I've had my chips.* □ *He'll have had his chips with me when I catch him!* **2.** *vb. phr.* to have died. □ *Just for a moment I was afraid I'd had my chips, but the moment passed.* □ *The parrot had had it's chips by the time I got home.*

have one's collar felt *vb. phr.* to be arrested. □ *If you want to have your collar felt, just keep on behaving like that.* □ *Harry's just had his collar felt.*

have one's feet under the table *vb. phr.* to be on very friendly terms. (*Have got* can replace *have*.) □ *Oh, he's really got his feet under the table there!* □ *Once you've got your feet under the table, you're OK for life.*

have one's mind in the gutter *vb. phr.* to think or suggest something obscene. (*Have got* can replace *have*.) □ *Tiffany has her mind in the gutter. That's why she laughs at all that dirty stuff.* □ *You always have your mind in the gutter.*

have one's wires crossed *vb. phr.* to be confused; to have misunderstood something. □ *I think we have our wires crossed.* □ *Let's try to avoid having our wires crossed again.*

haves *n.* the wealthy; those who have money. (Always with *the*. Compare with HAVE-NOTS.) □ *The haves seem to be able to take care of themselves.* □ *I live in the western suburbs with the rest of the haves.*

have seen better days *vb. phr.* showing signs of wear or exhaustion. □ *This coat has seen better days.* □ *The bowler has seen better days. He's about through in this team, I think.*

have someone *vb.* to swindle or cheat someone. □ *Don't try to have me. I know the score.* □ *Oh, in the end we'll have him out of all his money.*

have someone by the balls See GET SOMEONE BY THE BALLS.

have someone by the short and curlies See GET SOMEONE BY THE BALLS.

have someone for breakfast *vb. phr.* to defeat someone with ease. □ *Careful, she'll have you for breakfast.* □ *I'm afraid they had our team for breakfast again.*

have someone on *vb. phr.* to trick or delude someone. □ *You're having me on!* □ *Come on, we'll have her on.*

have someone over a barrel *vb. phr.* to have someone at a considerable disadvantage; to have someone where you want them. □ *All right, you have me over a barrel about this.* □ *Once we have him over a barrel the rest'll be easy.*

have someone's guts for garters *vb. phr.* to take extreme retribution against someone. (Normally uttered in the form of a threat.) □ *If you try anything like that again, I'll have your guts for garters.* □ *I told him I'd have his guts for garters.*

have someone up *vb. phr.* to bring someone to justice. □ *They'd have Mr Big up if they could just find the evidence.* □ *Why are they having up that poor guy? It's not his fault.*

have the decorators in *vb. phr.* to go through menstruation. □ *It's her time to have the decorators in. You know how she feels then.* □ *Sue doesn't go swimming when she's got the decorators in.*

have the dirt on someone *vb. phr.* to know some useful secret information about someone. □ *If you have the dirt on her, would you publish it?* □ *Sammy would love to have the dirt on Tom.*

have the hots for someone *vb. phr.* to lust after someone. (Crude.) □ *Otto has* the hots for you, Sandra. □ When Otto has the hots for someone, nothing is going to get in his way!

have too much on one's plate *vb. phr.* to be too busy. □ I'm sorry, I just have too much on my plate right now. □ If you have too much on your plate, can I help?

Hawaii *n.* fifty Pounds Sterling. (Rhyming slang, linked as follows: Hawaii [Five-0] ≈ [five-oh] = fifty pounds. From the 1970s TV show "Hawaii Five-0.") □ Burnside slipped him a Hawaii and faded into the fog. □ He put a Hawaii into the top pocket of my shirt and said that there were plenty more to be had if I asked no questions.

hay 1. *n.* money. □ I don't make enough hay to go on a trip like that! □ It takes a lot of hay to buy a car like that. **2.** *n.* marijuana. □ Got any hay, man? □ I always keep some hay at home, just in case I feel the need.

haywire 1. *mod.* chaotically disorganised; seriously out of control. □ The telephone system here is haywire today. □ The haywire traffic in town causes serious delays. **2.** *mod.* livid with anger; beside oneself with rage. □ Angry? He was haywire! □ The news drove Geoff haywire with fury.

haze *vb.* to physically assault or verbally insult or taunt a homosexual. (Crude.) □ I think they must have hazed a couple of queers last night, constable. □ Watch out! There's a lot of hazing going on around here.

head *n.* a member of the drug culture; a hippie or a person who drops out of mainstream society because of drug use. (From the 1960s and 1970s.) □ You still see a few heads around, even today. □ Some of the heads became very, very straight.

headache 1. *n.* an annoying person or thing. □ Here comes that Ken Johnson. He's a real headache. □ Cars can be such a headache. **2.** *n.* a problem. □ If we don't get this headache sorted out, the whole project will fail. □ This is a headache! What do we do now?

headbanger 1. *n.* an enthusiastic follower of heavy rock music. □ The typical headbanger shakes his or her head violently in time to the music. □ No, I am not a headbanger! **2.** *n.* a blatantly crazy person. (Derived from the Scots HEIDBANGER.) □ Don't let any headbangers in here. □ Some headbanger called to tell us that the sky is falling in. **3.** *n.* an extremist politician. □ You're not seriously considering voting for that headbanger, are you? □ Look at his policies! He's a headbanger!

headcase AND **heidcase** *n.* a crazy person. (Scots usage.) □ Dinny be a headcase. Use yer heid. (Don't be a crazy person. Use your head.) □ This guy must a real heidcase if he imagines he can get a taxi at this hour.

head cook and bottle washer AND **chief cook and bottle washer** *n.* someone who is in charge of something trivial. □ I'm the head cook and bottle washer around here. □ I want to see the chief cook and bottle washer.

head hunt *vb.* to search out and recruit executives for employment. (*Head* means "individual considered as a unit" here, as when employed in the expression "head of cattle.") □ He went to the conference to head hunt a new employee. □ All the managers were there to head hunt.

head hunter *n.* someone who searches out and recruits executives for employment. (*Head* means "individual considered as a unit" here, as when employed in the expression "head of cattle.") □ The board of directors asked a head hunter to get a new manager. □ The head hunter brought in a few candidates, but nobody promising.

head job AND **skull job** *n.* an act of oral sex. (Taboo.) □ That girl standing at the corner does provide a head job if you pay enough. □ The punter was looking for a skull job.

head off *vb. phr.* to begin a journey. □ We must head off now if we're going to get there on time. □ They headed off a few minutes ago.

head shrinker *n.* a psychiatrist. □ Well the head shrinker said he was nuts, but then we already knew that. □ Maybe a *good head shrinker can help get you sorted out in your head.*

heads will roll *phr.* "someone will be punished." □ *When I find out who did this, heads will roll.* □ *Heads will roll when I get back to the office.*

head trip *n.* self-obsessive behaviour, characterised by delusion and contemplation. □ *Willy is on another of his head trips.* □ *Come down from your head trip and see if you can get along with us mere mortals.*

healthy *mod.* large or considerable. (Especially of money.) □ *To me, £400 is healthy.* □ *She gets paid too healthily to have to worry about stuff like that.*

heap 1. *n.* an old car. □ *I've got to get my heap fixed up.* □ *Is this old heap yours?* **2.** *n.* lots; plenty. (Often in the plural. See LOAD.) □ *I have a whole heap of papers for you.* □ *Mr Wilson has heaps of money.* **3.** *n.* a slovenly person. □ *What's a heap like that doing around here?* □ *I'm sorry but we really don't need another heap working here.*

hear oneself think *vb. phr.* to be able to think clearly. (Always used in the negative.) □ *Shut up! I can't hear myself think in here!* □ *How can anyone hear themselves think with all that racket going on?*

hearth rug *n.* a dupe; a fool. (Rhyming slang, linked as follows: hearth rug ≈ [mug] = dupe/fool.) □ *That old hearth rug came past again, muttering something incoherent under his breath.* □ *Sometimes I'm such a hearth rug. I really messed the whole business up, didn't I?*

heart-throb 1. *n.* a glamorous show-business star. □ *Now that little tart is a heart-throb in Hollywood.* □ *All right, she's a heart-throb, but she still is a human being.* **2.** *n.* a person that one feels romantically inclined towards. □ *What does this heart-throb of hers actually want?* □ *Even heart-throbs have rights, Harry.*

heart-to-heart (talk) *n.* a serious and intimate discussion. □ *We sat down and had a nice heart-to-heart for about an hour.* □ *A little heart-to-heart talk is just what you need.*

hearty 1. *n.* a sporty or athletic sort of university undergraduate; an enthusiastic devotee of sports, but one lacking brainpower. □ *Arthur's a hearty, he's sure to volunteer for the team.* □ *Am I alone in finding hearties depressing?* **2.** *mod.* slightly intoxicated due to drink. (Irish usage.) □ *I felt a little hearty, but that didn't stop me from having more.* □ *The hostess was somewhat hearty but still, it was good party.*

heat 1. *n.* pressure. (Which is something those of us who can remember the Gas Laws—Boyle's Law and Charles' Law—from learning physics at school will already know: the pressure of a gas varies directly with its temperature.) □ *There's a lot of heat on Fred right now.* □ *The boss put some heat on Willy, and things are moving faster now.* **2.** *n.* the police. (Always with *the.*) □ *The heat frisked us all.* □ *The heat shouted, "Freeze, or you're dead meat!"*

heater *n.* a revolver. □ *Otto took out his heater and pointed it at the cashier.* □ *"Do you carry a heater?" asked Mr Big.*

heave *vb.* to empty one's stomach; to vomit. (Crude.) □ *He heaved and heaved and sounded like he was dying.* □ *I think I'm going to have to go and heave.*

heavens above *n.* love. (Rhyming slang.) □ *Just look at the two of them It's heavens above!* □ *It was obvious they were in heavens above.*

heavy 1. *n.* a large villain of threatening appearance. (Especially in the cinema, etc.) □ *He is well-known for playing heavies in films.* □ *Do I always have to be the heavy?* **2.** *mod.* important; profound; serious. □ *This is a very heavy matter.* □ *This matter is too heavy.* □ *I have some heavy things to talk over with you, Sam.* **3.** *mod.* sexually aroused. (Crude. Especially of the male, when this is not welcomed by the female.) □ *John was getting too heavy for June.* □ *Watch it buster! Don't get heavy with me!*

heavy date *n.* an important date with someone; a date with someone important. □ *Mary has a heavy date with Sam* tonight. □ *Pete and Sally were out on a heavy date at the time.*

heavy-duty *mod.* ardent and earnest. □ *Oh Nigel, why do you have to be so heavy-duty all the time?* □ *He's a heavy-duty sort of guy.*

heavy-handed 1. *mod.* tactless; forceful; unfair. □ *Paul is a little heavy-handed at times, but mostly he's reasonable.* □ *That was a pretty heavy-handed thing to do.* **2.** *mod.* [of drinks] too strong. □ *I think you were a bit heavy-handed there, Paul.* □ *I don't like a drink that's too heavy-handed.*

heavy metal 1. *n.* a type of rock music characterised by enormous volume and a throbbing beat. □ *I just don't care for that heavy metal.* □ *Heavy metal is just too loud.* **2.** *mod.* having to do with HEAVY METAL music or musicians. □ *Heavy metal stuff is a little harsh for my old ears.* □ *Those heavy metal guys must have made a fortune.*

heavy necking *n.* hugging and kissing, plus intimate caresses. (Crude. Compare with HEAVY PETTING.) □ *Mary and Sam are past heavy necking.* □ *The teacher caught them at some heavy necking in the closet.*

heavy petting *n.* carressing stopping just short of sexual intercourse. (Crude. Compare with HEAVY NECKING.) □ *Heavy petting often leads on to something more.* □ *You'll get kicked out of the cinema if they find you doing heavy petting.*

hedgehopper *n.* a trainee pilot. (From their reputed tendency to fly low.) □ *Oh, we get a lot of hedgehoppers around here, thanks to the local flying school.* □ *Look at that hedgehopper! Are you sure he's going to make it?*

heebie-jeebies AND **heeby-jeebies** *n.* very severe anxiety, depression or fear. (Compare with WILLIES.) □ *I have the heebie-jeebies whenever I go to the dentist.* □ *That kind of film gives me the heebie-jeebies.*

hee-haw *n.* nothing whatsoever; zilch. (Scots usage.) □ *We've got hee-haw for you here.* □ *He's brought hee-haw with him!*

heel *n.* a low and despicable man. □ *You are the most impossible heel!* □ *The guy is a heel, and he seems to work at it, too.*

heeled *mod.* in possession of drugs. □ *He was heeled when the cops stopped him.* □ *If you're heeled they'll book you.*

heidbanger 1. *n.* a violently insane person. (Scots usage. Compare with HEADBANGER.) □ *Watch that one; he's a heidbanger all right.* □ *Yon heidbanger canna be trusted to cross the road without thumping you.* **2.** *n.* a very stupid person. (Scots usage.) □ *He's just a heidbanger; ignore what he says.* □ *What a heidbanger!*

heid bummer *n.* an ironic or sarcastic name for anyone in a position of authority. (Scots usage.) □ *Have you heard the latest idea from the heid bummer?* □ *If he's the heid bummer then I'm Lady Mick.*

heidcase See HEADCASE.

heid-the-baw *n.* an affectionate nickname for someone considered none too smart. (Scots usage.) □ *Leave wee heid-the-baw alone, he's no gonna harm anyone.* □ *Have you ever noticed that this place is run by heid-the-baws?*

Heinz 57 (variety) *n.* a mongrel breed of dog. (From the trade name of a condiment company.) □ *We have one pedigreed dog and one Heinz 57 variety.* □ *My Heinz 57 is the greatest dog of all.*

hell 1. *n.* trouble. (Crude.) □ *I went through all sorts of hell to get this done on time.* □ *This day was real hell.* **2.** *exclam.* "Damn!" (Crude.) □ *Oh, hell. I'm late.* □ *Hell, I'm too early.*

hellhole *n.* a hot and crowded place; any unpleasant place. (Crude.) □ *I want out of this hellhole.* □ *The theatre was an over-crowded hellhole. Lucky there was no fire.*

hellish *mod.* very. (Crude.) □ *No, that's a hellish good idea!* □ *She's a hellish nice girl, really.*

hell of a mess *n.* a terrible mess. (Crude.) □ *This is really a hell of a mess you've got us into.* □ *I never* *dreamt I'd come back to such a hell of a mess.*

hell of a someone or something 1. *n.* a very bad person or thing. (Crude.) □ *That's a hell of a way to treat someone.* □ *He's a hell of a driver! Watch out!* **2.** *n.* a very good person or thing. (Crude.) □ *He is one hell of a guy. We really like him.* □ *We had a hell of a good time.*

Hell's bells (and buckets of blood)! AND **Hell's teeth!** *exclam.* "Dammit!" (Crude. An expression of surprise or annoyance.) □ *Oh, hell's bells and buckets of blood! I forgot my keys.* □ *Hell's teeth! I'm late.*

Hell's teeth! See HELL'S BELLS (AND BUCKETS OF BLOOD)!

Helluva Bellow Chorus AND **Hullabaloo Chorus** *n.* derisory names for the *Hallelujah Chorus* from Handel's oratorio, the *Messiah*. (Crude. Although no foreign language is involved, these terms bear much similarity to hobson-jobson. Always with *the*.) □ *When they played that recording of the Helluva Bellow Chorus at full volume for the fourth time, Paul phoned the police.* □ *If you like the Hullabaloo Chorus, fine. Me? No, I don't.*

hell week *n.* the time of a woman's menses. (Crude.) □ *You're right, it's my old woman's hell week again.* □ *Harry really hates my hell week. So do I.*

helmet *n.* a uniformed police officer. □ *We need some helmets down here urgently.* □ *I was never more pleased to see a helmet.*

helter-skelter 1. *n.* a slide spiralling down around a tower, typically at a amusement park. □ *We went down that helter-skelter I don't know how many times that day.* □ *The kids love the helter-skelter, you know.* **2.** *n.* a condition of confused and disorganised hurry. □ *It was all a last-minute helter-skelter.* □ *It must have got lost in that terrible helter-skelter last night.*

hemp *n.* cannabis. □ *The guy sort of smells like hemp.* □ *I smell hemp in here.*

hen *n.* a woman. (Scots usage. Also a term of address.) □ *Come on hen, vote for Glen!* □ *Are you all right, hen?*

hen party 1. *n.* a gossipy party attended by women. (Compare with STAG PARTY.) □ *I have a hen party every few weeks. We love to get together.* □ *I wouldn't be caught dead at one of those hen parties.* **2.** *n.* a pre-wedding party for the female participants in the forthcoming event, equivalent to an all-male STAG PARTY. □ *What time do we have to be at that hen party on Saturday night?* □ *What a fancy hen party! They even have glass glasses!*

Here's mud in your eye. *sent.* "I salute you." (A jocular drinking toast.) □ *Here's mud in your eye. Bottoms up!* □ *Well, here's mud in your eye. Care for another?*

her indoors *n.* a wife or girlfriend. □ *Her indoors is looking for you.* □ *I'll ask her indoors if we can come over this weekend.*

hetro *mod.* hetrosexual. □ *Of course I'm hetro! What the hell are you?* □ *Sorry. I'm hetro too, but there's a lot of fairies around here.*

het-up *mod.* excited. □ *She was really het-up, I tell you.* □ *Don't get so het-up. It's going to be all right.*

hey-diddle-diddle AND **hi-diddle-diddle 1.** *n.* the middle. (Rhyming slang.) □ *Not too big and not too small. Just in the hey-diddle-diddle.* □ *I appear in the hi-diddle-diddle of the play.* **2.** *n.* an act of urination. (Crude. Rhyming slang, linked as follows: hey/hi-diddle-diddle ≈ [piddle] = urinate.) □ *Where do you go around here for a hey-diddle-diddle?* □ *If you need a hi-diddle-diddle, go through there.*

hideously *mod.* very. □ *That one is hideously expensive.* □ *A hideously large man came to the house to see you.*

hide up *vb. phr.* to protect or shield someone wanted by the police. □ *I've got to hide up; the fuzz are after me.* □ *You can't hide up in here, son!*

hide-up *n.* a hiding place. □ *Where do you think his hide-up is?* □ *I think Otto's gone into his hide-up.*

hid(e)y-hole See FUNK-HOLE.

Hide your eyes. *phr.* "don't look." □ *What a mess. Hide your eyes.* □ *Please, hide your eyes.*

hi-diddle-diddle See HEY-DIDDLE-DID-DLE.

hi-diddler *n.* a violin player. (Scots usage.) □ *Where did you find such a great hi-diddler?* □ *There's a lot of hi-diddlers in an orchestra, you know.*

hiding to nothing *n.* a situation that can only lead to failure. □ *Let's face it, we're on a hiding to nothing here.* □ *I don't intend to let this become a hiding to nothing, thank you!*

hi-fi 1. *mod.* high fidelity. □ *Oh yes sir, these compact disk systems are really hi-fi.* □ *In fact, CDs are higher fidelity than the old hi-fi systems ever were.* **2.** *n.* a record-player or radio that reproduces sounds with high fidelity to the original. □ *Can I use the hi-fi in your room?* □ *She plays that hi-fi till very late every night.*

high *n.* a state of euphoria caused by drugs or alcohol. □ *His life is nothing but one high after another.* □ *Her only goal is a high.*

high and dry *mod.* abandoned; unsupported. (Like a ship beached or stranded ashore.) □ *He went off and left me high and dry.* □ *Here I sit high and dry—no food, no money, no nothing.*

high (as a kite) *mod.* intoxicated due to drink or drugs. □ *Willy is a little high for so early in the evening.* □ *They went out that evening to get as high as a kite, and for no other reason.*

highbrow 1. *n.* an intellectual person or one with such pretensions. (Compare with *lowbrow*.) □ *Sam used to be a highbrow, but he gave up his fancy ways.* □ *The highbrows usually congregate in there.* **2.** *mod.* concerning an intellectual person or one with such pretensions. (Compare with *lowbrow*.) □ *Ben asked how he could get rid of his highbrow image, but Tony said you can't get rid of what you don't have in the first place.* □ *Pete is sort of highbrow, but still he's okay, sort of.*

higher ups See HIGH UPS.

high-hatted *mod.* supercilious. □ *Tiffany can be high-hatted if she wants to, and she usually wants to.* □ *Don't be so high-hatted!* □ *What a high-hatted waiter!*

high heid yin *n.* an ironic or sarcastic name for anyone in a position of authority. (Scots usage.) □ *Yon high heid yin canna be trusted with anything.* □ *Oh, he's the high heid yin around here all right.*

highjinks *n.* tricks; capers. □ *Enough of your highjinks! Get busy.* □ *I like to hear about the kids and their latest highjinks.*

high jump 1. *n.* any severe punishment. □ *It's the high jump for you, my lad!* □ *What else but the high jump do you expect after what you've done?* **2.** *n.* a job dismissal; the sack. (Always with *the*.) □ *The high jump is what I am afraid of.* □ *The boss gave them all the high jump.* **3.** AND **long jump** *n.* an execution, particularly a hanging. □ *The high jump was carried out at dawn this morning.* □ *There's to be another long jump next week.*

high old time *n.* a very enjoyable experience. □ *Thank you for a high old time.* □ *Come on, we'll have a high old time.*

high spot *n.* the optimum or best part of something. □ *Winning that Oscar was the high spot.* □ *I don't believe I've got to my high spot yet.*

high-tech *mod.* used or associated with high technology or very innovative equipment, devices or techniques. □ *I don't understand any of this high-tech gibberish the young talk nowadays.* □ *A video recorder is too high-tech for me, thanks.*

high ups AND **higher ups** *n.* the people in charge or in positions of authority. □ *I have to speak to the high ups about the refund.* □ *One of the higher ups is coming down to talk to you.*

highway robbery See DAYLIGHT ROBBERY.

high, wide and handsome *mod.* going very well. □ *How are things? High, wide and handsome, of course!* □ *Well, that was high, wide and handsome, I must say.*

hike *n.* a long walk. □ *I went for a hike, just to get away from him.* □ *Go on! Get out! Take a hike!*

hillibilly *mod.* chilly. (Rhyming slang. Scots usage.) □ *My, it's getting fair* *hillibilly again, innit? (My, it's getting rather chilly again, isn't it?)* □ *Senga hates it when it's hillibilly like this.*

himie AND **hymie** *n.* a Jewish person. (Offensive.) □ *He said he was not a racist, he just hated this particular himie!* □ *Don't call Jewish people hymies, please. It is very offensive and racist.*

hip *mod.* informed; aware. □ *The guy is just not hip. He's a nerd.* □ *Get hip, Tom!*

hippy AND **hippie** *n.* a long-haired, drug-using youth of the 1960s and 1970s. □ *That guy looks like a hippy left over from the sixties.* □ *Who's that has-been hippie who just came in?*

hipster *n.* a youth of the 1950s, characterised by an interest in jazz and COOL things. □ *Can you imagine your father as a hipster?* □ *Were the hipsters the ones with the big shoulder pads?*

history *n.* someone or something in the past. (Compare with ANCIENT HISTORY.) □ *Dave? Oh, he's just history. I never go out with him anymore.* □ *Susan is just history. We're through.* □ *Don't make a move! If this gun goes off, you're history.*

hit **1.** *n.* a success; something that meets with approval. (Often with *with*.) □ *The play was a hit.* □ *The fudge with nuts in it was a great hit at the sale.* **2.** *n.* a successful result; something that is exactly as intended. □ *It was a hit—a real winner.* □ *Your idea was right on target—a hit for sure.* **3.** *vb.* to reach something; to achieve something. □ *The car hit ninety in no time at all.* □ *I hit sixty next month, and I'm going to retire.* **4.** *vb.* to kill someone; to assassinate someone. (Underworld.) □ *Bruno was told to hit Max.* □ *The thug set out to hit the mayor, but got nabbed first.* **5.** *n.* a dose of a drug; a puff of a marijuana cigarette. □ *He had a hit of Mary Jane and went out to finish his work.* □ *She took a hit by the water cooler.* **6.** *n.* intoxicated due to drink. (Rhyming slang, linked as follows: hit [and miss] ≈ [piss(ed)] = drunk.) □ *Boy, I was really hit. I'll never drink another drop.* □ *By morning they were all hit.*

hitch *vb.* to get married. □ *So they've finally got hitched, then?* □ *We got hitched in a little chapel in Wales.*

hitched *mod.* married. □ *Sam and Mary decided to get hitched.* □ *They went abroad to get hitched.*

hitch(-hike) *vb.* to travel by means of free lifts provided by passing traffic. □ *It used to be safe to hitch-hike around Europe, but now it's not.* □ *There she was, trying to hitch a lift to Leeds.*

hit list *n.* a list of people to whom something is going to happen. □ *Ralph is on my hit list for contributing money for the orphans.* □ *She's on our hit list for volunteers.*

hit man *n.* a hired killer. (Underworld.) □ *Bruno was the perfect hit man. Hardly any brains or conscience.* □ *To look at Rocko, you'd never believe he was a hit man.*

hit on something *vb. phr.* to discover something. □ *She hit on a new scheme for removing the impurities from drinking water.* □ *I hit on it when I wasn't able to sleep one night.*

hit pay dirt AND **strike pay dirt** **1.** *vb. phr.* to discover something of value. □ *At last, we hit pay dirt.* □ *When we opened the last trunk, we knew we had struck pay dirt.* **2.** *vb. phr.* to get to the basic facts of something. □ *Now we're beginning to hit pay dirt.* □ *When we figured out the code, we really struck pay dirt.*

hit (someone) below the belt *vb. phr.* to deal with someone unfairly. (Boxing.) □ *Don't hit below the belt!* □ *You were hitting Tom below the belt when you said that.*

hit someone with something *vb. phr.* to present someone with an idea, plan or proposal—usually unexpectedly. □ *Pete hit me with a great idea just before we left.* □ *Fred hit his boss with a plan to save a bundle in the front office.*

hit something for six **1.** *vb. phr.* to demolish an argument. □ *Your argument is easy to hit for six.* □ *Come on, that theory was hit for six ages ago.* **2.** *vb. phr.* to successfully subject someone or something to a sudden shock or attack. □ *We really were hit for six by the* *news.* □ *If he does that again I'll hit him for six all right.* **3.** *vb. phr.* to score six runs by hitting a cricket ball over the boundary of the playing field without touching the ground after leaving the bat. □ *Wonderful! He hit it for six!* □ *Hit the ball for six again!*

hit the booze See HIT THE BOTTLE.

hit the bottle AND **hit the booze** *vb. phr.* to go on a drinking bout; to get drunk. □ *Jed's hitting the bottle again.* □ *He's been hitting the booze for a week now.*

hit the deck *vb. phr.* to fall down; to drop down or lie down quickly. □ *Hit the deck. Don't let them see you.* □ *I hit the deck the minute I heard the shots.*

hit the dust AND **kiss the dust** *vb. phr.* to fall to the earth, because of death or because of being struck. (Western films.) □ *I'll see that you hit the dust before sunset, cowboy!* □ *You'll kiss the dust before I will, Sheriff.*

hit the hay AND **hit the sack** *vb. phr.* to go to bed. □ *I have to go home and hit the hay pretty soon.* □ *Let's hit the sack. We have to get an early start in the morning.*

hit the jackpot 1. *vb. phr.* to win a large amount of money. □ *I hit the jackpot in the big contest.* □ *Sally hit the jackpot in the lottery.* **2.** *vb. phr.* to have very good luck. □ *Sometimes you just hit the jackpot and it's great!* □ *Me hit the jackpot? Chance would be a fine thing.*

hit the panic button AND **press the panic button; push the panic button** *vb. phr.* to panic; to call for urgent help. □ *She hit the panic button and just went to pieces.* □ *Don't press the panic button. Relax and keep your eyes open.*

hit the pavement 1. *vb. phr.* to be thrown out of somewhere, such as a pub, club, etc. □ *It was late at night and all around the drunks were hitting the pavements.* □ *Right you; either leave quietly or allow my large bouncer friend here to help you hit the pavement. Get the picture?* **2.** *vb. phr.* to be thrown out of one's job. □ *A lot of us hit the pavement on that black Thursday.* □ *Do that again and you'll hit the pavement as fast as you can blink.*

hit the road *vb. phr.* to leave; to begin to travel along a road. □ *We plan to hit the road about dawn.* □ *Let's hit the road. We have a long way to go.*

hit the roof See GO THROUGH THE ROOF.

hit the sack See HIT THE HAY.

hive something off *vb. phr.* to separate something from a larger entity. □ *I hear they plan to hive off the pharmaceuticals division from the rest of the company.* □ *Why would I want to hive off that bit? It's the most profitable.*

hobby-bobby *n.* a part-time policeman. □ *The hobby-bobby broke up the fight.* □ *The government wants to recruit more hobby-bobbies, I hear.*

hobo *n.* a tramp. □ *The hobo asked politely for some work in exchange for food.* □ *Two old hobos wandered slowly down the lane.*

Hobson's choice 1. *n.* a choice that is no choice; take it or leave it. (From Thomas Hobson, a Cambridge carrier in the late 16th and early 17th century, who reputedly insisted that customers could either take the horse next to the door or none at all.) □ *I'm afraid it's Hobson's choice this evening, we're running short of alternatives.* □ *Well, if you don't like that room it's too bad. There are no others so you've got Hobson's choice.* **2.** *n.* a voice. (Rhyming slang. Theatrical.) □ *What a Hobson's choice that woman has! How it carries!* □ *Come on love, we need more Hobson's choice from you than that!*

hochmagandie *n.* fornication. (Scots usage. Pronounced HOOKK-ma-gan-dy.) □ *I think there's a wee spot of hochmagandie going on between these two, Archie.* □ *If I catch you at any more hochmagandie I'm leaving you!*

hock *n.* a male homosexual. (Crude. Rhyming slang, linked as follows: hock ≈ [cock] = homosexual.) □ *Why does he work so hard to look like he's a hock?* □ *He doesn't like being called a hock.*

hockshop AND **popshop** *n.* a pawnshop. □ *We took the watch to a hockshop, but couldn't get enough money for it.* □ *The police checked all the popshops in town for the murder weapon.*

hock something *vb.* to pawn something. □ *I tried to hock my watch to get some money.* □ *I've got nothing left to hock.*

hodden grey *n.* a simple, unaffected person. (Scots usage.) □ *Watch that one; he's a hodden grey all right.* □ *She dizny act like she's a hodden grey.*

hog 1. *n.* phencyclidine (P.C.P.), an animal tranquilliser used by drug addicts. □ *We are glad to learn that the demand for hog is tapering off.* □ *Max won't sell hog to kids these days.* **2.** *vb.* to acquire greedily; to hoard in a selfish way. □ *If you hog money, sooner or later someone will rob you.* □ *I wonder how he hogged all that money?*

hogwash *n.* nonsense. □ *Now that's just hogwash, and you know it.* □ *Hogwash! That's about enough of your lies!*

ho-hum 1. *mod.* uncertain; of doubtful value. □ *Clare gave another ho-hum performance at the concert hall last night.* □ *I feel rather ho-hum about his lecture.* **2.** *mod.* uninteresting; boring. □ *It was really ho-hum, I'm afraid!* □ *It really is a ho-hum sort of place.*

hoick *vb.* to spit. □ *Angry? I could've hoicked!* □ *None of your hoicking in here!*

hoist something *vb.* to steal something. □ *Someone's hoist my suitcase!* □ *If you leave your luggage in here, someone'll hoist it as sure as anything.*

hoity-toity *mod.* affectedly or condescendingly superior. □ *He's a real hoity-toity type; you know—a gutless wonder.* □ *Make a difficult choice? No, Jemima is far too hoity-toity for that.*

hokum *n.* sentimental or sensational nonsense. □ *All that is just hokum.* □ *No more hokum. I want the truth.*

hold down a job *vb. phr.* to perform satisfactorily in one's employment. □ *She has been holding down a job for over three years now.* □ *I too could hold down a job, if I just had one to hold down in the first place.*

Hold everything! *exclam.* "Stop everything!" □ *Hold everything! I forgot my wallet.* □ *Hold everything, my door isn't closed!*

Hold it! *exclam.* "Stop right there!" □ *Hold it! Stop!* □ *That's enough! Hold it!*

Hold it, Buster! *exclam.* "Stop that, mister!" (Sometimes said by women in repulsing an excessively amorous male.) □ *Hold it, Buster! Who do you think you are?* □ *Just hold it, Buster; who do you imagine I am?*

hold no brief for someone *vb. phr.* to fail to support or agree with someone. □ *No, no, I hold no brief for him!* □ *She says she holds no brief for him, but I'm not so sure.*

hold one's horses *vb. phr.* to wait; to relax and slow down; to be patient. (Usually a command.) □ *Hold your horses! Don't get in such a hurry.* □ *Now, just hold your horses and let me explain.*

hold out on someone *vb. phr.* to avoid supplying something (usually information or money) to someone. □ *Don't hold out on me! What happened?* □ *He's trying to hold out on me but I'll find out the truth, never you fear.*

hold the fort *vb. phr.* to remain behind and take care of things. □ *Hold the fort. I'll be there in a while.* □ *I left John there to hold the fort.*

hold water *vb. phr.* [for an idea, plan, etc.] to survive an evaluation or investigation. □ *Nothing you've said so far holds water.* □ *Her story doesn't hold water.*

hole 1. *n.* the anus. (Taboo.) □ *His doctor has just told him he needs an operation on his hole.* □ *Shift! Get your hole out of here now!* **2.** *n.* the female sexual organ. (Taboo.) □ *Who do think you are, going for my hole like that?* □ *Get your hand off my hole, Sunshine!*

hole in one 1. *n.* a golfing shot from the tee that goes directly into the hole without intermediate shots. □ *I once got a hole in one.* □ *I don't think a hole in one is ever likely for me.* **2.** *vb. phr.* to perform sexual intercourse on a first date, from the male perspective. (Taboo.) □ *I don't think you're going to manage to hole in one with her.* □ *Well, you're wrong. I holed in one last night.*

hole in the wall *n.* a tiny shop, office, workshop, etc., figuratively not much wider than its doorway. □ *I went into this tiny hole in the wall where they had* the nicest little gifts. □ *His office is just a hole in the wall.*

hole up *vb. phr.* to hide (somewhere). □ *It's too late to try to hole up, Boris. The police are already here.* □ *He's holed up somewhere to avoid his creditors.*

holier-than-thou *mod.* condescendingly, possibly hypocritically, self-righteous. □ *She has such a holier-than-thou attitude.* □ *Tracy can act so holier-than-thou sometimes.*

H.O.L.L.A.N.D. AND **HOLLAND** *phr.* "here our love lies and never dies." (The initialism is sometimes written on love letters. Also an acronym.) □ *Love and kisses. H.O.L.L.A.N.D.* □ *XXXX HOLLAND.*

hollow legs *n.* anyone who can eat or drink prodigious amounts. (Also a term of address.) □ *You'll see why he's called hollow legs when he starts to eat.* □ *I hope you've got enough food in the house Mavis; he's a real hollow legs.*

hols *n.* holidays. □ *I'm going to America for the hols.* □ *What are you doing for your hols this year, Charles?*

Holy cow! AND **Holy mackerel!; Holy Moses!** *exclam.* an expression of surprise or amazement. □ *Holy cow! A red one!* □ *Holy mackerel! What a day!* □ *Give me a chance! Holy Moses, don't rush me!*

holy friar *n.* a liar. (Rhyming slang.) □ *Anyone who told you that is a holy friar.* □ *The fact is, he's just a holy friar.*

Holy Ghost 1. *n.* the post. (Rhyming slang.) □ *The postman handed her her Holy Ghost.* □ *Anything in the Holy Ghost for me today?* **2.** *n.* the winning post. (Rhyming slang.) □ *Me horse was first past the Holy Ghost and that's all that matters, innit?* □ *He stood at the Holy Ghost and watched the horses rushing past.* **3.** *n.* toasted bread. (Rhyming slang.) □ *Any more of that Holy Ghost?* □ *I'm going to make myself some Holy Ghost. Fancy some?*

Holy Joe *n.* any ostentatiously pious man. □ *There's a Holy Joe running that office, so watch your language.* □ *I just cannot stand these Holy Joes.*

Holy mackerel! See HOLY COW!

Holy Moses! See HOLY COW!

holy nail AND **Royal Mail** *n.* court bail. (Rhyming slang.) □ *Any chance of holy nail, guv?* □ *If he gets Royal Mail again, I'll eat my hat.*

holy terror *n.* a formidable individual; an awkward person or one who is particularly difficult or demanding. □ *Jane has become a holy terror lately.* □ *The new boss is a real holy terror; he expects us to do actual work.*

home and dry *mod.* safe after taking a risk. □ *I don't feel home and dry here.* □ *Don't worry, you're home and dry now.*

home-brew *n.* homemade beer or wine. □ *Is this disgusting concoction your own home-brew, Willy?* □ *My uncle makes his own home-brew.*

home fixture *n.* a sporting event at a team's home base. □ *So, how do you think they'll do in the forthcoming home fixture?* □ *The next home fixture is on Saturday.*

Home of Lost Causes *n.* a sardonic nickname for Oxford University (Normally with *the*.) □ *Yes, I am a graduate of the Home of Lost Causes.* □ *Why do they call Oxford University the Home of Lost Causes?*

homework *n.* a girlfriend; a wife. □ *I wish I had as lovely homework as her to go back to every evening!* □ *I think I'm in love with Harry's new homework.*

homo 1. *mod.* homosexual, normally male but not exclusively. (Crude.) □ *Is this one of those homo bars?* □ *Where'd you get those homo-looking clothes?* **2.** *n.* a homosexual, normally male but not exclusively. (Crude.) □ *Somebody said she's one of these homos.* □ *So what if he's a homo? He can still vote, can't he?*

Honestly! *exclam.* an expression of surprise or amazement. □ *Honestly! What a day!* □ *I enjoyed our visit, honestly!*

honey 1. *n.* money. (Rhyming slang.) □ *Sorry, I can't afford it, I've no honey.* □ *How much honey do you need, then?* **2.** *mod.* excellent; wonderful. □ *Your news is really honey, you know.* □ *What a honey idea that was.*

honey cart See HONEY WAGON.

honeymoon (stage) *n.* an early stage in any activity, before problems set in. □ *Of course, this is still the honeymoon stage, but everything seems to be going all right.* □ *The honeymoon is over, Carl. You have to produce now.*

honey wagon AND **honey cart** *n.* any vehicle used for or designed for carrying excreta: a farm manure wagon; a tank truck used to pump out septic tanks; a tank truck used to pump out aircraft toilets; a portable latrine truck used in film making. (Crude.) □ *It may not be very romantic but someone has to drive the honey wagon.* □ *The honey cart was stuck in front of the plane due to a puncture.*

honk 1. *n.* a drinking spree; a wild party. □ *Jed's last honk lasted nearly a week.* □ *The guys went off on the honk to end all honks.* **2.** *vb.* to empty one's stomach; to vomit. (Crude. Scots usage. Onomatopoetic.) □ *I can hear someone in the cludge honking something awful. (I can hear someone in the toilet being violently sick.)* □ *Who honked on the driveway?* **3.** *n.* a bad smell; a stink. □ *Where is that terrible honk coming from?* □ *I just can't stand that honk.* **4.** *vb.* to smell badly; to stink. □ *If you've got to honk like a badger's backside, do so a long way from me.* □ *When we opened the room it honked very badly.*

honked AND **honking; honkers** *mod.* intoxicated due to drink or drugs. (Crude.) □ *Wally was too honked to stand up.* □ *Boy, is that guy honkers!*

Honkers *n.* Hong Kong. □ *Meet Simon, just back from Honkers.* □ *I'm off to Honkers on business next week.*

honkers See HONKED.

honkin *mod.* stinking; disgusting. (Scots usage.) □ *Oh my, what a honkin mess.* □ *I don't know what had been going on but the whole place was honkin.*

honking See HONKED.

honk (up) one's ring *vb. phr.* to vomit in a very bad way. (Crude. Scots usage.) □ *There must've been something wrong wi' yon beer 'cause I've been honkin up ma ring aw nicht. (There must have been something wrong with that beer because I've been vomiting in a very bad way all night.)* □ *Dinna you bother ta honk yer ring aw ower ma new carpet, ya bampot! (Don't you dare to be violently sick on my carpet, you fool!)*

hooch AND **hootch** *n.* hard liquor; any alcoholic beverage. □ *Let's go get ourselves some hooch.* □ *More hootch for you?*

hooey *n.* nonsense. □ *The whole newspaper is nothing but hooey today.* □ *What's all this hooey about getting a new car?*

hoof it AND **leg it 1.** *vb. phr.* to walk instead of to travel by other means. □ *My car's broken down, so I had to hoof it to work today.* □ *Let's leg it over to the library.* **2.** *vb. phr.* to run away. □ *I saw them coming and hoofed it home.* □ *Lefty legged it when he saw the uniform.*

Hoo Flung Dung *n.* a jocular name for a Chinese person. (Racially offensive. Compare with ONE HUNG LOW.) □ *Y'know, Otto, if you call a Chinese a Hoo Flung Dung, he's likely to get nasty.* □ *Why can you not be polite to Hoo Flung Dungs?*

hoo-ha 1. *n.* nonsense. □ *What is all this hoo-ha about your leaving the company?* □ *Stop talking hoo-ha and tell the truth.* **2.** *n.* a commotion; a fuss. □ *What is all this hoo-ha about?* □ *There was quite a hoo-ha when a terrified deer ran frantically through the department store.*

hooked AND **hooky** *mod.* stolen. □ *I know they must have hooked my handbag after I left it on the table, officer.* □ *I think these computer memory chips are hooky.*

hooked (on someone or something) *mod.* preferring someone or something; enamoured of someone or something. □ *I'm really hooked on chocolate anything.* □ *Sam is hooked on Mary for good.*

hooked (on something) *mod.* addicted (to a drug). □ *Gert is hooked on horse.* □ *Everybody knows she's been hooked for years.*

hookie *n.* a Jewish person. (Offensive.) □ *Don't call Jews hookies, please. It is very offensive and racist.* □ *He said he was not a racist, he just hated this particular hookie!*

hook, line and sinker *mod.* totally; entirely. □ *She fell for it hook, line and sinker.* □ *They believed every word hook, line and sinker.*

hook someone 1. *vb.* to hit someone. □ *Harry's livid and out to hook you for what you did.* □ *He hooked me as I walked over to my car.* **2.** *vb.* to addict someone (to something). (Not necessarily drugs.) □ *The constant use of bicarb hooked him to the stuff.* □ *Finally, the pot hooked him.*

hook something *vb.* to steal something. □ *Lefty hooked a couple of Mars bars just for the hell of it.* □ *What did they hook last night?*

hook up with someone 1. *vb. phr.* to meet with someone. □ *Fancy hooking up with you here, Bill. How have you been?* □ *Well, hello, Tom. I didn't think I'd hook up with you again so soon.* **2.** *n.* to join forces with someone. □ *If we hook up with each other it'll be easier to defeat the others.* □ *These two have hooked up together and we now have a real problem.*

hooky See HOOKED.

hoolie *n.* a wild party. (Scots and Irish usage.) □ *Shuggy ower likes a good hoolie an that. (Hugh always like as a wild party like that.)* □ *They're aw oot at some hoolie. (They're all out at some wild party.)*

hooligan *n.* a rough, wild, often criminal, youth. □ *A gang of hooligans were blocking the street.* □ *He's nothing better than a hooligan.*

hoolivan *n.* a police vehicle equipped with TV cameras and so forth in order to survey HOOLIGANS. □ *The hoolivans were out in force that day, recording everything they could of the riot.* □ *The police have got a new and improved hoolivan now, you know.*

Hooray Henry *n.* a rich, fashionable, loud-mouthed, conventional, dim-witted young man. □ *There's a Hooray Henry here looking for you.* □ *The Hooray Henry sat on the bench and waited for him.*

hoot 1. *vb.* to laugh loudly. □ *The audience screamed and hooted with their appreciation.* □ *They howled and hooted. I know they just loved it.* **2.** *n.* a joke; something very funny. □ *The whole business was a terrific hoot.* □ *The skit was a hoot, and everyone enjoyed it.* **3.** *n.* someone or something that is considered to be very amusing. □ *What a hoot you are!* □ *The whole evening was a total hoot.*

hootch See HOOCH.

hooter *n.* a nose, especially a big or protruding one. □ *I sort of wish my hooter wasn't so darned big.* □ *He blew his hooter and went back to his reading.*

Hoover *n.* a hovercraft. (A pun on the Hoover vacuum cleaner.) □ *We crossed the Channel on the Hoover.* □ *Crossing by Hoover is much faster than by conventional ferry.*

Hoover (up) *vb. (phr.)* to devour rapidly or greedily. □ *The children really Hoovered up the food put out for them.* □ *If you Hoover your food like that again Johnny, mummy will be angry.*

hop 1. *n.* a dancing party for young people. □ *The kids are out at the school hop.* □ *The hop was a lot of fun.* **2.** *n.* a lift in or on a vehicle. □ *He gave me a hop back last night.* □ *Can I give you a hop?*

Hop it! *exclam.* "Go away!"; "Get lost!" □ *Get out of there! Hop it!* □ *Why don't you just hop it?*

hop off (one's twig) 1. *vb. phr.* to leave very suddenly. □ *Well, I must hop off my twig now.* □ *Time for us to hop off now, I think.* **2.** See also DROP OFF THE TWIG.

hop on *vb. phr.* to get aboard a plane, train, etc. □ *I'll hop on a plane and be there in a couple of hours.* □ *Hop on a train or anything, but get here as soon as you can.*

hopping mad *mod.* very angry; livid. □ *I was hopping mad about the broken window.* □ *The boss was hopping mad at his secretary.*

Hop to it! *exclam.* "Get moving!"; "Hurry up!" □ *Hop to it! I don't pay* you to stand around. □ *I need it now! Hop to it!*

horizontal *mod.* intoxicated due to drink. □ *The boss was horizontal at the Christmas party.* □ *Stewed? No, he's totally horizontal!*

horizontal exercise 1. *n.* sexual intercourse. (Crude.) □ *They were talking about, you know, horizontal exercise.* □ *After that horizontal exercise, she felt cheap.* **2.** *n.* sleep. □ *You really need some horizontal exercise. Why don't you try a week of it and see if that works?* □ *I've got to get home and get my horizontal exercise.*

horn *n.* an erection. (Taboo.) □ *As long as you have a horn like that I'll love you, Frank.* □ *You can't walk along the street with a horn!*

horn-pill *n.* an aphrodisiac. (Taboo.) □ *What's this stuff you want me to take? A horn-pill?* □ *Now these ones are real horn-pills, he told me.*

hornswoggle *n.* nonsense. □ *What hornswoggle that is!* □ *You're talking hornswoggle again—as usual.*

horny *mod.* sexually aroused. (Taboo.) □ *Tom said he was horny.* □ *Who's that horny jerk?* □ *All the guys in that class are horny all the time.*

horrors 1. *n.* frightening hallucinations cause by drugs. (Always with *the.*) □ *Once he had gone through the horrors, he swore he was off the stuff for keeps.* □ *Pete had the horrors and had to be hospitalised.* **2.** *n.* menstruation. (Crude. Always with *the.*) □ *The horrors have struck again!* □ *It's her horrors. You know how she feels then.*

horrorscope *n.* a horoscope. □ *We all look at the horrorscope in the paper every morning when we have our coffee.* □ *Do you believe your horrorscope?*

horse 1. *n.* heroin. □ *Now, horse is all that Gert will touch.* □ *Horse is still very popular in the big cities.* **2.** *vb.* to defecate. (Taboo. Rhyming slang, linked as follows: horse [and trap] ≈ [crap] = defecate.) □ *I tried to chase the cat away as soon as it started horsing.* □ *Your dog horsed on my lawn.* **3.** *n.* gonorrhoea. (Taboo. Rhyming slang,

linked as follows: horse [and trap] ≈ [clap] = gonorrhoea. Normally with *the.*) □ *All right, it's true, I've got the horse.* □ *Getting the horse tends to restrict your love life, you know.* **4.** *n.* a prostitute. (Taboo. Rhyming slang, linked as follows: horse ≈ [whore(s)] = prostitute. Also from association with RIDE.) □ *There was a horse standing right on that corner.* □ *There are a lot of horses around here in the centre of town.*

horse and cart *n.* an anal release of intestinal gas; a noise or smell associated with this. (Crude. Rhyming slang.) □ *Oh lord! Who made that horse and cart?* □ *The pungent scent of a recent horse and cart hung in the air.*

horse's arse *n.* a despicable person. (Taboo.) □ *What a horse's arse that woman can be.* □ *Get out of here, you horse's arse!*

horses for courses *n.* capabilities and requirements that are well matched together. □ *You'll be fine; remember—horses for courses.* □ *Let's try to find horses for courses, people.*

horse's hoof *n.* a male homosexual. (Crude. Rhyming slang, linked as follows: horse's hoof ≈ [poof] = homosexual.) □ *Tom is getting to be such a horse's hoof.* □ *The last person who called him a horse's hoof ended up in hospital.*

hot 1. *mod.* stolen. □ *This watch is hot. I'm not buying it.* □ *Rich won't touch a hot watch or anything else hot.* **2.** *mod.* of great renown; doing well for the time being. □ *The opera tenor was hot, and even the lowbrows would pay to hear him.* □ *The dancer was hot and was offered film roles and all sorts of things.* **3.** *mod.* selling well. □ *These things are really hot this season.* □ *Now, here's a hot item.* **4.** *mod.* very skilled. □ *Look at that; she's really hot at this.* □ *We need a hot operator here.* **5.** *mod.* smuggled. □ *That stuff came in from the Far East and is hot.* □ *It's cheap because it's hot.* **6.** *mod.* attractive; popular. □ *We think we've got a hot way to solve that problem.* □ *Larry is really hot—at least to me he is.* **7.** *mod.* traceable, in the criminal sense. □ *Don't touch the stuff; it's still hot.* □ *If it's hot, stash it 'till the cops lose interest.*

hot air *n.* boasting; lies; nonsense. □ *I've heard enough of your hot air.* □ *That's just a lot of hot air. Ignore it.*

hot and bothered *mod.* excited; agitated nervously worried. □ *This is just not worth getting hot and bothered about, if you ask me.* □ *He was really hot and bothered by this time.*

hot-arsed AND **hot-panted; hot-tailed** *mod.* [of a woman] very lascivious. (Taboo.) □ *Now there's one really hot-arsed bitch!* □ *If Sarah was any more hot-panted, she'd melt!*

hotbed of something *n.* a place where the growth of something is encouraged or promoted. (The original meaning of the expression was a bed of plants in soil heated with fermenting manure.) □ *This office is a hotbed of gossip.* □ *That area of town is a hotbed of vice.*

hot bills *n.* newly issued Treasury bills. □ *The bank bought a lot of these hot bills.* □ *The government sometimes has trouble shifting hot bills.*

hot-head *n.* a person with a bad or quick temper. □ *Max is a hot-head. Watch out.* □ *Don't be such a hot-head, Charlie.*

hot item *n.* an item that sells well. □ *This little thing is a hot item this season.* □ *Now here's a hot item that everybody is looking for.*

hotkey *n.* a keyboard button that when pressed will cause a computer to perform some task that would otherwise require several keystrokes to implement. Also called a "function key." (Standard English.) □ *The hotkey for my thesaurus is "F2."* □ *Press the hotkey to bring up a calendar.*

hot money *n.* stolen money that can be identified as such. □ *I ain't going to touch that, it's hot money!* □ *There's an awful lot of hot money around these days.*

hot number *n.* an exciting piece of popular music. □ *Now here's a hot number by the Wanderers.* □ *Another hot number after the break, folks!*

hot on someone 1. *mod.* severe with someone. □ *I'm going to be very hot on*

anyone who steps the least way out of line. □ *She was very hot on me when she found out what I'd done.* **2.** *vb. phr.* to be very friendly towards someone. □ *Marti is hot on Stuart right now.* □ *These two are an item, really hot on each other.*

hot on something *vb. phr.* to be very skilled at something. □ *Can you find me someone who is hot on Quark Xpress?* □ *He's really hot on anything to do with cars.*

hot-panted See HOT-ARSED.

hot potato *n.* a difficult problem, usually with political or social implications. □ *I certainly don't want to have to deal with that hot potato.* □ *This one is a hot potato. Ignore it for a while and maybe it'll go away.*

hot rod *n.* a car that has been customised for power and speed by the owner. □ *My hot rod'll outrun yours any day.* □ *Is that a hot rod or a junk heap?*

hots *n.* lust. (Crude. Always with *the.*) □ *She's really got the hots for Bruno.* □ *Try to contain your hots for her, Harry. She's happily married with three kids.*

hot seat *n.* a position of particular difficulty or responsibility. □ *Harry's the one in the hot seat nowadays.* □ *Whoever is responsible for the factory is certainly in the hot seat.*

hot spot AND **jam** *n.* a difficult position; a predicament. □ *That's a hot spot; avoid it.* □ *Don't let yourself get into a jam like that.*

hot stuff *n.* an exceptional person or thing. □ *What makes you think you're such hot stuff?* □ *These new computers are really hot stuff!*

hot-tailed See HOT-ARSED.

hottie(-tottie) *n.* a hot water bottle. □ *Aunt Mary set off to bed with her hottie-tottie as usual.* □ *I'd prefer a hottie to an electric blanket.*

hotting *n.* joyriding in a stolen car. □ *The kids killed in the crash had been hotting.* □ *There's a lot of hotting going on in this area.*

hot tip *n.* a special bit of information that ought to be reliable. □ *Ted got a* *hot tip on a horse.* □ *I phoned in a hot tip about a news story to the papers.*

hot under the collar *mod.* angry, annoyed or embarrassed. □ *Joe was really hot under the collar when he discovered that someone had stolen the money.* □ *Don't get so hot under the collar; no one blames you for what happened.*

hot up *vb. phr.* to become lively. □ *It's good to see things hotting up at last.* □ *Try to hot up this business, for goodness sake!*

hot-wire *vb.* to start a car without a key. □ *Lefty hot-wired the car and used it for an hour or two.* □ *Isn't it illegal to hot-wire a car?*

hounds *n.* a pack of foxhounds. (Normally with *the.*) □ *Have the hounds come this way yet?* □ *The hounds are over in the next field.*

house 1. *n.* a form of electronic dance music. (Teens.) □ *What do you know about house?* □ *House? Nothing. What is house?* **2.** See also HOUSEY-HOUSEY.

household gods *n.* a figurative name for the essentials of domestic life. (An allusion to the *lares* and *penates*, the domestic gods of the Roman household.) □ *Everything has settled down again; the household gods are all in place.* □ *Do we have all the household gods ready for us to live there now?*

housekeeper *n.* a kept mistress. (A euphemism.) □ *Well, let's just call her his housekeeper.* □ *A housekeeper? Oh! I see what you mean!*

housekeeping *n.* housekeeping money. □ *It takes a lot of housekeeping to buy a car like that.* □ *I don't make enough housekeeping to go on a trip like that!*

housemaid's knee *n.* the sea. (Rhyming slang. Always with *the.*) □ *He looked out over the vastness of the housemaid's knee.* □ *His plane ditched right into the housemaid's knee, I'm afraid.*

House of Lords *n.* a men's toilet. (Crude. Normally with *the.* A euphemism.) □ *Can you tell me where I'll find the House of Lords?* □ *I need to use the House of Lords urgently!*

house to let *n.* a bet. (Rhyming slang.) □ *I'm placing a house to let on that*

horse. □ *Did you win your house to let?*

housey-housey AND **house** *n.* a version of bingo played by the military. □ *Housey-housey is very popular among squaddies when they are not otherwise kept busy.* □ *Anyone for a game of house?*

How come? *interrog.* "I don't understand; please explain?" □ *How come? Please explain that again.* □ *He asked how come, but I didn't know.*

How does that grab you? *interrog.* "What do you think of that?" □ *Looks good, okay? How does that grab you?* □ *How does that grab you? Enough salt?*

how-do-you-do AND **how-d'ye-do 1.** *n.* a difficult or embarrassing predicament. □ *Well, this is a right how-do-you-do we've to get out of now.* □ *How did you get us into a how-d'ye-do like this, eh?* **2.** *n.* a brawl or quarrel. □ *Who started this how-do-you-do anyway?* □ *I'm sorry about the how-d'ye-do we had yesterday, but it was all your fault.* **3.** *n.* a fuss; a commotion. □ *Why do you have to turn the simplest things into such a how-do-you-do?* □ *Don't make such a how-do-you-do! It's almost sorted.*

how-d'ye-do See HOW-DO-YOU-DO.

How goes it? *interrog.* "How are you?"; "How are things going?" □ *Nice to see you. How goes it?* □ *How goes it? Everything okay?*

howl 1. *n.* something funny. (Compare with SCREAM.) □ *What a howl the surprise party turned out to be when the guest of honour didn't show up.* □ *The gag was a real howl.* **2.** *vb.* to call out in pleasure. □ *Everybody howled at my mistake.* □ *John really howled when he heared that joke.*

howler 1. *n.* an amusing mistake. □ *Who is responsible for this howler on the Wilson account?* □ *That howler cost us plenty.* **2.** *n.* an obvious mistake. □ *I'm afraid that one is just too obviously a howler.* □ *If you make a howler on the title page, it's a biggie, right?* **3.** *n.* a baby; a young child. □ *I hope you like howlers. There are several here this afternoon.* □ *I wish she would try to control that howler of hers.*

How's tricks? *interrog.* "How are you?" □ *How's tricks with you?* □ *Hello, Jim! How's tricks?*

how the other half lives *n.* how the opposite portion of society lives. (That is, the poor in contrast with the rich, or the rich in contrast with the poor.) □ *Now I am beginning to understand how the other half lives.* □ *Most people don't care how the other half lives.*

hubby *n.* a diminutive alternative for "husband." □ *My hubby will be late tonight.* □ *Where is your hubby tonight?*

huffer *n.* someone who inhales glue vapours or some other solvent for a HIGH. □ *The age of the huffers has come to an end. Now they start out on crack.* □ *His school work suffered because he was a huffer.*

huffy *mod.* annoyed, hurt or irritated. □ *Now, don't get huffy. I said I was sorry, didn't I?* □ *Who's the huffy old lady?* □ *She was so huffy about it.*

Hullabaloo Chorus See HELLUVA BELLOW CHORUS.

hum 1. *n.* a bad smell. □ *There is a terrible hum in here.* □ *Let's see if we can get rid of this hum.* **2.** *vb.* to emit a bad smell. □ *The fact is, the tramp was humming badly.* □ *The food, which had been left to rot, hummed in a most offensive manner.*

humdinger 1. *n.* someone or something excellent. □ *Now, this idea is a real humdinger.* □ *Yup, he's a humdinger all right.* **2.** *n.* an especially loud anal release of intestinal gas. (Crude.) □ *I've told you before Joe—no more of these humdingers.* □ *The trouble with Joe is that he lets go of these humdingers all the time.*

hump 1. *n.* a fit of depression or bad temper. (Normally with *the.*) □ *I think it would be smart to leave him alone just now; he's got the hump.* □ *The hump? If you don't get yourself sorted out in short order I'll give you the hump all right!* **2.** *vb.* to perform sexual intercourse, from the male perspective. (Taboo.) □ *One look and he knew she had already been humped that evening.* □ *There were a couple of teenagers in the back room, humping away.*

hump(h) *vb.* to lift up or to carry upon the back. □ *Give it to me; I don't mind humphing the thing for a while.* □ *That was some load you asked me to hump.*

humungous *mod.* vast; terrifying. □ *She lives in that humungous house on the hill.* □ *This business plan is humungous; the implications could blow your mind.*

hundreds and thousands *n.* tiny coloured sweets sometimes sprinkled over food, such as cakes, in order to decorate them. □ *Johnny likes it when mum puts hundreds and thousands all over a cake.* □ *She spilt the hundreds and thousands, which then got into everything.*

hung on someone *mod.* emotionally dependent upon someone. □ *Look, she's become quite hung on you so you're going to have to be careful.* □ *It's important that your patients don't become hung on you.*

hungover *mod.* having a hangover caused by over-consumption of alcohol. □ *John is really hungover today.* □ *I can't eat when I'm hungover.*

hungry *mod.* ambitious. □ *He gets ahead because he's hungry.* □ *We like to employ the hungry ones.*

hung-up 1. *mod.* neurotic. □ *I'm a psychiatrist; it's my job to sort out hung-up people like you.* □ *The poor fellow is quite hung-up; I think he needs professional help.* **2.** *mod.* prevented from continuing. □ *Do you not realise that we are hung-up on this problem and need a solution urgently so we can move on?* □ *Try not to get hung-up on the details; just get the thing finished on time.*

hung-up on someone *mod.* obsessed with or in love with someone. □ *I think she's hung-up on him.* □ *If you must get hung-up on someone, make sure they're worth it.*

hunk *n.* a strong and sexually attractive male, from the female viewpoint. □ *Larry is a real hunk.* □ *Who was that big hunk I saw you with?*

hunky-dory *mod.* fine; okay. □ *As a matter of fact, everything is just hunky-dory.* □ *That is a hunky-dory idea all right.*

Huntley *n.* fate. (Rhyming slang, linked as follows: Huntley [and Palmer] ≈ [karma] = fate. (Huntley and Palmer™ make biscuits.) □ *Face it mate, it's just Huntley.* □ *If that's your Huntley, that's your Huntley.*

husband *n.* the dominant member of a homosexual couple. (Crude. Compare with WIFE.) □ *Somebody said she's her husband. Who do they mean?* □ *John's husband's a mean character; watch out!*

Hush! *exclam.* "Silence!"; "Be quiet!" □ *Hush! Don't let them know we're here!* □ *Be quiet. Hush!*

hush *n.* silence. □ *There was a hush in the close tonight.* □ *The hush was almost oppressive.*

hush-hush *mod.* secret; undercover. □ *The matter is so hush-hush I can't talk about it over the phone.* □ *What is all this hush-hush stuff?*

hush money *n.* money paid to buy someone's silence. □ *They paid enough hush money to silence an army.* □ *There was some hush money paid to someone in the local council.*

hush someone up *vb. phr.* to prevent someone from spreading a secret. □ *We just couldn't hush him up.* □ *We wanted to hush up these people, but there was no way to do it.*

hush something up *vb. phr.* to keep something a secret; to stop a rumour from spreading. □ *We just couldn't hush it up.* □ *We wanted to hush up the story, but there was no way to do it.*

hydro(pathic hotel) *n.* a health spa or a spa hotel. □ *There's a hydropathic hotel in these hills that's very popular.* □ *He takes a week's holiday in a hydro at this time every year.*

hymie See HIMIE.

hype 1. *vb.* to publicise or promote someone or something aggressively; to overpraise someone or something. □ *Don't hype the thing to death.* □ *Let's hype it until everyone in the country has heard about it.* **2.** *n.* a hypodermic syringe and needle. □ *She forgot to clean the hype.* □ *He got an infection from a dirty hype.* **3.** *n.* an injection of drugs. □ *Ernie needed a hype real bad.* □ *Max told him who could help him with a hype.* **4.** *n.* publicity or sales promotion, especially if blatant and aggressive. □ *There was so much hype before the picture was released that the picture itself was a letdown.* □ *There is hype for the election all over the place.*

hyped (up) 1. *mod.* excited; stimulated. □ *They were all hyped up before the game.* □ *She said she had to get hyped before the tennis match.* **2.** *mod.* contrived; heavily promoted; falsely advertised. □ *I just won't pay good money to see these hyped up movies.* □ *If it has to be hyped so much, it probably isn't very good.*

hyper 1. *n.* a drug user who injects drugs with a hypodermic syringe. □ *How long have you been a hyper, Gert?* □ *Max has been a hyper since he was twenty-four.* **2.** *n.* a person who hypes; a publicist or promoter. □ *She's a hyper, and she doesn't always tell things the way they are.* □ *If it's a hyper you want, she's the best.*

hype something up *vb. phr.* to overpraise something; to propagandise something. □ *They hyped it up too much.* □ *Why do they hype up an election?*

hypo 1. *n.* a hypochondriac. □ *Of course he's just a hypo.* □ *Get up, you lazy hypo!* **2.** *mod.* hypochondriac. □ *Get that lazy hypo out of his bed and back to work!* □ *Just because he's hypo does not mean he is not ill.*

ice cream *n.* a man. (Rhyming slang, linked as follows: ice cream [freezer] ≈ [geezer] = man.) □ *What does the ice cream want?* □ *He's a rather surprising ice cream.*

ice creamer *n.* an Italian person. (Offensive.) □ *Why can you not be polite to ice creamers?* □ *Y'know, Otto, if you call an Italian an ice creamer, he's likely to get nasty.*

ice-cream habit *n.* the irregular use of drugs, possibly the prelude to full addiction. □ *Ice-cream habits turn into full addiction before you realise what's happened.* □ *No, I'm no addict. I've just got a harmless ice-cream habit.*

ice-cream suit *n.* a white suit, supposedly typical of that worn by ice-cream salesmen, and a derisory term for such a suit when worn by other men. □ *Look at Otto in his ice-cream suit!* □ *Really, you don't suit an ice-cream suit.*

icing on the cake *n.* an extra enhancement. □ *Oh, great! A full tank of petrol in my new car. That's icing on the cake!* □ *Your coming home for a few days was the icing on the cake.*

icky 1. *mod.* distasteful; nasty. □ *What is this icky old stuff?* □ *What an icky day.* **2.** *mod.* excessively sentimental. □ *Harry always laughs at icky rubbish in a film.* □ *The love scenes were real out-and-out icky, but nobody laughed.*

icky-poo *mod.* unpleasant; cloyingly sentimental. □ *I don't like all this icky-poo talk.* □ *What is that icky-poo stuff in the soup bowl?*

I couldn't care less. *sent.* "I don't care!"; totally disinterested. □ *So you're late. I couldn't care less.* □ *I couldn't care less if you fell off a cliff.*

idiot board See IDIOT CARD.

idiot box AND **idiot's lantern; box** *n.* a television set. □ *You spend too much time watching the idiot box.* □ *What's on the box tonight?*

idiot broth *n.* cider. □ HE: *Have you ever drunk real West Country cyder?* SHE: *No.* HE: *Then you don't know why it's called idiot broth.* □ *Another pint of that idiot broth please, landlord!*

idiot card AND **idiot board** *n.* a large card that shows people on television what to say. □ *The floor director held up an idiot card so I could read out the telephone number.* □ *I couldn't read the number off the idiot board.*

idiot pills *n.* a street name for barbiturates. □ *Joan's back on the idiot pills again.* □ *She's really hooked on idiot pills.*

idiot's lantern See IDIOT BOX.

I don't believe this! **1.** *exclam.* "What is happening right now is unbelievable!" □ *That's grotesque! I don't believe this!* □ *I don't believe this! It can't be happening.* **2.** *exclam.* "What I am hearing is unbelievable!" □ *That's grotesque! I don't believe this!* □ *I don't believe this! That could never have happened!*

I don't know. 1. *sent.* "I disagree...I think." □ *I don't know. I like it. What's wrong with it?* □ *I don't know. It looks good to me.* **2.** *sent.* "I don't know what to decide." □ *If I don't know will you decide for me?* □ *I don't know. It looks good to me, but something's wrong all the same.*

I don't mean maybe! *exclam.* "I am not kidding!" □ *You get over here right now. I don't mean maybe!* □ *I'll spank* *you if you ever do that again, and I don't mean maybe.*

iffy *mod.* doubtful, uncertain or suspicious. □ *Things are still sort of iffy, but we'll know for sure in a few days.* □ *It's sort of an iffy matter, but things will get straightened out.*

if I've told you once, I've told you a thousand times. *phr.* "I know I have told you many, many times." □ *If I've told you once, I've told you a thousand times, don't lean back in that chair.* □ *Wipe your feet! If I've told you once, I've told you a thousand times!*

if one knows what's good for one *phr.* "one had better do what is expected of one." □ *You'd better be on time if you know what's good for you.* □ *If you know what's good for you, you'll phone up and apologise.*

if one's a day *phr.* a phrase attached to an expression of someone's age. □ *She's fifty if she's a day!* □ *I'm sure he's forty-five if he's a day.*

if push comes to shove See WHEN PUSH COMES TO SHOVE.

if the cap fits *phr.* "if it appears to be true." □ *If the cap fits, so be it.* □ *Well, maybe. But only if the cap fits very well indeed.*

if you'll pardon the expression *phr.* "please excuse the indelicate nature of the words I am using here." (Compare with PARDON MY FRENCH.) □ *This thing is—if you'll pardon the expression—totally screwed up.* □ *I'm really pissed-off, if you'll pardon the expression.*

ignorant *mod.* ill-mannered. □ *What an ignorant man he is.* □ *I cannot stand ignorant people like that.*

I haven't a clue. *sent.* "I have no idea." □ *Why ask me? I haven't a clue.* □ *I haven't a clue, but I'm still expected to know.*

I hear what you're saying. AND **I hear you. 1.** *sent.* "I hear and understand what you say but it is not worthy of an answer." (Scots usage.) □ *Is that so? Well, I hear what you are saying.* □ *I hear you. You don't expect an answer, do you?* **2.** *sent.* "I hear and understand what you say but do not feel obliged to agree with you." □ *I hear you. So do what you want?* □ *I hear you, but it*

doesn't matter. **3.** *sent.* "What you said was not true. Who do you think you are kidding?" (Scots usage.) □ *I hear what you are saying. Let's just leave it at that.* □ *A Martian UFO has landed in front of Buckingham Palace, you say? Oh yes, I hear you.* **4.** *sent.* "I hear and understand what you say and completely agree with you." □ *Yes, yes. I hear what you are saying, and I'm with you.* □ *Yes! I hear you!*

I hear you. See I HEAR WHAT YOU'RE SAYING.

I'll be there *n.* a chair. (Rhyming slang.) □ *Sit on that I'll be there and say not a word!* □ *He produced the strangest I'll be there from a cupboard.*

illegitimate glow-worm *n.* a know-all; a SMART ALEC. (Crude. A skittish derivation from BRIGHT BASTARD.) □ *Well, there goes another illegitimate glow-worm; a lot of good it'll do him where he's going.* □ *So this illegitimate glow-worm asks if I understand quantum mechanics...*

illegitimis non carborundum AND **nil carborundum illigitium** *phr.* "Don't let the bastards grind you down." (Crude. There are other versions of this sentiment, in various renditions of pseudo-Latin. Compare with PLUMBUM OSCILLANS.) □ *Just remember, whatever happens, illegitimis non carborundum!* □ *"Nil carborundum illigitium" is a thought that has sustained me through many a difficult time.*

(I) love it! *exclam.* "That is wonderful!" □ *It's wonderful, Ted. I love it!* □ *Love it! More, more!* □ *You're so clever! Love it! Love it!*

I.L.U.V.M. AND **ILUVM** *phr.* "I love (yo)u very much." (This initialism is sometimes written on love letters. Also an acronym.) □ *Love and kisses. I.L.U.V.M.* □ *XXXX ILUVM.*

I'm afloat *n.* a coat. (Rhyming slang.) □ *I've lost my I'm afloat.* □ *That's a ridiculous I'm afloat; I won't wear it.*

imaginary invalid *n.* a hypochondriac. □ *Get up, you imaginary invalid!* □ *Of course he's just a imaginary invalid.*

imaginitis 1. *n.* the "disease" of using one's imagination when this is not desirable. □ *Look, they don't want people with imaginitis like you, asking awkward questions.* □ *My problem was my imaginitis again; it would have been better just not to have thought about the thing.* **2.** *n.* the "disease" of imagining problems that are not there. □ *The trouble with you, Jack, is you suffer from acute imaginitis.* □ *We've got enough real problems, without your imaginitis at work as well.*

I'm listening. AND **Let's hear it.** *sent.* "Keep talking."; "I am waiting to hear your explanation, justification or apology." □ *You did it wrong. Let's hear it.* □ *I'm sure there's an explanation...well, I'm listening...*

I'm not kidding. *sent.* "I am telling the truth." □ *Get over here now! I'm not kidding.* □ *I'm not kidding. It was this big!*

impuritans *n.* those people who do not maintain a puritanical attitude to life, etc. □ *I would think you're a lot more likely to meet impuritans than puritans around this pub.* □ *Impuritans are my sort of people.*

I'm shaking (in fear). AND **I'm shaking with fright.** *sent.* "You don't really frighten me at all." (A mocking or ironic response to a threat.) □ *Oh, to say such things! I'm shaking.* □ *Your threats really scare me. I'm shaking with fright.*

I'm shaking with fright. See I'M SHAKING (IN FEAR).

I'm so *n.* whisky. (Rhyming slang, linked as follows: I'm so [frisky] ≈ whisky.) □ *Get out the I'm so; let's have a drink.* □ *The bottle was empty. More I'm so, I think!*

I'm willing *n.* five pence. (Rhyming slang, linked as follows: I'm willing ≈ [shilling] = five pence. Five pence in modern currency is equivalent to one shilling in pre-1971 currency units.) □ *An I'm willing? For what?* □ *That'll be an I'm willing, missus.*

in 1. *mod.* current; fashionable. (Compare with IN THING TO DO.) □ *This kind of thing is in now.* □ *What's in around here in the way of clothing?* **2.** *mod.* accepted. □ *All right. You're in.* □ *The idea's in, but you're not.*

in a bad way See IN BAD SHAPE.

in a big way *mod.* very much; urgently. □ *I'm really interested in her in a big way.* □ *He plays to win—in a big way.*

in a blue funk *mod.* in a state of blind panic or abject terror. □ *I've been in a blue funk ever since these noises from the loft began in the middle of the night.* □ *Don't get yourself in a blue funk. Sit down calmly and take deep breaths; you'll soon feel better.*

in a cold sweat *mod.* in a state of fear. □ *He stood there in a cold sweat, waiting for something to happen.* □ *I was in a cold sweat while they counted the ballots.*

in a dither *mod.* confused; undecided. (Compare with DITHER.) □ *Mary is sort of in a dither lately.* □ *Don't get yourself in a dither.*

in a flash *mod.* right away; immediately. □ *Jimmy had the answer in a flash; he's good at maths.* □ *I'll be there in a flash.*

in a hot spot AND **in a jam** *mod.* in a difficult situation or predicament. □ *I think I'm sort of in a hot spot.* □ *Sam is in a jam.*

in a jam See IN A HOT SPOT.

in a jiff(y) *mod.* right away; immediately. (Compare with JIFFY.) □ *I'll be there in a jiffy.* □ *The clerk'll be with you in a jiff.*

in a maxe *mod.* confused or bewildered. □ *Leave her be; she's completely in a maxe this afternoon.* □ *Don't tell me you're in a maxe yet again!*

in and out *n.* a nose. (Rhyming slang, linked as follows: in and out ≈ [snout] = nose.) □ *He threatened to punch me right on the in and out!* □ *How did you get an in and out like that?*

in a pig's ear *phr.* "emphatically never"; "on no account." (An extension of the rhyming slang term PIG'S EAR. Originally and more fully, this expression was "never in a pig's ear.") □ *Sell out to you? In a pig's ear!* □ *In a pig's ear would I give that particular sucker the slightest of even breaks, I assure you.*

in a state of nature *mod.* naked. □ *As proud as anything she was, standing* there in a state of nature! □ *People go to these naturist camps so they can go about in a state of nature, Lavinia.*

in a tizzy AND **of a tizz** *mod.* in a state of mental agitation. □ *Fred is all of a tizz.* □ *The whole office is in a tizzy today.*

in a twitter AND **of a twitter** *mod.* in a giddy state; silly. □ *Don't get yourself in a twitter.* □ *We were all of a twitter over the upcoming event.*

in bad shape AND **in a bad way** **1.** *mod.* injured or debilitated in any manner. □ *Fred had a little accident, and he's in bad shape.* □ *Tom needs to exercise. He's in a bad way.* **2.** *mod.* intoxicated due to drink or drugs. □ *Two glasses of that stuff and I'm in really bad shape.* □ *Fred is in a bad way. I think he's going off to honk.*

in business *mod.* operating; equipped to operate. □ *We're in business now, and things are running smoothly.* □ *Now it works. Now we're in business.*

in cahoots (together) *mod.* conspiring together □ *The plain fact, sir, is that these two have been in cahoots together for months.* □ *I don't see what they have been in cahoots about.*

in care *mod.* [of a child] residing in an orphanage or similar institution. (Usually one operated by a local authority under order of a court.) □ *That child is now in care, M'lud.* □ *Both her children had been in care since the mother went to prison four years ago.*

In Carey Street *mod.* bankrupt. (Carey Street in London was where the court that adjudicated bankruptcy cases was formerly located.) □ *Well that was it, I was in Carey Street.* □ *A lot of famous people have ended up in Carey Street in their time.*

in cold blood *mod.* intentionally and calculatedly; without feeling; with cruel intent. □ *Rocko kills in cold blood and never gives a thought to his victims.* □ *Apparently he had sat down and worked out in cold blood his chances of getting away with murdering her.*

income tax *n.* the frequent fines which street prostitutes have to pay for illegal soliciting. (Crude.) □ *If you're going to*

work the street, you've got to accept that you'll pay income tax, dear. □ *Are the fuzz short of money? That's the third time I've been touched for income tax this week already!*

in deep *mod.* deeply involved (with someone or something). □ *Mary and Sam are in deep.* □ *Max is in deep with the mob.*

in deep shit See IN THE SHIT.

in dock AND **in the dock** **1.** *mod.* in hospital. □ *I'm afraid Norman is in dock at the moment.* □ *What's he in the dock for?* **2.** *mod.* undergoing repairs. □ *My car's in dock at the moment.* □ *My car is in the dock, too.* **3.** *mod.* on trial in a court of law. □ *Otto's in dock again today.* □ *Not many weeks pass between Otto's appearances in the dock.*

in drag *mod.* wearing clothing normally used by the opposite sex. (Crude. Usually refers to women's clothing worn by men.) □ *Two actors in drag did a skit about life on the farm* □ *Gary looks better in drag than he does in a suit.*

in dribs and drabs *mod.* in small portions; bit by bit. □ *I'll have to pay you what I owe you in dribs and drabs.* □ *The whole story is being revealed in dribs and drabs.*

in fine feather AND **in fine fettle; in good nick** **1.** *mod.* in good form; in good spirits □ *Mary is really in fine feather tonight.* □ *I feel in good nick and ready to go!* **2.** *mod.* in good condition; looking good. □ *Well, you are certainly in fine feather today.* □ *I always try to be in fine fettle when I come here.*

in fine fettle See IN FINE FEATHER.

info *n.* information. □ *You can usually get all the info you want from there.* □ *I don't know why you're asking me; I have no info.*

Infobahn *n.* the information super highway. (From the German *Autobahn*, meaning "motorway" or "super highway.") □ *The Infobahn is where we will all work in the future.* □ *I think the Infobahn is just a fashion item; this too will pass.*

in for a penny, in for a pound 1. *phr.* "once started, there's no way out." □ *Well, in for a penny, in for a pound. We've no choice.* □ *If we must do it, let's do it: in for a penny, in for a pound!* 2. *phr.* "all or nothing." □ *In for a penny, in for a pound! We must succeed now!* □ *Once we pass that point it's in for a penny, in for a pound.*

in for the high jump AND **in for the long jump** 1. *mod.* facing very severe problems or punishment. □ *I'm in for the high jump; I just know it!* □ *If they catch you you're certainly in for the long jump.* 2. *mod.* due to be hanged; liable to be hanged. □ *There in the courtroom, for the first time, he really appreciated that he could be in for the high jump.* □ *They don't mess around in that country. Drug smugglers are in for the long jump.*

in for the long jump See IN FOR THE HIGH JUMP.

infotainment 1. *n.* information masquerading as entertainment. □ *Some kids learn an amazing amount when it's fed to them in the form of infotainment.* □ *Sometime infotainment seems to be the only form of information that goes in.* 2. *n.* entertainment masquerading as information. □ *It's all that infotainment—fiction dressed up as fact—that worries me.* □ *Infotainment presenting entertainment as truth is very dangerous, especially for children.*

in good nick See IN FINE FEATHER.

in great form See IN RARE FORM.

in hock 1. *mod.* in pawn. □ *My watch is already in hock.* □ *Get it out of hock or go and buy a new one.* 2. *mod.* in debt. □ *If we get too deep in hock, the company will collapse.* □ *So we're in hock again this month.*

in-joke *n.* a joke that can only be understood by a small group who are aware of certain facts. □ *I'm sorry. That was an in-joke, please.* □ *No more in-jokes, please.*

in marching order *mod.* organized and equipped; ready to go. (Originally military.) □ *Is the unit in marching order?* □ *We're in marching order and eager to go, sir.*

in mint condition *mod.* as if completely new. □ *It's not new, but it's in mint condition.* □ *This one looks in mint condition, I think.*

in mufti *mod.* not in uniform. (Military.) □ *Why was the man in mufti, sergeant?* □ *Although he was in mufti, he still saluted us.*

in my book *phr.* "in my opinion." □ *In my book, that can never be justified.* □ *We must sort this out now, in my book.*

in narrow circumstances *mod.* impoverished. □ *No, I can't lend you money. I'm in narrow circumstances myself.* □ *Since the factory closed, everyone in this town is in narrow circumstances.*

Innit? *Interrog.* "Isn't it?" (Eye-dialect, used in the examples in this dictionary.) □ *It's okay if I take one of these mum, innit?* □ *Innit cold today!*

in-off *vb.* to pocket one ball by bouncing it off another. (Billiards and Snooker.) □ *He did a brilliant in-off to pocket the black ball.* □ *I looked at the table and realised I was going to have to play the in-off of my life if I was to have any chance of winning the championship.*

in one's birthday suit AND **in the altogether** *mod.* naked. □ *It's called being in one's birthday suit because that's the way we are born.* □ *He actually came to the door in the altogether!*

in one's blood *mod.* inborn; part of one's genetic makeup. □ *It's in my blood. I can't help it.* □ *Running is in his blood. He loves it.*

in on something *mod.* participating; aware of. □ *Are you in on this deal?* □ *He's in on the first business but not the other one.*

in orbit 1. *mod.* ecstatic; euphoric. □ *She was just in orbit when she got the letter.* □ *Pete was in orbit over the promotion.* 2. *mod.* intoxicated due to drink or drugs. □ *Gary is so in orbit he couldn't see a hole in a ladder.* □ *After having a six-pack all to herself, Julie was in orbit, too.*

in play *mod.* being played; inbound. (Said of a ball in a game.) □ *The ball's in play, so you made the wrong move.* □ *No, it wasn't in play, you twit!*

in pop *mod.* in pawn. □ *Get it out of pop or go and buy a new one.* □ *My watch is already in pop.*

in Queer Street *mod.* in serious trouble, especially financial. □ *He business went bust and now he's in Queer Street.* □ *Not everyone in Queer Street is there by their own fault.*

in rare form AND **in great form** *mod.* in good condition; at one's best. □ *He is in rare form today.* □ *We are not exactly in great form on Monday mornings.*

ins and outs *n.* the fine points (of something); the details; the intricacies. □ *Learn the ins and outs of this before you try to tell us how do it better.* □ *My father taught me the ins and outs of our family business.*

insects (and ants) *n.* trousers, knickers or pants. (Rhyming slang.) □ *You're not properly dressed without insects and ants.* □ *She opened the drawer, removed all the insects there, and left the room with them.*

in service *mod.* employed as a servant. □ *My grandmother was in service with the Duke of Barchester.* □ *These grand families once had hundreds of people in service with them.*

inside *mod.* inside prison. □ *I really hate it inside.* □ *I'd like to see Mr Big being put inside for a good long time.*

inside a week **1.** *mod.* in less than a week □ *We must get all this sorted out inside a week; all right?* □ *We've got inside a week to get it right.* **2.** *mod.* in the middle of a week; mid-week. □ *We better do it inside a week; a Wednesday, say.* □ *No, weekends are useless. Keep to inside a week.*

inside job **1.** *n.* a crime committed by someone working or living at the scene of the crime. □ *There was little doubt that it was an inside job, thought the inspector.* □ *It's a particularly cunning way to carry out an inside job.* **2.** *n.* a crime perpetrated against a business or other organisation by someone associated with the victimised organisation. (Underworld.) □ *The cops figured that it was an inside job.* □ *It was an inside job all right. The butler did it.*

inspector of manholes *n.* a male homosexual. (Taboo.) □ *So what if he's an inspector of manholes? He can still vote, can't he?* □ *He doesn't like being called an inspector of manholes.*

instant mum *n.* a foster mother. □ *She was brought up by an instant mum.* □ *Henrietta is an instant mum.*

in stitches *mod.* very amused. □ *Funny? He had me in stitches!* □ *We were in stitches all evening.*

interesting *mod.* unusual; exotic. (Used as an ambiguously polite or sarcastic dismissive description of something that one has been asked to admire but in truth cannot. Compare with DIFFERENT and FABULOUS.) □ *"Well, it's...uh...interesting!"* □ *Let's just say that her dress sense is interesting.*

in the air **1.** *n.* gossip. □ *That may be what's in the air. Now, can we get down to some serious business?* □ *I've heard enough about what's in the air to last me a lifetime.* **2.** *n.* what is currently fashionable. □ *That seems to be the style that's in the air just now.* □ *So darling, what's in the air at the moment?*

in the altogether See IN ONE'S BIRTHDAY SUIT.

in the bag *mod.* clinched; achieved. □ *It's in the bag—as good as done.* □ *The election is in the bag unless the voters find out about my past.*

in the black *mod.* financially solvent; profitable; not in debt. (Compare with IN THE RED.) □ *Now that the company is in the black, there's a good chance it will become a take-over candidate.* □ *We're in the black now and making a profit.*

in the buff AND **in the raw; in the rude** *mod.* naked. □ *You-know-who sleeps in the buff.* □ *You can save hundreds of pounds in a lifetime by not buying pyjamas and sleeping in the rude instead.*

in the cart *mod.* in a losing, embarrassing or difficult situation or predicament. □ *Really, we're lucky not to be in the cart in a far worse way than we are.* □ *Let's be honest: we're in the cart.*

in the country *mod.* anywhere upon a cricket field that is a long way from the wickets. □ *Yes, I think we could say that that's in the country.* □ *Try to hit more of the balls out in the country.*

in the dirt See IN THE SHIT.

in the dock See IN DOCK.

in the dog-house *mod.* in disgrace. □ *I'm in the dog-house with my wife. I don't know why, but I am.* □ *Any more of that and you'll be in the dog-house, too!*

in the driver's seat *mod.* in control. □ *She's just not comfortable unless she's in the driver's seat.* □ *I'm in the driver's seat now, and I get to decide who gets pay rises.*

in the event 1. *mod.* as it turned out. □ *In the event, it did not matter.* □ *It made no difference in the event.* **2.** *mod.* as it may happen (in the future). □ *In the event, you better phone home.* □ *I don't know exactly what to do in the event.*

in the family way *mod.* pregnant. □ *I hear that Tracy is in the family way.* □ *Is she in the family way, again?*

in the frame *mod.* suspected of a crime by the police. □ *Otto's in the frame again.* □ *If you're not careful, you'll be in the frame, too.*

in the groove *mod.* COOL; GROOVY; pleasant and delightful. □ *Man, is that combo in the groove tonight!* □ *Get in the groove! Relax.*

in the home straight See IN THE HOME STRETCH.

in the home stretch AND **in the home straight** *mod.* in the last stage of the process. (From horse racing.) □ *They're in the home stretch with this project and will not change anything now.* □ *We're in the home straight. Only three more days till we graduate.*

in the know *mod.* knowledgeable (about something); having inside knowledge (about something). □ *Ask Harry. He's usually in the know.* □ *Of course I'm in the know. But I'm not telling.*

in the lurch *mod.* in church. (Rhyming slang.) □ *The whole party was waiting for us in the lurch.* □ *Come on, we've got to be in the lurch in time for the wedding.*

in the money *n.* rich. □ *Pete is in the money for life.* □ *Her father died and left her in the money.*

in the noddle See IN THE NOODLE.

in the noodle AND **in the noddle; in the nuddie** *mod.* naked. □ *All these nudists were running about playing volleyball or something in the noddle.* □ *It's the thought of barbecues in the nuddie that would put me off.*

in the nuddie See IN THE NOODLE.

in the nude *n.* food. (Rhyming slang.) □ *Joe likes his in the nude.* □ *No, no! He doesn't eat food naked; in the nude is the stuff he eats. All right?*

in the picture *mod.* well-informed; aware of what is going on. □ *Please, keep me fully in the picture.* □ *He's in the picture so take care.*

in the pink *mod.* in excellent health. □ *I'm in the pink today. Feeling great.* □ *When she's in the pink again, she'll give you a ring.*

in the pipeline *mod.* already in process; already in production; on its way. □ *There's so many goods already in the pipeline that we're taking no more orders for the moment.* □ *Your papers are in the pipeline somewhere. You'll just have to wait.*

in the (pudding) club *mod.* pregnant. □ *Then this woman, very obviously in the pudding club, started to complain, too.* □ *I can see she's in the club.*

in the raw See IN THE BUFF.

in the red *mod.* in debt; overdrawn on a bank account. (Shown in red ink on a financial statement. Compare with IN THE BLACK.) □ *So we're in the red again this month.* □ *If we get too deep in the red, the company will collapse.*

in the rude See IN THE BUFF.

in the shit AND **in the dirt; in deep shit** *mod.* in dire trouble. (SHIT is taboo.) □ *Well, now you're in the shit for sure.* □ *Otto's really in deep shit now.*

in the soup *mod.* in trouble. □ *Now you're in the soup.* □ *I'm in the soup with the boss.*

in the works *mod.* under preparation. □ *Don't worry, it's in the works.* □ *It may be in the works, but it should have been ready by now.*

in thing to do *n.* the fashionable or orthodox thing to do. (Always with *the.* Compare with IN.) □ *Cutting your hair short on the sides is the in thing to do.* □ *Smoking is no longer the in thing to do.*

in trade *mod.* owning and operating a shop or other retail business. □ *Mr Smith is in trade, I think.* □ *I'd rather be in trade that just have an ordinary nine-to-five job.*

intro *n.* an introduction. □ *He had a good intro but the rest was terrible.* □ *Harry, you've to organise an intro.*

in two ticks *mod.* very soon. □ *Hold on, I'll be there in two ticks.* □ *We'll be done in just two ticks!*

invincible ignorance *n.* ignorance which cannot be removed or overcome. □ *Invincible ignorance is what you get when someone declines to recognise that he or she indeed is or even may possibly be ignorant, and thus do not see why it is necessary to correct behaviour or learn anything new.* □ *I don't think he's so much suffering from invincible ignorance as irredeemable stupidity.*

in work *mod.* employed. □ *Of course I'm in work. I've got a good job.* □ *Willy was in work for a few weeks but it didn't last.*

IOW *interj.* "in other words." (Computer jargon. Written only. An initialism used in computer communications.) □ *IOW, you are angry at me.* □ *I have heard enough on this point. IOW, shut up.*

Irish *n.* a wig. (Rhyming slang, linked as follows. Irish [jig] ≈ wig.) □ *I wear just a little Irish to cover up a shiny spot.* □ *Is that guy wearing a Irish, or does his scalp really slide from side to side?*

Irish apple *n.* a potato. □ *There was a large dish of steaming Irish apples on the table.* □ *Any more Irish apples?*

Irish confetti *n.* rocks, bricks and other hard objects thrown in the course of a riot. □ *They were throwing Irish confetti at each other like it was going out of fashion.* □ *The ground was littered with Irish confetti after the fight was over.*

Irishman's rise *n.* a reduction in pay. (Potentially offensive.) □ *Wait a minute, that's almost a pound a week less than before! This is an Irishman's rise!* □ *I'm not having no Irishman's rise, no way!*

iron (hoof) *n.* a male homosexual. (Crude. Rhyming slang, linked as follows: iron (hoof) ≈ [poof] = homosexual.) □ *She came to the dance with an iron hoof.* □ *Why does he work so hard to look like he's an iron?*

ironmongery *n.* firearms. □ *OK, have you all got your ironmongery?* □ *Check all ironmongery before checking it out.*

iron tank AND **tin tank** *n.* a bank. (Rhyming slang. The kind of bank where money is kept.) □ *Otto asked the iron tank to lend him a quid or two because he was broke but they said they don't lend money to people with no money.* □ *When the tin tank said this it got Otto, who is a simple soul at heart, really confused.*

I say! 1. *exclam.* an expression of surprise. □ *I say, what do you think you are doing?* □ *I say! That's unexpected!* **2.** *interj.* something said to draw attention or to commence a discussion. □ *I say! Excuse me! I want to speak!* □ *I say, I think I should point out...*

Is it buggery! AND **Is it fuck!; Is it hell!** *exclam.* an emphatic denial. (Taboo.) □ *Get your facts right. Is it buggery!* □ *Is it hell! That's a lie!*

Is it fuck! See IS IT BUGGERY!

Is it hell! See IS IT BUGGERY!

I.T.A.L.Y. AND **ITALY** *phr.* "I trust and love you." (The initialism is sometimes written on love letters. Also an acronym.) □ *XXXX I.T.A.L.Y.* □ *Love and kisses. ITALY.*

It's a sair fecht. *sent.* "Life is a hard struggle." (Scots usage.) □ *Yes, it's a sair fecht, but we're getting there.* □ *It was a sair fecht, but well worth it.*

itsy-bitsy See ITTY-BITTY.

It's your funeral! *exclam.* "If you do it, you will suffer all the consequences!" □ *Go if you want. It's your funeral!* □ *Go ahead, swim to Cuba. It's your funeral!*

itty-bitty AND **itsy-bitsy** *mod.* tiny, insignificant. □ *What an itty-bitty car!* □ *Give me an itty-bitsy piece. I'm on a diet.*

it won't wash 1. *phr.* "it will not work." □ *Nope, it won't wash. Think up another story.* □ *It won't wash, whatever I try.* **2.** *phr.* "nobody will believe it." □ *Sorry, it won't wash. Try again.* □ *Don't be absurd; it won't wash.*

I've been there. *sent.* "I know from experience what you are talking about." □ *I know what you mean. I've been there.* □ *I've been there. You don't need to spell it out for me.*

I've got to fly. AND **Must fly.** *sent.* "I have to leave right now." □ *I've got to fly. See you later.* □ *Time's up. I've got to fly.* □ *I've no time. Must fly.*

ivories 1. *n.* piano keys. (From the time when piano keys were made from real elephant ivory.) □ *She can really tickle those ivories.* □ *I'd say she has mastered the ivories.* **2.** *n.* the teeth. □ *I've got to go and brush my ivories.* □ *Look at her nice white ivories!*

ivory tower *n.* an imaginary location where aloof academics are said to reside and work. □ *Why don't you come out of your ivory tower and see what the world is really like?* □ *Better yet, stay in your ivory tower.*

IYHO *interj.* "in your humble opinion." (Computer jargon. Written only. An initialism used in computer communications.) □ *Things are in bad shape IYHO, but I think they are great.* □ *IYHO, everyone else is wrong!*

J

J AND **jay** *n.* a marijuana cigarette; marijuana. (From the initial letter of JOINT.) □ *Toss me a J, eh?* □ *A jay is two quid.*

jab AND **jag** *n.* a medicinal injection, especially a vaccination. □ *Right Mary, time for a little jab.* □ *Don't worry, this tiny jag won't hurt.*

jabber *vb.* to chatter. □ *Come over and we'll jabber about things over coffee.* □ *What are those kids jabbering on about?*

jabber AND **jabbering** *n.* mindless chatter. □ *Stop all this jabber and get to work.* □ *I've heard enough of your jabbering.*

jabbering See JABBER.

jack 1. *n.* a policeman or detective. □ *See that jack over there? He lifted me once.* □ *The jacks will catch up with you some day.* **2.** *n.* an odd-job man. □ *Ask the jack if he needs any help.* □ *Why do we need this jack?* **3.** *n.* money. □ *I don't make enough jack to go on a trip like that!* □ *It takes a lot of jack to buy a car like that.*

jack all AND **naff all** *n.* nothing. □ *We've got jack all for you here. Shove off.* □ *Nice words, but worth naff all.*

Jack and Jill 1. *n.* a hill. (Rhyming slang.) □ *There's a castle on that Jack and Jill.* □ *Let's climb the Jack and Jill and look at the castle.* **2.** *n.* a pill. (Rhyming slang.) □ *Come on mum, you know you've got to take your Jack and Jill.* □ *Get mum her Jacks and Jills please, love.*

jack ashore *mod.* intoxicated due to drink. (From the drunken reputation of sailors, or JACK TARS, on shore leave.) □ *Joe and Arthur kept on knocking them back till they were both jack ashore.* □ *You came in completely jack ashore again last night. What's going on?*

jacked-off AND **naffed-off** *mod.* fed up; annoyed. □ *Now you've got me really jacked-off.* □ *Have you noticed yet that you seem to be able to get everyone naffed-off?*

Jack Horner *n.* a corner. (Rhyming slang.) □ *There was a nice-looking chair in the Jack Horner.* □ *As the car came round the Jack Horner it rolled over twice.*

jack-in office *n.* a self-important, minor civil servant. □ *Oh, he's just another jack-in-office; he's not important.* □ *If you must be a jack-in-office, could you please at least be an efficient one?*

Jack-in-the-box *n.* syphilis. (Rhyming slang, linked as follows: Jack-in-the-box ≈ [pox] = syphilis.) □ *People who get Jack-in-the-box are unlikely to tell everybody about it!* □ *I hear Margy's got the Jack-in-the-box again.*

jack (it) in AND **jack up; pack (it) in 1.** *vb. phr.* to give up or abandon an activity or attempt before it is completed. □ *Walter was just about ready to jack it in when he had a big win.* □ *If you pack in now, everything will have been for nothing.* **2.** *vb. phr.* to die. □ *The cat jacked it in last night.* □ *I'm too young to jack up just yet.*

jack someone or something in AND **pack someone or something in 1.** *vb. phr.* to ruin or destroy someone or something. □ *I think he's trying to jack us in.* □ *Why should anyone jack this great venture in?* **2.** *vb. phr.* to abandon someone or something. □ *Oh, I jacked that idea in some time ago.* □ *We have* *had to pack in our expansion plans, I'm afraid.*

jack something up *vb. phr.* to raise the price of something. □ *They kept jacking the price up with various charges, so I walked out.* □ *How can they jack up the published price now?*

Jack Straw *n.* a worthless man. □ *I like the look of this Jack Straw.* □ *The Jack Straw was not there.*

jack(sy) *n.* the anus; the buttocks. (Taboo.) □ *Someone kicked him on the jacksy.* □ *With luck, his jack will hurt for a long time, that creep!*

jack tar *n.* a sailor. (It used to be that sailor's hands were regularly covered in tar from tar-encrusted rigging.) □ *I've sailed a little, but you could hardly call me an old jack tar.* □ *A couple of jack tars came ashore and asked if they could buy some beer.*

Jack-the-Lad 1. *n.* a popular rogue. □ *I don't know why, but he's quite a Jack-the-Lad.* □ *Harry's always been seen as a Jack-the-Lad by some women.* **2.** *n.* a wanted criminal. □ *Harry's just another Jack-the-Lad, now he's on the run.* □ *Sometimes these Jack-the-Lad's don't care who they hurt.*

Jack the Ripper *n.* a kipper. (Rhyming slang. A kipper is a herring which has been cured by smoking.) □ *He likes a Jack the Ripper for breakfast.* □ *I could never see the attraction of Jack the Rippers.*

jack up See JACK (IT) IN.

Jag *n.* a Jaguar car. □ *What I really want is a Jag.* □ *So, how much will a Jag set me back?*

jag 1. *n.* a drinking bout; a prolonged state of alcoholic or drug-related intoxication. □ *Is he off on another jag, or is this the same one?* □ *One more jag will kill her. Try to keep her away from the stuff.* **2.** See also JAB.

jailer *n.* a policeman. (Scots usage.) □ *The jailer broke up the fight.* □ *These two jailers drove around in their car picking on innocent people like me.*

jake *n.* methylated spirits when drunk by down-and-outs. (Methylated spirits is alcohol which has been denatured by the addition of methanol. See METHS.)

□ *There they are, drinking jake again.* □ *By the time you're drinking jake, it's pretty late in the day.*

jakes *n.* a men's toilet, especially a public one. (Crude. Normally with *the*.) □ *Where's the jakes?* □ *The jakes is around the corner.*

jalopy *n.* an old and dilapidated car. □ *Is this old jalopy yours?* □ *I've got to get my jalopy fixed up.*

jam 1. *n.* a problem; trouble; difficulty. □ *I hear you're in a bit of a jam.* □ *Well, it's not as bad a jam as all that.* **2.** *vb.* [for musicians] to play together, improvising. □ *They jammed until the neighbours complained.* □ *Come over and let's jam, okay?* **3.** *n.* a pleasure or joy. □ *What a wonderful jam yesterday turned out to be.* □ *The world needs more jam like that.* **4.** See also HOT SPOT.

jamboree bags *n.* the female breasts. (Crude. Normally with *the* and in the plural.) □ *Cor, look at the jamboree bags on that, Fred!* □ *With jamboree bags like that, she can go anywhere she likes.*

jam-jar *n.* a tram-car. (Rhyming slang.) □ *There used to be jam-jars in every major British city but now there are very few.* □ *They've built a new jam-jar system in Manchester.*

jammies AND **jim-jams** *n.* pyjamas. □ *Where are my jammies?* □ *I can't go to bed without my jim-jams!*

jammy 1. *mod.* easy. □ *I did not think that opening a bank vault could be so jammy.* □ *What a jammy little job that was!* **2.** *mod.* lucky. □ *Why, you jammy sod!* □ *You were really, really jammy that time!* **3.** *mod.* profitable. □ *This is a jammy little business you have here.* □ *If you must work, make it jammy, I always say.*

jam-packed See JAMPACKED.

jampacked AND **jam-packed** *mod.* full. □ *This day has been jampacked with surprises.* □ *The box was jam-packed with goodies.*

jam roll *n.* parole. (Rhyming slang.) □ *He smiled. It was jam roll time, at last!* □ *Now this lot are really well-behaved 'cause they're all hoping for jam roll.*

jam sandwich *n.* a police car. (Many are white with a conspicuous horizontal red band along each side.) □ *The jam sandwich drove forward, blocking my exit.* □ *Watch it! That's a jam sandwich!*

jam tart 1. *n.* heart. (Rhyming slang.) □ *How's your jam tart, Bert?* □ *I hear Harry's got a weak jam tart.* **2.** *n.* an anal release of intestinal gas; a noise or smell associated with this. (Crude. Rhyming slang, linked as follows: jam tart ≈ [fart] = intestinal gas.) □ *The pungent scent of a recent jam tart hung in the air.* □ *Oh lord! Who made that jam tart?*

jam tomorrow *n.* a promise of future riches or pleasantness that never arrives. □ *I see the politicians are still promising jam tomorrow, as usual.* □ *Don't count on that; it's all jam tomorrow.*

jane 1. *n.* a prostitute. (Crude. Rhyming slang, linked as follows: Jane [Shore] ≈ [whore] = prostitute. Jane Shore was a mistress of Edward IV, in the 15th century.) □ *The Old Bill hauled her in because she looked like a jane.* □ *Clare dresses like a jane.* **2.** *n.* a woman's toilet. (Crude.) □ *Joan's visiting the jane.* □ *That jane's busy. Is there another one?*

jangle *vb.* to chat or gossip. □ *My, isn't Mary jangling a lot today?* □ *He's always jangling on about something or other, but I like him.*

jank *n.* cheek; impudence. □ *What jank! Who does she think she is?* □ *Any more jank like that and he'll get everything he deserves.*

jankers *n.* military punishment. □ *Otto spent most of his time in the army experiencing jankers.* □ *If you think civilian jail's bad, try jankers.*

janky *mod.* impudent. □ *Kids get some pretty janky ideas.* □ *Ken can be rather janky sometimes.*

Jap *n.* a Japanese person. (Racially offensive.) □ *He said he was not a racist, he just hated this particular Jap!* □ *Don't call Japanese people Japs, please. It is very offensive and racist.*

jar 1. *n.* a glass, usually a pint, of beer. □ *I do like this jar they have in here.* □ *Can I have jar please?* **2.** *n.* imitation jewellery manufactured convincingly enough to be able to be sold to the unwary as if real. □ *I think that's jar she's wearing.* □ *If it's really jar you'd not be able to tell, would you?* **3.** *n.* a stoneware hot-water bottle. (Irish usage.) □ *Once jars were very common.* □ *You can pay a fortune for old jars now.*

J. Arthur (Rank) 1. *n.* a bank. (Rhyming slang. The kind of bank where money is kept. J. Arthur Rank was a former British filmmaker.) □ *That's the J. Arthur where I keep my money.* □ *When does yer J. Arthur Rank open today, then?* **2.** *n.* masturbation. (Taboo. Rhyming slang, linked as follows: J. Arthur Rank ≈ [wank] = masturbation.) □ *At least with a J. Arthur Rank you don't have to be polite first.* □ *A J. Arthur is a very popular teenage pastime, you know.*

jaw AND **jaw-jaw 1.** *n.* a chat; a discussion. □ *Come over for a jaw this weekend.* □ *I could use a good jaw-jaw with my old friend.* **2.** *vb.* to chat; to discuss. □ *Stop jawing and get to work.* □ *"Talking jaw-jaw is better that war-war." (Winston Churchill, in 1954.)*

jaw-jaw See JAW.

jay See J.

jazzed (up) *mod.* enhanced; with something added; having been made more enticing. □ *The third act was jazzed up with a little skin.* □ *It was jazzed enough to have the police around asking questions.*

jazz someone or something up *vb.* to make someone or something more exciting or sexy; to make someone or something appeal more to contemporary and youthful tastes. □ *Let's jazz this up a little bit.* □ *They jazzed up the old girl till she looked like a teenager.* □ *Don't jazz up the first number too much.*

jazzy *mod.* vivid; loud-coloured. □ *It was a jazzy sort of place, but I liked it.* □ *Where did she find that jazzy material?*

Jeanie-boy *n.* an effeminate man; a passive male homosexual. (Crude.) □ *So what if he's a Jeanie-boy? He can* *still vote, can't he?* □ *He doesn't like being called a Jeanie-boy.*

jeer *n.* a male homosexual. (Crude. Rhyming slang, linked as follows: jeer ≈ [queer] = homosexual.) □ *He doesn't like being called a jeer.* □ *She came to the dance with a jeer.*

Jeez! See JESUS!

jellies *n.* cheap, brightly-coloured plastic shoes or sandals. □ *It's too cold to wear jellies.* □ *These jellies of yours will crack in this cold weather.*

jelly See GELLY.

jelly babies AND **jelly beans** *n.* an amphetamine tablet or capsule. (From the name of a popular brand of sweet.) □ *Have you got any jelly babies?* □ *Are there any jelly beans available around here?*

jelly beans See JELLY BABIES.

jelly belly *n.* a seriously obese person. (Offensive. Also a term of address.) □ *Have you seen Margaret lately? She's turning into a real jelly belly.* □ *Then this really gross jelly belly tried to get into one of these tiny seats they have at the back of the plane.*

Jenny (Willocks) AND **jessie** *n.* an effeminate man; a passive male homosexual. (Taboo. Scots usage.) □ *He doesn't like being called a Jenny Willocks.* □ *Oh, you can see that you-know-who is a jessie.*

Jeremiah *n.* a fire. (Rhyming slang.) □ *I told him to put more coal on the Jeremiah.* □ *There was a big Jeremiah near here last night.*

jerk *n.* a stupid or worthless person. (Now used for both males and females.) □ *What a loony jerk!* □ *You are such a classic jerk!*

jerk off *vb. phr.* to masturbate. □ *Girls jerk off as well as boys, you know.* □ *Someone has jerked off in here!*

jerks See PHYSICAL JERKS.

jerrican *n.* a petrol can. (Originally one captured from the German Army in North Africa during World War II. Now any such can.) □ *We always carry a jerrican of petrol in the boot in case the car runs out.* □ *Is it safe to carry a jerrican full of petrol in your car?*

jerry *n.* a chamber pot. □ *Where's your jerry?* □ *The jerry's through that way.*

Jerry 1. *n.* a German. (Offensive.) □ *There's a Jerry here to see you.* □ *Uncle Simon was in the war and has never trusted Jerries.* **2.** *n.* the German nation. (Offensive.) □ *Uncle Simon was in the war and has never trusted Jerry.* □ *England plays Jerry at soccer tonight.*

jerry-built *mod.* carelessly and awkwardly built. (The origin of this term is uncertain, but the most probable explanation is that is a corruption of the nautical term "jury," as in "jury-mast"—that is, a temporary mast—which is in turn derived from the French *jour*, meaning "day." Compare with KLUDGE, LASH-UP, QUICK FIX and STOP-GAP.) □ *Yes indeed, this is an old and jerry-built house, but we love it.* □ *The lawyer's case was jerry-built, but the jury bought it anyway.*

jessie See JENNY (WILLOCKS).

Jesus! AND **Jeez!** *exclam.* "That is a surprise!" (Taboo. An expression of surprise or annoyance. Use caution with JESUS in profane senses, as this is potentially offensive.) □ *Jesus, what a jerk!* □ *Jeez! I'm late.*

Jesus boots *n.* sandals. (Use caution with JESUS in profane senses, as this is potentially offensive.) □ *Jesus boots are okay in the summer.* □ *Who is the nut in Jesus boots?*

Jesus factor *n.* an extra safety margin (in the design of a machine, for example) provided to allow for the unlikely. (Use caution with JESUS in profane senses, as this is potentially offensive.) □ *I'd hate to fly in any aircraft that did not have a large Jesus factor built in.* □ *I can't believe there's much of a Jesus factor left in this old thing.*

Jesus nut *n.* the nut that keeps a helicopter attached to its rotor. (Use caution with JESUS in profane senses, as this is potentially offensive.) □ *As you fly along in your helicopter, you try not to think about the Jesus nut and what happens if it breaks.* □ *Just how often do Jesus nuts shear?*

Jesus wept! *exclam.* an exclamation of annoyance or despair. (Taboo. An expression of surprise or annoyance. Use caution with JESUS in profane senses, as this is potentially offensive.) □ *Jesus wept! How could anyone be so stupid?* □ *Jesus wept, he's done it again!*

jet *vb.* to travel in a jet-propelled aircraft. □ *We jetted down to the Canary Islands for Christmas.* □ *People jet back and forth over the Atlantic nowadays and think nothing of it.*

jet-jockey *n.* the pilot of a jet-powered aircraft. □ *These jet-jockeys think they know it all, don't they?* □ *Well, you have to be good to be a jet-jockey.*

jet-set(ters) *n.* young and wealthy people who fly by jet from resort to resort. □ *The jet-set doesn't come here anymore.* □ *Jet-setters have turned to other kinds of excitement.*

Jewie *n.* a Jewish person. (Offensive. Irish usage.) □ *Y'know, Otto, if you call a Jew a Jewie, he's likely to get nasty.* □ *Why can you not be polite to Jewies?*

Jewish piano AND **Jewish typewriter; Yiddish piano** *n.* a cash register. (Offensive. Compare with PIANO.) □ *I don't think referring to the cash register as a "Yiddish piano" is a good idea when you're talking to Mr Cohen, Walter.* □ *Walter says Mr Cohen himself calls it a Jewish typewriter!*

Jewish typewriter See JEWISH PIANO.

jiffy *n.* a very short time. (Compare with IN A JIFF(Y).) □ *That was a pretty long "jiffy" I had to wait!* □ *Please wait just a jiffy, I'll be there.*

jig-a-lig AND **jiggady-jig** *n.* sexual intercourse. (Taboo.) □ *After that jig-a-lig, she felt cheap.* □ *They were talking about, you know, jiggady-jig.*

jiggady-jig See JIG-A-LIG.

jigger *n.* the male sexual organ. (Taboo.) □ *The doctor said Paul's got something wrong with his jigger.* □ *That's all very well Myra, but where would the world be without jiggers?*

jiggery-pokery *n.* trickery or dishonesty. □ *None of your jiggery-pokery, now!* □ *I don't like people who go in for jiggery-pokery like that.*

jiggin *n.* dancing. (Scots usage.) □ *They're aw oot at the jiggin. (They're all out at the dancing.)* □ *Shuggy ower likes the jiggin an that. (Hugh always*

likes dancing and everything associated with that.)

jiggle and jog *n.* a French person. (Offensive. Rhyming slang, linked as follows: jiggle and jog ≈ [Frog] = French.) □ *Why can you never be polite to jiggles and jogs?* □ *Y'know, Otto, if you call a French person a jiggle and jog, he's likely to get nasty.*

jiggy *n.* a jigsaw puzzle. □ *This jiggy is a real tough one.* □ *Can you help me with this jiggy?*

jill 1. *n.* a girl. (Probably from the nursery rhyme "Jack and Jill.") □ *What a beautiful jill she is.* □ *Hands off her! She's my jill!* **2.** *n.* a policewoman. □ *He still found it difficult to take jills, especially pretty ones, seriously.* □ *Otto could not believe that this tiny little jill had actually arrested him.*

jim *n.* men who watch street prostitutes transact business with their clients. (Taboo.) □ *The jim just stood there at the corner, watching everything with unblinking eyes.* □ *As soon as the minder turned towards him, the jim ran off.*

jim-jams See JAMMIES.

Jimmy 1. *n.* a familiar form of address for a man, especially if his correct name is not known. (Scots usage. See JOHN, KIDDO, MOOSH, TOSH, WHACKER, WHACK and WACK.) □ *See you Jimmy, ah'll get you, ye'll see, so ye will!* □ *Got a light Jimmy?* **2.** *n.* a Scotsman. (Offensive. In imitation of Scots slang usage.) □ *Why can you not be polite to Jimmies?* □ *Y'know, Otto, if you call a Scotsman a Jimmy, he's likely to get nasty.*

jimmy 1. *n.* one Pound Sterling. (Rhyming slang, linked as follows: Jimmy [Goblin] ≈ [Sovereign] = one Pound Sterling. A Sovereign is a former coin with a face value equal to one Pound.) □ *There's a thousand jimmies in this for you. But do it now!* □ *I could use a jimmy if you can spare one, guv.* **2.** *vb.* to obtain entry to a place of public entertainment such as a sports stadium, cinema, etc., by trickery or deceit. □ *We jimmied our way into the stadium and saw the game.* □ *How did you ever jimmy your way in there?*

Jimmy Prescott *n.* a waistcoat. (Rhyming slang.) □ *He had the strangest, garishly-coloured Jimmy Prescott you've ever seen in your life.* □ *Are Jimmy Prescotts not kinda dated nowadays?*

jimmy (riddle) *n.* an act of urination. (Crude. Rhyming slang, linked as follows: jimmy (riddle) ≈ [piddle] = urination.) □ *He went out to take a jimmy riddle.* □ *I've just got to go for a jimmy.*

Jim(my) Skinner AND **Lilley and Skinner** *n.* dinner. (Rhyming slang. Lilly and Skinner is a well-known store in London. Goodness knows who Jimmy Skinner was.) □ *Hey, where's me Jimmy Skinner?* □ *Right love, where are we going for our Lilley and Skinner tonight?*

jinx *n.* someone or something that brings bad luck. □ *I think there must be some sort of jinx on us.* □ *I wish I could find out what our jinx is.*

jinxed *mod.* cursed with bad luck. □ *We've been jinxed.* □ *How did we get jinxed?*

jinx someone or something *vb. phr.* to cause someone or something to suffer bad luck. □ *Something must be jinxing the company.* □ *He says he's jinxed us!*

jitters *n.* a feeling of extreme nervousness; edginess. (Always with *the*.) □ *I get the jitters when I have to talk in public.* □ *Too much booze gives me the jitters.*

jittery *mod.* nervous; on edge. □ *Don't let yourself get so jittery.* □ *I'm just a jittery fellow.*

job *n.* a theft; a criminal act. (Police and underworld. Compare with PULL A JOB.) □ *Max and Lefty planned a bank job over in Bristol.* □ *Who did that job at the old mansion last week?*

jobbie AND **jobby** *n.* a bowel movement. (Crude. Juvenile.) □ *Don't forget to do a jobbie, Jimmy.* □ *Mummy, I've got to do a jobby.*

jober as a sudge *mod.* sober. (A deliberate spoonerism on "sober as a judge.") □ *Me? I'm as jober as a sudge.* □ *What I mean to shay is that I am shertainly as jober as a sudge!*

jobsworth *n.* an official or employee who insists on strict adherence to petty rules. (From the phrase, "It's more than my job's worth...") □ *Oh, forget him. He's a real jobsworth if ever I saw one.* □ *I hate these petty jobsworth types.*

jock 1. *n.* a Scotsman. (Offensive.) □ *Don't call Scotsmen jocks, please. It is very offensive and racist.* □ *He said he was not a racist, he just hated this particular jock!* **2.** *n.* an athlete; a sportsman. □ *Am I alone in finding jocks depressing?* □ *Arthur's a real jock, he's sure to get on the team.* **3.** See also DISK JOCKEY.

jockey *n.* a prostitute's client. (Crude.) □ *Another jockey went off with her in his car.* □ *Oh, there's always another jockey, Charlotte.*

Jock's trap *n.* a wheel clamp used on illegally-parked vehicles. (Named after Assistant Commissioner Jock Wilson of the Metropolitan Police, who ordered their use in London. Rhyming slang from JOCKSTRAP.) □ *I came back to the car to find a Jock's trap on the wheel.* □ *Don't you hate these Jock's trap things?*

jockstrap *n.* an athletic support garment. □ *Before you go out there on the rugger field, make sure you've got your jockstrap on.* □ *You can wash your own jockstrap.*

Jock Tamson's bairns *n.* the human race. (Scots usage.) □ *When you get right down to it, we're all Jock Tamson's bairns.* □ *We're aw Jock Tamson's bairns, and dinny forget it!*

Joe Bloggs AND **Joe Public; Joe Soap** *n.* the average British man. □ *You may go for that choice, but do you really imagine Joe Bloggs would?* □ *Just because I'm only a Joe Soap doesn't mean I don't have an opinion, you know.*

Joe Public See JOE BLOGGS.

Joe Soap 1. *n.* a dim-witted drudge. □ *Ignore him, he's just another Joe Soap.* □ *It's these Joe Soaps over there I pity.* **2.** See also JOE BLOGGS.

joey 1. *n.* an illegal package or parcel sent in or out of prison. □ *Is that a joey you've got there, Otto?* □ *How can he get a joey out to me?* **2.** *n.* a dupe, weakling or fool. □ *Why do you have* *to be such a joey?* □ *That poor joey thinks he can convince them.*

Jo(h)anna *n.* a piano. (Rhyming slang.) □ *There she was, playing the old Johanna.* □ *There used to be a Joanna in that corner.*

John *n.* a familiar form of address for a man, especially if his correct name is not known. (Most common in and around London. See JIMMY, KIDDO, MOOSH, TOSH, WHACKER, WHACK and WACK.) □ *You all right, John? Can I help?* □ *Why don't you do the smart thing and clear off, John?*

john *n.* a prostitute's client. (Crude.) □ *She led the john into an alley where Lefty robbed him.* □ *The john looked a little embarrassed.*

John Armstrong *n.* a sailor's name for the personification of human effort. □ *What we need to see from you, me lad, is a lot more of John Armstrong.* □ *He's pleasant but does not over-display the John Armstrong.*

John Barleycorn *n.* the personification of Scotch whisky. (Scots usage.) □ *Inspiring bold John Barleycorn, What danger thou canst make us scorn! (Robert Burns.)* □ *There is little doubt that Willie is a keen friend of John Barleycorn.*

John Bull *n.* a policeman. □ *Think about how the John Bull on the beat is affected by this cold.* □ *The John Bull stopped at the door, tried the lock and moved on.*

John Collins *n.* a tall drink with a gin base. □ *I do like this John Collins.* □ *Can I have a John Collins, please?*

john(darm) *n.* a policeman. (From the French *gendarme*, meaning "policeman.") □ *The johndarm stopped at the door, tried the lock and moved on.* □ *Think about how the john on the beat is affected by this cold.*

John Hop *n.* a policeman. (Rhyming slang, linked as follows: John Hop ≈ [cop] = policeman.) □ *The John Hops are here looking for you again, Joe.* □ *What have you been doing to interest that John Hop this time?*

Johnnie-come-lately *n.* someone new to an already-well-established situation

or status. □ *This Johnnie-come-lately doesn't know what it was like in the old days.* □ *Maybe I'm just a Johnnie-come-lately, but I'm eager.*

Johnny Rutter *n.* butter. (Rhyming slang.) □ *Half a pound of Johnny Rutter, please.* □ *I like Johnny Rutter on me bread. Don't you?*

Johnston *n.* an American sailor. □ *There were a group of Johnstons in our pub last night.* □ *The Johnstons were all right. They bought everyone a round of drinks.*

John Thomas *n.* the male sexual organ. (Taboo.) □ *Unlike Myra, Sharon thinks of little else but John Thomases.* □ *Men keep their brains in their John Thomases!*

joint *n.* a marijuana cigarette. □ *He always has a joint with him.* □ *The joint wasn't enough to carry him very long.*

joker *n.* a man; a guy. □ *Who was that joker I saw you with last night?* □ *Some joker was at the door selling something.*

jokey *mod.* funny, in the sense of "unusual" rather than "comical." □ *What a jokey sort of place this is.* □ *I better warn you; Otto's a bit jokey right now.*

jollies *n.* a charge or thrill; a sexual thrill; a KICK. (Crude.) □ *He got his jollies from skin flicks.* □ *This reefer gives Ernie all the jollies he wants.*

jolly 1. *mod.* somewhat intoxicated due to drink □ *Everybody was jolly and singing by the time the food arrived.* □ *Kelly was a little too jolly, and her sister told her to slow down.* **2.** *n.* a pleasant visit or journey. □ *Well that was jolly, that journey was.* □ *We're all going to Sally's for a jolly. Coming?*

jolly D. See JOLLY DEE.

jolly decent See JOLLY DEE.

jolly dee AND **jolly decent; jolly D.** *mod.* considerate; helpful. □ *Thanks, that's jolly dee of you.* □ *You know, you're being jolly decent about this.*

jolly-well *mod.* certainly. □ *You jolly-well better be there on time.* □ *I jolly-well will be, buster!*

jolt 1. *n.* a drink of strong liquor. □ *Can you give me a little jolt of booze?* □ *He knocked back a jolt and asked for* *another.* **2.** *n.* a portion or dose of a drug. □ *How about a little jolt as a taste?* □ *A jolt costs.* **3.** *n.* the RUSH from an injection of drugs. □ *This stuff doesn't have much jolt.* □ *What kind of jolt do you want?*

josser *n.* a foolish person. □ *Then this josser comes up and asks her for a dance.* □ *You right josser! You've buttered the tablecloth!*

jotters *n.* an employee's documents that are held by his or her employer. (Scots usage.) □ *I've been given my jotters! I've been sacked!* □ *She handed her jotters over to her new employer.*

journey *n.* a prison term. □ *How long a journey did the judge give you this time?* □ *We call it a journey because that name sort of kids you into thinking you're getting somewhere.*

joy *n.* success. □ *I'm sure it's going to be a great joy.* □ *What a joy! The whole thing was just wonderful.*

joy-bag AND **joy-sock** *n.* a condom. (Taboo.) □ *There's a machine selling joy-bags through the back.* □ *He bought a packet of joy-socks and left.*

joy pop 1. *vb.* to take drugs infrequently. □ *She just joy pops at weekends, sometimes.* □ *Joy popping is how addicts get started.* **2.** AND **skin pop** *vb.* to inject drugs intramuscularly. □ *Let's joy pop.* □ *I think people who skin pop are very strange.*

joy (powder) *n.* heroin. □ *She's been all over town looking for joy powder.* □ *I've got a stash of joy here.*

joy-ride *n.* a car ride at high speed, for pleasure only. □ *I don't mind these kids going for a joy-ride, but did they have to steal my car to do it?* □ *Come on mother, let's go for a little joy-ride.*

joyride *vb.* to take and drive away a car without the owner's permission, done for pleasure rather than profit. □ *All these kids want to do is joyride.* □ *Someone has been joyriding in my car!*

joy-rider *n.* someone who goes on a JOY-RIDE. □ *Why do these joy-riders do it? It's suicidal.* □ *The joy-rider was killed when the stolen car collided with a train.*

joy-sock See JOY-BAG.

joy-stick *n.* the male sexual organ. (Taboo.) □ *The streaker covered his joy-stick as he ran across the field. What sort of streak is that?* □ *He made some joke about a joy-stick, but nobody laughed.*

jubber *n.* a burglar's iron bar, used to force open a door. □ *Otto found it rather difficult to explain to the policeman why he was carrying a jubber around at 3:00 a.m.* □ *He slipped the jubber in between the door and its frame, and in seconds the doorway was clear and they could enter.*

jubbies AND **jujubes** *n.* the female breasts. (Crude. Often with *the* and in the plural.) □ *My jubbies aren't all I might have wished for.* □ *Nice jubbies, eh?* □ *Cor, look at the jujubes on that, Fred!*

jubbly *n.* money. □ *How much jubbly do you need, then?* □ *Sorry, I can't afford it, I've no jubbly.* □ *Lovely jubbly!*

judy *n.* a woman. (From "Punch and Judy.") □ *I'm afraid I do not know the judy.* □ *Why is that judy walking through our office?*

judy scuffer *n.* a policewoman. □ *Otto could not believe that this tiny little judy scuffer had actually arrested him.* □ *He still found it difficult to take judy scuffers, especially pretty ones, seriously.*

jug *n.* a small pitcher used to serve beer. □ *Bring us a jug of beer, please.* □ *I think we need another jug over here.*

jug (and pail) *n.* jail. (Usually with *the*. Rhyming slang.) □ *Take it easy. I don't want to end up in the jug.* □ *A couple of days in the jug and pail would do you the power of good.*

jugged (up) *mod.* intoxicated due to drink. □ *I'm not jugged up. I'm not even tipsy.* □ *Fred was too jugged to drive home.*

juggernaut *n.* a very large or heavy truck. □ *We need a bypass built through that valley to divert these juggernauts away from our lovely village.* □ *We are never going to permit a new road that will send another juggernaut through our peaceful valley every few seconds.*

juggins *n.* an idiot or fool. □ *Who's the juggins in the bright orange trousers?*

□ *That juggins thinks he can convince them.*

juggler *n.* a drug addict selling drugs to finance his or her own habit. □ *Harry was a juggler for a while.* □ *We had a juggler living next door for a while. Now he's living in jail.*

jug handles AND **jug-lugs** *n.* protruding ears. (Usually in the plural.) □ *Pull back your jug handles, this is worth hearing!* □ *He was grabbed by the jug-lugs and forcibly removed from the premises.*

jug-lugs See JUG HANDLES.

jugs AND **milk-jugs** *n.* the female breasts. (Crude. Normally with *the* and in the plural.) □ *My jugs aren't all I might have wished for.* □ *With milk-jugs like that, she can go anywhere she likes.*

jug (up) *vb.* *(phr.)* to drink heavily. □ *Let's jug up and have a good time.* □ *We jugged till about noon and then went to sleep.*

juice 1. *n.* electricity. □ *The juice has been off since dawn* □ *Turn on the juice, and let's see if it runs.* 2. *n.* petrol. □ *Fill it up with juice, thanks.* □ *How much juice have we left?*

juicy 1. *mod.* excellent. □ *Mary's got herself a juicy new job.* □ *This is a really juicy day!* 2. *mod.* intoxicated due to drink. □ *Tracy gets a little juicy after a drink or two.* □ *Bruno's a really nice person when he's juicy.*

jujubes See JUBBIES.

jumble *n.* miscellaneous used or discarded articles. □ *There's a big pile of jumble over there in that corner.* □ *Why do you never throw out this jumble?*

jumble sale AND **jumbly** *n.* a special one-day sale where articles of JUMBLE are for sale. □ *The jumble sale raised a lot of money for the church.* □ *If the club needs funds, lets have a jumbly.*

jumbly See JUMBLE SALE.

jumbo 1. *mod.* intoxicated due to drink. (Rhyming slang, linked as follows: jumbo ≈ [elephant's trunk] = drunk.) □ *She seems a little jumbo. Must have had a few already.* □ *I felt a little jumbo, but that didn't stop me from having more.* 2. *n.* a drunk. (Rhyming slang, linked as follows: jumbo ≈ [elephant's trunk]

= drunk.) □ *There was an old jumbo asleep across the front entrance to the office when I got here this morning.* □ *You are going to turn into a jumbo if you don't let up on your drinking.* 3. *n.* a large, awkward man. □ *He's a rather surprising jumbo.* □ *What does the jumbo want?*

jumbo (jet) *n.* a large aircraft, especially a large civilian passenger aircraft. (Originally the Boeing 747, but now generic for this class of vehicle.) □ *We flew to Los Angeles in a jumbo.* □ *The jumbo jet was carrying over four hundred passengers.*

jump 1. *n.* an act of sexual intercourse, from the male perspective. (Taboo.) □ *He seemed to imagine that calling it a "jump" would make everything all right with her.* □ *They were talking about, you know, a jump.* 2. *vb.* to perform sexual intercourse, from the male perspective. (Taboo.) □ *They were jumping like it was going out of fashion* □ *I think you could soon be jumping there, Harry.* 3. *n.* an ambush; a surprise attack. □ *Don't jump him; he's not to blame.* □ *I think he was wrong to jump you.* 4. AND **good jump** *n.* a sexually attractive or willing girl or woman. (Taboo.) □ *She certainly looks like a good jump.* □ *Is it true that Mary is a jump?*

jump bail *vb. phr.* to fail to show up in court, forfeiting bail. □ *Lefty jumped bail, and now he's a fugitive.* □ *Once you've jumped bail, everybody is after you.*

jumped-up *mod.* presumptuous; self-important. □ *Look, you jumped-up little nothing, watch your tongue!* □ *Who's the jumped-up idiot who came up with this preposterous suggestion?*

jumper *n.* a ticket inspector on a train or bus. □ *We all had to produce our tickets when the jumper appeared.* □ *The jumper is asking for your ticket, Charlie.*

Jump in the lake! See GO AND TAKE A FLYING LEAP AT YOURSELF!

jump-jet *n.* a jet aircraft that can take off vertically and land in the same manner. □ *The beauty of the jump-jet is that it needs almost no runway.* □ *Jump-jets* *are also good in air-to-air combat, as they are so manoeuvrable.*

jump out of the window *vb. phr.* to parachute from an aircraft. □ *I used to jump out of the window during the war, you know.* □ *You won't catch me jumping out of the window!*

jump ship *vb. phr.* to desert. (Not necessarily from a ship.) □ *I've had enough, too. Let's jump ship.* □ *Three more men jumped ship today, sir.*

jump-start 1. *n.* the act of starting a car by taking electrical power—through jumper cables—from another car. □ *I got a jump-start from a friend.* □ *Who can give me a jump-start?* **2.** *vb. phr.* to start a car by taking electrical power—through jumper cables—from another car.* □ *I jump-started her car for her.* □ *Sorry, I can't jump-start your car. My battery is also flat.*

jump the gun *vb. phr.* to start too soon; to start before the starting signal. □ *Don't jump the gun again. Wait till I tell you.* □ *The secretary jumped the gun and gave out the letters too soon.*

jump the queue See QUEUE JUMP.

jumpy *mod.* nervous. □ *I'm a little jumpy today, and I don't know why.* □ *Now, don't be jumpy. Everything will be all right.*

jungle *n.* a place of bewilderment and confusion; the real world. □ *It really is a jungle out there. You'll grow up fast or not at all.* □ *Once you're out in that jungle, you'll appreciate home more.*

jungle-bunny *n.* a black person. (Racially offensive.) □ *Don't call black people jungle-bunnys, please. It is very offensive and racist.* □ *He said he was not a racist, he just hated jungle-bunnys!*

Jungle Jim *n.* a Roman Catholic. (Offensive. Also a term of address. Scots usage. Rhyming slang, linked as follows: Jungle Jim ≈ [Tim] = Roman Catholic. Compare with DAN and TIM.) □ *Don't call Roman Catholic people Jungle Jims, please. It is very offensive.* □ *He said he was not prejudiced, he just hated this particular Jungle Jim!*

jungle juice *n.* homemade liquor; any strong liquor of inferior quality. □ *This jungle juice will knock you for six.* □ *Jungle juice will do in a pinch.*

jungle telegraph See BUSH TELEGRAPH.

junk bond *n.* a low-rated corporate bond that pays higher interest because of greater risk. (Parallel to JUNK FOOD.) □ *Don't put all your money into junk bonds.* □ *Junk bonds pay a lot of interest.*

junk fax *n.* an unwanted or annoying advertisement sent by fax. (See JUNK MAIL.) □ *We got nothing but a whole lot of junk faxes today.* □ *I wish they would outlaw junk faxes.*

junk food *n.* food that is typically high in fats and salt and low in nutritional value; food from a fast-food restaurant. □ *Stay away from junk food. It's bad for you.* □ *Junk food tastes good no matter how greasy it is.*

junkie *n.* a drug user; an addict. □ *This is one junky who can be helped, you know.* □ *Junkies have to steal to support their habits.*

junk mail *n.* an unwanted or annoying postal advertisement. (See JUNK FAX.) □ *All we got was junk mail today.* □ *I read everything that comes in the post, even the junk mail.*

just *mod.* merely; only. □ *Barbara and I are just good friends.* □ *It's just a small yacht I own, you know.*

just a tick *phr.* "just a moment." □ *Just a tick. Can we have a word?* □ *Hold on! Just a tick!*

just so *interj.* "Exactly."; "I agree."; "It is splendid." □ *Just so; you're quite right.* □ *That looks, well, just so.*

just the job AND **just the ticket** *n.* the perfect thing. □ *A nice cup of tea will be just the job.* □ *This little thing is just the ticket.*

just the ticket See JUST THE JOB.

just what the doctor ordered *n.* exactly what is needed. □ *This nice cool beer is just what the doctor ordered.* □ *A nice chat with friends is just what the doctor ordered.*

K

K 1. *n.* a thousand (of anything, such as Pounds, bytes, etc.). (Originally from the Greek *khilioi*, meaning "thousand" via the French prefix *kilo-* that is widely used to represent 1,000 in the metric system of measurement. The form considered here is more directly derived from computing where strictly speaking it represents not 1,000 but 1,024, which is the tenth power of two. Compare with THOU.) □ *This car is worth at least twenty K.* □ *I have only 640 K memory in my computer.* **2.** *n.* a kilometre. □ *We've got about ten more Ks to go.* □ *A K is about five eighths of a mile.* **3.** *n.* a knighthood. □ *He's hoping to get a K in the next year or so.* □ *If he can get a K, anyone can.*

kafuffle AND **kerfuffle; cufuffle** *n.* a commotion; a brawl; a fuss. □ *Stop that kafuffle and get down to work!* □ *I've had about enough of your cufuffles.*

kahsi See CARSEY.

kak See CACK.

kaka See CACA.

kaliwater *n.* a sparkling wine, especially champagne. (Military slang, from the Arabic *kali*, meaning "alkali," which is the root of that English word also, by the way. Hobson-jobson.) □ *It was a pleasant reception, with kaliwater and all that sort of thing.* □ *Some kaliwater? Excellent!*

kalplonker *n.* a crowbar. □ *Why do you have a kalplonker on you, son?* □ *We need a kalplonker over here!*

kangaroo *n.* a Jewish person. (Offensive. Rhyming slang.) □ *You know, Otto, if you call a Jew a kangaroo, he's likely to get nasty.* □ *Why can you not be polite to kangaroos?*

kangaroo court *n.* a bogus or illegal court. □ *Is this a newspaper office or a kangaroo court?* □ *You have turned this interview into a kangaroo court.*

kangaroo petrol *n.* the supposed fuel of a car driven in a particularly jerky or jumpy manner. □ *Look at this. He seems to have got some of that kangaroo petrol in his car.* □ *You'd think he always bought kangaroo petrol, from the way he drives.*

Kangaroo Valley *n.* Earl's Court, an area in west London where itinerant Australians tend to congregate. □ *Earl's Court is called Kangaroo Valley because it's impossible to turn around without hitting an Aussie.* □ *One thing about Kangaroo Valley, you can get plenty of great Australian beer.*

Kango *n.* an Australian. (Offensive.) □ *Barry's a Kango from Woolamaloo.* □ *Why are there all these Kangos here today?*

kaput *mod.* damaged beyond repair; finished; dead. (From the German *kaputt*.) □ *That's it; it's really kaput now.* □ *If it's kaput because of something you did you're in serious trouble!*

Kate and Sidney *n.* steak and kidney pie. (Rhyming slang.) □ *Oh good. Kate and Sidney is always my favourite!* □ *Fancy some more Kate and Sidney?*

kay-pee See K.P.

kay-rop poches *n.* pork chops. (Backslang.) □ *Fancy some kay-rop poches, dead cheap?* □ Q: *Where've you got them kay-rop poches from?* A: *Don't ask.*

kecks *n.* trousers. (Always plural.) □ *Woman, what have you done with all me kecks?* □ *He pulled on his kecks and stood up.*

keel over *vb. phr.* to die. □ *Every fish in Greg's tank keeled over last night.* □ *The cat was friendly for a moment before she keeled over.*

keen as mustard *mod.* enthusiastic. □ *The young fellow was keen as mustard, but useless.* □ *The other guy was anything but keen as mustard, but very effective instead.*

keen on someone *mod.* very attracted to or fond of someone. □ *I think she's quite keen on him.* □ *Yes, I think he's lovely and I'm very keen on Patrick.*

keep *vb.* to reside, particularly at Cambridge University. □ *I was most unhappy when I started keeping at Cambridge.* □ *Do you intend to keep at the College?*

keep an ear to the ground *vb. phr.* be alert; be aware of what's happening. □ *I'm paying you to keep an ear to the ground, Harry.* □ *Thank goodness you keep an ear to the ground.*

keep cool *vb. phr.* to keep calm. (Compare with KEEP ONE'S COOL.) □ *Now, keep cool. It's going to be all right.* □ *Just keep cool, son. Calm down.*

keeping one's end up *mod.* doing what is required or expected, but no more. □ *Yes, you are keeping your end up but that's the best we could say.* □ *I must be seen to be keeping one's end up.*

Keep in touch. *sent.* "Good-bye." (Sometimes a sarcastic way of saying good-bye to someone one doesn't care about.) □ *Nice talking to you. Keep in touch.* □ *Sorry, we can't use you anymore. Keep in touch.*

Keep it out! See KEEP OUT OF THIS!

keep one's cool *vb. phr.* to remain calm and in control. (Compare with KEEP COOL and LOSE ONE'S COOL.) □ *Relax, Joe! Just keep your cool.* □ *It's hard to keep your cool when you've been cheated.*

keep oneself to oneself *vb. phr.* to remain aloof. □ *He does tend to keep himself to himself.* □ *Keep yourself to yourself, and you'll be all right there.*

keep one's end up 1. *vb. phr.* to continue to bat despite difficulties. (Cricket.) □ *Well, there's no doubt that he's doing a good job of keeping his end up.*

□ *Come on, you must try to keep your end up too; we need the runs.* **2.** *vb. phr.* to continue with the appearance of normality despite difficulties. □ *Despite the storm, we managed to keep our end up.* □ *It's very important to keep your end up if you want to stay in business.*

keep one's lips buttoned *vb. phr.* to remain silent; not to tell. □ *Will you be quiet! Just keep your lips buttoned!* □ *Keep your lips buttoned while I deal with this.*

keep one's nose clean *vb. phr.* to keep out of trouble, especially trouble with the law. □ *Okay, chum. Keep your nose clean.* □ *I can keep my nose clean. Don't worry.*

Keep out of this! AND **Keep it out!** *exclam.* "Mind your own business!" □ *This is not your affair. Keep out of this!* □ *Keep it out! I'll settle it.*

Keep shtoom! *exclam.* "Keep quiet!" □ *Be quiet. Keep shtoom!* □ *Keep shtoom! Don't let them know we're here!*

keep something under one's hat *vb. phr.* to keep a secret; not to tell. □ *Can you keep this under your hat?* □ *Keep it under your hat, but Samantha's pregnant.*

keep the ball rolling *vb. phr.* to keep things going. □ *If you can keep the ball rolling, it's going to be all right.* □ *Right you, keep the ball rolling over there!*

Keep your hair on! See KEEP YOUR SHIRT ON!

Keep your hands to yourself. 1. *sent.* "Do not touch things that are not yours."; "Do not touch breakable things." (Said to a child.) □ *You can look, but don't touch. Keep your hands to yourself.* □ *Put that down and keep your hands to yourself.* **2.** *sent.* "Don't poke or hit other children." (Said to a child.) □ *Jimmy! Leave him alone and keep your hands to yourself.* □ *Keep your hands to yourself when you go to school.* **3.** *sent.* "No intimate caressing is allowed." (Said to an adult, usually a male.) □ *Keep your hands to yourself, Sunshine.* □ *Just keep your hands to yourself or take me home.*

Keep your head down. *sent.* "Lie low, try not to be noticed." □ *My advice to you is to keep your head down for the moment.* □ *Keep your head down. It'll blow over.*

keep your pecker up 1. *phr.* "remain cheerful." □ *Keep your pecker up, it's not all that bad!* □ *Don't ruin everyone's fun, keep your pecker up!* **2.** *phr.* "don't give up hope." □ *Keep your pecker up, it's going to turn out all right.* □ *Don't loose hope, keep your pecker up.* **3.** *phr.* "don't lose courage." □ *Keep your pecker up, we're going to beat them!* □ *Be brave, keep your pecker up.*

Keep your shirt on! AND **Keep your hair on!** *exclam.* "Remain calm!"; "Don't panic!" □ *I'll be right with you. Keep your shirt on!* □ *"Keep your hair on!" said the barber, "You're next."*

kelly bow *n.* money. (Scots usage. Rhyming slang, linked as follows: kelly bow ≈ [dough] = money.) □ *Oany kelly bow spare Jimmy? Ah'm skint. (Can you spare me some money, sir? I am pennyless.)* □ *Where are aw the folk with the kelly bow?*

Kelper *n.* a native of the Falkland Islands. (The harvesting of kelp—seaweed—is a major component of the economy of these British-owned South Atlantic islands.) □ *We fought a war to keep the Falklands for the Kelpers.* □ *Most Kelpers went to the Falkland Islands from Scotland in the 19th century, I believe.*

kerb-crawl *vb.* to drive slowly around, looking for a street prostitute. (Crude.) □ *Kerb-crawling is becoming more and more of a nuisance in the centre of town.* □ *It's amazing who comes out kerb-crawling of an evening.*

kerb-crawler *n.* a man who drives slowly around, looking for a street prostitute. (Crude.) □ *There is a continual stream of kerb-crawlers here every night.* □ *The kerb-crawler could not believe it when he was arrested.*

kerfuffle See KAFUFFLE.

Kermit *n.* a French person. (Rhyming slang, linked as follows: Kermit [the Frog] ≈ [frog] = French.) □ *I'm sorry but we really don't need another Kermit working here.* □ *What's a Kermit like that doing around here?*

kettle *n.* a steam-powered locomotive. □ *We spend our weekends restoring old kettles.* □ *That kettle certainly produced lots of steam, smoke, noise...and everything.*

kettled *mod.* somewhat intoxicated due to drink. □ *The hostess was a little kettled, I suppose.* □ *My friend here is kettled and needs a lift, and can I have one, too?*

Kevin *n.* a brainless, vulgar youth. (See WAYNE.) □ *I don't like him, he's a Kevin!* □ *Who's that Kevin I saw Linda with?*

key *vb.* to own or drive a car. (Derived from the driver being the person who has its key.) □ *Yeh, he keys that car.* □ *Get out your car and key it over to Charlie's.*

keyed up *mod.* nervous; anxious. □ *Sally was a little keyed up before the meet.* □ *When I get keyed up, I meditate.*

key grip *n.* the head labourer on a film set. (Filmmaking.) □ *The key grip has a complaint that could hold up production.* □ *What is the key grip's problem?*

key money *n.* money paid by a new tenant for a key to his or her house or flat. □ *The landlord wants key money before we get into the flat. Is that legal?* □ *Key money is a form of illegal extortion.*

kharsie See CARSEY.

khazi See CARSEY.

khyber *n.* the buttocks. (Taboo. Rhyming slang, linked as follows: Khyber [Pass] ≈ [arse] = buttocks. The Khyber Pass is a route through the Himalayas from what is now Pakistan to Afghanistan. In the days of the British Raj it formed one of the key defensive points on the North West Frontier of Britain's Indian Empire.) □ *The dog bit her right in the khyber.* □ *She fell right on her khyber.*

kibosh AND **kybosh** to end something; to squelch something. □ *Please don't try to kibosh the scheme this time.* □ *Fred kyboshed our plan.*

kick 1. *n.* a charge or good feeling (from something); pleasure or enjoyment from something. □ *That song really gives me a kick. I love it!* □ *What a kick that gives me!* **2.** *n.* the RUSH from a drug or a drink of strong liquor. □ *This stuff really has a kick.* □ *The kick nearly knocked Harry over.*

kick back *n.* money received in return for a favour. (Usually KICK-BACK.) □ *The kick-back the counsellor got wasn't enough, as it turned out.* □ *You really don't believe that counsellors take kickbacks!*

kick in the arse See KICK IN THE (SEAT OF THE) PANTS.

kick in the backside See KICK IN THE (SEAT OF THE) PANTS.

kick in the guts AND **kick in the teeth** *n.* a severe setback or disappointment; a strong message of discouragement. □ *No business could ever survive a kick in the guts like that.* □ *That's not going to encourage her—it's more like a kick in the teeth.*

kick in the (seat of the) pants AND **kick in the arse; kick in the backside** *n.* a strong message of encouragement or demand. (All are crude. KICK IN THE ARSE is taboo.) □ *All he needs is a kick in the seat of the pants to get him going.* □ *A little kick in the backside will get her moving again.*

kick in the teeth See KICK IN THE GUTS.

kick it AND **kick the habit** *vb. phr.* to voluntarily end any habit or custom, especially a drug habit. □ *I knew I had the guts in me somewhere to kick it.* □ *She tried and tried to kick the habit.*

kick one's heels See COOL ONE'S HEELS.

kick the bucket *vb. phr.* to die. □ *I'm too young to kick the bucket.* □ *The cat kicked the bucket last night.*

kick the habit See KICK IT.

kick up a fuss AND **kick up a stink** *vb. phr.* to cause trouble. □ *Please, I don't want you to kick up a fuss.* □ *Why did you have to kick up a stink about this?*

kick up a stink See KICK UP A FUSS.

kid 1. *n.* a child; a teenager. □ *How many kids do you have now?* □ *My kid is playing in the garden.* **2.** *vb.* to lie; to

trick; to confuse. □ *Stop kidding me and tell me the truth.* □ *Why do you always feel the need to kid?*

Kiddo *n.* a familiar form of address for a man, especially if his correct name is not known. (See JOHN, JIMMY, MOOSH, TOSH, WHACKER, WHACK and WACK.) □ *Got a light, Kiddo?* □ *Look Kiddo, I'll get you, just you wait!*

kiddologist *n.* a practitioner of KIDDOLOGY. □ *Oh come on, you're just a kiddologist!* □ *Listen to that kiddologist; his patter's great!*

kiddology *n.* pretentious pseudo-scientific talk intended to confuse or deceive. □ *Oh, come on! That's just pure kiddology!* □ *The kiddology is not working this time, OK?*

kiddywinks *n.* an affectionate name for children. □ *So, how are all the kiddywinks today?* □ *Well, kiddywinks, what shall we do next?*

kidney-wiper *n.* the male sexual organ. (Taboo.) □ *Only small boys wave their kidney-wipers about like that, Wayne. Put it away!* □ *Myra says kidneywipers are disgusting but then Myra's strange.*

kid('s)-stuff *n.* that which is suitable for or associated with children. □ *Oh, he says these books are all kid's-stuff.* □ *I'm looking for some kid-stuff for my daughter.*

kidult *n.* a childish adult; a child that behaves like an adult. □ *It's difficult, but try to remember that that kidult is really thirty years old.* □ *By age ten, she was holding her own in serious discussions—a real kidult, in fact.*

kike *n.* a Jewish person. (Offensive.) □ *He said he was not a racist, he just hated this particular kike!* □ *Don't call Jewish people kikes, please. It is very offensive and racist.*

kill 1. *vb.* to be very successful with an audience; to perform very well for an audience. □ *She really killed them with that last joke.* □ *She killed them, and they died with laughter.* **2.** *vb.* to eat all of something; to drink all (of a bottle) of something. □ *Kill this bottle so we can get another.* □ *We finally killed the last of the turkey.* **3.** *vb.* to douse a light.

□ *Kill that light!* □ *Would you kill the light so they can't see we're home?* **4.** *vb.* to quash a story; to stop a story from being printed in a newspaper. □ *We must kill that story before it appears in print.* □ *It's too late to kill it; It's already on the TV.* **5.** *vb.* to stop or terminate something. □ *Management have just killed that project.* □ *They killed our plan yesterday.*

killick *n.* a leading seaman in the Royal Navy. (From the symbol of an anchor that appears on his badge; a killick is a kind of small anchor.) □ *I think a killick or two can sort that out, sir.* □ *How many killicks are there in the ship's company?*

killing *n.* a great financial success. □ *Sally made a real killing in the stock market.* □ *Fred made a killing in property speculation.*

killjoy *n.* a person who takes the fun out of things for other people; a PARTY-POOPER. □ *Don't be such a killjoy!* □ *Larry is such a killjoy when he gets nervous.*

kilted brickie *n.* a woman working on a building site. □ *I don't rate the chances for a kilted brickie on this site.* □ *All right, it's sexist, but I'm not having any of these kilted brickies on my building site.*

Kinell! *exclam.* an abbreviated form of "Fucking hell!" (Taboo.) □ *Kinell! It's broke again!* □ *Oh kinell! She'll probably fire us all!*

King AND **Queen** *n.* the British National Anthem. (Whether "King" or "Queen" is used depends upon the sex of the reigning monarch. Always with *the*.) □ *At the end of the evening we all stood for the Queen.* □ *Ladies and Gentlemen, the King!*

King Billy *n.* a nickname for King William III. (Scots and Northern Ireland usage. Still in daily use among Orangemen and others still reliving ancient religious wars and battles, especially in Northern Ireland.) □ *King Billy beat James II's army at the battle of the River Boyne in Ireland in 1690.* □ *"Hullo! Hullo! We are King Billy's boys!"—A Loyalist slogan heared in Northern Ireland.*

King Dicky *n.* a bricklayer. (Rhyming slang, linked as follows: King Dicky ≈ [brickie] = bricklayer.) □ *There's a King Dicky hear to see you.* □ *We need more King Dickys if we're to get this thing built on time.*

king kong *n.* a drink consisting of methylated spirits and lavender water—which combination is guaranteed to knock you out, we are told. □ *King kong? It sounds lethal.* □ *No, I do not fancy a tot of king kong, thank you very much!*

King Lear *n.* a male homosexual. (Crude. Rhyming slang, linked as follows: King Lear ≈ [queer] = homosexual.) □ *She came to the dance with a King Lear.* □ *Why does he work so hard to look like he's a King Lear?*

kingpin *n.* the major or leading individual in an organisation. □ HE: *Walter really likes to believe he's the kingpin around here. Don't disillusion him.* □ SHE: *The real kingpin in this place is Walter's secretary, Janice.* □ HE: *Shouldn't Janice be a queenpin?*

king-size(d) *mod.* very large; relatively large; the largest available. □ *Although we asked for a king-sized bed they supplied a much smaller one.* □ *We've got a king-size problem here, folks.*

kink 1. *n.* a strange person; a KINKY person. □ *The guy's a kink. Watch out for him.* □ *There are kinks all over this place.* **2.** *n.* a sexually deviant person. (Crude.) □ *He was a kink, and I broke up with him.* □ *The kinks congregate two streets over.* **3.** *n.* a clever idea. □ *No more kinks like that. They need solid answers.* □ *Well it's a kink, but I don't think you'll get away with it.*

kinky 1. *mod.* strange; eccentric or weird. □ *The guy is so kinky that everyone avoids him.* □ *Who is that kinky dame in the net stockings?* **2.** *mod.* having to do with unconventional sexual acts or people who perform them. (Crude.) □ *She seems to have a morbid interest in kinky stuff.* □ *He showed her a picture of some kind of kinky sex thing.* **3.** *mod.* concerning any clothing worn to heighten sexual interest in the wearer among the opposite sex. (Crude.) □ *There was no doubt that she wore really kinky clothes.* □ *Kinky underwear like that is asking for it, Myra.*

kip 1. *vb.* to sleep. □ *He's upstairs kipping. Can he phone you back later?* □ *He'll kip for about another hour.* **2.** *n.* a bed. □ *Well, it's time I was getting into the old kip.* □ *Get out of that kip and get up and get going!*

kip down *vb. phr.* to go to sleep. □ *I'm just going to kip down for half-an-hour.* □ *He's kipped down through there.*

kipper 1. *n.* an affectionate name for a small child. □ *It's all right, kipper, it's all right.* □ *What's wrong now, kipper?* **2.** *n.* a torpedo. □ *How many kippers does this submarine carry, Captain?* □ *They launched a kipper at the target, but missed.* **3.** *n.* the female sexual organ. (Taboo.) □ *What do you mean, you can see my kipper? Oh my god, I've forgotten my knickers!* □ *They dance completely nude in there, with kipper and everything on view.* **4.** *n.* a particularly wide necktie. □ *The attacker was wearing a bright kipper, officer.* □ *Pardon me sir, is this your kipper?*

kipper and bloater *n.* a car. (Rhyming slang, linked as follows: kipper and bloater ≈ [motor] car.) □ *Good lord, what sort of kipper and bloater do you call that?* □ *I don't think much of your kipper and bloater!*

kip shop 1. *n.* a cheap boarding-house. □ *He was wandering around the streets, looking for a kip shop.* □ *There are some real weirdos living in that kip shop.* **2.** *n.* a brothel. (Crude.) □ *The police raided the kip shop and took away the madam and all the girls.* □ *He was found dead in a cheap kip shop late last night.*

kirp See CURP.

kisser *n.* the face; the mouth. (Compare with RIGHT IN THE KISSER.) □ *I poked him right in the kisser.* □ *There he stood with a bloody kisser.*

kissing tackle *n.* the mouth. □ *Shut your kissing tackle!* □ *Put this in your kissing tackle and chew it up.*

kiss of death *n.* the direct cause of the end of someone or something. □ *That*

new contract was the kiss of death for our budding jazz band.* □ *Your attitude was the kiss of death for your employment here.*

kiss of life *n.* mouth-to-mouth resuscitation. □ *Quick, he's stopped breathing! Give him the kiss of life!* □ *Thousands of people are saved by the kiss of life every year.*

kiss something good-bye *vb. phr.* to face up to and accept the loss of something. □ *Well, you can kiss that 100 quid good-bye.* □ *I kissed my chance for success good-bye.*

kiss the dust See HIT THE DUST.

kit *n.* clothes. □ *I'll get on my kit, and we'll go out tonight.* □ *You look pretty good in your new kit.*

kitchen-sink *mod.* characteristic of an extremely realistic portrayal of some of the more squalid aspects of modern life in a play or movie. □ *It was a very kitchen-sink play.* □ *Jayce does not like kitchen-sink dramas; she says they are not anything like her own home life.*

kite 1. *vb.* to write worthless cheques; to increase the value on a cheque illegally. (Underworld.) □ *Chuck made a fortune kiting cheques.* □ *He kited a cheque for £50,000.* **2.** *n.* a worthless cheque. (Underworld.) □ *He finally wrote one kite too many, and they nabbed him.* □ *She passed kites from one end of town to the other, then dyed her hair, took off her glasses and did it all over again.* **3.** *vb.* to illegally alter a medical prescription to increase the number of drugs specified by the doctor. □ *He's been kiting; that's how he gets the stuff.* □ *The thing about kiting is that drugs are very cheap that way, so long as you don't get caught, of course.*

kitsch *n.* any kind of sentimental or trashily pretentious popular art or entertainment—films, books, paintings, furniture, plays, etc.—which is vulgar and worthless. (From the German *kitschig,* meaning "rubbishy," "trashy," "inartistic," or "vulgarly showy." Compare with CHOCOLATE BOX.) □ *Kitsch is selling like crazy these days.* □ *Most people prefer kitsch to real art.*

kitschy *mod.* of popular art or entertainment—films, books, paintings, furniture, plays, etc.—which is both sentimentally or trashily pretentious and vulgar and worthless too. □ *A lot of people like kitschy art.* □ *This stuff is too kitschy for me.*

kit someone out *vb. phr.* to provide someone with all they require for a particular purpose. □ *We've got to kit out these people properly.* □ *What do you want to kit me out for now?*

kitty 1. *n.* a pool of money held for a common purpose. □ *Have we got enough in the kitty for another round of drinks?* □ *We all put 10 into the kitty.* **2.** *n.* the female sexual organ. (Taboo. Derived from PUSSY.) □ *Get your hand off my kitty, Sunshine!* □ *Who do think you are, going for my kitty like that?*

Kiwi *n.* a New Zealander. (The kiwi is the national bird of New Zealand.) □ *Do you know a very tall, very muscular and very angry Kiwi?* □ *Well, there is just such a Kiwi outside looking for you.*

klondyke 1. *vb.* to obtain money with ease. □ *Come on, we're gonna klondyke here!* □ *He's always looking to klondyke.* **2.** *vb.* to catch herring in the North Sea, salt and barrel them at sea, and sail directly to Russia (previously Germany) to sell them. (From the huge profits made.) □ *He makes a lot of money klondyking.* □ *They klondyke because they make a great deal of profit.*

klondyker *n.* the owner or captain of a ship that KLONDYKES. □ *They say these klondykers can make a fortune.* □ *Ask that klondyker if it's true.*

kludge AND **cludge 1.** *vb.* to put together a roughly improvised or temporary arrangement that might possibly work. (Computers, especially software. Compare with JERRY-BUILT, LASH-UP, QUICK FIX and STOP GAP.) □ *I only have time to kludge this.* □ *The kid cludged a program together for us in about an hour.* **2.** *n.* a roughly improvised or temporary arrangement that might possibly work. (Computers, especially software.) □ *This is a messy kludge, but it'll do the job, with luck.* □ *Cludges which are invisible don't bother anybody.*

kludgy AND **cludgy** *mod.* concerning a roughly improvised or temporary arrangement that might possibly work. (Computers, especially software.) □ *This program is too kludgy to be acceptable.* □ *Who wrote this cludgy mess?* □ *I don't care if it's kludgy. Does it work?*

klutz *n.* a fool. □ *Those klutzes are at it again. Spend, spend, spend.* □ *How can you be such an utter klutz?*

knacker *vb.* to exhaust. □ *If he tries to do that all day he'll soon knacker himself.* □ *I'll knacker myself if I keep that up!*

knackered *mod.* exhausted. □ *Poor Ted really looks knackered.* □ *I feel too knackered to go to work today.*

knackers *n.* the testicles. (Taboo. Normally with *the* and in the plural.) □ *He got hit right in the knackers.* □ *The teacher preferred "testicles" to "knackers," if they had to be mentioned at all.*

knacker someone *vb. phr.* to kill someone. □ *Barlowe was sure he could keep Rocko from knackering him.* □ *The boss told Rocko to knacker Barlowe.*

knee *vb.* to strike or punch with the knee. □ *He wouldn't move, so I kneed him.* □ *Knee him in the guts!*

kneecap *vb.* to shoot through the kneecaps. (A common form of punishment that cripples but does not kill, employed by terrorists in Northern Ireland.) □ *They kneecapped another drug dealer last night.* □ *Would you rather be kneecapped or sent to jail?*

knee-deep in something *mod.* heavily involved in something; in plentiful supply of something. (Compare with UP TO ONE'S KNEES.) □ *We are knee-deep in orders and loving it.* □ *Right now, we are knee-deep in trouble.*

knee-high to a grasshopper *mod.* of very short stature because of extreme youth. □ *I knew you when you were knee-high to a grasshopper.* □ *I was knee-high to a grasshopper when I first heard that joke.*

knees-up *n.* a lively gathering or party. □ *I haven't had a knees-up like that in years.* □ *That was some knees-up at Tom's the other night.*

knee-trembler *n.* an act of sexual intercourse performed while standing up. (Taboo.) □ *Fancy a quick knee-trembler, darling?* □ *After that knee-trembler, she felt cheap.*

knicker bandit *n.* a small-time thief who steals from clothes lines. □ *Well, seems like we've got a knicker bandit at work in this area.* □ *It turned out the knicker bandit was not exactly a pervert; he was selling what he stole at a car boot sale!*

Knickers! *exclam.* a term of disgust or contempt. □ *"Knickers!" he said, and walked away, ignoring their cries.* □ *Knickers! There's no way I'm going to do that.*

knicks *n.* women's knickers. □ *All her knicks were there on display, drying in her bathroom.* □ *There's a little shop just round the corner where you can buy new knicks, Ella.*

knight of the road 1. *n.* a lorry driver. □ *You'll find a lot of knights of the road in this cafe.* □ *My old man's a knight of the road.* **2.** *n.* a taxi driver. □ *Another knight of the road'll be along soon.* □ *Most knights of the road are very knowledgeable and helpful.* **3.** *n.* a commercial traveller. □ *Oh no, here comes another knight of the road. I wonder what he wants to sell us?* □ *I do not fancy being a knight of the road.* **4.** See also GENTLEMAN OF THE ROAD.

knight of the shire *n.* a depreciative modern term for those MPs representing English rural constituencies. □ *An awful lot of these knight of the shires should be kicked out at the next election.* □ *I don't think much of any of these knights of the shire.*

Knit it! *interj.* "Shut up!" (Scots usage.) □ *Look you! Just knit it! Okay?* □ *Big Shuggy telt me to knit it, so I knitted it, right? (Big Hugh told me to shut up so I shut up, right?)*

knob 1. *n.* an aristocrat. □ *A knob was driven past in his Rolls-Royce.* □ *The knobs all live in the big houses on that hill over there.* **2.** *n.* the male sexual organ. (Taboo.) □ *That's all very well Myra, but where would the world be*

without knobs? □ *The doctor told him that he's got something wrong with his knob.*

knob-job 1. *n.* an act of male masturbation. (Taboo.) □ *If he gets frustrated enough, he does a knob-job.* □ *Timmy's mother caught him giving himself a knob-job in the garden shed.* **2.** *n.* an act of oral sex upon a man. (Taboo.) □ *If you want to have a knob-job you better find another girl, buster!* □ *Fancy a knob-job, darling?*

knobs *n.* the female breasts. (Crude. Normally with *the* and in the plural.) □ *Cor, look at the knobs on that, Fred!* □ *With knobs like that, she can go anywhere she likes.*

knock 1. *vb.* to disparage someone or something. □ *Don't knock it if you haven't tried it.* □ *The papers are knocking my favourite candidate again.* **2.** *n.* a cricket inning. □ *We did quite well that knock.* □ *The next knock will be tougher, I fear.* **3.** *vb.* to perform sexual intercourse. (Taboo.) □ *There were a couple of teenagers in the back room, knocking.* □ *One look and he knew she had already been knocked that evening.* **4.** *vb.* to astonish. □ *I was really knocked by your news.* □ *That should knock him!* **5.** *n.* an act of sexual intercourse. (Taboo.) □ *All the shipwrecked sailor could think about was knock.* □ *I could use a good knock about now.* **6.** *n.* a sexually available or willing woman. (Taboo.) □ *There is plenty of knock in the pubs of this town—if that's all you want.* □ *Oh, Maggy is a knock all right. You'll see!* **7.** *n.* stolen goods. □ *All right, then tell us where this knock came from?* □ *We found a huge pile of knock in his house.* **8.** *vb.* to sell at a loss. □ *I don't want to knock the things too much, but I don't think we have much choice.* □ *Knocking stuff is a good way to go bust.*

knock along *vb. phr.* to cope with life. □ *There's more to life that just knocking along, surely.* □ *Oh don't worry, we can knock along all right.*

knock along (together) with someone *vb. phr.* to get on with someone. □ *I* *know you two can knock along together with each other all right.* □ *If I have to knock along with him, I suppose I can.*

knock around 1. *vb. phr.* to hit repeatedly; to treat in a rough manner. □ *Well, that old car of yours looks as if it's been really knocked around in it's time.* □ *Tom had been knocking Sue around for ages before the cops arrived.* **2.** See also FLOAT AROUND.

knock around with someone *vb. phr.* to keep company with someone. □ *Joe and I have been knocking around together for some time now.* □ *I hear Mary's knocking around with Terry again.*

knock back 1. *vb. phr.* to eat very quickly. □ *What are you knocking back there in the restaurant?* □ *He knocked back his lunch in a couple of minutes.* **2.** *vb. phr.* to consume a drink rapidly. □ *He knocked back three beers in a row.* □ *Let's knock back another one or two and leave.* **3.** *vb. phr.* to disconcert. □ *Well, that really knocked me back.* □ *Are you trying to knock back these people?* **4.** *vb. phr.* to fine. □ *Being knocked back fifty quid for illegal parking seems a bit steep.* □ *How much did the court knock you back this time?* **5.** *vb. phr.* to refuse or reject. (Scots usage.) □ *Jimmy's offer has been knocked back again.* □ *Why do you keep knocking back every time I try to progress.*

knock-back *n.* a rejection or refusal. □ *It's just a knock-back; you'll survive!* □ *I just don't like being given a knock-back.*

knock-down price *n.* a low price; a bargain. □ *You can get them at a knock-down price there.* □ *50? That's not what I'd call a knock-down price!*

knocked about *mod.* battered; beaten. □ *Sally was a little knocked about by the accident.* □ *This book is a little knocked about, so I'll lower the price.*

knocked out *mod.* overwhelmed; impressed. □ *We were just knocked out when we heard your news.* □ *Were we surprised? We were knocked out—elated!*

knocker 1. *n.* a disparaging or discouraging person. □ *I don't think I could take another knocker like that today.* □ *This woman was one knocker just one too many, he thought.* **2.** *n.* a person who intentionally welshes on debts. □ *He's pleasant, but still a knocker.* □ *The knocker was waiting outside the office for him.* **3.** *n.* a welshing bookmaker. □ *When I find that knocker his life will not be worth living.* □ *There's nothing worse than a knocker.*

knockers *n.* the female breasts. (Crude. Normally with *the* and in the plural.) □ *Nice knockers, eh?* □ *All you think about is knockers.*

knocking company *n.* a hire purchase company, one that sells on the installment plan. □ *The knocking company wants to know when you intend to pay your next installment.* □ *The trouble with knocking companies is that they always want back the money they lend you.*

knocking copy *n.* comparative advertising. □ *Did you see the knocking copy? It made great reading!* □ *Knocking copy is dangerous; unless your facts can't be refuted, the other guys can sue.*

knocking-joint See KNOCKING-SHOP.

knocking on a bit *vb. phr.* to grow old. □ *Well, I suppose I am knocking on a bit now.* □ *I'll say she's knocking on a bit. She's almost 100!*

knocking-shop AND **knocking-joint** *n.* a brothel. (Crude.) □ *He was found dead in a knocking-shop late last night.* □ *The police raided the knocking-joint and took away the madam and all the girls.*

Knock it off! 1. *exclam.* "Be Quiet!"; "Shut up!" □ *Hey, you lot! Knock it off! I'm trying to sleep! Knock it off!* **2.** *exclam.* "Stop!" □ *That's enough! Knock it off!* □ *Okay, knock it off! Any more will just make things worse.*

knock-off *n.* a cheap, probably illegal, copy of something. □ *That's a knock-off? But it looks perfect!* □ *It's its perfection that gives it away as a knock-off. Real ones always have defects.*

knock off (from work) *vb. phr.* to quit work, either for the day or for a short rest-break. □ *What time do you knock off from work?* □ *I knock off about five-thirty.*

knock one back *vb. phr.* to take a drink of liquor. □ *He knocked one back right away and demanded another.* □ *He knocked back one and belched grossly.*

knock-on effect *n.* the effect that one event has on another, followed by the effect that that effect that has on the next, and so on and on...* □ *Look out for a knock-on effect.* □ *Knock-on effects can sometimes turn out to be knock-out effects in the long run.*

knock on the head *vb. phr.* to stop or prevent a process or plan from proceeding. □ *It is vital that this plan be knocked on the head right now.* □ *All my hopes have been knocked on the head by this development.*

knockout 1. *n.* something that is quite stunning. □ *Your new car is a knock-out.* □ *Isn't her dress a knockout?* **2.** *n.* a good-looking man or woman. □ *Your date is a real knockout.* □ *Who is that knockout I saw you with last weekend?*

knock someone back *vb. phr.* to cost. □ *That trip to Spain knocked me back almost £500.* □ *How much did that knock us back?*

knock someone cold AND **knock someone dead; knock someone out; knock someone for six 1.** *vb. phr.* to put on a stunning performance or display; to amaze someone. □ *She knocked us dead with her stunning performance.* □ *Go out on that stage and knock them cold, Sally.* **2.** *vb. phr.* to render someone unconscious by a violent blow. □ *One swipe, and he knocked him cold.* □ *If you touch her again I'll knock you for six.*

knock someone dead See KNOCK SOMEONE COLD.

knock someone for six See KNOCK SOMEONE COLD.

knock someone (off) *vb. (phr.)* to kill someone. (Underworld. Compare with BUMP SOMEONE OFF.) □ *I think the police would be quite happy if someone wanted to knock off Mr Big.* □ *Watch it! Otto would knock you as soon as look at you.*

knock someone off *vb. phr.* to seduce someone. □ *I think he's trying to knock off Felicity!* □ *Oh David, are you trying to knock me off?*

knock someone out See KNOCK SOMEONE COLD.

knock someone's block off *vb. phr.* to hit someone hard in the head. □ *Wilbur almost knocked Tom's block off by accident.* □ *He threatened to knock my block off if I didn't do as I was told.*

knock someone's socks off *vb. phr.* to surprise or startle someone; to overwhelm someone. □ *Wow, that explosion nearly knocked my socks off.* □ *This news'll knock your socks off.*

knock something into shape See LICK SOMETHING INTO SHAPE.

knock something (off) *vb. (phr.)* to steal something. □ *He knocked some valuable ornaments off from a little old lady.* □ *The policed warned that he was likely to try to knock things.*

knock something off 1. *vb. phr.* to manufacture or make something, especially in haste or as a cheap imitation. □ *I'll see if I can knock another one off before lunch.* □ *They knocked off four window frames in an hour.* **2.** *vb. phr.* to lower the price of something; to knock off some pounds or pennies from the price of something. □ *The store manager knocked 30 percent off the price of the coat.* □ *Can't you knock something off this damaged item?* **3.** See also KNOCK SOMETHING OUT.

knock something out AND **knock something off** *vb. phr.* to write something quickly. □ *Would you please knock a speech out for the minister?* □ *I'll knock out a letter explaining the whole thing.*

knock something together AND **throw something together** *vb. phr.* to assemble something hurriedly or at the last moment. □ *I'll see if I can throw something together.* □ *I knocked together a vegetable dish at the last minute.*

knock the starch out of someone See TAKE THE STARCH OUT OF SOMEONE.

knock the stuffing out of someone See TAKE THE STARCH OUT OF SOMEONE.

know-all *n.* someone who gives the impression of knowing everything; a SMART ALEC. (Compare with WISE GUY.) □ *Pete is such a know-all!* □ *That know-all isn't of much use to our committee.*

know all the angles *vb. phr.* to know all the tricks and artifices of dealing with someone or something. □ *Ask my mouthpiece about taxes. He knows all the angles.* □ *Rocko knows all the angles. That's how he keeps out of the slammer.*

know a thing or two *vb. phr.* to be knowledgeable. □ *Oh, I know a thing or two.* □ *If he says so, it's so; he knows a thing or two, you know.*

know-how *n.* the knowledge of how to do something. □ *I don't have the know-how to do this job.* □ *You'll get the know-how on the job.*

Knowledge *n.* the highly detailed knowledge of the streets of London that must be accurate enough to pass a very thorough examination set by the Metropolitan Police, before a license to drive a taxi for hire in London can be issued. (Normally with *the*.) □ *Gerry's trying to learn the Knowledge.* □ *It's not everyone who can get their mind around the Knowledge.*

know one's age *vb. phr.* to act in accord with one's age or maturity. (Often used in the negative.) □ *Why does he do this? He doesn't seem to know his age.* □ *Know your age! You're not a child any more.*

know one's arse from one's elbow *vb. phr.* to be competent. (Taboo. Usually in the negative.) □ *He's useless. He doesn't know his arse from his elbow.* □ *Next time, please find me someone who actually does know their arse from their elbow.*

know one's onions AND **know one's stuff** *vb. phr.* to be competent. □ *If you know your onions you'll know what to do in that situation.* □ *Now, these peo-*

ple know their stuff; there's nothing to worry about.

know one's stuff See KNOW ONE'S ONIONS.

know one thing *vb. phr.* to be certain of something. □ *If I know one thing, it's that there you are wrong.* □ *He knows one thing; it's worth more than that.*

know the score *vb. phr.* to know the way things work in the hard, cruel world. □ *Don't try to con me. I know the score.* □ *She knows the score. She wasn't born yesterday.*

know what's what *vb. phr.* to be aware of what is going on in the world. □ *Heidi knows what's what. She can help.* □ *We don't know what's what around here yet.*

know where one is coming from *vb. phr.* to understand someone's motivation; to understand and relate to someone's position. □ *I know where you're coming from. I've been there.* □ *We all know where he's coming from. That's why we are so worried.*

knuckle down (to something) *vb. phr.* to get busy doing something. □ *Please knuckle down to your studies.* □ *You have to knuckle down if you want to get ahead.*

knucklehead *n.* a stupid person. □ *Oh, I feel like such a knucklehead!* □ *Don't worry, you're not a knucklehead.*

knuckle pie AND **knuckle sandwich** *n.* a punch in the teeth, mouth or jaw. □ *How would you like a knuckle pie?* □ *He threatened to give me a knuckle sandwich.*

knuckle sandwich See KNUCKLE PIE.

knuckle under (to someone or something) *vb. phr.* to give in to or accept someone or something. □ *She always refused to knuckle under to anyone.* □ *You have to knuckle under to the system sometimes.*

konk See CONK.

kosher *mod.* acceptable; orthodox; CRICKET. (From Hebrew *kaser*, meaning "proper," via Yiddish.) □ *Is it kosher to do this?* □ *It's a kosher thing, okay.* □ *Of course, it's kosher. Everybody does it.*

K.P. AND **kay-pee** *n.* an insane person; a lunatic. (Rhyming slang, linked as follows: kay-pee/K.P. = [Peanuts] ≈ [nut(s)] = insane person. K.P.™ are manufacturers of foodstuffs, including peanuts.) □ *Watch it, he's a real K.P.* □ *These kay-pees from the hospital keep coming in here.*

Kremlin *n.* New Scotland Yard, the headquarters of the Metropolitan Police. (Always with *the*.) □ *That's the Kremlin over there, son, where the fuzz live.* □ *Do policemen really live in the Kremlin, dad?*

kybosh See KIBOSH.

lab *n.* a laboratory. □ *I've got to look in at the lab on the way back.* □ *What are these people doing in that lab?*

laced mutton AND **mutton** *n.* a prostitute. (Crude.) □ *There are always laced mutton standing right on that corner.* □ *There are lots of mutton to be found around here in the centre of town.*

lace something 1. *vb.* to add alcohol to coffee or tea; to add alcohol to any food or drink. □ *Who laced the punch?* □ *I think I'll lace my coffee with a little whisky.* **2.** *vb.* to add a portion of one drug to another; to add drugs to any food or drink.* □ *Somebody laced the ice cubes with acid.* □ *This fag is laced with opium.*

lackanookie *n.* masculine sexual frustration; the bachelor's disease. (Taboo. Compare with NOOKIE. Scots usage.) □ *Lackanookie is what they say you get if you are getting nothing, if you see what I mean.* □ *I've got to find a helpful female nurse to cure this lackanookie of mine soon!*

laddio *n.* a fellow; a familiar name for a man. (Irish usage.) □ *There's a laddio here looking for you.* □ *The laddio sat on the bench and waited for him.*

laddish *mod.* of childish or immature behaviour in a grown man. □ *Don't you think that's kind of laddish behaviour for a grown man, Walter?* □ *Well, he may be middle-aged, but his laddish side keeps on breaking through.*

ladies' (room) *n.* a woman's toilet. (Crude. Normally with *the*.) □ *Is there a ladies' room somewhere close?* □ *Sally has gone to the ladies'.*

lads *n.* the members of a group of men of approximately equal rank who go about together on a regular basis. (Also a term of address.) □ *Some of the lads are wanting to have a darts competition.* □ *I'm going out to the pub with the lads, darling.*

Lady Bountiful *n.* a benefactress who is condescending to those she helps. (Originally a character in George Farquhar's *The Beaux' Stratagem* play of 1707. Compare with LADY MUCK and LORD MUCK.) □ *Watch out lads, here comes Lady Bountiful again.* □ *She's so much the Lady Bountiful she actually does more harm than good.*

Lady Godiva *n.* five Pounds Sterling; a five pound note. (Rhyming slang, linked as follows: Lady Godiva ≈ [fiver] = five Pounds Sterling.) □ *Have you got a few Lady Godiva you can spare?* □ *These things cost more than just a few Lady Godivas, you know.*

lady-in-waiting *n.* a pregnant woman. □ *When I became a lady-in-waiting, I wondered what to do.* □ *I hear that Tracy is now a lady-in-waiting.*

lady-killer *n.* a man who is very successful with women. □ *Bert is not what you'd call your typical lady-killer.* □ *We saw an old-time lady-killer with a close-cut black moustache and everything.*

Lady Muck *n.* a self-important and pretentious woman. (Compare with LADY BOUNTIFUL and LORD MUCK.) □ *Oh, these two really do think they're Lord and Lady Muck.* □ *I cannot stand that Lady Muck.*

lady of the town *n.* a prostitute. (Crude.) □ *The Old Bill hauled her in because she looked like a lady of the town.* □ *Clare dresses like a lady of the town.*

Lady Snow *n.* cocaine. (See also SNOW.) □ *I spent the afternoon with Lady Snow.* □ *Lady Snow is about the only friend I have left.*

lady wife *n.* a pretentious and dated term of address for someone's wife. □ *My lady wife and I will be delighted to attend your little soiree.* □ *What can I get for your lady wife, sir?*

lag 1. *vb.* to go to prison. □ *I was lagged by the court.* □ *They've lagged me again!* **2.** *vb.* to serve a term in prison. □ *Otto's lagging these days.* □ *If you do that and get caught you'll lag for sure.* **3.** *n.* a convict. (See OLD LAG.) □ *OK, bring that lag through here.* □ *How's the lag in Cell 3?* **4.** *vb.* to arrest someone. □ *I lagged him as he came running round the corner, sir.* □ *When the police lagged Tom he still had the stolen watch on him.*

lager lout *n.* a disruptive, badly behaved, yet affluent youth. □ *There seem to be lager louts everywhere you look nowadays.* □ *I don't like lager louts at all.*

lagging *n.* a term of imprisonment; sometimes a prison term of three years. □ *The beak gave him a lagging, and quite right too.* □ *Well, here he was at the start of another lagging.*

la(h)-di-da(h) *mod.* affectedly fashionable or stylish. □ *He's always so, well, lah-di-dah.* □ *I can't stand that la-di-da creep.*

laid *mod.* subjected to sexual intercourse. (Taboo.) □ *Well, you certainly look laid, all right.* □ *If you come home laid, don't say I didn't warn you.*

laid back *mod.* calm and relaxed. □ *Bruno is not what I would call laid back.* □ *You are really one laid back guy!*

laid on *mod.* planned, organised and assured. □ *It's all been laid on and you've nothing more to do.* □ *She had it all laid on for us.*

lakes *mod.* crazy. (Rhyming slang, linked as follows: Lakes [O'Killarney] ≈ [barmy] = crazy.) □ *I'm not lakes. I just can't make it work.* □ *I'm beginning to feel more lakes the longer I stay around here.*

la-la-land *n.* a state of alcohol or drug-induced euphoria. □ *We were all far away in la-la-land.* □ *Sometimes I think I prefer la-la-land.*

lallies *n.* legs. (Always in the plural.) □ *Look at the lallies on that bird!* □ *Is she the one with the lovely lallies?*

lam *vb. phr.* to hit hard with a stick. □ *Stop! You can't lam away like that at your dog!* □ *After it was lammed, the dog ran away, yelping pitifully.*

lame *mod.* inept; inadequate; undesirable. □ *That fellow's so lame, it's pitiful.* □ *Your explanation is about as lame as they come; do you know that?*

lamebrain *n.* a foolish or slow-witted person. □ *Please don't call me a lamebrain. I do my best.* □ *What a lamebrain!*

lamp 1. *vb.* to strike; to hit. □ *Harry lamped him one right on the jaw.* □ *I got a heavy lamping from Harry yesterday.* **2.** *vb.* to look at someone or something. (The lamps are the eyes.) □ *I lamped the paper and then threw it away.* □ *Here, lamp this tyre for a minute. It's low isn't it?* **3.** *vb.* to throw. □ *When I said you should get rid of it I did not mean you should literally lamp it out the window.* □ *She was lamping all her old clothes away.*

lance-jack *n.* a lance-corporal. (Military.) □ *He's been made up to lance-jack.* □ *What does the lance-jack want?*

land a blow *vb. phr.* to strike someone. □ *He kept moving, and I found it almost impossible to land a blow.* □ *The boxer landed a blow to the face of his opponent.*

land a job *vb. phr.* to obtain employment. □ *As soon as I land a job and start to bring in some money, I'm going to get a stereo.* □ *I managed to land a job at a factory.*

land-crab *n.* a sailor who no longer goes to sea. □ *I suppose I'm a land-crab, now I've retired.* □ *I just want to keep on sailing 'till I drop. I'd hate to end up a land-crab.*

Land of Hope *n.* soap. (Rhyming slang, from the patriotic song *Land of Hope and Glory*.) □ *A bar of Land of Hope, please.* □ *What have you done with the Land of Hope, woman?*

land someone one *vb. phr.* to hit someone. □ *Harry's livid and out to land you one for what you did.* □ *He landed me one as I walked over to my car.*

land someone with something *vb. phr.* to impose some duty or burden upon someone. □ *Why have you landed me with all this trouble?* □ *They've landed me with these costs.*

language *n.* bad language or profanity. (A euphemism.) □ *Mind your language!* □ *We'll have none of that language in here, if you don't mind.*

lap it up *vb. phr.* to be susceptible to flattery. □ *Oh, she really lapped it up.* □ *Most people lap it up, in fact.*

lap of luxury *n.* a luxurious situation. □ *I rather enjoy living in the lap of luxury.* □ *You call this pigpen the lap of luxury?*

lardo *n.* a fat person. (Derogatory.) □ *What does the lardo want?* □ *Even a lardo like that has to earn a living.*

lark 1. *n.* an activity or occupation. □ *What sort of lark are you up to here?* □ *I've no time for that sort of lark.* **2.** *n.* a trivial escapade. □ *It's not important; just a lark, really.* □ *We don't have time for any more larks, Harry.* **3.** *vb.* to steal □ *Who larked my book?* □ *Someone has been larking the change out of the shop's till.*

lash-up *n.* a quick, probably temporary and unsatisfactory solution to a problem. (Compare with JERRY-BUILT, KLUDGE, QUICK FIX and STOP-GAP.) □ *Well, it's a lash-up but it should get us home.* □ *The lash-up looked like one, but it did the trick.*

lassie *n.* a diminutive, poetic or affectionate form of "lass." (Scots usage. Also a term of address.) □ *It's aw richt lassie, dinnie fash yersell. (It's all right girl, don't be concerned.)* □ *Ask the wee lassie what she wants, Shuggy.*

last but one *mod.* next to last. □ *You're last but one so you've got a long wait.* □ *No, I'm not last; last but one but not actually last.*

last straw *n.* the final act or insult; the act that finally calls for a response. □ *This is the last straw. I'm calling the police.* □ *Your leaving the egg shells in the sink was the last straw.*

latch onto something *vb. phr.* to begin to understand something. □ *When Fred finally latched onto the principles of algebra, he began to get better marks.* □ *Sue doesn't quite latch onto the proper stance in golf.*

laugh all the way to the bank *vb. phr.* to have made a great deal of money. □ *If we advertise, we'll soon be laughing all the way to the bank.* □ *The promoters laughed all the way to the bank on the product.*

laugh and joke *n.* a smoke. (Rhyming slang.) □ *He stopped for a minute for a laugh and joke.* □ *He had a laugh and joke and then went back to work.*

laughing academy See FUNNY-FARM.

laughing boy *n.* a serious, morose or sullen individual. (Ironic.) □ *Look out; here comes laughing boy.* □ *What a miserable individual he is; a regular laughing boy.*

laughing gear *n.* the mouth. □ *Why don't you just close your laughing gear for a moment and listen.* □ *How do we get her laughing gear closed so the rest can talk?*

laughing soup AND **laughing water** *n.* any alcoholic drink. □ *How about a drink of the laughing soup?* □ *No ice, please. I prefer my laughing water raw.*

laughing water See LAUGHING SOUP.

laugh like a drain *vb. phr.* to laugh loudly. □ *Funny? I laughed like a drain.* □ *The woman laughs like a drain at the least provocation.*

launder *vb.* to conceal the source and nature of stolen or illicitly obtained money by moving it in and out of different financial institutions. (Underworld.) □ *The woman's sole function was to launder the money from drug deals.* □ *When you finish laundering the last job, we want you to do another.*

lav *n.* a lavatory. □ *Where's your lav?* □ *Paul is in the lav, reading, I think.*

lavender *n.* an effeminate man; a passive male homosexual. (Crude.) □ *She came to the dance with a lavender.* □ *So what if he's a lavender? He can still vote, can't he?*

lavvy *n.* a lavatory. (Scots usage.) □ *Ah need the lavvy.* □ *Oor lavvy's through there.*

lavvy-diver *n.* a plumber. (Scots usage.) □ *Gauny get the lavvy-diver to fix yon flood? (Are you going to get the plumber to fix that flood?)* □ *The lavvy-diver's here to fix yer flooded bog. (The plumber is here to repair your flooded toilet.)*

law *n.* the police. (Always with *the*.) □ *She is in a little trouble with the law.* □ *Mrs Wilson has finally called the law in on her old man for beating her.*

lay *n.* a sailor's wages. □ *Don't ever go to sea for the lay, me lad.* □ *We used to get our lay when the ship docked, and a day or two later, when we sailed again, we were all broke again.*

lay-down *n.* a sleep. □ *I could use a lay-down before I have to get to work.* □ *I need a lay-down before I get started again.*

lay it on the line 1. *vb. phr.* to speak very frankly and directly. □ *I'm going to have to lay it on the line with you, I reckon.* □ *Go ahead; lay it on the line. I want to know exactly what you think.* **2.** *vb. phr.* to explain fully. □ *I think I better lay it on the line.* □ *Yes, he most certainly laid it on the line to us.*

Lay off (it)! AND **Leave it out!** *exclam.* "Stop!"; "Cease doing this!" □ *Lay off it! I'll get out of your way.* □ *Right, that's it! Leave it out!*

lay off (someone or something) *vb. phr.* to stop bothering or harming someone or something; to stop being concerned about someone or something. □ *Lay off the booze for a while, why don't you?* □ *Lay off me! I didn't do anything!*

lay someone out *vb. phr.* to knock someone down with a punch. □ *I can't wait to get into that ring and lay the guy out.* □ *The boxer laid out his opponent with a blow to the head.*

lazybones *n.* a lazy person. □ *I'm just a lazybones, but I don't eat much.* □ *That lazybones is through there sleeping, as usual.*

L-driver *n.* a person learning to drive a car. □ *You drive like an L-driver!* □ *I'm sorry but we really don't need another L driver working here.*

lead in one's pencil *phr.* a raffish term for sexual vitality or strength. (Crude.)

□ *Don't you worry my dear, there's plenty lead in my pencil!* □ *It's not lead in his pencil Boris needs, it's common sense.*

lead poisoning *n.* death caused by being shot with a bullet. (Underworld. Traditionally, bullets are made of lead.) □ *He expired due to a terminal case of lead poisoning.* □ *The fourth drug dealer to die of lead poisoning this month was buried today in a private service.*

lead someone a (merry) dance AND **lead someone up the garden path** *vb. phr.* to initiate a course of action that causes a lot of trouble and difficulty for someone else; to mislead someone. □ *You've been leading us all a merry dance, haven't you?* □ *I'm sorry but that one small piece of spurious information has lead the whole project up the garden path.*

lead someone up the garden path See LEAD SOMEONE A (MERRY) DANCE.

lead-swinger *n.* a malingerer or loafer. □ *Harry is such a lead-swinger!* □ *Get moving, you lead-swingers.*

lean and mean *mod.* capable and ready for hard, efficient work. □ *Ron got himself lean and mean and is ready to play in Saturday's game.* □ *The management is lean and mean and looks ready to turn a profit next year.*

lean on someone *vb. phr.* to put pressure on someone, in order that they agree to something or provide information. □ *Stop leaning on me!* □ *Don't lean on him, it'll just make him worse.*

lean over backwards See BEND OVER BACKWARDS.

leaper *n.* amphetamines or any other stimulant drug. (The name is derived from *sleepers*, such as barbiturates because they have the opposite effect.) □ *You can tell Bruno's on leapers. He's as wired as hell.* □ *He needs some barbs to balance the leapers, or maybe he just ought to try cold turkey and go straight.*

leather *n.* a middle-aged or elderly person who has acquired a lined, leathery skin by spending a great deal of time relaxing in the sun. □ *He could not understand why anyone would want to become a leather like that.* □

The hotel seemed to be populated by leathers like her.

Leave it out! See LAY OFF (IT)!

leave someone cold *vb. phr.* to leave someone unaffected. □ *He said it was dull and left him cold.* □ *The music's good, but the story left the producer cold.*

leave something at that *vb. phr.* to stop further activity or discussion on something. □ *I think we should leave it at that.* □ *But we can't just leave something as important as this at that.*

leave (something) over *vb. (phr.)* to leave someting for action or consideration later. □ *Leave it over. I'll take a look later.* □ *Oh leave over Charlie. I don't have time for this just yet.*

left and right *n.* a fight. (Rhyming slang.) □ *Well, if that's really how you feel, let's have a left and right!* □ *The left and right was a bit of a failure as the other side failed to show!*

Left-footer *n.* a Roman Catholic. (Offensive. Scots usage.) □ *Willy actually moved house because a Left-footer moved in next door!* □ *Willy thinks the Left-footers are taking over these days.*

lefty *n.* a member of a left-wing political party or group; a holder of left-wing views. (Compare with RIGHTY.) □ *I don't trust any lefty.* □ *Of course, no sane lefty would trust you either.*

legal *n.* a passenger who pays the exact taxi fare, without any tip. □ *I don't know if ah want a lot of legals; I live on me tips.* □ *Another miserable legal.*

legal-eagle *n.* a lawyer. □ *I've got a legal-eagle who can get me out of this scrape.* □ *She keeps a whole bunch of legal-eagles to handle that sort of thing.*

leg it See HOOF IT.

legit *mod.* honest; legal. □ *If she's not legit, I won't work with her.* □ *Is this deal legit?*

legless *mod.* very intoxicated due to drink or drugs. □ *They were both legless. They could only lie there and snore.* □ *Tipsy? Legless, more like!*

leg-opener *n.* a drink, especially of gin, reputed to make a woman more likely to be sexually accommodating. (Taboo.) □ *Barman, another whisky please, and a leg-opener for my lady-friend.* □ *He's been plying me with what he thinks are leg-openers all evening.*

leg-over *n.* an act of sexual intercourse. (Taboo.) □ *I think really, she's gasping for a leg-over, you know.* □ *A good leg-over would probably do her the power of good, in fact.*

leg-up *n.* assistance; help. □ *I could use a leg-up.* □ *Here, I'll give you a leg-up.*

lemons *n.* the female breasts. (Crude. Normally with *the* and in the plural.) □ *There she was, bold as brass, with her lemons on full display.* □ *My lemons aren't all I might have wished for.*

lemon squash *n.* a wash. (Rhyming slang.) □ *Well, I'm off for a lemon squash now.* □ *He certainly needed to have a lemon squash.*

lemon tea *n.* urine. (Taboo. Rhyming slang, linked as follows: lemon tea ≈ [pee] = urine.) □ *Don't step in the puppy's lemon tea!* □ *Where's the dog? There's lemon tea on the carpet.*

length 1. *n.* a prison term of six months. □ *I've only been given a length!* □ *I could not take another length.* **2.** *n.* the male sexual organ. (Taboo.) □ *Men keep their brains in their length!* □ *Unlike Myra, Sharon thinks of little else but lengths.*

lengths ahead 1. *mod.* leading a horse race by a considerable margin. (This refers to the length of a horse.) □ *One horse was lengths ahead of the rest. Unfortunately, it was not my one.* □ *The winning horse was lengths ahead at the winning post.* **2.** *mod.* superior in general. □ *Oh yes, that one's lengths ahead.* □ *Why is one so clearly lengths ahead of the other?*

les AND **leso; lezo** *n.* a lesbian. (Crude.) □ *Who's the les in the cowboy boots?* □ *Why does she work so hard to look like a lezo?*

leso See LES.

letch *n.* lust. (Crude.) □ *He's got the letch for you, Zoe!* □ *There's nothing like a touch of well-measured letch to make a romance bounce along.*

letch after someone AND **letch for someone; letch over someone** *vb. phr.* to lust after someone. (Crude.) □

Are you still letching after that girl? □ *It would be better to letch over someone you have a chance of winning.*

letch for someone See LETCH AFTER SOMEONE.

letch over someone See LETCH AFTER SOMEONE.

le(t)chy *mod.* lecherous. (Crude.) □ *Watch out girls, Paul's real letchy tonight.* □ *If you were less lechy and more sympathetic you'd get better results, Paul.*

Let her rip! *exclam.* "Let's do it, never mind the consequences!" □ *Time to start. Let her rip!* □ *There's the signal! Let her rip!*

let it all hang out *vb. phr.* to be yourself, assuming that you generally are not; tell the whole truth, never mind the consequences. □ *Come on. Relax! Let it all hang out.* □ *I let it all hang out, but I still feel rotten.*

let off (some) steam See BLOW OFF (SOME) STEAM.

let (one) off *vb. phr.* to release intestinal gas anally; to cause a noise or smell associated with this. (Crude.) □ *I could not believe it! He just let one off right there, without warning or apology.* □ *If you absolutely must let off, would you have the goodness to go somewhere else to do it?*

let one's hair down *vb. phr.* to enjoy oneself; to have a great time. □ *It was great! We really did let our hair down.* □ *Let's let our hair down tonight, and get back to work tomorrow.*

let-out *n.* an excuse; an alibi. □ *That's not a good reason. That's just a let-out.* □ *This is just a silly let-out.*

Let's be having it! *exclam.* "Give it to me!" □ *What have you done with it? Let's be having it!* □ *Let's be having it; we'll soon find it you know!*

Let's have it! *exclam.* "Please tell (us) the news!" □ *What's happened? Let's have it!* □ *Don't beat around the bush. Let's have it!*

Let's hear it. See I'M LISTENING.

let something ride *vb. phr.* to let something remain as it is; to ignore something (for a while). □ *Don't bother with*

it now. Let it ride for a day or two. □ *Let it ride. It's not that important.*

let's say *phr.* introduces an estimate or a speculation. □ *I need about—let's say—twenty pounds.* □ *Let's say I go over and talk to him. What do you think?*

letter-box *n.* an accommodation address. □ *He uses our house as a sort of letter-box.* □ *Do you have a letter-box I can send post to you at?*

letting *n.* a room, house or apartment that is rented or available to rent. □ *Are you interested in this letting?* □ *The letting is available from next week.*

lettuce *n.* money. (Compare with CABBAGE.) □ *Put your lettuce on the table; then we'll talk.* □ *How much lettuce do you have left?*

level best *n.* one's very best effort. □ *I will do my level best to find your husband.* □ *Don't go to a whole lot of trouble. Your level best is good enough.*

level peg with someone or something *vb. phr.* to perform equally well with someone or something. □ *Our software was level pegging with the others in the lab tests, but was much more expensive.* □ *Maria level pegged with the rest of the class in most subjects.*

lezo See LES.

lezzie AND **lizzie** *n.* a lesbian. (Crude.) □ *You'll find nothing but lezzies in that pub.* □ *Don't you know? Sandra's a lizzie.*

libber *n.* a woman who advocates woman's liberation movements; a feminist. (Usually derogatory.) □ *She certainly sounds like a libber.* □ *This libber on the radio says men are unnecessary. However, Otto reckons she is.*

liberate *vb.* to steal something. (Originally military.) □ *We liberated a few reams of paper and a box of pens.* □ *The privates liberated a jeep and went into town.*

lick and a promise *n.* a task performed in a hasty and perfunctory manner. (Always with *a*. Originally, a rapid and superficial act of washing.) □ *A lick and a promise is not good enough. Take some* *time and do it right.* □ *She gave it a lick and a promise and said she was done.*

licker *n.* a toady. □ *You are just a plain old licker.* □ *That licker actually gave the boss a bottle of wine for her birthday.*

lick something into shape AND **knock something into shape** *vb. phr.* to put something into presentable or working condition as rapidly as possible. □ *I've got about two days more to lick this place into shape so I can sell it.* □ *I want to knock this house into shape for Saturday night.*

lid 1. *n.* an eyelid. □ *Her lids began to close, and the professor raised his voice to a roar.* □ *Pop your lids open! It's morning!* **2.** *n.* the hatch cover of a submarine. □ *It's really rather important to ensure that the lid is properly sealed before diving in a submarine.* □ *A submarine's lid is usually on top of its conning tower.*

lie doggo *vb. phr.* to remain motionless; to wait patiently. □ *Terry lay doggo in the ditch, hoping the Bill would pass him by.* □ *I'm in no hurry to have this matter discussed; as far as I'm concerned, it can lie doggo for ever more.*

lie in *vb. phr.* to stay in bed after normal rising time. □ *I wanted to have a lie in that morning.* □ *Are you still lying in, you lazybones?*

life of Riley *n.* a luxurious life, free of worries or cares. (Irish usage. Always with *the*) □ *When I win the lottery, I'll live the life of Riley.* □ *I'm already living the life of Riley, without any lottery winnings.*

lifer *n.* a prisoner serving a life sentence. (Prisons and military.) □ *The lifers begin to accept their fate after a few years.* □ *Most of the lifers are kept in this cell block.*

Liffey water *n.* Guinness™ porter beer. (Rhyming slang, linked as follows: Liffey water ≈ [porter beer] = Guinness. Irish usage. The Liffey is the river in Dublin, Ireland, upon which the Guinness brewery is situated.) □ *Here, that's good Liffey water!* □ *Have a bottle of Liffey water, Charlie.*

LIFO *phr.* "last in, first out." (Computers. Acronym. Refers to the order of data put in and returned from the processor. Compare with FIFO and GIGO.) □ *I can't remember whether the stack is LIFO or FIFO.* □ *This one is LIFO.*

lift 1. *n.* a brief spiritual or ego-lifting occurrence. □ *Your kind words have given me quite a lift.* □ *I could use a lift today. I am glummer than usual.* **2.** *vb.* to steal something. □ *She had lifted this ring. We found it on her when we arrested her.* □ *Some of these really young kids will lift something just because they like it.*

lift one's elbow See BEND ONE'S ELBOW.

lift someone *vb.* to arrest someone. (Scots usage.) □ *The polis lifted Jimmy last night.* □ *What's he been lifted for this time?*

ligger *n.* a sponger. □ *Get out of here you ligger, and earn your keep.* □ *I do not like or trust that ligger.*

light *n.* an eye. (Usually plural.) □ *Do you want me to poke your lights out?* □ *Open your lights and look out for the street names.*

light and dark *n.* a park. (Rhyming slang.) □ *After lunch, we went for a stroll in the light and dark.* □ *I like being able to look out over the light and dark from my flat.*

light blue 1. *n.* a present or former student of Cambridge University. □ *He is a light blue, studying physics.* □ *I was not a light blue; I went to Oxford.* **2.** *n.* a present or former pupil of Eton College. □ *An awful lot of prime ministers have been light blues.* □ *Why are Eton College pupils called light blues?*

light of love *n.* the Governor of a prison. (Prisoner's slang. Rhyming slang, linked as follows: light of love ≈ [guv] = Governor.) □ *The light of love here is a right sod.* □ *I was there four years and never saw the light of love yet.*

lights out *n.* bedtime. □ *It's lights out, kids. Radios off, too!* □ *I was finished with it by lights out.*

lightweight 1. *mod.* inconsequential. □ *This is a fairly lightweight matter.* □ *We* need an executive here, not just some lightweight flunkey. **2.** *n.* an inconsequential person; someone who accomplishes very little. □ *Don't worry about her. She's just a lightweight.* □ *Those lightweights don't know how to run things right.*

lig off someone *vb. phr.* to sponge. □ *You're not going to lig off me. Get yourself a job.* □ *He's been ligging off us for months.*

like *interj.* as it were; so to speak. □ *Johnny got the things we asked for, like.* □ *You mean, like, she's a big-time lawyer?*

like a bat out of hell See LIKE THE CLAPPERS (OF HELL).

like a fart in a gale *phr.* insignificant; trivial. (Taboo.) □ *That matters like a fart in a gale: not at all, in other words.* □ *What's proposed here is like a fart in a gale and will make no difference.*

like as not *interj.* probably, most likely. □ *As like as not, we'll have to go there.* □ *You're going to lose this case, as like as not.*

like a spare prick (at a wedding) *vb. phr.* to be obviously surplus to requirements. (Taboo.) □ *There I was, left standing about like a spare prick at a wedding.* □ *He made it pretty obvious that he did not want to be left at a loose end, like a spare prick.*

like a tit in a trance *mod.* in a dream; half-awake; disconnected from reality. (Crude.) □ *Don't just stand there like a tit in a trance!* □ *He's like a tit in a trance, noticing nothing.*

like a ton of bricks *mod.* like something very ponderous and heavy. □ *The whole thing hit me like a ton of bricks.* □ *Hitting the rear of that lorry was like hitting a ton of bricks.*

like billy-o *mod.* with great vitality or speed. □ *I've been trying like billy-o to fix this machine all weekend.* □ *We were late and driving like billy-o when the accident happened.*

like blazes See LIKE THE CLAPPERS (OF HELL).

like crazy AND **like mad** *mod.* furiously; very much, fast, many or actively. □ *They're buying tickets like crazy.* □

Look at those people on that riverbank. They're catching fish like mad!

like death warmed up *mod.* unwell or hungover, and looking or feeling the part. □ *Oh my, what a night that was! I feel like death warmed up!* □ *A tall, black-garbed gentleman sat there, looking like death warmed up.*

Like fuck! AND **Like hell!** *exclam.* "That is not true!"; "I do not believe you!" (Both are crude; FUCK is taboo.) □ *You're going to a heavy metal concert? Like hell!* □ *Like fuck you are!*

like greased lightning *mod.* like something that is exceptionally rapid. □ *That little car is like greased lightning.* □ *That kid can run like greased lightning.*

Like hell! See LIKE FUCK!

Like it or lump it! *exclam.* "You have no choice about this, so make the best of it." (Compare with LUMP IT!) □ *Well tough; that's the way it'll be, like it or lump it.* □ *Like it or lump it, we're all going to see your aunt Mary this weekend.*

like it or lump it *phr.* "like it or not"; "love it or hate it." □ *Like it or lump it, that's the way things will be around here from now on.* □ *Since I'm the one running things here now and not you, I really don't care whether you like it or lump it.*

likely as an electric walking stick See LIKELY AS A THREE POUND NOTE.

likely as a nine bob note See LIKELY AS A THREE POUND NOTE.

likely as a three pound note AND **likely as a nine bob note; likely as an electric walking stick** *mod.* obviously worthless; absurd; bogus. □ *His explanation was as likely as an electric walking stick.* □ *The whole idea stinks. It's as queer as a three pound note.*

likely lad 1. *n.* a young man who is clever and alert. □ *Yes, he's a likely lad full of smart answers. But they are the right answers.* □ *Why do we need this likely lad?* **2.** *n.* a young man who is expected to have a successful career. □ *Now if ever I saw a likely lad, he's it.* □ *This likely lad's going to go to the very top. Just watch!*

likely story AND **likely tale** *phr.* an ironical expression of disbelief. (Always with *a.*) □ *A likely story! So, what really happened?* □ *Well that's a likely tale, I must say.*

likely tale See LIKELY STORY.

like mad See LIKE CRAZY.

like nobody's business *mod.* excellently; better than anyone else. □ *She can sing like nobody's business. What a voice!* □ *My mum can bake chocolate cakes like nobody's business.*

like stink *mod.* extremely rapid; extremely hard. □ *Those kids absorbed the topic like stink; they were the keenest I've seen.* □ *As long as she can run like stink, swim like stink and smell like a flower, she gets my support.*

like the clappers (of hell) AND **like blazes; like a bat out of hell** *mod.* very fast or sudden. (Crude. CLAPPERS is rhyming slang for HELL, linked as follows: clappers = [bells] ≈ hell['s bells]. See HELL'S BELLS.) □ *The cat took off like the clappers.* □ *The car pulled away from the curb like a bat out of hell.*

like there was no tomorrow *mod.* as if there would never be another opportunity. □ *She was drinking booze like there was no tomorrow.* □ *He lived like there was no tomorrow.*

Likewise. *sent.* "I agree." □ *Me likewise.* □ *Likewise. Let's do it, then.*

lilac *mod.* effeminate. (Crude.) □ *A lilac man does not have to be gay, you know!* □ *He may have been lilac but he gave us an amazing torrent of abuse.*

Lilley and Skinner 1. *n.* a beginner. (Rhyming slang. Lilly and Skinner is a well-known store in London.) □ *Come on, that's not fair. I'm just a Lilley and Skinner.* □ *You can't put a Lilley and Skinner like her on a case like this, sir.* **2.** See also JIM(MY) SKINNER.

lily-livered *mod.* cowardly. □ *Don't be so lily-livered. Give it a try.* □ *That lily-livered guy is up hiding under his bed till this blows over.*

limit *n.* the farthest possible extreme of a thing, action or person; the maximum which can be tolerated. (Always with *the*.) □ *That's the limit. Get out.* □ *Exceed the limit and you're finished.*

limp-wrist *n.* a male homosexual. (Crude.) □ *Tom is getting to be such a* limp-wrist. □ *He doesn't like being called a limp-wrist.*

line 1. *n.* a story or argument intended to persuade; a story intended to seduce someone. □ *I've heard that line before.* □ *Don't feed me that line. Do you think I was born yesterday?* **2.** *n.* a dose of finely cut cocaine arranged in a line, ready for insufflation or snorting. □ *Let's you and me go do some lines, okay?* □ *See these lines here? Watch what happens to them.*

linen draper *n.* a newspaper. (Rhyming slang.) □ *This linen draper's only good for putting in the bottom of bird cages!* □ *I'm tired of reading this linen draper day after day. Can't we get a different paper?*

line of country *n.* a field or area of knowledge or expertise. □ *Computers are my line of country, I suppose.* □ *What's your line of country, then?*

line one's own pocket(s) *vb. phr.* to make money for oneself in a greedy or dishonest fashion. □ *They are interested in lining their pockets first and serving the people second.* □ *You can't blame them for wanting to line their own pockets.*

lines *n.* text written out several times as a form of punishment imposed on a school pupil. □ *Johnny's busy writing out lines.* □ *Right, I'm going to give you lines for that!*

lingo *n.* language; a special vocabulary. □ *When you catch on to the lingo, everything becomes clear.* □ *If you don't like the lingo, don't listen.*

Lionel Blair *n.* a chair. (Rhyming slang. Lionel Blair is a popular entertainer.) □ *He produced the strangest Lionel Blair from a cupboard.* □ *Sit on that Lionel Blair and say not a word!*

Lionel Blair(-cut) *n.* a disastrous or seriously unsatisfactory hair-cut. (Rhyming slang. From a 1990s TV commercial for beer, believe it or not! Lionel Blair is a popular entertainer.) □ *Can you get your money back for that Lionel Blair-cut, mate?* □ *With a Lionel Blair like that, I don't suppose you'll want to appear in public for a week or two, then?*

lion's share *n.* the largest portion. □ *I earn a lot, but the lion's share goes for taxes.* □ *The lion's share of the surplus cheese goes to school cafeterias.*

lip *n.* back talk; impudent talk. □ *Don't give me any more of your lip!* □ *I've had enough of her lip.*

lippy *mod.* insolent. □ *Don't you get lippy with me, young lady!* □ *She's a lippy little brat.*

lip service *n.* an act of oral sex. (Taboo.) □ *The punter was looking for some lip service.* □ *That girl standing at the corner does provide lip service if you pay enough.*

liquidate someone *vb.* to kill someone. (Underworld.) □ *The boss wants me to liquidate Bruno.* □ *They used a machine gun to liquidate a few troublesome characters.*

liquid laugh *n.* vomit. (Crude.) □ *If you drink much more, you're gonna come out with a liquid laugh.* □ *There's some liquid laugh on your shoe.*

liquid lunch *n.* a jocular name for a midday repast consisting of alcoholic drink only. □ *Another day, another liquid lunch.* □ *Hey, Mart! Fancy a liquid lunch today?*

liquid sunshine *n.* rain. (Ironic.) □ *Ah, lovely liquid sunshine!* □ *Where would the farmers be without their share of liquid sunshine?*

listen in *vb. phr.* to listen to the radio. (Compare with LOOK IN.) □ *He's through there, listening in to the cricket commentary on the BBC.* □ *Listen in to Radio 1; you'll hear something interesting.*

Listen who's talking! See LOOK WHO'S TALKING!

lit 1. *n.* literature, as a school subject. □ *I'm flunking English lit again.* □ *I hate lit. Give me numbers any day.* **2.** AND **lit up** *mod.* intoxicated due to drink. □ *She was always lit by bedtime.* □ *Todd was lit up like a Christmas tree at our office party.*

little Audrey *n.* the bulls-eye of a dart board. □ *His first dart was right on little Audrey, Amazing!* □ *Some people never manage to hit little Audrey*

little black book *n.* a book containing the names and addresses of acquaintances, usually of women who are potential dates, usually put together by men. □ *I've got a nice collection in my little black book.* □ *Am I in your little black book, or can you already tell that I wouldn't go out with you?*

little boys' room *n.* the gent's; the men's toilet. (Compare with LITTLE GIRLS' ROOM.) □ *Can you tell me where the little boys' room is?* □ *Ted's in the little boys' room. He'll be right back.*

little devils AND **little horrors; little monsters; little terrors** *n.* disparaging names for young children. (Normally in the plural.) □ *I'm afraid they are all most irritating little devils.* □ *Are all these little terrors yours?*

little girls' room *n.* the lady's; the women's toilet. (Compare with LITTLE BOYS' ROOM.) □ *Can you please tell me where the little girls' room is?* □ *Is there an attendant in the little girls' room?*

little horrors See LITTLE DEVILS.

little man 1. *n.* a small boy. (Also a term of address.) □ *Well my little man, how are you today?* □ *What a fine little man he is now.* **2.** *n.* a middle-class woman's patronising term for a tradesman. □ *I know a little man who would be able to do these repairs for you, my dear.* □ *I could use a little man to repair our plumbing.* **3.** AND **(little) willy; (little) willie; winkle** *n.* the male sexual organ of a small boy. (Crude.) □ *The naked infant ran through the room, his little man wobbling up and down.* □ *Jonny! Put your willie away!*

little man in the boat *n.* the female sexual organ. (Taboo.) □ *If your dresses get any shorter, we'll all be able to see your little man in the boat.* □ *What do you mean, you can see my little man in the boat? Oh my god, I've forgotten my knickers!*

little monsters See LITTLE DEVILS.

little number 1. *n.* a dress. □ *You look really good in that little number.* □ *Now that's a sexy little number you got on.* **2.** *n.* a woman, viewed as a sex-object.

(Crude.) □ *Now there's a nice little number walking down the street.* □ *So this little number I'd been eyeing up came right up to me and said, "It's £20 for a short time, ducks."*

little something 1. *n.* a drink of spirits. (A euphemism.) □ *Can I interest you in a little something before lunch?* □ *We sat there, nursing our little somethings, in a long embarrassing silence.* **2.** *n.* a snack; something eaten between meals. □ *Can I offer you a little something before you go?* □ *I wonder if I could have a little something?*

little terrors See LITTLE DEVILS.

(little) willie See LITTLE MAN.

little woman 1. *n.* a man's condescending term for his wife. □ *Me little woman is angry with me.* □ *I've got to get home to my little woman.* **2.** *n.* a middle-class woman's patronising term for her dressmaker. □ *Ask the little woman when the dress will be ready, please.* □ *Your little woman's here asking if she can measure you.*

lit up See LIT.

live-in lover *n.* an unmarried person that is living with another as if married. □ *I'm sorry but we really don't need another pair of live-in lovers working together here.* □ *What's her live-in lover doing around here?*

live in one's suitcase AND **live out of one's suitcase** *vb. phr.* to be perpetually on the move; to lack a permanent place or residence. □ *My job requires me to live in my suitcase.* □ *I can't stand living out of my suitcase any longer.*

live it up *vb. phr.* to live well; to have an extravagant lifestyle. □ *I love living it up!* □ *I'll live it up when I've got this done.*

live out of one's suitcase See LIVE IN ONE'S SUITCASE.

live rough *vb. phr.* to sleep out-of-doors as a way of life. □ *I don't like living rough, but I do when I have to.* □ *Did you hear that Otto's living rough now?*

liveware *n.* the human component of computing. (Patterned on "software" and "hardware." Compare with FIRMWARE, VAPOURWARE, and WETWARE.) □ *The hardware is okay. It's the liveware that's bad.* □ *If I don't get some sleep, you're going to see a liveware crash.*

live wire *n.* an energetic and vivacious person. □ *Tracy is a real live wire.* □ *With a live wire like Tracy in charge, things will get done, that's for sure.*

lizzie See LEZZIE.

load 1. *n.* a cache of drugs; a STASH. □ *My load is up in the closet.* □ *If his load dwindles, he gets more easily.* **2.** *n.* lots; plenty. (Often in the plural. See HEAP.) □ *Mr Wilson has loads of money.* □ *I have a whole load of papers for you.*

loaded *mod.* very wealthy; possessing a lot of money. □ *Mr Wilson is loaded, but he is also generous with his money.* □ *My Uncle Fred is loaded, and he fully intends to take it all with him—if he can just figure out how.*

loaded question *n.* a question which has concealed or misleading implications. □ *Now, that's a loaded question, so don't expect an answer.* □ *I didn't mean it to be a loaded question.*

loaded remark *n.* a remark which has concealed or misleading implications. □ *Your loaded remark did not go over well with our host.* □ *In spite of your numerous loaded remarks, I do hope you will return sometime when it is convenient to us.*

loaded to the barrel AND **loaded to the earlobes; loaded to the gills; loaded to the gunnals; loaded to the gunwales; loaded to the hat; loaded to the muzzle; loaded to the Plimsole line** *mod.* very intoxicated due to drink. □ *He's loaded to the gills. Couldn't see a hole in a ladder.* □ *Boy, he's loaded to the earlobes and spoiling for a fight.*

loaded to the earlobes See LOADED TO THE BARREL.

loaded to the gills See LOADED TO THE BARREL.

loaded to the gunnals See LOADED TO THE BARREL.

loaded to the gunwales See LOADED TO THE BARREL.

loaded to the hat See LOADED TO THE BARREL.

loaded to the muzzle See LOADED TO THE BARREL.

loaded to the Plimsole line See LOADED TO THE BARREL.

load of cods(wallop) AND **load of old cobblers; load of crap; load of guff** *n.* utter nonsense. (See also COBBLERS.) □ *Don't give me that load of codswallop! I won't buy it.* □ *That's just a lot of load of guff.*

load of crap See LOAD OF CODS(WALLOP).

load of guff See LOAD OF CODS(WALLOP).

load of old cobblers See LOAD OF CODS(WALLOP).

Loadsamoney! 1. *exclam.* much wealth. (Eye-dialect.) □ *He may not look it but he's got loadsamoney.* □ *Loadsamoney; that's what I want!* **2.** *exclam.* "I have a lot of money; have you?" (Called out at the less fortunate by those flaunting their wealth.) □ *Loadsamoney! How about you, mate?* □ *Look at this! Loadsamoney!*

loaf *n.* the head; the brain. (Rhyming slang, linked as follows: loaf [of bread] ≈ head.) □ *That's using your loaf!* □ *Put your hat on your loaf, and let's go.*

local *n.* a neighbourhood pub. □ *You'll usually find our local is well-attended in the evenings.* □ *The local is where you go to pick up all the gossip.*

local talent AND **talent** *n.* "available" girls, as a group. (Normally with *the.*) □ *Where do you find the local talent around here?* □ *Is that the best there is in the way of local talent?*

lockjawed *mod.* intoxicated due to drink. □ *She's more than a little lockjawed. Must have had a good few already.* □ *Boy, I was really lockjawed. I'll never drink another drop.*

loco weed AND **love weed** *n.* marijuana. □ *Have you got any love weed?* □ *I certainly could use some loco weed right now.*

logbook *n.* a vehicle registration document. □ *If you are involved in an accident, the police will want to see your logbook.* □ *It's usual to keep the logbook at home and not in the car.*

LOL *interj.* "laughing out loud." (Computer jargon. Written only. An initialism used in computer communications. Indicates that one is laughing in response to a previous remark.) □ *I'm LOL about the last remark you made.* □ *LOL at your last message.*

lollipop 1. *n.* the police. (Rhyming slang, linked as follows: lollipop ≈ [cop] = policeman.) □ *See that lollipop over there? He lifted me once.* □ *The lollipop will catch up with you some day.* **2.** *vb.* to inform the police. (Rhyming slang, linked as follows: lollipop ≈ [shop] = inform.) □ *Are you going to lollipop on me?* □ *I don't lollipop on no one.*

lollipop lady AND **lollipop man; lollipop woman** *n.* a school crossing patrol person. (This person halts traffic by holding up a large circular sign on a pole resembling a lollipop; thus this name.) □ *The school is looking for a new lollipop man or woman.* □ *The lollipop woman outside the local school really looks after the children well.*

lollipop man See LOLLIPOP LADY.

lollipop woman See LOLLIPOP LADY.

lollop *vb.* to lounge about. □ *Don't lollop like that, Johnny.* □ *I don't like to see people lolloping instead of sitting correctly.*

lollos *n.* large, well-shaped female breasts. (Crude. Said to be derived from Gina Lollobrigida, the Italian film star, who possessed such attributes.) □ *"Nice lollos," he thought, as she walked past.* □ *My lollos aren't all I might have wished for.*

lolly 1. *n.* money. □ *Sorry, I can't afford it, I've no lolly.* □ *How much lolly do you need, then?* **2.** *n.* sweets. □ *Mummy, can I have a lolly?* □ *I love lollies. I always have, ever since I was little.* **3.** *n.* a lollipop. □ *Remember Kojak? He always used to be sucking on a lolly.* □ *Come on, let's both get lollies to suck on.*

lolly someone *vb.* to betray one's criminal colleague to the police. □ *Would you lolly me?* □ *I'd never lolly, Bruno.*

lombard *n.* a stupid but wealthy person. (An acronym: *l*oads *of* *m*oney *b*ut *a* *r*eal *d*ickhead. Lombard Street is where the Stock Exchange is located in the City of London. Compare with DICKHEAD.) □ *Mr Big really loves lombards, so easy to part from their money.* □ *So this lombard want to know if he could buy Tower Bridge?*

Lombard Street to a China orange *phr.* "very long odds indeed." (Lombard Street is where the Stock Exchange is located in the City of London.) □ *I'll give you Lombard Street to a China orange that it does not happen.* □ *Might the government fall? Lombard Street to a China orange against that!*

lommix See LUMMOX.

London fog *n.* a dog. (Rhyming slang.) □ *The London fog frightened the child.* □ *Why do you keep a London fog like that?*

lone wolf *n.* a man who keeps himself to himself. □ *Fred is sort of a lone wolf until he has a few drinks.* □ *It's the lone wolves you read about in the paper when they pull a drowning person from the river.*

long arm of the law *n.* the police; the legal system. □ *The long arm of the law is going to tap you on the shoulder some day, Lefty.* □ *The long arm of the law finally caught up with Gert.*

long-dated *mod.* [of an invoice or bill] not due for early payment. □ *Oh, this is a long-dated bill, don't worry about paying it yet.* □ *Why did you buy all this long-dated stock?*

long drink of water See BIG DRINK OF WATER.

long-eared *mod.* stupid. □ *I've very sorry, but the truth is that Otto is a long-eared oaf.* □ *Don't worry Otto, I don't think you're all that long-eared.*

long firm *n.* corporate swindlers. □ *Long firms operate by setting up a dummy company, ordering goods from trade suppliers, and then vanishing before they have to pay for them.* □ *Well, it seems these nice people who placed that big order last week were really a long firm.*

long-hair *n.* an intellectual person. □ *The long-hairs usually congregate in there.* □ *Sam is a long-hair, I suppose. I mean, he likes to think about things and he reads books.*

long-haired *mod.* intellectual. □ *So, what do the long-haired people have to say on this question?* □ *Then this long-haired professor type came in and talked about multi-dimensional space-time continuums or something, but by now Otto was sound asleep.*

long in the tooth *mod.* elderly; very old; ancient. □ *Oh, that story's long in the tooth!* □ *I did not think Brian was that long in the tooth.*

longjohns *n.* long-legged underpants. □ *I wear longjohns all winter as they are so comfortable and warm.* □ *Now it's getting colder, Harry's asking where his longjohns are.*

long jump See HIGH JUMP.

long-legged *mod.* very fast. □ *Now there's a long-legged filly for you* □ *You can have long-legged cars too, I suppose.*

long lie *n.* time spent lying in bed longer than usual. □ *On Saturday morning I usually have a long lie.* □ *He's a lazy individual, always taking long lies.*

long odds *n.* a very considerable improbability. □ *I'd give long odds against that ever happening.* □ *Unfortunately, long odds sometime come up.*

long paper *n.* an academic thesis. □ *I've had to spend the summer working on my long paper.* □ *His long paper is actually very good.*

long pockets and short arms *n.* a psychological inability to spend money. □ *You'll be lucky! He's a severe case of long pockets and short arms.* □ *People with long pockets and short arms are also called "mean."*

long shot *n.* a wild guess; an attempt at something that has little chance of succeeding. □ *Well, it was a long shot, but I had to try it.* □ *You shouldn't expect a long shot to pay off.*

longstop **1.** *n.* the area of a cricket field behind the wicket keeper. □ *I'd like you* *to field in the longstops this afternoon, please.* □ *Who's that fielding at longstop?* **2.** *n.* a final chance or opportunity. □ *It's only a longstop, but worth a try.* □ *All right, here's a longstop for you.*

long streak of piss See STREAK OF PISS.

Long time no see. *phr.* "I haven't seen you in a long time." □ *Hey, John! Long time no see!* □ *Long time no see! How've you been?*

long-tongued *mod.* long-winded; loquacious. □ *What a boring, long-tongued explanation that was.* □ *Could we have a less long-tongued story the next time?*

long-winded See WINDY.

loo *n.* a toilet. (Possibly from the French *l'eau*, meaning "water.") □ *Where's the loo?* □ *The loo? Oh, it's along that passageway.*

look after number one AND **take care of number one** *vb. phr.* to take care of oneself first. (Compare with NUMBER ONE.) □ *You've got to look after number one, right?* □ *It's a good idea to take care of number one. Who else will?*

Look alive! *exclam.* "Move faster!"; "Wake up!"; "Look and act alert!" □ *There's work to be done! Look alive!* □ *Look alive! It's a long, hard day ahead!*

look back *vb. phr.* to make a return visit. □ *Look back soon.* □ *Why don't you look back soon?*

looker *n.* a good-looking or attractive girl or young woman. □ *I like the looker you were with last night.* □ *What a looker! I want a piece of that one.*

look in *vb. phr.* to watch television. (Compare with LISTEN IN.) □ *I spent the evening look in.* □ *What's worth look in on tonight?*

look-in *n.* a chance or opportunity. (Normally used in the negative.) □ *I didn't have a look-in!* □ *Give the lad a look-in, fellows!*

look-see *n.* a look; a visual examination. □ *Let's go and have a look-see at this monster of yours.* □ *Take a look-see at this one and see if you like it.*

Looks good! *exclam.* "It seems very promising." □ *Great work, looks good!* □ *Looks good! Keep it up!*

Look sharpish! *exclam.* "Watch out!" □ *Look sharpish, that's a dangerous corner!* □ *If you don't look sharpish, they'll get you!*

look sharpish *vb. phr.* to keep awake. □ *Hey you! Look sharpish; no sleeping on the job!* □ *If you look sharpish most of the time, they won't bother you.*

look sharpish AND **look slippy** *vb. phr.* to get a move on. □ *Look sharpish! We're late!* □ *Come on, all of you! Look slippy!*

look slippy See LOOK SHARPISH.

look something out *vb. phr.* to search out or find. □ *I'm looking out for a new car.* □ *She went off to look out some clothes.*

Look who's talking! AND **Listen who's talking!** *exclam.* "You are in no position to criticise!"; "In the circumstances you would be wise to remain silent." □ *Me a tax cheat? Look who's talking!* □ *Listen who's talking. You were there before I was.*

loony AND **looney 1.** *mod.* crazy. (From *lunatic.*) □ *That is a loony idea. Forget it.* □ *I'm not really as loony as I seem.* **2.** *n.* a crazy person. □ *I'm beginning to feel more and more like a looney the longer I stay around here.* □ *Don't be a loony. Use your common sense, if you have any.*

loony bin *n.* an insane asylum; a mental hospital. □ *I feel like I'm about ready for the loony bin.* □ *Today's loony bins are far different from those of just a few decades ago.*

loop-legged *mod.* intoxicated due to drink. □ *He's too loop-legged to drive.* □ *She has this strange tendency to get a little loop-legged when she has four or five drinks.*

loop-the-loop *n.* soup. (Rhyming slang.) □ *There's nothing better than some loop-the-loop on a cold day.* □ *Fancy a bowl of loop-the-loop?*

loopy 1. *mod.* crazy; insane. □ *Jane's got this loopy idea that she's going to marry Frank.* □ *Anyone wanting to marry Frank would have to be loopy.* **2.** *mod.* irrational; illogical. □ *That's a loopy way to get the job done.* □ *Don't be so loopy! You can buy the same* *thing at half that price if you shop next door.*

loot 1. *n.* money received as wages. □ *So when I got my loot there was far more deducted than I'd expected.* □ *Have you collected this week's loot from the pay office yet?* **2.** *n.* money in general. □ *I left home without any loot.* □ *It takes too much loot to eat at that restaurant.*

Lor! See LORD ALMIGHTY!

Lord Almighty! AND **Lor!; Lummy!** *exclam.* an exclamation of surprise. □ *Lord Almighty! It's Mary!* □ *Lummy, I'm tired!*

Lord love a duck! AND **Lor love a duck!; Cor love a duck! Gawd love a duck!** *exclam.* an exclamation of surprise. □ *Lord love a duck! It's Mary!* □ *Gawd love a duck! That's amazing!*

Lord Muck *n.* a self-important and pretentious man. (Compare with LADY BOUNTIFUL and LADY MUCK.) □ *They've behaved like Lord and Lady Muck as long as we've known them.* □ *Lord Muck over there seems to think he can just summon you to his presence.*

lose a bundle *vb. phr.* to lose a lot of money. (Compare with BUNDLE and MAKE A BUNDLE.) □ *Don lost a bundle on that land deal.* □ *I know I would lose a bundle if I went to Monte Carlo and gambled.*

lose one's cool AND **lose one's hair; lose one's rag** *vb. phr.* to lose control; to become over-excited or angry. (Compare with KEEP ONE'S COOL.) □ *Now, don't lose your cool. Relax.* □ *I'm trying not to lose my hair, but it's hard.*

lose one's grip *vb. phr.* to lose one's control over events. □ *When I begin to lose my grip, I will just quit.* □ *I'm losing my grip. It must be time to chuck it.*

lose one's hair See LOSE ONE'S COOL.

lose one's marbles *vb. phr.* to lose one's sanity. (Compare with HAVE (GOT) ALL ONE'S MARBLES.) □ *Have you lost your marbles?* □ *She acts like she lost her marbles.*

lose one's rag See LOSE ONE'S COOL.

lose one's shirt *vb. phr.* to go broke; to lose everything of value, notionally even one's shirt. □ *I lost my shirt on*

that bank deal. □ *Try not to lose your shirt in the market again.*

loser *n.* someone or something that is an inveterate failure. □ *Dave is a real loser.* □ *Only losers wear clothes like that.* □ *Those guys are all losers. They'll never amount to anything.*

losing streak *n.* a period of bad luck, especially in gambling. □ *After a prolonged losing streak, the lady retired and opened a pedicure parlour for dogs in south London.* □ *I've been on a three-year losing streak in my business. I'm just about done.*

lost cause *n.* a hopeless or worthless thing or person. □ *The whole play began to come apart during the second act. It was a lost cause by the third.* □ *Max is just a lost cause. Forget about him.*

lotion *n.* an alcoholic drink. □ *Did you bring the lotion?* □ *Can't have a good party without lots of lotion.*

Lots of luck! 1. *exclam.* "Good luck!" □ *I'm glad you're giving it a try. Lots of luck!* □ *Lots of luck in your new job!* **2.** *exclam.* "You don't have a chance!"; "Good luck, you'll need it!" (Sarcastic.) □ *Think you stand a chance? Well, lots of luck!* □ *You a member of parliament? Ha! Lots of luck!*

loudmouth *n.* a person who talks too much or too loudly. □ *I try not to be a loudmouth, but I sometimes get carried away.* □ *There are a number of loudmouths in here who are competing with one another.*

louse *n.* a thoroughly repellent person, usually a male. □ *You can be such a louse!* □ *Max turned out to be a louse, and his wife of two weeks left him.*

louse-ladder *n.* a run in a woman's stocking. □ *Oh no, I've got another louse-ladder.* □ *Louse-ladders are so unsightly.*

louse something up *vb. phr.* to ruin something. □ *You seem to have loused this one up, too.* □ *Try not to louse things up this time.*

lousy *mod.* rotten; poor; bad. (Pronounced LAU-zee.) □ *This is a lousy day.* □ *This mushy stuff is lousy. Do I have to eat it?*

lousy with someone or something *mod.* having lots of someone or something. (In the fashion of an infestation of lice.) □ *Old Mr Wilson is lousy with money.* □ *Tiffany is lousy with jewels and furs, but she's got bad teeth.*

love AND **luv; luvvy** *n.* a casual term of endearment to a stranger, particularly to or from a woman. □ *Are you all right, love?* □ *Right luvvy, you can't stay here.*

love blobs See BLOBS.

(love) handles *n.* rolls of fat around the waist that raffishly, can supposedly be held on to during lovemaking. □ *Ted exercised daily, trying to get rid of his love handles.* □ *Not only did he grow a belly, but he's got handles on his handles.*

lovely **1.** *mod.* all right; acceptable. □ *Okay, that's lovely! Stop there!* □ *Yes, that's lovely.* **2.** *mod.* attractive; excellent. □ *Mary's got herself a lovely new job.* □ *This is such a lovely day!*

love weed See LOCO WEED.

Love you! *exclam.* "You are great!" (Almost meaningless patter.) □ *See you around, Martin. Let's do lunch! Love ya! Bye!* □ *Nice talking to you, babe. Love you!*

low-down *n.* inside information. □ *Come on then; what's the real low-down?* □ *If it's the low-down you want, try somewhere else.*

lowdown **1.** *mod.* rotten; bad. □ *What a dirty, lowdown thing to do.* □ *You are a lowdown rat!* **2.** *n.* the facts or the gossip about something. □ *What's the lowdown on that funny statue in the park?* □ *Give me the lowdown on the project we just started.*

Lower Regions *n.* Hell. (Normally with *the*.) □ *It's as hot as the Lower Regions down here in the engine room.* □ *You can go straight to the Lower Regions as far as I care.*

L.S.D. AND **LSD** **1.** *n.* money. (The three units of currency—pounds, shillings and pence—used in Britain prior to the introduction of decimal currency in 1971. An abbreviation of the Latin *librae, solidi, denarii*, which loosely translates as this.) □ *I don't make*

enough L.S.D. to go on a trip like that! □ *It takes a lot of LSD to buy a car like that.* **2.** *n.* lysergic acid diethylamide, an hallucinogenic drug. (Initialism. A mainstay of the 1960s and 1970s drug culture.) □ *Is there still much L.S.D. around here these days?* □ *LSD isn't the problem it used to be, but it's far from all gone away.*

lubricated *mod.* intoxicated due to drink. □ *They are sufficiently lubricated for the night.* □ *He's not fit to talk to until he's lubricated a bit.*

lubrication *n.* alcoholic drink. □ *A little lubrication would help this party a lot.* □ *Wally has had a little too much lubrication.*

luck of the draw **1.** *n.* the result of chance. □ *Why do I always end up having to take the luck of the draw?* □ *The team was assembled by chance. It was just the luck of the draw that we could work so well together.* **2.** *n.* the absence of any choice. (Normally with *the*.) □ *I'm sorry but there you are; it's just the luck of the draw.* □ *Who can tell; the luck of the draw may go for you this time.*

lucky budgie *n.* a lucky person. (Ironic. Also a term of address.) □ *For once, I really felt I'd been a lucky budgie.* □ *Here was one lucky budgie, he thought.*

lucky dog AND **lucky sod** *n.* a lucky person, perhaps undeserving. (Also a term of address.) □ *You lucky dog!* □ *Max was a lucky sod because he won the football pools.*

lucky sod See LUCKY DOG.

lucy *n.* lysergic acid diethylamide, or LSD, an hallucinogenic drug. (From the Beatles' song, "Lucy in the Sky with Diamonds," which is believed to describe a TRIP with LSD.) □ *You can get some good lucy in this part of town.* □ *What does lucy cost around here?*

Lucy Locket *n.* a pocket. (Rhyming slang.) □ *Have you any change in your Lucy Locket?* □ *Get yer hand out of yer Lucy Locket, son.*

lug(hole) *n.* an ear. (LUG is a proper Scots word for "ear"; and is neither slang nor colloquial there.) □ *Pin back your lugholes, this is worth hearing!* □

He was grabbed by the lug and forcibly removed from the premises.

lumber gaff *n.* the room or house where a prostitute takes her clients. (Crude.) □ *There are a lot of lumber gaffs along this street.* □ *So this seedy little room, smelling of stale urine and rotten food, was what they called a lumber gaff. He wanted to be sick.*

lumber someone *vb.* to date someone on a regular basis. □ *How long have you been lumbering Victor now, Gladys?* □ *I've been lumbering Gladys for a couple of months.*

lumber someone or something with someone or something *vb. phr.* to encumber someone or something with someone or something inconvenient or unwanted. □ *It would seem they have lumbered us with this problem, like it or not.* □ *Don't try to lumber me with that character again ever!*

lummox AND **lommix; lummux** *n.* a heavy, awkward, stupid person. □ *He looks like a big lummox, but he can really dance.* □ *Bruno is what you would call a lummux—but not to his face, of course.*

lummux See LUMMOX.

Lummy! See LORD ALMIGHTY!

lump 1. *n.* an automobile engine. □ *He's spent hours out there trying to figure out what's wrong with the lump.* □ *There's something wrong; the lump won't turn over.* **2.** *n.* a stupid clod of a man. □ *I am not a lump! I am just sedate and pensive.* □ *Who is that lump leaning over the bar?* **3.** *n.* the informal employment and payment of casual construction workers, without benefit of income tax and other such deductions. (Normally with *the*.) □ *People working the lump think they're getting one over the tax people, but I'm not so sure.* □ *The lump is much less common than it used to be.*

lumpectomy *n.* the surgical removal of an unspecified tumour. □ *This looks like being another lumpectomy, I think.* □ *How many of these lumpectomies are you doing these days?*

Lump it! *exclam.* "Make the best of it!" (Compare with LIKE IT OR LUMP IT!) □ *Well, you can just lump it!* □ *Lump it! Drop dead!*

Lumpy Gravy AND **Plain and Gravy; Pudding and Gravy; Soup and Gravy** *n.* the Royal Navy. (Rhyming slang. Always with *the*.) □ *The Lumpy Gravy are always looking for the right kind of people.* □ *Paul's joined the Soup and Gravy.*

lurker 1. *n.* an unauthorised street trader. □ *There are always plenty of lurkers working in this area.* □ *You don't see so many lurkers nowadays.* **2.** *n.* an unwelcome or unpleasant person. (Offensive.) □ *Just get out of my sight, you filthy lurker!* □ *What a dirty lurker you are!*

lush 1. *n.* a drunkard; an alcoholic. □ *I was afraid of it for some time, but now I know. Tracy is a lush.* □ *There were four confirmed lushes at the party, but they all passed out pretty soon and so didn't bother us much.* **2.** *n.* beer. □ *Give my friend here a lush.* □ *How about a lush before you go, Charlie?* **3.** *mod.* delicious. □ *Who made this lush cake?* □ *This stuff is really lush.*

lush bint *n.* a good-looking or attractive girl or young woman. (Crude. See BINT.) □ *Now there's a real lush bint.* □ *Look at her, isn't she a lush bint?*

lush someone up *vb. phr.* to cause someone to become intoxicated. □ *Me? Lush you up? Naw!* □ *After we got him lushed up, it was easy to persuade him to sign the contract.*

luv See LOVE.

luvvy 1. *n.* an actor's term of address for another actor, regardless of sex. (Also a term of address.) □ *Can you ask all the luvvies to come up on stage now, Nigel?* □ *Well hello luvvy! How have you been?* **2.** See also LOVE.

L.Y.K.A.H. AND **LYKAH** *phr.* "leave your knickers at home." (Crude. An initialism sometimes written on love letters. Also an acronym.) □ *I'll be waiting there! L.Y.K.A.H.* □ *I can't wait. LYKAH!*

M

Mac 1. *n.* an Apple Macintosh™ computer. □ *Joe says the Mac is the greatest computer ever invented.* □ *Because he was using a Mac, Joe had no problem delivering his work on time, and making it look good, too.* **2.** *n.* a Scotsman. (Offensive.) □ *Don't call a Scotsman a "Mac," please. It is sometimes considered offensive and racist.* □ *He said he was not a racist, he just hated this particular Mac!*

macaroni *n.* an Italian person. (Offensive.) □ *Y'know, Otto, if you call an Italian a macaroni, he's likely to get nasty.* □ *Why can you not be polite to macaronis?*

machine *vb.* to sew using a sewing machine. □ *It won't take long to machine these seams.* □ *My mother used to sit over her sewing machine, machining away all day long.*

machinery *n.* drug-injecting equipment. □ *Have you any machinery? I need a fix.* □ *There it was; all her machinery was laid out on the table for everyone to see.*

mac(k) *n.* a mackintosh raincoat. □ *You're not going out in that rain without your mack, are you?* □ *I flung on my mac and ran through the downpour.*

Maconochie *n.* the stomach. (Maconochie was a supplier of tinned stew to the British Army in the 19th century.) □ *I think large Maconochies are most unsightly.* □ *Fred's at home today with a bad pain in his Maconochie.*

madam 1. *n.* the female owner or keeper of a brothel. (Crude.) □ *The madam was caught in a sting operation.* □ *The cops led the madam away, followed by a parade of you-know-whats.* **2.** *n.* a conceited young woman. □ *Why are you always such a madam, Zoe?* □ *Just watch you lip, madam!*

mad (keen) on someone or something *mod.* very enthusiastic about someone or something. □ *I'm mad keen on Wagner.* □ *Samantha's mad on horses, but I'm sure she'll grow out of that as she grows up.*

mad money 1. *n.* money a girl takes with her on a date, in case she falls out with her companion and has to make her own way home. □ *Don't forget your mad money, Maddy!* □ *If you still feel the need for mad money after going with him this long, what's wrong?* **2.** *n.* money saved up for spending recklessly on a good time while on holiday, etc. □ *I've got my mad money and I'm all ready to go!* □ *Susan managed to blow all her mad money on her first day in Majorca.*

mad nurse *n.* a nurse who cares for insane people. □ *I think we're going to need a mad nurse here before much longer.* □ *Nurses who work at the asylum don't like being called mad nurses, Willy.*

mag *n.* magazine. □ *I stopped and got a computer mag.* □ *I've seen your face in the mags, haven't I?*

Maggie *n.* the £1 coin. (Given this name when introduced in 1983 during the premiership of Margaret Thatcher, on the grounds that it (and she) was "hard, rough at the edges and pretending to be a sovereign." The sovereign was a former British gold coin with a face value of £1.) □ *It's three Maggies for that, mate.* □ *Will you take a Maggie?*

maggot 1. *n.* a low and wretched person; a vile person. □ *You maggot! Take your hands off me!* □ *Only a maggot would do something like that.* **2.** *n.* money. □ *How much maggot do you need, then?* □ *Sorry, I can't afford it. I've no maggot.*

maggoty *mod.* very intoxicated due to drink. (Irish usage.) □ *They were both so maggoty all they could do was lie there and snore.* □ *Joe and Arthur kept on knocking them back till they were both maggoty.*

magic *mod.* wonderful or perfect. □ *Great, that's magic!* □ *It would be magic if you could do that.*

magic bus See BLACK MARIA.

magic mushrooms AND **sacred mushrooms** *n.* mushrooms of the genus *Psilocybe*, which cause visions or hallucinations when eaten. □ *Magic mushrooms are okay because they are natural, or something like that.* □ *This is the so-called "sacred mushroom," named for its use in the Aztec rituals of pre-Columbian Mexico.*

make 1. *vb.* to arrive at a place; to cover a distance. □ *Can we make Bristol by sunset?* □ *We made forty miles in thirty minutes.* **2.** *vb.* to achieve a specific speed. □ *See if this thing can make ninety.* □ *This buggy will make twice the speed of the old one.*

make a baby AND **make babies** *vb. phr.* to have sexual intercourse. (Crude. A euphemism.) □ *One look and he knew she had already been making babies that evening.* □ *There were a couple of teenagers in the back room, making a baby.*

make a bad fist of something *vb. phr.* to perform something badly. □ *I'm afraid I've make a bad fist of this.* □ *Don't make a bad fist of this one, too.*

make a bitch of something *vb. phr.* to spoil or ruin something. □ *Why must you make a bitch of everything?* □ *I suppose we've made a bitch of it again, as usual?*

make a bog of something *vb. phr.* to make a mess or muddle of something. □ *Well, we've really made a bog of things this time.* □ *Why did we let Otto*

make such a make a bog of everything?

make a bomb AND **make a bundle; make a pile** *vb. phr.* to make a great deal of money. (Compare with BUNDLE.) □ *I made a bomb out of that last deal.* □ *I want to buy a few stocks and make a pile in a few years.*

make a boo-boo *vb. phr.* to make an error. (Compare with BOO-BOO.) □ *Everybody makes a boo-boo every now and then.* □ *Whoops! I made a boo-boo.*

make a bundle See MAKE A BOMB.

make a dead set at someone *vb. phr.* to attempt to attract or interest someone romantically or sexually. □ *Charles has been making a dead set at Cynthia.* □ *If you must make a dead set at someone, try Robert.*

make a dead set at something *vb. phr.* to attack with vigour and determination. □ *The guerrillas make a dead set at capturing the outpost.* □ *"We're making a dead set at beating them in the field this time," said the general.*

make a fuck-up of something *vb. phr.* to make a complete mess of something. (Taboo.) □ *You make a fuck-up of everything you touch!* □ *If I make a fuck-up of something else I'll be fired.*

make a good fist *vb. phr.* to do a good job. □ *This time, I must make a good fist of things.* □ *If you can make a good fist, you'll get rewarded.*

make a go of something *vb. phr.* to succeed at something. □ *It's good to see you're making a go of this opportunity.* □ *Try to make a go of things this time, John.*

make a killing *vb. phr.* to make an huge profit; to become an enormous success. □ *The company made a killing from the sale of its subsidiary.* □ *I wanted to make a killing as a banker, but it didn't work out.*

make a meal (out) of something *vb. phr.* to make a major issue out of something. □ *Don't make a meal out of this but just get on with it.* □ *Why must they all make a meal of things like this?*

make a monkey of someone *vb. phr.* to make a fool of someone; to make someone look absurd. □ *You're not* going to make a monkey of me. □ Making a monkey of someone is not funny.

make a muck of something AND **make a poor fist of something** vb. phr. to bungle or to do a poor job of something. □ I hope I don't make a muck of things this time. □ I really made a poor fist of this before.

make a mull of something vb. phr. to perform badly. □ Please try not to make a mull of this as you seem to have of everything else. □ Why do I always make a mull of these things?

make a pass at someone vb. phr. to make a sexual advance at someone. □ "Men seldom make passes at girls who wear glasses."—Dorothy Parker. □ Are you making a pass at me?

make a pig of oneself vb. phr. to overeat; to take more of something than anyone else gets; to be selfish. □ Please don't make a pig out of yourself. □ I have a tendency to make a pig of myself at affairs like this.

make a pile See MAKE A BUNDLE.

make a poor fist of it See MAKE A MUCK OF IT.

make a stink (about someone or something) See RAISE A STINK (ABOUT SOMEONE OR SOMETHING).

make at someone vb. phr. to lunge towards someone. □ He make at me! □ Don't you make at me like that! Hands off!

make babies See MAKE A BABY.

make for somewhere vb. phr. to set out for somewhere; to run or travel to somewhere. □ Martin made for Liverpool when he heard the rozzers in the Big Smoke were after him. □ Barlowe made for the stairs, but two shots rang out, and he knew it was all over for Mary.

make good See MAKE IT.

make it AND **make good** vb. phr. to achieve one's goals. (Compare with MAKE IT BIG.) □ I can see by looking around this room that you have really made it. □ I hope I make good someday. But if not, I tried.

make it big vb. phr. to become very successful, especially financially. (Compare with MAKE IT.) □ I always

knew that someday I would make it big. □ My brother made it big, but it has just led to tax problems.

make it hot for someone vb. phr. to make things difficult for someone; to put someone under pressure. □ The rozzers were making it hot for him, so he went to ground. □ The boss is making it a little hot for me, so I had better get to work on time.

Make it snappy! exclam. "Hurry up!"; "Make it fast!" □ We're late, Tracy. Make it snappy! □ Make it snappy, Fred. The cops are coming up the path right now.

make like someone or something vb. phr. to behave like someone or something that one is not. □ Why don't you make like a bunny and run away? Skedaddle! □ Would you please make like a butler and hold the door open for me?

make mincemeat out of someone or something vb. phr. to beat someone or something to a pulp; to destroy someone or something utterly. □ The puppy made mincemeat of my newspaper. □ They threatened to make mincemeat of me.

make noises about something vb. phr. to talk about or hint at something. □ I'll make noises about that, just to see their reaction. □ He made noises about that situation, but got nowhere.

Make no mistake (about it)! sent. "There is no doubt about this." □ Make no mistake! This is the real thing. □ This is a very serious matter, make no mistake about it.

make one's hair curl vb. phr. to be greatly frightened. □ He told a wonderful ghost story that was terrifying enough to make your hair curl. □ I don't intend to go through any experience that makes my hair curl like that again, ever!

make polite noises vb. phr. to say something that is polite or soothing but without meaning it. □ Do we have to make polite noises all over again? □ Well, they're making polite noises, but everyone knows it's hopeless.

make someone up to something vb. phr. to promote someone in rank. □

Stewart has been made up to Captain. □ *We need to make a number of privates up to corporal very soon, sir.*

make the running *vb. phr.* to take charge; to establish the pace. □ *Are you making the running here?* □ *We need someone to make the running.*

make tracks *vb. phr.* to move away rapidly. □ *I've got to make tracks for home now.* □ *Let's make tracks. We've got to get to Manchester this morning.*

make waves *vb. phr.* to disturb or upset the normal or established way of doing things. □ *Just relax. Don't make waves.* □ *If you make waves too much around here, you won't last long.*

malarkey *n.* nonsense; absurd exaggeration. □ *Don't come that old malarkey.* □ *What ridiculous malarkey!*

male chauvinist pig *n.* a male who acts in a superior, condescending or aggressive way toward women. (From the woman's liberation movements of the 1970s. Now dated.) □ *The guy is just a male chauvinist pig, and he'll never change.* □ *Don't you just hate walking through a room filled with male chauvinist pigs and just knowing what they are thinking about you?*

malkie *n.* a razor, used as a weapon. (Scots usage. Rhyming slang, linked as follows: malkie = [Malcolm Frazer] ≈ razor.) □ *If you come any nearer I'm cut you with this malkie here!* □ *He got out his malkie and held it up for all to see.*

malkin 1. *n.* a careless or untidy woman. □ *Why is that malkin walking through our office?* □ *I'm afraid I do not know the malkin.* **2.** *n.* a cat. □ *Get that malkin out of the refrigerator!* □ *Is this your malkin here? What's he called?* **3.** *n.* a hare. □ *It's easy to confuse a malkin with a rabbit if you don't know these things.* □ *There are some malkins on our land.*

Malta dog *n.* a picturesque name for diarrhoea or similar, inflicted upon a visitor to a foreign land.(Maltese variety.) □ *I had a little touch of the Malta dog the second day, but other than that we had a wonderful time.* □ *Most people blame the Malta dog on the water.*

mam 1. *n.* mother. (Also a term of address.) □ *What does yer mam want with me?* □ *All right mam, I'll do it.* **2.** *n.* a lesbian. (Crude.) □ *Why does she work so hard to look like a mam?* □ *Who's the mam in the cowboy boots?*

mama *n.* a promiscuous woman. (Crude.) □ *That one's a real mama!* □ *Where are all the mamas around this town?*

mammy 1. *n.* mother. □ *Will your mammy let you out to the pub tonight?* □ *I'd better ask me mammy.* **2.** *n.* wine. (Rhyming slang, linked as follows: mammy [mine] ≈ wine.) □ *Oh, I like a glass of mammy now and again.* □ *Mrs Struther had one little glass of mammy and she was high as a kite!*

man and wife *n.* a knife. (Rhyming slang.) □ *Bring your man and wife over here and cut this loose.* □ *What are you carrying a man and wife for?*

man-drag *n.* men's clothing worn by women. (Crude.) □ *I don't understand why a woman would want to wear man-drag.* □ *I see Pauline is into man drag now.*

manhole cover *n.* a sanitary towel. (Taboo.) □ *Why do I need manhole covers? Why do you think?* □ *I've got a manhole cover on, you pig!*

man in the street *n.* the common man; an average person selected at random. □ *But what does the man in the street think about all this?* □ *The man in the street really doesn't care about most of what you think is important.*

manky 1. *mod.* naughty. (North of England usage.) □ *You are a manky pig!* □ *What a manky thing to do.* **2.** *mod.* dirty or disgusting. □ *What a manky day!* □ *Gosh, that is really manky!*

manor 1. *n.* the territory that an individual police station is responsible for. □ *The newly-appointed Station Superintendent went out to look over his new manor.* □ *The manor needed proper policing and was about to get it.* **2.** *n.* one's local area, which one knows and where one is known. □ *Yes, I think we can say this village is my manor; I've lived here all my days.* □ *It's good to come home to one's manor after travelling around the world.*

man-sized job *mod.* a considerable or difficult task; one that requires a proper man to complete. □ *This is a man-sized job. We better get a real man to do it.* □ *When there's a man-size job to be done, send for Smith & Son, the men who can.*

man upstairs *n.* God. (Always with the.) □ *Whatever you do, the man upstairs will know.* □ *What would the man upstairs expect you to do in these circumstances?*

marbles 1. *n.* money; one's income. □ *Oh, Mr Big's got plenty of marbles all right.* □ *Yes, your marbles are big enough to allow financing of this purchase.* **2.** *n.* sanity; common sense. □ *The problem with marbles is that so few have any.* □ *Anyone with any marbles worth mentioning should be able to do that, Otto.* **3.** *n.* the testicles. (Taboo. Normally with *the* and in the plural.) □ *Thud, right in the marbles. Ye gods, it hurt!* □ *He turned sideways to protect his marbles.*

marching orders 1. *n.* a military order to march. □ *Expect marching orders soon.* □ *Right, we've got our marching orders.* **2.** *n.* a job dismissal; the sack. □ *If you get your marching orders, phone this number.* □ *I've been given my marching orders.* **3.** *n.* a direction to depart. □ *The boss has given me my marching orders.* □ *If you got your marching orders what would you do?*

mardie *n.* an effeminate man or one who is ineffectual or weak-willed. (Crude.) □ *You must admit, he looks like a mardie.* □ *Why does he have to behave so like a mardie?*

mardy 1. *mod.* bad-tempered. □ *What a mardy person she can be.* □ *Do what I ask or I'll get really mardy with you.* **2.** *mod.* spoiled or over-indulged. □ *What a mardy little boy he is!* □ *Joan's so mardy, always ruining things for others.* **3.** *mod.* marred or ruined. □ *You really are mardy, you know.* □ *This is a really mardy mess.*

mare See COW.

marg *n.* margarine. □ *They say marg is better than butter, but I much prefer butter.* □ *Marg helps keep you fit.*

mark 1. *n.* a DUPE; a victim selected for a theft or a swindle. (Underworld.) □ *I bumped the mark on the shoulder, and he put his hand on his wallet just like always.* □ *We picked the marks out of the crowd in front of the shop window.* **2.** *n.* someone who gives generously to tramps, beggars, etc. □ *I think these tramps know I'm an easy mark.* □ *Once they think you're a mark, they'll never leave you in peace.*

mark someone's card 1. *vb. phr.* to warn someone off. (From the action of a soccer referee who records a breach of rules in the card which each professional player must carry.) □ *I'm marking your card; don't come back.* □ *He marked my card, I don't really know why.* **2.** *vb. phr.* to tell someone what they want to know. □ *All right, I'll mark your card. Buy shares in Acme Company.* □ *I tried to mark his card as he wanted, but I don't think he got the point.*

mark time *vb. phr.* to wait; to do nothing but wait. □ *I'll just mark time till things get better.* □ *Do you expect me just to stand here and mark time?*

marleys *n.* haemorrhoids. (Rhyming slang, linked as follows: Marley [Tile]s ≈ [piles] = haemorrhoids. "Marley Tiles™" is a brand of thermoplastic tiles.) □ *Me marleys is giving me gyp again.* □ *I'll have to get these marleys seen to.*

marmalise *vb.* to destroy utterly; to beat up severely. (Scots usage.) □ *See you? Ah'll marmalise you!* □ *They lads aw picked on ma wee Shuggie and marmalised him. (These lads all picked on my little Hugh and beat him to a pulp.)*

Marquess of Lorn *n.* an erection. (Taboo. Rhyming slang, linked as follows: Marquess of Lorn ≈ [horn] = erection.) □ *Here I come, complete with the Marquess of Lorn!* □ *Fear not my lovely, I shall have a Marquess of Lorn for you!*

marriage lines *n.* a marriage certificate. □ *He wants to see our marriage lines.* □ *I don't know where we keep our marriage lines.*

marry above oneself *vb. phr.* to marry someone of higher class than oneself.

□ *If you marry above yourself you'll regret it all your life, my lad.* □ *He's married above himself, of course.*

marry below oneself See MARRY BENEATH ONESELF.

marry beneath oneself AND **marry below oneself** *vb. phr.* to marry someone believed to be of lower class than oneself. □ *She's married beneath herself, of course.* □ *If you marry below yourself you'll regret it all your life, my girl.*

Mars Bar *n.* a scar. (Rhyming slang. Scots usage.) □ *That's a nasty Mars Bar, Jimmy.* □ *Some hard case with a malkie gave me that Mars Bar last year. (Some thug with a razor gave me that scar last year.)*

Mary Ann *n.* an effeminate man; a passive male homosexual. (Crude.) □ *So what if he's a Mary Ann? He can still vote, can't he?* □ *I hear that you-know-who is a Mary Ann.*

Mary Blane *n.* a train. (Rhyming slang.) □ *Get the Mary Blane—that's the easy way to get there from here.* □ *There are Mary Blanes passing here all the time.*

Mary J See MARY JANE.

Maryjane See MARY JANE.

Mary Jane AND **Mary J; Maryjane; Mary Warner; Mary Jane Warner** *n.* marijuana. (All are variants of the literal translation of the originally-Spanish word *marijuana*, which can, wrongly, be translated to mean "Mary Jane" in that language. There are also elements of hobson-jobson present here.) □ *I can't live another day without Mary Jane!* □ *I certainly could dance with Mary J about now.*

Mary Jane Warner See MARY JANE.

Mary Warner See MARY JANE.

marzipan *n.* a material used as bodywork filler on cars that removes—or rather, hides—the effects of accidents or corrosion. □ *Well, I'd say you've bought yourself some very expensive marzipan here.* □ *Marzipan, the cowboy car bodyworker's friend.*

mash *n.* mashed potatoes. □ *I like mash with my bangers.* □ *Pass me the mash, mum.*

masses *mod.* lots; plenty. □ *When I have spaghetti, I just love masses of*

noodles. □ *My uncle has just masses and masses of money.*

massy *mod.* massive, solid or bulky. □ *A truly massy man stood in the lobby.* □ *I don't want to live in such a massy house as this.*

mate *n.* a friend. (Also a term of address.) □ *The two mates left the pub, each one preventing the other from falling over.* □ *Who's your mate, Albert?*

matelot *n.* a sailor. □ *Two ships had docked that afternoon and now two groups of matelots were fighting outside the pub.* □ *If you want to die rich, fat and happy, don't become a matelot.*

matey 1. *mod.* friendly; sociable. (Sometimes used sarcastically.) □ *They're all real matey now, of course.* □ *I don't see what there is to be matey about, actually.* **2.** *n.* a friend. (Often used sarcastically.) □ *Come on matey! You can do better than that.* □ *You'd better do better than that, matey!*

maths *n.* mathematics. □ *Simon is very good at maths.* □ *He came first in maths at school.*

matiness *n.* friendliness. □ *I don't know I like all this matiness.* □ *He thinks too much matiness is unhealthy.*

matric 1. *n.* matriculation. □ *Matric is first week of term.* □ *Matric is necessary before you can attend degree examinations.* **2.** *vb.* to matriculate. □ *I've come to matric.* □ *Everyone matrics during the first week at university.*

mature *mod.* obscene; pornographic. (A euphemism. Crude.) □ *Otto has a large collection of mature videos and magazines.* □ *Do you have any mature videos for sale?*

maud *n.* a male prostitute. (Crude.) □ *There are a lot of mauds around here in the centre of town.* □ *So this maud comes up to me and acts like he's met me before.*

mauley 1. *n.* a fist; a hand. □ *Get your mauley off my car!* □ *If your mauleys so much as brush by my jacket again, you are finished!* **2.** *n.* handwriting; a signature. □ *Try to write in a reasonable mauley if you can.* □ *Well, I could read his mauley—just about.*

mau-mau *n.* a black person. (Offensive. The Mau-Mau was a terrorist liberation organisation in Kenya during the 1950s.) □ *He said he was not a racist, he just hated mau-maus!* □ *Don't call black people mau-maus, please. It is very offensive and racist.*

maxi 1. *mod.* large; major; significant. (Normally used as a prefix.) □ *I have a maxi-problem you can maybe help me with.* □ *He's maxi-important in advertising.* **2.** *n.* a maxi-skirt or dress. □ Q: *Don't I look pretty good in a maxi?* A: *Well Bruno, you do look better than you do in a mini.* □ *Are maxis coming back into fashion?*

max someone *vb.* to confuse someone. □ *Well, you've maxed me.* □ *I suspect you've maxed yourself into the bargain.*

me *mod.* my. (Eye-dialect. Typical spoken English. Used in writing only for effect. Used in the examples of this dictionary.) □ *Meet me wife.* □ *Me house is along that road.*

meal-ticket *n.* someone regarded by another as their main or sole financial support. □ *She certainly sees him as her meal-ticket.* □ *I'd like to think I'm more than just a meal-ticket to you, Lavinia.*

mean business *vb. phr.* to be in earnest. □ *Stop laughing! I mean business.* □ *I could tell from the look on her face that she meant business.*

meany AND **meanie 1.** *n.* a small-minded or mean person; someone reluctant to pay what is due. □ *Come on! Don't be such a meany! Pay up.* □ *I don't want to be a meany, but I don't think we got value for money and don't think I should pay.* **2.** *n.* a spoilsport. □ *Come on! Don't be such a meany! We were only having fun.* □ *I don't want to be a meanie, but if you don't turn down that radio, I'll take it away.*

measly *mod.* unacceptable; inferior in quality. □ *That sort of behaviour is just measly, you know.* □ *Sorry, you're too measly for me.*

measure one's length *vb. phr.* to fall flat upon the ground or floor by accident. □ *It was just a gentle tap, but still he measured his length.* □ *If you measure your length like that, something is wrong.*

meat 1. *n.* the female body, considered sexually by the male. (Taboo.) □ *I think that's one piece of meat I would like to investigate more closely.* □ *Hands off! She's my meat!* **2.** *n.* the sexual organ, either male or female. (Taboo.) □ *People who exhibit their meat for money are little better than prostitutes!* □ *Everywhere there was meat clearly on display. That was to be expected in a nudist camp.*

meat dagger See BEEF BAYONET.

meathead *n.* a stupid oaf. □ *Don't call him a meathead. He does his best.* □ *Is this meathead bothering you, miss?*

meathooks *n.* the hands. □ *Get your meathooks off my car!* □ *If your meathooks so much as brush by my jacket again, you are finished!*

meat injection See BIT OF MEAT.

meat-rack *n.* a public place where prostitutes gather to seek clients. (Crude.) □ *The area around the railway station is often the local meat-rack.* □ *Clare's taken to hanging around that meat-rack.*

meat wagon *n.* an ambulance. □ *The meat wagon showed up just as they were pulling what was left of Marty out of what was left of her car.* □ *When the meat wagon stops at all the traffic lights on the way to the hospital, you know somebody's snuffed it.*

meat-wagon See BLACK MARIA.

meaty *mod.* obscene. □ *The movie was too meaty for me.* □ *How would you know what's meaty and what's not?*

medic *n.* a medical doctor. □ *I went to the surgery, but the medic wasn't in.* □ *That medic wouldn't renew my prescription.*

meet *n.* a meeting or an appointment. (Mostly underworld.) □ *If this meet works out, we could net a cool million.* □ *What time is the meet?*

meeting of minds *n.* a consensus; an agreement. □ *At last we've reached a meeting of minds.* □ *This so-called meeting of minds is nothing more than a truce.*

meet up with someone *vb. phr.* to meet with someone. □ *I met up with Alan in London yesterday.* □ *If we can meet up with him at the hotel later, that would be good.*

meet up with something *vb. phr.* to link or connect something (such as roads or rivers) together. □ *That tributary meets up with the Thames about here.* □ *This is where the two motorways meet up with each other.*

mega *mod.* overpowering; huge. □ *Some mega beast boogied down to the front of the auditorium and started screaming.* □ *But the music was real mega, y'know.*

mellow *mod.* slightly intoxicated due to drink or drugs. □ *I got mellow and stopped drinking right there.* □ *I'm only mellow, but you drive anyway.*

mellow out **1.** *vb. phr.* to calm down; to get less angry. □ *When you mellow out, maybe we can talk.* □ *Come on, man, mellow out!* **2.** *vb. phr.* to become generally more relaxed; to grow less contentious. □ *Gary was nearly forty before he started to mellow out a little and take life less seriously.* □ *After his illness, he mellowed out and seemed more glad to be alive.*

men in grey suits *n.* those Establishment figures who are rarely if ever seen in the light of day but who supposedly control events. (Normally with *the.*) □ *Supposedly the men in grey suits are like puppeteers who manipulate things from behind the scenes, pulling at the rest of us upon strings.* □ *When the men in grey suits arrived to see the prime minister, we knew his time was nearly over.*

meno *mod.* menopausal. (Crude.) □ *A warning: Susan's meno this week.* □ *Meno women can be temperamental.*

mental **1.** *mod.* crazy, uncontrollable or eccentric. □ *You're mental if you think I care.* □ *Frank's mental. Really odd.* **2.** *mod.* insane; crazy. (Offensive.) □ *The poor girl's mental. Leave her alone.* □ *Everybody in this ward is mental.* **3.** *n.* an insane or crazy person. (Offensive.) □ *He's a mental. He'll need some help.* □ *Who doesn't need help? Mentals are normal about that.* **4.** *n.* eccentric or ex-cessively enthusiastic. (Offensive.) □ *He's mental about heavy metal music.* □ *Joe's more than just enthusiastic about sport, he's mental about it.*

me old cock *phr.* a term of friendly address to a male acquaintance. □ *Come on, me old cock! I'll buy you a pint.* □ *I told me old cock here not to worry. It'll be all right in the end.*

mercy blow-through AND **mercy bucket(s)** *phr.* "thank you very much." (From the French *merci beaucoup*, which means this. An example of hobson-jobson.) □ *Mercy buckets! That was great!* □ *If she had just said so much as "mercy blow-through" it would have been nice.*

mercy bucket(s) See MERCY BLOW-THROUGH.

mere bagatelle *n.* a trivial or unimportant thing. □ *It was not of any significance, a mere bagatelle.* □ *If it's mere bagatelle, why are you so worked up about it?*

merger-mania *n.* an perceived need for companies to merge with one another. (Stock markets and journalese.) □ *Merger-mania is in the news again tonight with Apple's bid to take over IBM.* □ *The market meltdown put an end to merger-mania.*

merries *n.* fairground rides. (Often with *the.*) □ *Harry always likes going on the merries.* □ *I see there are some new merries this year.*

merry *mod.* somewhat intoxicated due to drink. □ *I felt a little merry, but that didn't stop me from having more.* □ *Tracy gets a little merry after a drink or two.*

merry dancers *n.* the aurora borealis or northern lights. (Normally with *the.*) □ *Have you ever seen the merry dancers?* □ *The merry dancers can be spectacular, especially from Northern Scotland.*

Merry Widow *n.* champagne. (A pun on the name of the leading brand, *Veuve Clicquot*, as *veuve* means "widow" in French; there is also a second pun on Lehar's opera, the *Merry Widow.* Always with *the.*) □ *My dad sent us a bottle of the Merry Widow.* □ *I could live on nothing but Merry Widow.*

mess 1. *n.* a hopelessly ineffectual person. □ *Harry has turned into a mess.* □ *He's a total mess!* **2.** *n.* excreta. (Crude. Usually with *a*.) □ *There's another dog mess on the lawn again this morning.* □ *There's a mess in Jimmy's nappy, Mum.*

mess about (with someone) See MESS AROUND (WITH SOMEONE).

mess about (with something) See MESS AROUND (WITH SOMETHING).

mess around (with someone) AND **mess about (with someone); monkey around (with someone) 1.** *vb. phr.* to waste someone's time. □ *Don't mess around with me. Just answer the question, if you please.* □ *I don't have the time for this. Stop messing around.* **2.** *vb. phr.* to waste time with someone else. □ *I was messing around with John.* □ *John and I were just monkeying around.*

mess around (with something) AND **mess about (with something); monkey around (with something)** *vb. phr.* to play with or interfere with something. □ *Don't mess around with the ashtray.* □ *You'll break it if you don't stop monkeying around with it.*

mess someone or something up *vb. phr.* to confuse, distract or disorder someone or something. (See MESS UP.) □ *You messed me up a little bit, but I know you didn't mean to bump into me.* □ *Who messed up this place?*

mess up *vb. phr.* to make an error; to do something wrong. □ *I hope I don't mess up the quiz.* □ *You really messed this one up!*

Met 1. *n.* the Metropolitan Police, London's police force. (Always with *the*.) □ *The Met are after me!* □ *Get away, get away! The Met are outside!* **2.** *n.* the Meteorological Office, which issues the official weather forecasts daily. (Always with *the*.) □ *What does the Met say the weather is going to be?* □ *Met forecasts are usually quite good.*

meter maid *n.* a female traffic warden or parking-meter attendant. □ *Meter maids must get insulted by drivers all day long.* □ *I was only one minute over, but still the meter maid issued the ticket.*

meth 1. *n.* methamphetamine. □ *Usually meth is injected, giving it an almost immediate effect.* □ *Meth comes in little glass tubes.* **2.** *n.* methadone. □ *Sometimes meth means methadone, a drug used in drug treatment.* □ *Jerry gets meth from a clinic in the city.*

meths *n.* methylated spirits. □ *This is where they come to drink meths.* □ *Meths is really a form of poison.*

meths drinker *n.* a tramp or degenerate of some sort, who drinks methylated spirits. □ *This is where the meths drinkers gather.* □ *Meths drinkers are a serious problem around this part of town.*

Metropolis *n.* London. (Normally with *the*.) □ *He likes it in the Metropolis, where he's anonymous.* □ *The Metropolis is where everything happens.*

Mick((e)y) 1. *n.* a Roman Catholic. (Offensive. Also a term of address.) □ *When he said there was a church for Mickies near his home, I knew there could be a problem.* □ *He seems to think I'm a Mick, as he puts it. Well, if so, so what?* **2.** *n.* an Irishman. (Offensive.) □ *He said he was not a racist, he just hated this particular Mickey!* □ *Don't call an Irishman a Micky, please. It is very offensive and racist.*

Mick(e)y (Finn) 1. *n.* a drink adulterated with a narcotic such as chloral hydrate. (Underworld.) □ *He slipped her a Mickey Finn, but she switched glasses.* □ *Once you've had a Mickey, you'll never forget it—provided you can remember it in the first place.* **2.** *n.* a narcotic such as chloral hydrate that is sometimes put in drinks to knock people out. (Underworld.) □ *There was a Mickey Finn in this drink, wasn't there?* □ *Now where would I get a Micky Finn?*

Mick(e)y Mouse 1. *n.* a house, particularly a small one. (Rhyming slang. Probably from the world-famous mouse character by the same name, owned by The Walt Disney™ Company.) □ *This is silly little mickey mouse.* □ *This mickey mouse may be small, but it's all mine.* **2.** *vb. phr.* to have a conversation with yourself. □ *Look at him; I think* *he's Mickey Mousing!* □ *Don't Micky Mouse! People will think you're crazy!*

mick(e)y-mouse-money See FUNNY-MONEY.

Mickey Rooney *n.* macaroni. (Hobson-jobson.) □ *I can't stand Mickey Rooney!* □ *A nice plate of Mickey Rooney would go down well right now.*

Mick Jagger *n.* lager. (Rhyming slang. Scots usage.) □ *Ah could go a pint or three of the old Mick Jagger.* □ *The Mick Jagger was fair flowing that evening, I can tell you.*

middlebrow 1. *mod.* having to do with average or mediocre intellect or average or mediocre tastes. (Between HIGHBROW and LOWBROW.) □ *No, he's not lowbrow but not highbrow either; just middlebrow.* □ *There are some who look down on middlebrow interests as trivial.* **2.** *n.* a person of average or mediocre intellect; a person of average or mediocre tastes. (Between HIGHBROW and LOWBROW.) □ *No, he's not a lowbrow but he's not a highbrow either; just a middlebrow.* □ *There are some who look down on middlebrows as trivial people.*

Middle for diddle! *exclam.* a call to choose who is first to play in a game of darts by throwing one dart as close as possible to the centre of a board. □ *Right, let's play now. Middle for diddle?* □ *Middle for diddle! You throw first!*

middle leg AND **third leg** *n.* the male sexual organ. (Taboo.) □ *He made some joke about a middle leg, but nobody laughed.* □ *The streaker covered his middle leg as he ran across the cricket field. What sort of streak is that?*

middle of nowhere *n.* an isolated place. □ *I don't want to stay out here in the middle of nowhere.* □ *I was stranded in the middle of nowhere for an hour with a punctured tyre.*

midi 1. *mod.* having to do with a mid-length woman's garment. □ *This midi style is out, and the mini is back in.* □ *The midi length was just transitional. Who decides on these things anyway?* **2.** *n.* a mid-length woman's garment. □ *Shall I wear my midi, or is it too hot?* □ *The midi is okay.*

mike 1. *n.* a period spent not working. □ *Oh, him? He's having some mike.* □ *Mike's on the mike again.* **2.** *vb.* to avoid work. □ *Mike goes to great lengths to mike, of course.* □ *Mike your work just once more and you're out. Is that clear?* **3.** *n.* a microphone. □ *Can we have another mike over here? This one's not working.* □ *If the singer had held the mike any closer it would have been inside her mouth.* **4.** *n.* a microscope. □ *At the end of the bench stood the large mike the scientist used to view samples.* □ *Come here and look at this through the mike!* **5.** *vb.* to hang about hopefully. □ *Oh, he's just miking.* □ *Don't waste your time miking; nothing ever happens here.*

mild and bitter *n.* a mixture of mild beer and bitter beer. □ *Can I have mild and bitter, please?* □ *I do like this mild and bitter they have in here.*

mileage *n.* additional profit or advantage. □ *I think there's still a lot of mileage in this deal.* □ *He found another million or two of mileage in it, you know.*

miles away *phr.* "day-dreaming"; "lost in thought." □ *Sorry, I was miles away. What did you say?* □ *He did not hear you as he's miles away.*

milk-bar *n.* the female breasts. (Crude. Normally with *the* and in the plural.) □ *There she was, bold as brass, with her milk-bar on full display.* □ *"Nice milk-bars," he thought, as she walked past.*

milkie AND **milko** *n.* a milkman. □ *The milkie delivers here about five every morning.* □ *We don't have a milko where we are.*

milk-jug *n.* a dupe. (Rhyming slang, linked as follows: milk-jug ≈ [mug] = dupe.) □ *I think we've found the milk-jug we need, boss.* □ *I'm not sure you'll be glad you chose Otto for milk-jug when he eventually finds out.*

milk-jugs See JUGS.

milko See MILKIE.

mill *n.* an automobile engine. □ *There's something wrong; the mill won't turn over.* □ *He's spent hours out there trying to figure out what's wrong with the mill.*

mince pie *n.* an eye. (Rhyming slang.) □ *He looked me right in the mince pie and assured me again that he was telling the truth.* □ *I think there's something wrong with me mince pies.*

mind-bender *n.* something that can alter one's state of mind. □ *Now here's a terrific mind-bender of an idea to chew over.* □ *That stuff's a real mind-bender, especially if swallowed.*

mind-bending *mod.* having to do with altering one's state of mind. □ *That particular problem is truly mind-bending in various ways.* □ *If you take mind-bending drugs, you're dicing with real danger.*

mind-blowing *mod.* amazing; unbelievable. □ *That's fantastic! It's mind-blowing!* □ *This is really mind-blowing news you bring us!*

Mind boggles! *exclam.* "This is amazing!"; "This is unbelievable!" (Always with *the*.) □ *Oh boy! The mind boggles!* □ *The mind boggles! I don't know how that's possible!*

minder 1. *n.* a bodyguard, particularly of a criminal. □ *Mr Big is tiny, but his minder is huge.* □ *I don't think you want to meet his minder.* **2.** *n.* a pickpocket's assistant, who keeps the victim occupied and unaware. □ *Look how they operate! I'm sure that guy's the minder.* □ *The police caught the minder, but the dip got away.* **3.** *n.* a prostitute's protector or bodyguard. □ *Zoe's minder is right over there.* □ *That six foot six guy? He's her minder?* **4.** See also BOUNCER.

ming 1. *vb.* to stink. (Scots usage.) □ *The whole house was minging by this time.* □ *You would not ming nearly so much if you just washed occasionally.* **2.** *n.* a stink. (Scots usage.) □ *Where on earth is that ming coming from?* □ *I don't think I can take too much of this ming.*

minge *n.* the female sexual organ. (Taboo.) □ *The door to the shower room flew open and the girl screamed, trying to cover her minge.* □ *If your dresses get any shorter, we'll all be able to see your minge.*

minging *mod.* stinking. (Scots usage.) □ *Oh my, what a minging mess.* □ *I don't know what had been going on but the whole place was minging.*

mini 1. *mod.* small; miniature; minor; trivial. (Normally used as a prefix.) □ *I have a mini-problem you can maybe help me with.* □ *This is just a mini-office. I'll get a bigger one later.* **2.** *n.* a miniskirt. □ *"I look pretty good in a mini." "No Bruno, you don't."* □ *I'll try a mini this time. I was too plump the last time they were in style.*

minibreak *n.* a quick or short holiday trip. □ *What you need is a weekend minibreak.* □ *We took a little minibreak to Greece.*

mint 1. *n.* a lot of money. □ *He makes a mint. He can afford a little generosity.* □ *That kind of car costs a mint!* **2.** *mod.* completely new. □ *Oh yes madam, it's completely mint.* □ *I want a mint one.*

mish-mash *n.* a mixture; a disorderly conglomeration. □ *What a mish-mash of colours and designs!* □ *There's no theme or focus. It's just a mish-mash.*

miss a trick *vb. phr.* to miss an opportunity or chance. (Always used in the negative.) □ *Mr Big never misses a trick.* □ *How did a smart cooky like you miss a trick like that?*

Miss Goody Two-shoes See GOODY TWO-SHOES.

missis AND **missus** *n.* a wife. □ *Will your missis let you out to the pub tonight?* □ *I'd better ask the missus.*

miss off AND **miss out** *vb. phr.* to avoid or omit. □ *I should be on the guest list. How did I come to be missed off?* □ *We'll miss out that stop as we are so short of time.*

miss out See MISS OFF.

miss the boat 1. *vb. phr.* to be too late. □ *If you don't get here right now you'll have missed the boat.* □ *Basil's missed the boat again. He can never get himself going fast enough.* **2.** *vb. phr.* to have failed to understand; to miss the point. □ *If you think that's what's wanted, you've missed the boat.* □ *This guy's completely missed the boat. I don't think he understands simple English.*

miss the bus *vb. phr.* to lose an opportunity. □ *"One thing is certain: Hitler missed the bus." —Prime Minister Neville Chamberlain in May 1940. (The following month, Hitler invaded France and Chamberlain was replaced by Churchill.)* □ *Move now or miss the bus!*

missus See MISSIS.

mitt *n.* a hand. □ *Get your mitts off my glass.* □ *The kid's got mitts on him like a gorilla.*

mittens 1. *n.* boxing gloves. □ *He pulled on his mittens and climbed into the ring.* □ *He held up his mittens for the umpire to inspect them.* **2.** *n.* handcuffs. □ *He slip the mittens onto the arrested thief.* □ *The policeman clipped a spare set of mittens on his belt.*

mixed up *mod.* confused; mentally troubled. (This is hyphenated before a nominal.) □ *I was a little mixed up after the accident.* □ *This kid's just a little mixed-up. She'll straighten out.* □ *She's a crazy mixed-up kid.*

mix it with someone *vb. phr.* to provoke trouble or start a fight with someone. □ *Mike and Barry mixed it for a while, but then things calmed down.* □ *Mike came out of the shop and began to mix it with Barry.*

mizzle *vb.* to decamp or abscond. □ *Now don't you try to mizzle again, Sammy.* □ *The dog mizzled for a while but came back on her own accord.*

M'lud *n.* a barrister's term of respectful address to the judge when addressing him or her in open court; an abbreviation of "My Lord." □ *M'lud, I believe my learned colleague may be in error on this point.* □ *I should like to bring the following evidence to the court's attention, M'lud.*

moaning minnie *n.* someone who is continually lamenting or complaining. □ *Sometimes I think you actually enjoy being a moaning minnie!* □ *You really are terrible moaning minnie, you know.*

mob-handed *mod.* in a group. □ *If we go in there mob-handed it should not be a problem.* □ *They turned up mob-handed and I was not going to argue.*

mock *n.* a trial or rehearsal of an examination. □ *How did you get on in your mock?* □ *The mocks are next week, you know.*

mocker *n.* a jinx. □ *All that character can utter is a string of mockers, it seems.* □ *Now there was a charming mocker!*

mod cons *n.* the facilities expected in modern property. (Estate agents jargon.) □ *House for sale with all mod cons.* □ *We're only interested in houses that have all the usual mod cons and things.*

Modern Athens See ATHENS OF THE NORTH.

mog See MOGGIE.

mogger See MOGGIE.

moggie AND **mogger; mog** *n.* a cat. □ *Is this your moggie here? What's he called?* □ *Get that mog out of the refrigerator!*

moist round the edges *mod.* slightly intoxicated due to drink or drugs. □ *Bruno's a really nice person when he's moist round the edges.* □ *She's usually moist round the edges by noon.*

moke *n.* a donkey. □ *The kids went for a ride on a moke along the seashore.* □ *There's a sanctuary for old and ill mokes near here.*

mole 1. *n.* the male sexual organ. (Crude.) □ *Myra says moles are disgusting but then Myra's strange.* □ *Only small boys wave their moles about like that, Wayne. Put it away!* **2.** *n.* a girl willing to have sexual intercourse with whoever asks. (Crude.) □ *Know of any moles in the pub tonight?* □ *Oh, Maggy is a mole all right. You'll see!* **3.** *n.* a secret agent, hidden within an enemy organisation in order to subvert or spy upon it. □ *Don't be absurd! How can there be a mole in here?* □ *They've found a mole in the organisation.*

mole-catcher *n.* the female sexual organ. (Taboo.) □ *A woman who shows her mole-catcher is just the lowest.* □ *The door to the shower room flew open and the girl screamed, trying to cover her mole-catcher.*

moley *n.* a weapon consisting of a potato with razor blades stuck into it. □

Someone attacked a kid with a moley at school. □ A moley is a nasty weapon because no one expects it.

Molly Malone *n.* a telephone. (Rhyming slang.) □ *The Molly Malone's been very busy all day today.* □ *The Molly Malone was ringing off the hook when I came in.*

moneybags *n.* a wealthy person. (Also a term of address. Derogatory. Use with caution.) □ *When old moneybags does finally buy the farm, who gets the loot?* □ *When you get to be a big moneybags, don't forget those you left behind.*

money for jam AND **money for old rope** *n.* a profit for little or no effort or cost. □ *This is so easy, it's money for jam.* □ *Why is this so much money for old rope? What are we missing?*

money for old rope See MONEY FOR JAM.

money grubber *n.* a person obsessed with gathering money. (Derogatory; use with caution.) □ *Why is he such a money grubber? Is he going to take it with him?* □ *The boss is such a money grubber. He makes customers pay for each paper clip.*

money talks *phr.* "money can buy co-operation"; "having money makes one influential." □ *I know money talks, but I don't have enough loot to say anything.* □ *Like they say, money talks, but don't try making it talk to a policeman.*

mongy *mod.* stupid. □ *Mike is so mongy when he's been drinking.* □ *What a mongy idiot I was!*

moniker AND **monicker; monniker** *n.* a name. □ *What's your moniker, mate?* □ *With a monniker like that, you must get into a lot of fights.*

monkey 1. *n.* five hundred Pounds Sterling. (Compare with GORILLA, PONY and SCORE.) □ *He put a monkey into the top pocket of my shirt and said that there were plenty more to be had if I asked no questions.* □ *Who the blazes is going to be daft enough to give you a monkey for that?* **2.** *n.* a dismissive term for a menial person. (Crude.) □ *Get out of here, you monkey!* □ *What a monkey that woman can be.*

monkey around (with someone) See MESS AROUND (WITH SOMEONE).

monkey around (with something) See MESS AROUND (WITH SOMETHING).

monkey business 1. AND **funny business; funny stuff** *n.* shady dealings; dishonest tricks. □ *No more monkey business; from now on, straight deals only, okay?* □ *The funny business has got to stop. I think the cops are on to us.* **2.** AND **monkey tricks** *n.* sexual play; flirting. (Crude.) □ *Stop it, John! That's enough of your monkey business!* □ *Come on, John! We've no time for monkey tricks just now.*

monkey suit *n.* an absurd or demeaning uniform. □ *I'm not wearing that monkey suit!* □ *Who thought up this ridiculous monkey suit?*

monkey tricks 1. *n.* mischievious activities. □ *I see you're up to your old monkey tricks again.* □ *He does not like these monkey tricks.* **2.** See also MONKEY BUSINESS.

monniker See MONIKER.

monthlies *n.* menstruation. (Crude.) □ *It's her monthlies. You know how she feels then.* □ *The monthlies have struck again!*

moo(-cow) See COW.

moody 1. *mod.* fake, pretended or counterfeit. □ *Sorry, it's a moody one.* □ *Watch out for more moody products.* **2.** *n.* a period or outburst of bad temper. □ *Don't work yourself up into a moody.* □ *You only have to look at them to see that they've been having a terrible moody.* **3.** *n.* meaningless or non-sensical talk; lies. □ *Boy, he can certainly churn out moody by the hour!* □ *That's just so much moody. Ignore it.* **4.** *mod.* counterfeited; faked. □ *I think that was a moody fight last night.* □ *Otto's taken to selling moody jewellery.*

moody someone *vb.* to delude someone with clever words or flattery. □ *Are you trying to moody me?* □ *I'm just not going to be moodied.*

mooey *mod.* [of fruit or vegetables] rotten or overripe. □ *Get ride of these vegetables; they're mooey!* □ *No mooey stuff here thank you.*

moolah *n.* money. □ *I don't make enough moolah to go on a trip like that!* □ *It takes a lot of moolah to buy a car like that.*

moon *n.* a month. □ *It'll take a moon to finish our work here.* □ *Every moon he went to visit his mother in Brighton.*

moon AND **do a moon job** *vb. (phr.)* to exhibit one's naked buttocks through a window (such as a car window) as a form of insult. □ *When the plane flew over Cuba, a guy named Victor actually mooned a Russian Mig interceptor that flew by.* □ *The kids who did a moon job in front of the mayor's wife got arrested for indecent exposure.*

moonlight *vb.* to work at a second job. □ *Larry had to moonlight to earn enough to feed his family.* □ *A lot of people have to moonlight to make ends meet.*

moonlight flitting AND **flit(ting)** *n.* an overnight house move made in order to avoid paying rent or other debts. □ *If you can't pay your rent, you can always do a moonlight flitting.* □ *We've done about six flittings in the last year already.*

Moosh 1. *n.* a familiar form of address for a man, especially if his correct name is not known. (See JOHN, KIDDO, JIMMY, TOSH, WHACKER, WHACK and WACK.) □ *Why don't you do the smart thing and clear off, Moosh?* □ *You all right, Moosh? Can I help?* **2.** *n.* the mouth. □ *Shut your moosh and get on with your work.* □ *Have I ever told you that you have a really ugly moosh?* **3.** *n.* the face. □ *Put some paint on your moosh, and let's get going.* □ *With a moosh like that, you ought to be in pictures. Maybe another King Kong remake.*

moosh 1. *vb.* to crush or squeeze. □ *I sat on my biscuits and mooshed them up into crumbs.* □ *He mooshed up the note and threw it upon the fire.* **2.** *vb.* to kiss. □ *Let's go somewhere quiet and moosh.* □ *There are some teenagers in the back room, mooshing and so on.*

mope *n.* a tired and ineffectual person. □ *I can't afford to pay mopes around here. Get to work or get out!* □ *I feel like such a mope today.*

mope (around) *vb. (phr.)* to wander about in a gloomy, sulky or sad manner. □ *I don't want to do anything but mope these days.* □ *He just mopes around all day and won't eat anything.*

mopper See WINE MOPPER.

mop something up *vb. phr.* to absorb knowledge or news rapidly and enthusiastically. □ *Oh, I'll soon mop up what's wanted.* □ *He could mop up new ideas like they were going out of fashion.*

more than one bargained for *n.* more than one expected or wanted. □ *This is certainly more than I bargained for!* □ *Trouble and more trouble. I'm getting more than I bargained for when I took on the job.*

Morgue *n.* the department of a newspaper where obituaries are prepared. (Always with *the.*) □ *I work in the Morgue, writing obituaries.* □ *Is life exciting in the Morgue?*

morning after (the night before) *n.* a hangover. (Always with *the.*) □ *Do worries about the morning after keep you from having a good time at parties?* □ *She's suffering from the morning after the night before.*

moron *n.* a very stupid person. (Offensive. Also a term of address.) □ *What a moron you are!* □ *Just get out of my sight, you moron!*

mosher *n.* an enthusiastic follower of heavy metal music. □ *You'll find moshers dancing in a very crowded space with whatever small movements are possible.* □ *I don't know any moshers.*

mosk something *vb.* to pawn something. □ *Why did you ever think to mosk that?* □ *He had no money and had to mosk something.*

most *n.* something that is superlative; the very best. (Always with *the.*) □ *This noodle stuff is the most, Mom!* □ *Sally is the most! Can she dance!*

MOT'd *mod.* concerning a vehicle tested and granted a MOT TEST certificate. □ *Has your car been MOT'd yet?* □ *Take that MOT'd car over there.*

mothball *vb.* to place to one side; to store for future use. □ *It's where the air force keeps some of its aircraft that* *have been mothballed.* □ *I think we'll have to mothball that plan.*

Mother Bunch *n.* a fat old woman. □ *This Mother Bunch is looking for help, I think.* □ *Please get that Mother Bunch out of here!*

Mother Hubbard *n.* a cupboard. (Rhyming slang.) □ *What do you have in that Mother Hubbard?* □ *She looked in the Mother Hubbard but it was empty.*

mother of pearl *n.* a wife. (Rhyming slang, linked as follows: mother of pearl ≈ [girl] = wife.) □ *Will your mother of pearl let you out to the pub tonight?* □ *I'd better ask me mother of pearl.*

mother's boy *n.* an effeminate or weak-willed man. (Crude.) □ *So this supposed mother's boy turned to us and gave us an amazing torrent of abuse.* □ *Just because he's a mother's boy does not make him gay, you know!*

mother's meeting 1. *n.* a gathering of the women of a parish. □ *I have to attend the mother's meeting tonight, dear.* □ *Oh, I'm sorry. I'd forgotten about the mother's meeting.* **2.** *n.* a discussion of trivial matters considered very important by the participants in the discussion but to no one else. □ *It was very mother's meeting; we ended up discussing the kind of jam to put on the sandwiches.* □ *I can't take any more of these mother's meetings.*

mother's ruin *n.* gin. □ *The bottle was empty. More mother's ruin, I think!* □ *Get out the mother's ruin; let's have a drink.*

motor 1. *n.* a motor car. □ *Like my new motor, darling?* □ *I'm rather partial to fast motors.* **2.** *vb.* to get along excellently; to proceed without trouble; to make good progress. □ *Look at them. Are they not really motoring?* □ *Well, we're really motoring now; it shouldn't take so long to get there.*

motorway madness *n.* dangerous driving upon a motorway in bad weather, especially when fog reduces visibility. □ *That pile up was the direct result of motorway madness.* □ *Motorway madness kills.*

mott *n.* the female sexual organ. (Taboo.) □ *He got arrested trying to look up women's skirts in the hope of seeing their motts.* □ *What do you mean, you can see my mott? Oh my god, I've forgotten my knickers!*

MOT Test *n.* a compulsory annual road-worthiness test for all automobiles more than three years old. □ *MOT Test is an abbreviation of "Ministry of Transport Test."* □ *I don't know how my car ever passed it's MOT Test.*

mouch *n.* someone who owes money to a bank. *(Irish usage.)* □ *How much does the mouch owe them?* □ *If you must be a mouch, make sure you owe the bank plenty. That way, they are beholden to you!*

mouldies *n.* copper coins. □ *He chucked her a few mouldies and left.* □ *Sorry, I don't have any mouldies with me. Can you pay?*

mouldy 1. *n.* a torpedo. □ *They launched a mouldy at the ship, but missed.* □ *How many mouldies does this submarine carry, Captain?* **2.** *mod.* very intoxicated due to drink. (Irish usage.) □ *Boy, he's mouldy and spoiling for a fight.* □ *They were both mouldy. They could only lie there and snore.*

mount the box *vb. phr.* to give evidence in court, from the witness box. □ *I've been asked to mount the box next.* □ *I hate mounting the box.*

mouse 1. *n.* a man who does not consummate his marriage on the first night. (Crude.) □ *They call Mike Mickey Mouse because he was a mouse when it mattered.* □ *It was his wife that let it be known he was a mouse.* **2.** *n.* a shy girl or young woman. □ *The little mouse sat there, not saying a word.* □ *Why are you such a mouse, Maureen?*

mouth music *n.* oral sex. (Taboo.) □ *Fancy some mouth music, darling?* □ *If you're looking for mouth music you better look for another girl, buster!*

mouthpiece *n.* a lawyer. □ *The one over there with the beard's me mouthpiece.* □ *I'm not saying a word more without my mouthpiece here.*

mover *n.* a dynamic, extroverted or enthusiastic person. □ *He's an effective* mover. □ *A real mover was not likely to be waiting for him.*

mow the lawn *vb. phr.* to shave with an electric razor. □ *He's just mowing the lawn and won't be long.* □ *I was standing in front of the mirror mowing the lawn when she arrived.*

Mozart *mod.* intoxicated due to drink. (Crude. Rhyming slang, linked as follows: Mozart [and Liszt] ≈ [pissed] = intoxicated. Compare with BOOED AND HISSED, and BRAHMS AND LISZT.) □ *The hostess was really Mozart.* □ *My Mozart friend here needs a lift, and can I have one, too?*

Mr Big *n.* the leader of a criminal gang. (Police slang.) □ *So you're Mr Big. I thought you'd be taller.* □ *Mr Big's office was cold and ostentatious, as was Mr Big.*

Mr Nice Guy *n.* a friendly, forgiving fellow. □ *You'll find that I'm Mr Nice Guy as long as you play fair with me.* □ *Screw up again and it's no more Mr Nice Guy.*

Mr Right *n.* the man that a woman is fated to marry. □ *Some day Mr Right will come along and sweep you off your feet.* □ *I'm tired of waiting for Mr Right. Where is Mr Maybe?*

Mr Sausage *n.* the male sexual organ. (Taboo.) □ *The doctor told him that he'd got something wrong with his Mr Sausage.* □ *That's all very well Myra, but where would the world be without Mr Sausages?*

Mrs Duckett! *exclam.* "Fuck it!" (Crude. Rhyming slang.) □ *Mrs Duckett! I've screwed up again.* □ *Oh Mrs Duckett, I don't care any more!*

Mrs Duckett *n.* a bucket. (Rhyming slang.) □ *Bring your Mrs Duckett over here and fill it with water.* □ *Someone has helped themself to my Mrs Duckett.*

Mrs Greenfield *n.* a place to sleep in the open. □ *Here's my Mrs Greenfield for tonight.* □ *This looks like a likely Mrs Greenfield.*

Mrs Mop(p) *n.* a nickname for a cleaning lady. □ *I was at the office so late, I met the Mrs Mop coming in as I was leaving.* □ *The Mrs Mopp we have here does not do a very great job, you know!*

muck about AND **muck around 1.** *vb. phr.* to fool around. □ *We'll muck about for a while, then get over there.* □ *That's enough mucking about for now, you two.* **2.** *vb. phr.* to potter about. □ *Instead of mucking about, could you try working for a change?* □ *Look, you can't just muck around like this all the time.*

muck around See MUCK ABOUT.

mucker 1. *n.* a bad fall. □ *My aunt took a mucker last week and is in hospital.* □ *Take care in there, it's easy to trip and have a mucker.* **2.** *n.* a fellow worker. □ *What are your muckers like there?* □ *I work on my own. I have no muckers.* **3.** *n.* a pal; a friend. □ *Who's your mucker, Albert?* □ *The two muckers left the pub, each one preventing the other from falling over.*

muck in with something *vb. phr.* to share something. □ *We all mucked in with together and soon had the tent erected.* □ *The sooner we all muck in with this, the sooner we can all go home.*

muck something out *vb. phr.* to clean out something. □ *The farmer mucked out the cowshed every day.* □ *Right you lot! Today is the day you muck out your rooms.*

muck something up *vb. phr.* to make a mess of something; to ruin something. □ *Try not to muck things up this time.* □ *You seem to have mucked up this one, too.*

muck sweat *n.* a heavy sweat. □ *Yes it was really hard physical work, and that's why I have this muck sweat.* □ *Don't get worked up into a muck sweat over this.*

mucky duck AND **mucky pup 1.** *n.* a raffishly, sexually promiscuous man. (Crude.) □ *Why, you mucky duck, you didn't...did you?* □ *The mucky pup was at it with his secretary, right there in his office.* **2.** *n.* a dirty or ill-behaved child. □ *That mucky duck is playing in the garden at this very moment.* □ *How many mucky pups like that do you think you can cope with at once?*

mucky pup See MUCKY DUCK.

muesli belt *n.* where middle-class food-faddists live. (Usually with *the*.) □ *They live in the muesli belt.* □ *If they are in the muesli belt, they can't be too near the poverty line.*

muesli belt malnutrition *n.* undernourishment among MUESLI BELT children. □ *These rich little children are typical victims of muesli belt malnutrition.* □ *Yes, I know it sounds absurd, but muesli belt malnutrition exists.*

muff *n.* the female sexual organ. (Taboo.) □ *They dance completely nude in there, with muff and everything on view.* □ *What do you mean, you can see my muff? Oh my god, I've forgotten my knickers!*

muff-diver *n.* a practitioner of oral sex upon a woman. (Taboo.) □ *Well, let's just say he has a reputation as a muff-diver.* □ *I think Marty prefers muff-divers, actually.*

mug 1. *n.* a face, especially an unattractive one. (Crude.) □ *Wipe that smile off your mug!* □ *What an ugly mug!* **2.** *vb.* to attack and rob someone. □ *Somebody jumped out of an alley and tried to mug me.* □ *Some scruff mugged Mrs Lopez last night.* **3.** *vb.* to buy someone a drink. □ *Come on, I'll mug you one.* □ *What can I mug for you?* **4.** See also MUG (PUNTER).

mugger *n.* someone, usually male, who attacks and robs people. □ *I clobbered the mugger with a tyre lever I carry just for such occasions.* □ *The muggers have the town centre almost to themselves after dark.*

muggins See MUG (PUNTER).

muggo *n.* a cup of tea. (Rhyming slang, linked as follows: muggo ≈ [mug of tea] = cup of tea. Compare with CUPPA.) □ *A muggo is always welcome.* □ *I sat down and had a lovely muggo.*

mug (punter) AND **muggins** *n.* a swindler's name for his victim. □ *I don't want to be anyone's mug punter.* □ *The con men found a handy muggins and started their scheme.*

mug's game *n.* a foolish or pointless activity. □ *Using drugs is a mug's game.* □ *Why do you fall for every mugs game going?*

mug shot *n.* a photograph of one's face taken for police records. (Underworld.) □ *I'm going to have to ask you to come down to the station and go through some mug shots.* □ *How can a professional photographer take a portrait that looks like a mug shot?*

mug up *vb. phr.* to learn by rapid, intensive study. □ *If you studied regularly all the time, you wouldn't need to mug up at the last moment like this.* □ *She spent the night mugging up for the test.*

mule *n.* someone who delivers or smuggles drugs for a drug dealer. □ *These creeps use a twelve-year-old kid for a mule!* □ *A car drove by, and suddenly the mule was riddled with machine gun bullets.*

mumper *n.* a beggar. □ *There's a mumper here who says he knows you!* □ *Tell that mumper to get out of here!*

mumping *n.* the taking of bribes by the police. □ *There's absolutely no mumping among our officers.* □ *I doubt there's ever been a police force anywhere with absolutely no mumping ever.*

munch *vb.* to eat a lot of food. □ *Munching; is that all you ever do?* □ *You certainly like to munch, eh?*

munchies *n.* hunger. (Always with *the*.) □ *What's to eat? I've got the munchies.* □ *The munchies are really gnawing at my tummy!*

mung 1. *n.* something that is filthy or disgusting. □ *I don't think Joe has ever tidied his room; it's just full of the most awful mung.* □ *I don't know how you can eat the mung that passes for food around here?* **2.** *vb.* to beg. □ *There were a number of kids munging from passers-by.* □ *Martin reckoned he could get by munging, but then he's never actually tried it.* **3.** *n.* dirt; earth; mud; filth. □ *The car was covered in the mung accumulated in thirty years of unwashed life.* □ *Looking around the room, she said she could never live with all the munge.*

mungy *n.* food. □ *Let's go get some mungy; I'm starved.* □ *He was pushing the mungy down his neck as if there was no tomorrow.*

muppet 1. *n.* a patient in a hospital for the mentally ill. □ *A lot of muppets seem quite like ordinary people at first.* □ *You'd never know, but in fact Stewart is a muppet.* 2. *n.* an unpopular teenager. □ *It's no fun being a muppet.* □ *It's the muppets who tend to suicide.* 3. *n.* a person with severe physical deformity or a grotesque appearance. (Offensive. Also a term of address.) □ *What a muppet that woman is.* □ *Get out of here, you muppet!*

murder AND **slaughter** *vb.* to overwhelm; to beat someone in a sports contest. □ *The other team murdered us.* □ *We went out on the field prepared to slaughter them.*

murder bag *n.* a bag containing all the equipment required by the police when they are investigating a murder. □ *The van drew up and out came the murder bag.* □ *These murder bags always give me the creeps.*

murg *n.* a telegram. (Backslang, from *(tele)gram*.) □ *I don't like getting no murg.* □ *Folks around here still remember murgs bring bad news during the War.*

murky *mod.* secret; mysterious. □ *What happened is all a bit murky, I'm afraid.* □ *There were murky goings-on at that time.*

Murphy's Law AND **Sod's Law; Spode's Law** *n.* a law that states: that which can go wrong will; that which can't go wrong just might. □ *Buttered bread always lands butter-side down; that's Murphy's Law.* □ *In accordance with Spode's Law we arrived at the station just after the last train of the day had left.*

muscle in *vb. phr.* to force one's way in upon the business or territory of another. □ *Don't you muscle in on my business.* □ *He keeps trying to muscle in on things that have nothing to do with him.*

mush 1. *n.* romance; lovemaking; kissing. □ *I can't stand movies with lots of mush in them.* □ *When an actor looks at an actress like that, you just know that there's gonna be some mush.* 2. *n.* military prison. □ *Civvy jail may be*

bad, but I promise mush is worse. □ *I served two years in mush for lightly tapping an officer on the shoulder. Well all right, I knocked him cold.* 3. *n.* a prostitute's client. (Crude.) □ *Another mush went off with her in his car.* □ *The mush didn't want to pay but Zoe slashed his face with an open razor she carried for such eventualities.*

mushroom *n.* a person who considers him- or herself to be ill-informed. □ *We're just mushrooms, kept in the dark and fed bullshit.* □ *I don't want to be a mushroom any more.*

mushy 1. *n.* mushrooms of the genus *Psilocybe*, which cause visions or hallucinations when eaten. □ *Mushy is okay because it's natural, or something like that.* □ *Mushies are also called "magic mushrooms" because they're supposed to give you visions.* 2. *mod.* badly thought out; sentimental. □ *The love scenes were real out-and-out mushy, but nobody laughed.* □ *Harry always laughs at mushy rubbish in a film.*

mushy peas *n.* boiled and mashed peas. □ *Mushy peas are particularly popular in Northern England.* □ *A portion of fish and chips with mushy peas, please.*

muskra *n.* a policeman. □ *Think about how the muskra on the beat is affected by this cold.* □ *The muskra stopped at the door, tried the lock, and moved on.*

must (do) *n.* something that one ought to do. (Always with *a*.) □ *Going up the Eiffel Tower is a must do in Paris.* □ *This is a must when you're in town.*

Must fly. See I'VE GOT TO FLY.

mutter and stutter See COUGH AND STUTTER.

mutton 1. *n.* an eye. (Rhyming slang, linked as follows: mutton [pie] ≈ eye.) □ *That man has very strange muttons, mummy.* □ *What do you mean? His muttons are bright red.* 2. See also LACED MUTTON.

mutton dagger See BEEF BAYONET.

mutton dressed as lamb *n.* a middle-aged or older woman who attempts by dress and make-up to make herself look like a young woman. □ *Here she* *comes, mutton dressed as lamb as usual.* □ *Women who are mutton dressed as lamb are usually objects of ridicule.*

muzzy 1. *mod.* befuddled due to drink. □ *Harry's a bit muzzy. As usual.* □ *Drink enough, you'll get muzzy.* **2.** *mod.* dull, uninspiring or poorly thought out. □ *Marvin is not really muzzy. He just looks, behaves and talks that way.* □ *You can be so muzzy without even trying.*

My Aunt Fanny! *exclam.* "I don't believe you!" □ *My Aunt Fanny, that's a pack of lies!* □ *Rubbish! My Aunt Fanny!*

My goodness! *exclam.* a mild exclamation of amazement, shock, etc. □ *My goodness! I didn't expect you to be here.* □ *My goodness! There's a man at the window!*

My (left) foot! *exclam.* "I do not believe it!"; "Like hell!" (An exclamation of contradiction.) □ *You're the best in town? My foot!* □ *What! My left foot! She's going to marry you?*

N

nabbed *mod.* caught by the police; arrested. □ *He got nabbed last night with a stolen watch on him.* □ *He was nabbed as he tried to run away.*

nab someone *vb.* to arrest someone; to catch someone. □ *When the police nabbed Tom he had the stolen watch on him.* □ *The policeman nabbed him as he came running round the corner.*

nadgers *n.* small problems or difficulties. (Always plural.) □ *Where are all these nadgers coming from?* □ *They say nadgers come out of the woodwork.*

nadgery *n.* a place where NADGERS happen. □ *Oh no, not another problem. This place is such a nadgery!* □ *Every time I go to that nadgery something else goes wrong.*

naff 1. *mod.* unfashionable; tasteless; shoddy. □ *This place is really naff. Let's get out of here.* □ *Oh, what an naff weirdo!* **2.** *mod.* useless. □ *Get out of here, you naff clot!* □ *I don't think he's naff at all.* **3.** *n.* the female sexual organ. (Taboo. Backslang of FANNY.) □ *The door to the shower room flew open and the girl screamed, trying to cover her naff.* □ *A woman who shows her naff is just the lowest.*

naff all See JACK ALL.

naffed-off See JACKED-OFF.

naffing *mod.* FUCKING. (Crude. A euphemism and disguise.) □ *That was a naffing stupid thing to do.* □ *Where's the naffing remote control for the naffing telly?*

Naff off! *exclam.* "Fuck off!" (Crude. A euphemism.) □ *Why don't you just naff off!* □ *Naff off! We don't want your like here!*

nag *n.* a horse suitable for riding. (Not a worn-out or old horse, which is the Standard English meaning of this word.) □ *I bet a week's pay on that nag yesterday but won nothing.* □ *There were a number of healthy-looking nags in the stables.*

nags *n.* horse racing. (Always with *the*) □ *He spent all his money on the nags and now he's broke.* □ *I'm off to the nags tomorrow. Wish me luck!*

nailed 1. *mod.* correctly identified. □ *The thugs certainly got nailed fast.* □ *The killer was nailed with the help of Scotland Yard.* **2.** *mod.* arrested. □ *Okay, chum. You are nailed. Let's go.* □ *Why am I nailed? I didn't do anything.* **3.** *vb.* to punish. □ *I've been nailed with a £100 fine.* □ *They nailed him all right: two years in the slammer.*

nail someone 1. *vb.* to identify someone. (Compare with NAILED.) □ *They nailed him from his picture.* □ *The officer nailed Freddy, thanks to the description the victim provided.* **2.** *vb.* to punish someone. (Compare with NAILED.) □ *The beak nailed me with a £100 fine.* □ *He nailed me all right: two years in the slammer.* **3.** *vb.* to arrest someone. □ *The cops nailed him right in his own doorway.* □ *"I'm gonna nail you," said the copper.*

namby(-pamby) *mod.* affected; effeminate and weak. (Said of a man.) □ *Fred is far too namby-pamby ever to make a difficult choice.* □ *He's a real namby-pamby type; you know—a gutless wonder.*

name of the game *n.* the way things are; the way things can be expected to be. (Always with *the*.) □ *The name of the game is money, money, money.* □ *I can't help it. That's the name of the game.*

Name your poison. *sent.* "State what you want to drink." (Refers to alcoholic drinks only.) □ *Okay, name your poison, Charlie.* □ *Step up to the bar and name your poison.*

Name yours. See WHAT'S YOURS?

namoh *n.* a woman. (Backslang.) □ *There's a namoh here asking for you.* □ *Ask the namoh what she wants, please.*

nana *n.* a foolish person. (An abbreviation of BANANA.) □ *I felt like such a bloody nana when I found out that I'd got onto the wrong train.* □ *Who's the nana in the bright orange trousers?*

nance See NANCY (BOY).

nancy (boy) AND **nance** *n.* an effeminate man; a passive male homosexual. (Crude.) □ *He doesn't like being called a nancy.* □ *Why does he work so hard to look like he's a nance?*

nan(ny) *n.* grandmother. (Childish.) □ *I love my nanny.* □ *The kids love visiting their nan.*

nanny *n.* a boat. (Rhyming slang, linked as follows: nanny [goat] ≈ boat.) □ *Three men sat in the nanny out there for hours, fishing.* □ *We sailed out into the middle of the bay in the little nanny.*

nanny state *n.* a welfare state. □ *The over-protective nanny state is sometimes blamed for suppressing initiative.* □ *It is disparaging to call the state social security system a nanny state.*

Nantee! *exclam.* "Watch out!"; "Beware!" □ *Nantee! They're after you!* □ *If you want my advice, it's just this: nantee!*

nantee AND **nantwas** *n.* absolutely nothing. □ *Nice words, but worth nantee.* □ *We've got nantwas for you here. Shove off.*

nantwas See NANTEE.

nap hand *n.* a situation that justifies an expectation of winning. □ *This looks good! We've a nap hand here, I think.* □ *Remember telling us we had a nap hand? Well, the other side has won.*

napoo *n.* something that either does not exist or is of no use whatsoever. (Said to be an abbreviation of the French *il n'y en a plus*, meaning "there is no more of it." If so, this is an example of hobson-jobson.) □ *Forget it. It's napoo.* □ *It may be napoo to you, but that does not mean it's unimportant to someone else.*

napper *n.* the head. □ *He's distinctive because he has a particularly large napper.* □ *Turn your napper around and take a look at this.*

nark 1. *vb.* to inform (on someone) to the police; to SQUEAL. (Often with *on*.) □ *Don't nark on me!* □ *All right. Who narked?* **2.** *vb.* to annoy someone. □ *Stop narking me!* □ *Why do you always have to be narking away at someone?* **3.** *n.* a spoil-sport or nagging person. □ *Joan's such a nark, always ruining things for others.* □ *Why do you have to be a nark all the time? Leave me in peace!* **4.** *n.* a police informer or decoy. (Compare with PIMP.) □ *Fred is a nark. He squealed.* □ *I'm going to get that nark for squealing.* **5.** *n.* a policeman. □ *The nark stopped at the door, tried the lock and moved on.* □ *Think about how the nark on the beat is affected by this cold.*

narked *mod.* annoyed or angered. (Usually with *at* or *with*.) □ *Just walk away. Don't let him cause you to become narked.* □ *Now that gets me really narked, you know.*

Nark it! 1. *exclam.* "Shut up!" □ *Nark it! I can't hear the music!* □ *Why don't you just nark it!* **2.** *exclam.* "Fuck it!" (Crude.) □ *Nark it, I'm going anyway.* □ *Nark it! I don't care any more.*

narky AND **sarky** *n.* sarcastic. (NARKY is rhyming slang from SARKY.) □ *There's no need to be narky.* □ *I'm not being sarky.*

narrow bed *n.* a grave. □ *Old Bert's been in his narrow bed a year now.* □ *The narrow bed lay open in the graveyard, waiting for some poor soul as its tenant.*

narrow squeak *n.* a success almost not achieved; a lucky or marginal success; a problem almost not surmounted; a lucky escape. □ *That was a narrow squeak. I don't know how I survived.* □ *Another narrow squeak like that and I'll give up.*

nasty 1. *n.* something unpleasant. □ *Do what I ask or I'll give you a nasty to remember.* □ *If you want another nasty, just keep annoying Mr Big like that.* **2.** *mod.* bad-tempered; unpleasant. □ *Do what I ask or I'll get really nasty with you.* □ *What a nasty person she can be.* **3.** *mod.* dangerous. □ *We had a nasty experience on the road today.* □ *Boy, that was a nasty thing to happen.*

nasty piece of work *n.* an unpleasant person. (Offensive. Also a term of address.) □ *Just get out of my sight, you nasty piece of work!* □ *What a nasty piece of work you are!*

Nat *n.* a Nationalist; an advocate of Scottish or Welsh independence. □ *Yon Nats canna be trusted to cross the road.* □ *Angus is okay; he's a Nat all right.*

natch *interj.* "yes"; "naturally." □ *I'm sure it's okay. She said natch.* □ *Natch, you can borrow my car.*

natter *vb.* to talk aimlessly; to chatter endlessly. □ *Instead of standing there nattering, do something useful.* □ *They seem to natter all day long.*

natty *mod.* admirable; attractive; neat. □ *That's a natty suit.* □ *We've got a natty way to solve that problem.*

natural 1. *n.* someone with obvious natural talent or skill in some activity or other. □ *That guy is a natural!* □ *Brother, can she dance! What a natural!* **2.** *n.* one's lifespan. □ *In all my natural, I never thought I'd see that!* □ *She spent her entire natural living in that one small village.*

natural-born *mod.* born with talent or skill. □ *She is really a natural-born dancer.* □ *Mary is a natural-born artist.*

Nature calls. *phr.* "I must relieve myself." (Crude.) □ *Just a moment; nature calls.* □ *Nature calls. I'll be back in a moment!*

nature's call AND **call of nature** *n.* the feeling of a need to go to the toilet. (Crude.) □ *I think I feel nature's call coming on.* □ *A call of nature forced us to stop along the way.*

naughty 1. *n.* an illegal act; a crime. □ *So, who have we caught in the middle of a naughty here then?* □ *I think there's a naughty going on there.* **2.** *n.* sexual intercourse. (Taboo.) □ *After that naughty, she felt cheap.* □ *They were talking about, you know, naughties.*

nauticals *n.* haemorrhoids. (Taboo. Rhyming slang, linked as follows: nautical [mile]s ≈ [piles] = haemorrhoids.) □ *The wife's got the nauticals and is in a foul mood.* □ *She's got to go into hospital to get her nauticals dealt with.*

navel engagement *n.* sexual intercourse. (Taboo.) □ *They were talking about, you know, navel engagements.* □ *After what Walter called a navel engagement, she felt cheap.*

navvy *n.* a nautical or aerial navigator. □ *Ask the navvy where we are!* □ *He's the navvy on a jumbo jet.*

nay say bad *mod.* rather good. (Scots usage.) □ *Oh, I suppose the play was nay say bad.* □ *That was nay say bad a meal, Morag.*

N.B.G. See NO BLOODY GOOD.

near and far *n.* a car. (Rhyming slang.) □ *I'm rather partial to nears and fars.* □ *Like my new near and far, darling?*

near (to) the knuckle See CLOSE TO THE KNUCKLE.

near thing 1. *n.* a narrow escape. □ *Wow, that was a near thing!* □ *Yes, it was a near thing but we made it.* **2.** *n.* a close victory. □ *The Battle of Waterloo is the classic example of a military near thing.* □ *That game was a really near thing.*

neaters *n.* a drink of neat spirits. □ *Sam usually has one or two neaters on the way home.* □ *I'll take a neaters—just the way it is now.*

nebbish AND **nebesh; nebech 1.** *n.* a foolish, clumsy, dull or pathetic person; a loser. (From Yiddish.) □ *Tracy is such a nebbish. Why doesn't she just give up?* □ *You are such a nebech!* **2.** *mod.* foolish, clumsy, dull or pathetic. (From Yiddish.) □ *Don't always be nebbish, Tracy! Pull yourself together!* □ *You lose because you are so nebech!*

nebech See NEBBISH.

necessaries *n.* the male sexual organ. (Taboo. Always with *the*, always in the plural.) □ *The streaker covered his necessaries as he ran across the cricket field. What sort of streak is that?* □ *He made some joke about necessaries, but nobody laughed.*

neck 1. *vb.* to cuddle, kiss and pet, short of sexual intercourse. (Crude. Typically in reference to teenagers.) □ *There are some teenagers in the back room, necking.* □ *Let's go somewhere quiet and neck.* **2.** See also BRASS NECK.

neck and neck AND **neck in neck** *mod.* so close as to be almost the same. □ *The horses were neck and neck at the finish line.* □ *They ran neck in neck for the entire race.*

neck in neck See NECK AND NECK.

ned *n.* a hooligan. (Scots usage.) □ *He dizny act like he's a ned.* □ *Watch that one; he's a ned all right.*

neddy *n.* a donkey. □ *There's a sanctuary for old and ill neddies near here.* □ *The kids went for a ride on a neddy along the seashore.*

needful *n.* money. (Normally with *the*.) □ *Sorry, I can't afford it, I've not enough of the needful.* □ *How much of the needful do you need, then?*

needle 1. *vb.* to tease or irritate someone. □ *Tom is always needling Frank.* □ *Stop needling me!* **2.** *n.* an injection. □ *Don't worry, this tiny needle won't hurt.* □ *Right Mary, time for a little needle.* **3.** *n.* an irritating person. (Offensive. Also a term of address.) □ *Get out of here, you needle!* □ *What a needle that woman can be.* **4.** *n.* resentment. (Always with *the*.) □ *Don't take the needle over what he says; it's not directed at you.* □ *Otto would have really taken the needle at that, if he'd been able to understand what was going on.* **5.** *n.* a nitwit; a stupid person. (Offensive. Also a term of address.) □ *Some needle forgot to get petrol today and the car has run dry.* □ *You needle! Why have you done that!*

needle and pin *n.* gin. (Rhyming slang.) □ *Can I have a needle and pin, please?* □ *I do like this needle and pin.*

needle and thread *n.* bread. (Rhyming slang.) □ *Even a few slices of needle and thread would be good.* □ *Any needle and thread, love?*

needle fight AND **needle game; needle match** *n.* a contest or game where the outcome is important and finely balanced. □ *What do think will happen at the needle fight tonight?* □ *The needle match has gone into extra time, so it must be close.*

needle game See NEEDLE FIGHT.

needle match See NEEDLE FIGHT.

needle something from someone *vb. phr.* to prise information from someone. □ *I wish you would stop trying to needle that information from me.* □ *I'm afraid there's nothing to needle from him.*

need something like a hole in the head *vb. phr.* to have no need whatever for something; to be much better off without something than with it. □ *Oh no! We need this new problem like a hole in the head.* □ *Since you ask, I feel like I need a visit from your Aunt Gladys like a hole in the head.*

negative capital *n.* debt. (A euphemism.) □ *There is the small matter of our negative capital.* □ *Unfortunately all we have to our name is, well, negative capital.*

negligible quantity *n.* a person or thing that does not matter. □ *What's a negligible quantity like that doing around here?* □ *I'm sorry but we really don't need another negligible quantity working here.*

negroid AND **groid** *n.* a black person. (Racially offensive.) □ *So this negroid drives away in a BMW!* □ *Why should a BMW not belong to a groid?*

Nellie AND **Nelly** *n.* an effeminate man; a passive male homosexual. (Crude.) □ *He doesn't like being called a Nellie.* □ *So what if he's a Nelly? He can still vote, can't he?*

Nellie Blight *n.* an eye. (Rhyming slang, linked as follows: Nellie Blight ≈ [sight] = eye.) □ *I think there's something wrong with me Nellie Blights.* □ *He looked me right in the Nellie Blight and assured me again that he was telling the truth.*

Nelson *n.* beer. (Rhyming slang, linked as follows: Nelson [Mandela] ≈ [Stella (Artios)] = beer. Stella Artios™ is a well-known brand of Belgian beer; Nelson Mandela is President of South Africa.) □ *How about a Nelson before you go, Charlie?* □ *Give my friend here a Nelson.*

Nelson touch *n.* a brilliantly effective way of resolving problems. (After the example of Admiral Lord Nelson.) □ *It's not often that you see the Nelson touch used so well these days.* □ *Great! That was pure Nelson touch!*

nerd 1. *n.* a dull and bookish person, usually male. (Rhymes with "bird.") □ *Fred can be such a nerd!* □ *That whole gang of boys is just a bunch of nerds.* **2.** *n.* someone, usually male, who appears to get on better with technical devices than people. (Computer jargon, originally and still especially but not exclusively applied to computers.) □ *I wouldn't say he was a nerd, but he never speaks to anyone except his computer.* □ *These nerds can certainly make their computers sing!*

nerk *n.* a fool. □ *Those nerks are at it again. Spend, spend, spend.* □ *Try not to be more of a nerk than you can help.*

nerve *n.* cheek; impudence. □ *Any more nerve like that and he'll get everything he deserves.* □ *The nerve of the woman! Who does she think she is?*

nervy *mod.* nervous. □ *Mary is so nervy. Anything will set her off.* □ *Now, don't get nervy.*

Nessie *n.* the supposed Loch Ness Monster. (Also a term of address.) □ *We went to Loch Ness to look for Nessie.* □ *Unfortunately Nessie was not on view that day.*

nest egg *n.* money saved for some important future purpose, such as retirement. □ *I lost most of my nest egg in the market crash.* □ *It takes years to build up a nest egg.*

netiquette *n.* the accepted or polite way to behave on a computer network. □ *If you don't want to get flamed, you better watch your netiquette!* □ *Netiquette is useful, because it keeps things under control.*

net result *n.* the final result after all the assets and liabilities have balanced out. □ *The net result was that I was fired.* □ *I don't care about the little things. What is the net result?*

netsurf *vb.* to explore the Internet. □ *He seems to spend every moment of the day and night netsurfing.* □ *How do you netsurf, anyway?*

Never fash yer hied. See DINNA FASH YERSEL.

never hatchy *n.* nonsense. (From the Japanese *abu hachi*, which means this, by hobson-jobson.) □ *Never hatchy, that can't be right.* □ *Oh no, not more of your never hatchy!*

never mind *phr.* "Forget it."; "It doesn't matter anymore." □ *Never mind. I forget what I was going to say.* □ *Oh, never mind. Nobody really cares anyway.*

newbie *n.* a neophyte or novice, usually in online computer communications. □ *Oh, he's a newbie and just doesn't know how to run it properly.* □ *Remember Harry, we were all newbies once!*

new boy AND **new girl** *n.* a new recruit (of any age) to an organisation; a new arrival. □ *We've got some new boys starting today. Treat them nicely.* □ *I don't think much of the new girl. Do you?*

Newgate fringe *n.* hair that has grown under the chin. (Because the style mimics the appearance of a hangman's rope around the neck.) □ *Charlie reckoned that until that moment, the only person wearing a Newgate fringe he'd ever seen was Gregory Peck in the film of "Moby Dick."* □ *They are called Newgate fringes because in London public hangings used to take place outside Newgate Prison.*

new girl See NEW BOY.

Newingtons *n.* the abdomen. (Rhyming slang, linked as follows: Newington [Butts] ≈ [guts] = abdomen. Newington Butts is a road in south London.) □ *Cor! I've been kicked right in the Newingtons!* □ *He's got some bug in the Newingtons but I'm sure he'll be okay in a day or so.*

new penny *n.* the penny that has been in circulation since decimalisation of the currency in 1971. (It is worth 1/100th of a Pound. Compare with OLD PENNY.) □ *What can you buy for one new penny?* □ *You get very little for a new penny, but even less for an old penny.*

News of the Screws *n.* the *News of the World*, a Sunday newspaper published in London which is famous for the extensive coverage it gives to sexual matters. (Crude. Always with *the*. See SCREW.) □ *Sunday morning, and time to buy the latest News of the Screws.* □ *The News of the Screws is a source of endless harmless titillation across the land.*

newted See PISSED AS A NEWT.

next (door) but one *mod.* following the next; two ahead. □ *These people don't live in the house next door but next door but one.* □ *We're next but one after the greengrocer's.*

Niagara (Falls) *n.* the testicles. (Taboo. Rhyming slang, linked as follows: Niagara (Falls) ≈ [balls] = testicles. Normally with *the* and in the plural.) □ *The teacher preferred "testicles" to "Niagaras," if they had to be mentioned at all.* □ *He got hit right in the Niagara Falls.*

nibble 1. *n.* the tentative or slight interest by a possible purchaser. □ *Well, I think there may be a bit of a nibble from that lady in the red dress over there.* □ Q: *Anything?* A: *Not a nibble from anyone, all day.* **2.** AND **nybble** *n.* half of one BYTE, which is to say, four BITS. (Computer jargon, based on the concept of a "nibble" being half of a "bite.") □ *My program wouldn't work just because I had one silly little nibble wrong!* □ *You don't program a nybble! It's just half a bite.*

nice as ninepence *mod.* very tidy; attractive. □ *Yes, very good. It's as nice as ninepence.* □ *I want every thing in here nice as ninepence before we leave, ladies.*

nice as pie *mod.* very agreeable; very polite. □ *What a lovely girl, as nice as pie she is.* □ *I'm pleased it's all ended up as nice as pie like this.*

nice little earner 1. *n.* that which makes easy profits. (Compare with EARNER.) □ *Now this operation is a nice little earner.* □ *I can see you've got yourself a nice little earner here.* **2.** *n.* a well-paid job. □ *I think she's got herself a nice little earner there.* □ *I could use a nice little earner, you know.*

nice little runner *n.* a car that drives well. (A used car dealer's expression; now often ironic.) □ *Now this is a nice little runner, sir.* □ *So that's your idea of a nice little runner. I see.*

nick 1. *n.* the state or condition of something. □ *What sort of nick is it in?* □ *We must know what nick he's in before we know what to do.* **2.** *n.* a police station. (Normally with *the*.) □ *Right, let's get you to the nick.* □ *I don't want to go to the nick!* **3.** *n.* a jail. (Normally with *the*.) □ *Welcome to the nick. Now, strip!* □ *If you're looking for Otto, try the nick.*

nicked *mod.* arrested. □ *Paul was nicked last night.* □ *"Now I'm nicked,"* he said.

nicker *n.* one Pound Sterling. □ *These things cost more than just a few nicker.* □ *Have you got a few nicker you can spare?*

nick off *vb. phr.* to play truant, especially from school. □ *By the time the class resumed after lunch, almost half the pupils appeared to have nicked off.* □ *Where are the children nicking off to, the teacher wondered?*

nick someone *vb.* to arrest someone. □ *The Old Bill nicked Paul outside his house.* □ *They are going to nick Joe, too.*

nick something *vb.* to steal something. □ *The thugs nicked a couple of apples from the fruit stand.* □ *Don't you never nick nufink! Do you 'ear me?*

niff 1. *n.* a bad smell. □ *I just can't stand that niff.* □ *Where is that terrible niff coming from?* **2.** *vb.* to smell badly. □ *The food, which had been left to rot, niffed in a most offensive manner.* □ *The fact is, the tramp was niffing badly.*

niffy *mod.* smelly. □ *If you must be niffy, be so somewhere else thank you.* □ *That's really niffy, don't go in there.*

nifty 1. *mod.* neat; smart. □ *That is a pretty nifty car you have there.* □ *Yes, it is nifty.* **2.** *mod.* agile; speedy. □ *Now here's a nifty little vehicle for you, sir.* □ *The nifty pickpocket ran off through the crowds and was gone in seconds.*

niggle 1. *vb.* to irritate; to nag. □ *Niggling her is not going to correct the mistake.* □ *So I made a mistake! I wish you'd stop niggling me.* **2.** *n.* an irritant or small complaint or worry. □ *Niggle, niggle! You're always niggling about something.* □ *What's your niggle today?*

niggling *mod.* irritating because much detail is involved. □ *Yes, it's niggling work.* □ *I hate jobs that are so niggling.*

night bird *n.* someone up and about at night. □ *What does that night bird get up to?* □ *I hate living next door to a night bird like that because I can't get to sleep.*

night person *n.* a person who prefers to be active at night. (Compare with DAY PERSON. The plural is NIGHT PEO-PLE.) □ *I can't function in the morning. I'm strictly a night person.* □ *Night people prefer to sleep in the daytime.*

night starvation *n.* sexual deprivation. (Crude.) □ *Hello my dear, can you help a young man with a severe case of night starvation?* □ *Night starvation? More like he's oversexed.*

nig-nog 1. *n.* a raw recruit to the army. □ *He may be a nig-nog but he knows how to look like a soldier.* □ *Tom? Oh, he's a nig-nog now.* **2.** *n.* a fool. □ *That nig-nog thinks he can convince them.* □ *I felt like such a bloody nig-nog when I found out that I'd got onto the wrong train.*

nil carborundum illigitium See ILLIGITIMIS NON CARBORUNDUM.

nimby *n.* "not in my back yard." (An acronym applied to anyone objecting to a new road, airport, power station, etc., that they do not wish to have intruding on their own neighbourhood, but would not object to intruding on someone else's.) □ *Me? A nimby? Naw. But I don't want that sewage plant built next door to my property.* □ *I think the nimbies have won again here.*

ninepence to the shilling *mod.* lacking intelligence or common sense; simple-minded. (In pre-1971 currency, there were 12 pennies in one shilling.) □ *Yes, clearly he's ninepence to the shilling.* □ *He may be ninepence to the shilling, but he's a really nice person.*

nineteenth hole *n.* the bar or clubroom of a golf club. (Likely to be filled with golfers who have played eighteen holes of golf.) □ *All of us gathered at the nineteenth hole to celebrate a great match.* □ *I hit a hole-in-one on the first hole and went straight to the nineteenth hole to celebrate.*

nine-to-five *mod.* typical working hours; structured and scheduled, starting and ending at set times. (From the expression *from nine to five*, normal working hours.) □ *I work nine-to-five.* □ *I can't stand the nine-to-five rat race.* □ *I really wanted a nine-to-five job until I finally got one.*

Nip *n.* a Japanese person. (Racially offensive.) □ *Why can you never be polite to Nips, eh?* □ *Y'know, Otto, if you call a Jap a Nip, he's likely to get nasty.*

nip *n.* a small, quickly-consumed measure of spirits. □ *Here, have a nip of this stuff.* □ *One nip is enough. That is powerful!*

nip out AND **pop out** *vb. phr.* to depart or exit briefly with the intention of returning. □ *I'm just nipping out to the shops.* □ *She's just popped out for a few minutes.*

nipper 1. *n.* a young child, particularly a boy. □ *I wish she would try to control that nipper of hers.* □ *I hope you like nippers. There are several here this afternoon.* **2.** *n.* a boy or youth assisting an adult workman. □ *Once, every tradesman worth his hire has to have his own nipper.* □ *Nippers are really rare nowadays.*

nipple count *n.* a measure of the down-market or prurience level of a newspaper. (Crude. Literally, the number of unencumbered female breasts visible upon perusal of the publication. Compare with PAGE THREE GIRL.) □ *On a typical day, some of these tabloids manage a nipple count well into double* *figures.* □ *What a disgusting idea! A nipple count! Really!*

nippy 1. *mod.* cold; chilly. □ *In nippy weather like this he prefers to stay indoors.* □ *Cor! Real nippy weather today, innit?* **2.** *mod.* fast; nimble. □ *It's a very nippy little car, especially when overtaking.* □ *We have some very nippy workers in here.* **3.** *mod.* irritable; bad-tempered. □ *Watch out, he's really nippy today.* □ *That's the sort of stupidity that makes me nippy!*

nit-picker *n.* someone who is hypercritical or pedantic. □ *Mary is always such a nit-picker.* □ *Nit-pickers drive me crazy.*

nit-picking *n.* minor criticism; pedantic fault-finding. □ *I am tired of all your nit-picking.* □ *Enough nit-picking! What are the major problems?*

nitty *mod.* foolish. □ *Don't be nitty. That's impossible.* □ *That was a nitty idea.*

nitty-gritty *n.* the fundamentals; the essential truth. (Compare with GET DOWN TO THE NITTY-GRITTY.) □ *What's the nitty-gritty about the broken window?* □ *Once we are down to the nitty-gritty, we can begin to sort things out.*

nitwit *n.* a stupid or foolish person. (Also a term of address.) □ *You are such a nitwit!* □ *Please stop acting like a nitwit all the time.*

nix 1. *n.* nothing. (From the German *nichts,* meaning "nothing.") □ *What did I get for all my trouble? Nix!* □ *I got nix for a tip. And after I was so helpful!* **2.** *exclam.* a warning to hide or take care. (Childish.) □ *Quick! Nix!* □ *Nix! They're looking for you.* **3.** *n.* no. □ *The man said nix, and he means nix.* □ *Nix, I won't do that.*

n.o. *mod.* not out. (In cricket.) □ *No, it's an n.o.* □ *Oh surely the umpire can't call that one another n.o.*

Noah's Ark 1. *n.* the dark. (Rhyming slang.) □ *It usually is Noah's Ark in the country at night when the Moon's not up.* □ *It's really Noah's Ark out there, you know.* **2.** *n.* a park. (Rhyming slang.) □ *I like being able to look out over the Noah's Ark from my flat.* □ *After lunch, we went for a stroll in the Noah's Ark.* **3.** *n.* an informer. (Rhym-

ing slang, linked as follows: Noah's Ark ≈ [nark] = informer.) □ *This new Noah's Ark gives me good info. OK?* □ *I don't trust Noah's Arks.*

nob 1. *n.* a wealthy or high-class person. □ *Here was one nob that was different from the others, he thought.* □ *I don't think I could take another nob like that today.* **2.** *n.* the head. □ *Harry's distinctive hairy nob hove into view.* □ *Where'd you get that nasty bump on your nob?* **3.** *n.* the male sexual organ. (Taboo.) □ *Unlike Myra, Sharon thinks of little else but nobs.* □ *Most men keep their brains in their nobs!* **4.** *vb.* to perform sexual intercourse. (Taboo.) □ *One look and he knew she had already been nobbed that evening.* □ *There were a couple of teenagers in the back room, nobbing away.*

nobble 1. *vb.* to acquire money by dishonest means. □ *I wonder how he nobbled that money?* □ *If you nobble money, sooner or later someone will nobble you.* **2.** *vb.* to catch or arrest a criminal. (Police.) □ *If I'm nobbled, I'll get ten years.* □ *The police nobbled him as he went to buy a newspaper.* **3.** *vb.* to secure support by cheating. □ *Somehow or other she nobbled their support away from me.* □ *Right, can we do this without any nobbling this time?* **4.** *vb.* to tamper with a racehorse to prevent it from winning. □ *I think someone must have nobbled the favourite.* □ *Why would anyone want to nobble that horse?* **5.** *vb.* to influence or attempt to influence a jury or an individual member of a jury. □ *If they catch you trying to nobble the jury they'll throw away the key.* □ *Nobbling is a very serious offence.*

no bloody good AND **N.B.G.; NBG** *mod.* useless, a waste of time. (Crude.) □ *That man is just no bloody good.* □ *My radio's NBG, Sarge.*

nobody *n.* an insignificant person. (Always with *a.* Compare with SOMEBODY.) □ *Don't pay any attention to him. He's just a nobody.* □ *That silly girl is a nobody and a pest.*

NOCD *phr.* "not our class, dear." (An initialism used to indicate that the person or thing referred to is not considered to be sufficiently high class for the speaker. Compare with NTD and PLU.) □ *Darling, let's face it. She is just NOCD, is she?* □ *He's pleasant enough, but NOCD.*

no cop *mod.* useless. □ *Sorry, that computer is no cop.* □ *All of them were no cop, as it turned out.*

noddle 1. *n.* the head. □ *That's using your noddle.* □ *Put your hat on your noddle, and let's go.* **2.** *n.* a fool or half-wit. (Use with caution. Also a form of address.) □ *Martin can be a complete noddle at times.* □ *Ignore them, Mary. These boys are just noddles.*

noddy *n.* a police officer on foot patrol. (Derived from WOODENTOP. "Noddy" is a well-known nursery character made of wood, who nods his head when speaking.) □ *The burglar was caught red-handed by the local noddy.* □ *What does the noddy want?*

noddy bike *n.* a small, underpowered motorcycle once used by police officers. (See NODDY.) □ *I saw a copper on a noddy bike the other day.* □ *Naw. The police haven't used noddy bikes for years.*

noddy car *n.* a small car. (See NODDY.) □ *I need a car, not a big one. A noddy car would do.* □ *You look ridiculous in that noddy car.*

noddy suit *n.* an NCB (nuclear, chemical and bacteriological) protection suit sometimes worn by military personnel. (It makes its wearers look foolish. Compare with NODDY.) □ *Noddy suits are exceptionally uncomfortable.* □ *We all had to sit there in our noddy suits for over an hour until the all clear sounded.*

nod through *vb. phr.* to agree without comment. □ *In the end, the scheme was just nodded through!* □ *There's no way that'll get nodded through.*

no earthly reason *n.* no conceivable reason. □ *There is no earthly reason for your behaviour.* □ *I can think of no earthly reason why the repairs should cost so much.*

noel *n.* a coward. (Rhyming slang, based on "Noel Coward.") □ *Well, are*

we all just noels, or are we going to do this? □ *I knew it, you're just a noel like all the rest.*

no end of something *n.* an endless supply of something. □ *Have some chocolate drops. I have no end of them.* □ *I've had no end of trouble ever since I bought this car.*

no-go area *n.* an area where entry is impossible or prohibited. □ *That's a no-go area, you can't go in there.* □ *They turned a number of streets around the area of the fire into a sort of no-go area.*

no great shakes *n.* someone or something that is not very good. (There is no affirmative version of this.) □ *Your idea is no great shakes, but we'll try it anyway.* □ *Ted is no great shakes in the brains department.*

no holds barred *mod.* without any moral or legal restrictions or limits. (There is no affirmative version of this.) □ *I want you to get that contract. Do anything—no holds barred.* □ *Try anything that will work, no holds barred.*

no-hoper 1. *n.* a hopeless case. □ *He's a total no-hoper, I'm sorry to say.* □ *Harry has become a no-hoper.* **2.** *n.* a person lacking the ability, drive or opportunity necessary to succeed. □ *What does the no-hoper want?* □ *Even a no-hoper like that has to earn a living.*

no joke *mod.* very serious. □ *I'm afraid this is no joke; we have a serious problem.* □ *It was no joke when he heard the news.*

no joy *n.* a failure. □ *Sorry, no joy.* □ *It's true. It was no joy again.*

No kidding! *exclam.* "I am telling the truth."; "I am not joking." □ *No kidding! I never thought she would do that.* □ *No kidding, he's really going to join the Air Force.*

No kidding? *interrog.* "Are you telling the truth?"; "Are you serious?" □ *No kidding? Are you telling me the truth?* □ *No kidding? Are you really going to join the Air Force?*

no names, no pack-drill *phr.* "with discretion, retribution can be avoided." □ *No names, no pack-drill, but I hear he's in deep trouble.* □ *Don't ask who told* *me that; no names, no pack-drill, you know!*

nonce 1. *n.* a worthless or useless person. (Offensive. Also a term of address.) □ *What a nonce that woman can be.* □ *Get out of here, you nonce!* **2.** *n.* a sexual pervert. (Crude.) □ *You would not believe what that nonce suggested!* □ *Most nonces are either sad or disgusting; a lot a both.* **3.** *n.* a prisoner convicted of a sexual offence. (Crude.) □ *Nonces are segregated from other prisoners for their own safety.* □ *Here is the special wing where we keep the nonces.* **4.** *n.* a lunatic. □ *Don't be a nonce. Use common sense.* □ *I'm beginning to feel more and more like a nonce the longer I stay around here.*

none-skid *n.* a Jewish person. (Offensive. Rhyming slang, linked as follows: none-skid ≈ [yid] = Jew.) □ *Don't call Jewish people none-skids, please. It is very offensive and racist.* □ *He said he was not a racist, he just hated this particular none-skid!*

none too clever See NOT SO CLEVER.

none too smart See NOT SO CLEVER.

no-no *n.* something that is not possible or permitted. □ *You can't smoke in here. That's a no-no.* □ *She seems to delight in doing all the no-no things.*

no object *n.* not a problem or a consideration. □ *I just want the best, Bruno; price no object!* □ *Oh, that's no object.*

no oil painting *n.* an ugly person. (Offensive.) □ *Bert's no oil painting; that's for sure.* □ *OK, I agree she's no oil painting, but she does have a lovely personality.*

nookie 1. *n.* sexual intercourse. (Taboo. Scots usage. Compare with LACK-ANOOKIE.) □ *Fancy a bit of nookie, gorgeous?* □ *I'm hoping to get some nookie tonight.* **2.** *n.* a woman viewed as a sex object. (Taboo.) □ *This particular nookie will break your fingers if you touch her again. Is that clear, you creep?* □ *Look at the nookie in this place, Martin!*

nooner *n.* sex in the middle of the day. (Taboo.) □ *Fancy a nooner, my angel?* □ *Their son, aged ten, walked right in on their nooner!*

nope *interj.* "no." □ *I won't do it! Nope. I won't!* □ *She asked him to do it, but he said, "Nope."*

norm *n.* a heterosexual, from the homosexual perspective. (Crude.) □ *Ignore him Sandy. He's just a norm.* □ *So this norm comes up and kicks Sandy in the stomach.*

Norman Normal *n.* a very conventional person. □ *I'm sorry but we really don't need another Norman Normal working here.* □ *What's a Norman Normal like that doing around here?*

north and south *n.* the mouth. (Rhyming slang.) □ *Have I ever told you that you have an ugly north and south?* □ *Shut your north and south and get on with your work.*

North Countryman *n.* a male native, citizen or inhabitant of northern England. □ *I'm a North Countryman and don't take to your soft southern ways.* □ *North Countryman can seem gruff but really, they are very kind and helpful.*

N.O.R.W.I.C.H. AND **NORWICH** *phr.* "(k)nickers off ready when I come home." (Crude. The initialism is sometimes written on love letters. Also an acronym.) □ *Don't forget, N.O.R.W.I.C.H.* □ *NORWICH! See you soon my love!*

nose 1. *n.* a criminal's informant. (Underworld.) □ *My nose told me about you.* □ *Mr Big has many noses.* **2.** *vb.* to spy. □ *I think there's someone nosing around outside the house.* □ *If you want to nose in my business, why not just ask? I've no secrets.*

nose and chin *vb.* to win. (Rhyming slang.) □ *Sally nosed and chinned in the lottery.* □ *He's convinced he'll nose and chin the big prize.*

nose candy *n.* cocaine. □ *Where do you buy nose candy around here?* □ *My sister's using nose candy, and I want to help her.*

nose job *n.* a plastic surgery operation to change the appearance of one's nose. □ *How much does a nose job cost?* □ *I don't want a nose job. What I've got is good enough.*

noserag *n.* a handkerchief. □ *He removed his noserag and blew his nose.*

□ *There was a noserag sticking out of his top pocket.*

nose-to-tail *mod.* of closely packed-together traffic. □ *The traffic was nose-to-tail on the by-pass this morning.* □ *I've been stuck in this nose-to-tail stuff for hours.*

Nosey Parker *n.* a meddlesome, inquisitive or prying person. (Also a term of address.) □ *Mary can be such a Nosy Parker.* □ *Look, you Nosy Parker, mind your own business.*

nosh 1. *vb.* to eat. (From the German *naschen*, meaning "to nibble," via Yiddish.) □ *You nosh too much.* □ *Every time I see you, you're noshing.* **2.** *n.* food. □ *How about some nosh?* □ *It's lunchtime. Let's go and find some nosh.*

nosher *n.* a greedy person. □ *Even a nosher like that has to earn a living.* □ *What does the nosher want?*

noshery *n.* a restaurant. □ *Do you know a good Indian noshery around here?* □ *There's a good noshery down the street so you won't starve.*

nosh on something *vb. phr.* to eat something. □ *After Christmas, we noshed on turkey for three days.* □ *Who's been noshing on the chocolate cake?*

no shortage of something *mod.* lots; plenty. □ *Oh, don't worry about that. I have no shortage of money!* □ *We've no shortage of fried chicken, so help yourself.*

no-show See NO SHOW.

no show AND **no-show** *n.* someone who doesn't show up for something, especially an airline flight. □ *My flight was cancelled because there were too many no-shows.* □ *I was bumped off my flight because it was over-booked and there were not enough no shows.*

nosh-up *n.* a big meal. □ *That was a great nosh-up at Tom's the other night.* □ *I haven't had a nosh-up like that in years.*

no skin off one's nose *mod.* no difference; immaterial. □ *It's no skin off my nose whether you go or I go.* □ *Pink, fuchsia, what does it matter? It's no skin off our nose.*

no sweat *interj.* "no problem;" "Don't worry; it is no problem." (Compare

with SWEAT.) □ *It's no big deal. No sweat.* □ *No sweat, don't fret about it.*

not a bean *mod.* without any money. □ *Me? Lend you money? I've not a bean.* □ *I had not a bean by the end of the week, but it was well worth it.*

not a bleeding thing AND **not a blind thing; not a dicky (bird); not a sausage** *n.* absolutely nothing. (NOT A DICKY (BIRD) is Rhyming slang, linked as follows: not a dicky bird ≈ [not a word] = [silence] = nothing.) □ *Sorry, this story is not a bleeding thing to do with me, all right?* □ *Say nothing, not a dicky bird.* □ *Okay, not a sausage, mate.*

not a blind thing See NOT A BLEEDING THING.

not a chance *interj.* "There is no possibility of this happening." □ *Me, lend you money? Not a chance!* □ *I won't go, not a chance. Don't ask.*

Not a clue. See NOT A GLIMMER (OF AN IDEA).

not a dicky (bird) See NOT A BLEEDING THING.

Not a glimmer (of an idea). AND **Not a clue.; Not the foggiest.** *sent.* "I have no idea."; "I do not have an answer." □ *Sorry. Not a glimmer of an idea.* □ *Not the foggiest. That's all I can say.*

not a hope in hell AND **not an earthly (chance); not a snowball's (chance in hell)** *phr.* "no hope or chance whatever." (Crude.) □ *I think we have to face the truth, which is that there is not a hope in hell for these people now.* □ *You have not a snowball's of the nomination.*

not all it's cracked up to be *phr.* "disappointing"; "not as good as promised." □ *Let's face it, this thing is not all it's cracked up to be.* □ *If it's not all it's cracked up to be, why do we continue to pretend it is?*

not all there *mod.* crazy; behaving strangely. □ *Tom's not all there. Really odd.* □ *You can't depend on Paul for much help. He's really not all there.*

not an earthly (chance) See NOT A HOPE IN HELL.

not a sausage See NOT A BLEEDING THING.

not a snowball's (chance in hell) See NOT A HOPE IN HELL.

not a soul *n.* nobody. □ *There was nobody there. Not a soul.* □ *Not a soul was awake, not even a mouse.*

not before time *mod.* late; at last. □ *Well, there you are—and not before time!* □ *Not before time, he got the situation back under control.*

Not (bloody) likely! AND **Not fucking likely!** *sent.* "Under no circumstances would I agree!" (Both are crude; NOT FUCKING LIKELY! is also taboo.) □ *Me join the army? Not bloody likely!* □ *It's not fucking likely that we're suddenly going to sprout wings and fly away.*

not bothered AND **not fussy** *phr.* "unconcerned"; "indifferent." □ *She seems to be not bothered by his fate.* □ *This is what you get for the money. I'm not fussy whether you like it or not.*

not care a brass farthing See NOT CARE A (TUPPENNY) DAMN.

not care a button See NOT CARE A (TUPPENNY) DAMN.

not care a fart See NOT CARE A (TUPPENNY) DAMN.

not care a fuck See NOT CARE A (TUPPENNY) DAMN.

not care a monkey's (fuck) See NOT CARE A (TUPPENNY) DAMN.

not care a toss See NOT CARE A (TUPPENNY) DAMN.

not care a (tuppenny) damn AND **not care a button; not care a brass farthing; not care a fart; not care a fuck; not care a monkey's (fuck); not care a toss; not care two hoots; not give a (tuppenny) damn; not give a button; not give a brass farthing; not give a fart; not give a fuck; not give a hoot; not give a monkey's (fuck); not give a toss; not give two hoots** *vb. phr.* to be completely disinterested; to not care in the least. (Expressions using FART or FUCK are taboo. All others are crude.) □ *Do what you like; really, I do not care a tuppenny damn.* □ *He really does not give two hoots, so take care.*

not care two hoots See NOT CARE A (TUPPENNY) DAMN.

notch something up AND **tote something up** *vb. phr.* to count up something; to add up or score something. □ *Well, it looks like we notched up another victory.* □ *The crooks were able to tote up just one more theft before they were caught.*

not cricket *mod.* unfair; unreasonable; unacceptable. (See affirmative examples at CRICKET.) □ *You can't do that! It's not cricket!* □ *What do you mean it's not cricket? You do it.*

not for toffee *mod.* under no circumstances. □ *No, not for toffee!* □ *I would not go there, not for toffee.*

Not fucking likely! See NOT (BLOODY) LIKELY!

not fussy 1. *mod.* not especially eager; unwilling. □ *I'm not fussy; do what you like.* □ *I don't think it matters; it would seem that he's not fussy.* **2.** *mod.* disinterested. □ *Suit yourself, I'm not fussy.* □ *If you're not fussy, can we go now?* **3.** See also NOT BOTHERED.

not give a brass farthing See NOT CARE A (TUPPENNY) DAMN.

not give a button See NOT CARE A (TUPPENNY) DAMN.

not give a fart See NOT CARE A (TUPPENNY) DAMN.

not give a fuck See NOT CARE A (TUPPENNY) DAMN.

not give a hoot See NOT CARE A (TUPPENNY) DAMN.

not give a monkey's (fuck) See NOT CARE A (TUPPENNY) DAMN.

not give a toss See NOT CARE A (TUPPENNY) DAMN.

not give a (tuppenny) damn See NOT CARE A (TUPPENNY) DAMN.

not give two hoots See NOT CARE A (TUPPENNY) DAMN.

not go much on someone *vb. phr.* to dislike someone, somewhat. □ *You don't go much on her, do you?* □ *The plain truth is she does not go much on her.*

not grow on trees *vb. phr.* not to be abundant; not to be expendable. (Usually said about money.) □ *I can't afford that. Money doesn't grow on trees, you know.* □ *Don't waste the apples; they don't grow on trees, you know.*

not half bad *mod.* really rather good. □ *That meal was not half bad, Mary.* □

Oh, I suppose the play was not half bad.

Nothing doing! *exclam.* "I refuse to do this!" □ *Me, go to the opera? Nothing doing!* □ *Nothing doing! I won't do this.*

nothing doing *phr.* "there is no sign of activity"; "nothing is happening." □ *It's very quiet at work this week; nothing doing.* □ *If there's nothing doing, go and get a cup of tea.*

Nothing in it. See (THERE'S) NOTHING IN IT.

nothing loath *mod.* willing. □ *Well, nothing loath, here goes!* □ *Certainly he has a very nothing loath attitude.*

Nothing to it. See (THERE'S) NOTHING IN IT.

nothing to sneeze at *n.* no small amount of money; something not inconsequential. □ *It's not a fortune, but it's nothing to sneeze at either.* □ *She worked hard and did not accomplish much, but it's nothing to sneeze at.*

nothing to write home about *n.* something small or inconsequential. □ *I got a little bit of a pay rise this year, but it was nothing to write home about.* □ *The party was nothing to write home about.*

nothing upstairs *phr.* no brains; stupid. (See BE A BIT SLOW UPSTAIRS.) □ *Tom is sort of stupid. You know—nothing upstairs.* □ *I know what's wrong with you. Nothing upstairs.*

not long arrived AND **not long here** *mod.* newly arrived. □ *We're not long arrived and don't yet know our way around.* □ *They have not long here so show them what to do, where to go, and so on.*

not long here See NOT LONG ARRIVED.

not much cop *mod.* of little use. □ *Simon's not much cop when it comes to thinking, I'm afraid.* □ *The original idea was not much cop so we've come up with another.*

not on *mod.* not acceptable; not possible. □ *I'm afraid that's just not on.* □ *What you suggest is not on. Please come up with an acceptable alternative.*

Not on your nelly! *exclam.* "Not on your life!" "Emphatically, absolutely not!"; "On no account whatsoever!" (Rhyming slang, linked as follows: not on your nelly [duff] ≈ [puff] = [breath] = not on your life. Who is "Nelly Duff?" Goodness knows. It is sufficient that her name rhymes with "puff.") □ *Work for him? Not on your nelly!* □ *Not on your nelly, I'm just not interested.*

not proper *mod.* not socially acceptable. □ *That is not proper behaviour.* □ *If what you do is considered to be not proper you'll be asked to leave.*

not quite *mod.* almost. □ *I know we're not quite there, but it's awfully close.* □ *I'm afraid what you say is not quite, and little things mean a lot in this.*

not short of a bob or two *mod.* prosperous. □ *Oh yes, he's not short of a bob or two.* □ *Anyone who can afford a house like that must be not short of a bob or two.*

not so clever AND **not very clever; not too clever; none too clever; not so smart; not very smart; none too smart; not too smart** **1.** *mod.* unwell. □ *Mike's not so clever this morning, but I think he'll be well again soon.* □ *Oh dear, I feel not so smart today.* □ *She took ill at work and was still not too clever by the time she got home.* □ *Carol is none too smart today, I'm afraid.* **2.** *mod.* unlikeable; unpleasant. □ *Well, the weather was not very clever over the weekend, was it?* □ *Letting yourself turn into a drug addict is none too clever—and it's not very smart either.* **3.** *mod.* broken; unusable. □ *The TV set's not so clever today; we'll have to get it fixed.* □ *Oh dear, the computer's not so smart today.* □ *Maggie's car was not looking too clever after she drove it into that tree.*

not so dusty *mod.* just about acceptable. □ *Well all right, that's not so dusty I suppose.* □ *Try to keep things not so dusty.*

not so smart See NOT SO CLEVER.

not take a blind bit of notice of someone or something *phr.* to completely disregard someone or something; to deliberately ignore someone or something. □ *My advice to you is to not take a blind bit of notice of the defect and* *the chances are no one else will either.* □ *Are you deliberately not taking a blind bit of notice of me in the hope I'll go away?*

Not the foggiest. See NOT A GLIMMER (OF AN IDEA).

not to know *mod.* could not know. □ *It's all right. You were not to know that.* □ *We caught him out because he was not to know that sort of thing unless he was genuine.*

not too clever See NOT SO CLEVER.

not too smart See NOT SO CLEVER.

Not to worry. *phr.* "Don't worry." □ *You lost your ticket? Not to worry. I'll give you mine.* □ *Not to worry. Everything will be all right.*

not very clever See NOT SO CLEVER.

not very smart See NOT SO CLEVER.

not want to know *vb. phr.* to refuse to listen or take notice. □ *We can't convince him. He just does not want to know.* □ *You may not want to know, but it's true anyway.*

not worth a brass farthing See NOT WORTH A (TUPPENNY) DAMN.

not worth a button See NOT WORTH A (TUPPENNY) DAMN.

not worth a damn *mod.* worthless. (Crude.) □ *This pen is not worth a damn.* □ *When it comes to keeping score, she's not worth a damn.*

not worth a fart See NOT WORTH A (TUPPENNY) DAMN.

not worth a fuck See NOT WORTH A (TUPPENNY) DAMN.

not worth a monkey's (fuck) See NOT WORTH A (TUPPENNY) DAMN.

not worth a toss See NOT WORTH A (TUPPENNY) DAMN.

not worth a (tuppenny) damn AND **not worth a button; not worth a brass farthing; not worth a fart; not worth a fuck; not worth a monkey's (fuck); not worth a toss; not worth two hoots** *mod.* utterly worthless; of no value whatever. (Expressions using FART or FUCK are taboo. All others are crude.) □ *He said he thought the idea was not worth a tuppenny damn.* □ *I'm sorry, your jewellery is not worth two hoots.*

not worth two hoots See NOT WORTH A (TUPPENNY) DAMN.

nous *n.* common sense, initiative or gumption. □ *Anyone with an ounce of nous should be able to do that, Otto.* □ *The problem with nous is that so few have any.*

No way! *exclam.* "This is impossible!" □ *Me join the Army? No way!* □ *She can't do that. No way!*

no-win situation *n.* a situation in which there is no hope of success. □ *I find myself in a no-win situation again.* □ *Realising he was in a no-win situation, Ted did the only rational thing; he panicked.*

Now what? *interrog.* "What is wrong now?"; "What happens next?" □ *I ran into the room and stopped in front of Tom. "Now what?" asked Tom.* □ *I see you're standing there. So, now what?*

Now you're talking! *exclam.* "What you are saying now makes sense!" □ *Now you're talking! You've got a great idea!* □ *"Now you're talking!" said the coach when I told him I was going to win.*

nozzer *n.* a new member of a ship's crew. □ *Who's the nozzer?* □ *How many nozzers are coming on board then?*

NTD *phr.* "not top drawer." (An initialism used to indicate that the person or thing referred to is not considered to be sufficiently high class for the speaker. Compare with NOCD and PLU. See TOP DRAWER.) □ *I don't think I want to talk to any more NTD people today.* □ *He's pleasant enough, but NTD.*

nub *n.* a cigarette end. □ *I threw my nub away and turned to look him in the eye.* □ *He produced a nub from his pocket and relit it.*

nuddie AND **nuddy 1.** *n.* a film featuring nudes. (Compare with SKIN FLICK.) □ *There is a nuddie showing at the Odeon.* □ *I didn't know this film was a nuddy!* **2.** *n.* a person who is naked; a nudist. □ *We walked through the woods and there was this nuddy standing there!* □ *How were we supposed to know there was a club for nuddies in the woods?*

3. *mod.* naked. □ *We walked through the woods and we saw a few nuddie people amongst the trees.* □ *How were we supposed to know there was a club for nuddy people in the woods?*

nudger *n.* the male sexual organ. (Taboo.) □ *The streaker covered his nudger as he ran across the field. What sort of streak is that?* □ *He made some joke about a nudger, but nobody laughed.*

nuffink *n.* nothing. (Eye-dialect. Typical spoken English in London and surrounding area. Used in writing only for effect. Used in the examples of this dictionary.) □ *I didn't swipe nuffink, sir.* □ *He's nuffink but a little toe-rag, and there's the truth!*

nuke 1. *n.* a nuclear weapon. □ *Are there nukes aboard that ship?* □ *The military establishment is working on a number of new nukes.* **2.** *vb.* to utterly destroy or annihilate someone or something. (As if with a nuclear weapon.) □ *Your cat ran through my garden and totally nuked my flowers!* □ *I'm going to nuke that cat the next time I see it.*

number 1. *n.* a good-looking or attractive girl or young woman. □ *Who is that cute little number I saw you with?* □ *She is really some number.* **2.** *n.* a marijuana cigarette. □ *Max lit up a number just as the boss came in.* □ *Can I have a hit off your number?* **3.** *n.* an act or performance; a theatrical act. □ *Ann did her number and left the stage.* □ *I'll talk to you after my number.*

number-cruncher *n.* a large and powerful computer. (Computer jargon.) □ *They traded in the old computer for a powerful number-cruncher.* □ *The small one is reserved for minor projects. The really big and important jobs are run on the number-cruncher.*

number crunching *n.* using a computer to solve enormously complicated or complex mathematical problems. (Computer jargon.) □ *I don't do a lot of number crunching, so I don't need a terribly fast machine.* □ *I use the big mainframe computer for number crunching.*

number one *n.* oneself. (Compare with LOOK AFTER NUMBER ONE.) □ *I don't know who will pay for the broken window, but old number one is not that person!* □ *Everything always comes back to number one. I have to solve everybody's problems.*

nuppence *n.* no money. □ *I'm broke. I've nuppence!* □ *Nuppence is all I pay for that thing.*

nut 1. *n.* (one's) head. □ *A brick fell and hit him on the nut.* □ *The cricket ball came in fast. Clonk! Right on the nut!* **2.** *n.* an enthusiast (about something). □ *Paul is a nut about chocolate cake.* □ *Mary is a party nut.*

nut (case) 1. *n.* an odd or strange person; a crazy person. (Compare with NUTTER.) □ *Who is that nut case over there in the corner?* □ *Some nut is going to try to fly from the top of one building to another.* **2.** *n.* a patient in a lunatic asylum. □ *Sorry, I think the guy's a real nut case.* □ *Who's that nut with Candy?*

nuthatch See NUTHOUSE.

nuthouse AND **nuthatch** *n.* an insane asylum. □ *That judge spent three years in the nuthouse, y'know.* □ *They're going to send you to the nuthatch one fine day.*

nutmeg *vb.* to kick a soccer ball between the legs of a member of the opposing team. (Crude.) □ *He nutmegged me!* □ *Did you see how he nutmegged that ball there?*

nut-rock *n.* a bald person. □ *He's a pleasant nut-rock.* □ *The nut-rock was waiting outside the office for him.*

Nuts! 1. *exclam.* "crazy." □ *You're nuts if you think I care!* □ *That whole idea is just nuts!* **2.** *n.* the testicles. (Taboo. Normally with *the* and in the plural.) □ *Thud, right in the nuts. Ye gods, it hurt!* □ *He turned sideways to protect his nuts.*

nuts and bolts *n.* the mundane workings of something; the basics of something. □ *I want you to learn how to write well. You have to get down to the nuts and bolts of writing.* □ *She's got a lot of good, general ideas, but when it* comes to the nuts and bolts of getting something done, she's no good.

nutter *n.* an odd or strange person; a crazy person. (Compare with NUT (CASE).) □ *Sally is such a nutter. She would forget her head if it wasn't screwed on.* □ *That guy is a real nutter if he thinks he can get a taxi at this hour.*

nuttery *n.* an insane asylum; the place where NUTTERS live. □ *If you keep acting so oddly, we'll have to put you in a nuttery.* □ *This place is a nuttery! I've never seen so many nutters!*

nutty *mod.* silly; giddy; stupid. □ *What a nutty idea!* □ *That's just nutty, you know.* □ *Mary is a real nutty girl, but she is my best friend.*

nyaff *n.* an insignificant or worthless person. (Scots usage. Ironic.) □ *Just get lost, ye wee nyaff!* □ *Who's that nyaff that keeps pestering Sheila?*

nybble See NIBBLE.

nympho 1. *mod.* nymphomaniacal. (Crude.) □ *I do not exaggerate; she behaved in a most nympho way with every man who crossed her path.* □ *Do you know what nympho behaviour is really like?* **2.** *n.* AND **nymph** a nymphomaniac. (Crude.) □ *I hear nymphos are found more often in male fantasies than real life.* □ *Oh, I don't know. There was this woman at work who we all reckoned had to be a nymph.*

O See ORAL.

oak *vb.* to fool around. (Rhyming slang, linked as follows: oak ≈ [joke] = fool around.) □ *Stop oaking and start working.* □ *Their kids just oak around all day.*

obie man *n.* a burglar who reads obituaries so that he knows which houses will be empty while the occupants are attending a funeral. □ *Otto thought being an obie man was smart.* □ *Unfortunately, Otto discovered that to be an obie man you have to be able to read.*

ocean wave *n.* a shave. (Rhyming slang.) □ *I need an ocean wave.* □ *He asked the barber to give him an ocean wave.*

O.D. AND **o.d.; OD 1.** *vb.* to purposely or accidentally give oneself a fatal dose of drugs. □ *Max O.D.'d on heroin.* □ *I knew he would OD someday.* **2.** *vb.* to die from an overdose of drugs. □ *Two kids at my school OD'd last weekend.* □ *I think Max may O.D. soon if nothing is done.* **3.** *n.* an overdose of a drug. (Initialism.) □ *Max took an O.D. and was sent to the hospital.* □ *If you take an o.d. and no one is around, you may end up dead.*

oddball 1. *n.* an eccentric person. □ *Tom really is an oddball. He ordered a pineapple and strawberry milkshake.* □ *We oddballs love concoctions like that.* **2.** *mod.* strange; peculiar. □ *It's too oddball for me.* □ *Your oddball ideas have cost us too much money.*

odd-bod *n.* a strange person. □ *Who is that odd-bod over in the corner?* □ *Ralph can be sort of an odd-bod now and then.*

odds and sods *n.* miscellaneous items. □ *Why do you never sort out these odds and sods?* □ *There's an even bigger pile of odds and sods over there in that corner.*

odds-on *mod.* referring to betting odds that are better than even. □ *My horse is an odds-on favourite to win.* □ *My plan is odds-on to be selected.*

Oedipus Rex *vb.* to perform sexual intercourse. (Taboo. Both rhyming slang—with "sex"—and a classical allusion.) □ *One look and he knew she had already Oedipus Rexed that evening.* □ *There were a couple of teenagers in the back room, Oedipus Rexing.*

of account *mod.* significant; important. (Often used in the negative.) □ *Now you may consider this news to be of no account...* □ *A major character, an individual of account.*

of a tizz See IN A TIZZY.

of a twitter See IN A TWITTER.

off *n.* the commencement of a horse race. (Always with *the*.) □ *At the off, my horse was in the lead.* □ *Right up to the off, I thought he might not run.*

off-beat *mod.* strange; unconventional. □ *That is really an offbeat idea.* □ *Tom is sort of offbeat. Well, he's weird.*

off by heart *mod.* memorized; known by heart. □ *In my day we had to learn our tables off by heart.* □ *Some people still think learning off by heart is the best way to learn.*

off colour *mod.* in poor health. □ *Carol is a bit off colour today, I'm afraid.* □ *Oh dear, I feel rather off colour.*

off-colour *mod.* slightly improper; somewhat pornographic. □ *That's not* *just off-colour, it's pure filth!* □ *What they were doing was disgusting! It was just like watching an off-colour film!...I suppose... I've never seen one, of course.*

off form *mod.* performing worse than usual. (Compare with ON FORM.) □ *That was terrible! She must be off form tonight.* □ *Try not to be off form again tomorrow.*

off-line *mod.* not connected to a computer, by direct connection or via the telephone system, etc. (Computer jargon. Compare with ON-LINE.) □ *When he's off-line he's sort of lost.* □ *The system was off-line all day, so we could get nothing done.*

off-load something *vb. phr.* to get rid of something burdensome by transferring it elsewhere. □ *Don't try to off-load your problems on me.* □ *Otto's trying to off-load his stash of stolen goods before the cops catch up with him.*

off one's block See OFF ONE'S CHUMP.

off one's chump AND **off one's rocker; off one's trolley; off one's block; off one's head; off one's nut; off the chump; off the head; off the scone** *mod.* crazy; insane; eccentric. □ *Just ignore Uncle Charles. He's off his chump.* □ *Am I off my trolley, or did that car suddenly disappear?*

off one's head See OFF ONE'S CHUMP.

off one's nut See OFF ONE'S CHUMP.

off one's rocker See OFF ONE'S CHUMP.

off one's trolley See OFF ONE'S CHUMP.

off the chump See OFF ONE'S CHUMP.

off the crust *mod.* insane. □ *Pay no attention to her. She's off the crust.* □ *You must really be off the crust if you think I'll put up with that kind of stuff.*

off the cuff **1.** *mod.* spontaneous; without delay. □ *He agreed, off the cuff.* □ *Off the cuff, it's not very likely.* **2.** See also OFF THE TOP OF ONE'S HEAD.

off the head See OFF ONE'S CHUMP.

off the hook **1.** *mod.* no longer in jeopardy; no longer obligated. □ *I'll let you off the hook this time, but never again.* □ *We're off the hook. We don't need to worry anymore.* **2.** *mod.* dead. □ *Well, that's him off the hook.* □ *I don't like to see anyone I knew off the hooks.*

off-the-peg *mod.* [of clothes] ready-made. □ *We came across this shop selling nothing but off-the-peg dresses.* □ *Only common people wear off-the-peg clothes, Mother!*

off the scone See OFF ONE'S CHUMP.

off-the-shelf *mod.* readily available; purchasable without any special difficulties or delays. □ *This is just plain old off-the-shelf hand lotion. Isn't it great?* □ *Is it off-the-shelf?* □ EANI: *I don't use off-the-shelf software in my computer. I write my own.* MEANI: *Ahah! That's why nothing ever works.*

off the top of one's head AND **off the cuff** *mod.* as first thought; without checking. □ *Just off the top of one's head, I think that's right.* □ *He gave an off the cuff response, but it turned out to be almost entirely correct.*

off the wagon *mod.* drinking again after a period of abstinence. □ *Poor John fell off the wagon again. Drunk as a skunk.* □ *He was off the wagon for a year the last time before he sobered up.*

off the wall *mod.* unusual; odd. □ *I better warn you; Otto's a bit off the wall.* □ *What an off the wall sort of place this is.*

off you go *phr.* "begin now." □ *Right, this is it. Off you go!* □ *Off you go, and good luck.*

off your own bat *mod.* without help. □ *If you can manage all that off your own bat I'll be impressed.* □ *You did this? Off your own bat? Great!*

of great age *mod.* very old. □ *This stately home is of great age.* □ *Mr Thurso is of great age.*

of sorts *mod.* inferior; substandard. □ *Well, it's a solution of sorts, I suppose.* □ *It was beer of sorts, but not what I'd ever have chosen.*

Oh, boy! AND **Boy, oh boy!** **1.** *exclam.* "This is surprising!"; "That was or will be very pleasing!" □ *Oh, boy! That was a great play!* □ *Boy, oh boy! What a party!* **2.** *exclam.* "What a mess!"; "We've got a real problem here!" □ *Oh, boy! That was a terrible play!* □ *Boy, oh boy! What a mess!*

oh my dear *n.* beer. (Rhyming slang.) □ *I do like this oh my dear they have* *in here.* □ *Can I have oh my dear, please?*

Oh, yeah? *interrog.* "You think you know about this but you don't."; "You are not just wrong but stupid, too."; "Are you trying to start a fight?" □ *Oh, yeah? What makes you think so?* □ *Oh, yeah? Do you want to start something?* □ *Tom said, "Bill, you are a numbskull." Bill whirled around, saying, "Oh, yeah?"*

oi(c)k *n.* an uncultured or boorish person; a country yokel. □ *What's an oick like that doing around here?* □ *I'm sorry but we really don't need another oik working here.*

oiled *mod.* intoxicated due to drink. □ *You came in oiled last night. What's going on?* □ *She was always oiled by bedtime.*

oiled, oiled story *n.* nonsense spoken by an intoxicated person. (With *the.*) □ *Oh no, here's Olly, straight from the pub with more of his oiled, oiled story.* □ *Please find some way to shut up that drunk and his oiled, oiled story, Mary.*

oiler *n.* a drunkard. □ *You are going to turn into a oiler if you don't let up on your drinking.* □ *There was an oiler asleep across the front entrance to the office when I got here this morning.*

oil the knocker *vb. phr.* to bribe or to tip a doorman. □ *Why do you want to oil the knocker?* □ *I'm sure you can oil the knocker of at least one doorman, if you try hard enough.*

oily lamp *n.* a tramp. (Rhyming slang.) □ *Even a oily lamp like that needs some money.* □ *The oily lamp was waiting outside the office for him.*

oily rag 1. *n.* an incompetent car mechanic. □ *Where's that oily rag friend of yours who serviced my car so it's worse than before he started, then?* □ *I would not say Joe's an oily rag. Not the world's greatest car mechanic, yes. But not an oily rag, no.* **2.** *n.* a cigarette. (Rhyming slang, linked as follows: oily rag ≈ [fag] = cigarette.) □ *Hey, mate, gimme an oily rag.* □ *Go and buy your own oily rags!*

OK AND **O.K.; okay 1.** *interj.* "accepted." (This may be an initialism derived

from a misspelling of "all correct" ("oll kerrect.") Alternatively, it may have developed from the Scots "och aye" which both means and sounds almost the same. There are many other theories but no one really knows its origin, except that it was first recorded in 19th century America.) □ *O.K., I'll do it.* □ Q: *I'd like you to lend me £100.* A: *Okay.* □ *So, he said, like, "okay," and, like, I go "okay." So we both go "okay." O.K.?* **2.** *mod.* acceptable. □ *Fred is an O.K. guy.* □ *This cake is okay, but not what I would call first rate.* **3.** *mod.* acceptably. □ *She ran okay—nothing spectacular.* □ *They usually do it okay.* **4.** *n.* [someone's] acceptance. □ *I won't give the final O.K. until I see the plans.* □ *We got her OK and went on with the job.* **5.** *vb.* to approve something. □ *She refused to okay our plans.* □ *Please OK this bill so I can pay it.*

okay See OK.

okay, yah *phr.* an indication of agreement, as uttered by a SLOANE RANGER. (See THAT'S BRILL.) □ *Okay, yah. That's brill.* □ *If you like, okay, yah.*

okey-dokey *interj.* "yes"; "OK." □ *Okey-dokey, I'll be there at noon.* □ *Okey-dokey. You certainly can.*

old and bitter *n.* a mother-in-law. (A pun on MILD AND BITTER.) □ *I'll ask my old and bitter if I can go.* □ *What time does your old and bitter get home?*

Old Bailey *n.* the popular name for the Central Criminal Court, London. (Normally with *the.* From the name of the street it is upon.) □ *Otto's up in the Old Bailey next week.* □ *All big criminal trials in London go to the Old Bailey.*

old battle-axe *n.* an elderly but aggressive and unpleasant woman. □ *I'm afraid I do know that old battle-axe.* □ *Why is that old battle-axe walking through our office?*

old bean AND **old boy; old chap; old fellow; old fruit; old stick** *n.* a friendly greeting between men. □ *What can I do for you today, old bean?* □ *The old stick's in a bad way, you know.*

Old Bill *n.* the police. (Normally with *the.* See BILL SHOP.) □ *Get away, get* *away! The Old Bill are outside! □ The Old Bill are after me!*

old boy See OLD BEAN.

old boy network *n.* an informal preferment network for men from similar backgrounds such as school, army, college, etc. □ *There's always an old boy network behind these things, isn't there? □ Well, the old boy network certainly did me no good.*

old bubble *n.* a wife. (Rhyming slang, linked as follows: old bubble ≈ [trouble and strife] ≈ wife. Compare with TROUBLE AND STRIFE.) □ *I've got to go home to my old bubble. □ My old bubble disapproved of the film.*

old buffer AND **buffer** *n.* a foolish but harmless old man. □ *There's an old buffer asking for you at the door. □ That poor buffer thinks he can convince them.*

old chap See OLD BEAN.

old fashioned look *n.* a sceptical or disapproving look. □ *Why the old fashioned look? □ I gave her an old fashioned look, but she winked back!*

old fellow 1. *n.* the male sexual organ. (Taboo.) □ *Only small boys wave their old fellows about like that, Wayne. Put it away! □ Myra says old fellows are disgusting but then Myra's strange.* 2. *n.* a man. (Also a term of greeting between men.) □ *Why do we need this old fellow? □ Come on old fellow; time to go home.* 3. See also OLD BEAN.

old flame *n.* a former sweetheart or lover. □ *Mary's old flame, Tom, will be at the party. □ It is best to forget an old flame.*

old fogey AND **old fogy** *n.* an old-fashioned person. □ *My uncle is an old fogey. He must be the most old-fashioned man in the world. □ Don't be such an old fogy.*

old fruit See OLD BEAN.

old girl *n.* an old lady; a lively older woman. □ *That old girl is still going strong. □ What makes an old girl like that so high-spirited?*

old hand (at something) *n.* someone experienced at doing something. □ *I'm an old hand at fixing cars. □ Do you need help with your painting? I'm an old hand.*

old hat *n.* an old-fashioned thing or person; an outmoded thing or person. □ *That's just old hat. This is the modern world! □ Her latest work is nothing but old hat. She's through.*

oldie 1. *n.* an old story, song, trick, etc. □ *Oh that song's an oldie but a goody. □ It's an oldie, and it was lousy the first time.* 2. *n.* an old person. □ *Here was one oldie that was different from the others, he thought. □ I don't think I could take another oldie like that today.*

old King Cole *n.* the dole. (Rhyming slang.) □ *I'm off to collect my old King Cole. □ How long have you been on the old King Cole now?*

old lady AND **old woman** 1. *n.* [one's] mother. □ *I'll ask my old lady if I can go. □ What time does your old lady get home?* 2. *n.* [one's] wife. □ *I wonder what my old lady is cooking for dinner tonight. □ My old lady doesn't like for me to go out without her.* 3. *n.* [one's] girlfriend. □ *My old lady and I are getting married next week. □ I got my old lady a bracelet for her birthday.*

old lag 1. *n.* a habitual convict. □ *An old lag has certain informal privileges denied to new prisoners. □ All the old lags are kept in that wing.* 2. *n.* a former convict. □ *You'd never guess Charlie's an old lag, would you? □ Watch out, he's an old lag, you know.*

old man 1. *n.* [one's] father. □ *I'll ask my old man if I can go. □ What time does your old man get home?* 2. *n.* [one's] husband. □ *My old man is downstairs fixing the furnace. □ My old man is sick and can't come with me.* 3. *n.* [one's] boyfriend. □ *Ask your old man to come to the party, too. □ I got my old man to take me to see that film I told you about.* 4. *n.* the boss; a high-ranking officer. (Always with *the.*) □ *The old man says do it, so you had better just do it. □ Quiet! Here comes the old man.*

old Mick *mod.* nauseous; sick. (Rhyming slang.) □ *Paul was feeling a bit of the old Mick so he went home. □ If you're old Mick, we better stop.*

old one-two 1. *n.* a series of two punches delivered quickly, one after another. (Boxing. Always with *the*.) □ *Tom gave Bill the old one-two, and the argument was ended right there.* □ *Watch out for Tom. He's a master of the old one-two.* **2.** *n.* a series of passes reciprocating between two players advancing up the field. (Soccer. Always with *the*.) □ *Tom and Bill did the old one-two right up to the goal-mouth.* □ *The other team specialises in that old one-two business. Watch out for it!* **3.** *n.* sexual intercourse. (Crude. Always with *the*.) □ *There were Bill and Mary doing the old one-two right there on the sofa.* □ *I think he's hoping for a little bit of the old one-two when he takes her home.*

Old Pals Act *n.* a mythical law or principle that old friends should help each other. (Always with *the*.) □ *Please, I'm desperate. Do I have to invoke the Old Pals Act?* □ *We'll have none of this Old Pals Act around here. Earn your keep or clear off!*

old penny *n.* the penny that was in circulation before decimalisation of the currency in 1971. (It was worth 1/240th of a Pound. Compare with NEW PENNY.) □ *You get very little for a new penny, but even less for an old penny.* □ *What were you able to buy for one old penny?*

old school tie 1. *n.* a necktie carrying a specific pattern or design that only former students of a particular school or college are entitled to wear. □ *The old school tie is there to remind you of your youth.* □ *But the school I went to has no old school tie.* **2.** *n.* a sentimental code of loyalty to traditional ways and values. □ *Can we rely upon the old school tie with him?* □ *The old school tie is always worth something.*

Old Scratch *n.* the Devil. □ *If you children are bad, Old Scratch will get you!* □ *Don't frighten the children with stories about Old Scratch.*

old soldier *n.* an empty liquor bottle; an empty beer bottle or can. □ *Larry hid all his old soldiers under the bed.* □ *Bill hit Tom over the head with an old soldier.*

old stick See OLD BEAN.

old sweat 1. *n.* an old soldier. □ *Old sweats, like old soldiers, never die. They just fade away.* □ *Who's the old sweat sitting in the corner?* **2.** *n.* an experienced individual. □ *Don't worry, he's an old sweat. John'll be all right with him.* □ *I suppose I'm a bit of an old sweat, having been working here for over twenty years now.*

old thing *n.* an affectionate term of address to someone of either sex, not necessarily old. □ *Don't worry old thing, we won't let you down.* □ *The poor old thing needs our help.*

old trout *n.* an unpleasant old woman. □ *Please get that old trout out of here!* □ *This old trout is looking for work, I think.*

old woman See OLD LADY.

O-levels See ORAL.

oliver *n.* a fist. (Rhyming slang, linked as follows: Oliver [Twist] ≈ fist. Oliver Twist was a character in Dickens's novel of the same name.) □ *Put up your olivers, you young whippersnapper!* □ *His olivers were about twice the size of mine!*

on a loser *mod.* in a position or situation from which winning is not possible. □ *I think you're on a loser if you really think that will happen.* □ *Old Harold's been on a loser for most of his life.*

on appro *mod.* on approval. □ *I brought the computer home on appro, but my dad didn't, so it went back.* □ *Of course you can have it on appro, sir.*

on a shoestring *mod.* on practically no money; on a very tight budget. (Compare with SHOESTRING.) □ *I run my business on a shoestring. I never know from day to day whether I will survive.* □ *We live on a shoestring—hardly any money at all.*

on a short leash See ON A TIGHT LEASH.

on a tight leash AND **on a short leash** *mod.* under very careful control. □ *My father keeps my brother on a tight leash.* □ *We can't do much around here. The boss has us all on a short leash.*

on camera *mod.* live on television. □ *I saw it happen! Right there, on camera!*

□ *The whole thing was there, right on camera.*

once (and) for all See FOR GOOD AND ALL.

once a week *n.* a judge or magistrate. (Rhyming slang, linked as follows: once a week ≈ [beak] = judge/magistrate.) □ *The once a week ain't wearing a wig!* □ *I'll be up before the once a week tomorrow.*

once in a blue moon *mod.* very rarely. □ *I do this only once in a blue moon.* □ *Once in a blue moon I have a little wine with dinner.*

once(-over) AND **oncer** *n.* a quick visual examination, especially of or by a person of the opposite sex. (Always with *the.*) □ *The way she was giving him the once-over, I knew she would say something to him.* □ *Tom, you're always giving the girls the oncer!*

on(c)er *n.* that which happens only once. □ *Winning the lottery must be a oncer for you, Brian. Make the most of it!* □ *I suppose a hole in one is a oner for most golfers.*

oncer **1.** *n.* impudence. (Rhyming slang, linked as follows: oncer = [once a week] ≈ [cheek] = impudence.) □ *What a oncer that is! Who does that woman think she is?* □ *Any more oncers like that and he'll get everything he deserves.* **2.** *n.* a unique person, object or event. □ *The oncer was still waiting outside the office for him.* □ *He really is a oncer.* **3.** See also ONCE(-OVER).

one-acter *n.* a short play, consisting of one act only. □ *The village drama club are putting on a one-acter next week.* □ *Oh come to the play. It's just a one-acter and not too long for you.*

one and a half *n.* a prison sentence of 18 months. □ *I could not take another one and a half.* □ *I've only been given a one and a half!*

one-and-one *n.* a portion of fish and chips suitable for one person. (Irish usage.) □ *That's him over there, eating the one-and-one.* □ *Do you sell one-and-one's in here, love?*

one and t'other **1.** *n.* brother. (Rhyming slang.) □ *Can I bring me one and t'other?* □ *Terry's here; he's brought his one and t'other with him.* **2.** *n.* mother. (Rhyming slang.) □ *I'd better ask me one and t'other.* □ *Will your one and t'other let you out to the pub tonight?*

one another *mod.* each other. □ *People should help one another.* □ *They give one another support when things are difficult.*

one-armed bandit *n.* a fruit machine; a slot machine. □ *Did you know that almost all the one-armed bandits in the world are made in Britain?* □ *Why do people waste their time and money on one-armed bandits?*

on(e)cer *n.* a one Pound coin; formerly, a one Pound note. □ *It'll takes a lot of your onecers to buy a car like that.* □ *Burnside slipped him a oncer and faded into the fog.*

one-eyed Bob See TROUSER-SNAKE.

one-eyed trouser-snake See TROUSER-SNAKE.

one (fine) day *n.* an unspecified future day. □ *One fine day, we'll be rich, respected and happy.* □ *One day all this will be yours, son.*

one for the road *n.* a final or extra drink before commencing a journey. □ *Let's have one for the road.* □ *Don't have one for the road if you are going to be the driver.*

One Hung Low *n.* a jocular name for a Chinese person. (Racially offensive. Compare with HOO FLUNG DUNG.) □ *Y'know, Otto, if you call a Chinaman a One Hung Low, he's likely to get nasty.* □ *Why can you not be polite to One Hung Lows?*

one jump ahead of someone or something *n.* a position in advance of someone or something; a step ahead of someone or something. □ *I try to be one jump ahead of the problems.* □ *You have to keep one jump ahead of the boss in order to succeed.*

one-man band *n.* a man who takes all responsibilities or duties upon himself. □ *He really is a sort of one-man band.* □ *I like the look of this one-man band; for a guy to do all that by himself takes real organisation.*

one-man show **1.** *n.* a theatrical performance put on by one person, of either sex. □ *It was a one-man show, but it was very entertaining.* □ *For a one-man show, it was very long.* **2.** *n.* an exhibition of the artistic works of one person. □ *She is having a one-man show at the Northside Gallery.* □ *I'm having a one-man show next weekend. Come and see what I have done.*

one-night stand 1. *n.* a performance lasting only one night. □ *The band did a series of one-night stands in the North.* □ *You can't make a living doing one-night stands.* **2.** *n.* a romance or sexual relationship that lasts just one night. □ *It was not a romance, just a one-night stand.* □ *It looked like something that would last longer than a one-night stand.*

one over the eight *mod.* slightly intoxicated due to drink. □ *I felt a little one over the eight, but that didn't stop me from having more.* □ *Bruno's a really nice person when he's one over the eight.*

one too many *n.* one drink of liquor too many, implying drunkenness. □ *I think I've had one too many. It's time to stop drinking.* □ *Don't drive if you've had one too many.*

one-track mind *n.* a (person's) mind obsessed with only one thing. □ *When it comes to food, Tom has a one-track mind.* □ *Mary has a one-track mind. All she thinks about is Tom.*

one under *n.* a suicide committed on a railway line. (Police.) □ *The police were called to a one under at the station.* □ *It was a very messy one under.*

one up on someone *mod.* at a comparative advantage to someone. □ *I'm sorry but we really don't try to get one up on people around here.* □ *Why are you always out to get one up on me?*

on form AND **on song** *mod.* performing as expected; performing well. (Compare with OFF FORM.) □ *When she's on form she's the best there is.* □ *Wonderful! She really was on song tonight.*

on ice *mod.* in reserve. □ *That's a great idea, but we'll have to put it on ice until we can afford to put it into action.* □ *I have two boyfriends. One I see every weekend, and the other I keep on ice for a rainy day.*

on-line *mod.* connected to a computer, by direct connection or via the telephone system, etc. (Computer jargon. Compare with OFF-LINE.) □ *When Harry's on-line he's like a different person.* □ *People will write things to you on-line they'd never say to your face.*

only here for the beer *mod.* present but not really interested in what's happening. (Originally a popular advertising slogan for Double Diamond™ beer in the 1960s.) □ *Don't mind me, I'm only here for the beer.* □ *If you're only here for the beer, take the beer and leave now, please.*

only way to go *n.* the best way to do something; the best choice to make. □ *Get a four-wheel drive car. It's the only way to go.* □ *That's it! A new house. It's the only way to go.*

ono See OR NEAR OFFER.

on oath *mod.* under oath, as in a court of law. □ *Oh yes, he said that on oath.* □ *It is serious to lie when on oath, Otto.*

on offer *mod.* for sale at a reduced price. □ *I see his car's on offer now.* □ *I'm looking for a bargain—one that's on offer.*

on one's high horse *mod.* in a haughty manner or mood. □ *Larry is on his high horse again, bossing people around.* □ *The boss is on her high horse about the number of paper clips we use.*

on one's Jack (Jones) *mod.* alone. (Rhyming slang.) □ *Since Mary left me, I've been on my Jack Jones.* □ *I'll be coming along my on my Jack, I'm afraid.*

on one's last legs *mod.* about to die. □ *Your mother is on her last legs, so please hurry home.* □ *Poor old Bert is on his last legs.*

on one's pea pod *mod.* alone. (Scots usage. Rhyming slang, linked as follows: on one's pea pod ≈ on one's tod = alone. An example of double rhyming, as ON ONE'S TOD is already rhyming slang in its own right.) □ *Since the wife passed on I'm on ma pea pod.* □ *Why are you sitting there on yer pea pod? Come over and join us!*

on one's tod *mod.* alone. (Rhyming slang, linked as follows: on one's Tod

[Sloan] ≈ alone. Compare with ON ONE'S PEA POD.) □ *Now he's left you, you'll be on your tod again I imagine, Jane.* □ *I'll be coming to the meeting on my tod.*

on pins *mod.* nervous or agitated. □ *When I get on pins, I meditate.* □ *Sally was really on pins before the meeting.*

on remand *mod.* held in custody awaiting trial. □ *They're holding Otto on remand until the trial.* □ *The court normally only keeps dangerous people or those thought likely to disappear on remand.*

on (someone's) plate *mod.* requiring to be done. □ *I'm sorry but I already have a lot of things on my plate.* □ *Do you have much on your plate just at the moment?*

on something's last legs *mod.* about to cease to function. □ *This car is on its last legs. We have to get a new one.* □ *The government is on its last legs.*

on song See ON FORM.

on spec **1.** *mod.* using money risked in the hope of profit. □ *He lives by buying and selling houses on spec.* □ *I think it might be an idea to build a few yachts on spec just now.* **2.** *mod.* as specified. □ *This has been built exactly on spec—just as you asked.* □ *It's important to make sure the design is on spec or the customer will not pay.*

on suss *mod.* on suspicion. □ *You're arresting me on suss! Nothing more!* □ *You can't arrest people on nothing but suss.*

on tap *mod.* immediately available. (From beer available on tap.) □ *By coincidence, I have on tap just the kind of person you're talking about.* □ *The cook has any kind of food you might want on tap.*

on-target *mod.* timely; exact; incisive. (Compare with OTE.) □ *Your criticism is exactly on-target.* □ *We are on-target for a December completion date.*

on the back boiler See ON THE BACK BURNER.

on the back burner AND **on the back boiler** *mod.* receiving little or no attention or consideration. (Compare with ON THE FRONT BURNER.) □ *We will have to put this on the back burner for a while.* □ *She thought she could keep her boyfriend on the back boiler until she decided what to do about him.*

on the ball *mod.* knowledgeable; competent; attentive. □ *This guy is really on the ball.* □ *If you were on the ball, this wouldn't have happened.*

on the bandwagon *mod.* with the majority; following the latest fad. (Often with *hop, get, climb,* or *jump.*) □ *Come on! Hop on the bandwagon! Everyone else is joining.* □ *Tom always has to climb on the bandwagon. He does no independent thinking.*

on the bash **1.** AND **on the batter; on the business; on the game; on the knock; on the nose** *mod.* engaging in prostitution. (Crude.) □ *All along this street there are dozens of girls on the bash every night.* □ *Well, the change of heart didn't last. She's on the knock again.* □ *When unemployment increases, so does the number of girls on the game.* **2.** AND **on the sauce** *mod.* drinking regularly; engaging in an extensive drinking session. □ *I think you'll find they're on the bash just now.* □ *On the sauce with Mike, anything can happen.*

on the batter **1.** AND **on the skite** *mod.* on a drinking spree; having a good time. (Scots usage.) □ *They're aw oot oan the batter again. (They're all out getting drunk again.)* □ *Shuggy ower likes being on the skite, an that. (Hugh always likes having a good time and so on.)* **2.** See ON THE BASH.

on the beam **1.** *mod.* honing in on an aviation radio beam. (No longer a major navigational device.) □ *The plane was on the beam and landed safely in the fog.* □ *I couldn't get on the beam, and I flew right over the airfield.* **2.** *mod.* on the right course or track. (From sense 1.) □ *That is exactly right. You are right on the beam.* □ *You're on the beam. You will finish this with no problems.* **3.** *mod.* smart; clever. □ *That was well done, Tom. You're on the beam.* □ *She is really on the beam. Glad she came along.*

on the blink AND **on the bum** **1.** *mod.* [of a person] unwell. □ *I was a little on the blink yesterday and decided to stay at home.* □ *She was feeling a bit on the* bum so I told her to go home. **2.** *mod.* [of a machine] out of order. □ *My phone's on the blink, so I'd like to ring the phone company from here, please.* □ *My refrigerator is on the bum again.*

on the boil 1. *mod.* busily active. □ *Things are really on the boil at the factory.* □ *Those teenagers are always on the boil!* **2.** *mod.* requiring urgent attention.* □ *Come on! This thing is really on the boil now!* □ *Once the process gets on the boil, you can't leave it.*

on the booze AND **on the ooze** *mod.* drinking. □ *Lets go on the booze tonight.* □ *He's always going on the ooze.*

on the box *mod.* appearing on television. □ *He's on the box tonight.* □ *Is there anything worth seeing on the box?*

on the bum See ON THE BLINK.

on the buroo *mod.* unemployed. (Scots usage.) □ *I'm on the buroo these day I'm afraid.* □ *There are a lot of good people on the buroo.*

on the business See ON THE BASH.

on the button *mod.* exactly the right time or place. □ *He was there on time, right on the button.* □ *I want to see you here at noon—on the button.*

on the cards *mod.* probable. □ *Yes, it's on the cards. It could happen.* □ *I had never thought such a thing was on the cards.*

on the carpet *phr.* being reprimanded. □ *If the boss finds out you'll be on the carpet.* □ *So, what are you on the carpet for now?*

on the coat and badge *phr.* begging. (Rhyming slang, linked as follows: on the coat and badge ≈ [cadge] = beg(ging). See CADGE.) □ *I think there are more people on the coat and badge than ever nowadays.* □ *Why are you on the coat and badge? Get a job!*

on the credit *mod.* on credit. □ *He bought the car on the credit.* □ *Some people go on the credit for everything they buy.*

on the dole *mod.* unemployed. □ *I'm on the dole, I'm afraid.* □ *If you're on the dole, go over there.*

on the dot AND **on the nose** *mod.* exactly on time; exactly as planned. □ *I want you there at noon on the dot.* □

All three of them were at the appointed place right on the nose.

on the double *mod.* very fast; twice as fast. (Originally military. Refers to "double time" in marching.) □ *Get over here right now—on the double!* □ *She wants to see you in her office on the double.*

on the fiddle *mod.* working a swindle. □ *I'm sure Harry's on the fiddle again.* □ *At least Otto's too thick to be on the fiddle. Isn't he?*

on the floor *mod.* poor. (Rhyming slang.) □ *Since the factory closed, everyone in this town is on the floor.* □ *No, I can't lend you money. I'm on the floor myself.*

on the fly *mod.* while something or someone is operating or moving. □ *I'll try to capture the data on the fly.* □ *Please try to buy some aspirin somewhere on the fly today.*

on the front boiler See ON THE FRONT BURNER.

on the front burner AND **on the front boiler** *mod.* receiving particular attention or consideration. (Compare with ON THE BACK BURNER.) □ *So, what's on the front burner for us this week?* □ *The Smith problem is back on the front boiler again it seems.*

on the game See ON THE BASH.

on the job *phr.* indulging in sexual intercourse. (Taboo.) □ *I'm hoping to get on the job tonight.* □ *I fancy getting on the job with the missus tonight.*

on the knock See ON THE BASH.

on the knocker *mod.* selling from door to door. □ *There's someone here on the knocker.* □ *I see Harry's on the knocker nowadays.*

on the lam *mod.* on the run from the police. □ *Otto's on the lam again.* □ *Can you live all your life on the lam?*

on the level *mod.* honest; straightforward. □ *Come on now. Be on the level with me.* □ *Is the ad on the level?*

on the (lifting) game *mod.* engaging in stealing. □ *Otto's on the game again, stealing whatever he can find.* □ *I am not on the lifting game, Inspector!*

on the mains *mod.* connected to the public electricity supply. □ *Of course we're on the mains! Where do you think* *this is? Outer Mongolia? □ Even remote parts of Scotland have been on the mains for over fifty years, you know.*

on the make 1. *mod.* ambitious; attempting to be great. □ *That young lawyer is sure on the make.* □ *This university is on the make.* **2.** AND **on the pull; on the prowl** *mod.* of a man looking for a female sexual partner. (Crude. Usually refers to a male seeking a female.) □ *Joe was on the make again at that party last night.* □ *That whole gang of boys is on the prowl. Watch out.*

on the mike *mod.* with nothing to do. □ *He's just hanging around, on the mike.* □ *They'll just have to stay on the mike until this is over.*

on the needle *mod.* addicted to injectable drugs. □ *My sister's on the needle, and I want to help her.* □ *Once you're on the needle, you've had it.*

on the never-never *mod.* purchasing by hire purchase, on the installment plan. □ *Buying things on the never-never is always expensive.* □ *We bought the new car on the never-never, you know.*

on the nod *mod.* agreed without comment. □ *There's no way that'll get passed on the nod.* □ *In the end, the scheme was agreed on the nod!*

on the nose 1. *mod.* smelly; stinking; offensive. □ *The place had not been cleaned for years, I think; it was really on the nose.* □ *It may be on the nose but it's a great cheese. Or so they told me in the cheese shop.* **2.** *mod.* objectionable; annoying. □ *Being so on the nose is bad for business.* □ *Mike said that he did not pay taxes to take an on the nose attitude like that from a civil servant.* **3.** See also ON THE BASH, ON THE DOT.

on the ooze See ON THE BOOZE.

on the phone 1. *mod.* connected to the telephone system. □ *Yes, I'm on the phone. Here's my number.* □ *If you're on the phone there, perhaps I could call you?* **2.** *mod.* speaking on the telephone. □ *She's on the phone but won't be long.* □ *Please take a seat while I'm on the phone.*

on the pill *mod.* taking birth control pills. □ *Is it true that Mary is on the pill?* □ *She was on the pill, but she isn't now.*

on the piss *mod.* drinking; intoxicated due to drink. (Taboo.) □ *My friend here is on the piss and needs a lift, and can I have one, too?* □ *He's been on the piss all evening and spoiling for a fight.*

on the prowl See ON THE MAKE.

on the pull See ON THE MAKE.

on the q.t. AND **on the quiet** *mod.* discretely. □ *I think I may be able to let you in later, on the q.t.* □ *On the quiet, I'm letting you know the result now.*

on the quiet See ON THE Q.T.

on the rag(s) *mod.* menstruating. (Crude.) □ *Kim's on the rag and in a foul mood.* □ *Sue doesn't go swimming when she's on the rags.*

on the ramp *mod.* participating in or conducting a swindle. □ *Are you on the ramp, too?* □ *The police are looking for a couple on some sort of ramp involving visiting old folks in this area.*

on the razzle *mod.* having a good time. □ *They're out on the razzle again.* □ *Come on, let's go on the razzle!*

on the road *mod.* traveling from place to place, not necessarily on the highways. (Compare with GET THE SHOW ON THE ROAD.) □ *I was on the road with the circus for six months.* □ *I don't work in the main office anymore, now I'm on the road.*

on the run 1. *mod.* while one is moving from place to place. □ *I will try to get some aspirin today on the run.* □ *I will think about it on the run.* **2.** *mod.* evading capture or arrest; attempting to escape. □ *Max is on the run from the cops.* □ *The gang of crooks is on the run. Probably somewhere in Spain by now.*

on the safe side *mod.* taking the risk-free path. □ *Let's be on the safe side and ring first.* □ *I think you should stay on the safe side and call the doctor about this fever.*

on the same wavelength *mod.* thinking in the same pattern. □ *We're not on the same wavelength. Let's try again.* □ *We kept talking it over until we were on the same wavelength.*

on the sauce See ON THE BASH.

on the scrounge for something *vb. phr.* to be searching for or attempting to obtain something. (Compare with SCROUNGE SOMEONE OR SOMETHING UP.) □ *Here she comes, on the scrounge for something again.* □ *Sorry to trouble you, but I'm on the scrounge for some sugar.*

on the shelf *mod.* not active socially; left to oneself in social matters. □ *I've been on the shelf long enough. I'm going to make some friends.* □ *She likes being on the shelf.*

on the side **1.** *mod.* extra or additional, such as a second job or a sideline activity. □ *He has a nice little business on the side, selling curtains.* □ *She is a bank teller and works as a waitress on the side.* **2.** *mod.* extramarital; in addition to one's spouse. □ *He is married, but also has a woman on the side.* □ *She has boyfriends on the side, but her husband knows about them.*

on the skite See ON THE BATTER.

on the sly *mod.* secretly and deceptively. □ *She was stealing little bits of money on the sly.* □ *Martin was having an affair with the maid on the sly.*

on the square *mod.* belonging to a Masonic lodge. □ *I hear the Police Superintendent is on the square.* □ *Are you on the square, Albert?*

on the strap *mod.* purchasing by hire purchase, on the installment plan. □ *We bought the new car on the strap, you know.* □ *Buying things on the strap is always expensive.*

on the street(s) **1.** *mod.* engaging in prostitution as a streetwalker. (Crude.) □ *Mary said, "What am I supposed to do—go on the street?"* □ *All three of them went on the streets to earn enough money to live.* **2.** *mod.* homeless. □ *How can you put mothers and young children on the streets like that just for a few pounds of rent?* □ *There are not that many homeless actually on the street any more, I suppose.*

on the strength **1.** *mod.* on the payroll. □ *Right, you're on the strength.* □ *I was hoping to get on the strength here.* **2.** *mod.* a member of the team. □ *Well, welcome aboard. Now you're on the strength. □ Everyone on the strength will have to help.*

on the take *mod.* taking bribes. (Underworld.) □ *I heard that the mayor is on the take.* □ *Everyone on the local council is on the take.*

on the thumb *mod.* hitchhiking. □ *I think it's too dangerous to travel on the thumb nowadays.* □ *A couple of teenagers on the thumb were standing at the next intersection.*

on the trot **1.** *mod.* busily occupied. □ *I'll talk to you later when I'm not so much on the trot.* □ *I was on the trot and couldn't get to the phone.* **2.** *mod.* in rapid succession. □ *Why are all these things happening on the trot like this?* □ *I've got a whole lot of things to attend to on the trot today.*

on the up-and-up *mod.* steadily getting better and better. □ *Yes, our business is really on the up-and-up these days.* □ *It's good to see an honest businessman on the up-and-up.*

on the wagon *mod.* no longer drinking alcohol. □ *How long has John been on the wagon this time?* □ *He's on the wagon again.*

on the warpath *mod.* very angry. □ *The boss is on the warpath again. Watch out!* □ *I am on the warpath about setting goals and standards again.*

on the whine *mod.* complaining. □ *There you are, always on the whine.* □ *I would be surprised if she was not on the whine.*

onto a good thing *mod.* having found something that is to one's advantage, such as something easy, profitable, inexpensive, etc. □ *I think that Bill got onto a good thing when he opened his own shop.* □ *I won't quit now. I'm onto a good thing, and I know it.*

on to someone or something *mod.* alerted to or aware of a deceitful plan or person. □ *The cops are on to your little game here.* □ *Max thought he was safe, but the rozzers was on to him from the beginning.*

On yer bike! AND **On your bike!** **1.** *exclam.* "Get on with things." □ *We don't have all day. On yer bike!* □ *On your* *bike, we don't have much time left.* **2.** *exclam.* "Exert yourself." □ *On your bike! Try working for a change.* □ *The job can be done; just get on yer bike!* **3.** *exclam.* "Get lost"; "Get out of here!" □ *What a bad joke! No puns allowed here! On yer bike!* □ *That's it! On your bike! We're not going to put up with that sort of behaviour around here.*

oodles of something *n.* lots of something. □ *My uncle has just oodles and oodles of money.* □ *I don't have oodles, but I have enough to keep me happy.* □ *When I have spaghetti, I just love oodles of noodles.*

oof *n.* cash. (This is derived from *ooftisch,* a Yiddish term derived from the German *auf (dem) tische,* meaning "on (the) table" in English. In other words, OOF is money actually placed on the table; which is to say, cash.) □ *I don't make enough oof to go on a trip like that!* □ *It takes a lot of oof to buy a car like that.*

oofy *mod.* rich. (Derived from OOF.) □ *The Wilmington-Thorpes are oofy.* □ *Well, what do you think? He won the lottery and of course he's oofy.*

oojahs *n.* the female breasts. (Crude. Normally with *the* and in the plural.) □ *All you think about is oojahs!* □ *Cor, look at the oojahs on that, Fred!*

oomph 1. *n.* sex appeal. (Crude.) □ *She had a lot of oomph, but didn't wish to become a film star.* □ *No amount of oomph can make up for a total lack of talent.* **2.** *n.* energy; drive and vitality. □ *Come on, you guys. Let's get some oomph behind it. PUSH!* □ *You need more oomph if you want to make a career in this business.*

op 1. *n.* a surgical operation. □ *When is your op due, mum?* □ *It was a very easy op, in the end.* **2.** *n.* a military operation. □ *Here are the details of the op, gentlemen.* □ *When does the op start?*

O.P. AND **o.p.; OP** *n.* that which belongs to "Other People," especially when it's a cigarette. □ ME: *"I only smoke O.P."* HE: *"An O.P.?"* ME: *"Why yes thank you, I'll take one since you're offer-*

ing." □ *My favourite kind of cigarettes are OPs. They're the cheapest, too.*

opener *n.* a remark made to commence a conversation or discussion. □ *He made a great opener, but then drifted off the point a bit.* □ *So, what's your opener?*

opening time(s) *n.* the hours during which public houses may legally open for business. □ *Our opening times are displayed on a notice besides the main entrance.* □ *Is it opening time yet?*

oppo *n.* an associate or colleague. □ *This is Harry; he's my oppo.* □ *Your oppo phoned. There's a problem at your office.*

opposite number *n.* one's partner or equal at work. □ *My opposite number will not like this.* □ *I do not like my opposite number and look forward to it when she's on holiday.*

oral AND **O; O-levels** *n.* an act of oral sex. (Taboo.) □ *That girl standing at the corner does provide oral if you pay enough.* □ *The punter was looking for his O-levels.*

orange pip *n.* a Japanese person. (Racially offensive. Rhyming slang, linked as follows: orange pip ≈ [Nip] = Japanese.) □ *He said he was not a racist, he just hated this particular orange pip!* □ *Don't call Japanese people orange pips, please. It is very offensive and racist.*

orbital *n.* a party occurring just outside London. (In other words, just beyond the M25 motorway, which "orbits" London.) □ *Sam invited us to an orbital, but we're getting a little old for that kind of thing.* □ *Fred knows how to put on a real orbital!*

orchestras *n.* the testicles. (Taboo. Rhyming slang, linked as follows: orchestra [stall]s ≈ [balls] = testicles. Normally with *the* and in the plural.) □ *He turned sideways to protect his orchestra.* □ *He got hit right in the orchestra.*

order of the boot AND **order of the wellie 1.** *n.* a dismissal; a rejection. □ *I've just been given the order of the boot.* □ *Shape up fast, or it's the order of the wellie for you, son.* **2.** *n.* a job dismissal; the sack. (Always with *the.*)

□ *Give him the order of the boot; he's no use.* □ *The firm just gave me the order of the wellie!*

order of the wellie See ORDER OF THE BOOT.

organise something *vb.* to arrange something; to obtain something by devious means. □ *We're going to have to organise something to celebrate the centenary of the founding of the school next year.* □ *Oh, I'm sure Mr Big can organise a good supply of tobacco and alcohol for your business.*

or near offer AND **ono** *mod.* of a price close to, but not quite as large as one referred to. (Words found in small advertisements for items on sale by individuals.) □ *For sale at £500 or near offer.* □ *Bicycle: £100 ono.*

orthodox *mod.* legitimate; legal. □ *I won't touch this deal if it's not orthodox.* □ *If she's not orthodox, I won't work with her.*

Oscar 1. *vb.* to practice homosexuality. (Crude. Oscar Wilde was a flamboyant and famous Irish wit and playwright who was imprisoned in 1895 for homosexual offences. Compare with OSCAR WILDING and OSCARISE SOMEONE.) □ *I think they've gone off for a spot of quiet Oscaring, if you know what I mean.* □ *They're always Oscaring! It's disgusting!* **2.** *mod.* out of control. (Rhyming slang, linked as follows: = Oscar [Wilde] ≈ [(running) wild] = out of control.) □ *Take it easy, man. Don't go Oscar.* □ *I was afraid he would soon be Oscar if we stayed any longer.*

Oscarise someone *vb.* to turn someone into a homosexual. (Crude. Compare with OSCAR.) □ *I don't think Bruno's a good choice to try a little Oscarising on.* □ *He tried to Oscarise Bruno, and now he's on life support in the hospital.*

Oscar Wilding *mod.* actively homosexual. (Crude. Compare with OSCAR.) □ *Of course he's Oscar Wilding. Why do you thing he hangs around in gay bars?* □ *There's a lot of Oscar Wilding people in this area.*

o.t.e. AND **OTE** *n.* on-target earnings. (An initialism used to describe the money that a successful salesperson paid on a commission basis is expected to earn. Compare with ON-TARGET.) □ *The OTE looked good but I'd've had to work twenty-four hours a day, every day, so I said no thanks.* □ *Even the o.t.e. he mentioned wasn't enough to pay the mortgage.*

Other Place *n.* a name used in Oxford for Cambridge University, and vice versa. (Always with *the.*) □ *In Cambridge, they don't think too highly of the Other Place.* □ *They don't think too highly of the Other Place in Oxford, either.*

OTOH *phr.* "on the other hand." (Computer jargon. Written only. An initialism used in computer communications.) □ *That's one good idea. OTOH, there must be many other satisfactory procedures.* □ *OTOH, everyone is a little forgetful now and then.*

OTT See OVER THE TOP.

out-and-out *mod.* complete or total; blatant. □ *Fred was an out-and-out liar.* □ *Don't be such an out-and-out stinker!*

out cold *mod.* unconscious. □ *Paul was out cold when we found him.* □ *Who knocked him out cold?*

outer *n.* a convenient explanation for why something went wrong; an excuse. □ *This outer that we have all been getting from Kevin is just too much.* □ *I listened to her outer without saying anything.*

outfit 1. *n.* a group of people forming an organisation; a company. □ *That outfit cheated me of my money.* □ *I will never deal with that outfit again.* **2.** *n.* a set of clothing. □ *You look lovely in that outfit.* □ *Should I wear my grey wool outfit?* **3.** *n.* a set of things; the items needed for some task. □ *I got a fine chemistry outfit for my birthday.* □ *My tool kit has everything I need. It's the whole outfit.*

out for the count *mod.* down for the count; inactive for the duration (of something). (From boxing.) □ *I've got a terrible cold, and I think I'm down for the count.* □ *Fred is down for the count. He's in jail.*

out like a light *mod.* unconscious; sleeping soundly. □ *I fell and hit my head. I* *was out like a light for two minutes, they tell me.* □ *I closed my eyes and was out like a light in no time at all.*

out of it *mod.* intoxicated due to drink or drugs. □ *Four beers and he was out of it.* □ *He sat in his chair, completely out of it once more.*

out of kilter *mod.* not functioning properly. (Compare with OUT OF WHACK.) □ *My car's engine is out of kilter and needs some repair work.* □ *My coffee-pot is out of kilter, so I have to make coffee in a pan.*

out of line *mod.* not in accord with what is appropriate or expected, especially in price or behaviour. □ *Your behaviour is quite out of line and I'll have to report you.* □ *Your price is out of line with the other shops.*

out of one's skull AND **out of one's tree 1.** *mod.* intoxicated due to drink or drugs. □ *Oh boy, I drank till I was out of my skull.* □ *Two beers and he was out of his tree.* **2.** *mod.* crazy; insane; behaving in an insane way. □ *He's out of his skull, I tell you; completely bananas.* □ *Ever since the operation, Joe's been out of his tree.*

out of one's tree See OUT OF ONE'S SKULL.

out of order 1. *n.* dishonest. □ *Hey! That's out of order! I'm getting the police!* □ *You are completely out of order and I want my money back!* **2.** *n.* not following the customary rules. (See BIT PREVIOUS.) □ *Come on, that's out of order! Do it the right way.* □ *I'm sorry but I did not realise that was out of order.* **3.** *n.* intoxicated due to drink or drugs. □ *Tracy gets a little out of order after a drink or two.* □ *She was out of order for a week.*

out of sight 1. *mod.* very expensive; high in price. □ *Prices at that restaurant are out of sight.* □ *The cost of housing is out of sight.* **2.** *mod.* excellent; wonderful. □ *Boy, this fishing rod is out of sight.* □ *This wine is really out of sight!*

out of sync *mod.* incompatible. □ *Our lives are out of sync.* □ *This sort of activity is out of sync with our other interests.*

out of the blue *mod.* unexpected; surprising. □ *My parents arrived last night to stay, out of the blue!* □ *Then, out of the blue, we got this huge phone bill.*

out of the picture *mod.* no longer relevant to a situation; departed; dead. □ *Now that Tom is out of the picture, we needn't concern ourselves about his objections.* □ *With her husband out of the picture, she can begin living.*

out (of) the window *mod.* absurd; no longer considered. □ *The whole idea is out the window now.* □ *Come back with a new plan that's not out of the window and we'll consider it.*

out of the woods *mod.* freed from a previous state of uncertainty or danger; no longer critical. □ *As soon as her temperature is down, she'll be out of the woods.* □ *We're out of the woods now, and things aren't so chancy.*

out of this world *mod.* wonderful or exciting; in other words, "heavenly." □ *This pie is out of this world.* □ *My boyfriend is just out of this world.*

out of whack 1. *mod.* unwell. □ *Carol is a bit out of whack today, I'm afraid.* □ *Oh dear, I feel really out of whack.* **2.** *mod.* misaligned. □ *No, it's still out of whack. We're going to have to re-align this thing.* □ *So long as the wheels are out of whack, this car is too dangerous to drive.* **3.** *mod.* not working properly. □ *No, try again. It's still out of whack.* □ *If it's out of whack, we can't use it.* **4.** *mod.* out of adjustment; inoperative. (Compare with OUT OF KILTER.) □ *My watch is out of whack.* □ *I think my left eye is out of wack a little. Maybe I need glasses.*

out on one's ear *mod.* thrown out. □ *Do that again and you'll be out on your ear as fast as you can blink.* □ *A lot of us were out on our ears that black Thursday.*

outside *n.* civilan life, seen from a military viewpoint. □ *Outside is not so wonderful as all that, you know.* □ *So what do you know about outside, private?*

out someone 1. *vb.* to reveal someone to be homosexual. (Crude.) □ *If you want to out Oscar, I don't want to be close to you at the time.* □ *But the* *person you out is supposed to be gay in the first place, Max.* **2.** *vb.* to sack someone. □ *I want you to out this guy.* □ *Why was I outed?* **3.** *vb.* to suspend someone from membership of a club, society, etc. □ *The Rake's Club outed old Smithers, y'know!* □ *They outed him because he was damaging the club's reputation by behaving too respectibly.*

out to lunch 1. *mod.* completely incorrect; wrong. □ *Oh, that's completely out to lunch.* □ *He's just wrong; out to lunch.* **2.** *mod.* crazy; insane. □ *You're out to lunch if you think I care.* □ *Tom's out to lunch. Really odd.*

Over my dead body! *exclam.* "Absolutely not!"; "Under no circumstances will I agree!" □ *You'll drop out of school over my dead body!* □ *Get married and move to Australia? Over my dead body!*

over one's head *mod.* confusing; too difficult to understand. □ *This stuff is too hard. It's over my head.* □ *Calculus is all over my head.*

over the edge *mod.* unreasonable; excessive. □ *The way they behaved was certainly over the edge.* □ *People who are over the edge deserve trouble, I say.*

over the hill 1. *mod.* deserted from the army. □ *Two privates went over the hill last night.* □ *They broke out of military prison and went over the hill.* **2.** *mod.* too old (for something). □ *You're only fifty! You're not over the hill yet.* □ *Some people seem over the hill at thirty.*

over the hump *mod.* over the hard part; past the midpoint. □ *Things should be easy from now on. We are over the hump.* □ *When you get over the hump, life is much better.*

over the moon *mod.* very pleased indeed. □ *She was over the moon when she heard the news.* □ *I did point out that it was a bit soon to be over the moon. There was still work to be done.*

over the road AND **over the way** *mod.* upon the other side of the street. □ *She waved to her friend over the road.* □ *Over the way she could see the shop she was looking for.*

over the top AND **OTT** *mod.* exceeding reasonable limits; beyond a joke. (See GO OVER THE TOP.) □ *It really was over the top.* □ *Why do you always have to let the situation get OTT?*

over the way See OVER THE ROAD.

owner *n.* the captain of a ship or aircraft. (Always with *the*.) □ *I don't think the owner will take kindly to your suggested diversion to Cuba, sir.* □ *Don't forget, I'm the owner of this ship and what I say goes.*

own goal 1. *n.* a soccer goal scored in error against one's own side. □ *Well yes, you scored. A pity it had to be an own goal.* □ *I don't think it's a good idea to boast about own goals.* **2.** *n.* an accidental action that hurts oneself or one's own side. □ *I'm afraid I had an own goal with the car last night.* □ *He accidently topped himself, which you might say is the ultimate own goal.* **3.** *n.* a suicide. (Police slang.) □ *The station sergeant has to be informed as soon as we think we've found an own goal.* □ *What a messy own goal that was.* **4.** *n.* a terrorist blown up by his or her own bomb. (Police slang.) □ *I think you'll find the police don't weep too long over an own goal.* □ *I'd not object if they all became own goals, the officer thought.*

Oxbridge *n.* Oxford and Cambridge taken together; what they have in common. (Compare with CAM AND ISIS and CAMFORD.) □ *There is a sort of Oxbridge mentality which some think is bad for British business.* □ *I don't know whether he went to Oxford or Cambridge but it was one or the other. Let's just settle for Oxbridge, eh?*

Oxford *n.* twenty-five pence; previously five shillings. (Rhyming slang, linked as follows: Oxford [scholar] ≈ [dollar] = five shillings. This originated in the 19th century, when £1 = $4 for a great many years, so that five shillings equalled $1.00.) □ *Thanks for the Oxford, guv.* □ *An Oxford? Is that all?*

Oz *n.* Australia. □ *We've off to visit our relatives in Oz.* □ *I've always wanted to visit Oz.*

Ozzie See AUSSIE.

P

P AND **p.; pee** *n.* a penny; a NEW PENNY. (Since decimalisation in 1971.) □ *That will cost you five P, mate.* □ *Have you got twenty pee on you?*

package *vb.* to position or display someone or something, as in marketing, to good advantage. □ *The agent packaged the actress so that everyone thought she only did dramatic roles.* □ *If you package your plan correctly, the committee will accept it.*

package deal *n.* a collection or group of related goods or services sold as a unit. □ *I got all these tools in a package deal for only £39.95.* □ *What about giving me all three shirts as a package deal?*

pack a punch *vb. phr.* to be powerful. □ *Here, take a drop of this—it really packs a punch!* □ *If this measure is to pack a punch, we're going to have to beef it up.*

packet *n.* a lot of money won or lost. □ *Somebody is going to collect a packet on this one.* □ *If we advertise, we can make a packet here.*

pack in AND **pack up 1.** *vb. phr.* [for people] to give up. □ *Why did you pack in just as it was starting to work?* □ *Oh, he packed up long ago.* **2.** *vb. phr.* [for machines] to cease to function. □ *My computer packed in today.* □ *He car packed up half way here.* **3.** *vb. phr.* to retire; to cease to be employed. □ *Well, I'll soon be 65 and it'll be time to pack in.* □ *I want to pack up well before I'm 65, if I can.*

pack (it) in See JACK (IT) IN.

pack of lies *n.* a whole collection or series of lies. □ *I've heard you talk about this before, and it's all a pack of lies.* □ *Her story is nothing but a pack of lies.*

pack out somewhere *vb. phr.* to fill some venue or event completely with people. □ *They certainly managed to pack out that reception!* □ *If they pack out the theatre they'll make a fortune.*

pack someone off *vb. phr.* to send someone away peremptorily. □ *Oh, he was packed off to our Belfast office after that disgraceful episode at the annual office dinner.* □ *Why am I being packed off to the backwoods like this?*

pack someone or something in See JACK SOMEONE OR SOMETHING IN.

pack up See PACK IN.

pad *n.* a place to live, particularly a flat. □ *Why don't you come over to my pad for a while?* □ *This is a nice pad you've got here.*

Paddy AND **Pat** *n.* an Irishman. (Offensive. From "Patrick," a common name in Ireland. Compare with TIM.) □ *Why can you never be polite to Paddies?* □ *Y'know, Otto, if you call an Irishman Pat, he's likely to get nasty.*

Paddy's taxi *n.* a police car. □ *Watch it! That's a Paddy's taxi!* □ *The Paddy's taxi drove forward, blocking my exit.*

paddy(wack) *n.* a burst of anger or excitement. □ *Don't start another paddywack; you'll get fired.* □ *Otto really had a terrible paddy when he was told.*

paddy wagon See BLACK MARIA.

padlock *n.* the male sexual organ. (Taboo. Rhyming slang, linked as follows: padlock ≈ [cock] = male sexual organ.) □ *That's all very well Myra, but where would the world be without padlocks?* □ *The doctor told him that he'd got something wrong with his padlock.*

padnag *n.* an unwilling or slow horse. □ *Why do I always put my money on a* *real padnag?* □ *The padnag they gave me was completely hopeless; I'd have been out there for ever if I had kept it.*

padre *n.* any male religious cleric: priest, monk or chaplain. (From Spanish. Typically military. Also a term of address.) □ *I went to see the padre for some advice.* □ *Hey, padre, anything new on the religion front?*

pad the hoof *vb. phr.* to walk. □ *Stop padding the hoof long enough to eat some dinner.* □ *I padded the hoof all day, looking for a present for Sarah.*

page three girl *n.* a nubile young lady photographed in a state of undress. (Traditionally found displayed upon page three of the *Sun*, a nationally-available daily tabloid publication loosely described as a newspaper. Compare with NIPPLE COUNT.) □ *Did you know that Samantha was once a page three girl?* □ *Come on, these page three girls are not real people. Are they?*

pain *n.* a difficult or annoying thing or person. (See PAIN IN THE ARSE.) □ *That woman is such a pain.* □ *Those long meetings are a real pain.*

pain in the arse AND **pain in the back; pain in the backside; pain in the balls; pain in the bum; pain in the neck** *n.* a difficult or annoying thing or person. (All are crude and PAIN IN THE ARSE and PAIN IN THE BALLS are taboo. See PAIN.) □ *This tax form is a pain in the arse.* □ *My boss is a pain in the neck.*

pain in the back See PAIN IN THE ARSE.

pain in the backside See PAIN IN THE ARSE.

pain in the balls See PAIN IN THE ARSE.

pain in the bum See PAIN IN THE ARSE.

pain in the neck See PAIN IN THE ARSE.

paint the Forth Bridge *vb. phr.* to perform an endless task. □ *I feel I've taken on painting the Forth Bridge with this job; it's endless!* □ *The Forth Rail Bridge, near Edinburgh in Scotland, is famous for being so vast that as soon as the bridge has been painted from one end to the other, it's time to start again. In other words, painting the Forth Bridge is an endless task.*

paint the town (red) *vb. phr.* to go out and celebrate; to go on a drinking bout; to get drunk. □ *I feel great. Let's go out and paint the town.* □ *They were out painting the town red last night.*

Paki *n.* a Pakistani or the descendant of one, living in Britain. (Racially offensive.) □ *Don't call Pakistani people Pakis, please. It is very offensive and racist.* □ *He said he was not a racist, he just hated this particular Paki!*

Paki bashing *n.* the victimisation of Pakistanis and other Asian residents in Britain. (Racially offensive.) □ *Paki bashing is a growing problem in inner city areas.* □ *What is the answer to Paki bashing?*

pal 1. *n.* a term of address for a stranger, usually male. (Scots usage.) □ *Hey pal, gauny geeza light? (Excuse me sir, could you let me have a light?)* □ *Look, pal, Ah wis here afore ye! (Pardon me my friend, but I was here first.)* **2.** *n.* a close friend. (Usually but not always a person of the same sex.) □ *Be nice to him. He's my pal.* □ *Don't take offence, Willy. We're all pals here.*

pally *mod.* friendly or excessively friendly with someone. □ *I don't know why Sue acts so pally. I hardly know her.* □ *She doesn't seem pally with me.*

palsy-walsy *mod.* excessively friendly. (Often with *with*.) □ *Why is Tom so palsy-walsy with everyone?* □ *That guy is a little too palsy-walsy for my liking.*

pan 1. *n.* the head; the face. (Compare with DEADPAN.) □ *Look at that guy! I've never seen such an ugly pan in my life.* □ *I stared her right in the pan and told her to shut up.* **2.** *n.* a lavatory bowl. □ *Flush the pan when you're finished, please.* □ *Don't put your goldfish in the pan, Jimmy!* **3.** *vb.* to criticise severely; to disparage to the point of destruction. □ *Oh, that play was panned by all the critics.* □ *Why do you have to pan everything I try to do?*

panda (car) *n.* a police patrol car, called this because of broad white stripes reminiscent of the panda. □ *The panda drove past slowly, but did not stop.* □ *Mike ran out into the road to wave down the panda.*

pan-flasher *n.* a short-lived success; someone or something that is a flash in the pan. □ *It was all right but really no more than a pan-flasher.* □ *We don't need pan-flashers, but real successes.*

panhandler *n.* a hospital orderly. □ *Ask the panhandler to help.* □ *I'm a panhandler in the hospital.*

panic merchant 1. *n.* someone inclined to panic. □ *Tell that panic merchant to calm down.* □ *Don't be a panic merchant; everything is fine.* **2.** *n.* someone whose panic induces similar behaviour among others. □ *Oh just ignore him; he's a panic merchant.* □ *That's all we need: a panic merchant.*

pan out *vb. phr.* [for something] to work out or turn out all right. □ *Don't worry. Everything will pan out okay.* □ *Nothing seems to pan out for me anymore.*

pansy *n.* an effeminate man; a passive male homosexual. (Crude.) □ *He doesn't like being called a pansy.* □ *So what if he's a pansy? He can still vote, can't he?*

pansy oneself up *vb. phr.* [for a man] to smarten up his appearance in an effeminate way. (Crude.) □ *When I said to smarten yourself up, I did not mean you to pansy yourself up!* □ *Here he comes, all pansied up again.*

pantomime *n.* absurd or outrageous behaviour. □ *The whole episode rapidly turned into a pantomime.* □ *Right, that's enough of this pantomime!*

papa *n.* father. (Childish. Also a term of address.) □ *Papa, what are you doing over there?* □ *I've come to see my papa.*

pape AND **papist** *n.* a Roman Catholic. (Offensive. Also a term of address. Scots usage.) □ *Willy thinks the papes are taking over these days.* □ *Willy actually moved house because a papist moved in next door!*

paper 1. *n.* cigarette paper. □ *Any paper? I need to roll me a cigarette.* □ *He bought a pack of papers and some tobacco.* **2.** *n.* a prescription. □ *There's enough on that paper to last us over the weekend.* □ *He's got a whole stack of papers. Just don't ask how!*

paper over something *vb. phr.* to try to conceal something unpleasant; to try to cover up a misdeed. □ *You can't*

paper this over. It has to be dealt with now! □ *This is a severe social problem. Don't try to paper over it.*

papist See PAPE.

paraffin *n.* sartorial elegance. (Scots usage. Rhyming slang, linked as follows: paraffin ≈ [paraphernalia] = sartorial elegance. See PARAPHERNALIA.) □ *Oh, look at the paraffin on him. Is he going to a wedding?* □ *There's nothing like a bit of paraffin to impress the lassies, Shuggy.*

paraffin budgie *n.* a helicopter. (See BUDGIE.) □ *I never want to fly in a paraffin budgie. Those things scare me.* □ *See that paraffin budgie up there? It's measuring your driving speed. Slow down.*

paralytic *mod.* very intoxicated due to drink. (Scots usage.) □ *Most men around here seem to set out to make themselves paralytic as rapidly as they can whenever they get paid.* □ *Of course he was paralytic! What would you be after twelve double whiskies?*

paraphernalia *n.* an excessively smart style of dress; over-grand clothes. (Scots usage. See PARAFFIN.) □ *Wullie, you don't think you could be overdoing the paraphernalia just a tad?* □ *Apart from anything else, where did Wullie come by all that paraphernalia?*

parcel *n.* stolen goods that have been passed on to a receiver. □ *We found a huge pile of parcels.* □ *All right, then tell us where this parcel came from?*

Pardon my French. AND **Excuse my French.** *sent.* "Excuse my use of swear words or taboo words." (Does not refer to real French. Compare with IF YOU'LL PARDON THE EXPRESSION.) □ *Pardon my French, but this has been one fucking awful day.* □ *What she needs is a kick in the arse, if you'll excuse my French.*

parish lantern *n.* the moon. (Usually with *the*.) □ *There was a full parish lantern for us to walk home under last night.* □ *He looked up at the parish lantern and smiled.*

parish pump 1. *mod.* trivial. □ *It was all just a parish pump thing really. Nothing to worry about.* □ *I'm really not interested in these parish pump* *problems. Sort them out yourself.* **2.** *mod.* very local. □ *It was all very parish pump stuff, I'm afraid.* □ *Can we try to get above the parish pump level and on to something that matters?*

park a custard *vb. phr.* to empty one's stomach; to vomit. (Crude.) □ *Harry is in the loo parking a custard.* □ *Who parked a custard on the floor?*

parkin *n.* a variety of gingerbread that contains oatmeal and treacle. □ *I've always loved parkin! Any more?* □ *There's always more parkin in this house.*

park one's arse AND **park one's bum; park one's carcass; park one's stern** *vb. phr.* to sit oneself down. (PARK ONE'S ARSE is taboo. Other expressions are crude.) □ *Just park your arse right there, and we'll have our little talk.* □ *Come in, Fred. Just park your arse anywhere you see a chair. This place is a mess.*

park one's bum See PARK ONE'S ARSE.

park one's carcass See PARK ONE'S ARSE.

park oneself *vb.* to position oneself. □ *Park yourself over there and wait your turn.* □ *I was told to park myself here!*

park one's stern See PARK ONE'S ARSE.

park something *vb.* to place something safely. □ *Will it be all right to park my car here.* □ *She parked all her valuables with us.*

park up *vb. phr.* to park vehicles close to each other. (Probably derived from "close up.") □ *"Park up please, sir; there's not much space."* □ *We were expected to park up because there was so little room.*

parky *mod.* bitterly cold. (Particularly with reference to mornings, the air, etc.) □ *Cor! Real parky today, innit?* □ *In parky weather like this he prefers to stay indoors.*

parlivue *n.* an informal discussion or chat. (From the French *parlez-vous,* meaning "you speak." Produced by hobson-jobson.) □ *Can we have that little parlivue just now please?* □ *Oh, we were just having a parlivue.*

parting shot *n.* the last word; a final comment before departing. □ *For her*

parting shot, she called me a miser. □ *His parting shot was some offensive remark about my inability to understand simple arithmetic.*

party *n.* a combining form used in expressions to refer to certain kinds of activity carried on in groups or in pairs. (See BOTTLE PARTY, HEN PARTY, STAG PARTY and SWING PARTY.)

party animal *n.* someone who loves parties. □ *My boyfriend and I are real party animals. Let's party!* □ *If you weren't such a party animal, you'd have more time for studying.*

party line *n.* the official version of events. (Always with *the.*) □ *I think we better know the party line before we meet the public.* □ *What is the party line on these products, anyway?*

party-pooper *n.* a spoilsport; a wet blanket; someone who ruins a party because of dullness or by leaving early. □ *Don't be a party-pooper!* □ *Don't invite Martha. She's such a party-pooper.*

pash *n.* a childish passion or infatuation. □ *She's always having a pash for some pop idol or other.* □ *These pashes are becoming serious, I fear.*

pass 1. *n.* a passing grade or mark on an examination test. (Compare with FAIL.) □ *Did you get a pass or a fail?* □ *This is my third pass this term.* **2.** *vb.* to decline something; to decline to participate in something. □ *No, thanks. I pass.* □ *I'll have to pass. I'm just not ready for this.* **3.** *n.* a sexual advance or invitation. (Crude. Usually with *make.*) □ *He made a pass at me, so I slapped him.* □ *When he made a pass at me, he got a pass right back.* **4.** *vb.* to succeed in spending counterfeit money; to succeed in cashing a bad check. □ *Beavis passed one bad check after another.* □ *He was arrested for passing bad checks.*

pass a comment *vb. phr.* to comment. □ *All I did was to pass a comment on her new dress.* □ *If you want to pass a comment, check it with me first, please.*

passion killers *n.* "sensible" female underwear constructed, intentionally or not, in such a way as to discourage or prevent sexual intimacy. (Crude.) □ *I* *thought I had a chance until I spotted her passion killers! □ They were real, 100% genuine brushed nylon passion killers.*

passion-wagon AND **shaggin'-wagon** *n.* a young man's car. (Crude.) □ *Harry drove past slowly in his brand-new passion-wagon. □ As soon as he saw it, he knew he too had to have a shaggin'-wagon like that.*

pass the buck *vb. phr.* to shift the responsibility for something to someone else; to evade responsibility. □ *When things get a little tough, do what I do. Pass the buck. □ Don't pass the buck. Stand up and admit you were wrong.*

pass the catheter See TAKE THE PISS.

paste 1. *vb.* to strike someone, especially in the face. □ *I pasted him right in the face. □ He tried to paste me, but I ducked.* **2.** *vb.* to defeat a person or a team, usually in a game of some type. (Compare with PASTING.) □ *Rangers pasted Rovers, by 8 goals to 2. □ They really pasted our team in last week's game.*

pasted *mod.* beaten; outscored. □ *Our team really got pasted. □ He certainly looked pasted the last time I saw him.*

pasting *n.* a beating; a defeat in a game. (Compare with PASTE.) □ *Our team took quite a pasting last weekend. □ I gave him a pasting.*

past it *mod.* unable to continue because of age. □ *Old Willie is clearly past it, I'm afraid. □ Once you're past it, you should retire.*

Pat See PADDY.

patch See GROUND.

patches *n.* pieces sewn onto a prisoner's uniform. □ *Prisoner's uniforms have patches to enable easy identification in the event of escape. □ Is that the police? There's a man wearing patches trying to hide at the bottom of our garden.*

patchy *mod.* inconsistent; variable. □ *I'm afraid the results are a bit patchy so far. □ If it's too patchy we'll have to replace it.*

pater *n.* a father. (Also a term of address. Latin.) □ *What time does pater get home? □ I'll ask pater if I can go.*

pathetic *mod.* contemptibly or pitifully insufficient or inadequate. □ *You are pathetic. □ What a pathetic exhibition.*

path lab *n.* a pathology laboratory in a hospital, etc. □ *The path lab is along there. □ I've got to look in at the path lab on the way back.*

patsy *n.* a victim of a SCAM; a DUPE. (Underworld. Compare with PIGEON.) □ *That guy over there looks like a perfect patsy. □ We got nearly twenty-five hundred quid off that patsy.*

patter *n.* the persuasive or glib talk of someone trying to sell or persuade. □ *Come on Harry; we all like you but your patter is really awful. □ I think her patter is good but can still be improved.*

patter merchant *n.* a person who gets into or out of situations by fast talking. □ *This patter merchant never seems to give up. □ As a patter merchant I was a failure.*

paw 1. *n.* someone's hand. (Jocular.) □ *Get your paws off me! □ That dog bit my paw.* **2.** *vb.* to fondle or handle someone sexually. (Crude.) □ *If you paw me again, I'll slap you! □ I can't stand men who paw you to pieces.* **3.** *vb. phr.* to touch someone clumsily or awkwardly, but not sexually. □ *I don't like for people to paw me while they're shaking hands. There is no reason to shake my shoulder, too. □ Tom doesn't realise that he paws people and that it annoys them.*

Pax! *exclam.* a call for a truce. (Childish. Latin for *peace*.) □ *Pax! Let's talk! □ Okay, pax.*

pay *n.* a military paymaster. (Compare with PAYBOB.) □ *If you've got a complaint about your money, go and see the pay. □ The pay's in that office across the parade ground.*

paybob *n.* a naval paymaster. (Compare with PAY.) □ *The paybob's in his cabin on the second deck. □ If you've got a complaint about your money, go and see the paybob.*

pay off *vb. phr.* to succeed. □ *It's going to pay off! □ It paid off this time.*

pay-off *n.* a punishment. □ *All right, I know I was wrong. What's the pay-off? □ Your pay-off will be settled now.*

pay round *n.* a recurring discussion about pay between trade union and employer. □ *Time for the annual pay round again, I think.* □ *How much of a fight do you expect during this pay round?*

pay scot and lot *vb. phr.* to share in a financial burden. □ *I do not see why I should have to pay scot and lot with the rest of you.* □ *We're all paying scot and lot, and that's that!*

pay the earth *vb. phr.* to pay a very high price. □ *If you sincerely want to pay the earth, that's the place to buy.* □ *I'm certainly not prepared to pay the earth for one, but if it's cheap enough...*

PC *n.* a Police Constable. □ *PCs are responsible for upholding the law.* □ *Surprising, Nigel is a PC.*

p.d.q. AND **PDQ** *mod.* "pretty damn quick"; very fast; very soon. (Initialism.) □ *You get those papers over here PDQ!* □ *They had better get this mess straightened out p.d.q. if they know what's good for them.*

pea-brained *mod.* stupid. □ *Whoever was the pea-brained clown who came up with that moronic idea?* □ *Tom has nothing upstairs. If you prefer, he's peabrained.*

peach *n.* a good-looking or attractive girl or young woman. □ *She's a real peach.* □ *Mary really is a peach of a girl.*

peanuts *n.* practically no money at all. (Compare with CHICKEN FEED.) □ *They want me to do everything, but they only pay peanuts.* □ *The cost is just peanuts compared to what you get for the money.* □ *If you pay peanuts, you get monkeys.*

pear-shaped *mod.* out of control; wrong. □ *My stereo's gone pear-shaped again.* □ *I'm afraid my car's steering's gone pear-shaped. It's too dangerous to drive.*

peas *mod.* hot. (Rhyming slang, linked as follows: peas [in the pot] ≈ hot.) □ *I can't take another peas day like this.* □ *Cor, it's really peas in there!*

pea-souper *n.* a dense, choking fog. □ *Formerly a common event in London, pea-soupers were heavy and dangerous fogs which once killed thousands of people each winter. Nowadays they are virtually unknown, as (relatively clean) internal combustion road travel has replaced (relatively filthy) steam-powered rail travel.* □ *Sherlock Holmes is supposed by many to have conducted his detecting business entirely from within a pea-souper.*

pebble-glass *n.* an especially thick lens. (Used in reading glasses, for example.) □ *We use a pebble-glass here, as magnification is more important than refractive precision.* □ *You can tell they're my specs because of their pebble-glass lenses.*

pecker *n.* the mouth. □ *Put this in your pecker and chew it up.* □ *Shut your pecker!*

Peckham Rye *n.* a necktie. (Rhyming slang. Peckham is a district in eastern London.) □ *The attacker was wearing a bright Peckham Rye, officer.* □ *Pardon me sir, is this your Peckham Rye?*

peckish *mod.* hungry. □ *I'm just a little peckish right now. I need a bite to eat.* □ *Well, you do look peckish!*

peculiar *mod.* eccentric; somewhat crazy. □ *Ever since the operation, Joe's been a bit peculiar.* □ *I'm not peculiar. I just can't make it work.*

pee 1. *vb.* to urinate. (Crude.) □ *He just went out to pee.* □ *I've got to pee. Back in a minute.* **2.** *n.* an act of urination. (Crude.) □ *If you need a pee, go through there.* □ *Where do you go around here for a pee?* **3.** *n.* urine. (Crude.) □ *That's disgusting! There's pee on your trouser-leg.* □ *There's pee on the rug. Where's that cat?* **4.** See also P.

peechy *mod.* soon. (From the Hindustani *pichhe*, which means this, by hobson-jobson.) □ *Peechy, peechy! We'll soon be there.* □ *It won't be long. Peechy, okay?*

peed off *mod.* extremely angry. (Crude. Euphemistic for PISSED OFF.) □ *I certainly was peed off!* □ *I've never been so peed off in my life!*

peel off *vb. phr.* to strip off one's clothing. □ *I had to peel off for my physical examination.* □ *She stood up on the* *stage and peeled off right down to nothing!*

peep *n.* a noise; an utterance. (Usually used in the negative only.) □ *Don't you make another peep!* □ *I don't want to hear another peep out of you.*

peep-toe *n.* an open-toed shoe. □ *She looked rather good in her peep-toes.* □ *Samantha used to love peep-toes.*

peeve *vb.* to irritate or annoy. □ *Stop peeving me!* □ *Tom is always peeving Frank.*

peg 1. *n.* a clothes peg or pin. □ *She went out into the garden with the pegs.* □ *He handed the pegs to her, one after another.* 2. *vb.* to pin laundry up on a clothesline. □ *I have to go and peg out the laundry.* □ *She was there, pegging up the washing on the line.* 3. *vb.* to drink. □ *What would you like to peg?* □ *Let's peg and talk.* 4. *n.* a leg. (Rhyming slang.) □ *I think I've hurt me peg.* □ *You've got great pegs, love!*

peg-leg AND **peg-the-leg** *n.* anyone with a wooden leg. (Now used primarily in reference to theatrical pirates, but otherwise offensive. Also a term of address.) □ *See that peg-leg over there? He lost his foot to a shark.* □ *Hey, peg-the-leg. Race you to the bar!*

peg-legger *n.* a beggar. (Rhyming slang. Scots usage.) □ *Yon peg-legger canna be trusted to cross the road without thumping you.* □ *Watch that one; he's a peg-legger all right.*

peg out AND **pip out** *vb. phr.* to collapse; to die. □ *I was so sick they thought I was going to peg out.* □ *The dog leapt straight up in the air and pipped out.*

peg someone down *vb. phr.* to restrict with rules, regulations, laws, etc. □ *Why are they trying to peg down everybody with these stupid new rules?* □ *If you think that regulation's going to peg down the real crooks, think again.*

peg-the-leg See PEG-LEG.

pelf *n.* money. □ *How much pelf do you need, then?* □ *Sorry, I can't afford it, I've no pelf.*

pen and ink 1. *n.* a stink. (Rhyming slang.) □ *I just can't stand that pen and ink.* □ *Where is that terrible pen and*

ink coming from? 2. *vb.* to yell; to make trouble. (Rhyming slang, linked as follows: pen and ink ≈ [kick up a stink] = yell/cause trouble. See KICK UP A STINK.) □ *I don't see what you have to pen and ink about.* □ *Just cut out all that pen and inking, thank you!* 3. *vb.* to stink. □ *If you've got to pen and ink like a badger's backside, do so a long way from me.* □ *When we opened the room it pen and inked like you would not believe.*

pen and inker *n.* an untrustworthy person. (Rhyming slang, linked as follows: pen and inker ≈ [stinker] = untrustworthy person. See STINKER.) □ *I don't think I could take another pen and inker like that today.* □ *Here was one pen and inker that was different from the others, he thought.*

penguin *n.* a non-flying flying machine. □ *Sorry, that particular crate's a penguin for the time being, Sir.* □ *I don't want a penguin; I want to do real actual flying.*

penguin suit See CLAW-HAMMER SUIT.

pennif *n.* a banknote. (Backslang of "five Pound," hence a five Pound note, hence any banknote.) □ *Sorry, I don't have any penniffs with me. Can you pay?* □ *He put a number of penniffs into the top pocket of my shirt and said that there were plenty more to be had if I asked no questions.*

penn'orth (of chalk) AND **ball o' chalk; ball of chalk** *n.* a walk. (Rhyming slang.) □ *Go on! Get out! Take a penn'orth!* □ *I went for a ball of chalk, just to get away from him.*

penny *n.* a smile. (Rhyming slang, linked as follows: penny[-a-mile] ≈ smile.) □ *Was that a penny?* □ *What a pretty penny she has.*

penny drops *phr.* "Finally there is understanding." (Normally with *the*.) □ *At last, the penny drops.* □ *Eventually the penny drops and we are able to move on.*

Penny for your thoughts? *interrog.* "What you are thinking?" (Always with *a*.) □ *You look lost in dreams...a penny for your thoughts?* □ *A penny for your thoughts, Martin?*

penny-pincher *n.* someone who is very miserly; someone who objects to the spending of every last penny. □ *If you weren't such a penny-pincher, you'd have some decent clothes.* □ *Let's elect some penny-pinchers to Parliament, just for a change.*

penny steamboat *n.* a ferry. □ *We crossed the Channel on one of these penny steamboats.* □ *I think they're trying to tell us that the penny steamboat is ready to leave, Sir.*

pep pill *n.* a stimulant pill or capsule, such as an amphetamine. □ *The doctor prescribed some kind of pep pills, but I refused to take them.* □ *Got any pep pills or anything?*

pep someone up *vb. phr.* to encourage; to revitalise; to invigorate. □ *That news really pepped me up.* □ *I could do with a little pepping up, now and again.*

pep talk *n.* a speech intended to encourage. □ *The trainer gave the team an excellent pep talk, but they lost anyway.* □ *The pep talk grew into a real gripe session.*

perc *n.* a coffee percolator. □ *The perc is through in the hall.* □ *Get the perc, will you?*

percentage *n.* profit. □ *Yeh, but what's the percentage in this for me?* □ *A little effort and you'll make a good percentage here.*

Percy *n.* the male sexual organ. (Taboo.) □ *Men keep their brains in their Percys!* □ *Unlike Myra, Sharon thinks of little else but Percys.*

perfect *mod.* delightful; amusing. □ *What a perfect little scene.* □ *He did what?...Oh, that's perfect!*

Period! See FULL STOP!

perisher *n.* an irritating person, especially a child. □ *She's an infuriating little perisher.* □ *If you can't control that perisher of yours, you can't stay here.*

perishing 1. *mod.* extremely cold. □ *I know it's perishing out, but someone has to do it.* □ *In perishing weather like this, I try to avoid going outdoors.* **2.** *mod.* confounded. □ *The perishing thing is broken.* □ *That is a perishing nuisance.*

perk *n.* an extra financial benefit; a monetary inducement or reward. (An abbreviation of *perquisite*.) □ *I don't get paid much, but the perks are good.* □ *I don't get paid much, and I don't get any perks!*

perky *mod.* energetic; alert. □ *Most poodles are quite perky.* □ *A perky hostess keeps parties alive.*

perm 1. *n.* a permanent wave in the hair. □ *She's off to the hair salon for a perm.* □ *I came home with a new perm and he didn't even notice!* **2.** *vb.* to apply a permanent wave to the hair. □ *She's having her hair permed just now.* □ *How much would you charge to perm my hair?*

perv *n.* a sexual pervert; a male homosexual. (Crude.) □ *I hear that you-know-who is an perv.* □ *He doesn't like being called a perv. Who would?*

petal *n.* an effeminate man; a passive male homosexual. (Crude.) □ *So what if he's a petal? He can still vote, can't he?* □ *Tom is getting to be such a petal.*

peter 1. *n.* a prison cell. □ *He would have paced up and down in his peter—if there had been room.* □ *Every time he returned to the peter his heart sank again.* **2.** *n.* the male sexual organ. (Taboo.) □ *Myra says peters are disgusting but then Myra's strange.* □ *Only small boys wave their peters about like that, Wayne. Put it away!*

pet peeve *n.* a major or principal annoyance or complaint. □ *Dirty dishes in restaurants are my pet peeve.* □ *He has no pet peeve. He hates everything equally.*

pew *n.* a seat. □ *Take a pew and wait your turn.* □ *Sit on that pew and say not a word!*

pheasant plucker *n.* an odious individual. (Crude. A deliberate spoonerism of "pleasant fucker." Compare with BAR STEWARD.) □ *I don't care if that pheasant plucker is the Pope in person. Get him out of here!* □ *You really can be a pheasant plucker at times, Rodney!*

phiz(og) *n.* a face. (Derived from "physiognomy.") □ *Why are you looking at me like that? Is there something wrong with my phizog?* □ *The woman* *had a very unusual phiz, you know.*

phone through AND **ring through; ring up** *vb. phr.* to call on the telephone. □ *I'll just phone through now.* □ *You'd better ring up to find out what she wants.*

phoney AND **phony 1.** *mod.* bogus; fake. □ *This money looks phony to me.* □ *I can't stand phony vanilla flavouring.* **2.** *n.* someone or something bogus. □ *That guy is a real phony!* □ *Look here, you phony, get out of my office!* □ *This is a phony. Get me a real one.*

phony See PHONEY.

phooey 1. *n.* nonsense. □ *Your story is just a lot of phooey.* □ *I've heard enough phooey. Let's get out of here.* **2.** *exclam.* an expression of disgust, disagreement or resignation. (Usually PHOOEY! Used typically when something smells or tastes bad.) □ *Who died in here? Phooey!* □ *This is the worst food I ever ate. Phooey!*

photo *n.* Guinness™ porter beer. (Rhyming slang, linked as follows: photo [finish] ≈ Guinness.) □ *Give my friend here a photo.* □ *How about a photo before you go, Charlie?*

Phyllis *n.* syphilis. (Crude. Rhyming slang.) □ *Get out of here, you Phyllis-infected slut!* □ *Getting Phyllis does nothing for your sex life.*

physical jerks AND **jerks** *n.* physical exercises. □ *Do we have to participate in these physical jerks every morning?* □ *He takes about ten minutes of jerks every day before breakfast.*

pi *mod.* pious. □ *Why does he always have to be so darned pi?* □ *Do you find that pi people like that make you suspicious?*

piano 1. *n.* a cash register. (Irish usage. So-called because it plays a cheerful tune. Compare with JEWISH PIANO and its variants.) □ *Even from the rear of the building, we could hear the ring of the piano every time my uncle made another sale in his little shop.* □ *The piano was playing loudly all day long as the goods were sold and the money rolled in.* **2.** *n.* a chamber-pot. □ *Oh, and there's a piano under the bed.* □ *I discovered what she meant by that*

when I had cause to use the piano in the wee small hours.

pick and choose *n.* beer or spirits. (Rhyming slang, linked as follows: pick and choose ≈ [booze] = beer/spirits.) □ *Here, that's good pick and choose!* □ *Have a can of pick and choose, Charlie.*

pickle *n.* a troublesome child. □ *Is this pickle yours?* □ *She is a most irritating pickle.*

pickled *mod.* intoxicated due to drink. □ *She's usually pickled by noon.* □ *It only takes a few drinks to get him pickled.*

pick-me-up *n.* any food or drink that boosts energy, such as alcohol, sweets, soft drink, etc. □ *I'm exhausted. I really need a pick-me-up.* □ *I can't get through my day without a little pick-me-up at lunch.*

pick on someone *vb. phr.* to intentionally and actively annoy or irritate someone. □ *So I made a mistake! I wish you'd stop picking on me.* □ *Picking on them is not going to correct the mistake.*

pick someone up 1. *vb. phr.* to arrest someone. □ *The Bill picked up everybody in sight.* □ *Don't argue with me, or I'll pick you up, too.* **2.** *vb. phr.* to befriend someone for ulterior sexual reasons. (Crude.) □ *Well, he picked up a tart and off they went.* □ *She's in the pub, hoping to pick someone up.*

pickup 1. *n.* a sudden increase in something, such as speed or tempo in music. □ *We need a bit of a pickup after the second interval.* □ *There will be a pickup in sales during the Christmas season.* **2.** *n.* someone befriended solely for ulterior sexual reasons. (Crude.) □ *She's no date. She's just a pickup.* □ *She had the gall to show up at the ball with some pickup in street clothes.*

pick up the tab for something *vb. phr.* to pay for something. □ *Oh, I'll pick up the tab for that.* □ *I can't afford to pick up the tab for a round of drinks this week, I'm afraid.*

picky *mod.* too choosy or critical. □ *Don't be so picky. They're all the same.* □ *I have to do it exactly right. My boss is very picky.*

picnic *n.* a good time; an easy time. □ *What a great class! Every day was a real picnic.* □ *Nothing to it. A real picnic.* □ *It wasn't a terrible day, but it was no picnic.*

picture perfect *mod.* looking exactly correct or right. □ *At last, everything was picture perfect.* □ *Nothing less than picture perfect will do.*

picture-skew *mod.* a humorous, often ironic, distortion of "picturesque." □ *Oh yes, I see your new house. Very picture-skew.* □ *Try to get something less picture-skew and more practical next time, eh?*

piddle 1. *vb.* to urinate. (Crude. Used euphemistically in reference to children and pets.) □ *Mommy! Jimmy's got to piddle!* □ *Please, Jimmy, don't piddle on the floor.* **2.** *n.* urine. (Crude. Used euphemistically in reference to children and pets.) □ *Where's the dog? There's piddle on the carpet.* □ *Don't step in the puppy's piddle.*

piddle about *vb. phr.* to fuss around, but achieve either very little or nothing. □ *Quit piddling about there and come and give me a hand!* □ *As usual, he's just piddling about.*

piddling *mod.* trivial; meagre; tiny. (Compare with PISS POOR. See also PIDDLE.) □ *What a piddling amount of money! I can't live on that.* □ *That is a piddling little steak. I ordered a big one.*

piddling AND **piffling; potty** *mod.* insignificant; trivial; feeble. □ *What a piddling little issue this is. Why are we making so much of it?* □ *Sort that potty thing out yourself.*

pie and liquor *n.* a clergyman. (Rhyming slang, linked as follows: pie and liquor ≈ [vicar] = clergyman.) □ *I went to see the pie and liquor for some advice.* □ *Most of the time, pie and liquors don't seem to have much to do.*

pie and mash *n.* an act of urination. (Crude. Rhyming slang, linked as follows: pie and mash ≈ [slash] = urination. See SLASH.) □ *Where do you go around here for a pie and mash?* □ *If you need a pie and mash, go through there.*

piece of cake AND **piece of piss 1.** *n.* something easy to do. □ *No problem. When you know what you're doing, it's a piece of cake.* □ *Glad to help. It was a piece of piss.* **2.** *exclam.* "It's a piece of cake!"; "It's easy!" (Usually PIECE OF CAKE!) □ *No problem, piece of cake!* □ *Rescuing drowning cats is my speciality. Piece of piss!*

piece of goods AND **piece of skirt** *n.* a woman. (Crude.) □ *Ask that piece of goods at the door what she wants, Bill.* □ *Who's that piece of skirt you're running around with these days?*

piece of piss See PIECE OF CAKE.

piece of skirt See PIECE OF GOODS.

piece (of the action) AND **bit of the action; slice of the action** *n.* a share in the activity or the profits. (Especially gambling activity.) □ *If you get in on that real estate deal, I want a piece, too.* □ *Don't be selfish. Give me a slice of the action.*

pie-eyed *mod.* intoxicated due to drink. □ *That guy is really pie-eyed. Send him home.* □ *We've got a pie-eyed bus driver. I want to get off!*

pie in the sky *mod.* a fantastic, unrealisable vision of future success or happiness. (This is hyphenated before a nominal.) □ *Get rid of your pie-in-the-sky ideas!* □ *What these pie-in-the-sky people really want is money.*

piffle 1. *exclam.* a mild exclamation or expression of distress. (Usually PIFFLE!) □ *You a stockbroker? Piffle!* □ *She finished her story, and I looked her straight in the eye and said, "Piffle!"* **2.** *n.* nonsense. □ *What utter piffle!* □ *The entire report was piffle from beginning to end.*

piffling See PIDDLING.

piffy *mod.* unlikely; improbable; suspect. □ *It's really piffy, but if you think so...* □ *That is a really piffy suggestion; it's absurd!*

pig (All senses are usually derogatory.) **1.** *n.* someone who eats too much; a glutton. □ *Stop being a pig! Save some for other people.* □ *I try to cut down on calories, but whenever I see red meat I make a pig of myself.* **2.** *n.* a dirty or slovenly person. □ *Max is a pig. I don't* *think he bathes enough.* □ *Jimmy, change your clothes. Look at that mud, you little pig!* **3.** *n.* a police officer. (Although widely known only since the 1960s, this sense of the word was in fact quite common in 19th century London.) □ *The pig did break up the fight.* □ *These two pigs drove around in their pigmobile aggravating innocent people like me.* **4.** *n.* a naval officer. □ *"What did the pig want?" the seaman asked his mate.* □ *You have to obey a pig in this navy.* **5.** *n.* a rugby football. □ *He grabbed the pig as it flew out of the scrum and ran with it all the way.* □ *He hoisted the pig with one fine kick right over the cross-bar.* **6.** *n.* a portion of an orange. □ *She peeled and opened up the orange, offering each of us a pig.* □ *He took each pig, one by one, and swallowed it whole.*

pigeon *n.* a DUPE; a SUCKER; someone singled out to be cheated. (Compare with PATSY.) □ *There's our pigeon now. Don't let him see us sizing him up.* □ *Be alert for pickpockets. Don't be some crook's pigeon.*

pigeon-hearted *mod.* cowardly. □ *He's pigeon-hearted, but I still love him.* □ *What a pigeon-hearted individual he turned out to be.*

piggery AND **pigsty** *n.* a house or a room that is in a filthy or slovenly condition. (Compare with PIG'S BREAKFAST.) □ *It really is a piggery, Simon.* □ *What a pigsty you've turned this place into!*

piggy-bank *n.* one's savings. □ *I'll have to see if I've got enough in my piggy-bank for that.* □ *Take a look in your piggy-bank and let me know if you can afford to come in on this.*

pig(gy)-in-the-middle 1. *n.* a children's game. □ *In the pig-in-the-middle, two players throw a ball back and forth while a third person in the middle tries to catch it.* □ *Now children, what about a game of piggy-in-the-middle?* **2.** *n.* someone placed in a difficult situation between two others. □ *How come I always end up as piggy-in-the-middle?* □ *I just will not be pig-in-the-middle again!*

pigheaded *mod.* stupidly stubborn. (From the notion that pigs are immovable.) □ *You are unbelievably pigheaded!* □ *What a stupid pigheaded position to take.*

pig-ignorant *mod.* very ignorant, especially of what is acceptable social behaviour. □ *Stupid? He's more like pig-ignorant, I'd say.* □ *Yes, he's pig-ignorant but we need him, OK?*

pig it *vb. phr.* to live in squalor. □ *Without doubt, they are pigging it.* □ *Why do you have to pig it like this all the time?*

pigmobile *n.* a police car. (See PIG.) □ *Look out, here comes the pigmobile.* □ *They took Jane away in a pigmobile.*

pigs See PIG'S EAR.

pig's arse See PIG'S BREAKFAST.

pig's breakfast AND **pig's ear; pig's arse** *n.* a chaotic mess; a complete disaster; a total failure. (PIG'S ARSE is taboo. Other expressions are crude. Compare with PIGGERY and PIGSTY.) □ *Why do have to make a pig's breakfast of every thing you touch?* □ *What a pig's arse this place have become.*

pig's ear 1. *n.* year. (Rhyming slang.) □ *Look, I've been working on this for a whole pig's ear and I'm fed up with it.* □ *It'll take more than one pig's ear to put that right.* **2.** See also PIG'S BREAKFAST. **3.** AND **pigs** *n.* beer. (Rhyming slang.) □ *Give my friend here a pig's ear.* □ *How about a pigs before you go, Charlie?*

pigsty See PIGGERY.

pile *n.* a large amount of money. □ *She really made a pile in the stock market.* □ *That old lady has a pile of money stashed in the bank.*

pileup *n.* a multi-vehicle road accident. □ *There is a serious pileup on the motorway.* □ *My car was ruined in a pileup on the bypass.*

pill 1. *n.* nonsense. □ *Boy, he can certainly churn out pill by the ton!* □ *That's just a lot of pill. Ignore it.* **2.** *n.* a birth control pill. (Always with *the*.) □ *Is Sally on the pill?* □ *The pill has really changed my life.* **3.** *n.* a ball. □ *The kids went outside to kick around the pill.* □ *Johnny lost his pill and wants a* *new one.* **4.** *n.* a tobacco or marijuana cigarette. □ *Hey, give me a pill, eh?* □ *I'll trade you a pill for a light.* **5.** *n.* an army doctor. □ *The pill wouldn't renew my prescription.* □ *I went to his office, but the pill wasn't in.* **6.** *vb.* to fail in an examination at college, etc. □ *I pilled all my exams except history.* □ *I pilled history again.* **7.** *n.* a boring individual. (From PILLOCK.) □ *Boy, are you a pill!* □ *Who's the pill in the tartan trousers?*

Pill Avenue *n.* Harley Street in London, where the leading members of the medical profession are to be found. □ *She's off to see her favourite quack on Pill Avenue again today.* □ *They reckon that once a doctor hangs up his plate on Pill Avenue, he has a licence to print money.*

pill bosun *n.* a ship's doctor. □ *Most of the time, pill bosuns don't have all that much to do.* □ *He had to go see the pill bosun because he felt unwell.*

pillock 1. *n.* a fool; an idiot. □ *I felt like a pillock when I found out that I'd got onto the wrong train.* □ *Those pillocks are at it again. Spend, spend, spend.* **2.** *n.* the male sexual organ. (Taboo.) □ *The doctor told him that he'd got something wrong with his pillock.* □ *That's all very well Myra, but where would the world be without pillocks?* **3.** *n.* an objectionable person. □ *What a pillock you are!* □ *Just get out of my sight, you pillock!*

pill opera *n.* any TV soap opera about life in a hospital. □ *She just loves all these pill operas on the TV.* □ *There are several pill operas on tonight, dear.*

pillow-biter *n.* a passive male homosexual. (Taboo.) □ *He doesn't like being called a pillow-biter.* □ *Why does he work so hard to look like he's a pillow-biter?*

pill-peddler See PILL-PUSHER.

pill-popper *n.* anyone who takes pills frequently or habitually. □ *Poor Sue is a pill-popper.* □ *I knew she was always ill, but I didn't know she was a pill-popper.* □ *The pill-popper thought she wouldn't get hooked.*

pill-pusher AND **pill-roller; pill-peddler** *n.* a medical doctor. □ *That pill-peddler wouldn't renew my prescription.* □ *I*

went to the surgery, but the pill-pusher wasn't in.

pill-roller See PILL-PUSHER.

pills *n.* the testicles. (Taboo. Normally with *the* and in the plural.) □ *He got hit right in the pills.* □ *The teacher preferred "testicles" to "pills," if they had to be mentioned at all.*

pimp 1. *n.* a man who solicits business for and lives off the earnings of one or more prostitutes. (Crude.) □ *The guy with the diamond rings looks like a pimp.* □ *The cops took in three hookers and their pimp.* **2.** *n.* a police informer. (Compare with NARK.) □ *The detective paid his pimp £30 for the information.* □ *No matter how useful to the police, a pimp has few friends on either side.*

pimple *n.* a hill. □ *There's a castle on that pimple.* □ *Let's climb the pimple and look at the castle.*

pimple and blotch *n.* whisky. (Rhyming slang, linked as follows: pimple and blotch ≈ [Scotch] = whisky.) □ *The pimple and blotch was certainly flowing that evening, I can tell you.* □ *I could go a glass or three of the old pimple and blotch.*

pin back your lugholes See PIN YOUR EARS BACK.

pinch *vb. phr.* to steal something. □ *The kid pinched a chocolate bar right off the counter.* □ *I pinched these paper clips from my office.*

pinched *mod.* arrested. (Compare with COP.) □ *I got pinched for speeding.* □ *Sam got pinched for breaking his parole conditions.*

pinch someone *vb.* to arrest someone. (Compare with COP.) □ *The cops pinched her in front of her house.* □ *The police inspector pinched her for passing bad cheques.*

pineapple *n.* a male homosexual. (Crude.) □ *He doesn't like being called a pineapple.* □ *Tom is getting to be such a pineapple.*

pinhead *n.* a fool; someone of very low intelligence. □ *That pinhead thinks he can convince them.* □ *You pinhead! You've buttered the tablecloth!*

pink elephants *n.* hallucinatory creatures seen during the *delirium tremens.*

□ *He said pink elephants were trying to kill him. He's really drunk.* □ *If you ever find yourself surrounded with pink elephants, you've got the D.T.s.*

pinkers *n.* pink gin. □ *Would you like another pinkers, sir?* □ *He gave me a pinkers and left me alone.*

pinko *n.* someone who holds vaguely left-wing/liberal opinions; an advocate of political correctness, feminism and similar views. □ *I hate that slimy little pinko.* □ *Where have all the pinkos gone?*

pink'un *n.* a newspaper, such as the *Financial Times*, that is printed upon pink paper. □ *Every morning he bought a pink'un and read it on the train taking him to work.* □ *So why should newspapers not be pink'uns?*

pinky 1. *n.* a white person. (Racially offensive. Called this by black people.) □ *Winston wondered what the pinky wanted.* □ *He thinks all pinkies are racist pigs.* **2.** *n.* a lesbian. (Crude.) □ *Don't you know? Sandra's a pinky.* □ *You'll find nothing but pinkys in that pub.*

pinny *n.* an apron. (From "pinafore.") □ *Doesn't he look sweet, standing there in his pinny!* □ *She put on her pinny and went to tidy up the house.*

pint *n.* this quantity of beer, especially as an order in a pub. □ *How about a pint?* □ *Make mine a pint, thanks.*

pinta *n.* a pint of milk. (A corruption of "pint of" invented for a campaign to encourage milk consumption in the 1960s.) □ *Ask the milkman to leave an extra pinta, please.* □ *She went into the dairy and asked for a pinta.*

pint-sized *mod.* small; miniature. □ *I won't fit into one of those pint-sized cars.* □ *My car is not pint-sized.* □ *Tell that little pint-sized guy to get lost.*

pin-up *n.* the likeness of a pretty girl, upon a wall where it may be appreciated by passing males. □ *You could not see the rough-hewn wall of the prison cell for the many pin-ups that covered it.* □ *Otto has a huge collection of pin-ups.*

pin your ears back AND **pin back your ears; pin back your lugholes** *vb. phr.* to listen very carefully. □ *That news re-*

ally got their ears pinned back. □ *Pin back your lugholes. This is going to be worth hearing.*

pip 1. *vb.* to blackball someone. □ *You can't join the club; I'm afraid you've been pipped.* □ *Why should anyone want to pip me?* **2.** *vb.* to defeat someone. □ *Oh, we'll pip them.* □ *How did we get pipped again?* **3.** *vb.* to hit someone or some creature with a shell from a gun.* □ *The trench was pipped, killing everyone in it.* □ *I bet you can't pip that pigeon over there.* **4.** *n.* a strong feeling of irritation or disgust. (Normally with *the*.) □ *That really gives me the pip.* □ *No wonder we got the pip.*

pip at the post *vb. phr.* to defeat at the very last moment. □ *We were pipped at the post.* □ *Don't try to pip them at the post.*

Pipe *n.* the underground railway system of London. (Normally with *the*. Compare with TUBE, which is much more commonly heard.) □ *Does the Pipe go to Crystal Palace?* □ *He likes using the Pipe because it's so quick.*

pipe down *vb. phr.* to become quiet; to cease making noise; to shut up. (Especially as a forceful command.) □ *Pipe down! I'm trying to sleep.* □ *Come on! Pipe down and get back to work!*

pipe off (about something) See SOUND OFF (ABOUT SOMETHING).

pipe one's eyes *vb. phr.* to weep. □ *When I heard, I had to pipe my eyes.* □ *Stop piping your eyes and act like a man!*

pip out See PEG OUT.

pipped *mod.* annoyed. □ *The whole business got her pipped after a while.* □ *That remark pipped her, once she realised what it meant.*

pipsqueak *n.* a small, unimportant or timid man or boy. (Also a term of address.) □ *Shut up you little pipsqueak, or I'll hit you.* □ *I may be a pipsqueak, but I am a gentleman.*

piss 1. *vb.* to urinate. (Taboo. An offensive word to most people. There are many additional meanings and constructions using this word. It is in fact Standard English, but virtually all applications of it are not.) □ *He went out* *and pissed in the woods.* □ *Don't piss on the floor.* **2.** *n.* urine. (Taboo.) □ *There's piss on the rug. Where's that cat?* □ *That's disgusting! There's piss on your trouser-leg.* **3.** *n.* an act of urination. (Taboo. Especially with *take*.) □ *He went out to take a piss.* □ *Come on, I've gotta stop here for a piss.* **4.** *n.* any drink of poor quality. (Taboo.) □ *Where did you get this disgusting piss, bartender?* □ *You don't really expect us to drink this piss, do you?*

piss about See PISS AROUND.

piss around AND **piss about** *vb. phr.* to mess about; to delay. (Taboo.) □ *If they didn't piss around, they'd get it done with time to spare.* □ *Stop pissing about and get on with your work!*

piss artist 1. *n.* a drunkard. (Taboo.) □ *There was some piss artist asleep across the front entrance to the office when I got here this morning.* □ *You are going to turn into a piss artist if you don't let up on your drinking.* **2.** *n.* a person who boasts of knowledge or skills that they do not have. (Taboo.) □ *We had a real piss artist here today, claiming he was an astronaut!* □ *That was no piss artist, that was my uncle who just happens to be a real live astronaut!*

pissed *mod.* intoxicated due to drink. (Taboo. This does *not* mean "angry" in Britain, although PISSED OFF does.) □ *He was really pissed.* □ *He was so pissed he could hardly stand up.*

pissed as a newt AND **newted** *mod.* very intoxicated due to drink. (Both are crude; PISSED AS A NEWT is taboo.) □ *Tipsy? Pissed as a newt, more like!* □ *Joe and Arthur kept on knocking them back till they were both completely newted.*

pissed off *mod.* angry. (Taboo. Compare with PISS SOMEONE OFF.) □ *I was so pissed off I could have screamed.* □ *He's come back, and he's really pissed off.*

piss-hole *n.* a urinal; a public toilet. (Taboo.) □ *What a piss-hole!* □ *What do you expect a toilet to be except a piss-hole?*

piss-hole bandit *n.* a homosexual who hangs around public toilets. (Taboo.) □

Why does he work so hard to look like he's a piss-hole bandit? □ *So what if he's a piss-hole bandit? He can still vote, can't he?*

pissing down *mod.* raining heavily. (Taboo.) □ *It was really pissing down and we went to the pictures.* □ *I hate driving when it's pissing down.*

piss in the wind *vb. phr.* to attempt something certain to fail; to make a futile gesture. (Taboo.) □ *We're just pissing in the wind; this will never work.* □ *Instead of trying to piss in the wind again, let's try do it this way for a change.*

piss it *vb. phr.* to succeed easily. (Taboo.) □ *There! We pissed it!* □ *If you can piss it here, you're either very clever or very lucky.*

Piss off! See FUCK OFF!

piss off 1. *vb. phr.* to depart rapidly and immediately. (Taboo.) □ *Look, just piss off. All right?* □ *It's all right. He's pissed off now.* **2.** See also FUCK OFF.

piss oneself *vb. phr.* to wet one's pants. (Taboo.) □ *Johnny's pissed himself again.* □ *He had drunk so much he was actually pissing himself.*

piss poor 1. *mod.* very inadequate; feeble. (Taboo. An elaboration of *poor*. Compare with PIDDLING.) □ *This is a piss poor excuse for fried chicken.* □ *It is really piss poor.* □ *That was a piss poor performance for a professional musician.* **2.** *mod.* poverty-stricken; without any money. (Taboo. An elaboration of *poor*.) □ *Since the factory closed, everyone in this town is piss-poor.* □ *No, I can't lend you money. I'm piss-poor myself.*

piss someone off *vb. phr.* to make someone angry. (Taboo. Compare with PISSED OFF.) □ *She really pissed me off!* □ *That's enough to piss off anybody.*

piss-taker *n.* one who mocks. (Taboo.) □ *Now Paul is a real piss-taker.* □ *All right you piss-takers! Get off your backsides and come and help instead!*

piss-up 1. *n.* a session of extensive drinking. (Taboo.) □ *That was one hell of a piss-up last night, Barry.* □ *Let's have another piss-up this weekend.* **2.** *vb. phr.* to mess up; to fail. (Taboo.) □ *I* *just hope I don't piss up again.* □ *Oh no, you've pissed up yet again!* **3.** See also ARSE-UP.

pissy *mod.* tawdry; third-rate; unacceptable. (Taboo.) □ *I'm sorry, but your entire exhibit is really pissy.* □ *What a pissy outfit this is.*

pit *n.* a bed. □ *Somebody put a spider in my pit.* □ *I was so tired I could hardly find my pit.*

pitch in *vb. phr.* to work hard to complete a task. □ *Come on, you guys! Pitch in.* □ *If more people would pitch in and help, we could get this job done in no time at all.*

pits 1. *n.* that which is the worst; that which is very bad indeed. (Always with *the*.) □ *Life is the pits.* □ *This whole day was the pits from beginning to end.* **2.** *n.* the depths of despair. (Always with *the*. Often with *in*.) □ *It's always the pits with him.* □ *She's depressed and in the pits.*

pit stop *n.* a pause in a journey (usually by car) to urinate. (From the name of a service stop in motor racing.) □ *I think we'll pull in at the next service area. I need a pit stop.* □ *Why do you need a pit stop every thirty miles?*

pix *n.* pictures; photographs. □ *I got my pix back from the chemist's.* □ *Hold still and let me get your pix taken. Then you can jump around.*

pixilated 1. *mod.* bewildered; confused. □ *That little old lady is pixilated.* □ *She seems a bit young to be so pixilated.* **2.** *mod.* intoxicated due to drink. □ *She seems a bit pixilated. She's probably been drinking.* □ *Martha, you musn't drive. I think you are pixilated.*

place-bet *n.* a bet that the horse backed will be in any one of the first three or four finishing positions in a race. □ *I want to put a place-bet on "Iolantha" in the 3:30 today.* □ *The thing about a place bet is that you stand to win less but you are less likely to lose.*

placed *mod.* occupying any one of the first three or four finishing positions in a race, particularly a horse race. □ *Her horse was not first, but at least it was placed.* □ *If it was placed, then I at least made some money on the transaction.*

Plain and Gravy See LUMPY GRAVY.

plain as a pikestaff *mod.* glaringly obvious. □ *Well, now it's plain as a pikestaff that we cannot continue as before.* □ *Surely you can see that church steeple over there? It's plain as a pikestaff!*

plain sailing *mod.* smooth, trouble-free or easy going. □ *It'll be plain sailing from now on.* □ *When this is finished, it'll be plain sailing.*

plain vanilla See VANILLA.

planky *mod.* dull-witted; stupid. (From "as thick as a plank.") □ *Oh come on, he must be the plankiest person on the planet.* □ *How planky can you get?*

plant 1. *vb.* to deliver a blow (to a particular spot on someone's body). □ *I planted one right on his nose.* □ *The boxer planted a good blow on his opponent's shoulder.* **2.** *n.* incriminating evidence secretly placed upon a putative criminal or on his property in order to incriminate him. (Allegedly done by police to entrap drug offenders.) □ *He was still protesting that it was a plant as they wheeled him off to the clink.* □ *The drugs the cops found on Harry were a plant.*

plant something on someone *vb. phr.* to hide incriminating evidence on a person for later discovery and use in prosecution. (Allegedly a police practice used to entrap drug offenders.) □ *The cops planted snow on Max and then arrested him for carrying it.* □ *Don't touch me! You'll plant something on me!*

plastered *mod.* intoxicated due to drink. □ *She's really plastered.* □ *She's so plastered she can't see.*

plastic 1. *mod.* PHONY; false. □ *She wears too much makeup and looks totally plastic.* □ *I'm tired of living in such a plastic society.* **2.** *n.* a credit card; credit cards in general. □ *Our economy depends on plastic.* □ *I don't carry any cash, just plastic.* **3.** *mod.* having to do with credit cards and their use. □ *This plastic economy is dangerous.* □ *There is too much plastic debt in most households.*

plates and dishes 1. *n.* kisses. (Rhyming slang. Always in the plural.) □ *Barlowe* *was greeted at the door by a lovely, cuddly bird in a nightie—eyes closed and lips parted for some better than average plates and dishes. He really wished—just for a moment—that he hadn't rung the wrong doorbell.* □ *He planted a series of quick plates and dishes square on her lips. She kicked him in the shins for his trouble.* **2.** *n.* wife. (Rhyming slang, linked as follows: plates and dishes ≈ [missus] = wife.) □ *I've got to get home to the plates and dishes.* □ *The plates and dishes is angry with me.*

plates of meat *n.* the feet. (Rhyming slang. Always plural.) □ *My plates of meat are aching after all that walking.* □ *Sit down and give your plates of meat a rest.*

plate someone *vb.* to perform oral sex on someone. (Taboo.) □ *He actually came right out and asked, you know, for me to plate him!* □ *So did you plate him then?*

play a hunch *vb. phr.* to act on intuition. □ *I'm going to play a hunch here and give you a chance.* □ *I've played a hunch and lost, you know.*

play around *vb. phr.* to waste time. □ *Stop playing around and get to work.* □ *We don't have time to play around.*

play around with someone 1. *vb. phr.* to flirt or have an affair with someone. □ *Those two have been playing around for months.* □ *She only wants to play around with me.* **2.** *vb. phr.* to tease, deceive or try to trick someone. □ *You're playing around with me. Leave me alone.* □ *Don't pay any attention to them. They're just playing around.* **3.** *vb. phr.* to waste someone's time. □ *Stop playing around with Mary and get back to work.* □ *Don't play around with me!*

play away *vb. phr.* to consort with someone other than one's regular partner. □ *I'm certain Nigel's playing away with some trollop!* □ *He found out she was playing away with just about every male that crossed her path, and so divorced her.*

play ball with someone *vb. phr.* to cooperate with someone. □ *Are you going* to play ball, or do I have to report you to the boss? □ *You will be better off if you will play ball with me.*

play bouncy-bouncy AND **bump tummies** *vb. phr.* to indulge in sexual intercourse. (Crude. Juvenile-sounding euphemisms employed by adults.) □ *Want to play bouncy-bouncy?* □ *All right, you smooth talker, let's bump tummies.*

play fast and loose with someone or something *vb. phr.* to treat someone or something carelessly or unfairly. □ *The broker played fast and loose with our money. Now we are nearly broke.* □ *He was playing fast and loose with his girl, so she left him.*

play for keeps *vb. phr.* to take serious and permanent actions. (Refers to playing a game where the money won is not returned at the end of the game.) □ *Wake up and face the fact that she's playing for keeps. She wants to get married.* □ *I always play for keeps.*

play for time *vb. phr.* to procrastinate. □ *Don't you try to play for time with me. I want your answer now!* □ *I think they're still trying to play for time on this decision.*

play gooseberry *vb. phr.* to be a third person present when the other two wish to be alone. □ *Why must she always play gooseberry?* □ *I think Aunt Martha actually does not even realise she's playing gooseberry.*

play hard to get *vb. phr.* to resist romantic advances, with the intent of ultimately succumbing. □ *I'm sure she's still just playing hard to get.* □ *If you play hard to get, they appreciate you more in the end.*

play hide the sausage *vb. phr.* to perform sexual intercourse. (Crude. A juvenile-sounding euphemism employed by adults.) □ *They were playing hide the sausage like it was going out of fashion.* □ *I think you could play hide the sausage there, Barry.*

play it cool 1. *vb. phr.* to do something while not revealing insecurities or incompetence. (Compare with COOL.) □ *Play it cool, Joe. Look as if you belong there.* □ *If the boss walks in, just play it* cool. **2.** *vb. phr.* to hold one's temper; to keep calm. □ *Come on now. Let it pass. Play it cool.* □ *Don't let them get you angry. Play it cool.*

play leapfrog *vb. phr.* to participate in male homosexual activities. (Crude.) □ *I think he's off to that pub—you know the one I mean—hoping to play leapfrog later.* □ *He's always playing leapfrog! It's disgusting!*

play lighthouses *vb. phr.* to have an erection while in the bath. (Taboo.) □ *Oh, he'll be in there, playing lighthouses as usual.* □ *Don't you think playing lighthouses is a bit juvenile, Harry?*

play (merry) hell with someone or something *vb. phr.* to cause difficulty for someone or something. (Crude.) □ *You know that this cake is going to play hell with my diet.* □ *Your decision plays merry hell with all my friends.*

play silly buggers *vb. phr.* to refuse to be serious when frivolity is not appropriate. (Taboo.) □ *Don't play silly buggers with me! I'm serious!* □ *If he is still playing silly buggers when you get back, sack him on the spot.*

play something by ear *vb. phr.* to handle a situation piece by piece, as it develops. □ *Don't you worry, I can play this one by ear.* □ *If you're going to play it by ear, please be careful.*

play something close (to one's chest) *vb. phr.* to be secretive. □ *We must play this close to one's chest for the time being.* □ *How did you manage to play something like that close for so long?*

play the goat *vb. phr.* to fool around. □ *That's enough of playing the goat.* □ *Stop playing the goat and get on with your work.*

play the wag See WAG (IT) OFF.

play with fire *vb. phr.* to take a foolish chance or risk. □ *When you talk to me like that, you're playing with fire.* □ *Going out at night in that part of town is playing with fire.*

plod 1. *n.* the police force; especially the uniformed section. (Always with the.) □ *The plod are after me!* □ *Get away, get away! The plod are outside!* **2.** *n.* a uniformed police officer, espe-

cially when on foot patrol. □ *There's a plod walking down the passage towards us.* □ *Get rid of that plod before he finds out what's really going on here.*

plonk 1. *n.* a cheap, poor-quality wine. (Possibly from French *blanc*, but now applied to wine of any colour or place of origin. If indeed from the French, then by hobson-jobson.) □ *That plonk is really hard on the gut.* □ *How about a bottle of plonk?* **2.** *n.* the male sexual organ. (Taboo.) □ *Unlike Myra, Sharon thinks of little else but plonks.* □ *Men keep their brains in their plonks!*

plonker 1. *n.* a big, loud, wet kiss. □ *His aunt gave him a plonker on his forehead and he cringed.* □ *Jimmy hates aunts who give their young nephews plonkers.* **2.** *n.* a stupid mistake. □ *Oh no, you've made another plonker.* □ *Any more plonkers like that and you're out!* **3.** *n.* a foolish or unimaginative person. □ *Those plonkers are at it again. Spend, spend, spend.* □ *You plonker! You've buttered the tablecloth!*

plonkers *n.* the feet. (Always plural.) □ *Sit down and give your plonkers a rest.* □ *My plonkers are aching after all that walking.*

plonk something down *vb. phr.* to put or place down something. □ *He plonked down a great wad of notes and asked if that was enough?* □ *Don't you plonk your filthy clothes down in here!*

plonk something out *vb. phr.* to hand out something. (Typically money.) □ *You expect me to plonk this out, but what's in it for me?* □ *I'm just not going to plonk out this just for your convenience.*

plop 1. *n.* the sound of dropping something soft and bulky, such as a hunk of meat. □ *When the roast fell on the floor, it made a nasty plop.* □ *When I heard the plop, I looked up and saw our dinner on the floor.* **2.** *vb.* to put or place something (somewhere). □ *I don't mind cooking a turkey. You only have to plop it in the oven and forget about it.* □ *I plopped my books on the table and went straight to my room.*

plop it down *vb. phr.* to sit oneself down somewhere; to place one's buttocks somewhere. (The *it* is the but-tocks.) □ *Come in, Fred. Just plop it anywhere you see a chair. This place is a mess.* □ *I just plopped it down beside him and we had our little talk.*

plough *vb.* to fail an academic examination. □ *I ploughed history again.* □ *I ploughed all my exams except history.*

ploughed *mod.* intoxicated due to drink or drugs. □ *She was ploughed for a week.* □ *They went out and got ploughed.*

PLU *n.* "people like us." (A code word for someone who is considered socially acceptable. Compare with NOCD and NTD.) □ *Oh, she's quite clearly PLU, my dear.* □ *We only want PLUs to join us here, don't we now?*

plug 1. *n.* a bite-sized, pressed mass of chewing tobacco. □ *He put a plug in his cheek and walked away.* □ *Let's have a piece of that plug!* **2.** *n.* free publicity, an advertisement or a commercial boost for a product or person. □ *I managed to get a plug on the Mike Michael show.* □ *How about a plug during your introduction?* **3.** *vb.* to give an advertisement or a commercial a boost for something without having to pay for it in the manner of a paid advertisment. □ *I want to get on that TV programme and plug my new book.* □ *I can't plug your product until I have a sample I can test.*

plug in both ways *vb. phr.* [for a male] to be bisexual. (Taboo.) □ *Since he plugs in both ways, I suppose he may stand a better chance at finding a date.* □ *I wouldn't say he was bisexual; let's just say he plugs in both ways.*

plum *n.* the best of something, especially when considered as a prize or reward. □ *That appointment was quite a plum.* □ *What did you have to do to get a plum job like that?*

plumber *n.* a surgeon. (Derogatory.) □ *I'd not want to let a plumber touch my insides.* □ *We really do need a plumber now. This is an emergency.*

plumbum oscillans *n.* malingering. (Pseudo-Latin. Literally, "the swinging of lead." Compare with ILLEGITIMIS NON CARBORUNDUM, NIL CARBORUNDUM IL-

LIGITIUM.) □ *That's enough. There shall be no more plumbum oscillans around here!* □ *I think we could say that plumbum oscillans was the principle activity in that department.*

plummy *mod.* of a form of affected speech which sounds as if the speaker has a plum in his or her mouth. □ *Who's the geezer with the plummy accent on the phone?* □ *Some people might say your voice is plummy, you know.*

plums *n.* the testicles. (Taboo. Normally with *the* and in the plural.) □ *The teacher preferred "testicles" to "plums," if they had to be mentioned at all.* □ *Thud, right in the plums. Ye gods, it hurt!*

PMJI *interj.* "Pardon me for jumping in." (Computer jargon. Written only. An initialism used in computer communications. Indicates that someone is responding to a message directed to someone else.) □ *PMJI, but I have some information that would help you with your problem.* □ *PMJI. As long as we are talking about holidays, does anyone know the price of admission to EuroDisney in Paris?*

po *n.* a chamber pot. (Childish.) □ *Mummy, I need the po!* □ *Get your po out, Tommy.*

poach *vb.* to recruit someone by enticing him or her away from a current employer. □ *Someone's poaching our best workers.* □ *Can you poach any more people from the other factory?*

pocket AND **trouser** *vb.* to put money into one's (trouser) pocket. □ *He pocketed the money and ran.* □ *Trouser that and get out of here.*

podged *mod.* replete; too full. □ *No more! I'm completely podged!* □ *Eat 'till you're podged!*

poggled See PUGGLED.

pogue AND **poke** *n.* a purse; a wallet. □ *Get out your pogue and give some money to this worthy cause.* □ *My poke's gone! I've been robbed!*

point Percy at the porcelain AND **aim Archy at the Armitage** *vb. phr.* to urinate. (Taboo. "Armitage Shanks" is a well-known British manufacturer of toilet fittings.) □ *I'm going to point Percy at the porcelain.* □ *Well, aiming Archy at the Armitage does relieve the pressure of all that beer!*

Point taken. *sent.* "I see what you mean." □ *Point taken. What do we do about it?* □ *Point taken. Let's get on with it.*

poison 1. *mod.* wicked; evil. □ *Stay away from her. She's poison.* □ *His plan was pure poison, and I realised he had to be stopped.* **2.** *n.* an alcoholic drink. □ *Name your poison.* □ *How about a drink of that poison there?*

poison dwarf *n.* a person of small stature and obnoxious nature. (Offensive.) □ *Now Short Albert over there is your real poison dwarf.* □ *She was only little but she was certainly a poison dwarf!*

poisonous *mod.* evil; corrupting; deadly. □ *Get out, you poisonous little creep!* □ *That one really is poisonous.*

poke 1. *vb.* to perform sexual intercourse, from the male perspective. (Taboo.) □ *They say he poked her.* □ *Your dog poked my dog, then ran away.* **2.** *n.* a paper bag. (Scots usage.) □ *The minister gave each of the weans a poke with their snack in it when they arrived. (The minister gave each of the children a bag with their snack in it when they arrived.)* □ *Sees a poke a chips, right? (Can I have a bag of chips, please?)* **3.** See also POGUE.

po(ker)-faced *mod.* with a blank inscrutable expression upon one's face. □ *As he spoke I sat there, poker-faced.* □ *Her po-faced look fooled no one.*

pole *vb.* to perform sexual intercourse, from the male perspective. (Taboo. Irish usage.) □ *I think you could pole there, Barry.* □ *They were poling like it was going out of fashion.*

polis *n.* the police. (Scots usage. Always with *the*.) □ *Whar's the polis when ye want them?* □ *The polis are after Willy again.*

polish someone off *vb. phr.* to defeat someone completely or finally. □ *You've polished off me!* □ *Why did you polish off all of them?*

polish something off *vb. phr.* to get rid of something completely. □ *He polished off the meal in minutes.* □ *Polish off that work quickly, and we'll sort you out.*

polis-man *n.* a policeman. (Scots usage.) □ *The polis-man are here looking for you again, Rab.* □ *What have yous yins been doing to interest the polis-man this time? (What have you people being doing to interest the policeman this time?)*

politico *n.* a politician; anyone interested in politics. □ *Why would anyone want to be a politico?* □ *Why should a politico want to talk to me?*

poll *n.* students who obtain no more than a pass degree from Cambridge University. (Normally with *the*.) □ *Come on! You can do better than just be a poll!* □ *I suppose most students have to end up as polls.*

Pom(my) *n.* an English person; particularly, an English immigrant in Australia or New Zealand. (Offensive. In origin and preponderant application this term is not British but Australian, yet it is well-known in Britain and so included here. It's origin is obscure, but is possibly rhyming slang that could be linked as follows: Pom(my) = [pomegranate]/[Jimmy Grant] ≈ immigrant.) □ *One Pommy was no different from the others, Bruce thought.* □ *I don't think I could take another whinging Pom like that today.*

Pompey *n.* the city of Portsmouth. □ *Pompey is the home port of the Royal Navy.* □ *Pompey was once a name for the old naval prison in Portsmouth.*

ponce 1. *n.* an effeminate man; a passive male homosexual. (Crude.) □ *I hear that you-know-who is a ponce.* □ *He doesn't like being called a ponce.* **2.** *n.* a pimp. (Crude.) □ *Oh, she has a ponce all right!* □ *They found the ponce the next morning, face-down in the river.* **3.** *vb.* to scrounge; to importune; to beg. □ *So, how much did you ponce out of the punters today?* □ *There seem to be more and more people poncing every year.*

ponce about *vb. phr.* to act in an affected or effeminate manner. (Crude.) □ *Stop poncing about like that.* □ *If they want to ponce about, what harm is it doing?*

poncy *mod.* flashy; garish. □ *If you did not dress so poncy you would not attract so many comments from passersby.* □ *Look at her! Have you ever seen anyone looking as poncy?*

pong *n.* a stink or unpleasant smell. □ *Where is that terrible pong coming from?* □ *I just can't stand that pong.*

pongo 1. *n.* a soldier. □ *I'd never be a pongo if I could help it!* □ *Who's the pongo Mart's with tonight?* **2.** *n.* an orangutan. □ *Originally, pongos were thought to be sort of cave men.* □ *That's why a pongo is called an orangutan, which means "wild man" in Malay.* **3.** *n.* a foreigner. (Offensive.) □ *Otto did not like that pongo, so he made that clear to the poor guy in the clearest possible way.* □ *There seem to be a lot of pongos around here these days.* **4.** *n.* a monkey. □ *My uncle has a pet pongo; it's a chimpanzee.* □ *Pongos are supposed to eat peanuts and bananas.* **5.** *n.* a black person. (Racially offensive.) □ *He said he was not a racist, he just hated pongos!* □ *Don't call black people pongos, please. It is very offensive and racist.*

ponies *n.* horse racing. (Always with *the*.) □ *I'm off to the ponies tomorrow. Wish me luck!* □ *He spent all his money on the ponies and now he's broke.*

pony 1. *vb.* to defecate. (Crude. Rhyming slang, linked as follows: pony [and trap] ≈ [crap] = defecate.) □ *Where do you pony around here?* □ *He had to go to pony.* **2.** *n.* £25 (twenty-five pounds). (See GORILLA, MONKEY and SCORE.) □ *All right, here's a pony. Don't spend it all in one shop.* □ *Can you lend me a pony 'till pay-day?*

poo *n.* champagne. (From SHAMPOO.) □ *How about another glass of poo?* □ *Oh, I just love poo!*

poodle-faker *n.* a young man of effete or over-refined manners, who appears to cultivate the company of older ladies.

The implication is that he is faking the behaviour of a lapdog. □ *Anthony looks like a real poodle-faker to me.* □ *I can't stand poodle-fakers like that.*

poof AND **poofter; pooftah; poove; pouffe; puff** *n.* a male homosexual. (Crude.) □ *So what if he's a poof? He can still vote, can't he?* □ *He doesn't like being called a pooftah.*

pooftah See POOF.

poofter See POOF.

poofy *mod.* smelly. □ *What a poofy place this is!* □ *The trouble is that while he's poofy his information is usually kosher.*

pooh-pooh AND **poo-poo** *vb.* to belittle someone or something. □ *He tends to pooh-pooh things he doesn't understand.* □ *Don't always poo-poo me when I express my opinions!*

Pool *n.* Liverpool. (Always with *the*.) □ *The Beatles came from the Pool.* □ *The Pool is on the Mersey, in northwestern England.*

poop 1. *vb.* to defecate. □ *Your dog pooped on my lawn.* □ *I tried to chase the cat away while it was pooping.* **2.** *n.* a foolish old man. □ *Martin can be a poop at times.* □ *You old poop! You've buttered the tablecloth!* **3.** See also POO.

pooped (out) *mod.* exhausted; worn out. (Said of a person or an animal.) □ *I'm really pooped out.* □ *The horse looked sort of pooped in the final stretch.*

poo(-poo) 1. *vb.* to defecate. (Crude.) □ *That old dog pooed on our lawn.* □ *Don't let your dog poo-poo here!* **2.** *n.* fecal material. (Crude. Euphemistic and often juvenile.) □ *Don't step in that dog poo!* □ *There's poo-poo on your shoe, I think.* □ *There's poo on the pavement.* **3.** See also POOH-POOH.

poor man's something *n.* a pale imitation of something; a poor substitute for something. □ *Yes, he's a sort of poor man's Frank Sinatra.* □ *Harry calls his 20-year old mini-car his poor man's Rolls-Royce, and he's right.*

poor show *mod.* not good enough; disappointing. □ *If it's a poor show, why do we continue to pretend it is not?* □

Let's face it, this thing has turned out to be a pretty poor show.

poove See POOF.

pop 1. *vb.* to inject a drug. □ *They all sat around, popping.* □ *Fancy a pop?* **2.** *vb.* to hit or strike someone. □ *Please, don't pop me again.* □ *She popped him lightly on the shoulder.* **3.** *mod.* popular. □ *This is a very pop style.* □ *I don't care for pop stuff.* **4.** *n.* popular music. □ *I like most pop, but not if it's too loud.* □ *Pop is the only music I like.* **5.** *n.* a fizzy soft drink. □ *I often enjoy a glass of pop in the evening.* □ *You know how pop disagrees with you, my dear.* **6.** *n.* a father. (Also a term of address.) □ *My pop insisted I took this job.* □ *Pop, what are you doing over there?* **7.** *n.* a turn; an occasion. □ *Well, that set me back five quid a pop.* □ *I don't think I'll be here for the next pop.* **8.** *vb.* to carry out a burglary. □ *Bruno and Max left town after they popped that house.* □ *Max decided that it was not a good time to do any more popping.*

pop in on someone *vb. phr.* to visit someone briefly. □ *I'll pop in on you when I'm passing.* □ *She popped in on me yesterday.*

pop it See POP ONE'S CLOGS.

pop off 1. AND **shoot off** *vb. phr.* to leave; to depart in haste. □ *Bye, I must pop off.* □ *Got to shoot off. I'm late.* **2.** SEE POP ONE'S CLOGS.

pop one's cherry *vb. phr.* to lose one's virginity, from the female viewpoint. (Taboo.) □ *I think Sue is rather eager to pop her cherry, you know.* □ *Well, I've popped my cherry good and proper now!*

pop one's clogs AND **pop it; pop off** *vb. phr.* to die. □ *My uncle popped his clogs last week.* □ *I hope I'm asleep when I pop it.*

pop out See NIP OUT.

popper 1. *n.* an ampoule of amyl nitrite, a drug that is inhaled when the ampoule is broken. □ *Have you a popper I can have?* □ *He had a popper in his pocket that broke when he sat down.* **2.** See also PILL-POPPER.

poppet 1. *n.* a small or dainty person. □ *The poppet was still waiting ouside the office for him.* □ *She's a pleasant little poppet.* **2.** *n.* a term of endearment for a woman or a man. (Also a term of address, often considered sexist.) □ *Now poppet, you know you can't stay here.* □ *Are you all right, poppet?*

poppycock AND **cock** *n.* nonsense. (From Dutch.) □ *I've heard enough of your poppycock.* □ *That's nothing but cock.*

pop round to see someone *vb. phr.* to briefly visit someone nearby. □ *I'm just popping round to see Mrs Smith.* □ *She popped round to see someone in the shop.*

pop-shop *n.* a pawn shop. □ *That place with the three balls above the door is a pop-shop, Victoria.* □ *Uncle's off to the pop-shop again.*

popshop See HOCKSHOP.

popsie AND **popsy** *n.* a good-looking or attractive girl or young woman. (Also a term of address, often considered sexist.) □ *Look at her, isn't she a popsie?* □ *What is it, my little popsy?*

pop someone's cherry *vb. phr.* to take someone's virginity, from the male viewpoint. (Taboo.) □ *I fully intend to pop her cherry at the first opportunity.* □ *He popped her cherry and then just walked out on her.*

pop something *vb.* to pawn something. □ *I've got nothing left to pop.* □ *I tried to pop my watch to get some money.*

pop the question *vb. phr.* to ask a someone to marry one. □ *She waited for years for him to pop the question.* □ *Finally, she popped the question.*

porker *n.* a policeman. (Derived from PIG.) □ *That porker will catch up with you some day.* □ *See that porker over there? He lifted me once.*

porking *n.* sexual intercourse. (Taboo.) □ *She seems to think that calling it "porking" is all right.* □ *They were talking about, you know, porking.*

porky *mod.* fat; obese; pig-like. □ *You are beginning to look a little porky.* □ *See that porky man over there?*

porky (pie) *n.* a lie. (Rhyming slang.) □ *That's not another of your porky pies, is it Johnny?* □ *A porky is only going to work if people believe it, you know.*

pornbroker *n.* someone who sells pornographic books, films, and so forth. □ *When you look at the stuff he sells in his shop, I suppose you could call him a pornbroker.* □ *Pornbrokers make a lot of money, you know.*

porn(o) *n.* obscenity; pornography. (A euphemism.) □ *There is more and more porno on satellite television.* □ *They keep the real porn in a secret room at the back of the shop.*

porn(o) AND **porny** *mod.* obscene; pornographic. (A euphemism.) □ *Otto has a large collection of porno videos and magazines.* □ *What they were doing was disgusting! It was just like watching a porny film!...I suppose... I've never seen one, of course.*

porny See PORN(O).

porridge *n.* time spent in jail. □ *Otto's been given a year's porridge.* □ *How much porridge did you get?*

porridge education *n.* education in the Scottish manner. (Where porridge is presumed to be the staple breakfast diet.) □ *Porridge education still has a lot going for it.* □ *I had a porridge education and never regretted it.*

Portsmouth defence *n.* a legal stratagem by which a man accused of assault pleads guilty but claims in mitigation that he was outraged by the homosexual advances made to him by the man he assaulted. (Portsmouth is the chief port of the Royal Navy, so such incidents are reputedly commoner there than most places. Normally with *the*.) □ *I hear Oscar is pleading the Portsmouth defence again.* □ *Oscar uses the Portsmouth defence to justify himself every time he beats someone up.*

Portuguese parliament *n.* an out-of-control discussion where everyone talks at once and no one listens. □ *Instead of a friendly chat it had turned into a Portuguese parliament; I left.* □ *Look, calm down! We don't want a Portuguese parliament, but a reasoned discussion.*

posh 1. *n.* a dandy; a rich and fashionable person. □ *He's a bit of posh, but all right really.* □ *Who's that posh you were with last night, Harry?* **2.** *n.* money. □ *It takes a lot of posh to buy a car like that.* □ *I don't make enough posh to go on a trip like that!* **3.** *mod.* stylish; grand; fine. □ *The building was so posh, I felt quite out of place.* □ *It was a very posh do and we had a great time.*

posh up *vb. phr.* to smarten up. □ *I'm glad to see you've poshed yourself up at last.* □ *If we got it poshed up, maybe we might just get it sold.*

post 1. *n.* mail collection. □ *Has the post been collected yet?* □ *No, you've ten minutes to the post.* **2.** *n.* mail delivery. □ *Has the post been delivered yet?* □ *No, here comes the post now.*

postie *n.* a postman or postwoman. □ *The postie usually is here before 8 a.m.* □ *We've had the same postie in this village for years.*

pot 1. *n.* a drinking vessel. (Old but still heard.) □ *How about a pot of beer?* □ *Care for another pot?* **2.** *n.* a vessel, hat, basket, etc., used to collect or receive contributions. □ *Please pass the pot.* □ *How much is left in the pot?* **3.** *n.* a sum of money collected; a pool of money. □ *Clare won the whole pot.* □ *How large is the pot this month?* **4.** *n.* cannabis; marijuana. □ *She had pot on her when she was arrested.* □ *The cops found pot growing next to the cop shop.* **5.** *n.* a microphone. □ *If the singer had held the pot any closer it would have been inside her mouth.* □ *Can we have another pot over here? This one's not working.*

pot and pan *n.* a father or husband. (Rhyming slang, linked as follows: pot and pan ≈ [(old) man] = father.) □ *The boy's pot and pan is here looking for you.* □ *The pot and pan sat on the bench and waited for him.*

potatohead 1. *n.* a stupid person. □ *Stop acting like a potatohead.* □ *Look potatohead, please just go home!* **2.** *n.* someone with very rough, large or unrefined facial features. (Cruel. Use with caution.) □ *Bert's no oil painting for sure; a potatohead, more like.* □ *So this potatohead pushes through the crowd and says, "What's wrong with me appearance?"*

pot-belly AND **pot-gut** *n.* a large belly. □ *He got a pot-belly from eating fried chicken.* □ *Everyone in her family has a pot-gut.*

pot boiler *n.* a book or other literary work of no value except for the money it earns. □ *I can write one pot boiler every six months or so.* □ *Can you produce anything but pot boilers?*

pot-gut See POT-BELLY.

pot-head *n.* a smoker of marijuana. □ *Harry's just another pot-head, you know.* □ *What are you so dismissive of pot-heads?*

potshot *n.* a sharp criticism; a wild shot of criticism. (Usually with *take*.) □ *Please stop taking potshots at me!* □ *He took a potshot at my old car.*

potty 1. *n.* a small portable toilet bowl. (Usually juvenile.) □ *Mummy, I've got to go to the potty.* □ *I need to use the potty.* **2.** *mod.* crazy. □ *She is acting a little potty.* □ *Who is that potty old man?* □ *He got more potty as he grew older.* **3.** See also PIDDLING.

pouffe See POOF.

pour cold water on something *vb. phr.* to put an end to something; to cool or subdue speculation or hope. □ *I hate to pour cold water on your plan, but it won't work.* □ *I wanted to go to the party, but my brother poured cold water on that by taking the car.*

pour oneself into something *vb. phr.* [for a woman] to dress in very close-fitting clothes. □ *Did you pour yourself into that dress?* □ *I'll just pour myself into something slinky.*

powder one's nose *vb. phr.* to visit the bathroom or toilet; to relieve oneself. (Said euphemistically or jocularly by both sexes, but most commonly by women.) □ *Excuse me, I have to powder my nose.* □ *She just went out to powder her nose.*

powder room *n.* the ladies' lavatory in a public place such as a restaurant. (A euphemism. So named because together with all its other less-mentionable functions, it is also the place women go to powder their noses.) □ *The ladies went to the powder room. They'll be back in a minute.* □ *She went to the powder room to clean the spill off her dress.*

power dress *vb. phr.* to dress in a manner intended to impart an appearance of authority and importance to the wearer. (Said more of women than men.) □ *Power dressing makes a difference at work.* □ *Power dressing is one thing, but knowing what you're talking about is another.*

powerhouse *n.* a very big strong person, usually a male. □ *Ted is a real powerhouse. I'm just glad he's on our side.* □ *Every member of that rugby team is a powerhouse.*

power suit *n.* a dress style intended to impart an appearance of authority and importance to the wearer. (Said more of women than men.) □ *Another important day at the office, I see; Jemima has her power suit on again.* □ *Wearing a power suit is one thing, but knowing what you're talking about is another.*

pox *n.* syphilis. (Crude. Often with *the*.) □ *People who get the pox are unlikely to tell everybody about it!* □ *If you've got the pox I want nothing more to do with you.*

pox on someone or something *exclam.* a curse on someone or something. (Crude.) □ *A pox on you! I hope you rot!* □ *I've been trying to make this computer work all day. A pox on it!*

prang 1. *vb.* to bomb accurately. □ *I think we really pranged the target this time.* □ *It's not so easy to prang, you know.* **2.** *vb.* to collide with a vehicle. □ *Did you see these cars prang?* □ *Careful! You nearly pranged!* **3.** *vb.* to crash one's own aircraft or car. □ *Woops! Pranged another one, sir?* □ *To prang once is unfortunate; twice is unlucky, but thrice is getting to be careless.* **4.** *vb.* to shoot down an enemy aircraft. □ *He says he pranged another two today but I'm not sure.* □ *Yes! I've just pranged another!*

prannet AND **pranny** *n.* a fool. □ *How can you be such a prannet?* □ *I felt like* *a pranny when I found out that I'd got onto the wrong train.*

pranny See PRANNET.

prat about *vb. phr.* to behave in a foolish manner. □ *Stop pratting about and get on with your work.* □ *That's enough pratting about.*

prat away AND **prat on; rabbit away; rabbit on** *vb. phr.* to talk or chatter at length without purpose or to come to the point. □ *Oh, they're always pratting away about something.* □ *Why must you rabbit on like that?*

prat on See PRAT AWAY.

prat(t) 1. *n.* a silly person. □ *I'm sorry but we really don't need another pratt working here.* □ *What's a prat like that doing around here?* **2.** *n.* the female sexual organ. (Taboo.) □ *They dance completely nude in there, with pratt and everything on view.* □ *What do you mean, you can see my prat? Oh my god, I've forgotten my panties!* **3.** *n.* a girl or young woman. (Taboo.) □ *Tell that stupid pratt to go home. We don't want her here!* □ *What did the little prat ever do to annoy you so much, Margaret?*

pray to the enamel god See PRAY TO THE PORCELAIN GOD.

pray to the porcelain god AND **pray to the enamel god; talk into the big white telephone; talk on the big white telephone.** *vb. phr.* to empty one's stomach; to vomit. (Crude. Refers to being on one's knees apparently praying in front of a porcelain toilet bowl.) □ *Boy, was I sick. I was praying to the porcelain god for two hours.* □ *Wayne was in the loo, talking on the big white telephone.*

preggers *mod.* pregnant. □ *Had you heard? Cynthia's preggers again.* □ *I can see she's preggers again.*

prelims *n.* preliminary examinations. (School or University.) □ *I hope I pass my prelims.* □ *What do you have to do to get to the actual degree once you pass your prelims?*

prep 1. *n.* school preparation; school homework. □ *No play until you've completed your prep, Nathanial!* □ *We get prep every night.* **2.** *n.* time set aside for school homework. □ *We have prep every evening from six until eight.* □ *I don't have any fixed period for prep.*

prep someone *vb.* to prepare someone for a surgical operation. □ *Have you prepped the next patient yet?* □ *Right, let's prep Mr Smith.*

press the panic button See HIT THE PANIC BUTTON.

pretty *mod.* moderately; somewhat. □ *Bob's a pretty nice guy.* □ *I'm pretty busy at the moment.*

pretty penny *n.* a sizeable amount of money. □ *I imagine that your jacket cost you a pretty penny.* □ *This watch cost me a pretty penny, and I intend to take care of it.*

Pretty please? *interrog.* an emphasised form of "please?" □ *Pretty please? I need an answer!* □ *Can I have my purse back? Pretty please?*

previous *n.* a previous conviction. (Police.) □ *Has Bruno got a previous?* □ *Watch him, he's got a list of previouses as long as your arm.*

prezzie *n.* a present or gift. □ *What a lovely prezzie, darling. Thank you.* □ *This will make the perfect prezzie.*

price *n.* a chance. (From the habit of bookies of assigning starting prices only upon horses they believe have a significant chance of being PLACED.) □ *There's a price here if you would just take it.* □ *He's just looking for the right price.*

pric(e)y *mod.* expensive. □ *This stuff is too pricey.* □ *That's a pretty pricy car.* □ *Do you have anything less pricy?*

prick 1. *n.* the male sexual organ. (Taboo.) □ *Only small boys wave their pricks about like that, Wayne. Put yours away!* □ *Myra says pricks are disgusting but then Myra's strange.* **2.** *n.* a term of contempt for a man. (Taboo. Also a term of address.) □ *Get the little prick away from that machine.* □ *You really are an utterly contemptible prick, Wilson.*

prick-tease See COCK-TEASE.

prick-teasing See COCK-TEASING.

priest of the blue bag *n.* a barrister. □ *Barristers are called priests of the blue bag from the colour of robe-bags once carried by junior counsel.* □ *Who's Otto's priest of the blue bag?*

prissy *mod.* effeminate. (Offensive.) □ *You must admit, he looks very prissy.* □ *So the prissy one turned to us and gave us an amazing torrent of abuse.*

private hire *n.* a car rented together with a driver. □ *It must be posh. They've arrived in a private hire.* □ *The private hire is here. Are you ready?*

private property *n.* a married woman; any girl already with a steady boyfriend. □ *Get away! She's private property!* □ *Here's Otto with his new private property.*

prize *mod.* exceptionally bad. □ *Oh Otto, you really are a prize fool!* □ *Unfortunately it turned out to be a prize example of how not to do that sort of thing.*

prize idiot *n.* an exceptionally foolish person. □ *You prize idiot! You've buttered the tablecloth!* □ *How can you be such a prize idiot?*

pro **1.** *n.* a "professional" (at anything); someone as good as a professional. □ *I'm a pro at photography.* □ *When it comes to typing, he's a pro.* **2.** *n.* a prostitute. (Crude.) □ *Do you think she's a pro or just excessively friendly?* □ *This pro comes up to me and acts like she's met me before.*

prod(dy) AND **prot** *n.* a Protestant. (Taboo. Scots and Irish usage.) □ *Don't call Protestant people proddies, please. It is very offensive.* □ *He said he was not prejudiced, he just hated this particular prot!*

prof *n.* a professor. (University.) □ *The prof was dull and the room was hot, and I kept closing my eyes.* □ *Who's the prof for that course?*

professor *n.* a professional cricketer. □ *You know the rules; no professors on either team.* □ *I'm sorry, but we are strictly amateur and a professor would be against the club rules.*

prog *n.* a proctor at Oxford or Cambridge Universities. □ *The responsibility of the prog is to maintain discipline in their college.* □ *Who would be a prog in this day and age?*

promo *n.* publicity material; advertising. □ *We need new ideas for promos.* □ *The publicity manager's promo was a*

disaster and now he's looking for another job.

prong *n.* the male sexual organ. (Taboo.) □ *That's all very well Myra, but where would the world be without prongs?* □ *The doctor told him that he'd got something wrong with his prong.*

pronk *n.* a fool. □ *That pronk thinks he can convince them.* □ *I felt like such a bloody pronk when I found out that I'd got onto the wrong train.*

proper **1.** *mod.* total, complete or very. □ *This is a proper mess.* □ *That girl is becoming a proper little madam.* **2.** *mod.* in a correct and polite way of speaking. □ *Please talk proper, Mary.* □ *They tell you to speak proper in there.*

proper bastard AND **proper bugger** *n.* a thoroughly unpleasant person or thing. (Taboo.) □ *Get that proper bastard out of here now!* □ *What a proper bugger that woman can be.*

proper bugger See PROPER BASTARD.

proper charlie AND **right charlie** *n.* a complete fool; someone who looks foolish. □ *Who's the proper charlie in the bright orange trousers?* □ *Martin can be a right charlie at times.*

proper do *n.* a first-class party or other social event. □ *Fred knows how to put on a proper do!* □ *Now that really was a proper do!*

proposition someone *vb.* to propose a sexual relationship with someone. (Taboo.) □ *She smiled slowly. Silence for a moment. Then, "Are you propositioning me, Albert?"* □ *I don't mind being propositioned, as long as I'm allowed to say no.*

prossie AND **prosso** *n.* a prostitute. (Taboo.) □ *There was a prossie standing right on that corner.* □ *There are a lot of prossos around here in the centre of town.*

prosso See PROSSIE.

prot See PROD(DY).

proverbial **1.** *n.* the buttocks. (A euphemism. Always with *the* and always in the plural.) □ *If that boy does not get a move on, give him a kick in the proverbials for me.* □ *I slipped on some* ice and landed on my proverbials. **2.** *n.* faeces. (A euphemism. Always with *the.*) □ *Watch out, there's a pile of the proverbial over there, left by some dog.* □ *Get this sorted out or we'll all end up in the proverbial.*

Provisionals AND **Provos** *n.* the Provisional IRA (Irish Republican Army). (Normally with *the.*) □ *The Provisionals may be quiet just now, but they're still around, you know.* □ *Were you ever a member of the Provos?*

Provo *n.* a member of the Provisional IRA (Irish Republican Army). □ *They say Sean is a Provo, but I don't know.* □ *There are a number of Provos living around here, I think.*

Provos See PROVISIONALS.

prune *n.* a stupid person. (Offensive. Also a term of address.) □ *You prune! Why have you done that!* □ *Some prune forgot to get petrol today and his car has run dry.*

pseud *n.* a person with pretensions to be cleverer than is the actual case; a phoney or make-believe intellectual; a *poseur.* □ *Even a pseud like that has to earn a living, I suppose. Probably. Well, maybe.* □ *What does the pseud expect? The Nobel Prize?*

pseudery *n.* the fatuous opinions or comments expressed by a PSEUD. □ *That's just pure pseudery.* □ *I've got no time for pseudery like that.*

pseudo *mod.* false; bogus; insincere. □ *This is a very pseudo position that you are taking.* □ *She is just too pseudo.* □ *What a pseudo hairdo!*

psycho *n.* a psychopathic person; a crazy person □ *Get that psycho out of here!* □ *Pat is turning into a real psycho.*

psych (oneself) up *vb. phr.* to prepare oneself mentally for something. □ *I've really psyched myself up for this test.* □ *The team has not psyched themselves up enough to do a good job yet.*

psych (someone) out *vb. phr.* to unnerve or mentally overwhelm someone. □ *We psyched her out by telling her what happened to the other candidates.* □ *Another day like this one and he'll be psyched out for sure.*

pub-crawl *vb.* a tour made of all the pubs in a district, with additional refreshment consumed at each one. □ *Go away! We went on a pub-crawl last night.* □ *Usually, people grow out of pub-crawls by the time they leave university.*

pubes *n.* the pubic hair. (Taboo.) □ *Get your hand off my pubes, Sunshine!* □ *Who do think you are, going for my pubes like that?*

public convenience *n.* a prostitute. (Taboo.) □ *The Old Bill hauled her in because she looked like a public convenience.* □ *Clare dresses like a public convenience.*

Pudding and Gravy See LUMPY GRAVY.

puff See POOF.

puff-adder *n.* an accountant. (Offensive. Derived as follows: puff-adder ≈ [addition] = [accounts] = accountant.) □ *The puff-adder says we've got to do something about our cash flow problem.* □ *When the puff-adders get finished with the numbers, you won't recognise them.*

puff and dart *vb.* to start or commence. (Rhyming slang.) □ *Time to puff and dart, eh?* □ *We puffed and darted, and it was not so bad as I thought.*

puggled 1. *mod.* stupid. (Scots usage.) □ *Watch that one; he's puggled all right.* □ *He dizny act like he's puggled.* **2.** *mod.* very intoxicated due to drink or drugs. (Scots usage.) □ *Look at him over there! Puggled already, an' it's just ten in the morning!* □ *When Shuggy gets puggled he likes to sing.* **3.** AND **poggled** *mod.* exhausted; bewildered. □ *I have had a long day, and I'm really puggled.* □ *Who is that poggled old man?*

puke 1. *n.* vomit. (Crude.) □ *There's puke on the floor!* □ *Good grief, Tom. Is that puke on your shoe, or what?* **2.** *vb.* to empty one's stomach; to vomit. (Crude.) □ *I think I am going to puke.* □ *Max went home and puked for an hour.*

pukey AND **puky** *mod.* disgusting; repellent. □ *Who is that pukey-looking guy?* □ *Gosh, it's puky!* □ *What a pukey day!*

pukka 1. *mod.* authentic. (From Hindi, meaning "well cooked" or "substantial.") □ *I'm afraid his pukka Porsche turns out to be a ringer.* □ *Of course it's pukka fake gold leaf.* **2.** *mod.* reliable. □ *Harry said to make sure we've only got pukka people on the team.* □ *This is a pukka piece of machinery; when you need it, it will work.* **3.** *mod.* of full measure. □ *Oh no, this is the full, pukka version.* □ *But I ordered the pukka one!*

pull 1. *n.* a mouthful of smoke from a cigarette; a DRAG on a cigarette. □ *A couple of pulls and she crushed out the cigarette.* □ *After a big pull, she blew an enormous smoke ring.* **2.** *vb.* to smoke a cigarette. □ *He pulled a long filter job and then went back to work.* □ *He stopped for a minute and pulled once again.* **3.** *vb.* to PULL ONE'S PUNCHES. (Martial arts.) □ *See, he pulled just at the last minute.* □ *If you pull during a fight, you're through as a fighter.* **4.** *vb.* to earn; to make a profit. □ *I was pulling good money there until the place went bust.* □ *Harry reckoned he could pull more selling used cars than new ones.* **5.** *vb.* to attract sexually. (Crude.) □ *Let's go down the pub and see if we can pull a couple of birds.* □ *Harry used to reckon he could pull more girls than any of his mates.* **6.** *vb.* to hit a cricket ball to the left. □ *We better reorganise the fielder since this batsman's pulling quite badly.* □ *We'll sort that out if he keeps pulling.* **7.** *vb.* to masturbate. (Taboo.) □ *You're not going to pull here!* □ *Well, pulling may be enough for you, but I want the real thing.*

pull about 1. *vb. phr.* to treat roughly. □ *The thugs pulled me about a bit but I'm all right.* □ *Come on, you don't have to pull him about like that.* **2.** *vb. phr.* to knock from side to side. □ *The little yacht was pulled about in the storm and I worried if we were going to make it.* □ *The vibrations really pulled about the aircraft for a while.*

pull a face *vb. phr.* to grimace. □ *Why are you pulling a face? What's up?* □ *He pulled a face at me and I just knew.*

pull a fast one 1. *vb. phr.* to outwit or outsmart someone by a clever and time-ly manoeuvre. (Compare with FAST ONE.) □ *Don't try to pull a fast one on me.* □ *So you think you can pull a fast one?* **2.** See also DO A FLANKER.

pull a flanker See DO A FLANKER.

pull a job *vb. phr.* to carry out a crime, especially a robbery. (Police and underworld. Compare with JOB.) □ *Max decided that it was not a good time to pull a bank job.* □ *Bruno and Max left town after they pulled the job.*

pull a stroke 1. *vb. phr.* to commit a successful crime. □ *Mr Big can work out how to pull a stroke.* □ *Otto actually pulls the strokes that Mr Big plans.* **2.** *vb. phr.* to successfully carry out a deception or trick. □ *I think we can pull a stroke here.* □ *Why do you keep pulling these cruel strokes on me?* **3.** See also DO A FLANKER.

pull down an amount of money *vb. phr.* to earn a stated amount of money. ("An amount of money" is expressed as a figure or other indication of an actual amount.) □ *She pulls down about £40,000 a year.* □ *They pull down pretty good salaries.*

pulling power 1. *n.* sexual attractiveness. (Crude.) □ *He seems to have the pulling power; look at the way the girls queue up!* □ *I wonder if he could spare some of that pulling power for me?* **2.** *n.* commercial or political attractiveness. □ *I think your advert has pulling power.* □ *We need a plan that has the pulling power to bring in enough customers.*

pull one's punches 1. *vb. phr.* to pull back during a boxing punch just before the full force of a blow is felt; to land lighter blows than normal upon an opponent. (Boxing and related sports.) □ *The boxer started pulling his punches, and the ref ended the fight.* □ *He got fined for pulling his punches.* **2.** *vb. phr.* to hold back in one's criticism; to attenuate the intensity of one's remarks. (Also with *any* in the negative.) □ *I won't pull my punches with you. This is lousy.* □ *He never pulls any punches. He always talks straight.*

pull out all the stops *vb. phr.* to use everything available; to not hold back. (Refers to pulling out all of the stops on an organ so that it will sound as loud as possible.) □ *Then the mayor decided to pull out all the stops.* □ *Don't pull out all the stops in the first round. Wait till he's tired in the third and clobber him good.*

pull rank on someone *vb. phr.* to use superior rank to achieve a desired effect on someone. □ *Sir, if you have to pull rank on someone like that, something's's wrong I think.* □ *He pulled rank on me! On me!*

pull someone 1. *vb.* to arrest someone. □ *Max got pulled as soon as he walked into the pub.* □ *The detective pulled both suspects.* **2.** *vb.* to interest or attract someone sexually. □ *How does he always manage to pull the best-looking women all the time?* □ *Cor! I'd like to pull her!*

pull someone's leg *vb. phr.* to kid someone; to tease someone. □ *They're just pulling your leg. Relax!* □ *Stop it! I don't believe you! You're pulling my leg.*

pull someone up (sharpish) *vb. phr.* to reprimand or criticise someone severely. □ *I think he was wrong to pull you up sharply like that.* □ *If you call him that, he'll pull you up.*

pull something down *vb. phr.* to earn some money. □ *The only reason he works is to pull down something.* □ *I have to pull down a lot of money so that we can continue to live like this.*

pull something off *vb. phr.* to make something happen. □ *I didn't think he could pull it off.* □ *It takes a lot of skill to pull off something like that.*

pull strings AND **pull wires** *vb.* to use one's influence with others. □ *Don't worry, Uncle James always managed to pull strings in the end, somehow or other.* □ *How do you expect me to pull wires for you when I don't have anything to do with the place any more?*

pull the moody *vb. phr.* to sulk. □ *I'm not pulling the moody, Lavinia.* □ *Oh, why must you always pull the moody on me, Albert?*

Pull the other one! *exclam.* "I don't believe you!" □ *Yeh, right, pull the other one!* □ *Pull the other one! It's got bells on it!*

pull the plug *vb. phr.* to commit suicide. □ *I could not believe it when I heard she had actually pulled the plug.* □ *It was an exceptionally messy way to pull the plug.*

pull the plug (on someone or something) *vb. phr.* to put an end to someone or something as a problem; to defuse a problem caused by someone or something. (As if one were disconnecting an electrical appliance.) □ *It's time to pull the plug on this problem.* □ *I've heard enough from Mr Jones. It's time to pull the plug on him.*

pull the plug out *vb. phr.* to cause a submarine to submerge. □ *All right Number One, let's pull the plug out and get this boat out of sight.* □ *We had to pull the plug out quickly or we would have been spotted.*

pull the rug (out) from (under) someone or something *vb. phr.* to seriously disrupt the equanimity or status quo of someone or something. □ *Thanks, you've just managed to pull the rug out from under the whole project we've been working on for months.* □ *Why do you have to pull the rug from me every time I think things are working out?*

pull wires See PULL STRINGS.

pulpit *n.* the cockpit of an aircraft. □ *When he climbs into that pulpit he becomes a different person.* □ *He's never been in a fighter's pulpit before and was surprised to find it so claustrophobic.*

pump *vb.* to release intestinal gas anally; to cause a noise or smell associated with this. (Crude.) □ *If you absolutely must pump, would you have the goodness to go somewhere else to do it?* □ *I could not believe it! He just pumped right there, without warning or apology.*

pump (some) iron *vb. phr.* to lift weights. □ *Andy went down to the gym to pump some iron.* □ *Mary's hobbies are pumping iron and running.*

punch-drunk AND **slap-happy** *mod.* unstable; stupid-acting; bewildered. (Originally a term describing a boxer suffering from brain damage.) □ *Roller coaster rides make me sort of punch-*

drunk. □ *I feel slap-happy when I drink too much coffee.*

punch-up *n.* a fistfight. □ *Stop that punch-up now.* □ *I will not tolerate punch-ups around here.*

punch up the bracket *phr.* a punch upon an imprecisely-specified part of the body, probably the nose. (Often incorporated into a threat. Usually with *a.*) □ *If you don't get out of here right now, you're going to get a punch up the bracket.* □ *Just when we all thought he'd lost, he gave Bruno an almighty punch up the bracket that laid him flat.*

punchy *mod.* energetic; vigorous; eager. □ *I feel really punchy after that rest.* □ *Who is that punchy guy? He really gets things moving around here.*

punk *mod.* having to do with PUNKS, or their mode of dress. (See PUNK (ROCKER).) □ *I am tired of your red punk hair. Try it brown for a change.* □ *This music sounds too punk for me.*

punk (rock) *n.* a form of popular music characterised by an amateurish level of musical accomplishment together with a punk mode of dress. □ *Well, punks may think punk rock is music, but I beg to differ.* □ *I think punk is a wonderful sound, and a wonderful way to dress, too.*

punk (rocker) *n.* a young person who favours a mode of dress featuring spiky, brightly-coloured hair, the wearing of chains and leathers, and the adornment of ears, noses, etc., with safety pins and similar. □ *It's not safe to walk on the street with all those weird punks rockers out there.* □ *These punks don't even have a sense of rhythm.*

punt 1. *vb.* to bet upon a race. □ *I've got a punt on the next race.* □ *Don't put a punt on that one!* **2.** *vb.* to make a purchase. □ *Come on, are you going to punt this thing or not?* □ *People were punting like it was going out of fashion.*

punter 1. *n.* an ordinary person. □ *I don't think I could take another punter like that today.* □ *Here was one punter that was different from the others, he thought.* **2.** *n.* a customer. □ *The punters have been pouring into that new supermarket ever since it opened last*

week. □ *If you can't get punters to buy the stuff, you're a pretty useless salesperson.* **3.** *n.* a gambler. □ *The casino was full of punters. He liked it that way.* □ *When yet another punter came up to bet on "Green Banana," he began to think they must know something he did not.* **4.** *n.* a prostitute's client. (Crude.) □ *Any punter who tries to avoid paying is in for a nasty shock.* □ *Don't worry, there's always another punter.*

pup *n.* an unpleasantly aggressive young man. □ *What does the pup want?* □ *He's a rather surprising pup.*

puppy-love See CALF-LOVE.

pure *mod.* completely; entirely. (Scots usage.) □ *Maggie, you are a pure brilliant cook.* □ *What a pure bit o scum yon yin is. (What complete scum that person is.)*

pure and simple *mod.* basically; simply; essentially. □ *Max is a crook, pure and simple.* □ *It's a pure and simple fact. The guy is no good.*

pure dead brilliant *mod.* wonderful; marvellous. (Scots usage.) □ *What a pure dead brilliant idea!* □ *Ah think that singer's pure dead brilliant, so Ah do!*

purler *n.* a blow that causes the victim to fall head first. □ *He delivered a violent purler, and Joe fell.* □ *Did you see how he fell? That was some purler!*

purr (like a cat) *vb. phr.* [for an internal combustion engine or other similar engine] to run well and smoothly. □ *My car really purred after I got it tuned up.* □ *New spark plugs and this old heap will really purr like a cat.*

push 1. *vb.* to approach a particular age (in years). □ *She looked like she was pushing forty-eight or fifty.* □ *He's only pushing thirty, but he looks much older.* **2.** *vb.* to recruit new drug users and sell drugs to them; to deal in drugs. □ *He was pushing for two years before the cops got him.* □ *Boy, look at that guy push. He hooks two new kids every day.* **3.** *vb.* to HYPE something or someone; to pressure something or someone. □ *She's always pushing her own interests.* □ *The salesman was pushing one brand so hard that I finally bought it.*

push bicycle See PUSH BIKE.

push bike AND **push bicycle** *n.* a pedal-powered bike. □ *I'm rather chuffed with my new push bike.* □ *What do you want with a push bicycle like that?*

pusher *n.* a drug dealer who works hard to establish new addicts and customers. (See PUSH.) □ *That pusher over on Walton Street has just been mobbed by a group of angry parents.* □ *They said that pushers should be locked up forever.*

pushing up daisies *mod.* dead and buried. (Usually in the future tense.) □ *I'll be pushing up daisies before this problem is solved.* □ *If you talk to me like that again, you'll be pushing up daisies.*

push in the truck *n.* sexual intercourse. (Taboo. Rhyming slang, linked as follows: push in the truck ≈ [fuck] = sexual intercourse.) □ *I fancy a bit of push in the truck with the missus tonight.* □ *All right, you smooth talker, let's push in the truck.*

push off AND **shove off** *vb. phr.* to leave. (As if one were pushing away from a dock.) □ *Well, it looks like it's time to push off.* □ *It's time to go. Let's shove off.*

push one's luck *vb. phr.* to take a risk. □ *I think you're pushing your luck.* □ *When you talk to me like that, you're pushing your luck.*

pushover 1. *n.* something that is easy to do. □ *Getting the result we wanted turned out to be a pushover.* □ *I did not think that opening the bank vault could be such a pushover.* **2.** *n.* a woman who is easy to seduce. (Crude.) □ *I'm afraid Norah was a real pushover last night.* □ *If you're looking for a pushover, try Norah.* **3.** *n.* someone who is easy to persuade. □ *He was a pushover for the insurance sales pitch.* □ *Go on, sell that old car to this guy; he looks like a real pushover.*

push-start *vb.* to start a car by pushing it along in order to turn over the engine and get it firing. □ *The middle of the night in the middle of nowhere and I'm out in the rain push-starting your car. Oh yes, I'm impressed I must say.* □ *If*

all else fails we'll just have to push-start it.

push the boat out *vb. phr.* to celebrate in a big way. □ *We're planning on pushing the boat out again tonight.* □ *We pushed the boat out 'till 4 a.m.*

push the panic button See HIT THE PANIC BUTTON.

pushy *mod.* very aggressive in dealing with other people. □ *Stop being so pushy! Who do you think you are?* □ *Who is that pushy dame?* □ *If she weren't so pushy, she would get more co-operation.*

puss(y) *n.* a passive, feminine lesbian. (Taboo.) □ *That little quiet one is Donna's new puss.* □ *It's not obvious to most people that these pussies are lesbians.*

pussy 1. *n.* the female sexual organ. (Taboo.) □ *If your dresses get any shorter, we'll all be able to see your pussy.* □ *The door to the shower room flew open and the girl screamed, trying to cover her pussy.* **2.** *n.* a woman viewed as a sex object. (Taboo.) □ *The pretty little pussy came over to him to ask for a light.* □ *Any pussy around here, mate?*

pussycat *n.* a weak or timid man. □ *Ask the pussycat if he needs any help.* □ *Why do we need this pussycat?*

puss(y) pelmet See FAN(NY) BELT.

put about *vb. phr.* to spread a rumour. □ *What's this story you're putting about about me?* □ *If you put about lies, people will get very angry indeed.*

put a damper on something *vb. phr.* to reduce the intensity of something, such as a problem. □ *The death of the chief put a damper on the ceremony.* □ *I hate to put a damper on your party, but you are too loud!*

Put a lid on it! *vb. phr.* to be silent. □ *Put a lid on it while I deal with this!* □ *Will you be quiet! Just put a lid on it.*

put a lid on something AND **put a sock in something** *vb. phr.* to stop something. □ *Right that enough! Put a lid on it!* □ *I wish you'd put a sock in it.*

put-and-take *n.* sexual intercourse. (Taboo. Raffish: the male puts, the female takes.) □ *After that put-and-take,* *she felt cheap.* □ *They were talking about, you know, put-and-take.*

put a smile on someone's face *vb. phr.* to please someone; to make someone happy. □ *We are going to give Andy a pretty good pay rise, and I know that'll put a smile on his face.* □ *I was able to pay a few pounds down, and that put a smile on the clerk's face.*

Put a sock in it! *exclam.* "Shut up!" □ *I've heard enough. Put a sock in it!* □ *Put a sock in it! You're a pain.*

put a sock on something See PUT A LID ON SOMETHING.

put a spoke in someone's wheel(s) *vb. phr.* to prevent or delay someone's intended action. □ *I wish they would not continually try to put a spoke in our wheels.* □ *The time to put a spoke in her wheel has come, I think.*

put-down 1. *n.* an insult; an intentionally cruel and deflating insult; a snub. □ *Another put-down like that and I'm going home.* □ *Don't cry. It was just a little friendly put-down.* **2.** *n.* something that brings someone back to reality; a humiliation. □ *The bill for the week's stay was a real put-down.* □ *I've had one put-down after another today.*

put it about AND **put it out** *vb. phr.* [for a woman] to permit sexual intercourse; to be sexually promiscuous. (Crude.) □ *There's Tanya, putting it about as usual.* □ *Come on, you put out too!*

put it on 1. *vb. phr.* to overcharge. □ *I'm sure that plumber put it on me, but how can you tell?* □ *He made a lot as a waiter because he put it on all his customers and kept the extra for himself.* **2.** *vb. phr.* to show off. □ *You don't have to put it on for me; I'm already impressed.* □ *There she is, putting it on as usual.*

put one out of (one's) misery *vb. phr.* to end a suspenseful situation. □ *Please, put me out of misery; what happened?* □ *I put her out of her misery and told her.*

put oneself upon someone *vb. phr.* to impose oneself upon someone. □ *I'm very sorry to put myself upon you like this, but I had no choice.* □ *How can you put yourself upon someone like that?*

put one's face on *vb. phr.* [for a woman] to apply cosmetics. □ *Martha's gone to put her face on.* □ *We'll be on our way once my wife has put her face on.*

put one's feet up *vb. phr.* to rest; to sleep. □ *He was knackered and had to go put his feet up.* □ *Time to put my feet up, I think.*

put one's foot to the floor *vb. phr.* to accelerate the vehicle one is driving. □ *Hurry up! Put your foot to the floor!* □ *So I put my foot to the floor and overtook the other car.*

put one's hand down AND **put one's hand in one's pocket** *vb. phr.* to pay; to stand one's round. □ *I can't afford to put my hand down for a round of drinks this week, I'm afraid.* □ *Oh, I'll put my hand in my pocket for that.*

put one's hand in one's pocket See PUT ONE'S HAND DOWN.

put one's wind up See GET ONE'S WIND UP.

put on the ritz *vb. phr.* to make things extra special for an important event. □ *Frank's really putting on the ritz for the big party on Friday night.* □ *They really put on the ritz for us.*

put out See PUT IT ABOUT.

put over *vb. phr.* to persuade. □ *Look, just what are you trying to put over onto me?* □ *He's good at putting over an argument.*

put paid to something *vb. phr.* to finish off, end or kill something. □ *The boss told Rocko to put paid to Barlowe.* □ *Barlowe was sure he could keep Rocko from putting paid to him.*

putrid *mod.* intoxicated due to drink or drugs. (Compare with ROTTEN.) □ *That guy is stinking drunk. Putrid, in fact.* □ *They went out last night and got putrid.*

put some distance between someone and someone or something else *vb. phr.* to lengthen the distance between oneself and someone or something (including a place). □ *I've got to put some distance between me and that cop, fast.* □ *She needed enough money to put some distance between herself and her home town.*

put someone away *vb. phr.* to put someone in prison for a long time. (Underworld.) □ *They put Max away for fifteen years.* □ *The judge put away the whole gang.*

put someone in the pudding club *vb. phr.* to make someone pregnant. (Crude.) □ *I don't think he intended to put her in the pudding club, you know.* □ *I put her in the pudding club, and now the baby's due next month.*

put someone on *vb. phr.* to tease or deceive someone innocently and in fun. □ *Come on! You're just putting me on!* □ *He got really livid even though they were only putting him on.*

put someone on hold *vb. phr.* to be delayed; to be made to wait. □ *Would you believe, we've been put on hold again!* □ *If you put me on hold once more you're in serious trouble.*

put someone on the mat *vb. phr.* to reprimand someone severely. □ *I must really put you on the mat this morning.* □ *I'm afraid that after that little exhibition, we will have put you on the mat.*

put (someone) out to grass *vb. phr.* to retire someone. □ *Old Albert's being put out to grass at the end of the month.* □ *This organisation puts everyone out to grass at 60, like it or not.*

put someone's gas at a peep *vb. phr.* to humiliate or cut someone down to size. (Scots usage.) □ *Well, that should have put her gas at a peep!* □ *You may have put her gas at a peep, but it does not solve the real problem.*

put someone's nose out of joint *vb. phr.* to cause someone to feel slighted; to cause someone to take offence. (Compare with GET ONE'S NOSE OUT OF JOINT.) □ *I'm sorry we didn't invite you. We didn't mean to put your nose out of joint.* □ *Now, now, that shouldn't put your nose out of joint. We're sorry.*

put someone up *vb. phr.* to provide someone with temporary shelter; to let someone stay the night. □ *Can you put me up for a few days?* □ *I could put up a football team, there's so much room here.*

put something away *vb. phr.* to eat something. □ *Are you going to put this cake away?* □ *Did you put away that whole pizza?*

put something on the slate *vb. phr.* to record a debt. □ *Put it on the slate, Jerry.* □ *I'll just put that on the slate, will I?*

put something out of (its) misery *vb. phr.* to kill an animal in a humane manner. □ *The vet put that dog with cancer out of its misery.* □ *Please, put my sick goldfish out of misery.*

Put that in your pipe and smoke it! *exclam.* "Take that!"; "See how you like that!" □ *Everybody thinks you're a phony! Put that in your pipe and smoke it!* □ *You are the one who made the error, and we all know it. Put that in your pipe and smoke it!*

put the black on someone *vb. phr.* to threaten to blackmail someone. □ *Otto threatened to put the black on him.* □ *I don't want anyone to put the black on me.*

put the boot in AND **sink the boot in 1.** *vb. phr.* to attack unnecessarily after victory is certain. □ *Otto certainly knows how to put the boot in.* □ *He did not hesitate to sink the boot in.* **2.** *vb. phr.* to kick an opponent who is already on the floor. □ *He was down, but still they put the boot in.* □ *To sink the boot in after the guy is downed is considered rather wicked.*

put the frighteners on someone *vb. phr.* to scare or frighten someone. □ *Otto's been putting the frighteners on the witnesses for the prosecution.* □ *Don't you try to put the frighteners on me, Sunshine!*

put the kibosh on something *vb. phr.* to finally dispose of or finish off something. □ *The mayor put the kibosh on the whole deal.* □ *Tom was starting his presentation when Bob put the kibosh on the plan.*

put the lid on something *vb. phr.* to terminate something. □ *They put the lid on our plan yesterday.* □ *Management have just put the lid on that project.*

put the mockers on someone 1. *vb. phr.* to curse someone. □ *I think she's put the mockers on me.* □ *He threatened to put the mockers on her.* **2.** *vb. phr.* to ruin or stop someone. □ *Some fool put the mockers on us today.* □

Don't try to put the mockers on me son, if you know what's good for you.

put the skids under someone or something *vb. phr.* to cause someone or something to fail. (Compare with *on the skids.*) □ *The mayor put the skids under my plan.* □ *Tom tried to talk, but the boss put the skids under him.*

put the squeeze on someone *vb. phr.* to pressure someone; to threaten someone to achieve something. □ *He told everything about the plan when they put the squeeze on him.* □ *The cops put the squeeze on Harry, and he soon spilt the beans.*

putty medal *n.* a trivial or humorous reward for a small service. □ *He got a putty medal for that, would you believe.* □ *I didn't think there was enough even for a putty medal.*

put-up job *n.* a fraudulent or deceptive event. □ *That's really phony. A put-up job if I ever saw one.* □ *No put-up job is clever enough to fool me.*

put up one's dukes *vb. phr.* to be prepared to fight. □ *He's telling you to put up your dukes.* □ *Put up your dukes and be a man!*

Put up or shut up! *exclam.* "Prove your claim or back down!" □ *I'm tired of your silly ideas. Where's your evidence? Put up or shut up!* □ *Put up or shut up! This is your chance to show you're right.*

put up the shutters *vb. phr.* to go out of business; to quit. □ *They put up the shutters last week.* □ *We'll all be putting up the shutters soon if the economy doesn't pick up.*

Put your money where your mouth is! *exclam.* "Back what you say with your own money!" (Originally from gambling. Can also be said to someone giving investment advice.) □ *If you want me to bet on that horse, why don't you put your money where your mouth is?* □ *If this is such a good stock, you buy it. Put your money where your mouth is!*

Pythonesque *mod.* a surreal event reminiscent of the bizarre TV series, *Monty Python's Flying Circus.* □ *The whole business was, well, Pythonesque.* □ *What a Pythonesque farce the meeting turned into!*

Q

quack 1. *n.* a fraudulent physician. (Offensive.) □ *I won't go back to that quack ever again!* □ *Tell that quack to heal himself!* **2.** *n.* any medical doctor. (Offensive.) □ *He had to go see the quack because he felt unwell.* □ *I don't think most quacks know what they're doing to you.*

quacker *n.* a duck. (Normally in the plural. Childish.) □ *Look at the nice quakers!* □ *There are a lot of quackers who live in and around that pond.*

quaggy *mod.* shaky or difficult. □ *Calculus is too quaggy for me.* □ *This arrangement is still very quaggy.*

quagmire *n.* a tricky situation or predicament that is difficult to get out of. □ *We're in a bit of a quagmire here.* □ *How did we get into a quagmire like this?*

Quaker Oat(s) *n.* a coat. (Rhyming slang.) □ *That's a ridiculous Quaker Oats; I won't wear it.* □ *I've lost my Quaker Oat.*

Qualities *n.* the better-class newspapers (as a group) as opposed to the downmarket tabloids. (Always with *the*.) □ *All the Qualities are saying the government will fall this week.* □ *What do the Qualities have to say about the situation in South America?*

Quango AND **QUANGO** *n.* a QUAsi Non-Governmental Organisation. (These are agencies set up under government authority, and largely funded from public funds, to supervise various matters of public concern. An initialism.) □ *This new Quango will oversee the way Quangos are run.* □ *Sir Simon is on the board of over fifty QUANGOs but knows nothing about any of them.*

quantum leap *n.* an instantaneous, highly significant and large change to or growth of something. (This term is borrowed from modern physics, where a *real* "quantum leap" is indeed abrupt, but anything but large. It is in fact the *smallest possible* change of energy, position or velocity of a subatomic particle. The expression's colloquial use has come about through popular misunderstanding, at a fundamental level, of the terminology of quantum mechanics.) □ *The Government has made a quantum leap forward with it's radical new social policy.* □ *I think your new hairstyle is a quantum leap, darling—at least, for you, maybe.*

quarter-bloke *n.* a quartermaster. □ *Go and see the quarter-bloke about that, soldier.* □ *The squaddies are at the quarter-bloke, getting fitted out for uniforms.*

quean(ie) 1. *n.* an elderly passive male homosexual. (Crude. The term is sometimes used by homosexuals to describe each other.) □ *Tom is getting to be such an old quean.* □ *He doesn't like being called a queanie.* **2.** *n.* a lesbian. (Crude. The term is sometimes used by lesbians to describe each other.) □ *Who's the queanie in the cowboy boots?* □ *Why does she work so hard to look like a quean?*

quean up 1. *vb. phr.* to fall in with homosexual company. (Crude.) □ *He's always queaning up! It's disgusting!* □ *I think he's off to that pub—you know the one I mean—to quean up for the evening.* **2.** *vb. phr.* [for a male or female homosexual] to acquire girlish characteristics, such as wearing cosmetics, etc.

(Crude.) □ *I'm getting rather worried by the extent to which Tom is queaning up nowadays.* □ *If Tom wants to quean up, that's his privilege, surely.*

queen 1. *n.* a flamboyantly effeminate male homosexual. (Crude.) □ *Tom is getting to be such a queen.* □ *What kind of a queen is Tom?*

Queen 1. *n.* the woman in charge. (Always with *the*.) □ *Believe me, Mrs Thomson is definitely Queen around this place!* □ *Who's Queen around here?* 2. See also KING.

Queen Anne is dead. *sent.* "That's very old news." □ *Yes, we won World War II, and Queen Anne is dead, too.* □ *Where have you been all this time? Queen Anne is dead.*

Queen's Park Ranger See GLASGOW RANGER.

queer 1. *mod.* counterfeit. □ *This bill is queer.* □ *I don't want any queer money.* 2. *mod.* intoxicated due to drink or drugs. □ *After a glass or two, he got a little queer.* □ *She was so queer she could hardly stagger home.* 3. *vb.* to spoil something. □ *Please don't queer the deal.* □ *I was afraid his dirty look would queer his chances.* 4. *mod.* homosexual; normally male but not exclusively. (Crude.) □ *Who is that queer character?* □ *Isn't he queer?* □ *She doesn't like being called queer.* 5. *n.* a homosexual; normally male but not exclusively. (Crude.) □ *Tell that queer to get out of here.* □ *She came to the dance with a queer.* 6. *mod.* unwell, faint or giddy. □ *She took ill at work and was still pretty queer by the time she got home.* □ *Mike's rather queer this morning, but I think he'll be okay again soon.*

queer as an electric walking stick See QUEER AS A THREE POUND NOTE.

queer as a nine bob note See QUEER AS A THREE POUND NOTE.

queer as a three pound note AND **queer as a nine bob note; queer as an electric walking stick** *mod.* definitely or obviously homosexual, normally male but not exclusively. (Crude.) □ *That guy is as queer as a three pound note.* □ *He's wearing* makeup. *He's as queer as a nine bob note.*

queer-bash AND **queer-roll** *vb. phr.* to assault a homosexual, normally male but not exclusively, for fun or profit. (Crude.) □ *Watch out! There's a lot of queer-bashing going on around here.* □ *I think they must have queer-rolled a couple of pooves last night, constable.*

queer fish *n.* a strange person; an aloof person. □ *She's a bit odd. Sort of a queer fish.* □ *He's a queer fish, don't you agree?*

queer in the head *mod.* slightly crazy. □ *I'm not queer in the head. I just can't make it work.* □ *You're queer in the head if you think I care.*

queer roll See QUEER-BASH.

Queer Street AND **Slump Alley** *n.* Carey Street in London. (See IN QUEER STREET.) □ *That's Queer Street, where the Bankruptcy Court is to be found.* □ *It's Slump Alley for you, my lad.*

queer the pitch *vb. phr.* to secretly spoil or ruin an opportunity. □ *Don't queer the pitch for me son, if you know what's good for you.* □ *Some fool queered our pitch today.*

queue-barge See QUEUE JUMP.

queue jump AND **jump the queue; queue-barge** *vb.* to move in front of those waiting in a queue. □ *Walter is an expert at queue jumping.* □ *Anyone who queue-barges goes to the rear to start again. OK?*

quick-and-dirty *mod.* rapidly and carelessly done. □ *I'm selling this car, so all I want is a quick-and-dirty repair job.* □ *They only do quick-and-dirty work at that garage.*

quick fix 1. *n.* a quick, probably temporary and unsatisfactory solution to a problem. (Compare with JERRY-BUILT, KLUDGE, LASH-UP and STOP-GAP.) □ *A quick fix isn't good enough in this case.* □ *He's a master of the quick fix.* 2. *mod.* having to do with a temporary or unsatisfactory solution or repair. (Often QUICK-FIX, especially before a nominal. Compare with JERRY-BUILT, KLUDGE, LASH-UP and STOP-GAP.) □ *Frank is a master of the quick-fix solution.* □ *This is no time for quick-fix efforts.*

quickie 1. *n.* a bet placed after the result of a race is known. (Scots usage.) □ *Shuggy reckons a quickie's the only sort of bet worth placing.* □ *If he'll just be good enough to tell me how to manage how to work a quickie, I'll stick to them, too!* **2.** See also QUICK ONE.

quick off the mark *mod.* quick starting or reacting. (Compare with SLOW OFF THE MARK.) □ *Boy, you were quick off the mark there!* □ *If you can be really quick off the mark you can soon find the answer.*

quick one AND **quickie; quick snort; quicky 1.** *n.* a rapidly consumed drink. □ *Come on! Just a quick snort before you leave?* □ *Oh, all right, but just a quicky, mind.* **2.** *n.* a rapidly completed act of sexual intercourse. (Taboo.) □ *After the quick one she got up and walked away as if she did not know him.* □ *I think really, she's gasping for a quicky, you know.* **3.** a brief visit to the toilet. (Crude.) □ *Gotta do a quick one!* □ *Sorry, I need a quicky.*

quick snort See QUICK ONE.

quid *n.* one Pound Sterling. □ *Have you got a few quid you can spare?* □ *These things cost more than just a few quid.*

quids in 1. *mod.* going well. □ *Well, things are quids in now, I must say.* □ *How are things? Quids in of course!* **2.** *mod.* making a profit. □ *Now we're quids in!* □ *Exert yourself and you'll be quids in with ease.*

quiff 1. *n.* an effeminate man; a passive male homosexual. (Crude.) □ *He doesn't like being called a quiff.* □ *Why does he work so hard to look like he's a quiff?* **2.** *n.* a clever trick. □ *Well it's a quiff, but I don't think you'll get away with it.* □ *No more quiffs. They need solid answers.*

quim AND **twim** *n.* the female sexual organ. (Taboo.) □ *A woman who shows her quim is just the lowest.* □ *They dance completely nude in there, with twim and everything on view.*

quite a lad See BIT OF A LAD.

quite an event *n.* an important or significant event. □ *What a party! It was quite an event.* □ *That was a quite an event at Tom's the other night.*

quite a while *n.* a long period of time. □ *We must keep doing this for quite a while.* □ *It's been quite a while since anyone tried to do that.*

quite so 1. *phr.* "it is agreed." □ *Quite so; that's the way it has to be.* □ *Yes. Quite so.* **2.** *phr.* "that is true." □ *Quite so; it really happened.* □ *Quite so. We really do have a problem.*

quite the thing *mod.* excellent; first class. □ *This day is quite the thing!* □ *Mary's new job is quite the thing.*

quitter *n.* someone who gives up easily. □ *Don't be a quitter. Get in there and finish the job.* □ *Dave has a reputation as a quitter.*

quit while one is ahead *vb. phr.* to stop doing something while one is still successful. □ *When will I learn to quit while I'm ahead?* □ *Get into the market. Make some money and get out. Quit while you're ahead.*

quod *n.* prison. □ *Otto's in quod, and will be there for some time I think.* □ *Have you ever been in the quod?*

quote-unquote *phr.* a parenthetical expression said before a word or short phrase indicating that the word or phrase would be in quotation marks if in writing. □ *So I said to her, quote-unquote, it's time we had a little talk.* □ *I think my quote-unquote reputation is ruined.*

R

rabbit *n.* inconsequential chatter. (Rhyming slang, linked as follows: rabbit [and pork] ≈ [talk] = chatter. Compare with BUNNY.) □ *There's never anything but rabbit between these two.* □ *Why do you always have to make such trivial rabbit all the time?*

rabbit away See PRAT AWAY.

rabbit hutch *n.* the crutch (= crotch). (Rhyming slang.) □ *He tried to grab me by the rabbit hutch.* □ *These trousers are far too tight around the rabbit hutch.*

rabbit on See PRAT AWAY.

rabbit punch *n.* a short blow to the nape of the neck, usually with the edge of the hand. (So-called because such a blow is used to kill a rabbit by breaking its neck.) □ *One rabbit punch and he was out cold!* □ *She is tiny and he is huge, but she gave him one almighty rabbit punch that he'll never forget—if he ever wakes up!*

rabbit('s) food *n.* lettuce; green salad; green vegetables. □ *I think I need a little more rabbit food in my diet.* □ *Rabbit food tends to have a lot of vitamin C.*

rabbit something *vb.* to borrow but fail to return something. □ *What does she want to rabbit this time?* □ *That's not fair. She does not mean to rabbit things; it's just that she forgets to bring them back.*

racket 1. *n.* noise. □ *Cut out that racket! Shut up!* □ *Who's making all that racket?* **2.** *n.* a trick or deception, usually criminal. □ *He worked a racket robbing old ladies of their savings.* □ *This is not a genuine ticket for Wimbledon Central Court; you're the victim of some racket.* **3.** *n.* any job. □ *I've been in this racket for twenty years and never made any money.* □ *I'm a stockbroker. What's your racket?*

rack something up *vb. phr.* to accumulate something; to collect or acquire something. □ *They all racked up a lot of profits.* □ *We racked up twenty points in the game last Saturday.*

Raddie *n.* an Italian person. (Offensive.) □ *Y'know, Otto, if you call an Italian a Raddie, he's likely to get nasty.* □ *Why can you not be polite to Raddies?*

radical *mod.* excellent. □ *What a radical idea that was.* □ *Your news is really radical, you know.*

rads *n.* the police. (Always with *the*.) □ *The rads broke up the fight.* □ *The rads finally caught up with Gert.*

Raff *n.* the Royal Air Force. (A near-acronym from "RAF." Always with *the*.) □ *Brian was a pilot in the Raff for a number of years.* □ *There's a Raff base near here.*

raft *n.* a large number. □ *There are a raft of measures to be enacted this year, ladies and gentlemen.* □ *He made a raft of proposals, but none were really serious.*

rag 1. *n.* a newspaper. □ *I'm tired of reading this rag day after day. Can't we get a different paper?* □ *What a rag! It's only good for putting in the bottom of bird cages!* **2.** *n.* ugly or badly-styled clothing; an ugly garment. (Compare with GLAD RAGS.) □ *I can't wear that rag!* □ *I wouldn't be seen in last season's rags.* □ *I need some new clothes. I can't go around wearing rags like these.* **3.** *n.* any clothing, even the best.

(Always plural.) □ *Man, I got some new rags that will knock your eyes out!* □ *You got coffee all over my new rags!* **4.** *n.* a rowdy celebration. □ *After that rag, I couldn't keep my eyes open the following day.* □ *Sam invited us to his rag, but we're getting a little old for that kind of thing.*

rag-head 1. *n.* a male Arab person. (Offensive. From the appearance of their traditional head-dress.) □ *Don't call Arabs rag-heads, please. It is very offensive and racist.* □ *He said he was not a racist, he just hated this particular rag-head!* **2.** *n.* a male Sikh person. (Offensive.) □ *Why can you not be polite to rag-heads?* □ *Y'know, Otto, if you call a Sikh a rag-head, he's likely to get nasty.*

raging queer *n.* a blatant or ostentatious male homosexual. (Crude.) □ *Tom is getting to be such a raging queer.* □ *So what if he's a raging queer? He can still vote, can't he?*

rag order *n.* a chaotic mess. □ *How did you create such a rag order here?* □ *What a rag order you've made of this!*

rags See CURSE RAG.

rag trade *n.* the clothing trade, in every aspect from the finest to the grubbiest. (Always with *the*.) □ *The biggest industry in this area of the city is the rag trade.* □ *The rag trade employs vast numbers of very low-paid people.*

rain stair-rods *vb. phr.* to rain very heavily. □ *It was really raining stair-rods so we went to the pictures.* □ *I hate driving when it's raining stair-rods like that.*

raise a gallop See GET THE HORN.

raise a stink (about someone or something) AND **make a stink (about someone or something)** *vb. phr.* to make a big issue about someone or something. (Compare with STINK.) □ *You can depend on Fred to raise a stink.* □ *I hope you don't plan to make a stink about the problem.*

raise Cain *vb. phr.* to make a lot of trouble; to RAISE HELL. (A Biblical reference, from Genesis 4.) □ *Fred was really raising Cain about the whole matter.* □ *Let's stop raising Cain.*

raise hell 1. *vb. phr.* to make a lot of trouble; to go on a rampage. (Crude.) □ *Stop raising hell so much of the time!* □ *Quiet! Don't raise hell around here.* **2.** *vb. phr.* to go on a drinking spree and get drunk. (Crude.) □ *Let's go out and really raise hell.* □ *The boys went out to raise hell.*

raise hell (with someone) 1. *vb. phr.* to confront someone in order to complain or scold. (Crude.) □ *I really raised hell with my brother for being late.* □ *It won't do any good to raise hell with me.* **2.** *vb. phr.* to cause trouble with something. (Crude.) □ *That development has raised hell with the client.* □ *Patrick raised hell with the boss when he learnt what had happened.*

raise the wind *vb. phr.* to raise money required for a particular purpose. □ *I'm still trying to raise the wind for the development.* □ *How much wind do you still have to raise?*

rake-off *n.* an illicit profit. □ *He's looking for a huge rake-off.* □ *In the end, his rake-off was rather small.*

rake something in *vb. phr.* to take in a lot of something, typically money. □ *Our candidate will rake votes in by the thousand.* □ *They were raking in money like it was going out of fashion.*

rake something off *vb. phr.* to make an illicit profit. □ *How much can we rake off?* □ *You can rake off a heck of a lot from this racket.*

ralph *vb.* to empty one's stomach; to vomit. (Crude. Youth usage. See also CRY HUGHIE.) □ *She went home and ralphed for an hour.* □ *I think I'm going to ralph.*

ralph something up *vb. phr.* to vomit something up. (Crude. Youth usage. See also CRY HUGHIE.) □ *The doctor gave him some stuff that made him ralph it up.* □ *He ralphed up his dinner.*

rammy 1. *n.* a brawl or fight. (Scots usage.) □ *They're aw awa oot at some rammy. (They're all out at some fight.)* □ *Shuggy ower likes a good rammy an that. (Hugh always like a good fight and all that sort of thing.)* **2.** *n.* a busy, struggling crowd. (Scots usage.) □ *They were all struggling to get through* the rammy coming out of the football match. □ That's a huge rammy there tonight, she thought.

ramp 1. vb. to swindle. □ Watch it, he's trying to ramp you. □ I think they are trying to ramp us in some way or other. **2.** n. a swindle. □ This is an okay ramp you've got going here. □ They pulled a real dirty ramp on that old lady. **3.** n. the counter of the bar in a public house. □ All the regulars have their own places along the ramp in here. □ He pushed his way through the crowd to the ramp in order to place an order with the barman.

ram-raid n. a SMASH-AND-GRAB robbery where access is made into a store by ramming into its front with a vehicle. □ The gang chose the electrical store for their next ram-raid. □ Right, you go and nick a Range Rover for the ram-raid.

ram something down someone's throat vb. phr. to force something upon someone. (Not literal.) □ Don't try to ram that nonsense down my throat. □ They're always trying to ram something down our throats.

randan n. a spree. □ That was some randan at Tom's the other night. □ I haven't had a randan like that in years.

randy mod. sexually excited or aroused. (Crude. Compare with RAUNCHY.) □ The town is full of randy sailors when the fleet's in. □ You're in luck, Joan— there's a randy-looking guy at the door asking for you.

rank and file n. the ordinary members of an organisation or association of some sort. □ What will the rank and file think of the proposal? □ The rank and file will vote on it tomorrow.

rap 1. vb. to talk or chat about something. □ Something wrong? Let's rap about it. □ The kids sat down and rapped for an hour or so. **2.** n. a conversation; a chat. □ How about a rap? □ Let's have a rap sometime. **3.** n. a criminal charge or case. □ What's the rap? □ Why am I up on that rap?

rap session n. an informal conversation session. □ The kids settled down for a long rap session. □ The rap session was interrupted by a fire drill.

rapt mod. delighted. □ I was really rapt with her news. □ Don't get too rapt just yet. There's more.

Raquel Welch n. a belch. (Rhyming slang.) □ She released a discrete Raquel Welch behind her hanky, thinking no one would notice. □ Try not to do a Raquel Welch at table, Johnny.

rare bird n. an unusual person; a person with rare talents or abilities. □ An interesting kind of rare bird is the man who can take long holidays and still make money. □ She is a rare bird who enjoys opera and can understand most of it, too.

rare old time n. a fine and enjoyable time at a party or something similar. □ That was a rare old time at Tom's the other night. □ I haven't had a rare old time like that in years.

rare tear n. a good time. (Scots usage.) □ Shuggy ower likes a rare tear an that. (Hugh is always keen on a good time and so forth.) □ They're aw oot having a rare tear. (They're all out having a good time.)

raring to go mod. anxious and eager to go. □ Come on, I'm raring to go! □ The whole family is raring to go on vacation.

raspberry 1. n. a rude noise signifying disapproval or derision, made by blowing through closed lips. (Rhyming slang, linked as follows: raspberry [tart] ≈ [fart] = rude noise. Compare with GIVE SOMEONE THE RASPBERRY.) □ The entire audience gave the performer the raspberry. □ The performer gave them a raspberry right back. **2.** n. a reprimand. □ Is it really necessary to give these people as much raspberry as you do? □ That tyke! I'll give him a raspberry he won't forget in a hurry!

rat n. a despicable or disgusting person. □ You dirty rat, you! □ Stop acting like the rat you are, just for once!

rat-arsed AND **ratted; rattled** mod. very intoxicated due to drink or drugs. (Taboo.) □ After an hour of that stuff, Bill was more than a little rattled. □ Once rattled from beer, I stopped that and began on the rum.

ratbag *n.* a disgusting or very unpleasant person. (Offensive. Also a term of address.) ☐ *What a ratbag that woman can be.* ☐ *Get out of here, you ratbag!*

rate of knots *n.* a high speed. ☐ *The Concorde really does move at a rate of knots.* ☐ *If you really want to drive at a rate of knots, try the German autobahnen where there is no speed limit.*

rathole *n.* a disgusting, run-down place; a DUMP. ☐ *I refuse to live in this rathole any longer.* ☐ *Why don't you clean up this rathole?*

rat on someone *vb. phr.* to inform on someone. ☐ *Bill said he was going to rat on that creep.* ☐ *If you rat on me, I'll get you!* ☐ *Who ratted?*

rat out *vb. phr.* to quit; to cease to cooperate (with someone or something). ☐ *It's too late to rat out.* ☐ *He tried to rat out at the last minute.*

rat race *n.* fierce competition between individuals workers to make a living. (Compare with DAILY GRIND.) ☐ *I am really tired of this rat race, day after day after day.* ☐ *She dropped out of the rat race and moved to the Isle of Skye, where she makes and sells paper flowers.*

rat-run 1. *n.* a passage, back alley or other narrow or informal route between buildings. ☐ *This passage has become quite a rat-run since the old pedestrian exit was closed off.* ☐ *You can hardly move through that rat-run now, so many people are using it.* **2.** *n.* an informal or illegal route used by vehicles attempting to by-pass congested parts of principle highways by means of minor roads, especially in urban areas.* ☐ *This quiet residential street has been turned into a rat-run ever since they introduced traffic-calming measures in that other street that used to be a rat-run.* ☐ *Living on a rat-run is not pleasant and is certainly dangerous.*

ratted See RAT-ARSED.

rattle and clank *n.* a bank. (Rhyming slang. This refers to the sort of bank where money is kept.) ☐ *When does that rattle and clank open today, please?* ☐ *That's the rattle and clank where I keep my money.*

rattled 1. *mod.* confused; bewildered. ☐ *He tends to get a little rattled at minor things.* ☐ *Try not to get her rattled.* **2.** See also RAT-ARSED.

rattler *n.* a bicycle. ☐ *How much did that rattler set you back?* ☐ *You have to wear a helmet with a rattler that size, don't you?*

rattling good *mod.* excellent. ☐ *Her party was really rattling good.* ☐ *What a rattling good place to live!*

raunchy 1. *mod.* crude; tasteless; coarse. (Offensive.) ☐ *He told a very raunchy story at the party.* ☐ *Stop being so raunchy all the time and act cultured, just for once.* **2.** *mod.* sexually explicit; risqué; lusty. (Compare with RANDY.) ☐ *Once he got a few drinks in him, Martin started acting very raunchy with Margaret.* ☐ *I like you when you're raunchy like this.*

raver *n.* a dedicated party-goer. ☐ *Now Sally is your right little raver, all right!* ☐ *There go these ravers at last. What time of night do they think this is?*

rave(-up) *n.* a party; a wild party or celebration. ☐ *What a rave-up! A really fine party.* ☐ *What a fancy rave-up! They even have glass glasses!* ☐ *What time do we have to be at that rave up on Saturday night?*

raw 1. *mod.* inexperienced; brand new. ☐ *The raw recruit did as well as could be expected.* ☐ *She'll get better. She's just a little raw.* **2.** *mod.* vulgar; crude; raucous; untamed. (Offensive.) ☐ *I've had enough of your raw humour.* ☐ *That joke was a little raw.* **3.** *mod.* [of alcoholic spirits] undiluted; neat. ☐ *No ice, please. I prefer it raw.* ☐ *I'll drink it raw—just the way it is now.* **4.** *mod.* [of alcoholic spirits] immature; fiery and strong. ☐ *My gosh, this stuff is raw! It'll burn a hole in me.* ☐ *Give me something to drink that isn't quite so raw.*

razor blade *n.* a black person. (Racially offensive. Rhyming slang, linked as follows: razor blade ≈ [spade] = black person. See SPADE.) ☐ *Don't call black people razor blades, please. It is very offensive and racist.* ☐ *He said he was not a racist, he just hated razor blades!*

razor-edge 1. *n.* a very sharp edge. □ *Watch out that's a real razor-edge there.* □ *I had not realised the corner was such a razor-edge.* **2.** *n.* a critical situation. □ *We've got a bit of a razor-edge here; take care.* □ *When it's razor-edge like this, it's very difficult.* **3.** *n.* a mountain ridge which forms a distinct dividing line. □ *If you look over there to the mountains you can see the razor-edge quite clearly.* □ *We actually stood on the razor-edge for a while and took in the spectacular views of both valleys.* **4.** *n.* a boundary line marking a sharp division. □ *Here's the razor-edge. Don't even think of crossing it!* □ *The division between the two areas of the factory was quite obvious; everyone could see the razor-edge.*

razor-edged *mod.* [of a disagreement] sharp. □ *Oh, not another razor-edged argument like last night!* □ *The disagreement has been razor-edged for weeks now.*

razor-slasher *n.* a criminal who attacks with a straight razor. □ *The razor-slasher took a particular delight in doing a thorough job.* □ *Razor-slashers can be particularly vicious.*

razor someone *vb.* to slash or cut someone with an open razor. (Scots usage.) □ *Someone razored Jock outside his house yesterday.* □ *Watch him, he'll razor you as soon as look at you.*

razz *vb.* to tease or harangue someone. (Juvenile. Originally an abbreviated form of RASPBERRY.) □ *Please stop razzing me.* □ *I was just razzing you. I didn't mean any harm.*

razzle-dazzle 1. *n.* flamboyant publicity; HYPE. □ *After all the razzle-dazzle dies down, we'll see what things are really like.* □ *Sometimes a lot of razzle-dazzle helps to sell, sometimes not.* **2.** *n.* exciting bustle and glamour. □ *I really liked all that razzle-dazzle at the party last night.* □ *A little razzle-dazzle is enough for Jack's weak heart.*

razzmatazz AND **razzamatazz** *n.* deceptive talk; HYPE. □ *Cut out the razzamatazz. How dumb do you think I am?* □ *Don't give me all that razzmatazz!*

reach for the stars See AIM FOR THE STARS.

reach-me-down 1. *mod.* [of clothes] inherited; hand-me-down. □ *I'm not going to wear reach-me-downs!* □ *I'd wear reach-me-downs, but not ones that look like reach-me-downs.* **2.** *mod.* [of clothes] ready-made. □ *Only poor people wear reach-me-down clothes, Mum!* □ *We came across this shop selling nothing but reach-me-down dresses.*

read and write *vb.* to fight. (Rhyming slang.) □ *The read and write was a bit of a failure as the other side failed to show!* □ *Well, if that's really how you feel, let's arrange another read and write!*

reader *n.* a prescription. □ *He's got a whole stack of readers. Don't ask!* □ *There's enough on that reader to last us over the weekend.*

readers *n.* reading-glasses. □ Q: *What have I done with my readers?* A: *You're wearing them.* □ *I broke my readers.*

readies *n.* cash or ready money. (Normally with *the*.) □ *Sorry, I can't afford it, I've no readies.* □ *How much readies do you need, then?*

Read my lips! AND **Watch my lips!** *exclam.* "What I'm about to say is important and true. Listen very carefully." (From the remark by President Bush during the 1988 US Presidential election.) □ *Read my lips! No new taxes!* □ *It's important you get this right first time. Read my lips!*

ready-made *mod.* [of a horse race] likely to win. □ *Now here's a horse that's ready-made for you, Joan.* □ *The last ready-made horse you chose for me came last.*

real bitch *n.* a very difficult or annoying thing or (female) person. (Crude.) □ *This maths problem is a real bitch.* □ *Fiona is a real bitch.*

real chuffed See DEAD CHUFFED.

Really! *exclam.* "I am surprised!"; "I am shocked!" □ *There's a little green man at the front door! Really!* □ *Really, are we supposed to believe that?*

Really? *interrog.* "Is that true?" □ *Really? Did it happen like that?* □ *Really? So what?*

real Mackay AND **real McCoy** *n.* something authentic. (Always with *the*.) □ *This is the real Mackay. Nothing else like it.* □ *This is no copy. It's the real McCoy.*

real McCoy See REAL MACKAY.

real money *n.* actual physical banknotes or cash. □ *He put a lot of real money into the top pocket of my shirt and said that there's plenty more to be had if I asked no questions.* □ *Sorry, I don't have any real money with me. Can you pay?*

rear (end) *n.* the tail end; the buttocks. (Crude. Euphemistic.) □ *She fell right on her rear.* □ *The dog bit her in the rear end.*

rear(s) *n.* institutional toilets. (Crude. At a school, military base, hospital, etc.) □ *Where are the rears in this place?* □ *The rear is along that passageway and to your right.*

recess *n.* a prison toilet. (Crude.) □ *Some very strange things happen in prison recesses.* □ *This is the recess. Good luck!*

reckon oneself *vb. phr.* to be conceited. □ *Oh, that one reckons herself, you know.* □ *I have never known anyone to reckon themselves more than he does.*

reckon someone or something *vb. phr.* to consider someone or something worthwhile; to count someone or something as significant. □ *Naw, I don't reckon Bruno. He's past it now.* □ *Do you reckon that's so important? I don't.*

red-arse *n.* a new recruit to the army. (Taboo.) □ *I don't think much of this red-arse. Do you?* □ *We've got some red-arses starting today. Treat them nicely.*

red biddy *n.* cheap wine. □ *Let's get out the red biddy and have a good time.* □ *That red biddy is just gut-rot.*

redcap *n.* a military policeman. (From the colour of their caps.) □ *That redcap is after me!* □ *These two redcaps drove around in their car picking on innocent people like me.*

redhat *n.* a military staff officer. □ *There's a redhat here to see you.* □ *I don't like redhats, but they have their uses.*

red hot 1. *mod.* important; in great demand. □ *This is a red hot item. Everybody wants one.* □ *The stock market is a red hot issue right now.* **2.** *mod.* sexually aroused. (Crude.) □ *Oh yes, I'm red hot now!* □ *Always make your move once they're red hot, lad.*

red-inker *n.* an arrest which has been officially recorded. (Police.) □ *Is that arrest a red-inker yet?* □ *Once it's a red-inker it's too late for any deals like that.*

red-letter day *n.* an important day that might well be marked in red on the calendar. □ *Today was a red-letter day in our history.* □ *It was a red-letter day for our club.*

red rag *n.* an object or idea that infuriates. □ *Your suggestion was like a red rag to him.* □ *Don't come up with any more red rags like that, thank you very much.*

red sails in the sunset *n.* menstruation. (Crude.) □ *The red sails in the sunset are here again.* □ *It's time for her red sails in the sunset again. You know how she feels then.*

red tape *n.* bureaucratic annoyances; bureaucratic forms and procedures (Typically with *cut*. Originally from the red tape used by lawyers and government officials to tie together bundles of official papers in 19th century London.) □ *If you deal with the government, you will have to put up with lots of red tape.* □ *I have a friend who knows how to cut through red tape.*

red, white and blue *n.* a shoe. (Rhyming slang.) □ *I find these red, white and blues uncomfortable.* □ *Why are you in these red, white and blues? Are you going somewhere?*

reeb *n.* beer. (Backslang.) □ *Can I have reeb, please?* □ *I do like this reeb they have in here.*

reefer *n.* cannabis; a marijuana cigarette. □ *He had a reefer in his hand when he was busted.* □ *Don't stall the reefer. Pass it on.*

ref 1. *vb.* to referee something, such as a game. □ *Are you going to ref this one, or am I?* □ *I don't like to ref night games.* **2.** *n.* a referee. (Also a term of address.) □ *Hey, ref! Get some glasses!* □ *The ref did a fine job.* □ *What use is a blind ref?*

regs *n.* regulations. (Military.) □ *Follow the regs or pay the penalty.* □ *There are a list of the regs posted on the back of your door.*

rehab *n.* a rehabilitation department, ward, etc., of a hospital. □ *I must be getting better if I'm being moved to the rehab.* □ *The rehab is over in that building.*

reinvent the wheel *vb. phr.* to make unnecessary or redundant preparations. □ *You don't need to reinvent the wheel. Read up on what others have done.* □ *I don't have time to reinvent the wheel.*

remotest See FAINTEST.

rent 1. *n.* money acquired by criminal means. □ *Harry could never make much rent from that racket.* □ *He's got a new racket with more rent now.* **2.** *n.* money earned from homosexual prostitution. (Crude.) □ *He's out on the streets, earning his rent every night.* □ *He fluttered his long artificial eyelashes and said some rent would always be handy.* **3.** *n.* a male prostitute. (Crude.) □ *That little creep is a real rent. I wouldn't trust him at all.* □ *Do you think he's a rent or just excessively friendly?*

rentacrowd AND **rentamob** *n.* a crowd of people gathered to demonstrate on some political topic, who do not appear to have any deep or personal involvement in the issue, but instead have been paid to be there to swell the numbers. □ *"Oh no," he thought as he looked over the sea of familiar faces. "Rentacrowd!"* □ *That rentamob was waiting ouside the office for him.*

rentamob See RENTACROWD.

rent boy AND **renter** *n.* a young male prostitute. (Crude.) □ *This rent boy comes up to me and acts like he's met me before.* □ *The police brought him in because he looked like a renter.*

renter 1. *n.* a part-time prostitute; a person of either sex who offers sexual favours for presents or money. (Crude.) □ *There was a renter standing right on that corner.* □ *There are a lot of renters*

around here in the centre of town. **2.** See also RENT BOY.

rep 1. *n.* repertory theatre. □ *He spent a year in rep in the North.* □ *Rep is the best place to get experience, but not to make money.* **2.** *n.* a representative, usually a sales representative. □ *Please ask your rep to stop by my office.* □ *Our rep will be in your area tomorrow.*

repat someone *vb.* to repatriate someone. □ *The government is going to repat that refugee back to where he came.* □ *How can they repat someone in danger like that?*

rep someone or something *vb. phr.* to represent someone or something. □ *I'm here to rep my company.* □ *If you don't want to rep that client, you have to tell him.*

resit *vb.* to sit an examination again after failing to pass it previously. □ *I'm having to resit all my degree exams except history.* □ *History is the only degree exam I don't have to resit.*

rest one's eyes *vb. phr.* to take a short sleep; to nap. □ *I'm just going to rest my eyes for an hour or two.* □ *There's a bed in here if you want to rest your eyes.*

rest on one's oar(s) *vb. phr.* to relax one's efforts. □ *If you rest on your oars right now, all you've gained will be lost.* □ *Don't rest on your oar! We've lots still to do.*

result *n.* a favourable outcome. (Police.) □ *We're looking for a result this time, as we expect to get one.* □ *There's been a result on that murder.*

return unopened *vb. phr.* to die an old maid. (To "return" to God a virgin. The first example was seen on a Scottish tombstone.) □ *Miss Struthers, retired post-mistress aged 81, returned unopened.* □ *My aunt use to worry that she would never marry and so return unopened, as she put it.*

Reverend (Ronald Knox) *n.* venereal disease. (Crude. Rhyming slang, linked as follows: Reverend (Ronald Knox) ≈ [pox] = venereal disease.) □ *A visit from the Reverend Ronald Knox is not really funny, you know.* □ *All right, it's true, I've got the Reverend.*

rev something up *vb. phr.* to speed up an engine in short bursts. □ *Rev it up a few times and see if it stalls.* □ *Tom sat at the traffic light revving up his engine.*

revved up *mod.* excited, perhaps by drugs. □ *Max is revved up from too much dope.* □ *The kids were all revved up, ready to party.*

rhino *n.* money. □ *I don't make enough rhino to go on a trip like that!* □ *It takes a lot of rhino to buy a car like that.*

rhubarb *n.* nonsense. □ *You're talking rhubarb again—as usual.* □ *What rhubarb that is!*

rhubarb and custard *n.* lysergic acid diethylamide, or LSD, an hallucinogenic drug. □ *You can get some good rhubarb and custard in this part of town.* □ *What does rhubarb and custard cost around here?*

rhubarb (pill) *n.* a bill. (Rhyming slang. This refers to the sort of bill that has to be paid.) □ *How much did the rhubarb pill come to?* □ *No no, it's my rhubarb; I insist on paying.*

riah AND **riha** *n.* hair. (Backslang. Most common among male homosexuals.) □ *Oh I do like your riah today, darling.* □ *I just can't do a thing with my riha!*

rib *vb.* to tease someone. □ *Please don't rib me any more tonight. I've had it.* □ *Let's go and rib Jennifer.*

ribbing *n.* a joke; an act of teasing. □ *I didn't mean any harm. It was just a little ribbing.* □ *That's a great ribbing, Sam!*

Richard (the Third) *n.* a dismissive response from an audience. (Theatrical. Rhyming slang, linked as follows: Richard (the Third) ≈ [bird] = dismissive response. Compare with BIRD.) □ *If you get the Richard the Third again, it's all over, right?* □ *The audience is giving everybody the Richard tonight, I think.*

ride 1. *n.* an act of sexual intercourse. (Taboo.) □ *I think really, she's gasping for a ride, you know.* □ *A good ride would probably do her the power of good, in fact.* **2.** *n.* a woman seen as a sex object. (Taboo.) □ *I don't think many women would consider being called a "ride" is much of a compli-*

ment. □ *Joan is a good ride.* **3.** *vb.* to perform sexual intercourse. (Taboo.) □ *Let's go somewhere quiet and ride.* □ *Want to ride?*

ride shotgun *vb. phr.* to escort. □ *All right, you ride shotgun but come right back.* □ *Do you really need someone to ride shotgun for you?*

ride someone 1. *vb.* to indulge in sexual intercourse with someone, from the male perspective. (Taboo.) □ *I'm hoping to ride her tonight.* □ *You'll always get to ride Fiona, the girl who can't say no.* **2.** *vb. phr.* to persistently and deliberately irritate or pester someone. □ *So I made a mistake! I wish you'd stop riding me.* □ *Stop riding me!*

riff *n.* a short, repeated line of music played by a particular performer. □ *Jim just sat there and forgot his riff.* □ *Listen to this riff, Tom.*

rig 1. *vb. phr.* to arrange or tamper with the results of something. □ *The crooks rigged the election.* □ *Somebody rigged the contest so no one got first prize.* **2.** *n.* an articulated lorry; a trailer truck. □ *That's Maggie's new boyfriend's rig.* □ *There's an rig parked outside our front door.* **3.** *n.* the equipment used by a group of pop musicians. □ *The crew were busy setting up the rig all day for the concert.* □ *The sort of rig these groups have costs a fortune.*

right as ninepence *mod.* in perfect condition. □ *I'm fine, as right as ninepence!* □ *If you're as right as ninepence, why are you here?*

right as rain *mod.* completely correct. (Often with *as.*) □ *Yes, indeed! You are right as rain!* □ *She was right as rain about the score.*

right charlie See PROPER CHARLIE.

right down to the ground *mod.* complete in every last respect. □ *That girl is becoming a little madam, right down to the ground.* □ *Let's face it: right down to the ground, this is a mess.*

right-ho *exclam.* a term of agreement. □ *Right-ho, I'll go right away.* □ *Right-ho! I'm very pleased with that.*

right in the kisser *mod.* right in the mouth or face. (Compare with KISSER.) □ *Max poked the cop right in the* *kisser.* □ *He caught one right in the kisser.*

right one *n.* a foolish person. □ *Well! We've got a right one here!* □ *You're not going to make a right one out of me.*

right shut *mod.* completely shut. □ *Make sure that door's right shut!* □ *The door was not right shut and a cold draught blew into the house.*

right smart *mod.* very clever. □ *You think you're right smart, don't you?* □ *That was a right smart thing to do.*

right up one's street AND **up one's street** *mod.* exactly one's kind of thing; exactly what one is best equipped to do. □ *That job is right up her street.* □ *It's not exactly up my street, but I'll try it.*

righty *n.* a member of a right-wing political party or group; a holder of right-wing views. (Compare with LEFTY.) □ *I don't trust any righty.* □ *Of course, no sane righty would trust you either.*

rigout *n.* a set of clothes. □ *I feel sort of funny in this rigout.* □ *Where did you get a rigout like that to wear?*

riha See RIAH.

ring 1. *n.* bookmakers as a class. (Normally with *the.*) □ *They're all the same, bookmakers; the ring looks after their own.* □ *I do not like the ring.* **2.** *n.* the anus. (Taboo.) □ *Shift! Get your ring out of here now!* □ *His doctor has just told him he needs an operation on his ring.* **3.** *vb.* to make a telephone call. □ *All right, I'll ring you later.* □ *Harry wants you to ring him as soon as you get in.* **4.** *n.* a telephone call. □ *All right, I'll give you a ring later.* □ *Harry wants you to give him a ring as soon as you get in.*

ring a bell *vb. phr.* to stir something in someone's memory. □ *Yes, that rings a bell. I seem to remember it.* □ *Maybe the name Marsha will ring a bell!*

ring back *vb. phr.* to return a telephone call. □ *You better ring back; it seemed important.* □ *Hello, I'm just ringing back.*

ringer 1. *n.* a person who can change their disguise quickly. □ *We think the con man must be a real ringer to have pulled this off.* □ *Whoever takes on this* part is going to have to be a ringer; there are seven costume changes in the first act alone. **2.** *n.* one who steals cars and alters their appearance so that they cannot be traced. □ *Watch that tyke, he's a ringer I'm sure.* □ *The professional ringer can transform a stolen car in a couple of hours.* **3.** *n.* a fake that looks genuine. □ *That car's a ringer.* □ *How can they make such convincing ringers?* **4.** *n.* a stolen car which has been altered to make deception easier. □ *Of course it's a ringer! Here, I'll show you the signs.* □ *Even the police can have difficulty identifying some well-put-together ringers.*

ringer (for someone) See DEAD RINGER (FOR SOMEONE).

ring off the hook *vb. phr.* [for a telephone] to ring endlessly or constantly. □ *The phone was ringing off the hook when I came in.* □ *We've been busy today. The phone's been ringing off the hook.*

ring-snatcher *n.* a male homosexual. (Taboo.) □ *So what if he's a ring-snatcher? He can still vote, can't he?* □ *I hear that you-know-who is a ring-snatcher.*

ring someone's bell 1. *vb. phr.* to make a woman pregnant. (Taboo.) □ *I don't think he intended to ring her bell, you know.* □ *I rang her bell, and the baby's due next month.* **2.** *vb. phr.* to induce an orgasm in a woman. (Taboo.) □ *Oh god, he's ringing my bell!* □ *Just let me ring your bell, my love.*

ring through See PHONE THROUGH.

ring up See PHONE THROUGH.

rinky-dink *mod.* neat; pretty. □ *Yes, it is rinky-dink.* □ *That is a pretty rinky-dink car you have there.*

riot *n.* someone or something entertaining or funny. □ *Tom was a riot last night.* □ *Her joke was a real riot.*

rip-off 1. *n.* a theft by deception; an exploitation. □ *This is a rip-off! That's my contract!* □ *What a rip-off! I want my money back.* **2.** *n.* a swindle or theft. □ *That little rip-off the kids did with the statue from the town square was a dandy.* □ *Another rip-off like that and I call your parents.*

rip-off artist *n.* a con artist. □ *Fred is such an rip-off artist.* □ *Beware of the rip-off artist who runs that shop.*

rip someone off *vb. phr.* to steal from someone by trickery; to cheat someone. □ *They ripped them all off.* □ *Harry was ripped off for three hundred pounds.*

rise *n.* an erection. (Taboo.) □ *Fear not my lovely, I shall have a rise for you!* □ *As long as you have a rise like that I'll love you, Frank.*

Rise and shine! *exclam.* "Get up and get going!" □ *Get up! Rise and shine! It's late.* □ *Okay, you guys, rise and shine!*

ritzy *mod.* elegant; flamboyant. □ *That is a real ritzy car.* □ *What a ritzy coat! Is it new?*

River Ouze *n.* an alcoholic drink. (Rhyming slang, linked as follows: River Ouze ≈ [booze] = alcoholic drink. The Ouse is a river that flows into the Wash on the eastern coast of England.) □ *Now that's what I'd call River Ouze.* □ *Any more of that River Ouze?*

riveted See GRIPPED.

riveting See GRIPPING.

roach *n.* the stub of a marijuana cigarette. □ *The cops found a roach on the bathroom floor.* □ *Here, gimme that roach!*

road hog *n.* someone who takes too much space on a road; someone who seems to run other people off the road. □ *Get over! Road hog!* □ *A road hog nearly ran me into the ditch.*

roadie *n.* a young person who helps rock groups set up for performances. □ *I want to be a roadie when I grow up.* □ *I was a roadie for a while, but didn't like it.*

road tax *n.* the excise tax which must be paid by all powered vehicles travelling on the public highway. □ *It's time to pay my road tax again, I see.* □ *Have you paid your road tax, sir?*

roaring poof(ter) *n.* an outrageous male homosexual. (Crude. Australianism.) □ *I hear that you-know-who is a roaring poofter.* □ *Why does he work so hard to look like he's a roaring poof?*

roast *vb.* to assault verbally; to criticise severely. □ *If you call him that, he'll roast you.* □ *I think he was wrong to roast you.*

roasting *n.* a verbal assault; a severe criticism. □ *Receiving an e-mail roasting can be a rather strange experience, and not a pleasant one.* □ *I think you earned your roasting.*

rob someone blind AND **steal someone blind 1.** *vb.* *phr.* to steal freely from someone. □ *Her maid was robbing her blind.* □ *I don't want them to steal me blind. Keep an eye on them.* **2.** *vb. phr.* to overcharge someone. □ *You are trying to steal me blind. I won't pay it!* □ *Those car repair places can rob you blind if you don't watch out.*

Rock *n.* Gibraltar. (Normally with *the.* See GIB.) □ *Well, at least the Rock's still British.* □ *Have you ever been to the Rock?*

rock 1. *n.* CRACK, a crystallised form of cocaine. □ *Some call it rock, and some call it crack.* □ *Rock is pretty expensive.* **2.** *n.* a diamond or other gemstone. □ *Look at the size of that rock in her ring.* □ *How many rocks are there decorating the edges of your watch?*

rock bottom 1. *n.* the lowest point or level. □ *The value of the goods is at rock bottom right now.* □ *Prices have reached rock bottom.* **2.** *mod.* as low as possible, especially in reference to price. □ *Prices are rock bottom this month.* □ *I am offering you the rock bottom price.* □ *You can't beat these rock bottom deals.*

rocker *n.* a rock and roll singer, song or fan. □ *Do all rockers have red hair?* □ *Let's listen to a good rocker.*

rocket(ing) *n.* a strong reprimand. □ *You're just asking for a rocketing.* □ *What was that rocket for?*

rocking *mod.* excellent. □ *Boy, what a rocking party!* □ *This set is really rocking.* □ *We had a rocking time!*

rocking-horse manure AND **rocking-horse shit** *n.* something exceptionally rare or non-existent. (ROCKING-HORSE MANURE is crude; ROCKING-HORSE SHIT is taboo.) □ *A genuine apology from Mr Big must be about as common as rocking-horse manure.* □ *If you've won the* *lottery that's a pile of rocking-horse shit out in the yard.*

rocking-horse shit See ROCKING-HORSE MANURE.

rock of ages *n.* wages. (Rhyming slang.) □ *Have you collected this week's rock of ages from the pay office yet?* □ *So when I got my rock of ages there was far more deducted than I'd expected.*

rod See HOT ROD.

rod in pickle *n.* trouble in store. □ *I'm sure you're going to find the rod in pickle for you, Sunshine.* □ *I know I've got a rod in pickle waiting when I get home.*

roger 1. *interj.* "okay."; "That is correct." (Originally military.) □ *Roger, I'll do it.* □ *Roger. Wilco!* **2.** *vb.* to perform sexual intercourse. (Taboo.) □ *I think really, she's gasping to roger, you know.* □ *Fred can't think about anything but rogering Martha.*

roll 1. *vb.* to rob a drunkard, a sleeping man or one absorbed in sexual activity. (Crude.) □ *The muggers found a drunk and rolled him.* □ *Some arsehole's taking to rolling the meths drinkers sleeping it off in the park.* **2.** *n.* a sustained period of luck or productivity. □ *I'm doing great! What a roll!* □ *The fantastic roll that this performer is on is truly exciting.* **3.** *n.* an act of sexual intercourse. (Taboo.) □ *Fred can't think about anything but rolling Martha.* □ *After the roll she got up and walked away as if she did not know him.*

Roller *n.* a Rolls-Royce car. □ *Like my new Roller, darling?* □ *I'm rather partial to Rollers.*

roll in *vb. phr.* to pull in; to drive up; to arrive. □ *The car rolled into the parking lot at a high speed.* □ *Four hatchbacks rolled in at the same time.*

rolling (in it) AND **swimming (in it)** *mod.* very rich indeed. (The word "it" refers to money.) □ *Oh, she's rolling in it!* □ *Well, what do you think? He won the lottery and of course he's rolling.* □ *The Wilmington-Thorpes are just swimming in it.*

rolling stone *n.* a person who does not remain long at the same address, job,

etc. □ *A rolling stone will never get rich...unless he can sing, of course.* □ *I'm sorry but we don't employ rolling stones around here.*

roll in the aisles *vb. phr.* to cause an audience to be helpless with laughter. □ *I really had them rolling in the aisles.* □ *That's the way to succeed as a comic; get them all to roll in the aisles.*

rollock *vb.* to chastise someone severely. □ *Did the lad really deserve being rollocked like that?* □ *Mr Big really knows how to rollock someone.*

rollocking See BOLLOCKING.

roly-poly pudding *n.* a dessert consisting of a strip or sheet of suet pastry covered with jam or fruit, then rolled and baked or steamed. □ *Bill loves his mother's roly-poly pudding.* □ *Please can I have more roly-poly pudding, mum?*

roman candle *n.* the characteristic progress of a parachutist whose parachute fails to open. □ *If the parachute fails to open, you'll do what's called a roman candle.* □ *Don't worry sir. If you have a roman candle, the manufacturers will supply you with a new parachute free of charge.*

ronk 1. *vb.* to stink. □ *When we opened the room it ronked very badly.* □ *If you've got to ronk like a badger's backside, do so a long way from me.* **2.** *n.* a stink. □ *I just can't stand that ronk.* □ *Where is that terrible ronk coming from?*

rook *vb.* to cheat someone; to overcharge extortionately. □ *She tried to rook me when I came to pay my bill.* □ *Don't go into that shop. They'll rook you.*

rooky 1. *n.* a raw recruit; a neophyte. (Originally military.) □ *Tom is a rooky in the police force.* □ *He may be a rooky but he knows how to put a ball through a goalmouth.* **2.** *mod.* new; inexperienced. (Particularly in the armed forces or the police.) □ *Fred is a rooky in the army now.* □ *A rooky cop can make arrests just like the other cops.*

rope someone in *vb. phr.* to recruit or involve someone in an organisation or project. □ *She's always trying to rope* me into her club. □ *Let's rope in some-one to help with cleaning up.* □ *A strange ropey ambience pervaded the whole area.*

rop(e)y 1. *mod.* low-grade or substandard. □ *The stuff in today's delivery was very ropey so we sent it back.* □ *Sorry, these products are too ropy for us.* **2.** *mod.* somewhat unwell. □ *Oh dear, I feel really ropey.* □ *Carol is a bit ropy today, I'm afraid.* **3.** *mod.* unreliable; untrustworthy. □ *He's got a ropey heart, you know.* □ *I'm afraid this car of mine's a bit ropy.* **4.** *mod.* smelly; unpleasant. □ *The trouble is that although he's ropey his information is usually kosher.* □ *A strange ropy ambience pervaded the whole area.*

rorty 1. *n.* enjoyable; boisterous. □ *The men always used to have a great rorty time after the harvest was all in.* □ *The party became a bit loud and rorty later on.* **2.** *n.* fond of amusement. □ *Oh, old Bert is rorty all right. What sort of entertainment are you thinking of?* □ *There were several rorty busloads in the theatre that night.* **3.** *n.* unsophisticated or crude. □ *She's a bit like that; anything in the least rorty is disapproved of.* □ *I think this pub may be a bit too rorty for me.* **4.** *n.* down to earth. □ *All right, let's keep this discussion rorty.* □ *To be completely rorty, what I really want is money. Lots of money.*

Roseland *n.* southeastern England apart from London. □ *The Roseland is the most pleasant part of England to live in, if you like that sort of thing of course.* □ *I'd rather live in London than Roseland. At least there are real people in London.*

roses *n,* a woman's period. (Crude. Irish usage.) □ *Marie is coming up roses this week, so forget it!* □ *It's my roses. Go away!*

Rosie Lee *n.* a flea. (Rhyming slang.) □ *Is that...no, it couldn't be...a Rosie Lee on your coat?* □ *There were Rosie Lees everywhere throughout the old house.*

Rosie Loader *n.* a whisky and soda. (Rhyming slang.) □ *The Rosie Loaders were certainly flowing that evening, I*

can tell you. □ *I could use a Rosie Louder.*

Rossies *n.* socks. (Scots usage. Rhyming slang, linked as follows: Rossies = [Rossay Docks] ≈ [Rothesay Docks] = socks. Rothesay Docks, now demolished, were located upon the River Clyde west of Glasgow. Always plural.) □ *Haw hen, whar's ma Rossies? (Where are my socks, my dear?)* □ *Ha yous yins seen yon tartan Rossies Shuggie's wearing? (Have any of you seen the tartan socks that Charles is wearing?)*

rosy *mod.* good; satisfactory. □ *Things are looking rosy now that the economy is improving.* □ *Doesn't look like a very rosy future.*

rot 1. *n.* nonsense. □ *Don't give me any more of your rot. Speak straight or shut up.* □ *What utter rot! Don't believe any of it!* **2.** *vb.* to joke. □ *Those people just rot around all day.* □ *Stop rotting and start working.* **3.** *vb.* to tease or annoy. □ *Stop rotting him, Johnny.* □ *Why do children always rot each other?*

RO(T)F(L) *interj.* "rolling on (the) floor (laughing)." (Computer jargon. Written only. An initialism used in computer communications.) □ *I was ROTFL when I read your note. That was too much.* □ *Your comment had me ROF.*

rotgut 1. *n.* strong or inferior liquor, especially whisky. □ *Where is that jug of rotgut you used to keep around here?* □ *The old man nearly went blind drinking all that rotgut.* **2.** *mod.* [of liquor] strong or fiery. □ *You've got to stop drinking that rotgut liquor and think of your health.* □ *I won't pay for this rotgut whisky. Give me something better.*

rotten 1. *mod.* concerning illness which is particularly unpleasant. □ *I've been feeling rotten all day.* □ *Try to shake off that rotten cold, won't you?* **2.** *mod.* intoxicated due to drink or drugs. (From sense 1. Compare with PUTRID.) □ *It takes a whole case of beer to get Wilbur rotten.* □ *When he gets rotten, he's sort of dangerous.* **3.** *mod.* unpleasant, poor or bad. □ *We have nothing but one* *rotten problem after another.* □ *This is the most rotten mess I've ever been in.*

rotten apple *n.* a single bad person or thing. (Compare with ROTTEN TO THE CORE.) □ *There always is a rotten apple to spoil it for the rest of us.* □ *Tom certainly has turned out to be the rotten apple.*

rotten egg *n.* a bad or despised person; a STINKER. □ *He is a real rotten egg.* □ *She has turned out to be a rotten egg after all.*

rotten luck AND **rough luck** *n.* bad luck. □ *Of all the rotten luck!* □ *I've had nothing but rough luck all day.*

rotten to the core *mod.* really bad. (Compare with ROTTEN APPLE.) □ *That lousy creep is rotten to the core.* □ *The entire government is rotten to the core.*

rotter *n.* an objectionable person. (Offensive. Also a term of address.) □ *What a rotter you are!* □ *Just get out of my sight, you rotter!*

rouf AND **ruof** *n.* four. (Criminal backslang. See FRENCH LOAF.) □ Q: *How much did you get?* A: *Just a measly rouf quid, mate.* □ *I could use ruof right now; I'm broke.*

rough *mod.* unwell. □ *Oh dear, I feel rather rough.* □ *Carol is a bit rough today, I'm afraid.*

rough and ready *mod.* crude but able; unrefined but ready. □ *Well, your idea's rough and ready, but there's no better one and it might just work.* □ *My friend is the rough and ready type. I'd rather sit and think about things.*

rough as a badger's arse AND **rough as a badger's bum** *mod.* coarse and bristly. (ARSE is taboo; BUM is crude.) □ *He hadn't shaved that morning and his skin was as rough as a badger's arse.* □ *God, he felt as rough as a badger's bum—and looked it, too!*

rough as a badger's bum See ROUGH AS A BADGER'S ARSE.

rough diamond *n.* someone who is wonderful despite a rough exterior; someone with great potential that has yet to develop. □ *Although Sam looks a little tacky, really he's a rough diamond.*

□ *He's a rough diamond—a little hard to take at times, but okay mostly.*

rough house *n.* a noisy or disorderly quarrel. □ *I've had about enough of that rough house you've been having for the last week or so.* □ *Stop that rough house and get down to work!*

rough it *vb. phr.* to live without those things that are normally available to make life easier or more pleasant. □ *We went camping and had to rough it for a week.* □ *After the storm we had to rough it as there was no electricity supply to the house.*

rough justice *n.* treatment that is approximately fair. □ *Under the circumstances, the best you can hope for is some sort of rough justice.* □ *Yes, I know it's only rough justice but if I were you I'd accept it.*

rough luck See ROTTEN LUCK.

roughneck 1. *n.* an ignorant, strong and violent male. □ *We try to stop the children behaving like roughnecks.* □ *Tell that young roughneck to behave in here or get out!* **2.** *n.* a labourer on an oil rig. □ *The roughnecks worked all night trying to cut off the gusher.* □ *We need more roughnecks to work this rig properly.*

rough riding See BAREBACK RIDING.

rough someone up *vb. phr.* to beat someone up; to maltreat someone. □ *Am I going to have to rough you up, or will you co-operate?* □ *The muggers roughed up the old lady before taking her purse.*

rough stuff AND **rough work** *n.* unnecessary roughness; physical violence or threats of violence. □ *Okay, let's cut out the rough stuff!* □ *There was too much rough work in Friday's game.*

rough time *n.* a hard time; a bad time. □ *I didn't mean to give you such a rough time. I'm sorry.* □ *What a rough time we had getting the car started!*

rough tongue *n.* rude or harsh language. □ *What a rough tongue that man has!* □ *She felt the strength of my rough tongue, I fear.*

rough trade AND **trade** *n.* sexual business with a homosexual prostitute.

(Taboo.) □ *There's a lot of rough trade in that park every night.* □ *This is where they hang around, looking for trade.*

rough work See ROUGH STUFF.

round *mod.* upon. □ *Harry hit him good and hard round the nose.* □ *Behave or I'll clout you round the ear-hole!*

roundeyes *n.* a white person. (Racially offensive.) □ *He thinks all roundeyes are racist pigs.* □ *Winston wondered what the roundeyes wanted.*

Roundhead *n.* a circumscribed male. (Taboo. Compare with CAVALIER.) □ *Is it true that all Jews are Roundheads?* □ *I've not looked, but I'm sure not all Roundheads are Jewish.*

round heeled *mod.* characteristic of a sexually co-operative girl. (Crude. She is assumed to have heels rounded from the frequency of occasions she lies on her back.) □ *Take my word for it; Mavis is as round heeled a little miss as you'll find.* □ *Willing? She's positively round heeled!*

round the bend See AROUND THE BEND.

round the houses *n.* trousers. (Rhyming slang. This is a rather poor rhyme that has to be worked at a bit.) □ *Why are you wearing bright green round the houses?* □ *These round the houses look ridiculous on you.*

round the twist See AROUND THE BEND.

rousting *n.* a beating-up. □ *What a rousting I gave Joan at tennis this afternoon!* □ *Harry took a rousting from someone on his way back from the pub last night.*

Royal Mail See HOLY NAIL.

rozzer *n.* a policeman. □ *Think about how the rozzer on the beat is affected by this cold.* □ *The rozzer stopped at the door, tried the lock, and moved on.*

RTFM *exclam.* "Read The Fucking Manual!" (Taboo. Computer jargon. Written only. An initialism used in computer communications. A cry of exasperation found on computer networks, addressed to people who ask stupid questions about the operation of the system.) □ *I refuse to tell you how to print something. RTFM!* □ *So I sug-*

gested that she RTFM, and she got huffy.

rub-a-dub-dub *n.* a pub. (Rhyming slang.) □ *That's not a bad little rub-a-dub-dub you've got there, mate.* □ *He's down the rub-a-dub-dub, as usual.*

rub along *vb. phr.* to get by or manage without too much difficulty. □ *We'll just have to try to rub along somehow.* □ *Mary and I have been rubbing along okay for months.*

rubber cheque *n.* a cheque that is worthless. (Because, like rubber, it bounces. Compare with BOUNCE.) □ *The bank says I wrote a rubber cheque, but I'm sure there was enough money in my account.* □ *One rubber cheque after another! Can't you add?*

rubbish 1. *vb.* to criticise someone with exceptional severity. □ *I'm tired of listening to you rubbishing every idea I come out with.* □ *Your ideas are rubbished because they are rubbish!* □ *I do wish you would not rubbish people like that.* **2.** *vb.* to discard something as useless. □ *Why do you have to rubbish everything?* □ *I'm afraid I'm going to have to rubbish that plan, too.*

rub someone out *vb. phr.* to kill someone. (Underworld.) □ *The gunman was eager to rub someone—anyone, he wasn't at all fussy—out.* □ *The crooks tried to rub out the witness.*

rub someone's nose in something *vb. phr.* to repeatedly embarrass or irritate someone by reminding them of some error or mistake they made earlier. (From the practice of house training a puppy by rubbing its nose in the messes it makes.) □ *So I made a mistake! I wish you'd stop rubbing my nose in it.* □ *Rubbing my nose in it is not going to correct the mistake.*

ruby *n.* curry. (Rhyming slang, linked as follows: Ruby [Murray] ≈ curry. Ruby Murray was a popular singer in the 1960s.) □ *Fancy a ruby to eat tonight.* □ *I always love a ruby, especially a Vindaloo!*

ruby red *n.* the head. (Rhyming slang.) □ *Put your hat on your ruby red, and let's go.* □ *That's using your ruby red!*

ruck 1. *n.* a heated argument. □ *Who started this ruck anyway?* □ *I'm sorry about that ruck we had yesterday, but it was all your fault.* **2.** *n.* a fight between gangs. □ *That was some ruck last night.* □ *Who's going to win the ruck, I ask?*

rucker *n.* a gang fighter. □ *I'd be nice to him, he's a rucker.* □ *Why are we trying to talk to ruckers?*

rucking *n.* a severe criticism. □ *You are going to get a terrible rucking after that remark.* □ *Did they really deserve a rucking like that?*

ruck (up) *vb. (phr.)* to become angry. □ *He had rucked himself up so much, I was afraid he would have a stroke.* □ *Now, now, don't get rucked over this!*

ruddy *mod.* BLOODY. (Crude. A euphemism or disguise.) □ *Why should I stop ruddy swearing just 'cos you ruddy tell me?* □ *Who the ruddy hell do you ruddy well think you are?*

rude *mod.* lewd; sexually improper. □ *They sat around in the pub swapping rude jokes.* □ *What a rude suggestion! I like it!*

rude bits *n.* the sexual organs, either male or female; female breasts. (Crude. Always with *the*. Euphemistic.) □ *Timmy! Hide your rude bits!* □ *What's wrong with my rude bits, mummy?*

rudery *n.* a rude remark. □ *Now there was some rudery that was not called for, I think.* □ *Try to cut out the rudery when speaking to clients, Otto.*

rug *n.* a wig or toupee. □ *Is that guy wearing a rug, or does his scalp really slide from side to side?* □ *I wear just a little rug to cover up a shiny spot.*

rugged *mod.* uncomfortable. □ *It was a bit rugged in that primitive hotel, y'know.* □ *Cynthia's not good with rugged things.*

ruined *mod.* intoxicated due to drink or drugs. □ *You came in last night ruined for the third time this week. What's going on?* □ *Tipsy? Ruined, more like!*

Rule OK! *exclam.* to dominate; to be the best. □ *Provos Rule OK!* (Graffiti slogan seen in Northern Ireland. See entry for PROVOS.) □ *Gers Rule OK!* (Graffi-

ti slogan seen in Glasgow and west-central Scotland. "Gers" is the common abbreviated name for Glasgow Rangers soccer club.)

rumble *vb.* to discover something that had been deliberately hidden. □ *I think I've rumbled what you're up to!* □ *They've rumbled it.*

rum-bum *n.* a drunkard. (Crude.) □ *You are going to turn into a right rum-bum if you don't let up on your drinking.* □ *There was a rum-bum asleep across the front entrance to the office when I got here this morning.*

rum customer *n.* a difficult person, one not to meddle with. □ *I don't want that rum customer working here.* □ *Even a rum customer like that has to earn a living.*

rum(my) 1. *mod.* strange or peculiar. □ *Tom is sort of rummy. Well, he's weird.* □ *That is really a rum idea.* **2.** *mod.* difficult or risky. □ *That sounds like a really rummy way of going about things.* □ *We've got a rum mess down there, I can tell you.*

rumpo 1. *n.* a good-looking or attractive girl or young woman. □ *Now there's a really attractive piece of rumpo.* □ *Look at her, isn't she a real rumpo?* **2.** AND **rumpy-pumpy; rumpty-tumpty** *n.* an act of sexual intercourse. (Taboo. Euphemistic.) □ *Fancy a bit of rumpo?* □ *Where can we go for some rumpty-tumpty around here?*

rumpty-tumpty See RUMPO.

rumpus *n.* a commotion, uproar or row. □ *Please don't make such a rumpus.* □ *There was quite a rumpus in Jim's room.*

rumpy-pumpy See RUMPO.

run amok AND **run amuck** *vb. phr.* to run wild in a violent frenzy. (From a Malay word meaning this.) □ *Someone ran amok with a machete next door and a lot of people ended up in hospital.* □ *The whole company ran amuck after the market crashed.*

run amuck See RUN AMOK.

runaround *n.* a wild goose chase. (Especially with *give*.) □ *The Inland*

Revenue gave us the runaround when we asked them to reconsider their tax assessment. □ *The customer will never get a runaround in my shop!*

run a skirt *vb. phr.* to have a mistress. (Crude.) □ *Mr Big runs a skirt, you know.* □ *Oh, I think you might find that Mr Big runs a lot more than just one skirt!*

run-in *n.* a quarrel. □ *Who's going to win the run-in, I ask?* □ *That was some run-in last night.*

runner 1. *n.* a person who transports contraband. (Underworld.) □ *The cops caught the runner red-handed.* □ *The runners got away, but we have the goods.* **2.** *n.* a police officer. (An historical reference to the Bow Street Runners, London's first full-time police force, from the 1740s to the founding of the modern Metropolitan Police in 1829.) □ *I was never more pleased to see a runner.* □ *We need some runners down here urgently.* **3.** *n.* a vehicle that is in working order. □ *Take the Ford. At least it's a runner.* □ *Oh, I've got a good little runner here.* **4.** *n.* an arrested person that the police consider likely to abscond if given bail. □ *Of course we'll oppose bail; he's a known runner.* □ *Why did the magistrate give a runner like him bail?* **5.** *n.* a person who is on the run from the police, etc. □ *Otto's usually a runner, for one reason or another.* □ *The cops reckon he's always either a runner or in jail.* **6.** *n.* a scheme or plan that is likely to work. □ *I think your idea is a runner, you know.* □ *It may be a runner, but I still don't like it.*

run-of-the-mill *mod.* average; typical. (Originally referring to the typical quality of a product that comes out of a mill.) □ *He is just a run-of-the-mill guy.* □ *I don't want just run-of-the-mill ice cream.* □ *This stuff is just run-of-the-mill.*

run ragged *mod.* exhausted. □ *I've been working at this all night and I'm really run ragged now.* □ *We sent Pete home. He'd been here all night and was run ragged.*

runs *n.* diarrhoea. (Always with *the*.) □ *That stuff we ate gave me the runs.* □ *I can't believe those tasty little hamburgers could give anybody the runs.*

run scared *vb. phr.* to behave in a frightened manner. □ *All the politicians are running scared.* □ *Don't panic. There is no reason to run scared.*

run someone in *vb. phr.* to arrest someone; to take someone to the police station. □ *Don't argue with me, or I'll run you in.* □ *The cops ran in everybody in sight.*

run something 1. *vb.* to smuggle something, usually across a border.. □ *Max used to run drugs into Spain from North Africa.* □ *The soldiers were caught running guns.* **2.** *n.* an act of smuggling. □ *Four soldiers were killed during a run.* □ *In their final run the cocaine smugglers made over four million pounds.*

runt *n.* a small person; someone who is vertically challenged. (Also a rude term of address. Originally, the smallest pig of a litter.) □ *He can't play basketball. He's just a runt.* □ *Hey, runt. Come here!*

Run that by (me) again. AND **Run that by (me) one more time.** *sent.* "Please tell it to me again." □ *I can't believe my own ears. Can you run that by again, please?* □ *It's noisy in here. Please run that by me one more time.*

Run that by (me) one more time. See RUN THAT BY (ME) AGAIN.

run the show *vb. phr.* to be in charge; to be in command. □ *Who's running this show?* □ *No, I don't want to have to run the show again.*

ruof See ROUF.

rush 1. *vb.* to overcharge or cheat someone. □ *He makes a lot as a waiter because he rushes all his customers and keeps the extra for himself.* □ *I'm sure that plumber rushed me, but how can you tell?* **2.** *n.* a burst of energy or good feeling from a drug; the explosive euphoria of some kinds of drugs. □ *Oh yes, this stuff really gives me a rush.* □ *What kind of rush does this have?* **3.** *n.* any excitement; any burst of good feeling. (From sense 2.) □ *I got a real rush* *from helping out.* □ *The wonderful ending to the film gave me a rush.*

rush one's fences *vb. phr.* to attempt to move or work too fast. □ *Please, don't rush your fences; we may be wrong.* □ *If you rush your fences you may miss something important.*

Rusky *n.* a Russian person. (Offensive.) □ *He said he was not a racist, he just hated this particular Rusky!* □ *Don't call Russian people Ruskys, please. It is very offensive and racist.*

rust-bucket *n* a seriously rusty car. □ *I've got to get my rust-bucket fixed up.* □ *Is this rust-bucket yours?*

rustle something up *vb. phr.* to organise something; to obtain something. □ *Oh, I'm sure Mr Big can rustle up a good supply of tobacco and alcohol for your business.* □ *We're going to have to rustle up something to celebrate the centenary of the founding of the school next year.*

S

sab *n.* someone who attempts to disrupt or sabotage hunting or other blood sports. □ *I suppose the sabs will be out trying to stop tomorrow's hunt?* □ *The sab sounded off a very loud klaxon, causing the horse to rear up, throwing the rider.*

sack 1. *n.* a bed. □ *I was so tired I could hardly find my sack.* □ *Somebody put a spider in my sack.* **2.** *vb.* to dismiss someone from employment; to fire someone. □ *The boss sacked the whole office staff last week.* □ *If I do that again, they'll sack me.* **3.** *n.* a job dismissal; the sack. (Always with *the*.) □ *The boss gave them all the sack.* □ *The sack is what I am afraid of.*

sacred mushrooms See MAGIC MUSHROOMS.

sad 1. *mod.* [of a person] pathetic; pitiable. □ *What a sad character he is! All that matters to Jack is collecting beer mats.* □ *She was vigorous once, but is just so sad now.* **2.** *mod.* [of a thing] poor; undesirable. □ *This is a sad excuse for a car!* □ *That was a sad inning there at the end of the afternoon's play.* □ *This steak is really sad.*

saddled with someone or something *mod.* burdened with someone or something. □ *I've been saddled with the children all day. Let's go out tonight.* □ *I don't want to be saddled with your work.*

sad sack *n.* a spoilsport. □ *I don't want to be a sad sack, but if you don't turn down that radio, I'll take it away.* □ *Come on! Don't be such a sad sack! We were only having fun.*

safe 1. *n.* a condom. (Crude.) □ *"Forget it without a safe!" she said.* □ *I've*

got a safe somewhere. **2.** *mod.* good; excellent. □ *This wine is really safe!* □ *Boy, this fishing rod is safe.*

sag *vb.* to play truant, especially from school. (North of England usage.) □ *No, no one sags here.* □ *Do you have a problem with kids sagging at this school?*

sailor's blessing *n.* a curse. □ *Now there was a charming sailor's blessing!* □ *All that character can utter is a string of sailor's blessings, it seems.*

sailor's farewell *n.* a parting curse. □ *He gave us all a sailor's farewell, and left.* □ *That was a sailor's farewell to remember, I'd say.*

sailors (on the sea) *n.* a cup of tea. (Rhyming slang, linked as follows: sailors (on the sea) ≈ [tea] = cup of tea.) □ *There was a big mug of sailors on the sea.* □ *The sailors was hot and wet and very welcome.*

sail (right) through something *vb. phr.* to achieve something with ease. □ *I sailed right through my homework.* □ *We sailed through the examination with no difficulty.*

Saint Grouse's Day *n.* August 12th. (A facetious name for the first day of the grouse shooting season.) □ *The laird always looked forward to Saint Grouse's Day.* □ *It was on Saint Grouse's Day that life picked up on the estate.*

Saint Partridge's Day *n.* September 1st. (A facetious name for the first day of the partridge shooting season.) □ *Every Saint Partridge's Day the lord of the manor organised a large shooting party.* □ *The whole village was looked forward to Saint Partridge's Day.*

Sally AND **Sally Army; Sally-Ann** *n.* the Salvation Army. (Normally with *the.*) □ *Mary plays a tambourine in the Sally band.* □ *The Sally-Ann have a hostel for homeless people along this street.*

Sally-Ann See SALLY.

Sally Army See SALLY.

salmon and trout *n.* stout beer. (Rhyming slang.) □ *How about a salmon and trout before you go, Charlie?* □ *Give my friend here a salmon and trout.*

salt *n.* a sailor. (Especially with *old.*) □ *A couple of salts came ashore and asked if they could buy some beer.* □ *I've sailed a little, but you could hardly call me an old salt.*

salt and batter *n.* assault and battery. □ *There's been another salt and batter reported outside the* Crown *pub, sarge.* □ *They've charged Otto with salt and batter.*

Saltash luck *n.* a grim or very depressing task that involves becoming thoroughly wet. □ *Saltash luck comes from Saltash, a port in Cornwall that is said to be home to some very wet and very unlucky—that is fishless—fishermen.* □ *Come on, I know it's Saltash luck but it just has to be done.*

salt horse *n.* a naval officer who performs general duties only. □ *I think he's really sort of a salt horse.* □ *No, he's not a specialist; just a salt horse.*

sambo *n.* a black person. (Racially offensive.) □ *So this sambo drives away in a BMW!* □ *Why should a BMW not belong to a sambo?*

same difference *n.* the same; no difference at all. □ *Pink, fuchsia, what does it matter? Same difference.* □ *Whether you go or I go, it's the same difference.*

same here *phr.* "me too"; "I agree." □ MARY: *I think I'll have the grilled halibut.* JANE: *Same here.* □ BILL: *I feel sort of cold. What about you?* SUE: *Same here.*

same old story *n.* an often repeated story or situation. □ *It's the same old story. Boy meets girl, girl gets consumption, girl dies.* □ *One after the other they come in. It's the same old*

story with each of them, "Not enough time to do my homework."

Sandy McNab *n.* a taxi-cab. (Rhyming slang.) □ *We hailed a Sandy McNab and got on board.* □ *There are never any Sandy McNabs when it rains.*

san fairy ann *phr.* "nothing to it." (Hobson-jobson, from the French *ca ne fait rien,* meaning much the same thing.) □ *"There, san fairy ann!" he said with a smile.* □ *You may say san fairy ann but I don't think it's that simple.*

sap *n.* a fool; a stupid person. □ *That poor sap thinks he can convince them.* □ *Who's that miserable-looking sap in the corner?*

Sarah Soo *n.* a Jewish woman. (Offensive. Rhyming slang.) □ *Y'know, Otto, if you call a Jewish woman a Sarah Soo, she's likely to get nasty.* □ *Why can you not be polite to Sarah Soos?*

sarbut *n.* a police informer. □ *I don't trust sarbuts.* □ *This new sarbut gives me good info. OK?*

sarky See NARKY.

sarnie *n.* a sandwich. □ *Fancy a bacon and tomato sarnie?* □ *Once we had to live on sarnies, being too poor for anything fancier.*

satin and silk *n.* milk. (Rhyming slang. Scots usage.) □ *Gimme ower the satin and silk, Wullie. (Pass me the milk please, William.)* □ *Have you any satin and silk?*

sauce 1. *n.* liquor; any alcoholic beverage. (See also ON THE SAUCE.) □ *Those fellows have had too much sauce again.* □ *Did you bring the sauce? Can't have a good party without lots of sauce.* **2.** *vb.* to perform sexual intercourse. (Taboo.) □ *One look and he knew she had already sauced that evening.* □ *There were a couple of teenagers in the back room, saucing.*

sauced (out) *mod.* intoxicated due to drink. □ *She went out and got herself sauced.* □ *Boy, do you look sauced out.*

saucepan lid *n.* a one pound note or coin. (Rhyming slang, linked as follows: saucepan lid ≈ [quid] = pound note. The pound note has now been replaced by the one pound coin, except in Scotland.) □ *Is that all you can manage? One miserable saucepan lid?* □ *I handed him a saucepan lid and he looked back at me, smiling.*

sausage *n.* a role of material placed at the foot of a door to exclude draughts. □ *We've got a sausage we put at the door in winter.* □ *The sausage does a great job keeping the cold out.*

sausage a goose *vb. phr.* to cash a cheque. □ *Where can I sausage a goose round here, mate?* □ *Harry'll sausage a goose, I think.*

sausage and mash 1. *n.* cash. (Rhyming slang.) □ *I don't have any sausage and mash.* □ *What do you want sausage and mash for, anyway?* **2.** *n.* marijuana; hashish. (Rhyming slang, linked as follows: sausage and mash ≈ [hash] = marijuana/hashish.) □ *Got any sausage and mash, man?* □ *Where can I get sausage and mash around here?* **3.** *n.* a crash. (Rhyming slang.) □ *There's been a bad sausage and mash at the road intersection.* □ *What caused the sausage and mash to your computer this time?*

sausage dog *n.* a dachshund. □ *My aunty has a sausage dog.* □ *I don't like sausage dogs 'cos I think they look silly.*

sausage roll *n.* the dole. (Rhyming slang.) □ *How long have you been on the sausage roll now?* □ *I'm off to collect my sausage roll.*

saved by the bell *mod.* saved by the timely intervention of someone or something. □ *I was going to have to do my part, but someone knocked on the door and I didn't have to do it. I was saved by the bell.* □ *I wish I'd been saved by the bell.*

saveloy *n.* a boy. (Rhyming slang.) □ *I hope you like saveloys. There are several here this afternoon.* □ *I wish she would try to control that saveloy of hers.*

savvy 1. *n.* knowledge; know-how; common sense. □ *She really has savvy when it comes to clocks.* □ *I don't have the savvy necessary to do that sort of job.* **2.** *mod.* knowledgeable. □ *What a savvy gal!* □ *She is truly savvy!* □ *He is*

one of the most savvy directors in London.

sawbones *n.* a surgeon. (Referring to someone who amputates limbs.) □ *We need a sawbones now. This is an emergency.* □ *Is there a decent sawbones in this town?*

Say cheese! *exclam.* "Please smile!" (A phrase said by a photographer who is trying to get someone to smile for a photograph.) □ *Come on, now. Say cheese!* □ *Say cheese for the camera, please.*

say one's piece *vb. phr.* to say what one must say. □ *Look, just say your piece and get out of here.* □ *I said my piece and left.*

Says me! AND **Sez me!** *exclam.* a formulaic answer to SAYS WHO? □ TOM: *Says who?* FRED: *Says me, that's who!* □ TOM: *You?* FRED: *You got it, sunshine. Sez me!*

say-so *n.* a command; an authorisation. (Compare with GO-AHEAD.) □ *I can't do it just on your say-so.* □ *We can begin as soon as we get the boss's say-so.*

Says who? AND **Sez who?** *interrog.* a formulaic challenge indicating disagreement with someone who has said something. (Compare with SAYS YOU!) □ *"Says who?" "Says me, that's who!"* □ *She drew herself up to her full height, looked him straight in the chest, and said, "Sez who?"*

Says you! *exclam.* "That's just what you say!"; "You don't know what you are talking about!" (Compare with SAYS WHO?) □ FRED: *You are fat and ugly.* TOM: *Says you!* □ MARY: *People who go around correcting other people were found to be very annoying in a recent survey.* BILL: *Says you!*

scag See SKAG.

scally *n.* a reprobate. □ *Pay that scally no attention.* □ *Look, we are going to have to get rid of this scally somehow.*

scaly *mod.* beset with difficulties. □ *Now there's one scaly fellow.* □ *How did we ever get so scaly so suddenly?*

scam 1. *vb.* to swindle someone; to deceive someone. □ *They were scammed by a sweet-talking little old lady who* took all their money. □ *She scammed them for every penny they had.* **2.** *n.* a swindle, deception or fraud. □ *I lost a fortune in that share scam.* □ *What a scam! I'm calling the police.*

scamp *n.* a mischievous small child. □ *Come here, you little scamp!* □ *There are three little scamps at the door asking if Paul can come out to play.*

scanties *n.* a woman's very short or flimsy panties or knickers. □ *There's a little shop just round the corner where you can buy new scanties, Ella.* □ *All her scanties were there on display, drying in her bathroom.*

Scapa Flow *vb.* to go. (Rhyming slang.) □ *Look, why don't you just Scapa Flow?* □ *She told him to Scapa Flow and he did!*

Scarborough warning *n.* no warning whatsoever. □ *A Scarborough warning is the approximate judicial equivalent of shooting first and asking questions afterwards.* □ *The Scarborough warning derives from the summary justice reputedly handed out by the magistrates of Scarborough.*

scared shitless AND **shit-scared** *mod.* very frightened. (Taboo.) □ *He wasn't just frightened. He was scared shitless!* □ *He had to go to court and was shit-scared about it.*

scared stiff *mod.* frightened; petrified with fear. □ *The poor little kid stood there, scared stiff.* □ *I was scared stiff for hours after the accident.*

scare the hell out of someone See FRIGHTEN THE HELL OUT OF SOMEONE.

scare the living daylights out of someone See FRIGHTEN THE HELL OUT OF SOMEONE.

scare the pants off someone See FRIGHTEN THE HELL OUT OF SOMEONE.

scare the shit out of someone See FRIGHTEN THE HELL OUT OF SOMEONE.

scarper *vb.* to escape, flee or run away. □ *There was no time to scarper, so we had to talk to Mrs Wilson.* □ *Lefty tried to scarper.*

Scat! *interj.* "Go away!"; "Get lost!" □ *Go away! Scat!* □ *Scat, cat! I can't work with you sitting on the keyboard.*

scatty *mod.* scatterbrained. □ *Who is that scatty girl in the red dress?* □ *That sweet little old lady is completely scatty, you do realise.*

scene 1. *n.* the drug-use environment; the drug scene. □ *The longer you spend in a scene like this, the harder it is to sober up and go straight.* □ *This coke scene is a bad one. It will shorten your life.* **2.** *n.* one's preference. □ *This nine-to-five stuff just isn't my scene. I quit.* □ *Your scene doesn't seem to involve much in the way of hard work.* **3.** *n.* a place; a setting. □ *This scene is no good. Let's split.* □ *I need a different scene. Life is too hectic here.*

schizo 1. *n.* a schizophrenic person. □ *That guy is an absolute schizo!* □ *Keep that schizo away from me.* **2.** *mod.* schizophrenic. □ *That gal is sort of schizo, isn't she?* □ *I have never dealt with such a schizo type before.*

schlep AND **shlep 1.** *n.* a journey; a distance to travel or carry something. (From German *schleppen* via Yiddish.) □ *It takes about twenty minutes to make the schlep from here to there.* □ *That's a ten-mile schlep, and I won't go by myself.* **2.** *n.* a stupid person; an irritating or annoying person. (Literally, a DRAG.) □ *What a schlep! The guy's a real pain.* □ *Ask that shlep to wait in the hall until I am free. I'll sneak out the back way.* **3.** *vb.* to drag or carry someone or something. □ *Am I supposed to schlep this whole thing all the way back to the shop?* □ *I am tired of shlepping kids from one place to another.*

schmaltz AND **shmaltz** *n.* extreme sentimentality; corny sweetness. (From a Yiddish word meaning fat or oil. Compare with SCHMALTZY.) □ *I didn't like that film. Too much schmaltz.* □ *You aren't playing this piece right. It needs a little shmaltz.*

schmaltzy AND **shmaltzy** *mod.* excessively sweet and sentimental. (Compare with SCHMALTZ.) □ *This film is too schmaltzy for me.* □ *What a shmaltzy play that was!*

schmuck AND **shmuck** *n.* a fool. □ *You schmuck! You've buttered the table-*

cloth! □ *Who's the shmuck in the bright orange trousers?*

schnozz(le) *n.* a nose, particularly a very large or protruding one. (From German *Schnauze* via Yiddish.) □ *Look at the schnozz on that guy!* □ *With a schnozzle like that he should be in the circus.*

schwartz(e) AND **schwartz; swartzer** *n.* a black person; an Indian or Pakistani; a person of mixed race. (Racially offensive. From the German *schwarz* meaning "black," via Yiddish.) □ *A schwartze came into the restaurant and asked for Harry.* □ *What did the swartzer do when he was told Harry was not there?*

schyster AND **shyster 1.** *n.* a dishonest, disreputable or unscrupulous lawyer. (From the German *Scheisser* meaning "shitter," via Yiddish. Compare with SHICER.) □ *He's got some schyster working on his case now; it's going to be a dirty battle.* □ *You mean, there are some lawyers who are* not *shysters?* □ *As long as our shyster is better than their shyster...* **2.** *n.* anyone conducting business by dubious means. (From the German *Scheisser* meaning "shitter," via Yiddish. Compare with SHICER.) □ *The guy is a real shyster; don't trust him an inch.* □ *What a dirty schyster you are!*

scoff 1. *n.* food. □ *This scoff is grim!* □ *I want some good old British scoff.* **2.** *vb.* to eat voraciously. □ *He sat down and scoffed the lot.* □ *If they're that hungry, they'll scoff this stuff.*

scoff (up) *vb. (phr.)* to eat ravenously. □ *He's scoffing up all the food he can find.* □ *She scoffed three hamburgers and a large portion of chips.*

scone *n.* the head. □ *Turn your scone around and take a look at this.* □ *He's distinctive because he has a particularly large scone.*

scoobs *n.* beer. (Rhyming slang. Military slang derived from the children's TV show, "Scooby Doo, where are you?" The usage dates from the 1991 Gulf War in Saudi Arabia, land of no alcohol. Compare with SCOOBY (DOO).)

□ *Have a can of scoobs, Charlie.* □ *Here, that's good scoobs!*

Scooby (Doo) *n.* a idea; a clue. (Scots usage. Always used in the negative. Compare with SCOOBS.) □ *Ah havney a Scooby what happened to yer heavy, pal; okay? (I have no idea what happened to your beer, my friend; is that all right?)* □ *That guy hasney a Scooby whit's going on here. (He does not have a clue about what's going on here.)*

scoop 1. *n.* news obtained and published by one newspaper, or broadcast by one TV channel, etc., before any other one. □ *We got a great scoop! Our reporter was right there when it happened.* □ *That was no scoop at all. It was on live television. Didn't you see the cameras?* **2.** *vb.* to obtain and publish news in just one newspaper, or broadcast it on just one TV channel, etc., before any other. □ *They scooped the other paper on both stories.* □ *Channel 4 scooped me twice last month.*

scoop the pool 1. *vb.* to make a financial killing. □ *She's dreamt of scooping the pool for decades.* □ *So, how do we scoop the pool?* **2.** *vb.* to win a bet in a big way. □ *Yippee! I've scooped the pool!* □ *If you scoop the pool again, a lot of people will not speak to you.*

scoot *vb.* to run or scurry quickly from one place to another. □ *I scooted from the bank to the cleaners and then on to the dentist's.* □ *The shoppers scooted from store to store spending money like it was going out of style.*

scorcher *n.* a very hot day. □ *This is really a scorcher, isn't it?* □ *Boy! What a scorcher!*

score 1. *vb.* to succeed in debate, battle, sport, business, etc. □ *I knew if I kept trying I could score.* □ *It takes hard work and luck to score.* **2.** *vb.* to obtain something; to obtain drugs or sex. □ *Max spent an hour trying to score some pot.* □ *Fred is always trying to score with women.* **3.** *n.* the result of a scoring: drugs, loot, winnings, etc. □ *Where's the score? How much did you get?* □ *The crooks dropped the score as* *they made their getaway.* **4.** *n.* a summary; a conclusion; the sum total; the BOTTOM LINE. □ *The score? Oh, the score is that you are in dire trouble with the Inland Revenue.* □ *Okay, waiter, what's the score?* **5.** *n.* twenty Pounds Sterling. (See GORILLA, MONKEY and PONY.) □ *Burnside slipped him a score and faded into the fog.* □ *Sorry, I don't have a score on me. Can you pay?*

score (with) *vb. (phr.)* to perform sexual intercourse, from the male perspective. (Taboo.) □ *Fred can't think about anything but scoring with Martha.* □ *He will spend his whole holidays trying to score.*

scorpion *n.* a native or citizen of Gibraltar. (Military.) □ *Manuel's a scorpion, you know.* □ *These people are called scorpions because they live on a rock under the hot sun.*

Scotch egg *n.* a woman's leg. (Rhyming slang.) □ *You've got great Scotch eggs, love!* □ *Cor, get a look at the Scotch eggs on that!*

Scotch mist *mod.* intoxicated due to drink. (Crude. Rhyming slang, linked as follows: Scotch mist ≈ [pissed] = intoxicated.) □ *They were both very Scotch mist. They could only lie there and snore.* □ *Tracy gets quite Scotch mist after just a drink or two.*

scot-free *mod.* without harm or cost. □ *She got away with it scot-free.* □ *It may be scot-free, but then it's worthless.*

Scottie *mod.* a nickname for a Scotsman. (Offensive, except when applied to dogs.) □ *How are things today, Scottie?* □ *Scottie's not here today, Joe.*

Scouse *n.* the dialect spoken in Liverpool. (Offensive.) □ *Scouse is a dialect unique to Liverpool.* □ *He was speaking Scouse, I think. I understood nothing.*

Scouser *n.* a native or inhabitant of Liverpool. □ *All the Beatles were Scousers.* □ *I can't understand a Scouser speaking in dialect.*

scrag *vb.* to tease someone; to torture someone; to attack someone. □ *I think he was wrong to scrag you.* □ *Don't scrag him; he can't answer back.*

scram *vb.* to exit fast; to get out of a place in a hurry. □ *I've got to scram.*

I'm late. □ *Go on, scram! Get out of here fast!*

scrambled eggs *n.* decorations on a military officer's uniform. □ *I know his rank is high because of the scrambled eggs, but I don't know how high.* □ *I'll be glad when I get some scrambled eggs on me.*

scran *n.* military rations. □ *Is that all we've got here? Scran?* □ *I once lived on nothing but scran for over a week.*

scrape the bottom of the barrel *vb. phr.* to utilise the last or only things or people available, even if unsatisfactory. (Compare with BOTTOM OF THE BARREL.) □ *They were really scraping the bottom of the barrel when they picked you.* □ *You scraped the bottom of the barrel for this one. I want something better.*

scratch 1. *n.* paper money; banknotes; money in general. □ *I just don't have enough scratch.* □ *How much scratch does it take to buy a car like this one?* **2.** *vb.* to eliminate something or someone from a list; to cancel something. □ *Scratch Fred. He can't make it to the party.* □ *We decided to scratch the idea of a new car. The old one will have to do.* **3.** *mod.* impromptu; temporary, made up of whatever or whoever is on hand at the time. □ *We started a scratch game of basketball, but most of the girls had to leave at lunchtime.* □ *This is just a scratch disk. After you use it for your computer program, someone else will overwrite it with something else.*

scratcher *n.* a bed. (Scots usage.) □ *Am aff ta ma scratcher fur a kip. (I'm off to my bed for a sleep.)* □ *You can use that scratcher over there.*

scream 1. *n.* someone or something very funny. (Always with *a*. Compare with HOWL.) □ *The joke Tom told was really a scream.* □ *Tom is always a scream at parties.* **2.** *vb.* to turn into a police informer; to become King's or Queen's evidence. □ *There's no chance of Otto screaming.* □ *Have you heard? Otto screams in the High Court today!* **3.** *n.* a very obvious male homosexual. (Crude.) □ *He doesn't like being called* *a scream.* □ *Why does he work so hard to look like he's a scream?*

scream bloody murder *vb. phr.* to scream very loudly; to complain or protest loudly. □ *She screams bloody murder every time I get near her.* □ *Those guys scream bloody murder long before they're hurt.*

screw 1. *n.* a miserable or mean person. □ *Here was one screw that was different from the others, he thought.* □ *I don't think I could take another screw like that today.* **2.** *n.* a jailer. (Underworld.) □ *See if you can get the screw's attention.* □ *I'm ill, screw! Let me out!* **3.** *n.* the value of salary or wages. □ *Do they give you a decent screw there?* □ *OK, what screw do you pay?* **4.** *vb.* to perform sexual intercourse. (Taboo.) □ *He's telling everybody that he screwed her.* □ *They screw all the time, just like bunnies.* **5.** *n.* the curved motion of a billiard ball which has been hit eccentrically.* □ *I don't know how he managed to put such a powerful and yet accurate screw on the ball.* □ *"Screw the ball to the left to avoid being snookered," I advised.* **6.** *vb.* to cheat someone. □ *That salesman tried to screw me, but I just walked out on him.* □ *They didn't screw me. I got good value for my money.* **7.** *vb.* to commit a burglary. □ *He was actually screwing the house when we arrived, sarge.* □ *Before you screw a house, make sure it's empty, especially of dogs.* **8.** *vb.* to keep watch while another commits a burglary.* □ *You screw out here while we go in, OK?* □ *We need someone who can screw for us, Henry, while we get the stuff.* **9.** *n.* a prison guard. □ *Some screws are friendly. Watch them especially!* □ *Never trust a screw.* **10.** *n.* an act of sexual intercourse. (Taboo.) □ *After that screw, she felt cheap.* □ *I think you could get a screw there, Barry.* **11.** *n.* a woman viewed as a sex object. (Taboo.) □ *So this little screw I'd been eyeing up came right up to me and said, "It's £20 if you want a short time."* □ *Now there's a nice screw walking down the street.* **12.** AND **twist** *n.* a small paper packet with screwed

up ends, used as a container. (Typically used to hold small quantities of tobacco, sugar, salt, etc.) □ *The prisoner slipped a screw into my hand as I left.* □ *I opened the twist to see what it contained.*

screw around 1. *vb. phr.* to waste time. □ *Stop screwing around and get on with things.* □ *John's always screwing around and never does anything on time.* **2.** *vb. phr.* to have sex on a casual basis. (Taboo.) □ *Apparently she screws around with just about everyone.* □ *It was one of these parties—you know, everyone was screwing around.*

screw around with someone or something *vb. phr.* to tinker or fiddle around with someone or something. □ *Andy screwed around with his clock until he broke it.* □ *Look, chum! Don't you screw around with me!*

screwdriver 1. *n.* a drink consisting of vodka or gin, together with orange juice. □ *Can I have a screwdriver please?* □ *I do like this screwdriver.* **2.** *n.* a senior prison guard; the commander of the guards in a prison. □ *I want to see the screwdriver!* □ *The screwdriver here's the worst of the lot.*

screwed *mod.* bested; defeated; cheated. □ *I really got screwed at the garage.* □ *If you don't want to get screwed by somebody, you have to do it yourself.*

screwed up 1. *mod.* ruined; messed up. □ *This is a really screwed up timetable. Let's start over again.* □ *Your plan is completely screwed up.* **2.** *mod.* neurotic; confused. □ *The poor fellow is quite screwed up; I think he needs professional help.* □ *I'm a psychiatrist; it's my job to sort out screwed up people.*

screw someone or something up *vb. phr.* to interfere with someone or something; to mess up someone or something. □ *Try again and don't screw it up this time.* □ *You really screwed up my brother by not being on time.*

screw someone out of something *vb. phr.* to cheat someone of something. □ *You are trying to screw me out of what is rightfully mine!* □ *I'm not trying to screw anybody out of anything!*

screw the arse off someone *vb. phr.* to perform sexual intercourse vigorously or repeatedly with someone. (Taboo.) □ *There they were, screwing the arse off each other.* □ *One look and he knew she had already screwed the arse off someone that evening.*

screw up See ARSE UP.

screw-up See ARSE-UP.

screwy *mod.* crazy. □ *I've never heard such a screwy idea.* □ *You are really screwy!* □ *That's the screwiest looking hat I've ever seen.*

scribe **1.** *n.* a clerk. (Military.) □ *Give the scribe your name and number, son.* □ *Did you give the scribe the information he wanted?* **2.** *n.* a forger. (Police.) □ *CID brought in a scribe tonight.* □ *There seems to be more scribes every year.*

scrimshank *vb.* to malinger or otherwise avoid military duty or responsibility. □ *Don't think you're going to get away with your scrimshanking.* □ *Scrimshanking? Naw, we never scrimshank, sarge.*

scroat AND **scrote** *n.* a despicable person. □ *Get out of here, you scroat!* □ *What a scrote that woman can be.*

Scrooge *n.* a miserly individual; a PENNY-PINCHER. (From the character in Dickens's *A Christmas Carol.* Also a term of address.) □ *Ask Scrooge over there if you can borrow a quid for a cup of coffee.* □ *Don't be such a Scrooge! All I want is a quid!*

scrote See SCROAT.

scrounge *n.* a hunt; a search. □ *There's some sort of scrounge going on out there. I wonder what they're looking for?* □ *Did your scrounge turn up anything useful?*

scrounge (around (for someone or something)) *vb. phr.* to look around for someone or something; to seek someone or something in every likely place. □ *Try to scrounge around for somebody to go to the party with, why don't you?* □ *I don't think there is anybody who will go with me, but I'll scrounge around.* □ *Ask John to scrounge around for a spanner.*

scrounger *n.* someone who obtains things by cadging or scrounging. □ *Here comes that miserable scrounger again.* □ *Ask that scrounger what he wants.*

scrounge someone or something up *vb. phr.* to get someone or something somehow. (Compare with ON THE SCROUNGE FOR SOMETHING.) □ *I scrounged a doctor up in the middle of the night.* □ *See if you can scrounge up a new carburetor by noon.*

scrounging *mod.* searching around to obtain things illegally or without payment. □ *The dog's been scrounging at the rubbish tip again.* □ *What are you scrounging for, anyway?*

scrub **1.** *vb.* to cancel something. □ *We had to scrub the whole plan because of the weather.* □ *The manager scrubbed the party because people wouldn't co-operate.* **2.** *vb.* to participate in a surgical operation. □ *I'm scrubbing with the professor this afternoon.* □ *Could you scrub with me on this one?* **3.** *vb.* to prepare for participation in a surgical operation. □ *I've got to scrub now. The rest of the firm are waiting.* □ *Is everyone scrubbed?*

scrubber **1.** *n.* a slut; a prostitute. (Crude.) □ *The Old Bill hauled her in because she looked like a scrubber.* □ *Clare dresses like a scrubber.* **2.** *n.* an unappealing or unpleasant girl or young woman. □ *The little scrubber came out and made a face at me!* □ *If it's scrubbers you want, you've come to the right place.*

Scrub it! *sent.* "Forget it!"; "Cancel it!" □ *All right, scrub it!* □ *I'm scrubbing it, and we'll try a different way.*

scruff *n.* a scruffy or untidy person. □ *Her boyfriend is a little scruff, but he's a rich little scruff!* □ *He says scruffs like us don't dress well enough for his restaurant!*

scruffy *mod.* sloppy; unkempt; shabby; messy. □ *Her boyfriend may be a little scruffy, but he's got loadsamoney!* □ *Why don't you clean up this scruffy car? It's disgusting!*

scrummage **1.** *n.* a frenetic crowd. □ *That's a huge scrummage there tonight, she thought.* □ *They were all struggling to get through the scrummage coming* *out of the football match.* **2.** *n.* a place of confusion. □ *The place was just a huge scrummage.* □ *I'm not going to go to a scrummage like that again.*

scrummy AND **yummy** *mod.* delicious; delightful. □ *What a scrummy cake!* □ *She said she had a yummy idea for the weekend.*

scrump *vb.* to steal fruit from an orchard. □ *I was only scrumping, officer!* □ *It's still a crime to scrump, son.*

scrumptious *mod.* excellent; tasty. □ *That cake is just scrumptious, Mary. What's in it?* □ *Who makes the most scrumptious chocolate chip cookies in the world—besides me, that is?*

scrunch something up *vb. phr.* to crush or crunch up. □ *He scrunched up the note and threw it upon the fire.* □ *I sat on my biscuits and scrunched them up into crumbs.*

SCSI AND **scuzzy** *n.* "small computer system interface." (Computers. An acronym. Rhymes with "fuzzy.") □ *With its built-in SCSI port, it's easy to attach external peripherals to a Macintosh.* □ *Why do they call it a scuzzy? Why not just say what it is?*

scuffer *n.* a policeman. □ *The scuffer stopped at the door, tried the lock, and moved on.* □ *Think about how the scuffer on the beat is affected by this cold.*

scum *n.* an utterly worthless person; someone lacking any merit. (Also a rude and provocative term of address.) □ *Who is that scum? Who does she think she is?* □ *Look, you scum, I'm gonna sort you out once and for all!*

scunner *n.* a despicable person. (Scots usage.) □ *What a scunner!* □ *He's just a scunner; ignore what he says.*

scupper **1.** *vb.* to sink a ship; to drown a ship's crew. □ *Uncle Mike's tanker was scuppered by a U-boat during the war.* □ *Almost all the crew was scuppered, too.* **2.** *vb.* to stop or wreck a project. □ *Well, that scuppers that!* □ *Why did you scupper my scheme?*

scupper someone *vb.* to kill someone. □ *Watch it! Otto would scupper you as soon as look at you.* □ *I'm gonna scupper you once and for all.*

scuzzy See SCSI.

sealed (up) *mod.* settled; secured; CINCHED. □ *The matter was sealed by Monday morning.* □ *The contract was sealed up just in time.*

Search me. *sent.* "I don't know." (There is a heavy stress on both words.) □ TOM: *How do crickets make that chirping noise?* BILL: *Search me.* □ *You can search me. How should I know?*

seat (of the pants) *n.* the buttocks. □ *Someone kicked him on the seat of the pants.* □ *With luck, his seat will hurt for a long time, that creep!*

sec *n.* a second. (Compare with TICK.) □ *I'll be with you in a sec. Keep your hair on!* □ *Just a sec. I'm on the phone.*

second fiddle *n.* a person in a secondary role; the second best. (Frequently with *play*.) □ *I won't stay around here playing second fiddle for someone half my age and ability!* □ *There are worse things than being second fiddle.*

second-hand dartboard *n.* a very promiscuous woman. (Crude.) □ *Promiscuous? She's a second-hand dartboard!* □ *Now that girl there is a real second-hand dartboard.*

see *vb.* to equal or raise someone's bet in poker. □ *I see your five and raise you ten.* □ *Well, can you see me or not?*

see a man about a dog *vb. phr.* to leave a place for a mysterious reason, presumed to be to go to the toilet. (A euphemism.) □ *I've got to see a man about a dog.* □ *Fred went to see a man about a dog. I hope he remembers to put the seat up first this time.*

see eye to eye *vb. phr.* [for two or more people] to agree on something or view something the same way. □ *We never seem to see eye to eye.* □ *Gary and Walter see eye to eye on this question.*

seeing double See SEEING PINK ELEPHANTS.

seeing pink elephants AND **seeing double** *mod.* intoxicated due to drink; recovering from a drinking bout; having the delirium tremens. □ *When I got to the point of seeing pink elephants, I knew that something had to be done.* □ *The old one who's shaking—he's probably seeing double.*

seeing-to 1. *n.* an act of sexual intercourse. (Taboo.) □ *A good seeing-to would probably do her the power of good, in fact.* □ *I think really, she's gasping for a seeing-to, you know.* **2.** *n.* an assault. □ *I was given the most terrible seeing-to that put me into hospital.* □ *If you call him that, he'll give you a seeing-to.*

see no further than the end of one's nose AND **cannot see (any) further than the end of one's nose** *vb. phr.* to be narrow-minded; to lack understanding and perception. □ *She is so selfish she can see no further than the end of her nose.* □ *You don't care about anyone but yourself. You can't see any further than the end of your nose.*

see over something *vb. phr.* to inspect something, a house for example. □ *We went to see over that house we're thinking of buying.* □ *Can I see over this car you have for sale?*

see red *vb. phr.* to be livid with rage. □ *When she hung up the phone, I saw red. I've never been so angry in my life.* □ *As he continued to talk, she began to see red.*

sees AND **sees us** *phr.* "give me"; "pass to me." (Scots usage.) □ *Sees me a dod o yon meat, mister. (Pass me a portion of that meat, sir.)* □ *Sees us a kiss afore ye go, hen. (Give me a kiss before you leave, dear.)*

see someone off *vb. phr.* to reprimand someone severely. □ *The boss really saw off Charlie!* □ *When I catch him I'll see him off so he'll never forget. That's a promise!*

see someone or something (all) right *vb. phr.* to make sure someone or something is all right. □ *Look, could you see her right for me?* □ *Don't worry about it Joan, I'll see you all right.*

see someone or something off *vb. phr.* to remove something; to evict someone. □ *I'm asking security to come and see you off my property.* □ *Oh, I'll soon see that one off!*

see stars *vb. phr.* to be (knocked) unconscious. □ *If you talk to me like that again, you'll be seeing stars.* □ *I saw stars for a few seconds, and then someone threw cold water in my face.*

sees us See SEES.

See you. *interj.* "Good-bye." □ *Good game, Tom. See you.* □ *See you, old chum. Give me a ring.*

See you later. *interj.* "Good-bye." (Common colloquial. Also said to people one knows one will never see again.) □ *Nice talking to you. See you later.* □ *Have a great trip, Mary. See you later.*

sell a pup *vb. phr.* to swindle by selling that which is worthless. □ *That lot sold you a pup. They must have seen you coming.* □ *Hey! Give me my money back! I've been sold a pup!*

sell out *n.* a betrayal. (Compare with SELL SOMEONE OR SOMETHING OUT.) □ *Any one of you could have stood up for me. What a sell out!* □ *How can you put up with a sell out like that?*

sell-out 1. *n.* the complete sale of all available tickets for a theatrical, etc., event. □ *From the first night it was a complete sell-out.* □ *He's hoping for a sell-out, but with that play he'll be lucky to sell any seats at all.* **2.** *n.* a theatrical, etc., event full to capacity. □ *The play's a sell-out.* □ *One sell-out and we're made!*

sell short *vb. phr.* to sell short-dated stock. (Securities markets.) □ *I wouldn't sell short on IBM. It's a long-term hold.* □ *The way the economy is heading, I'd sell short the whole market.*

sell someone or something out *vb. phr.* to betray a person or a cause or one's nation for profit. (Compare with SELL OUT.) □ *How could you sell the Party out like that?* □ *She would sell out her mother.*

sell someone or something short *vb. phr.* to disparage. □ *Why does Mary have to sell Joan short all the time?* □ *She's just like that. She sells short everyone whenever she gets the chance.*

sell under guise AND **sug** *vb. phr.* to attempt to sell while pretending to carry out market research. □ *Selling under guise is, let's face it, sneaky.* □ *Are you planning to sug in this area?*

semi *n.* a semi-detached house. □ *I've always lived in a semi.* □ *Some semis are actually very roomy and comfortable.*

semi-detached *mod.* not paying proper attention. □ *Wake up! You were semi-detached again.* □ *Try to be less semi-detached all the time and you might learn something.*

send someone down 1. *vb. phr.* to expel from a university. □ *He's been sent down for theft.* □ *Not so many people get sent down from university nowadays.* **2.** *vb. phr.* to sentence someone to a term of imprisonment. □ *I am sending you down for a period of two years.* □ *I got sent down for assault.*

send someone from pillar to post *vb. phr.* to send someone from place to place; to give someone the run-around. □ *Red tape everywhere I went. They sent me from pillar to post until closing time.* □ *Nobody is in charge there. They send you from pillar to post, and you don't complain for fear they'll start you all over again.*

send someone to Coventry *vb. phr.* to ostracise someone. □ *After what he did, it was hardly surprising they sent him to Coventry.* □ *It's not often that the men send someone to Coventry.*

send someone up *vb. phr.* to mock or ridicule, particularly by imitation. □ *Last week, he sent the prime minister up.* □ *In his act, he sends up famous people.*

send-up *n.* a parody. □ *It was clear the government was in real trouble when almost every time you switched on the TV or opened a paper there there was another send-up of its leading members.* □ *I enjoy a good send-up, even if it is about me.*

sent *mod.* made ecstatic, especially by music. □ *She's really sent. Look at her as she listens.* □ *All the musicians were sent. Or maybe they were on something.*

September morn *n.* an erection. (Taboo. Rhyming slang, linked as follows: September morn ≈ [horn] = erection. Compare with HAIL SMILING MORN.) □ *As long as you have a September morn like that I'll love you,*

Frank. □ *Here I come, complete with a real fine September morn!*

septic *mod.* offensive; disagreeable. (A jocular derivative from "sceptic.") □ *I'm afraid he really is a septic little person.* □ *That was a septic thing to do.*

Septic (Tank) *n.* an American. (Rhyming slang, linked as follows: Septic (Tank) ≈ [Yank] = American.) □ *Mr Big's talking to a Septic Tank just now.* □ *Some Septic was here looking for you this afternoon.*

sergeant-major 1. *n.* tea laced with rum. (Military slang.) □ *A nice cup of sergeant-major will set you up!* □ *I sipped at the sergeant-major and tasted the rum.* **2.** *n.* very strong, well-sugared tea. (Military slang.) □ *Right, sergeant-major time. Put the kettle on.* □ *That sergeant-major was the strongest tea I'd ever tasted.*

serious about someone *mod.* in love, or almost in love, with someone. □ *I'm afraid I'm getting serious about Bill.* □ *Bill, unfortunately, is pretty serious about Mary.*

seriously *mod.* a general intensifier, without any specific meaning beyond this. □ *Do you seriously expect to get away with that?* □ *He seriously imagined no one would guess.*

serve someone right *vb. phr.* to be just the bad luck or punishment that someone deserves. □ *It would serve you right if you lost your money.* □ *He fell down. It serves him right.*

sesh See SESSION.

session AND **sesh 1.** *n.* a drinking bout. □ *Your father's off on another session again.* □ *He was just sobering up from a sesh with the bottle.* **2.** *n.* a marijuana-smoking session; time spent on a drug high. (Youth usage.) □ *What a fine sesh that was!* □ *Max was terribly hungry after the session.*

set about someone *vb. phr.* to set upon or to attack someone. □ *He set about me for no reason!* □ *The tribe set about their neighbours with a will.*

set of wheels *n.* a car. □ *I need a new set of wheels.* □ *Boy, look at the set of wheels that bird has!*

set someone back *vb. phr.* to cost someone. □ *That must have set you back a mint!* □ *This bracelet set me back plenty.*

set someone up (for something) *vb. phr.* to contrive to place someone in a dangerous or vulnerable situation. □ *His so-called pals set him up for the practical joke—which ended up injuring two of them severely.* □ *Who set me up for this anyway?*

set something to one side *vb. phr.* to disregard something. □ *Set that to one side for the moment; it's not so urgent.* □ *Don't bother me with that now. Set it to one side.*

set the Thames on fire *vb. phr.* to make a great success in life, etc. □ *Well, you've not exactly set the Thames on fire so far, have you?* □ *I don't want to set the Thames on fire, but just to live quietly.*

settle someone's hash *vb. phr.* to silence, subdue, defeat or kill someone. □ *If he comes in here, I'll settle his hash all right.* □ *Now, that ought to settle your hash.*

setup *n.* a plan or arrangement. □ *Okay, what's the setup around here?* □ *I've got me a nice little setup for earning some money.*

Seven Dials *n.* haemorrhoids. (Rhyming slang, linked as follows: Seven Dials ≈ [piles] = haemorrhoids. Seven Dials is a district in London.) □ *A bad dose of the Seven Dials is sheer hell.* □ *Our Bert suffers terribly from the Seven Dials, you know.*

Severn capon *n.* a sole; a flatfish. □ *Do you enjoy Severn capon?* □ *He asked for Severn capon, but the restaurant was unable to oblige.*

sewed up See SEWN UP.

sewer *n.* a despicable person. □ *Just get out of my sight, you sewer!* □ *What a sewer you are!*

sewer press See GUTTER PRESS.

sewn up AND **sewed up; buttoned up; tied up** *mod.* completed in a satisfactory manner. (Compare with SEW SOMETHING UP.) □ *I've just about got this contract sewn up.* □ *When we get it tied up, we'll go out for a drink.*

sew something up AND **stitch something up; button something up; tie something up** *vb. phr.* to finalise or conclude something in a satisfactory manner. (Compare with SEWN UP.) □ *Let's sew this up and get out of here.* □ *I'm about ready to tie up this matter.*

sex 1. *vb.* to perform sexual intercourse. (Crude. Euphemistic.) □ *There were a couple of teenagers in the back room, sexing.* □ *One look and he knew she had already sexed that evening.* **2.** *n.* sexual intercourse. (Crude. Euphemistic.) □ *She seems to think that calling it "sex" makes it all right.* □ *They were talking about, you know, sex.* **3.** *n.* the sexual organ, male or female. (Crude. Euphemistic.) □ *What's wrong with my sex?* □ *Doctor, my sex hurts.*

sexiness *n.* agreeableness or attractiveness. □ *She oozes sexiness.* □ *Sexiness is not everything.*

sexing-piece *n.* the male sexual organ. (Crude. Euphemistic.) □ *He's very proud of what he always calls his sexing-piece, for some reason.* □ *She could not see what was so wonderful about a two-inch sexing-piece.*

sex kitten *n.* a young woman who makes the most of her sexual attractiveness to men. □ *He thought he was getting a sex kitten, but she turned out to be just a plain cat.* □ *Clare does everything she can to look like a sex kitten, which is difficult by the time you're on the wrong side of fifty.*

sexpot AND **sex-pot** *n.* a female who is not merely sexually appealing, but apparently willing, too. (Crude.) □ *Tiffany is such a sexpot.* □ *There are plenty of sexpots in the pubs of this town—if that's all you want.*

sexy 1. *mod.* fashionable; exciting. (Compare with TRENDY.) □ *Right now it's sexy to drive a Porsche.* □ *He always made the sexy investments and now he's broke. Maybe that's sexy now, too?* **2.** *mod.* effective; clever; agreeable. □ *That's a sexy solution to our little difficulty.* □ *Your idea is really sexy.* **3.** *mod.* agreeable or attractive. □ *What a sexy girl!* □ *It's a sexy idea, I'll say that.*

Sez me! See SAYS ME!

Sez who? See SAYS WHO?

s.f.a. AND **S.F.A.; sfa; SFA** *n.* absolutely nothing. (Literally, an abbreviation of Sweet Fuck All. Compare with SWEET FANNY ADAMS.) □ *There is just s.f.a. there.* □ *SFA, I tell you; nothing!*

shackie *n.* a white woman living with a coloured man. (Racially offensive.) □ *She was just a shackie, no one cared.* □ *The trouble with shackies is that they have no friends on either side.*

shackles *n.* a thick soup made from leftovers. □ *Fancy a bowl of shackles?* □ *There's nothing better than some shackles on a cold day.*

shack up (with someone) AND **get shacked 1.** *vb. phr.* to live with someone as if married but without bothering with the formality of a marriage ceremony. □ *They shacked up for over a year until her parents found out and stopped sending her money.* □ *More and more couples are getting shacked nowadays rather than getting married.* **2.** *vb. phr.* to marry someone. □ TOM: *Will you shack up with me?* MARY: *And I thought you'd never ask me to marry you! Of course I will!* □ *Mary and Tom are getting shacked at last!*

shades AND **sunshades** *n.* dark glasses; sun glasses. □ *Where are my shades? The sun is too bright.* □ *The guy stood there—wearing sunshades and carrying a violin case. Barlowe grimaced.*

shaft 1. *n.* an exceptionally bad deal; ruinous treatment. □ *He really gave me the shaft.* □ *It's the shaft every time you go into that place.* **2.** *vb.* to ruin or severely damage someone. □ *That jerk really shafted me this time.* □ *We are going to shaft this guy in a way that he will remember.* **3.** *vb.* to perform sexual intercourse. (Taboo.) □ *They were shafting like it was going out of fashion.* □ *I think you could soon be shafting there, Barry.* **4.** *n.* a woman seen as a sex object. (Taboo.) □ *Any shaft around here, mate?* □ *The pretty little shaft came over to him to ask for a light.* **5.** *n.* the male sexual organ. (Taboo.) □ *Men keep their brains in their shafts!* □ *Unlike Myra, Sharon thinks of little else but shafts.*

shaftable *mod.* [of a woman] worthy of performing sexual intercourse with. (Taboo. From a male perspective.) □ *Now she's shaftable, all right!* □ *The most shaftable woman in the world came into the room.*

shafted *mod.* ruined; destroyed; cheated. □ *I really got shafted in that deal.* □ *I've been shafted!*

shafting 1. *n.* an act of sexual intercourse. (Taboo.) □ *After that shafting, she felt cheap.* □ *They were talking about, you know, shafting.* **2.** *n.* an occasion of particularly harsh or unfair treatment. □ *Well, we got a right shafting there!* □ *I could only call it a shafting and you can be sure I will complain.*

shag 1. *vb.* to perform sexual intercourse. (Taboo.) □ *One look and he knew she had already been shagged that evening.* □ *There were a couple of teenagers in the back room, shagging.* **2.** *n.* a woman seen as a sex object. (Taboo.) □ *Joan is a good shag.* □ *I don't think many women would consider being called a "shag" is much of a compliment.* **3.** *n.* a whore; a prostitute. (Taboo.) □ *There are a lot of shags around here in the centre of town.* □ *The Old Bill hauled her in because she looked like a shag.*

shagged (out) *mod.* exhausted. □ *What a day! I'm shagged out!* □ *You people look sort of shagged.*

shagging *n.* an act of sexual intercourse. (Taboo.) □ *I think really, she's gasping for a shagging, you know.* □ *A good shagging would probably do her the power of good, in fact.*

shaggin'-wagon See PASSION-WAGON.

shag oneself *vb.* to masturbate. (Taboo.) □ *Someone has shagged themselves or something in here!* □ *Girls shag themselves as well as boys, you know.*

shake *n.* a milkshake. □ *I'd like a chocolate shake, please.* □ *A shake only costs sixty pence.*

Shake a leg! *exclam.* "Get started!"; "Hurry up!" □ *Shake a leg! We've got* *to be there in twenty minutes.* □ *She told me to shake a leg, so I hurried the best I could.*

shake a leg *vb. phr.* to dance. □ *Let's shake a leg. The music's great.* □ *Tracy, do you want to shake a leg with me?*

shake-out See SHAKE-UP.

shakes 1. *n.* the DELIRIUM TREMENS. (Always with *the.*) □ *I got the shakes again. That's what I get for putting soda water in my whisky.* □ *In the last stages, alcoholics have the shakes all the time.* **2.** *n.* a condition of extreme nervousness. (Always with *the.*) □ *I get the shakes every time I have to speak in public.* □ *He has the shakes so bad you could actually see his knees trembling.*

shake-up 1. *n.* a frightening or disheartening experience. □ *When you experience a shake-up like that, you must take it easy for a while.* □ *Fred and Clare both survived their shake-up.* **2.** AND **shake-out** *n.* a drastic change or reorganisation. □ *After a shake-up like the one we've just been through, everybody's a little upset.* □ *After a shakeout that lasted a month, we went into full production.*

shaky *mod.* risky; dangerous. □ *You really are in a shaky situation here, you know.* □ *Your plan is, let's say, shaky.*

shamateur *n.* a player or participant in any sport who claims amateur status but nevertheless makes money from the sport. □ *Rugby is one sport that used to be full of shamateurs.* □ *There goes one very rich shamateur.*

shambles *n.* a state of uproar, confusion or chaos. □ *I'm in such a shambles; I don't know what to do next.* □ *It's hard to sort out a shambles like that.*

shambolic *mod.* chaotic; in a shambles. □ *That shambolic traffic in town causes serious delays.* □ *The telephone system here is shambolic today.*

shampers See CHAMPERS.

shampoo *n.* champagne. (Compare with CHAMPERS and POO.) □ *I just love this bubbly shampoo!* □ *There is nothing like shampoo to liven up a party!*

shamrock tea *n.* very weak tea. (Figuratively, tea with just three leaves in it.)

□ *Now this was real shamrock tea, barely distinguishable from hot water.* □ *I can't stand shamrock tea!*

shank's mare See SHANK'S PONY.

shank's nag See SHANK'S PONY.

shank's pony AND **shank's mare; shank's nag** *n.* one's own legs, used as a method of transportation. (Compare with TAMSON'S MARE.) □ *You'll find that shank's pony is the quickest way to get around in this town.* □ *Is there a bus, or are we using shank's nag?*

shape up 1. *vb. phr.* to show promise of improvement or reform. □ *Come on you lot! Shape up!* □ *I guess I'd better shape up if I want to stay in school.* **2.** *vb. phr.* to assume a final form or structure. □ *Our scheme for winning the election was beginning to shape up.* □ *Her objectives began to shape up in her final year.*

shark 1. *n.* a swindler; a confidence trickster. (Underworld.) □ *The sharks were lined up ten deep to get at the blue-eyed new owner of the club.* □ *The guy's a shark, and he's after your hard-earned money!* **2.** *n.* a lawyer. (Derogatory.) □ *Some shark is trying to squeeze a few thousand out of me.* □ *Hire another shark to go after him.* **3.** *n.* a professional punter. □ *Bookies don't like to take bets from a shark.* □ *"You're a shark," said the bookie, "I'm not accepting your bet."*

sharon *n.* a supposedly-typical young working-class woman. □ *All these sharons look the same to me.* □ *They're called sharons because Sharon is a very common name among them.*

sharp *mod.* good-looking; well-dressed. □ *You really look sharp today.* □ *That's a sharp set of wheels you've got there.*

sharp as a tennis ball AND **sharp as the corners of a round table** *mod.* exceptionally dumb; very slow-witted. (Ironic.) □ *Yes, I'm afraid Tony is about as sharp as a tennis ball.* □ *The guy's as sharp as the corners of a round table, but very friendly.*

sharp as the corners of a round table See SHARP AS A TENNIS BALL.

sharp end *n.* a jocular or landlubber's term for the bow of a ship. (Compare with BLUNT END.) □ *The two of them stood at the sharp end, watching the island appear from over the horizon.* □ *I think the sharp end is the bit at the front of the boat.*

sharp end (of something) *n.* a critical point in the decision-making process. (See also BUSINESS END OF SOMETHING.) □ *We're at the sharp end now. There's no one else to pass the decision-making onto.* □ *Right at the sharp end of the process, Harry gets himself sacked!*

sharpish 1. *mod.* quite rapidly. □ *Move sharpish!* □ *Get a sharpish move on, you lot.* **2.** *mod.* quite sharp. □ *Oh yes, he's sharpish all right.* □ *That's a sharpish knife you have there.*

shattered 1. *mod.* very intoxicated due to drink or drugs. □ *It takes a whole case of beer to get Walter shattered.* □ *Well, you see, he's shattered and can't come to the phone.* **2.** *mod.* utterly exhausted. □ *After the game, the whole team was shattered.* □ *I feel too shattered to go to work today.*

shawl *n.* a prostitute. (Crude. Irish usage.) □ *This shawl comes up to me and acts like she's met me before.* □ *Do you think she's a shawl or just very friendly?*

shed *n.* an aircraft hangar. □ *There were three planes in the shed.* □ *Use the second shed over there please, Sir.*

shed a tear *vb. phr.* to urinate. (Crude.) □ *Well, shedding a tear does relieve the pressure of all that beer!* □ *I'm just going to shed a tear.*

sheen(e)y AND **shonk(y)** *n.* a Jewish person. (Offensive.) □ *Why can you not be polite to sheenies?* □ *Y'know, Otto, if you call a Jew a shonk, he's likely to get nasty.*

sheep in wolf's clothing *n.* a young man too timid to approach a girl. (A deliberate spoonerism of "wolf in sheep's clothing.") □ *The reason Albert never gets the girl is that he really is a sheep in wolf's clothing.* □ *Sometimes being a sheep in wolf's clothing makes the guy more attractive to a girl.*

sheepshagger *n.* a rustic individual; a country bumpkin. (Taboo.) □ *How, thought Smythe, had he ever ended up living among these sheepshaggers?* □ *The old sheepshagger looked down on him as he lay on the ground and smiled.*

sheet *n.* a banknote. □ *Sorry, I don't have any sheets with me. Can you pay?* □ *He put a number of sheets into the top pocket of my shirt and said that there's plenty more to be had if I asked no questions.*

Sheffield (handicap) *n.* an act of defecation. (Taboo. Rhyming slang, linked as follows: Sheffield (handicap) ≈ [crap] = defecation.) □ *He said he needed a Sheffield handicap.* □ *He took a Sheffield and then came back.*

shekels *n.* Pounds Sterling; money. □ *Have you got a few shekels you can spare?* □ *These things cost plenty of shekels.*

shell-like *n.* an ear. □ *Allow me to take you to one side and have a word in your shell-like, sonny.* □ *Look at the huge shell-likes on her!*

sherbet *n.* liquor or beer. □ *I could use a little sherbet with this soft stuff.* □ *Larry hid all his sherbet under the bed.*

sherracking AND **shirricking** *n.* a severe dressing-down; a public humiliation. (Scots usage.) □ *Are you just gonna stand there like a big wean and let her give me a sherracking like that? (Are you just going to stand there like an overgrown child and let her give me a public humiliation like that?)* □ *But I think you deserve a right shirricking, Archie.*

sherrack someone AND **shirrick someone** *vb.* to subject someone to a severe public humiliation or dressing-down. (Scots usage.) □ *Don't you sherrack me, you little tyke!* □ *She was really shirricking her.*

Sherwood Forest *n.* the rows of vertical missile tubes which fill a large part of the interior of a nuclear missile submarine. □ *I had to pass through Sherwood Forest several times every day.* □ *You try not to think about the destructive power contained in Sherwood Forest.*

shice 1. *n.* counterfeit money. (From the German *Scheisse*, meaning "shit.") □ *Get the cops! This stuffs all shice!* □ *Mr Big's got a lot of shice to offload.* **2.** *n.* nothing. □ *He said there was shice there.* □ *No, shice.*

shicer *n.* a despicable person. (From the German *Scheisser*, meaning "shitter." Compare with SCHYSTER.) □ *Stop acting like the shicer you are, just for once!* □ *You dirty shicer, you!*

shickered *mod.* bankrupt. □ *A lot of famous people have ended up shickered in their time.* □ *Well that was it, I was shickered.*

shift *vb.* to rapidly gulp down large quantities of food. □ *You should see how he can shift that stuff.* □ *They were shifting it like food was going out of fashion.*

Shift it! See SHIFT YER BARROW!

Shift yer barrow! AND **Shift it!** *exclam.* "Get out of the way!"; "Move on!" (Scots usage.) □ *Come oan! Shift yer barrow! Ah canny get past!* □ *Shift it! Yer car's blocking the street!*

shill *n.* a salesman's confederate or decoy planted in the crowd to urge others to purchase, bet or otherwise hand over money for whatever is on offer. □ *The guy's a shill! Don't fall for this setup!* □ *There were more shills than suckers in the crowd that day.*

shindig *n.* a lively party. (Irish usage.) □ *What a fancy shindig! They even have glass glasses!* □ *What time do we have to be at that shindig Saturday night?*

shiner 1. *n.* a black eye. □ *Take a look at Marty's shiner!* □ *I got this shiner by walking into a door.* **2.** AND **sparkler** *n.* a diamond or other gemstone. □ *Look at the shiners on that old lady!* □ *Janice has a new sparkler on her finger.*

shin off *vb. phr.* to go away. □ *You know, I told him to shin off and he did!* □ *Look, why don't you just shin off?*

ship a sea *vb. phr.* to ship a lot of water. □ *We're shipping a sea, cap'n.* □ *If we ship a sea like that for long we're in trouble.*

shipshape and Bristol fashion AND **Bristol fashion** *mod.* everything in perfect order. □ *He won't quit until everything is shipshape and Bristol fashion.* □ *It's very important that we get it all Bristol fashion.*

shirricking See SHERRACKING.

shirrick someone See SHERRACK SOMEONE.

shirt-lifter *n.* a male homosexual. (Taboo.) □ *Why does he work so hard to look like he's a shirt-lifter?* □ *Tom is getting to be such a shirt-lifter.*

shit a brick AND **shit bricks** *vb. phr.* to be terrified. (Taboo.) □ *Terrified? I shat a brick!* □ *He's so frightened he's shitting bricks.*

shit and derision *n.* confusion or despair. (Taboo.) □ *The whole place has been thrown into shit and derision.* □ *If people would just stop all the shit and derision, we might be able to sort out the mess.*

shit bricks See SHIT A BRICK.

shit(e) 1. *n.* faeces. (Taboo. A highly offensive word to most people. There are many additional meanings and constructions using this word. It is in fact Standard English, but virtually all applications of it are not.) □ *Don't step in that shit there.* □ *There's dog shite in my garden!* **2.** *n.* something poor in quality; junk. (Taboo.) □ *This stuff is shit. Show me something better.* □ *What do you keep all this shit around here for?* **3.** *n.* nonsense. (Taboo. Compare with *bullshit*.) □ *Don't give me that shite! I know you're lying.* □ *I'm tired of your shit!* **4.** *n.* drugs in general; heroin; marijuana. (Taboo.) □ *Lay off the shit, Harry! You'll end up hooked.* □ *So Marty scores a bag of shit—you know, H.—and we get out the stuff to shoot.* **5.** *n.* a despicable person. (Taboo.) □ *Tell that stupid shit to get out of here, or I'll land him one.* □ *What a shite you are!* **6.** *exclam.* a general expression of disgust. (Taboo.) □ *Oh, shit! What a mess!* □ *Shit! That's terrible.* **7.** *n.* foul weather. (Taboo.) □ *The weather is real shit out there tonight.* □ *He drove through shite for hours to be at her side.* **8.** *n.* abuse; unreasonable, severe or unpleasant treatment. (Taboo.) □ *I'm not* taking any more of your shite, Otto. I'm leaving you. □ How does he get away with all that shit he heaps on these people? **9.** vb. to defecate. (Taboo.) □ Jimmy shat in his nappy! □ It's time you learnt to shite in the potty.

shit-eating n. the practice of sycophancy; servility. (Taboo.) □ Keeping your job will involve a large dollop of shit-eating now, Jack. □ If shit-eating is the key to a successful political career, why is Albert not Prime Minister by now?

shite-hawk 1. n. a seagull. (Taboo.) □ The shite-hawks wheeled and cried overhead at the stern as the dirty lugger pulled away from the quay. □ If you wonder why seagulls are sometimes called shite-hawks, just watch how they behave over a sewage works. **2.** n. a despicable person. (Taboo.) □ Get out of here, you shite-hawk! □ What a shite-hawk that woman can be.

shit(e)-house n. a toilet; a public convenience. (Taboo.) □ My Lord! This place looks like a shite-house! □ That's because it is a shite-house.

shit-faced mod. extremely intoxicated due to drink or drugs. (Taboo.) □ Come to the phone? He's completely shit-faced! □ How can anybody get so shit-faced in so little time?

shithead 1. n. a despicable person. (Taboo.) □ You lousy shithead! □ The guy is somewhere between an arsehole and a shithead. **2.** n. a very stupid person. (Taboo.) □ Just get out of my sight, you idiotic shithead! □ What a fool of a shithead you are!

shit-hot mod. enthusiastic in a disagreeable way. (Taboo.) □ They're really shit-hot on this crazy idea. □ So this creep got shit-hot on Mary and she had a problem until he got too drunk to stand up.

shit-house mod. a disgusting or filthy place. (Taboo.) □ Sort out this shit-house now! □ I don't know how you can stand this shit-house.

shit-list n. a supposed list of those who are out of favour. (Taboo.) □ I think that after my remarks yesterday, I'm on her shit-list. □ Mr Big's shit-list is not a healthy place to be.

shit or bust phr. "no matter what it takes." (Taboo.) □ Shit or bust, we'll make it this time! □ We must get there today, shit or bust.

shits n. nervous diarrhoea. (Taboo. Always with the.) □ He's so worried about the interview, he's got the shits. □ I had a little touch of the shits the second day, but after that it was OK.

shit-scared See SCARED SHITLESS.

shitter n. a toilet. (Taboo.) □ Where's the shitter? □ The shitter? Oh, it's along that passageway.

shitty mod. inferior; substandard; shabby. (Taboo.) □ What a shitty place. □ Oh, that's really shitty!

shit (up)on someone from a (very) great height vb. phr. to reprimand someone with very great severity; to land someone in a great deal of trouble. (Taboo.) □ After what he did, are you surprised that the boss shit on him from a very great height? □ Being shat upon from a great height is a just reward for that screw-up, don't you agree?

shiv AND **chiv 1.** vb. to stab someone. (Underworld.) □ He shivved Rocko, and Rocko deserved it. □ The boss told Bruno to get Rocko one way or the other—chiv him, shoot him, clobber him—but get him. **2.** n. a knife. (Underworld.) □ Swiftly and silently his shiv found its way up under Rocko's ribs. All over a silly bit of skirt. □ I could tell from the way his cuff broke that there was a chiv strapped to his leg.

shlep See SCHLEP.

shmaltz See SCHMALTZ.

shmaltzy See SCHMALTZY.

shmuck See SCHMUCK.

shock absorbers n. the female breasts. (Crude. Normally with the and in the plural.) □ There she was, bold as brass, with her shock absorbers on full display. □ Nice shock absorbers, eh?

shocker n. an unacceptable, horrifying or shocking person. □ Have you seen her new boyfriend? He's a real shocker, I can tell you! □ There are a number of shockers attending that school.

shoebox *n.* a very small or tight space. □ *Well, I've got myself and all my stuff into this shoebox, goodness knows how.* □ *If you think I'm satisfied with this shoebox, then you've got another thing coming.*

shoestring *mod.* low-cost; cheap. (Compare with ON A SHOESTRING.) □ *This is just a shoestring operation. There is no capital involved.* □ *We have nothing but a shoestring budget this year.*

shonk *n.* a nose. □ *What a shonk on that guy!* □ *I want some glasses that sit in just the right place on my wonderful shonk.*

shonk(y) See SHEEN(E)Y.

shoot AND **shoot up 1.** *n.* an injection of heroin. (Usually SHOOT-UP.) □ *The way Ernie was yawning, I knew he needed a shoot-up.* □ *"Just one more shoot. That's all. Then, never again!" moaned Ernie, rather unconvincingly.* **2.** *vb.* to inject a specific drug into the bloodstream. □ *He actually had to leave the meeting to shoot.* □ *The two of them were shooting up smack.*

shoot a cat *vb. phr.* to empty one's stomach; to vomit. (Crude.) □ *Oh Lord, I've gotta shoot a cat.* □ *Harry is in the loo shooting a cat.*

shoot a line 1. *vb. phr.* to tell a lie. □ *She certainly can shoot a line, can't she?* □ *I don't believe a word of it. You're shooting a line.* **2.** *vb. phr.* to talk in a pretentious manner. □ *Oh, he's just shooting a line, as usual.* □ *We don't want you to shoot a line but to confine yourself to the proven facts.*

shooter *n.* a gun, especially a handgun of some sort. □ *Otto removed a shooter from his coat pocket and held it at the clerk's temple.* □ *Nice shooter! Where did you get it?*

shooting gallery *n.* a place where drug users meet to inject and share needles. □ *That derelict factory has become a shooting galley, I'm afraid.* □ *You can tell where the shooting galleries are by the discarded needles on the ground.*

shoot off See POP OFF.

shoot off one's mouth AND **shoot one's mouth off** *vb. phr.* to brag; to tell secrets. □ *Stop shooting off your mouth. Nobody believes you anymore.* □ *So you had to go and shoot your mouth off about the bankruptcy proceedings!*

shoot oneself in the foot *vb. phr.* to cause oneself difficulty; to be the author of one's own misfortune. □ *I am a bit of an expert at shooting myself in the foot, it seems.* □ *Once more, he shot himself in the foot by his open and honest dealings with the press.*

shoot one's mouth off See SHOOT OFF ONE'S MOUTH.

shoot-out *n.* a gunfight. □ *There was a big shoot-out at the end of the film.* □ *In this shoot-out, there were no survivors—not even a horse!*

shoot someone or something down from a great height See SHOOT SOMEONE OR SOMETHING DOWN IN FLAMES.

shoot someone or something down in flames AND **shoot someone or something down from a great height** *vb. phr.* to defeat someone utterly in argument; to completely crush an opposing point of view. □ *It was a bad idea, okay, but you didn't have to shoot it down in flames like that.* □ *I didn't mean to shoot you down from a great height.*

shoot the breeze *vb. phr.* to chat casually and without purpose. □ *We spent the entire afternoon just shooting the breeze.* □ *It was good to shoot the breeze with you, Mary.*

shoot the craw AND **shuit the craw** *vb. phr.* to depart without ceremony; to go home. (Scots usage.) □ *Well, I'm shooting the craw now. See you!* □ *If yous want to, yous can shuit the craw richt the noo. (If you people want to, you can all go right now.)*

shoot the lights *vb. phr.* to cross a junction when the red "stop" light is showing. □ *He shot the lights and was booked.* □ *Don't try shooting the lights. It's not worth it.*

shoot the shit *vb. phr.* to boast. (Taboo.) □ *Oh, he's always shooting the shit about this or that.* □ *I wish I could stop him shooting the shit as he does.*

shoot up See SHOOT.

shop *vb.* to inform against someone, especially to the police. □ *Who shopped me?* □ *I didn't shop you!*

shop around *vb. phr.* to comparison-shop, seeking the best bargains. □ *Always shop around, and you'll save a fortune.* □ *That's right. If you shop around enough, you'll never buy anything.*

shopfloor *n.* workers as a group, as distinct from management. □ *The shopfloor is not happy, boss.* □ *If there's much more grumbling by the shopfloor we could soon have a strike on our hands.*

shopping list *n.* a list of questions requiring answers. □ *I have a shopping list of absolute must-knows.* □ *He showed up for the interview with a shopping list so long that it took two pages.*

shop-window *n.* any opportunity to exhibit products, talents, etc. □ *You've got a great shop-window there; use it!* □ *I'd like a shop-window for my talents.*

short 1. *n.* a small drink of spirits (not beer or wine) that is undiluted or almost so. □ *One short of Scotch please, bartender.* □ *I'll have a short and a packet of cigarettes.* **2.** *n.* short-dated stock. (Stock markets. Always in the plural.) □ *Actually, I think that holding IBM shorts is the right way to go right now.* □ *There is a lot of covering of shorts this week. After that, the market is in for a steady decline, I'm sure.*

short-and-curlies AND **short hairs** *n.* pubic hairs. (Taboo. Always plural, always with *the.*) □ *Let's face it, he has them by the short-and-curlies.* □ *Uh Donna, we can see your short hairs round the side of your bikini bottom.*

short arm *n.* the male sexual organ. (Taboo.) □ *Myra says short arms are disgusting but then Myra's strange.* □ *Only small boys wave their short arms about like that, Wayne. Put it away!*

shortarse *n.* a small person. (Taboo.) □ *What a shortarse that woman is.* □ *Get out of here, you shortarse!*

short back and sides *n.* a man's hair, cut short at both the back and the sides

of the head. □ *Just a short back and sides then, sir?* □ *Yes, a short back and sides is exactly what I want.*

short commons *n.* insufficient food to go around. □ *Well folks, it's short commons until the supplies get through.* □ *Short commons is not much fun.*

short fuse *n.* a quick temper. □ *Fred's got a short fuse. Watch out.* □ *I knew she'd blow up. She's got such a short fuse.*

short hairs See SHORT-AND-CURLIES.

short one *n.* a small or quickly drunk measure of liquor, including beer. □ *How about a short one before you go, Charlie?* □ *Give my friend here a short one.*

short time *n.* a brief time with a prostitute, for a single act of sexual intercourse only. (Crude.) □ *Fancy a short time, dear?* □ *How much do you want for a short time?*

short-timer *n.* a prostitute's client who comes straight to the point. (Crude.) □ *The short-timer didn't want to pay but Zoe slashed his face with an open razor she carried for such eventualities.* □ *Another short-timer, the fourth that hour, went off with her in his car.*

shot 1. *n.* a try at something. □ *Go ahead. Give it another shot.* □ *Have a shot at this problem.* **2.** *n.* a small or quickly drunk drink of spirits, typically whisky. □ *Here, have a shot of this stuff.* □ *He stopped at every pub along the street for a quick shot.* **3.** *n.* an injection of drugs. □ *Just one shot of that stuff and you're hooked for life.* □ *A shot of H put the poor guy straight for a while.* **4.** *n.* a bill in a restaurant, etc. □ *No no, it's my shot; I insist on paying.* □ *How much did the shot come to?* **5.** *mod.* exhausted. □ *I feel too shot to go to work today.* □ *Poor Ted really looks shot.*

shot down 1. *mod.* demolished; destroyed. □ *Her idea was shot down after all her work.* □ *I felt shot down, even though I was sure of what I was getting into.* **2.** *mod.* to be under the influence of drugs. □ *Go away. I'm shot down.* □ *Well, I wouldn't like to say she was shot down, but she couldn't stand up.*

shot full of holes AND **shot to ribbons** **1.** *mod.* [of an argument that is] demolish or comprehensively destroyed. □ *Come on, that theory was shot full of holes ages ago.* □ *Your argument is easy to shoot to ribbons.* **2.** *vb. phr.* to be very intoxicated due to drink or drugs. □ *Tipsy? Shot to ribbons, more like!* □ *"Boy, I was really shot full of holes. I'll never drink another drop." "Right."*

shotgun marriage AND **shotgun wedding** *n.* a forced wedding, necessary because the bride is pregnant. (Traditionally because the bride's father forces the groom to go through with the ceremony by holding a shotgun at him.) □ *It was a shotgun wedding, but they really are in love.* □ *I thought shotgun marriages went out with feuds and things like that.*

shotgun wedding See SHOTGUN MARRIAGE.

shot in the arm **1.** *n.* a drink of spirits. □ *I could use a shot in the arm right now.* □ *How about a little shot in the arm, landlord?* **2.** *n.* an act or sign of encouragement. □ *That pep talk was a real shot in the arm for all of us.* □ *The good exam result was a shot in the arm for Gerry.*

shot in the dark *n.* a wild guess. □ *It was just a shot in the dark. I had no idea I was exactly correct.* □ *Come on, try it. Even a shot in the dark may just be right.*

shot to ribbons See SHOT FULL OF HOLES.

shot up **1.** *mod.* severely injured by gunshots. □ *Tom got himself shot up in a hunting accident.* □ *He was pretty badly shot up in the police action.* **2.** *mod.* very intoxicated due to drink or drugs. □ *You see, he's far too shot up to come to the phone just now.* □ *Simon went off on a pub-crawl with Harry hours ago. He'll be well shot up by now, I'm sure.*

shouldn't happen to a dog AND **shouldn't happen to one's worst enemy** *phr.* of fate so bad that no creature deserves it. □ *Poor guy. That shouldn't happen to a dog.* □ *This cold I got shouldn't happen to my worst enemy.*

shouldn't happen to one's worst enemy See SHOULDN'T HAPPEN TO A DOG.

shout *n.* the purchase of a round of drinks. □ *Come on! It's your shout!* □ *All right, all right; it's my shout. What do you want to drink this time?*

shout and holler *n.* a collar. (Rhyming slang.) □ *He hates wearing a shout and holler.* □ *You've got to have on a shout and holler to get in there.*

Shove it! *exclam.* "Get lost!"; "Forget it!"; "Give up!" □ *No way! Shove it!* □ *Shove it, it's not worth the trouble.*

shove(l) along *vb. phr.* to move along without fuss. □ *Shovel along, please.* □ *They shoved along, making room for the others.*

shovel and broom *n.* a room. (Rhyming slang.) □ *This is my shovel and broom. Sod off!* □ *I got back to me shovel and broom and shut the door.*

shovel and tank *n.* a bank. (Rhyming slang. This refers to the kind of bank where money is kept.) □ *That's the shovel and tank where I keep my money.* □ *When does that shovel and tank open today, please?*

shove off See PUSH OFF.

Show a leg! *exclam.* "Get out of bed!" □ *Come on you lot! Show a leg!* □ *Show a leg! It's time to get up!*

showbiz *n.* show business; the entertainment industry. □ *Susan has always wanted to be in showbiz, but unfortunately has absolutely no talent whatsoever.* □ *What's so attractive about a life in showbiz anyway?*

show-down *n.* a decisive test or trial of strength or support. □ *Right, are you ready for the show-down?* □ *Now for the show-down!*

shower **1.** *n.* an objectionable or unacceptable person or group of people. □ *The same shower was waiting outside the office for him as he left.* □ *They're just a shower.* **2.** *n.* a pre-wedding party at which the bride is given presents by her female friends and relatives. □ *That was a shower at Mary's the other night.* □ *I haven't been to a shower like that in years.*

show one's cards *vb. phr.* to show one's hand; to declare one's intentions. □ *Why did you show your cards so soon?* □ *Try not to show our cards if possible.*

show the flag *vb. phr.* to make an appearance for the sake of form. □ *I can't cancel my visit; I've got to show the flag.* □ *I think she's just here to show the flag.*

show willing *vb. phr.* to demonstrate willingness. □ *I'll show willing all right, as soon as I can see the point.* □ *Look, just tell what you want me to show willing about?*

shreddies *n.* torn, tattered or otherwise disgusting underwear. □ *How could anyone wear shreddies like that?* □ *First, let's get you out of these terrible shreddies.*

shrimp *n.* a very small person. □ *Who's the little shrimp over by the door?* □ *I'm such a shrimp. I just have short genes.*

shrink *n.* a psychoanalyst or psychotherapist. □ *I spent a lot of time with a shrink, but it didn't help me.* □ *The shrink says I have to take these pills to help me get off the drug habit.*

shtik *n.* a routine or act that is the trademark of an entertainer, especially in variety. (Yiddish.) □ *His shtick was a trained dog and cat act.* □ *Their shtik is so old! Maybe nobody will remember whose it was originally.*

shufti AND **shufty** *n.* a glimpse or quick glance. □ *He took a shufti but saw nothing unusual.* □ *Take a shufty at that!*

shuit the craw See SHOOT THE CRAW.

shunt *n.* a traffic accident involving two or more vehicles. □ *There was a bad shunt outside the office this morning.* □ *Several people were injured in the shunt.*

shunt something onto someone *vb. phr.* to shift responsibility for something onto someone. □ *Look, I know you're trying to shunt something onto me. What is it?* □ *He'd managed to shunt responsibility for the crash onto Otto, he thought.*

Shush! *exclam.* "Be quiet!" □ *Shush! I want to hear the weather forecast.* □

Shush! Listen to the lecture, or at least go quietly to sleep.

shut-eye *n.* sleep. □ *It's about time to get some shut-eye.* □ *I could use about another hour of shut-eye.*

Shut it! See SHUT UP!

Shut up! AND **Shut your face!; Shut your gab!; Shut it!; Wrap it!; Wrap up!** *exclam.* "Be silent!" □ *Shut up and listen!* □ *Oh, shut your face! I've heard enough.* □ *Wrap it yourself, you two!*

Shut your face! See SHUT UP!

Shut your gab! See SHUT UP!

shy *mod.* without, lacking or lost. □ *We're shy a couple of essential components.* □ *Make sure the machine is not shy of anything that matters.*

shyster See SCHYSTER.

sick *n.* vomit. □ *Mummy, there's sick all over the carpet.* □ *I think it's cat sick, Jimmy.*

sickening *mod.* loathsome. □ *I'm afraid I think this whole business is really quite sickening.* □ *What a sickening little tyke he is.*

sick to death (of someone or something) *mod.* totally disgusted with someone or something. □ *I am sick to death of your constant bickering.* □ *This whole bribery business just has me sick to death.*

sick up *vb. phr.* to empty one's stomach; to vomit. (Crude.) □ *I think I'm going to sick up. Isn't there supposed to be a sick bag in one of these seat pockets?* □ *He's got to sick up, and there's no air sickness bag. Help!*

side 1. *n.* a sideways spin placed on a cricket ball. □ *Watch out for side from that bowler.* □ *He likes to add side just when you think it's not going to happen.* **2.** *n.* a television channel. □ *It's the news next on this side.* □ *Let's see what's on some of the other sides.* **3.** *n.* pomposity or boastfulness. □ *He's a genuine fellow; no side about him.* □ *Every time he speaks, he oozes side.*

side-bet *n.* a bet on a subsidiary matter. □ *All right. For a side-bet, how many riders will fall off during the race?* □ *Otto took a side-bet that he would win the main bet.*

sideboards *n.* side-whiskers or side-burns. □ *I don't trust men with sideboards.* □ *He's the fellow with the great big sideboards.*

sidekick *n.* deputy; assistant. □ *Harry, if Mr Big's sidekick says "jump," you jump. Clear?* □ *He's got a new sidekick that I don't think'll last too long.*

sidley *mod.* stylishly furtive; hypocritically arrogant. □ *If you were less sidley, you'd get more done.* □ *Why do you always have to be so sidley?*

sidy *mod.* affected with pomposity or boastfulness. □ *What a sidy character he is!* □ *Why does he always have to be so sidy?*

siff AND **syph** *n.* syphilis. (Crude. Normally with *the.*) □ *I hear Margy's got the siff again.* □ *People who get the syph are unlikely to tell everybody about it!*

signing *n.* a sportsman who has signed a contract to play for a particular team. □ *The team's new singing cost 4 million.* □ *I don't know why anyone would want that useless clown as a signing.*

sign off *vb. phr.* to cease to be unemployed. (Compare with SIGN ON.) □ *It's great to sign off!* □ *I'm signing off on Monday.*

sign on *vb. phr.* to register as unemployed. (Compare with SIGN OFF.) □ *He's a way signing on.* □ *Sign on through there.*

silk 1. *n.* a King's or Queen's Counsel. □ *The silk entered the court and bowed before the judge.* □ *What does the silk think Harry's chances are?* **2.** *n.* the silk gown worn by a King's or Queen's Counsel. □ *The silk pulled on his silk and left his chambers.* □ *"Where is my silk?" the QC asked.*

silly billy *n.* a foolish or clown-like person, a figure of fun. (Originally, a nickname for King William IV.) □ *That silly billy thinks he can convince them.* □ *Those silly billies are at it again. Spend, spend, spend.*

silly (old) moo *n.* a stupid woman. □ *What a silly old moo! You can't do that, love.* □ *What does the silly moo want now?*

silly prick AND **stupid prick** *n.* a term of contempt for a man. (Taboo. Also a term of address.) □ *Tell that silly prick the jobs been taken.* □ *Oh, he's really no more than a stupid prick.*

silver moon *n.* a black person. (Racially offensive. Rhyming slang, linked as follows: silver moon ≈ [coon] = black person.) □ *Don't call black people silver moons, please. It is very offensive and racist.* □ *He said he was not a racist, he just hated silver moons!*

silver plate *interj.* "please." (From the French *s'il vous plait*, which means this, by hobson-jobson.) □ *Can I have my purse back? Silver plate?* □ *Silver plate! I need an answer!*

simmer down *vb. phr.* to calm down. □ *Now, now! Just simmer down!* □ *Simmer down, you people.*

simp *n.* a simpleton. □ *You are such a simp!* □ *Why did some simp feel it necessary to do this?*

sin bin *n.* where offenders are put. □ *Keep that up and you're heading straight for the sin bin, son!* □ *A few weeks in the sin bin might concentrate his mind.*

sin bosun *n.* a ship's chaplain. □ *He had to go to see the sin bosun about something or other.* □ *Most of the time, sin bosuns don't have much to do.*

since Adam was a boy AND **since the year dot** *phr.* "since a very long time ago." □ *I think old Robert has worked here since Adam was a boy.* □ *We have not changed that since the year dot!*

since the year dot See SINCE ADAM WAS A BOY.

sing *vb.* to inform (on someone). (Underworld.) □ *Barry knew the nark would sing. He had to do something to stop her.* □ *Bruno would never sing. He's a champ.*

Singapore tummy *n.* a picturesque name for diarrhoea or similar, inflicted upon a visitor to a foreign land. (Singaporean variety.) □ *Most people blame Singapore tummy on the water.* □ *I had a little touch of Singapore tummy the second day, but other than that we had a wonderful time.*

Singers *n.* Singapore. □ *I'm off to Singers on business next week.* □ *Meet Simon, just back from Singers.*

single *n.* a single, or one-way, travel ticket. □ *A single to Manchester, please.* □ *How much is a single from here to London?*

single-decker *n.* a bus with one deck only, as distinct from a DOUBLE-DECK-ER. □ *Single-deckers don't have stairs. Obviously.* □ *I feel safer travelling in a single-decker.*

sink *vb.* to drink alcohol. ⊔ *Let's go round the pub and sink a few jars.* □ *Len stopped at a pub to sink a pint before going home.*

sink the boot in See PUT THE BOOT IN.

sippers *n.* an additional sip of rum offered to a Royal Navy ship's crew as a reward or in celebration. □ *Well done, people. Sippers, I think!* □ *Now that result certainly should earn some sippers, don't you think?*

Sir Galahad *n.* a noble, pure and unselfish man. □ *I like the look of this Sir Galahad.* □ *Samantha's Sir Galahad was not there.*

Sir John *n.* the male sexual organ. (Taboo.) □ *The doctor told him that he'd got something wrong with his Sir John.* ⊔ *That's all very well Myra, but where would the world be without Sir Johns?*

sis *n.* sister. (Also a term of address and a common pet name for one's sister.) □ *Come on, sis. We're going to be late.* □ *Well, sis, good luck.*

sissie See CISSIE.

sissified *mod.* effeminate. (Crude.) □ *Do you have to be so sissified all the time?* □ *I'm not comfortable in a sissified place like that.*

sissy See CISSIE.

sister *n.* a male homosexual's male homosexual friend who is not his lover. (Crude.) □ *Paul is his sister, not his lover.* □ *The thing is, Simon has many sisters among the brotherhood.*

sitcom *n.* a situation comedy as found on television. □ *These sitcoms are made for juvenile minds.* □ *Sitcoms can be fun.*

sit-down *n.* a rest period; a lull. □ *As soon as we've had a sit-down, it's back to work.* □ *I really need a sit-down.*

sit on the fence *vb. phr.* to fail to support either side of an issue; to be unable to decide which side of an issue to support. (See STRADDLE THE FENCE.) □ *The government is sitting on the fence on this issue, hoping the public will forget it.* □ *Our candidate wanted to sit on the fence until the last minute, and that alone cost her a lot of votes.*

sitting duck AND **sitting target** *n.* someone or something that is vulnerable or an easy target. □ *Get out of the way! You're a sitting duck.* □ *The guy was a sitting target for a mugging.*

sitting member *n.* an incumbent Member of Parliament. □ *He is the sitting member for our constituency.* □ *An awful lot of these sitting members should be kicked out at the next election.*

sitting target See SITTING DUCK.

sitting tenant *n.* an incumbent tenant. □ *It's not usually a smart idea to buy a flat with a sitting tenant.* □ *The sitting tenant is a little old lady, and she's not going anywhere soon.*

sit-upon *n.* the buttocks. □ *She needs some jeans that will flatter her sit-upon.* □ *With her sit-upon, they'll have to be flattened a lot before jeans will do any flattering.*

six-and-eight AND **two-and-eight 1.** *mod.* honest. (Rhyming slang, linked as follows: six-and-eight/two-and-eight ≈ [straight] = honest. SIX-AND-EIGHT, meaning six shillings and eight pence, is a typical example of the way money was described, particularly in speech, prior to decimalisation in 1971. Similarly, "two-and-eight" means "two shillings and eight pence.") □ *Walter's as two-and-eight as they come.* □ *Six-and-eight, guv! It's true!* **2.** *n.* a condition of excitement or distress. (Rhyming slang, linked as follows: six-and-eight/two-and-eight ≈ [state] = condition of excitement/distress.) □ *Calm down! There's no need to be in such a six-and-eight!* □ *She was in a terrible two-and-eight, I tell you.*

six feet under *mod.* dead and buried. □ *Fred died and is six feet under.* □ *They put him six feet under two days after he keeled over.*

six months hard *n.* a card. (Rhyming slang.) □ *He turned over the six months hard saying, "My game, I think!"* □ *Holding out the fanned-out pack, he asked Otto to pick a six months hard.*

six moon *n.* a prison sentence of six months. □ *I could not take another six moon.* □ *I've only been given a six moon!*

six-to-four *n.* a prostitute. (Crude. Rhyming slang, linked as follows: six-to-four ≈ [whore] = prostitute. SIX-TO-FOUR is a way of expressing racing odds.) □ *A lot of six-to-fours are hooked on something or other.* □ *Joan almost became a six-to-four to pay for a habit.*

sixty-nine 1. *n.* mutual oral sex; the sexual activity known as *soixante-neuf* in France. (Taboo.) □ *If you want to have a sixty-nine you better find another girl, buster!* □ *Fancy a sixty-nine, darling?* **2.** *vb.* to perform mutual oral sex. (Taboo.) □ *I'm serious, I opened the door and there they were, sixty-nining away!* □ *Maya thinks that sixty-nining is revolting.*

sizzler *n.* a steak served on a plate so hot that the meat sizzles while at the table. □ *Sarah served us all sizzlers again. Delicious!* □ *I just love a sizzler. That's the way to serve a steak!*

skag AND **scag** *n.* heroin, especially poor quality heroin; any powerful drug. □ *Just lay off the skag—if you can.* □ *Scag has sent a lot of my friends to the bone orchard.*

skate *vb.* to leave rapidly. □ *I thought I better skate before they discovered I was not supposed to have been there in the first place.* □ *I wish that pest would be good enough to skate and leave me in peace.*

skating rink *n.* a bald head. □ *You'll recognise him because of his skating rink.* □ *I like men with skating rinks.*

skedaddle *vb.* to get out; to leave in a hurry; to flee. □ *Go on, skedaddle! Out!* □ *Well, I'd better skedaddle on home.*

sketch 1. *n.* an amusing sight. □ *The whole exhibition was a total sketch.* □ *What a sketch you are, Frank!* **2.** *n.* a comical or humorous person. □ *I'm sorry but we really don't need another sketch working here.* □ *What's a sketch like that doing around here?*

skew-whiff *mod.* out of alignment. □ *You've hung this door skew-whiff.* □ *I'm afraid a skew-whiff machine like that is quite useless.*

skid-lid *n.* a motorcycle helmet. □ *The law has no business telling me I gotta wear a skid-lid.* □ *Don't you use a skid-lid?*

skid marks *n.* unclean, brownish marks on one's underpants. (Crude.) □ *Just looking at him, you know he's the type who has skid marks and enjoys popping zits.* □ *There is hardly anything a genteel person can say about skid marks that is acceptable in public.*

skim *vb.* to take money illegally; to fail to declare income for tax. □ *Everyone around here is skimming all the time.* □ *He skimmed just a little too deep and the income tax people came down on him like a ton of bricks.*

skin *vb.* to cheat or overcharge someone; to fleece someone, hence to SKIN them. □ *The guy who sold me this car really skinned me.* □ *We skinned him on that stock deal.*

skin and blister *n.* a sister. (Rhyming slang.) □ *Terry's here; he's brought his skin and blister with him.* □ *Can I bring me skin and blister?*

skin flick *n.* a film featuring nudity. (Crude. Compare with NUDDIE.) □ *We took in a skin flick when we were in the city.* □ *Max likes skin flicks better than real girls.*

skinful *n.* enough beer, wine or spirits to induce intoxication. (Compare with HAVE (GOT) A SKINFUL.) □ *He's had a skinful and can't drive.* □ *She knows enough to stop drinking before she gets a skinful.*

skin(head) *n.* a teenage working-class hoodlum with very close-cropped hair or a shaved head. □ *Who's the skin with the earrings?* □ *That skinhead looks stoned.*

skinnamalink AND **skinnymalink** *n.* a thin, skinny person. (Scots usage.) □ *What a skinnamalink Shuggie has become since he took ill.* □ *When people are skinnymalinks like that, they canny be eating right.*

skinny dip 1. *vb. phr.* to swim in the nude. (Crude.) □ *We used to go skinny dipping there when I was a kid.* □ *There was a little stream on the farm where we used to skinny dip.* **2.** *n.* a swim in the nude. (Crude.) □ *A nice skinny dip in a quiet glade takes you back to nature.* □ *Randolph, who fears fish, didn't take a skinny dip with the others.*

skinnymalink See SKINNAMALINK.

skin pop See JOY POP.

skins *n.* drums. (Always plural.) □ *Someone gave Jimmy a set of skins for Christmas. This was a pity.* □ *The soldiers marched off to the beat of the sticks on his skins.*

skint *mod.* completely without money. □ *I was skint by the end of the week, but it was well worth it.* □ *Me? Lend you money? I'm skint!*

skip 1. *vb.* to escape; to jump bail. □ *I'm going to skip now.* □ *He tried to skip but was caught at the gate.* **2.** *n.* a large metal container for rubbish. □ *Someone tried to block the entrance-way with a skip.* □ *You can usually see skips at the foot of these tower blocks.* **3.** *n.* a very old and dilapidated car. □ *My lord, that's a real skip you've got there.* □ *You don't seriously propose to drive that skip on the public highway?*

Skip it! *exclam.* "Forget it!"; "Never mind!" □ *I won't bother you with my question again. Skip it!* □ *Oh, skip it! It doesn't matter.*

skip(per) 1. *n.* an officer commanding an army unit. □ *The skipper has told us to be ready to march by four tomorrow morning.* □ *The skip's been hit by a sniper and I'm in command.* **2.** *n.* the captain of a sporting team. □ *The skipper was pleased with the result.* □ *Unless we do better, there'll be a new skip*

around here. **3.** *n.* the captain of an aircraft. □ *Don't forget, I'm the skipper of this plane and what I say goes.* □ *I don't think the skip will take kindly to your suggested diversion to Cuba, sir.* **4.** *n.* a police sergeant. □ *Can we collar this guy, skipper?* □ *The skip's come over to see what to do.* **5.** *n.* a rough, hidden shelter, suitable for sleeping in. □ *He was pleased with the skipper he'd found.* □ *I just wanted to find a good skip and go to sleep.*

skipper *vb.* to sleep rough. □ *I've been skippering for some time now.* □ *If you don't have a choice, you skipper.*

skippering *n.* sleeping rough. □ *Some people like skippering.* □ *Other people would rather die than end up skippering.*

skirt *n.* a woman. (Crude.) □ *Some skirt comes up to me and asks where the police station is.* □ *Who's the skirt I saw you with last night?*

skit *n.* a large crowd. □ *It was strange that there was such a skit today of all days.* □ *The skit was pressing in towards the stadium and Brian was swept along with them.*

skive *n.* a ploy or ruse to shirk duty or responsibility. □ *Yes, It's a cunning skive, but I don't think it'll work.* □ *Who thought up that skive, Otto?*

skive (off) *vb. (phr.)* to evade or shirk duty or responsibility. □ *Hoy! Where do you think you're skiving off to?* □ *No more skiving. There's work to be done here.*

skiver *n.* someone who avoids duty or responsibility □ *I don't want that skiver on my team.* □ *If you want to be a skiver, go and be one somewhere else.*

skivvy *n.* a female drudge or servant. □ *Why does everybody treat me like a skivvy?* □ *Because you are a skivvy, that's why.*

skoosh *n.* any sort of carbonated soft drink. (Scots usage. Compare with GINGER.) □ *See's a boatle o that skoosh, hen. (Might I have a bottle of that soft drink, miss?)* □ *Give the weans some more skoosh, then.*

skull *n.* a passenger. □ *Fourteen skulls and crew of fifteen? I don't think this is* *a profitable route for a 747.* □ *Driving busses would be great fun if we didn't have to carry skulls.*

skullduggery *n.* deceitful doings; villainy in general. (Originally 18th or 19th century Scots *sculduddery*, meaning "fornication" or "obscenity"; evolved to present spelling and meaning via "misappropriation of funds" in late 19th century US.) □ *There's a lot of skullduggery goes on down at the club; just don't ask any awkward questions.* □ *Without skullduggery, politics wouldn't be interesting.*

skulled *mod.* intoxicated due to drink or drugs. □ *He's too skulled to drive.* □ *He had got himself skulled in less than twenty minutes.*

skull job See HEAD JOB.

skunk 1. *n.* a derivative of cannabis suitable for smoking. □ *He's smoking skunk now.* □ *Once you start on skunk, there's not much hope left.* **2.** *n.* a mean and hateful person. (Compare with STINKER.) □ *What a skunk!* □ *Must you be such a skunk in front of my friends?*

sky-artist *n.* a psychiatrist. (Rhyming slang.) □ *Maybe the sky-artist can help you get sorted out in your head.* □ *Well the sky-artist said he was nuts, but then we already knew that.*

sky hook *n.* a very useful, but unfortunately imaginary, tool. □ *I can't get this thing outa here without a sky hook.* □ *Go get me a sky hook would you, son?*

sky-pilot *n.* a chaplain, especially one working with sailors or military personnel. □ *When Walter was in hospital, the sky-pilot sat with him for hours every day.* □ *The sky-pilot's a good guy.*

sky-rocket *n.* a pocket. (Rhyming slang.) □ *Get yer hand out of yer sky-rocket, son.* □ *Have you any change in your sky-rocket?*

sky's the limit *phr.* "there is no upper limit." (Always with *the*.) □ *I can afford it. The sky's the limit.* □ *You can do anything you set your mind to, Billy. The sky's the limit.*

slabs-pu *n.* confusion; muddle. (Backslang from BALLS-UP.) □ *No more slabs-pus like that, thank you very*

much. □ *The slabs-pus was so bad, we just had to leave.*

slag 1. *n.* a slut; a prostitute. (Crude.) □ *Joan almost became a slag to pay for a habit.* □ *A lot of slags are hooked on something or other.* **2.** *n.* an unimportant or worthless person. (Offensive. Also a term of address.) □ *What a slag you are!* □ *Just get out of my sight, you slag!* **3.** *n.* a tramp. □ *Slags are a serious problem around this part of town.* □ *This is where the slags gather.* **4.** *n.* a petty criminal. □ *Get out, you slag!* □ *I'm not a slag; I'm Mr Big!* **5.** *n.* a coward. □ *If you're a slag, you don't take many risks.* □ *I think that Wally is a slag. That's what's wrong.* **6.** *n.* a layabout; a time-waster. □ *Tell that slag to get himself a job.* □ *I've no time for slags like them.* **7.** *n.* women in general. (Offensive. Always in the plural.) □ *Otto does not really like slags in general.* □ *That woman is just an out-and-out slag!* **8.** *n.* an insulting remark. (Scots usage.) □ *I hear you've been making slags about me to my friends.* □ *I'm not going to stand for a slag like that from a nyaff like him.*

slagging *n.* a severe criticism. □ *Did they really deserve a slagging like that?* □ *You are going to get a terrible slagging after that remark.*

slaggy *mod.* low, in the pejorative sense. □ *Why, you slaggy little tyke!* □ *I don't want anything to do with that sort of slaggy deal.*

slag-name *n.* an insulting nickname. (Scots usage.) □ *His slag-name is Rasputin but really he's just a harmless wee fellow.* □ *You're not really popular at school if you don't have a slag-name.*

slag someone (off) *vb. (phr.)* to slander or criticise someone pejoratively. □ *I do wish you would not slag off people like that.* □ *Otto's always slagging him.*

slammed *mod.* intoxicated due to drink or drugs. □ *The hostess was so slammed she could hardly stand.* □ *He's slammed and spoiling for a fight.*

slammer *n.* a jail. □ *I got out of the slammer on Monday and was back in* *by Wednesday.* □ *The slammer in this town is like a hotel.*

slam someone *vb.* to hit someone hard. □ *Tom slammed Fred on the hooter.* □ *Fred got slammed, and that really made him angry.*

slanging match *n.* an extended and loud exchange of insults. □ *There was a great, long, loud slanging match next door.* □ *Now let's not have another slanging match, please.*

slant *n.* a biased point of view; a unique, unusual or unexpected perception. □ *You will probably give us yet another slant on this problem, I suppose.* □ *He provided us with a fresh slant on this question.*

slant(y) *n.* an oriental person, especially one who is Japanese or Chinese. (Racially offensive.) □ *Y'know, Otto, if you call a Chinaman a slanty, he's likely to get nasty.* □ *Why can you not be polite to slants?*

slap and tickle *n.* good-humored mild sexual banter or teasing. □ *Stop your slap and tickle, Albert Tamworth!* □ *Well, the slap and tickle led on and now the baby's due next month.*

slap-dash AND **slap-happy** *mod.* fast and careless. □ *I wish you hadn't done it in such a slap-dash fashion.* □ *This is a very slap-happy way to do something.*

slap-happy 1. *mod.* boisterously or recklessly happy. □ *I get slap-happy when I have anything to drink with alcohol in it.* □ *She's a little slap-happy, but a tremendous dear.* **2.** See also SLAP-DASH; PUNCH-DRUNK.

slap in the face *n.* an insult; a rejection. □ *That remark was a real slap in the face.* □ *Her departure was a slap in the face to the manager who had refused to give her a raise.*

slapper *n.* a prostitute. (Crude.) □ *The Old Bill hauled her in because she looked like a slapper.* □ *Clare dresses like a slapper.*

slap someone on the wrist See SLAP SOMEONE'S WRIST.

slap someone's wrist AND **slap someone on the wrist** *vb. phr.* to administer a minor reprimand. □ *The judge only*

slapped her wrist. □ *These days the courts just slaps them on the wrist and sends them back out on the streets.*

slap-up 1. *mod.* [of a meal] first-rate or lavish. □ *What a slap-up meal that was.* □ *You always get a slap-up dinner from Mary.* **2.** *mod.* lavish; extravagant. □ *They're planning a really slap-up do for Donna's retirement.* □ *Well, that was a slap-up meal!*

slash *n.* an act of urination. (Crude.) □ *I'm just going to have a slash.* □ *He went out to take a slash.*

slate someone for something *vb.* to assign someone to a task. □ *I've slated Stuart for the Lonnock job.* □ *Who do you think we should slate for that one?*

slate someone off *vb. phr.* to disparage someone. □ *Don't just slate him off! He's right!* □ *To slate off people all the time is not a good way to be popular with the folks closest to you.*

slating *n.* a strong reprimand. □ *What was that slating for?* □ *You're just asking for a slating.*

slaughter 1. *vb.* to entirely defeat someone or a team. □ *What a game! We really slaughtered the other side!* □ *Bill is out to slaughter the other people bidding for that contract.* **2.** *n.* a wholesale dismissal of employees. □ *There's been a slaughter at the factory; hundreds have been sacked.* □ *If we don't get that contract, we can't keep the workforce. There would have to be a slaughter.* **3.** *n.* a hideout where criminals go to divide up, pass on, sell or otherwise dispose of the proceeds of their nefarious activities. □ *You'll find Willy in his slaughter, so long as you know where it is!* □ *No, I don't know where his slaughter is.* **4.** See also MURDER.

slay *vb.* to overwhelm someone with one's performance or other excellence. □ *These jokes always slay the audience.* □ *Oh, you slay me with your silly remarks.*

sleaze *n.* a low and despicable person. □ *God, what a sleaze! How can anybody be so repellent?* □ *You'd expect to find a sleaze like that in a sleazy joint like this.*

sleazebag AND **sleazeball; sleaze-bucket** *n.* a repellent person or place. □ *I don't want anything to do with a sleazebag like that.* □ *Who is the sleaze-bucket leaning against the wall?*

sleazeball See SLEAZEBAG.

sleaze-bucket See SLEAZEBAG.

sleazy 1. *mod.* delapidated; inferior; slatternly. □ *The place is so sleazy; I don't want to go back.* □ *I don't understand why you always want to go to such sleazy clubs.* **2.** *mod.* garish; tawdry. □ *What a sleazy little outfit this is.* □ *I'm sorry but I think your entire exhibition is really sleazy, since you ask.*

sleep around *vb. phr.* to behave promiscuously. (Crude.) □ *Sleeping around used to be a good way to destroy a girl's reputation; now it seems to make her reputation if some people are to be believed.* □ *That tramp is always willing to sleep around.*

sleeper *n.* someone or something that achieves fame or other forms of success after having failed to achieve good results for some time. □ *The film "Red Willow" was undoubtedly the sleeper of the year, winning six awards.* □ *My candidate had been a sleeper for ages, but he finally began to pull ahead in the polls.*

sleeping policeman *n.* a ramp or hump placed across a road to slow down traffic. □ *They say sleeping policemen makes traffic safer.* □ *Well maybe, but a sleeping policeman doesn't do your car any good.*

slice of the action See PIECE (OF THE ACTION).

slick 1. *mod.* clever; glib. □ *He is a slick operator.* □ *His talk is slick, but his action is zilch.* **2.** *mod.* excellent. □ *This is a really slick setup you've got here.* □ *That's a slick idea.* **3.** *n.* a smooth tyre used in motor racing. □ *That set of wheels has slicks. I wonder why.* □ *I have some slicks at home in the garage.*

slider *n.* a wafer of ice cream. (Scots usage.) □ *Ma mammy bought aw us weans sliders frae the tally doon the street. (My mother bought all of us children ice-cream wafers from the Italian cafe along the street.)* □ *Sliders is dead good on hot days. (Ice-cream wafers are very acceptable on hot days.)*

slightly rattled *mod.* somewhat upset or confused. □ *Tom was slightly rattled by the trouble at the door.* □ *I'm slightly rattled. I'll get over it.*

slime 1. *n.* a worthless person; a low and wretched person. □ *What a slime that guy is!* □ *Who is the slime over there with the greasy hair?* **2.** *vb.* to behave in an unpleasantly devious or ingratiating manner. □ *Do you have to slime all the time?* □ *Just cut out your disgusting sliming, thank you!*

slime bag AND **slime bucket; slime-bag; slimeball** *n.* a despicable person, usually male. □ *To think, a slime bag like that in the same room with me! Yuck!* □ *Who's the slime bucket in the naff car?*

slimeball See SLIME BAG.

slime bucket See SLIME BAG.

sling one's drizzle *vb. phr.* to urinate. (Crude.) □ *I'm just going to sling my drizzle.* □ *Don't sling your drizzle on the floor.*

sling one's hook *vb. phr.* to go away; to depart. □ *Look, why don't you just sling your hook?* □ *You know, I told him to sling his hook and he did!*

Sling yer hook! *exclam.* "Go away!"; "Get lost!" □ *Sling yer hook!* □ *Sling yer hook! We don't want your like here!*

slinky 1. *mod.* sneaky; sly; furtive. □ *That was very slinky. How did you do it?* □ *Well, you're a slinky one!* **2.** *mod.* smooth; sensuous; clinging. □ *What a lovely slinky dress you are wearing this evening, Mary.* □ *Just feel the slinky texture of this material.*

slip in the gutter *n.* bread and butter. (Rhyming slang, linked as follows: slip in the gutter ≈ [butter] = bread and butter.) □ *She gave me a few slices of slip in the gutter.* □ *I'd rather like some slip in the gutter.*

slip it to someone *vb. phr.* to perform sexual intercourse, from the male perspective. (Taboo.) □ *I'm hoping to slip it to her tonight.* □ *You'll get to slip it to Fiona, the girl who can't say no.*

slip one's trolley *vb. phr.* to go insane; to lose one's self-control. □ *I'll slip my trolley if I have to take much more of this.* □ *Aunt May's already slipped her trolley, I think.*

slip someone a fatty See SLIP SOMEONE A LENGTH.

slip someone a length AND **slip someone a fatty** *vb. phr.* to perform sexual intercourse upon another, from the male perspective. (Taboo.) □ *Let's find somewhere quiet and I'll slip you a length.* □ *Want to slip me your fatty?*

slip (someone) up *vb. phr.* to cause a girl to become pregnant by accident. (Taboo.) □ *When her brother found out I'd slipped Sophia up, I had to run!* □ *If you slip my sister up I'll kill you.*

slip (up) *vb. (phr.)* to make an error. □ *Don't slip up and pay this bill twice, please.* □ *I slipped and gave the guy a 35 percent tip.*

slip(-up) *n.* an accident or error. □ *That was a silly slip-up. I'm sorry.* □ *That slip cost us nearly £2,000 and its coming out of your pay.*

slit *n.* the female sexual organ. (Taboo.) □ *What do you mean, you can see my slit? Oh my god, I've forgotten my knickers!* □ *They dance completely nude in there, with their slits and everything on view.*

Sloane Ranger AND **Sloanie** *n.* an upper-class, non-intellectual, conventional, fashion-obsessed, wealthy, green welly-wearing young person, especially in and around London. (An amalgam of "Sloane" Square—a fashionable area in London—with the Lone "Ranger" of Western TV series fame. Leading members of the group have included the Duchess of York and the Princess of Wales.) □ *Even a Sloane Ranger like that has to earn a living. No they don't actually.* □ *What does a Sloanie want in a place like this?*

Sloanie See SLOANE RANGER.

slob 1. *n.* a rude, fat, dim-witted and unpleasant person. □ *What a slob! Comb your hair, if you can get a comb through it!* □ *Why doesn't that slob go on a diet or something? Anything!* **2.** *n.* a fat, lazy, simple-minded child. (Irish usage.) □ *How many slobs do you have here now?* □ *We could see the slob was playing in the garden.*

slog *n.* an extended spell of hard work. □ *Look, I know it's a slog, but it just has to be done.* □ *Once the slog is over, you'll enjoy things here more.*

slop AND **esclop** *n.* the police. (Backslang.) □ *Get away, get away! The slop are outside!* □ *The esclop are after me!*

slopperati *n.* a class of prosperous young people who flaunt a SLOPPY appearance. □ *Some of these people are not derelicts, Cynthia, but members of the slopperati.* □ *"Why do the slopperati do it? I don't understand their thinking." "What thinking?"*

sloppy *mod.* negligent; careless. □ *This is a very sloppy way to do something.* □ *I wish you hadn't done it in such a sloppy fashion.*

slops *n.* beer. □ *Well, Tom certainly has plenty of slops at his bash tonight.* □ *Yes, they have pretty reasonable slops in this pub.*

slosh *n.* sentimental nonsense. □ *That's just a lot of slosh.* □ *Don't give me that slosh! I won't buy it.*

sloshed *mod.* intoxicated due to drink. □ *Boy, is he sloshed!* □ *He's already as sloshed as they come.*

slosh someone *vb.* to hit someone hard. □ *Harry sloshed him one right on the jaw.* □ *I got heavily sloshed by Harry yesterday.*

slot *n.* the female sexual organ. (Taboo.) □ *The door to the shower room flew open and the girl screamed, trying to cover her slot.* □ *If your dresses get any shorter, we'll all be able to see your slot.*

slotted job *n.* a woman. (Taboo.) □ *Who's that slotted job sitting over there?* □ *So the new slotted job looked me in the eye and told me to sod off.*

sloughed *mod.* dead. (A hospital euphemism.) □ *Another sloughed one just came in.* □ *That's three sloughed customers already tonight.*

slow off the mark 1. *mod.* slow starting or reacting. (Compare with QUICK OFF THE MARK.) □ *If you are always that slow off the mark you will never get* *there in time.* □ *Boy, you were slow off the mark there!* **2.** *mod.* slow-witted. □ *The guy's slow off the mark, but very friendly.* □ *Yes, I'm afraid Tony is a bit slow off the mark when it comes to maths.*

slubber *vb.* to stain or spoil something. □ *Don't you dare slubber my best table-cloth!* □ *Oh no! Someone has slubbered all over these things.*

slug it out *vb. phr.* to fight something out; to endure something until success-ful. □ *They finally went outside to slug it out.* □ *We'll just have to sit down in the conference room and slug it out.*

sluice 1. *n.* the female sexual organ. (Taboo.) □ *Get your hand off my sluice, Sunshine!* □ *Who do think you are, going for my sluice like that?* **2.** *n.* sexual intercourse. (Taboo.) □ *They were talking about, you know, sluice.* □ *After the sluice, she felt cheap.*

Slump Alley See QUEER STREET.

slurp *vb.* to eat or drink in a noisy and messy manner. □ *Do you have to slurp in that disgusting manner.* □ *Look at the way he slurps!*

slush 1. *n.* counterfeit banknotes. □ *The police have been warning of a rash of slush in this area, so watch out.* □ *She held the note up to the light and said, "If you want to pass slush you'll have to make better forgeries than that!"* **2.** *n.* unsolicited manuscripts received by book publishers. □ *Every day, more slush arrived. Mostly, it was badly written and very depressing.* □ *Her job was to read slush.* **3.** *n.* unsolicited tapes received by record publishers. □ *He looked at all the tapes of slush and thought, "I've got to listen to all of them."* □ *Once in every while in among the slush there was a musical gem.*

slusher *n.* a counterfeiter. □ *Out there, some slusher is making a lot of very good fake coins.* □ *The police picked up a slusher tonight.*

slush fund *n.* a secret fund of money that can be used for various unofficial or illegal purposes. □ *How much is left in the slush fund?* □ *The slush fund is empty.*

slushy *mod.* cloyingly sentimental. □ *Harry always laughs at slushy rubbish in a film.* □ *The love scenes were real out-and-out slushy, but nobody laughed.*

smack *n.* heroin. □ *I spent the after-noon shooting smack.* □ *You can get some good smack in this part of town.*

smack-bang in the middle *mod.* exact-ly in the middle. □ *I arrived smack-bang in the middle of the play.* □ *Not too big and not too small. Just smack-bang in the middle.*

smacker 1. *n.* a loud or dramatic kiss. □ *He planted a smacker square on her lips. She kicked him in the shins for his trouble.* □ *Barlowe was greeted at the door by a lovely, cuddly bird in a night-ie—eyes closed and lips parted for a better than average smacker. He really wished—just for a moment—that he hadn't rung the wrong doorbell.* **2.** *n.* one Pound Sterling; formerly, a pound note. □ *There's a thousand smackers in this for you. But do it now!* □ *Frank opened the suitcase and we all stared at the contents. "Yes," he said, break-ing the silence, "That's what a million smackers looks like."*

smack-head *n.* a heroin addict. □ *The place was crawling with smack-heads.* □ *The two of them are real smack-heads now, you know.*

smack on See BANG ON.

small ad *n.* a classified advertisement. (Compare with SMALLS.) □ *Mike placed a small ad for his old wardrobe among the smalls in the newspaper.* □ *Joan read the small ad and thought it sound-ed just like the sort of furniture she was looking for.*

small beer *n.* nothing or next to noth-ing; an insignificant person. □ *He's just small beer. Pay him no mind.* □ *Small beer or not, he's my customer, and I will see that he is taken care of.*

small bundle *n.* a new-born baby. □ *When your small bundle arrives, things will be a little hectic for a while.* □ *We are expecting a small bundle next September.*

small change *n.* an insignificant issue. □ *Oh, that's just small change. We can* deal with it later. □ *You may think it's small change; I happen to know it's the most important point of all.*

small fortune *n.* a rather sizeable amount of money. □ *This set of wheels cost me a small fortune.* □ *I've got a small fortune tied up in test equipment.*

small fry AND **small potatoes** *n.* anything or anyone small or unimportant. (*Fry* are juvenile fish.) □ *Forget the small fry. I'm going after Mr Big.* □ *This contract is small potatoes, but it'll keep us in business till we get into the real money.* □ *Don't worry about the small fry. It's the fat cats you've got to please!*

small potatoes See SMALL FRY.

small print See FINE PRINT.

smalls 1. *n.* small items of underclothing. □ *I spent the evening washing my smalls.* □ *She looked out the smalls she wanted to wear that evening and left.* **2.** *n.* classified advertisements. (Compare with SMALL AD.) □ *You can find all sorts of interesting products and services for sale when you read the smalls.* □ *Mike placed a small ad for his old wardrobe among the other smalls in the newspaper.*

small-time *mod.* insignificant; petty. □ *I was into a lot of small-time stuff at home, but never a West End hit before.* □ *The West End is not small-time.* □ *Max was already involved in a lot of small-time crime by the time he was twelve.*

smarm *vb.* to behave in an insincere, obsequious or toadying manner. □ *He always smarms when he wants something. Do you have to smarm like that all the time?*

smarmy *mod.* insincerely obsequious; toadying. □ *He's obnoxious certainly, but brazen rather than smarmy.* □ *He's a smarmy creep.* □ *The guy is so smarmy, I can't stand him.*

smart Alec AND **smarty; smarty-pants; smart-arse** *n.* a know-all; someone who flaunts their knowledge; a smugly clever person. (ARSE is taboo.) □ *A smart Alec like you ought to have no trouble at all getting his face smashed in.* □ *Don't be such a smarty-pants if you know what's good for you.*

smart-arse See SMART ALEC.

smartish *mod.* rapidly. □ *Move smartish please; we don't have all day!* □ *Mike was in the pub right smartish as soon as the doors opened.*

smarts *n.* intelligence. □ *She's got plenty of smarts but no spunk.* □ *I've got the smarts to do the job. All I need is someone to trust me.*

smarty See SMART ALEC.

smarty-pants See SMART ALEC.

smash-and-grab raid *n.* a robbery where the thief smashes a store window and grabs what is displayed there. □ *Traditionally, smash-and-grab raids are done to jeweller's shops.* □ *There was a smash-and-grab raid at the jewellers in the High Street.*

smashed *mod.* intoxicated due to drink or drugs. □ *He was so smashed he couldn't stand up.* □ *Tracy can drink a lot without ever getting smashed.*

smasher *n.* a good-looking or attractive girl or young woman. □ *What a smasher! I want that one.* □ *I like the smasher you were with last night.*

smash hit *n.* a play, movie, musical, etc., which is a big success. □ *Her first book was a smash hit. The second was a disaster.* □ *A smash hit doesn't always make people rich.*

smashing 1. *n.* beautiful or attractive, especially of a girl or woman. □ *Joanne looked really smashing in her wedding dress.* □ *What a smashing girl that is.* **2.** *n.* exactly suitable. □ *That's smashing. It's just ideal.* □ *What a smashing answer to that problem!* **3.** *mod.* excellent; really tremendous. □ *We had a smashing time at your little do.* □ *This whole meal has been smashing.*

smell a rat *vb. phr.* to suspect or sense that something is wrong. □ *He smelt a rat the minute he came into the room.* □ *Keep everything normal. I don't want her to smell a rat. She has never had a surprise party before.*

smell fishy *vb. phr.* to seem suspicious. (Compare with FISHY.) □ *Barlowe squinted a bit. Something smells fishy here, he thought.* □ *Something about the deal smelt fishy.*

smell like a rose *vb. phr.* to seem innocent. □ *I came out of the whole mess smelling like a rose, even though I caused all the trouble.* □ *Tiffany pretended that she was the only one who should smell like a rose, but I knew different.*

smidgen *n.* a tiny bit or portion. □ *I just want a smidgen of cake. I'm on a diet.* □ *Oh, come on, more than a smidgen. Just a little?*

Smiley *n.* a circular, smiling yellow face. (The face appears in many forms, stick-on labels, pin-on buttons, hand-drawn, etc. It is possible to recreate the smiling face on any keyboard through the use of the punctuation symbols, as with :) or :-). All computer Smileys and their variants appear sideways. A major variant is the *Unsmiley,* which is basically :(or :-(. The following faces are a sample of the variants that can be seen in computer bulletin board messages and informal typewritten or word processed notes. This type of symbol is called an EMOTICON because it is intended to show "emotion" in what is otherwise a rather cold medium of communication. The typical use is to show that the writer is just joking or writing in good, well-intentioned spirits. The following Smileys are separated by slashes, and an equal sign separates the actual Smiley from its explanation.) :-] = Squarejaw Smiley / :-o = Singing Smiley; Shocked Smiley; Surprised Smiley / :-(= Sad Smiley / :-) = Happy Smiley / :-=) = Smiley with a Big Moustache / :-)' = Drooling Smiley; Smoking Smiley / :-)8 = Smiley Wearing a Bow Tie / :-D = Bigmouth Smiley / :-# = Smiley with Sealed Lips / :-" = Pursed-lips Smiley; Shocked Smiley / :-s = Twisted-mouth Smiley (after hearing or saying something strange) / :-" = Smiley with Walrus Moustache / :-| = Smiley Making Dull Response; "Have-a-dull-day" Smiley / :-> Wry-faced Smiley / :-0 = Loudmouth Smiley; Big-mouth Smiley / :-x = Sealed-lips Smiley / :-Q = Smoking Smiley; Drooling Smiley / :> = Midget Smiley / ;-) = Winking Smiley / (-) = Smiley Needing a Haircut / ":-) Smiley with its Hair Parted in the Middle / :-) Smiley Priest / "-(= Smiley Cyclops, Poked in the Eye / ":o) Bozo Smiley / <:I = Dunce Smiley / #-) = Cyclops Smiley / #:I = Smiley Wearing a Turban / |-) = Gleeful Smiley / |-| = Sleeping Smiley; Bored Smiley / 0-) = Smiley Wearing a Scuba Mask / 8-) = Smiley in Glasses / 8:-) A Smiley with Glasses on its Forehead / B-) = Smiley Wearing Horn-rim Glasses / o-) = Cyclops Smiley / [:-) = Smiley Happily Listening to a Walkman / [:|] = Robot Smiley; Squarejaw Smiley Listening to a Walkman.

smithereens *n.* many tiny pieces or splinters. □ *The mirror was broken to smithereens.* □ *I broke my crystal ball into smithereens.*

smitten *mod.* infatuated. □ *Mark is really smitten with Lavinia.* □ *Unfortunately Lavinia is anything but smitten by Mark.*

smoke *n.* a cigarette; a pipe; a cigar. □ *I think I'll have a smoke now.* □ *Have you got a smoke I can owe you?*

Smoke See BIG SMOKE.

smoked haddock *n.* the paddock of a racecourse. (Rhyming slang. Always with *the.*) □ *I can't see no horses in the smoked haddock, Bert.* □ *That's cause that's not the smoked haddock, you clown.*

smoke like a chimney *vb. phr.* to smoke very heavily and at every opportunity. □ *My uncle smoked like a chimney when he was living.* □ *Anybody who smokes like a chimney in a restaurant ought to be thrown out.*

smoker *n.* a high-mileage car. □ *Is this old smoker yours?* □ *I've got to get my smoker fixed up.*

smoking gun *n.* direct, indisputable, obvious and incriminating evidence. □ *Mr South was left holding the smoking gun.* □ *The chief of staff decided that the Admiral should be found with the smoking gun.*

smooch *vb.* to kiss and cuddle in an amorous manner. □ *Too much smooching in a film ruins it for me.* □ *I like to smooch myself, but I don't enjoy watching somebody else.*

smooth-faced *mod.* falsely friendly. □ *Watch that smooth-faced creep! □ He's a smooth-faced one, isn't he?*

smoothie See SMOOTH OPERATOR.

smooth move *n.* a clever or well-thought-out action or piece of work. □ *Hey, that was a smooth move! How did you come up with that one! □ A few more smooth moves like that and you've got it made!*

smooth operator 1. AND **smooth talker; smoothie** *n.* a clever, suave, flattering and unruffled person, especially in reference to romantic involvement. □ *Clare is an old smoothie till she thinks she's got everything the way she wants. Then you see the real Clare. □ Harry is a really smooth operator. He has the girls eating out of his hand.* **2.** AND **smoothie** *n.* a plausible but untrustworthy character. □ *He was a really smooth operator. He talked old Mrs Jones out of £5,000 before anyone caught on. □ What a smoothie! Every night he has a different girl!*

smooth talker See SMOOTH OPERATOR.

smudge *n.* pornographic photographs; magazines containing these. (Crude.) □ *Otto has a large collection of really strong smudge. □ They keep the smudge on the top shelf.*

smudger *n.* a friend. □ *This is my smudger, Wally. □ We've been smudgers for years. Went to school together.*

snake bite *n.* a drink consisting of cider and lager in equal portions. □ *You know how snake bite disagrees with you, my dear. □ I often enjoy a snake bite in the evening.*

Snap! *exclam.* "That's a coincidence!" (From the children's card game of this name.) □ *Snap! What a coincidence meeting you here now! □ When the twins met for the first time since childhood some clown called out, "Snap!"*

snap 1. *vb.* to go crazy. □ *Suddenly Rocko snapped and began beating her savagely. □ His mind snapped, and he's never been right since.* **2.** *n.* a snack. □ *I wonder if I could have a snap? □ Can I offer you a snap before you go?*

Snap out of it! *exclam.* "Wake up!"; "Realise what's really happening!" □ *Come on, snap out of it! We need your attention over here. □ Snap out of it, Paul. Can't you see how they're ripping you off?*

snap out of something *vb. phr.* to recover from something. □ *I'll snap out of it in a while. □ It was an emotional blow, but he'll snap out of it soon.*

snappin *n.* packed food. (North of England usage.) □ *All she ever buys is snappin. □ Snappin food is expensive.*

snappy AND **snippy 1.** *mod.* quick-witted; intelligent. □ *You're certainly full of snappy answers today, Mary. □ Bright? Oh yes, she's snippy all right.* **2.** *mod.* smartly-dressed. □ *That's a really snappy outfit you're wearing. □ You'll know her right away. She's the one who's the snippy dresser.* **3.** *mod.* irritable; sharp-tongued. □ *Just take care what you say to her. She's really snappy today. □ Come on Harry! Don't be so snippy all the time.*

snap something up *vb. phr.* to buy up something. □ *People were snapping these things up like hot cakes. □ The customers snapped up all the air-conditioners on the second day of the heat wave.*

snare *vb.* to win something; to steal something; to acquire something. □ *What did you manage to snare for us today? □ Would you be good enough to go back out and snare some food, as it will soon be time to eat.*

snatch 1. *n.* a rapidly-completed act of sexual intercourse. (Taboo.) □ *It was really just a snatch, and not very satisfying. □ Even a snatch would be welcome just now, he thought.* **2.** *n.* the female sexual organ. (Taboo.) □ *They dance completely nude in there, with snatch and everything on view. □ A woman who shows her snatch is just the lowest.* **3.** *n.* a woman viewed as a sex object. (Taboo.) □ *Look at the snatch in this place, Martin! □ This particular snatch with break your fingers if you touch her again. Is that clear, you creep?*

snazzy *mod.* elegant; classy. □ *This is a snazzy place all right. □ This place is really snazzy. □ Whose snazzy new car is this?*

sneak *n.* an informer. □ *No matter how useful his information, a sneak makes no friends in either camp.* □ *Fred is a sneak. He told the teacher.*

sneaky *mod.* unfair and sly. □ *That was a sneaky thing to do!* □ *Jerry is sneaky. Don't trust him.*

snibley *n.* sexual intercourse. (Taboo.) □ *A good bit of snibley would probably do her the power of good, in fact.* □ *I think really, she's gasping for some snibley, you know.*

snide 1. *mod.* unacceptable; inferior in quality. □ *Sorry, it's too snide for me.* □ *That sort of behaviour is just snide, you know.* **2.** *mod.* counterfeit; dishonest; illegal; stolen. □ *All right Harry, where did this snide stuff come from?* □ *We found a huge stock of snide coins.*

snide remark *n.* a caustic, haughty or insulting remark. □ *You're really quick with the snide remarks. Ever say anything nice to anybody?* □ *I did not appreciate that snide remark.*

sniff 1. *vb.* to inhale fumes from such substances as glue, for the intoxicating effect. □ *The police came around the corner and found three twelve-year-olds, absorbed in sniffing.* □ *"Well I'm sorry, but Johnny has sniffed himself into an early grave," said the doctor.* **2.** *n.* a male desire for sexual relations with a woman. (Crude.) □ *He's been away for two years and has more sniff than you would know how to handle, Mavis.* □ *I like a man with plenty of sniff.* **3.** *vb.* to drink spirits. □ *He's been sniffing gin since early morning.* □ *Actually, he's been sniffing the stuff since 1943.*

sniffer 1. *n.* a woman viewed as a sex object. (Taboo.) □ *Now there's a nice sniffer walking down the street.* □ *So this sniffer I'd been eyeing up came right over to me and said, "It's £20 if you want a short time."* **2.** *n.* a man who persistently attempts to establish a sexual relationship with any convenient woman. (Crude.) □ *Watch out girls, the sniffer's back.* □ *I suppose sniffers are rather sad, really.*

sniffles *n.* a runny nose caused by a cold in the head. (Always with *the*.) □ *I've got the sniffles today, I'm afraid.* □ *If you've got the sniffles, go home. We don't all want them!*

snifter *n.* a small measure of spirits. □ *Fancy a snifter?* □ *Don't mind if I do have a snifter.*

snig *n.* a policeman. (Childish.) □ *The snigs are here looking for you again, Joe.* □ *What have you been doing to interest that snig this time?*

snip 1. *n.* a bargain. □ *They'd be a snip at twice the price.* □ *£50? That's not what I'd call a snip!* **2.** *n.* a good racing tip. □ *I've got a great snip here.* □ *None of your snips are ever of any use, Charlie.*

snipcock *n.* a Jewish person. (Offensive. The reference to circumcision is obvious.) □ *He said he was not a racist, he just hated this particular snipcock!* □ *Don't call Jewish people snipcocks, please. It is very offensive and racist.*

snipe *n.* an ambush by a sniper. (Irish usage. Called this by the Provisional IRA, of such events organised by themselves.) □ *They killed two in a snipe last night.* □ *There used to be a lot of snipes around this part of the county.*

snippy See SNAPPY.

snips *n.* a pair of scissors. □ *She cut up the paper with her snips.* □ *Where are my snips? I can't make this dress without them.*

snit 1. *n.* an unpleasant or devious person. (Offensive. Also a term of address.) □ *Get out of here, you snit!* □ *What a snit that woman can be.* **2.** *n.* a tantrum or bout of agitated irritation. (Normally with *the*, normally in the plural.) □ *She exposed us to a terrible dose of the snits.* □ *If she wants to have the snits, count me out.*

snitch 1. *n.* a nose. □ *He scratched the side of his snitch and smiled.* □ *Jack's easy to recognise. He's the one with the big, red snitch.* **2.** *n.* an informer. (From SNITCH, meaning "nose.") □ *Who needs a snitch? If he can't keep his mouth shut, he can shove off.* □ *The snitch went and told the teacher.* **3.** *vb.* to inform (on someone). (Often with *on*.) □ *The cops were waiting for us. Who* *snitched?* □ *Tracy snitched on Bruno, and he nearly snuffed her.* **4.** *vb.* to steal. □ *Someone snitched Harry's wallet while he was in that restaurant.* □ *He's good at snitching your ideas without you noticing it, so take care what you tell him.*

snitcher 1. *n.* a thief. □ *Some snitcher took Harry's wallet while he was in that restaurant.* □ *He's s snitcher of other people's ideas, so take care what you tell him.* **2.** *n.* an informer. (Originally underworld.) □ *There's nothing worse than a snitcher.* □ *Clare is a snitcher. Watch what you say around her.*

snitch someone *vb.* to arrest someone. □ *The police have snitched the person who stole Harry's wallet.* □ *If you do that again, I'll snitch you!*

snog 1. *vb.* to kiss and caress in an amorous way. □ *Let's go somewhere quiet and snog.* □ *There are some teenagers in the back room, snogging.* **2.** *vb.* to flirt. □ *Those two have been snogging like that for months.* □ *She only wants to snog with me.*

snood-hood AND **willie-warmer** *n.* a knitted woolen cover for the male sexual parts (Crude.) □ *Are you really supposed to wear this snood-hood?* □ *She gave him a willie-warmer for his birthday.*

snooker *vb.* to prevent a continuation; to thwart. (From the game of snooker, where the purpose is to do this to one's opponent.) □ *It seems my entire career has been snookered.* □ *Why are you trying to snooker this development?*

snooks AND **snookums** *n.* a nickname for a child or a pet such as a lap-dog. (Also a term of address.) □ *Now, now, snooks, it's all right.* □ *Does my little snookums want to play?*

snookums See SNOOKS.

snoop (around) *vb.* *(phr.)* to pry; to go around in a sly manner. □ *What are you snooping here for?* □ *Somebody was here snooping around and asking questions about you.*

snooper *n.* someone who snoops. □ *Don't be a snooper.* □ *Fred is such a snooper. I'm sure he went through my desk!*

snoot *n.* a nose. (Variant of SNOUT.) □ *Do you want to get yourself thumped on the snoot?* □ *That's a fine zit you've got yourself on your snoot.*

snooty AND **snottie; snotty** *mod.* haughty; supercilious. □ *Don't be so snooty!* □ *What a snooty waiter!* □ *Tiffany can be snottie if she wants to, and she usually wants to.*

snooze 1. *n.* a sleep, especially a little nap. □ *I need a little snooze.* □ *Why not go up and take a little snooze?* **2.** *vb.* to sleep; to take a little nap. □ *You can't snooze every afternoon!* □ *I snoozed a little bit before the party.*

snort 1. *vb.* to sniff (insufflate) a powdered drug, now usually cocaine. □ *Here, snort this.* □ *You're snorting every time I see you.* **2.** *n.* a nasal dose of a drug, usually cocaine. □ *Here, take a snort.* □ *I don't want a snort. I'm clean, and I'm going to stay that way.* **3.** *n.* a short drink of spirits. □ *I'd not say no to a snort, y'know.* □ *Here, have a snort of this stuff.*

snot 1. *n.* a nasty person; an obnoxious person. □ *You needn't be such a snot about it.* □ *What a snot!* **2.** *n.* nasal mucus, (Crude.) □ *Oh, God, there's snot on your cheek.* □ *He sneezed and got snot all over the newspaper.*

snotrag *n.* a handkerchief. (Crude.) □ *I suppose I should use my snotrag.* □ *Don't you carry a snotrag?*

snotty 1. *mod.* foul with nasal mucus. (Crude.) □ *Keep your snotty old handkerchief to yourself, thank you very much!* □ *Don't leave your snotty tissues all over the house!* **2.** *n.* a midshipman. □ *A snotty is the lowest officer's rank in the navy.* □ *Well, to be more accurate, a snotty is half-cadet, half-officer.* **3.** See also SNOOTY.

snout 1. *n.* a cigarette; tobacco. (Prison slang.) □ *Prisoners are always desperate for snout.* □ *Any snout, mate?* **2.** *n.* a police informer. (Criminal's slang.) □ *Otto a snout? Come on!* □ *He is a snout, y'know.* **3.** *n.* a detective. (Scots usage.) □ *Yon snout is always out to get me.* □ *Watch that one; he's a snout all right.* **4.** *vb.* to discover or reveal something. □ *You take delight in snouting* *people's embarrassing secrets, don't you?* □ *Why did you have to snout that?*

snouter *n.* a tobacconist's shop. □ *My aunt used to have a snouter, but it's closed now.* □ *Is there a snouter around here?*

snow 1. *vb.* to attempt to deceive someone. □ *Don't try to snow me!* □ *You can try to snow me if you want, but I'm onto your tricks.* **2.** AND **Lady Snow** *n.* a powdered or crystalline narcotic: morphine, heroin or cocaine. (Now almost always the latter.) □ *Now, snow is almost old-fashioned.* □ *The price of Lady Snow has come down a lot as South America exports more of it.*

snowball 1. *vb.* to grow at an increasing rate. (As a snowball rolling down a hill might increase in size.) □ *The problem began to snowball, and we had to close down for a while.* □ *Offers to help with money and prayers began to snowball, and we had to get volunteers to help answer the phones.* **2.** *n.* a black person. (Racially offensive. Ironic.) □ *Although I've spoken to Terry many times on the phone, I never knew he was a snowball.* □ *So these two snowballs came into the shop and asked for Walter.*

snowball's chance in hell *n.* a very small chance indeed. (Crude. Usually employed in the negative.) □ *She doesn't have a snowball's chance in hell of getting it done on time.* □ *I know I don't have a snowball's chance in hell, but I'll try anyway.*

snow bunny *n.* the young female companion of a male skier. □ *Some cute little snow bunny came over and sat beside me.* □ *This resort is swarming with snow bunnies who have never even seen a ski.*

snowdrop *vb.* to steal clothes, often from a clothes line. □ *Clearly someone is snowdropping around here.* □ *Why should anyone want to snowdrop?*

snowed under *mod.* over-worked; exceptionally busy. □ *Look, I'm really snowed under at the moment. Can this wait?* □ *He really has been snowed under with work.*

snow job 1. *n.* a deception; a cover-up. □ *No snow jobs; just the plain truth, OK?* □ *That whole report was nothing more than a snow job.* **2.** *n.* insincere charm; flattery. □ *If it's a snow job you want, Harry'll give you one like you've never seen.* □ *Look, cut out the snow job and give me the raw facts.*

snuffer *n.* a veterinary surgeon. □ *Is there a decent snuffer for my dog in this town?* □ *We need a snuffer now. This is a really sick cat.*

snuff film *n.* a film in which someone is really killed. □ *Who would watch a snuff film anyway?* □ *Some of these snuff films have a loyal following of real sickies.*

snuff (it) *vb.* *(phr.)* to die. □ *The dog leapt straight up in the air and snuffed it.* □ *I was so sick they thought I was going to snuff.*

soak 1. *n.* a drunkard. □ *Some old soak lay moaning in the gutter.* □ *Hank is getting to be a real soak.* **2.** *vb.* to overcharge someone; to extort large sums of money from someone. □ *They soaked me for twenty pounds for the parts, but at least it runs now. For the moment.* □ *The cleaners soaked me for the cleaning job.*

soak(ing) *n.* a very heavy fall of rain. □ *We all got caught out in that soaking and had to return home to dry out.* □ *There was a very heavy soak last night which will help to revive the flowers in my garden.*

soak someone *vb.* to borrow money from someone. □ *He's trying to soak everyone.* □ *Can I soak you for a fiver?*

so-and-so *n.* a despicable individual; a "bastard," "bitch," etc., as the context requires. (A euphemism. However, the expression can also be used between well-established good friends, especially male to male, to show affection.) □ *This lousy so-and-so tried to take me for four hundred quid.* □ *Terry, you old so-and-so, how have you been?*

soapy *mod.* silly and sentimental. □ *Come on, don't be so soapy.* □ *Y'know, maybe that's not all that soapy.*

sob *n.* one Pound Sterling. □ *These things cost more than just a few sobs.* □ *Have you got a sob you can spare?*

sob story *n.* a hard-luck story. □ *I've heard nothing but sob stories today. Isn't anybody happy?* □ *She had quite a sob story, and I listened to the whole thing.*

socked out *mod.* out of commission; not functioning. □ *That machine is socked out, I'm afraid.* □ *Harry got the socked out unit working again.*

sod 1. *n.* a male homosexual. (Crude. Originally, an abbreviation of "sodomite.") □ *I hear that you-know-who is a sod.* □ *So what if he's a sod? He can still vote, can't he?* **2.** *n.* a worthless or despised person, usually male. (Crude.) □ *Why do we employ that useless sod?* □ *The sod has just written off another company car.* **3.** *n.* an average or typical man. □ *The poor sod sat on the bench, just waiting.* □ *What is that sod here for, anyway.*

sod all *n.* absolutely nothing. (Crude.) □ *Sod all, I tell you; nothing!* □ *There is just sod all there.*

sodding *mod.* damned. (Crude. A euphemism or disguise.) □ *Cut out that sodding bad language!* □ *What's the sodding meaning of this?*

sodger-clad but major-minded *mod.* of a strong sense of duty despite a lowly rank. (Scots usage.) □ *Now there's one man who's sodger-clad but major-minded.* □ *Being sodger-clad but major-minded used to be much more common than nowadays, I'm afraid.*

Sod it! *exclam.* "Damn it!" (Crude.) □ *Sod it, it's not working again!* □ *No, I can't fix it...oh, sod it!*

Sod off! *exclam.* "Go away!"; "Get lost!" (Crude.) □ *I've told you before. Sod off!* □ *Sod off! How often do you have to be told?*

sods' holiday See BUGGER'S MUDDLE.

Sod's Law See MURPHY'S LAW.

Sod them! *exclam.* "Damn them!" (Crude.) □ *Sod them, I'm going to do it!* □ *I won't give up! Sod them!*

Sod this for a game of soldiers! See FUCK THIS FOR A GAME OF SOLDIERS!

soft 1. *mod.* having to do with drugs which are reputedly non-addictive. (Which is something of an oxymoron as one definition of a drug is that which causes addiction. Compare with HARD.) □ *The soft stuff just leads to hard stuff.* □ *This acid is not exactly soft.* □ *Soft drugs just take longer to turn you into a zombie.* **2.** *mod.* stupid. □ *The guy's soft in the head. He just can't think straight.* □ *She may seem a little soft, but she's really bright.*

soft core 1. *mod.* of mild pornography. (Crude. Compare with HARD CORE.) □ *There are more and more soft core movies on cable and satellite television.* □ *This stuff I saw was just soft core.* □ *Now even the soft core stuff is getting harder to find these days.* **2.** AND **soft porn** *n.* mild pornography. (Crude. Compare with HARD CORE.) □ *They keep the soft core on the top shelf.* □ *The film was just a bit of soft porn, but people still walked out.*

softie AND **softy 1.** *n.* a compassionate person; someone who is easily moved to pity. □ *He shouldn't give you much trouble. He's such a softie.* □ *The judge who tried the case was anything but a softie.* **2.** *n.* a weakling; a coward. □ *He's too much of a softie to fight back.* □ *Don't worry—he's a softie.* **3.** *n.* a silly person. □ *I don't think I could take another softie like that today.* □ *Here was one softy that was different from the others, he thought.*

soft in the head *mod.* stupid; witless. □ *George is just soft in the head. He'll never get away with his little plan.* □ *You're soft in the head if you think I'll go along with that.*

soft-nosed *mod.* stupid. (Compare with HARD-NOSED.) □ *What a soft-nosed idiot I was!* □ *Don't call him soft-nosed. He does his best.*

soft number *n.* a easy task. □ *Well, you've got a real soft number here!* □ *How come you get all the soft numbers?*

soft on someone *mod.* romantically attracted to someone. □ *Fred is soft on Martha, I've heard.* □ *He looked like he was getting a little soft on Sally.*

soft on someone or something *mod.* too easy on someone or something. □ *The judge was viewed as being too soft on pushers.* □ *The cops are soft on speeders in this town.*

soft option *n.* the easiest or most comfortable of a number of choices available. □ *Trust you to choose the soft option every time!* □ *So, which one's the soft option, eh?*

soft pedal something *vb. phr.* to tone down or subdue something. (Refers to the soft pedal on the piano.) □ *Try to soft pedal the problems we have with the cooling system.* □ *I won't soft pedal anything. Everyone must know the truth.*

soft porn See SOFT CORE.

soft roll *n.* a woman easily persuaded to indulge in sexual intercourse. (Crude.) □ *Oh, Maggy is a soft roll all right. You'll see!* □ *Know any soft rolls in the pub tonight?*

soft sell *n.* a restrained, gentle or subtle way to sell. □ *Some people won't bother listening to a soft sell. You've got to let them know you believe in what you are selling.* □ *I tried the soft sell, but that didn't work.*

soft soap 1. *n.* persuasive flattery. □ *I don't mind a little soft soap. It won't affect what I do, of course.* □ *Don't waste my time with soft soap. I know you don't mean it.* **2.** *vb.* to persuade by flattery. □ *We couldn't soft soap her into it.* □ *Don't try to soft soap her. She's an old battle-axe.*

soft touch *n.* a gullible person; someone particularly easy to persuade to lend money. (Compare with TOUCH.) □ *John is a soft touch for a few quid.* □ *Here comes the perfect soft touch—a nerd with a gleam in his eye.*

soft tyre *n.* a partially deflated tyre. □ *Take a look here; I think you've got a soft tyre.* □ *A soft tyre's dangerous and must be attended to.*

soggies *n.* breakfast cereals. □ *Where are my usual soggies?* □ *I like my soggies at breakfast.*

soldier *n.* a bottle of spirits or beer. (Compare with DEAD SOLDIER.) □ *Throw your empty soldiers in the rubbish bin, please.* □ *There was a broken soldier on the floor and a cap on the table.*

soldier on *vb. phr.* to persevere in the face of hardships and difficulties. □ *I suppose we just have to soldier on, whatever happens.* □ *It can be hard to soldier on, but we will, never fear.*

soldiers *n.* toast cut into thin strips, coated in yolk by dipping in a soft-boiled egg, and then eaten. □ *There is nothing nicer than a soft-boiled egg and soldiers for breakfast.* □ *He sat there at the table and cut his toast into soldiers.*

sold on something *mod.* enthusiastic about or attracted to something. □ *I think I'm sold on that idea.* □ *Now, can we sell everyone else on this?*

solid 1. *mod.* staunch; reliable. □ *Harry said to make sure we've only got solid people on the team.* □ *I know he's personable, but is he solid?* **2.** *mod.* consecutive; consecutively. □ *Larry ate for four solid days.* □ *Then he "had the flu" for three days solid.* **3.** *mod.* stupid. □ *Why are you always so solid about money?* □ *She's sort of solid, although she means well.*

somebody *n.* an important person. (Often with *a.* Compare with NOBODY.) □ *Aren't you a somebody?* □ *If she was a somebody, you wouldn't have to ask.*

something awful *mod.* terrible or frightful. (Here "something" was originally a euphemism for BLOODY.) □ *This is really something awful; what can be done about it?* □ *The mess they left behind in that place was something awful.*

something cruel *mod.* exceptionally cruel. (Here "something" was originally a euphemism for BLOODY.) □ *What they do to their horses there is something cruel, it really is.* □ *Apparently he had been treating the poor girl something cruel, until she ran away from him.*

something else *mod.* excellent or wonderful. □ *Your news is really something else.* □ *That cake is just something else, Mary. What's in it?*

Something's got to give. *sent.* "Things cannot go on like this."; "The stalemate will be broken." □ *The pressure on me is getting to be too much. Something's got to give.* □ *Something's got to give as they keep on arguing about money.*

something to be going on with See ENOUGH TO BE GOING ON WITH.

song of the thrush *n.* a brush. (Rhyming slang.) □ *He took out a large song of the thrush and swept the driveway clear of leaves.* □ *Look at that delicate song of the thrush her Ladyship uses on her hair.*

Sonny *n.* a small boy. (Also a form of address to a small boy or, disparagingly, to a youth.) □ *Just watch yourself, Sonny!* □ *Well Sonny, how are you today?*

son of a gun *n.* an affectionate term of address. (Formerly, a euphemism for "bastard.") □ *Well you son of a gun, where have you been?* □ *How's life treating you, you old son of a gun?*

son of something or someone *n.* the successor to something. (A jocular name, derived from the title of many films.) □ *Well here he comes, son of Mr Big—he thinks!* □ *So what does he imagine this invention of his is? Son of television or something?*

soon as dammit See AS QUICK AS DAMMIT.

sooner *mod.* better; best. □ *Mary had sooner go see what's ailing Tom.* □ *I'd sooner you got sorted out as soon as you can.*

soor *n.* an unpleasant person. (Offensive. Also a term of address. From the Hindi *suar*, meaning "pig," by hobson-jobson.) □ *Just get out of my sight, you soor!* □ *What a soor you are!*

soothing noises *n.* calming or comforting words. □ *Make some soothing noises and get them out of here.* □ *He plied us with soothing noises but nothing more.*

sootie AND **sooty** *n.* a black person. (Racially offensive.) □ *He said he was not a racist, he just hated sooties!* □ *Don't call a black person a sooty, please. It is very offensive and racist.*

soppy **1.** *mod.* foolishly sentimental. □ *Don't always be so soppy.* □ *What a*

soppy idea! **2.** *mod.* puerilely infatuated. □ *The girl is really soppy about someone.* □ *She'll eventually realise he's not worth being soppy about.*

sorry about that AND **sorry 'bout that** *interj.* "sorry"; "whoops." (A gross understatement, said more as a self-deprecating joke than as an apology.) □ *You spill hot cocoa on my coat, and all you can say is "Sorry 'bout that"?* □ *When the passenger stepped on my toe, she said lightly, as if it was a joke, "Sorry about that."*

sorry and sad *mod.* bad. (Rhyming slang.) □ *This entire government is sorry and sad.* □ *That sorry and sad creep is asking for you again.*

sorry 'bout that See SORRY ABOUT THAT.

sorted *mod.* satisfactory; contented. □ *Don't worry, it's all sorted again now.* □ *It's fine; it's all sorted.*

sort someone or something out **1.** *vb. phr.* to disentangle or separate people or things; to resolve a problem. □ *Let's see if we can sort out you two.* □ *It would be good to sort out this mess and let the two of them go their own ways.* **2.** *vb. phr.* to reprimand or punish someone. □ *Misbehave and he'll sort you out all right.* □ *The teacher sorted out the wayward pupil.*

so sharp one could cut oneself *phr.* "too clever for one's own good." □ *That was well done, Tom. You're so sharp you could cut yourself.* □ *She is really so sharp she could cut herself. Glad she came along.*

so-so *mod.* average; mediocre. □ *It was just so-so. Nothing to write home about.* □ *I don't need to pay £7.50 to see a so-so film.*

sound off (about something) AND **pipe off (about something)** **1.** *vb. phr.* to complain or protest loudly about something. □ *You always have to be piping off about something or other, don't you?* □ *Just sound off if you've got a problem.* **2.** *vb. phr.* to boast about something; to say more than is wise. □ *Why did you have to go and sound off about your pay rise?* □ *Don't pipe off about the surprise party.*

sounds 1. *n.* popular music; hit records. □ *I got some new sounds. Do you want to come over and listen?* □ *Yeh, these sounds are fab!* **2.** *n.* music. (Teenagers.) □ *Let's hear this week's top sounds.* □ *I like these sounds.*

soup *n.* bad weather. (Aviation.) □ *There's no way we can fly through soup like this.* □ *Somewhere, far away through the soup, we could hear an aircraft. I was glad I was not in it.*

Soup and Gravy See LUMPY GRAVY.

souped up *mod.* made more powerful. □ *That souped up car of John's certainly makes a lot of noise.* □ *Why do all cars driven by males under the age of twenty have to be souped up?*

souper *n.* a traitor; a defector. (Irish usage.) □ *If Mick weren't such a souper, I could stand him.* □ *You slimy little souper! How could you?*

soup something up *vb. phr.* to increase the power of something. □ *He souped his car up so it will do nearly 120.* □ *If only I could soup up this computer to run just a little faster.*

sourpuss *n.* a morose or foul-tempered person. □ *What a sourpuss! He makes King Kong look sweet.* □ *Don't be such a sourpuss, love.*

souse *vb.* to drink with the intention of becoming drunk. (Compare with SOUSED.) □ *Of course he's sousing! What else is there to do in a place like this?* □ *I'm sure they went off with every intention of sousing.*

soused *mod.* somewhat intoxicated due to drink. (Compare with SOUSE.) □ *We were all getting soused.* □ *All we need right now is a soused bus driver.*

Southend kiss See GLASGOW KISS.

South of France *n.* a dance. (Rhyming slang.) □ *We're off to the South of France this evening.* □ Q: *Eh?* A: *The South of France—you know, the dance.*

southpaw *n.* a left-handed person. (Originally descriptive of such a boxer.) □ *Micky's a southpaw so his writing looks sort of funny.* □ *My sister is a southpaw, but I'm not.*

sow See COW.

So what? *interrog.* "What is important or significant about this?" □ *So what if*

I'm older than the other guy? What has that got to do with this? □ *I'm a crook. So what?*

So what else is new? See WHAT ELSE IS NEW?

sozzle *vb.* to drink to excess. □ *They're sozzling over at the pub.* □ *I wish you'd stop sozzling yourself to sleep every night.*

sozzled *mod.* very intoxicated due to drink. □ *Boy, was she sozzled.* □ *She was so sozzled she didn't even know her name, or my name, or anybody's name.*

s.p. AND **S.P.; sp; SP** *n.* inside information; the low-down. (Literally, an abbreviation of "starting price," the odds ruling at the beginning of a horse race.) □ *The inspector asked the constable what the s.p. was on this fellow that had been arrested.* □ *Have you got the SP, mate?*

spade *n.* a black person. (Racially offensive.) □ *So this spade drives away in a BMW!* □ *Why should a BMW not belong to a spade?*

spag bol AND **spaggers** *n.* spaghetti Bolognese; a way of serving spaghetti with chopped beef, onion and tomato. (Originally from the city of Bologna in Italy.) □ *Fancy some spag bol for lunch?* □ *Spaggers is always a popular eating choice.*

spaggers See SPAG BOL.

Spanish custom *n.* a shady or illegal practice. □ *Mike and Jack have a few handy Spanish customs working for them among the local street traders that bring them in a nice steady income.* □ *Well, Spanish customs are all very fine, so long as the rozzers don't get to hear about them!*

Spanish tummy *n.* a picturesque name for diarrhoea or similar, inflicted upon a visitor to a foreign land. (Spanish variety.) □ *I had a little touch of Spanish tummy the second day, but other than that we had a wonderful time.* □ *Most people blame Spanish tummy on the water.*

spank(ing) *n.* a severe beating. □ *After a spanking like that, the guy spent two weeks in the hospital.* □ *Bruno gave the guy a terrible spank.*

spanking new See BRAND SPANKING NEW.

spank the plank *vb. phr.* to play a guitar. □ *Manuel spanked the plank for a while.* □ *The teenagers were spanking the plank and making a terrible noise that they considered passed for music.*

spanner in the works *n.* a problem or delay. □ *I'm afraid there is one spanner in the works.* □ *I don't want to hear about more spanners in the works.*

spare 1. *mod.* idle; at a loose end. □ *Just looking at him you could see he was spare.* □ *Try not to look so spare all the time.* **2.** *mod.* livid with rage. □ *So she went spare. Why should that affect you so much?* □ *I just knew you'd go spare.* **3.** *mod.* crazy; insane. □ *Any more of this and I'll go spare.* □ *I'm spare with worry.* **4.** *n.* an unattached member of the opposite sex. (Crude.) □ *There's always a lot a spare at Harry's place.* □ *The only spare was Tony's maiden aunt, which did not really count.*

spare tyre *n.* a thickness in the waist; a roll of fat around one's waist. □ *I've got to get rid of this spare tyre.* □ *The spare tyre started when I was twenty-six.*

sparked out AND **sparko 1.** *mod.* asleep. □ *He's sparked out, and I can't rouse him.* □ *After all that exercise, he's sparko.* **2.** *mod.* intoxicated from drink or drugs. □ *He's in his room, sparked out again.* □ *Try not to get sparko again this time!* **3.** *mod.* dead. □ *I don't know why but my dog just went and sparked out.* □ *What you do with a sparko dog around here?*

sparkers *mod.* unconscious; deeply asleep. □ *Who is that sparkers gal by the window?* □ *I'm still more than a bit sparkers. Give me a minute or two to wake up.*

sparkler 1. *n.* an electric train. □ *There are sparklers passing here all the time.* □ *Get the sparkler— that's the easy way to get there from here.* **2.** *n.* a helpful lie. □ *A lie is only a sparkler if people believe it, you know.* □ *That's not another of your sparklers, is it Johnny?* **3.** See also SHINER.

sparko See SPARKED OUT.

spark out 1. *vb. phr.* to fall into a deep sleep. □ *He sparked out in seconds.* □ *I'm just going to spark out, all right?* **2.** *vb. phr.* to become unconscious through drink or drugs. □ *He sparked out half-way through the session.* □ *I don't know what was in that stuff but we all sparked out in no time.* **3.** *vb. phr.* to die. □ *For a minute, I thought I was going to spark out, too.* □ *He sparked out when his plane crashed during a training flight.*

sparks 1. *n.* an electrician. □ *Not another power failure! We need a sparks here in a hurry.* □ *The sparks says that building needs a complete re-wiring.* **2.** *n.* a hospital X-ray department. □ *Right, it's the sparks for you today, George.* □ *Here are the pictures from sparks, doctor.*

sparks AND **sparky** *n.* a radio operator. (Naval and aviation. Also a term of address.) □ *Sparks, keep trying to raise the tower.* □ *The sparky has a coded message from base for the captain.*

sparky See SPARKS.

sparring partner *n.* one's friend; one's husband or wife. □ *I'd better ask the sparring partner.* □ *Will your sparring partner let you out to the pub tonight?*

sparrow-fart 1. *n.* someone of no significance. (Taboo. Irish usage.) □ *Him? Oh, he's just another sparrow-fart.* □ *Tell these sparrow-farts the job's been taken.* **2.** *n.* dawn. (Taboo.) □ *The word "sparrow-fart" is a humorous "reinterpretation" of "cock-crow."* □ *Oh my goodness, sparrow-fart again so soon!*

spastic AND **spaz(z)** *n.* a very foolish or clumsy individual; a bungler. (Offensive. Also a term of address.) □ *Get lost, you spastic!* □ *Billy is just a little spaz.*

spat *n.* a quarrel. □ *That was some spat last night.* □ *Who's going to win the spat, I ask?*

spaz(z) See SPASTIC.

spazzmobile *n.* an invalid carriage. (Offensive, as the term is clearly derived from SPASTIC.) □ *Spazzmobile is a pretty sick term derived from "spastic."* □ *Who's the guy on the spazzmobile?*

speak of the devil AND **talk of the devil** *phr.* said when someone whose name has just been mentioned appears or is heard from. (A catch phrase.) □ *And speak of the devil, here's Ted now.* □ *Talk of the devil, that was Mary on the phone.*

speak proper AND **talk proper** *vb. phr.* to speak Standard English. □ *Try to speak proper, can't you?* □ *The man said we should talk proper when we spoke to him.*

specs *n.* glasses or spectacles. □ *I broke my specs.* □ *I need specs to find where I left my specs.*

speed *n.* methamphetamine; amphetamines in general. □ *Speed is a monstrous problem in some cities.* □ *Kids think that speed won't get them into trouble.*

speed freak *n.* a drug user who injects methamphetamine; an amphetamine user. (Drugs and general slang.) □ *Hank is a speed freak, but he's not on skag.* □ *Speed freaks, not heroin addicts, account for a high proportion of drug-related crime.*

speed merchant 1. *n.* someone who is a very fast bowler. (Cricket.) □ *Watch out when you're batting against Smith. He's a real speed merchant.* □ *The visiting team put on their speed merchant to bowl right at the end in a last desperate attempt to recover the game.* **2.** *n.* someone who drives a vehicle or rides a bicycle at great speed. □ *Look at her move that little Honda! What a speed merchant!* □ *Watch out for speed merchants here—they loves this wide straight length of road. So do the speed cops.*

speedo *n.* a speedometer. □ *He tapped the speedo again. "Nope!" he said, "It's broken."* □ *According to the speedo he was exceeding the speed limit by forty miles per hour. Could that have anything to do with the police car on his tail with siren blaring and lights flashing?*

spend a penny *vb. phr.* to go to the toilet. (Crude. A euphemism. From the former necessity to put a penny into the lock in order to gain access to a stall in a public toilet.) □ *Timmy has to spend a penny.* □ *Just a moment while I spend a penny.*

spending money *n.* pocket money; spare money, available for discretionary spending after essentials are taken care of. □ *I'm a little short of spending money at the present. Could I borrow ten pounds?* □ *I don't have any spending money either.*

spend money like it's going out of fashion AND **spend money like it's going out of style; spend money like there's no tomorrow** *vb. phr.* to spend money recklessly; to spend money as if it were worthless or will soon be worthless. □ *Extravagant? She's spending money like it's going out of fashion!* □ *Spending money like there's no tomorrow is a common reaction to bad news.*

spend money like it's going out of style See SPEND MONEY LIKE IT'S GOING OUT OF FASHION.

spend money like there's no tomorrow See SPEND MONEY LIKE IT'S GOING OUT OF FASHION.

spew *vb.* to empty one's stomach; to vomit. (Crude.) □ *After dinner, I suddenly had the urge to spew.* □ *Fred is up in the loo spewing like mad.*

spew one's guts (out) 1. *vb. phr.* to tell everything that one knows; to confess everything. (Underworld.) □ *Lefty was sitting there in the cop-shop spewing his guts out about the bank job.* □ *If he really is spewing his guts, Max will cancel his Christmas.* **2.** AND **spew one's ring (up)** *vb. phr.* to empty one's stomach; to vomit. (Crude. Compare with SPILL ONE'S GUTS.) □ *Fred is spewing his guts out because of that lousy fish you served.* □ *He's spewing his ring because he has the flu, cabbagehead.*

spew one's ring (up) See SPEW ONE'S GUTS (OUT).

Spic(k) *mod.* a Spanish person. (Offensive.) □ *Why can you not be polite to Spicks?* □ *Y'know, Otto, if you call a Spaniard a Spic, he's likely to get nasty.*

spiderman *n.* a construction worker who works high up on tall buildings. □ *I could never work as a spiderman.* □ *I* *don't think they want spidermen with vertigo.*

spiel *n.* a hard-luck story. □ *I don't find your spiel very convincing, I'm afraid.* □ *All right, what's the spiel today?*

spiffed out 1. *mod.* dressed up, brushed up and polished up nicely. □ *See if you can get yourself a little spiffed out before we get to the front door. We wouldn't want the Wilmington-Thorpes to think you only have one suit.* □ *The house doesn't have to be too spiffed out for the Franklins. They are used to clutter.* **2.** *mod.* nicely dressed up; decked out. □ *I like to get all spiffed out every now and then.* □ *Wow, you look spiffed out! Where are you going?*

spiffing *mod.* excellent. □ *This is a really spiffing place you've got here, Sally.* □ *Come have a look at my spiffing new car.* □ *Doesn't look so spiffing to me.*

spiffy *mod.* clean and tidy; excellent. □ *Mary's got herself a spiffy new job.* □ *This is a spiffy day!*

spike 1. *n.* a hypodermic needle; a hypodermic syringe and needle; a medicine dropper and a needle. □ *The addict caught some strange disease from a dirty spike.* □ *What'll I do? I broke my spike.* **2.** *vb.* to add ether or alcohol to beer, originally by injecting it through the cork with a hypodermic needle; to add alcohol to a non-alcoholic drink. (From prohibition times in the US.) □ *He found a man who would spike his beer for a small fee.* □ *He spiked the beer with ether, which is a dangerous thing to do.* **3.** *n.* a flophouse or cheap rooming house. □ *It's just a spike, but it's where I live just now.* □ *That's the spike over there, across the street.* **4.** *n.* a High Church Anglican promoting or practising Anglo-Catholic forms of worship. □ *I suppose the archdeacon is a spike.* □ *We don't want a spike as our vicar, please.*

spiked 1. *mod.* having to do with a drink with alcohol added to it; having to do with a punch with an alcoholic content. □ *Is the punch spiked? I want some without.* □ *We only have spiked punch.* □ *Max's breakfast orange juice*

is usually spiked. **2.** *mod.* having to do with hair that stands up straight. □ *His spiked hair wouldn't look so bad if it wasn't orange.* □ *Is spiked hair a fad or the way of the future?*

spike up 1. *vb. phr.* to inject oneself with a narcotic drug. □ *Max is in the back room, spiking up with his pals.* □ *You could see they were all well spiked up as soon as you came into the room.* **2.** *vb. phr.* to make Anglican worship more ritualistic or High Church in form. □ *Our archdeacon has been trying to spike up services around here for some time but the bishop resists this.* □ *I like my services to be spiked up somewhat.*

spiky *mod.* of Anglican worship which is very ritualistic or High Church in form. □ *The local parish church has a very spiky form of service.* □ *I'm afraid spiky worship is not for me.*

spill *vb.* to confess; to reveal secrets. (Underworld. Probably derived from SPILL THE BEANS.) □ *The rozzers tried to get her to spill, but she just sat there.* □ *The gang was afraid she would spill, but she's a tough old thing.*

spill one's guts *vb. phr.* to tell all; to confess. (Compare with SPEW ONE'S GUTS (OUT).) □ *I had to spill my guts about the broken window. I didn't want you to take the blame.* □ *Mary spilled her guts about the window. She confessed that she was trying to shield Bob.*

spill the beans *vb. phr.* to give away a secret or a surprise. □ *There is a surprise party for Heidi on Wednesday. Please don't spill the beans.* □ *Paul spilled the beans about Heidi's party.*

spin 1. *vb.* to bestow a partial or biased interpretation upon events. (From the spin imparted upon a ball thrown in sports such as cricket. Compare with SPIN DOCTOR.) □ *To say that Max's death is "inconvenient" is one way to spin that news, I suppose.* □ *If anyone could spin things to look good for herself, it's Henrietta.* **2.** *vb.* to search a suspect. (Police.) □ *Ok, constable, spin him.* □ *Why are you spinning me?*

spin doctor *n.* someone who is skilled in the art of bestowing a partial or biased interpretation upon events. (Usually in the context of manipulating the news for political reasons. Compare with SPIN.) □ *Things were going bad for the candidate, so he got himself a new spin doctor.* □ *A good spin doctor could have made the incident appear far less damaging.*

spin-off 1. *n.* a significant secondary effect or result. □ *Now here's an interesting spin-off!* □ *What sort of spin-off would you expect, professor?* **2.** *n.* an unexpected benefit. □ *A few good spin-offs would make all the difference for the funding of this project.* □ *That spin-off was a real turn up for the books!*

spit and a drag *n.* a cigarette. (Rhyming slang, linked as follows: spit and a drag ≈ [fag] = cigarette.) □ *Have you got a spit and a drag I can owe you?* □ *I think I'll have a spit and a drag now.*

spit and polish *n.* excessive orderliness; precision and neatness taken to extreme. (From the standards expected of a soldier.) □ *I like spit and polish. It comes from being in the military.* □ *There is no such thing as too much spit and polish.*

Spithead pheasant *n.* a bloater. (The fish.) □ *Oh yes, Otto has been known to eat Spithead pheasant.* □ *I think I'd pass on the Spithead pheasant.*

Spit it out! *exclam.* "Say it!"; "Confess!" □ *Come on, don't be shy! Spit it out!* □ *Say what you have to say and leave. Hurry up! Spit it out!*

spitting distance *n.* a short distance. □ *Oh, they live within spitting distance of here.* □ *Just spitting distance, there's a superb library.*

splash *n.* a small quantity of soda water or some other dilutant added to spirits. □ *Just a splash!* □ *Yes, any more than a splash ruins these single malts.*

splash out on something *vb. phr.* to spend money extravagantly. □ *I just feel like splashing out on something.* □ *Splash out on me, if you like!*

splash the boots *vb. phr.* to urinate. (Crude.) □ *He just went out to splash the boots.* □ *I've got to splash the boots. Back in a minute.*

spliff *n.* a marijuana cigarette. (Originally Jamaican.) □ *They consume an enormous number of spliffs and try to sell them to the tourists.* □ *It's really high-quality spliff.*

split 1. *vb.* to leave. □ *Look at the clock. Time to split.* □ *Let's split. We're late.* **2.** *n.* a division of money, especially that acquired as the result of a crime. □ *We all gathered at Harry's for the split, but Harry never showed—and he had the money.* □ *Yes, there was some trouble at the split. The cops arrived.*

split new *mod.* brand new. □ *How did Otto ever get hold of a split new BMW?* □ *How does Otto get a split new anything, do you think?*

split pea *n.* tea. (Rhyming slang.) □ *I could go some split pea.* □ *Where do you get a cup of split pea around here?*

split the vote *vb. phr.* to attract voters from one choice to vote for a second, possibly in the secret hope or intention that a third may then win the election. □ *I'm sure he's only standing so as to split the vote.* □ *If you stand, you do realise you'll split the vote?*

splosh 1. *n.* women in general; one specific woman. (Crude.) □ *I don't want that stuck-up splosh in here!* □ *Look, you stupid splosh, I don't care!* **2.** *n.* sexual intercourse. (Taboo.) □ *After that splosh, she felt cheap.* □ *They were talking about, you know, splosh.*

splurge *vb.* to indulge oneself with much spending or eating. □ *I like to splurge every now and then. I deserve it.* □ *I splurge every weekend, and then regret it all the following week.*

Spode's Law See MURPHY'S LAW.

spoiled rotten *mod.* indulged in; greatly spoiled. □ *This kid is spoiled rotten!* □ *I was spoiled rotten when I was a child, so I'm used to this kind of wasteful luxury.*

spoiling for a fight *phr.* argumentative; asking for a fight. □ *They were just spoiling for a fight, and they went outside to settle the matter.* □ *She was really grumpy, and you could tell she had been spoiling for a fight all day.*

spondulicks AND **spondulics; spondulix** *n.* money. □ *How much spon-*

dulicks will this set me back? □ *I don't have enough spondulix to pull of the deal.*

spondulics See SPONDULICKS.

sponge 1. *n.* a parasitic person. □ *Of course he's a sponge. He's never out of the pub.* □ *There were so many drunks all together it looked like a sponges convention.* **2.** *vb.* to live parasitically off others while offering nothing in return. □ *Stop sponging all the time. Get your own!* □ *Here comes Willy. Hide your wallet, pencils, glasses and anything else not nailed down before he sponges them off you.*

sponger *n.* a heavy drinker. (From an apparent ability to absorb the stuff like a sponge.) □ *This pub is full of spongers, any night of the week.* □ *Well, you may be no use whatever at anything else, Willy, but you certainly are a genuine sponger!*

spoof 1. *vb.* to parody someone or something. □ *The comedian spoofed the government by sitting in a big chair and going to sleep.* □ *I like to spoof myself. It can help break the ice at parties.* **2.** *n.* a parody. □ *The first act was a spoof of a Parliamentary investigation.* □ *The second act was a spoof of the first act.*

spool *n.* a roll of film or tape. □ *He took the spool in to get developed.* □ *There are several spools of film right here.*

spoon *vb.* to behave in a foolishly or sentimentally amorous fashion. □ *They like to go out and spoon under the stars.* □ *Do you remember spooning with me years ago?*

sport *n.* friend; chum. (A term of address.) □ *Well, sport, looks like we have a little problem here.* □ *So what's new, sport?*

sports *n.* a gathering for the purpose of participating in or observing a sporting activity, particularly athletics. □ *The annual school sports are next week.* □ *Jimmy ran a race in the sports but came last.*

spot 1. *n.* a small quantity of drink or food; more generally, an entire (small) meal. (Compare with SPOT OF LUNCH.)

□ *I'll just have a spot of that brandy, please.* □ *You must have a spot to eat before you go.* **2.** *n.* a nightclub; a night spot. □ *It was a nice little spot, with a combo and a canary.* □ *We went to a spot with a jukebox for entertainment.* **3.** *n.* a spotlight. □ *The spot illuminated her clearly on the darkened stage.* □ *The two spots converged on the singer during her solo.* **4.** *n.* a short period allocated at a certain point in a TV programme, theatrical entertainment, church service, etc. □ *I've been given a five-minute spot at the end of the second act.* □ *He said that he knew it was short, but at this stage in my career I should be pleased to get any sort of spot at all.* **5.** *n.* a small quantity. □ *Would you like a spot of whisky?* □ *He took a spot of salt and sprinkled it over the food.*

spot market *n.* the open market where deals are made on the spot. (Securities markets.) □ *Oil reached nearly twenty-five dollars a barrel on the spot market.* □ *Gold prices on the spot market finally reached £600 per ounce and then promptly collapsed.*

spot of bother *n.* some slight trouble. □ *It looks as if there's a spot of bother ahead.* □ *Sorry for that spot of bother, folks.*

spot of lunch *n.* a small amount of lunch. (Compare with SPOT.) □ *How about a spot of lunch?* □ *I had a spot of lunch at my desk, thanks.*

spot on *mod.* exact or perfect. □ *Don't move! That's spot on!* □ *No, try to get it spot on this time.*

spout off *vb. phr.* to talk at length, loudly or out of context. □ *As usual, Harry spouted off about something he knew nothing about.* □ *I don't have much time for people who spout off about things they are ignorant of.*

sprat to catch a mackerel *n.* a small risk that promises a large reward. □ *It's worth a sprat to catch a mackerel this time, I think.* □ *For such a large mackerel, it's well worth risking such a tiny sprat.*

sprauncy *mod.* well-presented, flashy or showy. □ *Look at her! Have you* *ever seen anyone looking as sprauncy?* □ *If you did not dress so sprauncy you would not attract so many comments from passers-by.*

spread oneself *vb.* to make oneself available for sexual intercourse, from the female perspective. (Taboo.) □ *She just spread herself and smiled at him.* □ *Oh, she'll spread herself for you, you'll see!*

spring chicken *n.* a young and naive person, especially a young woman. (Often in the negative.) □ *Well, I may not be a spring chicken, but I've still got some life left in me.* □ *I'm a bit of a spring chicken still, but I lie about my age to get served in pubs.*

spring someone *vb.* to get someone out of jail on a technicality; to get someone out of jail illegally—in other words, to help that person to escape. □ *My wife came down and sprung me; otherwise, I'd still be in the slammer.* □ *His sidekick tried to spring him by throwing a rope over the wall, but the screws caught them both, even though they found it so funny they couldn't stop laughing.*

sprog 1. *n.* a new military recruit. □ *Who is that sprog over there?* □ *There's a new intake of sprogs today.* **2.** *n.* a baby or young child. □ *I hope you like sprogs. There are several here this afternoon.* □ *I wish she would try to control that sprog of hers.* **3.** *n.* a new prisoner, especially a young one. □ *Try to keep the sprogs away from Otto.* □ *What does Otto want with that sprog?* **4.** *vb.* to give birth; to become a parent. □ *When do you sprog?* □ *Samantha sprogged a pup last week.*

sprout wings *vb. phr.* to become so good as to resemble an angel. □ *The kid is not about to sprout wings, but he probably won't get into jail again.* □ *He was so good and helpful, I thought he would sprout wings.*

spruce *vb.* to evade work or responsibility. □ *Mike's on the spruce again.* □ *Mike goes to great lengths to spruce, of course.*

spruce someone *vb.* to deceive or confuse someone. □ *Don't spruce me!*

What happened? □ *If you're going to spruce someone, don't get caught.*

spud *n.* a potato. □ *I'd like a few more spuds.* □ *Mashed spuds are the best of all.*

spud bash *vb.* to peel large numbers of potatoes as a military duty or punishment. (Derived from "square bash.") □ *He spent a week spud bashing. It was clear after an hour or so why this was considered a punishment.* □ *Watch it, son! Or do you actually want to spud bash?*

spud-grinder *n.* the gullet. □ *Otto grabbed him by the spud-grinder. He nearly croaked.* □ *What you say really does stick in my spud-grinder a bit.*

spunk *n.* courage; spirit; pluck. □ *Show some spunk. Get in there and stand up for your rights.* □ *I have the spunk, but I don't have the brains.*

spunky *mod.* plucky; courageous. □ *I like a spunky girl—one who can really dance.* □ *The guy's tiny, but he's spunky.*

spurter *n.* a severed artery. (Medical slang. Because it spurts blood.) □ *Woops! We've got a real a spurter here!* □ *Now the one thing we really don't want to do is make the wrong cut and give ourselves a spurter to deal with.*

squaddie 1. *n.* a private soldier. □ *Who's the squaddie Mart's with tonight?* □ *I'd never be a squaddie if I could help it!* **2.** *n.* a new recruit to the army. □ *Tom has just become a squaddie.* □ *He may just be a squaddie but he already looks a soldier.*

square 1. *mod.* conventional; old-fashioned; stodgy. □ *Oh boy, you are really square.* □ *I come from a very square family.* **2.** *n.* a person who is conventional, old-fashioned or stodgy. □ *You are a square if I ever saw one.* □ *Ask that square what her favourite kind of music is.* **3.** *vb.* to settle something or to make something right. □ *Let's talk about squaring this matter up.* □ *Will twenty quid square things?*

square bash *vb. phr.* to drill and exercise upon a parade ground. (Military.) □ *Right you lot! Now it's time for you to square bash!* □ *We seemed to be square bashing for hours.*

square-eyed *mod.* concerning a reputed effect of watching too much TV. □ *I'm afraid Jimmy's becoming square-eyed from watching too much television.* □ *Another classroom of square-eyed little monsters again, the teacher thought.*

square-head *n.* a German person. (Offensive.) □ *Don't call Germans square-heads, please. It is very offensive and racist.* □ *He said he was not a racist, he just hated this particular square-head!*

square meal *n.* a good and nutritious meal. □ *I need three square meals a day—at least.* □ *The old soak looks like he could use a square meal.*

square peg (in a round hole) *n.* someone who does not fit in. □ *I'm a square peg in a round hole. Maybe I am meant to be eccentric.* □ *Kelly seems to be a square peg. What'll we do with him?*

square-rig *n.* a naval rating's uniform. □ *Susie is always a sucker for a sailor in a square-rig.* □ *Some people think the traditional square-rig looks rather silly.*

square with someone *vb. phr.* to become honest with someone after earlier dishonesty. □ *I want you to square with me. Tell the truth this time.* □ *Okay, I'll square with you. Terry did it.*

squashy bits *n.* a feminine euphemism for the breasts. (Crude. Normally with *the* and in the plural.) □ *Hey! Mind my squashy bits with that door!* □ *There I stood, my hands trying to hide my squashy bits, screaming at him to get out of the room.*

squat 1. *n.* a building occupied by squatters. □ *That old block of flats on Dover Street has been turned into a squat.* □ *We don't want any squats around here as they'll drive down property prices.* **2.** *vb.* to move into a building and live there illegally. □ *There are people squatting in that old block of flats on Dover Street.* □ *No, you can't squat there.*

squatter *n.* a person who squats. □ *There are squatters in that old block of flats on Dover Street.* □ *The cops moved into Dover street and arrested all the squatters.*

squawk 1. *vb.* to complain. □ *Come on, don't squawk all the time!* □ *Some people squawk because they don't have anything else to do.* **2.** *n.* a complaint. □ *Here's another squawk from the lady on the third floor.* □ *I have a list of squawks from the town hall.* **3.** *n.* a radio transmission. □ *There were a number of squawks from the expedition last week, but since then just silence.* □ *Let's see if we can pick up another squawk from them.*

squawk box *n.* a public address system; a loudspeaker, especially if installed in a box or other housing. □ *A raspy voice came over the squawk box announcing the arrival of what we had been waiting for.* □ *The squawk box was strangely quiet through the night.*

squeaky clean *mod.* obviously honest, legitimate and correct; entirely innocent. □ *Of course Mary had nothing to do with the robbery. She's as squeaky clean as you can get.* □ *This police force is squeaky clean; all the corrupt officers are in jail now.*

squeal *vb.* to inform or betray. □ *Who squealed to the cops?* □ *Tracy squealed on us.*

squealer 1. *n.* an informer or betrayer. (Underworld.) □ *Tracy is a terrible squealer.* □ *Some squealer let the cops know what was going to happen.* **2.** *n.* a pig; a piglet. □ *They sent their squealers to market at just the right time.* □ *Myra was horrified to learn that bacon comes from nice little squealers.*

squeeze 1. *n.* a tight or difficult financial situation; a situation where there is a shortage of money. □ *I'm in a sort of a squeeze. Can you wait a month?* □ *When the squeeze is over, we'll be able to sort out our debts.* **2.** *n.* cash. □ *What do you want the squeeze for, anyway?* □ *I don't have any squeeze.*

squeeze-box *n.* an accordion. □ *My brother plays the squeeze-box—not very well, but who can tell?* □ *The band consisted of drums, clarinet and a squeeze-box. A real winner.*

squeeze the lemon *vb. phr.* to urinate. (Crude.) □ *Well, squeezing the lemon does relieve the pressure of all that* *beer!* □ *I'm just going to squeeze the lemon.*

squew-whiff *mod.* somewhat intoxicated due to drink. □ *Tracy gets a little squew-whiff after a drink or two.* □ *You came in squew-whiff last night. What's going on?*

squib *n.* a professional gambler. □ *Take care playing cards with a squib.* □ *A squib will take you for every penny you have, and then some.*

squidgy 1. *mod.* soggy or damp. □ *Jimmy! How did you get all your clothes all squidgy like this?* □ *It was another horrible, squidgy day.* **2.** *mod.* squeezable. □ *This new material is very squidgy, as you will see.* □ *Squidgy things are more "friendly" than hard ones.*

squiffed AND **squiffy** *mod.* intoxicated due to drink. □ *She was a little squiffed, but still entertaining.* □ *The hostess was so squiffed she could hardly stand.*

squiffy 1. *mod.* out of alignment or disordered. □ *I'm afraid a squiffy machine like that is too dangerous to use.* □ *You've hung up this door sort of squiffy.* **2.** See also SQUIFFED.

squiffy doo *mod.* doubtful; questionable. □ *It's sort of squiffy doo, but things will get straightened out.* □ *Things are still sort of squiffy doo, but we'll know better in a few days.*

squillion *n.* an unimaginably vast number. □ *Mummy, there are a squillion cats in our garden!* □ Q: *A squillion cats?* A: *Well all right; our cat and the one from next door.*

squillionaire *n.* someone who is unimaginably rich. □ *Her father died and left her a squillionaire.* □ *Pete is practically a squillionaire, you know.*

Squire *n.* a jocular term of address between men. □ *Morning, Squire!* □ *How can I help you today, Squire?*

squirrelly *mod.* demented; crazy; irrational. □ *Who wrote this squirrelly play?* □ Q: *Good old squirrelly Tom! Isn't he a wonder?* A: *No, he's just squirrelly.*

squirrel something away *vb. phr.* to hide something in reserve. (In the manner of a squirrel hiding away nuts.) □

Here is some food. I squirreled it away in my suitcase. □ *She had squirreled away quite a fortune.*

squirt *n.* a person who is of little significance but is excessively presumptuous; a self-important nobody. □ *Who is that squirt asking all these dumb questions?* □ *He likes to think he's important but really he's nothing, just a squirt.*

squit 1. *n.* a small or unimportant person. □ *He's a pleasant little squit.* □ *The squit was waiting outside the office for him.* **2.** *vb.* to exterminate; to destroy. □ *Why should anyone want to squit this great venture?* □ *I think he's trying to squit us.*

squits AND **squitters** *n.* diarrhoea; a case of diarrhoea. (Always with *the.*) □ *Most people blame the squits on the water.* □ *I've got the squitters and can't go out tonight.*

squitters See SQUITS.

squiz *n.* a brief glance. □ *He took a squiz but saw nothing unusual.* □ *Take a squiz at that!*

stab at something *vb. phr.* to make an attempt at doing something. □ *Although he's been stabbing at it all day long he's no closer to a solution.* □ *Stab at it even if you don't know what you are doing!*

stable-companion *n.* a member of the same group, class, etc. □ *This vintage car does have a stable-companion. Come next door.* □ *Harry's my stable-companion.*

stag 1. *mod.* having to do with a gathering for men only. □ *The party is stag, so Tom and I are going together.* □ *Stag parties cease to be fun after a while.* **2.** *n.* a purchaser of newly issued stock, for immediate resale at a profit. □ *I'm looking for a stag.* □ *I think I might be a stag on this one.* **3.** *n.* military sentry-go. (*Sentry-go* is the process of marching up and down along a fixed path in the manner of a military sentry.) □ *Smith, you're on stag tonight.* □ *I hated stag on cold winter nights.*

stagger-through *n.* a preliminary, approximate, dress rehearsal. (Theatrical.) □ *The first stagger-through is tomor-*

row. □ *You could say we barely staggered through that stagger-through.*

stag party *n.* a party for men only. (Typically held in honour of the groom on the eve of his wedding day. Compare with HEN PARTY.) □ *Sally and Joe's wedding had to be cancelled after Joe was arrested when his stag party got just a tiny bit out of hand.* □ *I've just got a job as an exotic dancer at stag parties. No, there's no costume provided.*

stag someone *vb.* to deride or disparage someone. (Irish usage.) □ *If you just stopped stagging folks for a moment and listened, you just might learn something.* □ *Do you have to go around stagging him?*

stain *n.* someone who is not one of the social elite at Oxford University. □ *Oh, he doesn't count, being a mere stain.* □ *What makes you think you're so much more wonderful than a stain?*

stake something out *vb. phr.* to place some location under surveillance. (By the police, for example.) □ *We have to stake out his house tonight.* □ *Harry was staked out but they got nothing.*

stalk *n.* an erection. (Taboo.) □ *You can't walk along the street with a stalk like that!* □ *As long as you have a stalk like that I'll love you, Frank.*

stamping ground 1. *n.* one's favourite or customary location. □ *Manchester is my old stamping ground. I was born there, you know.* □ *I like to go back and look at my old stamping ground every now and then.* **2.** *n.* a military parade ground. □ *The men stood on the stamping ground, shivering.* □ *We could hear the sergeant major's commands being called, even when far from the stamping ground.*

stand-by *n.* a passenger hoping to board a plane if another passenger cancels. □ *All stand-bys please wait over there.* □ *Are you a stand-by, too?*

standee *n.* someone who must stand because there is nowhere to sit. □ *Not only was every seat in the theatre occupied, but there were about forty standees at the back of the auditorium.* □ *Can I get in as a standee, or do I have to wait for the next showing?*

stand-in *n.* a substitute; a temporary replacement. □ *I was a stand-in for the lead soprano, who had the sniffles.* □ *The audience booed the stand-in. They had paid to hear a star.*

standoffish *mod.* distant or cool in manner. □ *Bob is sort of standoffish until he gets to know you.* □ *Don't be so standoffish! Join in the fun!* □ *I am just a standoffish sort of guy, I suppose.*

stand(-on) *n.* an erection. (Taboo.) □ *Fear not my lovely, I shall always have a stand-on ready for you!* □ *You can't walk along the street with a stand like that!*

stand pat (on something) *vb. phr.* to stick firmly to one's position or opinions. □ *I am going to stand pat on this issue.* □ *I thought you would stand pat in the absence of new information.*

stand someone off *vb. phr.* to lay off an employee. □ *Times are hard and we're just going to have to stand off some of these people.* □ *They stood off the whole workforce!*

stand someone up *vb. phr.* to break a date or appointment by not showing up. □ *She stood him up, and he was really angry.* □ *He stood up his date while he played cricket with his pals.*

stand to something *vb. phr.* to abide with something such as the terms or conditions of an agreement or proposal. □ *I stand to what I agreed.* □ *Will you stand to that?*

star See STAR PRISONER.

starbolic naked See STARK NAKED.

stark bollock (naked) See STARK NAKED.

starkers 1. *mod.* entirely crazy. □ *She's frightened of starkers people.* □ *Tom's starkers. Really odd.* **2.** See also STARK NAKED.

stark naked AND **bollocky starkers; starbolic naked; stark bollock (naked); starko; starkers** *mod.* entirely naked. (Crude.) □ *Some creepy character asked Sally if she would pose stark naked for a girlie magazine.* □ *We walked through the woods and there were all these starkers people!*

starko See STARK NAKED.

stark staring bonkers *mod.* completely crazy. □ *Tom's stark staring bonkers.*

Really odd. □ *That's the most stark staring bonkers idea I've ever heard.*

star man See STAR PRISONER.

star prisoner AND **star man; star** *n.* a first-time prisoner. □ *Just because you're a star prisoner does not give you any special rights, you know.* □ *I hear a bunch of stars arrived today.*

starter(s) *n.* the first course of a meal. □ *We had soup for starters.* □ *What would you like as a starter?*

start something 1. *vb. phr.* to be the instigator of something significant. □ *I don't want to start something, but...* □ *I see you've managed to start something here all right!* **2.** *vb. phr.* to cause a woman to become pregnant. (Crude.) □ *I started something, and now the baby's due next month.* □ *I don't think he intended to start something, you know.*

star turn 1. *n.* the leading or most significant individual. □ *I don't know if he's really all that important, but he certainly sees himself as the star turn.* □ *I hear you're the star turn in court tomorrow, Otto.* **2.** *n.* someone who is very good at their job, or is greatly admired.* □ *Now, him; he's a real star turn!* □ *I wish I were a star turn like him.*

starver *n.* a man; a fellow. (Also a term of address.) □ *How are you this fine day, you old starver?* □ *Whatever does that starver want this time?*

stash 1. *n.* a hiding place. □ *Fred always used a cavity behind the wash-basin in the kitchen as his stash.* □ *I could use a good stash to hide away all this stuff from prying eyes.* **2.** *n.* a cache; that which is hidden. □ *Fred always puts his stash behind the washbasin in the kitchen.* □ *I must hide away my stash from prying eyes.*

stash (away) *vb. (phr.)* to hide something (somewhere). □ *Stash away this under the chair until I can think of a safer place to put it.* □ *Fred stashed his cut behind the wash-basin in the kitchen.*

Stash it! *exclam.* a request to stop some activity. □ *Jimmy! Stash it! Now!* □ *Stash it, or I'll stash it for you!*

state *n.* an excited or agitated condition; a disordered or chaotic condition. □ *She was in a terrible state, I tell you.* □ *Calm down! There's no need to be in such a state!*

state of nature 1. *mod.* naked; unclothed. (Euphemistic.) □ *If you want to go about the house in a state of nature, then kindly go and find your own house to do it in.* □ *Well, I found them all out in their garden, sunbathing in a state of nature.* **2.** *n.* the condition of an uncivilised or uneducated person. □ *You seem to be reverting to a state of nature here; it's got to stop.* □ *He's pretty primitive, almost in a state of nature.* **3.** *n.* the condition of a wild animal or plant. □ *The whole garden had reverted to a state of nature.* □ *He looked over the chaotic mess. "Clearly people who want us to go back to a state of nature have never seen a real one," he muttered.*

stats *n.* statistics. □ *They're working out the stats now.* □ *The stats are expected to show that the trade balance is growing steadily worse.*

staunch *n.* someone very keen on sports and other outdoors activities, and who makes life unpleasant for those who are not so inclined. □ *Why do I seem to be surrounded by staunches in this place?* □ *A staunch? Me? You're joking!*

steady *n.* a long-term boyfriend or girlfriend. □ *She showed up with her steady, Tom.* □ *My steady is laid up with a cold. I'll come alone.*

steal someone blind See ROB SOMEONE BLIND.

steal the show *vb. phr.* to be the most popular entertainer or act in a theatre, etc. □ *That song really stole the show.* □ *You steal the show every evening, my dear.*

steam 1. *vb.* to rush through a public place or vehicle such as a train, robbing all there. □ *A gang steamed the tube train and got away with a few hundred quid.* □ *Have you ever steamed anywhere?* **2.** *vb.* to work very hard. □ *We must really steam this one right now. There is no time to lose!* □ *If you steam* *like crazy you should be finished on time.* **3.** *vb.* to travel rapidly, by any means of transportation. □ *If you must steam like that you'll get booked.* □ *Ton-up boys steam around on motor-bikes.* **4.** *mod.* old-fashioned; tradition-al; trustworthy. □ *Why do we have to deal with steam people all the time?* □ *I don't know why, but I prefer the steam railway to the modern electric one.*

steamboats *mod.* very intoxicated due to drink. (Compare with STEAMED (UP).) □ *By 3:00 in the morning, everyone was completely steamboats.* □ *Joe and Arthur kept on knocking them back till they were both steamboats.*

steam chicken *n.* a carrier-born air-craft. □ *Right, let's get our steam chick-ens airborne!* □ *In rapid succession one steam chicken after the other was catapulted off the deck.*

steamed (up) AND **steaming 1.** *mod.* angry. □ *Now, now, don't get so steamed up!* □ *She is really steaming about all this, you know.* **2.** *mod.* intox-icated due to drink. (Scots usage. Com-pare with STEAMBOATS.) □ *By the time Willy got home that evening, he was re-ally steaming.* □ *You can imagine how steamed up they were after spending the entire day in the pub.*

steamer 1. *n.* one who robs by STEAM-ING. □ *I think he's one of the steamers who did the tube train, sir.* □ *When did you become a steamer then, son?* **2.** *n.* a cigarette. (Teens.) □ *He produced a steamer and lit it.* □ *I threw my steam-er away and turned to look him in the eye.*

steam in *vb. phr.* to join an existing fight or start a new one. □ *Everyone just steamed in; there was nothing I could do.* □ *The two gangs were all for steaming in at each other.*

steamin *mod.* very intoxicated due to drink. (Scots usage.) □ *Shuggy got home late, as usual; and steamin, as usual.* □ *To say they were steamin seemed like a bit of an understatement, she thought.*

steaming See STEAMED (UP).

steam navigation *n.* navigation of a ship or aircraft that relies on the old

methods involving charts, slide-rules, sextants and so forth. □ *When all else fails, we can try good old-fashioned steam navigation I suppose.* □ *It's sur-prising just how accurate steam navi-gation can be if done right.*

steam radio *n.* a jocular name for radio since the arrival of television. □ *Yes he's broadcast, but only on steam radio.* □ *An amazing number remain loyal to steam radio, you know.*

steamroller *vb. phr.* to force something to be approved despite significant op-position; to force something to happen despite significant resistance. □ *He thinks he can steamroller this bill through Parliament, but it just won't work.* □ *When you can't steamroller something, try some soft soap instead.*

steam tug *n.* a foolish person. (Rhym-ing slang, linked as follows: steam tug ≈ [mug] = fool.) □ *How can you be such a steam tug?* □ *Making a steam tug like that of someone is not funny.*

steamy *mod.* lewd; sensuous; erotic. □ *They cut a couple of steamy scenes out of the film because of complaints.* □ *Henry and Bess were having a steamy time on the couch.*

steekit nieve *n.* a clenched fist. (Scots usage.) □ *See this? It's ma steekit nieve. See that? It's your nose. Now, do as I ask or watch the two meet at high speed.* □ *Haw maw, a big boy threat-ened me wi' his steekit nieve! (Mummy, a big boy threatened me with his clenched fist!)*

steep *mod.* overpriced; expensive. □ *Isn't £100 sort of steep?* □ *I don't have steep prices here.* □ *Their prices are pretty steep, but their goods are of high quality.*

steever *n.* five pence; originally, a one shilling coin. □ *That'll be a steever, missus.* □ *A steever? For what?*

steno(g(gy)) *n.* a stenographer. □ *Where's my stenoggy? I've got letters to dictate.* □ *There are fewer stenos these days, it seems.*

Stephens See EVEN-STEPHEN(S).

stereo *mod.* stereophonic. □ *The stereo sound effect on this disk is really good.* □ *If you're buying a good stereo sys-*

tem, make sure you can place the speakers in the right locations, or you're wasting your money.

Stevens See EVEN-STEPHEN(S).

stew 1. *vb.* to become agitated or angry. □ *It's bad, but don't stew about it.* □ *I spent most of last night stewing about my job.* **2.** *n.* a state of agitation or anger. (Compare with WORK ONESELF UP INTO A LATHER.) □ *Don't work yourself up into a stew.* □ *You only have to look at them to see that they've been in a terrible stew.* **3.** *n.* a state of prolonged frustration, embarrassment, etc. □ *Let's be honest: we're in a stew.* □ *Well, I'm really glad that stew's behind us now.* **4.** *vb.* to suffer from a state of prolonged frustration, embarrassment, etc. □ *We have no choice but to stew until this sorts itself out.* □ *I hate being left to stew like that.* **5.** *vb.* to be oppressed by excessive heat or humidity, particularly within a room or other enclosed space. □ *Everyone stewed after the air conditioning broke down during the second act.* □ *We really stewed in that tiny room during the heatwave.*

stewed *mod.* somewhat intoxicated due to drink. □ *I've never seen a bartender get stewed like that before.* □ *I felt a little stewed, but that didn't stop me from having more.*

stewed as a prune See STEWED TO THE EYEBALLS.

stewed to the ears See STEWED TO THE EYEBALLS.

stewed to the eyeballs AND **stewed to the eyebrows; stewed as a prune; stewed to the ears; stewed to the gills** *mod.* very intoxicated due to drink. □ *Gerry was stewed to the eyeballs; he couldn't remember his own name.* □ *The kid was stewed to the gills and scared to death of what his parents were going to do to him.* □ *He was stewed to the ears; in fact, he couldn't remember what his own name was.*

stewed to the eyebrows See STEWED TO THE EYEBALLS.

stewed to the gills See STEWED TO THE EYEBALLS.

stick 1. *n.* the device used to propel the ball in various games, such as golf, hockey, billiards, etc. □ *These aren't my sticks, and you aren't my caddy. What's going on around this golf club today?* □ *Joan wanted a new hockey stick for Christmas, but she got a dolls house instead.* **2.** *n.* a joystick. (The principle attitude control column of an aircraft.) □ *The pilot pulled back on the stick, and the plane did nothing—being that he hadn't even started the engine or anything yet.* □ *You pull back on the stick, which lowers the tail and raises the nose, and up you go.* **3.** *n.* punishment; censure; criticism. □ *That tyke! I'll give him some stick he won't forget in a hurry!* □ *Is it really necessary to dole out as much stick as you do?* **4.** *n.* a marijuana cigarette. □ *Harry had to stop for a stick.* □ *The kids found an old stick in Fred's car.* **5.** *n.* a police truncheon. □ *We knew it was going to be bad as the rozzers already had their sticks out.* □ *Max held up his trophy from last night—a copper's stick!* **6.** *n.* the backwoods; the provinces; remote country areas. (Always with *the* and always plural.) □ *I hated living in the sticks.* □ *You hear a lot about how things are in the sticks. They're worse.* **7.** *n.* a stupid, awkward or strange person. □ *Harry is a difficult old stick.* □ *Oh, I don't think Harry is such a bad old stick.* □ *Tell that stick to get a move on.* **8.** *n.* a small glass of beer. □ *Give my friend here a stick.* □ *How about a stick before you go, Charlie?* **9.** *n.* a radio or television transmission mast; an antenna. □ *We don't want another great ugly stick around here, thank you.* □ *Do you think that one day cable and satellite transmission will mean they can pull down all these sticks?* **10.** *n.* a conductor's baton. □ *When the conductor waves his stick, the players are supposed to know what to play.* □ *That new conductor broke about a dozen sticks during rehearsals.* **11.** *n.* the male sexual organ. (Taboo.) □ *Unlike Myra, Sharon thinks of little else but sticks.* □ *Men keep their brains in their sticks!* **12.** *n.* the mast of a ship. □ *The ship had just one stick, but it was unusually tall.* □ *At the top of the stick was the* *crows nest.* **13.** *n.* a ladder. □ *I got onto the stick and climbed up to the roof.* □ *We need a longer stick, I think.*

stickability *n.* perseverance; endurance. □ *Well, Pete has lots of stickability. We must give him that.* □ *It takes a lot of stickability to do something like that.*

stick around *vb. phr.* to remain nearby. □ *Stick around. Things are bound to get better.* □ *I think if you'll stick around, you'll get a seat sooner or later.*

stick at trifles *vb. phr.* to let small details get in the way of a larger issue; to become bogged down with trivia. □ *There are important matters here and we don't want to stick at trifles.* □ *Many a major deal has come unstuck by sticking at trifles.*

Stick 'em up! See HANDS UP!

sticker 1. *n.* a reliable and efficient worker. (Scots usage.) □ *He dizny act like he's a sticker.* □ *Watch that one; he's a sticker all right.* **2.** *n.* a small poster with a sticky back. □ *It's terrible the way the walls are covered with stickers.* □ *Put a sticker there. Everyone will see it there.* **3.** *n.* a prisoner remanded in custody awaiting trial. □ *All the stickers are kept in that wing.* □ *A sticker has privileges denied to convicted prisoners.*

stickie *n.* a member of the Official IRA or Sinn Fein. (Irish usage.) □ *There are a number of stickies living around here, I think.* □ *They say Sean is a stickie, but I don't know.*

stickie-willy *n.* goosegrass or cleavers. (Scots usage.) □ *Why does the cat always come in covered in stickie-willies?* □ *There was a large patch of stickie-willy at the back of the house.*

stick in at something AND **stick in with something** *vb. phr.* to persevere or work hard and doggedly at something. (Scots usage.) □ *I was told that if you stick in at school you'll get a good job.* □ *Morag's sticking in with the Uni to get a good degree.* *(Morag is studying assiduously at University in order to obtain a good degree.)*

stick-in-the-mud *n.* a dull and old-fashioned person. □ *Don't be such an old stick-in-the-mud.* □ *Some stick-in-the-*

mud objected to the kind of music we wanted to play in church.

stick in with something See STICK IN AT SOMETHING.

stick it on someone *vb. phr.* to punch someone. □ *Tom stuck it on Fred on the hooter.* □ *She tried to stick it on me!*

stick man *n.* a constantly lustful man. (Crude.) □ *He doesn't like being called a stick man.* □ *Tom is getting to be such a stick man.*

stick one's neck out *vb. phr.* to take a chance; to invite trouble. □ *Me? Oh no, I'm not sticking my neck out on that!* □ *If you must stick your neck out, try something you have at least some slight chance of being right about.*

stick one's nose in (where it's not wanted) *vb. phr.* to interfere in someone else's business. □ *Why do you always have to stick your nose in?* □ *Please don't stick your nose in where it's not wanted!*

stick out like a sore thumb *vb. phr.* to be very obvious □ *That zit really sticks out like a sore thumb.* □ *Do you think I would stick out like a sore thumb at the party if I wear this coat?*

sticks 1. *n.* a drummer. □ *The soldiers marched off to the beat of the sticks on his skins.* □ *Jimmy says he wants to be a sticks when he grow up, so meantime he has to practice all day long, right?* **2.** *n.* a wooded area. □ *We were walking through the sticks when we found the body, officer.* □ *My land stretches to these sticks over there.*

stick someone on *vb. phr.* to put someone on a criminal charge. (Police.) □ *The pigs are really out to stick Mr Big on for something major this time.* □ *Naw, they'll never stick Mr Big on.*

stick-up *n.* a robbery in the form of a hold-up. □ *This is a stick-up!* □ *Telling people it's a stick-up will normally be more effective if you have a gun in your hand instead of that banana.*

sticky 1. *mod.* [of a person] difficult; unhelpful. □ *He's being very sticky about this, you know.* □ *Why do you have to be so sticky over every new idea presented to you?* **2.** *mod.* [of a problem] requiring much effort or skill to resolve; awkward. □ *Things began to get a little sticky, and Barlowe began to move toward the door.* □ *When the going got sticky, Freddy disappeared.* **3.** *mod.* having to do with hot and humid weather. □ *It's so sticky today!* □ *I can't take another sticky day like this.* **4.** *n.* a liqueur. □ *A wonderful meal! And now...a sticky?* □ *I'm afraid Otto would prefer a pint of beer to a sticky.*

sticky (bun) *n.* a sweet bun covered with icing. □ *Would you like a sticky bun?* □ *Let's have a sticky bun with our coffee.*

sticky end *n.* an unpleasant or messy way to die. □ *Julius Caesar came to a sticky end on the steps of the Capitol.* □ *If you don't get that report on my desk by morning, you'll be coming to a sticky end, too!*

sticky fingers *n.* a tendency to steal. □ *Bruno has sticky fingers and especially likes wallets.* □ *Watch these young kids with sticky fingers who come in here "just looking."*

sticky wicket 1. *n.* a cricket pitch that has not yet dried after rain and so is difficult to play. □ *I think we'll have a sticky wicket after that rain.* □ *The sticky wicket made the game slow for the rest of the day.* **2.** *n.* a difficult situation. □ *How did we get into a sticky wicket like this?* □ *We're got a bit of a sticky wicket here.*

stiff 1. *mod.* dead. (Originally underworld.) □ *He's stiff. There's nothing that can be done.* □ *Yeah, he's stiff. Don't hit him no more.* **2.** *n.* a corpse. (Underworld.) □ *They pulled another stiff out of the river last night. Looks like another gang killing.* □ *They took me into a room full of stiffs to identify Rocko's body.* **3.** *n.* a non-tipping customer. □ *I just knew, the moment he came into the restaurant, that he was another stiff.* □ *There seemed to have been an awful lot a stiffs in the cafe that day, she thought.* **4.** *n.* a conformist; a conventional person. (Teens.) □ *What does the stiff want?* □ *Even a stiff like that has to earn a living.* **5.** *n.* any illicit document within a prison. □ *The*

screws found a whole lot of stiffs in Mr Big's cell.* □ *Where did you get these stiffs?* **6.** *vb.* to participate in sexual intercourse, from the male perspective. (Taboo.) □ *One look and he knew she had already been stiffed that evening.* □ *There were a couple of teenagers in the back room, stiffing.* **7.** *mod.* [of drink that is] potent; strong. □ *I could use a stiff drink.* □ *Here, see if this one's stiff enough for you.*

stiff-arsed 1. *mod.* constipated. (Taboo.) □ *I hate being stiff-arsed like this.* □ *Some of this stuff may stop you being stiff-arsed.* **2.** *mod.* stiff-necked or unbending. (Taboo.) □ *Try unbending, you stiff-arsed clown.* □ *No, this guy is really stiff-arsed.*

stiffener 1. *n.* a short drink of spirits. □ *I'll have a stiffener and a packet of cigarettes.* □ *One Scotch stiffener please, bartender.* **2.** *n.* a reviving drink. □ *I do like this stiffener.* □ *Can I have a stiffener, please?*

stiff someone 1. *vb.* to extort something from someone. □ *He's always stiffing someone. That's his thing.* □ *Lefty tried to stiff forty quid out of me.* **2.** *vb.* to kill someone. □ *Barlowe was sure he could keep Rocko from stiffing him.* □ *The boss told Rocko to stiff Barlowe.*

stiffy 1. *n.* a formal, engraved invitation card. □ *See who we got a stiffy from today, dear!* □ *The mantelpiece carried a number of stiffies from the very top people in London society.* **2.** *n.* an erection. (Taboo.) □ *Here I come, stiffy and all!* □ *Fear not my lovely, I'll have a stiffy for you!*

still and all *mod.* nevertheless. □ *Really? Still and all, you could be right...* □ *I did not believe it at the time, but still and all later on, when I saw some of the lab results, I began to have doubts.*

sting 1. *n.* a confidence trick. □ *That street trader caught me in a very neat sting. Unfortunately.* □ *Take care, most pawnshops work some kind of sting on their punters.* **2.** *n.* a scheme intended to entrap criminals. □ *The sting came off without a hitch.* □ *It was a well-*

planned sting and shouldn't have failed.
3. *n.* the male sexual organ. (Taboo.) □
Only small boys wave their stings about like that, Wayne. Put it away! □ *Myra says stings are disgusting but then Myra's strange.* **4.** *n.* any short burst of music, a logo, or other sign used as a station identifier by a TV or radio station.* □ *Here comes the sting for your soap, mum!* □ *I like the programme but hate the sting. Sorry.*

stink 1. *vb.* to be repellent. □ *This whole setup stinks.* □ *Your act stinks. Try another agent.* **2.** *n.* a commotion. (Compare with RAISE A STINK (ABOUT SOMEONE OR SOMETHING).) □ *The stink you made about money has done no good at all. You're fired.* □ *One more stink like that and out you go.*

stinker 1. *n.* an unpleasant or untrustworthy person. (Compare with SKUNK.) □ *Jerry is a real stinker. Look what he did!* □ *What stinker messed up my desk?* **2.** *n.* a serious problem. □ *This whole business is a real stinker.* □ *What a stinker of a problem.* **3.** *n.* an offensive letter; a crushing criticism or severe rebuke. □ *Well! I'll write a real stinker about this.* □ *After the story in the paper, he got twenty letters of thanks and one stinker.*

stinking *mod.* lousy; rotten; disgusting. □ *What a stinking mess you've got yourself into now.* □ *That was a lousy stinking thing to do. Really stinking!*

stinking (drunk) AND **stinko** *mod.* very intoxicated due to drink. □ *He was really stinko.* □ *She came within an inch of getting stinking drunk.*

stinking rich AND **stinking with (money)** *mod.* very rich. □ *I'd like to be stinking rich for the rest of my life.* □ *Tiffany is stinking with, and she acts like it.*

stinking with (money) See STINKING RICH.

stinko See STINKING (DRUNK).

stinkpot *n.* an unpleasant or wicked person. (Also a term of address. Juvenile. Offensive.) □ *Who is the stinkpot who has ruined all my work?* □ *Jerry is a real stinkpot. Look what he did!*

stink to (high) heaven 1. *vb. phr.* to have a very offensive smell. □ *This kitchen stinks to high heaven. What besides garlic are you cooking?* □ *Where has this dog been? It stinks to heaven.* **2.** *vb. phr.* to be obviously wrong or suspicious. □ *This deal is messed up. It stinks to high heaven.* □ *Something's wrong here. Somebody blabbed. This setup stinks to high heaven.*

stink-wagon *n.* any road vehicle powered by petrol or diesel. (From the point-of-view of the cyclist.) □ *I hate driving among these stink-wagons.* □ *The stink-wagon almost forced me off the road!*

stinky *mod.* bad. (Juvenile.) □ *That was a stinky thing to do.* □ *You have a very stinky attitude. Really stinky.*

stir *n.* prison. (Underworld.) □ *I can't stand being in stir!* □ *Stir is very dull—and dangerous.*

stir the shit *vb. phr.* to cause trouble. (Taboo.) □ *There's Harry, stirring the shit as usual.* □ *Why do people have to stir the shit like that?*

stitch *n.* a sharp pain, usually in the side. □ *I got a stitch and had to drop out of the marathon.* □ *A stitch in the side can be very painful.*

stitch something up See SEW SOMETHING UP.

Stitch this! *exclam.* a cry of defiance, said when attacking someone. (Refers to the damage caused to the recipient.) □ *Oh yeh? Well, stitch this!* □ *"Stitch this!" he yelled, and then punched me on the nose.*

stitch up someone or something *vb. phr.* to deal with someone or something in an effective, thorough, final, but ruthless way. □ *They've really stitched me up now; that's for sure.* □ *We found a way to stitch up that little difficulty once and for all.*

St. Louis blues 1. *n.* shoes. (Rhyming slang.) □ *Why are you in your St. Louis blues? Are you going somewhere?* □ *I find these St. Louis blues uncomfortable.* **2.** *n.* news. (Rhyming slang. Scots usage.) □ *What's the St. Louis blues, Wullie?* □ *You could tell he was the bearer of bad St. Louis blues.*

stoater AND **stotter 1.** *n.* anything that is brilliant or impressive. (Scots usage.) □ *Now that is one stoater of an idea!* □ *What a stotter! Where can I get one?* **2.** *n.* a particularly attractive woman. (Scots usage.) □ *Have yous seen Shuggie's new wumman? She's a right wee stoater, I tell yous! (Have you people seen Hugh's new girlfriend? She's small but really very attractive, you know.)* □ *Look at her! Whit a stotter!*

stocious AND **stoshers; stoshious; stotious** *mod.* very intoxicated due to drink. (Scots usage.) □ *Clearly there had been a little something extra in the wine. Everyone in the church was stocious.* □ *If yer stotious yer no gonna bide in ma howff; oot richt noo, the hale jing-bang o' yous! (If you are very drunk you're not going to stay in my public house; out right now, all of you!)*

stockbroker belt *n.* the prosperous suburbs where stockbrokers live. □ *He's got a huge house in the stockbroker belt, you know.* □ *We're moving to the stockbroker belt ourselves, you know.*

Stockbroker Tudor *n.* expensive, but tasteless, reproduction architecture. □ *As you might expect, Gloria lives in a typical example of Stockbroker Tudor.* □ *Stockbroker Tudor may not be to your taste, but it is not cheap.*

stocking-filler AND **stocking-stuffer** *n.* a small gift that is suitable for putting inside a Christmas stocking. □ *This will make the perfect stocking-filler.* □ *I got some little stocking-stuffers for the kids.*

stocking-stuffer See STOCKING-FILLER.

stodge *n.* thick, heavy, unappetising food. □ *This stuff is just stodge.* □ *Have you nothing but stodge in this place?*

stoked *mod.* delighted; excited. □ *I was really stoked with her news.* □ *Don't get too stoked just yet. There's more.*

stoke up *vb. phr.* to eat well. □ *Who's been stoking up on the chocolate cake?* □ *After Christmas, we stoked up on turkey for three days.*

stomach *vb.* to tolerate someone or something. (Usually negative.) □ *Bruno couldn't stomach the opera, and he left after the first ten minutes.* □ *I can't stomach films like that.*

stone (cold) sober *mod.* absolutely sober. □ *I am stone cold sober, or I will be by morning anyway.* □ *I found the secret to being stone sober. Don't drink.*

stoned *mod.* very intoxicated due to drink or drugs. □ *Bruno's a really nice person when he's stoned.* □ *Tipsy? Stoned, more like!*

stone dead *mod.* dead; unquestionably dead; long dead. □ *The cat was stone dead and stiff as a board by the time we got to him.* □ *Old Tom is stone dead and in the ground.*

stoned out of one's head AND **stoned out of one's mind** *mod.* under the effects of marijuana. □ *Tiffany was stoned out of her head and started giggling.* □ *The guy was stoned out of his mind and should never have been driving.*

stone frigate *n.* a shore establishment of the Royal Navy. □ *I've been posted to a stone frigate!* □ *There are a lot of stone frigates in the Portsmouth area.*

Stone me! AND **Stone the crows!** *exclam.* an exclamation of surprise. □ *Stone me! He didn't, did he?* □ *Well stone the crows, what do you expect!*

stones *n.* the testicles. (Taboo. Normally with *the* and in the plural.) □ *He turned sideways to protect his stones.* □ *Thud, right in the stones. Ye gods, it hurt!*

Stone the crows! See STONE ME!

stonewall *vb.* to obstruct something or someone. □ *And again, the chairman tried to stonewall the investigation.* □ *If you continue to stonewall like this, we'll have to call in the police.*

stonewall bonkers *mod.* absolutely certain. □ *It's stonewall bonkers; everything is now settled.* □ *Can you have two? For stonewall bonkers you can!*

stonewall(ing) *n.* an act of obstruction. □ *His answer to the committee was another stonewall that caught them all by surprise.* □ *The stonewalling they were faced with was almost too much.*

stonie *n.* a stonemason. □ *When you look at the work they have left behind, you can see that there have been some very fine stonies in these parts.* □ *Is there much work for a stonie today?*

stonk *n.* a large artillery bombardment. □ *There was a huge stonk, so we knew a major attack was coming soon.* □ *A stonk like that involves literally millions of shells.*

stonker *vb.* to defeat, kill or outwit someone. □ *I'm gonna stonker you once and for all.* □ *Watch it! Otto would stonker you as soon as look at you.*

stonkered 1. *mod.* very exhausted or tired. (Australian.) □ *I feel too stonkered to go to work today.* □ *After the game, the whole team was stonkered.* **2.** *mod.* very intoxicated due to drink or drugs. □ *My friend here is stonkered and needs a lift, and can I have one, too?* □ *Wally was stonkered beyond any kind of help.*

stonkers *n.* the female breasts. (Crude. Normally with *the* and in the plural.) □ *My stonkers aren't all I might have wished for.* □ *There she was, bold as brass, with her stonkers on full display.*

stonking *mod.* wonderful or fantastic. (Australian.) □ *This wine is really stonking!* □ *Boy, this fishing rod is stonking.*

stony (broke) *mod.* completely without money. □ *I'm sorry, I'm stony broke. Can I send you a cheque?* □ *What could I do? She was stony.*

stooge *n.* someone who is a compliant subordinate; a puppet. □ *I'm not going to be your stooge!* □ *The guy's a stooge for Mr Big. Ignore him.*

stoolie See STOOL (PIGEON).

stool (pigeon) AND **stoolie** *n.* an informer. (Originally underworld.) □ *Some stool spilled the works to the boys in blue.* □ *There's nothing I hate worse than a stoolie.*

stooshie *n.* a loud argument; a brawl. (Scots usage.) □ *Shut up! Ah dinna want to know about yer stooshie! (Shut up! I don't want to know about your brawl.)* □ *Shuggy ower likes a good stooshie an that. (Hugh always like a good loud argument and all that sort of thing.)*

stop a packet *vb. phr.* to be killed or wounded, especially by a bullet. □ *My great uncle stopped a packet during the Battle of the Somme.* □ *If you go out into that firefight, you're almost sure to stop a packet.*

stop at home *vb. phr.* to stay at home. □ *No, I'm not going. I'm stopping at home tonight.* □ *Can we not both stop at home tomorrow, dear?*

stop-gap *n.* a quick, probably temporary and unsatisfactory solution to a problem. (Compare with JERRY-BUILT, KLUDGE, LASH-UP and QUICK FIX.) □ *It's crude, but we've got a stop-gap here for you.* □ *I don't want a stop-gap, I want a proper cure.*

stop-go economics *n.* the use—or rather, the misuse—of government economic regulations and controls in such a way that there are alternate periods of fast and slow growth of business, employment, prices, etc. □ *Stop-go economics has been the curse of the British economy since the end of the Second World War.* □ *Oh no, stop-go economics has been a British problem for much longer than that.*

stop press *n.* last-minute news; space left in a newspaper for any last-minute news. □ *There is nothing about that in the stop press.* □ *Not many newspapers still have a stop press, do they?*

stormer *n.* a large or impressive entity. □ *Boy, there's a real stormer!* □ *We're looking for a stormer here.*

storm in a teacup *n.* much excitement over very little. □ *Oh it's nothing; a storm in a teacup.* □ *Now we don't want another storm in a teacup, do we?*

stoshers See STOCIOUS.

stoshious See STOCIOUS.

stotious See STOCIOUS.

stotter See STOATER.

stottin fou *mod.* spectacularly intoxicated due to drink. (Scots usage.) □ *Wee Shuggy's stottin fou agin!* □ *How can anybody get stottin fou like that in so little time?*

stout fellow *n.* a reliable, worthy man. □ *He's a real great, stout fellow.* □ *What does the stout fellow expect?*

stove *n.* a car heater. □ *Cor, it's freezing. Let's put on the stove.* □ *The stove is on, but it takes a minute or two for the heat to come through.*

Stow it! *exclam.* "Shut up!" □ *Okay, stow it! I've heard enough.* □ *Stow it! That is enough of your winging.*

straddle the fence *vb. phr.* to support (or attempt to support) both sides of an issue. (See SIT ON THE FENCE.) □ *The government is straddling the fence on this, hoping the public will forget it come election time.* □ *Our candidate wanted to straddle the fence until the last minute, and that alone cost her a lot of votes.*

straight 1. *mod.* honest; unembellished. □ *This is the straight truth.* □ *Have I ever been anything but straight with you?* **2.** *n.* a tobacco cigarette; a tobacco cigarette butt. (As opposed to a marijuana cigarette.) □ *No, I want a straight. That spliff makes me sneeze.* □ *Can I borrow a straight from you?* **3.** *mod.* having to do with undiluted spirits. □ *I'll take mine straight.* □ *Make one straight with a little ice.* **4.** *mod.* relieved and satisfied by a dose of drugs. □ *It only takes a few bucks and a little time to get straight.* □ *She will be straight for a few hours, and then the same struggle all over again—all through the night.* **5.** *mod.* off drugs; no longer using drugs. □ *I'm straight now, and I'm gonna stay that way.* □ *See how long you can stay straight, how about it?* **6.** *n.* someone who does not use drugs. □ *The guy's a straight. He's going to turn us over to the cops!* □ *The straights are putting pressure on the local police to clean up this area.* **7.** *n.* a non-homosexual; a heterosexual person, especially from the homosexual viewpoint. □ *Walter invited a few straights to the affair, just to keep things calm.* □ *The straights really get upset if you camp it up too much.*

straight and narrow *n.* the path of true virtue. □ *Just you stick to the straight and narrow, and you can't go too far wrong.* □ *Sometimes it's hard keeping to the straight and narrow, especially if you can't find it.*

straighten oneself up *vb. phr.* to become honest. □ *Well, you've served your time. Now go out there and straighten yourself up, eh?* □ *I've just got to straighten myself up this time.*

straighten someone out *vb. phr.* to enlighten someone as to the true nature of something. □ *I can see I better straighten him out.* □ *Okay, let me straighten you out about this business.*

straight-faced *mod.* with a serious, unsmiling face. □ *Mary couldn't stay straight-faced very long. It was just too funny.* □ *He appears to be a very straight-faced guy, but really he has a tremendous sense of humour.*

straight from the bog AND **straight off the turnips** *mod.* "as Irish as can be." (Offensive.) □ *Here they are, more Irish straight from the bog!* □ *They don't all come straight off the turnips, you know. They are intelligent and well-educated.*

straight from the horse's mouth *mod.* directly from the source. (As if a racehorse were giving racing tips.) □ *Of course it's true. I got it straight from the horse's mouth.* □ *This came straight from the horse's mouth. It's Zeerocks Copy in the sixth race.*

straight from the shoulder *mod.* frankly; directly, without attenuation or embellishment. □ *Okay, I'll give it to you straight from the shoulder.* □ *All right, here it is straight from the shoulder: clean out your desk; you're finished here.*

straight man *n.* a comedian's partner or stooge, who supplies him with remarks that are replied to humorously. □ *I need a straight man to feed me all my jokes.* □ *I'm tired of being a straight man for a has-been comic.*

straight off the turnips See STRAIGHT FROM THE BOG.

straight out of the trees *mod.* refers to black persons. (Racially offensive.) □ *To accuse blacks of being straight out of the trees is highly insulting.* □ *He's not straight out of the trees, but is straight out of Oxford University.*

straight talk(ing) *n.* direct and honest talk. □ *It's about time for a little straight talking around here.* □ *If they want straight talk and can handle straight talk, give 'em straight talk.*

Straight-up! *exclam.* "Honestly!"; "It's true!" □ *But it's true, straight-up!* □ *Straight-up! That's what happened!*

straight-up 1. *mod.* true; correct. □ *Don't worry, it's all straight-up again now.* □ *It's fine; it's all straight-up.* **2.** *mod.* honest. □ *He's always been straight-up with me.* □ *Jack's a completely straight-up man in my experience.*

strain one's greens AND **strain one's taters** *vb. phr.* to urinate. (Crude.) □ *I've got to strain my greens. Back in a minute.* □ *Well, straining my taters does make room for some more beer!*

strain one's taters See STRAIN ONE'S GREENS.

strangler *n.* a necktie. □ *Pardon me sir, is this your strangler?* □ *The attacker was wearing a bright strangler, constable.*

straphanger *n.* a passenger on public transport such as bus, train or underground, who has to stand. (Typically during rush hour, when there are more passengers than seats available.) □ *I didn't think I could ever get used to being a straphanger.* □ *Straphangers learn to blot out their surroundings.*

strapped (for cash) *mod.* broke; short of money. □ *I'm sorry I can't pay you right now. I'm strapped.* □ *They're really strapped for cash at the present time.*

strawberry 1. *n.* a red nose. □ *How did you get a strawberry like that?* □ *He threatened to punch me right on my big strawberry!* **2.** *n.* a cripple. (Rhyming slang, linked as follows: strawberry [ripple] ~ cripple. *Strawberry ripple* is a variety of ice cream.) □ *You can't go around calling people with walking difficulties strawberries!* □ *I would not say he's a strawberry, but he has great difficulty with walking.*

streak 1. *vb.* to run about in a public place naked, as a stunt. □ *So this girl streaked back and forth over the pitch for quite a while until the cops caught her.* □ *He streaked round the park as a dare.* **2.** *n.* a naked run in a public place, carried out as a stunt. □ *There was a streak at the end of the game, but peo-*ple were leaving then and didn't see it. □ *That was no streak; that was the trainer in his longjohns being chased by the owner of the team.*

streaker *n.* someone who runs naked in public places as a stunt. □ *The streaker ran through a glass door and was severely injured.* □ *Streakers seemed to take over the whole country in the '70s.*

streak of piss AND **long streak of piss** *n.* someone who considers themself more important than other people do. (Taboo.) □ *Oh, he's really just a streak of piss.* □ *Tell that long streak of piss to get lost.*

street accident *n.* a mongrel dog. □ *Why do you keep a street accident like him?* □ *The ugly old street accident frightened me.*

street cred(ibility) *n.* the ability to relate with ordinary people or with the currently fashionable urban subculture. □ *He certainly got lots of street credibility.* □ *You won't have much street cred if you go around dressed like that.*

streets ahead *mod.* much superior. □ *What Jones Co. has to offer is streets ahead of anything from Smith Ltd.* □ *Don't worry, you're streets ahead of the competition.*

street-smart AND **street-wise** *mod.* wise in the ways of urban life; imbued with the low cunning of a dweller in a deprived city area. □ *Freddy was street-smart at the age of eight.* □ *Bess wasn't street-wise enough to survive by herself.*

street-walker *n.* a street prostitute. (Crude.) □ *There was a street-walker standing right on that corner.* □ *There are a lot of street-walkers around here in the centre of town.*

street-wise See STREET-SMART.

stretch 1. *n.* a prison term. □ *I was away for a stretch of about seven years.* □ *That's quite a stretch for tax evasion.* **2.** *vb.* to be hanged (that is, executed). □ *You'll stretch for this, Lefty!* □ *I'll live to see you stretched, you rat!* **3.** *vb.* to outlast or out-endure an opponent. (Irish usage.) □ *You've nothing to worry about as you're easily going to* stretch the rest of them. □ I thought I could stretch her, but I was wrong.

stretcher n. a liar. □ The fact is, he's just a stretcher. □ Anyone who told you that is a stretcher.

stretch one's legs vb. phr. to take a walk, principally for the purpose of exercising oneself. □ I need to get out of here and stretch my legs for a while. □ Most of us got up to go and stretch our legs during the intermission.

Strewth! exclam. a variant of "God's truth." □ Strewth! What next! □ Strewth, what did they expect?

strides n. trousers. □ He pulled on his strides and stood up. □ Woman, what have you done with all my strides?

Strike a light! exclam. an exclamation of surprise. □ Well strike a light, what do you expect! □ Strike a light! He didn't, did he?

strike it rich vb. phr. to discover riches or a source of prosperity or success. □ I never thought I would strike it rich. □ "Pete is the kind of guy who just wants to strike it rich and live in the lap of luxury for the rest of his life." "So. He's pretty ordinary, then?"

strike(-me) n. bread. (Rhyming slang, linked as follows: strike(-me) [dead] ≈ bread.) □ Any strike-me, love? □ Even a few slices of strike would be good.

strike pay dirt See HIT PAY DIRT.

Strine n. Australian English. (Australian.) □ Oh yes, she's an Aussie all right; listen to her talking Strine! □ Can you understand Strine?

string n. a surgical ligature. □ We will apply a string to stem the flow in that artery now. □ There were some very interesting strings there, the surgeon thought.

string along with someone or something AND **tag along with someone or something** vb. phr. to accompany someone. □ I strung along with him to the exhibition. □ All right, I'll tag along with that.

stringer n. a journalist who is paid by the number of words published. □ She's got three stringers working for her now on her local newspaper. □ Being a

stringer is a pretty soulless occupation, I would think.

String (of Beads) n. Leeds. (Rhyming slang. Leeds is a city in the north of England.) □ String of Beads is the largest city in Yorkshire. □ I come from String; have you got a problem with that?

string of ponies n. a "stable" of prostitutes controlled by one PIMP. (Crude.) □ Mr Big keeps a string of ponies, you know. □ The real surprise would have been if he had not had a string of ponies.

string someone along vb. phr. to mislead someone. (See LEAD SOMEONE A (MERRY) DANCE.) □ I'm being strung along again. □ No, I'm not stringing you along. This is the plain truth.

string someone up vb. phr. to hang someone. □ They just strung the bandit up without ceremony. □ Of course, stringing him up was exactly what he deserved.

strip lighting n. fluorescent lighting. □ I don't like strip lighting; it's too garish. □ I like to have strip lighting in my house because it makes everything so bright.

stripper n. a strip-tease artist. □ Tracy worked for a while as a stripper. □ Strippers from all over the world assembled here for their fourth annual convention and immediately got down to the bare essentials.

strip-tease n. a slow, tantalising removal of clothes, performed as a theatrical act. (Normally, but not exclusively, performed by a female.) □ They had a strip-tease at the party, but it was exceptionally boring, if you really want to know. □ Why is it that are strip-teases are so un-sexy?

stroke n. a trick or deception. □ No more strokes. They need solid answers. □ Well it's a stroke, but I don't think you'll get away with it.

strong vb. to impose a heavy sentence. □ The judge really stronged it on Otto there! □ Any one who did something like that really deserves to be stronged.

strong-arm 1. vb. phr. to force or bully someone to do something. □ Bruno tried to strong-arm Frank into co-op-erating. □ *Don't you try to strong-arm me, you slob!* **2.** *mod.* forceful; by phys-ical force. □ *The strong-arm approach got him nowhere.* □ *Too much strong-arm stuff isn't good.*

strong-arm man *n.* a bully; a man who is employed to use physical power to force someone to do some-thing. □ *Bruno is Mr Big's strong-arm man.* □ *You can take your pick from hundreds of strong-arm men in this part of town.*

strong-arm tactics *n.* the use of force. □ *No more strong-arm tactics. You need to be more subtle.* □ *Strong-arm tactics are out. The boss says be gentle and don't break anybody.*

strongbox *n.* a solitary confinement cell in a prison. □ *Right! It's the strong-box for you!* □ *He was in the strongbox for almost half his sentence.*

strong it *vb. phr.* to behave in an exces-sively aggressive manner. □ *Oh, he's always stronging it.* □ *Instead of stronging it, think first.*

stroppy *mod.* obstreperous. □ *Oh, he's always being stroppy about something or other.* □ *I don't want that stroppy character working here.*

struggle and strife *n.* a wife. (Rhyming slang.) □ *My struggle and strife disap-proved of the film.* □ *I've got to go home to me struggle and strife.*

strung out **1.** *mod.* intoxicated and be-wildered due to drugs. □ *Bruno is re-ally strung out lately. What's he shooting now?* □ *Tim is sort of strung out and doesn't even remember what he took.* **2.** *mod.* physically weak; weak-willed; dissipated. □ *Harry's still badly strung out all this time after his illness.* □ *Clare is strung out and so easily con-fused.* **3.** *mod.* depressed; nervous. □ *I get strung out before exams and other traumatic things.* □ *I'm a little strung out—because of the accident, I sup-pose.*

stubs *n.* the teeth. □ *Look at her nice white stubs!* □ *I've got to go and brush my stubs.*

stuck-up *mod.* pretentious or snobbish-ly conceited. □ *Tom is really stuck-up.*

□ *What a stuck-up old fart!* □ *Don't be so stuck-up. Unbend a little.*

stuck with someone or something *mod.* burdened with someone or some-thing; left with the burden of someone or something. □ *It's your problem, and you're stuck with it.* □ *Am I stuck with this kid forever?*

stud *n.* a young man considered to be particularly successful sexually. (Crude. From the Standard English sense of a male horse kept for breeding purposes.) □ *Fred likes to think he's a real stud.* □ *Susan, do you see that stud over there? Think he's going steady with anyone?*

stuff **1.** *n.* an anaesthetic. □ *You won't feel a thing once you're given the stuff.* □ *I don't like having stuff given to me.* **2.** *n.* a woman viewed as a sex object. (Taboo.) □ *The pretty little stuff came over to him to ask for a light.* □ *Any stuff available around here, mate?*

stuffed shirt *n.* pretentious or snob-bishly foolish man. □ *Mr Wilson is a stuffed shirt, and people would tell him so if he didn't have so much money.* □ *I don't want to listen to that stuffed shirt anymore.*

Stuff it! *exclam.* "I am not interested in that!", "Get rid of that!" □ *Stuff it! I'm going home.* □ *Stuff it, I don't want to see it again.*

stuff someone *vb. phr.* to perform sex-ual intercourse, from the male perspec-tive. (Taboo.) □ *I'm hoping to stuff someone tonight.* □ *He was stuffing her like it was going out of fashion.*

stuffy **1.** *mod.* straight-laced; conven-tional. □ *Sometimes the stuffy ones get the best degrees.* □ *Exciting? Let's just say everyone thought he was really stuffy.* **2.** *mod.* wealthy. □ *Ken is stuffy because of the money his uncle left him.* □ *I wouldn't mind being stuffy like him.* **3.** *mod.* obstinate; sulky; awkward. □ *Oh, why must you always be so stuffy, Albert?* □ *I'm not being stuffy, Lavinia.*

stumer **1.** *n.* a failure or bad bargain. □ *Brilliant! You do realise that's another stumer you've got us, Harry?* □ *Stumers are the last thing we need right now. How about a success, just for a change?* **2.** *n.* a counterfeit coin, forged banknote or bad check. □ *I don't want these coins! They're all stumers, and not even very good ones!* □ *The bank returned another of Otto's cheques, making that ten stumers he's tried to pass this week.* **3.** *n.* an imaginary horse race, devised to alter the public perception of a horse's chances of winning in a real race so that its odds are run up and a killing can be made by those operating the deception. □ *It turns out they had "raced" that horse in a dozen stumers over the last few months.* □ *How can they get away with stumers, anyway?* **4.** *n.* a swindle. □ *Gerry has a new plan for a money-making stumer, but he hasn't actually tried it out yet.* □ *What sort of stumer did you get ripped off with?* **5.** *n.* a swindler. □ *What an obvious stumer that fellow is.* □ *I don't want anything to do with a stumer like him.* **6.** *n.* a foolish person. □ *Who's the stumer in the bright orange trousers?* □ *Don't be a stumer. That's impossible.* **7.** *n.* a mess; a mistake or error. □ *Any more stumers like that and you're out!* □ *Oh no, you've made another stumer.*

stumped for an answer *mod.* unable to reply. □ *Well, now you got me completely stumped for an answer.* □ *If you're ever stumped for an answer, try "Knickers."*

stumper *n.* a wicket keeper. (Cricket.) □ *Who's to be stumper?* □ *The stumper caught him!*

stumps *n.* a person's legs. □ *My stumps are sore from all that walking.* □ *You need good strong stumps to do that kind of climbing.*

stump someone *vb.* to confuse or puzzle someone. □ *That one really stumped me.* □ *I like to stump people with hard questions.*

stump up *vb. phr.* to pay up. □ *I refuse to stump up for someone else's stupidity.* □ *You know, you're going to have to stump up anyway in the long run.*

stung for something *vb. phr.* to be cheated of something, usually a smallish sum of money or other minor loss. □ *The taxi driver stung me for £10!* □ *Harry reckons he got stung for a few quid by his bookie.*

stunned *mod.* slightly intoxicated due to drink. (Scots usage.) □ *No, no, it's not too bad. He's just somewhat stunned.* □ *One pint and he's stunned; two and he's stocious!*

stunner *n.* a spectacularly good-looking woman. □ *Did you see that stunner who just came in?* □ *I think that she is a real stunner, and I go to all her films—again and again.*

stupid arse See STUPID ASS.

stupid ass AND **stupid arse** *n.* a stupid person. (STUPID ARSE is taboo.) □ *That was the sort of thing only a stupid ass would do.* □ *You can be such a stupid arse!*

stupid prick See SILLY PRICK.

sub 1. *n.* a subaltern. (Military.) □ *I was a sub under Colonel Smith for a while.* □ *The subs in this regiment are all of the very finest character.* **2.** *n.* a sub-editor, especially on a newspaper. □ *The sub had made a complete hash of my story as it appeared in the paper.* □ *I'm a sub on the Daily Grind.* **3.** *n.* a submarine. □ *I was aboard a sub for twenty minutes—and that was at Disney World.* □ *You have to have a special kind of personality to live on a sub.* **4.** *n.* a subscription, as to a magazine. □ *I got a sub to a computer magazine for my birthday.* □ *Would you like to buy a sub to the local newspaper?* **5.** *n.* a subvention, a loan made in anticipation of future income. □ *Can I have a sub until pay day, please?* □ *He asked for a sub because he's broke.*

subcheese *n.* everything; the lot. (From the Hindi words *sab* and *chiz*, meaning "all" and "thing" respectively, by hobson-jobson.) □ *Yes. Everything, the lot, subcheese.* □ *You can have the subcheese so far as I care.*

subtopia *n.* ugly and unplanned urban or suburban sprawl. □ *Everywhere there was subtopia, to the horizon.* □ *He hated living in subtopia but everyone did. What could he do?*

Subway *n.* the popular name for Glasgow's underground railway system. (Scots usage. Normally with *the*.) □ *The Glasgow underground railway is the only one in Europe which is com-*

monly called a "subway" by the local people and not just visiting Americans. □ *I met him on the Subway this morning.*

sucker 1. *n.* a gullible person; a simpleton. □ *See if you can sell that sucker Tower Bridge.* □ *The sucker says he doesn't need another bridge, thank you. He's already bought London Bridge.* **2.** *n.* a prospective victim. (Criminals.) □ *Here comes another sucker.* □ *There's another sucker born every minute.*

sucker for someone or something *n.* someone who is strongly predisposed to like or be in favour of someone or something. □ *I'm always a sucker for a pretty girl.* □ *Ted is a sucker for any dessert with whipped cream on it.*

sucker someone *vb.* to delude someone. □ *Are you trying to sucker me?* □ *You're suckering me!*

suck someone off *vb. phr.* to perform oral sex upon a man. (Taboo.) □ *Prostitutes make most of their money by sucking men off, you know.* □ *She'll suck you off for £20.*

suck up to someone *vb. phr.* to attempt to gain influence with or favour from someone. □ *In school, Max was always sucking up to the teacher.* □ *Don't suck up to me. It won't do any good.*

sudden death *mod.* of a decision or choice that is made quickly, decisively and without recourse to reconsideration. □ *The game ended in a sudden death playoff.* □ *Okay, you've got just one more sudden death chance.*

suds *n.* beer. □ *I do like the suds they have in this place.* □ *Can I have suds, please?*

sug See SELL UNDER GUISE.

Sugar! *exclam.* SHIT and BUGGER, which two words it might be concatenated from. (Crude. A euphemism and disguise.) □ *Sugar! They found out!* □ *Oh sugar, what do I do now?*

sugar 1. *n.* a good-looking or attractive girl or young woman. □ *Look at her, isn't she a sugar?* □ *Now there's a really attractive sugar.* **2.** *n.* banknotes that are without value. □ *Old East German Ost Marks are just sugar nowa-*

days, you know. □ *If inflation keeps up long enough, every banknote becomes sugar eventually.* **3.** *n.* granulated snow, good for skiing. □ *They say there's always plenty of sugar at that resort.* □ *There was not a single particle of sugar to be seen anywhere.*

sugar-coated *mod.* concerning something which has been made palatable or easy to digest. (Figurative.) □ *Maths is so sugar-coated these days, even I could learn it.* □ *Stop giving them nothing but sugar-coated snippets of knowledge.*

sugar daddy *n.* an older man who is both guardian and lover of a younger woman. □ *Old Mr Wilson? He's Caroline's new sugar daddy, of course.* □ *I thought sugar daddies were illegal.*

suicide blonde *n.* a woman or girl whose hair was dyed by her own hand. □ *What a mess her hair is; definitely a suicide blonde, I'd say.* □ *He reckons he can tell the suicide blondes quite easily.*

suit *n.* a bureaucrat; a management person; a functionary within a corporate or government hierarchy. (From the habit of such people of dressing more formally than those in less exalted positions. A dismissive term implying mild contempt, so use with caution.) □ *So this suit comes up and asks to be taken to the airport.* □ *A couple of suits checked into a working-class hotel and caused some eyebrows to be raised.*

sulph *n.* amphetamines. □ *You can get some good sulph in this part of town.* □ *What does sulph cost around here?*

Sunday best *n.* one's best clothing, such as one would wear to church. □ *We are in our Sunday best, ready to go.* □ *I got mud on my Sunday best.*

Sunday driver *n.* a slow and leisurely driver who appears to be sightseeing and enjoying the view, holding up traffic in the process. (Also a term of address.) □ *Yes, I'm a Sunday driver and sorry, but I do feel it's dangerous to go faster than 25 mph.* □ *Then move over, you Sunday driver!*

sundowner *n.* a drink taken at sunset. □ *Fancy a sundowner?* □ *We're in here having a sundowner.*

sunny south *n.* the mouth. (Rhyming slang.) □ *How do we get her sunny south closed so the rest can talk?* □ *Why don't you just close your sunny south for a moment and listen.*

sunshades See SHADES.

Sunshine *n.* a jocular form of address for a man or boy. (The term has no racial implications and is derived from "son.") □ *You think you're so smart, don't you Sunshine?* □ *Look Sunshine, just watch yourself; all right?*

super 1. *mod.* superfluous; unnecessary. □ *All these tables are super. Get rid of them.* □ *If you are super you can go home now.* **2.** *n.* superintendent. □ *The super comes by every now and then to check on things.* □ *Call the super and ask for some help.*

super-dooper See SUPER-DUPER.

super-duper AND **super-dooper** *mod.* excellent. □ *That's just super-duper. Couldn't have asked for better.* □ *Where is this super-dooper car of yours?*

supergrass *n.* a police informer supplying information or evidence that is especially incriminating or concerns a large number of people. □ *They say that after giving evidence, the supergrass had plastic surgery, was provided with a new identity, and relocated to Australia.* □ *One supergrass and we could get the lot, sir.*

supremo *n.* an overall or "supreme" commander. (The Spanish word for "supreme.") □ *Dr Wilson has been appointed supremo for the whole operation.* □ *We urgently need a new military supremo in that area.*

sure-fire *mod.* certain; infallible; fail-safe. □ *I've got a sure-fire way to fix cracks in drywall.* □ *Good, yes; sure-fire, no.* □ *This stuff is a sure-fire cure.*

sure thing *n.* something that is absolutely certain. □ *It's a sure thing! You can't lose!* □ *Well, it looks like the sure thing didn't turn out to be so sure, after all.*

surf *vb.* to joyride by clinging to the side or roof of a train, car, etc. □ *He was killed surfing on a train that went into a tunnel.* □ *Why do these kids surf? It's suicidal.*

surface *vb.* to wake up. □ *You're going to have to surface before noon if you want to be able to keep a job like that.* □ *When did you surface today?*

surfboard 1. *n.* a girl possessing tiny or very flat breasts. (Crude.) □ *Harriet hates being called a surfboard.* □ *It's mostly other girls who call them surfboards, you know.* **2.** *n.* a sexually willing or promiscuous girl or woman. (Crude.) □ *I wouldn't say Susan's a surfboard, but you never know your luck.* □ *She's a surfboard, I'm sure.*

surf the (Inter)net *vb. phr.* to explore the world-wide electronic network by means of a personal computer, briefly dipping in and out of items of possible interest. (Computer jargon.) □ *Paul spends most weekends surfing the Internet.* □ *I once tried to surf the net but nearly drowned in a tidal wave of irrelevant or trivial data.*

Surprise, surprise! *exclaim.* "Well, that's no surprise!" (Ironic.) □ *Oh, surprise, surprise! Did you expect anything else?* □ *He's not prepared to leave, eh? Surprise, surprise!*

Surrey Docks *n.* venereal disease. (Crude. Rhyming slang, linked as follows: Surrey Docks ≈ [pox] = venereal disease.) □ *Getting the Surrey Docks tends to restrict your love life, you know.* □ *All right, it's true, I've got the Surrey Docks.*

surtitles *n.* words projected onto a screen above the stage in a theatre where an opera is being sung in a foreign language. □ *They had surtitles at that Italian opera we went to last night.* □ *I'd rather have an opera with surtitles than one sung in English when it was supposed to be sung in German or Italian or something.*

suss 1. *n.* a suspect. □ *Right, let's interview our suss.* □ *Bring the suss in now, constable.* **2.** *n.* suspicion. □ *There's something really suss about their stories, Inspector.* □ *If you've got good grounds for your suss, we'll take this further.* **3.** *n.* suspicious behaviour. (Police terminology.) □ *It looks kinda suss to me, sarge.* □ *If you think it's really suss, pull them in.* **4.** *vb.* to suspect something. □ *Keep everything normal. I don't want her to suss anything. She has never had a surprise party before.* □ *He sussed something the minute he came into the room.*

suss something out 1. *vb. phr.* to investigate. □ *Please go and suss out this situation immediately.* □ *It's very important that this is sussed out properly.* **2.** *vb. phr.* to work out or come to understand something. □ *I'm glad you suss out that at last.* □ *If you can't suss out what's been happening you can't be too smart.*

sussy *mod.* suspicious. □ *Something about the deal seemed sussy.* □ *Barlowe squinted a bit. Something was sussy here, he thought.*

swag *n.* the profits of a crime; a thief's booty. □ *Where do you suppose Mr Big might have hidden the swag?* □ *The cellar was full to the ceiling with swag from numerous jobs.*

swag someone away *vb. phr.* to kidnap or abduct someone. (Police.) □ *Looks like they've managed to swag her away after all.* □ *No one's going to get off with swagging anyone away while I'm in charge around here.*

swailer *n.* a cosh; a bludgeon. □ *The police stopped Otto and found he was carrying a swailer.* □ *That's a vicious-looking swailer you have there.*

swakking *n.* the censorship of mail in the military. (From S.W.A.(L.)K.) □ *Swakking is normal in the Army when you're on operations and there is information to keep from the enemy.* □ *I don't like swakking.*

S.W.A.L.C.A.K.W.S. AND **SWALCAK-WS** *mod.* "sealed with a lick 'cos a kiss won't stick" : written and sent with love and care. (This initialism is sometimes written on love letters. Also an acronym, it is a jocular elaboration of S.W.A.(L.)K.) □ *Love and kisses. S.W.A.L.C.A.K.W.S.* □ *XXXX SWALCAKWS.*

S.W.A.(L.)K. AND **SWA(L)K** *mod.* "sealed with a (loving) kiss." (This initialism is sometimes written on love letters. Also an acronym. Compare with S.W.A.L.C.A.K.W.S. and SWAKKING.)

□ *All her letters come SWAK.* □ *I know they are S.W.A.L.K., because she says so.*

swallow 1. *n.* a puff of cigarette smoke. □ *He took just one swallow and started coughing.* □ *Can I have a swallow of your fag?* **2.** *vb.* to be credulous; to believe or accept something that is most unlikely to be true. (Compare with GO DOWN.) □ *Did they actually swallow that?* □ *Nobody's gonna swallow that nonsense.*

swallow and sigh *n.* a collar and tie. (Rhyming slang.) □ *You've got to have on a swallow and sigh to get in there.* □ *He hates wearing a swallow and sigh.*

swallow the dictionary *vb. phr.* to have acquired an enormous vocabulary; to use numerous long or obscure words. □ *My uncle says I've swallowed the dictionary. That's because I know so many big words.* □ *Did you just go to university to swallow a dictionary?*

swamped *mod.* overwhelmed with something. □ *I can't handle it now. I'm swamped with orders.* □ *We're always swamped at this time of the year.*

swan around *vb. phr.* to move around in a casual way while presenting a superior attitude to others. □ *I could not swan around like that all day long.* □ *There he was, swanning around as usual.*

swankpot *n.* someone who behaves in an ostentatious manner. □ *Why do we need this swankpot?* □ *Ask the swankpot if he needs any help.*

swanky *mod.* ostentatiously classy; boastful. □ *What a swanky place this is!* □ *This place is too swanky for me. I like to eat where I can pronounce the names of the stuff in the menu.*

swap spit *vb. phr.* to kiss passionately. □ *The teenage couple were swapping spit as if their lives depended upon it.* □ *Keep an eye on those kids. They aren't going to be satisfied with just swapping spit forever, you know.*

swartzer See SCHWARTZ(E).

swear and cuss *n.* a bus. (Rhyming slang.) □ *Waiting for the swear and cuss, eh?* □ *I met him on the swear and cuss this morning.*

swear blind *vb. phr.* to affirm in a very forceful and convincing manner. □ *I swear blind I had nothing to do with it!* □ *You can swear blind if you like; your fingerprints say different.*

swear like a trooper *vb. phr.* to curse and swear with great facility. (In the supposed manner of a soldier.) □ *Mrs Wilson has been known to swear like a trooper on occasion.* □ *The sales assistant started swearing like a trooper, and the customer started crying.*

swear off something *vb. phr.* to promise to cease or desist. □ *He's sworn off the booze.* □ *Otto swears off the booze every week, regular as clockwork.*

sweat 1. *vb.* to worry; to become bothered. (Compare with NO SWEAT.) □ *I can handle this fine. Don't sweat.* □ *You really had us sweating a lot around here for a while.* **2.** *n.* a long-distance run. (Childish.) □ *The school is having a sweat for us all tomorrow.* □ *He does not like going on sweats.*

sweat blood *vb. phr.* to work very hard at something; to endure distress in the process of accomplishing something. □ *I sweated blood to get the best education, and now you treat me like a stranger.* □ *Everybody in the office had to sweat blood that week.*

sweat-room 1. *n.* the interrogation room at a police station. □ *Well, who have we got in the sweat-room this fine day?* □ *I think it's time for Otto to come with us to the sweat-room for a little talk.* **2.** *n.* the cell where criminals wait before appearing in court. □ *Mr Big did not like it in the sweat-room.* □ *I don't think he's ever been in a sweat-room before.*

sweat something out *vb. phr.* to endure some difficult event or experience until it is complete. □ *You'll just have to sweat it out. There's no way to hurry this up.* □ *We'll just have to wait and sweat it out like everybody else.*

Sweeney (Todd) *n.* a police flying squad, especially in London. (Rhyming slang, derived from Sweeney Todd, an early 19th century London barber convicted of murdering his clients. Normally with *the*.) □ *The Sweeney Todd is London's top crime-busting unit.* □ *Send for the Sweeney!*

sweenie *n.* a member of the police flying squad. □ *That sweenie is after me!* □ *That plod is a sweenie now, y'know.*

sweep something under the carpet *vb. phr.* to hide something, especially in the hope that it will be forgotten about. □ *He tried to sweep the evidence under the carpet, but it came out anyway.* □ *Sweeping the truth under the carpet never works in the long run.*

sweet *mod.* good; profitable; excellent. □ *I got involved in a real sweet deal that was supposed to lead to a better job.* □ *Fred offered Bill a sweet contract, but he turned it down all the same.*

sweet and sours *n.* flowers. (Rhyming slang.) □ *What does it say when it's the girl who brings the boy sweet and sours?* □ *A huge bunch of sweet and sours were waiting for her when she got home.*

sweet B.A. See SWEET FANNY ADAMS.

sweet bugger all See SWEET FANNY ADAMS.

sweeten *vb.* to make a bargain or agreement better or more attractive. □ *Okay, I'll sweeten the deal. I'll throw in go-faster stripes.* □ *He tried to sweeten his offer with another £1,000, but I think that just made Mike suspicious.*

sweetener *n.* extra encouragement, usually in the form of money. □ *Money makes the best sweetener around.* □ *Let me add a little sweetener, and we'll see if he goes for it.*

sweet evening *n.* cheese. (Rhyming slang, linked as follows: sweet evening [breeze] ≈ cheese.) □ *Can I have some sweet evening, please?* □ *He likes a few biscuits with his sweet evening.*

sweet FA See SWEET FANNY ADAMS.

sweet fanny adams 1. AND **sweet FA; fanny adams; FA.** *n.* tinned mutton. (In 1867 an eight-year-old girl called Fanny Adams was brutally murdered, and there was much publicity over the matter. At about the same time, sailors in the Royal Navy were issued tinned mutton for the first time, which with gallows humour they dubbed with her name.) □ *They sat us down to a plate of sweet fanny adams and I nearly retched.* □ *I don't like FA. Do you?* **2.** AND **sweet FA; fanny adams; FA; sweet F.A.; F.A.; sweet bugger all; sweet B.A.; B.A.** *n.* absolutely nothing whatsoever; that which is worthless. (Crude. Here FANNY ADAMS is used as a euphemism for "fuck all." Of course, FA could be an abbreviation of either "fanny adams" or "fuck all." Compare with S.F.A.) □ *There is nothing in that room; just sweet fanny adams.* □ *No, nothing! Sweet B.A.! Clear off!*

sweetheart agreement AND **sweetheart deal** *n.* a private agreement reached between a public agency or government department on the one hand, and a private company on the other, that is to the mutual interests of both but may be against the interests of everyone else, or unethical, or illegal, or all three. □ *They found that the minister was involved in a number of sweetheart agreements.* □ *Most of the building contractors in town would be out of business if they didn't offer sweetheart deals to the local politicians.*

sweetheart deal See SWEETHEART AGREEMENT.

sweetie *n.* a small item of sweet confectionery. □ *Mummy, can I have a sweetie?* □ *I love sweeties. I always have, ever since I was little.*

sweetie(-pie) *n.* [one's] dear child, husband, wife, lover, etc. (A diminutive form of *sweetheart.* Often a term of address.) □ *Look, sweetie, can't we afford a new car?* □ *Pick up your toys, sweetie-pie. Aunt Matilda is coming over for a visit.*

sweet nothings *n.* loving comments; pleasant remarks between lovers. □ *They are out on the porch swing whispering sweet nothings in each other's ears.* □ *Thank heavens most married people never remember the sweet nothings they were once told.*

swift *mod.* unfair. □ *Hey, that's swift!* □ *I'm not letting you be swift like that.*

swift half *n.* a half pint of beer, taken quickly. □ *Can I have swift half,*

please? □ *Well, a swift half if you're going to insist.*

swiftie AND **swift one** *n.* a quick drink. □ *You know how a swiftie disagrees with you, my dear.* □ *I often enjoy a swift one in the evening.*

swift one See SWIFTIE.

swig 1. *n.* a deep swallow of liquid. □ *She took a swig of rum and leaped into the lagoon.* □ *One swig of that stuff was enough for me.* **2.** *vb.* to drink deeply. □ *He nearly swigged the whole bottle before he stopped to take a breath.* □ *She swigged a big gulp and just stood there—bottle in her hand—as if she had been paralysed.*

swill 1. *n.* inferior drink. □ *Let's not go to that pub again. They serve disgusting swill and call it beer.* □ *Man does not live by swill alone. Let's go to McDonald's first.* **2.** *vb.* to drink beer as rapidly as possible and with little concern for decorum. □ *Ted was in the pub swilling like the stuff was going out of fashion.* □ *He swilled a whole case of beer yesterday. Isn't he satisfied yet?*

swill something out *vb. phr.* to rinse or flush with water in order to clean or clear. □ *He was swilling out the sluice room when I got there.* □ *This place is such a mess I think we may have to swill it out!*

swimming (in it) See ROLLING (IN IT).

swimmingly *mod.* moving forward excellently; proceeding without problems. □ *I'm having a fine time here. Everything is going along just swimmingly.* □ *The plans are moving ahead swimmingly.*

swindle sheet *n.* an expense account record sheet or book. □ *I turned in my swindle sheet yesterday, and no one challenged the £400 for new shoes.* □ *The government makes it harder and harder to get away with really creative swindle sheets these days.*

swing 1. *vb.* [for a person] to be up-to-date and modern. □ *Does Tom really swing, you ask? Well, just look at those blue suede shoes!* □ *I used to swing, but then age and good taste overtook me.* **2.** *vb.* [for a party or other social occasion] to be fun or exciting. □ *This* party really swings! □ I've never been to a gathering that swings like this one. **3.** vb. to participate in group sex or the swapping of sexual partners. (Crude. Compare with SWINGER.) □ Carol says that Tom, Ted, and Heidi swing. So how does she know? □ There is a lot less swinging going on since AIDS appeared on the scene. **4.** vb. to bring something off; to execute a deal. □ This is a very important deal. I hope I can swing it. □ They want to elect me president of the club. I hope they can swing it.

swing a free leg vb. phr. to be unmarried. □ It's great to be swinging a free leg: don't get married! □ Is it true that he swings a free leg?

swing both ways vb. phr. to be bisexual. (Crude.) □ They say that Gary swings both ways, but I wouldn't know. □ Since he swings both ways, he may stand a better chance at finding a date.

swinger 1. n. a person who indulges in group sex or the swapping of sexual partners. (Crude. Compare with SWING.) □ Is Gary a swinger? I've heard talk about him. □ We watched a film about a swinger, but everything interesting happened in dim blue light. Is that why they're called "blue movies"? **2.** n. a youthful, socially active and knowledgeable person. □ Those kids are real swingers. □ Tom is a swinger. He knows everyone who matters.

swinging mod. great. □ We had a swinging time at John's rally. □ The concert was swinging—nothing like it, ever.

swing into high gear vb. phr. to begin operating at a fast pace; to increase the rate of activity. □ During the winter season we swing into high gear around here. □ The chef swings into high gear around eight o'clock in preparation for the theatre crowd.

swing it AND **swing the lead** vb. phr. to malinger; to evade responsibilities or work. (See PLUMBUM OSCILLANS.) □ Mike is swinging it, of course. □ Mike's swinging the lead as usual.

swing party n. a sexual orgy. (Crude.) □ I've heard you're having a swing

party at your place this weekend. □ A swing party? Me? You're sadly mislead there, I fear!

swing the lead See SWING IT.

swipe n. a hard blow or an act of striking someone or something heavily. (Compare with TAKE A SWIPE AT SOMEONE OR SOMETHING.) □ Bob got a nasty swipe across the face. □ The cat gave the mouse a swipe with its paw.

swipe something vb. to steal something. □ Max swiped a pack of cigarettes from the counter. □ Somebody swiped my wallet!

swish 1. mod. elegant; fashionable; attractive and smart. □ Oh, you do look swish today! □ What a swish dress that is. **2.** mod. effeminate. (Crude.) □ Why does he have to behave in such a swish way? □ A swish man does not have to be gay, you know!

switched on 1. mod. up-to-date; fashionable. □ My brother is switched on and has lots of friends. □ I'm not switched on. In fact, I'm pretty dull. **2.** mod. excited. □ I get switched on by that kind of music. □ I am never switched on by raucous music.

switch off vb. phr. to become oblivious to everything. □ I want to go home and switch off—just forget this whole day. □ I have to switch off when I go home.

swizz(le) 1. n. something that is unfair. □ My last job was a swizz. I hope this is better. □ You really got a swizzle there. **2.** n. a swindle. □ They pulled a real dirty swizz on that old lady. □ This is an okay swizzle you've got going here.

swot n. a hard-working, serious pupil or student. □ Yes, he's a swot, and he passes his exams, too. □ I wouldn't like to be a swot.

swot (up) vb. (phr.) to study hard or learn quickly. □ He's swottting hard to pass his exams. □ I've got to swot up on this.

syph See SIFF.

syphon the python vb. phr. to urinate. (Crude.) □ He just went out to syphon the python. □ I've got to syphon the python. Back in a minute.

syrup n. a wig. (Rhyming slang, linked as follows: syrup [of figs] ≈ wig.) □ I *wear just a little syrup to cover up a shiny spot.* □ *Is that guy wearing a syrup, or does his scalp really slide from side to side?*

syrupy *mod.* excessive sentimentality or sweetness of manner. □ *I can't stand syrupy films.* □ *That music is too syrupy.* □ *All this syrupy talk is making me feel sick.*

SYSOP *n.* "system operator," the person who manages a computer system or bulletin board. (An acronym. Pronounced SIS-op.) □ *The SYSOP tried to bring order to the bulletin board discussion but failed.* □ *I sent a message to the SYSOP complaining about the number of personal messages on the board.*

2IC *n.* the second in command. □ *I hear he's 2IC now.* □ *Wilson? He's a good choice for 2IC.*

T AND **tea** *n.* marijuana. (From TEA.) □ *Can't you stay off that T?* □ *All she thinks about is smoking tea and where she's gonna get more of it.*

ta *interj.* an infantile form of "thank you," sometimes used informally by adults. □ *Ta for the coffee.* □ *Yes, the meal you bought. Ta.*

tab 1. *n.* a cigarette. □ *I'll trade you a tab for a light.* □ *Give me a tab mate, will you?* **2.** *n.* an old woman. □ *Why is that tab walking through our office?* □ *I'm afraid I don't know the tab.* **3.** *n.* lysergic acid diethylamide, or LSD, an hallucinogenic drug. □ *You can get some good tab in this part of town.* □ *What does tab cost around here?* **4.** *n.* a member of Cambridge University. □ *Are you a tab? No, I'm at Oxford.* □ *If you want to be a tab, you've got to be at Cambridge.* **5.** *vb.* to walk. □ *Let's tab over to the library.* □ *My car's broken down, so I had to tab to work today.* **6.** See also YOMP.

tabby *n.* a good-looking or attractive girl or young woman. □ *I liked the look of the tabby you were with last night.* □ *What a tabby! I want that one.*

tab(hole) *n.* an ear. □ *Allow me to take you to one side and have a word in your tabhole, sonny.* □ *Look at the huge tabs on that man over there!*

tach *n.* a moustache. □ *I don't trust men with a tach.* □ *I was amazed at the size of his tach.*

tack attack *n.* a short burst of bad taste. (See TACK(INESS).) □ *Did you have a tack attack while you were choosing*

that dress, dear? □ *The whole evening was ghastly; I'm sure the hostess must have had a tack attack or something.*

tacker *n.* a child. □ *She is a most irritating tacker, I'm afraid.* □ *Is this tacker yours?*

tackety boot *n.* hob-nailed boot. (Scots usage. Normally in the plural.) □ *Get they tackety boots oot o ma hoose! (Get these hob-nailed boots out of my house!)* □ *The noise these weans make charging aboot, ye'd think they aw wear tackety boots! (The noise the children make as they run about was such you would think they all wear hob-nailed boots.)*

tack(iness) *n.* bad taste; squalor; seediness. □ *Unfortunately the whole evening turned out to be a sort of celebration of tackiness.* □ *What a collection of tack there is there!*

tacky 1. *mod.* crude; unrefined; vulgar. □ *That was a tacky thing to do to her.* □ *It was all so tacky!* □ *This is sort of a tacky gift for a wedding.* **2.** *mod.* tasteless; squalid; seedy. □ *Oh, what a tacky weirdo!* □ *This place is really tacky. Let's get out of here.*

tad *n.* a bit; a small bit. □ *I'll take just a tad. I'm on a diet.* □ *That's a little more than a tad, but all right then.*

tadger *n.* the male sexual organ. (Taboo.) □ *That's all very well Myra, but where would the world be without tadgers?* □ *The doctor told him that he'd got something wrong with his tadger.*

Taffia *n.* a supposed Welsh Mafia. (Offensive. Normally with *the*. Derived from TAFF(Y).) □ *Do you really think there is a Taffia?* □ *I suppose I'll be* *accused of being in the Taffia just because I'm Welsh, too!*

Taff(y) *n.* a Welshman. (Offensive. Said to be from the Welsh pronunciation of "David," which is spelt *Dafydd* in Welsh.) □ *Y'know, Otto, if you call a Welshman a Taffy, he's likely to get nasty.* □ *Why can you not be polite to Taffs?*

tag along with someone or something See STRING ALONG WITH SOMEONE OR SOMETHING.

taggy *n.* a girl or woman. □ *The taggy entered the police station and asked to speak to the inspector.* □ *What does the taggy want with me, sergeant?*

tag on to something AND **twig (on to) something; take something on board** *vb. phr.* to comprehend something. □ *Don't worry, he'll tug on to this eventually.* □ *I think I've taken this on board now.*

Taig *n.* an Irish Protestant's nickname for a Roman Catholic. (Offensive. Also a term of address. Irish usage.) □ *He said he was not prejudiced, he just hated this particular Taig!* □ *Don't call Roman Catholic people Taigs, please. It is very offensive.*

tail 1. *n.* the male sexual organ. (Taboo.) □ *Men keep their brains in their tails!* □ *Unlike Myra, Sharon thinks of little else but tails.* **2.** *n.* sexual intercourse. (Taboo.) □ *I think really, she's gasping for tail, you know.* □ *A good bit of tail would probably do her the power of good, in fact.* **3.** *n.* a prostitute. (Crude.) □ *This tail comes up to me and acts like she's met me before.* □ *Do you think she's a tail or just too friendly?* **4.** *n.* someone who follows another person. □ *Why was there a tail following him, he wondered.* □ *The tail was still waiting ouside the office when he left.* **5.** *n.* women in general. (Crude.) □ *Are there no tail in this town?* □ *All Otto's ever after is tail.* **6.** *vb.* to perform sexual intercourse. (Taboo.) □ *Let's go somewhere quiet and tail.* □ *Want to tail?* **7.** *vb.* to follow someone or something. □ *We're being tailed.* □ *Why would anyone want to tail us?*

tail-end *n.* the rearmost part of something or someone. □ *He was at the tail-*

end of a long queue. □ *Tracy fell down on her tail-end.*

tail-end Charlie 1. *n.* someone bringing up the rear. □ *Why do I always end up being tail-end Charlie when we go somewhere together.* □ *The tail-end Charlie pays for the parking.* **2.** *n.* the rear gunner in a bomber. □ *My Uncle Willy was tail-end Charlie in a Lancaster during the war.* □ *Being tail-end Charlie is not a healthy occupation.* **3.** *n.* the rear aircraft of a group. □ *I hate flying tail-end Charlie.* □ *Who's tail-end Charlie this time?*

tail (it) *vb. (phr.)* to die. □ *Come on, mister, don't tail it!* □ *Get that medicine over here fast before this guy tails on us.*

tails *n.* a tailcoat. □ *Shall I wear my tails?* □ *Ralph had to rent tails for the evening.*

tail-wagger *n.* a dog. □ *Why do you keep a tail-wagger like that?* □ *The tail-wagger frightened the child.*

take 1. *n.* a section of a film that is pronounced acceptable just after it is shot. □ *It's a take. Get it over to the lab.* □ *After seven straight takes the crew demanded a break.* **2.** *n.* the amount of money taken in at some event; the money received for the tickets that have been purchased. □ *What was the take for the concert?* □ *The take was much larger than we expected.*

take a bath on something *vb. phr.* to make a large financial loss on an investment. □ *Fred took a bath on these gold mining shares.* □ *The broker warned me that I might take a bath if I bought this stuff.*

take a beating *vb. phr.* to be beaten, bested or defeated. □ *Our candidate took a beating in the election.* □ *The team took quite a beating.*

take a break *vb. phr.* to stop working for a rest period. □ *Let's take a break here. Be back in five minutes.* □ *I've got to take a break before I drop.*

take a crack at something AND **have a crack at something** *vb. phr.* to make an attempt at something. □ *She had a crack at food preparation, but that wasn't for her.* □ *Let me take a crack at it.*

take a dim view of something AND **take a poor view of something** *vb. phr.* to disapprove of something. □ *The teacher took a dim view of your behaviour yesterday.* □ *I must take a poor view of something as stupid as that.*

take a dive See TAKE A FALL.

take advantage of someone *vb. phr.* to seduce a woman. (Crude.) □ *Oh David, you're taking advantage of me!* □ *I think he's trying to take advantage of Felicity.*

take a fall AND **take a dive; take a tumble** *vb. phr.* to fake being knocked out in a boxing match. □ *Wilbur wouldn't take a fall. He doesn't have it in him.* □ *The boxer took a dive in the second round and made everyone suspicious.*

take a flyer (on something) *vb. phr.* to take a chance on something. □ *Kim was very reckless when she took a flyer on these shares in Flybynight Airlines.* □ *Fred is too wise an investor to take a flyer on a funny outfit like that.*

Take a flying leap! See GO AND TAKE A FLYING LEAP AT YOURSELF!

Take a flying leap at yourself! See GO AND TAKE A FLYING LEAP AT YOURSELF!

take against something *vb. phr.* to start to dislike something. □ *Mr Big has taken against that one.* □ *If you take against this, what will you do instead?*

take a gander (at someone or something) *vb. phr.* to look at someone or something. (Compare with GANDER.) □ *Hey, take a gander at this bit of skirt!* □ *I wanted to take a gander at the new computer before they started using it.*

take a hike AND **take a walk** *vb. phr.* to leave; to go away. □ *Okay, I've had it with you. Take a hike! Shove off!* □ *I had enough of the boss and the whole place, so I cleaned out my desk and took a walk.*

take a leak AND **take a slash** *vb. phr.* to urinate. (Crude.) □ *I've got to take a leak. Back in a minute.* □ *He just went out to take a leak.* □ *Well, taking a slash does relieve the pressure of all that beer!*

take a lot of nerve 1. *vb. phr.* to be very rude; to require a lot of rudeness (to behave so badly). □ *He walked out on her, and that took a lot of nerve!* □ *That took a lot of nerve! You took my parking place!* **2.** *vb. phr.* to require courage. □ *He climbed the mountain with a bruised foot. That took a lot of nerve.* □ *It took a lot of nerve to go into business for himself.*

take an early bath *vb. phr.* to depart from some location or cease some activity before this would normally be expected. (Originally a sporting metaphor for departing a game before it is finished.) □ *I wish that pest would be good enough to take an early bath and leave me in peace.* □ *I thought I better take an early bath before they discovered that I was not supposed to have been there in the first place.*

take a nosy around *vb. phr.* to take a look around. □ *I think I'll take a nosy around.* □ *The detective inspector is just taking a nosy around, sir.*

take a note *vb. phr.* to write something down. □ *Just a moment while I take a note.* □ *What are you taking a note about now?*

take a page from someone's book *vb. phr.* to copy or emulate. □ *I took a page from Edison's book and began inventing useful little things myself.* □ *Mind if I take a page from your book and apply for a job here?*

take a pew See GRAB A PEW.

take a poor view of something See TAKE A DIM VIEW OF SOMETHING.

take a pop at someone *vb. phr.* to attack someone physically. □ *Harry took a pop at me, but I ducked.* □ *The drunk took a pop at the cop—which was the wrong thing to do.*

take a powder *vb. phr.* to leave; to leave town. (Underworld.) □ *Why don't you take a powder? Go on! Beat it!* □ *Bruno took a powder and will lie low for a while.*

take a purler *vb. phr.* to be hit in such a way as to fall lengthways. □ *I took a purler and was in hospital for a week.* □ *Clear off, or I'll make sure you take a purler you won't forget in a hurry!*

take a quickie See HAVE A QUICKIE.

Take a running jump (at yourself)! *exclam.* "Go away!"; "Get away from me!" □ *You know what you can do? You can take a running jump. Sod off!* □ *Why don't you go and take a running jump at yourself, you creep!*

take a shine to someone *vb. phr.* to take a liking to someone. □ *I think he's taken a shine to her!* □ *It's hard to see why she would take a shine to anyone like that.*

take a shot (at something) *vb. phr.* to make an attempt at something. □ *I don't think I can do it, but I'll take a shot at it.* □ *Go ahead. Take a shot.*

take a shufti *vb. phr.* to take a look. (See SHUFTI.) □ *Cor! Take a shufti at this!* □ *We each took a shufti, but really there was little to see.*

take a slash See TAKE A LEAK.

take a stab at something *vb. phr.* to take a try at doing something. □ *Please take a stab at fixing this.* □ *If you want to take another stab at it come through here.*

take a swing at someone *vb. phr.* to attempt to punch someone. □ *He took a swing at me!* □ *Try that once again buster, and I'll be taking a swing at you.*

take a swipe at someone or something AND **take a whack at someone or something** *vb. phr.* to hit out at someone or something. (Compare with SWIPE.) □ *Max took a swipe at Bruno.* □ *Jerry got an axe and took a whack at the tree, but didn't do much damage.*

take a tumble See TAKE A FALL.

take a walk See TAKE A HIKE.

take-away (food) *n.* food purchased at a restaurant or shop to be removed and eaten elsewhere. □ *I like some take-away food.* □ *Some take-away is okay, some is not.*

take-away (restaurant) *n.* a restaurant specialising in TAKE-AWAY FOOD. □ *There's a take-away restaurant down the street so you won't starve.* □ *Does the take-away do Indian food?*

take a whack at someone or something See TAKE A SWIPE AT SOMEONE OR SOMETHING.

take a whack at something *vb. phr.* to make an attempt at something. □ *Let me take a whack at it.* □ *Why don't you*

practice for a little while and take a whack at it again tomorrow?

Take care. *phr.* "Good-bye, be careful." □ *See you later. Take care.* □ *Take care. See you next week.*

take care of number one See LOOK AFTER NUMBER ONE.

take care of someone *vb. phr.* to kill someone. (Underworld.) □ *Watch it! Otto would take care of you as soon as look at you.* □ *I'm gonna take care of you once and for all.*

take ill *vb. phr.* to become sick. □ *He took ill and went home.* □ *If you take ill, tell us. That's an order!*

take in something *vb. phr.* to buy or have delivered something, such as a newspaper, at regular intervals. □ *He takes in several newspapers every day.* □ *Would you like to take in a daily paper?*

take it *vb. phr.* to endure something, physically or mentally. (Compare with TAKE IT ON THE CHIN.) □ *I just can't take it anymore.* □ *If you can't take it, quit.*

take it easy AND **take things easy 1.** *phr.* "relax"; "don't strain yourself." □ *See you later. Take it easy.* □ *They told me to take things easy for a few days.* **2.** *exclam.* "Proceed with care."; "Go forward gently." □ *Take things easy! That hurts!* □ *Take it easy; he's just a kid!*

take it like a man See TAKE IT ON THE CHIN.

take it on the chin AND **take it like a man 1.** *vb. phr.* to suffer misfortune stoically. (Compare with TAKE IT.) □ *They said some really cutting things to him, but he took it on the chin.* □ *I knew he could take it like a man.* **2.** *vb. phr.* to receive the full brunt of something. □ *Why do I have to take it on the chin for something I didn't do?* □ *If you did it, you have to learn to take it like a man.*

Take it or leave it. *sent.* "That's the only offer available. I am indifferent as to whether you accept it or not." □ *This is what you get for the money. Take it or leave it.* □ *I told her that there was a shortage of these things and she had to take it or leave it.*

take it out on someone or something *vb. phr.* to punish or harm someone or something because one is angry or disturbed about something. □ *I'm sorry about your difficulty, but don't take it out on me.* □ *Don't take it out on the cat.*

take it slow(ly) *vb. phr.* to proceed slowly and carefully. □ *Just relax and take it slowly. You've got a good chance.* □ *You'll make it. Take it slow and keep your spirits up.*

take legal advice *vb. phr.* to consult a lawyer. □ *I'm taking legal advice before I say another word.* □ *It's going to cost you to take legal advice, of course.*

taken AND **had; took 1.** *mod.* cheated; deceived; fooled. □ *"I've been taken!" he cried, running down the street after the boy.* □ *You were really took that time, all right.* **2.** *mod.* [of a woman] already participated in sexual intercourse with a man. (Taboo.) □ *One look and he knew she had already been had by another.* □ *After he had taken her, she felt cheap.*

take no harm *vb. phr.* to survive or endure without being damaged or hurt. □ *Oh, he'll take no harm.* □ *I just hope his camera took no harm when it fell off the train.*

take off 1. *vb. phr.* [for someone] to leave in a hurry. □ *She really took off out of there.* □ *I've got to take off—I'm late.* **2.** *vb. phr.* [for something] to become successful or popular. □ *The fluffy dog dolls began to take off, and we sold out the lot.* □ *Ticket sales really took off after the first performance.*

take-off *n.* a mimicking or parody of someone or something. (Usually in a mocking fashion. Usually with *of.*) □ *The comedian did a take-off of the wealthy politician.* □ *The take-off of the dean didn't go over too well.*

take on *vb. phr.* to accept a bribe. □ *Well, I've found one who'll take on, but his price is very high.* □ *He took on all right, but then informed the police.*

take oneself out of oneself *vb. phr.* to shrug off or brush aside excessive introspection. □ *Try to take yourself out of yourself; things are not so bad as you seem to think.* □ *I don't know why I'm so depressed. I've tried to take myself*

out of myself, but have been unable to so far.

taker 1. *n.* one who accepts an offer; a buyer. □ *Are there any takers for this fine, almost new caddy?* □ *Here's a taker. You'll not be sorry, sir.* **2.** *n.* one who takes a bet. □ *Okay, I'm offering five to one on Straight Arrow at the Three O'clock tomorrow. Are there any takers?* □ *There were so many takers I soon had to change the odds.*

take some doing *vb. phr.* to require considerable effort and care. □ *It'll take some doing, but it'll get done.* □ *It's not impossible. It'll just take some doing.*

take someone 1. *vb.* to cheat or deceive someone. □ *That clerk tried to take me.* □ *When they think you're going to count your change, they won't try to take you.* **2.** *vb.* to defeat someone, as in a fight. □ *Max thought he could take the guy, but he wasn't sure.* □ *I know I can take you. Make my day!*

take someone for a ride *vb. phr.* to trick or delude someone. □ *The scoundrel took me for a ride!* □ *Don't let him take you for a ride.*

take someone in *vb. phr.* to cheat or deceive someone. □ *He might try to take you in. Keep an eye on him and count your change.* □ *The con artists tried to take in the old lady, but she was too clever.*

take someone or something apart 1. *vb. phr.* to criticise someone very severely. □ *They really took me apart, but what the hell?* □ *The editorial took the whole board apart.* **2.** *vb. phr.* to injure someone severely by means of physical violence. □ *The mugger really took the old lady apart.* □ *The cops then caught the mugger and took him apart.*

take someone or something off *vb. phr.* to mimic or parody someone or something. (Usually in a mocking fashion.) □ *The comedian took off the wealthy politician.* □ *Well, I took off the dean, but it didn't go down too well.*

take someone or something on *vb. phr.* to accept the task of handling a difficult person or thing. □ *I'll take it on if nobody else will.* □ *Nobody wanted to* *take on Mrs Franklin, but it had to be done.*

take someone out 1. *vb. phr.* to date someone. □ *I hope he'll take me out soon.* □ *She wanted to take him out for an evening.* **2.** *vb. phr.* to kill someone. (Underworld.) □ *The boss told Rocko to take out Barlowe.* □ *Barlowe was sure he could keep Rocko from taking him out.*

take someone to the cleaners 1. *vb. phr.* to defeat someone utterly. □ *We took the other team to the cleaners.* □ *Look at the height they've got! They'll take us to the cleaners!* **2.** *vb. phr.* to severely criticise someone. □ *My boss gave me my annual appraisal today and he took me to the cleaners.* □ *The Daily Grind's drama critic took Sarah to the cleaners over her so-called acting.*

take someone up on something *vb. phr.* to interrupt or question a speaker, especially at a public meeting. □ *I'd like to take up the speaker on that last comment.* □ *Could you wait until I am finished before taking me up on that point?*

take something as read *vb. phr.* to accept something as true or already known. □ *All right, we'll take what you say as read.* □ *Even if we do take what they say as read, how does that help us decide what we have to know?*

take something in turns *vb. phr.* to take turns at something. □ *All right, we'll take this in turns.* □ *If we take it in turns, we'll both get a chance to go.*

take something lying down *vb. phr.* to accept one's fate passively. □ *If you think we're going to take this lying down, you could not be more wrong.* □ *Well, up to now you've taken everything else lying down. Why make an exception now?*

take something on board 1. *vb. phr.* to accept or seriously consider an idea. □ *I don't think she had ever seriously taken that idea on board until now.* □ *Try to take this point on board; it may save your business.* **2.** *vb. phr.* to accept responsibility for something. □ *Please take it on board; after all, you*

did it. □ *All right I've taken it on board; it's my fault.* **3.** See also TAG ON TO SOMETHING.

take something out *vb. phr.* to bomb or destroy something. (Military.) □ *The enemy took out one of the tanks, but not the one carrying the medicine.* □ *The last flight took out two enemy bunkers and a radar installation.*

take something public *vb. phr.* to sell shares in a company to the general public. (Securities markets. Compare with GO PUBLIC.) □ *The board decided not to take the company public.* □ *We're going to take it public whenever the market looks good.*

take stick *n.* severe criticism or censorious advice. (Compare with GIVE SOMEONE STICK.) □ *Well, I took a lot of stick for that comment I made.* □ *Do that again and you'll take stick all right!*

takes two to tango *phr.* "requires two people to do certain things." □ *No, he didn't do it all by himself. Takes two to tango, you know.* □ *There's no such thing as a one-sided argument. It takes two to tango.*

take tea 1. *vb. phr.* to drink a cup of tea. □ *I took tea and got on with my work.* □ *Would you like to take tea while we discuss this?* **2.** *vb. phr.* to indulge in a meal such as afternoon tea, high tea, etc. □ *I took tea with Lady Simpson this afternoon.* □ *Why not come round one afternoon and we'll take tea?*

take the biscuit AND **take the bun; take the cake** *vb. phr.* to be exceptional or remarkable. □ *I think that idea really must take the biscuit.* □ *It takes the cake for him to say a thing like that.*

take the bun See TAKE THE BISCUIT.

take the cake See TAKE THE BISCUIT.

take the dick *vb. phr.* to swear or affirm that something is true. (A corrupted abbreviation of "declaration.") □ *He's taken the dick in court this morning.* □ *You will be required to take the dick too, you know.*

take the heat off someone *vb. phr.* to relieve the pressure on someone; to free someone from suspicion, responsibility, a deadline, etc. □ *The confession by*

Rocko took the heat off the cop shop for a while. □ *They took the heat off us by moving the deadline.*

take the high jump AND **take the long jump** *vb. phr.* to be hanged. □ *He's sure to take the high jump, you know.* □ *I'll be taking the long jump soon.*

take the huff *vb. phr.* to take offence. (Scots usage.) □ *The wife's taken the huff again. (My wife has taken offence again.)* □ *Come on hen, don't take the huff with me. (Come on dear, don't take offence with me.)*

take the long jump See TAKE THE HIGH JUMP.

take the Michael See TAKE THE PISS.

take the Mick(e)y See TAKE THE PISS.

take the Mike See TAKE THE PISS.

take the piss AND **take the Mick(e)y; take the Michael; extract the Michael; take the Mike; extract the urine; pass the catheter** *vb. phr.* to disparage or mock. (All are crude; TAKE THE PISS is taboo.) □ *Don't take the piss! He's right!* □ *If you just stopped passing the catheter for a moment and listened, you just might learn something.* □ *Don't you try to extract the urine from me!*

take the pledge *vb. phr.* to promise to abstain from alcohol. □ *I'm not ready to take the pledge yet, but I will cut down.* □ *My aunt tried to get me to take the pledge.*

take the plunge *vb. phr.* to marry someone. □ *I'm not ready to take the plunge yet.* □ *Sam and Mary took the plunge.*

take the shame *vb. phr.* to take the entire blame. □ *I won't take the shame for something I did not do.* □ *You did it, you take the shame.*

take (the) silk See CALL WITHIN THE BAR.

take the starch out of someone AND **take the stuffing out of someone; knock the starch out of someone; knock the stuffing out of someone** *vb. phr.* to humiliate or reduce the self-confidence of someone, especially someone haughty or conceited. □ *I took the starch out of Kelly by telling him where he was heading if he didn't change his ways.* □ *That remark really*

knocked the stuffing out of him.

take the stuffing out of someone See TAKE THE STARCH OUT OF SOMEONE.

take the wind out of someone's sails *vb. phr.* to frustrate someone by doing what they plan to do or saying what they plan to say, but doing or saying it first. □ *When Amundsen got to the South Pole just ahead of him in 1911, it must have taken the wind out of Scott's sails.* □ *It really took the wind out of his sails when he found out that Jane had already done the work.*

take things easy 1. *vb. phr.* to relax temporarily and recuperate. □ *The doctor says I'm supposed to take things easy for a while.* □ *I want you to take it easy until the stitches heal.* **2.** See also TAKE IT EASY.

take to the hills *vb. phr.* to escape from danger; to go into hiding. □ *Oh, they've all taken to the hills, well out of the way of danger.* □ *If I were you, I'd take to the hills before the other guys get here.*

talent See LOCAL TALENT.

Tale of Two Cities AND **two cities** *n.* the female breasts. (Crude. Rhyming slang, linked as follows: (Tale of) Two Cities ≈ [titties] = female breasts. Normally with *the* and in the plural. Compare with BRISTOLS. *A Tale of Two Cities* is the title of a novel by Charles Dickens.) □ *There she was, bold as brass, with her Tale of Two Cities on full display.* □ *Cor, look at the two cities on that, Fred!*

tale of woe *n.* a sad story; a list of personal problems; an excuse for failing to do something. □ *I listened to her tale of woe without saying anything.* □ *This tale of woe that we have all been getting from Kelly is just too much.*

Taliano AND **Tally** *n.* an Italian person. (Offensive.) □ *Why can you not be polite to Talianos?* □ *Y'know, Otto, if you call an Italian a Tally, he's likely to get nasty.*

talk (a)round something *vb. phr.* to avoid the issue; to talk of everything except what matters. □ *I'm afraid she would only talk round the problem.* □ *We must not just talk around this, but face it head on.*

talk big *vb. phr.* to brag; to make grandiose statements. □ *She talks big, but can't produce anything.* □ *He has some deep need to talk big. He can't do anything.*

talk Billingsgate *vb. phr.* to speak in a foul or abusive manner. (Billingsgate is London's 1,000-year-old fish market.) □ *They were talking Billingsgate with a vengeance in there.* □ *I hate it when people talk Billingsgate like that.*

talk funny *vb. phr.* to speak in a strange or odd manner; to speak English in any non-local accent. □ *Oh, you don't half talk funny!* □ *Why do foreigners talk funny, daddy?*

talking head *n.* someone on television who does nothing but talk. □ *Oh, it's just another of these talking heads.* □ *Who watches these boring talking heads?*

talking-shop *n.* somewhere, such as a legislature, considered to be a place where talk is substituted for action. □ *Some people say Parliament is no more than a talking-shop nowadays.* □ *We don't want a talking-shop, we want an effective system that delivers.*

talk into the big white telephone See PRAY TO THE PORCELAIN GOD.

talk like a nut *vb. phr.* to say stupid things. □ *You're talking like a nut! You don't know what you are saying.* □ *Don't talk like a nut! We can't afford a trip to Florida!*

talk nineteen to the dozen *vb. phr.* to talk in a rapid and continuous stream. □ *They were all talking nineteen to the dozen when we arrived.* □ *If we all talk nineteen to the dozen nothing will get done.*

talk of the devil See SPEAK OF THE DEVIL.

talk one's head off *vb. phr.* to talk endlessly; to argue at length or vigorously. □ *I talked my head off trying to convince them.* □ *Don't waste time talking your head off to them.*

talk on the big white telephone See PRAY TO THE PORCELAIN GOD.

talk proper See SPEAK PROPER.

talk someone (a)round *vb. phr.* to persuade someone by talking. □ *I think*

we've talked him around. □ *See if you can talk him round to that point of view.*

talk someone ragged *vb. phr.* to talk to someone to the point of exhaustion; to bore someone with excessive talking. □ *That was not an interview. She talked me ragged.* □ *He always talks me ragged, but I always listen.*

talk someone's ear off *vb. phr.* to talk ceaselessly to someone; to bore someone with excessive talking. □ *My aunt always talks my ear off when she comes to visit.* □ *Stay away from Mr Jones. He will talk your ear off if he gets a chance.*

talk something up *vb. phr.* to extol the virtues of something. □ *Oh, she's always talking up her latest fad.* □ *He talked up the scheme so well, I almost bought it.*

talk through one's hat AND **talk through (the back of) one's neck** *vb. phr.* to exaggerate greatly; to talk nonsense or in a wild manner. □ *Pay no attention to my friend here. He's just talking through his hat.* □ *You don't know what you are talking about. You're just talking through the back of your neck.*

talk through (the back of) one's neck See TALK THROUGH ONE'S HAT.

talk turkey *vb. phr.* to talk serious business; to talk frankly. □ *We've got to sit down and talk turkey—get this thing wrapped up.* □ *It's time to talk turkey and quit messing around.*

talk until one is blue in the face *vb. phr.* to talk until one is exhausted. □ *You can talk till you're blue in the face, but it won't do any good.* □ *She talked until she was blue in the face, but could not change their minds.*

talk wet *vb. phr.* to speak in a foolishly sentimental way. □ *Don't talk wet!* □ *Talking wet like that is stupid.*

tall order *n.* a request that is difficult to fulfill. □ *That's a tall order. Do you think anyone can do it?* □ *Well, it's a tall order, but I'll do it.*

Tally See TALIANO.

Tamson's mare *n.* one's own legs, used as a method of transportation. (Scots usage. Compare with SHANKS'S PONY and JOCK TAMSON'S BAIRNS.) □ *Here he comes along the road now, using Tamson's mare.* □ *Tamson's mare may be slow, but it's cheap and keeps you fit.*

tangle with someone or something *vb. phr.* to quarrel or fight with someone or something. □ *I didn't want to tangle with her, so I did what she wanted.* □ *It's like tangling with a grizzly bear.*

tank 1. *n.* a drink of beer, usually a pint. □ *Can I have a tank please?* □ *I do like this tank they have in here.* **2.** *vb.* to travel a high speed. □ *We were tanking along the motorway when this cop car spotted us.* □ *She tanked past me a few miles back. What's up?*

tanked AND **tanked up 1.** *mod.* intoxicated due to drink. □ *She was too tanked to drive.* □ *That old codger is really tanked.* **2.** *mod.* defeated; outscored. □ *The team was completely tanked again—40-7.* □ *I just knew we'd get tanked today.*

tanked up See TANKED.

tanker *n.* a heavy drinker. □ *I can see that he's a real tanker.* □ *Don't let yourself turn into a tanker like him.*

tank (something) up *vb. phr.* to fill up a vehicle with petrol. □ *Let's tank up and get on our way.* □ *We tanked up the car before we left.*

tank (up) *vb. (phr.)* to drink too much beer; to drink to excess. □ *The two brothers were busily tanking up and didn't hear me come in.* □ *Let's go out this Friday and get really tanked.*

Tanky *n.* a member of the Communist Party of Great Britain who supports the Stalinist worldview. □ *Tankies are Communists who think Stalin was a nice guy.* □ *There are not many Tankies around these days.*

tan someone's hide *vb. phr.* to beat someone as a punishment. □ *I'll tan his hide as soon as he comes in.* □ *If I catch you I'll tan your hide, you little rascal!*

tape *n.* the sleeve chevrons worn on military and other uniforms to indicate rank. □ *Judging by his tapes, this guy is a sergeant.* □ *Sew on another tape; you've been promoted!*

taped 1. *mod.* finalized; settled; tied up. (As if one were tying up a package.) □ *I'll have this all taped by Thursday. Then we can relax for a while.* □ *Until this thing is taped, we can't do anything.* **2.** *mod.* sized up; seen through. □ *I suspect she's got us all taped.* □ *Don't concern yourself, it's all taped.*

tapper *n.* a beggar or scrounger. □ *The tappers who hang around outside the railway station were rounded up by the police today.* □ *Since John lost his job he's turned into a terrible tapper.*

tappers *n.* overtime. □ *I'm working tappers tonight again.* □ *There's lots of tappers while this rush lasts.*

tap someone *vb.* to ask someone for money. □ *The tramp tapped Harry for a pound as he came out of the hotel.* □ *I was going to tap Sally but in the end I was too embarrassed.*

ta-ra AND **ta-ta** *interj.* an infantile form of "good-bye," sometimes used informally by adults. □ *Be seeing you. Ta-ra!* □ *Ta-ta! I've got to go.*

tart *n.* a slut; a prostitute; a vulgar or coarse-mannered woman. (Crude. Rhyming slang, linked as follows: tart ≈ [(sweet)heart] = prostitute. The word "sweetheart" was formerly descriptive of an illicit lover, mistress or whore.) □ *The tart said business was so good these days, if she'd another pair of legs she'd open them in the next town.* □ *There are a lot of tarts around here in the centre of town.*

tart around *vb. phr.* to behave in a promiscuous or ostentatious or tasteless manner or style. (Crude.) □ *If you keep tarting around like that you'll get kicked out of here.* □ *I do wish she would not tart around in that manner.*

tart's delight *n.* a certain kind of lacy curtaining which is often considered to appear cheap and tasteless. (Crude.) □ *It was a really over-the-top room, with lots of tart's delight.* □ *Right, we'll start by removing all that terrible tart's delight.*

tart something up *vb. phr.* to smarten something up in an ostentatious or tasteless manner or style. (Crude.) □ *If we got it tarted up, maybe we might just* get it sold. □ *Why are you tarting up that ancient car?*

tarty *mod.* in the manner of a prostitute. (Crude.) □ *Why does Clare have to dress so tarty?* □ *She looked so tarty a man came up and asked her if she was looking for business!*

taste blood *vb. phr.* to be encouraged to continue or go further by an initial success. □ *She tasted blood once early on and after that was really driven to win.* □ *Once you taste blood, you're hooked.*

tasty 1. *mod.* having a criminal record. □ *Well, we've got a real tasty one here, Sergeant.* □ *Otto's tasty, all right.* **2.** *mod.* of a good-looking or attractive girl or young woman. □ *Now that's what I'd call a tasty young lady!* □ *I liked that tasty woman you were with last night.*

tat 1. *n.* a grubby individual. □ *The guy is a real tat, I'm afraid.* □ *You stupid tat!* **2.** *n.* garbage or junk. □ *She looked around the room and said she could never live with all that tat.* □ *This stuff is just tat. Show me something better.* **3.** *n.* clothes lacking taste. □ *He's the one dressed in tat.* □ *Why are you always dressed in such terrible tat?*

ta-ta See TA-RA

tater *n.* a potato. □ *Any more taters?* □ *There was a large dish of steaming taters on the table.*

taters *n.* cold weather. (Rhyming slang, linked as follows: taters = [potatoes in the mold] ≈ cold weather.) □ *When it's taters like this, I try to avoid going outdoors.* □ *I know it's taters, but someone has to do it.*

tatt *n.* odds and ends of dress or furnishing material. □ *Don't throw out your tatt! You never know when it'll be useful.* □ *There was a huge pile of tatt in the corner of the room.*

tatty 1. *mod.* inferior; worn; shabby. □ *Oh that's really tatty!* □ *What a tatty place.* **2.** *mod.* trivial; unimportant; neglected. □ *Sort that tatty thing out yourself.* □ *What a tatty little issue this is. Why are we making so much of it?*

taut ship *n.* a well-run, efficient ship. □ *Now men, I like to run a taut ship.* □ *This is not what I'd call a taut ship but I promise, it soon will be.*

tax disc *n.* a small paper disk that is a certificate of payment of the *Road Fund Licence.* □ *It is a legal requirement to display a tax disc upon a vehicle's windshield.* □ *Why is there no tax disc on your car, sir?*

taxi *n.* a pubic louse. (Taboo. Rhyming slang, linked as follows: taxi[-cab] ≈ [crab] = pubic louse.) □ *The old wino and his taxis wandered into the flophouse for a little peace and quiet.* □ *He's scratching like he's got taxis.*

taxing *n.* the collection of protection money. □ *Otto is into taxing now, I hear.* □ *Taxing is one of the more disgusting rackets.*

tea 1. *n.* high tea. □ *Time for tea, I think.* □ *We all sat down for tea at six o'clock.* **2.** See also T.

tea grout *n.* a boy scout. (Rhyming slang.) □ *What is that tea grout doing?* □ *Were you ever a tea grout?*

tea lady *n.* a woman who goes around an office with tea, coffee, etc., on a tea trolley. □ *The tea lady usually appears about 10 a.m.* □ *Hello, I'm Gladys, your new tea lady.*

tea leaf *n.* a thief. (Rhyming slang.) □ *We are the police. We are here to catch tea leaves, madam.* □ *This little toe-rag is just another tea leaf.*

team *n.* a criminal gang. □ *Mr Big's team is getting really dangerous these days.* □ *Keep clear of the team if you know what's good for you.*

tear *n.* a spree; a lark; a joke. (Scots usage.) □ *That was a great tear we had in the pub last night!* □ *Joe always likes to have a tear with any new employees, but he means no harm by it.*

tear-arse 1. *n.* cheese. (Taboo.) □ *They call cheese "tear-arse" because it can cause constipation.* □ *Fancy a bit more tear-arse, love?* **2.** *n.* a very hard worker. (Taboo.) □ *Joe's a real tear-arse, always busy.* □ *We could use more tear-arses like him.*

tear-arse about *vb. phr.* to rush about; to behave recklessly. (Taboo.) □ *Stop tear-arseing about and just listen for a moment!* □ *If you tear-arse about like that you'll miss something important.*

tear a strip off someone *vb. phr.* to reprimand someone. □ *Misbehave and he'll tear a strip off you for sure.* □ *The teacher tore a strip off the wayward pupil.*

tearaway **1.** *n.* a juvenile delinquent. □ *Jerry is a real tearaway. Look what he did!* □ *Who's the tearaway who has ruined all my work?* **2.** *n.* an unthinking or careless youth. □ *Who's that tearaway I saw Linda with?* □ *I don't like him, he's nothing but a tearaway!*

tear into someone *vb. phr.* to scold someone severely; to attack someone. □ *I was late, and the boss tore into me like crazy.* □ *I don't know why she tore into me. I was at work when the window was broken.*

tear into something **1.** *vb. phr.* to begin eating food with gusto. □ *The family tore into the mountain of food like they hadn't eaten since breakfast—which was true, in fact.* □ *Jimmy tore into the turkey leg and cleaned it off in no time.* **2.** *vb. phr.* to rush into a place. □ *I tore into the office and answered the phone.* □ *They tore into town and held up the bank.*

tear-jerker *n.* a very sentimental story or film. □ *That film was a real tear-jerker.* □ *I don't care to read a steady diet of tear-jerkers.*

tear off a piece *vb. phr.* to perform sexual intercourse. (Taboo.) □ *They were tearing off a piece like it was going out of fashion.* □ *I think you could tear off a piece there, Barry.*

tear one's arse off *vb. phr.* to work at a furious pace. (Taboo.) □ *I've been tearing my arse off all week and now you tell me it was not necessary!* □ *If you tear your arse off you can still get done in time.*

tear someone or something apart *vb. phr.* to criticise someone or something severely. □ *I was late, and the boss tore me apart.* □ *I thought my paper was good, but the prof tore it apart.*

tear somewhere apart *vb. phr.* to search somewhere to the point of destruction. □ *The cops came with a search warrant and tore your room apart.* □ *If you don't come up with the*

money you kept for us, we'll tear your house apart.

tear the arse out of something *vb. phr.* to utterly demolish something. (Taboo.) □ *Frank does not appreciate having someone tear the arse out of something he has worked on for over a year.* □ *Well, he really tore the arse out of that!*

tear the tartan *vb. phr.* to speak in Gaelic. (Scots usage.) □ *Can you tear the tartan?* □ *No I can't, but Angus can tear the tartan, I hear.*

teaser **1.** *n.* a brief sample of something, such as a film, record or book, intended to tempt people to buy the complete product. □ *The teaser didn't look very promising, but the reviews were great.* □ *The teasers they showed before the main film were the best part of the evening.* **2.** *n.* a particularly difficult question to answer. □ *All the way there Mike kept asking a series of teasers that had my brain hurting by the time we arrived.* □ *Well, that's a real teaser of a question. I don't know the answer.*

tea's up *phr.* "Here is tea ready to drink." □ *Tea's up! Come and get it!* □ *Come on, tea's up.*

tech **1.** *n.* a technician; a person with technical skills or knowledge. □ *We'll have to take this problem to the techs.* □ *Get hold of a tech who can sort this thing out!* **2.** *n.* a technical or engineering college. □ *He's an engineering student at the local tech.* □ *That's the tech over there, but you're supposed to call it a university now.*

techie *mod.* having to do with technical people or things. □ *I don't like this techie jargon.* □ *This is the techie lounge. See how messy it is?*

technicolor yawn *n.* projectile vomiting. (Crude. Compare with THROW A TECHNICOLOR YAWN.) □ *This garbage will bring on a few technicolor yawns if we serve it.* □ *Who did the technicolor yawn in the bushes?*

technofreak *n.* someone who is obsessed with technology. □ *Young Colin is turning into a complete technofreak.* □ *It's the technofreaks who will keep* *the rest of us prosperous in the years to come.*

ted *n.* a tearaway; an uncouth youth. □ *What a ted he's turned into.* □ *A ted came in and asked about buying one of these very expensive houses!*

Ted Frazer *n.* a cut-throat razor. (Rhyming slang.) □ *How can you use a Ted Frazer? They look deadly.* □ *A Ted Frazer can be deadly in the wrong hands.*

teeming and lading *n.* the practice of using money received today to hide money embezzled yesterday. (Accountants.) □ *Once a business has to resort to teeming and lading, the end is usually only a matter of time away.* □ *Teeming and lading gets very complex very quickly.*

teeny-weeny AND **teensy-weensy** *mod.* tiny. □ *It was just a teeny-weeny sin.* □ *This one is too teeny-weeny.* □ *Could you move just a teensy-weensy bit to the left?*

teeth *n.* a hospital's dental clinic. □ *I think you should pay a visit to teeth, Mrs Gavin.* □ *Teeth is over that way, madam.*

teething troubles *n.* initial difficulties with any new product or service. □ *Don't worry. Every new product has its teething troubles.* □ *Are the teething troubles getting sorted out?*

telephone numbers *n.* vast sums of money. □ *She gets paid telephone numbers to worry about stuff like that.* □ *To me, £400 is almost telephone numbers!*

Tell me another (one)! *exclam.* "I don't believe you!" □ *You a stockbroker? Tell me another one!* □ *Did you seriously imagine that this solution would work? Tell me another!*

tell someone where to get off *vb. phr.* to tell someone when enough is enough; to tell someone it is time to cease being a nuisance. □ *I was fed up with her bossiness. I finally told her where to get off.* □ *He told me where to get off, so I walked out on him.*

tell the (whole) world *vb. phr.* to make someone's private business public knowledge. □ *Well, you don't have to tell the whole world.* □ *Go ahead, tell the world!*

Telly *n.* the *Daily Telegraph.* (A leading London newspaper.) □ *So, what's in the Telly today?* □ *The Telly has the most amazing details of that court case, you know.*

telly 1. *n.* a television set. □ *Have you seen the rubbish they put on the telly these days?* □ *What's showing on the telly tonight?* **2.** *n.* television. (The medium.) □ *The influence of telly is almost impossible to exaggerate.* □ *I like the telly.*

temp 1. *n.* temperature. □ *What's the temp now?* □ *It's important the temp's right.* **2.** *n.* a temporary employee, especially secretarial. □ *We don't need any more temps in here.* □ *Can we get another temp to help with this busy period?*

ten a penny AND **two a penny** *mod.* very common. □ *Skirts like that are ten a penny.* □ *Her type are as common as they come—two a penny.*

ten-bob bit *n.* a fifty-pence coin. (From this value in pre-1971 currency.) □ *He chucked her a ten-bob bit and left.* □ *I hate these ten-bob bit, they're so big and bulky.*

tenner *n.* a ten Pound note. (Compare with FIVER.) □ *For a tenner, the tramp led Barlowe to the place where the crate still lay in the alley.* □ *Barlowe slipped him a tenner and faded into the fog.*

ten penn'orth *n.* a prison sentence of ten years. □ *Oh no, ten penn'orth. I could not believe I could be so unlucky.* □ *The judge said he was sorry he wasn't able to send him away for more than a ten penn'orth.*

ten-to-two *n.* a Jewish person. (Offensive. Rhyming slang.) □ *Y'know, Otto, if you call a Jew a ten-to-two, he's likely to get nasty.* □ *Why can you not be polite to ten-to-twos?*

tenuc *n.* the female sexual organ. (Taboo. Backslang.) □ *The door to the shower room flew open and the girl screamed, trying to cover her tenuc.* □ *If your dresses get any shorter, we'll all be able to see your tenuc.*

terminal boredom *n.* boredom so intense or long-lasting, it feels as if it may either prove directly fatal (as if it were a disease) or drive the sufferer to suicide. □ *If we don't get away from this soon, terminal boredom will set in.* □ *Another minute of him and we would all have had terminal boredom.*

Terrier *n.* a member of the Territorial Army. □ *I used to be Terrier, and it was great!* □ *A number of Terriers went past on a route march.*

Terriers AND **Terries** *n.* the Territorial Army. (Always with *the*.) □ *If you want to help defend your country, consider joining the Terriers.* □ *Most people who join the Terries have a great time.*

Terries See TERRIERS.

terrific **1.** *mod.* excellent. □ *Glad to hear it. That's just terrific.* □ *What a terrific idea!* **2.** *mod.* large; excessive. □ *He made a terrific fuss about this when he heard.* □ *A terrific amount of time and money has been wasted on this project.* **3.** *phr.* "wonderful." (Often used in a sarcastic sense.) □ *Oh that's just terrific. What are we supposed to do now?* □ *That's terrific news, Jane. I'm very pleased for you.*

test *n.* a cricket test match. □ *Harry likes to watch tests on the TV.* □ *When is the next test?*

testiculation *n.* the practice of waving one's arms about and talking a lot of BALLS. (Crude.) □ *Less testiculation, madam, and more calm explanation.* □ *Let's cut out all this pointless testiculation, shall we?*

Thai sticks *n.* cannabis. □ *Max has Thai sticks on him now. No dust.* □ *Can't you lay off the Thai sticks stuff a while?*

thalidomide *n.* unarmed combat. (Offensive.) □ *Calling unarmed combat "thalidomide" is extremely sick and cruel.* □ *There was a little spot of thalidomide outside the pub last night.*

thanks a bunch *phr.* "thank you." (Often used in a sarcastic sense. Often used when there is really nothing to thank anyone for.) □ *Thanks a bunch for your help.* □ *He said "thanks a bunch," and walked out, slamming the door behind him.*

thank you very much *phr.* "thank you." (Often used in a sarcastic sense. Often used when there is really nothing to thank anyone for.) □ *I think I can manage somehow to find my own way out, thank you very much.* □ *You've been quite annoying enough already, thank you very much!*

That'll be the day! AND **That will be the day!** *exclam.* "That is most unlikely ever to happen." (Often used in a sarcastic sense.) □ *You win a medal? That'll be the day!* □ *When he gets his own car—that will be the day!*

That'll teach someone. *sent.* "That is what someone deserves." □ *That'll teach you to pull out in front of me.* □ *I hit him on the head. That'll teach him.*

That's about the size of it. *sent.* "That is the way things are."; "That's all there is to tell." □ *Well, that's about the size of it. See you tomorrow.* □ *That's about the size of it. You've understood it perfectly.*

That's all someone needs. *sent.* "That is too much."; "That is the last straw." □ *Now the sewer's backing up. That's all I need.* □ *A new mouth to feed. That's all we need!*

That's a new one on me. *sent.* "I did not know that."; "I have never heard of such a thing." □ *A machine that copies in four colours. That's a new one on me.* □ *A talking camera? That's a new one on me.*

that's brill *phr.* an indication of agreement, as uttered by a SLOANE RANGER. □ *Okay, yah. That's brill.* □ *That's brill, let's do it.*

That's (gone and) torn it! See THAT TEARS IT!

That's my boy! AND **Thattaboy!; Attaboy!** *sent.* "That is my son of whom I am proud."; "I'm proud of this young man." □ *After the game, Tom's dad said, "That's my boy!"* □ *Attaboy! Always a winner!*

That's that! *exclam.* "That is final!"; "That is the end of it!" □ *I said no, and that's that!* □ *I won't go, and that's that!*

That's the stuff (to give the troops)! *exclam.* "This is even better than expected!" □ *Good shot, Willy! That's the* *stuff!* □ *What an excellent meal! That's the stuff to give the troops!*

That's the ticket! *exclam.* "That is exactly what is needed!" □ *Good! That's the ticket! Now you're doing it right.* □ *That's the ticket! Perfect!*

That's torn it! *exclam.* "That's wrecked things!" □ *Well, that's torn it!* □ *That's torn it! It's too late now!*

That's what I say (too). *sent.* "I agree with you." □ *Of course, Mary. That's what I say.* □ *That's what I say, too. The way to cut spending is just to do it.*

Thattaboy! See THAT'S MY BOY!

That tears it! AND That's (gone and) torn it! *exclam.* "That has ruined everything!"; "Everything is wrecked now!" □ *Well, that tears it! I'm leaving!* □ *I thought yesterday's error was bad enough, but that's gone and torn it now!*

that way *mod.* homosexual. (Crude.) □ *Well, really...I didn't know he was, you know, that way.* □ *Brian's been that way for years, in case you don't know.*

That will be the day! See THAT'LL BE THE DAY!

then and there See THERE AND THEN.

there and then AND then and there *mod.* without delay and without moving. □ *He dropped the box right there and then and walked out on us.* □ *Right then and there, he pulled up his shirt and showed everyone the jagged scar.*

there it is 1. *phr.* "that's what's been decided." □ *I'm sorry, but there it is.* □ *There it is, that's the way it will be done.* **2.** *phr.* "this is the problem." □ *Well I'm sorry, but there it is.* □ *There it is. What can we do about it?*

(There's) nothing in it. AND (There's) nothing to it. *sent.* simple; easy. □ *Oh don't worry, there's nothing in it.* □ *Changing a light bulb is easy; there's nothing to it!* □ *I think there's nothing in it; it's not a problem.*

there you are *n.* a public house or pub. (Rhyming slang, linked as follows: there you are ≈ [bar] = pub(lic house).) □ *He's down the there you are, as usual.* □ *That's not a bad little there you are you've got there, mate.*

There you are. AND There you go. 1. *sent.* "This is the result."; "This is the way things turned out." □ *There you are. Didn't I warn you?* □ *Well, there you go. Another first-class mess.* **2.** *sent.* "Well done, you did it correctly!" (Usually THERE YOU GO!) □ *There you are! That's the way!* □ *Good shot, Charlie! There you go!*

There you go (again)! 1. *exclam.* "You are doing again that which you should not do!" □ *There you go! You said it again.* □ *I just told you not to put that junk on the table, but there you go again!* **2.** See THERE YOU ARE.

The (very) idea! *exclam.* an expression of strong disapproval. □ *Resignation? The very idea!* □ *The idea! Absolutely not!*

thick AND thickie; thicko; thicky *n.* an exceptionally stupid person. (Crude.) □ *What a thick that woman can be.* □ *Get out of here, you thicko!*

thick (as thieves) *mod.* involved or very friendly with someone. □ *Sam and Mary are really thick together.* □ *These two are as thick as thieves, y'know.*

thick ear *n.* an ear swollen because of a blow upon it. □ *There! Now you've got one thick ear.* □ *And if you say or do anything like that again, you'll have another thick ear. Got it?*

thick(headed) *mod.* stupid. □ *She's sort of thick, but means well.* □ *Why are you always so thickheaded about money?*

thickie See THICK.

thicko See THICK.

thick on the ground 1. *mod.* in large numbers. □ *Suits in that style were indeed thick on the ground once sir, but I have no personal recollection of the fashions of the 1920s.* □ *You should have no difficulty. People like that are always thick on the ground.* **2.** *mod.* present everywhere. □ *Opportunities like that are not exactly thick on the ground.* □ *Problems like that usually are pretty thick on the ground just when you don't want them.*

thick-skinned *mod.* insensitive to criticism. (Compare with THIN-SKINNED.) □ *You've got to be more thick-skinned if* *you want to be a copper.* □ *He's really thick-skinned, is that one.*

thicky See THICK.

thimble and thumb *n.* rum. (Rhyming slang.) □ *I could use a thimble and thumb.* □ *The thimble and thumb were certainly flowing that evening, I can tell you.*

thing 1. *n.* an obsession. □ *I can see he's got a thing about this, but we'll just have to work it out.* □ *She's got a thing about cats.* **2.** *n.* someone's interest or preference; what someone is skilled at. □ *This isn't exactly my thing, but I'll give it a try.* □ *This is just your thing! Enjoy it!* **3.** *n.* drugs. □ *You can get some good thing in this part of town.* □ *What sort of thing do you take?* **4.** AND **thingie; thingy** *n.* one's sexual organs, either male or female. (Crude. Euphemistic.) □ *Doctor, my thing hurts.* □ *What's wrong with my thingie?*

thingamajig AND **thingumajig; thingumabob; thingy; thingummy; thingamy** *n.* someone or something for which the correct name has been forgotten or was never known. □ *Hand me that thingamajig with the copper base, will you?* □ *What're you supposed to do with this thingumabob?* □ *Did you know thingamy is looking for you?*

thingamy See THINGAMAJIG.

thingie See THING.

thingumabob See THINGAMAJIG.

thingummy See THINGAMAJIG.

thingy See THINGAMAJIG; THING.

think-tank *n.* a place where great minds are assembled to try to think up solutions to problems or to envisage the future. □ *She spent a few months in one of those think-tanks, but quit when she couldn't think of anything to think about.* □ *What sort of solutions are coming out of the think-tanks of the nation?*

thin on the ground 1. *mod.* in very small numbers. □ *I'm afraid that model is rather thin on the ground nowadays, sir.* □ *Tickets for the concert were thin on the ground by this time.* **2.** *mod.* absent everywhere. □ *That stuff is thin on the ground, you'll find.* □ *Good ideas are always thin on the ground.*

thin-skinned *mod.* sensitive to criticism. (Compare with THICK-SKINNED.) □ *Don't be so thin-skinned. You can't expect everyone to like you.* □ *I'm too thin-skinned to be a debt collector.*

third leg See MIDDLE LEG.

third wicket partnership *n.* a pair of cricketing batsman working together to make runs. □ *The two of them made a magnificent third wicket partnership.* □ *That was a terrible performance. These two are no more a third wicket partnership than my aunt and the cat next door.*

this and that 1. *vb.* to bat (in cricket). (Rhyming slang.) □ *It's your turn to this and that.* □ *I'm just no use at thising and thating.* **2.** *n.* a selection of various trivial things. □ *We've got this and that, but not what you want.* □ *There was a huge collection of this and that in the barn.* **3.** See also BALL AND BAT.

this day week *n.* a week from today. (This might be in either future or past sense, which the listener or reader must determine from the context.) □ *We have to have all this ready this day week.* □ *This day week, we'll be sunning ourselves on a Spanish beach.*

This is it! 1. *exclam.* "This is exactly what I have been looking for!"; "I have found it!" □ *This is it! I got it right this time.* □ *This is it! The world's best pizza!* **2.** *exclam.* "This is the crucial moment!"; "The time has come!" □ *Okay, this is it, the last chance!* □ *Get ready, this is it! Jump now!*

This is where I came in. *sent.* "This all seems very familiar."; "One has been through all this before." □ *Okay, that's enough. This is where I came in.* □ *This is where I came in. It's the same thing all over again.*

this weather *n.* today; at this time; now. (Scots usage.) □ *What are you doing this weather, Willie?* □ *Willie's no weel this weather. (William is not well today.)*

thorny wire *n.* an easily-riled person. (Irish usage.) □ *I don't think I could take another thorny wire like that today.* □ *He's a real thorny wire; take care.*

thou *n.* one thousand. (Compare with

K.) □ *I managed to get a couple of thou from the bank, but I need a little more than that.* □ *It only costs four thou. I could borrow it from my uncle.*

thought plickens *phr.* "things are getting harder to understand." (A comical inversion of *the plot thickens*; normally with *the*.) □ *So, the thought plickens!* □ *Well I don't understand what's going on; you might say, the thought plickens.*

thrash 1. *n.* a lavish party. □ *What time do we have to be at that thrash on Saturday night?* □ *What a fancy thrash! They even have glass glasses!* **2.** *n.* a tough fight or battle. □ *It's going to be some thrash but we'll win.* □ *That was some tough thrash. Don't feel so bad about losing.* **3.** AND **towel** *vb.* to hit forcibly. □ *He thrashed me as I walked over to my car.* □ *Harry's livid and out to towel you for what you did.* **4.** *vb.* to defeat thoroughly. □ *The team was completely thrashed.* □ *Our candidate was comprehensively towelled in the election.*

threads *n.* clothes. □ *You look pretty good in your new threads.* □ *I'll get on my threads, and we'll go out tonight.*

thread (the needle) *vb. phr.* to perform sexual intercourse, from the male perspective. (Taboo. Irish usage.) □ *One look and he knew he had already threaded the needle with her that evening.* □ *There were a couple of teenagers in the back room, threading away.*

three bricks shy of a load AND **two sandwiches short of a picnic** *mod.* stupid; dense; short-changed on intelligence. (The *two* and *three* are interchangeable in both expressions.) □ *I would never say she was dense. Just three bricks shy of a load.* □ *Why do you always act like you're two sandwiches short of a picnic?*

three-cornered fight *n.* an election contest with three candidates. □ *When it's a three-cornered fight it's much harder to predict the result.* □ *Three-cornered fights can be much more fun.*

three-decker *n.* a novel or other literary work that is published in three volumes. □ *I'm reading the first part of that new three-decker.* □ *Do you like reading three-deckers?*

three'd up *mod.* concerns the condition of having three prisoners in one cell. (Prison.) □ *Yes, we were three'd up for a few months. It was pretty grim.* □ *Prison is bad always, but three'd up it becomes much worse still.*

three-piece suite *n.* the male sexual organ. (Taboo.) □ *The doctor told him that he'd got something wrong with his three-piece suite.* □ *Only small boys wave their three-piece suites about like that, Wayne. Put it away!*

three sheets in(to) the wind See BOTH SHEETS IN(TO) THE WIND.

thrill *n.* an orgasm. (Taboo.) □ *After I gave her one thrill she wanted another, and then another.* □ *Did you have a thrill too, my love?*

thrilled *mod.* pleased; content. □ *I was really thrilled to hear your news.* □ *I was so thrilled for you.*

thrilled to bits *mod.* utterly content. □ *She was thrilled to bits to win.* □ *I would really be thrilled to bits if that were true.*

throne *n.* a toilet or lavatory seat. (Crude.) □ *And there was the cat—sitting on the throne and just staring at me as cats do.* □ *The only place where I could get any solitude in that house was when I sat on the throne.*

throne room *n.* a toilet or lavatory. (Crude.) □ *Paul is in the throne room, reading, I think.* □ *Where's your throne room?*

through and through 1. *mod.* repeatedly; again and again. □ *We have discussed this through and through. How long before you understand?* □ *He kept on asking the same question through and through.* **2.** *mod.* thoroughly; throughout. □ *She's a born fighter, through and through.* □ *He is totally dishonest. A crook through and through.*

through the mill *mod.* subjected to hard work, intensive pressure, etc. □ *If you've been a marine, you've been through the mill.* □ *I feel like I've gone through the mill. I'm pooped.*

through (with) something or someone. 1. *vb. phr.* to be finished or completed with something or someone. □ *When Harry was through with the* book, he passed it over to Claire. □ *Are you through yet? We are all waiting.* **2.** *vb. phr.* to have nothing further to do with something or someone. □ *I'm through with you, Harry. Get lost!* □ *Joan says she's through with crack for good. We'll see.*

throw 1. *n.* a round; a turn; the price of a round. (In a bar or such.) □ *Right, it's my throw. What do you want?* □ *Don't imagine you're getting away from here before you pay for another throw, you miserable sod!* **2.** *vb.* to earn as wages. (Scots usage.) □ *How much do yous throw at yon place? (How much do you people earn at that place?)* □ *If Ah can throw enough Ah'd come ta work wi' yous yins there. (If I can earn enough I'd come to work with you people there.)*

throw a fight *vb. phr.* to lose a boxing match on purpose. (Boxing. Other words can replace *a*. Compare with THROW A GAME.) □ *I just know that Wilbur didn't throw that fight.* □ *The guy would never throw a fight.*

throw a fit AND **throw forty fits; have a fit.** *vb. phr.* to become extremely angry or bad-tempered. □ *I knew you'd throw a fit when I told you.* □ *Oh, boy, did she throw forty fits!* □ *If she does that, I think I'll have a fit.*

throw a game *vb. phr.* to lose a game on purpose. (Compare with THROW A FIGHT.) □ *I know Wilbur. He could never throw a game.* □ *There's a couple of those guys who would throw a game if they got enough money to do it.*

throw a party *vb. phr.* to give a party. □ *I hear Tom's throwing a party on Saturday night.* □ *If I threw a party, would you come?*

throw a technicolor yawn *vb. phr.* to indulge in projectile vomiting. (Crude. Compare with TECHNICOLOR YAWN.) □ *One look at the food, and I almost threw a technicolor yawn.* □ *John stumbled into the living-room and threw a technicolor yawn all over the new carpet.*

throw (away) *vb. (phr.)* to deliberately lose a battle, competition or game. □ *Don't throw away the game now!*

You've almost won! □ *He threw that game, you know.*

throw-away 1. *mod.* of that which is not important or which can be discarded. □ *He threw away the throw-away cigarette lighter.* □ *Some people seem to think they have throw-away families.* **2.** *n.* a leaflet. □ *There was a woman giving away these throw-aways at the street corner.* □ *Let's print a throw-away about this.*

throw-away (line) *n.* an aside or extempore remark, usually witty. □ *The comedian tossed off his best throw-away line of the evening just as the curtain fell.* □ *She was an expert at the one-line throw-away.*

throw a wobbly *vb. phr.* to suddenly or unexpectedly behave irrationally. □ *Well the opposition have really thrown a wobbly this time.* □ *I wonder what caused him to throw a wobbly like that?*

throw forty fits See THROW A FIT.

throw in the sponge See THROW IN THE TOWEL.

throw in the towel AND **throw in the sponge; toss in the sponge; throw it in** *vb. phr.* to quit; to give up. (From boxing where a towel or sponge thrown into the ring indicates that a boxer has given up. Compare with CHUCK IT IN.) □ *I can tell when it's time to throw in the towel, and this is that time.* □ *The candidate who was exposed by the press as a former pickpocket tossed in the sponge at a tearful press conference.*

throw it in See THROW IN THE TOWEL.

throw money at something *vb. phr.* to try to solve a problem by spending money on it. □ *This government has thrown billions at the housing problem, but it has been nothing but a long-term disaster.* □ *Don't just throw money at it.*

throw one out on one's ear *vb. phr.* to remove someone from a place forcibly. □ *Behave yourself, or I'll throw you out on your ear.* □ *The caretaker caught us and threw us out on our ears.*

throw one's hat in(to) the ring *vb. phr.* to let it be known that one is to be a contestant or a candidate. □ *All the big* developers in the area have thrown their hats in the ring for our land. □ I won't throw my hat into the ring until the last minute.

throw one's lines vb. phr. to fail to make the proper impact with one's lines in a play. (Theatrical.) □ It was terrible. The leading actor was throwing his lines right through the play. □ Don't come on my stage if you're going to throw your lines.

throw one's weight around vb. phr. to behave in an assertive and unattractive manner. □ The managing director was throwing his weight around, but that had little effect on anything. □ Just because she's throwing her weight around doesn't mean she'll get any better service.

throw someone vb. to disconcert or confuse someone. □ He threw all of us with that explanation. □ Every time he opens his mouth he throws me, you know.

throw something together See KNOCK SOMETHING TOGETHER.

Throw the baby out with the bathwater. vb. phr. to carry some process too far, resulting in more being lost than gained. (Normally used in the negative.) □ If you go that far you'll throw the baby out with the bathwater. □ Don't throw the baby out with the bathwater by going all the way with that measure.

throw the book at someone 1. vb. phr. to be charged (by the police) or punished (by the court) for as many crimes as possible or to the maximum possible extent permitted by the law or both. □ The judge wanted to throw the book at Bruno, but the prosecutor convinced him to go easy in hope that Bruno would lead them to Mr Big. □ The police sergeant smiled at Rocky and said, "Right, now it's our turn. We're going to throw the book at you." **2.** vb. phr. to be required to pay the maximum possible legal price. (As a form of retribution for some real or imagined offence.) □ Yes, I know the person, always complaining about poor service. Okay, throw the book at her this time. □ Some solicitors have a reputation for throwing the book at unsuspecting clients.

throw (up) vb. (phr.) to empty one's stomach; to vomit. (Crude.) □ I'm gonna throw up! □ Don't you dare throw in here!

thumb a lift vb. phr. to beg a lift; to stand at the side of the road and signal to cars with one's thumb that one is seeking a lift. □ I'll thumb a lift to get there if I have to. □ I thumbed a lift in the hope of speeding things up.

thumbnail sketch n. a quick and concise description. (Figuratively, one that could be written on someone's thumbnail.) □ Let me give you a thumbnail sketch of what happened. □ The story—in a thumbnail sketch—deals with a family of storks and what happens to them during each of the four seasons.

thumbs down 1. n. a sign of disapproval. (Compare with THUMBS UP.) □ The board gave our proposal a thumbs down. □ Oh no, not another thumbs down! **2.** mod. disapproving; negative. □ It was thumbs down, and I was disappointed. □ That thumbs down decision was a victory for good sense.

thumbs up 1. n. a sign of approval. (Compare with THUMBS DOWN.) □ It was a thumbs up on the new filtration plant at Thursday's village board meeting. □ There was no thumbs up for the mayor as she faced certain defeat in today's vote. **2.** mod. approving; positive. □ The new filtration plant got a thumbs up decision at the board meeting. □ A thumbs up vote assured another three years of financial assistance.

thunderbox n. a chamber pot. (Crude.) □ Where's your thunderbox? □ The thunderbox's through that way.

thundering mod. vast or considerable. □ Why are lawyer's fees always so thundering big? □ A thundering great aircraft flew low over the village.

thunder-thighs n. someone who is grossly overweight. (Crude.) □ Here comes old thunder-thighs. □ Here, thunder-thighs, let me get you a chair or two.

tick 1. n. a minute; a second; a brief interval of time. (Originally, the time between two ticks of a clock. Compare with SEC.) □ *I'll be with you in a tick.* □ *This won't take a tick. Sit tight.* **2.** *n.* credit. □ *I suppose we could buy it on tick.* □ *It costs more on tick, you know.*

ticker 1. *n.* a heart. □ *I've got a good strong ticker.* □ *His ticker finally gave out.* **2.** *n.* a watch. □ *My ticker stopped. The battery must be dead.* □ *If your watch runs on a battery, can you really call it a ticker?* **3.** *n.* a taxi-meter. □ *"Look squire," said the cabbie, "the ticker says £20, so you pay me £20. Get it?"* □ *We sat in the traffic jam, and still the ticker ticked up larger and larger sums.*

ticket 1. *n.* the exact thing required; the needed thing. □ *Her smile was her ticket to a new career.* □ *"That's the very ticket!" he said, pleased with my present.* □ *This degree will be your ticket to a bright and prosperous future.* **2.** *n.* a military certificate of discharge. □ *When do you get your ticket, mate?* □ *I've just got my ticket!* **3.** *n.* a trade union membership card. □ *You've got to have your ticket to work here.* □ *Don't ever loose your ticket, son; it's your meal ticket.* **4.** *n.* a playing-card, especially for bridge. □ *What do you like to play with your tickets?* □ *Get out the tickets and we'll have a game.* **5.** *n.* an arrest or search warrant. (Police.) □ *We've got the ticket, sir.* □ *A search warrant? Yes sir, here's the ticket.* **6.** *n.* a person. (Scots usage.) □ *What a ticket he is!* □ *He's just an ordinary ticket; ignore what he says.* **7.** *mod.* physically or mentally fit. (Always with *the*.) □ *Well, I can see you're the ticket again.* □ *You've got to be the ticket to work here, you know.*

tickety-boo AND **ticketty-boo; tiggerty-boo** *mod.* all right; okay; correct; satisfactory. (Possibly from the Hindustani *tikai babu*, meaning "it is all right, sir," in which case the expression is an example of hobson-jobson.) □ *It's fine; it's all tickety-boo.* □ *Don't worry, it's all tiggerty-boo again now.*

tickled (pink) *mod.* amused; utterly delighted; pleased. □ *I am tickled pink*

you could come this evening. □ *We were tickled that you thought of us.*

tickle the ivories *vb. phr.* to play the piano. □ *I used to be able to tickle the ivories real nice.* □ *She sat down to tickle the ivories for a while.*

tickle-you-fancy *n.* a male homosexual. (Crude. Rhyming slang, linked as follows: tickle-you-fancy ≈ [nancy] = homosexual.) □ *He doesn't like being called a tickle-you-fancy.* □ *Tom is getting to be such a tickle-you-fancy.*

tick over *vb. phr.* [for a person, business, machine, etc.] to operate at a minimal level. □ *After his illness he's really just ticking over.* □ *Let the car tick over until we're ready to go.*

tick someone off *vb. phr.* to reprimand or scold someone. □ *When she caught the child she ticked her off right there, in front of the whole class.* □ *Do you have to tick me off in public like this?*

tick-tack See TIC-TAC.

tick-tock 1. *n.* a watch or clock. (Juvenile.) □ *Wind your tick-tock before you forget.* □ *The tick-tock in the kitchen has broken.* **2.** *n.* a clock. (Juvenile.) □ *See the tick-tock, see the big hand and the little hand?* □ *We have a big tick-tock in our house.*

tic-tac AND **tick-tack** *n.* a manual semaphore-like signalling system used by race-course bookmakers. □ *Bookies use tic-tac to communicate odds and other information between each other.* □ *Fewer and fewer use tick-tack now. Cellular phone have a lot to do with this.*

tiddle *vb.* to urinate. (Crude. Juvenile.) □ *I'm just going to tiddle.* □ *Well, tiddling does relieve the pressure of all that beer!*

tiddled *mod.* slightly intoxicated due to drink. □ *He had a tendency to get a little tiddled.* □ *Jack's too tiddled to drive.*

tiddler 1. *n.* a small fish such as a minnow. □ *It's just a tiddler. Throw it back!* □ *He took the tiddler off the end of his line and threw it back in.* **2.** *n.* an especially small person or thing. □ *I don't think I could take another tiddler like that today.* □ *Here was one tiddler that was different from the others, he thought.*

tiddly 1. *mod.* very small. □ *"Well," she giggled, "holding it gently, as if it might break, "it's very tiddly."* □ *"It may be tiddly now," he said, "but with careful handling it will grow to full size soon enough."* **2.** *mod.* slightly intoxicated due to drink. (Rhyming slang, linked as follows: tiddly[wink] ≈ [drink] = [drunk] = intoxicated.) □ *I felt a little tiddly, but that didn't stop me from having more.* □ *Tracy gets a little tiddly after a drink or two.*

tiddlywink 1. *n.* a drink. (Rhyming slang.) □ *I'm down the pub for a tiddlywink.* □ *Let's have a tiddlywink.* **2.** *n.* a Chinese person. (Racially offensive. Rhyming slang, linked as follows: tiddlywink ≈ [chink] = Chinese.) □ *He said he was not a racist, he just hated this particular tiddlywink!* □ *Don't call Chinese people tiddlywinks, please. It is very offensive and racist.*

tidemark 1. *n.* a mark, often in the form of a ring, upon someone's body indicating the extent of the washed area. □ *Mum says if you leave a tidemark again she'll make you lick it clean!* □ *That tidemark is a dead give-away as to how far you washed, Otto.* **2.** *n.* a mark left around the inside of a bathtub by the dirty water that had been in it. □ *Hey, who left the tidemark in the bath?* □ *This time, no tidemark. OK?*

tidy sum *n.* a large sum of money. □ *To me, £400 is a tidy sum.* □ *She gets paid a tidy sum to worry about stuff like that.*

tied up 1. *mod.* busy. □ *I was tied up and couldn't get to the phone.* □ *The phone was tied up for more than an hour.* **2.** See also SEWN UP.

tie-in *n.* a connection; a link. □ *And just what is your tie-in with the Acme Cat Food Corporation, Mr Tiddles?* □ *The video game will make a really good tie-in with the film when it's released.*

tie in with someone or something *vb. phr.* to link up with or co-operate with someone or something. □ *We're planning to tie in with these people to launch the new product.* □ *Are you sure you would want to tie in with someone like that?*

tie one on *vb. phr.* to become intoxicated from drink. □ *The boys went out to tie one on.* □ *They really tied one on.*

tie something up See SEW SOMETHING UP.

tie the knot 1. *vb. phr.* to get married. □ *We tied the knot in a little chapel in Wales.* □ *So they've finally tied the knot, then?* **2.** *vb. phr.* [for someone such as priest, registrar, ship's captain, etc.] to officiate at a marriage ceremony. □ *It was hard to find somebody to tie the knot at that hour.* □ *It only took a few minutes for the ship's captain to tie the knot.*

tiger 1. *n.* a strong, aggressive, awe-inspiring person. (Usually male.) □ *The guy's a tiger. Take care.* □ *Isn't Brian a tiger when he's roused!* **2.** *n.* a wife. □ *The tiger is angry with me.* □ *I've got to get home to the tiger.*

tiger's milk See TIGER'S SWEAT.

tiger's sweat AND **tiger's milk** *n.* bad liquor; strong liquor; any beer or liquor. □ *How about some more of that tiger's sweat?* □ *This tiger's milk would kill a tiger of any age or disposition.*

tiggerty-boo See TICKETY-BOO.

tight 1. *mod.* intoxicated due to drink. □ *Frank was tight and didn't want to drive.* □ *The host got tight and had to go to bed.* **2.** *mod.* tense; with little margin for error. □ *In a tight situation Martin can turn sort of wet.* □ *You can bet that when time is tight and we are busy as can be, the telephone won't stop ringing.*

tight-arsed *mod.* very mean. (Taboo.) □ *"Good riddance," he thought, "you always were a tight-arsed git."* □ *Do we really have to be so tight-arsed about this?*

tight as a badger's bum See TIGHT AS A DUCK'S ARSE(HOLE).

tight as a crab's bum See TIGHT AS A DUCK'S ARSE(HOLE).

tight as a drum AND **tight as a fart; tight as a tick** *mod.* very intoxicated due to drink. (FART is taboo; the rest are crude.) □ *Geoff was tight as a drum by midnight.* □ *Oh boy, I drank till I was tight as a fart.*

tight as a duck's arse(hole) AND **tight as a badger's bum; tight as a crab's**

bum; **tight as a fish's arse(hole); tight as a gnat's arse(hole); tight as a mouse's ear(hole)** *mod.* very mean. (ARSE is taboo; the rest are crude.) □ *Mean? He's tight as a duck's arsehole!* □ *Being as tight as a mouse's ear does not impress the girls, Harry.*

tight as a fart See TIGHT AS A DRUM.

tight as a fish's arse(hole) See TIGHT AS A DUCK'S ARSE(HOLE).

tight as a gnat's arse(hole) See TIGHT AS A DUCK'S ARSE(HOLE).

tight as a mouse's ear(hole) See TIGHT AS A DUCK'S ARSE(HOLE).

tight as a tick See TIGHT AS A DRUM.

tighten one's belt *vb. phr.* to economise. (As if unable to afford enough food to cause one's stomach to press against one's belt.) □ *Get ready to tighten your belt. I lost my job.* □ *The entire country will have to tighten its belt now.*

tighter than a nun's cunt See TIGHTER THAN A WITCH'S CUNT.

tighter than a witch's cunt AND **tighter than a nun's cunt** *mod.* very tight; very hard to remove or withdraw from. (Taboo.) □ *The screw was embedded tighter than a witch's cunt.* □ *I don't think it'll fit in there, it's tighter than a nun's cunt.*

tight-(fisted) *mod.* stingy. □ *She's really tight with her cash.* □ *You're just too tight-fisted. Give me a fiver, Dad, come on!*

tight money *n.* money that is hard to get. □ *This is tight money. Go easy on it. There's no more after this.* □ *In these days of tight money, no new expenditures will be approved.*

tight spot *n.* a difficulty; a predicament. □ *I'm in a sort of tight spot and wondered if you could help out?* □ *Of course, I like helping people out of tight spots as long as it doesn't cost me any money.*

till hell freezes over AND **until hell freezes over** *mod.* forever. (Crude.) □ *That's all right, boss; I can wait till hell freezes over for your answer.* □ *I'll be here until hell freezes over.*

till kingdom come AND **until kingdom come** *mod.* forever. □ *Do I have to*

keep assembling these units till kingdom come? □ *I'll hate her guts until kingdom come.*

till the fat lady sings AND **until the fat lady sings; when the fat lady sings** *mod.* at the end; a long time from now. (Supposedly from a tale about a child—sitting through an opera—who asks a parent when it will be over. "Not until the fat lady sings" is the answer.) □ *Relax. It won't be over till the fat lady sings.* □ *We can leave with everybody else when the fat lady sings.*

Tim *n.* a Roman Catholic. (Offensive. Also a term of address. Scots usage. From "Timothy," a given name once common among Irish Roman Catholics. Compare with PADDY, DAN and JUNGLE JIM.) □ *Willy actually moved house because a Tim moved in next door!* □ *Willy thinks the Tims are taking over these days.*

timbers *n.* cricket stumps or wickets. □ *The ball went clean through the timbers.* □ *At close of play we pull the timbers and bring them back to the clubhouse.*

tin *n.* money. □ *How much tin do you need, then?* □ *Sorry, I can't afford it, I've no tin.*

tin budgie *n.* an aircraft. (See BUDGIE.) □ *She's scared of getting into a tin budgie.* □ *We flew half-way around the world in this huge tin budgie.*

tincture *n.* an alcoholic drink. □ *Len stopped at a pub for a tincture before going home.* □ *How about a tincture?*

tin fish *n.* a torpedo. □ *How many tin fish does this submarine carry, Captain?* □ *They launched a tin fish at the target, but missed.*

tin hat *n.* a steel helmet. (Military.) □ *Where's my tin hat?* □ *You use your tin hat for everything—washing, carrying water—you name it.*

tinkerbelle *n.* a male homosexual. (Crude.) □ *He doesn't like being called a tinkerbelle.* □ *Why does he work so hard to look like he's a tinkerbelle?*

tinkle 1. *vb.* to urinate. (Crude. Juvenile.) □ *I've got to tinkle!* □ *Jimmy, be sure and tinkle before we leave.* **2.** *n.* a telephone call. □ *You will give me a tin-*

kle, won't you? □ *It's just a tinkle to ask how you are.*

tinkler *n.* the male sexual organ. (Taboo.) □ *Myra says tinklers are disgusting but then Myra's strange.* □ *Only small boys wave their tinklers about like that, Wayne. Put it away!*

tin lid 1. *n.* the last straw. (Normally with *the*.) □ *When she poured her drink down my back, that was the tin lid.* □ *This is just the tin lid. I'm leaving.* **2.** *n.* a child. (Rhyming slang, linked as follows: tin lid ≈ [kid] = child.) □ *Our tin lid is playing in the garden.* □ *How many tin lids do you have now?*

tin-lid *n.* a Jewish person. (Offensive. Rhyming slang, linked as follows: tin-lid ≈ [Yid] = Jew.) □ *Why can you not be polite to tin-lids?* □ *Y'know, Otto, if you call a Jew a tin-lid, he's likely to get nasty.*

tinnie AND **tube** *n.* a can of beer. □ *Have a tinnie, Charlie.* □ *Here, that's a good tube!*

tin plate *n.* a friend. (Rhyming slang, linked as follows: tin plate ≈ [mate] = friend.) □ *The two tin plates left the pub, each one preventing the other from falling over.* □ *Who's your tin plate, Albert?*

Tinseltown *n.* Hollywood, California, USA. □ *Tinseltown is a very glitzy place.* □ *She's talented and has set her sights on Tinseltown.*

tin tack 1. *n.* a sack. (Rhyming slang.) □ *He opened the tin tack and looked inside.* □ *What's in yer tin tack, mate?* **2.** *n.* a job dismissal; the sack. (Rhyming slang.) □ *The boss gave them all the tin tack.* □ *The tin tack is what I am afraid of.*

tin tacks See BRASS TACKS.

tin tank See IRON TANK.

tin termites *n.* rust (on a car). □ *I see the thing's infested with tin termites.* □ *Everywhere you looked, the tin termites had eaten away at the bodywork.*

tiny tots *n.* small children. □ *I wish she would try to control these tiny tots of hers.* □ *I hope you like tiny tots. There are several here this afternoon.*

tip *n.* a very untidy room. □ *What a tip you've turned this place into!* □ *It really is a tip, Simon.*

tip-off *n.* a warning; a hint; a clue. □ *The tip-off was when the dog started wagging his tail. We knew you were hiding somewhere close.* □ *The broken twig was just the tip-off Barlowe needed.*

tipple 1. *n.* a drink, especially of spirits. □ *This is a really fine tipple.* □ *Another little tipple, Tom?* **2.** *vb.* to drink spirits; to take small sips of spirits continuously over a long period. □ *He's been tippling whisky since early morning.* □ *Actually, he's been tippling since 1943.*

tippler *n.* one who drinks spirits. □ *Uncle Ben was a tippler, but a harmless one.* □ *He started drinking at fifteen and has been a tippler ever since.*

tipply AND **tipsy** *mod.* intoxicated due to drink. □ *Ben is too tipply to drive home.* □ *I feel a little tipsy.*

tip someone off *vb. phr.* to warn or hint privately. □ *I tipped him off but I think he ignored me.* □ *Tip Otto off; the cops are on to him.*

tipster *n.* someone who provides information, particularly about horse-racing. □ *We got this from a tipster who has usually proven reliable in the past.* □ *Well, I just hope your "reliable" tipster put his own money on his "reliable" information, too.*

tipsy See TIPPY.

tired and emotional *n.* intoxicated due to drink. (A euphemism.) □ *They said on TV that the politician was tired and emotional. So he'd been at the sauce again, it seems.* □ *They were both tired and emotional. They could only lie there and snore, in fact.*

tiswas *n.* a state of chaos or confusion. □ *No more tiswas like that, thank you very much.* □ *What a tiswas there is in that office. I don't know how they can ever get anything done.*

tit 1. *n.* a teat or nipple. (Crude. This probably originated as a misspelling of "teat." Normally used in the plural.) □ *Frank could see her tits through the thin material of her dress.* □ *If you go* out without a bra, everyone will see your tits, Mary. **2.** n. a foolish or insignificant person. □ *That poor tit thinks he can convince them.* □ *You tit! You've buttered the tablecloth!*

titbag See TIT-HAMMOCK.

ti(t)ch n. a tiny or insignificant person. □ *I'm sorry but we really don't need another tich working here.* □ *What's a titch like that doing around here?*

ti(t)chy mod. tiny. □ *That is a titchy little steak. I ordered a big one.* □ *What a tichy amount of money! I can't live on that.*

titfer n. a hat. (Rhyming slang, linked as follows: titfer ≈ [tit-for-tat] ≈ hat.) □ *I'm going to buy myself a new titfer.* □ *Why are you wearing that ridiculous titfer?*

tit-hammock AND **tit-sling; titbag** n. a brassiere. (Crude.) □ *Susan's huge tits require huge tit-hammocks, too.* □ *With tiny boobs like mine, I hardly need a titbag at all.*

titless wonder n. a flat-chested woman. (Crude.) □ *Robin's new woman is a real titless wonder, I hear.* □ *Men just don't go for titless wonders, my dear.*

tits n. the female breasts. (Crude. Normally with *the* and in the plural. Compare with TITTIE.) □ *Cor, look at the tits on that, Fred!* □ *All you think about is tits!*

tit-sling See TIT-HAMMOCK.

tit(s)-man n. a man particularly interested in women's breasts. (Crude.) □ *Joe is definitely a tits-man.* □ *All these tit-men make me sick.*

tittie n. a female breast. (Crude. Normally with *the* and in the plural. Compare with TITS.) □ *"Nice titties," he thought, as she walked past.* □ *There she was, bold as brass, with her titties on full display.*

tit willow AND **weeping willow** n. a pillow. (Rhyming slang.) □ *As soon as her head hit the tit willow she was sound asleep.* □ *Can I have another weeping willow, please?*

tiz(z) See TIZZY.

tizzy AND **tiz(z)** n. a state of confusion or nervous anxiety. □ *The kind of tizzy that this place gets into drives me up*

the wall. □ *The office was in a right tiz by the time I left.*

t.l.c. AND **TLC** n. tender loving care. (Initialism.) □ *Lots of t.l.c., and he'll pull through.* □ *TLC is the best medicine.*

toad n. a despicable person. (Compare with WEASEL.) □ *He's a disgusting toad.* □ *The toad was waiting outside the office for him.*

to boot mod. in addition; what's more. □ *For graduation, I got a new suit and a coat to boot.* □ *She failed her finals and then crashed her father's car to boot.*

toby 1. n. a tramp. □ *Two old tobies wandered slowly down the lane.* □ *The toby asked politely for some work that he would be paid for in food.* **2.** n. a young child. (Also a term of address.) □ *Is this toby yours?* □ *She is a most irritating toby.*

toddle AND **todge** vb. to walk slowly and with difficulty. □ *He can toddle along to the shops but that's about his limit.* □ *Why are you todging around like that?*

toddle off vb. phr. to depart; to walk away. □ *She said good-bye and toddled off.* □ *The old man toddled off somewhere and got lost.*

todge See TODDLE.

todger n. the male sexual organ. (Taboo.) □ *The doctor told him that he'd got something wrong with his todger.* □ *That's all very well Myra, but where would the world be without todgers?*

to-do n. a commotion. □ *Don't make such a to-do when you come in late.* □ *They made quite a to-do about the broken window.*

toe-rag 1. n. a vagrant; a beggar. (Offensive. Supposedly, from a habit vagrants have of keeping their feet warm by wrapping them in rags rather than wearing socks, which of course they don't possess.) □ *The toe-rags who hang around outside the railway station were rounded up by the police today.* □ *It was a cold night and no one was to be seen but a lonely toe-rag slowly making her way along the street.*

2. *n.* a contemptible person. (Offensive. Also a term of address.) □ *What a toe-rag you are!* □ *Just get out of my sight, you toe-rag!* **3.** *n.* rubbish. □ *That's just a lot of toe-rag. Ignore it.* □ *Boy, he can certainly churn out toe-rag by the ton!* **4.** *n.* a cigarette. (Rhyming slang, linked as follows: toe-rag ≈ [fag] = cigarette.) □ *He got out the toe-rags and passed them around.* □ *Got a toe-rag, pal?*

toff 1. *n.* a dandy. □ *Who's that toff you were with last night, Susan?* □ *He's a bit of a toff, but all right really.* **2.** *n.* a well-dressed or upper-class person. □ *What's a toff like that doing around here?* □ *I'm sorry but we really don't need another toff working here.*

toffee 1. *n.* gelignite. (A form of dynamite.) □ *The toffee was packed into a tight crate at the back of the van, and sweating dangerously.* □ *Pat's the one who knows how to get the best results with toffee.* **2.** *n.* nonsense. □ *That's just a lot of toffee. Ignore it.* □ *Boy, he can certainly churn out toffee by the ton!*

toffee-nosed *mod.* pretentious; supercilious. □ *Don't be so toffee-nosed. Unbend a little.* □ *Tom is really toffee-nosed.* □ *What a toffee-nosed old fart!*

together *mod.* organized; under control. □ *I'm not together yet. I'll phone you back.* □ *That girl's really got it together.*

togs *n.* clothes. □ *Where did you get togs like that to wear?* □ *I feel sort of funny in these togs.*

tog up *vb. phr.* to dress up. □ *Oh good, I like togging up.* □ *We all got togged up before the party.*

To hell with that! *exclam.* "No way!"; "Get lost!"; "I refuse!" (Crude. The expression is an abbreviation of *go to hell with that.*) □ *To hell with that! That's not acceptable!* □ *I'm not prepared to go along with this absurd order. To hell with that.*

toke 1. *vb.* to puff a marijuana cigarette. □ *He sat on a stone to toke one before eating.* □ *He tokes for a good bit of every day.* **2.** *n.* a puff of marijuana smoke. □ *After a big toke, he settled back to drift.* □ *Harry took a big toke and sighed.*

to let *phr.* "available for rent." □ *Flat to Let.* □ *Yes, this house is to let.*

tom 1. *n.* a prostitute. (Crude.) □ *The Old Bill hauled her in because she looked like a tom.* □ *Clare dresses like a tom.* **2.** *vb.* to practice prostitution. (Crude.) □ *Just how many years do you think you can tom for?* □ *Zoe's out tomming on Smith Street again tonight.*

tom-cat *n.* door-mat. (Rhyming slang.) □ *Clean your feet on the tom-cat.* □ *Someone had removed the tom-cat.*

tom(foolery) *n.* jewellery. (Rhyming slang.) □ *She's out tonight with all the tomfoolery on.* □ *Don't wear your tom out in the street, love. You'll lose it.*

Tom(, Harry) and Dick *n.* sick. (Rhyming slang.) □ *If you're old Tom, Harry and Dick, we better stop.* □ *I told you that curry would make you Tom and Dick.*

Tommy Rabbit *n.* a pomegranate. (Rhyming slang.) □ *The costermonger's stall was laden with every sort of fruit, even the occasional Tommy Rabbit.* □ *Have you ever tasted a Tommy Rabbit?*

tomorrow week *n.* one week from tomorrow. □ *Will you be ready tomorrow week?* □ *Tomorrow week, it will all be over.*

Tom Thumb *n.* the buttocks. (Rhyming slang, linked as follows: Tom Thumb ≈ [bum] = buttocks.) □ *He got arrested trying to look up women's skirts in the hope of seeing their Tom Thumbs.* □ *If your dresses get any shorter, we'll all be able to see your Tom Thumb.*

tom-tit *vb.* to defecate. (Taboo. Rhyming slang, linked as follows: tom-tit ≈ [shit] = defecate.) □ *He had to go to tom-tit.* □ *Where do you tom-tit around here?*

ton 1. *n.* a score of 100 in a game such as darts. □ *I bet he can't make a ton in one turn.* □ *Two double twenties and a single one. Just like that, he scored a ton!* **2.** *n.* one hundred Pounds Sterling. □ *Can you lend me ton 'till pay-day?* □ *All right, here's a ton. Don't spend it all in one shop.*

tongue wrestling *n.* passionate kissing. □ *He tried tongue wrestling with me,* *but I stopped him.* □ *Kids like to try tongue wrestling at an early age. It's part of growing up.*

tonic *n.* an alcoholic drink, especially an aperitif. □ *How about a little tonic before we eat?* □ *Oh well, I'm cutting down, but one tonic should be fine.*

tons of something *n.* lots of something. □ *We've got tons of fried chicken, so help yourself.* □ *You are in tons of trouble.*

ton(-up) *n.* a speed of 100 miles per hour. □ *We managed a ton-up for several miles but lost time again when we got stuck in a huge tail-back near Birmingham.* □ *If you try to do a ton here the cops will book you for sure.*

ton-up boy *n.* a motorcyclist who makes a habit of travelling at 100 miles per hour. □ *Ton-up boys steam around on motorbikes.* □ *She says her son has become one of these ton-up boys.*

Toodaloo! AND **Tooraloo!** *interj.* an informal parting greeting; "Good-bye." (Irish usage.) □ *Be seeing you. Toodaloo.* □ *Tooraloo! Have a good trip home.*

too funny for words *mod.* extremely funny. □ *Tom is usually too funny for words at parties.* □ *The joke Tom told was really too funny for words.*

too Irish *mod.* too true. (Rhyming slang, linked as follows: Irish = [Irish stew] ≈ true.) □ *Yes, that's just too Irish.* □ *It's certainly too Irish but you can't tell her, of course.*

took See TAKEN.

tool *n.* the male sexual organ. (Taboo.) □ *Unlike Myra, Sharon thinks of little else but tools.* □ *Men keep their brains in their tools!*

tool around *vb. phr.* to idle or fool around. □ *Tooling around like that will get you into trouble.* □ *Please don't tool around around here.*

tooled-up 1. *mod.* in possession of house-breaking equipment. (Police.) □ *The police found him all tooled-up.* □ *If they catch when you're tooled-up, it's much harder to talk your way out of it.* **2.** *mod.* in possession of a gun. (Police.) □ *A tooled-up gang robbed the bank at*

the corner of the High Street. □ *Watch out, this one's tooled-up for sure.*

tool someone *vb.* to attack someone with a razor. □ *The thug tooled the passer-by, just because he was there.* □ *If you try to tool Otto, you'll be sorry.*

too much *mod.* overwhelming; excellent. □ *It's wonderful. It's just too much!* □ *You are so kind. This is too much.*

too much by half *mod.* far too much. □ *Oh no, that's too much by half for me.* □ *Gloria is always too much by half, I think you're going to find.*

too muchly *phr.* a humorous rendition of "thank you very much." □ *Well, too muchly. I could not possibly accept.* □ *Look this is all being far too muchly.*

Tooraloo! See TOODALOO!

toot 1. *n.* a BINGE; a drinking spree. □ *Harry's on a toot again.* □ *He's not on a new one. It's the same old toot.* **2.** *vb.* to drink copiously. □ *She could toot booze from dusk to dawn.* □ *They tooted and tooted till they could toot no more.* **3.** *n.* a line or dose of cocaine; cocaine. □ *These tootheads get sort of frantic when they can't get a toot.* □ *What do you spend on a toot, anyway?* **4.** *vb.* to SNORT a portion of cocaine. □ *She had to leave the office to toot.* □ *She tooted a couple of lines and came back.* **5.** *n.* money. (Rhyming slang, linked as follows: toot ≈ [loot] = money.) □ *It takes a lot of toot to buy a car like that.* □ *I don't make enough toot to go on a trip like that!*

toot AND **tootoo** *n.* excreta. (Crude.) □ *Don't worry. It's dog toot.* □ *There's fresh tootoo in the front garden.*

toothead *n.* a user of cocaine. □ *She's become a real toothead since she moved in with that circle.* □ *I looked around the room and saw nobody there who was not a toothead.*

tootle along AND **tootle off** *vb. phr.* to depart. □ *I think I'd better tootle off now.* □ *Nice talking to you. Must tootle along.*

tootle off See TOOTLE ALONG.

toot one's own horn See BLOW ONE'S OWN HORN.

tootoo See TOOT.

Too true! *sent.* "That is absolutely correct!"; "There is no doubt about this!" □ *Too true! He did say that!* □ *Too true I won't be letting the matter rest there!*

top and tail 1. *vb. phr.* to cook and preserve fruit, etc. □ *It's important to top and tail fruit when it's ready; it won't wait.* □ *My wife is in the kitchen, topping and tailing the fruit from our garden.* **2.** *vb. phr.* to wash and check over a bedridden patient. (Hospital.) □ *Nurse Smith, top and tail that patient, please.* □ *I'm exhausted! I've been topping and tailing patients all day!*

top ballocks AND **top buttocks; top set; top 'uns** *n.* the female breasts. (Taboo. Normally with *the* and in the plural.) □ *Cor, look at the top ballocks on that, Fred!* □ *With top 'uns like that, she can go anywhere she likes.*

top buttocks See TOP BALLOCKS.

top dog 1. *n.* the person in charge; the boss. □ *The reporter tried to get hold of the top dog, but couldn't get past the secretary.* □ *The company's top dog read a prepared statement.* **2.** *n.* the winner, especially of a sporting competition. □ *After winning that match, the Rovers are top dogs again.* □ *Harry is usually top dog in this golf club.*

top drawer *mod.* of high social status. (See NTD.) □ *I'm afraid he's just not top drawer.* □ *Whoever does this has to be really top drawer, you know.*

top-drawer *mod.* of the best quality available. □ *Oxford is a really top-drawer university.* □ *I want to hire a young graduate who's top-drawer.*

top heavy *mod.* intoxicated due to drink. □ *Tracy gets a little top heavy after a drink or two.* □ *Don't you dare come back from the pub top heavy tonight again!*

top-hole *mod.* excellent. □ *Boy, this fishing rod is top-hole.* □ *This wine is really top-hole!*

topless *mod.* naked above the waist, specifically with the breasts exposed. (Crude. Usually a woman.) □ *Everyone goes topless on Spanish beaches nowa-days.* □ *There's a topless dancer at the local pub now.*

top of the shop 1. *n.* the highest number called in a game of bingo, lotto, tombola or other lottery-like games. □ *Harry got the top of the shop in that game.* □ *There's a prize for the top of the shop this time.* **2.** *n.* the very best quality item on sale in a shop. □ *Only the top of the shop for you, my dear!* □ *Shopkeeper, bring out the top of the shop for us to see!*

top of the world *mod.* prosperous; content and cheerful. □ *Everything's wonderful and I'm on top of the world.* □ *I felt on top of the world last night; now I've got a hangover.*

top set See TOP BALLOCKS.

topside *mod.* [of an aircraft] airborne. □ *Now we're topside, we can turn off the seatbelt sign.* □ *The view from topside is great!*

top someone 1. *vb.* to kill someone. □ *Max was out to top Bruno.* □ *Bruno was gonna top Max first.* **2.** *vb.* to behead someone. □ *Of course, topping him was exactly what he deserved.* □ *They just topped the bandit without ceremony.*

top something up *vb. phr.* to refill a partially depleted container of liquid, especially drink. □ *Let me top up your drink.* □ *The girl topped up all our drinks several times.*

top storey AND **upper storey (department)** *n.* the brain. □ *A little lightweight in the upper storey department, but other than that, a great guy.* □ *He has nothing for a top storey.*

topsy-turvy *mod.* upside down; in disarray. □ *The whole office is topsy-turvy.* □ *He came in and turned everything topsy-turvy.*

top 'uns See TOP BALLOCKS.

Tosh *n.* a familiar form of address for a man, especially if his correct name is not known. (See JOHN, KIDDO, MOOSH, JIMMY, WHACKER, WHACK, and WACK.) □ *You all right, Tosh? Can I help?* □ *Why don't you do the smart thing and clear off, Tosh?*

tosh 1. *n.* money. □ *Sorry, I can't afford it, I've no tosh.* □ *How much tosh* *do you need, then?* **2.** *n.* nonsense. □ *What tosh that is!* □ *You're talking tosh again—as usual.*

tosser *n.* an undesirable or unpleasant person, especially a man. (Crude. Compare with TOSS OFF.) □ *Get out of here, you tosser!* □ *What a tosser that man can be.*

toss in the sponge See THROW IN THE TOWEL.

toss off *vb. phr.* to masturbate. (Taboo. Compare with TOSSER.) □ *Timmy's mother caught him tossing off in the garden shed.* □ *If he gets frustrated enough, he tosses off.*

toss-pot *n.* a drunkard. □ *There was some toss-pot asleep across the front entrance to the office when I got here this morning.* □ *You are going to turn into a regular toss-pot if you don't let up on your drinking.*

toss something back *vb. phr.* to gulp down a drink. □ *Did you toss that whole pint of beer back in one?* □ *Jed tossed back a quick snifter and went on with his complaining.*

toss something off 1. *vb. phr.* to do something quickly without much time or effort. □ *It was nothing special. I tossed it off in thirty minutes.* □ *We can toss off the entire order in—let's say—three hours.* **2.** *vb. phr.* to drink down in a single draught. □ *He tossed it off and ordered another.* □ *She tossed off her scotch and walked out on him.*

toss-up *n.* a difficult choice; an even bet. (As unpredictable as the outcome of the toss of a coin.) □ *Nobody knew which way to go. It was a toss-up.* □ *Who knows if he'll pull it off or not? It's a toss-up.*

tot 1. *n.* a shot of liquor. □ *Fancy a tot?* □ *He knocked back one tot and asked for another.* **2.** *n.* discarded items rescued by a rubbish collector for his own delectation. □ *And just what are you going to do with all this tot?* □ *You've certainly got a lot of tot in here.*

totalled *mod.* killed outright. □ *This guy was totalled.* □ *Who would want to have him totalled?*

total loss *n.* someone or something that is useless. □ *All of them were total loss-*

es, as it turned out. □ *What a total loss that woman can be.*

total someone *vb.* to kill someone. □ *I'm gonna total you once and for all.* □ *Watch it! Otto would total you as soon as look at you.*

tote something up See NOTCH SOMETHING UP.

to the tune of something *phr.* a large but approximate sum of money. □ *The whole thing set me back to the tune of £400.* □ *You will end up paying out to the tune of twenty pounds a month.*

totter *n.* a rag and bone man. □ *There's a totter here looking for you.* □ *The totter sat on the bench and waited for him.*

totty 1. *n.* a small child or infant. □ *How many totties do you have now?* □ *The totty was playing in the garden.* **2.** *n.* a promiscuous young woman. (Crude.) □ *Well, if she's out with someone new every night, I think that makes her a totty.* □ *The totty looked her prim girlfriend in the eye and smiled.*

touch 1. *n.* a likely target for begging; someone who is asked for a loan. (Compare with SOFT TOUCH.) □ *He was just the kind of touch we were looking for, not too bright and not too poor.* □ *The touch looked around him and gave the dosser twenty pence.* **2.** *n.* a request for money (from a beggar); a request for a loan. □ *I ignored the touch and walked on by.* □ *Here comes Fred, and he looks like he wants to make a touch.* **3.** *vb.* to ask someone for a loan. □ *He touched me for a hundred quid.* □ *The down-and-out touched Martin for a fiver.* **4.** *n.* a small portion of something to eat or drink. □ *I'll have just a touch. I'm on a diet, you know.* □ *Can I have another touch of that pie, please?*

touch and go *mod.* chancy. □ *It was touch and go for a while, but we are out of the woods now.* □ *The place was in a real tizzy. Everything was touch and go.*

touch of the tarbrush *n.* a person who is partially of coloured race. (Offensive.) □ *So what if he is a touch of the tarbrush?* □ *"Touch of the tarbrush" is considered to be a most offensive phrase.*

touch (on) a sore point *vb. phr.* to mention something that upsets someone. □ *I touched a sore point with Larry when I mentioned taxes.* □ *That touched on a real sore point for me.*

touch someone for money *vb. phr.* to importune or beg money from someone. □ *You're wasting your time to try to touch her for money.* □ *If you tried to help everyone who wants to touch you for money in the streets of Calcutta, you'd very rapidly go insane, broke or both.*

touch someone or something with a bargepole *vb. phr.* to deal with or handle someone or something. (Always in the negative.) □ *I wouldn't touch that problem with a bargepole.* □ *Mr Wilson is a real pain, and I wouldn't touch his account with a bargepole. Find somebody else to handle it.*

touch someone up *vb. phr.* to touch in a sexually exciting or provocative way. (Taboo.) □ *She actually said he could touch her up if he liked!* □ *He touched her up, yet she said nothing.*

touch wood *vb. phr.* to knock on wood, as a talisman of good luck. □ *We should be all right now, touch wood.* □ *Touch wood, and then let's get going again.*

tough 1. *mod.* unfortunate. □ *Tough, but you should have thought of that earlier.* □ *I'm sorry to hear that; it's really tough for you.* **2.** *mod.* severe; harsh. □ *I think you're being too tough with him.* □ *If I'm not tough now, it'll be worse for him later.* **3.** *mod.* criminally violent. □ *You bet he's tough. Watch yourself!* □ *If you want to find out just how tough Bruno can be, keep this up.* **4.** AND **toughie** *n.* a violent criminal. □ *This tough appeared and demanded £100.* □ *There were two toughies with Mr Big.*

tough customer *n.* someone who is difficult to deal with. □ *Some of those bikers are really tough customers.* □ *Bruno is a tough customer. Just keep away from him.*

tough guy *n.* a man who is—or has pretensions to be—powerful and violent. □ *He was your typical tough guy—jutting chin, gruff voice—but re-*

ally he was just our decorator checking up on the curtains. □ *So, you want to be a tough guy, eh?*

toughie See TOUGH.

tough luck AND **tough titty; tough titties** *interj.* "That is too bad." (TOUGH TITTY and TOUGH TITTIES are crude.) □ *Tough luck, but that's the way the cookie crumbles.* □ *That's too bad, tough titties.*

tough nut (to crack) *n.* someone or something that is difficult to understand or deal with. □ *This problem is a tough nut to crack.* □ *I wish Jill wasn't such a tough nut.*

tough row to hoe *n.* a difficult task to carry out; an onerous duty or responsibility. □ *It's a tough row to hoe, but hoe it you will.* □ *This is not an easy task. This is a tough row to hoe.*

Tough shit! AND **Tough (titty)!** *exclam.* an unsympathetic recognition of another person's misfortune or difficulty. (TOUGH SHIT! is taboo and TOUGH (TITTY)! is crude.) □ *Tough shit! I told you it wouldn't be easy.* □ *So you missed the bus. Well, tough titty!*

tough something out *vb. phr.* to endure something unpleasant or difficult to the end. □ *We'll just have to tough this problem out, I'm afraid.* □ *If you can tough this out, you'll be fine.*

tough titties See TOUGH LUCK.

Tough titty! See TOUGH SHIT.

tough titty See TOUGH LUCK.

tourist trap *n.* a place set up to lure tourists in to spend their money. (Can be a shop, a town or a whole country.) □ *It looked like a tourist trap, so we didn't even stop the car.* □ *"What keeps these tourists traps going?" "Would you believe, tourists?"*

touristy *mod.* full of tourists. □ *I hate these touristy places.* □ *Touristy places are where we make our money.*

towel See THRASH.

tower block *n.* a skyscraper; any tall modern building containing flats or offices. □ *She lived on the twentieth floor of a tower block.* □ *The company has moved it's main office into a new tower block in the city centre.*

Town *n.* London. □ *I don't like going up to Town, but when I must, I must.* □ *I'm off to Town for a business meeting.*

town bike See BICYCLE.

townee AND **townie 1.** *n.* a permanent, non-academic citizen or resident of a city or town that has a university within or associated with it. □ *The townees get upset when we make a lot of noise on Sundays.* □ *A couple of townies won the bicycle race.* **2.** *n.* a town or city dweller. □ *People in the countryside can be suspicious of townees buying up the local properties.* □ *I like being a townie!*

toyboy *n.* a younger man who is the kept lover of an older woman. □ *Would you believe it, she brought her toyboy to the church social?* □ *"If that's her toyboy," said Norah, "I can see the attraction all right."*

track record *n.* the career record of someone or something. □ *Harry's proud of his track record; he's always been a productive worker.* □ *It's not so much your track record I'm interested in as what you are like now.*

trad *mod.* "traditional." (An abbreviation.) □ *The approach is sort of trad, but so what?* □ *A more trad style might make the grownups more comfortable.*

trade 1. *n.* espionage. (Normally with *the*.) □ *The trade is a dirty business, and not very glamorous.* □ *Is there still much trade after the end of the Cold War?* **2.** *n.* enemy aircraft available to be attacked. □ *Wing Leader, Wing Leader, we've got twenty trade for you at angles twenty five.* □ *Roger, this is Wing Leader, we see our trade 3,000 feet below us.* **3.** *n.* the submarine service of the Royal Navy. (Always with *the*.) □ *He's a submariner, in other words, he in the trade.* □ *It requires a special sort of crewman for a life in the trade.* **4.** See also ROUGH TRADE.

trade-in 1. *n.* a car given to a car dealer as partial payment for a new one. □ *What's that one worth to you as a trade-in?* □ *Have you got a trade-in, sir?* **2.** *n.* the price or valuation placed on a car traded in for a new one. □ *I'll give you £2,500 as a trade-in on you old car, squire.* □ *I want a better trade-in than that.*

tradesman's entrance *n.* the anus. (Taboo. Always with *the*.) □ *Someone kicked him on the tradesman's entrance.* □ *With luck, his tradesman's entrance will hurt for a long time, that creep!*

trade (something) in *vb. phr.* to give a car to a car dealer as partial payment for a new one. □ *Dave's talking of trading in his car for a new one.* □ *It depends how much he can get when he trades in.*

traf *n.* an anal release of intestinal gas; a noise or smell associated with this. (Crude. Backslang, from FART.) □ *Who let off the traf?* □ *This place smells like a traf.*

tragic *mod.* useless. □ *Our side were really tragic in that game last night.* □ *What a tragic waste of time that turned out to be.*

trail one's coat *vb. phr.* to go around looking for a quarrel or fight. □ *Why are you going around trailing your coat here?* □ *Trail your coat like that and you may get more than you bargained for.*

tramp *n.* a sexually promiscuous woman. (Crude.) □ *She's just a tramp, who will throw herself at any man who happens to be handy.* □ *The little tramp actually accused me of being a stuck-up old bitch!*

trannie 1. *n.* a photographic transparency. □ *I've got a lot of trannies taken on my holidays.* □ *He wants me to go and look at all his trannies.* **2.** *n.* a transsexual. (Crude.) □ *Neither trannies nor TVs need be homosexual, you know.* □ *A T.V. is not the same as a trannie, and we're not talking about radio transmission receiving apparatus here.* **3.** *n.* a transistor radio. □ *Do you have to play that trannie all day long?* □ *Sometimes she thought her trannie was the only thing keeping her sane.* **4.** *n.* a transport cafe. □ *The trannie was deserted; when we ordered our food we discovered* *why.* □ *I'm hungry and here's a trannie; let's use it.*

transatlantic *mod.* American. □ *What's the transatlantic answer to this sort of problem?* □ *Do you like these latest transatlantic films?*

trap 1. *vb. phr.* to be hired. (Said by a taxi-driver.) □ *Oh, Harry was trapped just a minute or two ago.* □ *I could use being trapped right now.* **2.** *vb. phr.* to meet a desirable person of the opposite sex.* □ *I'd like to trap a nice girl tonight.* □ *Where do you go to trap around here?* **3.** See also CLAPTRAP.

traps *n.* one's personal effects or trappings. □ *I've come to collect my traps.* □ *All my traps will fit into one small suitcase.*

trash someone or something *vb.* to destroy or wreck someone or something. □ *They threatened to trash me.* □ *The puppy trashed my newspaper.*

treat *n.* anything considered enjoyable, well done or good. □ *That visit to the opera yesterday evening was a real treat.* □ *I've got another treat for you this weekend.*

treat someone like shit *vb. phr.* to treat someone in a humiliating manner. (Taboo.) □ *If you treat someone like shit it's likely that he'll return the compliment.* □ *I'm not going there again ever; they treat everyone like shit.*

treat (someone or something) with kid gloves See HANDLE (SOMEONE OR SOMETHING) WITH KID GLOVES.

trekkie *n.* a fan of *Star Trek.* (The science fiction television series and associated films.) □ *There is a convention of trekkies in Glasgow this weekend.* □ *These trekkies seem to have their own language.*

trendiness *n.* the quality of being trendy. □ *Sorry, I'm not interested in trendiness, just effectiveness.* □ *If you can't see beyond trendiness, we don't need you here.*

trendy 1. *mod.* fashionable. (Compare with SEXY.) □ *He always made the trendy investments and now he's broke. Maybe that's trendy now, too?* □ *Right now it's trendy to drive a*

Porsche. **2.** *n.* a person who is dedicated to following current fashions. □ *The trendy was waiting outside the office for him.* □ *She's pleasant, but a real trendy.*

trick *n.* a prostitute's client. (Crude.) □ *The trick didn't want to pay but Zoe slashed his face with an open razor she carried for such eventualities.* □ *Another trick went off with her in his car.*

trick cyclist *n.* a psychiatrist. (Rhyming slang.) □ *Well the trick cyclist said he was nuts, but then we already knew that.* □ *Maybe the trick cyclist can help you get sorted out in your head.*

tricks of the trade *n.* special skills and knowledge associated with a trade or profession. □ *I know a few tricks of the trade that make things easier.* □ *I learnt the tricks of the trade from my uncle.*

trigger *vb.* to start something; to set something off. □ *The noise triggered an avalanche.* □ *Some little detail triggered that software crash, and we must find out what it is.*

trigger-happy *mod.* liable to fire a gun at the least provocation or without warning. □ *Richard is sort of trigger-happy. Watch out.* □ *Ask your trigger-happy shooters to be careful when out on the moor this year.*

trimmer *n.* a prevaricator; an equivocator. □ *He's always been a trimmer and won't change now.* □ *We don't want a trimmer but someone who can make decisions.*

trip *n.* a HIGH from a drug. □ *Me and Sid went on a little trip.* □ *The trip was great, but once was enough.*

tripe 1. *n.* nonsense. □ *I don't want to hear any more of that tripe.* □ *That's just tripe. Pay no attention.* **2.** *n.* a bad performance; something worthless. □ *I know tripe when I see tripe, and that was tripe.* □ *The reviewer thought your play was tripe.* **3.** *n.* anything considered nonsensical or useless. □ *Oh please! Not that tripe again!* □ *I think your work is tripe. Don't come back.*

triple *n.* a large alcoholic drink containing three measures of spirits. □ *It was a hard day. Make it a triple, John.* □ *One* *triple, but no more. You're cutting down, remember?*

trip (out) *vb. (phr.)* to experience a HIGH from a drug, especially L.S.D. □ *Don't bother Max. He's tripping.* □ *He trips out about every other day.*

trog *n.* a lout. □ *Tell that trog we don't want him here any more.* □ *Who's that trog kicking at the side of your car?*

trog along *vb. phr.* to trudge or plod, as when carrying a heavy load. □ *We had to help; she was trogging along in the rain with two heavy suitcases.* □ *I do feel sorry for anyone having to trog along like that.*

trog(lodyte) *n.* a very stupid person. (Crude.) □ *Just get out of my sight, you troglodyte!* □ *What a trog you are!*

trog off *vb. phr.* to walk away. □ *We had a horrible fight, but still when it was over I could just trog off.* □ *It couldn't have been much of an accident. Both drivers trogged off.*

troll 1. *vb.* to go seeking clients; to streetwalk. (Crude. Refers to prostitutes.) □ *Mary? She's trolling this evening.* □ *A lot of girls troll in this part of town.* **2.** *vb.* to wander about in an aimless fashion. □ *Why must you just troll around?* □ *Don't troll! Look as if you've got something to do.*

troller *n.* a street-walking prostitute. (Crude.) □ *This troller comes up to me and acts like she's met me before.* □ *Do you think she's a troller or just too friendly?*

trollies AND **trolleys 1.** *n.* a woman's panties or knickers. (Crude. Always in the plural.) □ *She went to the shops and bought herself some new trollies.* □ *Oh heavens she thought, as she stepped off the bus. I've forgotten my trolleys!* **2.** *n.* a man's underpants. (Always in the plural.) □ *Truly! He was wearing luminous, glow-in-the-dark trollies!* □ *There's a whole drawer there just full of my trolleys.*

trollop *n.* a prostitute. (Crude.) □ *There was a trollop standing right on that corner.* □ *There are a lot of trollops around here in the centre of town.*

trombone *n.* a telephone. (Rhyming slang.) □ *He's got one of them portable*

trombones. □ *You'll find a trombone over in that corner.*

tronk *n.* an idiot. □ *Don't be a tronk. That's impossible.* □ *Who's the tronk in the bright orange trousers?*

troopie groupie *n.* a war reporter; a military correspondent. □ *Watch out lads, here comes another of these troopie groupies.* □ *This is no place for a troopie groupie; there's real fighting going on here.*

troops *n.* police officers as a group. (Police jargon.) □ *We need some troops down here urgently.* □ *I was never more pleased to see the troops.*

trophy *n.* a convert. (Salvation Army.) □ *Does the Army get many trophies these days?* □ *She's been with the Salvation Army since becoming a trophy over twenty years ago.*

tross *vb.* to walk. (Post Office.) □ *The postman trosses his round here.* □ *This delivery route is too long to tross.*

Trot *n.* a Trotskyist; hence any left-wing political extremist. □ *Sheldon used to be a Trot at college.* □ *How come there are any Trots left nowadays?*

trot *n.* nonsense. □ *Don't give me that trot! I won't buy it.* □ *That's just a lot of trot.*

trots *n.* diarrhoea; a case of diarrhoea. (Always with *the.*) □ *I've got the trots and can't go out tonight.* □ *There's a lot of the trots going around just now.*

trotter *n.* a military deserter. □ *The military police were here looking for a trotter.* □ *Mrs Sutton's son is supposed to have become a trotter. They say.*

trotters *n.* the feet. □ *My trotters are aching after all that walking.* □ *Sit down and give your trotters a rest.*

trouble and strife AND **worry and strife** *n.* one's wife. (Rhyming slang. Compare with OLD BUBBLE.) □ *Will your trouble and strife let you out to the pub tonight?* □ *I'd better ask the worry and strife.*

trouble at t'mill *n.* trouble at work. (North of England usage.) □ *Come quick! There's trouble at t'mill!* □ *I suppose you're going to tell me there's trouble at t'mill?*

trouper *n.* a reliable friend or fellow-worker. □ *Now Sally is a real trouper.* □ *She's a trouper; she'll come good.*

trouser See POCKET.

trouser-bandit See ARSE-BANDIT.

trouser chuff *n.* an anal release of intestinal gas; a noise or smell associated with this. (Crude.) □ *Oh lord! Who made that trouser chuff?* □ *The pungent scent of a recent trouser chuff hung in the air.*

trouser-snake AND **one-eyed trouser-snake; one-eyed Bob** *n.* the male sexual organ. (Taboo.) □ *Only small boys wave their trouser-snakes about like that, Wayne. Put it away!* □ *Myra says one-eyed Bobs are disgusting but then Myra's strange.*

truck *vb.* to go searching for a sexual partner. (Crude.) □ *He's out there somewhere, on the truck again.* □ *Where are you trucking these days, Otto?*

trumped up *mod.* made up; contrived. □ *They put Larry in the slammer on some trumped up charge.* □ *The whole story was trumped up simply to embarrass her. Just forget it.*

trundlie *n.* a shopping trolley. □ *There's a whole line of trundlies outside the supermarket, silly!* □ *I pushed my trundlie round the aisles, looking for the items on the shopping list.*

try-on *n.* an attempt to deceive or delude; an attempt to avoid responsibility. □ *Ignore it, it's just a try-on.* □ *I don't think your try-on is going to work.*

TTFN *phr.* "ta-ta for now." (Compare with BBFN.) □ *TTFN! See you next week.* □ *I'm away now. TTFN.*

tub *n.* a boat. □ *We sailed out into the middle of the bay in the little tub.* □ *Three men sat in the tub out there for hours, fishing.*

Tube *n.* London's underground railway system. (Normally with *the.* Compare with PIPE.) □ *Millions of Londoners depend on the Tube to get to work every morning.* □ *The Tube is one of the most extensive underground railway systems in the world.*

tube 1. *n.* a television set. (Always with *the.*) □ *What's on the tube tonight?* □ *The tube is on the blink, so I read a book.* **2.** *n.* a submarine. □ *That's my tube, against that jetty over there.* □ *There is something rather sinister about*

the black hull of a nuclear tube gliding silently through the water. **3.** *n.* a foolish person. (Scots usage.) □ *Yon poor tube thinks he can talk them into it.* □ *Here comes that tube again. Be nice to him, now!* **4.** See also TINNIE.

tub of lard *n.* a fat person. (Crude.) □ *Who's that tub of lard who just came in?* □ *That tub of lard can hardly get through the door.*

tuck *n.* food, especially confectionery and cakes eaten by children. (An abbreviation of the obsolete British—but contemporary Australian—slang word *tucker,* meaning "food.") □ *What tuck have you got today?* □ *I'm not sharing my tuck with anyone.*

tuck in *vb. phr.* to eat up eagerly. □ *After Christmas, we tucked in to turkey for three days.* □ *Who's been tucking in on the chocolate cake?*

tuck-in *n.* an extensive meal. □ *I haven't had a tuck-in like that in years.* □ *That was a great tuck-in at Tom's the other night.*

tuck someone up *vb. phr.* to imprison someone. □ *They'll tuck him up for that; you'll see.* □ *That judge just loves tucking up people.*

tuft *n.* a woman's pubic hair. (Taboo.) □ *What do you mean, you can see my tuft? Oh my god, I've forgotten my knickers!* □ *He got arrested trying to look up women's skirts in the hope of seeing their tuft.*

tug 1. *n.* an academic student. (At Eton College.) □ *Are there many tugs at Eton?* □ *I think the new boy's a tug.* **2.** *n.* that which is normal or common. (At Winchester School.) □ *Come on! What we're asking of you is just tug.* □ *How do I know if it's tug or not?*

tumble down the sink *n.* a drink. (Rhyming slang.) □ *I was in the pub having a quiet tumble down the sink when he came in.* □ *Let a man finish his tumble down the sink in peace first, okay?*

tumble in the hay *n.* a pleasant sexual dalliance. (Crude.) □ *What more pleasant way to spend a summer evening than a tumble in the hay.* □ *You may call it a tumble in the hay, my dear. I call it adultery!*

tum(my) *n.* the stomach. □ *Fred has been developing a huge tummy in recent years.* □ *Hold your tum in! There, that makes you look much better.*

tummy-ache *n.* abdominal pain. □ *If you have a bad, persistent tummy-ache, go and see your doctor.* □ *I really can't stand much more of this tummy-ache.*

tummy banana See BANANA.

tummy-tickling *n.* sexual intercourse. (Crude.) □ *After that tummy-tickling, she felt cheap.* □ *They were talking about, you know, tummy-tickling.*

tuned in *mod.* aware; up-to-date. □ *Jan is tuned in and alert to what is going on around her.* □ *Come on, Jill! Get yourself tuned in, just for once.*

tuppenny-halfpenny *mod.* [of something that is] practically worthless, almost without value. □ *Why are you bothering with such tuppenny-halfpenny stuff?* □ *Oh, he's just another tuppenny-halfpenny guy. Forget him.*

tup with someone *vb. phr.* to perform sexual intercourse with someone. (Taboo.) □ *I burst in on him tupping with Margaret.* □ *I fully intend to tup with her at the first opportunity I get.*

turd 1. *n.* a lump of excreta. (Taboo.) □ *There is a dog turd on the lawn.* □ *...and there are also some little mouse turds in the kitchen. Where's the cat?* **2.** *n.* a despicable person. (Taboo.) □ *What a total turd he is.* □ *Get that turd out of my house!*

turd-burglar *n.* a male homosexual. (Taboo.) □ *I hear that you-know-who is a turd-burglar.* □ *Why does he work so hard to look like he's a turd-burglar?*

turd-features *n.* an exceptionally ugly person. (Taboo.) □ *I don't think a turd-features like her has much of a future in glamour modelling.* □ *The guy is a real turd-features; look at him!*

turf 1. *n.* [one's] ground or territory. □ *When you're on my turf, you do what I say—savvy?* □ *This is my turf, and what I say goes.* **2.** *n.* a police precinct; the area or district that a police station is responsible for. □ *This station looks after a really tough turf. Let's not kid ourselves!* □ *It's the tough turves that are the interesting ones, policing-wise.*

turf someone out See BOOT SOMEONE OUT.

Turkey Trots *n.* a picturesque name for diarrhoea or similar, inflicted upon a visitor to a foreign land. (Turkish variety.) □ *I had a little touch of the Turkey Trots the second day, but other than that we had a wonderful time.* □ *Turkey Trots ruined Fred's entire holiday.*

turn 1. *vb.* to defect (as in espionage); to change from criminal into law-abiding citizen; to turn from law-abiding citizen (especially a police officer) into criminal. □ *Is there a chance that Max would turn?* □ *Max turn? Ha!* **2.** *n.* an act of sexual intercourse, especially when performed by a prostitute. (Crude.) □ *Maggie's not fussy, she'll give anyone a turn. Anyone with the money, that is.* □ *Bold as brass, she looked him in the eye and said, "It's twenty quid a turn, mister."*

turn an honest penny 1. *vb. phr.* to work honestly. □ *All I ask is a chance to turn an honest penny, Gov.* □ *He's turned an honest penny in that job all his days and has very little to show for it.* **2.** *vb. phr.* to make an honest profit. □ *Mr Big could not turn an honest penny if his life depended upon it.* □ *I think he's less interested in turning an honest penny than in turning a very large penny.* **3.** *vb. phr.* to pimp. (Crude. Ironic.) □ *Wally has a new career, turning an honest penny after a fashion.* □ *That man over there is the one who turns an honest penny on this street, and no one else better try.*

turn around *vb. phr.* [for a person] to undergo a major, dynamic change. □ *Things turned around for Willard and went okay for a while.* □ *When life turned around and things went more smoothly, Frank was happier.*

turn a trick *vb. phr.* to perform an act of prostitution. (Crude.) □ *She can turn a trick and be on the streets again in six minutes flat.* □ *Maggie's upstairs, turning a trick.*

turn belly up See GO BELLY UP.

turn copper *vb. phr.* to inform to the police. □ *He turned copper as soon as* *he heard about the reward money.* □ *If he's turned copper I'll kill him!*

turn in *vb. phr.* to go to bed. □ *Well, it's about time to turn in.* □ *I can't wait to turn in tonight.*

turnip-basher *n.* a rustic individual; a country bumpkin. □ *The old turnip-basher looked down on him as he lay on the ground and smiled.* □ *How, thought Smythe, had he ever ended up living among these turnip-bashers?*

turn it on *vb. phr.* to be charming. (The implication being that this is false, as it can be switched on and off at will.) □ *Yes, he can certainly turn it on.* □ *He'll turn it on to you and even you will begin to wonder if he's right.*

turn off *vb. phr.* to become sexually disinterested or repelled. (Crude.) □ *It was fine till she smiled and flashed her rotten teeth. Lord, did that turn me off fast!* □ *Sorry, he does nothing for me except turn me off.*

turn-off *n.* something that repels someone. □ *The film was a complete turn-off. I couldn't stand it.* □ *What a turn-off!*

turn on **1.** *vb. phr.* to become inspired or excited. (Compare with TURN SOMEONE ON.) □ *He always gets turned on by Wagnerian operas.* □ *He really was turned on by your new book.* **2.** *vb. phr.* to take a drug. □ *Pete just can't wait to light up and turn on.* □ *He will turn on with anybody at the drop of a hat.* **3.** *n.* someone or something that excites someone. (Usually TURN-ON.) □ *The concert was a real turn-on.* □ *David can be a real turn-on when he's in a good mood.* **4.** *vb. phr.* to become sexually excited or receptive. (Crude.) □ *Just one look from him and I'm really turned on—ready for anything!* □ *The girl was really turned on, going at it like crazy.*

turn on a sixpence *vb. phr.* to turn sharply; to turn in a small radius. □ *This vehicle will turn on a sixpence.* □ *A car that will turn on a sixpence at high speed without turning turtle is what I want.*

turn on the waterworks *vb. phr.* to begin to cry. □ *His lower lip was quiv-*

ering, and I knew he was going to turn on the waterworks. □ *Now, now! Don't turn on the waterworks. Cheer up!*

turn on, tune in, drop out *phr.* a slogan promoting the use of L.S.D. among young people. □ *The key phrase in the heyday of acid was "turn on, tune in, drop out."* □ *Millions heard "turn on, tune in, drop out" and did just that.*

turn queer *vb. phr.* to become somewhat unwell. □ *Something she ate turned her queer.* □ *Thinking of that could make me turn queer.*

turn someone off *vb. phr.* to disgust someone. □ *What happened really turned off everyone.* □ *Are you trying to turn us off?*

turn someone off *vb. phr.* to dull someone's interest in someone or something. □ *That teacher really turned me off the subject.* □ *The vicar set out to turn off the congregation to sin.*

turn someone on **1.** *vb. phr.* to excite or interest someone. (Compare with TURN ON.) □ *Fast music with a good beat turns me on.* □ *That stuff doesn't turn on anyone.* **2.** *vb. phr.* to excite or interest someone sexually. (Crude. Compare with TURN ON.) □ *Jane, you're turning every male for miles on with that tiny skirt and tight T-shirt.* □ *Yup. Turning them on is the idea!*

turn someone or something over See TURN SOMEONE OR SOMETHING UPSIDE DOWN.

turn someone or something upside down AND **turn someone or something over** *vb. phr.* to search someone or something in a disruptive manner. □ *We turned his place upside down, but never found the gun.* □ *The cops turned all three of us over when they got us back to the station.*

turn someone's stomach *vb. phr.* to nauseate someone. □ *That stuff turns my stomach. Do I have to eat it?* □ *Whatever that smell is, it's turning my stomach.*

turn somewhere over *vb. phr.* to search a building. (Police.) □ *Turn the place over, men.* □ *Someone got here and turned it over first.*

turn tail (and run) *vb. phr.* to flee; to run away in fright. □ *I couldn't just turn tail and run, but I wasn't going to fight that monster either.* □ *Sometimes turning tail is the only sensible thing to do.*

turn the corner *vb. phr.* to pass the critical point of some problem or task. □ *By the third week, we had turned the corner.* □ *If we can't turn the corner soon, it'll be too late.*

turn turtle *vb. phr.* [for a person or animal] to die; [for a machine or process] to cease to work permanently. (Figuratively, to roll over or capsize.) □ *Our old dog finally turned turtle last week, so that's that.* □ *Dave's car turned turtle in an accident the other day.*

turn up (for the books) *n.* an unexpected but welcome event or discovery. □ *That discovery was a real turn up for the books!* □ *What a pleasant event that turn up was!*

turn up one's nose at someone or something *vb. phr.* to show disdain or disgust at someone or something. □ *This is good, wholesome food. Don't turn your nose up at it.* □ *She turned up her nose at Max, which was probably a good idea.*

turn up trumps 1. *vb. phr.* to be very helpful. □ *Thank you. You've turned up trumps!* □ *Thank you for turning up trumps yet again.* **2.** *vb. phr.* to unexpectedly resolve difficulties. □ *Well, I did not think he would turn up trumps like that.* □ *We certainly turn up trumps that time!* **3.** *vb. phr.* to perform better than expected. □ *As I might have expected, Walter has turned up trumps again.* □ *You had better turn up trumps this time, or face serious trouble.*

turtle-dove *n.* a glove. (Rhyming slang.) □ *Here she comes, wearing her turtle-doves as usual.* □ *If you're going to do that sort of heavy and dirty work, turtle-doves would be an excellent idea.*

T.V. AND **TV** *n.* a transvestite. (Crude.) □ *A T.V. is not the same as a trannie, and we're not talking about radio transmission receiving apparatus here.* □ *Neither trannies nor TVs need be homosexual either.*

twallop AND **twollop** *n.* a fool. □ *Those twallops are at it again. Spend, spend, spend.* □ *How can you be such a twollop?*

twam(my) *n.* the female sexual organ. (Taboo.) □ *What do you mean, you can see my twammy? Oh my god, I've forgotten my knickers!* □ *He got arrested trying to look up women's skirts in the hope of seeing their twams.*

twank *n.* an effeminate man; a passive male homosexual. (Crude.) □ *So what if he's a twank? He can still vote, can't he?* □ *He doesn't like being called a twank.*

twat 1. AND **twit** *n.* a fool. □ *I felt like such a twat when I found out that I'd got onto the wrong train.* □ *Who's the twit in the bright orange trousers?* **2.** *n.* an insignificant person. (Crude.) □ *What a twat that woman is!* □ *Get out of here, you twit!* **3.** AND **twot** *n.* the female sexual organ. (Taboo.) □ *Who do think you are, going for my twat like that?* □ *Get your hand off my twot, Sunshine!*

twat-faker AND **twat-masher** *n.* a pimp. (Crude.) □ *the twat-faker turned and came after the punter.* □ *They found the twat-masher the following morning, face-down in the river.*

twat-hooks See CUNT-HOOKS.

twat-masher See TWAT-FAKER.

tweak *vb.* to adjust something slightly; to fine-tune. □ *I just need to tweak this program a little bit; then I'll be with you.* □ *Tweak the tuner a little and see if you can get that station just a little bit clearer.*

twee 1. *mod.* affected; over-dainty; quaint. (Usually referring to a woman.) □ *She's a real twee type; you know—untouched by real life in any way.* □ *Fiona's far too twee ever to make a difficult choice.* **2.** *mod.* excessively fastidious about neatness; disdainful of normal standards. □ *You will find that Lavinia is really very twee.* □ *I can't stand twee people.*

tweedler *n.* a disreputable salesman or agent; a confidence trickster. □ *What a despicable little tweedler he is.* □ *The man is no more than a tweedler, I think.*

Twelfth See GLORIOUS TWELFTH.

twenty-spot *n.* a twenty Pound note. □ *For a twenty-spot, the tramp led Burnside to the place where the crate still lay in the alley.* □ *Burnside slipped him a twenty-spot and faded into the fog.*

twerp See TWIRP.

twicer 1. *n.* a widow or widower who remarries. □ *Well Marie, I suppose that makes you a twicer now.* □ *Sorry, I did not know you were a twicer.* **2.** *n.* a two-year prison sentence. □ *There's Bert. He's got a twicer.* □ *He was lucky not to get much more than a twicer.*

twiddle one's thumbs *vb. phr.* to do nothing but wait. (Figuratively, to wait nervously, playing with one's fingers.) □ *I was left here twiddling my thumbs while you were away doing I don't know what!* □ *Don't just sit there twiddling your thumbs!*

twig *n.* a style or custom. □ *I don't think that twig suits her.* □ *That is a strange twig they have around here.*

twig (on to) something See TAG ON TO SOMETHING.

twim See QUIM.

twink 1. *n.* a moment. □ *It only took a twink, but it was enough.* □ *A twink later it was all over.* **2.** *mod.* an effeminate man; a passive male homosexual. (Crude.) □ *He doesn't like being called a twink.* □ *I hear that you-know-who is a twink.*

twinkle *n.* jewellery. □ *Don't wear your twinkles out in the street, love. You'll loose the stuff.* □ *She's out tonight with all the twinkle on.*

twirp AND **twerp** *n.* an irritating or stupid or unpleasant person, usually male. (Also a term of address.) □ *Look, you twirp, get out of here while you still can!* □ *Some little twerp threatened to kick me in the shin.*

twist 1. *n.* a fraud or swindle. □ *Frank has a new money-making twist, although he hasn't actually made any money with it yet.* □ *What sort of lowdown twist did you get ripped off with this time?* **2.** *n.* a drink made by mixing two or more ingredients. □ *I do like this twist.* □ *Can I have a twist, please?* **3.** *n.* to cheat or swindle. □ *Some scum*

twisted that poor old woman out of £50. □ *No officer, I didn't twist this money. I won it on the horses.* **4.** See also SCREW.

twisted 1. *mod.* perverted; distorted. □ *That's a very twisted way of looking at things. Why can't you learn to think straight?* □ *Watch out for Harry. He's got a really twisted sense of humour.* **2.** *mod.* suffering from drug withdrawal. □ *Frank was twisted and hurting bad.* □ *When you're twisted, your head spins, and you feel like screaming.*

twister 1. *n.* a key. (Underworld.) □ *Did you get the twister for this place, Max?* □ *Bruno lifted the jailer's twisters and hid them until midnight before trying anything.* **2.** *n.* a cheat or swindle. □ *Another twister like that and I call your parents.* □ *That little twister the kids did with the statue from the town square was a dandy.* **3.** *n.* a cricket ball bowled with a spin. □ *You're going to get twisters from this bowler.* □ *The bowler sent him a vicious twister.*

twist someone's arm *vb. phr.* to exert pressure, especially moral pressure, on someone. □ *I had to twist her arm a little, but finally she agreed.* □ *Do I have to twist your arm, or will you co-operate?*

twit See TWAT.

twitcher *n.* an ornithologist who attempts to view rare birds. □ *There's a convention of twitchers in town this week.* □ *My Uncle Harold's a twitcher.*

twitters 1. *n.* menstruation. (Crude. Always with *the*.) □ *Kim's having the twitters and in a bad mood.* □ *Sue doesn't go swimming when it's time for the twitters.* **2.** *n.* nervousness. (Always with *the*.) □ *She was full of the twitters, quite unable to concentrate.* □ *Now try to avoid getting the twitters again, Cynthia.*

two-and-eight See SIX-AND-EIGHT.

two a penny See TEN A PENNY.

two cities See TALE OF TWO CITIES.

two eyes of blue *mod.* absolutely correct. (Rhyming slang, linked as follows: two eyes of blue ≈ [(too) true] = absolutely correct.) □ *That's two eyes of blue, mate.* □ *You really expect us to believe that's two eyes of blue?*

twofer *n.* a cigarette. (From the slot machines that once—long ago—issued two cigarettes for one penny.) □ *Hey, give me a twofer, eh?* □ *I'll trade you a twofer for a light.*

twollop See TWALLOP.

twopenny *n.* the head. (Rhyming slang, linked as follows: twopenny [loaf] = [loaf of bread] ≈ head. It's a long time since a loaf cost two pennies; this expression is showing its age.) □ *Where'd you get that nasty bump on your twopenny?* □ *Harry's distinctive hairy twopenny hove into view.*

twopenny damn *n.* that which is worthless. (Crude.) □ *I don't give a twopenny damn what you think.* □ *It's just not worth a twopenny damn. OK?*

(two) pins *n.* someone's legs. □ *My pins are a little wobbly.* □ *Stand up on your two pins and speak your mind.*

two sandwiches short of a picnic See THREE BRICKS SHY OF A LOAD.

two shakes of a dog's tail See TWO SHAKES OF A LAMB'S TAIL.

two shakes of a lamb's tail AND **two shakes of a dog's tail** *mod.* quickly; rapidly. □ *I'll be there in two shakes of a lamb's tail.* □ *In two shakes of a dog's tail, the entire pile of bricks had collapsed.*

two sheets in(to) the wind See BOTH SHEETS IN (TO) THE WIND.

twot See TWAT.

two-time 1. *vb.* to deceive one's lover. □ *Sam wouldn't two-time Martha. He just wouldn't!* □ *Sam would and did two-time Martha!* **2.** *vb.* to double-cross or swindle someone. □ *Harry two-timed me out of my share of the haul from the bank job.* □ *What's more, he two-timed me and told the cops where I was.*

two-time loser *n.* someone who keeps on losing. □ *Poor Max really has been a two-time loser this week.* □ *Martin is a two-time loser, or at least he looks like one.*

two-timer 1. *n.* one who deceives one's lover. □ *Sam just isn't my idea of the typical two-timer.* □ *Of course not. Two-timers rarely look like two-timers.* **2.** *n.* a double-crosser or swindler. □ *Harry is a certified two-timer. Don't trust him with a penny!* □ *That filthy two-timer told the cops where I was.*

two-up, two-down *n.* a house with two rooms on each of its two floors. □ *We bought a little two-up, two-down because it was all we could afford at the time.* □ *It may be no more than a two-up, two-down, but it's a very nice two-up, two-down.*

two-way street *n.* a reciprocal situation. □ *This is a two-way street, you know. You will have to help me someday in return.* □ *Friendship is a two-way street.*

tyke 1. *n.* a churlish or offensive man. (Offensive. Also a term of address.) □ *What does the tyke want?* □ *He's a rather offensive tyke.* **2.** *n.* a small child. □ *I hope you like tykes. There are several here this afternoon.* □ *I wish she would try to control that tyke of hers.* **3.** *n.* a Roman Catholic. (Offensive. Also a term of address.) □ *Don't call Roman Catholic people tykes, please. It is very offensive.* □ *He said he was not prejudiced, he just hated this particular tyke!*

type *n.* a combining form indicating a specified type of person. □ *He's a cave man type. You know, sort of hairy and smelly.* □ *Ted's the brainy type, but has no guts.*

typewriter *n.* a fighter; a boxer. (Rhyming slang, linked as follows: typewriter ≈ [fighter] = boxer.) □ *I tell you, Mr Big, this one is a real typewriter.* □ *With a typewriter like him we can make serious money.*

typo *n.* a typographical error. □ *If you keep making typos we'll have to replace you.* □ *Can you find a typist who makes fewer typos?*

U

U(c)kers See U(C)KIE.

U(c)kie AND **U(c)ky; U(c)kers** *n.* the United Kingdom. (Often with *the.* Eye-dialect.) □ *Like most expats, we'd like to be back in the Uckie a lot of the time.* □ *I wonder what the folks back home in Ukers are doing right now.*

Ugandan affairs AND **Ugandan discussions** *n.* sexual intercourse. (Racially offensive. Euphemistic. From the reputed discovery, in *flagrante delicto*, of the (female) Ugandan Foreign Minister in a public toilet at London's Heathrow Airport in the early 1970s. However, it is now thought this story may have been invented in the columns of the satirical magazine *Private Eye.* Whatever the truth, the euphemism remains.) □ *Charles and Mary are upstairs discussing Ugandan affairs.* □ *Would you care for us to participate in Ugandan discussions, too?*

Ugandan discussions See UGANDAN AFFAIRS.

ugsome *mod.* unpleasant without any redeeming features. □ *Now that was one ugsome film.* □ *He stood before the ugsome building and shuddered.*

umpteen *n.* a very large but indeterminate number. □ *I've told you umpteen times not to feed the cat right out of the can.* □ *There are umpteen ways to do this right. Can you manage just one of them?*

umpteenth *mod.* concerns a very large but indeterminate sequence of numbers. □ *This is the umpteenth time I've told you to keep your dog out of my garden.* □ *This is the umpteenth meeting of the joint conference committee, but still there is no budget.*

uncle 1. *n.* a pawnbroker. □ *I have to go and see uncle.* □ *He didn't get much out of uncle this time.* **2.** *n.* the financial backer of a theatrical production. □ *All we need now to get this play on stage is an uncle.* □ *I wonder if my agent can find an uncle for our play?*

Uncle (Dick) 1. *mod.* sick. (Rhyming slang.) □ *God, I feel really Uncle Dick!* □ *Paul was feeling Uncle so I sent him home.* **2.** *n.* the male sexual organ. (Taboo. Rhyming slang, linked as follows: Uncle (Dick) ≈ [prick] = male sexual organ.) □ *Men keep their brains in their Uncle Dicks!* □ *Unlike Myra, Sharon thinks of little else but Uncles.*

Uncle Fred *n.* bread. (Rhyming slang.) □ *What, there's nothing to eat? Not even Uncle Fred?* □ *She got out the Uncle Fred and cut off a few slices.*

Uncle Ned 1. *n.* a bed. (Rhyming slang.) □ *Somebody put a spider in my Uncle Ned.* □ *I was so tired I could hardly find my Uncle Ned.* **2.** *n.* a head. (Rhyming slang.) □ *He's distinctive because he has a particularly large Uncle Ned.* □ *Turn your Uncle Ned around and take a look at this.*

Uncle Willy 1. *mod.* silly. (Rhyming slang.) □ *Y'know, maybe that's not so Uncle Willy.* □ *Come on, don't be Uncle Willy.* **2.** *mod.* chilly. (Rhyming slang.) □ *Sonia hates it when it's Uncle Willy like this.* □ *In Uncle Willy weather he prefers to stay indoors.*

uncomfy *mod.* uncomfortable. □ *Mummy, I'm all uncomfy.* □ *There are uncomfy clothes.*

uncool 1. *mod.* unfashionable; dull and orthodox. □ *Oh, what an uncool weirdo!* □ *This place is uncool. Let's* *get out of here.* **2.** *mod.* unable to keep calm; overexcited. □ *She's far too uncool for her own good.* □ *How do we calm down someone as uncool as that?*

under 1. *mod.* unconscious. □ *I was under seconds after the anaesthetic was administered.* □ *It's important to make sure the patient is properly under before the operation begins.* **2.** See also UNDER (THE INFLUENCE).

under-arm *mod.* obscene; pornographic. (A euphemism.) □ *You can't sell under-arm stuff like that in a shop like this!* □ *There are more and more under-arm movies on satellite television.*

under-book *mod.* [of a used car] priced less than usual. □ *When business is slow cars go under-book.* □ *Under-book sales are bad news for the company profits.*

undercart *n.* an aircraft's undercarriage. □ *Lower the undercart, we're about to land.* □ *The undercart would not lock into the down position. We had a problem.*

underfug *n.* underclothes. (Childish.) □ *Johnny, put your underfug back on.* □ *I don't like my underfug.*

undergricer *n.* an enthusiastic watcher of underground trains. (See GRICER.) □ *Being an undergricer is even stranger than just being a gricer, I would think.* □ *Sometimes undergricers congregate near where Tube trains come out of their tunnels to run on the surface through the suburbs.*

underground *n.* the anti-establishment counter-culture. (Always with *the*.) □ *He was a member of the underground in the sixties, but now he's a judge.* □ *I think the underground has emerged into the overground and has taken over by now.*

underkecks *n.* underpants. □ *First, let's get you out of these tattered underkecks.* □ *How could anyone wear dirty, worn-out underkecks like that?*

under one's belt *mod.* to one's credit. □ *He's got the Struthers case under his belt, and now he wants this other one.* □ *Let's look at your record; let's see what you have under your belt, eh?*

under one's own steam *mod.* unaided; without external help. □ *You did this? Under your own steam? Great!* □ *If you can manage all that under your own steam I'll be impressed.*

under someone's thumb *mod.* under someone's complete control. □ *You can't keep your kids under your thumb all their lives.* □ *Mr Big reckons he now has the corporation completely under his thumb.*

under starter's orders 1. *mod.* ready to commence a horse race. □ *It's too late to bet; they're under starter's orders now.* □ *Now they're under starter's orders, shut up and watch the race.* **2.** *mod.* in general, ready to begin. □ *Right, we're under starter's orders now.* □ *Let me know when you're all under starter's orders.*

under the affluence of incohol *mod.* intoxicated due to drink. (A deliberate spoonerism on UNDER (THE INFLUENCE) of alcohol.) □ *Perhaps I am under the affluence of incohol just a teeny-weeny little bit.* □ *You are very, very much under the affluence of incohol, as you have so aptly put it.*

under the doctor *mod.* under the professional care of a medical doctor. □ *You look terrible! Are you under the doctor?* □ *She's under the doctor for her back.*

under (the influence) *mod.* intoxicated due to drink. □ *Yes, I think that to say that Mary was under the influence last night would be accurate; she passed out in the hallway, you know.* □ *Bruno's a really nice person once he's under.*

under the table 1. *mod.* very intoxicated due to drink. □ *Geoff was under the table by midnight.* □ *By 3:00 in the morning, everyone was under the table.* **2.** *mod.* secret; clandestine. (This is hyphenated before a nominal.) □ *It was strictly an under-the-table deal.* □ *The politician made a few quid under the table, too, I bet.*

under the weather 1. *mod.* somewhat drunk. □ *Daddy's under the weather again.* □ *Willy's just a tad under the weather just now.* **2.** *mod.* somewhat unwell. □ *I feel sort of under the weather today.* □ *Whatever I ate for lunch is making me feel a bit under the weather.*

underthings *n.* underwear. □ *There's a whole drawer there just full of my underthings.* □ *Honestly! He was wearing luminous, glow-in-the-dark underthings!*

underwhelm *vb.* to fail to impress (someone). □ *As we were being underwhelmed by a buxom soprano, my thoughts drifted to more pleasant matters.* □ *Your talents simply underwhelm me.* □ *We know you really tried, but I'm afraid you just underwhelm.*

under wraps *mod.* secret. □ *We kept it under wraps until after the election.* □ *The plan we had under wraps had to be scrapped anyway.*

undies *n.* underwear, especially women's. □ *I like red undies.* □ *Where are my clean undies?*

unearthly *mod.* weird; terrible. □ *What was that unearthly noise?* □ *There was an unearthly smell coming out of the kitchen.* □ *That's not an unearthly smell, it's a heavenly one!*

unflappable *mod.* not subject to distraction; imperturbable. □ *Isn't he great? Truly unflappable.* □ *She is totally unflappable.* □ *I wish I was that unflappable.*

unfunny *mod.* not funny, although that may have been the intent. □ *I'm afraid that's just unfunny.* □ *No more of your unfunny jokes, Otto.*

ungodly *mod.* ridiculous; preposterous. □ *What is that ungodly noise?* □ *What do you want at this ungodly hour?*

unhappy chappie *n.* someone, usually male, who is extremely displeased. □ *There's an extremely unhappy chappie in the front office asking for you, Cynthia.* □ *Being Complaints Officer does mean that it's you that deals with unhappy chappies, you know.*

unhealthy *mod.* dangerous. □ *Your plan is, let's say, unhealthy.* □ *You really are in a unhealthy situation here, you know.*

unholy *mod.* outrageous; terrible. □ *I never dreamt I'd come back to such an* unholy mess. □ *This really is an unholy predicament you've got us into.*

uni *n.* university. □ *What are you reading at uni?* □ *He's a prof at the uni.*

union-bash *vb.* to attack or criticise trade unions, their members and their rights. □ *Union-bashing is a popular pastime in the Tory Party.* □ *In the past the unions have done a lot that deservedly brought union-bashing down upon themselves.*

unload 1. *vb.* to defecate. (Taboo.) □ *I tried to chase the cat away while it was unloading.* □ *Your dog unloaded on my lawn.* **2.** *vb.* to release intestinal gas anally; to cause a noise or smell associated with this. (Taboo.) □ *I could not believe it! He just unloaded right there, without warning or apology.* □ *If you absolutely must unload, would you have the goodness to go somewhere else to do it?*

unmentionables AND **unthinkables 1.** *n.* underwear. (A euphemism.) □ *Her unmentionables were strewn all over the room.* □ *I'm thinking of buying some new unthinkables.* **2.** *n.* the sexual organs. (Crude. A euphemism.) □ *They were almost naked and you could see their, well, you know, unmentionables!* □ *But surely you must have expected to see people's unthinkables in a nudist camp?*

unpack (something) *vb.* to empty one's stomach; to vomit something up. (Crude.) □ *He unpacked his dinner.* □ *One more mouthful of this beer and I'm gonna have to unpack.*

unputdownable *mod.* of a book that is too exciting to stop reading. □ *What a great, unputdownable book!* □ *Do you think his book is unputdownable too?*

unreal 1. *mod.* outrageous; irrational. □ *Your hairdo is so...well...unreal.* □ *Who started this unreal argument?* **2.** *mod.* exceptionally or surprisingly good or excellent. □ *Your news is re unreal.* □ *What an unreal idea that was.*

unthinkables See UNMENTIONABLES.

until hell freezes over See TILL HELL FREEZES OVER.

until kingdom come See TILL KINGDOM COME.

until the fat lady sings See TILL THE FAT LADY SINGS.

unwaged 1. *mod.* unemployed. □ *If you're unwaged, go over there.* □ *I'm unwaged, I'm afraid.* 2. *mod.* unpaid. □ *I don't do unwaged work.* □ *Why are we unwaged for this?*

unwind *vb.* to relax. □ *Sit down and try to unwind, please.* □ *I do need to unwind for a while.*

up *vb.* to increase something. □ *She tried to up the price on me, thinking I wouldn't notice.* □ *The bank upped its rates again.*

up against it *mod.* having serious problems. □ *I'm really up against it right now, and just hope I'll make it through.* □ *Can I borrow a few quid? I'm up against it this week.*

up against the wall *mod.* in serious difficulties. □ *Let's face it, we're up against the wall this time.* □ *It's when you're up against the wall that your character shows.*

up a gum tree *mod.* in serious trouble or difficulty. □ *Yes, we are up a gum tree, and we must do something or it will just get worse.* □ *Let's face it, we're up a gum tree here.*

up an' at 'em See UP AND AT THEM.

up and at them AND **up an' at 'em** *phr.* to get up and go at people or things; to get active and get busy. □ *Come on, you guys! Up and at them! Can't sleep all day.* □ *Up an' at 'em! The sun is shining.*

upbeat *mod.* bright and cheery; optimistic. □ *I'd prefer to open the conference on an upbeat note.* □ *That topic is not upbeat enough.* □ *This piece of music has an upbeat flavour to it.*

upchuck 1. *n.* vomit. (Crude.) □ *Is that upchuck on your shoe?* □ *There is still some upchuck on the bathroom floor.* 2. *vb.* to empty one's stomach; to vomit. (Crude. Compare with CHUCK (UP).) □ *Willy upchucked his whole dinner.* □ *Who upchucked over there?*

up for grabs *mod.* easily available; awaiting capture. □ *It's still up for grabs. Go for it and you'll get it!* □ *I*

don't know who will get it, but it's up for grabs.

up front 1. *mod.* at the beginning; in advance. □ *She wanted £200 up front.* □ *The more you pay up front, the less you have to pay later.* 2. *mod.* open; honest; forthcoming. □ *She is a very up front girl. You can trust her.* □ *I wish the salesman had been more up front about these problems.* 3. *mod.* in the forefront; under fire (at the front). (Military slang.) □ *You guys who are up front are going to take the most fire.* □ *You two go up front and see if you can help.*

up in arms *mod.* angry; furious. (Usually with *about*.) □ *The whole town was up in arms about the planned by-pass road.* □ *Now, don't get up in arms about this.*

up in the air (about someone or something) *mod.* undecided about someone or something. □ *I'm sort of up in the air about whether to marry Mary or not.* □ *Mary's up in the air about this, too.*

upload *vb.* to transfer data from a local computer to a remote one by electronic means. (Computer jargon. Compare with DOWNLOAD.) □ *We need that data right now. Can you upload it?* □ *Okay, we'll upload that file to you now.*

up one's street See RIGHT UP ONE'S STREET.

upper 1. *n.* amphetamines. □ *You can get some good uppers in this part of town.* □ *What does upper cost around here?* 2. *n.* an upper-class person. □ *I'm sorry but we really don't need any more uppers working here.* □ *What's a upper like that doing around here?* 3. *n.* a student in the upper school of an English public school. □ *Now that you're an upper, you have to shoulder more responsibility, Jones.* □ *The uppers are to be found in the upper school.*

uppers and downers *n.* the teeth. (Because they move in just this way.) □ *That horse has a nice set of uppers and downers.* □ *I may be on my last legs, but my uppers and downers are still my own.*

upper school *n.* that part of an English public school where the oldest students are taught. □ *The uppers are to be found in the upper school.* □ *The large building at the rear of the main complex is where the upper school is.*

upper storey (department) See TOP STOREY.

uppity *mod.* arrogant; conceited. □ *Why do you always have to be so uppity?* □ *If you were less uppity you'd get more done.*

up shit creek See UP THE CREEK (WITHOUT A PADDLE).

upsides with something or someone *mod.* equivalent or equal to something or someone. □ *So you think that's the way to be upsides with Roger?* □ *You'll never get upsides with him because you're not half the man.*

upstairs 1. *mod.* in or concerning the brain or the head. □ *What's going on upstairs, Mike?* □ *Oh, I wasn't think of very much upstairs just now.* **2.** *mod.* concerning a woman's breasts. (Crude.) □ *The trouble with Susan is that she may be very intelligent, but she has almost nothing upstairs.* □ *Why are men more interested in what women have upstairs than anything else?*

up stickers See UP THE DUFF.

up sticks *vb. phr.* to leave one location in order to go and live at another. (*Up* has the force of a verb here. US *up stakes.*) □ *They just upped sticks and left without saying good-bye.* □ *It's that time of the year when I feel like upping sticks and moving to the country.*

up the ante 1. *vb. phr.* to increase a price. □ *Sensing how keen the people looking at the house were, Jerry upped the ante another £1,000.* □ *"Don't try to up the ante on us," said the man, "We know what the asking price is."* **2.** *vb. phr.* to raise the stakes in a bet. □ *Pete upped his ante on that horse by another £10.* □ *I wouldn't up the ante any more; you're betting far too much money already.*

up the creek (without a paddle) AND **up shit creek** *mod.* in an awkward position with no easy way out. (UP SHIT CREEK is taboo.) □ *I'm sort of up the creek without a paddle and don't know*

what to do. □ *Yes, you are up shit creek! You got yourself into this, so get yourself out of this!*

up the duff AND **up the pole; up the stick; up the spout; up stickers** *mod.* pregnant. (Crude.) □ *I can see she's up the duff.* □ *Then this woman, very obviously up stickers, started to complain, too.*

up the pole See UP THE DUFF.

up the shute 1. *mod.* worthless; damaged beyond repair. □ *Your car is up the shute.* □ *The whole play began to come apart during the second act. It was up the shute by the third.* **2.** *mod.* [of people] in serious error; wrong. □ *It's all up the shute; we'll have to start again.* □ *Are you sure everything is up the shute?*

up the something *mod.* towards something; at something. □ *I'm just going up the shops, okay?* □ *Hello, John. It's good to see you up the town again after your illness.*

up the spout 1. *mod.* hopeless. □ *The cause is gone, lost, up the spout.* □ *Let's not say it's up the spout just yet. Ken's making one more try.* **2.** *mod.* useless. □ *I am afraid the plan is completely up the spout. We must think again.* □ *Well, that's it. The car's up the spout.* **3.** *mod.* pawned. □ *You'd be amazed at some of the things you'd find up the spout.* □ *Everything I have is already up the spout.* **4.** *mod.* destroyed. □ *It's all useless, all up the spout!* □ *It's all up the spout again.* **5.** See also UP THE DUFF.

up the stick 1. *mod.* crazy; insane. □ *Tom's up the stick. Really odd.* □ *She's frightened of up the stick people.* **2.** See also UP THE DUFF.

up the Swanee *mod.* not working; useless. □ *It's up the Swanee. Get a new one.* □ *I don't think it's up the Swanee at all. Here, I'll fix it.*

uptight 1. *mod.* anxious; nervous. □ *Dave always seems uptight about something.* □ *Don't get uptight before the exam.* **2.** *mod.* tense and nervous. □ *I'm a little uptight—because of the accident, I suppose.* □ *I get uptight before exams and other traumatic things.*

up time *n.* the time when a computer is running. (Now dated. Compare with DOWN TIME.) □ *You'll get maximum up time with this machine.* □ *On some systems the down time is longer than the up time.*

up to here *mod.* to a considerable degree or extent. □ *I've had it up to here with your excuses!* □ *We are all up to here with work just now.*

up to no good *mod.* doing harm. □ *He's clearly up to no good.* □ *I know you're up to no good and I'm calling the police.*

up to one's arse in alligators *mod.* in really deep trouble. (Taboo.) □ *When you're up to your arse in alligators it's difficult to remember that you're there to drain the swamp.* □ *If we don't sort this mess out soon we'll be up to our arses in alligators, too.*

up to one's ears See UP TO ONE'S EYEBALLS.

up to one's eyeballs AND **up to one's ears** *mod.* almost or completely involved. □ *She's up to her ears in marriage proposals.* □ *We're up to our eyeballs in spare parts.*

up to one's knees AND **up to one's neck** *mod.* involved deeply in something, such as paperwork or water. (Compare with KNEE-DEEP IN SOMETHING.) □ *We're up to our knees with orders and getting more all the time.* □ *I am up to my neck in other people's grief and anguish.* □ *We are all up to our necks in your problems.*

up to one's neck See UP TO ONE'S KNEES.

up to scratch AND **up to snuff** *mod.* up to the necessary or required standard. □ *This just isn't up to scratch. You'll have to do it again.* □ *The food was up to snuff, but the hotel staff wasn't.*

up to snuff See UP TO SCRATCH.

up to the knocker AND **up to the mark** **1.** *mod.* of an acceptable standard. □ *I'm sorry but I don't think this stuff is up to the knocker.* □ *You must get up to the mark if you want to make it.* **2.** *mod.* in good condition or unspoiled. □ *I always try to be up to the knocker when I*

come here. □ *Well, you are certainly up to the mark today.*

up to the mark See UP TO THE KNOCKER.

up West *mod.* in London's West End. □ *We're going up West to see a play.* □ *Up West is where you'll find all the best—or at least, most expensive—restaurants.*

Up you! AND **Up your arse!; Up your bum!; Up your pipe!; Up your jacksie!** *exclam.* ways of saying "No!" with maximum contempt. (Taboo. The possible permutations are almost endless...here we have but a flavour.) □ *Up you! I'm all right.* □ *Get lost! Up your jacksie!*

Up your arse! See UP YOU!

Up your bum! See UP YOU!

Up your jacksie! See UP YOU!

Up your pipe! See UP YOU!

use 1. *vb.* to use drugs; to take drugs habitually. □ *I tried to stop using, but I couldn't.* □ *I couldn't face myself if I started using the stuff again.* **2.** *vb.* to enjoy. □ *I could use a pint right now!* □ *Could you use a break for a few minutes?*

useless ticket *n.* a good-for-nothing man. (Scots usage.) □ *Watch that one; he's a useless ticket all right.* □ *He dizny act like he's a useless ticket.*

user *n.* a drug user; a drug addict. □ *I want to stop being a user, but I can't do it by myself.* □ *I'm no user! Maybe a joint now and then, and an upper on a dreary morning—but I'm no user!*

user-friendly *mod.* easy-to-use. □ *Now this is what we call a user-friendly computer system.* □ *The bank tried to operate a user-friendly business area until they discovered it was bank-robber-friendly, too.*

Use the head! See USE YOUR BEAN!

Use the loaf! See USE YOUR BEAN!

Use the noggin! See USE YOUR BEAN!

Use the noodle! See USE YOUR BEAN!

Use the skull! See USE YOUR BEAN!

Use the turnip! See USE YOUR BEAN!

Use your bean! AND **Use your head!; Use the head!; Use your loaf!; Use the loaf!; Use your noodle!; Use the noodle!; Use your noggin!; Use the**

noggin!; **Use your skull!; Use the skull!; Use your turnip!; Use the turnip!** *exclam.* "Think!"; "Think it through!" □ *You know the answer. Use your head!* □ *Use the turnip! It's there for more than hanging your hat on.* □ *Just think about that again, but this time use your skull before answering!*

Use your head! See USE YOUR BEAN!

Use your loaf! See USE YOUR BEAN!

Use your noggin! See USE YOUR BEAN!

Use your noodle! See USE YOUR BEAN!

Use your skull! See USE YOUR BEAN!

Use your turnip! See USE YOUR BEAN!

usual offices *n.* those things like kitchens, toilets, storage space and so forth, which turn a building into a suitable dwelling for human beings. □ *The house seems to have all the usual offices.* □ *The usual offices is basic. What else does it have to offer?*

U-turn *n.* a complete and rapid reversal of policy. (Political.) □ *There's been a government U-turn on that since then.* □ *Oh no, not another U-turn!*

vac *n.* a university vacation. □ *What are you doing during the vac, Charles?* □ *I'm going to America during the vac.*

value-added entertainment *n.* a commercial break on TV or radio. (A euphemism.) □ *She made herself a cup of tea during the value-added entertainment.* □ *Mary is strange; she actually thinks value-added entertainment is.*

vanilla AND **plain vanilla** *mod.* plain; dull; unexciting. □ *The entire production was sort of vanilla, but it was okay, I suppose.* □ *No more vanilla music, please.* □ *The holiday was plain vanilla, but restful.*

vapourware *n.* new software that been announced by its manufacturer but has failed to appear at the promised time. (Computer jargon. Compare with FIRMWARE, LIVEWARE and WETWARE.) □ *SuperDuperWriter? Oh, that's been vapourware for almost a year now.* □ *Once your new program becomes vapourware, fewer and fewer people take it seriously.*

varnish *n.* liquid nail polish. □ *There was a very glamorous secretary who seemed to spend all her time applying varnish to her nails.* □ *Do you have any varnish, Maggy?*

Vatican roulette *n.* the "rhythm method" of birth control, recommended by the Roman Catholic Church, which is to avoid intercourse except during so-called "safe" times of the menstrual cycle. □ *Susan and Jim trusted in Vatican roulette. They now have five beautiful children!* □ *"Vatican roulette can be made to work," said the priest. "How do you know?" asked Sheila, "Have you tried it personally?"*

Vatman *n.* an official responsible for assessing and collecting value added tax. □ *Why does everyone fear the Vatman?* □ *My uncle got a job as a Vatman and loves it.*

veg 1. *n.* the vegetable components of a dish to be eaten. (Note this is an abbreviation of the plural form. Compare with VEGGY.) □ *I'd like a steak with two veg.* □ *Today's vegs are peas and boiled spuds.* **2.** See also VEGGY.

vegetable 1. *n.* someone who has suffered severe brain damage, making normal intellectual activity impossible. (Compare with VEGGY.) □ *Alf has been a vegetable ever since the accident.* □ *The doctor said it was time for us to recognise that he'll be never be anything but a vegetable again.* **2.** *n.* someone who appears never to perform any physical activity or exert themselves mentally. (Offensive. Also a term of address.) □ *Get up off your backside, you vegetable, and do something useful just for once!* □ *Sitting there staring at TV all day long was turning me into a vegetable.* **3.** *n.* someone almost totally destroyed by drugs. (Offensive. Also a term of address.) □ *You want to end up a vegetable? Just keep shooting that stuff.* □ *There are lots of people turned into vegetables by drugs nowadays. It's very sad.*

veggy AND **veggie; veg 1.** *n.* a vegetable. (Usually plural.) □ *Do you want any veggies with this?* □ *Come on Timmy, you must eat your veggies!* **2.** *n.* a comatose patient in a hospital. (Medical. Compare with VEGETABLE.) □ *Mary's aunt has been a veggie in the hospital for more than a year.* □ *I don't* *want to lie there and rot as a veggie. I want someone to pull the plug.* **3.** *n.* a vegetarian. □ *We have a lovely salad bar for the veggies among you.* □ *She's a veggy, so make sure there's a nice selection of appropriate goodies.*

vehicle licence *n.* a certificate of payment of vehicle excise tax. □ *I've got to go to buy a new vehicle licence.* □ *Don't forget to display your new vehicle licence.*

velcro-head *n.* a black person. (Racially offensive.) □ *Don't call black people velcro-heads, please. It is very offensive and racist.* □ *He said he was not a racist, he just hated velcro-heads!*

velvet glove AND **velvet vice** *n.* the female sexual organ. (Taboo.) □ *If your dresses get any shorter, we'll all be able to see your velvet glove.* □ *The door to the shower room flew open and the girl screamed, trying to cover her velvet vice.*

velvet vice See VELVET GLOVE.

vent one's spleen *vb. phr.* to rebuke or abuse someone without justification. (Usually followed by *on*.) □ *No need to vent your spleen on me. I wasn't in on it.* □ *Sorry, I just felt I had to vent my spleen on somebody.*

verbal *n.* a verbal admission of guilt made by a criminal to the police. □ *They've got my verbal! It's hopeless.* □ *Rubbish! All they've got is your verbal.*

verboten *mod.* strongly forbidden on pain of severe retribution. (From German, where it means just "forbidden.") □ *That is strictly verboten.* □ *You said a verboten word around here.*

versemonger *n.* a poet. □ *He's a rather fine versemonger, I think.* □ *No one appreciates versemongers any more.*

vet someone or something *vb.* to check over carefully and thoroughly. □ *Well, vet it and let me know what you think.* □ *He's been very thoroughly vetted, I can assure you.*

vibes *n.* mood; atmosphere; feelings. (Usually with *good* or *bad*.) □ *I just don't get good vibes about this deal.* □ *The vibes are just plain bad.*

vicious *mod.* great; excellent; impressive. (Teens.) □ *Yes, this burger is real-ly vicious.* □ *That guy is a vicious driver, all right.* □ *That was a really vicious concert last night.*

video nasty *n.* a particularly violent or pornographic film on videotape. □ *When Harry got home, the kids were sitting there, watching a video nasty!* □ *Video nasties are becoming a serious problem these days.*

villain *n.* a professional criminal; any criminal. □ *Otto is a real villain.* □ *Mr Big is a bigger villain.*

vim and vigour *n.* energy; enthusiasm. □ *Show more vim and vigour! Let us know you're alive.* □ *She's certainly got lots of vim and vigour.*

vino *n.* wine. □ *We drank too much vino while in Spain, I think.* □ *Brian goes to Italy every year just for the vino.*

vinyl *n.* a generic term for recorded music. (From old-style gramophone records made with vinyl plastic, which are now almost entirely supplanted by cassette tapes and compact discs.) □ *This is one of the best tunes on vinyl.* □ *I've got some new vinyl. Come over and listen.*

v.i.p. AND **VIP; V.I.P. 1.** *n.* a "very important person." (Initialism.) □ *Who's the V.I.P. in the Mercedes?* □ *That's no V.I.P.; that's the boss.* **2.** *mod.* concerning something reserved for a V.I.P. (Initialism.) □ *My smile and casual manner didn't get me into the V.I.P. lounge.* □ *They gave us the V.I.P. treatment.*

visit the plumbing See CHECK OUT THE PLUMBING.

vital statistics *n.* the measurements of a person's body. □ *Her vital statistics must require higher maths to work out!* □ *Here are his vital statistics for those who are interested.*

vote with one's feet *vb. phr.* to show one's displeasure by walking out. □ *A lot of people are voting with their feet. Customers clearly don't like our goods.* □ *When the audience votes with its feet, you know you don't have a hit.*

vox pop *n.* comments made by individual members of the public, purporting to represent public opinion on a radio or TV show. (From the Latin *vox pop-uli*, meaning "voice of the people.") □ *We got a lot of vox pop on this show, and it was 100% negative.* □ *Who cares what the vox pop says? I loved it!*

vroom *interj.* the noise of a loud engine. (Onomatopoetic.) □ *Vroom, vroom went the engine as Vic raced it again* *and again.* □ *Suddenly, a loud vroom as a plane passed low overhead.*

vulture *vb.* to borrow from someone's collection of books, tapes, etc., without permission. □ *What are you hoping to vulture from me now, Marti?* □ *Yes, every day she vultures something from her friends.*

W

Wack See WHACKER.

wacky AND **wonky** *mod.* unreliable; untrustworthy. □ *Careful! That chair's kinda wacky and may collapse under you.* □ *The whole plan looks very wonky to me.*

wad 1. *n.* a roll of banknotes; a large sum of money. (Originally underworld.) □ *I lost a whole wad on a rotten horse in the seventh race.* □ *You'd better not flash a wad like that around here. You won't have it long.* **2.** *n.* a sandwich. (Military.) □ *Once we had to live on wads, being too poor for anything fancier.* □ *Fancy a bacon and tomato wad?*

waffle *n.* nonsensical talk. □ *Don't talk waffle.* □ *If you just come out with waffle, you'll be ignored.*

waffle (around) *vb. (phr.)* to be indecisive; to dither. □ *Don't waffle around so long. Make up your mind.* □ *She spent three days waffling over the colour of the car and finally decided on red.*

waffler 1. *n.* a person who cannot make up their mind; a ditherer. (Offensive.) □ *There he is, unable to decide. Alf really is a prize waffler.* □ *There was one waffler ahead of me who took forever to decide what to buy.* **2.** *n.* a person who talks nonsense. (Crude.) □ *What a waffler you are!* □ *Just get out of my sight, you waffler!*

wage round *n.* a general increase in wages or salaries. □ *There's to be a wage round soon, I hear.* □ *That wage round was pathetic.*

wages *n.* illegal or illicit income; the proceeds of prostitution, thieving, etc. □ *The thing about tomming is that the wages are rather nice.* □ *The trouble is that by the time you fence the stuff, the wages you make from break-ins ain't all that great.*

wages snatch *n.* a payroll robbery. □ *The so-called wages snatch turned out to be a bit of a fiasco because no one gets paid cash nowadays and all they got was a bundle of unsigned cheques.* □ *Whoever organised this wages snatch can't have been too bright, Inspector.*

wagger *n.* a rubbish bin. □ *Occassionally your wagger has to be emptied, you know.* □ *We've got five waggers now.*

wag (it) off AND **play the wag** *vb. phr.* to play truant, especially from school. □ *Do you have a problem with kids wagging it off at this school?* □ *No, no one plays the wag here.*

wah-wah *n.* a difficult-to-start car. (Onomatopoetic.) □ *I've got to get my wah-wah fixed up.* □ *Is this old wah-wah yours?*

Wait a mo! *exclam.* "Wait a moment!" □ *Wait a mo! You can't leave it like that!* □ *Wait a mo! Something is happening!*

Wake up your Ideas! *exclam.* "Get your thinking sorted out!"; "Think more clearly!" □ *If you want this to work, wake up your ideas!* □ *Wake up your ideas or let someone else have a go!*

Wakey-wakey! *intej.* "Wake up!" □ *Wakey-wakey! It's a long, hard day ahead!* □ *There's work to be done! Wakey-wakey!*

walk 1. *vb.* to walk out on someone. □ *They had a big fight, and he just got up and walked.* □ *Much more of this and*

I'm going to walk. **2.** *vb.* to walk away from something unharmed. □ *It couldn't have been much of an accident. Both drivers walked.* □ *We had a horrible fight, but still when it was over I just walked.* **3.** *vb.* to get out of prison; to get off from a criminal charge. (Underworld.) □ *They thought they could stick Bruno with a vice conviction, but he walked.* □ *I walked from prison last week, and now I'm looking for Bruno.* **4.** See also FADE.

Walkies! *exclam.* "Time to take a walk!" (To a pet or small child.) □ *Come on Rover! Walkies!* □ *Come on, let's go walkies!*

walking disaster area *n.* a person who is especially prone to accidents or ineptness. □ *Even a walking disaster area like that has to earn a living but will do so somewhere else, thank you.* □ *What does that walking disaster area want now?*

walking wounded *n.* a person with psychological difficulties who nevertheless continues to try to live a normal life. □ *As one of the walking wounded who has suffered the things you described, I have to disagree with you.* □ *The outpatient clinic was filled with the walking wounded.*

walk it *vb. phr.* to win with ease. (Originally of a horse race.) □ *Come on! You'll walk it!* □ *I knew you would walk it.*

walk on eggs AND **walk on thin ice** *vb. phr.* to walk very cautiously; to be in a very precarious position. □ *I have to remember that I'm walking on eggs when I give this speech.* □ *Careful with ideas like that. You're walking on thin ice.*

walk on thin ice See WALK ON EGGS.

walkover *n.* an easy victory; an easy task. (From sports.) □ *The game was a walkover. No problem.* □ *Learning the computer's operating system was no walkover for me.*

walk the streets **1.** *vb. phr.* to engage in street prostitution. (Crude.) □ *I think she sees walking the streets as an ever-present help in times of financial stringency, which in her case is all the time.* □ *You're never going to stop toms walking the streets.* **2.** *vb. phr.* to walk around looking for work. □ *Harry's walking the streets looking for a job.* □ *I never thought walking the streets was a particularly smart way to get a job.*

wallah *n.* a man in charge of or responsible for the operation of an office, business or service. (From the Hindi *wala*, meaning "protector," by hobson-jobson.) □ *Ask the wallah if he needs any help.* □ *Why do we need this wallah?*

wallflower **1.** *n.* a shy or neglected person, particularly a woman lacking partners at a dance. □ *Clare was sort of a wallflower until she graduated.* □ *Don't be a wallflower, Nancy. I'd love to dance with you.* **2.** *n.* a prisoner who is obsessed with escaping. □ *You'll find the wallflowers over there at that table.* □ *So, I see you're a wallflower, too.*

wallie close *n.* an entranceway into an apartment building which has tiled walls. (Scots usage. "Wallie" means "glazed" or "made of porcelain.") □ *Posh people live up wallie closes.* □ *Wullie lives up a wallie close and he's no posh.*

wallie dug *n.* an ornamental porcelain dog. (Scots usage.) □ *Ma grannie collects wallie dugs.* □ *There is a very nice wallie dug on the shelf over there.*

wallies *n.* false teeth. (Scots usage. Always in the plural.) □ *Ah've lost ma wallies!* □ *Ma Uncle Hamish canny chew his grub properly since he got his new wallies.*

wallop **1.** *vb.* to strike someone or something especially severely. □ *I walloped him hard on the shoulder, but he kept on laughing.* □ *The door swung open and walloped me in the back.* **2.** *n.* an especially severe blow. (Compare with CLOUT.) □ *She planted a hard wallop on his right shoulder.* □ *I got quite a wallop when I walked into the door.* **3.** *n.* beer or other drink containing alcohol. □ *Have a can of wallop, Charlie.* □ *Here, that's good wallop!* **4.** *vb.* to dance. □ *We walloped for hours, yet somehow were not exhausted.* □ *Come on darling, let's wallop.*

walloper *n.* a dancer. □ *Martin is a really great walloper.* □ *She's a great* *walloper, but otherwise as dumb as they come.*

walloping 1. *mod.* big; heavy. □ *He arrived last night with this great walloping box.* □ *Mary has got to get more exercise—she's turning into a walloping great lump.* **2.** *n.* a heavy beating; a convincing defeat. □ *Harry took a walloping from someone on his way back from the pub last night.* □ *What a walloping I gave Joan at tennis this afternoon!*

wall-to-wall *mod.* plentiful and comprehensive. (From "wall-to-wall carpeting.") □ *The guy doesn't exactly have wall-to-wall generosity.* □ *Old Tom is giving me wall-to-wall hostility these days. What's wrong?*

wally 1. *n.* an incompetent or silly person. (Crude.) □ *Get out of here, you wally!* □ *What a wally that woman can be.* **2.** *n.* a pickled cucumber. □ *How can you just sit there eating wallies like that?* □ *He likes a wally with his salad.* **3.** *n.* the male sexual organ. (Taboo.) □ *Myra says wallies are disgusting but then Myra's strange.* □ *Only small boys wave their wallies about like that, Wayne. Put it away!* **4.** *n.* a uniformed policeman. □ *See that wally over there? He lifted me once.* □ *The wallies will catch up with you some day.* **5.** *vb.* to parody. □ *Don't you wally me, young man!* □ *Harold wallies everyone, you know.*

waltz off (with something) *vb. phr.* to remove something with ease. □ *The thieves waltzed off with a giant screen television in broad daylight.* □ *They just picked the thing up and waltzed off. Nobody asked them any questions.*

waltz through something *vb. phr.* to get through something easily. □ *I waltzed through my first year, but second year was a tougher proposition.* □ *I thought I could waltz through my assignment, but it was too hard for that.*

wamba *n.* money. □ *I don't make enough wamba to go on a trip like that!* □ *It takes a lot of wamba to buy a car like that.*

wammers AND **whammers** *n.* the female breasts. (Crude. Normally with

the and in the plural.) □ *There she was, bold as brass, with her wammers on full display.* □ *"Nice whammers," he thought, as she walked past.*

wang *n.* disgusting food. □ *That stuff is just wang.* □ *Call that wang food?*

wang(er) AND **whang(er)** *n.* the male sexual organ. (Taboo.) □ *The doctor said Brian's got something wrong with his wanger.* □ *That's all very well Myra, but where would the world be without whangs?*

wangle *n.* an illicit favour. □ *Can you work a wangle for me, mate?* □ *I don't like all these wangles; one day we'll be caught.*

wangler *n.* someone who obtains illicit favours. □ *We need a good wangler to work this one.* □ *Otto's a great wangler.*

wank 1. *vb.* to masturbate. (Taboo.) □ *Well, wanking may be enough for you, but I want the real thing.* □ *You're not going to wank here!* **2.** *n.* rubbish; nonsense. (Crude.) □ *Boy, he can certainly churn out wank by the ton!* □ *That's just a lot of wank. Ignore it.* **3.** *n.* an act of masturbation. (Taboo.) □ *Timmy's mother caught him giving himself a wank in the garden shed.* □ *If he gets frustrated enough, he does a wank.*

wanker 1. *n.* a foolish or trivial person. (Crude.) □ *You wanker! You've buttered the tablecloth!* □ *Those wankers are at it again. Spend, spend, spend.* **2.** *n.* a masturbator. (Taboo.) □ *These cinemas showing dirty films are full of wankers.* □ *Some filthy wanker has been here before us!* **3.** *n.* an untrustworthy person. (Crude.) □ *Just get out of my sight, you wanker!* □ *What a wanker you are!*

want out *vb. phr.* to be completely fed up with one's present situation or circumstances and wanting to leave it for some other one. □ *Ted had had as much as he could stand, and he wanted out.* □ *I want out. This relationship is stifling me.*

Want to make something of it? *interrog.* a response to an insulting comment or criticism which implies willingness to respond with physical assault upon the critic. □ *So, I'm an ugly little runt. Want to make something of it?* □ *I see.*

You don't agree with my opinion of Harry. Want to make something of it?

warhorse *n.* a reliable or tough person, usually old. □ *Yes, the conductor is a warhorse all right, but he knows how to get the best out of the orchestra.* □ *What time does the old warhorse's train get in, and how long is she staying this time?*

warmer *n.* an exasperating or disgusting person. (Scots usage.) □ *He dizny act like he's a warmer.* □ *Watch that one; he's a warmer all right.*

warm shop *n.* a brothel. (Crude.) □ *The police raided the warm shop and took away the madam and all the girls.* □ *He was found dead in a cheap warm shop late last night.*

warm someone up *vb. phr.* to prepare an audience for another—more famous—performer. □ *A famous singer came out to warm us up for Benny Hill.* □ *This man Bennett is a superb choice to warm up the audience.*

war-paint *n.* female cosmetics. □ *We knew Samantha was serious when she arrived there with her full war-paint on.* □ *All the girls were in the powder-room getting their war-paint in order.*

warriors bold 1. *n.* the cold. (Rhyming slang.) □ *I hate the warriors bold.* □ *There is something very bracing about the warriors bold.* **2.** *mod.* cold. (Rhyming slang.) □ *In warriors bold weather like this he prefers to stay indoors.* □ *Cor! Real warriors bold today, innit?* **3.** *n.* a cold. (Rhyming slang.) □ *I'm afraid I've got a dose of the warriors bold.* □ *Everyone seems to be down with the warriors bold.*

wart *n.* an annoying person. (Also a rude term of address.) □ *Who is that wart with the inch-thick glasses?* □ *Tell the wart to leave, or we will be forced to call Bruno, who doesn't care for such persons.*

warts and all *mod.* with no attempt made to hide flaws. (From a remark by Oliver Cromwell to the painter of his portrait, that he wanted it to be completely honest and accurate.) □ *It's a great performance—warts and all.* □ *Yes, we love each other very much, warts and all.*

wash 1. *vb.* to be believed. (Always used in a negative context. As if untruth were a stain that will not COME OUT IN THE WASH.) □ *It sounds phony. It won't wash.* □ *That'll never wash! It's totally unbelievable.* **2.** *n.* beer. (Compare with CHASER.) □ *Here, that's good wash!* □ *Have a can of wash, Charlie.*

was had See BEEN HAD.

washed out *mod.* exhausted; tired. □ *I feel too washed out to go to work today.* □ *Poor Ted really looks washed out.*

washer-upper *n.* someone who washes cutlery and crockery. □ *It ain't glamorous, but someone's got to be a washer-upper and it pays the bills.* □ *I'm a washer-upper at the Ritz.*

washout *n.* a failure; a fiasco. □ *The whole project was a washout. A lost cause from beginning to end.* □ *I am beginning to think that Sally's specialty is washouts.*

wash someone out *vb. phr.* to exhaust; to tire. □ *That activity today really washed me out.* □ *He was washed out by all the excitement.*

wash something out *vb. phr.* to cancel. □ *Had you not heard that it's been washed out?* □ *Right, we'll wash out that one.*

wasp *n.* a traffic warden. □ *I was only one minute over, but still the wasp issued the ticket.* □ *Wasps must get insulted by drivers all day long.*

wass *vb.* to urinate. (Crude.) □ *He just went out to wass.* □ *I've got to wass. Back in a minute.*

was(s)er *n.* a girl or woman. □ *See what that wasser wants, Harry.* □ *The young waser crossed the road and entered the shop.*

wasted 1. *mod.* dead; killed. □ *Max didn't want to end up wasted.* □ *That's silly. We all end up wasted, one way or another.* **2.** *mod.* intoxicated due to drink or drugs. □ *I really feel wasted. What did I drink?* □ *I've never seen a bartender get wasted before.* **3.** *mod.* exhausted. □ *I worked two shifts and I'm totally wasted.* □ *Mary was wasted and went to bed.*

waste of space 1. *n.* someone who is completely useless. (Scots usage.) □

Yon Shuggy is a waste of space; fire him! □ *Get out of here, you waste of space!* **2.** *n.* something that is completely without value. (Scots usage.) □ *The wrecked furniture in here is just a waste of space.* □ *Yon whole place is a waste of space, too.*

waste someone *vb.* to kill someone. (Underworld.) □ *Bruno had orders to waste Max.* □ *The rival gang's hit men sped by in a car and wasted four pushers.*

Watcher! *interj.* "Look out!" □ *Watcher, mate! You all right?* □ *Watcher! Mind that ladder!*

Watch it! *exclam.* "Be careful!"; "Watch your step!"; "Careful of what you say!" (Often uttered as a threat or with threatening undertones.) □ *Watch it, buster!* □ *You're walking on thin ice. Just watch it!*

Watch my lips! See READ MY LIPS!

Watch your mouth! AND **Watch your tongue!** *exclam.* "Pay attention to what you are saying!"; "Do not say anything rude!" □ *Hey, don't talk that way! Watch your mouth!* □ *Watch your tongue, you little creep!*

Watch your tongue! See WATCH YOUR MOUTH!

water-hen *n.* ten. (Rhyming slang.) □ *A water-hen? You've got that many?* □ *I'll give you a quid for water-hen of them.*

water-hole See WATERING HOLE.

watering hole AND **water-hole** *n.* a pub or bar. □ *Now this place is one of my favourite watering holes.* □ *I think you live down at that water-hole.*

waterworks 1. *n.* the human urinary system. (A euphemism. Normally with *the.* A term used by doctors patronising their patients.) □ *Well, Mrs McTavish, how are your waterworks today?* □ *I'm afraid the waterworks is no better, doctor.* **2.** *n.* rain. □ *Don't just stand out there in the waterworks!* □ *Oh no, waterworks again.*

wax *n.* a phonograph recording; a substance onto which a recording is put. (Never singular or plural. Now dated, but still used.) □ *This is one of the finest pieces of music ever put on wax.*

□ *Now here's some wax I'll bet you've never heard before.*

waxy *mod.* bad-tempered. □ *That's the sort of stupidity that makes me waxy!* □ *Watch out, he's really waxy today.*

Wayne *n.* a brainless, vulgar youth. (See KEVIN.) □ *I don't like him, he's just another Wayne!* □ *Who's that Wayne I saw Linda with?*

way-out 1. *mod.* unusual; excellent. □ *Some of your clothes are really way-out.* □ *What a way-out hairdo.* **2.** *mod.* innovative; avant-garde. □ *That exhibition of modern art is really way-out.* □ *Now that really is a way-out idea.* **3.** *mod.* disconnected from the real world; very eccentric. □ *I love this way-out music.* □ *I'm afraid it's just too way-out for me.*

wazzock 1. *n.* a stupid or incapable person. (Offensive. Also a term of address.) □ *What a wazzock that woman can be.* □ *Get out of here, you wazzock!* **2.** *n.* a drunkard. □ *You are going to turn into a real wazzock if you don't let up on your drinking.* □ *There was some wazzock asleep across the front entrance to the office when I got here this morning.*

wazzocked *mod.* intoxicated due to drink. □ *I felt a little wazzocked, but that didn't stop me from having more.* □ *Ben is too wazzocked to drive home.*

WBMTTP *interj.* "Which brings me to the point." (Computer jargon. Written only. An initialism used in computer communications.) □ *Of course, you may not like that approach. WBMTTP. You need someone to help you choose the proper method.* □ *I agree with what Tom said. WBMTTP. I think we spend too much time worrying about these matters.*

weapon *n.* the male sexual organ. (Taboo.) □ *Unlike Myra, Sharon thinks of little else but men's weapons.* □ *The streaker covered his weapon as he ran across the field. What sort of streak is that?*

wear something *vb.* to tolerate or put up with something. (Usually negative.) □ *That's no good. I won't wear it.* □ *I don't mind, but my wife won't wear it.*

wear the trousers *vb. phr.* to be the boss in the house; to run a household. □ *All right, if you have to wear the trousers in the house, have it your way.* □ *Well, somebody has to wear the trousers around here.*

wear two hats *vb. phr.* to have two responsibilities or jobs. □ *It's not so easy to wear two hats, you know.* □ *I really hate having to wear two hats like this.*

weasel 1. *n.* a traitor; a liar; generally, a despicable person. (Compare with TOAD.) □ *You slimy little weasel! How could you!* □ *If Fred weren't such a weasel, I could stand him.* **2.** *n.* a trick or expedient used to avoid work, responsibility or cost. □ *Well, it's certainly an original weasel, I'll say that.* □ *None of your weasels; we expect work from you in here.* **3.** *vb.* to behave in a sly or devious manner. □ *Do you have to weasel like that all the time!* □ *Just cut out your weaseling, thank you!*

weasel out of something *vb. phr.* to get out of doing something; to wriggle out of a responsibility. □ *I know how to weasel out of something like that. You get a headache.* □ *You can't just weasel out now when we need you!*

weasel words *n.* words said, or more likely, written (as in a formal contract, for example) in such an ambiguous manner as to enable one party to evade some obligation or commitment that had been assumed by the other party to have been contracted by the first. □ *Always read the weasel words. That's how they'll try to get out of this.* □ *Well, I've got to say these were very clever weasel words indeed. But they don't hold water; we've got you!*

weasle and stoat *n.* a coat. (Rhyming slang.) □ *I've lost my weasle and stoat.* □ *That's a ridiculous weasel and stoat; I won't wear it.*

wedding kit See FAMILY JEWELS.

wedding tackle See FAMILY JEWELS.

wedge *n.* a sandwich. □ *Can I have a wedge, mum?* □ *He sat there, eating a wedge.*

weed 1. *n.* tobacco; a cigarette or cigar. (Often with *the*.) □ *I've about given up the weed.* □ *The weed is going to be the death of me.* **2.** *n.* marijuana; a marijuana cigarette. □ *This is good weed, man.* □ *This weed is green but decent.* **3.** *vb.* to pilfer; to steal small things. □ *I don't know why you waste your time weeding; you could steal much bigger things. Where's your ambition?* □ *What did you weed for us today?* **4.** *n.* a weak and feeble-willed person. (Offensive. Also a term of address.) □ *What a weed you are!* □ *Just get out of my sight, you weed!*

weedhead *n.* a smoker of marijuana. □ *Max is a confirmed weedhead.* □ *The weedheads are taking over this neighbourhood.*

weedy *mod.* ineffective; weak-willed; irresolute. □ *My last one looked weedy at first, but it worked, didn't it?* □ *Don't bring me any more of your weedy efforts.*

wee goldie AND **wee hauf; wee tottie** *n.* a small measure of Scotch whisky. (Scots usage.) □ *Ah could go a wee goldie.* □ *The wee totties wur fair flowing yon evening, ah can tell you. (Small measures of whisky were poured very frequently that evening, I can tell you.)*

wee hauf See WEE GOLDIE.

wee heavy *n.* a small bottle containing about half a pint of heavy beer. (Scots usage.) □ *Bring me back some wee heavies from the pub, will you Bill?* □ *He emptied the wee heavy and got up to leave.*

wee hoose *n.* a toilet. (A euphemism. Scots usage.) □ *Where's yer wee hoose?* □ *The wee hoose? Oh, it's along that passageway.*

weelfaured *mod.* handsome; attractive. (Scots usage.) □ *He's a weelfaured person and I love what he says.* □ *What a weelfaured man he is!*

Wee Man *n.* the Devil. (Scots usage. Normally with *the*.) □ *If you wains are no good the Wee Man'll get you. (If you children are not good the Devil will get you.)* □ *Don't frighten the wains with tales of the Wee Man, Sandy. (Don't frighten the children with tales of the Devil, Sandy.)*

wee man *n.* the male sexual organ. (Taboo. Scots usage. Normally with *the.*) □ *Only wee boys wave their wee men about like that, Willie. Put it away!* □ *Morag says wee men are disgusting but then Morag's strange.*

ween(s)y *mod.* tiny; minute. □ *Just give me an weensy piece. I'm on a diet.* □ *What an weeny car!*

weepie *n.* a sentimental film. □ *My wife always loves a good weepie.* □ *There's a weepie on the tellie.*

weeping willow See TIT WILLOW.

wee small hours *n.* the time just after midnight. □ *The party went onto the wee small hours.* □ *What were you doing up in the wee small hours?*

wee tottie See WEE GOLDIE.

wee-wee *n.* an act of urination, (Crude. Juvenile.) □ *If you need a wee-wee, go through there.* □ *Where do you go around here for a wee-wee?*

weigh into someone *vb. phr.* to attack someone. □ *Why can't you leave people alone? Why do you always have to weigh into someone who does not agree with you?* □ *There's Otto, weighing into some poor sod again.*

weigh someone off *vb. phr.* to get one's own back on someone. □ *The pig! I'll weigh him off all right.* □ *Why weigh off people? It does no good.*

weirdo AND **weirdy 1.** *n.* a strange person; an eccentric. □ *She is certainly a weirdo lately.* □ *Don't be such a weirdy!* **2.** *mod.* strange; eccentric. □ *She is certainly in a weirdo mood lately.* □ *Don't be so weirdy!* **3.** *n.* a male homosexual. (Crude.) □ *Tom is getting to be such a weirdo.* □ *He doesn't like being called a weirdy.*

weirdy See WEIRDO.

welcher AND **welsher** *n.* someone who does not pay their debts, especially gambling debts; someone who evades their responsibilities. □ *It was Bruno's job to let the welchers know that Mr Big was angry.* □ *Harry goes to great lengths to avoid his responsibilities. In other words, he's a welsher.*

welch on someone AND **welsh on someone** *vb. phr.* to fail to pay debts, especially gambling debts; to evade responsibility. (Objected to by the Welsh.) □ *It was Bruno's job to let people know*

that it was a bad idea to welsh on Mr Big. □ *Harry goes to great lengths to welsh on his responsibilities.*

well *mod.* very. □ *Old Alf was well gone by closing time, I'm afraid.* □ *The bank says we're well over our limit and we must cut back.*

well and truly *mod.* thoroughly or completely. □ *By now, everyone was well and truly fed up with Simon.* □ *I'm well and truly satisfied that it was not his fault.*

well away AND **well gone; well lit; well on; well oiled** *mod.* very intoxicated due to drink. □ *Joe and Arthur kept on knocking them back till they were both well away.* □ *That guy is really well oiled. Send him home.*

well-endowed See (WELL) STACKED.

well-endowed AND **well-equipped; well-furnished; well-hung; well-loaded** *mod.* of a man with a large sexual organ. (Taboo.) □ *She just wanted to go with him because she'd heard he was well-endowed.* □ *Susan would prefer him to have a well-loaded bank account than just to be well-loaded.*

well-equipped See WELL-ENDOWED.

well-furnished See WELL-ENDOWED.

well gone See WELL AWAY.

well-heeled AND **well-lined; well-loaded** *mod.* rich. □ *His father died and left him pretty well-heeled.* □ *Her well-loaded uncle left her a lot of money.* □ *Pete is well-lined for life.*

well-hung See WELL-ENDOWED.

wellie AND **welly 1.** *n.* a wellington boot. (Normally in the plural.) □ *Well, pull on your wellies and lets go for a walk across the field.* □ *Jimmy lost a welly when it got stuck in the mud.* **2.** See also FRENCH LETTER; WILLIE-WELLIE.

wellied *mod.* very intoxicated due to drink. (Scots usage.) □ *Tipsy? Wellied, more like!* □ *Well, eh, I suppose you could say we were wellied again.*

wellie someone *vb.* to defeat or break someone or a team. (Derived from PUT THE BOOT IN.) □ *Come on! We'll wellie them!* □ *Well, they were well and truly wellie yesterday!*

wellie-wanging *n.* the competitive throwing of wellington boots as far as possible. □ *Willy flung one over 100 feet to win the wellie-wanging championship.* □ *Don't laugh; wellie-wanging is definitely a growing sport, you know.*

well-in *mod.* popular. □ *She's a very well-in young lady around here, you know.* □ *If you're that well-in, you've nothing to worry about.*

well-lined See WELL-HEELED.

well lit See WELL AWAY.

well-loaded See WELL-ENDOWED; WELL-HEELED.

well oiled See WELL AWAY.

well on See WELL AWAY.

well shod *mod.* [of a car] with tyres in good condition. □ *Now here's a well shod motor, squire.* □ *At least the car was well shod. Everything else about it was rotten except the tyres.*

(well) stacked AND **well-endowed; well-equipped** *mod.* of a woman with large and well-formed breasts. (Crude.) □ *That girl really is stacked!* □ *Now Mary is what you'd call well-endowed.* □ *Boy, does she come really well-equipped!*

welly 1. *vb.* to kick forcefully. □ *Stop these children wellying that dog!* □ *They knocked him down and started to welly him.* **2.** See also WELLIE.

welsher See WELCHER.

welsh on someone See WELCH ON SOMEONE.

Welshy *n.* a Welsh person. (Offensive.) □ *Don't call Welsh people Welshies, please. It is very offensive and racist.* □ *He said he was not a racist, he just hated this particular Welshy!*

wench *n.* a facetious word for a girl or woman. □ *Well, my pretty wench, what say you to some rumpy-pumpy?* □ *The wench was remarkably unwilling to succumb to my undoubted charms.*

wendy *n.* a particularly weak or small boy. (Childish.) □ *Although he's a poor wendy, he's still an irritating one at times.* □ *Her son is really just a wendy, I'm afraid.*

Were you born in a barn? *interrog.* "Don't you know doors can be closed as well as opened?"; or more simply, just "Shut the door!" □ *Close the door! Were you born in a barn?* □ *Do you always leave doors open? Were you born in a barn?*

Western (Ocean) *n.* the Atlantic Ocean. (Nautical. Always with *the*.) □ *I sailed all those years on the Western Ocean and have little to show for it, me lad.* □ *The Western is the second-largest ocean on the surface of the globe.*

wet 1. *mod.* having to do with an area where is it legal to sell alcohol. (Compare with DRY.) □ *Most Welsh counties became wet just a few years ago.* □ *Is it wet or dry in this county?* **2.** *n.* a drink. □ *I often enjoy a wet in the evening.* □ *You know how a wet disagrees with you, my dear.* **3.** AND **damp** *mod.* feeble; spineless; over-sentimental. □ *Why do you have to be so wet all the time? Show some backbone!* □ *He really is a terribly damp, indecisive individual.* **4.** *n.* a Conservative politician who has a liberal stance. (Compare with DRY.) □ *Him? Oh yes, he's a really damp damp.* □ *Being wet was particularly unpopular during the Prime Ministership of Margaret Thatcher, who is reputed to have invented the usage.* **5.** *mod.* unrealistic; ineffectual. □ *That decision was just wet and will never work.* □ *Don't be so damp—there's no way we can do that.* **6.** *mod.* of a sexually aroused woman. (Taboo.) □ *It does not take a lot to get Joan wet.* □ *I don't know if she liked it, but I can tell you she was certainly damp.*

wet AND **wet rag** *n.* a WIMP; a useless JERK. □ *Don't be such a wet! Stand up for your rights!* □ *Well, in a tight situation, Martin is sort of a wet rag.*

wet behind the ears *mod.* young; untrained; unskilled; naive. □ *Although he's still wet behind the ears, he's bright and he'll learn.* □ *I don't think you know what's what, and you're really wet behind the ears.*

wet blanket *n.* a person with a gloomy or depressing manner which spoils the pleasure of others. (In the way that a wet blanket is used to put out a fire.) □ *Oh, Martin! Why do you have to be such a wet blanket?* □ *Don't be a wet blanket! Have some fun!*

wet rag See WET.

wet the baby's head *vb. phr.* to celebrate the birth of a baby with an alcoholic drink. □ *We wetted the baby's head 'till 4 a.m.* □ *We're planning on wetting the baby's head again tonight.*

wetware *n.* living matter, particularly the human brain, in the context of computer hardware and software. (From the supposed soft and damp nature of protoplasmic matter. Compare with FIRMWARE, LIVEWARE and VAPOURWARE.) □ *When your computer screws up, wetware proves it's worth once more.* □ *Wetware has it's place, but for massive number-crunching you need a number-cruncher.*

wet weekend *n.* a depressed or depressing person. □ *I don't think I could take another wet weekend like that today.* □ *One wet weekend was little different from the others, he thought.*

w(h)ack 1. *vb.* to strike hard at someone or something. □ *Jed whacked the kid on the head.* □ *Larry reached down and wacked the dog across the snout.* **2.** *n.* a heavy blow or hit (at someone or something). □ *She tried to take a whack at me!* □ *She landed a nasty wack on his thigh.* **3.** *n.* a share. □ *I've come here for me whack and I'm not leaving without it.* □ *Is that all? I expected a bigger wack than that.* **4.** *n.* a worried a confused condition. □ *He was in a real whack by this time.* □ *This is just not worth the wack, if you ask me.* **5.** *n.* food and board. (Irish usage.) □ *I'm looking for somewhere I can get good whack.* □ *Mrs O'Reilly always does excellent wack.*

Whack See WHACKER.

whacked *mod.* exhausted or worn-out. □ *Poor Ted really looks whacked.* □ *I feel too whacked to go to work today.*

w(h)acker *n.* a crazy or eccentric person. □ *Ever since the operation, Joe's been a real wacker.* □ *Sally is a real whacker. She'd forget her head if it wasn't screwed on.*

Whacker AND **Whack; Wack** *n.* a familiar form of address for a man, especially if his correct name is not known. (Most common in and around Liverpool. Compare with JOHN, KIDDO, MOOSH, TOSH and JIMMY.) □ *Look Whacker, I'll get you, you wait!* □ *Got a light, Wack?*

whacking 1. *mod.* whopping; huge. □ *A whacking great aircraft flew low over the village.* □ *Why are lawyer's fees always so whacking big?* **2.** *mod.* very; very large. □ *What's that whacking great lorry doing parked outside my house?* □ *Can you explain this whacking telephone bill, my young lady?*

whack off *vb. phr.* to masturbate. (Taboo.) □ *Someone has whacked off or something in here!* □ *Girls whack off as well as boys, you know.*

whack someone or something *vb.* to defeat or better an adversary. □ *We certainly whacked that lot; they won't be back in a hurry.* □ *We just have to whack the next lot or we're done for.*

w(h)acky *mod.* crazy; eccentric; very unusual. □ *I've never heard such a wacky idea.* □ *It's really whacky.* □ *I better warn you; Otto's a bit wacky.*

w(h)acky-baccy *n.* marijuana. (Humorous.) □ *Have you got any of that wacky-baccy?* □ *He gets that silly look in his eye from smoking whacky-baccy.*

whammers See WAMMERS.

whang(er) See WANG(ER).

whang someting *vb.* to throw hard. □ *Go one, whang it!* □ *I think he whanged it over there.*

What! AND **What?** *exclam.* a terminating emphasiser. □ *Jolly good idea, what!* □ *I think I won that time, what?*

What (a) nerve! *exclam.* "What insolence!"; "How rude and presumptuous!" □ *Did you hear what she said? What nerve!* □ *What a nerve! Have you ever seen such gall?*

What can I do you for? *interrog.* "How can I help you?"; "How can I serve you?" □ *Good morning. What can I do for you?* □ *Now it's your turn. What can I do for you?*

whatchamacallit See WHAT-D'YOU-CALL-IT.

What do you say? *interrog.* "What is your answer?" □ *Well, what do you say?* □ *Come on, I need an answer now. What do you say?*

what-d'you-call-it AND **whatchamacallit; whatsit; whatzit** *n.* a name for a person or thing whose real name has been forgotten or is being avoided. □ *Did you invite whatchamacallit to the party?* □ *Put this little whatsit on the top and another on the bottom.* □ *I lost my—you know—my whatzit—my watch!*

What else is new? AND **So what else is new?** *interrog.* "But isn't that what you expect?"; "What you said isn't new, so what is?" □ *Yes, there is trouble around the world. So what else is new?* □ *So, there's not enough money this week. What else is new?*

whatever turns you on *phr.* "It's all right if it excites you or interests you." (Said originally about sexual matters, but now much more general in application.) □ *You really like pickled pigs feet? Whatever turns you on.* □ *I can't stand that kind of music, but whatever turns you on.*

what for *n.* trouble or retribution. □ *Right my lad, you're going to get what for!* □ *I knew I faced what for when I returned.*

What for why? *interrog.* "What is the purpose?"; "What is going on?" (Scots usage.) □ *What for why are us yins here, mammy? (What is the reason for our being here, mother?)* □ *The wain wanted to ken what for why he got a jeely piece. (The child wanted to know why he got a jam sandwich.)*

What gives? *interrog.* "What is going on?"; "What is happening?" (Probably from German, where *was gibt's* has almost exactly the same sound and meaning; if so, by hobson-jobson.) □ *Hey! What gives? Who left this here?* □ *What gives, Harry? How are you today?*

what-have-you *n.* anything similar. □ *I'm seeking a computer; a Macintosh or what-have-you would be just right.* □ *All right, let's go to the theatre, cinema or what-have-you this evening.*

What is it? *interrog.* "Hello, what is happening?" □ *What is it? Are you okay?* □ *What is it? What's happening?*

What is something in aid of? AND **What's (all) something in aid of?** *in-*terrog. "What is something for?"; "Why is something happening?" □ *Can someone tell me what is all this in aid of?* □ *Just what's our work in aid of, eh?*

What'll it be? See WHAT'S YOURS?

What'll you have? See WHAT'S YOURS?

what makes someone tick *n.* someone's driving force or chief motivation. □ *Oh, what makes her tick is just money, plain and simple.* □ *He's always wanting to know what makes people tick.*

What's (all) something in aid of? See WHAT IS SOMETHING IN AID OF?

What's cooking? *interrog.* "What is happening?"; "What's about to happen?" □ *What's cooking? Anything interesting?* □ *What's cooking anyway?*

What's eating someone? *interrog.* "What is bothering someone?" □ *Come on, Tom, what's eating you?* □ *What's eating Fred? He's in a rotten humour.*

What's going on? *interrog.* "What is happening here?" □ *I hear a lot of noise. What's going on?* □ *What's all this broken glass? What's going on?*

What's happening? *interrog.* "Hello, what's new?" □ *Hello there! What's happening?* □ *What's happening? How's it going?*

what's-his-face AND **what's-his-name** *n.* someone whose name has been forgotten or was never known; someone whose name is being avoided. □ *Was what's-his-name there? I never can remember his name.* □ *I can't remember what's-his-face's name either.*

what's-his-name See WHAT'S-HIS-FACE.

What's in it for me? *interrog.* "How do I benefit or profit from this?" □ *I might help out. What's in it for me?* □ *I might be able to contribute a little. What's in it for me?*

whatsit See WHAT-D'YOU-CALL-IT.

What's it to be? See WHAT'S YOURS?

What's it to you? *interrog.* "What does it matter to you?"; "Is it any of your business?" □ *What's it to you if I don't do it?* □ *So I broke my glasses. What's it to you?*

What's new? *interrog.* "Hello, how are you?"; "What has happened since I last saw you?"; "What's the news?" □ *Hello, Jim! What's new?* □ *What's new with you?*

What's the (big) deal? 1. *interrog.* "What is going on here?"; "What is the problem?" □ *There's a big rumpus down the hall. What's the deal?* □ *I give you £20 and you gave me £5 back. What's the deal?* □ *What's the big deal? Where's my other five?* **2.** *interrog.* "Calm down. What are you getting so excited about?" □ *It's all right, it's nothing to do with us. What's the big deal?* □ *What's the deal? It makes no difference to our plans.*

What's the catch? *interrog.* "What is the drawback?"; "It sounds good. Are there any hidden problems?" □ *Sounds too good to be true. What's the catch?* □ *What's the catch? This looks like a good deal.*

What's up? *interrog.* "What is going on?"; "What is happening?" □ *Hello, Jim! What's up?* □ *Haven't seen you in a month of Sundays. What's up?*

What's with someone? *interrog.* "Why is someone doing something?"; "Why is someone behaving in such a manner?" □ *What's with Harry? Why is he doing this to me?* □ *I want to know what's with these people around here. Is it something I've said?*

What's yours? AND **What'll you have?; Name yours; What's it to be?; What'll it be?** *interrog.* "What would you like to drink?" (Typically said on offering drinks.) □ *"What's yours?" said the bartender.* □ *Okay, pal, name yours?* □ *What'll it be, mate?*

What the deuce? AND **What the dickens?** *interrog.* "What has happened?"; "What?"; a variation of "What the devil?" (DEUCE and DICKENS are euphemisms for DEVIL.) □ *What the deuce! Who are you?* □ *What the dickens are you doing here?*

What the devil? AND **What the fuck?; What the hell?; What the shit?** *interrog.* "What has happened?"; "What?" (Often with the force of an exclamation. WHAT THE FUCK? and WHAT THE SHIT? are taboo.) □ *What the devil? Who put sugar in the salt shaker?* □

What the fuck? Who are you? What are you doing in my room? □ *What the shit are you doing here? You're supposed to be at work.*

What the dickens? See WHAT THE DEUCE?

What the fuck? See WHAT THE DEVIL?

What the heck! See WHAT THE HELL!

What the hell? 1. *interrog.* "What does it matter?" (Crude. Usually with the force of an exclamation.) □ *Give her a new one. What the hell!* □ *Don't be such a cheapskate. Get the nice one. What the hell!* **2.** See also WHAT THE DEVIL?

What the hell! AND **What the heck!** *exclam.* "It doesn't matter!" (Crude. Often with the force of an exclamation.) □ *Oh, what the hell! Come on in. It doesn't matter.* □ *Oh, what the heck! I'll have another beer. Nobody's counting.*

What the shit? See WHAT THE DEVIL?

What you see is what you get. *sent.* "The product you are looking at is exactly what you get if you buy it." (Compare with WYSIWYG.) □ *It comes just like this. What you see is what you get.* □ *What you see is what you get. The ones in the box are just like this one.*

whatzit See WHAT-D'YOU-CALL-IT.

wheeler-dealer *n.* a cunning, aggressive person who always appears to be involved in large and multiple business deals. □ *She has turned into a real wheeler-dealer.* □ *Who's the wheeler-dealer who set up this deal?*

wheelie bin *n.* a large, wheeled rubbish can, sometimes issued by garbage-collection agencies to simplify their work. □ *You can usually see wheelie bins at the foot of these tower blocks.* □ *Someone tried to block the entranceway with a wheelie bin.*

wheels *n.* a car; transportation by car. □ *I've got to get some wheels pretty soon.* □ *I'll need a lift. I don't have any wheels.*

wheely AND **wheelie** *n.* an act of rearing up on a bike or motorcycle, balancing it on the rear wheel. □ *Can you do wheelies?* □ *The kid did a wheelie and scared his mother to death.*

wheeze *n.* a clever idea. □ *A few more wheezes like that and you've got it made!* □ *Here, that was a clever wheeze! How did you come up with that one!*

when Dover and Calais meet *mod.* never. □ *I'll agree to that when Dover and Calais meet.* □ *When Dover and Calais meet, we'll agree to your demands.*

whenever *mod.* at any time that you wish. □ *Do it whenever; I don't care.* □ Q: *When can I come to see you?* A: *Whenever.*

whennie *n.* someone who bores listeners with tales of their past exploits. (From regular use of the expression, "When I...") □ *Oh, he's a real whennie.* □ *That whennie has three basic stories, but they seem to bear endless repetition.*

when one's ship comes in *mod.* when one becomes rich and successful. □ *When my ship comes in, we'll live in one of these huge mansions on the hill, my lass.* □ *When your ship comes in, Otto, I'll probably die of amazement!*

when push comes to shove AND **if push comes to shove** *phr.* "when things get a little pressed"; "when the situation gets more active or intense." □ *When push comes to shove, you know I'll be on your side.* □ *If push comes to shove, the front office can help with some statistics.*

when the balloon goes up *phr.* when trouble starts. □ *When the balloon goes up I intend to be long gone.* □ *Are you ready for when the balloon goes up?*

when the fat lady sings See TILL THE FAT LADY SINGS.

Where have you been hiding? See WHERE (HAVE) YOU BEEN KEEPING YOURSELF?

Where (have) you been keeping yourself? AND **Where have you been hiding?** *interrog.* "I haven't seen you in a long time. Where have you been?" □ *Long time no see. Where've you been keeping yourself?* □ *I haven't seen you in a long time. Where have you been hiding?*

Where in the world? *interrog.* "Where?" (An intensive form of *where*. See examples for variations.) □ *Where in the world have you been?* □ *Where in the world did I put my glasses?*

Where on earth? *interrog.* "(Exactly) where?" (An intensive form of *where*. See examples for variations.) □ *Where on earth did you get that ridiculous hat?* □ *Where on earth is my book?* □ *Where on earth were you?*

Where's the fire? *interrog.* "Why are you going so fast?"; "What's the hurry?" □ *Going a little fast there, weren't you? Where's the fire?* □ *Where's the fire? We have an hour to get there.*

where the action is *phr.* "where important things are happening." □ *I want to be where the action is.* □ *Right there in the House of Commons. That's where the action is.*

where the shoe pinches *mod.* where there are problems or difficulties. □ *I want to know where the shoe pinches.* □ *Where the shoe pinches, we'll come up with the answers.*

where the sun don't shine *phr.* in a dark place, namely the anus. (Crude. Often with *put it* or *shove it*. Part of the answer to the question "Where shall I put it?" Always with *don't*; never with *doesn't*.) □ *I don't care what you do with it. Just put it where the sun don't shine.* □ *For all I care you can shove it where the sun don't shine.*

wherewithal *n.* the money necessary for a specific purpose. □ *I don't have the wherewithal to invest in anything like that.* □ *I've got the interest but not the wherewithal.*

whiff *n.* a smell, especially an unpleasant one. □ *I just can't stand that whiff.* □ *Where is that terrible whiff coming from?*

whiffy *mod.* possessing an unpleasant smell. □ *That's really whiffy, don't go in there.* □ *If you must be whiffy, do so somewhere else than here.*

whinge AND **winge** *vb.* to complain repeatedly or continuously. □ *Some people whinge because they don't have* *anything else to do.* □ *Come on, don't winge all the time!*

whip-round *n.* an informal collection of money for a charitable cause of some sort. □ *Oh, you've got to put something into a whip-round for the hospice.* □ *Amazingly, the whip-round collected almost £1,000.*

whip someone up *vb. phr.* to excite or stir up someone. □ *Well, you've certainly whipped them up with that speech.* □ *Harry got really whipped up when he heard what Max had been playing at.*

whip something *vb.* to steal something. □ *Someone whipped my handbag!* □ *I told him they would whip anything not nailed down.*

whip something off *vb. phr.* to finish something quickly, especially food or drink. □ *Did you just whip that whole pizza off?* □ *Let me whip off this sandwich, and I'll be right with you.* □ *She whipped off the dishes in ten minutes.*

whip something up *vb. phr.* to prepare something (typically food) very quickly. □ *It's no problem. I can whip a meal up in no time.* □ *She whipped up something to eat in a few minutes.*

whirlybird *n.* a helicopter. □ *See that whirlybird up there? It's measuring your driving speed. Slow down.* □ *The whirlybird landed on the roof of the hospital.*

whisky Mac(Donald) *n.* a drink consisting of whisky and ginger wine. (Originally Scots usage.) □ *The whisky MacDonalds were fair flowing that evening, I can tell you.* □ *Yes, ah could go a whisky Mac, since you ask.*

whisper (and talk) *n.* a walk. (Rhyming slang.) □ *Go on! Get out! Take a whisper and talk!* □ *I went for a whisper, just to get away from him.*

whistle *n.* a suit of clothes. (Rhyming slang, linked as follows: whistle [and flute] ≈ suit of clothes.) □ *I'll get on my whistle, and we'll go out tonight.* □ *You look pretty good in your new whistle.*

whistle-bait *n.* a good-looking or attractive girl or young woman. □ *Now there's a really attractive piece of whis-*tle-bait. □ *Look at her, isn't she real whistle-bait?*

whistle-blow AND **blow the whistle** *vb.* to call a halt to or make public something improper. □ *Someone has whistle-blown us about this.* □ *I was afraid some rat would blow the whistle and get us all into trouble.*

whistle-blower *n.* someone who calls a halt to or makes public something improper; an informer. □ *I don't know who the whistle-blower was, but a good time was really ruined.* □ *Some whistle-blower put Max behind bars for a few days.*

whistled *mod.* intoxicated due to drink. □ *Frank was whistled and didn't want to drive.* □ *Geoff was entirely whistled by midnight.*

whistle in the dark *vb. phr.* to falsely profess fearlessness—perhaps to oneself for the purpose of self-encouragement—as well as others. □ *Come on, you're as scared as the rest of us. You're just whistling in the dark.* □ *Although Harry told everyone he wasn't scared of Max, the truth was that he was whistling in the dark and refusing to admit his fear—even to himself.*

white-arsed 1. *mod.* despicable. (Taboo.) □ *Why, you white-arsed little tyke! Get out!* □ *That is a really white-arsed thing to do.* **2.** *mod.* scared. (Taboo.) □ *When he saw Otto coming at him, you could tell he was really white-arsed.* □ *Flying always makes me white-arsed.*

white elephant *n.* a useless or unwanted object. □ *How can I get rid of this white elephant?* □ *Take all those white elephants to the flea market.*

Whitehall warrior 1. *n.* a civil servant. □ *Whitehall warriors have a reputation for being out of touch, interfering and overpaid.* □ *Wilbur got a job in London as a Whitehall warrior.* **2.** *n.* a military officer engaged in clerical duties rather than on active service. □ *Wilbur has been a Whitehall warrior for his entire military career.* □ *I don't want to be a Whitehall warrior! I joined the army to fight!*

White Highlands *n.* the affluent suburbs that surround many deprived and multi-racial inner cities. (Racially offensive.) □ *He made his money, bought a big property in the White Highlands and has never been seen here again.* □ *The White Highlands is where the money is.*

white-knuckle *mod.* having to do with an event, such as an aircraft flight, that may cause a lot of tension or fear for some people. □ *I had a real white-knuckle session with the boss today.* □ *We came in during the storm on a white-knuckle flight from Rome.*

white night *n.* a night when sleep does not come. □ *Another white night! I've got to get something from the doctor.* □ *A white night can seem to last forever.*

whitey *n.* a white person. (Racially offensive.) □ *Winston wondered what the whitey wanted.* □ *He thinks all whities are racist pigs.*

whizz *n.* amphetamines. □ *You can get some good whizz in this part of town.* □ *What does whizz cost around here?*

whiz(z)-kid **1.** *n.* a precociously intelligent boy or young man, especially one highly skilled in high technology, typically computing. □ *Martin is turning out to be a real software whizz-kid.* □ *Hire a few twelve-year-old whiz-kids to write the sort of games kids want to play, and make a fortune...* **2.** *n.* a young man rising rapidly in an organisation by means of intelligence and will-power. □ *I like the look of this whizz-kid.* □ *This whiz-kid is really going places.*

whizzo *mod.* splendid; excellent. □ *This has been a whizzo day!* □ *Mary's got herself a whizzo new job.*

Whoa! *exclam.* "Stop!" (Originally said to a horse, but now to any person or thing.) □ *You've gone about far enough. Whoa!* □ *Whoa, you've made your point.*

whochamaflip See WHO-D'YA-MA-FLIP.

whodunit *n.* a detective story. □ *I love to read a good whodunit every now and then.* □ *I go through about three whodunits a week.*

who-d'ya-ma-flip AND **whochamaflip** *n.* someone whose name has been forgotten or was never known; someone whose name is being avoided. □ *Did you invite who-d'ya-ma-flip to the party?* □ *If you didn't invite whochamaflip then who did?*

whole bag of tricks *n.* everything; every possibility. □ *Well now. I've used my whole bag of tricks, and we still haven't solved this.* □ *It may take my whole bag of tricks to do it, but I'll try.*

whole kit and caboodle See WHOLE SHEBANG.

whole shebang AND **whole shoot; whole shooting match; whole kit and caboodle** *n.* the whole affair; everything and everyone. (Always with *the*.) □ *The whole shebang is just about washed up.* □ *I'm fed up with the whole kit and caboodle.*

whole shoot See WHOLE SHEBANG.

whole shooting match See WHOLE SHEBANG.

whole time *mod.* full time. □ *She's in whole time work now.* □ *That's a whole time business nowadays, you know.*

whole wide world *n.* everywhere; everywhere and everything. (Always with *the*.) □ *It's the best in the whole wide world.* □ *I've searched the whole wide world for just the right hat.*

whomp See WHUMP.

whoosh *vb.* to move with great rapidity. □ *Stop whooshing like that and think about this for a moment, please.* □ *He's always whooshing here and there.*

whop it up someone *vb. phr.* to perform sexual intercourse, from the male perspective. (Taboo.) □ *I'm hoping to whop it up her tonight.* □ *You'll always get to whop it up Fiona, the girl who can't say no.*

whopper **1.** *n.* something that is of relatively great size. □ *That thing's really a whopper!* □ *It was a whopper of an argument.* **2.** *n.* a very big lie. □ *That one's a whopper. I don't believe a word of it.* □ *She certainly told a whopper, didn't she?*

whopping (great) *mod.* enormous. □ *Somebody showed up with a whopping* great basin of chunks of pickled fish. Yummy! □ What a whopping fool he is!

whore n. a promiscuous woman; a prostitute. (Crude. An unacceptable word to many people. There are many additional meanings and constructions using this word. It is in fact Standard English, but most applications of it are not.) □ Joan almost became a whore to pay for a habit. □ A lot of whores are hooked on something or other.

whore-house AND **whore-shop** n. a brothel. (Crude.) □ He was found dead in a cheap whore-house late last night. □ The police raided the whore-shop and took away the madam and all the girls.

whore-shop See WHORE-HOUSE.

Who the deuce? interrog. "Who?" (An elaboration of who. The DEUCE is the devil. Compare with examples for variations.) □ Who the deuce do you think you are? □ Who the deuce is making all that noise?

Who the devil? See WHO THE HELL?

Who the hell? AND **Who the devil?** interrog. "Who?" (Crude. An elaboration of who. See examples for variations.) □ Who the hell was that masked man? □ Who the hell are you?

whump AND **whomp** n. the sound made when two flat surfaces collide. □ I heard the whump when the shed collapsed. □ The whomp woke everyone up.

wick n. the male sexual organ. (Taboo. Rhyming slang, linked as follows: wick ≈ [prick] = male sexual organ. Compare with DIP ONE'S WICK and GET ON SOMEONE'S WICK.) □ That's all very well Myra, but where would the world be without wicks? □ The doctor told him that he'd got something wrong with his wick.

wicked mod. excellent; impressive. □ Now this is what I call a wicked guitar. □ Boy, this wine is wicked!

widdle vb. to urinate. (Crude. Juvenile.) □ Well, widdling does relieve the pressure of all that beer! □ I'm just going to widdle.

wide 1. mod. shrewd or knowing, in a derogatory sense. □ We don't need a wide individual in that job. □ Simon is a wide one all right; he knows all the tricks of the trade, which is just what worries me. **2.** mod. dishonest. □ He's a wide one all right; check your wallet before you leave. □ Get that wide boy out of here.

wide (boy) n. a small-time crook. □ Why do you hang around with these wide boys. □ He's just a wide, not worth worrying over.

widget 1. n. a hypothetical product made by a hypothetical company. □ Someone said that your company is manufacturing widgets. □ No, we stopped making widgets last year. Too much foreign competition. **2.** n. any small gadget or device. □ Do you have any more of these widgets? □ We need a special widget to make this work.

widow's wink n. a Chinese person. (Racially offensive. Rhyming slang, linked as follows: widow's wink ≈ [Chink] = Chinese person.) □ Y'know, Otto, if you call a Chinese a widow's wink, he's likely to get nasty. □ Why can you not be polite to widow's winks?

wife 1. n. a girlfriend; a fiancee; a mistress. □ Me and my wife are going to Fred's this Friday. □ Ask your wife if she wants to come along. **2.** n the passive member of a homosexual couple. (Crude. Compare with HUSBAND.) □ Somebody said he's his wife. Who do they mean? □ Jennifer's wife's really attractive; you'd never guess she's like that.

wigged out 1. mod. alcohol or drug intoxicated. □ How did you get so wigged out? □ The kid got a little wigged out and slipped under the table. **2.** mod. having lost control of oneself; having flipped one's wig. □ The kid is just too wigged out to do anything these days. □ After the bad news, she was totally wigged out.

wigging n. a scolding. □ Her mother gave her a wigging when she finally got home. □ Tom got a wigging for his part in the prank.

wiggle out of something *vb. phr.* to successfully avoid doing something. □ *We wiggled out of the appointment.* □ *Don't try to wiggle out of it. I saw you with her.*

wiggy *mod.* eccentric; irresponsible. □ *Watch Harry, he's really wiggy these days.* □ *You can't expect people to take you seriously if you're so wiggy all the time.*

wig out 1. *vb. phr.* to lose control of oneself; to FLIP ONE'S WIG. □ *I was afraid I would wig out if I stayed any longer.* □ *Take it easy, man. Don't wig out.* **2.** *vb. phr.* to have a good time at a party, etc. □ *We wigged out at John's do.* □ *Come on, let's wig out!*

Wilco. *interj.* "I will comply." (Military.) □ *Roger. Wilco!* □ *Wilco on that. We're ready now.*

wild *mod.* exciting; eccentric; COOL. □ *Things are really wild here.* □ *We had a wild time.*

wild-cat (strike) *n.* an unofficial strike; a strike called without notice. □ *There's a wild-cat strike at the factory.* □ *Some people think wild-cats are the most effective strikes.*

Will do. *phr.* "I will do it." □ *Will do. I'll get right on it.* □ *Fix the stuck window? Will do.*

William *n.* a policeman; the police. (Derived from BILL.) □ *The William broke up the fight.* □ *These two Williams drove around in their car picking on innocent people like me.*

Will I buggery! See WILL I HELL!

willie AND **willy** *n.* the male sexual organ. (Taboo. Sometimes juvenile.) □ *The streaker covered his willy as he ran across the field. What sort of streak is that?* □ *Unlike Myra, Sharon thinks of little else but willies.*

willies *n.* a sensation of fear or anxiety. (Always with *the*. Compare with HEE-BIE-JEEBIES.) □ *That kind of film always gives me the willies.* □ *I got the willies before the exam.*

willie-warmer See SNOOD-HOOD.

willie-wellie AND **wellie; welly** *n.* a condom. (Taboo.) □ HE: *What's the point, with a willie-wellie?* □ SHE: *No welly, no willie: that's my point!*

Will I fuck! See WILL I HELL!

Will I hell! AND **Will I buggery!; Will I fuck!; Will I shit!** *exclam.* "I will not do something!" (All are crude; All except WILL I HELL! are also taboo.) □ *Resign? Will I hell!* □ *Will I shit help that little creep!*

Will I shit! See WILL I HELL!

will-o'-the-wisp 1. *n.* an illusory hope or hopeless dream. □ *Don't waste your time over that will-o'-the-wisp of a plan.* □ *Soon it became clear the plan was a mere will-o'-the-wisp.* **2.** *n.* someone hard to find. □ *That boy is a real will-o'-the-wisp.* □ *Where has that will-o'-the-wisp got to now?*

willow *n.* a cricket bat, because that's the wood it's made of. □ *He took his willow and walked out onto the field.* □ *The leather of the ball made a sharp "crack" as it hit his willow.*

wiltshire *n.* impotence. (Crude.) □ *It's a long time since old Walter moved on into wiltshire.* □ *Wiltshire? Of course not, I've no problem there!*

wimp 1. *mod.* "windows, icons, mouse, pointer." (Computer jargon and an acronym. Refers to a computer system, such as Macintosh or Microsoft Windows, with an elaborate user interface including resizable windows, clever icons and a movable mouse. The term is sometimes taken to imply that such systems are for "computer weaklings." See the following definition of the term.) □ *Being a masochist, I am happier with a computer system that doesn't have all that wimp stuff.* □ *I want a computer with as many wimp features as I can get!* **2.** *n.* a weak and feeble-willed person. □ *Don't be a wimp. Stand up for your rights.* □ *What a wimp. People walk all over her.* **3.** *n.* an old-fashioned person; a square. □ *He's a terrible wimp.* □ *The wimp was waiting outside the office for him.* **4.** *n.* a spotty, immature youth. □ *Who's that wimp I saw Linda with?* □ *I don't like him, he's nothing but a wimp!* **5.** *n.* a "weakly interacting massive particle." (Acronym. An astronomical term for a hypothetical particle which must exist if certain cosmological theories of the formation of the universe are true.) □ *He's attending a seminar on wimps this week.* □ *I'm not convinced by theories that depend on wimps.*

wimpish AND **wimpy** *mod.* weak; inept. □ *You are just a wimpy nerd!* □ *Come on, don't be so wimpy.*

wimpy See WIMPISH.

winch *vb.* to go courting. (Scots usage.) □ *Are you winchin? (Do you have a steady boy- (or girl-)friend?)* □ *Oh, they have been winching as long as I can remember.*

windbag AND **bag of wind** *n.* someone who speaks much but says nothing of value. □ *Oh just be quiet, you windbag!* □ *Talk, talk, talk! She's nothing but a big bag of wind.*

window (of opportunity) *n.* a short-lived opportunity. □ *We've got a window here; let's use it.* □ *I think we'll have a window of opportunity soon.*

wind-pills *n.* beans. □ *I gather you've been eating wind-pills again, Otto.* □ *They say wind-pills are good for you, despite everything.*

wind someone up 1. *vb. phr.* to irritate or provoke someone. □ *That remark really wound her up, once she realised what it meant.* □ *The whole business began to wind me up after a while.* **2.** *vb. phr.* to play a practical joke on someone. □ *Come on, you're winding me up.* □ *Would I wind you up? It's gospel!*

wind something up *vb. phr.* to bring something to a conclusion; to end something. □ *OK folks, it's time to wind this meeting up.* □ *The bank stepped in and wound the company up.*

wind-up *n.* a practical joke. □ *No more wind-ups, please.* □ *I'm sorry. That was a wind-up that went wrong.*

windy 1. *mod.* nervous; frightened. (From the supposed tendency of such feelings to cause flatulence.) □ *I feel a little windy every time I have to fly.* □ *She's a very windy individual; try not to frighten her off.* **2. long-winded** *mod.* verbose; boring. □ *She's so long-winded! Won't she ever let up?* □ *Here comes old long-winded Charlie. Once he gets started, he never stops.*

wine grape *n.* a Roman Catholic. (Offensive. Also a term of address. Scots usage. Rhyming slang, derived as follows: wine grape ≈ [pape] = Roman Catholic.) □ *Willy thinks the wine grapes are taking over these days.* □ *Willy actually moved house because a wine grape moved in next door!*

wine mopper AND **mopper** *n.* an alcoholic who drinks cheap reinforced wine. □ *Some wine mopper came in and asked for twenty pence.* □ *You see mopper after mopper all up and down Maxwell Street.*

winge See WHINGE.

winger 1. *n.* a friend. □ *We've been wingers for years. Went to school together.* □ *This is my winger, Wally.* **2.** *n.* a steward or attendant on board a ship. □ *Ask the winger to bring me another whisky and soda.* □ *Winger! Can you come to Cabin 37, please?* **3.** *n.* a team player in a wing position. □ *Brian is an excellent winger and we think he's done real good.* □ *Clive is our new winger.* **4.** *n.* an effeminate man; a passive male homosexual. (Crude.) □ *Tom is getting to be such a winger.* □ *Why does he work so hard to look like he's a winger?*

wing it *vb. phr.* to improvise something; to extemporise. □ *I lost my lecture notes, so I had to wing it.* □ *Don't worry. Just go out there and wing it.*

wings *n.* the boards carried by a sandwich-board man. (Normally plural.) □ *Once, he was reduced to walking around with wings advertising a barber's shop to make some money.* □ *What people don't realise is that wings are actually very heavy.*

winker *n.* the female sexual organ. (Taboo.) □ *They dance completely nude in there, with winker and everything on view.* □ *A woman who shows her winker is just the lowest.*

winkie AND **winky** *n.* the male sexual organ. (Taboo.) □ *Myra says winkies are disgusting but then Myra's strange.* □ *Only small boys wave their winkies about like that, Wayne. Put it away!*

winkle See LITTLE MAN.

winkle-picker *n.* a shoe with a long pointed toe. □ *Have you ever seen any-*

thing as ridiculous as these winkle-pickers? □ *Winkle-pickers are pretty rare nowadays.*

winkle someone or something out *vb. phr.* to displace, extract or evict someone or something. □ *Oh, I'll winkle it out soon enough.* □ *Go and winkle him out and get him back here!*

winkle something out *vb. phr.* to discover something. □ *They've winkled it out at last.* □ *I think I've winkled out what you're up to!*

winner 1. *n.* an excellent person or thing. □ *This one is a real winner.* □ *He's no winner, but he'll do.* **2.** *n.* someone or something that is a success. □ *Congratulations on your great winner.* □ *One more winner like that and we'll be happy.*

winners and losers *n.* trousers. (Rhyming slang. Scots usage, where *trousers* is pronounced TROO-serz.) □ *There he was, kicked out into the street wi' no winners and losers!* □ *What have ye done wi' ma winners and losers, wumman? (What have you done with my trousers, woman?)*

wino *n.* a degenerate alcoholic; an excessively drunk vagrant. (Crude. Originally one who drank cheap wine, but now broadened to cover other forms of alcoholic beverage that deliver a similar effect.) □ *By midnight the winos had gone into their stupors, and we got that part of town to ourselves.* □ *I gave the wino some money to help him stop the shakes.*

win some, lose some *phr.* "Sometimes one wins; other times one loses." □ *Too bad. Sorry about that. Win some, lose some.* □ *"Win some, lose some" doesn't mean you never win at all.*

wiped out 1. *mod.* alcohol or drug intoxicated. □ *Harry was too wiped out to drive.* □ *Oh Lord, I'm really wiped out.* **2.** *mod.* [of a person or thing] exhausted. □ *I'm so wiped out that I just want to go home and go to bed.* □ *Boy, am I wiped out!* **3.** *mod.* broke. □ *I'm totally wiped out. Not enough bread for grub.* □ *Repair bills left us totally wiped out.*

wipe someone out 1. *vb. phr.* to eliminate or kill someone. (Underworld.

See also WIPED OUT.) □ *Max almost wiped Bruno out.* □ *Who wiped out Lefty?* **2.** *vb. phr.* to exhaust or tire someone. □ *The game wiped me out.* □ *Jogging always wipes me out.* **3.** *vb. phr.* to ruin someone financially. □ *The loss of my job wiped us out.* □ *The new regulations ruined the fishing industry and wiped out everyone in the region.*

wipe something *vb.* to wipe out or destroy information, especially data, stored on a computer. (Computer jargon.) □ *If you do that you'll wipe all the data.* □ *That kid who was playing on the computer seems to have wiped the entire hard disk!*

wipe something out *vb. phr.* to use up all of something. □ *I wiped the biscuits out—not all at once, of course.* □ *Who wiped out the strawberry jam?*

wipe the deck with someone AND **wipe the floor with someone 1.** *vb. phr.* to defeat humiliatingly or totally. □ *It was a real one-sided contest. Harry wiped the floor with Bruno.* □ *If it comes to a fight, he'll wipe the deck with you.* **2.** *vb. phr.* to entirely defeat or devastate; to wipe out. □ *Charlie was great! He wiped the deck with the other guy.* □ *Since we wiped the floor against Iraq in 1990, how come Saddam is still there in Bagdad?*

wipe the floor with someone See WIPE THE DECK WITH SOMEONE.

wipe the slate clean 1. *vb. phr.* to cancel a debt. □ *Please, can you wipe the slate clean?* □ *I'm not going to wipe the slate clean for you!* **2.** *vb. phr.* to forget or forgive an earlier misdemeanour. □ *Could you possibly see your way to wipe the slate clean?* □ *If I wipe the slate clean, what's in it for me?*

wire *vb.* to install electronic eavesdropping equipment. □ *Somebody wired the ambassador's office.* □ *They say the minister wired his own office to make himself look like a victim.*

wired *mod.* nervous; over-alert; hyperactive. □ *He's pretty wired because of the election.* □ *I get wired before an exam.*

wired for sound *mod.* wearing earphones. □ *He won't hear you while he's wired for sound.* □ *I don't think I've ever seen him not wired for sound.*

wiseacre See WISE GUY.

wise-arse *n.* a presumptuous SMART ALEC. (Taboo.) □ *Who's the wise-arse who put sugar in the salt shaker?* □ *Look, wise-arse, watch your tongue!*

wisecrack *n.* a smart or witty saying or remark. □ *Fewer wisecracks and more work would be appreciated, Walter.* □ *All right, who came up with that wisecrack?*

wise guy AND **wiseacre** *n.* someone who seems to know better than everyone else on every topic. (Often used in an ironic or negative sense. Compare with KNOW-ALL. Also a term of address.) □ *Look, wise guy, mind your own business!* □ *If you're such a wiseacre, you can tell us what the solution to this almighty mess is.*

wise to something or someone *mod.* aware of the situation, particularly any problems, associated with someone or something. □ *He was wise to that before he met us.* □ *I want to be wise to the situation before I meet with them.*

wishy-washy *mod.* indecisive; insipid; weak. □ *Don't be such a wishy-washy wimp.* □ *She is so wishy-washy!*

witch's hat *n.* a portable, plastic traffic cone. □ *There were thousands of witch's hats along the side of the road, ready for use.* □ *The car ran out of control into the work area, sending dozens of witch's hats flying in every direction.*

with a bang *mod.* In a flamboyant or exciting manner. (Especially with *go out, quit* and *finish*.) □ *The party started off with a bang.* □ *The old year went out with a bang.*

with bells on AND **with (brass) knobs on** *mod.* emphatically; without any doubt whatsoever; enthusiastically. □ *Do I want to go? With bells on I do!* □ *I assured Mac that if he tried any more funny stuff he'd get repaid with brass knobs on.*

with (brass) knobs on See WITH BELLS ON.

with flying colours *mod.* flamboyantly; boldly. □ *Heidi won first place with flying colours.* □ *Paul came home with flying colours after the match.*

within a hair(s-breadth) of something See WITHIN AN ACE OF SOMETHING.

within an ace of something AND **within a hair(s-breadth) of something** *mod.* very close to something. □ *I came within an ace of getting into Parliament.* □ *We were within a hairs-breadth of beating the all-time record.*

with it *mod.* alert; on the ball. □ *Martin is not exactly with it.* □ *Come on, mate. Get with it.*

with (one's) eyes (wide) open *mod.* totally aware of what is going on. □ *I went into this with my eyes open.* □ *We all started out with our eyes open but didn't realise what could happen to us.*

With or without? *interrog.* "Do you wish your tea or coffee to be with or without sugar or with or without milk?" □ *How do you like your tea? With or without?* □ *Do you drink your coffee with or without?*

without a hitch *mod.* with no problem(s). □ *Everything went off without a hitch.* □ *We hoped the job would go off without a hitch.*

without (so much as) a for or by your leave AND **without (so much as) a with or by your leave** *phr.* "without (the least hint of) permission." □ *Without so much as a for or by your leave, they just walked into our house.* □ *He left, without a with or by your leave.*

without (so much as) a with or by your leave See WITHOUT (SO MUCH AS) A FOR OR BY YOUR LEAVE.

with someone *mod.* in agreement with someone. □ *Are you with me?* □ *We are all with you, John.*

witter on *vb. phr.* to speak at great length to no purpose or without coming to any sort of point. □ *There she was, wittering on as usual.* □ *If you did not witter on all the time but tried listening occasionally, you might just learn something.*

wizard *mod.* remarkable or outstanding. □ *You have a really wizard idea there, Harry.* □ *She's a really wizard girl.*

wodge *n.* a lump or clump. □ *There was a wodge of the stuff on the plate, but I wasn't going to eat it.* □ *All right, give me a wodge.*

Wog 1. *n.* any non-white or foreign person. (Racially offensive. Applies especially to someone from the Middle or Far East; reputedly the word is an abbreviation of "Worthy Oriental Gentlemen," but this is apocryphal.) □ *A Wog came into the restaurant and asked for Harry.* □ *Harry asked what the Wog wanted, but no one knew.* **2.** *n.* the Arabic language. (Racially offensive.) □ *Do you speak Wog?* □ *Why bother learning Wog? Most Arabs seem to speak some English.*

wolf *n.* a sexually bold and aggressive male; a would-be seducer. (Crude.) □ *He sees himself as a lady-killer. The girls see him more like an old-fashioned wolf.* □ *And then this wolf comes up to me and without a word starts holding my hand!*

wolf something down AND **woof something down** *vb. phr.* to gobble something up; to bolt down food or drink. □ *Enjoy your food. Don't just wolf it down.* □ *But I enjoy woofing down food more than anything.*

wolf-whistle *n.* a whistle made by a man to show appreciation of a sexually-attractive woman. □ *He gave me a wolf-whistle! A real wolf-whistle! That's sexist and disgusting!* □ *He gave me a wolf-whistle! A real wolf-whistle! What a morale booster for any girl!*

wolly *n.* a policeman in uniform. □ *Think about how the wolly on the beat is affected by this cold.* □ *The wolly stopped at the door, tried the lock, and moved on.*

womble *n.* anyone considered unfashionably dressed or uninteresting. (From a TV puppet show popular with young children in the 1970s.) □ *Oh, Sammy's just a womble.* □ *I don't want to be a womble; I want nice things to wear!*

wonk 1. *n.* a cadet or new recruit. □ *I don't think much of the wonk. Do you?* □ *We've got some wonks starting today. Treat them nicely.* **2.** *n.* an ineffective person. □ *What's a wonk like that doing around here?* □ *I'm sorry but we really don't need another wonk working here.* **3.** *n.* a male homosexual. (Crude.) □ *I hear that you-know-who is a wonk.* □ *He doesn't like being called a wonk.*

wonky 1. *n.* shaky or unsteady. □ *We've got a wonky mess down there, I can tell you.* □ *That sounds like a really wonky way of organising things.* **2.** *n.* incorrect or wrong. □ *No, no, that's all wonky. Let me show you the right way...* □ *He's just wrong; completely wonky.* **3.** *mod.* obscene; pornographic. (A euphemism.) (Crude.) □ *Have a look at this wonky video.* □ *Otto has a large collection of wonky videos and magazines.* **4.** See also WACKY.

wooden-eared See CLOTH-EARED.

wooden ears See CLOTH EARS.

wooden spoon See BOOBY-PRIZE.

woodentop 1. *n.* a policeman in uniform. (See WOOLLY.) □ *The woodentop stopped at the door, tried the lock, and moved on.* □ *Think about how the woodentop on the beat is affected by this cold.* **2.** *n.* a slow-witted person. (Offensive. Also a term of address.) □ *Get out of here, you woodentop!* □ *What a woodentop that woman can be.*

woodman *n.* a prison sentence of one month. □ *A woodman can be bad enough, if you've never been banged up before.* □ *I don't think I fancy prison at all, not even for a woodman.*

woodwork *n.* soccer goalpost frames. □ *The idea is to kick the ball between the woodwork, you see.* □ *The goalkeeper's job is to stop you getting the ball between the woodwork.*

woof one's custard *vb. phr.* to empty one's stomach; to vomit. (Crude.) □ *Fred is woofing his custard because of that lousy fish she served.* □ *One look at that food, and I wanted to woof my custard, too.*

woof something down See WOLF SOMETHING DOWN.

woof(ter) *n.* a male homosexual. (Crude.) □ *So what if he's a woofter? He can still vote, can't he?* □ *Tom is getting to be such a woofter.*

woollies *n.* woollen underwear. □ *Now it's getting colder, Harry's asking where his woollies are.* □ *I wear woollies all winter as they are so comfortable and warm.*

Woollies *n.* Woolworth's chain store. □ *Is there a Woollies near here?* □ *He could spend hours in Woollies just looking, never buying anything.*

woolly 1. *n.* a woollen garment such as a sweater. □ *It's winter, and time for my woollies.* □ *He's sitting over there, wearing a woolly.* **2.** *n.* a policeman in uniform. (See WOODENTOP.) □ *The woollies are here looking for you again, Joe.* □ *What have you been doing to interest that woolly this time?*

woopsie *n.* an embarrassing error. □ *Woops! I've done another woopsie!* □ *That was a silly woopsie. I'm sorry.*

woozled AND **woozy 1.** *mod.* intoxicated due to drink. □ *I felt a little woozy, but that didn't stop me from having more.* □ *Woozled as I am, I can still drive. Now, give me back my bees.* **2.** *mod.* dizzy or confused, perhaps due to lack of sleep. □ *Aren't you always woozy at this time of day?* □ *I'm still sort of woozy. Give me a minute or two to wake up.*

woozy See WOOZLED.

Wop *n.* an Italian person. (Offensive.) □ *He said he was not a racist, he just hated this particular Wop!* □ *Don't call Italian people Wops, please. It is very offensive and racist.*

words *n.* an argument. □ *I'm sorry about these words we had yesterday, but it was all your fault.* □ *Who started these words anyway?*

work a flanker See DO A FLANKER.

workaholic *n.* someone who is obsessed with work. □ *Jerry is a workaholic. He can't enjoy going on holiday.* □ *Are workaholics really productive?*

working girl *n.* a prostitute. (Crude.) □ *The Old Bill hauled her in because she looked like a working girl.* □ *Clare dresses like a working girl.*

work oneself up (into a lather) AND **work oneself up (into a sweat) 1.** *vb. phr.* to work very hard and sweat very much. (In the manner that a horse works up a lather.) □ *Don't work yourself up into a lather. We don't need to finish this today.* □ *I worked myself into a sweat getting this stuff ready.* **2.** *vb. phr.* to get excited or angry. (An elaboration of WORK ONESELF UP TO SOMETHING.) □ *Now, now, don't work yourself up over this!* □ *He had worked himself into such a sweat, I was afraid he would have a stroke.* **3.** *vb. phr.* to allow oneself to become emotionally upset. (Compare with STEW.) □ *Terry worked himself up, until I thought he would scream.* □ *Don't work yourself up into a lather over Tracy. She's just not worth it.*

work oneself up (into a sweat) See WORK ONESELF UP (INTO A LATHER).

work oneself up to something *vb. phr.* to get oneself mentally ready to do something. □ *I spent all morning working myself up to taking the driver's test.* □ *I had to work myself up to it little by little.*

works 1. *n.* a hypodermic syringe used to inject drugs. (Always with *the.*) □ *He got out the works and did it right there—I mean, in front of everybody in the cafe.* □ *Got the works, pal? I need a fix.* **2.** *n.* the entire amount; everything. (Always with *the.*) □ *I'd like my hamburger with onions, pickles, tomato sauce, mustard—the works.* □ *She's getting the works at the beauty shop—cut, wash, dye and set.*

work someone over *vb. phr.* to threaten, intimidate or beat up someone. □ *Bruno threatened to work Sam over.* □ *Bruno had worked over Terry, and Sam knew that this was no idle threat.*

works outing *n.* a short pleasure-trip for employees, organised and usually paid for by their employer. □ *We're off on the works outing tomorrow.* □ *The annual works outing was a disaster. As usual.*

work the oracle 1. *vb. phr.* to influence events in secret or without being noticed. □ *How do you expect me to work the oracle for you when I don't have anything to do with the place any more?* □ *Don't worry, Uncle James always managed to work the oracle in* *the end, somehow or other.* **2.** See also VERBAL.

work the streets *vb. phr.* to work as a street prostitute. (Crude.) □ *A lot of them work the streets in this part of town.* □ *If you work the streets around here the cops will pick you up.*

world and his wife *n.* everybody. (Normally with *the.*) □ *It was as if the world and his wife were in our garden that afternoon.* □ *I thought this was a secret, but if you feel the world and his wife should know all about our private business, feel free...*

world is one's oyster *phr.* one rules the world; one is in charge of everying; everything in the world is going one's way. (Always with *the.*) □ *I feel like the world is my oyster, today.* □ *The world is my oyster! I'm in love!*

worm *n.* a repellent person, usually a male. □ *Lord, you're a worm, Tom.* □ *I'd like Fred better if he wasn't such a worm.*

worry and strife See TROUBLE AND STRIFE.

worse for wear 1. *mod.* quite intoxicated due to drink. (Normally with *the.*) □ *You were the worse for wear last night. What's up?* □ *The three came in, the worse for wear again.* **2.** *mod.* damaged through use. (Normally with *the.*) □ *Eventually, every machine becomes worse for wear, you know.* □ *The truth is it's the worse for wear; you will just have to get a new one.* **3.** *mod.* injured. (Normally with *the.*) □ *Tom needs exercise. He's the worse for wear.* □ *Fred had a little accident, and he's the worse for wear.*

worst-case scenario *n.* the worse outcome considered. (Compare with BEST-CASE SCENARIO.) □ *Now, let's look at the worst-case scenario.* □ *In the worst-case scenario, we're all dead—but then that's true of the best-case scenario also.*

worth a bob or two 1. *mod.* [of things] valuable. □ *Now this painting must be worth a bob or two.* □ *Look at that house over there! It must be worth a bob or two.* **2.** *mod.* [of people]

wealthy. □ *My Uncle Fred is worth a bob or two, and he fully intends to take it all with him, if he can just figure out how.* □ *Mr Wilson is worth a bob or two, but he is also generous with his money.*

Wotcher! *interj.* a friendly greeting between men. □ *Wotcher mate, how are you?* □ *Wotcher! OK, are you?*

would not be seen dead *phr.* would not do something under any circumstances. □ *I wouldn't be seen dead going out with Bruno!* □ *Martha would not be seen dead going into a place like that.*

wouldn't touch someone or something with a bargepole See WOULDN'T TOUCH SOMEONE OR SOMETHING WITH A TEN-FOOT POLE.

wouldn't touch someone or something with a ten-foot pole AND **wouldn't touch someone or something with a bargepole** *phr.* would not get involved with someone or something under any circumstances. □ *Forget it. I wouldn't touch it with a bargepole.* □ *Tom said he wouldn't touch Tracy with a ten-foot pole.*

Would you believe (it)? *interrog.* amazing; unbelievable. □ *He actually tried to get me to scratch his bare back! Would you believe?* □ *Would you believe it? A half-per-cent pay rise?*

WPC *n.* a Woman Police Constable. □ *Ask the WPC what she wants, please.* □ *There's a WPC here asking for you.*

Wrap it! See SHUT UP!

wrapped up (in someone or something) *mod.* concerned or obsessed with someone or something. □ *Sally is pretty wrapped up in herself.* □ *I'm too wrapped up in my charity work to get a job.*

wrapped up (with someone or something) *mod.* busy with someone or something. □ *He's wrapped up with a client right now.* □ *I'll talk to you when I'm not so wrapped up.*

Wrap up! 1. *exclam.* "Shut up!" □ *Look Barry, take some advice. Wrap up!* □ *Wrap up! You sound ridiculous.* **2.** See also SHUT UP!

wrinkle *n.* a useful idea; a clever tip. □

Fred came up with a new wrinkle for the ad campaign. □ *Here's a wrinkle for you. Nobody has ever tried this one.*

wrinkly *n.* an old person. (Offensive. Also a term of address.) □ *Just remember we'll each of us be a wrinkly ourselves one day, with luck.* □ *Take care where there are wrinklies crossing the road.*

writer See CROAKER.

wrong 'un *n.* a dishonest person. □ *Let's face it, he's a wrong 'un.* □ *Even*

a wrong 'un has to earn a living, but honestly!

WYSIWYG *phr.* "What you see on the screen is what will print on the printer." (Computer jargon and an acronym. Compare with WHAT YOU SEE IS WHAT YOU GET.) □ *This computer gives you these WYSIWYG features that everyone wants.* □ *I need a system that's WYSIWYG. I have no imagination.*

X

X *n.* a written symbol of a kiss, sometimes found at the end of a letter sent between lovers. □ *I love you. XXXXXXX.* □ *Lots of love and Xs.*

X marks the spot. *sent.* "This is the exact place!" (A catch phrase.) □ *This is where it happened. X marks the spot.* □ *X marks the spot where we first met.*

Xmas *n.* Christmas. □ *Well, it's October, and time to buy Xmas presents again.* □ *Xmas Trees For Sale Here!*

x-rated *mod.* sexually explicit; pornographic. (From the former classification of such films.) □ *When I arrived home, Willy and his pals were in the living room, watching an x-rated video.* □ *What they were doing was disgusting! It was just like watching an x-rated film!...I suppose...I've never seen one, of course.*

Y

yack See YAK.

yacker(s) See ACKER(S).

yackety-yack See YACKING.

yacking AND **yack-yack; yackety-yack** *n.* idle chatter; meaningless talk; loud, stupid talk; gossip. □ *I've heard enough yacking to last me a lifetime.* □ *That's enough yackety-yack. Can we get down to some serious business now?*

yack (on) *vb. (phr.)* to chatter in an idle or meaningless fashion; to gossip. □ *He's always yacking on about something or other, but I like him.* □ *My, isn't Mary yacking a lot today?*

yack-yack See YACKING.

yak AND **yack 1.** *n.* a chat. □ *We had a nice little yack and then left for work.* □ *Drop by for a yak sometime.* **2.** *vb.* to talk. □ *Stop yakking for a minute.* □ *I need to yack with you about something.*

Yank(ee) 1. *n.* an American. □ *Some Yankee was here looking for you this afternoon.* □ *Mr Big's talking to a Yank just now.* **2.** *mod.* American. □ *These roads are too narrow for Yankee cars.* □ *We flew to America in a Yank plane.*

Yankee *n.* a form of bet that involves backing four horses in one race. □ *A Yankee on the three o'clock race, please.* □ *I don't like placing a Yankee.*

yank off *vb. phr.* to masturbate. (Taboo.) □ *If he gets frustrated enough, he yanks off.* □ *Timmy's mother caught him yanking off in the garden shed.*

yank someone's chain *vb. phr.* to irritate or annoy someone. □ *Yanking her chain is not going to correct the mistake.* □ *So I made a mistake! I wish you'd stop yanking my chain over it.*

yank-tank *n.* a large American car. □ *Like my new yank-tank, darling?* □ *I'm rather partial to yank-tanks.*

yap 1. *vb.* to chatter; to gossip. □ *Who's yapping so much in here?* □ *Did you just come here to yap?* **2.** *n.* idle chatter. □ *Have you ever listened to her yap?* □ *Why all this yap?* **3.** *n.* the mouth. □ *Why don't you just close your yap for a moment and listen?* □ *How do we get her yap closed so the rest can talk?*

yard *n.* the male sexual organ. (Taboo.) □ *The doctor told him that he'd got something wrong with his yard.* □ *That's all very well Myra, but where would the world be without yards?*

Yard 1. *n.* New Scotland Yard, the headquarters of the Metropolitan Police. (Always with *the*.) □ *Do all the policemen really live in the Yard, dad?* □ *That's the Yard over there, son, where the fuzz live.* **2.** *n.* the Metropolitan Police. (Normally with *the*.) □ *The Yard are after me!* □ *The Yard finally caught up with the Streatham Strangler.*

Yardies *n.* gangs of criminals, originally from Jamaica or the descendants of Jamaican immigrants in Britain. (Normally in the plural. Always with *the*.) □ *The Yardies own the drug business around here.* □ *Don't get mixed up with the Yardies, whatever you do.*

Yardy *n.* an individual member of the YARDIES. □ *Look at him at the corner; I'm sure he's a Yardy.* □ *Don't mess with a Yardy.*

Yarmouth capon See BILLINGSGATE PHEASANT.

yatter *vb.* to chatter at length about nothing much. □ *What are you yattering about now, woman?* □ *Yatter, yatter! That's all you ever do!*

yeah *interj.* yes. □ HARRY: *Are you okay?* BRUNO: *Yeah.* □ HARRY: *Yeah?* BRUNO: *Yeah! I said yeah! Did you hear me say yeah?*

Yec(c)h! AND **Yuc(c)h!** *exclam.* a theatrically expression of disgust or horror. □ *Oh, yech! What's that stuff?* □ *Yucch! It's moving!*

Ye gods (and little fishes)! *exclam.* a theatrically humorous expression of astonishment or surprise. □ *Ye gods! What is this stuff here?* □ *Ye gods and little fishes! Now my hair is falling out!*

yellow *mod.* cowardly. □ *Who says I'm yellow?* □ *Bruno says you're yellow. D'you want to make something of it?*

yellow-bellied *mod.* cowardly. □ *You are a yellow-bellied coward!* □ *I'm not yellow-bellied!* □ *What yellow-bellied low-life ran off with my horse?*

yellow duster AND **yellow flag; yellow jack** *n.* a sick-flag flown from a ship. □ *You could see the yellow duster fluttering from her yardarm.* □ *The ship was flying the yellow jack.*

yellow flag See YELLOW DUSTER.

yellow jack See YELLOW DUSTER.

yellow (satin) AND **yellow silk; yellow velvet 1.** *n.* an oriental woman considered as a sex object. (Racially offensive.) □ *They are not yellow satin! They are people!* □ *What a luscious piece of yellow velvet that woman was!* **2.** *n.* sexual intercourse with an oriental woman. (Racially offensive.) □ *Harry always likes some yellow satin.* □ *I think talking about yellow velvet like that is disgusting.*

yellow silk See YELLOW (SATIN).

yellow streak (down someone's back) *n.* a tendency toward cowardice. □ *Tim's got a yellow streak down his back a mile wide.* □ *Get rid of that yellow streak. Show some courage.*

yellow stuff *n.* gold. (Always with *the*.) □ *He opened the small bag. "Look," he said, "That's real yellow stuff."* □ *So this guy put all his money into yellow stuff and lost a fortune.*

yellow velvet See YELLOW (SATIN)

yer *poss. pro.* "your. " (Eye-dialect, used in the examples in this dictionary.) □ *Yer old woman's looking for you, Bert.* □ *What's that you've got in yer hand, mate?*

yer actual something *n.* the genuine, real or true something. □ *Look mate, it's yer actual genuine fake gold leaf.* □ *I'm afraid yer actual real Porsche turns out to be a ringer.*

Yer hied's aw full o mince! *exclam.* "What you say is complete nonsense!" (Scots usage.) □ *Yer hied's aw full o mince, son! Try again!* □ *I don't care what you say, yer hied's aw full o mince!*

yes-girl *n.* a girl who can't say no. (Crude.) □ *Sandra is the office yes-girl.* □ *Otto says yes-girls provide a necessary public service.*

yes-man *n.* a sycophant; a creep. □ *You are just a plain old yes-man.* □ *That yes-man actually gave the boss a bottle of wine for her birthday.*

Yid *n.* a Jewish person. (Offensive.) □ *Why can you not be polite to Yids?* □ *Y'know, Otto, if you call a Jew a Yid, he's likely to get nasty.*

Yiddish piano See JEWISH PIANO.

Yippee! *exclam.* a cry of pleasure. □ *Yippee! We've won!* □ *Yippee, that's great news!*

Y'know (what I mean)? *phr.* a request for assurance added to the end of statements. (Compare with AN' THAT.) □ *So we sorted out these things okay, y'know?* □ *So we gave Otto what he deserved, y'know what I mean?*

Yo! *interj.* "Hello!"; "Emphatically yes!" □ *Yo, Michael! What's happening?* □ *Yo! That's it! We've won!*

yobbery *n.* hooliganism. □ *Something has to be done about all the yobbery we're getting around here nowadays.* □ *The police are determined to wipe out yobbery.*

yobbish *mod.* in the manner of a hooligan. □ *Yobbish behaviour like that will get you in jail.* □ *We don't want yobbish youths like that in here.*

yob(bo) *n.* a lout or hooligan. (Back-slang from "boy.") □ *Who's that yobbo* *kicking at the side of your car?* □ *Tell that yob we don't want him here any more.*

yodel *vb.* to empty one's stomach; to vomit. (Crude.) □ *I've been yodelling because I have the flu.* □ *I've got to go and yodel!*

yomp AND **tab** *n.* a forced military march in full kit. □ *It was the British Army yomp across the Falkland Islands that won that war.* □ *Right lads, there's a tab tomorrow.*

yoni *n.* the female sexual organ. (Taboo.) □ *He got arrested trying to look up women's skirts in the hope of seeing their yoni.* □ *What do you mean, you can see my yoni? Oh my god, I've forgotten to put on panties!*

yonks *n.* a very long time; ages. □ *It's been like that for yonks.* □ *Just because it's not been changed for yonks is no reason not to change it now.*

yon time *n.* very late at night. (Scots usage.) □ *Come on, yous yins, it's yon time and Ah want to get some kip. (Come on you lot, it's very late and I want to sleep.)* □ *What are you doing coming home at yon time?*

yop on someone AND **bubble on someone** *vb. phr.* to inform on someone. (Scots usage.) □ *Shuggy yopped to the polis on Wullie. (Hugh informed on William to the police.)* □ *Anyone who bubbles on someone is scum; okay pal? (Anyone who informs on someone is beneath contempt, okay friend?)*

you and me 1. *n.* a cup of tea. (Rhyming slang.) □ *Ah, you and me! Always welcome.* □ *A cup of you and me was just what she needed.* **2.** *n.* an act of urination. (Crude. Rhyming slang, linked as follows: you and me ≈ [pee] = urination.) □ *Where do you go around here for a you and me?* □ *If you need a you and me, go through there.*

You and who else? AND **You and whose army?** *interrog.* "Who besides you are threatening me?"; "You're going to have be more impressive than that before I take you seriously." □ *You're gonna beat me up? You and who else?* □ *You and whose army are gonna yank my chain?*

You and whose army? See YOU AND WHO ELSE?

You asked for it! *exclam.* "Here comes the trouble you deserve!" □ *So you want the full treatment? You asked for it!* □ *So, you wanted to hear both sides of the story? Well, you asked for it!*

you bet *interj.* "certainly"; "without doubt." □ *Can you have two? You bet.* □ *You bet; it's all settled.*

You bet your boots! *exclam.* "Absolutely certain!"; "Without any doubt!" □ *Am I happy? You bet your boots!* □ *You bet your boots I'm angry about this.*

You bet your sweet life! *exclam.* "That is absolutely correct!" □ *Happy? You bet your sweet life!* □ *You bet your sweet life I'm glad!*

You can say that again! *exclam.* "I agree absolutely!" □ *You can say that again! It's really hot!* □ *You can say that again! You hit the nail right on the head.*

You can't get there from here. *sent.* "There is no solution to this problem." □ *I'm sure you can't get there from here, the problem as stated cannot be solved.* □ *Sorry, perpetual motion is not possible. You can't get there from here.*

You can't take it with you. *sent.* "You cannot take wealth with you when you die." □ *Enjoy it now. You can't take it with you.* □ *My uncle doesn't believe that you can't take it with you. He's going to try very hard.*

You can't win 'em all. See YOU CAN'T WIN THEM ALL.

You can't win them all. AND **You can't win 'em all.** *sent.* "No one succeeds all the time." (Said as consolation when someone fails.) □ *Don't fret about it, Tom. You can't win them all.* □ *You can't win 'em all, but then you can't lose 'em all, either.*

You could have knocked me down with a feather. *sent.* "I was completely surprised." □ *I was shocked. You could have knocked me down with a feather.* □ *You could have knocked me down with a feather, I was so surprised!*

You don't know the half of it. *sent.* "Things are far more complicated than you think."; "Things are far worse than you think." □ *You think that's bad? You don't know the half of it.* □ *You don't know the half of it, and I'm too much a lady to tell.*

You (had) better believe it! *exclam.* "Absolutely correct!" □ *It's true. You better believe it.* □ *Yes, this is the best, and you had better believe it!*

you lot *n.* all of you. □ *Right, you lot. Listen to what I have to say.* □ *You lot have got a lot of work to do.*

young fogey *n.* a young person with old-fashioned ideas, particularly if those tend toward the right wing in politics. □ *Here was one young fogey that was different from the others, he thought.* □ *I don't think I could take another young fogey like that today.*

young Turk *n.* a young person eager to improve or change things. □ *That young Turk is causing difficulties again.* □ *Not another young Turk!*

You reckon? *interrog.* "Do you believe that to be true?" □ *Really? You reckon?* □ *If you reckon that, you'll reckon anything.*

you reckon *interj.* "So you say, but I am not convinced." □ *Well, you reckon. We'll see.* □ *You reckon, but you're wrong. Try again.*

Your guess is as good as mine. *sent.* "I don't know either." □ *I don't know. Your guess is as good as mine.* □ *Your guess is as good as mine as to when the train will get in.*

Your place or mine? *interrog.* "Shall we carry on an affair at your dwelling or mine?" □ *Then I said to her, "Your place or mine?" Then she clobbered me.* □ *Your place or mine? It doesn't matter.*

yours truly *n.* "me," the speaker. □ *If yours truly had a problem like that, it would be settled by nightfall.* □ *If it was*

up to yours truly, there wouldn't be any such problem.

You've got another think coming. *sent.* "You are absolutely wrong. Think again." □ *If you think I'm going to let you get away with that, you've got another think coming.* □ *You've got another think coming if you think I'll do it.*

You what? *interrog.* "I do not understand you."; "What are you saying?" □ *You what? Eh? Say that again.* □ *You what? That can't be right.*

yoyo **1.** *mod.* stupid. □ *Ask that yoyo creep to move along.* □ *That is the world's yoyoest joke!* **2.** *n.* a fool; a silly person. □ *Who's the yoyo in the bright orange trousers?* □ *Some yoyo wants to talk to you on the phone.*

Yuc(c)h! See YEC(C)H!

yuck AND **yuk** **1.** *exclam.* "Horrible!" (Usually YUCK!) □ *Oh, yuck! Get that horrible thing out of here!* □ *Yuck! It looks alive!* **2.** *n.* someone or something disgusting. (Also a term of address.) □ *I don't want any of that yuck on my plate!* □ *Who is that yuk in the red bandana?*

yucky *mod.* nasty. □ *What is this yucky pink stuff on my plate?* □ *This tastes yucky.*

yummy **1.** *mod.* delightful; beautiful. □ *Who is that yummy blonde?* □ *This evening was just yummy.* **2.** See also SCRUMMY.

Yum-yum! *exclam.* "excellent!"; "wonderful!" □ *This wine is really yum-yum!* □ *Boy, this fishing rod is yum-yum!*

yuppie **1.** *n.* a young urban professional. (Acronym.) □ *These yuppies are taking a lot of stick these days.* □ *Why pick on yuppies?* **2.** *mod.* having to do with YUPPIES. □ *I don't want to drive one of those yuppie cars.* □ *Have you got something against yuppie bummers?*

zap someone 1. *vb.* to kill someone. □ *The stress from it all nearly zapped him.* □ *I was afraid that one of those thugs would zap me.* **2.** *vb.* to pretend to stun someone with an toy gun of some sort. □ *Jimmy swung around the corner and zapped me.* □ *He zapped me with a water gun.* **3.** *vb.* to defeat someone heavily. □ *They zapped us 10-8.* □ *Fred zapped Tracy in the spelling bee.* **4.** *vb.* to criticise someone with extreme severity. □ *I thought my paper was good, but the prof zapped me for it.* □ *I was late, and the boss zapped me.*

zap something *vb.* to erase or destroy a program or data stored on a computer. (Computer jargon.) □ *To reset things, you have to zap the parameter RAM like this.* □ *That kid who was playing on the computer seems to have zapped all my work!*

zero *n.* an insignificant person; a nobody. □ *Ignore her. She's a zero around here.* □ *I want to be more in life than just another zero.*

zilch *n.* nothing. □ *And what do I get? Zilch, that's what!* □ *"Even zilch is too much," said the clerk.*

zing *n.* vigour; enthusiasm. □ *She's certainly got lots of zing.* □ *Show more zing! Let us know you're alive.*

zip(po) *n.* nothing. □ *There was nothing in the post today. Nothing. Zippo.* □ *I got zip from the booking agency all week.*

zippy 1. *mod.* bright; vigorous; lively. □ *It's wonderful to see John so zippy again after the difficult time he had.* □ *I feel zippy this morning!* **2.** *mod.* speedy; rapid. □ *Now here's a zippy little vehicle for you, sir.* □ *The car was moving along at a very zippy pace.*

zit *n.* a pimple. □ *Don't squeeze your zits on my mirror!* □ *That is one prize-winning zit on your nose.*

zit doctor *n.* a dermatologist. □ *The zit doctor I went to was a crater face!* □ *My zit doctor wears rubber gloves and has for years.*

zizz *n.* a snooze or nap. □ *I need some zizz before I get started again.* □ *I could use a zizz before I have to get to work.*

zombie *n.* someone with a corpse-like demeanour or vacant expression; a weird and frightening person. □ *Martin is practically a zombie. Doesn't he ever go out—in the daylight, I mean?* □ *Tracy's getting to look like a zombie. Is she well?*

zonked (out) 1. *mod.* intoxicated due to drink or drugs. □ *She's too zonked to drive.* □ *Jed was almost zonked out to unconsciousness.* **2.** *mod.* exhausted; asleep. □ *She was totally zonked out by the time I got home.* □ *I'm zonked. Good night.*

zonkey *n.* a cross between a donkey and a zebra. □ *We went to the zoo to see the zonkey.* □ *There are not too many zonkeys around, you know.*

zonk out *vb. phr.* to collapse from exhaustion; to go into a stupor from drugs or exhaustion. □ *I'm going to go home and zonk out.* □ *I went home after the trip and just zonked out.*

zulu *n.* a black person. (Racially offensive.) □ *So this zulu drives away in a BMW!* □ *Why should a BMW not belong to a zulu?*

PHRASE-FINDER INDEX

This is an index of the *non-initial* words that are found in the entry heads of this dictionary. Always try looking up an expression in the body of the dictionary first. If you do not find it, this index will help you locate it.

First, pick out any main word [except the first word] in the phrase you are seeking. Second, look that word up in this index to find the form of the phrase used in this dictionary. Third, look up the phrase in the main body of this dictionary. See *Hints* below.

Some of the words occurring in this dictionary do not occur as entries in this index. Single word entries are not indexed here and should be looked up in the dictionary directly. The initial words of compounds and phrases are not always listed in the index and should be looked up directly. Some words are omitted because they occur so frequently that their lists would cover many pages. Most prepositions, most personal pronouns, and other short words do not occur as entries in the index.

Hints

1. This is an index of forms, not meanings. The expressions in an index entry do not necessarily have any meaning in common. Consult the dictionary definitions for information about meaning.

2. When you are trying to find a slang or colloquial expression in this index, try first to look up any nouns that may be part of the expression.

3. In most expressions where a noun or pronoun is a variable part of the expression, it will be represented by the words *someone* or *some thing*. If you do not find the noun you want in the index, it may, in fact, be a variable word and you should look up another word.

4. When you locate the phrase you want, look it up in the main body of the dictionary.

ABSORBERS
shock absorbers
ACADEMY
laughing academy
ACCIDENT
street accident
ACCOUNT
of account
ACE
ace up one's sleeve □ cherry ace □
have (got) an ace up one's sleeve □
within an ace of something
ACID
acid house (party) □ acid test
ACRE
God's acre
ACROSS
come across
ACT
act a part □ clean one's act up □ get in
on the act □ get one's act together □
Old Pals Act
ACTION
action man □ back in action □ bit of
the action □ piece (of the action) □
slice of the action □ where the action is
ACTUAL
yer actual something
AD
small ad
ADAM
Adam and Eve □ Adam's ale □
Adam's wine □ fanny adams □ since
Adam was a boy □ sweet fanny adams
ADD
value-added entertainment
ADVANTAGE
take advantage of someone
ADVENTURE
denture adventure
ADVICE
take legal advice
AFFAIRS
Ugandan affairs
AFFLUENCE
under the affluence of incohol
AFLOAT
I'm afloat
AFRICAN
African lager □ African Woodbine
AFTER
day after the fair □ letch after some-
one □ look after number one □ morn-
ing after (the night before)

AGAIN
Alf's peed again. □ Come again? □
Run that by (me) again. □ There you
go (again)! □ You can say that again!
AGAINST
take against something □ up against it
□ up against the wall
AGE
donkey's ages □ know one's age □ of
great age □ rock of ages
AGONY
agony aunt □ agony column
AGREE
agree to disagree □ sweetheart
agreement
AHEAD
ahead of the game □ come out ahead
□ lengths ahead □ one jump ahead of
someone or something □ quit while
one is ahead □ streets ahead
AID
What is something in aid of? □
What's (all) something in aid of?
AIM
aim Archy at the Armitage □ aim for
the stars
AIR
air dancing □ airs and graces □
come up for air □ full of hot air □ give
one's bum an airing □ hot air □ in the
air □ up in the air (about someone or
something)
AISLES
roll in the aisles
ALE
Adam's ale
ALEC
smart Alec
ALIVE
Look alive!
ALL
all gas and gaiters □ all mouth and
trousers □ all of a doodah □ all over
bar the shouting □ all over someone
□ all over the place □ all over the shop
□ all piss and wind □ All right. □ all
serene □ all set □ all the best □ all the
hours God gives us □ all the rage □
all to buggery □ all to cock □ bit of
all right □ bugger all □ can't win
(th)em all □ carry all before one □
daddy of them all □ damn all □ Dash
it all! □ for all I know □ for (all) one's
trouble □ for good and all □ free for

500

all □ go all the way □ grand-daddy of them all □ Hang it all! □ have (got) all one's marbles □ jack all □ know all the angles □ laugh all the way to the bank □ let it all hang out □ naff all □ not all it's cracked up to be □ not all there □ once (and) for all □ pull out all the stops □ see someone or something (all) right □ sod all □ still and all □ sweet bugger all □ That's all someone needs. □ warts and all □ What's (all) something in aid of? □ You can't win 'em all. □ You can't win them all.

ALLEY

alley cat □ Slump Alley

ALLIGATORS

up to one's arse in alligators

ALMIGHTY

Lord Almighty!

ALONG

barrel (along) □ blind (along) □ buzz along □ cut along □ get along with you □ knock along □ rub along □ shove(l) along □ string along with someone or something □ string someone along □ tag along with someone or something □ tootle along □ trog along

ALTOGETHER

in the altogether

AMATEUR

enthusiastic amateur

AMOK

run amok

AMONG

down among the dead men

AMOUNT

any amount □ pull down an amount of money

AMUCK

run amuck

ANGEL

angel dust □ angels on horseback

ANGLE

know all the angles

ANIMAL

party animal

ANN

Mary Ann □ san fairy ann

ANNE

Queen Anne is dead.

ANNEXE

granny annexe

ANOTHER

another peep (out of you) □ one another □ Tell me another (one)! □ You've got another think coming.

ANSWER

dusty answer □ stumped for an answer

ANTE

up the ante

ANTS

have (got) ants in one's pants □ insects (and ants)

ANY

any amount □ Any joy? □ any road □ Any work going? □ cannot see (any) further than the end of one's nose

APART

come apart (at the seams) □ take someone or something apart □ tear someone or something apart □ tear somewhere apart

APE

ape hangers □ go ape (over someone or something)

APPLE

apple core □ apple fritter □ apple-pie bed □ apple-pie order □ apples and pears □ apples and rice □ as sure as God made little green apples □ Irish apple □ rotten apple

APPRO

on appro

ARCHY

aim Archy at the Armitage

ARE

Are we away? □ there you are □ There you are.

AREA

grey area □ no-go area □ walking disaster area

ARK

Noah's Ark

ARM

arm and a leg □ as long as one's arm □ long arm of the law □ long pockets and short arms □ one-armed bandit □ short arm □ shot in the arm □ strong-arm man □ strong-arm tactics □ twist someone's arm □ up in arms

ARMITAGE

aim Archy at the Armitage

ARMSTRONG

John Armstrong

ARMY

army and navy □ army rocks □ Sally Army □ You and whose army?

AROUND

(a)round the bend □ arse around □ bat around □ blue around the gills □ clown around □ drive someone around the bend □ faff around □ fart-arse around □ fat-arse around □ flaff around □ flap around □ float around □ galumph (around) □ go (a)round the houses □ green around the gills □ hang around □ knock around □ mess around (with someone) □ mess around (with something) □ monkey around (with someone) □ monkey around (with something) □ mope (around) □ muck around □ piss around □ play around □ screw around □ scrounge (around (for someone or something)) □ shop around □ sleep around □ snoop (around) □ stick around □ swan around □ take a nosy around □ talk (a)round something □ talk someone (a)round □ tart around □ throw one's weight around □ tool around □ turn around □ waffle (around)

ARRIVED

not long arrived

ARROW

bow and arrow

ARSE

arse about □ arse around □ arse over elbow □ arse over tits □ arse up □ fart-arse around □ fat-arse around □ horse's arse □ kick in the arse □ know one's arse from one's elbow □ pain in the arse □ park one's arse □ pig's arse □ rough as a badger's arse □ screw the arse off someone □ stupid arse □ tear-arse about □ tear one's arse off □ tear the arse out of something □ up to one's arse in alligators □ Up your arse!

ARSEHOLE

Fucking arseholes! □ tight as a duck's arse(hole) □ tight as a fish's arse(hole) □ tight as a gnat's arse(hole)

ARTHUR

J. Arthur (Rank)

ARTICLE

genuine article

ARTIST

con artist □ piss artist □ rip-off artist

ASH

fag-ash Lil □ flash the ash

ASHORE

jack ashore

ASK

ask for it □ ask for trouble □ Don't ask me. □ Don't ask. □ You asked for it!

ASS

stupid ass

ASSIST

assist the police with their enquiries

ASTHMA

dock asthma

ATHENS

Athens of the North □ Modern Athens

ATTACK

tack attack

AU

cafe au lait

AUDREY

little Audrey

AULD

Auld Reekie

AUNT

agony aunt □ Aunt Nelly □ Aunt Sally □ Aunt(y) Beeb □ My Aunt Fanny!

AURORA

aurora metropolis

AVENUE

Pill Avenue

AW

Yer hied's aw full o mince!

AWAY

Are we away? □ Away an bile yer heid! □ Away an raffle yer doughnut! □ Away an take a running jump at yersel! □ away fixture □ away team □ beaver away at something □ blow someone away □ blown away □ come away □ fire away □ Get away! □ get away with something □ get away with you □ get one's end away □ give away (the) change □ give it away □ give the game away □ have it away □ have it (away) with someone □ miles away □ play away □ prat away □ put someone away □ put something away □ rabbit away □ squirrel something away □ stash (away) □ swag someone away □ take-away (food) □ take-away (restaurant) □ throw (away) □ throw-away (line) □ well away

AWFUL
something awful

AWKWARD
awkward customer □ awkward squad

AXE
old battle-axe

BA
sweet B.A.

BABY
baby blues □ baby's head □ baby's pram □ jelly babies □ make a baby □ make babies □ Throw the baby out with the bathwater. □ wet the baby's head

BACK
back in action □ back of beyond □ back to square one □ back to the salt mines □ break the back of someone □ break the back of something □ come back □ face like the back (end) of a bus □ fed (up) to the back teeth with something or someone □ get off someone's back □ have (got) a monkey on one's back □ have (got) a yellow streak down one's back □ kick back □ knock back □ knock one back □ knock someone back □ laid back □ look back □ on the back boiler □ on the back burner □ pain in the back □ pin back your lugholes □ pin your ears back □ ring back □ set someone back □ short back and sides □ talk through (the back of) one's neck □ toss something back □ yellow streak (down someone's back)

BACKROOM
backroom boys □ boys in the backroom

BACKSIDE
kick in the backside □ pain in the backside

BACKWARD
backward about coming forward □ backward thought □ bend over backwards □ fall over backwards □ lean over backwards

BACON
bring home the bacon

BAD
Bad cess to you! □ bad egg □ bad fist □ bad form □ bad job □ bad news □ bad patch □ bad penny □ bad show □ bad trip □ get a bad name □ have (got) bad vibes □ in a bad way □ in

bad shape □ make a bad fist of something □ nay say bad □ not half bad

BADGE
on the coat and badge

BADGER
rough as a badger's arse □ tight as a badger's bum

BAFFLE
baffle someone with bullshit

BAG
bag of bones □ bag of wind □ bum bag □ in the bag □ jamboree bags □ murder bag □ priest of the blue bag □ slime bag □ whole bag of tricks

BAGATELLE
mere bagatelle

BAIL
bail out □ jump bail

BAILEY
Old Bailey

BAIRNS
Jock Tamson's bairns

BAKED
baked bean

BAKER
Baker day

BALL
ball and bat □ ball and chain □ ball is in someone's court □ ball o' chalk □ ball of chalk □ ballsed up □ blue balls □ drop the ball □ game ball □ get someone by the balls □ have a ball □ have someone by the balls □ keep the ball rolling □ on the ball □ pain in the balls □ play ball with someone □ sharp as a tennis ball

BALLISTIC
go ballistic

BALLOCKS
chew someone's ball(ocks) off □ top ballocks

BALLOON
balloon car □ go down like a lead balloon □ go over like a lead balloon □ when the balloon goes up

BANANA
go bananas □ tummy banana

BAND
band in the box □ brass band □ one-man band

BANDIT
knicker bandit □ one-armed bandit □ piss-hole bandit

BANDWAGON
on the bandwagon

BANG
bang like a shit-house door ☐ bang off ☐ bang on ☐ bang someone up ☐ bang the drum for someone or something ☐ bang to rights ☐ hail jing-bang ☐ hale jing-bang ☐ smack-bang in the middle ☐ with a bang

BANK
laugh all the way to the bank

BAR
all over bar the shouting ☐ bar steward ☐ behind bars ☐ bounty bar ☐ call someone to the bar ☐ call someone within the bar ☐ half (a) bar ☐ Mars Bar ☐ no holds barred

BARGEPOLE
touch someone or something with a bargepole ☐ wouldn't touch someone or something with a bargepole

BARLEYCORN
John Barleycorn

BARN
Were you born in a barn?

BARNEY
bit of a barney

BARREL
barrel (along) ☐ barrel of fun ☐ bottom of the barrel ☐ double-barrelled name ☐ have someone over a barrel ☐ loaded to the barrel ☐ scrape the bottom of the barrel

BARROW
Shift yer barrow!

BASH
bash someone up ☐ bash someone's head in ☐ ear basher ☐ give something a bash ☐ have a bash ☐ on the bash ☐ Paki bashing ☐ spud bash ☐ square bash

BASINFUL
had a basinful

BASKET
basket case ☐ dry as a basket

BASTARD
bright bastard ☐ proper bastard

BAT
at a good bat ☐ ball and bat ☐ bat an eyelid ☐ bat and wicket ☐ bat around ☐ carry one's bat ☐ have (got) bats in one's belfry ☐ like a bat out of hell ☐ off your own bat

BATH
early bath ☐ take a bath on something ☐ take an early bath

BATHWATER
Throw the baby out with the bathwater.

BATTER
battered fish ☐ on the batter ☐ salt and batter

BATTLE
battle cruiser ☐ old battle-axe

BAYONET
beef bayonet

BEADS
String (of Beads)

BEAM
on the beam

BEAN
baked bean ☐ full of beans ☐ jelly beans ☐ not a bean ☐ old bean ☐ spill the beans ☐ Use your bean!

BEAT
beat someone's brains out ☐ beat the drum for someone or something ☐ take a beating

BEAUTY
beauty sleep ☐ black beauties

BEAVER
beaver away at something

BED
apple-pie bed ☐ bed of roses ☐ come-to-bed eyes ☐ feather-bed someone ☐ get into bed with someone ☐ narrow bed

BEDPOST
between you, me and the bedpost

BEE
Bee Em ☐ bee's knees ☐ bees (and honey)

BEEB
Aunt(y) Beeb

BEEF
beef bayonet ☐ beef curtains ☐ beef something up ☐ corned (beef) ☐ corned beef

BEEN
been had ☐ Been there, done that, got the tee-shirt. ☐ I've been there. ☐ Where have you been hiding? ☐ Where (have) you been keeping yourself?

BEER
beer and skittles ☐ beer belly ☐ beer from the wood ☐ beer gut ☐ beer token

☐ beer voucher ☐ bottle of beer ☐ cry in one's beer ☐ do a beer ☐ ginger (beer) ☐ guest beer ☐ only here for the beer ☐ small beer

BEETLE
beetle about ☐ beetle off

BEFORE
carry all before one ☐ morning after (the night before) ☐ not before time

BEG
borrow and beg

BEGGAR
beggar belief ☐ beggar my neighbour

BEHIND
behind bars ☐ get behind someone or something ☐ wet behind the ears

BELFRY
have (got) bats in one's belfry

BELIEF
beggar belief

BELIEVE
Believe you me! ☐ I don't believe this! ☐ Would you believe (it)? ☐ You (had) better believe it!

BELL
Bell's palsy ☐ bells and whistles ☐ ding-dong (bell) ☐ give someone a bell ☐ Hell's bells (and buckets of blood)! ☐ ring a bell ☐ ring someone's bell ☐ saved by the bell ☐ with bells on

BELLOW
Helluva Bellow Chorus

BELLY
beer belly ☐ belly button ☐ belly flop ☐ belly laff ☐ belly laugh ☐ belly up ☐ Delhi belly ☐ go belly up ☐ jelly belly ☐ turn belly up

BELOW
hit (someone) below the belt ☐ marry below oneself

BELT
belt and braces ☐ belt (down) ☐ belt out ☐ belt up ☐ Belt up! ☐ fan(ny) belt ☐ full belt ☐ hit (someone) below the belt ☐ muesli belt ☐ stockbroker belt ☐ tighten one's belt ☐ under one's belt

BEN
big ben

BEND
(a)round the bend ☐ bend one's elbow ☐ bend over backwards ☐ bend

someone ☐ bend something ☐ bend the elbow ☐ bend the law ☐ drive someone around the bend ☐ round the bend

BENEATH
marry beneath oneself

BENEFIT
give someone the benefit of one's thoughts

BENNETT
Gordon Bennett!

BERETS
Green Berets

BERTIE
do a Bertie

BESS
Corgi and Bess

BEST
all the best ☐ best-case scenario ☐ Best of British (luck). ☐ for the best ☐ level best ☐ Sunday best

BET
both-way bet ☐ you bet

BETTER
better half ☐ Better luck next time. ☐ have seen better days ☐ You (had) better believe it!

BETWEEN
between hell and high water ☐ between you, me and the bedpost ☐ between you, me and the gatepost ☐ put some distance between someone and someone or something else

BEYOND
back of beyond ☐ beyond it ☐ beyond the pale

BICYCLE
push bicycle

BIDDY
red biddy

BIG
big ben ☐ Big Brother ☐ big cheese ☐ big deal ☐ Big deal! ☐ big drink of water ☐ big end ☐ big girl's blouse ☐ big H ☐ big league ☐ big M ☐ big mouth ☐ big name ☐ big noise ☐ big of someone ☐ big on someone or something ☐ big P ☐ big shot ☐ Big Smoke ☐ big spender ☐ big stink ☐ big talk ☐ big time ☐ big top ☐ big wean ☐ give someone the big E ☐ go over big ☐ have (got) a big mouth ☐ in a big way ☐ make it big ☐ Mr Big ☐ talk big ☐ talk into the big white telephone

☐ talk on the big white (tele)phone ☐ What's the (big) deal?

BIKE
bike it ☐ noddy bike ☐ On yer bike! ☐ push bike ☐ town bike

BILE
Away an bile yer heid!

BILL
bill and coo ☐ Bill shop ☐ Bungalow Bill ☐ fill the bill ☐ fit the bill ☐ go to pay the water bill ☐ hot bills ☐ Old Bill

BILLINGSGATE
Billingsgate pheasant ☐ Billingsgate talk ☐ talk Billingsgate

BILLY
King Billy ☐ like billy-o ☐ silly billy

BIN
bin end ☐ bin something ☐ loony bin ☐ sin bin ☐ wheelie bin

BINT
lush bint

BIRD
bird cage ☐ bird's nest ☐ do bird ☐ early bird ☐ night bird ☐ not a dicky (bird) ☐ rare bird

BIRTHDAY
in one's birthday suit

BISCUIT
take the biscuit

BIT
be a bit much ☐ be a bit off ☐ be a bit slow upstairs ☐ be a bit thick ☐ bit of a barney ☐ bit of a lad ☐ bit of all right ☐ bit of Braille ☐ bit of crackling ☐ bit of crumpet ☐ bit of fluff ☐ bit of homework ☐ bit of meat ☐ bit of nonsense ☐ bit of skirt ☐ bit of spare ☐ bit of stuff ☐ bit of tail ☐ bit of the action ☐ bit of the other ☐ bit of tickle ☐ bit of tit ☐ bit on the side ☐ bit previous ☐ bits and bobs ☐ get a bit ☐ go on a bit ☐ hair of the dog (that bit one) ☐ have a bit (off with someone) ☐ knocking on a bit ☐ not take a blind bit of notice of someone or something ☐ rude bits ☐ squashy bits ☐ ten-bob bit ☐ thrilled to bits

BITCH
bitch of a person or thing ☐ make a bitch of something ☐ real bitch

BITE
bite the bullet ☐ Bite your tongue! ☐ snake bite

BITTER
mild and bitter ☐ old and bitter

BLACK
black and blue ☐ black and tan ☐ black and white ☐ black beauties ☐ black bombers ☐ black-coated workers ☐ black maria ☐ Black or white? ☐ black velvet ☐ in the black ☐ little black book ☐ put the black on someone

BLADE
razor blade

BLAG
blag someone ☐ blag something

BLAIR
Lionel Blair ☐ Lionel Blair(-cut)

BLANE
Mary Blane

BLANKET
wet blanket

BLAST
Blast it! ☐ full blast

BLAZES
Go to blazes! ☐ like blazes

BLEED
bleed for someone ☐ bleed like a (stuck) pig ☐ bleed someone ☐ bleed someone dry ☐ bleed someone white ☐ not a bleeding thing

BLESSING
sailor's blessing

BLIGHT
Nellie Blight

BLIND
blind (along) ☐ blind drunk ☐ blind hedge ☐ blind man's holiday ☐ blind with science ☐ blindingly stupid ☐ easy as taking pennies from a blind man ☐ effing and blinding ☐ not a blind thing ☐ not take a blind bit of notice of someone or something ☐ rob someone blind ☐ steal someone blind ☐ swear blind

BLINK
on the blink

BLISS
bliss out ☐ blissed (out)

BLISTER
skin and blister

BLOATER
kipper and bloater

BLOBS
ove blobs

BLOCK
admin block □ knock someone's block off □ off one's block □ tower block
BLOGGS
Joe Bloggs
BLONDE
dumb blonde □ suicide blonde
BLOOD
bloody mary □ Hell's bells (and buckets of blood)! □ in cold blood □ in one's blood □ no bloody good □ Not (bloody) likely! □ scream bloody murder □ sweat blood □ taste blood
BLOTCH
pimple and blotch
BLOUSE
big girl's blouse
BLOW
blow (up) □ blow a fuse □ blow a gasket □ blow job □ blow off (some) steam □ blow one's fuse □ blow one's own horn □ blow one's top □ blow someone □ blow someone's cover □ blow someone's mind □ blow the gaff □ blow the lid off □ blow the lid off something □ blow the whistle □ blow up □ blown away □ land a blow □ mercy blow-through
BLUE
baby blues □ black and blue □ blue around the gills □ blue balls □ blue chip □ blue-eyed boy □ blue funk □ blue in the face □ blue moon □ blue murder □ blue o'clock □ boy in blue □ boys in blue □ dark blue □ in a blue funk □ light blue □ once in a blue moon □ out of the blue □ priest of the blue bag □ red, white and blue □ St. Louis blues □ talk until one is blue in the face □ two eyes of blue
BOARD
board of green cloth □ idiot board □ take something on board
BOAT
boat race □ Glasgow boat □ little man in the boat □ miss the boat □ push the boat out
BOB
bits and bobs □ bob (and dick) □ Bob's your uncle! □ couple of bob □ likely as a nine bob note □ not short of a bob or two □ one-eyed Bob □ queer as a nine bob note □ ten-bob bit □ worth a bob or two
BODY
body count □ body of the kirk □ Over my dead body!
BOFF
boff someone □ boffing (off)
BOG
bog off □ Bog off! □ bog seat □ make a bog of something □ straight from the bog
BOGGLES
Mind boggles!
BOIL
go off the boil □ on the boil
BOILER
dodgy boiler □ on the back boiler □ on the front boiler □ pot boiler
BOL
spag bol
BOLD
brave and bold □ warriors bold
BOLLOCK
bollocky starkers □ stark bollock (naked)
BOLTS
nuts and bolts
BOMB
bomb out □ dive bomb □ go down a bomb □ go like a bomb □ make a bomb
BOMBER
black bombers □ dive bomber
BOMBSHELL
drop a bombshell
BOND
granny bond □ junk bond
BONE
bag of bones □ bone box □ bone dome □ bone idle □ dog and bone □ ground bones
BONK
bonk oneself □ bonk someone □ bonk something
BONKERS
drive someone bonkers □ stark staring bonkers □ stonewall bonkers
BOO
booed and hissed □ can't say boo to a goose □ make a boo-boo
BOOB
boob job □ boob tube

BOOBY

booby hatch □ booby hutch □ booby trap

BOOK

bring someone to book □ cheque-book journalism □ cook the books □ get one's books □ go by the book □ in my book □ little black book □ take a page from someone's book □ throw the book at someone □ turn up (for the books)

BOOT

boot is on the other foot □ boot sale □ boot someone out □ bovver boot □ car boot sale □ Jesus boots □ order of the boot □ put the boot in □ sink the boot in □ splash the boots □ tackety boot □ to boot □ You bet your boots!

BOOZE

hit the booze □ on the booze

BORE

bore someone to tears □ bore the pants off someone □ boring old fart □ crashing bore □ full bore □ terminal boredom

BORN

Were you born in a barn?

BOSUN

fang bosun □ pill bosun □ sin bosun

BOTH

both sheets in(to) the wind □ both-way bet □ plug in both ways □ swing both ways

BOTHER

hot and bothered □ not bothered □ spot of bother

BOTTLE

bottle and stopper □ bottle of beer □ bottle of sauce □ bottle of Scotch □ bottle of water □ bottle out □ bottle party □ chief cook and bottle washer □ full bottle □ head cook and bottle washer □ hit the bottle

BOTTOM

bottom line □ bottom of the barrel □ bottom of the garden □ bottom out □ bottomless pit □ Bottoms up! □ front bottom □ rock bottom □ scrape the bottom of the barrel

BOUNCY

play bouncy-bouncy

BOUNTIFUL

Lady Bountiful

BOVVER

bovver boot □ bovver boy

BOW

bow and arrow □ dicky bow □ draw the bow □ draw the long bow □ kelly bow

BOWL

bowl someone out □ bowling green □ clean bowl someone

BOX

band in the box □ bone box □ box clever □ box someone in □ boxed in □ cardboard box □ chocolate box □ cog box □ ghetto box □ goggle box □ idiot box □ mount the box □ on the box □ squawk box

BOY

backroom boys □ blue-eyed boy □ bovver boy □ boy in blue □ Boy, oh boy! □ boys in blue □ boys in the backroom □ boys on ice □ bum boy □ laughing boy □ little boys' room □ mother's boy □ nancy (boy) □ new boy □ Oh, boy! □ old boy □ rent boy □ since Adam was a boy □ That's my boy! □ ton-up boy □ wide (boy)

BRACES

belt and braces

BRACKET

punch up the bracket

BRAILLE

bit of Braille

BRAIN

beat someone's brains out □ brain drain □ have (got) something on the brain

BRAND

brand new □ brand spanking new

BRASS

brass band □ brass farthing □ brass monkey's weather □ brass neck □ brass something out □ brass tacks □ brass up □ brassed (off) □ not care a brass farthing □ not give a brass farthing □ not worth a brass farthing □ with (brass) knobs on

BREAD

bread (and honey) □ bread and butter □ bread and lard □ brown bread

BREADTH

within a hair(s-breadth) of something

BREAK

Break a leg! □ Break it up! □ break the back of someone □ break the back of something □ break the ice □ broken reed □ Gimme a break! □ Give me a break! □ take a break

BREAKFAST
dog's breakfast □ have someone for breakfast □ pig's breakfast

BREATHE
as one lives and breathes □ breathe down someone's neck

BREED
Bulldog Breed

BREEZE
shoot the breeze

BREEZY
bright and breezy

BREWERY
could not organise a piss-up in a brewery

BRICK
built like a brick shithouse □ come down on someone like a ton of bricks □ drop a brick □ kilted brickie □ like a ton of bricks □ shit a brick □ shit bricks □ three bricks shy of a load

BRIDGE
bridge widow □ Forth Bridge job □ paint the Forth Bridge

BRIEF
hold no brief for someone

BRIEFCASE
Brixton briefcase

BRIGADE
dirty mac brigade □ green welly brigade

BRIGHT
bright and breezy □ bright as a button □ bright bastard □ bright-eyed and bushy-tailed □ bright spark

BRILL
that's brill

BRILLIANT
pure dead brilliant

BRING
bring home the bacon □ bring someone down □ bring someone low □ bring someone off □ bring someone on □ bring someone to book □ bring something up

BRISTOL
Bristol fashion □ shipshape and Bristol fashion

BRITISH
Best of British (luck).

BRIXTON
Brixton briefcase

BROKE
broken reed □ flat (broke) □ go for broke □ stony (broke)

BROOM
shovel and broom

BROTH
idiot broth

BROTHER
Big Brother

BROWN
brown bread □ brown hatter □ brown job □ brown someone off □ browned off □ brownie points

BRUMMAGEM
brummagem screwdriver

BRUSH
(as) daft as a brush □ broad brush □ daft as a brush □ give someone the brush-off

BUBBLE
Bubble (and Squeak) □ bubble and squeak □ bubble on someone □ double bubble □ old bubble

BUCK
Buck House □ buck up □ pass the buck

BUCKET
bucket and pail □ bucket shop □ Hell's bells (and buckets of blood)! □ kick the bucket □ mercy bucket(s) □ slime bucket

BUDDY
bosom buddy

BUDGIE
lucky budgie □ paraffin budgie □ tin budgie

BUFF
in the buff

BUFFER
old buffer

BUGGER
bugger about □ bugger all □ Bugger it! □ Bugger me! □ bugger off □ Bugger off! □ bugger (up) □ bugger's muddle □ buggeration factor □ buggered for something □ play silly buggers □ proper bugger □ sweet bugger all

BUGGERY
all to buggery □ Did one buggery! □ Is it buggery! □ Will I buggery!

BUILT
built for comfort □ built like a brick shithouse
BULGE
bulge the onionbag
BULL
bull and cow □ bull session □ John Bull
BULLET
bite the bullet □ get the bullet
BULLSHIT
baffle someone with bullshit
BUM
bum and tit □ bum bag □ bum boy □ bum chum □ bum trip □ bum's rush □ give one's bum an airing □ on the bum □ pain in the bum □ park one's bum □ rough as a badger's bum □ tight as a badger's bum □ tight as a crab's bum □ Up your bum!
BUMMER
heid bummer
BUMP
bump someone □ bump tummies □ duck(y) bumps
BUN
bun fight □ Currant Bun □ sticky (bun) □ take the bun
BUNCH
bunch of fives □ Mother Bunch □ thanks a bunch
BUNDLE
bundle of joy □ bundle of nerves □ go a bundle on someone □ lose a bundle □ make a bundle □ small bundle
BUNK
bunk off □ do a bunk
BUNNY
bugs bunny □ snow bunny
BURN
burnt offering □ burnt out □ Chinese burn □ have money to burn
BURNER
on the back burner □ on the front burner
BUROO
on the buroo
BURTON
go for a burton
BUS
face like the back (end) of a bus □ magic bus □ miss the bus
BUSH
bright-eyed and bushy-tailed □ bush telegraph

BUSINESS
business end of something □ business girl □ do the business □ funny business □ in business □ like nobody's business □ mean business □ monkey business □ on the business
BUST
bust a gut □ bust someone □ shit or bust
BUSTER
Hold it, Buster!
BUT
last but one □ next (door) but one □ sodger-clad but major-minded
BUTTER
bread and butter
BUTTOCKS
top buttocks
BUTTON
belly button □ bright as a button □ buttoned up □ Button it! □ button something up □ Button up! □ Button (up) your lip! □ hit the panic button □ keep one's lips buttoned □ not care a button □ not give a button □ not worth a button □ on the button □ press the panic button □ push the panic button
BUTTY
chip butty
BUY
buy it □ buy something □ buy the farm □ buy time
BUZZ
buzz along □ Buzz off!
BYE
kiss something good-bye
CABOODLE
whole kit and caboodle
CACKLE
Cut the cackle!
CAGE
bird cage
CAHOOTS
in cahoots (together)
CAIN
raise Cain
CAKE
icing on the cake □ piece of cake □ take the cake
CALAIS
when Dover and Calais meet
CALF
cow and calf

CALL
call Charlie □ call Earl □ call Hughie □ call it a day □ call of nature □ call Ralph □ call Ruth □ call someone to the bar □ call someone within the bar □ call up □ close call □ cold call □ Nature calls. □ nature's call

CALM
cool, calm and collected

CAME
This is where I came in.

CAMERA
on camera

CAMP
camp about □ camp it up □ happy camper

CAN
can of worms □ can't say boo to a goose □ can't say fairer □ can't win (th)em all □ carry the can □ What can I do you for? □ You can say that again! □ You can't get there from here. □ You can't take it with you. □ You can't win 'em all. □ You can't win them all.

CANDLE
roman candle

CANDY
nose candy

CANNOT
cannot see (any) further than the end of one's nose

CAP
if the cap fits

CAPE
Cape of Good Hope

CAPITAL
negative capital

CAPON
Glasgow capon □ Severn capon □ Yarmouth capon

CAPTAIN
Captain Cook □ captain of industry

CAR
balloon car □ car boot sale □ cop car □ dodgem car □ noddy car □ panda (car)

CARBORUNDUM
illegitimis non carborundum □ nil carborundum illigitium

CARCASS
park one's carcass

CARD
get one's cards □ idiot card □ mark someone's card □ on the cards □ show one's cards

CARE
don't care tuppence □ expensive care unit □ I couldn't care less. □ in care □ not care a (tuppenny) damn □ not care a brass farthing □ not care a button □ not care a fart □ not care a fuck □ not care a monkey's (fuck) □ not care a toss □ not care two hoots □ take care of number one □ take care of someone □ Take care.

CAREY
in Carey Street

CARPET
on the carpet □ sweep something under the carpet

CARRY
carry all before one □ carry one's bat □ carry someone □ carry the can □ carry weight

CART
cart someone □ honey cart □ horse and cart □ in the cart

CARTE
D'Oyly Carte

CARVE
carve someone □ carve something up □ carved in stone □ carving knife

CASE
basket case □ best-case scenario □ case the joint □ hard case □ nut (case) □ worst-case scenario

CASH
cash cow □ strapped (for cash)

CAT
alley cat □ cat and mouse □ cat's miaow □ cat's mother □ cat's pyjamas □ cat's whiskers □ enough to make a cat laugh □ purr (like a cat) □ shoot a cat □ wild-cat (strike)

CATCH
catch a cold □ catch (one) with one's trousers down □ catch someone on the rebound □ catch up □ sprat to catch a mackerel □ What's the catch?

CATHETER
pass the catheter

CATTLE
cattle (truck)

CAUSE
Home of Lost Causes □ lost cause

CEMETERY
flies' cemetery
CERT
dead cert
CESS
Bad cess to you!
CHAIN
ball and chain □ chain and locket □ yank someone's chain
CHALK
ball o' chalk □ ball of chalk □ by a long chalk □ chalk and cheese □ chalk up □ penn'orth (of chalk)
CHANCE
Chance would be a fine thing. □ fat chance □ not a chance □ not a snowball's (chance in hell) □ not an earthly (chance) □ snowball's chance in hell
CHANGE
and change □ chop and change □ get no change □ give away (the) change □ small change
CHANNEL
channel fleet □ channel hop □ channel hopper □ channel surf □ channel surfer □ channel zap □ channel zapper
CHAP
old chap
CHAPPIE
happy chappie □ unhappy chappie
CHARACTER
give one one's character
CHARGE
give someone in charge
CHARLIE
call Charlie □ proper charlie □ right charlie □ tail-end Charlie
CHARMING
Charming(, fucking charming)! □ charming wife
CHASE
(ambulance) chaser □ chase someone □ chase the dragon
CHAT
chat show □ chat someone up
CHAUVINIST
male chauvinist pig
CHEAP
cheap shot □ dirt cheap □ el cheapo
CHECK
check out the plumbing
CHEESE
big cheese □ chalk and cheese □

cheesed (off) □ cheesed off □ hard cheese □ Say cheese!
CHEQUE
cheque-book journalism □ rubber cheque
CHERRY
cherry ace □ pop one's cherry □ pop someone's cherry
CHEST
get something off one's chest □ play something close (to one's chest)
CHEW
chew someone's ball(ocks) off □ chew something over □ chew the fat □ chew the rag
CHICKEN
chicken feed □ chicken out (of something) □ for chicken feed □ spring chicken □ steam chicken
CHILD
easy as taking toffee from a child □ from a child
CHIMNEY
smoke like a chimney
CHIN
chin someone □ chinless wonder □ nose and chin □ take it on the chin
CHINA
China white □ Lombard Street to a China orange
CHINESE
Chinese burn □ Chinese screwdriver □ Chinese white
CHIP
bargaining chip □ blue chip □ chip butty □ have one's chips
CHOCOLATE
chocolate box □ chocolate drop
CHOICE
Hobson's choice
CHOKEY
do chokey
CHOOSE
pick and choose
CHOP
chop and change □ chop someone □ get the chop □ give someone the chop
CHORUS
Helluva Bellow Chorus □ Hullabaloo Chorus
CHRIST
For Christ's sake!

CHUCK
Chuck it! □ chuck it in □ chuck one's hand in □ chuck someone (out) □ chuck someone out □ chuck something (out) □ chuck (up).

CHUFF
dead chuffed □ real chuffed □ trouser chuff

CHUM
bum chum

CHUMP
off one's chump □ off the chump

CHUNTER
chunter (on)

CHUTE
down the chute

CIRCUMSTANCES
in narrow circumstances

CITY
City of Dreaming Spires □ city slicker □ Granite City □ Tale of Two Cities □ two cities

CLAD
sodger-clad but major-minded

CLANGER
drop a clanger

CLANK
rattle and clank

CLAPPERS
go like the clappers □ like the clappers (of hell)

CLAPPY
happy clappy

CLASSES
chattering classes

CLAUSE
get-out clause

CLEAN
clean bowl someone □ clean one's act up □ clean someone out □ clean sweep □ clean up (on something) □ cleaned out □ come clean with someone (about something) □ keep one's nose clean □ squeaky clean □ take someone to the cleaners □ wipe the slate clean

CLEAR
clear as mud □ clear out

CLEVER
box clever □ clever clogs □ clever dick □ clever Mike □ none too clever □ not so clever □ not too clever □ not very clever

CLIMB
climb the wall(s)

CLIMBER
curtain climber

CLOCK
clock in □ clock off □ clock on □ clock out □ clock someone □ clock watcher □ face that would stop a clock

CLOGS
clever clogs □ pop one's clogs

CLOSE
close call □ close shave □ close to the knuckle □ play something close (to one's chest) □ wallie close

CLOTH
board of green cloth □ cloth ears

CLOTHING
sheep in wolf's clothing

CLOVER
come a clover

CLUB
Darby and Joan club □ in the (pudding) club □ put someone in the pudding club

CLUE
clued up □ I haven't a clue. □ Not a clue.

COAL
coal and coke □ coals to Newcastle

COAT
black-coated workers □ on the coat and badge □ trail one's coat

COBBLERS
Cobblers to you! □ load of old cobblers

COCK
all to cock □ cock a snook (at someone) □ cock and hen □ cock someone up □ cock something up □ cock that won't fight □ cock up □ go off at half-cock □ me old cock

COCKTAIL
corporation cocktail

COD
cod roe □ cod's wallop □ load of cods(wallop)

CODSWALLOP
cod's wallop □ load of cods (wallop)

COKE
coal and coke

COLD
catch a cold □ cold call □ cold feet

□ cold fish □ cold-meat job □ cold shoulder □ cold sober □ cold steel □ cold turkey □ freezing cold □ go cold on someone or something □ in a cold sweat □ in cold blood □ knock someone cold □ leave someone cold □ out cold □ pour cold water on something □ stone (cold) sober

COLE
old King Cole

COLLAR
collar someone □ feel someone's collar □ have one's collar felt □ hot under the collar

COLLECT
collect a gong □ cool, calm and collected

COLLINS
John Collins

COLOUR
colour of someone's money □ off colour □ with flying colours

COLUMN
agony column

COME
backward about coming forward □ come a clover □ come across □ Come again? □ come apart (at the seams) □ come away □ come back □ come clean with someone (about something) □ come down □ come (down) hard □ come-hither look □ come it □ come (off) □ Come off it! □ come off something □ come on □ Come on! □ come out □ come over queer □ come round □ come the innocent □ come the old soldier with someone □ come through □ come to a sticky end □ come-to-bed eyes □ come to no harm □ come to stay □ Come to that. □ come to the wrong shop □ come under the hammer □ come undone □ come unglued □ come unravelled □ come unstrung □ come unstuck □ come up for air □ coming out of one's ears □ How come? □ if push comes to shove □ know where one is coming from □ till kingdom come □ until kingdom come □ when one's ship comes in □ when push comes to shove □ You've got another think coming.

COMEDY
Cut the comedy!

COMFORT
built for comfort

COMMENT
pass a comment

COMMON
common (dog) □ common or garden □ short commons

COMPANY
company man □ fit-up company □ knocking company

COMPLIMENT
backhanded compliment

CON
con artist □ con man □ con trick □ mod cons

CONDITION
in mint condition

CONFETTI
Irish confetti

CONVENIENCE
public convenience

COO
bill and coo

COOK
Captain Cook □ chief cook and bottle washer □ cook something up □ cook the books □ head cook and bottle washer

COOKING
What's cooking?

COOL
Cool it! □ cool off □ cool one's heels □ cool, calm and collected □ keep cool □ keep one's cool □ lose one's cool □ play it cool

COP
cop a feel on someone □ cop a packet □ cop a plea □ cop car □ cop it □ cop one's whack □ cop (on to) something □ cop out □ cop shop □ fair cop □ no cop □ not much cop

COPE
cope (with it) □ cope (with things)

COPPER
turn copper

COPY
knocking copy

COPYBOOK
blot one's copybook

CORE
apple core □ hard core □ rotten to the core □ soft core

CORNED
corned (beef) □ corned beef

CORNER
corner shop □ cut corners □ sharp as the corners of a round table □ three-cornered fight □ turn the corner

CORPORATION
corporation cocktail

COST
cost a packet □ cost the earth

COSTA
Costa del Crime □ Costa Geriatrica

COUGH
cough and stutter □ cough something up

COULD
could not organise a piss-up in a brewery □ couldn't half □ I couldn't care less. □ so sharp one could cut oneself □ You could have knocked me down with a feather.

COUNT
body count □ nipple count □ out for the count

COUNTRY
country cousin □ go to the country □ in the country □ line of country

COUNTRYMAN
North Countryman

COURAGE
Dutch courage

COURSE
crash course □ horses for courses

COURT
ball is in someone's court □ kangaroo court

COUSIN
country cousin □ Cousin Jack

COVENTRY
send someone to Coventry

COVER
blow someone's cover □ cover in □ manhole cover

COW
bull and cow □ cash cow □ cow and calf □ Holy cow!

CRAB
tight as a crab's bum

CRACK
crack a stiffie □ crack down on someone □ crack down on something □ crack house □ crack it □ crack on □ crack one's face □ crack up □ cracked up to be □ fair crack of the whip □ get cracking □ get something

cracked □ have a crack at something □ not all it's cracked up to be □ take a crack at something □ tough nut (to crack)

CRACKERED
Christmas crackered

CRACKLING
bit of crackling

CRAP
full of crap □ load of crap

CRASH
crash course □ crash pad □ crashing bore

CRAW
shoot the craw □ shuit the craw

CRAWLING
crawling with it □ crawling with someone or something

CRAZY
like crazy

CREAM
cream puff □ ice cream □ ice creamer □ ice-cream habit □ ice-cream suit

CREASE
at the crease

CREATE
create fuck □ create hell

CREDIBILITY
street cred(ibility)

CREDIT
on the credit

CREEK
up shit creek □ up the creek (without a paddle)

CREEPERS
brothel creepers

CRICKET
not cricket

CRIME
Costa del Crime

CROSS
double cross □ get one's wires crossed □ have one's wires crossed

CROWS
Stone the crows!

CRUEL
something cruel

CRUISER
battle cruiser

CRUMPET
bit of crumpet □ crumpet run

CRUNCHING
number crunching

CRUST
off the crust

CRY
cry hughie □ cry in one's beer □ cry ralph □ cry ruth □ cry stinking fish □ For crying out loud!

CUFF
off the cuff

CUNT
cunt face □ cunt hat □ tighter than a nun's cunt □ tighter than a witch's cunt

CURL
curl up and die □ get someone by the short and curlies □ have someone by the short and curlies □ make one's hair curl

CURTAIN
beef curtains □ curtain climber

CUSS
swear and cuss

CUSTARD
custard and jelly □ park a custard □ rhubarb and custard □ woof one's custard

CUSTOM
Spanish custom

CUSTOMER
awkward customer □ rum customer □ tough customer

CUT
cut along □ cut and run □ cut corners □ cut it □ cut loose □ cut no ice (with someone) □ cut off a slice □ cut one's losses □ cut one's own throat □ cut someone down to size □ cut someone in (on something) □ cut something fine □ cut something out □ Cut the cackle! □ Cut the comedy! □ cut the mustard □ cut up (about someone or something) □ cut up rough □ Lionel Blair(-cut) □ so sharp one could cut oneself

CYCLIST
trick cyclist

D
jolly D.

DABS
dibs and dabs

DADDY
daddy of them all □ grand-daddy of them all □ sugar daddy

DAFT
(as) daft as a brush □ daft as a brush □ daft as a yett (on a windy day)

DAGGER
meat dagger □ mutton dagger

DAILY
daily grind □ Daily (Mail)

DAISY
daisy roots □ pushing up daisies

DAMMIT
(as) near as dammit □ as quick as dammit □ soon as dammit

DAMN
damn all □ not care a (tuppenny) damn □ not give a (tuppenny) damn □ not worth a damn □ not worth a (tuppenny) damn □ twopenny damn

DAMPER
put a damper on something

DANCE
air dancing □ dance the Tyburn jig □ lead someone a (merry) dance □ merry dancers

DANDY
fine and dandy

DARK
dark blue □ dark horse □ light and dark □ shot in the dark □ whistle in the dark

DART
puff and dart

DARTBOARD
second-hand dartboard

DASH
Dash it! □ Dash it all!

DATE
heavy date

DAUGHTER
dirty daughter □ Gunga Din and squatter's daughter

DAWNING
day's a-dawning

DAY
Baker day □ call it a day □ daft as a yett (on a windy day) □ day after the fair □ day one □ day person □ day's a-dawning □ early days □ flag day □ forever and a day □ glory days □ have seen better days □ if one's a day □ one (fine) day □ red-letter day □ Saint Grouse's Day □ Saint Partridge's Day □ That'll be the day! □ That will be the day! □ this day week

DAYLIGHT
daylight robbery □ frighten the living daylights out of someone □ scare the living daylights out of someone

DEAD
dead and gone □ dead cert □ dead chuffed □ dead drunk □ dead duck □ dead easy □ dead-end kid □ dead from the neck up □ dead head □ dead in the water □ dead issue □ dead letter □ dead loss □ dead man □ dead marine □ dead meat □ dead on □ dead one □ dead ringer (for someone) □ dead soldier □ dead to rights □ dead to the world □ dead trouble □ deadly dull □ down among the dead men □ Drop dead! □ knock someone dead □ make a dead set at someone □ make a dead set at something □ Over my dead body! □ pure dead brilliant □ Queen Anne is dead. □ stone dead □ would not be seen dead

DEAL
big deal □ Big deal! □ dirty deal □ package deal □ sweetheart deal □ What's the (big) deal?

DEAR
Dear John letter □ oh my dear

DEATH
as sure as death □ death on someone or something □ feel like death warmed up □ kiss of death □ like death warmed up □ sick to death (of someone or something) □ sudden death

DECEIVERS
gay deceivers

DECENT
jolly decent

DECK
flight deck □ hit the deck □ wipe the deck with someone

DECORATORS
have the decorators in

DEE
jolly dee

DEEP
deep shit □ deep-sea diver □ deep-sea fisherman □ go off the deep end □ in deep □ knee-deep in something

DEFENCE
Portsmouth defence

DELIGHT
deb's delight □ tart's delight

DELL
flowery (dell)

DEPARTMENT
upper storey (department)

DERISION
shit and derision

DEUCE
deuce to pay □ What the deuce? □ Who the deuce?

DEVIL
Be a devil. □ devil of a time □ devil's own □ Go to the devil! □ little devils □ speak of the devil □ talk of the devil □ What the devil? □ Who the devil?

DIALS
Seven Dials

DIAMOND
rough diamond

DICK
bob (and dick) □ clever dick □ dickless Tracy □ take the dick □ Tom (, Harry) and Dick □ Uncle (Dick)

DICKENS
What the dickens?

DICKY
dicky bow □ dicky dido □ dicky (dirt) □ dicky seat □ King Dicky □ not a dicky (bird)

DICTIONARY
swallow the dictionary

DID
Did one buggery! □ Did one fuck! □ Did one hell!

DIDDLE
Middle for diddle!

DIE
curl up and die □ die laughing □ die on someone

DIFFERENCE
same difference

DIG
dig (at) someone

DIGGER
gold digger

DIM
take a dim view of something

DIN
Gunga Din and squatter's daughter

DING
ding-dong (bell)

DINNA
Dinna fash yersel.

DINNER
dinner lady □ dinner pail □ dog's dinner

DIP

dip one's wick □ dip out □ skinny dip

DIRT

dicky (dirt) □ dirt cheap □ have the dirt on someone □ hit pay dirt □ in the dirt □ strike pay dirt

DIRTY

dirty daughter □ dirty deal □ dirty dog □ dirty joke □ dirty laundry □ dirty linen □ dirty look □ dirty mac brigade □ dirty old man □ dirty washing □ dirty weekend □ dirty word □ dirty work □ do the dirty on someone □ get the dirty end

DISAGREE

agree to disagree

DISASTER

walking disaster area

DISC

disc jockey □ tax disc

DISCUSSIONS

Ugandan discussions

DISEASE

duck's disease □ English disease □ foot-and-mouth disease

DISH

dish someone or something □ dish someone out of something □ dish something out □ plates and dishes

DISHWATER

(as) dull as dishwater

DISTANCE

put some distance between someone and someone or something else □ spitting distance

DITHER

in a dither

DIVE

dive bomb □ dive bomber □ duck and dive □ gin dive □ take a dive

DIVER

deep-sea diver

DO

do a beer □ do a Bertie □ do a bunk □ do a drink □ do a drop □ do a flanker □ do a good turn to someone □ do a Houdini □ do a job on someone or something □ do a left □ do a line with someone □ do a message □ do a Michael □ do a mick(e)y □ do a mischief to someone □ do a moon job □ do a number on someone □ do a one

□ do a right □ do a runner □ do a show □ do a starry □ do as you like □ do bird □ do chokey □ do drugs □ do for someone □ do me good □ do one's fruit □ do one's nut □ do oneself proud □ do one's (own) thing □ do porridge □ do right by someone □ do someone □ do someone's head in □ do something up □ Do tell. □ do the (religious) dodge on someone □ do the business □ do the dirty on someone □ do the honours □ do the Knowledge □ do the lot □ do the messages □ do the ton □ do the trick □ do time □ do well □ Do you get my drift? □ do's and don'ts □ Easy does it. □ How does that grab you? □ in thing to do □ must (do) □ nothing doing □ Nothing doing! □ proper do □ take some doing □ What can I do you for? □ What do you say? □ Will do.

DOCK

dickory dock □ dock asthma □ go into dry dock □ in dock □ in the dock □ Surrey Docks

DOCTOR

just what the doctor ordered □ spin doctor □ under the doctor □ zit doctor

DODGE

do the (religious) dodge on someone

DODGER

Artful Dodger

DODGY

dodgy boiler □ dodgy gear □ dodgy kit

DOG

common (dog) □ dirty dog □ dog (end) □ dog and bone □ dog's breakfast □ dog's dinner □ hair of the dog (that bit one) □ in the dog-house □ lucky dog □ Malta dog □ sausage dog □ see a man about a dog □ shouldn't happen to a dog □ top dog □ two shakes of a dog's tail

DOGGO

lie doggo

DOLE

dole something out □ on the dole

DOLL

Barbie doll □ doll up

DOME

bone dome

DON'TS
do's and don'ts

DONE
Been there, done that, got the tee-shirt. □ done by mirrors □ done for □ done over □ done thing □ done to a turn □ done with mirrors □ hard done by

DONG
ding-dong (bell)

DONKEY
donkey's ages □ donkey's years

DOO
Scooby (Doo) □ squiffy doo

DOODAH
all of a doodah

DOOR
bang like a shit-house door □ door to door □ early door □ next (door) but one

DOSE
go through (something) like a dose of salts

DOT
dot someone □ from the year dot □ on the dot □ since the year dot

DOUBLE
double-barrelled name □ double bub-ble □ double cross □ double Dutch □ double event □ double take □ double up (with laughter) □ on the double □ seeing double

DOUGHNUT
Away an raffle yer doughnut!

DOVER
when Dover and Calais meet

DOWNERS
uppers and downers

DOWNHILL
go downhill

DOZEN
talk nineteen to the dozen

DRABS
in dribs and drabs

DRAG
be a drag (on someone) □ drag one's heels □ drag queen □ drag up □ dragged out □ in drag □ spit and a drag

DRAGON
chase the dragon

DRAIN
brain drain □ down the drain □ drain one's radiator □ drain one's snake □ laugh like a drain

DRAPER
linen draper

DRAW
draw the bow □ draw the long bow □ luck of the draw

DRAWER
top drawer

DREAMING
City of Dreaming Spires

DRESS
dressed to kill □ dressed to the nines □ mutton dressed as lamb □ power dress

DRIBS
in dribs and drabs

DRIFT
Do you get my drift? □ Get my drift? □ get the drift

DRILL
no names, no pack-drill

DRINK
big drink of water □ do a drink □ drinking token □ drinking voucher □ drink (money) □ Drink up! □ get down to some serious drinking □ long drink of water □ meths drinker

DRIVE
backseat driver □ drive someone around the bend □ drive someone bonkers □ drive someone nuts □ drive someone up the wall □ in the driver's seat □ Sunday driver

DRIZZLE
sling one's drizzle

DROP
chocolate drop □ do a drop □ drop (a pup) □ drop a bombshell □ drop a brick □ drop a clanger □ Drop dead! □ Drop it! □ drop of the hard stuff □ drop off the twig □ drop on someone (from a (very) great height) □ drop one □ drop one's guts □ drop one's lunch □ drop out □ drop someone □ drop the ball □ drop them □ get the drop on someone □ penny drops □ turn on, tune in, drop out

DRUG
do drugs

DRUM
bang the drum for someone or some-thing □ beat the drum for someone or

something □ drum and fife □ drum up □ fife and drum □ tight as a drum

DRUNK
blind drunk □ dead drunk □ falling-down drunk □ stinking (drunk)

DRY
(as) dry as dust □ bleed someone dry □ dry as a basket □ dry-as-dust □ dry old stick □ dry run □ dry up □ Dry up! □ go into dry dock □ high and dry □ home and dry

DUB
dub out □ dub someone up □ dub up

DUCK
Cor love a duck! □ dead duck □ Donald Duck □ duck (out) □ duck and dive □ duck's disease □ duck(y) bumps □ fine weather for ducks □ Gawd love a duck! □ goose and duck □ Lord love a duck! □ mucky duck □ sitting duck □ tight as a duck's arse(hole)

DUCKETT
Mrs Duckett □ Mrs Duckett!

DUFF
duff shot □ duff up □ fluff one's duff □ up the duff

DUG
wallie dug

DUKE
Duke of Kent □ put up one's dukes

DULL
(as) dull as dishwater □ deadly dull

DUMMY
dummy run □ dummy up

DUNG
Hoo Flung Dung

DUNLOP
dangle the Dunlops □ Dunlop (tyre)

DUNNIT
gone an' dunnit

DUST
angel dust □ (as) dry as dust □ dry-as-dust □ dusty answer □ gold dust □ hit the dust □ kiss the dust □ not so dusty

DUSTBIN
Dagenham dustbin □ dustbin lid

DUSTER
yellow duster

DUTCH
double Dutch □ Dutch courage □

Dutch kiss □ Dutch treat □ Dutch uncle □ go Dutch

DWARF
poison dwarf

E
give someone the big E

EAR
cloth ears □ coming out of one's ears □ ear basher □ in a pig's ear □ keep an ear to the ground □ loaded to the earlobes □ out on one's ear □ pig's ear □ pin your ears back □ play something by ear □ stewed to the ears □ talk someone's ear off □ thick ear □ throw one out on one's ear □ up to one's ears □ wet behind the ears □ wooden ears

EARFUL
give someone an earful

EARHOLE
tight as a mouse's ear(hole)

EARL
call Earl

EARLOBES
loaded to the earlobes

EARLY
early bath □ early bird □ early days □ early door □ have an early night □ take an early bath

EARNER
nice little earner

EARTH
cost the earth □ earth to someone □ feel like nothing on earth □ go to earth □ no earthly reason □ not an earthly (chance) □ pay the earth □ Where on earth?

EASY
dead easy □ easy as pie □ easy as taking pennies from a blind man □ easy as taking toffee from a child □ easy as you know how □ Easy does it. □ easy mark □ easy meat □ easy money □ take it easy □ take things easy

EAT
eat one's hat □ eat one's heart out □ eat shit □ eat someone out □ eat something up □ eat up □ What's eating someone?

ECO
eco freak □ eco nut

ECONOMICS
stop-go economics

EDGE
moist round the edges □ over the edge

EDUCATION
porridge education

EFF
effing and blinding □ Eff off!

EFFECT
knock-on effect

EGG
as sure as eggs is eggs □ bad egg □ egg and spoon □ egg someone on □ have (got) egg on one's face □ nest egg □ rotten egg □ Scotch egg □ scrambled eggs □ walk on eggs

EGO
ego trip □ ego tripper

EIGHT
one over the eight

ELBOW
arse over elbow □ bend one's elbow □ bend the elbow □ give someone the elbow □ know one's arse from one's elbow □ lift one's elbow

ELECTRIC
electric soup □ likely as an electric walking stick □ queer as an electric walking stick

ELEPHANT
pink elephants □ seeing pink elephants □ white elephant

ELSE
put some distance between someone and someone or something else □ something else □ So what else is new? □ What else is new? □ You and who else?

EM
Bee Em

EMBARRASSED
embarrassed

EMOTIONAL
tired and emotional

ENAMEL
pray to the enamel god

END
at a loose end □ big end □ bin end □ blunt end □ business end of something □ cannot see (any) further than the end of one's nose □ come to a sticky end □ dead-end kid □ dog (end) □ end to end □ face like the back (end) of a bus □ from Land's End to John O'Groats □

get one's end away □ get one's end in □ get the dirty end □ go off the deep end □ keep one's end up □ keeping one's end up □ no end of something □ rear (end) □ see no further than the end of one's nose □ sharp end □ sticky end □ tail-end Charlie

ENEMY
shouldn't happen to one's worst enemy

ENGAGEMENT
navel engagement

ENOUGH
enough to be going on with □ enough to make a cat laugh

ENQUIRIES
assist the police with their enquiries

ENTERTAINMENT
value-added entertainment

ENTRANCE
tradesman's entrance

ESSEX
Essex girl □ Essex man

EVE
Adam and Eve

EVENING
sweet evening

EVENT
double event □ in the event □ quite an event

EVER
as ever was □ ever so

EVERYTHING
Hold everything!

EXERCISE
horizontal exercise

EXPRESSION
if you'll pardon the expression

EXTRACT
extract the Michael □ extract the urine

EYE
bedroom eyes □ blue-eyed boy □ bright-eyed and bushy-tailed □ come-to-bed eyes □ get some shut-eye □ glad eye □ Here's mud in your eye. □ Hide your eyes. □ one-eyed Bob □ one-eyed trouser-snake □ pipe one's eyes □ rest one's eyes □ see eye to eye □ two eyes of blue □ with (one's) eyes (wide) open

EYEBALL
eyeball to eyeball □ stewed to the eyeballs □ up to one's eyeballs

EYEBROWS
stewed to the eyebrows
EYELID
bat an eyelid
FA
sweet FA
FACE
arse about face □ blue in the face
□ crack one's face □ cunt face □ face
fungus □ face like the back (end) of
a bus □ face like the side of a house □
face that would stop a clock □ face
the music □ feed one's face □ have
(got) egg on one's face □ pull a face
□ put a smile on someone's face □
put one's face on □ Shut your face! □
slap in the face □ talk until one is blue
in the face
FACTOR
buggeration factor □ Jesus factor
FACTORY
giggle factory
FACTS
facts of life
FAFF
faff about □ faff around
FAG
fag-ash Lil □ fagged out □ fag it □ fag
out
FAIR
can't say fairer □ day after the fair □
fair cop □ fair crack of the whip □
fair dos □ fair few □ fair jiggert □ fair
skint □ fair treat □ fair-weather friend
FAIRY
fairy glen □ fairy story □ fairy tale
□ san fairy ann
FALL
fall down on the job □ fall for it □
fall for someone □ fall guy □ fall over
backwards □ falling-down drunk □ Niagara (Falls) □ take a fall
FAMILY
family jewels □ in the family way
FANCY
Fancy meeting you here. □ fancy
parts □ Fancy that! □ fancy woman
FANNY
fanny adams □ fan(ny) belt □ fanny
hat □ My Aunt Fanny! □ sweet fanny
adams
FAR
far gone □ far out □ near and far

FAREWELL
sailor's farewell
FARM
buy the farm
FART
boring old fart □ fart about □ fart-
arse around □ farting shot □ like a
fart in a gale □ not care a fart □ not
give a fart □ not worth a fart □ tight
as a fart
FARTHING
brass farthing □ not care a brass farthing □ not give a brass farthing □ not
worth a brass farthing
FASH
Dinna fash yersel. □ Never fash yer
hied.
FASHION
Bristol fashion □ old fashioned look
□ shipshape and Bristol fashion □ spend
money like it's going out of fashion
FAST
fast one □ get nowhere fast □ play
fast and loose with someone or something □ pull a fast one
FAT
chew the fat □ fat-arse around □ fat
chance □ till the fat lady sings □ until the
fat lady sings □ when the fat lady sings
FATE
as sure as fate
FATTY
slip someone a fatty
FAX
junk fax
FEAR
frank and fearless □ I'm shaking (in
fear).
FEATHER
feather-bed someone □ in fine feather □ You could have knocked me down
with a feather.
FECHT
It's a sair fecht.
FED
fed (up) to the back teeth with something or someone □ fed up (with something or someone)
FEED
chicken feed □ fed (up) to the back
teeth with something or someone □ fed
up (with something or someone) □
feed one's face □ for chicken feed

FEEL

cop a feel on someone □ feel like death warmed up □ feel like nothing on earth □ feel like shit □ feel someone up □ feel someone's collar □ feeling no pain

FEET

cold feet □ find one's feet □ have one's collar felt □ have one's feet under the table □ put one's feet up □ six feet under □ vote with one's feet

FELLOW

old fellow □ stout fellow

FELT

have one's collar felt

FENCE

rush one's fences □ sit on the fence □ straddle the fence

FETTLE

in fine fettle

FEW

fair few □ good few

FIDDLE

on the fiddle □ second fiddle

FIFE

drum and fife □ fife and drum

FIGHT

bun fight □ cock that won't fight □ needle fight □ spoiling for a fight □ three-cornered fight □ throw a fight

FILE

(circular) file □ file 13 □ rank and file

FILL

fill someone in □ fill the bill

FILM

snuff film

FILTHY

filthy lucre □ filthy (rich)

FINANCIALLY

financially embarrassed

FIND

find one's feet □ find something

FINE

Chance would be a fine thing. □ cut something fine □ fine and dandy □ fine print □ fine weather for ducks □ in fine feather □ in fine fettle □ one (fine) day

FINGER

get your finger out □ green fingers □ sticky fingers

FINN

Mick(e)y (Finn)

FIRE

fire away □ play with fire □ set the Thames on fire □ Where's the fire?

FIRM

long firm

FISH

battered fish □ cold fish □ cry stinking fish □ queer fish □ smell fishy □ tight as a fish's arse(hole) □ tin fish □ Ye gods (and little fishes)!

FISHERMAN

deep-sea fisherman

FIST

bad fist □ hand over fist □ make a bad fist of something □ make a good fist □ make a poor fist of it

FIT

fainting fits □ fit someone up □ fit the bill □ fit-up company □ have a fit □ if the cap fits □ throw a fit □ throw forty fits

FITTINGS

fixtures and fittings

FIVES

bunch of fives

FIX

fix someone up □ fixed up □ get a fix □ quick fix

FIXTURE

away fixture □ fixtures and fittings □ home fixture

FLAG

flag day □ show the flag □ yellow flag

FLAKE

flaked out □ flake (out)

FLAME

Flaming heck! □ Flaming hell! □ go down in flames □ old flame □ shoot someone or something down in flames

FLANKER

do a flanker □ pull a flanker □ work a flanker

FLASH

Flash Harry □ flash (it) □ flash of light □ flash one's meat □ flash the ash □ in a flash

FLAT

flat (broke) □ flat out □ flat spin □ flat top □ granny flat

FLEET

channel fleet □ Fleet Street

FLICK

skin flick

FLIP
flip one's lid □ flip one's top □ flip one's wig □ flip side □ flip (out)

FLITTING
moonlight flitting

FLOOR
on the floor □ put one's foot to the floor □ wipe the floor with someone

FLOP
belly flop

FLOW
Scapa Flow

FLOWER
flowers (and frolics) □ flowery (dell)

FLUFF
bit of fluff □ Fluff off! □ fluff one's duff

FLUID
embalming fluid

FLUNG
Hoo Flung Dung

FLY
flies' cemetery □ fly a kite □ fly man □ Go and take a flying leap at yourself! □ I've got to fly. □ Must fly. □ on the fly □ Take a flying leap! □ Take a flying leap at yourself! □ with flying colours

FLYER
take a flyer (on something)

FLYNN
Errol (Flynn)

FOG
foggiest (idea) □ London fog □ Not the foggiest.

FOGEY
old fogey □ young fogey

FOGY
old fogy

FOLD
folding money □ folding stuff □ fold (up)

FOOD
junk food □ rabbit('s) food □ take-away (food)

FOOL
bloody fool □ festering fool □ flan-nelled fools

FOOT
boot is on the other foot □ foot-and-mouth disease □ have (got) one foot in the grave □ My (left) foot! □ put one's foot to the floor □ shoot oneself in the foot □ wouldn't touch someone or something with a ten-foot pole

FORBIDDEN
forbidden fruit

FOREST
Sherwood Forest

FORM
bad form □ current form □ good form □ in great form □ in rare form □ off form □ on form

FORT
hold the fort

FORTH
Forth Bridge job □ paint the Forth Bridge

FORTUNE
small fortune

FORTY
forty winks □ throw forty fits

FORWARD
backward about coming forward

FOU
stottin fou

FOUL
foul mouth □ foul up □ fouled up

FOUR
four-letter man □ four-letter word □ four sheets in(to) the wind

FRAME
frame someone □ in the frame

FRANCE
France and Spain □ South of France

FRAZER
Ted Frazer

FREAK
eco freak □ freak (out) □ freak someone out □ speed freak

FRED
Uncle Fred

FREE
or free □ free for all □ swing a free leg

FREEZE
freeze someone out □ freezing cold □ till hell freezes over □ until hell freezes over

FRENCH
Excuse my French. □ French kiss □ French leave □ French letter □ French loaf □ French someone □ Pardon my French.

FRIAR
Friar (Tuck) □ holy friar

FRIDAY
Girl Friday
FRIEND
fair-weather friend
FRIGATE
stone frigate
FRIGHT
frighten the hell out of someone □ frighten the living daylights out of someone □ frighten the pants off someone □ frighten the shit out of someone □ I'm shaking with fright. □ put the frighteners on someone
FRINGE
fringe theatre □ Newgate fringe
FRITTER
apple fritter
FROG
frog and toad □ frog in the throat □ play leapfrog
FROLICS
flowers (and frolics)
FRONT
front bottom □ front man □ front passage □ front runner □ on the front boiler □ on the front burner □ up front
FROST
degree of frost
FROZEN
give someone the frozen mitten
FRUIT
do one's fruit □ forbidden fruit □ old fruit
FRUITCAKE
(as) nutty as a fruitcake
FRY
fry someone (up) □ small fry
FUCK
Awa' tae fuck! □ Charming(, fucking charming)! □ create fuck □ Did one fuck! □ For fucks sake! □ Fucking arseholes! □ Fucking hell! □ fuck like a stoat □ Fuck me! □ Fuck me gently! □ fuck off □ Fuck off! □ Fuck this for a game of soldiers! □ fuck up □ Fuck you! □ Get to fuck (out of here)! □ Go (and) fuck yourself! □ Is it fuck! □ Like fuck! □ make a fuck-up of something □ not care a fuck □ not care a monkey's (fuck) □ Not fucking likely! □ not give a fuck □ not give a monkey's (fuck) □ not worth a fuck □ not worth a monkey's

(fuck) □ What the fuck? □ Will I fuck!
FULL
at full stretch □ full belt □ full blast □ full bore □ full bottle □ full marks □ full of beans □ full of crap □ full of hot air □ full of it □ full of shit □ full of wind □ Full stop! □ full tilt □ full whack □ shot full of holes □ Yer hied's aw full o mince!
FUN
barrel of fun □ fun and games
FUND
slush fund
FUNERAL
It's your funeral!
FUNGUS
face fungus
FUNK
blue funk □ funk hole □ funk something □ in a blue funk
FUNNY
funny business □ funny stuff □ talk funny □ too funny for words
FURTHER
cannot see (any) further than the end of one's nose □ see no further than the end of one's nose
FUSE
blow a fuse □ blow one's fuse □ have (got) a short fuse □ short fuse
FUSS
don't make a fuss □ kick up a fuss □ not fussy
GAB
gift of the gab □ Shut your gab!
GAFF
blow the gaff □ lumber gaff
GAITERS
all gas and gaiters
GALAHAD
Sir Galahad
GALE
ike a fart in a gale
GALLERY
shooting gallery
GALLOP
raise a gallop
GAME
ahead of the game □ Fuck this for a game of soldiers! □ fun and games □ game ball □ give the game away □ mug's game □ name of the game □

needle game □ on the game □ on the (lifting) game □ Sod this for a game of soldiers! □ throw a game

GANDER
take a gander (at someone or something)

GARDEN
bottom of the garden □ common or garden □ lead someone up the garden path

GARTERS
have someone's guts for garters

GAS
all gas and gaiters □ put someone's gas at a peep

GASKET
blow a gasket

GATE
creaking gate □ gates of Rome

GATEPOST
between you, me and the gatepost

GEAR
dodgy gear □ laughing gear □ swing into high gear

GENTLEMAN
gentleman of the road □ gentleman's gentleman

GENTLY
Fuck me gently!

GEORGE
George Raft □ George (the Third)

GERIATRICA
Costa Geriatrica

GHOST
Holy Ghost

GIDDY
giddy limit □ Giddy up!

GIFT
gift of the gab

GIGGLE
giggle (and titter) □ giggle factory □ good for a giggle

GILL
blue around the gills □ green around the gills □ loaded to the gills □ stewed to the gills

GIN
gin and It □ gin dive □ gin palace

GINGER
ginger (beer) □ ginger (girl)

GIRL
big girl's blouse □ business girl □ Essex girl □ ginger (girl) □ Girl Fri-

day □ girlie magazine □ girlie show □ go-go girl □ goose girl □ little girls' room □ new girl □ old girl □ page three girl □ working girl

GLAD
glad eye □ glad rags

GLASGOW
Glasgow boat □ Glasgow capon □ Glasgow kiss □ Glasgow Ranger

GLEN
fairy glen

GLIMMER
Not a glimmer (of an idea).

GLOVE
handle (someone or something) with kid gloves □ treat (someone or something) with kid gloves □ velvet glove

GLOW
illegitimate glow-worm

GNAT
gnat's piss □ tight as a gnat's arse(hole)

GOAL
own goal

GOAT
get someone's goat □ play the goat

GOD
all the hours God gives us □ as sure as God made little green apples □ God love her □ God rep □ God slot □ God's acre □ household gods □ pray to the enamel god □ pray to the porcelain god □ Ye gods (and little fishes)!

GODDESS
green goddess

GODIVA
Lady Godiva

GOLD
gold digger □ gold dust □ gold watch □ golden handcuffs □ golden handshake □ golden oldie □ golden opportunity □ wee goldie

GONE
dead and gone □ far gone □ gone an' dunnit □ gone by □ gone time □ That's (gone and) torn it! □ well gone

GONG
collect a gong

GOOD
at a good bat □ Cape of Good Hope □ do a good turn to someone □ do me good □ for good and all □ get (out) while the going is good □ get out while

the going's good □ get the goods on someone □ give someone a (good) talking to □ good few □ good for a giggle □ good for a laugh □ Good for you! □ good form □ Good heavens! □ good job □ good jump □ good kick □ good looker □ Good on you! □ Good show! □ good trip □ good wicket □ goody two-shoes □ have (got) good vibes □ if one knows what's good for one □ in good nick □ kiss something good-bye □ Looks good! □ make a good fist □ make good □ Miss Goody Two-shoes □ no bloody good □ onto a good thing □ piece of goods □ rattling good □ up to no good □ Your guess is as good as mine.

GOODNESS
My goodness!

GOOSE
can't say boo to a goose □ goose and duck □ goose girl □ goose('s neck) □ sausage a goose

GOOSEBERRY
play gooseberry

GRAB
grab a pew □ How does that grab you? □ smash-and-grab raid □ up for grabs

GRACES
airs and graces

GRAND
grand-daddy of them all □ grand slam

GRANITE
Granite City □ Granite Jug

GRANNY
granny annexe □ granny bond □ granny flat

GRAPE
wine grape

GRASS
grass on someone □ put (someone) out to grass

GRASSHOPPER
knee-high to a grasshopper

GRAVE
have (got) one foot in the grave

GRAVY
go down for the gravy □ gravy train □ Lumpy Gravy □ Plain and Gravy □ Pudding and Gravy □ Soup and Gravy

GREASE
grease monkey □ greasy spoon □ like greased lightning

GREAT
drop on someone (from a (very) great height) □ go great guns □ Great Scott! □ Great Smoke □ great unwashed □ Great Wen □ in great form □ no great shakes □ of great age □ shit (up)on someone from a (very) great height □ shoot someone or something down from a great height □ whopping (great)

GREEN
as sure as God made little green apples □ board of green cloth □ bowling green □ green around the gills □ Green Berets □ green fingers □ green goddess □ green light □ green welly □ strain one's greens

GREENFIELD
Mrs Greenfield

GREY
grey area □ hodden grey □ men in grey suits

GRIND
daily grind

GRIP
get a grip on one's knickers □ gripped at the knickers □ key grip □ lose one's grip

GRITTY
get down to the nitty-gritty

GROOVE
in the groove

GROUND
down to the ground □ ground bones □ keep an ear to the ground □ right down to the ground □ stamping ground □ thick on the ground □ thin on the ground

GROUPIE
troopie groupie

GROUSE
Saint Grouse's Day

GROUT
tea grout

GROW
not grow on trees

GROWTH
bungaloid growth

GRUBBER
money grubber

GRUNT
grumble and grunt

GUESS
Your guess is as good as mine,

GUEST
Be my guest. □ guest beer

GUFF
load of guff

GUISE
sell under guise

GUM
By gum! □ gum up the works □ up a gum tree

GUN
give (it) the gun □ go great guns □ gun for someone □ jump the gun □ smoking gun □ son of a gun

GUNWALES
loaded to the gunwales

GUT
beer gut □ bust a gut □ drop one's guts □ hate someone's guts □ have someone's guts for garters □ kick in the guts □ spew one's guts (out) □ spill one's guts

GUTTER
gutter press □ have one's mind in the gutter □ slip in the gutter

GUY
fall guy □ Mr Nice Guy □ tough guy □ wise guy

GYP
give someone gyp

GYPSY
Gypsy's (kiss) □ Gypsy's warning

H
big H

HABIT
ice-cream habit □ kick the habit

HACK
hack it □ hacked off

HAD
been had □ had a basinful □ have (had) it □ have had it □ was had □ You (had) better believe it!

HADDOCK
smoked haddock

HAIL
hail and hearty □ hail and rain □ hail jing-bang □ hail rickmatick □ hail smiling morn

HAIR
hair of the dog (that bit one) □ Keep your hair on! □ let one's hair down □ lose one's hair □ make one's hair curl □ short hairs □ within a hair(s-breadth) of something

HALE
hale jing-bang □ hale rickmatick

HALF
better half □ couldn't half □ go off at half-cock □ half (a) bar □ half a mo □ half a nicker □ half a stretch □ half a ton □ half under □ how the other half lives □ not half bad □ one and a half □ swift half □ too much by half □ You don't know the half of it.

HALT
Halt, tomatoes, turds!

HAMMER
claw-hammer suit □ come under the hammer

HAND
chuck one's hand in □ dab hand □ hand it to someone □ hand job □ hand over fist □ hands down □ Hands up! □ Keep your hands to yourself. □ nap hand □ old hand (at something) □ put one's hand down □ put one's hand in one's pocket □ second-hand dartboard

HANDCUFFS
golden handcuffs

HANDICAP
Sheffield (handicap)

HANDLE
handle (someone or something) with kid gloves □ jug handles □ (love) handles

HANDSHAKE
golden handshake

HANDSOME
high, wide and handsome

HANG
Hang about! □ hang around □ hang in there □ Hang it all! □ hang on □ hang one on □ hang up □ let it all hang out

HANGERS
ape hangers

HAPPEN
shouldn't happen to a dog □ shouldn't happen to one's worst enemy □ What's happening?

HAPPY
happy as a pig in shit □ happy as a sandboy □ happy as Larry □ happy camper □ happy chappie □ happy clappy □ happy pills

HARD
come (down) hard □ come down

hard □ come down on someone hard □ drop of the hard stuff □ hard at it □ hard case □ hard cheese □ hard core □ hard done by □ hard hit □ hard lines □ hard neck □ hard porn □ hard sell □ hard stuff □ hard ticket □ hard to swallow □ hard to take in □ hard up □ play hard to get □ six months hard

HARM
come to no harm □ take no harm

HARRY
'Arry Stottle □ Flash Harry □ Harry hoof □ Tom(, Harry) and Dick

HASH
settle someone's hash

HAT
brown hatter □ cunt hat □ eat one's hat □ fanny hat □ keep something under one's hat □ loaded to the hat □ old hat □ talk through one's hat □ throw one's hat in(to) the ring □ tin hat □ wear two hats □ witch's hat

HATCH
booby hatch □ Down the hatch!

HATCHET
bury the hatchet □ hatchet job □ hatchet man

HATCHY
never hatchy

HAUF
wee hauf

HAY
hit the hay □ tumble in the hay

HAYSTACK
go round the haystack

HAYWIRE
go haywire

HEAD
baby's head □ bash someone's head in □ by a short head □ dead head □ do someone's head in □ get one's head down □ give head □ head cook and bottle washer □ head hunt □ head hunter □ head job □ head off □ head shrinker □ head trip □ heads will roll □ Keep your head down. □ knock on the head □ need something like a hole in the head □ off one's head □ off the head □ off the top of one's head □ over one's head □ queer in the head □ soft in the head □ stoned out of one's head □ talk one's head off □ talking head □ Use the head! □ Use your head! □ wet the baby's head

HEAR
hear oneself think □ I hear what you're saying. □ I hear you. □ Let's hear it.

HEART
eat one's heart out □ have a heart □ Have a heart! □ heart-to-heart (talk) □ off by heart

HEARTY
hail and hearty

HEAT
take the heat off someone

HEAVE
give someone or something the (old) heave-ho

HEAVEN
Good heavens! □ heavens above □ stink to (high) heaven

HEAVY
heavy date □ heavy metal □ heavy necking □ heavy petting □ top heavy □ wee heavy

HECK
Flaming heck! □ What the heck!

HEDGE
blind hedge

HEEL
cool one's heels □ drag one's heels □ kick one's heels □ round heeled

HEID
Away an bile yer heid! □ heid bummer □ high heid yin

HEIGHT
drop on someone (from a (very) great height) □ shit (up)on someone from a (very) great height □ shoot someone or something down from a great height

HELL
as sure as hell □ between hell and high water □ create hell □ Did one hell! □ Flaming hell! □ for the hell of it □ frighten the hell out of someone □ Fucking hell! □ get the hell out (of here) □ give someone hell □ hell of a mess □ hell of a someone or something □ hell week □ Hell's bells (and buckets of blood)! □ Hell's teeth! □ Is it hell! □ like a bat out of hell □ Like hell! □ like the clappers (of hell) □ not a hope in hell □ not a snowball's (chance in hell) □ play (merry) hell with someone or something □ raise hell □ scare the hell

out of someone □ snowball's chance in hell □ till hell freezes over □ To hell with that! □ until hell freezes over □ What the hell! □ What the hell? □ Who the hell? □ Will I hell!

HEN
as rare as hen's teeth □ as scarce as hen's teeth □ cock and hen □ hen party

HENRY
Hooray Henry

HER
God love her □ her indoors □ Let her rip!

HERE
as sure as I'm standing here □ Fancy meeting you here. □ from here on in □ get one right here □ get the hell out (of here) □ Get to fuck (out of here)! □ have had it (up to here) (with someone or something) □ Here's mud in your eye. □ not long here □ only here for the beer □ same here □ up to here □ You can't get there from here.

HIDE
hide up □ Hide your eyes. □ hiding to nothing □ play hide the sausage □ tan someone's hide □ Where have you been hiding?

HIED
Never fash yer hied. □ Yer hied's aw full o mince!

HIGH
between hell and high water □ high (as a kite) □ high and dry □ high heid yin □ high jump □ high old time □ high spot □ high ups □ high, wide and handsome □ higher ups □ in for the high jump □ knee-high to a grasshopper □ on one's high horse □ stink to (high) heaven □ swing into high gear □ take the high jump

HIGHLANDS
White Highlands

HIKE
take a hike

HILL
over the hill □ take to the hills

HIRE
private hire

HISSED
booed and hissed

HISTORY
ancient history

HIT
hard hit □ hit list □ hit man □ hit on something □ hit pay dirt □ hit (someone) below the belt □ hit someone with something □ hit something for six □ hit the booze □ hit the bottle □ hit the deck □ hit the dust □ hit the hay □ hit the jackpot □ hit the panic button □ hit the pavement □ hit the road □ hit the roof □ hit the sack □ smash hit

HITCH
without a hitch

HITHER
come-hither look

HO
give someone or something the (old) heave-ho

HOCK
hock something □ in hock

HOE
tough row to hoe

HOG
road hog

HOLD
hold down a job □ Hold everything! □ Hold it! □ Hold it, Buster! □ hold no brief for someone □ hold one's horses □ hold out on someone □ hold the fort □ hold water □ no holds barred □ put someone on hold

HOLE
funk hole □ hole in one □ hole in the wall □ hole up □ need something like a hole in the head □ nineteenth hole □ piss-hole bandit □ shot full of holes □ square peg (in a round hole) □ watering hole

HOLIDAY
blind man's holiday □ sods' holiday

HOLLER
shout and holler

HOLY
Holy cow! □ holy friar □ Holy Ghost □ Holy Joe □ Holy mackerel! □ Holy Moses! □ holy nail □ holy terror

HOME
bring home the bacon □ home and dry □ home fixture □ Home of Lost Causes □ in the home straight □ in the home stretch □ nothing to write home about □ stop at home

HOMEWORK
bit of homework

HONEST
turn an honest penny
HONEY
bees (and honey) □ bread (and honey) □ honey cart □ honey wagon
HONOURS
do the honours
HOO
Hoo Flung Dung
HOOF
Harry hoof □ hoof it □ horse's hoof □ iron (hoof) □ pad the hoof
HOOK
hook someone □ hook something □ hook up with someone □ hook, line and sinker □ hooked (on someone or something) □ hooked (on something) □ off the hook □ ring off the hook □ sky hook □ sling one's hook □ Sling yer hook!
HOOSE
wee hoose
HOOT
not care two hoots □ not give a hoot □ not give two hoots □ not worth two hoots
HOP
channel hop □ channel hopper □ Hop it! □ hop off (one's twig) □ hop on □ Hop to it! □ hopping mad □ John Hop
HOPE
Cape of Good Hope □ Land of Hope □ not a hope in hell
HORN
blow one's own horn □ get the horn □ toot one's own horn
HORNER
Jack Horner
HORRORS
little horrors
HORSE
dark horse □ hold one's horses □ horse and cart □ horse's arse □ horse's hoof □ horses for courses □ on one's high horse □ rocking-horse manure □ rocking-horse shit □ salt horse □ straight from the horse's mouth
HORSEBACK
angels on horseback
HOSE
fireman's hose
HOT
drop someone or something like a

hot potato □ full of hot air □ get hot □ have the hots for someone □ hot air □ hot and bothered □ hot bills □ hot item □ hot money □ hot number □ hot on someone □ hot on something □ hot potato □ hot rod □ hot seat □ hot spot □ hot stuff □ hot tip □ hot under the collar □ hot up □ in a hot spot □ make it hot for someone □ red hot
HOTEL
hydro(pathic hotel)
HOUDINI
do a Houdini
HOURS
all the hours God gives us □ banker's hours □ wee small hours
HOUSE
acid house (party) □ as safe as houses □ bang like a shit-house door □ Buck House □ council house □ crack house □ face like the side of a house □ go (a)round the houses □ House of Lords □ house to let □ in the dog-house □ rough house □ round the houses
HOW
And how! □ easy as you know how □ How come? □ How does that grab you? □ How goes it? □ how the other half lives □ How's tricks?
HUBBARD
Mother Hubbard
HUDDLE
go into a huddle
HUFF
take the huff
HUGHIE
call Hughie □ cry hughie
HUMP
over the hump
HUNCH
play a hunch
HUNG
hung on someone □ hung-up on someone □ One Hung Low
HUNT
head hunt
HUNTER
head hunter
HUSH
hush money □ hush someone up □ hush something up
HUTCH
booby hutch □ rabbit hutch

HYPE
hype something up □ hyped (up)

ICE
boys on ice □ break the ice □ cut no ice (with someone) □ ice cream □ ice creamer □ ice-cream habit □ ice-cream suit □ on ice □ walk on thin ice

IDEA
foggiest (idea) □ Not a glimmer (of an idea). □ The (very) idea! □ Wake up your ideas!

IDIOT
blithering idiot □ festering idiot □ idiot board □ idiot box □ idiot broth □ idiot card □ idiot pills □ idiot's lantern □ prize idiot

IDLE
bone idle

IF
If I've told you once, I've told you a thousand times. □ if one knows what's good for one □ if one's a day □ if push comes to shove □ if the cap fits □ if you'll pardon the expression

IGNORANCE
invincible ignorance

ILL
take ill

ILLEGITIMATE
illegitimate glow-worm

ILLEGITIMIS
illegitimis non carborundum

ILLIGITIUM
nil carborundum illigitium

INCOHOL
under the affluence of incohol

INDOORS
her indoors

INDUSTRY
captain of industry

INFLUENCE
under (the influence)

INJECTION
meat injection

INK
pen and ink □ pen and inker

INNOCENT
come the innocent

INSIDE
inside a week □ inside job

INSPECTOR
ceiling inspector □ inspector of manholes

INTERNET
surf the (Inter)net

INTO
both sheets in(to) the wind □ four sheets in(to) the wind □ get into bed with someone □ get into something □ get one's teeth into something □ get tore into someone □ go into a huddle □ go into dry dock □ go into orbit □ knock something into shape □ lick something into shape □ pour oneself into something □ swing into high gear □ talk into the big white telephone □ tear into someone □ tear into something □ three sheets in(to) the wind □ throw one's hat in(to) the ring □ two sheets in(to) the wind □ weigh into someone □ work oneself up (into a lather) □ work oneself up (into a sweat)

INVALID
imaginary invalid

IRISH
Irish apple □ Irish confetti □ too Irish

IRON
iron (hoof) □ iron tank □ pump (some) iron

ISIS
Cam and Isis

ISSUE
dead issue

ITCH
have (got) an itch for something

ITEM
hot item

IVORY
ivory tower □ tickle the ivories

J
J. Arthur (Rank) □ Mary J

JACK
Cousin Jack □ jack (it) in □ jack all □ Jack and Jill □ jack ashore □ Jack Horner □ jack someone or something in □ jack something up □ Jack Straw □ jack tar □ Jack the Ripper □ jack up □ on one's Jack (Jones) □ yellow jack

JACKPOT
hit the jackpot

JACKSIE
Up your jacksie!

JAGGER
Mick Jagger

JAM
in a jam □ jam roll □ jam sandwich □ jam tart □ jam tomorrow □ money for jam

JANE
Mary Jane

JAZZ
jazz someone or something up □ jazzed (up)

JELLY
custard and jelly □ jelly babies □ jelly beans □ jelly belly

JERK
jerk off □ physical jerks

JESUS
Jesus boots □ Jesus factor □ Jesus nut □ Jesus wept!

JET
jumbo (jet)

JEWELS
family jewels

JEWISH
Jewish piano □ Jewish typewriter

JIFFY
in a jiff(y)

JIG
dance the Tyburn jig

JIGGERT
fair jiggert

JILL
Jack and Jill

JIM
Jungle Jim

JIMMY
Jimmy Prescott □ jimmy (riddle) □ Jim(my) Skinner

JING
hail jing-bang □ hale jing-bang

JOAN
Darby and Joan

JOB
bad job □ blow job □ boob job □ brown job □ cold-meat job □ conversion job □ do a job on someone or something □ do a moon job □ fall down on the job □ Forth Bridge job □ gob job □ good job □ hand job □ hatchet job □ head job □ hold down a job □ inside job □ just the job □ land a job □ man-sized job □ nose job □ on the job □ pull a job □ put-up job □ skull job □ slotted job □ snow job

JOBER
jober as a sudge

JOCK
Jock Tamson's bairns □ Jock's trap

JOCKEY
disc jockey □ disk jockey

JOE
Holy Joe □ Joe Bloggs □ Joe Public □ Joe Soap

JOG
jiggle and jog

JOHN
Dear John letter □ from Land's End to John O'Groats □ John Armstrong □ John Barleycorn □ John Bull □ John Collins □ John Hop □ John Thomas □ Sir John

JOINT
case the joint □ get one's nose out of joint □ put someone's nose out of joint

JOKE
dirty joke □ laugh and joke □ no joke

JOLLY
jolly D. □ jolly decent □ jolly dee

JONES
on one's Jack (Jones)

JOTTERS
get yin's jotters

JOURNALISM
cheque-book journalism

JOVE
By jove!

JOY
Any joy? □ bundle of joy □ joy pop □ joy (powder) □ no joy

JUG
Granite Jug □ jug (and pail) □ jug handles □ jug (up) □ jugged (up)

JUICE
jungle juice

JUMP
Away an take a running jump at yersel! □ get a jump □ Go (and) jump in the lake! □ good jump □ have a jump □ high jump □ in for the high jump □ in for the long jump □ jump bail □ Jump in the lake! □ jump out of the window □ jump ship □ jump the gun □ jump the queue □ long jump □ one jump ahead of someone or something □ queue jump □ Take a running jump (at yourself)! □ take the high jump □ take the long jump

JUNGLE
Jungle Jim □ jungle juice □ jungle telegraph

JUNK
junk bond □ junk fax □ junk food □ junk mail

JURY
designer jury

JUST
just a tick □ just so □ just the job □ just the ticket □ just what the doctor ordered

JUSTICE
rough justice

KANGAROO
kangaroo court □ kangaroo petrol □ Kangaroo Valley

KEEN
keen as mustard □ keen on someone □ mad (keen) on someone or something

KEEP
for keeps □ keep an ear to the ground □ keep cool □ Keep in touch. □ Keep it out! □ keep one's cool □ keep one's end up □ keep one's lips buttoned □ keep one's nose clean □ keep oneself to oneself □ Keep out of this! □ Keep shtoom! □ keep something under one's hat □ keep the ball rolling □ Keep your hair on! □ Keep your hands to yourself. □ Keep your head down. □ keep your pecker up □ Keep your shirt on! □ keeping one's end up □ play for keeps □ Where (have) you been keeping yourself?

KENT
Duke of Kent

KEY
key grip □ key money □ keyed up

KIBOSH
put the kibosh on something

KICK
for kicks □ good kick □ kick back □ kick in the arse □ kick in the backside □ kick in the guts □ kick in the (seat of the) pants □ kick in the teeth □ kick it □ kick one's heels □ kick the bucket □ kick the habit □ kick up a fuss □ kick up a stink

KID
dead-end kid □ handle (someone or something) with kid gloves □ I'm not

kidding. □ No kidding! □ No kidding? □ treat (someone or something) with kid gloves □ kid ('s)-stuff

KILL
dressed to kill □ make a killing □ passion killers

KILT
Go and piss up your kilt! □ kilted brickie

KILTER
out of kilter

KING
King Billy □ King Dicky □ king kong □ King Lear □ old King Cole

KINGDOM
till kingdom come □ until kingdom come

KIP
kip down □ kip shop

KIPPER
do someone up like a kipper □ kipper and bloater

KIRK
body of the kirk

KISS
cuddle and kiss □ Dutch kiss □ French kiss □ Glasgow kiss □ Gypsy's (kiss) □ kiss of death □ kiss of life □ kiss something good-bye □ kiss the dust □ kissing tackle □ Southend kiss

KISSER
right in the kisser

KIT
dodgy kit □ kit someone out □ wedding kit □ whole kit and caboodle

KITE
fly a kite □ high (as a kite)

KITTEN
have kittens □ sex kitten

KNEE
bee's knees □ housemaid's knee □ knee-deep in something □ knee-high to a grasshopper □ up to one's knees

KNICKER
get a grip on one's knickers □ get one's knickers in a twist □ gripped at the knickers □ knicker bandit

KNIFE
carving knife □ fork and knife

KNIGHT
knight of the road □ knight of the shire

KNOBS
with (brass) knobs on
KNOCK
knock along □ knock around □ knock back □ knock-down price □ Knock it off! □ knock off (from work) □ knock-on effect □ knock on the head □ knock one back □ knock someone (off) □ knock someone back □ knock someone cold □ knock someone dead □ knock someone for six □ knock someone off □ knock someone out □ knock someone's block off □ knock someone's socks off □ knock something into shape □ knock something (off) □ knock something off □ knock something out □ knock something together □ knock the starch out of someone □ knock the stuffing out of someone □ knocked about □ knocked out □ knocking company □ knocking copy □ knocking on a bit □ on the knock □ You could have knocked me down with a feather.
KNOCKER
oil the knocker □ on the knocker □ up to the knocker
KNOT
Get knotted! □ rate of knots □ tie the knot
KNOW
Don't I know it! □ easy as you know how □ for all I know □ I don't know. □ if one knows what's good for one □ in the know □ know a thing or two □ know all the angles □ know one thing □ know one's age □ know one's arse from one's elbow □ know one's onions □ know one's stuff □ know the score □ know what's what □ know where one is coming from □ not to know □ not want to know □ Y'know (what I mean)? □ You don't know the half of it.
KNOWLEDGE
do the Knowledge
KNOX
Reverend (Ronald Knox)
KNUCKLE
close to the knuckle □ knuckle down (to something) □ knuckle pie □ knuckle sandwich □ knuckle under (to someone or something) □ near the knuckle

KONG
king kong
LAB
path lab
LACE
lace something □ laced mutton
LAD
bit of a lad □ likely lad □ quite a lad
LADING
teeming and lading
LADY
dinner lady □ ladies' (room) □ Lady Bountiful □ Lady Godiva □ Lady Muck □ lady of the town □ Lady Snow □ lady wife □ lollipop lady □ old lady □ tea lady □ till the fat lady sings □ until the fat lady sings □ when the fat lady sings
LAFF
belly laff
LAG
old lag
LAGER
African lager □ lager lout
LAID
get laid □ laid back □ laid on
LAIT
cafe au lait
LAKE
Go (and) jump in the lake! □ Jump in the lake!
LAM
on the lam
LAMB
mutton dressed as lamb □ two shakes of a lamb's tail
LAMP
oily lamp
LAND
from Land's End to John O'Groats □ land a blow □ land a job □ Land of Hope □ land someone one □ land someone with something
LANTERN
idiot's lantern □ parish lantern
LAP
lap it up □ lap of luxury
LARD
bladder of lard □ bread and lard □ tub of lard
LARRY
happy as Larry

LAST

last but one □ last straw □ on one's last legs □ on something's last legs

LATCH

latch onto something

LATER

See you later.

LATHER

work oneself up (into a lather)

LAUGH

belly laugh □ die laughing □ Don't make me laugh! □ double up (with laughter) □ enough to make a cat laugh □ good for a laugh □ laugh all the way to the bank □ laugh and joke □ laugh like a drain □ laughing academy □ laughing boy □ laughing gear □ laughing soup □ laughing water □ liquid laugh

LAUNDRY

dirty laundry

LAW

bend the law □ long arm of the law □ Murphy's Law □ Sod's Law □ Spode's Law

LAWN

mow the lawn

LAY

lay it on the line □ Lay off (it)! □ lay off (someone or something) □ lay someone out

LEAD

go down like a lead balloon □ go over like a lead balloon □ lead in one's pencil □ lead poisoning □ lead someone a (merry) dance □ lead someone up the garden path □ swing the lead

LEAF

tea leaf

LEAGUE

big league

LEAK

take a leak

LEAN

lean and mean □ lean on someone □ lean over backwards

LEAP

Go and take a flying leap at yourself! □ quantum leap □ Take a flying leap! □ Take a flying leap at yourself!

LEAPFROG

play leapfrog

LEAR

King Lear

LEASH

on a short leash □ on a tight leash

LEAVE

French leave □ Leave it out! □ leave someone cold □ leave something at that □ leave (something) over □ Take it or leave it. □ without (so much as) a for or by your leave □ without (so much as) a with or by your leave

LEE

Rosie Lee

LEFT

do a left □ left and right □ My (left) foot!

LEG

arm and a leg □ Break a leg! □ get one's leg over □ hollow legs □ leg it □ middle leg □ on one's last legs □ on something's last legs □ pull someone's leg □ shake a leg □ Shake a leg! □ Show a leg! □ stretch one's legs □ swing a free leg □ third leg

LEGAL

take legal advice

LEMON

lemon squash □ lemon tea □ squeeze the lemon

LENGTH

lengths ahead □ measure one's length □ slip someone a length

LESS

I couldn't care less.

LET

house to let □ Let her rip! □ let it all hang out □ let off (some) steam □ let (one) off □ let one's hair down □ let something ride □ Let's be having it! □ Let's have it! □ Let's hear it. □ let's say □ to let

LETCH

letch after someone □ letch for someone □ letch over someone

LETTER

bread and butter letter □ dead letter □ Dear John letter □ four-letter man □ four-letter word □ French letter □ red-letter day

LEVEL

level best □ level peg with someone or something □ on the level

LIBERTINE
chartered libertine
LICENCE
vehicle licence
LICK
lick and a promise □ lick something into shape
LID
blow the lid off □ blow the lid off something □ dustbin lid □ flip one's lid □ Put a lid on it! □ put a lid on something □ put the lid on something □ saucepan lid □ tin lid
LIE
lie doggo □ lie in □ long lie □ pack of lies
LIFE
facts of life □ go for one's life □ kiss of life □ life of Riley □ You bet your sweet life!
LIFT
lift one's elbow □ lift someone □ on the (lifting) game □ thumb a lift
LIGHT
be light (of) something □ flash of light □ go out like a light □ green light □ light and dark □ light blue □ light of love □ lights out □ out like a light □ shoot the lights □ Strike a light! □ strip lighting
LIGHTHOUSES
play lighthouses
LIGHTNING
like greased lightning
LIKELY
likely as a nine bob note □ likely as a three pound note □ likely as an electric walking stick □ likely lad □ likely story □ likely tale □ Not (bloody) likely! □ Not fucking likely!
LIL
fag-ash Lil
LIMIT
giddy limit □ sky's the limit
LINE
bottom line □ do a line with someone □ hard lines □ hook, line and sinker □ lay it on the line □ line of country □ line one's own pocket(s) □ loaded to the Plimsole line □ marriage lines □ out of line □ party line □ shoot a line □ throwaway (line) □ throw one's lines
LINEN

dirty linen □ linen draper
LIONEL
Lionel Blair □ Lionel Blair(-cut)
LIP
Button (up) your lip! □ keep one's lips buttoned □ lip service □ Read my lips! □ Watch my lips!
LIQUID
liquid laugh □ liquid lunch □ liquid sunshine
LIQUOR
pie and liquor
LIST
hit list □ shopping list
LISTEN
I'm listening. □ listen in □ Listen who's talking!
LISZT
Brahms and Liszt
LIT
lit up □ well lit
LITTLE
as sure as God made little green apples □ little Audrey □ little black book □ little boys' room □ little devils □ little girls' room □ little horrors □ little man □ little monsters □ little number □ little something □ little terrors □ (little) willie □ little woman □ nice little earner □ nice little runner □ Ye gods (and little fishes)!
LIVE
as one lives and breathes □ as sure as you live □ frighten the living daylights out of someone □ how the other half lives □ live-in lover □ live in one's suitcase □ live it up □ live out of one's suitcase □ live rough □ live wire □ scare the living daylights out of someone
LOAD
get a load off one's mind □ load of cods(wallop) □ load of crap □ load of guff □ load of old cobblers □ loaded question □ loaded remark □ loaded to the barrel □ loaded to the earlobes □ loaded to the gills □ loaded to the gunnals □ loaded to the gunwales □ loaded to the hat □ loaded to the muzzle □ loaded to the Plimsole line □ off-load something □ three bricks shy of a load
LOADER
Rosie Loader

LOAF
French loaf □ Use the loaf! □ Use your loaf!

LOATH
nothing loath

LOCKET
chain and locket □ Lucy Locket

LOLLIPOP
lollipop lady □ lollipop man □ lollipop woman

LONG
as long as one's arm □ by a long chalk □ draw the long bow □ in for the long jump □ long arm of the law □ long drink of water □ long firm □ long in the tooth □ long jump □ long lie □ long odds □ long paper □ long pockets and short arms □ long shot □ long streak of piss □ Long time no see. □ not long arrived □ not long here □ take the long jump

LOO
go to the loo

LOOK
come-hither look □ dirty look □ look after number one □ Look alive! □ look back □ look in □ look sharpish □ Look sharpish! □ look slippy □ look something out □ Look who's talking! □ Looks good! □ old fashioned look

LOOKER
good looker

LOOSE
at a loose end □ cut loose □ have a slate loose □ have (got) a screw loose □ play fast and loose with someone or something

LORD
House of Lords □ Lord Almighty! □ Lord love a duck! □ Lord Muck

LORN
Marquess of Lorn

LOSE
lose a bundle □ lose one's cool □ lose one's grip □ lose one's hair □ lose one's marbles □ lose one's rag □ lose one's shirt □ losing streak □ on a loser □ two-time loser □ win some, lose some □ winners and losers

LOSS
cut one's losses □ dead loss □ total loss

LOST
Get lost! □ Home of Lost Causes □ lost cause

LOT
do the lot □ Lots of luck! □ pay scot and lot □ take a lot of nerve □ you lot

LOUD
For crying out loud!

LOUIS
St. Louis blues

LOUT
lager lout

LOVE
Cor love a duck! □ For the love of Mike! □ Gawd love a duck! □ God love her □ (I) love it! □ light of love □ live-in lover □ Lord love a duck! □ love blobs □ (love) handles □ love weed □ Love you!

LOW
bring someone low □ Lower Regions □ One Hung Low

LUCK
Best of British (luck). □ Better luck next time. □ Lots of luck! □ luck of the draw □ push one's luck □ rotten luck □ rough luck □ Saltash luck □ tough luck

LUCKY
lucky budgie □ lucky dog □ lucky sod

LUCRE
filthy lucre

LUCY
Lucy Locket

LUGHOLES
pin back your lugholes

LUMBER
lumber gaff □ lumber someone

LUMP
like it or lump it □ Like it or lump it! □ Lump it! □ Lumpy Gravy

LUNCH
drop one's lunch □ liquid lunch □ out to lunch □ spot of lunch

LURCH
in the lurch

LUSH
lush bint □ lush someone up

LUXURY
lap of luxury

LYING
take something lying down

M
big M
MAC
dirty mac brigade
MACDONALD
whisky Mac(Donald)
MACKAY
real Mackay
MACKEREL
Holy mackerel! □ sprat to catch a mackerel
MAD
barking (mad) □ hopping mad □ like mad □ mad (keen) on someone or something □ mad money □ mad nurse
MADE
as sure as God made little green apples □ have (got) it made
MADNESS
motorway madness
MAGAZINE
girlie magazine
MAGIC
magic bus □ magic mushrooms
MAIL
Daily (Mail) □ junk mail □ Royal Mail
MAINS
on the mains
MAJOR
sodger-clad but major-minded
MAKE
as sure as God made little green apples □ don't make a fuss □ Don't make me laugh! □ enough to make a cat laugh □ have (got) it made □ make a baby □ make a bad fist of something □ make a bitch of something □ make a bog of something □ make a bomb □ make a boo-boo □ make a bundle □ make a dead set at someone □ make a dead set at something □ make a fuck-up of something □ make a go of something □ make a good fist □ make a killing □ make a meal (out) of something □ make a monkey of someone □ make a muck of something □ make a mull of something □ make a pass at someone □ make a pig of oneself □ make a pile □ make a poor fist of it □ make a stink (about someone or something) □ make at someone □ make babies □ make for somewhere □ make

good □ make it □ make like someone or something □ make mincemeat out of someone or something □ make noises about something □ Make no mistake (about it)! □ make one's hair curl □ make polite noises □ make someone up to something □ make the running □ make tracks □ make waves □ on the make □ Want to make something of it? □ what makes someone tick
MALNUTRITION
muesli belt malnutrition
MALONE
Molly Malone
MAN
action man □ backdoor man □ blind man's holiday □ cave man □ company man □ con man □ dead man □ dirty old man □ down among the dead men □ easy as taking pennies from a blind man □ Essex man □ fly man □ four-letter man □ front man □ hatchet man □ hit man □ little man □ lollipop man □ man and wife □ man in the street □ man-sized job □ man upstairs □ men in grey suits □ obie man □ old man □ one-man band □ one-man show □ poor man's something □ see a man about a dog □ star man □ stick man □ straight man □ strong-arm man □ take it like a man □ Wee Man
MANHOLE
inspector of manholes □ manhole cover
MANURE
rocking-horse manure
MANY
one too many
MARBLES
have (got) all one's marbles □ lose one's marbles
MARCHING
in marching order □ marching orders
MARE
shank's mare □ Tamson's mare
MARIA
black maria
MARINE
dead marine
MARK
easy mark □ full marks □ mark someone's card □ mark time □ quick off the mark □ skid marks □ slow off

the mark □ up to the mark □ X marks the spot.

MARKET
spot market

MARRIAGE
marriage lines □ shotgun marriage

MARRY
marry above oneself □ marry below oneself □ marry beneath oneself

MARY
bloody mary □ Mary Ann □ Mary Blane □ Mary J □ Mary Jane □ Mary Warner

MASH
bangers and mash □ pie and mash □ sausage and mash

MAT
put someone on the mat

MATCH
needle match □ slanging match □ whole shooting match

MAXE
in a maxe

MAYBE
I don't mean maybe!

MCCOY
real McCoy

MCNAB
Sandy McNab

MEAL
make a meal (out) of something □ square meal

MEAN
I don't mean maybe! □ lean and mean □ mean business □ Y'know (what I mean)?

MEAT
bit of meat □ cold-meat job □ dead meat □ easy meat □ flash one's meat □ meat dagger □ meat injection □ meat wagon □ plates of meat

MEDAL
putty medal

MEET
Fancy meeting you here. □ meet up with someone □ meet up with something □ meeting of minds □ mother's meeting □ when Dover and Calais meet

MEMBER
sitting member

MEN
down among the dead men □ men in grey suits

MENACE
Dennis the Menace

MENTAL
go mental

MERCHANT
panic merchant □ patter merchant □ speed merchant

MERCY
mercy blow-through □ mercy bucket(s)

MERRY
lead someone a (merry) dance □ merry dancers □ Merry Widow □ play (merry) hell with someone or something

MESS
hell of a mess □ mess about (with someone) □ mess about (with something) □ mess around (with someone) □ mess around (with something) □ mess someone or something up □ mess up

MESSAGE
do a message □ do the messages □ Get the message?

METAL
heavy metal

METROPOLIS
aurora metropolis

MIAOW
cat's miaow

MICHAEL
do a Michael □ extract the Michael □ take the Michael

MICK
Mick Jagger □ old Mick

MICKEY
do a mick(e)y □ Mick(e)y (Finn) □ Mick(e)y Mouse □ Mickey Rooney □ take the Mick(e)y

MIDDLE
Middle for diddle! □ middle leg □ middle of nowhere □ smack-bang in the middle

MIKE
clever Mike □ For the love of Mike! □ on the mike □ take the Mike

MILK
tiger's milk

MILL
through the mill □ trouble at t'mill

MINCE
mince pie □ Yer hied's aw full o mince!

MINCEMEAT

make mincemeat out of someone or something

MIND

blow someone's mind □ get a load off one's mind □ have one's mind in the gutter □ meeting of minds □ Mind boggles! □ never mind □ one-track mind □ sodger-clad but major-minded □ stoned out of one's mind

MINE

back to the salt mines □ Your guess is as good as mine. □ Your place or mine?

MINNIE

moaning minnie

MINT

in mint condition

MINUTE

at the minute

MIRRORS

done by mirrors □ done with mirrors

MISCHIEF

do a mischief to someone

MISERY

put one out of (one's) misery □ put something out of (its) misery

MISS

give someone or something a miss □ give something a miss □ miss a trick □ Miss Goody Two-shoes □ miss off □ miss out □ miss the boat □ miss the bus

MIST

Scotch mist

MISTAKE

Make no mistake (about it)!

MITTEN

give someone the frozen mitten

MIX

mix it with someone □ mixed up

MO

half a mo □ Wait a mo!

MOCING

Ee-mocing pu!

MOCKERS

put the mockers on someone

MONEY

colour of someone's money □ drink (money) □ easy money □ folding money □ have money to burn □ hot money □ hush money □ in the money □ key money □ mad money □ money for jam □ money for old rope □ money grubber □ money talks □ pull down an amount of money □ Put your money where your mouth is! □ real money □ spend money like it's going out of fashion □ spend money like it's going out of style □ spend money like there's no tomorrow □ spending money □ stinking with (money) □ throw money at something □ tight money □ touch someone for money

MONKEY

brass monkey's weather □ get one's monkey up □ grease monkey □ have (got) a monkey on one's back □ make a monkey of someone □ monkey around (with someone) □ monkey around (with something) □ monkey business □ monkey suit □ monkey tricks □ not care a monkey's (fuck) □ not give a monkey's (fuck) □ not worth a monkey's (fuck)

MONSTERS

little monsters

MONTH

flavour of the month □ six months hard

MOO

silly (old) moo

MOODY

moody someone □ pull the moody

MOON

blue moon □ do a moon job □ Harvest Moon □ once in a blue moon □ over the moon □ silver moon □ six moon

MOPP

Mrs Mop(p)

MOPPER

wine mopper

MORE

more than one bargained for □ Run that by (me) one more time.

MORN

hail smiling morn □ morning after (the night before) □ September morn

MOSES

Holy Moses!

MOTHER

be mother □ cat's mother □ Mother Bunch □ Mother Hubbard □ mother of pearl □ mother's boy □ mother's meeting □ mother's ruin

MOTIONS

go through the motions

MOUSE

cat and mouse □ Mick(e)y Mouse □ tight as a mouse's ear(hole)

MOUTH

all mouth and trousers □ big mouth □ foaming (at the mouth) □ foot-and-mouth disease □ foul mouth □ have (got) a big mouth □ mouth music □ Put your money where your mouth is! □ shoot off one's mouth □ shoot one's mouth off □ straight from the horse's mouth □ Watch your mouth!

MOVE

smooth move

MR

Mr Big □ Mr Nice Guy □ Mr Right □ Mr Sausage

MRS

Mrs Duckett □ Mrs Duckett! □ Mrs Greenfield □ Mrs Mop(p)

MUCH

be a bit much □ ever so much of something □ have too much on one's plate □ not go much on someone □ not much cop □ thank you very much □ too much □ too muchly □ without (so much as) a for or by your leave □ without (so much as) a with or by your leave

MUCK

Lady Muck □ Lord Muck □ make a muck of something □ muck about □ muck around □ muck in with something □ muck something out □ muck something up □ muck sweat □ mucky duck □ mucky pup

MUD

clear as mud □ Here's mud in your eye.

MUDDLE

bugger's muddle

MUFTI

in mufti

MUG

mug (punter) □ mug shot □ mug up □ mug's game

MULL

make a mull of something

MUM

instant mum

MURDER

blue murder □ murder bag □ scream bloody murder

MUSHROOMS

magic mushrooms □ sacred mushrooms

MUSIC

face the music □ mouth music

MUST

must (do) □ Must fly.

MUSTARD

cut the mustard □ keen as mustard

MUTTON

laced mutton □ mutton dagger □ mutton dressed as lamb

MUZZLE

loaded to the muzzle

NAFF

naff all □ Naff off!

NAG

shank's nag

NAIL

coffin nail □ holy nail □ nail someone

NAKED

starbolic naked □ stark bollock (naked) □ stark naked

NAME

big name □ double-barrelled name □ get a bad name □ name of the game □ Name your poison. □ Name yours. □ no names, no pack-drill

NARROW

in narrow circumstances □ narrow bed □ narrow squeak □ straight and narrow

NASTY

nasty piece of work □ video nasty

NATIVE

go native

NATURE

call of nature □ in a state of nature □ Nature calls. □ nature's call □ state of nature

NAVIGATION

steam navigation

NAVY

army and navy

NEAR

(as) near as dammit □ near and far □ near thing □ near (to) the knuckle □ or near offer

NECK

brass neck □ breathe down someone's neck □ dead from the neck up □ get it in the neck □ goose('s neck) □ hard neck □ heavy necking □ neck and neck □ neck in neck □ pain in the neck □ stick one's neck out □ talk through (the back of) one's neck □ up to one's neck

NECTAR
amber nectar

NED
Uncle Ned

NEED
need something like a hole in the head □ That's all someone needs.

NEEDLE
needle and pin □ needle and thread □ needle fight □ needle game □ needle match □ needle something from someone □ on the needle □ thread (the needle)

NEIGHBOUR
beggar my neighbour

NELLY
Aunt Nelly □ Not on your nelly!

NERVE
bundle of nerves □ take a lot of nerve □ What (a) nerve!

NEST
bird's nest □ nest egg

NETWORK
old boy network

NEVER
Never fash yer hied. □ never hatchy □ never mind □ on the never-never

NEW
brand new □ brand spanking new □ new boy □ new girl □ new penny □ So what else is new? □ spanking new □ split new □ That's a new one on me. □ What else is new? □ What's new?

NEWCASTLE
coals to Newcastle

NEWS
bad news □ News of the Screws

NEWT
pissed as a newt

NEXT
Better luck next time. □ next (door) but one

NICE
Mr Nice Guy □ nice as ninepence □ nice as pie □ nice little earner □ nice

little runner

NICK
in good nick □ nick off □ nick someone □ nick something

NICKER
half a nicker

NIEVE
steekit nieve

NIGHT
have an early night □ morning after (the night before) □ night bird □ night person □ night starvation □ one-night stand □ white night

NIL
nil carborundum illigitium

NINE
likely as a nine bob note □ queer as a nine bob note

NINEPENCE
nice as ninepence □ ninepence to the shilling □ right as ninepence

NINES
dressed to the nines

NINETEEN
talk nineteen to the dozen

NITTY
get down to the nitty-gritty

NOBODY
like nobody's business

NOD
give someone the nod □ nod through □ on the nod

NODDLE
in the noddle

NODDY
noddy bike □ noddy car □ noddy suit

NOGGIN
Use the noggin! □ Use your noggin!

NOISE
big noise □ make noises about something □ make polite noises □ soothing noises

NON
illegitimis non carborundum

NONE
none too clever □ none too smart

NONSENSE
bit of nonsense

NOODIE
in the noodie

NOODLE
Use the noodle! □ Use your noodle!

NORTH

Athens of the North □ north and south □ North Countryman

NOSE

cannot see (any) further than the end of one's nose □ get one's nose out of joint □ get up someone's nose □ keep one's nose clean □ no skin off one's nose □ nose and chin □ nose candy □ nose job □ on the nose □ powder one's nose □ put someone's nose out of joint □ rub someone's nose in something □ see no further than the end of one's nose □ stick one's nose in (where it's not wanted) □ turn up one's nose at someone or something

NOSY

take a nosy around

NOTE

likely as a nine bob note □ likely as a three pound note □ queer as a nine bob note □ queer as a three pound note □ take a note

NOTHING

feel like nothing on earth □ hiding to nothing □ nothing doing □ Nothing doing! □ Nothing in it. □ nothing loath □ Nothing to it. □ nothing to sneeze at □ nothing to write home about □ nothing upstairs □ sweet nothings □ (There's) nothing in it. □ (There's) nothing to it.

NOTICE

not take a blind bit of notice of someone or something

NOW

Now what? □ Now you're talking!

NOWHERE

get nowhere fast □ middle of nowhere

NUDDIE

in the nuddie

NUDE

in the nude

NUMBER

do a number on someone □ hot number □ little number □ look after number one □ number crunching □ number one □ opposite number □ soft number □ take care of number one □ telephone numbers

NUN

tighter than a nun's cunt

NURSE

mad nurse

NUT

do one's nut □ drive someone nuts □ eco nut □ Jesus nut □ nut (case) □ nuts and bolts □ off one's nut □ talk like a nut □ tough nut (to crack)

NUTTY

(as) nutty as a fruitcake

O

ball o' chalk □ like billy-o □ Yer hied's aw full o mince!

O'CLOCK

blue o'clock

O'GROATS

from Land's End to John O'Groats

OARS

rest on one's oar(s)

OATH

on oath

OATS

get one's oats □ Quaker Oat(s)

OBJECT

no object

OCEAN

ocean wave □ Western (Ocean)

ODDS

long odds □ odds and sods

OFFER

burnt offering □ on offer □ or near offer

OFFICES

usual offices

OH

Boy, oh boy! □ Oh, boy! □ oh my dear □ Oh, yeah?

OIL

no oil painting □ oil the knocker □ oiled, oiled story □ oily lamp □ oily rag □ well oiled

OK

Rule OK!

OLD

boring old fart □ come the old soldier with someone □ dirty old man □ dry old stick □ give someone or something the (old) heave-ho □ golden oldie □ high old time □ load of old cobblers □ me old cock □ money for old rope □ old and bitter □ Old Bailey □ old battle-axe □ old bean □ Old Bill □ old boy □ old bubble □ old buffer □ old chap □ old fashioned look □ old fellow □ old flame □ old fogey □ old fogy □ old fruit □ old girl □ old hand (at something) □ old hat □ old King Cole □ old lady □ old lag □ old man □ old Mick □ old one-two □ Old Pals Act □ old penny □ old school tie □ Old Scratch □ old soldier □ old stick □ old sweat □ old thing □ old trout □ old woman □ rare old time □ same old story □ silly (old) moo

ONCE
If I've told you once, I've told you a thousand times. □ once (and) for all □ once a week □ once in a blue moon

ONIONBAG
bulge the onionbag

ONIONS
know one's onions

ONLY
only here for the beer □ only way to go

ONTO
latch onto something □ onto a good thing □ shunt something onto someone

OOZE
on the ooze

OPEN
for openers □ opening time(s) □ with (one's) eyes (wide) open

OPERA
pill opera

OPERATOR
smooth operator

OPPORTUNITY
golden opportunity □ window (of op-portunity)

OPTION
soft option

ORACLE
work the oracle

ORANGE
Lombard Street to a China orange □ orange pip

ORBIT
go into orbit □ in orbit

ORDER
apple-pie order □ in marching order □ just what the doctor ordered □ march-ing orders □ order of the boot □ order of the wellie □ out of order □ rag order □ tall order □ under starter's orders

ORGANISE
could not organise a piss-up in a

brewery □ get organised □ organise something

OSCAR
Oscar Wilding □ Oscarise someone

OSCILLANS
plumbum oscillans

OTHER
bit of the other □ boot is on the other foot □ how the other half lives □ one and t'other □ Other Place □ Pull the other one!

OUGHT
didn't oughter

OUTFIT
cowboy outfit

OUTING
works outing

OUTS
ins and outs

OUZE
River Ouze

OVEN
have one in the oven

OVERBOARD
go overboard

OWN
blow one's own horn □ cut one's own throat □ devil's own □ do one's (own) thing □ line one's own pocket(s) □ off your own bat □ own goal □ toot one's own horn □ under one's own steam

OYSTER
world is one's oyster

P
big P

PACE
at a snail's pace

PACK
no names, no pack-drill □ pack a punch □ pack in □ pack (it) in □ pack of lies □ pack out somewhere □ pack someone off □ pack someone or some-thing in □ pack up

PACKET
cop a packet □ cost a packet □ get a packet □ stop a packet

PAD
crash pad □ pad the hoof

PADDLE
up the creek (without a paddle)

PADDY
paddy wagon □ Paddy's taxi

PAGE
page three girl □ take a page from someone's book

PAID
carriage paid □ put paid to something

PAIL
bucket and pail □ dinner pail □ jug (and pail)

PAIN
feeling no pain □ pain in the arse □ pain in the back □ pain in the backside □ pain in the balls □ pain in the bum □ pain in the neck

PAINT
no oil painting □ paint the Forth Bridge □ paint the town (red)

PALACE
gin palace

PALE
beyond the pale

PALM
have (a) sticky palm

PALS
Old Pals Act

PALSY
Bell's palsy

PAN
down the pan □ pan out □ pot and pan

PANIC
hit the panic button □ panic merchant □ press the panic button □ push the panic button

PANTS
bore the pants off someone □ frighten the pants off someone □ have (got) ants in one's pants □ kick in the (seat of the) pants □ scare the pants off someone □ seat (of the pants)

PAPER
get one's walking papers □ long paper □ paper over something

PARDON
if you'll pardon the expression □ Pardon my French.

PARISH
parish lantern □ parish pump

PARK
park a custard □ park one's arse □ park one's bum □ park one's carcass □ park one's stern □ park oneself □

park something □ park up □ Queen's Park Ranger

PARKER
Nosey Parker

PARROT
(as) sick as a parrot □ (as) thick as a parrot

PART
act a part □ fancy parts □ parting shot

PARTNER
sparring partner

PARTNERSHIP
third wicket partnership

PARTRIDGE
Saint Partridge's Day

PARTY
acid house (party) □ bottle party □ hen party □ party animal □ party line □ stag party □ swing party □ throw a party

PASS
make a pass at someone □ pass a comment □ pass the buck □ pass the catheter

PASSAGE
front passage

PASTY
Cornish (pasty)

PAT
got something off pat □ stand pat (on something)

PATCH
bad patch □ cabbage patch

PATH
lead someone up the garden path □ path lab

PAVEMENT
hit the pavement

PAY
deuce to pay □ go to pay the water bill □ hit pay dirt □ pay off □ pay round □ pay scot and lot □ pay the earth □ put paid to something □ strike pay dirt

PEA
mushy peas □ on one's pea pod □ split pea

PEANUTS
for peanuts

PEARL
mother of pearl

PEARS
apples and pears

PECK
Gregory (Peck)
PECKER
keep your pecker up
PEDAL
soft pedal something
PEED
Alf's peed again. □ peed off
PEEP
another peep (out of you) □ put someone's gas at a peep
PEEVE
pet peeve
PEG
level peg with someone or something □ peg out □ peg someone down □ square peg (in a round hole)
PELMET
puss(y) pelmet
PEN
pen and ink □ pen and inker
PENCIL
lead in one's pencil
PENN'ORTH
penn'orth (of chalk) □ ten penn'orth
PENNY
bad penny □ easy as taking pennies from a blind man □ in for a penny, in for a pound □ new penny □ old penny □ penny drops □ Penny for your thoughts? □ penny steamboat □ pretty penny □ spend a penny □ ten a penny □ turn an honest penny □ two a penny
PEP
pep pill □ pep someone up □ pep talk
PER
as per usual
PERCY
point Percy at the porcelain
PERSON
bitch of a person or thing □ day person □ night person
PET
heavy petting □ pet peeve
PETE
For Pete's sake!
PETROL
kangaroo petrol
PEW
grab a pew □ take a pew
PHEASANT

Billingsgate pheasant □ pheasant plucker □ Spithead pheasant
PHONE
on the phone □ phone through
PIANO
Jewish piano □ Yiddish piano
PICK
pick and choose □ pick on someone □ pick someone up □ pick up the tab for something
PICKLE
rod in pickle
PICNIC
two sandwiches short of a picnic
PICTURE
in the picture □ out of the picture □ picture perfect
PIE
apple-pie bed □ apple-pie order □ easy as pie □ knuckle pie □ mince pie □ nice as pie □ pie and liquor □ pie and mash □ pie in the sky □ porky (pie)
PIECE
nasty piece of work □ piece of cake □ piece of goods □ piece of piss □ piece of skirt □ piece (of the action) □ say one's piece □ tear off a piece □ three-piece suite
PIER
Brighton Pier
PIG
bleed like a (stuck) pig □ essence of pig-shit □ happy as a pig in shit □ in a pig's ear □ make a pig of oneself □ male chauvinist pig □ pig it □ pig's arse □ pig's breakfast □ pig's ear
PIGEON
stool (pigeon)
PIKESTAFF
plain as a pikestaff
PILE
make a pile
PILL
happy pills □ idiot pills □ on the pill □ pep pill □ Pill Avenue □ pill bosun □ pill opera □ rhubarb (pill)
PILLAR
send someone from pillar to post
PIN
(two) pins □ needle and pin □ on pins □ pin back your lugholes □ pin your ears back

PINCH
at a pinch □ pinch someone □ where the shoe pinches

PINK
in the pink □ pink elephants □ seeing pink elephants □ tickled (pink)

PIP
give someone the pip □ orange pip □ pip at the post □ pip out

PIPE
pipe down □ pipe off (about something) □ pipe one's eyes □ Put that in your pipe and smoke it! □ Up your pipe!

PIPELINE
in the pipeline

PISS
all piss and wind □ could not organise a piss-up in a brewery □ gnat's piss □ Go and piss up your kilt! □ long streak of piss □ on the piss □ piece of piss □ piss about □ piss around □ piss artist □ piss-hole bandit □ piss in the wind □ piss it □ piss off □ Piss off! □ piss oneself □ piss poor □ piss someone off □ pissed as a newt □ pissed off □ pissing down □ streak of piss □ take the piss

PIT
bottomless pit □ pit stop

PITCH
pitch in □ queer the pitch

PITY
For pity's sake!

PLACE
all over the place □ go places □ Other Place □ Your place or mine?

PLAIN
Plain and Gravy □ plain as a pikestaff □ plain sailing □ plain vanilla

PLANK
as thick as a short plank □ as thick as two short planks □ spank the plank

PLATE
have too much on one's plate □ on (someone's) plate □ plate someone □ plates and dishes □ plates of meat □ silver plate □ tin plate

PLAY
in play □ play a hunch □ play around □ play away □ play ball with someone □ play bouncy-bouncy □ play fast and loose with someone or something □ play for keeps □ play for time □ play gooseberry □ play hard to get □ play hide the sausage □ play it cool □ play leapfrog □ play lighthouses □ play (merry) hell with someone or something □ play silly buggers □ play something by ear □ play something close (to one's chest) □ play the goat □ play the wag □ play with fire

PLEA
cop a plea

PLEASE
Pretty please?

PLEDGE
take the pledge

PLICKENS
thought plickens

PLIMSOLE
loaded to the Plimsole line

PLONK
plonk something down □ plonk something out

PLUCKER
pheasant plucker

PLUG
plug in both ways □ pull the plug

PLUMBING
check out the plumbing □ visit the plumbing

PLUNGE
take the plunge

POCHES
kay-rop poches

POCKET
line one's own pocket(s) □ long pockets and short arms □ put one's hand in one's pocket

POD
on one's pea pod

POINT
brownie points □ point Percy at the porcelain □ Point taken. □ touch (on) a sore point

POISON
lead poisoning □ Name your poison. □ poison dwarf

POLE
up the pole □ wouldn't touch someone or something with a ten-foot pole

POLICE
assist the police with their enquiries

POLICEMAN
sleeping policeman
POLISH
polish someone off □ polish something off □ spit and polish
POLITE
make polite noises
POLY
roly-poly pudding
PONY
shank's pony □ string of ponies
POOFTER
roaring poof(ter)
POOL
scoop the pool
POOR
make a poor fist of it □ piss poor □ poor man's something □ poor show □ take a poor view of something
POP
in pop □ joy pop □ pop in on someone □ pop it □ pop off □ pop one's cherry □ pop one's clogs □ pop out □ pop round to see someone □ pop someone's cherry □ pop something □ pop the question □ skin pop □ take a pop at someone □ vox pop
PORCELAIN
point Percy at the porcelain □ pray to the porcelain god
PORN
hard porn □ soft porn
PORRIDGE
do porridge □ porridge education
POST
pip at the post □ send someone from pillar to post
POT
pot and pan □ pot boiler
POTATO
couch potato □ drop someone or something like a hot potato □ hot potato □ small potatoes
POUND
in for a penny, in for a pound □ likely as a three pound note □ queer as a three pound note
POUR
pour cold water on something □ pour oneself into something
POWDER
flea powder □ joy (powder) □ powder one's nose □ powder room □ take a powder
POWER
corridors of power □ power dress □ power suit □ pulling power
PRAM
baby's pram □ get (someone) out of one's pram
PRAT
prat about □ prat away □ prat on
PRAY
pray to the enamel god □ pray to the porcelain god
PRESCOTT
Jimmy Prescott
PRESS
gutter press □ press the panic button □ sewer press □ stop press
PRETTY
be sitting pretty □ pretty penny □ Pretty please?
PREVIOUS
bit previous
PRICE
have a price □ knock-down price
PRICK
French letter on the prick of progress □ like a spare prick (at a wedding) □ silly prick □ stupid prick
PRIEST
priest of the blue bag
PRINT
fine print □ small print
PRISONER
star prisoner
PRIVATE
private hire □ private property
PROGRESS
French letter on the prick of progress
PROMISE
lick and a promise
PROPER
not proper □ proper bastard □ proper bugger □ proper charlie □ proper do □ speak proper □ talk proper
PROUD
do oneself proud
PROWL
on the prowl
PRUNE
stewed as a prune

PSYCH
psych (oneself) up □ psych (someone) out

PT
Egyptian PT

PU
Ee-mocing pu!

PUB
down the pub

PUBLIC
go public □ Joe Public □ public convenience □ take something public

PUDDING
in the (pudding) club □ Pudding and Gravy □ put someone in the pudding club □ roly-poly pudding

PUFF
cream puff □ puff and dart

PULL
on the pull □ pull a face □ pull a fast one □ pull a flanker □ pull a job □ pull a stroke □ pull about □ pull down an amount of money □ pull one's punches □ pull out all the stops □ pull rank on someone □ pull someone □ pull someone's leg □ pull something down □ pull something off □ pull strings □ pull the moody □ Pull the other one! □ pull the plug □ pull the rug (out) from (under) someone or something □ pull wires □ pulling power

PUMP
parish pump □ pump (some) iron

PUNCH
pack a punch □ pull one's punches □ punch up the bracket □ rabbit punch

PUNK
punk (rock) □ punk (rocker)

PUNTER
mug (punter)

PUP
drop (a pup) □ mucky pup □ sell a pup

PURE
pure and simple □ pure dead brilliant

PURLER
take a purler

PURR
purr (like a cat)

PUSH
get the push □ if push comes to shove □ push bicycle □ push bike □ push in the truck □ push off □ push one's luck □ push the boat out □ push the panic button □ pushing up daisies □ when push comes to shove

PUSSY
puss(y) pelmet

PUT
put a damper on something □ Put a lid on it! □ put a lid on something □ put a smile on someone's face □ Put a sock in it! □ put a sock on something □ put a spoke in someone's wheel(s) □ put about □ put it about □ put it on □ put on the ritz □ put one out of (one's) misery □ put one's face on □ put one's feet up □ put one's foot to the floor □ put one's hand down □ put one's hand in one's pocket □ put one's wind up □ put oneself upon someone □ put out □ put over □ put paid to something □ put some distance between someone and someone or something else □ put someone away □ put someone in the pudding club □ put someone on □ put (someone) out to grass □ put someone up □ put someone's gas at a peep □ put someone's nose out of joint □ put something away □ put something on the slate □ put something out of (its) misery □ Put that in your pipe and smoke it! □ put the black on someone □ put the boot in □ put the frighteners on someone □ put the kibosh on something □ put the lid on something □ put the mockers on someone □ put the skids under someone or something □ put the squeeze on someone □ put-up job □ put up one's dukes □ Put up or shut up! □ put up the shutters □ Put your money where your mouth is!

PYJAMAS
cat's pyjamas

PYTHON
syphon the python

QT
on the q.t.

QUANTITY
negligible quantity

QUEEN
closet queen □ drag queen □ Queen Anne is dead. □ Queen's Park Ranger

QUEER

come over queer □ in Queer Street □ queer as a nine bob note □ queer as a three pound note □ queer as an electric walking stick □ queer fish □ queer in the head □ queer roll □ Queer Street □ queer the pitch □ raging queer □ turn queer

QUESTION

loaded question □ pop the question

QUEUE

jump the queue □ queue jump

QUICK

as quick as dammit □ have a quickie □ quick fix □ quick off the mark □ quick one □ quick snort □ take a quickie

QUIET

on the quiet

QUITE

not quite □ quite a lad □ quite a while □ quite an event □ quite so □ quite the thing

RABBIT

go like a rabbit □ rabbit away □ rabbit hutch □ rabbit on □ rabbit punch □ rabbit something □ rabbit('s) food □ Tommy Rabbit

RACE

at the races □ boat race □ go racing □ rat race

RADIATOR

□ drain one's radiator

RADIO

□ steam radio

RAFFLE

Away an raffle yer doughnut!

RAFT

George Raft

RAG

chew the rag □ curse rag □ glad rags □ lose one's rag □ oily rag □ on the rag(s) □ rag order □ rag trade □ red rag □ run ragged □ talk someone ragged □ wet rag

RAGE

all the rage □ raging queer

RAID

smash-and-grab raid

RAIN

hail and rain □ rain stair-rods □ right as rain

RAISE

raise a gallop □ raise a stink (about someone or something) □ raise Cain □ raise hell □ raise the wind

RAKE

rake something in □ rake something off

RALPH

call Ralph □ cry ralph □ ralph something up

RAMP

□ on the ramp

RANGER

Glasgow Ranger □ Queen's Park Ranger □ Sloane Ranger

RANK

J. Arthur (Rank) □ pull rank on someone □ rank and file

RARE

as rare as hen's teeth □ in rare form □ rare bird □ rare old time □ rare tear □ raring to go

RASPBERRY

give someone the raspberry

RAT

rat on someone □ rat out □ rat race □ smell a rat

RATTLE

rattle and clank □ rattling good □ slightly rattled

RAW

in the raw

RAZOR

razor blade □ razor someone

RAZZLE

on the razzle

READ

read and write □ Read my lips! □ take something as read

READY

rough and ready

REAL

for real □ real bitch □ real chuffed □ real Mackay □ real McCoy □ real money

REASON

no earthly reason

REBOUND

catch someone on the rebound

RECKON

reckon oneself □ reckon someone or something □ you reckon □ You reckon?

RECORD

track record

RED

in the red □ paint the town (red) □

red biddy □ red hot □ red-letter day □ red rag □ red sails in the sunset □ red tape □ red, white and blue □ ruby red □ see red

REED
broken reed

REEKIE
Auld Reekie

REGIONS
Lower Regions

RELIGIOUS
do the (religious) dodge on someone

REMAND
on remand

REMARK
loaded remark □ snide remark

REP
God rep □ rep someone or something

RES
des res

REST
Give it a rest! □ Give me a rest! □ rest on one's oar(s) □ rest one's eyes

RESTAURANT
take-away (restaurant)

RESULT
net result

RETURN
by return □ return unopened

REVENGE
Gandhi's revenge

REX
Oedipus Rex

RHUBARB
rhubarb and custard □ rhubarb (pill)

RIBBONS
shot to ribbons

RICE
apples and rice

RICH
filthy (rich) □ stinking rich □ strike it rich

RICKMATIC
hail rickmatick □ hale rickmatick

RIDDLE
jimmy (riddle)

RIDE
bareback riding □ let something ride □ ride shotgun □ ride someone □ rough riding □ take someone for a ride

RIGHT
All right. □ bang to rights □ bit of all right □ dead to rights □ do a right □

do right by someone □ get one right here □ left and right □ Mr Right □ right as ninepence □ right as rain □ right charlie □ right down to the ground □ right in the kisser □ right one □ right shut □ right smart □ right up one's street □ sail (right) through something □ see someone or something (all) right □ serve someone right

RILEY
life of Riley

RING
honk (up) one's ring □ ring a bell □ ring back □ ring off the hook □ ring someone's bell □ ring through □ ring up □ spew one's ring (up) □ throw one's hat in(to) the ring

RINGER
dead ringer (for someone) □ ringer (for someone)

RINK
skating rink

RIP
bodice ripper □ Jack the Ripper □ Let her rip! □ rip-off artist □ rip someone off

RISE
get a rise □ have a rise □ Irishman's rise □ Rise and shine!

RITZ
put on the ritz

RIVER
River Ouze

ROAD
any road □ gentleman of the road □ get the road □ get the show on the road □ get this show on the road □ hit the road □ knight of the road □ on the road □ one for the road □ over the road □ road hog □ road tax

ROAR
Hampden roar □ roaring poof(ter)

ROBBERY
daylight robbery □ highway robbery

ROCK
almond (rocks) □ army rocks □ get one's rocks off □ punk (rock) □ rock bottom □ rock of ages □ rocking-horse manure □ rocking-horse shit

ROCKER
off one's rocker □ punk (rocker)

ROD
hot rod □ rain stair-rods □ rod in pickle

ROE
cod roe
ROLL
have a roll □ heads will roll □ jam roll □ keep the ball rolling □ queer roll □ roll in □ rolling (in it) □ rolling stone □ sausage roll □ soft roll
ROLY
roly-poly pudding
ROME
gates of Rome
RONALD
Reverend (Ronald Knox)
ROOF
go through the roof □ hit the roof
ROOM
ladies' (room) □ little boys' room □ little girls' room □ powder room □ throne room
ROONEY
Mickey Rooney
ROOTS
daisy roots
ROP
kay-rop poches
ROPE
money for old rope □ rope someone in
ROSE
bed of roses □ smell like a rose
ROSIE
Rosie Lee □ Rosie Loader
ROTTEN
rotten apple □ rotten egg □ rotten luck □ rotten to the core □ spoiled rotten
ROUGH
cut up rough □ live rough □ rough and ready □ rough as a badger's arse □ rough as a badger's bum □ rough diamond □ rough house □ rough it □ rough justice □ rough luck □ rough riding □ rough someone up □ rough stuff □ rough time □ rough tongue □ rough trade □ rough work
ROULETTE
Vatican roulette
ROUND
come round □ go round the haystack □ moist round the edges □ pay round □ pop round to see someone □ round heeled □ round the bend □ round the houses □ round the twist

□ sharp as the corners of a round table □ square peg (in a round hole) □ wage round
ROW
tough row to hoe
RUB
rub along □ rub someone out □ rub someone's nose in something
RUDE
in the rude □ rude bits
RUDGE
Barnaby Rudge
RUG
hearth rug □ pull the rug (out) from (under) someone or something
RUIN
mother's ruin
RUN
Away an take a running jump at yersel! □ crumpet run □ cut and run □ do a runner □ dry run □ dummy run □ front runner □ have a run off □ make the running □ nice little runner □ on the run □ run amok □ run amuck □ run a skirt □ run ragged □ run scared □ run someone in □ run something □ Run that by (me) again. □ Run that by (me) one more time. □ run the show □ Take a running jump (at yourself)! □ turn tail (and run)
RUSH
bum's rush □ rush one's fences
RUTH
call Ruth □ cry ruth
RUTTER
Johnny Rutter
RYE
Peckham Rye
SACK
get the sack □ give someone the sack □ hit the sack □ sad sack
SAD
sad sack □ sorry and sad
SAFE
as safe as houses □ on the safe side
SAIL
plain sailing □ red sails in the sunset □ sail (right) through something □ take the wind out of someone's sails
SAILOR
sailor's blessing □ sailor's farewell □ sailors (on the sea)

SAINT
Saint Grouse's Day □ Saint Partridge's Day

SAIR
It's a sair fecht.

SAKE
For Christ's sake! □ For fucks sake! □ For Pete's sake! □ For pity's sake!

SALE
boot sale □ car boot sale □ jumble sale

SALLY
Aunt Sally □ Sally Army

SALT
back to the salt mines □ go through (something) like a dose of salts □ salt and batter □ salt horse

SAME
on the same wavelength □ same difference □ same here □ same old story

SANDBOY
happy as a sandboy

SANDWICH
jam sandwich □ knuckle sandwich □ two sandwiches short of a picnic

SATIN
satin and silk □ yellow (satin)

SAUCE
bottle of sauce □ on the sauce □ sauced (out)

SAUSAGE
Mr Sausage □ not a sausage □ play hide the sausage □ sausage a goose □ sausage and mash □ sausage dog □ sausage roll

SAY
can't say boo to a goose □ can't say fairer □ I hear what you're saying. □ I say! □ let's say □ nay say bad □ Say cheese! □ say one's piece □ Says me! □ say-so □ Says who? □ Says you! □ That's what I say (too). □ What do you say? □ You can say that again!

SCARCE
as scarce as hen's teeth

SCARE
run scared □ scare the hell out of someone □ scare the living daylights out of someone □ scare the pants off someone □ scare the shit out of someone □ scared shitless □ scared stiff

SCENARIO
best-case scenario □ worst-case scenario

SCENE
have a scene with someone

SCHOOL
old school tie □ upper school

SCIENCE
blind with science

SCOFF
scoff (up)

SCONE
off the scone

SCORE
know the score □ score (with)

SCOT
pay scot and lot

SCOTCH
bottle of Scotch □ Scotch egg □ Scotch mist

SCOTT
Great Scott!

SCRATCH
Old Scratch □ up to scratch

SCREAM
constant screamer □ scream bloody murder

SCREW
have (got) a screw loose □ News of the Screws □ screw around □ screw someone or something up □ screw someone out of something □ screw the arse off someone □ screw up □ screwed up

SCREWDRIVER
brummagem screwdriver □ Chinese screwdriver

SCROUNGE
on the scrounge for something □ scrounge (around (for someone or something)) □ scrounge someone or something up

SCUFFER
judy scuffer

SEA
deep-sea diver □ deep-sea fisherman □ sailors (on the sea) □ ship a sea

SEAMS
come apart (at the seams)

SEAT
bog seat □ dicky seat □ hot seat □ in the driver's seat □ kick in the (seat of the) pants □ seat (of the pants)

SECOND
second fiddle □ second-hand dartboard

SEE

cannot see (any) further than the end of one's nose □ have seen better days □ Long time no see. □ pop round to see someone □ see a man about a dog □ see eye to eye □ see no further than the end of one's nose □ see over something □ see red □ see someone off □ see someone or something (all) right □ see someone or something off □ see stars □ See you. □ See you later. □ seeing double □ seeing pink elephants □ sees us □ What you see is what you get. □ would not be seen dead

SELL

hard sell □ sell a pup □ sell out □ sell short □ sell someone or something out □ sell someone or something short □ sell under guise □ soft sell

SEND

send someone down □ send someone from pillar to post □ send someone to Coventry □ send someone up

SERENE

all serene

SERIOUS

get down to some serious drinking □ serious about someone

SERVICE

in service □ lip service

SESSION

bull session □ rap session

SET

all set □ make a dead set at someone □ make a dead set at something □ set about someone □ set of wheels □ set someone back □ set someone up (for something) □ set something to one side □ set the Thames on fire □ top set

SEW

sew something up □ sewed up

SEZ

Sez me! □ Sez who?

SHACKED

get shacked

SHAG

shag oneself □ shagged (out)

SHAKE

I'm shaking (in fear). □ I'm shaking with fright. □ no great shakes □ shake a leg □ Shake a leg! □ two shakes of a dog's tail □ two shakes of a lamb's tail

SHAME

take the shame

SHANK

shank's mare □ shank's nag □ shank's pony

SHAPE

in bad shape □ knock something into shape □ lick something into shape □ shape up

SHARE

lion's share

SHARP

look sharpish □ Look sharpish! □ pull someone up (sharpish) □ sharp as a tennis ball □ sharp as the corners of a round table □ sharp end □ so sharp one could cut oneself

SHAVE

close shave

SHEBANG

whole shebang

SHEET

both sheets in(to) the wind □ four sheets in(to) the wind □ swindle sheet □ three sheets in(to) the wind □ two sheets in(to) the wind

SHELF

on the shelf

SHIFT

graveyard shift □ Shift it! □ Shift yer barrow!

SHILLING

ninepence to the shilling

SHINE

Rise and shine! □ take a shine to someone □ where the sun don't shine

SHIP

jump ship □ ship a sea □ taut ship □ when one's ship comes in

SHIPSHAPE

shipshape and Bristol fashion

SHIRE

knight of the shire

SHIRT

Been there, done that, got the tee-shirt. □ Keep your shirt on! □ lose one's shirt □ stuffed shirt

SHIT

bang like a shit-house door □ deep shit □ drop someone in the shit □ eat shit □ essence of pig-shit □ feel like shit □ frighten the shit out of someone □ full of shit □ get one's shit together □ give someone the shits □ happy as a pig in shit □ in deep shit □ in the shit □ rocking-horse shit □ scare the shit out of someone □ scared shitless □ shit a brick □ shit and derision □ shit bricks □ shit or bust □ shit (up) on someone from a (very) great height □ shoot the shit □ stir the shit □ Tough shit! □ treat someone like shit □ up shit creek □ What the shit? □ Will I shit!

SHITHOUSE
built like a brick shithouse

SHOD
well shod

SHOE
goody two-shoes □ Miss Goody Two-shoes □ where the shoe pinches

SHOESTRING
on a shoestring

SHOOT
shoot a cat □ shoot a line □ shoot off □ shoot oneself in the foot □ shoot one's mouth off □ shoot someone or something down from a great height □ shoot someone or something down in flames □ shoot the breeze □ shoot the craw □ shoot the lights □ shoot the shit □ shoot up □ shooting gallery □ whole shoot □ whole shooting match

SHOP
all over the shop □ Bill shop □ bucket shop □ come to the wrong shop □ cop shop □ corner shop □ grocer's shop □ kip shop □ shop around □ shopping list □ top of the shop □ warm shop

SHORT
as thick as a short plank □ as thick as two short planks □ by a short head □ get someone by the short and curlies □ go short of something □ have (got) a short fuse □ have someone by the short and curlies □ long pockets and short arms □ not short of a bob or two □ on a short leash □ sell short □ sell someone or something short □ short arm □ short back and sides □ short commons □ short fuse □ short hairs □ short one □ short time □ two sandwiches short of a picnic

SHORTAGE
no shortage of something

SHOT
bent shot □ big shot □ boss shot □ cheap shot □ duff shot □ farting shot □ get shot of someone or something □ long shot □ mug shot □ parting shot □ shot down □ shot full of holes □ shot in the arm □ shot in the dark □ shot to ribbons □ shot up □ take a shot (at something)

SHOTGUN
ride shotgun □ shotgun marriage □ shotgun wedding

SHOULDER
cold shoulder □ straight from the shoulder

SHOUT
all over bar the shouting □ give someone a shout □ shout and holler

SHOVE
if push comes to shove □ Shove it! □ shove off □ when push comes to shove

SHOVEL
shove(l) along □ shovel and broom □ shovel and tank

SHOW
bad show □ chat show □ do a show □ get the show on the road □ get this show on the road □ girlie show □ Good show! □ no show □ one-man show □ poor show □ run the show □ Show a leg! □ show one's cards □ show the flag □ show willing □ steal the show

SHOWERS
April showers

SHRINKER
head shrinker

SHTOOM
Keep shtoom!

SHUFTI
take a shufti

SHUT
get some shut-eye □ Put up or shut up! □ right shut □ Shut it! □ Shut up! □ Shut your face! □ Shut your gab!

SHUTE
up the shute

SHUTTERS
put up the shutters

SHY
three bricks shy of a load

SICK
(as) sick as a parrot □ sick to death
(of someone or something) □ sick up
SIDE
bit on the side □ face like the side
of a house □ flip side □ give someone
the side of one's tongue □ on the safe
side □ on the side □ set something to
one side □ short back and sides
SIDNEY
Kate and Sidney
SIGHT
out of sight
SIGN
sign off □ sign on
SILK
satin and silk □ take (the) silk □ yellow silk
SILLY
play silly buggers □ silly billy □ silly
(old) moo □ silly prick
SILVER
silver moon □ silver plate
SIMPLE
pure and simple
SIN
(as) ugly as sin □ sin bin □ sin
bosun
SINCE
since Adam was a boy □ since the
year dot
SING
till the fat lady sings □ until the fat
lady sings □ when the fat lady sings
SINK
hook, line and sinker □ sink the boot
in □ tumble down the sink
SIR
Sir Galahad □ Sir John
SIT
be sitting pretty □ sit on the fence □
sitting duck □ sitting member □ sitting
target □ sitting tenant
SITE
gap site
SITUATION
no-win situation
SIX
hit something for six □ knock someone for six □ six feet under □ six
months hard □ six moon
SIXPENCE
turn on a sixpence

SIZE
cut someone down to size □ man-
sized job □ That's about the size of it.
SKATE
get your skates on □ skating rink
SKETCH
thumbnail sketch
SKID
put the skids under someone or
something □ skid marks
SKIN
no skin off one's nose □ skin and
blister □ skin flick □ skin pop
SKINFUL
have (got) a skinful
SKINNER
Jim(my) Skinner □ Lilley and Skinner
SKINT
fair skint
SKIRT
bit of skirt □ piece of skirt □ run a
skirt
SKITE
on the skite
SKITTLES
beer and skittles
SKULL
out of one's skull □ skull job □ Use
the skull! □ Use your skull!
SKY
pie in the sky □ sky hook □ sky's
the limit
SLAM
grand slam □ slam someone
SLAP
slap and tickle □ slap in the face □
slap someone on the wrist □ slap
someone's wrist
SLASH
take a slash
SLATE
have a slate loose □ put something
on the slate □ slate someone for something □ slate someone off □ wipe the
slate clean
SLEEP
beauty sleep □ sleep around □ sleeping
policeman
SLEEVE
ace up one's sleeve □ have (got) an
ace up one's sleeve
SLICE
cut off a slice □ slice of the action

SLICKER
city slicker
SLIME
slime bag □ slime bucket
SLING
sling one's drizzle □ sling one's
hook □ Sling yer hook!
SLIP
give someone the slip □ look slippy
□ slip in the gutter □ slip it to someone
□ slip one's trolley □ slip someone a
fatty □ slip someone a length □ slip
(someone) up □ slip (up)
SLOT
God slot □ slotted job
SLOW
be a bit slow upstairs □ slow off the
mark □ take it slow(ly)
SLY
on the sly
SMACK
smack-bang in the middle □ smack on
SMALL
small ad □ small beer □ small bundle □ small change □ small fortune □
small fry □ small potatoes □ small
print □ wee small hours
SMART
get smart (with someone) □ none
too smart □ not so smart □ not too
smart □ not very smart □ right smart
□ smart Alec
SMASH
smash-and-grab raid □ smash hit
SMELL
smell a rat □ smell fishy □ smell
like a rose
SMILE
hail smiling morn □ put a smile on
someone's face
SMOKE
Big Smoke □ Great Smoke □ Put
that in your pipe and smoke it! □
smoke like a chimney □ smoked haddock □ smoking gun
SMOOTH
smooth move □ smooth operator □
smooth talker
SNAIL
at a snail's pace
SNAKE
drain one's snake □ one-eyed
trouser-snake □ snake bite

SNAP
Make it snappy! □ Snap out of it! □
snap out of something □ snap something up
SNATCH
wages snatch
SNEEZE
nothing to sneeze at
SNOOK
cock a snook (at someone)
SNORT
quick snort
SNOW
Lady Snow □ snow bunny □ snow
job □ snowed under
SNOWBALL
not a snowball's (chance in hell) □
snowball's chance in hell
SNUFF
snuff film □ snuff (it) □ up to snuff
SO
ever so □ I'm so □ just so □ not so
clever □ not so dusty □ not so smart
□ quite so □ so sharp one could cut
oneself □ So what? □ So what else is
new? □ without (so much as) a for or
by your leave □ without (so much as) a
with or by your leave
SOAP
Joe Soap □ soft soap
SOBER
cold sober □ stone (cold) sober
SOCK
American sock □ knock someone's
socks off □ Put a sock in it! □ put a
sock on something □ socked out
SOD
lucky sod □ odds and sods □ sod all
□ Sod it! □ Sod off! □ sods' holiday
□ Sod's Law □ Sod them! □ Sod this
for a game of soldiers!
SOFT
soft core □ soft in the head □ soft
number □ soft on someone □ soft option □ soft pedal something □ soft
porn □ soft roll □ soft sell □ soft soap
□ soft touch □ soft tyre
SOLDIER
come the old soldier with someone
□ dead soldier □ Fuck this for a
game of soldiers! □ old soldier □
Sod this for a game of soldiers! □
soldier on

SOME

blow off (some) steam □ get down to some serious drinking □ get some shut-eye □ let off (some) steam □ pump (some) iron □ put some distance between someone and someone or something else □ take some doing □ win some, lose some

SON

son of a gun □ son of something or someone

SONG

on song □ song of the thrush

SORE

stick out like a sore thumb □ touch (on) a sore point

SORRY

sorry about that □ sorry and sad □ sorry 'bout that

SORT

get sorted out □ of sorts □ sort someone or something out

SOUL

not a soul

SOUND

sound off (about something) □ wired for sound

SOUP

alphabet soup □ electric soup □ in the soup □ laughing soup □ Soup and Gravy □ soup something up □ souped up

SOUTH

north and south □ South of France □ sunny south

SPACE

waste of space

SPAIN

France and Spain

SPANISH

Spanish custom □ Spanish tummy

SPANK

brand spanking new □ spank the plank □ spanking new

SPARE

bit of spare □ go spare □ like a spare prick (at a wedding) □ spare tyre

SPARK

bright spark □ spark out □ sparked out

SPEAK

speak of the devil □ speak proper

SPEC

on spec

SPEED

speed freak □ speed merchant

SPEND

big spender □ spend a penny □ spend money like it's going out of fashion □ spend money like it's going out of style □ spend money like there's no tomorrow □ spending money

SPEW

spew one's guts (out) □ spew one's ring (up)

SPILL

spill one's guts □ spill the beans

SPIN

flat spin □ spin doctor

SPIRES

City of Dreaming Spires

SPIT

spit and a drag □ spit and polish □ Spit it out! □ spitting distance □ swap spit

SPLASH

splash out on something □ splash the boots

SPLEEN

vent one's spleen

SPLICED

get oneself spliced

SPLIT

split new □ split pea □ split the vote

SPOIL

spoiled rotten □ spoiling for a fight

SPOKE

put a spoke in someone's wheel(s)

SPONGE

throw in the sponge □ toss in the sponge

SPOON

egg and spoon □ greasy spoon □ wooden spoon

SPOT

high spot □ hot spot □ in a hot spot □ spot market □ spot of bother □ spot of lunch □ spot on □ tight spot □ X marks the spot.

SPOUT

spout off □ up the spout

SPRING

spring chicken □ spring someone

SPROUT

Brussels Sprout □ sprout wings

SQUAD

awkward squad

SQUARE
back to square one □ on the square □ square bash □ square meal □ square peg (in a round hole) □ square with someone

SQUASH
lemon squash

SQUATTER
Gunga Din and squatter's daughter

SQUEAK
Bubble (and Squeak) □ bubble and squeak □ narrow squeak

SQUEEZE
put the squeeze on someone □ squeeze the lemon

STAB
stab at something □ take a stab at something

STACKED
(well) stacked

STAG
go stag □ stag party □ stag someone

STAGE
honeymoon (stage)

STAGGERS
get the staggers

STAIR
above stairs □ rain stair-rods

STAND
as sure as I'm standing here □ one-night stand □ stand pat (on something) □ stand someone off □ stand someone up □ stand to something

STANK
doon the stank

STAR
aim for the stars □ do a starry □ reach for the stars □ see stars □ star man □ star prisoner □ star turn

STARCH
knock the starch out of someone □ take the starch out of someone

STARING
stark staring bonkers

STARK
stark bollock (naked) □ stark naked □ stark staring bonkers

STARKERS
bollocky starkers

START
Don't start! □ start something

STARTER
for starters □ under starter's orders

STARVATION
night starvation

STASH
stash (away) □ Stash it!

STATE
in a state of nature □ nanny state □ state of nature

STATISTICS
vital statistics

STAY
come to stay

STEADY
go steady

STEAL
steal someone blind □ steal the show

STEAM
blow off (some) steam □ let off (some) steam □ steam chicken □ steam in □ steam navigation □ steam radio □ steam tug □ steamed (up) □ under one's own steam

STEAMBOAT
penny steamboat

STEEL
cold steel

STEPS
go up the steps

STERN
park one's stern

STEWARD
bar steward

STEWED
stewed as a prune □ stewed to the ears □ stewed to the eyeballs □ stewed to the eyebrows □ stewed to the gills

STICK
cancer stick □ dry old stick □ give someone stick □ likely as an electric walking stick □ old stick □ queer as an electric walking stick □ stick around □ stick at trifles □ Stick 'em up! □ stick in at something □ stick in with something □ stick it on someone □ stick man □ stick one's neck out □ stick one's nose in (where it's not wanted) □ stick out like a sore thumb □ stick someone on □ take stick □ Thai sticks □ up sticks □ up the stick

STICKERS
up stickers

STICKY
come to a sticky end □ have (a)

sticky palm □ sticky (bun) □ sticky end □ sticky fingers □ sticky wicket

STIFF
crack a stiffie □ scared stiff □ stiff someone

STINK
big stink □ cry stinking fish □ kick up a stink □ like stink □ make a stink (about someone or something) □ raise a stink (about someone or something) □ stinking (drunk) □ stinking rich □ stinking with (money) □ stink to (high) heaven

STITCH
in stitches □ stitch something up □ Stitch this! □ stitch up someone or something

STOAT
fuck like a stoat □ weasle and stoat

STOCKBROKER
stockbroker belt □ Stockbroker Tudor

STOMACH
turn someone's stomach

STONE
carved in stone □ rolling stone □ stone (cold) sober □ stone dead □ stone frigate □ Stone me! □ Stone the crows! □ stoned out of one's head □ stoned out of one's mind

STOP
face that would stop a clock □ Full stop! □ pit stop □ pull out all the stops □ stop a packet □ stop at home □ stop-go economics □ stop press

STOPPER
bottle and stopper

STOREY
top storey □ upper storey (department)

STORY
fairy story □ likely story □ oiled, oiled story □ same old story □ sob story

STOTTLE
'Arry Stottle

STRAIGHT
go straight □ in the home straight □ straight and narrow □ straight from the bog □ straight from the horse's mouth □ straight from the shoulder □ straight man □ straight off the turnips □ straight out of the trees □ straight talk(ing) □ straighten oneself up □ straighten someone out

STRAIN
strain one's greens □ strain one's taters

STRAP
on the strap □ strapped (for cash)

STRAW
Jack Straw □ last straw

STREAK
have (got) a yellow streak down one's back □ long streak of piss □ losing streak □ streak of piss □ yellow streak (down someone's back)

STREET
civvy street □ Fleet Street □ Grub Street □ in Carey Street □ in Queer Street □ Lombard Street to a China orange □ man in the street □ on the street(s) □ Queer Street □ right up one's street □ street accident □ street cred(ibility) □ streets ahead □ two-way street □ up one's street □ walk the streets □ work the streets

STRENGTH
on the strength

STRETCH
at full stretch □ half a stretch □ in the home stretch □ stretch one's legs

STRIFE
struggle and strife □ trouble and strife □ worry and strife

STRIKE
Strike a light! □ strike it rich □ strike pay dirt □ wild-cat (strike)

STRING
pull strings □ string along with someone or something □ String (of Beads) □ string of ponies □ string someone along □ string someone up

STRIP
strip lighting □ tear a strip off someone

STROKE
pull a stroke

STRONG
come on strong □ strong-arm man □ strong-arm tactics □ strong it

STROPPY
get stroppy

STUCK
bleed like a (stuck) pig □ get stuck in □ stuck with someone or something

STUFF
bit of stuff □ drop of the hard stuff □

folding stuff □ funny stuff □ get one's stuff together □ Get stuffed! □ hard stuff □ hot stuff □ kid('s)-stuff □ knock the stuffing out of someone □ know one's stuff □ rough stuff □ Stuff it! □ stuff someone □ stuffed shirt □ take the stuffing out of someone □ That's the stuff (to give the troops)! □ yellow stuff

STUMP

stump someone □ stump up □ stumped for an answer

STUPID

blindingly stupid □ stupid arse □ stupid ass □ stupid prick

STUTTER

cough and stutter □ mutter and stutter

STYLE

cramp one's style □ spend money like it's going out of style

SUCK

suck someone off □ suck up to someone

SUCKER

sucker for someone or something □ sucker someone

SUDGE

jober as a sudge

SUIT

claw-hammer suit □ ice-cream suit □ in one's birthday suit □ men in grey suits □ monkey suit □ noddy suit □ penguin suit □ power suit

SUITCASE

live in one's suitcase □ live out of one's suitcase

SUITE

three-piece suite

SUM

tidy sum

SUN

sunny south □ where the sun don't shine

SUNDAY

Sunday best □ Sunday driver

SUNSET

red sails in the sunset

SUNSHINE

liquid sunshine

SURE

as sure as death □ as sure as eggs is eggs □ as sure as fate □ as sure as God made little green apples □ as sure as

hell □ as sure as I'm standing here □ as sure as you live □ for sure □ For sure! □ sure thing

SURF

channel surf □ channel surfer □ surf the (Inter)net

SUSS

on suss □ suss something out

SWALLOW

hard to swallow □ swallow and sigh □ swallow the dictionary

SWANEE

up the Swanee

SWEAR

swear and cuss □ swear blind □ swear like a trooper □ swear off something

SWEAT

in a cold sweat □ muck sweat □ no sweat □ old sweat □ sweat blood □ sweat something out □ tiger's sweat □ work oneself up (into a sweat)

SWEEP

clean sweep □ sweep something under the carpet

SWEET

sweet and sours □ sweet B.A. □ sweet bugger all □ sweet evening □ sweet FA □ sweet fanny adams □ sweet nothings □ You bet your sweet life!

SWEETHEART

sweetheart agreement □ sweetheart deal

SWIFT

swift half □ swift one

SWING

swing a free leg □ swing both ways □ swing into high gear □ swing it □ swing party □ swing the lead □ take a swing at someone

SWIPE

swipe something □ take a swipe at someone or something

SWITCH

switch off □ switched on

SYNC

out of sync

T

B and T

TAB

pick up the tab for something

TABLE

have one's feet under the table □

sharp as the corners of a round table □ under the table

TACK

brass tacks □ tack attack □ tin tack □ tin tacks

TACKLE

kissing tackle □ wedding tackle

TACTICS

strong-arm tactics

TAE

Awa' tae fuck!

TAG

tag along with someone or something □ tag on to something

TAIL

bit of tail □ bright-eyed and bushy-tailed □ have a tiger by the tail □ tail-end Charlie □ tail (it) □ top and tail □ turn tail (and run) □ two shakes of a dog's tail □ two shakes of a lamb's tail

TALE

fairy tale □ likely tale □ Tale of Two Cities □ tale of woe

TALENT

local talent

TALK

big talk □ Billingsgate talk □ give someone a (good) talking to □ heart-to-heart (talk) □ Listen who's talking! □ Look who's talking! □ money talks □ Now you're talking! □ pep talk □ smooth talker □ straight talk(ing) □ talk (a)round something □ talk big □ talk Billingsgate □ talk funny □ talk into the big white telephone □ talk like a nut □ talk nineteen to the dozen □ talk of the devil □ talk on the big white (tele)phone □ talk one's head off □ talk proper □ talk someone (a)round □ talk someone ragged □ talk someone's ear off □ talk something up □ talk through one's hat □ talk through (the back of) one's neck □ talk turkey □ talk until one is blue in the face □ talk wet □ talking head □ whisper (and talk)

TAMSON

Jock Tamson's bairns □ Tamson's mare

TAN

black and tan □ tan someone's hide

TANGO

takes two to tango

TANK

iron tank □ Septic (Tank) □ shovel and tank □ tank (something) up □ tank (up) □ tanked up □ tin tank

TAP

on tap □ tap someone

TAPE

have it taped □ red tape

TAR

jack tar

TARBRUSH

touch of the tarbrush

TART

jam tart □ tart around □ tart's delight □ tart something up

TARTAN

tear the tartan

TATERS

strain one's taters

TAX

income tax □ road tax □ tax disc

TAXI

Paddy's taxi

TEA

cup of tea □ lemon tea □ shamrock tea □ take tea □ tea grout □ tea lady □ tea leaf □ tea's up

TEACH

That'll teach someone.

TEACUP

storm in a teacup

TEAM

away team

TEAR

bore someone to tears □ get tore into someone □ get tore in to something □ rare tear □ shed a tear □ tear-arse about □ tear a strip off someone □ tear into someone □ tear into something □ tear off a piece □ tear one's arse off □ tear someone or something apart □ tear somewhere apart □ tear the arse out of something □ tear the tartan □ That tears it! □ That's (gone and) torn it! □ That's torn it!

TECHNICOLOR

technicolor yawn □ throw a technicolor yawn

TEE

Been there, done that, got the tee shirt.

TEETH

as rare as hen's teeth □ as scarce as

hen's teeth □ fed (up) to the back teeth with something or someone □ get one's teeth into something □ Hell's teeth! □ kick in the teeth □ teething troubles

TELEGRAPH
bush telegraph □ jungle telegraph

TELEPHONE
talk into the big white telephone □ talk on the big white (tele)phone □ telephone numbers

TELL
Do tell. ⊔ Tell me another (one)! □ tell someone where to get off □ tell the (whole) world

TEN
ten a penny □ ten-bob bit □ ten penn'orth □ wouldn't touch someone or something with a ten-foot pole

TENANT
sitting tenant

TENNIS
sharp as a tennis ball

TERMITES
tin termites

TERROR
holy terror □ little terrors

TEST
acid test □ MOT Test

THAMES
set the Thames on fire

THAN
cannot see (any) further than the end of one's nose □ more than one bargained for □ see no further than the end of one's nose □ tighter than a nun's cunt □ tighter than a witch's cunt

THANK
thank you very much □ thanks a bunch

THEM
Stick 'em up! □ up an' at 'em □ You can't win 'em all. □ You can't win them all.

THEN
then and there □ there and then

THERE
Been there, done that, got the tee-shirt. □ hang in there □ I'll be there □ I've been there. □ like there was no tomorrow □ not all there □ spend money like

there's no tomorrow □ then and there □ there and then □ there it is □ there you are □ There you are. □ There you go. □ There you go (again)! □ (There's) nothing in it. □ (There's) nothing to it. □ You can't get there from here.

THICK
(as) thick as a parrot □ as thick as a short plank □ as thick as two short planks □ be a bit thick □ thick (as thieves) □ thick ear □ thick on the ground

THIEVES
thick (as thieves)

THIN
thin on the ground □ walk on thin ice

THING
bitch of a person or thing □ Chance would be a fine thing. □ cope (with things) □ done thing □ do one's (own) thing □ in thing to do □ know a thing or two □ know one thing □ near thing □ not a bleeding thing □ not a blind thing □ old thing □ onto a good thing □ quite the thing □ sure thing □ take things easy

THINK
hear oneself think □ You've got another think coming.

THIRD
George (the Third) □ Richard (the Third) □ third leg □ third wicket partnership

THIRTEEN
file 13

THOMAS
□ John Thomas

THOUGHT
backward thought □ give someone the benefit of one's thoughts □ Penny for your thoughts? □ thought plickens

THOUSAND
hundreds and thousands □ If I've told you once, I've told you a thousand times.

THREAD
needle and thread □ thread (the needle)

THREE
likely as a three pound note □ page three girl □ queer as a three pound note

□ three bricks shy of a load □ three-cornered fight □ three'd up □ three-piece suite □ three sheets in(to) the wind

THRILL

give someone a thrill □ thrilled to bits

THROAT

cut one's own throat □ frog in the throat □ ram something down someone's throat

THROUGH

come through □ get through □ go through (something) like a dose of salts □ go through the motions □ go through the roof □ mercy blow-through □ nod through □ phone through □ ring through □ sail (right) through something □ talk through one's hat □ talk through (the back of) one's neck □ through and through □ through the mill □ through (with) something or someone. □ waltz through something

THROW

throw a fight □ throw a fit □ throw a game □ throw a party □ throw a technicolor yawn □ throw (away) □ throw-away line □ throw a wobbly □ throw forty fits □ throw in the sponge □ throw in the towel □ throw it in □ throw money at something □ throw one out on one's ear □ throw one's hat in(to) the ring □ throw one's lines □ throw one's weight around □ throw someone □ throw something together □ Throw the baby out with the bath-water. □ throw the book at someone □ throw (up)

THUMB

on the thumb □ stick out like a sore thumb □ thimble and thumb □ thumb a lift □ thumbs down □ thumbs up □ Tom Thumb □ twiddle one's thumbs □ under someone's thumb

TICK

in two ticks □ just a tick □ tick over □ tick someone off □ tight as a tick □ what makes someone tick

TICKET

hard ticket □ just the ticket □ That's the ticket! □ useless ticket

TICKLE

bit of tickle □ slap and tickle □ tickle the ivories □ tickled (pink)

TIE

old school tie □ tie in with someone or something □ tie one on □ tie something up □ tie the knot □ tied up

TIGER

have a tiger by the tail □ tiger's milk □ tiger's sweat

TIGHT

on a tight leash □ tight as a badger's bum □ tight as a crab's bum □ tight as a drum □ tight as a duck's arse(hole) □ tight as a fart □ tight as a fish's arse(hole) □ tight as a gnat's arse(hole) □ tight as a mouse's ear(hole) □ tight as a tick □ tight money □ tight spot □ tighten one's belt □ tighter than a nun's cunt □ tighter than a witch's cunt

TILL

till hell freezes over □ till kingdom come □ till the fat lady sings

TILT

full tilt

TIME

Better luck next time. □ big time □ buy time □ devil of a time □ do time □ down time □ gone time □ have a whale of a time □ high old time □ If I've told you once, I've told you a thousand times. □ Long time no see. □ mark time □ not before time □ opening time(s) □ play for time □ rare old time □ rough time □ Run that by (me) one more time. □ short time □ two-time loser □ up time □ whole time □ yon time

TIN

tin budgie □ tin fish □ tin hat □ tin lid □ tin plate □ tin tack □ tin tacks □ tin tank □ tin termites

TIP

hot tip □ tip someone off

TIT

arse over tits □ bit of tit □ bum and tit □ get on someone's tits □ like a tit in a trance □ tit willow □ titless wonder

TITTER

giggle (and titter)

TITTY
tough titty ☐ tough titties ☐ Tough titty!

TIZZ
in a tizzy ☐ of a tizz

TOAD
frog and toad

TOD
on one's tod

TODD
Sweeney (Todd)

TOEHOLD
get a toehold

TOFFEE
easy as taking toffee from a child ☐ not for toffee

TOGETHER
get it together ☐ get one's act together ☐ get one's shit together ☐ get one's stuff together ☐ go about together ☐ in cahoots (together) ☐ knock along (together) with someone ☐ knock something together ☐ throw something together

TOKEN
beer token ☐ drinking token

TOLD
If I've told you once, I've told you a thousand times.

TOM
Tom(, Harry) and Dick ☐ Tom Thumb

TOMATOES
Halt, tomatoes, turds!

TOMORROW
jam tomorrow ☐ like there was no tomorrow ☐ spend money like there's no tomorrow ☐ tomorrow week

TON
come down on someone like a ton of bricks ☐ do the ton ☐ half a ton ☐ like a ton of bricks ☐ tons of something ☐ ton-up boy

TONGUE
☐ Bite your tongue! ☐ give someone the side of one's tongue ☐ rough tongue ☐ tongue wrestling ☐ Watch your tongue!

TOO
have too much on one's plate ☐ none too clever ☐ none too smart ☐ not too clever ☐ not too smart ☐ one too many ☐ That's what I say (too). ☐ too funny for words ☐ too Irish ☐ too much ☐ too muchly ☐ Too true!

TOOL
down tools ☐ tool around ☐ tool someone

TOOTH
long in the tooth

TOOTLE
tootle along ☐ tootle off

TOP
big top ☐ blow one's top ☐ carrot top ☐ come out on top ☐ cotton wool on top ☐ flat top ☐ flip one's top ☐ go over the top ☐ off the top of one's head ☐ over the top ☐ top and tail ☐ top ballocks ☐ top buttocks ☐ top dog ☐ top drawer ☐ top heavy ☐ top of the shop ☐ top of the world ☐ top set ☐ top someone ☐ top something up ☐ top storey ☐ top 'uns

TORE
get tore into someone ☐ get tore in to something

TORN
That's (gone and) torn it! ☐ That's torn it!

TOSS
not care a toss ☐ not give a toss ☐ not worth a toss ☐ toss in the sponge ☐ toss off ☐ toss something back ☐ toss something off

TOTAL
total loss ☐ total someone

TOTS
tiny tots

TOTTIE
wee tottie

TOUCH
Keep in touch. ☐ Nelson touch ☐ soft touch ☐ touch and go ☐ touch of the tarbrush ☐ touch (on a sore point ☐ touch someone for money ☐ touch someone or something with a bargepole ☐ touch someone up ☐ touch wood ☐ wouldn't touch someone or something with a bargepole ☐ wouldn't touch someone or something with a ten-foot pole

TOUGH
tough customer ☐ tough guy ☐ tough luck ☐ tough nut (to crack) ☐ tough row to hoe ☐ Tough shit! ☐ tough something out ☐ tough titties ☐ tough titty ☐ Tough titty!

TOWEL
throw in the towel
TOWER
ivory tower □ tower block
TOWN
go to town □ go up to town □ lady of the town □ paint the town (red) □ town bike
TRACK
make tracks □ one-track mind □ track record
TRACY
dickless Tracy
TRADE
in trade □ rag trade □ rough trade □ trade (something) in □ tricks of the trade
TRADING
cease trading
TRAIN
going like a train □ gravy train
TRANCE
like a tit in a trance
TRAP
booby trap □ Jock's trap □ tourist trap
TREAT
Dutch treat □ fair treat □ go down a treat □ treat someone like shit □ treat (someone or something) with kid gloves
TREE
not grow on trees □ out of one's tree □ straight out of the trees □ up a gum tree
TRICK
con trick □ confidence trick □ do the trick □ How's tricks? □ miss a trick □ monkey tricks □ trick cyclist □ tricks of the trade □ turn a trick □ whole bag of tricks
TRIFLES
stick at trifles
TRIP
bad trip □ bum trip □ ego trip □ good trip □ head trip □ trip (out)
TRIPPER
ego tripper
TROG
trog along □ trog off
TROLLEY
off one's trolley □ slip one's trolley
TROOPER
swear like a trooper

TROOPS
That's the stuff (to give the troops)!
TROT
on the trot □ Turkey Trots
TROUBLE
ask for trouble □ dead trouble □ for (all) one's trouble □ teething troubles □ trouble and strife □ trouble at t'mill
TROUSER
all mouth and trousers □ catch (one) with one's trousers down □ one-eyed trouser-snake □ trouser chuff □ wear the trousers
TROUT
old trout □ salmon and trout
TRUCK
cattle (truck) □ push in the truck
TRUE
Too true!
TRULY
well and truly □ yours truly
TRUMP
trumped up □ turn up trumps
TRUTH
gospel (truth)
TUBE
boob tube □ down the tubes □ go down the tube(s)
TUCK
Friar (Tuck) □ tuck in □ tuck someone up
TUDOR
Stockbroker Tudor
TUG
steam tug
TUMBLE
give something a tumble □ take a tumble □ tumble down the sink □ tumble in the hay
TUMMY
bump tummies □ Gippy tummy □ Gyppo tummy □ Gyppy tummy □ Singapore tummy □ Spanish tummy □ tummy banana
TUNE
to the tune of something □ tuned in □ turn on, tune in, drop out
TUPPENCE
don't care tuppence
TUPPENNY
not care a (tuppenny) damn □ not give a (tuppenny) damn □ not worth a (tuppenny) damn

TURDS
Halt, tomatoes, turds!

TURK
young Turk

TURKEY
cold turkey □ talk turkey □ Turkey Trots

TURN
buggin's turn □ do a good turn to someone □ done to a turn □ star turn □ take something in turns □ turn a trick □ turn an honest penny □ turn around □ turn belly up □ turn copper □ turn in □ turn it on □ turn off □ turn on □ turn on, tune in, drop out □ turn queer □ turn someone off □ turn someone on □ turn someone or something over □ turn someone or something upside down □ turn someone's stomach □ turn somewhere over □ turn tail (and run) □ turn the corner □ turn turtle □ turn up (for the books) □ turn up one's nose at someone or something □ turn up trumps □ whatever turns you on

TURNIP
straight off the turnips □ Use the turnip! □ Use your turnip!

TURTLE
turn turtle

TWEED
Harris tweed

TWELFTH
Glorious Twelfth

TWIG
drop off the twig □ hop off (one's twig) □ twig (on to) something

TWIST
get one's knickers in a twist □ round the twist □ twist someone's arm

TWITTER
in a twitter □ of a twitter

TWO
as thick as two short planks □ goody two-shoes □ in two ticks □ know a thing or two □ Miss Goody Two-shoes □ not care two hoots □ not give two hoots □ not short of a bob or two □ not worth two hoots □ old one-two □ takes two to tango □ Tale of Two Cities □ two a penny □ two cities □ two eyes of blue □ (two) pins □ two sandwiches short of a picnic □ two shakes of a

dog's tail □ two shakes of a lamb's tail □ two sheets in(to) the wind □ two-time loser □ two-up, two-down □ two-way street □ wear two hats □ worth a bob or two

TYBURN
dance the Tyburn jig

TYPEWRITER
Jewish typewriter

TYRE
Dunlop (tyre) □ soft tyre □ spare tyre

UGANDAN
Ugandan affairs □ Ugandan discussions

UGLY
(as) ugly as sin

UNCLE
Bob's your uncle! □ Dutch uncle □ Uncle (Dick) □ Uncle Fred □ Uncle Ned □ Uncle Willy

UNDER
come under the hammer □ down under □ half under □ have one's feet under the table □ hot under the collar □ keep something under one's hat □ knuckle under (to someone or something) □ one under □ pull the rug (out) from (under) someone or something □ put the skids under someone or something □ sell under guise □ six feet under □ snowed under □ sweep something under the carpet □ under one's belt □ under one's own steam □ under someone's thumb □ under starter's orders □ under the affluence of incohol □ under the doctor □ under (the influence) □ under the table □ under the weather □ under wraps

UNDERGROUND
go underground

UNDONE
come undone

UNGLUED
come unglued

UNIT
expensive care unit

UNOPENED
return unopened

UNRAVELLED
come unravelled

UNSTRUNG
come unstrung

UNSTUCK
come unstuck

UNTIL

talk until one is blue in the face □ until hell freezes over □ until kingdom come □ until the fat lady sings

UNWASHED

great unwashed

UPPER

upper school □ upper storey (department) □ uppers and downers

UPS

high ups □ higher ups

UPSIDE

turn someone or something upside down □ upsides with something or someone

UPSTAIRS

be a bit slow upstairs □ man upstairs □ nothing upstairs

UPTAK

gleg in the uptak

URINE

extract the urine

USE

Use the head! □ Use the loaf! □ Use the noggin! □ Use the noodle! □ Use the skull! □ Use the turnip! □ Use your bean! □ Use your head! □ Use your loaf! □ Use your noggin! □ Use your noodle! □ Use your skull! □ Use your turnip! □ useless ticket

USUAL

as per usual □ usual offices

VALLEY

Kangaroo Valley

VANILLA

plain vanilla

VARIETY

Heinz 57 (variety)

VELVET

black velvet □ velvet glove □ velvet vice □ yellow velvet

VERSE

chapter and verse

VERY

drop on someone (from a (very) great height) □ not very clever □ not very smart □ shit (up)on someone from a (very) great height □ thank you very much □ The (very) idea!

VIBES

have (got) bad vibes □ have (got) good vibes

VICE

velvet vice

VIEW

take a dim view of something □ take a poor view of something

VIGOUR

vim and vigour

VOTE

split the vote □ vote with one's feet

VOUCHER

beer voucher □ drinking voucher

WAG

play the wag □ wag (it) off

WAGE

wage round □ wages snatch

WAGON

honey wagon □ meat wagon □ off the wagon □ on the wagon □ paddy wagon

WALK

get one's walking papers □ go walkies □ likely as an electric walking stick □ queer as an electric walking stick □ take a walk □ walk it □ walk on eggs □ walk on thin ice □ walk the streets □ walking disaster area □ walking wounded

WALL

climb the wall(s) □ drive someone up the wall □ hole in the wall □ off the wall □ up against the wall

WALLIE

wallie close □ wallie dug

WALLOP

cod's wallop □ get the wallop

WALTZ

waltz off (with something) □ waltz through something

WANT

not want to know □ stick one's nose in (where it's not wanted) □ want out □ Want to make something of it?

WARM

feel like death warmed up □ like death warmed up □ warm shop □ warm someone up

WARN

Gypsy's warning □ Scarborough warning

WARNER

Mary Jane Warner □ Mary Warner

WARPATH

on the warpath

WARRIOR
warriors bold □ Whitehall warrior
WASH
chief cook and bottle washer □
come out in the wash □ dirty washing
□ head cook and bottle washer □ it
won't wash □ wash someone out □
wash something out □ washed out
WASTE
waste of space □ waste someone
WATCH
clock watcher □ gold watch □
Watch it! □ Watch my lips! □ Watch
your mouth! □ Watch your tongue!
WATER
between hell and high water □ big
drink of water □ blow someone out of
the water □ bottle of water □ dead in
the water □ go to pay the water bill □
hold water □ laughing water □ Liffey
water □ long drink of water □ pour
cold water on something □ watering
hole
WATERWORKS
turn on the waterworks
WAVE
make waves □ ocean wave
WAVELENGTH
on the same wavelength
WAY
both-way bet □ get that way □ go
all the way □ in a bad way □ in a big
way □ in the family way □ laugh all
the way to the bank □ No way! □ only
way to go □ over the way □ plug in
both ways □ swing both ways □ that
way □ two-way street
WEAN
big wean
WEAR
wear something □ wear the trousers
□ wear two hats □ worse for wear
WEASEL
weasel out of something □ weasel
words
WEATHER
brass monkey's weather □ fair-
weather friend □ fine weather for ducks
□ this weather □ under the weather
WEAVE
get weaving □ Get weaving!
WEDDING
like a spare prick (at a wedding) □

shotgun wedding □ wedding kit □
wedding tackle
WEE
wee goldie □ wee hauf □ wee heavy
□ wee hoose □ Wee Man □ wee small
hours □ wee tottie
WEED
loco weed □ love weed
WEEK
hell week □ inside a week □ once a
week □ this day week □ tomorrow
week
WEEKEND
dirty weekend □ wet weekend
WEEP
Jesus wept! □ weeping willow
WEIGH
weigh into someone □ weigh someone
off
WEIGHT
above one's weight □ carry weight
□ throw one's weight around
WELCH
Raquel Welch □ welch on someone
WELL
do well □ go down well □ well and
truly □ well away □ well gone □ well
lit □ well oiled □ well on □ well shod
□ (well) stacked
WELLIE
order of the wellie □ wellie someone
WELLY
green welly
WEN
Great Wen
WEPT
Jesus wept!
WEST
easts and wests □ go west □ up West
□ Western (Ocean)
WET
talk wet □ wet behind the ears □ wet
blanket □ wet rag □ wet the baby's
head □ wet weekend
WHACK
cop one's whack □ full whack □ out
of whack □ take a whack at someone
or something □ take a whack at something □ whack off □ whack someone
or something
WHALE
have a whale of a time

WHEAT
field of wheat
WHEEL
put a spoke in someone's wheel(s)
□ reinvent the wheel ⊔ set of wheels
WHEEN
gey wheen
WHEN
when Dover and Calais meet □
when one's ship comes in □ when push
comes to shove □ when the balloon
goes up □ when the fat lady sings
WHERE
know where one is coming from □
Put your money where your mouth is!
□ stick one's nose in (where it's not
wanted) □ tell someone where to get
off □ This is where I came in. □
Where have you been hiding? □
Where (have) you been keeping yourself? □ Where in the world? □ Where
on earth? □ Where's the fire? □
where the action is □ where the shoe
pinches □ where the sun don't shine
WHILE
get (out) while the going is good □
get out while the going's good □ quit
while one is ahead □ quite a while
WHINE
on the whine
WHIP
fair crack of the whip □ whip someone up □ whip something
WHISKERS
cat's whiskers
WHISTLE
bells and whistles □ blow the whistle □ whistle in the dark
WHITE
black and white □ Black or white?
□ bleed someone white □ China white
□ Chinese white □ red, white and blue
□ talk into the big white telephone □
talk on the big white (tele)phone □
white elephant □ White Highlands □
white night
WHIZ
Gee (whiz)!
WHO
Listen who's talking! □ Look who's
talking! □ Says who? □ Sez who? □
Who the deuce? □ Who the devil? □
Who the hell? □ You and who else?

WHOLE
tell the (whole) world □ whole bag
of tricks □ whole kit and caboodle □
whole shebang □ whole shoot □ whole
shooting match □ whole time □ whole
wide world
WHOP
whop it up someone □ whopping
(great)
WHOSE
You and whose army?
WHY
What for why?
WICK
dip one's wick □ get on someone's
wick
WICKET
at the wicket □ bat and wicket □
good wicket □ sticky wicket □ third
wicket partnership
WIDE
high, wide and handsome □ whole
wide world □ wide (boy) □ with
(one's) eyes (wide) open
WIDOW
bridge widow □ computer widow □
golf widow □ Merry Widow □
widow's wink
WIFE
charming wife □ lady wife □ man
and wife □ world and his wife
WIG
flip one's wig □ wigged out □ wig out
WILDING
Oscar Wilding
WILL
heads will roll □ That will be the
day □ Will do. □ Will I buggery! □
Will I fuck! □ Will I hell! □ Will I shit!
WILLIE
(little) willie
WILLING
I'm willing □ show willing
WILLOCKS
Jenny (Willocks)
WILLOW
tit willow □ weeping willow
WILLY
Uncle Willy
WIN
can't win (th)em all □ no-win situa-
tion □ win some, lose some □ You can't
win 'em all. □ You can't win them all.

WIND

all piss and wind □ bag of wind □ both sheets in(to) the wind □ four sheets in(to) the wind □ full of wind □ get one's wind up □ piss in the wind □ put one's wind up □ raise the wind □ take the wind out of someone's sails □ three sheets in(to) the wind □ two sheets in(to) the wind □ wind someone up □ wind something up

WINDOW

jump out of the window □ out (of) the window □ window (of opportunity)

WINDY

daft as a yett (on a windy day)

WINE

Adam's wine □ wine grape □ wine mopper

WING

clip someone's wings □ sprout wings □ wing it

WINK

forty winks □ widow's wink

WINKLE

winkle someone or something out □ winkle something out

WIPE

wipe someone out □ wipe something □ wipe the deck with someone □ wipe the floor with someone □ wipe the slate clean □ wiped out

WIRE

get one's wires crossed □ have one's wires crossed □ live wire □ pull wires □ thorny wire □ wired for sound

WISE

wise guy □ wise to something or someone

WISH

Don't you wish!

WITCH

tighter than a witch's cunt □ witch's hat

WITHIN

call someone within the bar □ within a hair(s-breadth) of something □ within an ace of something

WITHOUT

up the creek (without a paddle) □ With or without? □ without a hitch □ without (so much as) a for or by your leave □ without (so much as) a with or by your leave

WOBBLY

throw a wobbly

WOE

tale of woe

WOLF

lone wolf □ sheep in wolf's clothing □ wolf something down

WOMAN

fancy woman □ little woman □ lollipop woman □ old woman

WON'T

cock that won't fight □ it won't wash

WONDER

chinless wonder □ titless wonder

WOOD

beer from the wood □ out of the woods □ touch wood □ wooden ears □ wooden spoon

WOODBINE

African Woodbine

WOOF

woof one's custard □ woof something down

WOOL

cotton wool on top

WORD

dirty word □ four-letter word □ give someone the word □ have a word with someone □ too funny for words □ weasel words

WORK

Any work going? □ dirty work □ gum up the works □ in the works □ in work □ knock off (from work) □ nasty piece of work □ rough work □ spanner in the works □ work a flanker □ work oneself up (into a lather) □ work oneself up (into a sweat) □ work oneself up to something □ work someone over □ work the oracle □ work the streets □ working girl □ works outing

WORKERS

black-coated workers

WORLD

dead to the world □ out of this world □ tell the (whole) world □ top of the world □ Where in the world? □ whole wide world □ world and his wife □ world is one's oyster

WORM

can of worms □ illegitimate glow-worm

WORRY

Not to worry. □ worry and strife

WORST

shouldn't happen to one's worst enemy □ worst-case scenario

WORTH

not worth a brass farthing □ not worth a button □ not worth a damn □ not worth a fart □ not worth a fuck □ not worth a monkey's (fuck) □ not worth a toss □ not worth a (tuppenny) damn □ not worth two hoots □ worth a bob or two

WOULD

Chance would be a fine thing. □ face that would stop a clock □ would not be seen dead □ wouldn't touch someone or something with a bargepole □ wouldn't touch someone or something with a ten-foot pole □ Would you believe (it)?

WOUNDED

walking wounded

WRAP

under wraps □ Wrap it! □ wrapped up (in someone or something) □ wrapped up (with someone or something) □ Wrap up!

WRESTLING

tongue wrestling

WRIST

slap someone on the wrist □ slap someone's wrist

WRITE

nothing to write home about □ read and write

WRONG

come to the wrong shop □ get it wrong □ wrong 'un

YAH

okay, yah

YANK

yank off □ yank someone's chain

YAWN

technicolor yawn □ throw a technicolor yawn

YEAH

Oh, yeah?

YEAR

donkey's years □ from the year dot □ since the year dot

YELLOW

have (got) a yellow streak down one's back □ yellow duster □ yellow flag □ yellow jack □ yellow (satin) □ yellow silk □ yellow streak (down someone's back) □ yellow stuff □ yellow velvet

YER

Away an bile yer heid! □ Away an raffle yer doughnut! □ Never fash yer hied. □ On yer bike! □ Shift yer barrow! □ Sling yer hook! □ yer actual something □ Yer hied's aw full o mince!

YERSEL

Away an take a running jump at yersel! □ Dinna fash yersel.

YETT

daft as a yett (on a windy day)

YIN

get yin's jotters □ high heid yin

YOUNG

young fogey □ young Turk

Z

from A to Z

ZAP

channel zap □ channel zapper □ zap someone □ zap something

ZONK

zonked (out) □ zonk out